Masterplots

Fourth Edition

Masterplots

Fourth Edition

Volume 3
Coningsby—Eat a Bowl of Tea

Editor

Laurence W. Mazzeno
Alvernia College

SALEM PRESS
Pasadena, California   Hackensack, New Jersey

Editor in Chief: Dawn P. Dawson

Editorial Director: Christina J. Moose *Editorial Assistant:* Brett S. Weisberg
Development Editor: Tracy Irons-Georges *Research Supervisor:* Jeffry Jensen
Project Editor: Desiree Dreeuws *Research Assistant:* Keli Trousdale
Manuscript Editors: Constance Pollock, *Production Editor:* Joyce I. Buchea
Judy Selhorst, Andy Perry *Design and Graphics:* James Hutson
Acquisitions Editor: Mark Rehn *Layout:* William Zimmerman

Cover photo: Erica Jong (Ulf Andersen/Getty Images)

Library of Congress Cataloging-in-Publication Data

Masterplots / editor, Laurence W. Mazzeno. — 4th ed.
    v.   cm.
Includes bibliographical references and indexes.
ISBN 978-1-58765-568-5 (set : alk. paper) — ISBN 978-1-58765-571-5 (v. 3 : alk. paper)
1. Literature—Stories, plots, etc.   2. Literature—History and criticism.   I. Mazzeno, Laurence W.
PN44.M33 2010
809—dc22

2010033931

Fourth Edition
First Printing

Contents

Contents

Complete List of Titles

Volume 1

Volume 2

Contents lvii
Complete List of Titles lxi

Volume 3

Volume 4

Volume 5

Contents clxxi
Complete List of Titles clxxv

Volume 6

Volume 7

Volume 8

Volume 9

Contents cccxxiii

Complete List of Titles cccxxvii

Volume 10

Contents ccclxi
Complete List of Titles ccclxv

Volume 11

Contents. cccxcix
Complete List of Titles. . . . . cdiii

Volume 12

Contents . . . . cdxxxvii

Masterplots

Fourth Edition

Coningsby
Or, The New Generation

Author: Benjamin Disraeli (1804-1881)
First published: 1844
Type of work: Novel
Type of plot: Bildungsroman
Time of plot: 1832-1840
Locale: England and Paris

Principal characters:
HARRY CONINGSBY, a young nobleman
MARQUIS OF MONMOUTH, his grandfather
SIDONIA, a wealthy young Jew and Coningsby's friend
EDITH MILLBANK, Coningsby's sweetheart
OSWALD MILLBANK, Edith's father
MR. RIGBY, a member of Parliament
LUCRETIA, a young Italian noblewoman and later Lord
    Monmouth's wife
FLORA, a member of a troupe of actors

The Story:

Harry Coningsby is fourteen years old when he meets his grandfather, the Marquis of Monmouth, for the first time. He was placed in his grandfather's charge when he was very young with the understanding that his widowed mother, a commoner, was never to see him again. He was turned over, sight unseen, to the care of Mr. Rigby, a member of Parliament who sat for one of Lord Monmouth's ten boroughs.

Lord Monmouth, who preferred to live abroad, returns to his native land in 1832 in order to help fight the Reform Bill. Hearing favorable reports of his grandson, he orders Mr. Rigby to bring the boy from Eton to Monmouth House. Unfortunately, young Coningsby is unable to put out of his mind thoughts of his mother, who died when he was nine years old, and he bursts into tears at the sight of his grandfather. Lord Monmouth, disgusted by this sign of weakness, orders him to be led away. He thinks to himself that the sentimental boy's future probably lies with the church. Fortunately, the boy becomes friendly with the marquis's guests, Princess Colonna and her stepdaughter, Lucretia. The princess passes on such glowing descriptions of Coningsby to his grandfather that they are on excellent terms by the time he returns to school.

At Eton, one of Coningsby's close friends is Oswald Millbank, a manufacturer's son. When Coningsby leaves Eton in 1835, he explores Manchester's factories before going to Coningsby Castle to join his grandfather. During his journey, he visits the Millbank mills. Oswald is abroad, but he is hospitably greeted by his friend's father. At the Millbank mansion, Coningsby meets beautiful but shy young Edith Millbank and learns from her Whig father that he favors the rise of a new force in government—a natural aristocracy of able men, not one composed of hereditary peers.

Before departing for Coningsby Castle, young Coningsby is tempted to inquire about the striking portrait of a woman that graces the dining room wall. His host, much upset by his question, makes a brusque, evasive answer.

Lord Monmouth, backing Mr. Rigby for reelection to Parliament, returns to his borough and schedules an elaborate program of dances, receptions, and plays to gain a following for his Conservative candidate. Princess Colonna and Lucretia are again his grandfather's guests. Coningsby has no need, however, to confine his attentions to them; as Lord Monmouth's kinsman and possible heir, he finds himself much sought after by society. He also finds time to encourage Flora, a member of the troupe of actors entertaining the marquis's guests. The girl is shy and suffers from stage fright.

Here Coningsby meets Sidonia, a fabulously wealthy young Jew. Coningsby finds his new friend impartial in his political judgments, not only because his fortune allows him to be just but also because his religion disqualifies him as a voter. During their lengthy discussions, Sidonia teaches him to look to the national character for England's salvation. He believes that the country's weakness lies in developing class conflicts.

Lucretia makes a brief effort to attract Coningsby when she observes the favor in which his grandfather holds him, but, before long, she finds Sidonia, a polished man of the world, more intriguing. Sidonia, however, is not to be captured. He is attracted by others' intellects, and Lucretia cannot meet him on his own level.

After his holiday, Coningsby goes to Cambridge for his last years of study. During his first year there, King William IV dies, and the Conservative cause falls in defeat. Mr. Rigby is, as he was for many years, the candidate from his borough, and with the marquis to back him, his victory seems certain until Mr. Millbank enters the field. The manufacturer and the marquis were enemies for many years, and their feud reaches a climax when Millbank not only buys Hellingsley, an adjoining estate that Lord Monmouth long coveted, but also defeats Monmouth's candidate.

Prepared for the worst, the defeated Mr. Rigby goes to Monmouth House, where the marquis is in residence. He is pleasantly disappointed, however, for his employer's thoughts are not on him. Lord Monmouth is preparing to marry Lucretia, who is determined at least to obtain power and riches through marriage even if she cannot have the man she desires. A year after the wedding, Coningsby is invited to join his grandfather and his bride in Paris for Christmas. Stopping at his banker's on his way through London, he is given a package of his mother's correspondence. In the packet is a locket with an exact copy of the portrait he saw at Millbank. It is a picture of his mother.

While visiting an art gallery in Paris with Sidonia, Coningsby again meets Edith, who is traveling with her relatives, Lord and Lady Wallinger. Coningsby, who falls in love with her immediately, is distressed to hear reports that Sidonia intends to marry her. Finding the couple conversing on familiar terms one evening, he regretfully decides to withdraw from the scene. He returns to England. Disappointed in love, Coningsby devotes himself to his studies for the remainder of his stay at Cambridge. Then, learning that Edith did not marry and that Sidonia is no more than an old family friend, he goes to Coningsby Castle in order to be near the Millbanks.

Coningsby spends every possible moment with Edith and her family during the next few weeks. When her father discovers the lovers' feelings, he asks Coningsby to leave. He will not, he explains, submit his daughter to the same fate the young man's mother suffered at Lord Monmouth's hands. In this manner, Coningsby learns that his mother was once Mr. Millbank's fiancé. Leaving Hellingsley, Coningsby goes on a sea voyage from which he is called home by the marquis. Parliament faces another crisis, and Lord Monmouth decides that Coningsby should stand as his candidate. Coningsby refuses, for he is of the opinion that men should cut across party lines to establish recognition of the bond between property and labor. The same day that Lord Monmouth faces his rebellious grandson, he separates from Lucretia, who proves unfaithful.

The marquis dies at Christmas of that year. He leaves most of his fortune to Flora, who turns out to be his natural daughter. Coningsby is cut off with the interest on ten thousand pounds. Deeply disappointed in his expectations,

Coningsby gives up his clubs and most of his friends and begins to study law. He resigns himself to the prospect of years of drudgery when Mr. Millbank repents his decision. The manufacturer withdraws his candidacy in the 1840 election to back Coningsby as the Tory candidate. Rigby is his rival candidate, but he is easily defeated. A few months later, Edith becomes Coningsby's bride and goes with him to live at Hellingsley, their wedding present from Mr. Millbank. As a final blessing, though not an unmixed one, Flora, who was always weak, dies, leaving the fortune she inherited to the man who befriended her many years before at Coningsby Castle.

Critical Evaluation:

Benjamin Disraeli had dual careers as a statesman and a novelist. He published several novels before entering Parliament, continued writing during his political career, and published one novel after completing his service as prime minister in 1880. *Coningsby* represents both the political and artistic interests of Disraeli. Politically, the novel is important because it documents the rise of Young England, a small group of young members of Parliament with which Disraeli was associated after the 1841 Tory victory. The novel provides a fictionalized account of the political climate the decade after the passage of the 1832 Reform Bill, which provided for somewhat wider voting privileges and for greater representation of the large manufacturing centers. Artistically, the novel is written as a traditional bildungsroman, a study of the maturation of the novel's hero. Harry Coningsby develops from a fourteen-year-old who, overcome by emotion, cries in an early scene, to a twenty-three-year-old newly elected member of Parliament. Disraeli intertwines his political and personal themes by having his protagonist involved with the politics of his day. An adolescent when the Reform Bill passes, Coningsby grows from an unquestioned acceptance of the conservative politics of his grandfather Lord Monmouth to a state of independence in which he accepts neither the Whig nor Tory Party politics. Instead, becoming the leader of the Young England group, he searches for principles that he believes should be the basis of life in England. *Coningsby* and two later novels, *Sybil* (1845) and *Tancred* (1847), function as a trilogy documenting the political, social, and religious views of the Young England group. The Young England trilogy is often considered the best of Disraeli's fiction.

Claiming to present impartially the various prevailing political views of the day, the narrator of *Coningsby* is intrusive. Through the narrator's characterizations and political wit, the Young England group is most often favored, while the established politicians, both Whig and Tory, are satirized. The political events and some of the characters in the novel so closely follow history that keys have been devised equating characters with their historic counterparts. So when the narrator openly judges the quality of the characters, he indirectly comments on some historical figures. Sidonia, an important influence on Coningsby and therefore in the Young England group, is valorized. "Sidonia, indeed, was exactly the character who would be welcomed in our circles." On the other hand, the narrator satirizes characters representing the established politicians. Rigby, a member of Parliament, the narrator tells us, "was not treacherous, [on a specific evening] only base, which he always was." Sometimes the wit is more general. "We live in an age of prudence. The leaders of the people, now, generally follow." In this way, the novel favors the upcoming generation of political leaders who accept neither the Whig nor the Tory Party lines.

A major theme of the novel is introduced in its subtitle: *The New Generation*. In promoting the cause of Young England, the novel argues for the virtues of youth, genius, and heroism. Along with these romantic virtues comes the belief in the importance of the individual. All these characteristics are inherent in the Young England group, but they have already reached fulfillment in the idealized character of Sidonia. His wealth, intelligence, international reputation, high connections, and virtue indicate the possibilities of life if only the proper course is followed. Outside formal government because he is Jewish, Sidonia nevertheless embodies the ideals that the Young England group professes. (In Sidonia, Disraeli champions his own Jewish background.)

The movement of the novel suggests Disraeli's view of history—more a spiral than a circle or a horizontal line. Tradition and the past were important in Disraeli's politics, yet he was aware that a static policy would not be successful in a changing world. The spiral figure suggests a constant move back to what has been proven good, while at the same time presenting an understanding that there must be a movement forward to keep up with the changing world. Coningsby, in his politics, reaches back to a belief in the responsibilities of the property owners, but he is ready to accept that the manufacturing cities in England are to play an important role. His marriage to Millbank's daughter Edith merges the aristocratic with the manufacturing segments of society. He does not proceed in a straight line, having the manufacturers overtake the aristocrats, or in a circle, coming back to the aristocracy without including the manufacturers. Coningsby, like Disraeli, wants to reinvigorate, not eradicate, the conservative perspective.

As Coningsby grows politically, he also matures socially and personally. Although much of the novel deals with politi-

cal views and intrigues, other passages describe the social life of the aristocracy. At first awkward in social situations and unable to tell the difference between genuine affection and idle flattery, Coningsby learns to judge character. He chooses his role models wisely. He is influenced by both Sidonia and Eustace Lyle, men who act with sensitivity and concern for others. Coningsby is never taken in, even at a young age, by Rigby's hypocrisy or self-interest. Although respectful of his grandfather, as a young man Coningsby refuses to act for Lord Monmouth's self-interest, acting instead according to his own principles, even when his inheritance is at stake. He falls in love with a manufacturer's daughter, someone of whom his wealthy grandfather and patron would certainly disapprove, but, by remaining steadfast in his choice and being willing to relinquish any inheritance and work in order to establish a living and a reputation, Coningsby manages to get everything—wealth, a seat in Parliament, and love. The rapid change in Coningsby's fortune from isolation and despair when he loses his inheritance to his final success marks the conclusion of the novel as improbable. Yet Coningsby's ultimate success is based on reward for his character. The ending fits an ideal if not a real world.

"Critical Evaluation" by Marion Petrillo

Further Reading

Bivona, Daniel. "Disraeli's Political Trilogy and the Antinomic Structure of Imperial Desire." *Novel: A Forum on Fiction* 22, no. 3 (Spring, 1989): 305-325. Sees *Coningsby* as addressing the problem of how to join aristocrats and bourgeoisie in order to renew England while maintaining a stable hierarchy. Views the answer provided in the novel—Coningsby's marriage to Edith—as a form of imperialism.

Cazamian, Louis. "Disraeli: Social Toryism." In *The Social Novel in England, 1830-1850*. Boston: Routledge & Kegan Paul, 1973. Places Disraeli's political trilogy—*Coningsby*, *Sybil*, and *Tancred*—in the context of his political position of social Toryism. Refers to *Coningsby* as a "hybrid," part political tract, part "fashionable novel."

Flavin, Michael. *Benjamin Disraeli: The Novel as Political Discourse*. Portland, Oreg.: Sussex Academic Press, 2005. Views Disraeli's novels as a "breeding ground" for his Conservative political ideas and activities.

Masefield, Muriel. *Peacocks and Primroses: A Survey of Disraeli's Novels*. London: Geoffrey Bles, 1963. Contains two chapters on *Coningsby* written for an audience not familiar with Disraeli's works. Provides plot, lengthy quotations from the novel, background historical information, and identifications of characters with historical figures.

O'Kell, Robert. "Disraeli's *Coningsby*: Political Manifesto or Psychological Romance?" *Victorian Studies* 23, no. 1 (Autumn, 1979): 57-78. Suggests *Coningsby* is more similar to Disraeli's earlier romance novels than is often accepted. Presents political portions of the novel as secondary to the theme of personal identity.

Schwarz, Daniel R. "Disraeli's Romanticism: Self-Fashioning in the Novels." In *The Self-Fashioning of Disraeli, 1818-1851*, edited by Charles Richmond and Paul Smith. New York: Cambridge University Press, 1998. Schwarz's analyses of Disraeli's novels are included in this collection of essays that examine the life and career of the young Disraeli.

The Conjure Woman

Author: Charles Waddell Chesnutt (1858-1932)
First published: 1899
Type of work: Short fiction
Type of plot: Regional
Time of plot: Post-Civil War
Locale: North Carolina

Principal characters:
THE NARRATOR, a potential buyer of the plantation
ANNIE, his wife
UNCLE JULIUS, his black coachman
AUNT PEGGY, the conjure woman

The Story:

When the Narrator's wife begins to suffer ill effects from the severe Great Lakes climate, he looks for a suitable place to take her. He was engaged in grape culture in Ohio, and when he learns of a small North Carolina town that seems to offer what he needs in climate and suitable land, he decides to buy an old, dilapidated plantation and settle there. An untended vineyard is already on the property; with a little care and expense, the vines will flourish once more. On the day that he takes his wife, Annie, to look at the plantation, they happen upon an ancient African American who calls himself Uncle Julius. He advises them not to buy the plantation because it is goophered. Realizing they do not know that anything goophered is bewitched (conjured), the old man asks permission to tell them the story of the vineyard.

Many years before the war, when Uncle Julius was still a slave, the plantation owner made many thousands of dollars from the grapes. Because the master could never keep the slaves from eating the rich grapes and stealing the wine made from them, he conceived the idea of having Aunt Peggy, a conjure woman living nearby, put a goopher on the vines. She made one that said that any black person eating the grapes would die within a year. Most of the slaves stayed away from the grapes, but a few tried them in spite of the conjure, and they all died. When a new slave came to the plantation, no one remembered to tell him about the conjure, and he ate some of the grapes. So that he would not die, Aunt Peggy

made him a counter-goopher. Then a strange thing happened. Every year, as the grapes ripened, this slave became so young and sprightly that he could do the work of several men, but in the fall, when the vines died, he withered and faded. This strange action went on for several years, until the master hit upon the idea of selling the slave every spring when he was strong and buying him back cheaply in the fall. By this transaction, he made money each year.

One year, the master hired an expert to prune his vines, but the expert cut them out too deeply and the vines were ruined. Soon afterward, the slave who bloomed and withered with the vines also died. Some said he died of old age, but Uncle Julius knew that it was the goopher that finally overcame him. Uncle Julius advises strongly against buying the land because the conjure is still on.

The Narrator buys the plantation, however, and it prospers. Later, he learns that Uncle Julius is living in a cabin on the place and sells the grapes. He always suspects that the story was told to prevent ruination of the old man's business. He gives Uncle Julius employment as a coachman, and so the former slave is well cared for.

When Annie wants a new kitchen, her husband decides to tear down an old schoolhouse on the place and use the lumber from it for the new building. Uncle Julius advises him against the plan. Strangely enough, that schoolhouse is goophered, too. Uncle Julius's story is that a slave called Sandy was borrowed by others so often that his woman was afraid they would be separated forever. She was a conjure woman, so she turned him into a tree. Each night, she would turn him back into a man, and they would slip into her cabin until morning, when she would again change him into a tree. One day, the woman was sent away from the plantation before she could change Sandy back into a man. While she was away, the master had the tree that was Sandy cut down to build a new kitchen. The slaves had a hard time felling the tree, which twisted and turned and tried to break loose from the chains. At last, they got it to the sawmill. Later the house was built, but it was never much used. The slaves refused to work there because at night they could hear moaning and groaning, as if someone were in great pain. Only Sandy's woman, when she returned, would stay in the building, and she, poor girl, went out of her mind.

Uncle Julius advises against using goophered lumber for the new kitchen. It seems that Uncle Julius needs the old schoolhouse for his church meetings. The goopher will not bother the worshipers; in fact, the preaching helps Sandy's roaming spirit. Because no one will use goophered wood, there is nothing for the wife and her husband to do but buy new lumber for her kitchen.

When the Narrator is about to buy a mule to use in cultivating some land, Uncle Julius warns him against mules because most of them are conjured. Uncle Julius does, however, know of a horse for sale. After his employer buys the horse, which dies within three months, Uncle Julius appears in a new suit he was admiring for some time.

One day, when Annie feels depressed and listless, Uncle Julius tells her and her husband about Becky, a slave who was traded for a horse. Taken away from her child, she grieved terribly. Aunt Peggy, the conjure woman, turned the baby into a hummingbird so that he could fly down to his mother and be near her and soothe her. Later the conjure woman arranged to have Becky and her baby reunited. Uncle Julius knew that she would never have had all that trouble if she owned the hindfoot of a rabbit to protect her from harm. The story seems to cheer Annie, and her husband is not surprised later to find Uncle Julius's rabbit's foot among her things.

When the Narrator prepares to clear a piece of land, Uncle Julius warns him that the land is goophered and tells him a harrowing tale about a slave turned into a gray wolf and tricked into killing his own wife, who was thereupon changed into a cat. Although the gray wolf is said to haunt the patch of land, it does not seem to bother a bee tree from which Uncle Julius gathers wild honey.

One day, Annie's sister Mabel and her fiancé quarrel bit-

terly. Uncle Julius has another story for them about Chloe, a slave who ruined her life because she was jealous. Chloe listened to a no-account rival and believed his story that her lover was meeting another woman. When she learned that she lost her lover because she allowed her jealousy to trick her, she sorrowed and died. Even the conjure woman could not help her. Mabel listens to the story and then runs to her fiancé, who just happens to be close to the spot where Julius stops their carriage. Later on, the young man develops a special fondness for Uncle Julius. After the wedding, he tries to persuade the old man to enter his service, but Uncle Julius remains faithful to his employers. He thinks they need his advice and help.

Critical Evaluation:

The Conjure Woman is Charles Waddell Chesnutt's first collection of short fiction. It includes seven short stories that are loosely connected but unified by parallel format, characters, and thematic similarities. Each story is presented against the unifying background of postbellum Southern life. The apparent model is the Joel Chandler Harris collection of Uncle Remus tales. Chesnutt's method differs from that of Harris by presenting an outside story providing the framework for the inside narrative, which is an original tale. Harris, on the other hand, based his inside material on existing folktales. An African American, Chesnutt places a distinctive black perspective on his folk material, which is liberally sprinkled with dialect. *The Conjure Woman* preserves a relatively inaccessible and easily overlooked portion of American social and literary history.

The outside narrative usually consists of some type of journey that offers an opportunity to relate the inside narrative in dialect by Uncle Julius. Each inside narrative, which usually involves a major change in a newly introduced character, can stand alone. Chesnutt uses the frame-within-a-frame technique to mute the racial implications of the inside narrative.

Chesnutt also contrasts *The Conjure Woman*'s outside and inside narratives. The outside narrative is solidly based in the real world, one that treats the weak harshly and rewards the wealthy and powerful. The inside narrative is more imaginative and entertaining than didactic. This complex method masks much of the intent to educate the reader about the plight of the African American without becoming offensive or maudlin.

Uncle Julius relates to his white employers in a manner that parallels that with which the artist relates to his audience. Using this paradigm, Chesnutt educates his white audience by correcting the flawed vision of the outside narrative. In a very real sense, Chesnutt conjures his readers by employing this complex methodology.

Some of these stories, in the author's words, "are quaintly humorous; others wildly extravagant, revealing the Oriental cast of the negro's imagination; while others . . . disclose many a tragic incident of the darker side of slavery." These tales are less amusing and more complex than the Uncle Remus stories: Both sets of tales recall the treasury of African American folklore, replete with birds and animals, witches and spells, spirits and haunts, horrors, wonders, protests, and fright.

The Conjure Woman presents several unique problems, one of which is the question of unity in the diversity of these seven stories. That unity is derived from Uncle Julius and consistently similar personas, plot development, and narrative thread, which concerns the trickster overcoming the deceptions of a hostile environment.

The exterior story is narrated in standard English by whites, and the interior story is narrated in dialect by Uncle Julius. The interior stories begin to develop after a catalyst such as an interrupted journey or task. The supernatural elements thereupon take over, with a full-blown story-within-a-story. The entire tale ends when the strands of all the outside plots are gathered up and brought to a satisfactory conclusion.

At the core of each of these seven stories is a desire to promote a better understanding of race relations in the antebellum South with which Chesnutt was so familiar. It also appears that Chesnutt was writing for the white audience a series of stories that appeal for more humane treatment of minorities in the United States.

All of the stories in *The Conjure Woman* are deftly and competently developed, but three are outstanding: "The Conjurer's Revenge," "The Goophered Grapevine," and "The Gray Wolf's Ha'nt." "The Goophered Grapevine" is the first story in the collection, deliberately placed to entice the reader to read the entire volume. It remains the most widely known and frequently anthologized of Chesnutt's short stories. At a seminal level, "The Goophered Grapevine" is about the economics of slavery; although Chesnutt masks his message, the story remains a powerful indictment.

"The Conjurer's Revenge" is properly placed as the fourth story in the collection. It is the centerpiece for unifying character and plot line and is the most complex of the seven stories. It concerns appearance versus reality, illustrated in many ways like Zora Neale Hurston's "The Gilded Six Bits."

"The Gray Wolf's Ha'nt," the sixth story in the collection, is a genuine sojourn in the world of the supernatural. Dan is evil personified; although he starts out with apparently good intentions, he develops a dangerous jealous streak and is transformed into a wolf and a multiple killer. It is a dark, brooding tale of act and revenge.

When *The Conjure Woman* was published in March, 1899, reviews were almost universally favorable. Chesnutt was given credit as the equal of Paul Laurence Dunbar, a new African American literary talent, and a master of the short story. All of these tributes inspired Chesnutt to continue writing short stories, many of which were collected in *The Wife of His Youth, and Other Stories of the Color Line* (1899).

"Critical Evaluation" by Joe Benson

Further Reading

Andrews, William L. "Dialect Stories." In *The Literary Career of Charles W. Chesnutt*. Baton Rouge: Louisiana State University Press, 1980. Focuses on the literary tradition of *The Conjure Woman*. Chesnutt wrote *The Conjure Woman* in the popular local-color tradition of the 1880's. The dialect, cultural habits, and terrain of the Cape Fear area of North Carolina are faithfully represented in the collection's stories.

Ashe, Bertram D. "'A Little Personal Attention': Storytelling and the Black Audience in Charles W. Chesnutt's *The Conjure Woman*." In *From Within the Frame: Storytelling in African-American Fiction*. New York: Routledge, 2002. Analyzes the written form of African American oral storytelling, comparing the frame tale, in which an inside-the-text storyteller narrates the tale to an inside-the-text listener, with an outside-the-text writer and reader. Begins with a discussion of Chesnutt's frame tales in *The Conjure Woman*.

Babb, Valerie. "Subversion and Repatriation in *The Conjure Woman*." *Southern Quarterly* 25 (Winter, 1987): 66-75. Compares Joel Chandler Harris's Uncle Remus stories to *The Conjure Woman*. Harris uses black dialect to reinforce his views of white supremacy; Chesnutt uses black dialect as a "subversive strategy to undo the ideology of white supremacy."

Frenberg, Lorne. "Charles W. Chesnutt and Uncle Julius: Black Storytellers at the Crossroads." *Studies in American Fiction* 15 (1987): 161-173. Focuses on *The Conjure Woman's* representation of the reconstructed South. Chesnutt establishes a barrier between his white narrator, John, and his black storyteller, Julius, that operates as both "mask" and "veil." John and Uncle Julius are at the "crossroads" of surviving during a transitional period in history.

Heermance, J. Noel. *Charles W. Chesnutt: America's First Great Black Novelist*. Hamden, Conn.: Archon Books, 1974. A fine overview of Chesnutt's life and a discussion of how his fiction emerged from his literary interests and social concerns. One chapter focuses on *The Conjure Woman* stories.

McElrath, Joseph R., Jr., ed. *Critical Essays on Charles W. Chesnutt*. New York: G. K. Hall, 1999. A broad compilation of materials, containing reviews of Chesnutt's work that appeared at the time of its initial publication, as well as essays, articles, and chapters, written between 1905 and 1997, that analyze his work. Includes "The Art of *The Conjure Woman*" by Richard E. Baldwin.

McWilliams, Dean. *Charles W. Chesnutt and the Fictions of Race*. Athens: University of Georgia Press, 2002. McWilliams examines Chesnutt's novels and short stories, describing how his fiction changed Americans' assumptions about race. Two of the chapters discuss the black vernacular and race in Chesnutt's short fiction.

Pickens, Ernestine Williams. *Charles W. Chesnutt and the Progressive Movement*. New York: Pace University Press, 1994. A biography focusing on Chesnutt's commitment to social equality for his fellow African Americans. Contains an excellent discussion of his use of fiction as a vehicle for African Americans to gain national recognition.

Render, Sylvia Lyons. "Business for Pleasure." In *Charles W. Chesnutt*. Boston: Twayne, 1980. Discusses character and theme in *The Conjure Woman*, arguing that Uncle Julius is a stereotype who carries unconventional messages about slavery. The stories are connected by a conjure woman and man who reflect the cultural practices of a region.

Wonham, Henry B. *Charles W. Chesnutt: A Study of the Short Fiction*. New York: Twayne, 1998. Wonham's chapter on Chesnutt's dialect tales devotes more than thirty pages to *The Conjure Woman*, and the index cites other references to the collection and its individual stories.

A Connecticut Yankee in King Arthur's Court

Author: Mark Twain (1835-1910)
First published: 1889
Type of work: Novel
Type of plot: Social satire
Time of plot: Late nineteenth and early sixth centuries
Locale: England

Principal characters:
HANK MORGAN, the Connecticut Yankee, known as the Boss
CLARENCE, his right-hand man, originally a young court page
KING ARTHUR, the legendary king of Britain
SANDY (ALISANDE), a young maiden, later Hank's wife
SIR SAGRAMOUR LE DESIROUS, a short-tempered knight
MERLIN, the court magician

The Story:

Struck on the head during a quarrel in a New England arms factory, a skilled Yankee mechanic (later identified as Hank Morgan) awakens to find himself being prodded by the lance of an armored knight on horseback. The knight is Sir Kay Seneschal of King Arthur's Round Table and the time is June, 528 C.E., in England. So a foppish young page named Clarence informs the incredulous Hank as the knight takes him to white-towered Camelot. Remembering that there was a total eclipse of the sun on June 21, 528, Hank decides that should the eclipse take place, he will know that he is indeed a lost traveler in time turned backward to the days of chivalry.

At Camelot, Hank listens to King Arthur's knights as they brag of their mighty exploits. The magician, Merlin, repeats his story of Arthur's coming. Finally, Sir Kay tells of his encounter with Hank, and Merlin advises that the prisoner be thrown into a dungeon to await burning at the stake on June 21.

In prison, Hank thinks about the coming eclipse. Merlin, he tells Clarence, is a humbug, and he sends the boy to the court with a message that on the day of his death, the sun will darken and the kingdom will be destroyed. Just as Hank is about to be burned, the sky begins to dim. Awed, the king orders the prisoner released. The people shout that Hank is a greater magician than Merlin, and the king makes him his prime minister. Soon, however, the populace demands another display of his powers. With the help of Clarence, Hank mines Merlin's tower with some crude explosives he makes and then tells everyone he will cause the tower to crumble and fall. When the explosion occurs, Hank is assured of his place as the new court magician. Merlin is thrown into prison temporarily.

The lack of mechanical devices in King Arthur's castle bothers the ingenious New Englander, and the illiteracy of the people hurts his American pride in education. He decides to raise the commoners above mere slaves to the nobility. After several years pass, he has a title of his own, for the people call him "The Boss." As the Boss, he intends to modernize the kingdom. His first act is to set up schools in small communities throughout the country. He has to work in secret, because he fears the interference of the Church. He trains workmen in mechanical arts. Believing that a nation needs a free press, he instructs Clarence in journalism. He has telephone wires stretched between hamlets, haphazardly, as it turns out, because there are no maps by which to be guided.

After Sir Sagramour challenges Hank to a duel, the king decides that Hank should go on some knightly quest to prepare himself for the encounter. His mission is to help a young woman named Alisande, whose precise story he is unable to get straight. With many misgivings, he puts on a burdensome suit of armor and on his heavy charger starts off with Alisande, whom he calls Sandy. Sandy tells endless tall tales as they travel through the land. Along the way, Hank marvels at the pitiable state of the people under the feudal system. Whenever he finds a man of unusual spirit, he sends him back to Clarence in Camelot, to be taught reading, writing, and a useful trade. He visits the dungeons of a castle at which he stays and releases prisoners unjustly held by the king's cruel sister, Morgan le Fay.

In the Valley of Holiness, he finds another opportunity to prove his magic skill. There a sacred well has gone dry because, according to legend, a sin was committed. When he arrives, Merlin, now released from prison, is attempting magic to make the spring flow. Hank repairs a leak in the masonry at the bottom of the well; then, with much pomp, he restarts the water flow. As the well fills, Merlin goes home in shame.

By chance, Hank finds one of his telephone installations in a cave nearby. He uses the phone to talk to Clarence, who tells him that King Arthur is on his way to the Valley of Holiness to see the flowing spring. He returns to the spring to find a fake magician assuring the gaping pilgrims that he can tell what anyone is doing at that moment. Hank asks him about

King Arthur. The magician says that he is asleep in his bed at Camelot. Hank grandly predicts that the king is on his way to the Valley of Holiness. When the king arrives, the people are again awed by Hank's magic.

Anxious to learn about the condition of the people, Hank proposes to disguise himself as a commoner and travel through the country. The king insists on joining him. Hank knows that Arthur is not to blame for his own social doctrines; he is a victim of his place in society. On their journey, the king proves to be courageous and kind. Misfortune overtakes them, however, when they are seized by an earl and sold as slaves because they are unable to prove themselves free men. As slaves they are taken to London, where Hank picks the lock that holds him, kills the slave driver, and escapes. After his escape, the rest of the slaves are ordered to be hanged, but Hank locates a telegraph office and sends a message to Clarence in Camelot, ordering him to send help. The next day, Sir Launcelot and five hundred knights mounted on bicycles arrive in time to save Hank and the king.

Hank returns to Camelot in glory, but he still has to fight a duel with Sir Sagramour—a fight that in reality will be a battle between him and Merlin. Merlin professes to cover Sir Sagramour with an invisible shield, but the credulous knight is invisible to no one but himself. Wearing no armor and riding a small pony, Hank meets the heavily armored Sir Sagramour on the tournament field, where he dodges the charging knight until the latter grows tired. Hank then lassoes Sagramour and pulls him from his horse. After Hank bests other knights in this manner, Sagramour returns to the field; this time, Merlin steals Hank's lasso. Seeing no alternative, Hank shoots Sir Sagramour with a revolver, after which he challenges all the knights of the land. He has only eleven rounds left in two revolvers, but after he kills nine charging knights, the line wavers and gives up.

Three years pass. By this time, Hank has married Sandy, and they have a little girl. He and Clarence plan to declare a republic after the death of Arthur, for the sixth century kingdom is now a nineteenth century land with schools, trains, factories, newspapers, telephones, and telegraph. Although the code of chivalry is abolished, the knights insist on wearing their armor. When little Hello-Central, Hank's daughter, becomes ill, he and Sandy take the child to France to recuperate. During a return visit to England, Hank finds Camelot in shambles. Clarence, his only follower who remains loyal, explains what has happened. King Arthur and Sir Launcelot fought over Queen Guenevere. Now the king is dead, and the Church destroys Hank's new civilization by Interdict.

Hank and Clarence fortify a cave, surrounding it with electrically charged barriers. In a battle with the massed chivalry of England, Hank is stabbed. When an old woman comes to the fortress from the enemy lines and offers to nurse him, no one recognizes her as Merlin in disguise. The magician casts a spell on Hank and declares that he will sleep for thirteen hundred years. Hank awakens to find himself once more in the nineteenth century.

Critical Evaluation:

A Connecticut Yankee in King Arthur's Court should have offered Mark Twain one of his best opportunities to attack the repressive and antidemocratic forces that he saw in post-Civil War America as well as in sixth century England. That the attack becomes in large part an exposé of the very system he sought to vindicate reveals as much the deep division in the author's own nature as any problem inherent in the material itself. Ironically, much of the interest the work continues to hold for readers is based on the complications resulting from Twain's inability to set up a neat conflict between the forces of progress and those of repression. Hank Morgan's visit to King Arthur's court not only unveils the greed and superstition associated with the aristocracy and the established Church but also reveals some of the weaknesses in humans that enable oppressive parasitical institutions to exist. The industrial utopia Hank tries to establish in sixth century England is no more than a hopeless dream.

As a character, Hank is, in many respects, a worthy successor to Huckleberry Finn. Like Huck, Hank is representative of the common people and, at his best, he asserts the ideal qualities Twain associates with those who escape the corruption of hereditary wealth and power and the conditioning of tradition. Unlike Huck, however, who is largely an observer powerless to change the system, Hank is given the opportunity to make his values the basis of a utopian society. While Huck sees being "civilized" as an infringement on his individuality and freedom, Hank is, in his own way, fully civilized according to the standards of the world he represents. The pragmatic wit that enables Huck to survive against all odds becomes for Hank the basis of his rise in the industrial system to a position of authority and success. He fully accepts the nineteenth century doctrines of laissez-faire capitalism, progress, and technology as the best social and human principles. Hank represents Twain's vision of technological humankind as a social ideal, the greatest product of the greatest society.

Twain's choice of Arthur's court as the testing ground for Hank's ideas was not accidental. Most immediately, the author was offended by Matthew Arnold's attacks on the American glorification of the common man and the view of America as a cultural desert. In attacking the golden age of chivalry, Twain simultaneously seeks to expose English history, culture, and traditions of aristocratic privilege. At the same time, he associates the age of Arthur with the sort of romantic attitudes he exposes in *Adventures of Huckleberry Finn* (1884) as the ruin of the American South. Making his spokesman, Hank, a product of the society Arnold deplored, Twain mounts a two-pronged attack against Europeanism and sophistication and, in his own view, the dangerously reactionary attitudes that asserted the superiority of the "romantic" past over the present.

What begins for Hank, with his prediction of the moment of the eclipse, as a simple expedient for survival quickly becomes open war between Merlin (and the Church) and the Machine Age represented by Hank. Hank sees himself as a Promethean bringer of new knowledge and new order to the oppressed masses. Hank's humanitarian values are pitted against the selfishness and greed of the aristocracy and the Church, and his reason challenges their superstition. Based on Twain's view of technological human beings as the apex of human development, Hank naturally assumes that he is the rightful ruler of the world. Hank seems to assume that because he takes up the cause of the oppressed people against their oppressors, he necessarily has a moral superiority to those against whom he fights. Neither Hank nor Twain seems to give consideration to the question of ends and means.

It is particularly ironic that Hank, ostensibly the bringer of light to this benighted people, should rely no less than his archenemy Merlin on the power of superstition to gain ascendancy over the masses. From the moment he discovers the profound effect that his prediction of the eclipse has on the audience, Hank begins to challenge Merlin to ever greater miracles. Such episodes as the destruction of Merlin's tower or the restoring of the Holy Well represent Hank's use of technology to create the fear and awe that Merlin previously commanded. Recognizing that humans are essentially base and weak, Hank, like Merlin, maintains his power through exploitation of ignorance and gullibility.

It is humanity, not technology, that ultimately fails Hank. With the exception of the fifty-two young men who have never been exposed to the teachings of the Church, the society that Hank constructs through his technology reverts to its former state the minute his back is turned. Humans, as Hank perceives them, are no more than conditioned animals, and none of his modern miracles can change that fact. In the end, Hank's technology, too, fails him and his companions, and his dream of progress becomes a nightmare, a sacrifice to the very ignorance it would replace. Promethean Hank Morgan, the bringer of light and knowledge, finally vindicates only Mark Twain's pessimistic view of human nature.

The ending of *A Connecticut Yankee in King Arthur's Court* is as bleak as anything the author ever wrote. The scenes of Hank's utopia destroyed by perverse human nature, the destruction unleashed by the power of technology, and, finally, the prospect of Hank's forces being overcome by the pollution of the bodies piled in their trenches are frightening to contemplate. Twain, having apparently set out to affirm the nineteenth century doctrine of progress, finally comes full circle to suggest that something permanent within human nature makes such dreams hopeless. Clearly, there is here an anticipation of the author who, having lost hope in the human potential of his Huck Finn, would become a misanthropic voice crying out against the "damned human race."

"Critical Evaluation" by William E. Grant

Further Reading

Berkove, Lawrence I. "*Connecticut Yankee:* Twain's Other Masterpiece." In *Mark Twain*, edited by R. Kent Rasmussen. Pasadena, Calif.: Salem Press, 2010. Written for classroom use, this stimulating essay argues that *A Connecticut Yankee in King Arthur's Court* can be recognized as a great novel over which Twain had full control only when readers approach it with the understanding that everything in the book is designed to lead to its bleak ending.

Camfield, Gregg. *The Oxford Companion to Mark Twain.* New York: Oxford University Press, 2003. Collection of about three hundred original essays, including Camfield's piece on *A Connecticut Yankee in King Arthur's Court.* Some of the other essays analyze the themes, characters, and language in Twain's works and discuss subjects that interested the author. Contains an appendix on researching Twain, which lists useful secondary sources, and an annotated bibliography of Twain's novels, plays, poems, and other writings.

Emerson, Everett. *Mark Twain: A Literary Life.* Philadelphia: University of Pennsylvania Press, 2000. A complete revision of Emerson's *The Authentic Mark Twain* (1984), this masterful study traces the development of Twain's writing against the events in his life and provides illuminating discussions of many individual works.

Fulton, Joe B. *Mark Twain in the Margins: The Quarry Farm Marginalia and "A Connecticut Yankee in King Arthur's Court."* Tuscaloosa: University of Alabama Press, 2000. An examination of the marginalia that Fulton finds revealing of the development of *Connecticut Yankee.*

Halliday, Sam. "History, 'Civilization,' and *A Connecticut Yankee in King Arthur's Court.*" In *A Companion to Mark Twain*, edited by Peter Messent and Louis J. Budd. Malden, Mass.: Blackwell, 2005. An analysis of the novel by a professor and a scholar of nineteenth and early twentieth century American literature.

Rasmussen, R. Kent. *Critical Companion to Mark Twain: A Literary Reference to His Life and Work.* 2 vols. New York: Facts On File, 2007. Alphabetically arranged entries about the plots, characters, places, and other subjects relating to Twain's writings and life. The revised edition features extended analytical essays on Twain's major works, an expanded and fully annotated bibliography of books about Twain, and a glossary explaining unusual words in Twain's vocabulary.

Sloane, David E. E. *Mark Twain as a Literary Comedian.* Baton Rouge: Louisiana State University Press, 1979. Defines, with many examples, the traditions of American humor, seeing *A Connecticut Yankee in King Arthur's Court* as their literary culmination. Identifies the novel's allusions to persons, events, and conditions in Twain's time. Discusses the book's diction, combining humorous caricature with corrective satire. Includes a bibliography.

Smith, Henry Nash. *Mark Twain's Fable of Progress: Political and Economic Ideas in "A Connecticut Yankee."* New Brunswick, N.J.: Rutgers University Press, 1966. Compares Twain's novel to works by Charles Dudley Warner, William Dean Howells, and Henry Adams, contemporary authors who treated problems of changing American values during post-Civil War industrialization. Discusses Twain's ambivalence as a critic of political corruption in the United States and a defender of entrepreneurship over feudalism.

Twain, Mark. *A Connecticut Yankee in King Arthur's Court.* Edited by Bernard Stein. Berkeley: University of California Press, 1979. The definitive, corrected edition of the novel, prepared by the Mark Twain Project in Berkeley. Contains all of Dan Beard's original illustrations, as well as extensive annotations and an elaborate editorial apparatus.

The Conscience of the Rich

Author: C. P. Snow (1905-1980)
First published: 1958
Type of work: Novel
Type of plot: Psychological realism
Time of plot: Early twentieth century
Locale: England

Principal characters:
LEWIS ELIOT, a young lawyer
CHARLES MARCH, a friend of Lewis
LEONARD MARCH, Charles's father
SIR PHILIP MARCH, Leonard's older brother
KATHERINE MARCH, Charles's sister
ANN SIMON, a young activist
HERBERT GETLIFFE, the lawyer with whom Lewis studies
FRANCIS GETLIFFE, Herbert's brother, a scientist

The Story:

After they finish writing their final examinations for the British Bar, Lewis Eliot and Charles March go out together to celebrate. A month later, both of the young men learn that they passed the test, and they begin a year of apprenticeship in London. They see each other often and soon become the closest of friends. Although Lewis often speaks about personal matters as well as his problems with Herbert Getliffe, with whom he is studying, Charles remains secretive for a long time. One day, he invites Lewis to dinner at his father's London house and mentions that his family is Jewish.

Lewis is dazzled by the March establishment and charmed by both Charles's vivacious sister, Katherine, and his father, Leonard, a wonderful storyteller. When Katherine balks at attending one of the dances where wealthy Jewish young people are supposed to meet their future mates, Leonard becomes extremely angry. When Charles takes his sister's side, Leonard turns on him as well.

Charles later tells Lewis that he intends to leave the law, so that he will no longer be trapped in the small society of which his family is a part. Both Leonard and his brother, Sir Philip March, find it hard to believe that this is not just a passing fancy. Leonard threatens action if Charles persists in his plan.

During the summer, Herbert's brother Francis, a likable, sensible young scientist, is a frequent guest at the March country house, even though, like Lewis, he is a Gentile and therefore presumably not a marital possibility. When Ann Simon, an attractive Jewish girl, comes to visit, she argues with Charles about Herbert. Her antipathy is based on what she was told by Ronald Porson, an unsuccessful lawyer. At dinner, Leonard is shocked to discover that Ann is a political radical, but when he finds that she has good family connections, he is somewhat reassured.

Now desperately in love, Ann and Charles begin meeting secretly in Lewis's room. Ann urges Charles to become a doctor, like her father, and Charles becomes convinced that it is a good idea. Leonard thinks it is ridiculous and informs Charles that he changed his mind about making him financially independent. He will continue paying an allowance, but otherwise Charles can fend for himself.

Ironically, Katherine, not Charles, is in love with someone outside the faith. When she announces her engagement to Francis, Leonard puts up only a token struggle and then proceeds with wedding plans. His brother is marrying into the March family, so Herbert warns them, through Lewis, that Porson is agitating for a government inquiry into Herbert's financial affairs. Porson alleges that Herbert used insider information, obtained in dealings with the government, for his own advantage. Katherine and Francis are married, and Charles and Ann begin to make their own wedding plans. With Charles's permission, Katherine approaches their father, hoping he will now change his mind and make Charles independent, but Leonard remains adamant.

Five years later, the family celebrates Leonard's seventieth birthday. Katherine and Francis have two children and are expecting a third. Charles and Ann have none, but Charles has completed his medical studies and has a good practice.

Porson is still hoping for revenge, not only on Herbert but also on the family of the man who took Ann away from him. This time the rumors about government leaks involve several officials, including Philip, a parliamentary secretary with hopes of a ministry. Lewis discovers that Ann is working for the Communist newspaper that is leading this new attack, and that she gathered the information they intend to print. He begs Ann to get the story stopped, if only out of consideration for Charles. Ann tries, but wins only a postponement.

At Charles's insistence, Ann accepts Leonard's invitation to dinner, although she does not feel well. During the evening, she becomes much worse, and her illness is diagnosed as pneumonia. She has to remain at the March home. When she realizes that she might die, Ann tells Charles where she secreted some documents that, if published, will result in the newspaper's being suppressed. Charles, she says, can decide whether or not to use them.

During Ann's long illness, Leonard faces the fact that he wants her to die; however, she survives. Shortly before Ann is finally well enough to leave the March home, Francis and Katherine confront Charles and ask him what he intends to do. If he asks her, they point out, Ann will stop the newspaper. Charles says that he would never ask that of his wife, not even to spare his father and the family reputation. In that case, Katherine and Francis say they never want to see Ann again, and Charles regretfully replies that also means a complete break with him.

When the final article in the series appears, Philip is dismissed from his government post. His career is finished. Leonard calls Charles to his home in order to inform him that from now on, there will be no monthly allowance. Lewis continues to attend Leonard's parties. One evening after he leaves the March house, Lewis looks back. Before long, he thinks, the lights will go out and Leonard will be left alone.

Critical Evaluation:

C. P. Snow was one of the most important intellectuals of his time. As a physicist, he was involved in the important molecular research that was being conducted at Cambridge University during the 1930's. As a wartime government official, he so distinguished himself that he was made Commander of the Order of the British Empire. Snow is best remembered, however, for his third career, that of a writer. *Strangers and Brothers*, a series of eleven novels published over a period of thirty years, brilliantly illuminates the crucial issues of the modern era.

As Snow points out in his introduction to *The Conscience of the Rich*, the publication dates of his novels do not indicate their actual order in the series. In fact, he says, although a number of the novels appeared before *The Conscience of the Rich*, it should be the second in the *Strangers and Brothers* sequence. It can also be considered singly, as a work complete in itself.

Although Lewis Eliot appears in every book of the *Strangers and Brothers* series, either as protagonist or as an observer, in *The Conscience of the Rich* he serves a special purpose. Lewis is no more a part of elite Anglo-Jewish society than the author himself; by telling his story from Lewis's point of view, instead of writing as an insider, Snow makes sure that it will ring true.

The primary conflict in the novel is a familiar one: the struggle between those who wish to preserve a highly traditional society and those who work for change or at least welcome it. As head of the extended family, Sir Philip feels it is

his duty to direct the younger members in the right path, and Leonard feels a similar obligation toward his own offspring. Two of the most important decisions that a young person makes are the choice of a career, which in the early years of the twentieth century applied only to men, and the choice of a mate. In offering guidance to Katherine and Charles, their elders believe that they are not only being helpful but also perhaps even averting tragedy.

On Lewis's first visit to the March household, however, he sees that Katherine and Charles do not have the reverence for tradition that their elders do. The dance that Leonard expects Katherine to attend is not just a casual social function; it is one of the periodic gatherings at which the members of the Jewish elite can meet suitable marriage partners. Katherine does not wish to be so circumscribed, and Charles voices his own understanding of her attitude. As it turns out, Katherine and Charles both marry people whom their elders consider unsuitable. Francis is a Gentile, and Ann, although Jewish, is a Communist, dedicated to overturning the social order and, as events prove, quite willing to destroy Charles's own family in the process.

On one level, *The Conscience of the Rich* describes a conflict between two philosophies; however, the characters' actions and reactions are motivated as much by emotion as by rationality. Leonard is likable, kind, and generous, but he is also domineering. He is not interested merely in the welfare of his children; he is also bent on demonstrating his power over them. One can understand his disappointment when Charles leaves the law and merely loafs; clearly this is the waste of a good mind and an embarrassment to the family. Charles's decision to become a doctor, however, cannot injure the family; Leonard is furious simply because the career choice was Ann's idea, not his.

Leonard hates Ann because he sees her as his enemy in a battle for control over Charles. What he never realizes is that, in Lewis's terms, Ann is really not Charles's master but his slave. If Charles tries to please her, it is only because he recognizes her total devotion to him. Leonard loses his son because he does not understand either himself or anyone else. In contrast, Charles achieves happiness because he recognizes the truth. His problem is not his Jewish blood but his sense of guilt, which arises from the realization that his wealth is not being used to benefit society (hence the title of the book) and from his recognition of a defect in his character, a tendency to be heartless and cruel. In his new career, Charles suppresses his evil propensities and dedicates himself to the service of others. Ironically, Leonard contributes to his son's happiness by disinheriting him.

Although Snow himself was of the party of change, not

that of tradition, it is a measure of his genius that none of the characters in his story is totally unsympathetic. What is tragic about *The Conscience of the Rich* is that it shows how basically good people, operating from principle and motivated by honest concern, can do so much harm to those they love.

Rosemary M. Canfield Reisman

Further Reading

De la Mothe, John. *C. P. Snow and the Struggle of Modernity.* Austin: University of Texas Press, 1992. Argues that Snow's primary concern is the need for "mediation between the private and the public spheres." A demanding study in intellectual history, but worth the effort. Includes photographs and bibliography.

Eriksson, Bo H. T. *The "Structuring Forces" of Detection: The Cases of C. P. Snow and John Fowles.* Uppsala, Sweden: University of Uppsala, 1995. Analyzes the novels in the *Strangers and Brothers* series as mystery and detective fiction.

Halperin, John. *C. P. Snow: An Oral Biography.* New York: St. Martin's Press, 1983. A series of interviews conducted during the last two years of Snow's life. Not indexed, but contains frequent references to *The Conscience of the Rich* and related matters. A brief conversation with Lady Snow (Pamela Hansford Johnson) is recorded in an appendix. Includes some photographs.

Heptonstall, Geoffrey. "Venturing the Real: The Significance of C. P. Snow." *Contemporary Review* 290, no. 1689 (Summer, 2008): 224-232. Offers a brief overview of Snow's life and literary career. Critiques some of his novels and defines his style as a combination of scientific realism and the description of sensory experience that is typical of modernist literature.

Karl, Frederick F. *C. P. Snow: The Politics of Conscience.* Carbondale: Southern Illinois University Press, 1965. The chapter on *The Conscience of the Rich* concentrates primarily on three characters: Charles and Lewis are discussed as "Snow's alternatives to the typical existential hero," and Leonard as a reactionary who, although charming, is essentially a fool. Includes a fictional chronology based on the first eight books of the *Strangers and Brothers* series.

Ramanathan, Suguna. *The Novels of C. P. Snow: A Critical Introduction.* London: Macmillan, 1978. Short but insightful. Although references to *The Conscience of the Rich* are scattered, provides a good overview of Snow's novels and useful comments about his originality. Includes bibliography.

Shusterman, David. *C. P. Snow.* Rev. ed. Boston: Twayne, 1991. A good starting point for the study of Snow. Three chapters are devoted to the *Strangers and Brothers* series. Contains biographical information, including a chronology, extensive notes and references, and a select bibliography, with annotations for secondary sources.

The Conscious Lovers

Author: Sir Richard Steele (1672-1729)
First produced: 1722; first published, 1723
Type of work: Drama
Type of plot: Sentimental
Time of plot: Early eighteenth century
Locale: London

Principal characters:
YOUNG BEVIL, a young gentleman of fortune
SIR JOHN BEVIL, young Bevil's father
INDIANA DANVERS, a young woman befriended by young Bevil
LUCINDA SEALAND, engaged to young Bevil
MR. SEALAND, Lucinda's father
MR. MYRTLE, young Bevil's friend, in love with Lucinda Sealand
MR. CIMBERTON, a suitor for Lucinda Sealand's hand

The Story:

Young Bevil, a gentleman of some fortune, is engaged to marry the daughter of Mr. Sealand. Although he is not in love with the woman, he agrees to marry her at his father's request. On the day of the marriage, however, there is some doubt that the marriage will take place, for the bride's father discovers that Bevil is paying the bills of a young woman he brought back from France. Fearing that the young woman, called Indiana, is Bevil's mistress, Mr. Sealand does not want his daughter to marry a man who keeps another woman.

The father does not know that Bevil sent a letter to Lucinda Sealand that gives her his permission to break off the marriage at that late date. Bevil did so because he knows that Lucinda is really in love with his friend, Mr. Myrtle, and because he himself wants to marry Indiana. After the letter is sent, Sir John's valet tells young Bevil that the marriage will probably be broken by Mr. Sealand. Bevil then confides in the servant that Indiana is the daughter of the British merchant named Danvers, who disappeared in the Indies soon after the ship in which Indiana, her mother, and her aunt were traveling to join him was captured by French privateers.

Myrtle then arrives at Bevil's apartment and tells his friend that a third marriage arrangement is in the wind that day. Mrs. Sealand is trying to wed her daughter to Mr. Cimberton, a queer fellow with peculiar ideas about wives and a great deal of money; Mrs. Sealand is willing to overlook strange notions in favor of the fortune her daughter might marry. The only thing that prevents the marriage contract from being settled that day is the nonappearance of Cimberton's wealthy uncle. Bevil suggests to Myrtle that he and Bevil's servant Tom, an artful rascal, disguise themselves as lawyers and go to the Sealand house in an attempt to prevent the marriage or, at least, to find out what can be done to keep the contract from being signed.

Meanwhile Indiana's aunt cautions her against the attentions of Bevil. The aunt cannot believe, despite Indiana's reports of Bevil's behavior, that the young man is helping Indiana and paying her bills without intending to make her his mistress. As they continue to argue, Bevil appears. Indiana tries to learn in private conversation what his intentions are, for she loves him very much. He replies only that he does everything for her because he finds pleasure in doing good. Wanting him to love her, she feels rather hurt. Secretly, Bevil promised himself that he would never tell her of his affection as long as his father did not give permission for a marriage to her.

At the Sealand house, in the meantime, Lucinda is subjected to the humiliation of an inspection by Cimberton, who in company with Mrs. Sealand looks at Lucinda as he might look at a prize mare he is buying for his stable. While they talk over her good and bad points, Myrtle and Bevil's servant, disguised as lawyers, put in their appearance. They learn very little, except that Mrs. Sealand is determined to wed her daughter to Cimberton as soon as possible. Upon leaving the house, Bevil's servant receives a letter from Lucinda for his master. Myrtle, who suspects duplicity on Bevil's part, sends him a challenge to a duel.

Myrtle appears at Bevil's apartment a few minutes after his challenge. Bevil refuses at first to be a party to a duel, but when Myrtle heaps many insults upon Bevil and Indiana, calling the latter Bevil's whore, his language so enrages Bevil that he says he will fight. A moment later Bevil regains control of himself. Realizing how foolish a duel will be, he shows Myrtle the letter from Lucinda, which only thanks Bevil for giving her permission to break off the wedding.

Sir John and Mr. Sealand meet. Mr. Sealand refuses to go on with the marriage that day until he satisfies himself as to the relationship between Indiana and Bevil. Sir John agrees to wait until the investigation is complete.

Bevil and Myrtle decide to make one more attempt to terminate the possible marital arrangements of Mrs. Sealand for her daughter. Myrtle disguises himself as Cimberton's uncle and goes to the Sealand house. There Lucinda discovers his identity, but she keeps it from her mother and the unwelcome suitor.

At the same time Mr. Sealand goes to Indiana's home. As soon as he enters the house Indiana's aunt recognizes him as someone she knew before, but she decides not to reveal herself to him. Questioned, Indiana says that she was befriended by Bevil but that he made no effort to seduce her. Her deportment and her narrative assure Mr. Sealand that there is no illicit relationship between the two. When she finishes her story, telling of her lost father and the capture of herself, her mother, and her aunt by French privateers, he asks her father's name. She tells him it is Danvers. Mr. Sealand then announces that Indiana is his long-lost daughter, and he identifies some trinkets she has as those belonging to his first wife and their child. When Indiana's aunt appears, identifying herself as Mr. Sealand's sister, he recognizes her at once. He tells them that he changed his name after undergoing certain difficulties in the Indies.

Mr. Sealand readily agrees to a marriage between his newfound daughter and Bevil. At that moment Sir John, young Bevil, and a group from the Sealand house arrive. Sir John, hearing the news, is pleased at the prospect of a marriage between Indiana and his son. Bevil, anxious to aid his friend Myrtle, then requests that a marriage be arranged between his friend and Lucinda. Cimberton tries to intercede on his own behalf until Mr. Sealand informs him that only half his fortune will now go to Lucinda. Cimberton, more anxious for the money than for the woman, departs in a huff, whereupon Myrtle, who still disguised as Cimberton's uncle, throws off the disguise and claims Lucinda for his bride.

Critical Evaluation:
The opening night on November 7, 1722, at Drury Lane of *The Conscious Lovers* proved to be an important event in

the development of English drama, marking the end of Restoration comedy and the beginning of sentimental comedy. The play was a success as indicated by what was then considered a long initial run—eighteen nights.

Sir Richard Steele is probably most widely acclaimed for his journalism in *The Tatler*, *The Spectator*, *The Guardian*, and *The Theatre* and for his contribution to the periodical essay. His appointment to the governorship of Drury Lane by George I enabled him, however, to maintain close contact with theatrical affairs. When Steele in this controlling position came under attack for failing to support new plays, he undertook *The Theatre*, which appeared twice weekly from January 2, 1720, to April 5, 1720. This periodical was closely allied to *The Conscious Lovers*, which was at that time called *Sir John Edgar*.

For his spokesman in *The Theatre*, Steele chose Sir John Edgar, the title character of the unfinished play on which he was working for approximately ten years. Sir John Edgar's son Harry, who appears in the periodical, is taken from his counterpart in the drama. Like the dramatic character, Harry has an overwhelming filial devotion and a reckless friend named Myrtle. In No. 3 of *The Theatre*, Steele again borrows from the play when he proposes a board of theatrical visitors that parallels in description several of the dramatic characters of the play—Mr. Sealand and his daughter Lucinda, Charles Myrtle, and Humphrey. *Sir John Edgar* was titled *The Conscious Lovers* shortly before it was produced, and Sir John Edgar and his son were renamed Sir John Bevil and Bevil Junior.

The Conscious Lovers has a threefold purpose. The first purpose, probably the least significant, is to attack the practice of dueling. That this was a subject of concern for Steele is apparent by its frequency as a topic in his periodical essays. Steele wished to promote the idea that a man who refused to duel was not a coward or a knave. A scene in act 4 between Bevil and Myrtle is designed to exemplify this theory.

Steele's second purpose is to justify the merchant as worthy of a high position in social circles. The merchant was much abused by Restoration dramatists. Steele was not the earliest author to make this point in dramatic form. *The Beaux Merchant*, a play "by a Clothier" identified as John Blanch, published in 1714, crusades for just recognition for merchants and precedes the production of *The Conscious Lovers*. In *The Conscious Lovers*, Steele's mouthpiece for this issue is apparently Mr. Sealand, who says in act 4: "We Merchants are a Species of Gentry, that have grown into the World this last Century, and are as honourable, and almost as useful, as you landed Folks, that have thought yourselves so much above us." Indeed, the two most despicable characters

of the play, Mr. Cimberton and Mrs. Sealand, suffer from the flaw Mr. Sealand points out—assumption of superiority by right of gentle birth.

The third purpose for writing *The Conscious Lovers* was, as Steele states in the prologue, "To chasten wit, and moralize the stage." In this endeavor Steele was taking up the cry for dramatic reform that was precipitated by the bawdiness and cynicism of Restoration comedy. Jeremy Collier's attack on the theater in 1698, titled *A Short View of the Immorality and Profaneness of the English Stage*, was widely read. Steele, however, held that the stage could serve a beneficial, educational purpose. On April 16, 1709, he wrote in *The Tatler* (No. 3), "I cannot be of the same opinion with my friends and fellow laborers, the Reformers of Manners, in their severity towards plays; but must allow, that a good play, acted before a well-bred audience, must raise very proper incitements to good behaviour, and be the most quick and most prevailing method of giving young people a turn of sense and breeding." Steele put his theory in motion with the production of *The Conscious Lovers*. That it was thought to achieve its purpose can be seen among other things in King George I's gift to Steele of five hundred guineas for the play's contribution to the reform of the stage.

The reform of the stage that Steele achieved came by replacing Restoration comedy with another type—sentimental comedy. The first attempt at this variety of comedy was made in 1696 with Colley Cibber's *Love's Last Shift*. The play, however, was tainted by bawdy Restoration dialogue and hypocrisy. Although Steele wrote other plays in this vein, it was not until *The Conscious Lovers* that a decisive turning point occurred and the sentimental drama seemed to find its place in the history of English drama. Sentimental drama is marked by a number of elements. One is the idea of the innate goodness of people rather than the idea of the depravity of the self that marks Restoration comedy. Second, sentimental comedy makes appeal to the emotions that surpasses the appeal to the intellect, again in direct opposition to Restoration comedy. Third, in sentimental comedy there is an obvious moral. Fourth, sentimental comedy makes an attempt to place the ideal in a realistic setting, which leads to a certain amount of improbability and exaggeration. Fifth, there is a stress upon pity and the evocation of tears. Sixth, there is a tendency to serious discussion of ethical questions. Seventh, there is an element of mystery, such as the lost child recovered, and, eighth, there are romantic love scenes.

Steele is also credited with establishing several character types that regularly appear in sentimental comedy: a man and maiden whose concepts of marriage are untainted by cynicism or contempt for the institution; the loyal friend; the debauchee redeemed in time for the fifth-act curtain; the rejected mistress who is reunited with her lover in marriage; and the loyal wife who, though tempted, remains virtuous. *The Conscious Lovers* has hints, if not fully formed representations, of both the characteristics and the characters of the sentimental comedy.

Steele's model for the new dramatic hero is young Bevil, who exudes innate goodness by his filial devotion, romantic love, gentlemanly behavior, and lack of narcissistic tendencies. He provides quite a contrast to the Restoration comedy hero. The comedy of the play is provided by Tom and Phillis, whom Steele worked into a farcical subplot at the suggestion of Cibber. Tom and Phillis imitate their social betters and thus provide a satirical look at the manners and customs of the time. More humor is provided by Cimberton, a character who recalls Restoration comedy. He boldly exhibits a self-love that blinds him to the true virtues of Lucinda and enables him to see her only as a means to his self-improvement. Steele's new play does not release itself completely from previous models, for Cimberton is the epitome of a Restoration character.

The influence of Steele's *The Conscious Lovers* went beyond England. When the first professional company of actors in America decided to move to New York from Williamsburg, they confronted considerable difficulty in obtaining a license to perform because of the Puritan influence in the area. Once they obtained the license, they chose a play from their repertory that they felt would satisfy the moral ethics of the Puritan community. Steele's *The Conscious Lovers*, billed as "a moral comedy," opened on September 17, 1753, was a success, and thus contributed to the beginning of theater in New York City. *The Conscious Lovers* was also significant to American theater in another way. The first play written by an American on a native subject and produced by professional actors was Royall Tyler's *The Contrast*, produced at the John Street Theatre on April 16, 1787, by the American Company. For the context of the play, Tyler borrowed heavily from *The Conscious Lovers*. Thus, *The Conscious Lovers* became not only noteworthy in the history of English theater but also instrumental in beginning the history of American theater.

"Critical Evaluation" by Phyllis E. Allran

Further Reading

Aitken, G. A. Introduction to *Richard Steele*, edited by G. A. Aitken. Westport, Conn.: Greenwood Press, 1968. Section 9 of this introduction to a collection of Steele's plays focuses on *The Conscious Lovers*, providing a production history and accounts of early performances. Discusses eighteenth century philosophical debates about the play.

Bernbaum, Ernest. *The Drama of Sensibility*. Gloucester, Mass.: Peter Smith, 1958. Traces eighteenth century English drama from the rakish Restoration comedy to the sentimental comedy exemplified by Steele's plays. Discusses *The Conscious Lovers* as a cultural artifact and provides interesting information about the play's debt to Terence.

Hynes, Peter. "Richard Steele and the Genealogy of Sentimental Drama: A Reading of *The Conscious Lovers*." *Papers on Language and Literature* 40, no. 2 (Spring, 2004): 142-166. Argues that in its time, the play was a significant departure from traditional comic forms. Analyzes the innovative structure and metaphorical resources of the play. Recounts the debate that was engendered by Steele's determination to change the ground rules of contemporary drama.

Loftis, John. *Comedy and Society from Congreve to Fielding*. Stanford, Calif.: Stanford University Press, 1959. Discusses the changes in English comedy resulting from social upheavals in eighteenth century England. Places *The Conscious Lovers* in the middle of this social change. Treats the play as a comedy of ideas with a definite Whiggish bias and suggests that political ideas interfere with the dramatic development of the play.

_____. *Steele at Drury Lane*. Westport, Conn.: Greenwood Press, 1973. Detailed discussion of *The Conscious Lovers*. Discusses the play as the culmination of Steele's efforts to reform the English stage. Examines the play's origins and production history, analyzes the controversy over the play, and defines sentimental comedy as a genre best exemplified by *The Conscious Lovers*.

Steele, Richard. *The Conscious Lovers*. Edited and with an introduction by Shirley Strum Kenny. Lincoln: University of Nebraska Press, 1968. The introduction places the play in its cultural, historical, philosophical, and theatrical contexts. Describes the play as a moral comedy that features good-natured characters and shows the influence of Steele's work on the plays of Oliver Goldsmith and Richard Sheridan.

Zunshine, Lisa. "Bastard Daughters and Foundling Heroines: Rewriting Illegitimacy in *The Conscious Lovers*." In *Bastards and Foundlings: Illegitimacy in Eighteenth-Century England*. Columbus: Ohio State University Press, 2005. Discusses the depiction of foundling heroines in the play within the context of Enlightenment England's obsessive attempts to justify, regulate, and modify the social practices surrounding bastardy.

The Conservationist

Author: Nadine Gordimer (1923-   )
First published: 1974
Type of work: Novel
Type of plot: Psychological realism
Time of plot: 1970's
Locale: South Africa

Principal characters:
MEHRING, a white pig-iron magnate and owner of a farm
TERRY MEHRING, his son
JACOBUS, the black foreman of the farm
THE DEBEERS, Mehring's Afrikaner neighbors
ANTONIA, Mehring's liberal lover

The Story:

South African pig-iron industrialist Mehring returns for a weekend visit to his farm on the Transvaal to find, to his dismay, a group of children playing with a clutch of guinea eggs. Suddenly, his foreman, Jacobus, rushes up to tell him that the body of a black man has been discovered on the farm.

Mehring bought his farm because owning land is something a person of his race and class should do; the farm would be an investment, and it also could be a place for amorous escapades. Mehring would rather not be bothered with the problem of a dead body, which is simply covered and placed in a shallow, unmarked grave by white police. The police tell Mehring they will deal with the matter later.

With an image of the dead body always in the back of his mind, Mehring begins to reflect on his relationship with his former lover, Antonia, the leftist he had to spirit out of the country when her life had become endangered. He is haughty about the misdirected energies of her liberalism, yet he continues to ruminate about her. Though he dismisses her honest evaluations of his society—for whom money and industrial development are the only gods—his recalling her evaluations so vividly seems to imply a growing inability to obliterate the truth.

Mehring encounters his Afrikaner neighbors, the DeBeers, who borrow his truck for a trip into town. During their visit, he grudgingly contrasts their solidity and good-naturedness with his own solitude.

Mehring begins to reflect on the farmworkers' homes and the "illegal" Indian shanty store. The store is illegal because it is on land set aside for whites. In one of these stores a farmworker named Solomon is attacked by two men and left for dead in Mehring's third pasture, the same place the dead body lies buried, thus establishing a frightening mythology for the third pasture. Then a fire erupts on the farm, devastating everything from the store to the DeBeers's land. Mehring returns to the farm after the fire and finds himself morbidly curious about what happened to the dead body in the fire. He tries to accept the idea that his surviving possessions are sufficient for him.

William, an African who has been patiently saving his money in a Christmas club, confronts the South African Indians who employ his wife, Dorcas, because they have taken money from her paycheck, presumably to pay for her purchases. William's frustration bursts forth when he says that all "Indias" must leave the country, that they will be tossed away with the whites. Juxtaposed with William's righteous indignation is Mehring's molestation of a Portuguese girl aboard an airliner in flight between Europe and South Africa. Though he occasionally expresses fear that his degenerate act will be revealed, he never expresses guilt or remorse.

Mehring's sixteen-year-old son, Terry, visits the farm. Clearly liked by the farmworkers, and not his father's son in terms of his sexuality or his feelings about required military service, Terry's stay is something of a failure for Mehring. In fact, the only communion Mehring seems to experience is a delusory oneness with the ancestors and the land, after Terry leaves.

Mehring encounters the daughter of one of his friends in a coffee bar, beginning his downturn. His weak attempt to seduce her is followed by his discovery that her father has just committed suicide. To avoid the funeral, Mehring escapes to his farm for the holidays. There, he manufactures an illusory New Year's Eve meeting in the veld with the farm foreman, Jacobus, a meeting in which the two share a moment of closeness, albeit one in which Mehring is undoubtedly the superior.

A cyclone hits while Mehring is in Johannesburg. The flooding is widespread, killing a couple who float away in their car on the same road Mehring frequents. The farm has been isolated from everyone for some time, but Mehring, upon his return, finds that Jacobus and his crew have handled everything well. Mehring believes the farmhands should be able to manipulate the water somehow so it will drain more quickly, but Jacobus knows this to be impossible. In their survey of the damage, they discover that the body in the third pasture had risen from its grave because of the floodwaters.

The image of the body takes hold of Mehring's imagination once again as he drives back to town. He reluctantly picks up a young hitchhiker. Eventually, they arrive at an old mine dump and begin to have sex. A man encounters them, frightening Mehring. Suddenly, lost in his fear, he runs, abandoning the hitchhiker to save himself. While running, he thinks to himself, "they can have it, the whole four hundred acres."

Mehring, flying off to some foreign country, abandons Jacobus and the farmworkers, leaving them to deal with the body. The farmworkers find a coffin and a cloth covering, conduct a beautiful ritual with dance and hymns, and shed tears for a man they did not even know.

Critical Evaluation:

Near the end of *The Conservationist*, Mehring is sitting outside on his farm on New Year's Eve. As he watches the fireworks of the DeBeers and hears the raucous celebrations of his own farmworkers, he also perches precariously on the edge of a tremendous storm—both literally and figuratively. He reflects that

> it's possible, just once, on a night like this, to sit at the point where its [the night's] element ends and the absolutely calm, full-moon-lit element begins. It is really two nights at once; just as midnight will bisect two years.

This moment in the novel perfectly captures the Bakhtinian dialogic quality that many critics see in Nadine Gordimer's fiction. It is the fault line that anthropologist Claude Lévi-Strauss sees as simultaneously bifurcating and bringing together past and present and time and space, illuminating and making sense of the real and psychological landscapes. For this work, Gordimer was awarded the Nobel Prize in Literature in 1991, and for *The Conservationist*, she earned a Booker Prize in Fiction in 1974.

Momentarily teetering on the fulcrum of history, Mehring becomes representative of the pragmatic, coldhearted South African who can see the coming change but has no need or desire to end the injustice of apartheid. Indeed, he becomes the colonizer, the capitalist, and the possessor, a relatively bloodless twentieth century Kurtz. Like novelist Joseph Conrad's demonic character, Mehring (whose name is German in origin) sees everything as his, though the progress of the novel chronicles the loss of each of these possessions: his wife, mistress, son, and land. Also like Kurtz, Mehring has a complete lack of sexual restraint, seen most vividly in his molestation of the Portuguese girl on the flight from Europe to South Africa.

Ironically, the final two encounters with women (or girls) in *The Conservationist* are both complete failures for Mehring. His attempt in the coffee bar to pick up the daughter of his associate, and his reluctant encounter with the female hitchhiker who takes him to the cyanide dump to have sex, is foiled by the appearance of either police officers and thugs, who each question Mehring's reasons for being with the women/girls. In the end, his failed sexual encounter with an aggressive prostitute (he even imagines her to be "coloured") leads him to spiral into a momentary lunacy and to realize that he is incapable of blocking the incipient changes about to upset the balance of power in his world. Before leaving South Africa, Mehring's final injunction to Jacobus is to deal with the dead body on the farm, symbolizing Mehring's relinquishing of real power to the Africans.

Symbols are significant in this novel, which is structured to a great degree as an interior monologue, or an interior dialogue between Mehring and any number of other characters. The major symbol in the book is Mehring's futile attempt to possess the landscape. The dead body found on the farm becomes the final and most profound symbol of the Africans' relationship to nature and to Mehring's own disconnect. Through the course of the novel, the body is buried in a shallow grave and seemingly forgotten for months, only to reemerge after devastating floods engulf the farm and cut it off from the rest of the landscape. In the end, the farmworkers give the body a dignified, ritualistic funeral. "He took possession of this earth, theirs," Gordimer writes, and the body is now "one of them," reestablishing a hierarchy that many critics maintain is a prophecy of the end of apartheid.

Another important symbol is the egg, a symbol that appears throughout the novel: the guinea eggs; the peace sign in the shape of an egg that a young Indian painted on a store wall; and the useless alabaster egg Terry buys for his mother. Other symbols include roads and cars: Whereas whites own cars, Africans and Afrikaners lack access to reliable modes of transportation.

Nature, another significant symbol in the novel, takes control and even reveals the unstable dominance of whites. Because of the terrible storm, Mehring's farm is damaged and roads are washed out, leading to the drowning of a white couple in their car (a symbol of white power). Also, the flood that replenishes nature after first destroying it brings back to life the repressed forces that will not remain buried.

Jaquelyn Weeks Walsh

Further Reading

Clingman, Stephen. *The Novels of Nadine Gordimer: History from the Inside.* 2d ed. Amherst: University of Massachusetts Press, 1992. Considered one of the most important book-length studies of Gordimer's work, this book examines Gordimer's novels in light of her earlier South African works. Focuses on the historical consciousness that characterizes her novels.

Cooke, John. *The Novels of Nadine Gordimer: Private Lives/ Public Landscapes*. Baton Rouge: Louisiana State University Press, 1985. Cooke claims that Gordimer moved from a Eurocentric writing style to one in which the African landscape takes on a life of its own. This represents a psychological movement in Gordimer, which Cooke believes had its beginnings in her mother's possessiveness.

Ettin, Andre Vogel. *Betrayals of the Body Politic: The Literary Commitments of Nadine Gordimer*. Charlottesville: University Press of Virginia, 1995. Examines all of Gordimer's genres of writing and addresses the recurring themes: betrayal, politics of the family, the concept of homeland, ethnicity, and feminism. Also discusses her belief that the personal and the political are inseparable.

Head, Dominic. *Nadine Gordimer*. New York: Cambridge University Press, 1994. Contextualizes Gordimer's body of work historically and politically. Finds in her work an increasing literary quality and an emphasis on the politicization of the body and the geopolitical ramifications of apartheid.

Newman, Judie. *Nadine Gordimer*. 2d ed. London: Routledge and Kegan Paul, 1990. The first book-length study of Gordimer by a woman. Addresses the theme of gender in Gordimer's works in light of her insistence that she is not a "feminist" writer. Newman also examines the significant themes and motifs that link Gordimer's novels, including racism, the abuse of political power, and sex.

Smith, Rowland. *Critical Essays on Nadine Gordimer*. Boston: G. K. Hall, 1990. Smith's introduction examines early reviews of Gordimer's work. The sixteen essays here trace the history of Gordimer as a writer and discuss how her work addresses the topics of women and women's roles.

Temple-Thurston, Barbara. *Nadine Gordimer Revisited*. New York: Twayne, 1999. Good introductory study of the author and her works. *The Conservationist* is among the novels discussed. Includes a chronology, a bibliography, and an index.

Uledi-Kamanga, Brighton J. *Cracks in the Wall: Nadine Gordimer's Fiction and the Irony of Apartheid*. Trenton, N.J.: Africa World Press, 2002. Presents a generally chronological discussion of Gordimer's works, with emphasis on the novels. Focuses on Gordimer's use of irony and her work in the context of South African politics.

Uraizee, Joya. *This Is No Place for a Woman: Nadine Gordimer, Nayantara Saghal, Buchi Emecheta, and the Politics of Gender*. Trenton, N.J.: Africa World Press, 2000. Places Gordimer within the context of postcolonial writing. Thematically organized chapters address the works, including *The Conservationist*.

The Consolation of Philosophy

Author: Boethius (c. 480-524)

First transcribed: De consolatione philosophiae,
    523 C.E. (English translation, late ninth century)

Type of work: Philosophy

The Consolation of Philosophy by Anicius Manlius Severinus Boethius is the most significant and final work to come from the thinker known as the last of the Romans, the first of the Scholastics. It is the author's most significant work because it draws on a lifetime of studying the writings of Plato, Aristotle, Porphyry, Proclus, Plotinus, and other classical figures; it is a piece, therefore, that proved to be critical to medieval philosophers of Christianity throughout Europe, as well as to such literary figures as Dante Alighieri and Geoffrey Chaucer. For, while *The Consolation of Philosophy* contains elements of Aristotelianism, Stoicism, and Neoplatonism, it is also ruled by the concept of a personal God to whom one can pray and from whom one might seek salvation.

It is Boethius's final work, written during his imprisonment in Pavia as he awaited execution under the authority of the Ostrogothic king Theodoric for the crime of treason against Pope John I. *The Consolation of Philosophy*, then, belongs to the ancient genre of Greek and Roman philosophy known as the *consolatio*, which is designed to provide the soul with a kind of moral and spiritual medication in times of distress. This aspect of the work had an influence on a number of literary masterworks of the Middle Ages, including Dante's *La divina commedia* (c. 1320; *The Divine Comedy*, 1802) and the fourteenth century Middle English *Piers Plowman*. Boethius's distress of the soul was extreme, since he had fallen from a position of favor in the Roman court to a position of disgrace after being unjustly accused of treason. This context of the work's authorship lends it an aspect of urgency and seriousness that many philosophical and literary texts do not have.

Divided into five books, with thirty-nine poems interspersed throughout the discourse, *The Consolation of Philosophy* is written in the form of a dialogue between Boethius and the feminine spirit of Philosophy, who visits him in his cell. The poems serve a purpose similar to that of the chorus in Greek tragedy: They summarize and at times advance the discussion between Boethius and the figure of Philosophy. In his commentaries on Porphyry, Boethius had maintained that philosophy, being the love of wisdom, brings to the mind the "reward of its own divinity" and thereby returns it to its own nature. This is the role of Philosophy in *The Consolation of Philosophy* as well, where Philosophy opens up to the author the path to God that belongs to the soul of the rational being. Philosophy conceives God to be the rational Being of all beings, belonging to the invisible and infinite realm of reason that transcends the finite realm of the material world. The soul that ascends to the realm of reason frees itself from the confines of matter—including the confines of prison walls— and therefore from suffering to enjoy the true freedom of the good that inheres in God alone.

Philosophy allows the soul to ascend through a process not only of education but also of remembering. This feature of the work reflects the influence on Boethius of Plato's doctrine of *anamnesis*, or recollection. Other important influences seen in the work include the idea of fate, as developed by Proclus, and the notion of God as the center of all things, which was expounded by Plotinus. This combination of Proclus and Plotinus proves to be especially important in Boethius's discussion of the distinction between fate and providence. Both of the earlier thinkers maintained that essential to the soul's approach to God is its divorce from material things: The movement toward is a movement inward, which philosophy reveals to be a movement upward.

Book 1 of *The Consolation of Philosophy* opens with a poem about the despair into which Boethius had fallen after fate robbed him of worldly power and position and cast him at death's door. The poem no sooner ends, however, than the awe-inspiring figure of Philosophy appears and casts out the muses of poetry. Boethius describes Philosophy as a "physician" who comes to heal him of the sickness in his soul by showing him who he truly is. He tries to justify himself before Philosophy by pointing out his good intentions and by complaining about the prosperity of the wicked. Philosophy answers him with an argument that true freedom and wellbeing come with the submission to God's will. Therefore, she says, the source of Boethius's illness lies not in having been abandoned by God but in having forgotten his own true, rational nature, which is not subject to the winds of fortune.

In book 2, Philosophy follows up her remarks with a discussion of the evils of turning to fortune as a basis for our understanding of ourselves and the world. It is not bad fortune that is at the root of his suffering, she explains to Boethius, but misguided belief (a principle held by the Stoic thinker Marcus Aurelius). To be happy, then he must alter his belief, for example, that the good amounts to good fortune. In order to do that, he must determine that happiness is to be found only within, not outside, himself. For Boethius, this "within oneself" means within one's rational nature as it comes from God. It is impossible to be happy without being who one is, a rational being created in the image of God. Since fortune pertains to what is external to one and external to one's nature, it is a false source of happiness.

The question of what characterizes genuine happiness is pursued further in book 3. Here, Philosophy affirms that the good and only the good distinguishes true happiness, since the good alone is inherently valuable. Neither money nor power, neither fame nor security, falls into the category of the good, because all of these derive their value from their relation to something else in the world; they are a means to something else, while the good is an end unto itself. As for the value of the good, it is determined by the God who alone is good and who alone is the source of all that is good. If the perfect good is true happiness, then, says Philosophy, true happiness is to be found only in God, who is the perfect good: God is the essence of happiness. From this claim it follows that happiness is possessed through the possession of divinity; where the divine image is manifest in the human being, happiness also is manifest. Therefore "the good itself and happiness are identical," and anyone who is happy is in possession of the divine image.

While Boethius is receptive to these arguments of Philosophy, in book 4 he is still unsettled by the fact that evil often goes unpunished. Philosophy assures him, however, that evil never goes unpunished or virtue unrewarded, suggesting that the world that has come from God's hand is the best of all possible worlds. She demonstrates her claim by arguing that all human activity derives from a combination of will and power and that all people will the good, since all people desire happiness. Those who fail to obtain the good do so because they lack a certain power; people who succumb to the lures of pleasure and vice, for example, do so because they are too weak to exercise self-control. Since to be good is to be who one is, those who are too weak to be good are too weak to be: To lose one's goodness is to lose one's being. Hence those who are so weak that they sink to doing evil are punished with non-being; similarly, those who have the power to do good are rewarded, for to be good is to be happy, and happiness is the greatest of all rewards. Philosophy thus responds to Boethius not by appealing to an external system of behavior modification but by positing a universal, internal, and necessary condition in which the soul suffers what it inflicts.

Having determined that reward and punishment are part of the inescapable condition of rational beings, Philosophy goes on to show that a good power rules the world, since, with the inevitable punishment of evil and rewarding of good, everything happens in a just and good manner. This design according to which all things transpire she calls providence, which is "divine reason itself." Providence, she explains, is the plan that derives from God's understanding, whereas fate is the unfolding of that plan through the order of things in the world. Human beings, according to this conception, may escape the rule of fate by divorcing themselves from the things of the world and using their own reason to draw near to divine reason. Those who cling to providence are free from ill fortune, since their happiness depends not on the twists and turns of fate but on the tranquillity and truth of reason.

In book 5, Boethius concludes *The Consolation of Philosophy* with a discussion of free will that arises from Philosophy's earlier remarks on fate and providence. Boethius begins by suggesting that there is a contradiction between God's foreknowledge and freedom of the will. Worse than a contradiction, he maintains, there is an injustice at work here, since it is unjust to punish people for doing evil when they cannot do otherwise. In addition, argues Boethius, such a condition renders prayer useless and hope pointless, since there is no hope of changing what is preordained. Philosophy replies by pointing out that foreknowledge does not result in predestination; to know what will happen is not to make it happen. Because God is eternal, she adds, all things and events from all times are simultaneously present; since God is above the realm of cause and effect, which is the realm of time, he does not cause anything to happen. What God knows, he knows necessarily, but the necessity of his knowing about the course of events does not imply the necessity of their happening.

Boethius ends his work by declaring that the key to understanding everything that Philosophy sets forth is the cultivation of virtue, for the cultivation of virtue takes people beyond the material world and into the realm of reason and divinity, where they become who they are by becoming good. The one necessity that God imposes upon humanity is the necessity to be good. In this, Boethius tells himself, lies the essence of humanity's being.

David Patterson

Further Reading

Barrett, Helen M. *Boethius: Some Aspects of His Times and Work.* 1940. Reprint. New York: Russell and Russell, 1965. This book, one of the older works on Boethius, provides a solid historical survey, sets Boethius firmly in this context, and interprets the scanty details of his life in a balanced and sensible way.

Chadwick, Henry. *Boethius: The Consolations of Music, Logic, Theology, and Philosophy.* New York: Oxford University Press, 1998. Unlike other writers, who have tended to concentrate on the Christian, the poet, the philosopher, or the educational theorist, Chadwick aims to show Boethius's career as a unified whole. He has succeeded in writing one of the most comprehensive books about Boethius's life and work.

Kaylor, Noel Harold, Jr., and Philip Edward Philips. *New Directions in Boethian Studies.* Kalamazoo: Medieval Institute Publications, Western Michigan University, 2007. Collection of essays analyzing both the Latin version and the vernacular translation of the text and assessing Boethius's place in art, literary history, religion, and mythography.

Lerer, Seth. *Boethius and Dialogue: Literary Method in "The Consolation of Philosophy."* Princeton, N.J.: Princeton University Press, 1985. Discusses the tradition of dialogue in the works of Cicero, Augustine, and Fulgentius and relates that tradition to *The Consolation of Philosophy.* Examines the function of the poems in that work and the use of dialogue as a means of arriving at truth.

Marenbon, John. *Boethius.* New York: Oxford University Press, 2003. Concise introduction to Boethius's works, with three chapters devoted to discussion and interpretation of *The Consolation of Philosophy.*

Means, Michael H. *The Consolatio Genre in Medieval English Literature.* Gainesville: University Press of Florida, 1972. Explores the significance of Boethius's *The Consolation of Philosophy* as a prototype for the consolatio genre in medieval English literature. Also examines the influence of the work on Dante's *Divine Comedy, Piers Plowman*, and other works.

Pieper, Josef. *Scholasticism: Personalities and Problems of Medieval Philosophy*. South Bend, Ind.: St. Augustine's Press, 2001. The author argues that Boethius, a century after Saint Augustine, still lived intellectually within classical philosophy and politically within the Roman Empire, although his listeners and readers did not. Boethius, Pieper notes, was the first thinker to turn to those who had come from the north into the ancient world.

Reiss, Edmund. *Boethius*. Boston: Twayne, 1982. Reiss argues the case against accepting too literally the autobiographical details in what he regards as a highly polished work of fictional art. He tends to reject the assumption that the quotations and other specific knowledge demonstrated in *The Consolation of Philosophy* constitute a feat of memory by a prisoner without access to a library.

Relihan, Joel C. *The Prisoner's Philosophy: Life and Death in Boethius's "Consolation."* With a contribution on the medieval Boethius by William E. Heise. Notre Dame, Ind.: University of Notre Dame Press, 2007. Reilhan maintains *The Consolation of Philosophy* is a Christian work in which Boetheius emphasizes the limits of pagan philosophy.

Scott, Jamie S. *Christians and Tyrants: The Prison Testimonies of Boethius, Thomas More, and Dietrich Bonhoeffer*. New York: Peter Lang, 1995. A collection of material from three philosophical giants that was produced while they were imprisoned.

Consuelo

Author: George Sand (1804-1876)
First published: 1842-1843 (English translation, 1846)
Type of work: Novel
Type of plot: Historical
Time of plot: Eighteenth century
Locale: Venice, Bohemia, and Vienna

Principal characters:
CONSUELO, a singer
ANZOLETO, her betrothed
PORPORA, her music master and godfather
COUNT RUDOLSTADT, a Bohemian nobleman
ALBERT, his son
CORILLA, Consuelo's rival
JOSEPH HAYDN, a composer

The Story:

At the church of the Mendicanti in Venice, Consuelo is the most gifted of all the pupils of the famous teacher, Porpora. Consuelo is a poor orphan child, and Porpora makes her his goddaughter. Before the death of her mother, Consuelo promises that she will one day become betrothed to Anzoleto, another poor musician of Venice.

Through the efforts of Anzoleto, Consuelo is engaged as the prima donna at the theater of Count Zustiniani, replacing Corilla, who also was Porpora's student. Consuelo is a great success, but Anzoleto, who was also engaged in the theater at the insistence of Consuelo, is not much of a musician and is not well received. Anzoleto, afraid that he will be discharged, pretends to be in love with Corilla, thinking that he will be safe if both singers are in love with him. Porpora never liked Anzoleto, and at last he contrives to have Consuelo visit Corilla's home. When they find Anzoleto there, Consuelo is so hurt that she leaves Venice at once, vowing that she will never set foot on the stage again and renouncing the false Anzoleto forever.

From Venice, Consuelo goes to Bohemia, where she is engaged by Count Rudolstadt as a companion for his niece, Amelia. This young noblewoman is betrothed to young Count Albert Rudolstadt, but she fears him because he seems to be insane. Albert often has visions in which he sees scenes of the past and often imagines himself to be the reincarnated body of some person long dead. When Albert first hears Consuelo sing, he calls her by her name, even though she took another name to hide her unhappy life in Venice. Albert tells Consuelo and the whole family that she is his salvation—that she was sent to remove the curse from him. Consuelo is bewildered.

Albert often disappears for many days at a time; no one knows where he goes. Consuelo follows him but can never find his hiding place until the night she descends into a deep well and finds steps leading to a grotto where Albert and an idiot called Zdenko spend many days together. Zdenko loves Albert more than his own life; when he sees Consuelo coming into the well, he thinks she wants to harm Albert, and he almost kills her. Consuelo escapes from Zdenko and finds Albert. After she speaks soothingly to him, he ceases his mad talk and seems to regain normal behavior. She persuades him to return to his family and not to go back to the grotto without her. Albert tells Consuelo that he loves her and needs her, but, although she no longer loves Anzoleto, she cannot forget how she once loved him, and she asks Albert to wait a while for her answer.

Albert's father and the rest of the family are grateful to Consuelo for helping restore Albert to his senses. The father, Count Rudolstadt, even tells Consuelo that he will give his consent to a marriage between his son and her, for the old gentleman believes that only Consuelo can keep his son sane. While Consuelo is debating whether she loves Albert and could accept the honor, Anzoleto, deserting Corilla, comes to the castle in search of her. Consuelo slips away from the castle, leaving a note for Albert. She goes to Vienna to rejoin Porpora.

Without funds, Consuelo has great difficulty in reaching Vienna and walks most of the way. In her travels, she meets Joseph Haydn, a young composer who is on his way to the castle to find her; he hopes he can persuade her to take him to Porpora, under whom he wishes to study. Dressed as a peasant boy, Consuelo accompanies Haydn to Vienna. One night they take refuge in the home of a canon of the church. While they are there, Corilla comes to the door, seeking a safe place to give birth to her child. Consuelo has pity on her former enemy and takes Corilla to an inn, where she helps to deliver the child. From a maid, Consuelo learns that Anzoleto is the father. Corilla does not recognize Consuelo, who continues to wear the disguise of a boy.

When Joseph and Consuelo finally reach Vienna, the girl finds Porpora overjoyed to see her again. Haydn becomes Porpora's pupil, and Consuelo sings for the empress. Then Corilla, who also comes to Vienna and learns that it is Consuelo who befriended her during the birth of her child, arranges for Consuelo to sing in the theater there. Corilla hopes to seal the lips of Consuelo, who knows of the illegitimate child and knows that Corilla abandoned the baby in the home of the canon who gave Consuelo and Joseph shelter. Anzoleto is never heard from again.

Consuelo writes to Albert, telling him that she is almost ready to return to him, but Porpora intercepts the letter and destroys it. Consuelo waits in vain for a reply from Albert. At last, Porpora tells her that he received a letter from the count,

saying that he does not wish his son to marry an actress and that Albert concurs in the decision. Consuelo so trusts her godfather that she believes him, not realizing how ambitious Porpora is for her musical career.

Porpora goes with Consuelo to accept a theater engagement in Berlin. On the way, they meet the brother of Count Rudolstadt. Albert asks his father to have someone at a certain place on the road on a specific day and at a specific hour, saying that the messenger is to bring the travelers he will meet there to the castle at once. Albert is very ill, and Consuelo persuades Porpora to allow her to go to Albert. When she arrives at the castle, she learns that his father received a letter from Porpora saying that he will never consent to a marriage between Consuelo and Albert and that Consuelo herself renounced Albert. It was the deathblow. Albert grows very weak and begs Consuelo to marry him before he dies so that his soul can find peace; he still believes that only through Consuelo can he find salvation. The marriage vows are repeated, and Albert, crying that he is now saved, dies in Consuelo's arms.

Consuelo stays with her husband all night, leaving him only when he is carried to his bier. She then bids Albert's family good-bye, refusing to accept any of the fortune that is now hers. Then she leaves the castle and goes to join Porpora in Berlin, where Frederick the Great himself worships both her beauty and her art.

Critical Evaluation:

George Sand is important in literary history for being a pioneer in the development of the category of fiction known as the romantic novel. Some modern classics in the genre are Daphne du Maurier's *Rebecca* (1938) and Margaret Mitchell's famous Civil War novel *Gone with the Wind* (1936). Earlier classics in the genre include Emily Brontë's *Wuthering Heights* (1847) and Charlotte Brontë's *Jane Eyre* (1847). It is interesting to note that *Consuelo* contains some of the elements that have come to be practically indispensable to such novels. Two of the most popular elements are the Cinderella theme and the theme of a woman torn between love for two different men. Sand uses both in *Consuelo*, the story of a poor girl who marries a handsome aristocrat and becomes a wealthy countess. The heroine is torn between love for the passionate but fickle Anzoleto and the noble but neurotic Albert.

The element of the vagabond in *Consuelo* undoubtedly appealed to female readers of Sand's time, many of whom lived housebound, dependent lives and could identify with a heroine who had the courage to live under the open sky, travel wherever she pleased, and obtain the necessities of life through her own wit and talent. The book is a powerful statement about the rights of the individual—male or female. It attacks corruption and hypocrisy and explores the difficulties that face an independent woman. Sand knew the pain of independence, and she steered her heroine through the traps waiting for any woman who tried to achieve success in her own right. Consuelo saves herself much suffering by avoiding financial or psychological dependence on men, subjugating her personality to no one. Her character explores the experience of a woman searching for personal integrity.

Her novels are often neglected because they have old-fashioned characteristics that annoy impatient readers. The modern reader may find *Consuelo* too long, too rambling, too digressive, too full of melodramatic events and inflated dialogue expressing impossibly noble sentiments. Some of the characters that were original creations in Sand's time have become stereotypes from too much copying by inferior writers. Consuelo herself is a slightly implausible character. She was raised on the streets of Venice but remains a chaste, high-minded girl throughout her harrowing adventures, which include attempts to seduce and rape her. Without any formal education, she has a huge vocabulary and impeccable grammar; she speaks Spanish, Italian, and German. She has the ability to pick up new languages practically overnight. Her voice captivates everyone who hears her. Men fall madly in love with her at first sight.

What saved Sand's best novels from oblivion was the keen mind of their author. Noteworthy in *Consuelo* are Sand's mini-essays contained in her many interesting digressions from the main thread of her tale. Chapter 56 contains an essay on folk art that displays Sand's intelligence, learning, and socialistic ideology. Chapter 74 contains a poetic essay on loneliness. Chapter 97 contains a moving description of the silence and the mystery of an empty theater. Chapter 101 contains a profound discussion of the function of art. *Consuelo* is also remarkable for its demonstration of Sand's musical knowledge, part of which she acquired during her famous love affair with the great Polish pianist and composer Frédéric Chopin. Perceptive readers are willing to overlook *Consuelo*'s faults in favor of its wealth of information about history, famous personalities of the eighteenth century, music, architecture, fashions, furnishings, social conditions, and human nature. The novel's portrait of the young Franz Joseph Haydn, founder of the symphony and teacher of the great Wolfgang Amadeus Mozart, is another of its interesting features.

Sand is regarded by contemporary feminists as an early heroine of the women's movement who outraged society by dressing in men's clothes, smoking cigars, and living a life of sexual freedom normally permitted only to men. This recognition of Sand as a dynamic personality has brought about a renewed interest in her fiction. *Consuelo* can be read as a protest against the suppressed condition of women. Sand's revolutionary concerns went beyond that, however; she wanted nothing less than a complete reconstruction of society based on evangelical love. She was appalled by the glaring contrast between the wealthy minority and the impoverished, overworked majority. *Consuelo* belongs to what has been called Sand's middle period. In later years, she withdrew from active life and wrote a number of pastoral romances that celebrate the virtues of a life of contemplation. Her life mirrored the turbulent period of history she lived through, which included the French revolution of 1848 and its reactionary aftermath. *Consuelo*, like most of Sand's novels, is intensely autobiographical and reveals the real-life courage as well as the lofty ideals and powerful emotions of a remarkable woman.

"Critical Evaluation" by Bill Delaney

Further Reading

Atwood, William G. *The Lioness and the Little One: The Liaison of George Sand and Frédéric Chopin.* New York: Columbia University Press, 1980. Chronicles Sand's famous love affair with Polish pianist and composer Frédéric Chopin, who helped her acquire the rich musical appreciation displayed in *Consuelo*.

Blount, Paul G. *George Sand and the Victorian World.* Athens: University of Georgia Press, 1979. This interesting short volume discusses the reaction of Victorians to Sand and her influence upon such famous writers as Robert Browning, Elizabeth Barrett Browning, Matthew Arnold, and George Eliot.

Datlof, Natalie, Jeanne Fuchs, and David A. Powell, eds. *The World of George Sand.* New York: Greenwood Press, 1991. A collection of penetrating essays on Sand's life, works, politics, contemporaries, and influence on world literature. Includes essays on *Consuelo* and its sequel, *La Comtesse de Rudolstadt* (1843-1844; *The Countess of Rudolstadt*, 1847). Chapter notes provide a wealth of reference material.

Eisler, Benita. *Naked in the Marketplace: The Lives of George Sand.* New York: Basic Books, 2006. Drawing on Sand's substantial body of correspondence, Eisler explores the complicated personality of the radical nineteenth century feminist. Particularly focuses on Sand's impressively active and lengthy love life and its impact on her literary output.

Harkness, Nigel. *Men of Their Words: The Poetics of Masculinity in George Sand's Fiction*. London: Legenda/Modern Humanities Research Association, 2007. Harkness examines questions of masculinity in Sand's fiction within the context of the nineteenth century French novel, describing how her novels repeatedly depict the connection of masculinity, power, and language.

James, Henry. *French Poets and Novelists*. New York: Grosset & Dunlap, 1964. One of the world's greatest novelists devotes a chapter in this authoritative book to the life and works of George Sand. Other chapters discuss Sand's other famous lover, poet Alfred de Musset, and her friend Gustave Flaubert.

Lewis, Linda M. *Germaine de Staël, George Sand, and the Victorian Woman Artist*. Columbia: University of Missouri Press, 2003. Describes how *Consuelo* created the myth of a Romantic female artist that influenced the work of George Eliot and three other Victorian women writers.

Massardier-Kenney, Françoise. *Gender in the Fiction of George Sand*. Atlanta: Rodopi, 2000. Argues that Sand's novels express a complex and extremely modern conception of gender, in which she questions prevalent patriarchal modes of discourse and redefines masculinity and femininity.

Powell, David A. *George Sand*. Boston: Twayne, 1990. This biography of Sand by an authority on her life and works provides a great deal of criticism and interpretation. Powell devotes many pages to discussions of both *Consuelo* and its sequel, *La Comtesse de Rudolstadt* (1843-1844; *The Countess of Rudolstadt*, 1847). The compact, functional volume contains considerable bibliographical material.

Sand, George. *Story of My Life: The Autobiography of George Sand*. Edited by Thelma Jurgrau. Albany: State University of New York Press, 1991. This excellent English-language edition of Sand's *Histoire de ma vie* (1854-1855; *History of My Life*, 1901) contains forty-five pages of introductory material as well as many pages of author's notes and editor's notes.

Continental Drift

Author: Russell Banks (1940-   )
First published: 1985
Type of work: Novel
Type of plot: Psychological realism
Time of plot: December, 1979, to February, 1981
Locale: Catamount, New Hampshire; Allanche, Haiti; Florida

Principal characters:
BOB DUBOIS, a blue-collar worker in search of the American Dream
ELAINE DUBOIS, his wife and the mother of their three children
EDDIE DUBOIS, his brother
MARGUERITE DILL, Bob's mistress
AVERY BOONE, Bob's former best friend
VANISE DORSINVILLE, a young Haitian woman with an infant son
CHARLES, her infant
CLAUDE, her nephew

The Story:

Bob Dubois has just gotten paid and heads for a beer in his home town of Catamount, New Hampshire, on a snowy Friday evening just before Christmas. After he drinks his beer, he intends to buy his young daughter a set of figure skates. Though self-reflection is not part of Bob's nature, he feels a building frustration with his life. He cheats on his wife and feels remorseful, especially when his infidelity leads him to be too late to buy the skates for his daughter. Bob's unhappiness with his life boils over, and he smashes out all the windows in his car. Finally home, he collapses with his wife

Elaine. They decide to try to improve their lives by moving to Florida, where Bob's brother Eddie lives.

Vanise Dorsinville lives in a small village in Haiti. As a hurricane rages, her family worries about Vanise's young nephew Claude, who is not at home. When the skies calm, he returns, carrying a ham. When he acknowledges looting it from an overturned truck, they become frightened that Claude will be arrested. The family decides that Vanise should take the boy to Miami, where his father lives.

Eddie arranges a job for Bob running a liquor store. Eddie

insists that Bob begin carrying a gun to work, which he can then leave behind the counter. At first Bob is happy with the changes in his life, and he takes a more active interest in his children. Bob is excited to learn that Elaine is carrying their third child.

Everything changes when Bob meets Marguerite Dill, an attractive African American woman who is the daughter of George, the part-time helper at the store. Bob flirts with Marguerite, and they eventually begin a sexual relationship. Late one night, after spending time with Marguerite, Bob interrupts two African American men robbing the store. Holding a shotgun to Bob, one man demands that Bob hand over the night deposit. In a moment of distraction, Bob gets the pistol from behind the counter and shoots dead the man with the shotgun. While Bob calls the police, the other robber runs away.

Vanise and Claude have given their money to a man named Victor, a boat owner. Though he has told a group of Haitians he will take them to Florida, his plan is to drop them off on North Caicos Island, 600 miles from the United States. Vanise prays according to her beliefs: first to the Christian Trinity and then to traditional Haitian powers. They follow a dog to a man named McKissick, who allows them to stay with him, for a price.

Bob Dubois once again feels lost in his life. Two weeks before his wife's due date, Bob is with his girlfriend when Elaine goes into labor. With the birth of his son, Bob once again vows to be a better husband. The next day, he plans to break things off with Marguerite, but she does not come to the store. He sees her sitting in a car with another man, and Bob is certain that the man was one of the robbers. Bob grabs his pistol and follows them, confronts the man on the street, then chases him into a bar.

Bob goes to his brother's house and gives him the gun. Bob is terrified at what he might do. Eddie describes how much money he needs each week and how much trouble he will be in if he does not pay his debts. Bob demands that Eddie take the gun; when Eddie refuses, Bob quits his job and leaves the weapon on the table. With no idea what to do next, Bob drives home to find a van belonging to Avery Boone, his former best friend. Avery proposes that Bob move down to Key West, where Bob can run a fishing boat.

Vanise, her baby, and Claude once more board a ship. They have no way to pay for their passage, so they are kept belowdecks. The crew members rape Vanise, as does a group of paying Haitians who later board the boat. Vanise and her charges are left at Nassau, Bahamas, and once again a man recognizes that they are refugees. He lets Vanise live upstairs from the store, prostituting her as well. One day,

Claude visits Vanise carrying a machete. The man who prostitutes her comes upstairs. Claude slashes the man's throat and steals a roll of money from his pocket, and the three take off again.

In Key West, Bob is soon taking vacationers on fishing trips. His friend Avery buys a bigger, faster boat and begins to disappear on mysterious, multiday trips. One night, Eddie calls Bob, asking to borrow money. Eddie says he knows Bob is smuggling drugs along with Avery. The bottom has fallen out for Eddie, his wife has left him, and unless he comes up with a hundred thousand dollars, he will lose everything he has.

Bob drives to see Eddie, only to discover that Eddie has committed suicide. The shock pushes Bob to try to get ahead in life. Bob asks Avery what he might do to further himself, and Avery tells him that he can ferry Haitians in from the Bahamas. Bob goes to the Bahamas and boards a group of Haitians that includes Vanise. He transports the group back toward Florida, approaching shore near dawn when the waves are high. A Coast Guard ship appears, and Tyrone, Bob's first mate, forces the Haitians overboard. Bob and Tyrone flee while the Coast Guard attempts to help the refugees in the water.

The next chapter shifts to Vanise, the only survivor. She is with her brother in Miami. She says her survival was due to the aid of an evil loa, or Voodoo spirit, who goes by the names Ghede and Baron Cimetier. She has lost her soul, and the loa has taken over.

Bob is haunted by the incident with the Haitian refugees. His fear and guilt grow even greater when he reads newspaper accounts of the bodies of Haitians washing up on the beach. He finally confesses to his wife, and they agree to leave that night for New Hampshire. Bob has one last task—Tyrone has given him a huge roll of money, taken from the Haitians.

Bob goes to Little Haiti, in Miami. He is led to a dark alley where he once again meets Vanise, who now has power over his soul. He begs her to take the money, but she turns her back on him, and he is attacked by a group of men with knives.

The book ends with a short chapter labeled "Envoi." In it, the narrator describes the fates of Bob's wife and children. The narrator explains why he wrote this book, in hopes that readers may come to understand the lives of people like Bob and Vanise and the effect greed has had on their lives.

Critical Evaluation:

Continental Drift is structured as a braided novel, where two stories alternate until their final collision. Over his career, Russell Banks has written a series of novels that attempt to describe America through careful, close looks at a variety of its challenges. He explores race relations (in *Cloudsplitter*, 1998), class relations (in *The Sweet Hereafter*, 1991, and the short-story collection *Trailerpark*, 1981), violence (in *Affliction*, 1989), and homelessness (in *Rule of the Bone*, 1995). In *Continental Drift*, questions of personal responsibility and the fantasy of the American Dream contribute to the power of the book.

The geological concept of continental drift is used in the book as an explanation for large-scale human behavior. The novel uses an overt first-person narrator to compare events such as the human migrations in Ethiopia and Somalia to the constant motion in the physical world—the shifting tectonic plates of continental drift, the endlessly moving currents of the ocean, and the swirl and change of the weather. If these events are natural and inevitable, then their real-world consequences—such as death and economic exploitation—cannot be helped, either.

Continental Drift also examines life on a micro level, describing what happens to the characters in their personal lives. Throughout the book, Vanise is exploited. When she is in her home village, the men of the family have left for the United States, so she has no protection from the chief of police, who abuses her sexually, becoming the father of Charles. The police chief does not help Varise or their son materially, but he does keep an eye on his son until they leave. Vanise is abused physically; she is not merely raped but beaten as well. She is lied to, told she will be taken to the United States but abandoned instead hundreds of miles from her destination. Bob and Tyrone agree to take Vanise and the other Haitians to Miami, but they abandon the Haitians to their death at the first sign of trouble.

Bob Dubois's exploitation is more difficult to describe. If it were up to him, he might well have allowed the the Coast Guard to board his ship, saving the Haitians. Bob, however, defers to Tyrone, who sees their cargo as merchandise. Bob simply stands by, as Tyrone, rifle in hand, chases them into huge waves.

In smaller ways, Bob uses his wife and family. For a while, he is a good husband and father, but then the boredom of his job drags him down. He ignores his children, fights with his wife, and lies while cheating on her. Bob and the other characters who exploit him see the truth as flexible. To them, acting badly at the expense of another person is not bad, so long as the other person does not know that he or she is being mistreated. Thus, when Bob's wife discovers he is cheating and is hurt by the discovery, his action is rendered bad. If she were never to find out, however, the same action would be acceptable.

Through this attitude toward the truth, Bob is exploited by his brother Eddie and his friend Avery. Bob comes to Florida on the assumption that Eddie will one day make him a business partner. Eddie, though, is just trying to stay one step ahead of his building financial problems. He looks rich, but his life is a house of cards, on the verge of collapse. He uses Bob as a one more way to make money. Avery treats Bob similarly. He leads Bob to believe that one day Bob will own a boat and make a living through it. (Ironically, Bob is far closer to attaining that dream in his abandoned life in New England, where he was just a few payments away from owning a boat). Bob dreams of the life Avery has—owning a bigger, faster boat, a fancy condo, and a van and enjoying the company of a beautiful and exotic girlfriend—but there appears no legal route to gaining these material things.

Continental Drift ends with its narrator talking to the reader about the purpose of the book. The ending is reminiscent of the ending of Charles Dickens's novel, *Hard Times* (1854; originally published as *Hard Times for These Times*), which also addresses its readers. Each ending calls to readers to recognize how personal greed has created such a terrible world. Each charges its readers to make the world a better place.

Brian L. Olson

Further Reading

Banks, Russell. "The Art of Fiction CLII: Russell Banks." Interview by Robert Faggen. *Paris Review* 40, no. 147 (Summer, 1998): 50-89. The novelist discusses his own work, as well as his ideas about the nature and project of literature generally.

_____. "Pariahs in America: A Conversation with Russell Banks." Interview by Loic Wacquant. *Salmagundi*, Spring, 2009, 148-159. An interview that explores Banks's views on outsiders and his interest in representing them in fiction.

Brown, Westley. "Who to Blame, Who to Forgive." *The New York Times Magazine*, September 10, 1989. Explores the questions of responsibility raised in Banks's work and the answers the novelist seeks to provide.

Deren, Maya. *Divine Horsemen: The Living Gods of Haiti.* New York: Documentext, 1953. A book about the rituals in which Vanise participates. *Continental Drift* is illustrated with drawings that can also be found in this book.

Maslin, Janet. "Newspaper Story Inspires *Drift.*" *The New York Times*, April 29, 1985. Describes the real-life events that provided Banks with the initial inspiration for his novel.

Conversation in the Cathedral

Author: Mario Vargas Llosa (1936-   )
First published: Conversación en la catedral, 1969
    (English translation, 1975)
Type of work: Novel
Type of plot: Social realism
Time of plot: 1960's
Locale: Lima, Peru

Principal characters:
SANTIAGO ZAVALA, a journalist
AMBROSIO PARDO, a dogcatcher and former chauffeur

The Story:

Santiago Zavala is the son of the late Peruvian industrialist Fermín Zavala. Lima is suffering an epidemic of rabies, and Zavala is writing editorials for the tabloid *La Crónica* attacking the city administration's handling of the stray-dog problem. Zavala sets out in search of his wife's dog, which was caught by dogcatchers eager to earn a commission, which, ironically, is part of the city's response to the crisis and to Zavala's editorials. While on his search, he encounters Ambrosio, a dogcatcher who once was Zavala's father's chauffeur as well as the chauffeur and the bodyguard of the notorious Cayo Bermudez, minister of security under the regime of the dictator Manuel Odría during Santiago's university days. The meeting of Santiago and Ambrosio initiates a four-hour conversation in The Cathedral, the bar-restaurant-brothel where Santiago and Ambrosio go to drink and reminisce.

The conversation drifts to the eight years of Odría's presidency, the time when Santiago and Ambrosio were young men on the verge of independence from their families. Both had fathers who were closely connected to the corrupt regime. Santiago's father was deeply involved in deals with Cayo Bermudez. Ambrosio's father worked as a member of the secret police. Ambrosio and Santiago attempted to separate themselves from their fathers' paths; both ultimately recognize that they failed.

During their conversation, Santiago asks Ambrosio several questions about the past. Santiago wants to discover the identity and motivation of a notorious prostitute's killer. On another level, however, Santiago seeks to unravel the puzzle of when and how his life and his country began to disintegrate.

Santiago's inquiry leads him to retrace his steps as a wealthy young man caught in an identity crisis that, metaphorically, was a historical crisis for his class. The favorite son of a wealthy upper-class family, Santiago was expected to enter a profession and have a lifestyle that continued to uphold the values and privileges of his predecessors. His older brother, Chispas, managed his father's pharmaceutical factories and continued his father's traditions. Neither Fermín nor Chispas ever appeared as cruel, arrogant, or oppressive men. Their mother, Zoila, however, adhered to strict class distinctions and had a fear and anxiety of "race mixtures." As far as she was concerned, Santiago adhered to the wrong values in his concern for the nation's, rather than his class's, destiny, and associated with the wrong people. Santiago rejected his family's wealth, ideology, and privileged position in Peruvian society. His mother's worst fears materialized when Santiago married his nurse, a simple, lower-class nonwhite woman.

Santiago defied his father's desire and mother's advice and chose to enter San Marcos University. There he became acquainted with an activist communist group whose members believed that only a Marxist revolution would enable Peruvians to set the nation on a road of development and justice. Santiago was unaware that the dictator's regime suspected his father of having joined a new alliance of rich men against General Odría. Santiago and his father were placed under surveillance, and the Zavala phone was tapped. Santiago's group was arrested, but Santiago's father used his connections, especially with Cayo Bermudez, to obtain Santiago's release.

Although he did not attempt to help any of the group members, Santiago viewed his father's actions as a final affront and broke with his parents. He went to live with a renegade bohemian uncle, who eventually found him a job with *La Crónica.* Santiago's writing skills were quickly recognized, and he was assigned to reporting on crime. As part of his duties, he performed an investigation into the murder of Lima's most famous prostitute, La Musa. In the course of the investigation Santiago discovered that his father was the famed homosexual Bola de Oro. Santiago knew that Ambrosio, as chauffeur to two powerful and corrupt men, shuffled between the sites of their domestic and public activities. Ambrosio witnessed the Zavala family's tensions as well as the political crisis that Fermín and Cayo Bermudez had to face and to surmount. Santiago assumes that Ambrosio holds the answer to the riddle of the Zavala family. Ambrosio, indifferent to Santiago's anxieties and obsessions, and unreflective himself, tells his story in his own way and in his own time.

Santiago learns from Ambrosio that Cayo Bermudez was groomed for advancement by Fermín, a senator in the dictator's mock parliament. Bermudez invited several of his old friends to his home, where La Musa and her lover, the mulatta Queta, played the roles of hosts and prostitutes to the group. Bermudez, observing that Fermín was a homosexual, procured for Fermín his somewhat reluctant chauffeur, Ambrosio. Ambrosio killed La Musa in order to protect Fermín (Ambrosio's much-admired employer) from scandal and blackmail at her hands. Santiago learns the truth, but this truth culminates in more riddles and no answers and no prospects for a brighter future. Santiago's quest ends with the despair and alienation with which it began.

Critical Evaluation:

Mario Vargas Llosa's major contribution to Latin American literature is his passionate, articulate literary denunciation of his society's ills. Vargas Llosa uses narrative structures and techniques that enable him to portray the multifaceted experiences of urban Peru. The life depicted in the Peru of his fiction is the life of a society in a furious process of urbanization. In this society, many of the existing social structures enter into a process of disintegration. The decay of the old order and the violence resulting from social alienation, class disparity, and racism stamp Vargas Llosa's fictional world with a terrifying sense of pain. Vargas Llosa's narrative structures encapsulate not only nostalgia for a beautiful and departing rural order but also the velocity of change in the everyday life of common individuals. Vargas Llosa captures a nation's movement from an unacceptable old order into the terrifying and relentless life of the city.

The length, complexity of plot, and subtlety of character motivation of *Conversation in the Cathedral* place great demands on the reader's memory and attention. Just as Santiago finds incredible the idea of his father's being the legendary Bola de Oro, the reader has difficulty making this same identification because information comes in bits and pieces, glimpses of scenes, and tails of gossipy conversations. Although the entire narrative is constituted out of the conversation between Santiago and Ambrosio, it has other conversations superimposed on it. One dialogue contains another dialogue that contains another dialogue, and so on. Each

dialogue involves different characters speaking at different times and different spaces.

In the middle of Ambrosio or Santiago's recollections, other voices intervene to tell their versions or contribute their information. Vargas Llosa presents a view that sensory perception is experienced in terms of memory and language. Sensory perception becomes the screen onto which all consciousness is projected in *Conversation in the Cathedral*.

By means of conversation, Vargas Llosa not only narrates the action in a series of crisscrossing retrospective scenes but also delves into complexity of character. In the novel, the author portrays the myriad complexities of Peru's social and racial class system, catching it in the middle of its process of decomposition. The dramatic, even melodramatic, experiences of the characters announce a farewell to Zoila's world. In the dictatorship there are no heroes or martyrs; it produces only failures.

In *Conversation in the Cathedral*, young university students have passed tests, their rites of initiation. They consider themselves autonomous, mature individuals responsible for themselves and for the future of their country. No longer isolated within the confines of their neighborhoods, they plunge into university life, defined by one of the characters as a microcosm of Peruvian political life. The novel takes university life as the point of departure for the story, but the total narrative breadth of *Conversation in the Cathedral* extends into other sectors and periods of Peru's social fabric. The plot chronicles the years of the Odría dictatorship (1948-1956) and the disastrous effects that this oppressive and corrupt regime had on Peruvian society as a whole. Directly (the planning of a student-labor uprising) and indirectly (the conversations of politicians, maids, prostitutes, and journalists), the novel's discourse is centered on the question of power. *Conversation in the Cathedral* is a quintessential political novel.

In *Conversation in the Cathedral*, the multiplicity of stories creates an overwhelming sense of circularity. At the end of each story there seems to be a connection with the beginning of another story of a previous time. The novel has four sections of roughly equal length. Each part is focused on a major event in the plot and theme of the story: the awakening of Santiago's social and moral consciousness, La Musa's settling in as Bermudez's lover and host, La Musa's murder, the defeat of Santiago's investigative consciousness.

At the end of the novel the reader, like Santiago, is persuaded that it is necessary to learn more about the nature of evil. The reader may even be tempted to try to find an answer to Santiago's initial question: "When did Peru get all screwed up?" It is the need to find an answer to this question that sustains the reader's interest as Santiago plunges through various sordid histories. The novel is an exhaustive inquiry into the nature and dynamics of evil in relation to the corrupting influence of power. It is considered by many critics to be Vargas Llosa's most pessimistic text.

Genevieve Slomski

Further Reading

Castro-Klaren, Sara. *Understanding Mario Vargas Llosa.* Columbia: University of South Carolina Press, 1990. Provides an introduction to the life and writings of Vargas Llosa and explicates his most important works. Includes bibliography.

Gerdes, Dick. *Mario Vargas Llosa.* Boston: Twayne, 1985. Good overview of Vargas Llosa's fiction in a historical and social context. Includes bibliography.

Köllmann, Sabine. *Vargas Llosa's Fiction and the Demons of Politics.* New York: Peter Lang, 2002. Provides a detailed reading of *Conversation in the Cathedral* in relation to Vargas Llosa's works of literary theory, political commentary, memoirs, and other fiction. Concludes that throughout his career, Vargas Llosa has expressed concern about political issues, including authoritarianism, corruption, ideology, and violence on the individual, and about the role of literature, writers, and intellectuals in society.

Kristal, Efraín. *Temptation of the Word: The Novels of Mario Vargas Llosa.* Nashville, Tenn.: Vanderbilt University Press, 1998. Traces the origin of the themes and the development of literary techniques in each of Vargas Llosa's novels published through 1996. Relates the novels to his literary influences and political activism.

Muñoz, Braulio. *A Storyteller: Mario Vargas Llosa Between Civilization and Barbarism.* Lanham, Md.: Rowman & Littlefield, 2000. Appraises Vargas Llosa's literary works and political involvement from a sociotheoretical perspective.

Rossman, Charles, and Alan Warren Friedman, eds. *Mario Vargas Llosa.* 2d ed. Austin: University of Texas Press, 1980. Examines individual novels, as well as major themes and concerns of Vargas Llosa's work.

Williams, Raymond L. *Mario Vargas Llosa.* New York: Frederick Ungar, 1986. An introduction to Vargas Llosa's works. Includes bibliography.

Coplas on the Death of His Father

Author: Jorge Manrique (c. 1440-1479)
First published: Coplas por la muerte de su padre,
    1492 (English translation, 1833)
Type of work: Poetry

Jorge Manrique, regarded as among the most accomplished of late medieval Spanish poets, belonged to an aristocratic Castilian family, one that left its mark upon the cultural as well as the political history of the fifteenth century. His father, Rodrigo, Count of Paredes, rose to be Master of Santiago and Constable of Castile. Jorge's uncle, Gómez Manrique, was one of the finest poets of the reign of King Enrique IV (1454-1474). Among more distant kinsmen, Jorge could claim as a great-uncle the celebrated writer Iñigo Lopez de Mendoza, Marquis of Santillana. Thus, Jorge Manrique was part of a brilliant vein of literary culture that marked at least certain individuals and families among the fifteenth century warrior aristocracy of Castile. Characteristic of his time, he was torn among the claims of a soldier's, a courtier's, and a poet's life, eventually dying in battle in 1479 fighting on behalf of Queen Isabel.

Coplas on the Death of His Father has been called the greatest poem in the Spanish language, but even without it, Manrique's approximately fifty *canciones* (lyric poems) and *decires* (narrative, panegyric, or satirical poems) would have established him among the leading poets of his time. As it was, *Coplas on the Death of His Father* so touched the imagination of subsequent generations that for more than two hundred years, criticism was written that sought to discover new and esoteric meanings in Manrique's masterpiece. Lope de Vega Carpio esteemed it so highly that he declared that it should have been written in letters of gold. Manrique's most eloquent English translator, Henry Wadsworth Longfellow, thought it to be the most beautiful "moral" poem in the Spanish language, and Pedro Salinas wrote that the poem represents the culmination of the elegiac lyric in Spanish. Manrique's critics concur that in this work he excels all other poets of the fifteenth century in Spain.

The poem, which consists of approximately five hundred lines divided into forty-two *coplas* (or stanzas), is a memorial to Manrique's father, Rodrigo, who died in 1476 at the height of his fame. An intensely emotional poem, it integrates the poet's personal loss, the medieval worldview, concern for the passing of time, the vagaries of fortune, the inevitability of death, and the hope of salvation. Its uniqueness lies in Manrique's ability to employ familiar and rather well-worn themes in such a way as to extend their aesthetic potential. A mark of Manrique's greatness is his ability to render the grief of one individual in such a way that it becomes a grief universally shared by his readers.

The poem uses the form known as the *copla de pie quebrado*, familiar in Spanish poetry from the time of Juan Ruiz, the Archpriest of Hita, in the fourteenth century. In the *pie quebrado*, the tetrasyllablic (four-syllable) line is used with the octosyllabic (eight-syllable) line, thus reducing some lines to half the metrical length of the others, in mixed trochaic meter. These half-lines, when handled by a master, create an effect of suspense or hesitation. Manrique's use of the *pie quebrado* form became so famous that thereafter the term *copla manriqueña* (after Manrique), or simply the *copla de Jorge Manrique*, became as distinctive as the Shakespearean sonnet became in English letters.

The dominant motifs in the *Coplas on the Death of His Father* reflect characteristic medieval themes: the *ubi sunt qui ante nos in mundo fuere?* (what has become of those who have gone before us?); the *memento mori* (in the middle of life we are in death); and the *contemptus mundi* (contempt for the things of this world); death personified; death as the great equalizer; the fleeting nature of fame and honor in this world; and the eternal promise of Christian salvation. Manrique, in presenting these well-known themes, achieves a rare intensity with his simple and direct vernacular Castilian. This was peculiarly significant for his time, because, in an age of classical translations, Castilian poets were increasingly abandoning vernacular forms of expression in favor of imitations of classical themes and forms. The poem, in exploiting every possibility of the vernacular language, demonstrates the fullest potentiality of Spanish versification. Furthermore, Manrique exemplifies the mood of his age, a period of profound pessimism and self-doubt. Such a mood is characteristic of an age of economic and demographic decay, as well as of plague and pestilence.

The poem can be divided into three sections. The first is a discussion of the theme of human mutability, the second pursues that of *ubi sunt*, while the third is an elegy for the late don Rodrigo. It begins by expressing a mood that is general and universal, meditating upon the transitory nature of this world, and then, following a series of examples taken from recent and ancient history, turns to the core of the poem, the reputation of the dead man himself.

In the first section, the poet contemplates the passage of time and the significance of memory. He explores the theme of life as a journey that eventually merges with death and thus returns to the source of all life: "Our lives are like rivers," he writes, gliding to the "boundless sea" that is the grave, in which "all earthly pomp and boast" are swallowed up. This section then develops the stock medieval theme of *contemptus mundi* as a prescription for attaining salvation: Things such as beauty and wealth, which are admired and esteemed in this temporal world, must perish, while those things that partake of the eternal, such as the human soul, endure. What men and women desire and pursue in this world are mere fleeting things that have no meaning and that offer no sustenance to the soul. At this point, death is introduced as the equalizer, for all are united in death. It is better, then, to regard this world as a journey until, in encountering death, one attains a better life beyond the grave. This present world is subject to mutability, chance, disaster, and decay, from which not even those in the highest places can escape. Manrique uses a favorite late medieval metaphor, the goddess Fortuna, ever inconstant, raising up men and women with the ascent of her wheel, only to cast them down again in despair.

Manrique turns to a second medieval theme, *ubi sunt*, posing several questions that ask, what happened to the men and women of the past? The answer is that they have all passed away because they are a part of this transitory and impermanent world, a theme that recalls the earlier theme of *contemptus mundi*. While the reiteration of the *ubi sunt* theme is ubiquitous in medieval literature, it is indicative of Manrique's inventiveness that in his use of it he is superior to all his contemporaries. He invokes those names associated with the life of his father, don Rodrigo, beginning with his king Juan II (1406-1454), the Infantes of Aragon, and don Alvaro de Luna, the notorious favorite of the king. He evokes the chivalric trappings of the royal court, the festivities and the tournaments, but in describing all this, he underscores the transitory nature of worldly splendor and of a life "false and full of guile," observing that "our happiest hour is when, at last,/ the soul is freed."

In the final section, the poet introduces don Rodrigo as "Spain's champion," implying for his readers a comparison with another Rodrigo, El Cid. He declares that there is no need for a eulogy because "ye saw his deeds!" His father's name "dwells on every tongue." There then follows an elaborate passage of comparisons with the Roman heroes of old—Caesar and Octavian, Titus, Trajan, and Hadrian, Antoninus Pius and Constantine—Manrique claims for his father "Scipio's virtue" and "the indomitable will/ of Hannibal."

In the last part of the poem, Death appears in person and courteously addresses don Rodrigo. Here, Death is not the typical macabre figure familiar to contemporaries from the dance of death but is a mediator assisting don Rodrigo in transcending the mortal state and attaining fame and immortality: "Let virtue nerve thy heart again," says Death, proclaiming the ideal of the "brave knight whose arm endures/ Fierce battle, and against the Moors/ His standard rears." Rodrigo replies: "O Death, no more, no more delay!/ My spirit longs to flee away/ And be at rest."

In its perfect use of medieval topics, the poem represents a high point, and thus a change, in medieval consciousness. In contrast with a work such as *The Poem of the Cid* (twelfth or early thirteenth century), which glorifies action, *Coplas on the Death of His Father* embodies the contemplative spirit. This treatment of examining the meaning of life and the nature of reality makes the poem distinctive. Although the poem is a traditional elegy, the genius of the poet transforms the experience of personal loss into a universal statement of the transitory nature of earthly happiness and an affirmation of the Christian ideal of salvation.

Donna Berliner

Further Reading

Bell, Alan S. "Tradition and Pedro Salinas's Original Approach to Jorge Manrique." *South Atlantic Bulletin* 39, no. 4 (November, 1974): 38-42. A critique of Salinas's widely read essay on Manrique.

Brenan, Gerald. *The Literature of the Spanish People from Roman Times to the Present Day.* New York: Cambridge University Press, 1976. A definitive study in English of Spanish literature.

Danker, Frederick E. "The *Coplas* of Jorge Manrique." *Boston Public Library Quarterly* 10 (July, 1958): 164-167. An introduction, including the poem's early printing history.

Deyermond, A. D. *A Literary History of Spain: The Middle Ages.* London: Ernest Benn, 1971. One of the best introductions to medieval Spanish literature.

Domínguez, Frank A. *Love and Remembrance: The Poetry of Jorge Manrique.* Lexington: University Press of Kentucky, 1988. Devotes two chapters to discussing the background and providing an interpretation of *Coplas on the Death of His Father.*

Dunn, Peter N. "Themes and Images in the *Coplas . . .* of Jorge Manrique." *Medium Aevum* 33 (1964): 169-183. A close reading of the poem, more concerned with aesthetic integrity than with literary history.

Krause, Anna. *Jorge Manrique and the Cult of Death in the Cuatrocientos.* Berkeley: University of California Press, 1937. Emphasizes late medieval attitudes toward mortality and death.

Longfellow, Henry Wadsworth, trans. "Ode on the Death of His Father," by Jorge Manrique. In *Ten Centuries of Spanish Poetry: An Anthology of English Verse with Original Texts from the Eleventh Century to the Generation of 1898*, edited by Eleanor L. Turnbull. Baltimore: Johns Hopkins University Press, 2002. Longfellow's translation remains highly readable. Pedro Salinas's introduction to this book also is valuable.

Vinci, Joseph. "The Petrarchan Source of Jorge Manrique's *Las coplas*." *Italica* 45 (1968): 314-328. Vinci makes a good case for Petrarch being a major influence on Manrique. Contains textual comparisons.

Coriolanus

Author: William Shakespeare (1564-1616)
First produced: c. 1607-1608; first published, 1623
Type of work: Drama
Type of plot: Tragedy
Time of plot: Third century
Locale: Rome, Corioli, and Antium

Principal characters:
CAIUS MARCIUS CORIOLANUS, a noble Roman
TITUS LARTIUS and COMINIUS, generals against the Volscians
MENENIUS AGRIPPA, a friend of Coriolanus
TULLUS AUFIDIUS, a general of the Volscians
SICINIUS VELUTUS and JUNIUS BRUTUS, tribunes of the people
VOLUMNIA, the mother of Coriolanus
VIRGILIA, the wife of Coriolanus

The Story:

Caius Marcius, a brilliant soldier, is attempting to subdue a mob in Rome when he is summoned to lead his troops against the Volscians from Corioli. The Volscians are headed by Tullus Aufidius, also a great soldier and perennial foe of Marcius. The hatred the two leaders have for each other fires their military ambitions. Marcius's daring as a warrior, known by all since he was sixteen, leads him to pursue the enemy inside the very gates of Corioli. Locked inside the city, he and his troops fight so valiantly that they overcome the Volscians. Twice wounded, the victorious general is garlanded and hailed as Caius Marcius Coriolanus.

On his return to Rome, Coriolanus is further proclaimed by patricians, consuls, and senators, and he is recommended for the office of consul, an appointment wholeheartedly approved by the nobles. Because the citizens, too, have to vote on his appointment, Coriolanus, accompanied by Menenius Agrippa, goes to Sicinius and Brutus, the plebeian tribunes, to seek their approval.

The people long held only contempt for Coriolanus because of his arrogance and inhumane attitude toward all commoners. Although coached and prompted by Menenius to make his appeal as a wound-scarred soldier of many wars, Coriolanus cannot bring himself to solicit the citizens' support but instead demands it. He is successful in this with individuals he approaches at random on the streets, but Brutus and Sicinius, who represent the common people, are not willing to endorse the elevation of Coriolanus to office. They voice the opinions of many citizens when they accuse Coriolanus of insolence and of abuses such as denying the people food from the public storehouses. Urging those citizens who voted for him to rescind their votes, Brutus and Sicinius point out that his military prowess is not to be denied but that this very attribute will result in further suppression and misery for the people. Coriolanus's ambitions, they pre-dict, will lead to his complete domination of the government and to the destruction of their democracy.

Menenius, Cominius, and the senators repeatedly plead with Coriolanus to approach the tribunes civilly, and Volumnia admonishes him that if he wants to realize his political ambitions he must follow their advice. Appealing to his responsibility as a Roman, Volumnia points out that service to one's country is not shown on the battlefield alone and that Coriolanus must use certain strategies and tactics for victory in peace as well as in war.

Coriolanus misconstrues his mother's suggestions. She taught him arrogance, nurtured his desires in military matters, and boasted of his strength and of her part in developing his dominating personality. Coriolanus now infers that his mother in her older years is asking for submissiveness and compliance. Although he promises Volumnia that he will deal kindly with the people, it is impossible for him to relent, even when his wife, Virgilia, who never condoned his soldiership, lends her pleas to those of the group and appeals to his vanity as a capable political leader and to his responsibility as a father and a husband.

Coriolanus's persistence in deriding and mocking the citizens leads to an uprising against him. Drawing his sword, he would have stood alone against the mob, but Menenius and Cominius, fearing that the demonstration might result in an overthrow of the government, prevail upon him to withdraw to his house before the crowd assembles. Coriolanus misinterprets the requests of his friends and family that he yield to the common people, and he displays such arrogance that he is banished from Rome. Tullus Aufidius, learning of these events, prepares his armies to take advantage of the civil unrest in Rome.

Coriolanus, in disguise to protect himself against those who want to avenge the deaths of the many he killed, goes to

Antium to offer his services to Aufidius against Rome. When Coriolanus removes his disguise, Aufidius, who knows the Roman's ability as a military leader, willingly accepts his offer to aid in the Volscian campaign. Aufidius divides his army in order that he and Coriolanus each can lead a unit, thereby broadening the scope of his efforts against the Romans. In this plan, Aufidius sees the possibility of avenging Coriolanus's earlier victories over him; once they take Rome, Aufidius thinks, the Romans' hatred for Coriolanus will make possible his dominance over the arrogant patrician.

The Romans hear with dismay of Coriolanus's affiliation with Aufidius; their only hope, some think, is to appeal to Coriolanus to spare the city. Although Menenius and Cominius blame the tribunes for Coriolanus's banishment, they go as messengers to the great general in his camp outside the gates of Rome. They are unsuccessful, and Cominius returns to inform the citizens that, in spite of old friendships, Coriolanus will not be swayed in his intentions to annihilate the city. Cominius reports that Coriolanus refuses to take the time to find the few grains who are his friends among the chaff he intends to burn.

Menenius, sent to appeal again to Coriolanus, meets with the same failure. Coriolanus maintains that his ears are stronger against the pleas than the city gates are against his might. Calling the attention of Aufidius to his firm stand against the Romans, he asks him to report his conduct to the Volscian lords. Aufidius promises to do so and praises the general for his stalwartness. While Coriolanus vows not to hear the pleas of any other Romans, he is interrupted by women's voices calling his name. The petitioners are Volumnia, Virgilia, and young Marcius, his son. Telling them that he will not be moved, he again urges Aufidius to observe his unyielding spirit. Then Volumnia speaks, saying that their requests for leniency and mercy are in vain, since he already proclaimed against kindliness, and that they will therefore not appeal to him. He also makes it impossible for them to appeal to the gods: They cannot pray for victory for Rome because such supplication will be against him, and they cannot pray for his success in the campaign because that would betray their country. Volumnia proclaims that she does not seek advantage for either the Romans or the Volscians but asks only for reconciliation. She predicts that Coriolanus will be a hero to both sides if he can arrange an honorable peace between them.

Finally moved by his mother's reasoning, Coriolanus announces to Aufidius that he will frame a peace agreeable to the two forces. Aufidius declares that he, too, is moved by Volumnia's solemn pleas and wise words. Volumnia, Virgilia, and young Marcius return to Rome, there to be welcomed for the success of their intercession with Coriolanus.

Aufidius withdraws to Antium to await the return of Coriolanus and their meeting with the Roman ambassadors, but as he reviews the situation, he realizes that peace will nullify his plan for revenge against Coriolanus. Moreover, knowing of the favorable regard the Volscians have for Coriolanus, he believes he has to remove the man who was his conqueror in war and who might become his subduer in peace. At a meeting of the Volscian lords, Aufidius announces that Coriolanus betrayed the Volscians by depriving them of victory. In the ensuing confusion, he stabs Coriolanus to death. Regretting his deed, he then eulogizes Coriolanus and says that he will live forever in men's memories. One of the Volscian lords pronounces Coriolanus the most noble corpse ever followed to the grave.

Critical Evaluation:

Coriolanus, which first appeared in 1607 or 1608, marked a vision quite distinct from and unlike the earlier great tragedies *Hamlet, Prince of Denmark* (pr. c. 1600-1601, pb. 1603), *King Lear* (pr. c. 1605-1606, pb. 1608), and *Macbeth* (pr. 1606, pb. 1623), which retain their appeal as much for their differences as for their likenesses to later ages. *Coriolanus*, on the other hand, remains modern in a number of significant ways. For one thing, there are no noble kings in the quasi-democratic society being portrayed, no amusing comic interludes with clowns and jesters that epitomize the jolly side of English sensibility, no fundamentally decent great men marred only by one tragic flaw, no declamatory soliloquies, no uplifting philosophical or poetic musings, no reassurances of a better future after the tragic hero's downfall. Instead, the landscape not only reflects the pessimism of Jacobean London but also distressingly resembles that of the twenty-first century. The play presents a proudly democratic and secular society marred by the corrosive effects of established wealth in tandem with rigid social class divisions, a populace easily distracted by concerns of the moment and appeals to narrow self-interest (which allow rabble-rousers and charlatans to use their false rhetoric to great effect), a guns-or-butter debate that pits military preparedness against social welfare, and a fundamental question about the role of the exceptional individual in a supposedly egalitarian society. These remained the concerns of later ages as well, and they give *Coriolanus* a political and social resonance with twenty-first century audiences that is not the case in those great Shakespearean tragedies that focus more exclusively on questions of individual morality.

Three related themes have particular resonance. In a society that at least tips its hat toward egalitarian ideals, the character of Coriolanus is a Shakespearean version of the

Nietzschean *Übermensch* or superman. This was a figure the Renaissance regarded with fear and fascination both in literature—as in Christopher Marlowe's characters Doctor Faustus and Tamburlaine and in John Milton's Satan—and in real life, as in such figures as Sir Francis Drake and Sir Walter Ralegh. These Renaissance overreachers took advantage of the new freedoms of their liberated age to accomplish wonders but in doing so shook the foundations of their society, which, though initially valuing what they represented, usually ended by destroying them. A Macbeth, a Lear, or a Richard III might temporarily threaten the state as a result of personal ambition, foolishness, or corruption, but these figures are not, like Coriolanus, a barely contained force whom those around him tolerate for his usefulness but never cease to regard nervously. (Othello comes closest to this description, but he is a basically good man led astray by personal weakness.) The dilemma William Shakespeare develops in *Coriolanus* anticipates the historical situations of individuals with a will to dominate, generals who accomplish what society wanted and who then turn on their own people with ferocity. Such strong personalities are needed in crisis but dangerous any other time, and from Napoleon to Adolf Hitler, Joseph Stalin to Mao Tse-tung, society has been terrorized by such figures. Whether the reader agrees with those critics who regard *Coriolanus* as a play about politics or see it, as Algernon Charles Swinburne did, as a "drama of individuality" focused on an outsize hero, the problem is timeless.

As perhaps nowhere else in his works, Shakespeare in *Coriolanus* ties the character of his hero to his upbringing. This is in contrast to the way he explores the forces that shape Prince Hal in the *Henry IV* (c. 1597-1598) and *Henry V* (pr. c. 1598-1599, pb. 1600) series, where it is shown how little power they had over the prince. Here, Shakespeare looks at Coriolanus's nature as peculiarly male rather than as simply natural for a great warrior, and in the scenes with his mother, Volumnia, and his wife, Virgilia, he suggests the power of upbringing. Volumnia, a stalwart Roman matron, is fiercely "masculine" in her martial virtues and has proudly raised Coriolanus in this model of manhood. Virgilia, more conventionally feminine, deplores her husband's violent ways and their influence on their son. Few other Shakespearean heroes have their natures so linked to environment, and nowhere else, saving in the frothy problems of the comedies, is the gender difference confronted so directly. As with the superman type, the male ego in its purest untamed form has practical uses for guarding the city, but Shakespeare asks what is to be done with it during peacetime. The easy answer, and the one the Romans first choose, is exile, but this backfires when Coriolanus thereupon embraces the worst enemy of those

who had rejected him. Critic John Holloway called Coriolanus a typical "scapegoat figure," a disturbing influence in the society to be symbolically driven out to restore peace. Yet such figures cannot easily be pushed into the desert permanently as were biblical scapegoats. Those like Coriolanus must be accepted as part of society itself, to be endured or dealt with.

Another concern in the play that surfaced during Shakespeare's Renaissance and continues to be relevant is that of mob psychology. It would be several generations before the English Civil War and almost two hundred years before the terrors of the French Revolution, but fear of mob rule was endemic in Britain since the earliest days of Elizabeth I's rule, during Shakespeare's childhood. This fear runs through *Coriolanus*, balancing the equally abhorrent specter of rule by an undisciplined general teetering on the edge of manic fury. The play offers no solution to this Hobson's choice between governance by the whim of the "many-headed multitude" and that by aristocratic contempt for the concerns of the commonality, but it establishes the problem. The world of *Coriolanus* exemplifies the dilemma between distrust of the failed values of a self-serving aristocracy and distrust in the alternative, the passions of a "democratic" mob, and it explores that problem in connection with ambition, social stratification, and gender roles. Shakespeare's entire tragic canon illuminates human nature as no other dramatist's has done, but in *Coriolanus* he also provides insight into the problems of an age that was just beginning.

"Critical Evaluation" by Gina Macdonald and Andrew Macdonald

Further Reading

Barton, Anne. "*Julius Caesar* and *Coriolanus*: Shakespeare's Roman War of Words." In *Shakespeare's Craft: Eight Lectures*, edited by Philip H. Highfill, Jr. Carbondale: Southern Illinois University Press, 1982. Barton points out that in a world dependent on verbal rhetorical persuasion, Coriolanus's distrust of language alienates and isolates him, as does his personal use of language without regard to audience response.

Blits, Jan H. *Spirit, Soul, and City: Shakespeare's "Coriolanus."* Lanham, Md.: Lexington Books, 2006. Provides a line-by-line commentary on the text, analyzing the play's characters, language, allusions, puzzles, and other literary devices and elements of the drama.

Crowley, Richard C. "*Coriolanus* and the Epic Genre." In *Shakespeare's Late Plays: Essays in Honor of Charles Crow*, edited by Richard Tobias and Paul Zolbrod. Athens: Ohio University Press, 1974. Argues that *Coriolanus* merges tragedy and epic and has at its heart the conflict between mercy and honor.

McAlindon, T. "*Coriolanus:* An Essentialist Tragedy." *Review of English Studies* 44 (November, 1993): 502-520. Rather than analyzing *Coriolanus* as a metaphor for England's problems, McAlindon regards the play as a political tragedy of class conflict and manipulation of power in a realistic, historically specific society.

McKenzie, Stanley D. "'Unshout the Noise That Banish'd Marcius': Structural Paradox and Dissembling in *Coriolanus.*" *Shakespeare Studies* 18 (1986): 189-204. Argues that in a world of chaotic reversals, betrayals, and paradoxes where only the adaptable survive, Coriolanus's unchanging consistency dooms him.

Miles, Geoffrey. "'I Play the Man I Am': *Coriolanus.*" In *Shakespeare and the Constant Romans.* New York: Oxford University Press, 1996. Examines the depiction of constancy in *Coriolanus* and Shakespeare's other Roman plays. The Romans considered constancy a virtue, and Miles traces the development of this ethical concept from ancient Rome through the Renaissance. He then analyzes the ambiguity of this virtue in Shakespeare's depiction of the obstinate Coriolanus.

Miller, Shannon. "Topicality and Subversion in William Shakespeare's *Coriolanus.*" *Studies in English Literature, 1500-1900* 32, no. 2 (Spring, 1992): 287-310. Dis-

cusses *Coriolanus*'s intricate structure of topical references and draws parallels with the career of James I, early seventeenth century issues of authority and monarchy, and other conflicts and contradictions of Shakespeare's age.

Rackin, Phyllis. "*Coriolanus:* Shakespeare's Anatomy of 'Virtus.'" *Modern Language Studies* 13, no. 2 (Spring, 1983): 68-79. Interprets *Coriolanus* as a cautionary illustration of the narrow, exclusive inadequacy of the Roman ideal. The hero's Roman virtues ironically are the vices that doom him.

Ripley, John. *"Coriolanus" on Stage in England and America, 1609-1994.* Madison, N.J.: Fairleigh Dickinson University Press, 1998. Chronicles how this play has been altered in performance to accommodate political and social ideologies, ideas about aesthetics, and changing theatrical practices at the time it was produced. Includes discussion of performances in the late seventeenth and early eighteenth centuries, the twentieth century interpretation of actor Laurence Olivier, and the influence of psychoanalysis, politics, and postmodernism in performances staged from 1961 through 1994.

Steible, Mary. *Coriolanus: A Guide to the Play.* Westport, Conn.: Greenwood Press, 2004. Describes the dramatic structure, themes, textual and performance history, critical approaches, and the historical, cultural, literary contexts of the play.

The Cornerstone

Author: Zoé Oldenbourg (1916-2002)
First published: La Pierre Angulaire, 1953 (English translation, 1955)
Type of work: Novel
Type of plot: Historical
Time of plot: Early thirteenth century
Locale: France and the Holy Land

Principal characters:
ANSIAU, the old lord of Linnières and a pilgrim to the Holy Land
LADY ALIS, his wife
HERBERT LE GROS, Ansiau's son and heir
DAME AELIS, his wife
HAGUENIER OF LINNIÈRES, Herbert's oldest son
EGLANTINE, Herbert's half sister and lover
ERNAUT, Herbert's bastard son
LADY MARIE DE MONGENOST, the object of Haguenier's chivalric love
AUBERI, Ansiau's young squire
RIQUET, a renegade monk and Ansiau's traveling companion
GAUCELM OF CASTANS, called Bertrand, another traveling companion

The Story:

Ansiau, an old crusader, leaves his fief in Champagne and his family to make a pilgrimage to the Holy Land. The half-blind lord hopes that at the grave of his eldest son and in the holy city of Jerusalem, he will find release from his grief. He is given a twelve-year-old boy, Auberi, as his squire.

The new lord of Linnières is another son, the licentious and unscrupulous Herbert le Gros. Herbert's mother, the Lady Alis, so disapproves of his behavior that she refuses to live with him. She moves to a farmhouse, along with her husband's illegitimate daughter Eglantine, who is having a clandestine affair with her half brother.

Herbert sends to Normandy for his son Haguenier, who for years was training to be a knight. On his way home, Haguenier meets the beautiful, bored Lady Marie of Mongenost and swears allegiance to her, hoping that devotion will propel her into his arms.

After ten years of absence, Haguenier feels like a stranger in his own home. However, he soon finds friends, including his brother Ernaut, who was refused the hand of a cousin's daughter because of his illegitimate birth. Ernaut is threatening to kill himself. Herbert decides to send Ernaut for a papal document that might help his case. Meanwhile, Herbert proceeds with his other plans. Haguenier and his two illegitimate brothers are knighted, and Haguenier is married to a wealthy, older widow. After Haguenier makes a poor showing in a tournament, Herbert sends him to prove himself in the crusade against the Albigensians.

On the road to Marseilles, Ansiau is joined by a light-hearted runaway monk, Riquet, and by Bertrand, or Gaucelm of Castans, who, because of his wife's Albigensian enthusiasm, was blinded as punishment for heresy. Riquet leaves the party to remain with a village girl, and the other three proceed through the war-ravaged countryside. At Pamiers, Bertrand is reunited with his son but finds him determined to die for his new faith. In despair, Bertrand departs.

Fearful of his mother and, to a lesser degree, of damnation, Herbert breaks off his affair with his half sister. Eglantine aborts their child and, bent on destroying Herbert, haunts the forest, experimenting with witchcraft.

After distinguishing himself in battle, Haguenier becomes ill and has to abandon the crusade. His wife produces a beautiful little girl. Haguenier is captivated, but because the child is not a male to carry on the line, Herbert is furious. Despite Haguenier's objections, Herbert has the marriage annulled. However, Haguenier says that unless Marie becomes available, he will not marry again. Marie continues to test her lover, pushing him into a battle with a rival, which Haguenier loses, then insisting that he fight in a tournament using only a

mirror for a shield. Amazingly, he survives and triumphs over four knights. By now, Haguenier is the complete chivalric lover. To show his devotion to Marie, he even forswears physical love.

One disaster after another comes upon Herbert and those associated with him. Ernaut is heartbroken when, despite the papal document, he is once again rejected and the girl he loves is betrothed to another man. Haguenier tries desperately to get his half brother through this crisis, but, when the marriage takes place, Ernaut hangs himself, just as he threatened to do.

Discovering his affair with Eglantine, the Lady Alis disowns Herbert and places a curse upon him. Then comes a bitter drought. When rain falls everywhere except on Herbert's lands, the peasants blame Eglantine's witchcraft. A mob sweeps down upon Lady Alis's farmhouse, injuring her and killing Eglantine. Convinced that his mother's curse is working, Herbert confesses his many sins to a priest and is given a number of penances. Herbert does make a fairly short pilgrimage. However, he hires someone else to go to the Holy Land in his place.

In Marseilles, Ansiau and his two friends are delighted to have Riquet rejoin them. The monk promptly begins making money to pay their way to the Holy Land and turning it over to Ansiau for safekeeping. When Ansiau is robbed, Riquet begins all over again. In desperation, he goes into a church to pray. While he is there, a woman leaves a necklace of precious stones at the shrine of Saint Mary Magdalene. Assuming that his prayer is answered, Riquet takes the necklace, sells it, and procures passages to the Holy Land for his friends and himself.

In Acre at last, Ansiau searches for his son's grave without success. He decides to continue on his way to Jerusalem. Unfortunately, Bertrand is now too ill to walk but, fearful of remaining behind alone. Ansiau and Riquet decide to take turns carrying him. The four leave Acre with a large convoy, accompanied by armed men. However, a band of Muslim warriors sweeps down from the hills, kills the guards, and takes the rest captive. Young, strong men such as Riquet are sent to be sold as slaves. Those not of much use, such as Bertrand, are marched until they die of exhaustion. In fact, Bertrand chooses to die; he leaves the line of prisoners and is decapitated. Seeing that Ansiau, though blind, still has considerable physical power, the Muslims set him to work turning a mill. Because they believe that Auberi is Ansiau's son, they permit the boy to remain with the old man.

While Herbert is away, his wife Aelis is so indiscreet that Haguenier is forced into a duel with her lover. On his return, when Herbert learns about the scandal, he begins beating his wife. Chivalrously, Haguenier goes to her defense. In the ensuing scuffle, Herbert's back is broken. During the days that follow, Herbert forgives his son, and the Lady Alis, regretting her curse upon him, forgives Herbert. On his deathbed, Herbert asks Haguenier to marry off his one-year-old daughter and turn over the family estates to her husband. Haguenier, he says, should enter a monastery. Haguenier obeys his father's wishes and becomes Brother Ernaut. When his wife dies, Haguenier has his daughter sent to Marie to be reared.

In the Holy Land, Ansiau persuades the faithful Auberi to make his escape, and, eventually, the boy finds his way to a group of Christian pilgrims. Among the Muslims, Ansiau gains the reputation of being a holy man and a healer. He dies on a hill above Jerusalem.

"The Story" by Rosemary M. Canfield Reisman

Critical Evaluation:

The Cornerstone is not so much a historical novel as a work of fiction in which medieval men and women live. This distinction is important. What now passes for the historical novel is little more than an adventure story filled with bombast or a record of bedroom escapades in fancy dress. Zoé Oldenbourg's book is the exception that justifies a literary form debased by most of her contemporaries. Her novel has all the qualities readers expect of a story enclosing long perspectives of time and change and the mysteries of life and death.

No small part of Oldenbourg's effectiveness is the result of her insight into the mind and heart of medieval people. Her characters come together, talk, and go about their intimate affairs, and, in so doing, they reveal themselves and their private concerns, loyalties, superstitions, hopes of heaven, and fears of hell. Nothing seems contrived or forced; situations arise as casually as they do in Geoffrey Chaucer's *The Canterbury Tales* (1387-1400) or the stories of Giovanni Boccaccio, but everything adds up to the stir and spirit of an age. Life is harsh, disappointing, and sad. Men seize at excitement or happiness in the pageantry of a tournament, the rituals of a court of love, an illicit passion, or the violence of war. Always, above everything else, Christian faith gives meaning and purpose to experience and guides humanity's quest for spiritual salvation. Through these matters, Oldenbourg brings to life and motion the gentry and the whole of medieval society—knights and their ladies, Crusaders, troubadours, wandering scholars, holy pilgrims, serfs, priests, merchants, clerks, and beggars—in the days when Philip Augustus reigned in Paris and Pope Innocent III summoned the chivalry of France to a new crusade against the Albigensian heretics of Provence and Toulouse.

In a novel so solid in construction, so varied in detail, certain comparisons are inevitable. There is something massive here, like the soaring bulk of a Gothic cathedral built in an age when people lived in daily intimacy with God and churches were powerful upsurges of buttressed masonry. In this connection, the title of Oldenbourg's book is symbolic, for Christian faith was the cornerstone on which rested the whole structure of the feudal period. Again, reading this novel is like inspecting at close hand a medieval tapestry, in which every figure, leafy tree, and symbolic beast is worked lovingly and with care, or like turning the pages of a beautifully limned Book of Hours, the figures of its decorative groupings a little stiff and archaic in their poses but believable and very human, with every face and gesture clear-cut and revealing.

Father, son, and grandson stand in the foreground of this landscape with figures. In his old age, Ansiau de Linnières, part of whose story was told in an earlier novel, *Argile et cendres* (1946; *The World Is Not Enough*, 1948), turns over his fiefs in Champagne to his heir and sets out on a pilgrimage to the Holy Land in order to win forgiveness for the sins of his rough life. A veteran of the Third Crusade, he hopes to see Jerusalem once more before he dies and to visit the grave of his oldest son, buried at Acre. His sight failing, he goes blind on the way and wanders through a countryside ravaged by the Albigensian wars in the company of a young squire, a blinded heretic, and a renegade monk. In Palestine, he is captured and forced into slave labor. His capacity for faith, however, allows him to overcome all agonies of the body and of the spirit, and, in his last hour, dying alone on a hillside near Jerusalem, he trustingly calls on God to be his priest.

His son Herbert, aptly nicknamed the Gross, is a man of brutal nature and prodigious physical appetites. Greedy, lecherous, cruel, disliked by his neighbors, and alienated from his children, he murdered, fornicated, and blasphemed his way into middle age. When he commits incest with his half sister Eglantine and is cursed by his mother, the Lady Alis, the pilgrimage he makes in expiation of his sins is little more than an impious fraud. On his return, he is fatally injured by his son, Haguenier, while he is trying to beat his wife to death.

Haguenier, the young knight of Linnières, represents the more tender and idealistic side of the medieval temperament. He might have become an even worthier son of an unworthy father if he had not been afflicted by physical weakness or come under the spell of Lady Marie de Mongenost, whom he serves faithfully but hopelessly, according to the rules of chivalric love. In repentance, after his sin of patricide, he leaves the older woman to whom he is married and his baby daughter and enters a religious order.

It is plain that the three Linnières of the novel illustrate three different facets of medieval life and belief. Bluff old Ansiau and Herbert le Gros stand at opposite poles of that age of contradictions and extremes. Haguenier, too sensitive for the rough life to which he was trained, confusing his adoration of the Virgin with his love for an earthly woman, dreamy, but manly in his capacity for fidelity and suffering, points to the more humanistic age that was soon to follow.

Oldenbourg expressed a belief that in the contemporary novel there is too little concern with what is great and eternal in man. In this somber, richly imagined, and starkly depicted story of thirteenth century France, she holds up a mirror of human conduct and faith that illumines the past to reflect the hopes and fears of the present.

Further Reading

Ames, Alfred C. "Mounting Power in Rare Novel." *Chicago Sunday Tribune*, January 9, 1955. Praises the author for her "proud lack of compromise" in treating a complicated subject. Even though the characters' way of life and modes of thought may be foreign to readers, they all come to life in this book and become objects of concern.

Christensen, Peter G. "Zoë Oldenbourg, the Albigensian Crusade, and Terrorist Repression." In *Correspondences: Medievalism in Scholarship and the Arts*, edited by Tom Shippey and Martin Arnold. Rochester, N.Y.: D. S. Brewer, 2005. Focuses on Oldenbourg's writings about the Albigensian Crusade, including two of her other novels, *Les Brûles* (1960; *Destiny of Fire*, 1961) and *Les Cités charnelles* (1961; *Cities of the Flesh*, 1963). Mentions her other works about the Middle Ages, including *The Cornerstone*.

Janeway, Elizabeth. "Courage and Faith in a Distracted Age." *The New York Times Book Review*, January 9, 1955. States that Oldenbourg's theme is the triumph of "courage and faith" in a period of conflict, violence, and rapid change. Although she reveals the worst side of Christianity, as well as the best, the author sees religion as the only sound basis for existence.

"Medieval Tapestry." *Time*, January 10, 1955. States that the novel is "artfully written." The accounts of vicious behavior and brutality are justified by Oldenbourg's intention to present a "huge and intricate tapestry" that shows clearly what life was like in the thirteenth century.

Pick, Robert. "Eros in a Wimple." *Saturday Review* 38 (January 8, 1955): 10. Argues that *The Cornerstone* is the first modern novel to re-create the world of chivalric love in all its subtlety and its innocent blasphemy. Additionally, the characters symbolize historical change; Herbert is a man of the Middle Ages, and the son who kills him is a Renaissance humanist.

Raymond, John. Review of *The Cornerstone*, by Zoé Oldenbourg. *New Statesman and Nation*, December 4, 1954. Raymond argues that by blending historical events with her characters' very human reactions to them, Oldenbourg produced a "great historical novel." The three major figures—Crusader, son, and grandson—are seen not merely as individuals but also as representatives of an era.

The Corsican Brothers

Author: Alexandre Dumas, *père* (1802-1870)
First published: Les Frères corses, 1844 (English translation, 1880)
Type of work: Novel
Type of plot: Adventure
Time of plot: 1841
Locale: Corsica and Paris

Principal characters:
ALEXANDRE DUMAS, *père*, the narrator
LUCIEN DE FRANCHI, a Corsican traditionalist
LOUIS DE FRANCHI, his twin brother, a law student in Paris
EMILY, a married woman with whom Louis is in love
MONSIEUR DE CHATEAU-RENAUD, a libertine ambitious to seduce Emily

The Story:

Alexandre Dumas, *père*, the story's narrator, explains that he has spent part of 1841 traveling on horseback in Corsica. One evening in March, he arrives at the top of a hill overlooking the towns of Olmeto and Sullacaro and surveys the scene in search of a house at which to seek hospitality for the night. The customs of the island guarantee that he will not be refused, and they specify that he must not offer any monetary recompense. He selects a home in Sullacaro that promises to be the most comfortable, taking note that all of the houses are fortified and many scarred by bullets. His guide informs him that the house is the property of Madame Savilia de Franchi.

Dumas is given the room of one of Madame de Franchi's twin sons, Louis, who has gone to Paris to study law. The other twin, Lucien, is determined to remain in Corsica and live as his forefathers had lived, although he regrets the gradual decline of ancient traditions, which he regards as an inexorable process of degeneration. Lucien even regrets the decline in the tradition of the vendetta, although such longstanding feuds are the principal factor requiring all the houses in Olmeto and Sullacaro to be fortified.

Although Lucien and Louis have chosen very different paths in life, according to their aptitudes—the bookish Louis has never handled a gun, while Lucien, a keen huntsman, is an expert marksman—they are very devoted to one other. While waiting for dinner to be served, Lucien shows Dumas his own room, furnished in a much more archaic manner then that of the absent Louis and decorated with weapons of various sorts, several of which have histories attached to them; they include matching rifles belonging to his father and his mother.

At dinner, Madame de Franchi asks Lucien, anxiously, if he has any news of Louis. Lucien explains to Dumas that he and his brother, having been born conjoined and having required surgical intervention to separate them, still "share the same body" and are thus aware of one another's sensations. He has felt sad for the past few days, so he knows that his brother must be in distress—but he can, at least, be certain that Louis is not dead.

Lucien also explains that he has a mission to undertake, as he has been appointed—rather reluctantly—to serve as a mediator in the vendetta between the Orlandi and Colona families. Lucien invites Dumas to accompany him, and they go to meet the present head of the Orlandi family at a remote spot to negotiate the terms for a formal agreement to be completed the following day. They visit the ruins of a house that once belonged to an ancestor of the Franchis, who had become involved some four hundred years before in a feud with the Guidices, which had only ended when the matching rifles in Lucien's room had simultaneously killed the two brothers who were the last survivors of the Guidices.

Lucien explains that the feud between the Orlandis and the Colonas began over a stray chicken, and the agreement that he has brokered between the present heads of the Orlandis and Colonas—which they are as reluctant to sign as he is to mediate—involves the symbolic return of a live chicken as well as the signing of a notarized document and the attendance of both families at a special mass. Dumas witnesses the conciliation; although he makes no explicit com-

ment, it is obvious to him that the agreement will not hold for long and that hostilities will be resumed in response to the slightest excuse.

Dumas has to leave later in the day to return to Paris. After a symbolic exchange of gifts, he sets off, bearing a letter that Lucien has given him to deliver to Louis. He attempts to do so immediately after arriving in Paris, but Louis is not at home. In response to the note he leaves, Louis calls on him the next day, surprising Dumas with the striking resemblance he bears to his identical twin. On being questioned, Louis admits that he has, indeed, been suffering personal distress, but has no time to explain further. He agrees to meet Dumas tomorrow night at a masked ball at the opera.

Louis is still distraught at the ball, and initially refuses Dumas's invitation to join him at a supper party to be given after the ball by his friend D——. When he discovers, however, that a man named Monsieur de Chateau-Renaud will be present, and that the gentleman in question has made a bet with the host that he will bring a certain unidentified person with him, Louis decides that he will come after all. At the party, Dumas discovers that Chateau-Renaud has wagered that he will bring a young married woman with him, and that he will do so before four o'clock; Louis is on tenterhooks, evidently having something at stake in the matter.

The couple arrive a matter of minutes before the appointed hour, with the man pressuring his reluctant companion. When she realizes that she had been the object of a wager, she insists on leaving immediately and asks Louis to take her home. When the young man readily agrees, he is challenged to a duel by Chateau-Renaud. Louis has no alternative but to accept the challenge.

Dumas agrees to serve as one of Louis's seconds, and Louis explains that Emily, the young woman whose champion he has become, has been entrusted to his guardianship by her husband, a sea captain. Deeply in love with her, Louis has made every effort to conceal his own passion, but when he had attempted to reproach her for encouraging Chateau-Renaud's advances, she had accused him of jealousy.

Louis writes a letter to his mother and brother, claiming that he is doing so during a lucid interval of a brain fever that is sure to kill him. He explains to Dumas that he has been visited by the ghost of his father and has been told that he is about to die. Not wishing his family to know the true circumstances of his death, he asks Dumas to send the letter, in order that Lucien will not come to Paris in search of vengeance, thus imperiling his own life. Again, Dumas makes no comment, but seems to know that Louis's gesture will be futile

Louis is shot dead by Chateau-Renaud, as he was always bound to be, having never before handled a pistol. Dumas sends the letter, but Lucien arrives before even receiving it, having felt the fatal bullet rip through his own flesh; he shows Dumas the mark that it has left on his own body. In the morning, he leaves for Paris immediately, with his mother's blessing. When he fights Chateau-Renaud in his turn, the result of the duel is quite different, Lucien being a crack shot.

Critical Evaluation:

The Corsican Brothers was probably written alongside or between the two novels that established Alexandre Dumas's reputation and transformed the fortunes of French popular fiction. These two novels, *Les Trois Mousquetaires* (1844; *The Three Musketeers*, 1846) and *Le Comte de Monte-Cristo* (1844-1845; *The Count of Monte-Cristo*, 1846), first ran as serials in daily newspapers, in direct opposition to Eugène Sue's *Les Mystères de Paris* (1842-1843; *The Mysteries of Paris*, 1843) and *The Wandering Jew*. Dumas's two exceedingly long novels also set the pattern for his own career and his future wealth. Their literary method also established a pattern that would dominate French popular fiction for the next half century.

At the time of writing *The Corsican Brothers*, Dumas had been attempting to establish himself in the more respectable arena of the theater and had imagined his endeavors in prose fiction as more akin to those of more upmarket writers; *The Corsican Brothers* explicitly acknowledges its influential debt to the work of its dedicatee, Prosper Mérimée, whose novella *Colomba* (1840; English translation, 1853) had helped romanticize Corsica.

Mérimée was by no means reluctant to incorporate melodramatic and supernatural elements into his own work; his other famous novella, *Carmen* (1845; revised, 1847; English translation, 1878), is unashamedly melodramatic, and *La Vénus d'Ille* (1837; *The Venus of Ille*, 1903) is one of the classics of French supernatural fiction, but he was careful to temper them with other literary qualities. Dumas, by contrast, was a writer whose success was always closely linked to excess, and *The Corsican Brothers* is no exception in that respect, even though it was probably intended to be excessive. At the time this novel was written, it was not exceptional to adopt the novella form, which Dumas had tried several times before. However, his future output was, inevitably, dominated by long serials improvised as he went along on a daily basis, which required a very different kind of discipline; he only returned to the shorter format on rare occasions.

The central challenge of serial fiction, which is at its most exaggerated in serials produced for daily newspapers, is to keep the reader hooked through long narrative distances by maintaining a relentless suspense. Novellas, by contrast,

have a much more definite shape; although their narrative method is similar to that of the novel in terms of scenic representation, they proceed with inexorable logic to a definite conclusion, which may (and hopefully will) seem surprising as well as inevitable and apt. Although *The Corsican Brothers* covers much narrative ground at a hectic pace—always one of Dumas's great assets, as befits a writer who composed his work at a similarly hectic pace—it does so with the same deadly accuracy of character Lucien's marksmanship and sense of honor, never losing its tight focus. It is a story obsessed with the relentlessness of fate, pretending to mirror the way of the world while actually mirroring, clearly and accurately, the principal respect in which the world within the text differs from the real world.

The period in which *The Corsican Brothers* was written was something of an interim in the history of supernatural fiction. German and English gothic novels had been very popular in France in the early years of the nineteenth century, and had spawned native imitations in the form of the *roman noir*, but their apparatus of ghosts, monsters, and curses had been subjected to such heavy usage that it seemed worn out, more appropriate for parody than continuation. Dumas loved this sort of fiction, and he continually tried to import gothic motifs into his work. His editors, though, had become wary of it, and it was squeezed out of his serials—but in his novellas, where he did not have to be so concerned about pleasing all the people all the time (or, more accurately, not offending anyone at any time), he felt free to give his idiosyncrasies freer rein. It is in this format that he wrote his best supernatural fiction, *The Corsican Brothers* as well as *Les Meneurs de loups* (1857; *The Wolf Leader*, 1904) and others.

The central motif of *The Corsican Brothers*—the supposed supernatural affinity existing between identical twins—was derived from folklore and would have been dramatized in fiction many times over even without the novella's example, but Dumas provides it with a dramatic frame that adds a useful narrative muscularity, which makes the story influential in its own right. He also adds an additional layer of complexity, which elevates his version to a higher literary level than crudely straightforward developments of the motif, in linking the carefully subverted mirror-imaging of the twins to the perverse mirror-imaging of the adversaries in long-enduring vendettas, balancing sympathy and antipathy in oddly similar ways.

Identical twins were a very rare phenomenon in Dumas's day—the most famous pair in nineteenth century France made a career out of exhibiting themselves on stage and in fairgrounds—and Dumas could not have had the opportunity to observe the now-commonplace phenomenon by which some identical twins deliberately differentiate themselves by cultivating contrasting abilities and interests. So, his characterization of Lucien and Louis displays unusual psychological insight, adding a further dimension to the story's interesting attributes and helping to secure its status as one of the landmarks of French supernatural fiction.

An English-language play by Dion Boucicault, an adaptation of Dumas's novel, premiered in 1852 and went on to become one of the standard pieces of Victorian theater. The play attracted great actors, such as Henry Irving, who rejoiced in the opportunity to play two parts.

"Critical Evaluation" by Brian Stableford

Further Reading

Davidson, Arthur F. *Alexandre Dumas (père): His Life and Works.* 1902. Reprint. Honolulu, Hawaii: University Press of the Pacific, 2002. A reprint of a classic biography of Dumas, *père*, who is described as "the property of all the world" because of his widespread fame, even by 1902. Includes a detailed bibliography and an index.

Dumas, Alexandre, *père. The Road to Monte-Cristo: A Condensation from "The Memoirs of Alexandre Dumas."* Translated by Jules Eckert Goodman. New York: Charles Scribner's Sons, 1956. An abridged translation of Dumas's memoirs that relate to his source material for his novels, including *The Corsican Brothers.*

Galan, F. W. "Bakhtiniada II, *The Corsican Brothers* in the Prague School: Or, The Reciprocity of Reception." *Poetics Today* 8, nos. 3/4 (1987): 565-577. Approaches *The Corsican Brothers* using the critical theories of Mikhail Bakhtin. While the reading is sometimes difficult, it is a rare English-language article on *The Corsican Brothers.*

Maurois, André. *The Titans: A Three-Generation Biography of the Dumas.* Translated by Gerard Hopkins. 1957. Reprint. Westport, Conn.: Greenwood Press, 1971. Considered the authoritative biography of Dumas, *père*, and his father and son. Discusses *The Corsican Brothers* in a cursory fashion. Includes an excellent bibliography.

Schopp, Claude. *Alexandre Dumas: Genius of Life.* Translated by A. J. Koch. New York: Franklin Watts, 1988. A biographical and critical approach to the life and works of Dumas, *père*. The volume contains a discussion on Dumas's adaptation of *The Corsican Brothers* into a drama to help pay his bills.

Stowe, Richard S. *Alexandre Dumas (père).* Boston: Twayne, 1976. An excellent starting place for an analysis of the life and works of Dumas, *père*, and one of the best sources in English. *The Corsican Brothers* is addressed in part 2 of chapter 10.

The Cossacks

Author: Leo Tolstoy (1828-1910)
First published: Kazaki, 1863 (English translation, 1878)
Type of work: Novel
Type of plot: Psychological realism
Time of plot: Nineteenth century
Locale: The Caucasus

Principal characters:
OLYENIN, a Russian aristocrat
MARYANKA, a Cossack woman
LUKASHKA, a young Cossack, betrothed to Maryanka
UNCLE YEROSHKA, an old Cossack retired from service

The Story:

Olyenin, a young Russian aristocrat, decides to leave the society of Moscow and enter the army as a junior officer for service in the Caucasus. There are a number of reasons for his decision. He squandered a large part of his estate, he is bored with what he considers an empty life, and he is in some embarrassment because of a love affair in which he could not reciprocate the woman's love.

Olyenin leaves the city after a farewell party one cold, wintry night. He and his servant, Vanyusha, travel steadily southward toward the Caucasus, land of the Cossacks. The farther Olyenin goes on his journey the better he feels about the new life he is about to begin. In a year's service, he sees the opportunity to save money, to rearrange his philosophy, and to escape from a mental state that does not permit him to love. He is sure that in a new environment he can become less egocentric and can learn to love others as he loves himself.

Shortly after he joins his unit, he is one of a force sent out along the Terek River to guard against depredations by the tribes who live in the mountains and on the steppes south of the river. The troops are to reinforce the Cossacks who live in the narrow strip of verdant land that borders the river. Olyenin's unit is stationed in the village of Novomlin, a small settlement of houses and farms with a population of less than two thousand people, mainly Cossacks.

The Cossack men spend their time in hunting and standing guard at posts along the Terek River, while the women tend the homes and farms. When Olyenin's unit moves into the village, he, as an aristocrat, is not assigned duties with the troops, and so his time is largely his own. The Cossacks do not like the Russian troops, for the tensions of differing cultures and the years of enmity between them are not assuaged. Olyenin is quartered in the house of a Cossack ensign and soon learns that he is not welcome. They are accepting him and his servant only because the household has to take them.

In the house lives an ensign, his wife, and their daughter Maryanka. Maryanka is spoken for in marriage by a young Cossack, Lukashka, a hero in his village because he saved a boy from death by drowning and killed a mountain tribesman who attempted to swim across the river during a raid. Olyenin quickly becomes infatuated with Maryanka. He does not know how to act in her presence, however, because he is bewildered by the possibility of a love affair between himself and the young, uncultured Cossack.

Olyenin makes friends with Lukashka, whom he meets at an outpost while hunting, and Uncle Yeroshka, an old Cossack whose days of service are over. In Yeroshka's company, Olyenin goes hunting almost every day. He dislikes drinking bouts, gambling at cards with the other officers, and the pleasure they find in pursuing the women of the village whose husbands and sweethearts are away on duty. Olyenin is happier alone or hunting with Yeroshka in the woods along the Terek, where he tries to work out his emotional problems.

At last, Olyenin begins to feel that he can be happy through generosity to others. He discovers that he enjoys giving a horse to Lukashka and presenting old Yeroshka with small gifts that mean little to Olyenin but a great deal to the old man. In addition, Olyenin wins the respect of the Cossacks by his ability to shoot pheasants on the wing, a new feat to the Cossacks, who never before saw it done.

As time passes, Olyenin becomes more and more aware of Maryanka's presence. When her parents announce that she is formally engaged to Lukashka, the announcement makes Olyenin decide that he, too, is really in love with her. He turns over in his mind the possibilities that such a love would entail. He cannot imagine taking her back to Moscow, into the society to which he was expected to return after his tour of duty, nor can he imagine settling down for life in the Cossack village. Although his stay there means a great deal to him, he knows that he can never be happy following the primitive life he sees there, for he has too many ties, both social and material, in the world he temporarily left.

While Olyenin helps Maryanka pick grapes in the vineyards, he has an opportunity to declare his love. Maryanka neither becomes angry nor repulses him, although she gives him little encouragement. Later Olyenin, able to press his suit at various times, promises to marry the Cossack woman. She, on her part, refuses to say that she will marry him, for she, too, realizes the difficulties of such a marriage. Unlike most of the Cossack women, she is not free with her favors and refuses to let either Olyenin or Lukashka share her bed. Lukashka is well aware of what is happening but is not worried; he believes that the situation will right itself because he is the better man.

One day a small band of marauders from across the Terek appear a short distance from the village. When the Cossacks, accompanied by Olyenin, make a sortie against them, the outlaws tie themselves together so that they cannot run away while they make a stand against the Cossacks. After the battle, Lukashka, wounded by a gunshot, is carried back to the village, where it is discovered that he cannot recover from his wound. Faced with the death of the man her parents chose to be her husband, Maryanka realizes that her life and her people are widely separated from Olyenin and the culture for which he stands. Deciding that she can never have any lasting affection for the Russian, she tells Olyenin bluntly of her decision. Olyenin requests a change of duty to another unit. After permission for the transfer is granted, he and his servant leave the village and the kind of life he can never learn to accept.

Critical Evaluation:

The character of Olyenin, the hero of *The Cossacks*, is largely autobiographical in origin. Like his young hero, Leo Tolstoy left Moscow in 1852 and joined an army regiment stationed in the Caucasus, the land of the Cossacks. Throughout his four years of service—during which he fought in expeditions in the Caucasus, the Danube, and the Crimea—Tolstoy kept very careful, detailed diaries, which years later were to provide invaluable material for his fiction. In the Caucasus diaries, he recorded all aspects of his life as a soldier, including not only the fighting but also the hunting and the drinking, the time spent reading and writing, and the periods of idleness and boredom. It is to this minute observation and recording of firsthand experience that *The Cossacks* owes much of its verisimilitude of plot and setting, its vividness of atmosphere and impression. In addition to using his army experiences in molding the character of Olyenin, Tolstoy provided his hero with a background nearly identical to his own; both Olyenin and his creator were young noblemen who left Moscow as a result of large debts and an unsuccessful love affair, and both were concerned with discovering new values amid a different way of life from that to which they were accustomed.

This escape from life in a teeming city, with its juxtaposition of culture and decadence, attractiveness and corruption, creativeness and stagnation, is at the thematic center of *The Cossacks*. The novel revolves around the concern for humanity's return to a more natural state from the debilitating influences of urban civilization. This idea is embodied in Olyenin's flight from the whirl of Moscow society to the Caucasus. The important question to be answered, however, is what Tolstoy does with the nature-versus-civilization hypothesis. Certainly, in the first chapters, it would appear that the hero is headed toward an environment that will heal and renew him. However, the extent to which the remaining course of the narrative proves the Caucasus to be the natural life that Olyenin is seeking remains in question.

Tolstoy is able to see both strengths and shortcomings in each way of life and condemns neither one. One illustration of his objectivity is seen in his characterization of old Yeroshka, who, if this novel were a polemic against civilization, would be the obvious candidate to represent Cossack wisdom and the superiority of the Cossack way of life. Instead, he is portrayed as a brave hunter and fighter but a fault-ridden and quite human individual; he is a lovable, if slightly lecherous old reprobate. Rather than dispensing profound insight and ancient wisdom to young Olyenin, Yeroshka simply rides, hunts, drinks, and encourages the youth to enjoy sensual pleasures without worrying about the future. Likewise, the other main Cossack figure, Lukashka, combines strength and virtue, weakness and pettiness. Yeroshka, Lukashka, and their people are admirable in their bravery, their energy, and their closeness to the land; yet at the same time they murder, steal, and lose themselves in drunkenness and debauchery.

In the same way, Tolstoy attacks all the evils of his own and his hero's class: idleness, selfishness, shortsightedness, hypocrisy, temper, and irresponsibility. Although he sees these vices in the nobility and includes many of them in Olyenin's personality, he does not lose sight of redeeming qualities in the aristocracy. Olyenin's merit lies in his basic morality, which will not allow him to be complacent about his weaknesses; he is dissatisfied with his faults and his former way of life and seeks, although in an imperfect fashion, to find remedies and to grow as a person.

Olyenin vacillates throughout the story in his opinion of what comprises happiness. In chapter 20, he exclaims to himself, "Happiness consists in living for others," while, in chapter 33, he is convinced that "Self-renunciation is all stuff and nonsense . . . in my heart there is nothing but love for myself and the desire to love her and live her life with her." Olyenin never finds the key to happiness throughout the novel, although he enjoys a brief period of unreflecting enjoyment with the Cossacks, but he does discover that the urban, aristocratic way of life and the Cossack culture are incompatible. He learns this lesson on the personal level when his attempt to form a relationship with Maryanka fails and on a more general level when he is unable ever to feel truly a part of Cossack culture.

In addition to the cohesiveness that Olyenin's search for happiness gives *The Cossacks*, the novel is strongly unified through its richly evocative descriptive passages. In a powerful style marked by its clarity and simplicity, Tolstoy paints an unforgettable picture of Cossack life and of the people who cultivate the land. In this early work, all the author's love of nature, farming, and country life emerges in scenes of riding, hunting, and harvesting to create a vividness of effect that foreshadows the genius of his later novels.

Tolstoy conceived the idea of writing *The Cossacks* in 1852, although it took him ten years of intermittent work to complete the novel. The basic idea for the work was inspired by the author's long talks with an old Cossack friend, Epishka. Tolstoy's projected plan, first jotted down in a brief diary entry, was for a story "(a) about hunting, (b) about the old way of life of the Cossacks, and (c) about his expeditions in the mountains." Tolstoy's original intention was to write a long and complex novel that would include a substantial background of Cossack history, faithful renditions of the folk customs of the Caucasus, and all the tales of the area told to him by Epishka. As it transpired, however, Tolstoy was forced, for financial reasons, to finish the novel hastily for a publication deadline in 1863; the final length was approximately two hundred pages, since much of the original plan for the work had either been altered over the years or sacrificed in the hurry to complete it. *The Cossacks* is therefore a work of many peculiarities of structure and style; nevertheless, it marks an important step in Tolstoy's development, being his first work to be translated into another language and to capture an enthusiastic audience abroad. Above all, it remains an unsurpassed description of Cossack life and an excellent psychological study of a young man casting about for values that will fill the moral void he fears has entered his life.

"Critical Evaluation" by Nancy G. Ballard

Further Reading

Bayley, John. *Tolstoy and the Novel*. Chicago: University of Chicago Press, 1988. For the nonspecialist, this book is the most readable survey of Tolstoy's long fiction in the English language. Compares *The Cossacks* with other examples of Tolstoy's fiction set in the Caucasus and finds it wanting.

Kornblatt, Judith Deutsch. *The Cossack Hero in Russian Literature: A Study in Cultural Mythology*. Madison: University of Wisconsin Press, 1992. Places *The Cossacks* in a Russian tradition that runs from early nineteenth century writer Alexander Pushkin through twentieth century novelist Mikhail Sholokhov.

McLean, Hugh. *In Quest of Tolstoy*. Boston: Academic Studies Press, 2008. McLean, a professor emeritus of Russian at the University of California, Berkeley, and longtime Tolstoy scholar, compiled this collection of essays that examine Tolstoy's writings and ideas and assess his influence on other writers and thinkers. Includes discussions of the young Tolstoy and women and Tolstoy and Jesus, Charles Darwin, Ernest Hemingway, and Maxim Gorky.

Orwin, Donna Tussig, ed. *The Cambridge Companion to Tolstoy*. New York: Cambridge University Press, 2002.

Collection of essays, including discussions of Tolstoy as a writer of popular literature, the development of his style and themes, his aesthetics, and Tolstoy in the twentieth century. The references to *The Cossacks* are listed in the index.

Turner, C. J. G. "Tolstoy's *The Cossacks*: The Question of Genre." *Modern Language Review* 73, no. 3 (July, 1978): 563-572. A detailed examination of Tolstoy's conflicting intentions in *The Cossacks*, which Turner declares "a hybrid" of such genres as sketch, tale, novel, idyll, and autobiography. Elucidates this position by recounting the decade-long process of the novel's composition.

Wasiolek, Edward. *Tolstoy's Major Fiction*. Chicago: University of Chicago Press, 1978. Notes that *The Cossacks* "has some clear deficiencies," particularly in terms of the point of view it presents, but differs with John Bayley (above) as to the nature and extent of the problem. Argues that Tolstoy needed to establish two points of view, subjective and objective, but did not handle their juxtaposition skillfully.

Wilson, A. N. *Tolstoy*. New York: W. W. Norton, 1988. A lengthy biography in which Wilson calls *The Cossacks* Tolstoy's "first masterpiece" and an example of his ability to make new, fresh use of clichéd material.

Cotton Comes to Harlem

Author: Chester Himes (1909-1984)
First published: Retour en Afrique, 1964 (English translation, 1965)
Type of work: Novel
Type of plot: Mystery and detective
Time of plot: Early 1960's
Locale: Harlem, New York City

Principal characters:
GRAVE DIGGER JONES, a black police detective in Harlem
COFFIN ED JOHNSON, a black police detective, Jones's partner
DEKE O'MALLEY, a former convict and a phony minister
IRIS, O'Malley's former girlfriend
MABEL HILL, O'Malley's new girlfriend
BARRY WATERFIELD, O'Malley's assistant
ROBERT L. CALHOUN, leader of a white supremacist group
LOBOY, a junky and thief
EARLY RISER, a con man and a thief
ABRAHAM GOODMAN, a Jewish junk dealer
UNCLE BUD, a rag picker

The Story:

A rally and barbecue in Harlem draws a crowd to listen to the Reverend Deke O'Malley speak about his new Back-to-Africa movement. For one thousand dollars, any family who signs up will receive transportation, tracts of land, a mule, and seed to farm in Africa, free from the racism that plagues the United States. Though one thousand dollars is a sizable investment for the poor families of Harlem, Deke and his cohorts nevertheless manage to collect eighty-seven thousand dollars, which is stacked in an armored car hired for the occasion.

During the rally, two black police detectives arrive, allegedly sent to bring Deke in to the station for questioning and to confiscate the money he has collected. Simultaneously, a meat truck drives up, apparently to replenish the rally barbecue. The back doors of the truck burst open, and masked white gunmen jump out and hijack the loot. One of Deke's cronies, John Hill, resists and is shot dead. The gunmen roar away in the meat truck. Deke and the detectives set off in pursuit in the armored car. As the meat truck turns a corner at high speed, a bale of cotton tumbles out the back. As the chase continues, a local rag picker, Uncle Bud, discovers the bale, loads it onto his cart, and hauls it to a nearby junkyard to sell.

At the same time, two thieves, Loboy and Early Riser, are sweet-talking a woman in an attempt to steal her purse. The woman becomes aware of their ruse and smacks Early Riser, who runs into the street to avoid her wrath. He is run over by the fleeing meat truck, which then crashes. Meanwhile, two other black detectives, Grave Digger Jones and Coffin Ed Johnson, learn of the robbery and set off to investigate. Jones and Johnson immediately suspect Deke, a known former convict, of a scam and question his girlfriend, Iris, in an attempt to locate him. Deke, in the meantime, calls home and learns that the detectives are waiting for him. Jones and Johnson are ordered to go to the meat truck crash site, and they leave a white police officer to guard Iris; she seduces the officer to escape.

Johnson and Jones examine the wrecked meat truck, discovering cotton fibers, and suspect the stolen money had been secreted in the bale that had fallen out of the fleeing truck. They then recognize the body of Early Riser and search for his known associate, Loboy.

Deke, in the interim, seeks refuge with Mabel Hill, the attractive widow of John Hill. Mabel and Deke inevitably sleep together, and Iris finds them. The two women fight. Iris then shoots Mabel dead, and Deke knocks her out before he flees. Iris is later arrested for homicide. Jones and Johnson, meanwhile, find Loboy, who identifies the meat truck driver as a white man.

The next day, a rival movement is afoot in Harlem. It is called Back-to-the-Southland, which is offering transportation and work to blacks willing to return to the South. The movement, the brainchild of white supremacist Robert L. Calhoun (known also as the Colonel), who epitomizes the white antebellum planter, is merely a front to retrieve the missing cotton bale and the money. An angry mob gathers to protest Calhoun's organization. Barry Waterfield, one of Deke's cronies, approaches Calhoun and offers to sell him a list of Back-to-Africa supporters ripe for the Back-to-the-Southland scheme. They agree to a rendezvous to exchange the list for money.

Jones and Johnson question Iris, who tells the detectives about Deke's scam. They have Waterfield followed and then allow Iris to leave so she can be followed, too. At the meeting with Calhoun, a gunfight breaks out, and Waterfield is killed, along with three of Calhoun's henchmen. Later, Joshua, an assistant of junk dealer Abraham Goodman, is found dead, and the bale of cotton is missing from Goodman's junkyard. Deke is taken into custody, but he does not remain behind bars long: Deke's former armored car drivers, Freddy and Four-Four, break him out, killing two police officers in the process, and remove him to a secret room in Deke's church to torture him until he reveals the whereabouts of the eighty-seven thousand dollars. Iris arrives at the church, followed by Jones and Johnson. She is captured by Freddy and Four-Four. Jones and Johnson engage in a shootout with the two men, killing them, and then recapture Deke and Iris.

The bale of cotton, meanwhile, surfaces at the Cotton Club, where exotic dancer Billie Belle uses it in her act. The bale is auctioned off to Calhoun. The bale is opened and examined, but it contains nothing. Jones and Johnson allow Calhoun to escape criminal charges in exchange for eighty-seven thousand dollars, which will be returned to the people who invested in the Back-to-Africa scam. Deke and Iris are indicted on a number of charges, including murder. The detectives later learn that Uncle Bud had found the money in the cotton bale. He then had flown to Africa and used the cash to purchase cattle to buy one hundred wives.

Critical Evaluation:

Chester Himes had originally intended to become a serious writer. Certain events, however, conspired to drive him toward genre fiction, and he is best remembered today for his series of noir-flavored, hard-boiled detective novels set in Harlem.

As an Ohio teenager, Himes ran afoul of the law, and he spent years in prison for armed robbery. During his incarceration, he passed the time reading pulp fiction and became a fan of such writers as Raymond Chandler, author of the highly regarded series of mystery novels featuring private detective Philip Marlowe. Himes began writing and then published some short fiction while still in prison.

Upon his release, Himes returned to old habits: associating with dubious friends, remaining jobless, and smoking marijuana. Faced with a return to prison, he found work and began writing again. By the mid-1940's, he had published two literary novels, but they failed to win him financial stability or critical acclaim. In the early 1950's, like African

American writers James Baldwin and Richard Wright before him, Himes relocated to Europe. In 1957, nearly broke, he connected with French actor-writer Marcel Duhamel, founder and editor of the publishing imprint *Série Noire*, who suggested that Himes write a pulp novel set in Harlem based on one simple principle: Start with action and keep up a blistering pace for more than two hundred pages. Himes took the advice to heart and wrote *For Love of Imabelle* (1957; revised as *A Rage in Harlem*, 1965; also known as *The Five-Cornered Square*). The novel introduced black detectives Coffin Ed Johnson and Grave Digger Jones; presented a new backdrop for crime—Harlem; established Himes's unique style of detective fiction; and brought him the recognition he sought, winning France's top literary honor for the 1957 novel.

Cotton Comes to Harlem, the eighth of ten Harlem-domestic novels by Himes, epitomizes the author's many strengths in the detective genre. For a person who had never lived in Harlem, Himes does a remarkable job of presenting the predominately black neighborhood in New York's borough of Manhattan as a living, breathing entity. Critical to understanding the dynamics of the entire detective series, and to *Cotton Comes to Harlem* in particular, is the colorful, vibrant setting populated with a full range of fully rounded human types. In Harlem are artists, thieves, junkies, prostitutes, and other lowlifes who take advantage of ordinary, honest folks trying to scrape together a living. Also in Harlem are the police, who must sometimes resort to brutality while serving and protecting the community.

Harlem symbolizes not only the potential of African American energy (as exemplified by reference to such remnants of the early twentieth century Harlem Renaissance as the Cotton Club) but also the realities of racism that prevailed at the time of the story. Blacks must dwell in this enclave because they are not allowed to live elsewhere. The neighborhood is thus a hotbed of resentment, and gullible residents are ripe for the pie-in-the-sky Back-to-Africa scam, around which *Cotton Comes to Harlem* revolves. It is up to the fully developed central and recurring characters Grave Digger and Coffin Ed to set things right.

Fast-moving plots are Himes's specialty. The author eschews a linear presentation, preferring instead a brisk cinematic format that cuts from scene to scene. This keeps the suspense high—since readers only view one piece of the overall puzzle at a time—and permits the omniscient, dispassionate third-person perspective necessary to show the foibles of characters, and the results of their flawed thinking, without making overt judgments about their actions.

Most of Himes's detective stories begin with an outra-

geous scheme that quickly spirals out of control into absurdity, resulting in sudden violence and bloody death for innocent and guilty alike. In *Cotton Comes to Harlem*, Deke O'Malley's con game generates a large sum of money, coveted by many, and the search for the money hidden in a bale of cotton propels the plot through a multitude of complications that leaves one dozen people dead and others facing imprisonment. Thematically, the breakdown of the Back-to-Africa con serves as the author's disapproval and rejection of the Marcus Garvey-inspired concept of modern African Americans returning to a place they have never been. The bale of cotton is a metaphor for the type of menial employment to which many blacks were once subjected.

Stylistically, Himes offers readers two interpretations of noir: bleak and black. In the traditional sense, the plans of protagonists and antagonists are doomed to failure; in the sense offered by Himes, black people are entitled to be just as human, to make the same mistakes, and to suffer the same consequences as whites. Himes's language is simple and straightforward, often mixing well-wrought, Chandler-like similes with profanity; blunt violence with lyric descriptive passages; and humorous incidents, which provide comic relief from the downbeat atmosphere that pervades the novel. The combination of quick action, well-drawn characters, crisp language, and sardonic humor made *Cotton Comes to Harlem* the first of Himes's detective series to draw attention and appreciation in the United States. In 1970, the novel was adapted into a popular film of the same name, a film that many believe launched the attitude-changing blaxploitation phenomenon, in which film audiences were shown African American role models who were strong and independent and no longer subservient to whites.

Jack Ewing

Further Reading

Bogle, Donald. *Toms, Coons, Mulattoes, Mammies, and Bucks: An Interpretive History of Blacks in American Films*. New York: Continuum, 2003. A new edition of a thirty-year-old study from a noted film critic and historian. Examines the changing roles of African Americans in motion pictures, from racist, stereotypical roles to positive roles in films such as *Cotton Comes to Harlem* (1970).

Fabre, Michel, and Robert Skinner. *Conversations with Chester Himes*. Jackson: University Press of Mississippi, 1995. This posthumous collection of interviews conducted over time with the author includes Himes's thoughts about blacks and Harlem, racism, detective fiction, and other subjects. Helps readers to understand the motivations behind his writing.

Lawrence, Novotny. *Blaxploitation Films of the 1970's: Blackness and Genre*. New York: Routledge, 2008. A critical examination of blaxploitation films, a series that many believe began in 1970 with the film *Cotton Comes to Harlem*, based on Himes's novel of the same name. The series, produced especially for blacks, depicts black protagonists in traditionally black milieus, not without controversy for stereotyping.

Margolies, Edward, and Michael Fabre. *The Several Lives of Chester Himes*. Jackson: University Press of Mississippi, 1997. A biography based on letters, memoirs, and Himes's fiction. Explores the cultural, socioeconomic, and family factors that shaped his views and writing. The authors knew Himes personally.

Sallis, James. *Chester Himes: A Life*. New York: Walker, 2001. A biography of Himes and an examination of his

writings. Sallis had been inspired by Himes to become a crime novelist. Supplemented with black-and-white photographs.

Skinner, Robert E. *Two Guns from Harlem: The Detective Fiction of Chester Himes*. Bowling Green, Ohio: Bowling Green State University Popular Press, 1989. An examination of Himes's fictional detectives Coffin Ed Johnson and Grave Digger Jones that traces their creation to Himes's early life, experience as a criminal, and firsthand experiences with racism.

Soitos, Stephen F. *The Blues Detective: A Study of African American Detective Fiction*. Amherst: University of Massachusetts Press, 1996. An analysis of the history, traditions, and themes found in mystery and detective novels featuring black protagonists, from such authors as Himes, Pauline Hopkins, J. E. Bruce, Rudolph Fisher, Ishmael Reed, and Clarence Major. Includes a detailed bibliography.

The Count of Monte-Cristo

Author: Alexandre Dumas, *père* (1802-1870)
First published: Le Comte de Monte-Cristo, 1844-1846, serial (English translation, 1846)
Type of work: Novel
Type of plot: Adventure
Time of plot: 1815-1838
Locale: France, Italy, the Mediterranean, and the Middle East

Principal characters:
EDMOND DANTÈS, a young sailor
MERCÉDÈS, his sweetheart
FERNAND MONDEGO, a rival
M. DANGLARS, an ambitious shipmate
M. VILLEFORT, a deputy magistrate
VALENTINE, his daughter
ABBÉ FARIA, a prisoner at Chateu D'If
CADEROUSSE, an innkeeper
M. MORREL, a shipping master
MAXIMILIAN, his son
ALBERT, Mondego's son
HAIDÉE, Edmond's lover

The Story:

Edmond Dantès, a competent and well-liked first mate, takes over command of the *Pharaon* after the ship's captain dies. The ship sails safely into Marseilles harbor in 1815. The pleasant, unassuming young man is unaware that enemies surround him. M. Danglars, the agent of the ship's owner, M. Morrel, is jealous of Morrel's affection for Edmond and covetous of the young sailor's impending appointment as captain of the *Pharaon*. A fisherman, Fernand Mondego, wishes to wed Mercédès, who is betrothed to Edmond.

Danglars and Fernand, under the guise of a jest, compose

a note accusing Edmond of conspiracy. They write that Edmond, in carrying out the last orders of his captain, had unwittingly conveyed a letter to the Bonapartist committee in Paris, which is trying to restore the exiled Napoleon Bonaparte to power. Caderousse, a drunkard, witnesses the writing of the note, but keeps silent out of cowardice. On his wedding day, Edmond is arrested and taken before an ambitious deputy king's attorney named M. Villefort, who, to protect himself from association with his Bonapartist father, Noirtier—implicated in the letter Edmond carries—has

Edmond secretly imprisoned in solitary confinement within the dank dungeons of the imposing Château D'If.

Napoleon escapes from Elba to reign briefly again, but Edmond lies forgotten in his cell as his psyche undergoes a series of changes: from hope, because he knows he is innocent of any crime; to despair, because the future looks hopeless; to anger at the people who placed him in his predicament. The cannonading at Waterloo dies away. Years pass. Then, one night, Edmond hears the sound of digging from an adjoining cell. He breaks a water jug and uses a fragment of the pottery to assist in the excavation. Soon, a narrow tunnel is completed, and Edmond meets an old man, a fellow prisoner named Abbé Faria, whose misguided attempt to dig his way to freedom has led him to Edmond's cell. Thereafter the two meet daily, and the old man teaches the uneducated Edmond history, mathematics, languages, and etiquette.

In Edmond's fourteenth year of imprisonment Faria, mortally ill, tells Edmond where to find a tremendous fortune should he escape after the old man's death. When death comes, Faria's body is placed into a sack prior to being heaved into the sea. Edmond, desperate to escape, changes places with the dead man, whom he drags through the tunnel into his own bed. Jailers throw the sack into the sea. Edmond rips the cloth and swims through the darkness to an islet in the bay.

At daybreak a gang of smugglers rescues him. Edmond works with the smugglers until a stroke of luck brings him to the island of Monte-Cristo, where Faria's fortune is supposedly concealed. He lands on the island with the crew of the ship and, feigning injury in a fall, persuades the crew to leave him behind until their return trip from a smuggling rendezvous. Edmond explores the island and finds the treasure hidden in an underground cavern. He stuffs his pockets with jewels and returns to the mainland to sell some of the precious stones and gain the money necessary to carry out his plans to bring the treasure from Monte-Cristo. Edmond buys a boat and a title and sets himself up as the fabulously wealthy count of Monte-Cristo, one of many aliases he will hold while putting together an elaborate plot to gain revenge against those who wronged him. Edmond soon learns that his father had died of starvation and that his intended bride, Mercédès, despairing of Edmond's return, had married Fernand.

Disguised as a priest, Edmond visits Caderousse to seek information about those who caused his imprisonment. Villefort had gained a fortune and risen in legal circles. Danglars is now a wealthy banker and baron. Fernand, formerly a humble fisherman, later a military general, has won wealth and a title in the Greek war and is now count de Morcerf. For this information, Edmond gives Caderousse a valuable diamond.

Edmond also learns that his old shipping master, Morrel, a true friend who frequently questioned the authorities about Edmond's fate, has suffered the loss at sea of most of his ships and is on the verge of bankruptcy. In gratitude, because Morrel had helped the elder Edmond, Edmond saves Morrel's shipping business and befriends Morrel's son, Maximilian.

Edmond—as the count of Monte-Cristo—moves to Paris, where he dazzles the upper echelons of the city's society with his mysterious background, fabulous wealth, and impeccable social graces. He and his protégé, a beautiful girl named Haidée, an Albanian slave he had bought during his travels in Greece, became the talk of the boulevards. He is invited into all the best homes and salons. Meanwhile, he slowly plots the ruin of those who caused him to be sent to prison.

Caderousse is first to be destroyed. His greed had awakened with Edmond's gift of the diamond. Soon, Caderousse had committed robbery and murder and had been condemned to the galleys. Now, he escapes with the assistance of Edmond in another guise as a wealthy Englishman, but Caderousse does not use the opportunity to become an honest citizen. Instead, he attempts to rob Monte-Cristo. An escaping accomplice mortally wounds him. As Caderousse lies dying, Monte-Cristo reveals his true identity.

In Paris, Monte-Cristo ingratiates himself with banker Danglars, who loses heavily by following the investing example of the count, and so faces bankruptcy. The next victim is Fernand, who gained his wealth by betraying Pasha Ali in the Greek revolution of 1823. Monte-Cristo persuades Danglars to send to Greece for confirmation of Fernand's operations there. Fernand is exposed, and at a trial conducted by his peers, Haidée, daughter of the Pasha Ali, confronts him with the story of her father's betrayal.

Albert, son of Mercédès and Fernand, challenges Monte-Cristo to a duel to avenge his father's disgrace. Monte-Cristo, an excellent shot, intends to make his revenge complete by killing the young man, but Mercédès visits him and begs for her son's life. Aware of Monte-Cristo's true identity, she intercedes with her son as well. When the duelists meet, Albert publicly declares that his father's downfall is justified and apologizes to Monte-Cristo. Fernand, with no way to salvage his name, commits suicide. Mercédès and her son renounce their ill-gotten fortune and leave Paris, almost penniless.

Monte-Cristo has also become an intimate of Madame Villefort and encourages her desire to possess the wealth of her stepdaughter, Valentine. The count has slyly directed Madame Villefort in the use of poisons, and the depraved woman murders three people. When Valentine, too, is poisoned, Maximilian Morrel, son of the shipping master and in love with Valentine, goes to Monte-Cristo for help. Monte-Cristo vows to save the young girl, but Madame Villefort has marked her for death, and Valentine apparently dies of poisoning. Despite this seemingly distressing turn of events, Monte-Cristo promises future happiness to a deeply depressed Maximilian, who is like a son to him.

Danglars's masculine daughter, Eugénie, rejects several potential matrimonial matches. Disguised as a man, she runs off with her female piano-teacher to seek her fortune. Danglars, facing ruin for misappropriating funds, deserts his wife and flees the country to escape prosecution. When Villefort discovers his wife's treachery and crimes, he threatens her with exposure. She then poisons herself and her young son, Edward, for whose sake she had poisoned the others. Monte-Cristo reveals his true name to the already unhinged Villefort, who subsequently goes completely insane. Edmond's revenge is complete.

Monte-Cristo sails to his rocky island with Maximilian, who is suicidal because he believes his beloved Valentine is dead; but she is not dead. Monte-Cristo has rescued Valentine through the use of a death-simulating drug and spirited her to safety from her tomb and away from the turmoil that arose in the wake of the count's machinations against his enemies. Now he reunites the two lovers, who become beneficiaries of the count's immense wealth. Edmond, with Haidée, who professes her love for him, sails away, never to be seen again.

"The Story" revised by Jack Ewing

Critical Evaluation:

The Count of Monte-Cristo is the best-known novel of Alexandre Dumas, *père*, after *The Three Musketeers* (1844). Improbable as it seems, the novel might be based on a true story that occurred some thirty years before the writing of the book, a story concerning a man named François Picaud who had been betrayed by friends and falsely imprisoned. He had inherited a large fortune from a fellow prisoner and, upon his release, successfully sought revenge against those who had denounced him.

Besides appealing to Dumas's instincts as a writer, the story also resonates with the author for other reasons: Dumas harbored many grievances against society in general and against individual enemies in particular. His father had been persecuted and he himself had been harassed by creditors and slandered. It is not unreasonable to believe that Dumas captured his own feelings of vengeance in this novel.

The twin themes of justice and revenge at the heart of *The*

Count of Monte-Cristo will always be understandable: Revenge as a driving force has figured prominently throughout literature, from the Bible to the works of such writers as William Shakespeare, Edgar Allan Poe, and Mickey Spillane. Dumas took the idea of revenge even further: The sins of the fathers are visited upon their children, so the downfall of Edmond's enemies is emphatic. Likewise, the idea of obtaining a vast fortune that makes anything possible is the stuff daydreams are made of. The resourcefulness and implacability of an Edmond Dantès, shaped by circumstances beyond his control into someone simultaneously capable of great charm and terrible cruelty, makes him a worthy protagonist; it is likely such scenes as that in which Edmond escapes from the forbidding Chateau d'If by sewing himself into a burial sack to be cast into the sea will long linger in the memory.

However, despite such inherent strengths, *The Count of Monte-Cristo* demands much from modern readers. Like most of Dumas's major novels—and like the works of other popular nineteenth century writers, such as Charles Dickens—the part-adventure, part-melodrama novel was first serialized in a daily newspaper. The author kept his public in a constant state of suspense by detailing romantic love affairs, intrigues involving impersonation, dastardly murders and betrayals, suggestion of perversions, and multiple other complications and subplots that increased tension and delayed denouement as long as possible. This methodology served two purposes. First, it kept the income flowing for the writer, who shamelessly padded his prose with asides and other details to flesh out the story installments (117 in all) to necessary length; second, it provided inexpensive and regular entertainment for a relatively captive readership.

Contemporary readers, more familiar with the blunter, faster-paced literary efforts of the twentieth and twenty-first centuries, may find *The Count of Monte-Cristo* slow reading. Because of nineteenth century conventions of writing, the prose of the novel is formal and convoluted, full of allusions, dense with layered meanings, and peppered with expressions and words now obsolete or obscure. Speeches in the mouths of characters will sound stilted to the ears of those attuned to modern colloquialisms, who live in a world where such strong concepts as justice and honor have been diluted since the time *The Count of Monte-Cristo* was written.

Another barrier to full enjoyment of the novel is the milieu in which the story is set. Students of history, aware of the conflicts between French royalty and Emperor Napoleon Bonaparte (often referred to in the book as "the usurper") that provide both backdrop and impetus to the story, will have greater appreciation of events as they unfold. Similarly, in the present world climate—more egalitarian in theory if not in fact—understanding the relationships and hierarchy and class distinctions of Parisian upper-class society (crowded with counts and barons and marquises both of the old aristocracy and newly created nobility) may cause readers some difficulties.

Though Edmond is a fully rounded, complex, and memorable character, most of the others who appear in *The Count of Monte-Cristo* are one-dimensional and more stereotypes than portraits of actual individuals; women uniformly swoon and weep, while men perspire freely and flush or blanch, unable to hide their emotions. Dumas, of impoverished aristocratic heritage though capable of describing the luxurious appointments and clothing of the wealthy, had a greater facility and more sympathy in depicting members of the lower classes.

The primary antagonists, against whom Edmond seeks revenge, represent facets of humanity's baser instincts. Fernand, who through subterfuge gains Edmond's intended love, symbolizes lust—for flesh, for power, for wealth—and suffers death, the ultimate price, as a result of his fatal flaw. Danglars, the eventual banker, stands for jealousy and avarice and is accordingly ruined financially, an outcome that will hurt him most. Villefort, the rational prosecutor who has subverted the law for his own ends, is a metaphor for blind ambition; in condemning his own murderous wife to death (she poisons herself and her young son), he condemns himself to madness, the loss of his rationality, as the result of a series of increasingly profound misfortunes that befalls him. Even Mercédès, whom Edmond once loved, as the faithless woman (by the hero's estimation), must be brought down. Though Edmond still has feelings for his former betrothed, and twice spares her son, she is made to give up everything she had gained by her desertion of Edmond and is returned to her common existence in the place where the story began, Marseilles.

While not as relevant now as when it was written, *The Count of Monte-Cristo* still has the capacity to thrill not only as a colorful, dramatic adventure story and a historical period piece, but also as a parable of the devastating effects of revenge, both on the victim and the perpetrator. The consequences of Edmond's careful, subtle plans, enacted over a decade, are more far-reaching than even he can imagine, and in destroying his tormentors there is considerable collateral damage: Innocents and guilty alike must perish when ends justify the means. Edmond himself is greatly changed in the process of wreaking his vengeance. The unsophisticated young man he was at the beginning of the story has by the end been forever transformed by suffering into a learned, well-traveled cosmopolite, capable of convincingly playing any

role to carry out his main task as an exterminating angel so consumed with his diabolical goals that he cannot relax and enjoy the fortune that has fallen into his lap. Though by the conclusion of the story Edmond is an empty shell distrustful of his own emotions, the reader is left with a ray of hope that Haidée's love can change him into the kinder, gentler person he once was.

These qualities—an exciting adventure, supported by a strong sense of morality and bolstered by the "what-if" possibilities of unlimited wealth; and a story set in a visually historical period and place and told from the perspective of a sympathetic hero fighting truly despicable villains—have kept *The Count of Monte-Cristo* (a work long in the public domain) a filmmaker's favorite. The best-known film version was released in 1934.

"Critical Evaluation" by Patricia Ann King;
revised by Jack Ewing

Further Reading

Bell, A. Craig. *Alexandre Dumas: A Biography and Study*. 1950. Reprint. Folcroft, Pa.: Folcroft Library Editions, 1979. Discusses the origins and the genesis of *The Count of Monte-Cristo*, including notes from Dumas to his collaborator Auguste Maquet. Provides a clear analysis of character, settings, and theme. Dated but still helpful.

Bell, David F. *Real Time: Accelerating Narrative from Balzac to Zola*. Urbana: University of Illinois Press, 2004. Bell cites examples from novels and short stories to explore how the accelerated movement of people and information in the nineteenth century was a crucial element in the work of Dumas and other French writers. Chapter 4 focuses on *The Count of Monte-Cristo*.

Dumas, Alexandre, *père*. *The Count of Monte-Cristo*. Rev. translation, with an introduction and notes by David Coward. New York: Oxford University Press, 2008. This new translation, based upon the novel's original serialization, includes revised notes, a new bibliography, and an introduction by Coward, the volume's translator and the editor of nine of Dumas's novels.

Hemmings, F. W. J. *Alexandre Dumas: The King of Romance*. New York: Charles Scribner's Sons, 1979. Good introductory source describing the origins of the plot of *The Count of Monte-Cristo* in an earlier story, "Georges," and in the imprisonment of François Picaud. Argues that the work is the greatest revenger's tragedy in the history of the novel and that it employs the hero as an instrument of divine providence. Offers a clear analysis of theme and character.

Schopp, Claude. *Alexandre Dumas: Genius of Life*. Translated by A. J. Koch. New York: Franklin Watts, 1988. Detailed biography that provides a good introduction to Dumas's life and work, including the events surrounding the creation of *The Count of Monte-Cristo* and an account of public response. Provides insights into Dumas's working methods.

Severson, Marilyn S. *Masterpieces of French Literature*. Westport, Conn.: Greenwood Press, 2004. An analysis of *The Count of Monte-Cristo*, discussing its plot, character development, style, and themes and placing the novel in its biographical and historical context. Designed for students.

Stowe, Richard. *Alexandre Dumas (père)*. Boston: Twayne, 1976. Provides a clear plot summary of *The Count of Monte-Cristo* and detailed analysis of character, setting, and atmosphere. Compares Dantès with other Dumas heroes and traces the novel's development, focusing on its blending of reality and fantasy.

The Counterfeiters

Author: André Gide (1869-1951)
First published: Les Faux-monnayeurs, 1925 (English translation, 1927)
Type of work: Novel
Type of plot: Psychological realism
Time of plot: Early 1920's
Locale: Paris

Principal characters:
ÉDOUARD, a writer
OLIVIER MOLINIER, his nephew
GEORGE MOLINIER, Olivier's younger brother
VINCENT MOLINIER, Olivier's older brother
BERNARD PROFITENDIEU, Olivier's friend and Édouard's secretary
LAURA DOUVIERS, Édouard's friend
COMTE ROBERT DE PASSAVANT, a libertine
ARMAND VEDEL, Laura's brother and Olivier's friend

The Story:

When seventeen-year-old Bernard Profitendieu discovers an old love letter of his mother and realizes that he is an illegitimate son, he leaves a scathing letter for the man whom he considered his real father and runs away from home. He spends that night with his friend, Olivier Molinier. Olivier tells him of his Uncle Édouard, a writer, who will be arriving from England the following day and also of a woman with whom his older brother Vincent is involved.

The next morning, Bernard leaves before Olivier awakens. For a time he wonders what to do. He idly decides to go to the station and watch Olivier meet his uncle. That same morning Vincent visits his friend, the notoriously gay Comte Robert de Passavant. Vincent is disturbed over his affair with Laura Douviers, a married woman he met while both were patients in a sanatorium. Upon her release, she followed Vincent to Paris.

Édouard returns to Paris because of a promise to Laura. He knew her before her marriage and told her to call upon him whenever necessary. He is also looking forward to seeing his nephew Olivier, of whom he is very fond. He is so excited, in fact, that, after checking his bag, he drops his checkroom ticket. The meeting with his nephew, however, proves unsatisfactory. Unobserved, Bernard watches the meeting between the two. He picks up the checkroom ticket Édouard dropped and claims the bag. In it he discovers a large sum of money, which he quickly pockets; Édouard's journal, which he reads without scruple; and Laura's supplicating letter.

With no definite plan in mind, Bernard calls on Laura. Laura is disturbed by the young man who knows so much about her affairs, but his actions become understandable when Édouard arrives and Bernard admits the theft of the bag. He says that he stole it as a means of getting in touch with Édouard. Édouard is impressed with the young man's impudent charm. When Bernard suggests that he might fill the role of a secretary, Édouard agrees. A few days later, with Bernard as his secretary, Édouard takes Laura to Switzerland. Bernard writes to Olivier in glowing terms about his new position. Olivier is jealous of Bernard, who, he believes, has taken his place in Édouard's affections. He decides to take an editorial assignment offered to him by de Passavant.

In the meantime, Bernard falls in love with Laura. When he confesses his love, Laura shows him a letter from her husband, begging her to come back to him with her child and Vincent's. She decides to return to him. Bernard and Édouard return to Paris. A letter then arrives from Olivier to Bernard. He is in Italy with de Passavant, and he writes complacently about the wonderful journal they intend to publish. Bernard shows the letter to Édouard, who fails to realize that the letter disguises the boy's real feelings of jealousy and hurt.

Although still serving as Édouard's secretary, Bernard enrolls in the Vedel School and is living in the Vedel household. The Vedels are Laura's parents and Édouard's close friends. Édouard is particularly fond of Rachel, Laura's older sister, and it distresses him to see that she is devoting all of her time and energy to managing the school. Bernard tells Édouard about some children, including George, Olivier's younger brother, who are engaged in some underhanded activities. The boys, as Bernard is soon to learn, are passing counterfeit coins.

Olivier returns to Paris to get in touch with Bernard. The meeting between the two is strained. As they part, Olivier invites Édouard and Bernard to a party that de Passavant is giving that evening. Olivier then visits another old friend, Armand Vedel, Laura's younger brother. Armand refuses the invitation to the party but suggests that Olivier ask his sister Sarah to go in his place. Bernard, who is living at the school, is to serve as her escort.

The party is an orgy. Olivier becomes drunk and quarrelsome. Édouard leads him from the room, and Olivier, ashamed, begs his uncle to take him away. Bernard escorts Sarah home. Her room is beyond Armand's, and her brother hands Bernard the candle to light the way. As soon as Bernard goes into her bedroom, Armand bolts the door. Bernard spends the night with Sarah.

The next morning, Bernard finds Édouard attempting to revive Olivier. After spending the night with his uncle, the boy rises early in the morning on the pretext that he wants to rest on the sofa. Getting up later, Édouard discovers his nephew lying on the bathroom floor unconscious, the gas jets turned on. Édouard nurses Olivier until the boy recovers. When Olivier's mother goes to see her son, she expresses to Édouard her concern for George and his wayward habits. Édouard promises to speak to George. He also learns that Vincent went away with Lady Griffith, a friend of de Passavant.

A few days later, Édouard receives a call from M. Pro-

fitendieu, the man Bernard thinks is his father. Ostensibly he calls in his office as magistrate to ask Édouard to speak to his nephew George, who is suspected of passing counterfeit coins. It soon becomes evident, however, that the real object of his visit is to inquire about Bernard. Since the boy left home, Profitendieu has been worried about him. He wants very much to have him home once more.

Meanwhile, Bernard's affair with Sarah attracts Rachel's attention, and she asks him to leave the school. Bernard goes to Édouard, who tells him of the interview with Profitendieu. For some time Bernard has regretted the harsh letter he wrote, and the hatred he felt for his foster father changes to sympathy and fondness. It is evident that Bernard is no longer needed as Édouard's secretary. He therefore decides to return home.

Armand succeeds Olivier as editor of de Passavant's journal. He goes to see Olivier and shows him a letter from an older brother in Egypt. The writer tells of a man with whom he is living who is almost out of his mind. From what he can gather from the fellow's ravings, the man was responsible for his female companion's death. Neither Armand nor Olivier guesses that the man is Olivier's brother Vincent.

George and his friends cause a tragedy at their school. Boris, the young grandson of an old friend of Édouard, is invited to join a secret society if he will perform the act of initiation—standing up before the class and shooting himself through the temple. It is understood that the cartridge will be a blank. Only one person knows there is a live cartridge in the gun; he tells no one. When Boris, pale but resolute, walks to the front of the class and shoots himself, the joke becomes a tragedy. The experience is terrible enough to bring George to his senses. Meanwhile, after Olivier completely recovers from his suicide attempt, Édouard settles down again to writing his book, with a great sense of peace and happiness.

Critical Evaluation:

One year after André Gide published *Corydon* (1924; English translation, 1950), which provoked a literary furor, he completed *The Counterfeiters* together with its complementary *Le Journal des "Faux-monnayeurs"* (1926; *Journal of "The Counterfeiters,"* 1951). Both books had taken six years to write. The idea for the novel, however, came to the author at least as early as 1906, when he cut out from the September 16 issue of the newspaper *Le Figaro* an article concerning a case of counterfeiting in which several children from respectable families had been involved. He also had on file a report of the suicide of Neny, a young student at the Lycée Blaise-Pascal. Furthermore, in 1907, news of a gang of anarchist counterfeiters was widely publicized. By 1919, Gide began a tentative draft of the novel, which he continued intermittently while he was writing his critical study *Dostoïevsky* (1923) and completing his sexual research. *The Counterfeiters*, a culmination of such long and careful thought, is generally regarded as Gide's masterpiece, although he preferred the more scandalous *Corydon*.

In a sense, *The Counterfeiters* summarizes the major ideas that Gide had presented up to that point in his career. Later, he would publish other major books—*Si le grain ne meurt* (1926; *If I Die...*, 1935), *L'École des femmes* (1929; *The School for Wives*, 1929), for example—but they would not break new ground. With *The Counterfeiters*, Gide's high place in European literature was assured. While its roots are in the tradition of the nineteenth century social novel and novel of ideas—for example, Gustave Flaubert's *L'Éducation sentimentale* (1869; *A Sentimental Education*, 1898) and Fyodor Dostoevski's *Besy* (1871-1872; *The Possessed*, 1913; also known as *The Devils*)—its influence, both in matters of style and in philosophy, is unmistakable in such important twentieth century novels as Aldous Huxley's *Point Counter Point* (1928) and Lawrence Durrell's *The Alexandria Quartet* (1962). Like these books, *The Counterfeiters* is at once a novel of ideas, of artistic development, and of psychological realism.

Gide's title, which is partly ironic, was the projected title of a yet unfinished—and, according to *The Journal of the Counterfeiters*, never-to-be-completed—novel by Édouard. Throughout the book, Édouard talks about his novel, describes its theme, and, at one point, allows George Molinier to read a selection from it; George not only fails to understand the meaning of the passage but also scorns the name of the protagonist. On reflection, Édouard agrees with his critic. Édouard is never satisfied with the direction that his writing takes. At first, he insists that his book has no subject, that it is a mere slice of life. Later, he catches sight of its "deep-lying subject," which is "the rivalry between the real world and the representation of it which we make to ourselves." That subject is expressed in the symbolism of a counterfeit coin. In the important chapter "Édouard Explains His Theory of the Novel," he shows Bernard Profitendieu a counterfeit ten-franc piece. If Bernard were to understand that the coin is not genuine, he would naturally despise it; if he were deluded into thinking that it is real, he would value it beyond its worth. Value, therefore, depends upon perception, but perception has nothing to do with reality. Later, the reader learns that the coin is more than a symbol of counterfeit values. George is suspected of passing counterfeit money.

Gide's trick upon the reader is characteristic of his artistic method, which is one of ironic contrast, of allowing his protagonists to play games that prove finally to be serious, or to turn their serious problems into farcical games. *The Counterfeiters* presents a wide diversity of ideas, exposes their absurdities, yet sometimes salvages their values. On one level, the book explores the risks along with the liberating energies of criminality. Bernard, who comes upon Édouard's checkroom ticket, takes the writer's bag, which contains money, a literary journal, and a letter from Laura Douviers. He keeps the money, at least for a while, excusing himself with the rationalization that he is not a thief, reads the confidential journal, and uses the letter as a pretext to involve himself in Laura's life as her protector. Thus, he commits a "gratuitous act," outrageous in its casual, motiveless interference in the lives of others. Yet the consequences, both for Bernard and for those concerned, are not as crass as the reader might expect. By exercising his total capacity for freedom, he has broken into life, enjoyed a more exciting and richer life experience than he might otherwise have known. To be sure, the ultimate consequences of his act are dangerous, and he learns that one's boldness may often cause other people unhappiness, but the lesson is not entirely cautionary. By the end of the book, more liberated than at the outset, Bernard makes his peace with his stepfather and returns to his family as a more responsible young man.

Bernard, though perhaps the most extraordinary example of this, is not the only character in the novel who asserts his philosophies by living them. Just as Bernard's fortunes rise because of his impetuosity, Vincent Molinier's decline. The seducer of Laura, whom he callously abandons, Vincent himself is destroyed by Lady Griffith. Her sensuality is greater and more destructive than his. Still other characters temporize, frozen in will, and allow the world to come to them. Gide's method is to provide brief scenes presenting encounters between characters, usually two characters at a time. The personalities express their ideas, sometimes debate, and at other times agree. Yet matched with a different partner, a different encounter, the characters change their minds, often subtly and without understanding the results of their actions. Thus, the sense of reality shifts, just as the circumstances appear to turn one direction or another. Reality is not absolute. The author, who is himself a voice in the novel, is not above suspicion of error. Surely Gide's major spokesman, the writer Édouard, is at times wise, at times foolish.

More than a complex novel of ideas that explores the limitations of perceiving reality, *The Counterfeiters* is an aesthetic novel that treats the development of the artist. To be sure, there are two novelists in the book. Édouard, the more important figure, is discreetly gay, stoic, troubled by problems of moral ambiguity, but generous, open-natured, and, like Gide, insistent that sincerity is his chief resource as an artist. His rival is Comte Robert de Passavant, also gay, more successful as a writer but more devious as a human being. The comte is also Édouard's rival for the affections of Olivier Molinier. As Édouard develops—through constantly changing and refining—his aesthetic, it becomes clear that his rivalry with Passavant is never far from the springs of his invention. Édouard explains his theory of art both in dialogues—or encounters—with other characters or, more fully, to himself in his journals. Like Gide's famous literary journals, Édouard's notebooks examine the philosophy and strategies of composition, relate anecdotes, puzzle over problems of structure, and attempt to analyze the writer's own motives. As an exploration both of art and of himself, the journals are filled with undigested, often contradictory, but urgent material for further investigation. It is a measure of Gide's excellence as an artist that he never exhausts but generally augments the subject he treats.

His understanding of the craft of fiction carries over to an interest in the artist's psychology. Perhaps this concern of Gide's novel is less satisfactory for most readers, because the writer's gay bias allows for only a partial, inadequate view of the subject. One theme of *The Counterfeiters* is the psychosexual development of the two university friends, Bernard and Olivier. At the beginning of the novel, both prepare for their *bachot*, the baccalaureate examinations at the Sorbonne. By the end, both pass. Similarly, they undergo a sensual education that results in a certain homosexual orientation for Olivier and a very nearly certain one for Bernard. Olivier is clearly disposed to homosexuality when he first encounters Bernard (and they share a bed), but he discovers, first through de Passavant and later through Édouard, that the relationship he prefers involves the companionship of an older patron. As for Édouard, a genteel and delicate pederast, the arrangement is ideal. Having achieved the satisfaction he has always craved from the love of Olivier, he is prepared to resume work on his novel.

Bernard's sexuality is more ambiguous, but without doubt it is mainly homoerotic. His sexual encounter with Sarah Vedel is almost farcical. Sarah, the aggressor throughout, is—incredible to say—assisted by her brother Armand, who bolts the bedroom door to make sure that the couple perform the act of love. As soon as Bernard wakes up, he runs from Sarah's chamber, never wishing to see her again. Bernard is capable only of veneration for women, as he idolizes Laura and admires Rachel, her sister, but feels for them nothing akin to desire. He is more finely attracted to Olivier. Yet, following Gide's homosexual fantasy, he bows out of the picture so that Édouard has the youth to himself. To complete

the fantasy, Gide allows Olivier's mother, Pauline, in a ludicrous scene, to bestow her blessings on the union. Curious though the scene is from the standpoint of heterosexual psychology, it is perfectly satisfactory in the context of the author's purpose in the novel. The description of the meeting, after all, is part of Édouard's journal. How much of it is imagined and how much real? Indeed, to what extent are the actions of the characters real or pretended? Gide, master of disguises, makes his characters speak their parts, cleverly or stupidly as may be, but withholds his own moral judgments.

"Critical Evaluation" by Leslie B. Mittleman

Further Reading

Brée, Germaine. *Gide.* Westport, Conn.: Greenwood Press, 1985. One of the best introductions to Gide and his work available in English. Brée's analysis of *The Counterfeiters* and *The Journal of "The Counterfeiters"* emphasizes sociological aspects, connections to Gide's life, and the importance of the reader's own participation in the novel's meaning.

Cordle, Thomas. *André Gide.* Updated ed. New York: Twayne, 1993. Contains a good analysis of *The Counterfeiters*, which Cordle considers Gide's greatest work. The social critique of early twentieth century petty bourgeoisie comes out as an important theme of the novel. Selected bibliography.

Gide, André. *Journal of "The Counterfeiters."* Translated by Justin O' Brien. In *The Counterfeiters* by André Gide. Translated by Dorothy Bussy. New York: Knopf, 1951. Gide's own account of his novel's genesis is a fascinating document in its own right and provides many insights into its meaning.

Goux, Jean-Joseph. *The Coiners of Language.* Translated by Jennifer Curtiss Gage. Norman: University of Oklahoma Press, 1994. Analyzes *The Counterfeiters* alongside the writings of Gide's uncle, political economist Charles Gide. Goux maintains that the demise of realism and the rise of modernism coincided with the disappearance of gold money, and that Gide and other modernists wrote with a new "token language" that expressed a new sensibility.

Guerard, Albert J. *André Gide.* Cambridge, Mass.: Harvard University Press, 1951. Still an important introduction to Gide's work. Places *The Counterfeiters* in the tradition of the modern novel of the turn of the century, and makes some interesting parallels with the work of Russian novelist Fyodor Dostoevski, who was an important influence on Gide.

Lucey, Michael. *Never Say I: Sexuality and the First Person in Colette, Gide, and Proust.* Durham, N.C.: Duke University Press, 2006. Lucey examines *The Counterfeiters* and Gide's other works to describe how he created characters, narrative techniques, and points of view that enabled him to write "about, for, or as" someone who was attracted to the same sex.

Sheridan, Alan. *André Gide: A Life in the Present.* Cambridge, Mass.: Harvard University Press, 1999. A comprehensive literary biography, which analyzes all of Gide's works and their relationships to one another and describes how Gide transformed his life into fiction. Chapter 13 focuses on *The Counterfeiters.*

Walker, David H. *André Gide.* New York: St. Martin's Press, 1990. Contrasts *The Counterfeiters* with Gide's earlier work. Analyzes the psychological aspects of the novel and the problem of causality.

_____, ed. *André Gide.* New York: Longman, 1996. A selection of criticism and interpretation of Gide's work, including pieces written during and after his lifetime. Each essay contains an introduction that places the piece in context. Includes bibliography and index.

The Countess Cathleen

Author: William Butler Yeats (1865-1939)
First produced: 1899; first published, 1892
Type of work: Drama
Type of plot: Allegory
Time of plot: Indeterminate
Locale: Ireland

Principal characters:
COUNTESS CATHLEEN, an Irish noblewoman
OONA, her childhood nurse and present companion
ALEEL, a visionary poet in love with Cathleen
SHEMUS RUA, a peasant
MARY, his wife
TEIGUE, their son
TWO DEMONS, disguised as merchants

The Story:

During a famine, an Irish peasant family talks about strange creatures that appear, portents that evil supernatural forces are abroad in the land. The Countess Cathleen and her companions arrive, searching for the way to her castle. The peasants bitterly complain to her of their state, and she gives them what she is left in her purse after previous charity to other starving folk. She invites the family to her castle the next day to receive more.

After her departure, Shemus and Teigue complain at the meagerness of her charity, while Mary scolds them for ingratitude. Irked by his wife's words, Shemus asserts his independence by rashly calling three times on the supernatural creatures of the woods to enter his house. Two traveling merchants appear, ostentatiously displaying their wealth. They offer money for souls and send Shemus and Teigue to broadcast their offer to the countryside. Cathleen arrives at her castle, where Aleel tries to distract her with a story about Queen Maeve of the fairies, who weeps for a mortal who died of love for her—not because she loved him, too, but because she forgot his name. Oona recalls her to the concerns of the day, earning a curse from Aleel for preventing him from relieving

Cathleen of distress for ten minutes. The castle steward tells Cathleen that men broke into the castle to steal food; to Oona's consternation, Cathleen declares the theft to be no sin, since the men must be starving. Shemus and Teigue then arrive with their tale of merchants buying souls; Cathleen, appalled, offers to buy their souls back. Father and son decline the offer, concluding that God turned his back on Ireland. Cathleen then instructs the steward to sell all her property, save only the house, and use the money to buy food for the starving, stating that she intends from that time forward to dedicate herself to others.

Aleel tries to get Cathleen to flee by telling her a dream he had of an angel who urges her to flee. She refuses, asserting that it was a pagan god, not an angel. She tenderly dismisses Aleel from her company to find the peace she cannot have herself and goes in to pray and sleep.

While she sleeps, the merchants enter and rob her treasury, then awaken Cathleen to tell her lies—that her relief efforts came to nothing—and to pass on rumors about their own appearance in the land. They explain men's willingness to sell their souls as a kind of joy in despair and tell her her own soul would be worth half a million crowns. She begins to suspect their true identities, and they depart as their pursuers close in on them.

Cathleen bids peasants fleeing the evil times welcome to a place where they will be safe, but at that moment, Oona discovers the empty treasury. Although close to personal despair, Cathleen urges all with her to pray for the souls of the famine victims. Meanwhile, other peasants pass the castle, talking about the power and beauty of gold as the merchants follow in silence. They move on, and a forlorn Aleel passes by, singing in a vain attempt to soothe his love-stricken heart.

The merchants set up shop in the house of Shemus and begin dealing for souls, with Shemus and Teigue as their lieutenants. Mary Rua refuses food bought with the devil's money and lies dead on her bed. Two peasants exchange their souls for money, finding themselves to be worth less than anticipated since the merchants have records of their darkest, most hidden secrets. Aleel, too, offers his soul—for free— since he has no need of it if it cannot help Cathleen. He is refused, since his soul already belongs to the countess. An old, nearly sinless woman sells her soul for a thousand crowns and wishes God's blessing on the merchants, whereupon she screams as a burning pain passes through her. This frightens the other peasants, who begin to shrink from the merchants.

Cathleen comes to the cottage, offering her soul for the half million crowns on the condition that the other bartered souls be returned to their owners. After the sale, the merchants follow her out, vowing to watch over her until her impending death from a broken heart allows them to take her soul.

Aleel has a vision of the old gods and heroes returning, and Oona arrives at the hut to be told that her mistress already had sold her soul. As they both kneel, in prayer or in despair, Cathleen is carried in to die. Outside, a ferocious storm brews, terrifying the peasants, whose fear is increased by Aleel's response to the storm: a curse on fate for leaving no hope. Aleel then describes a vision of angels and devils battling in the middle of the storm. He seizes one of the angels to demand word of Cathleen's fate. The angel describes her arrival in heaven, redeemed by her sacrifice despite the sin of having sold her soul. Aleel kneels before this revelation, while Oona begs for her own death, bemoaning her separation from Cathleen.

Critical Evaluation:

William Butler Yeats first published a version of the story of the Countess Kathleen O'Shea in his collection *Fairy and Folk Tales of the Irish Peasantry* (1888), and appears to have conceived of a play based on the story at around the same time. Although he later dismissed the play, his first and longest major dramatic work, as merely "a piece of tapestry," Yeats was unable to dismiss the idea from his imagination. For more than thirty years, he repeatedly revised *The Countess Cathleen* to bring it into line with his evolving vision of poetry and the theater.

Unable to fit the play into the formalized symbolism of Yeats's later drama, many writers have examined *The Countess Cathleen* only in terms of its role in the development of the Irish theater. Yeats published an early version in 1892. The play was not performed, however, until 1899, after at least one major revision, when it was half of the playlist of the inaugural season of the Irish National Theater.

The Dublin premiere was politically controversial; protesters objected to the play's unorthodox theology and allegedly slanderous depiction of Irish peasants—even before the play was staged. Religious authorities objected to Yeats's conclusion that, "The Light of Lights/ Looks always on the motive, not the deed"; while nationalists insisted no Irishman would ever sell his soul. These sorts of objections were prophetic of later conflicts between Irish playwrights and the public. Organized hecklers tried to disrupt the first performance, disgusting the young James Joyce, who was present. Despite these protests, however, the first performance was enthusiastically received by much of the audience.

The play's role in theater history has distracted attention from the play itself, which critics of Yeats's drama seldom treat favorably. The frequent revisions, none of which brought out the "personal thought and feeling" that Yeats claimed were his real goals in writing it, make it easy to see *The Countess Cathleen* as a failure. The more intense poetry and more accomplished drama of his later plays also contributed to a critical focus on the play's flaws, as did Yeats's own judgment.

Such dismissals obscure the play's thematic strengths: the patterned exposition of conflicts between private and public roles, between responsibility to the real world and fulfillment of the dream, between the motive and the deed. Yeats sought to portray this metaphysical conflict in the person of Cathleen and conceded that, insofar as she undergoes no dramatic transformation, the play does not succeed. The internal conflict is over almost before it begins. Cathleen vows in the second scene to place others' joys and sorrows before her own, and never thereafter appears seriously tempted to renege on the vow.

Even the play's detractors grant that its strength is lyric rather than dramatic. Linguistic expression, not plot and characterization, is what is most impressive and original about the play. In some versions, the play was subtitled "A

Mystery Play," suggesting another way to read it. Placing its story of sacrifice and redemption in the context of medieval religious mysteries shifts the emphasis from drama of character to the contrasts between the allegorical figures of the play. Each major figure occupies a different position in the debate between the demands of public and private life, highlighting different aspects of Cathleen's choices. Aleel, the poet, urges Cathleen to embrace his dream of love and thus to transfer (but not to abandon) her public responsibility to the peasantry to others. He fails to tempt Cathleen with his songs of fairyland, but his poetic vision enables him to see her final assumption into heaven, confirming her choice and his visionary perspective. Mary Rua, the peasant's wife, holds to orthodox theology. She will have no dealings with devils and so saves her soul even as her body dies. A countess, unlike a peasant, has a public as well as a private responsibility, so Cathleen's choice must be to compromise with evil in the interests of a greater good. Her compromise represents the triumph of public responsibility over personal satisfaction. It is a subtle reading of the relationship between good and evil.

Yeats's play can be seen as an allegory cataloging the forms of response to worldly concerns. Cathleen's willingness to sacrifice herself in the interest of her peasants contrasts to the selfish desperation of the peasants who sell their souls, to the distant refusal of Aleel to abandon hopeless love, and to the stern refusal to compromise of Mary, none of which prove useful in relieving suffering. Despite the objections of dogmatists, the play presents a fairly orthodox response to the problem of evil, a response from which Yeats would move away as his artistic vision developed.

A. Waller Hastings

Further Reading

Howes, Marjorie, and John Kelly, eds. *The Cambridge Companion to W. B. Yeats*. New York: Cambridge University Press, 2006. Collection of essays providing an overview of Yeats's work in all genres, including a discussion of Yeats and the drama.

Lucas, F. L. *The Drama of Chekhov, Synge, Yeats, and Pirandello*. New York: Phaeton Press, 1976. Places *The Countess Cathleen* in the context of European drama. Finds the play wanting.

Nathan, Leonard E. *The Tragic Drama of William Butler Yeats: Figures in a Dance*. New York: Columbia University Press, 1975. Examines Yeats's failure to realize completely his goal of a metaphysical drama about the conflict between the natural and supernatural worlds.

O'Connor, Ulick. *All the Olympians: A Biographical Portrait of the Irish Literary Renaissance*. Dublin: Town House and Country House, 1999. The chapter on *The Countess Cathleen* provides unusual detail about the play's first Dublin production in 1899 and its hostile reception by some segments of the Irish public.

Rajan, Balachandra. *W. B. Yeats: A Critical Introduction*. London: Hutchinson University Library, 1972. Includes a good, brief account of the play's failure to achieve Yeats's vision and places the work in the context of his later successes, arguing that these successes unfairly color critical vision of *The Countess Cathleen*.

Richman, David. *Passionate Action: Yeats's Mastery of Drama*. Newark: University of Delaware Press, 2000. Draws on Yeats's correspondence and the many drafts of his plays to chronicle his work as a playwright and theatrical producer.

Yeats, W. B. *The Countess Cathleen: Manuscript Materials*. Edited by Michael J. Sidnell and Wayne K. Chapman. Ithaca, N.Y.: Cornell University Press, 1999. Yeats frequently revised *The Countess Cathleen*, and these revisions reflect his relations with critics and audiences, his changing ideas about drama, and the status of his relationship with actress Maud Gonne. This book contains extant manuscripts and other materials that chronicle the play's writing and revision from 1889 through 1934.

A Country Doctor

Author: Sarah Orne Jewett (1849-1909)
First published: 1884
Type of work: Novel
Type of plot: Bildungsroman
Time of plot: Mid-nineteenth century
Locale: Oldfields, Maine

Principal characters:
NAN PRINCE, a student of medicine
MRS. THACHER, her grandmother
DR. LESLIE, her guardian
MISS NANCY PRINCE, her aunt

The Story:

One cold winter night, while Mrs. Thacher and two of her neighbors sit around the stove and gossip about neighborhood activities, they are interrupted by a noise at the door. Adeline Thacher Prince lies fallen on the doorstep. In her arms she holds her infant daughter, Nan. Dr. Leslie is sent for at once, but by the next day, Adeline is dead. According to her wishes, Dr. Leslie becomes the little child's guardian, though she lives with her maternal grandmother.

Nan's mother left home to work in a textile mill in Lowell. There she fell in love with a young man from Dunport, Maine, and after a short courtship, she married him. The marriage was far from happy. Adeline inherited a wild, rebellious tendency, and it was whispered in Dunport that she eventually started to drink. Furthermore, Adeline resented the strong opposition of her husband's family to the marriage, and, in particular, the views of her husband's sister, Miss Nancy Prince. After Adeline's husband died, she tried for a time to support both herself and the child. When she could do so no longer, she trudged back to Oldfields to die in her mother's home.

Nan seems to exhibit some of her mother's traits, for she is mischievous and inclined to pleasure. Her grandmother often thinks her a trial, but to Dr. Leslie she is something quite different. One day, Nan retrieves a fallen bird with a fractured leg and applies a splint, as she saw Dr. Leslie do to his patients. The doctor begins to wonder if Nan inherited some tendency toward medicine from her father. He does not insist that she go to school. He thinks that the training she receives in the woods and the fields is far more beneficial than any she would obtain in the schoolroom.

When Mrs. Thacher dies, Nan goes to live with Dr. Leslie. There is a great feeling of affection between the two. Nan, who continues to go out on calls with the doctor, exhibits much interest in his work. The time comes at last for her to be sent to boarding school. At first, she is shy and rather backward in her studies, but after a while, she makes admirable progress. She would have been completely satisfied with her life had she not wondered, from time to time, about the mys-

terious aunt of whom she heard only rumors. Mrs. Thacher never explained anything of the girl's family background to her, and Nan conjures up the figure of a wealthy aristocratic relative who will one day send for her. Miss Prince, who inherited a large estate, regularly sends money to Dr. Leslie to help provide for Nan's upkeep. The doctor never touches a penny of it. When Adeline died, Miss Prince asked for custody of the child, but Mrs. Thacher and Dr. Leslie refused her request.

When Nan grows older, she tells Dr. Leslie of her desire to study medicine. Although the doctor is aware of the difficulties she will face, he approves heartily of her interest. Yet, the town of Oldfields does not, and many are shocked at the idea of a woman doctor. Nan continues her studies using the doctor's books, however, and acts as his nurse. She is to continue training at a medical school in a nearby city.

When the time comes for her to leave Oldfields, Nan writes a brief note to her aunt, Miss Prince, and asks if she might visit her father's sister. Miss Prince, although she fears that Nan might be like her mother, consents to receive her niece. On Nan's arrival in Dunport, Miss Prince, genuinely pleased with her, helps Nan to make friends and openly acknowledges her young relative. Yet, when Nan expresses her wish to study medicine, everyone is shocked, even Miss Prince, who in a large measure blames Dr. Leslie for Nan's unladylike desire for a professional career. Nan, although made unhappy by her aunt's objections, remains adamant.

Her aunt and her friends, however, seek to lead her astray from her work. Miss Prince has a favorite friend, young George Gerry, to whom she intends to leave her money. When Nan grows fond of George, everyone hopes that they will marry. One day, during an outing, Nan and George stop at a farmhouse, and Nan treats a farmer who threw his arm out of joint. Sometime later, George asks Nan to marry him. She refuses, both because she wants to become a doctor and because she is afraid that her inherited characteristics might cause her to be a bad wife.

At last, she tells her aunt that she will return to Oldfields. On her arrival, the doctor, apprehensive that Nan was influenced by Miss Prince and her money, is pleasantly surprised. She is the same Nan as before and all the more ambitious for a successful medical career.

Nan goes away to study. When she returns, Dr. Leslie is older and needs more help in his practice. Nan settles down in Oldfields and slowly the community accepts her. Before many years pass, she succeeds Dr. Leslie in the affections of the men and women of the village.

Critical Evaluation:

Sarah Orne Jewett uses the conventional novel pattern of the development of a young person to explore why a nineteenth century woman may choose not to follow a traditional life path. The book further argues that a woman should be encouraged in an alternative path if her inclinations and talents lead her toward a career rather than a home life. Jewett subsumes a courtship plot into the novel of development and portrays the heroine's rejection of marriage as an important step in her growing up. In *A Country Doctor*, an independent career rather than a dependent marriage is the final goal.

The primary plot of the novel is Nan Prince's development, and Jewett intertwines exposition with event to demonstrate how a woman might grow into a vocation instead of into marriage. Nan's guardian and mentor, Dr. Leslie, makes her a test case with which to try out his theory that a child, like a plant, should be allowed to grow naturally rather than to be clipped, tied, and trained according to predetermined notions. Nan discovers her vocation rather than having Dr. Leslie or society choose it for her. The novel suggests that some combination of inheritance, environment, and the will of God makes people what they are. From her father, Nan inherits a talent for medicine and a determination to pursue goals. From her mother, she inherits a wild streak that, the novel suggests, is better channeled into a career than into domestic life. Nan has no inclination toward domestic pursuits or romantic love, and so she comes to believe that she should fulfill what she believes to be her God-given life purpose of practicing medicine.

After she decides to become a doctor, Nan confronts a series of hurdles that threaten to deter her, and when she has successfully cleared each one, she has proven she deserves the glorious future she thanks God for in the novel's final lines. Nan is first discouraged by people who persistently trivialize her goals. Many refuse to take her aspiration seriously, assuming that she will grow out of her fancy for working or that she will fall in love and give it up. She successfully maintains her own conviction, however, that her vocation is medicine and not marriage. When she goes to Dunport for an extended visit with her wealthy Aunt Nancy, whom she has

never seen before, she faces additional hurdles. She can become her aunt's heiress if she stays in Dunport, and not be obliged to work for a living at all. Mrs. Fraley, a friend of her aunt and a force to be reckoned with in Dunport society, invites Nan to tea in order to denounce her desire to be a doctor. Rather than buckle under the pressure, Nan politely but assertively defends her choices. The toughest obstacle of all, however, comes from within Nan. She surprises herself by falling in love with George Gerry, Aunt Nancy's young protégé. The courtship scenes are subsumed into the novel's overall purpose of tracing Nan's growth toward a career. Her knowledge of herself is strong, and she knows she cannot give herself entirely to George and to marriage. She knows her marriage will eventually prove to be unhappy, and she knows she will regret turning aside from her life's purpose, so she rejects George's marriage offer and her aunt's insistence that she make Dunport her home. Having successfully overcome these challenges and proven herself true to her convictions, Nan returns to her childhood home, Oldfields, to take up her study of medicine and to begin to establish a practice.

Jewett attempts to present Nan's rebellion against conventional roles for women as nonthreatening. The novel stresses several times that many women can and should find fulfillment in marriage and homemaking, and that a married woman should devote herself to her husband and home. Nan professes to regard marriage highly; that is one reason she rejects it for herself. Jewett never hints that Nan might both marry and practice medicine. The heroine must choose between those paths. Jewett's handling of the courtship between Nan and George unsettles the cultural dictate in favor of marriage nevertheless. In the key scene in which Nan, on a pleasure trip with George, confidently and successfully adjusts a separated shoulder for a suffering farmer, Jewett shows that a woman can have power to command men. The farmer and George obey Nan's directions because she offers them with such confidence, and while the farmer is astonished and grateful at the outcome, George is disturbed. He cannot conceive of a relationship with a woman in which she has superior command, and he begins to conceive of his courtship of Nan as a battle in which he is endeavoring to master her, to persuade her to give up her silly idea of becoming a doctor. When he is defeated, he is forced to recognize his inferiority to Nan, a self-awareness that Jewett suggests will inspire him to work harder toward his own goals. The novel claims on one hand to hold marriage sacred; it also reveals on the other hand that a woman might prove herself independent of romantic love, stronger than men, and fully satisfied with a career.

Jewett is frequently praised for her precise rendition of New England scenes, characters, and language, but the relevance of her work to American literature and culture goes beyond its successful representation of isolated rural communities. *A Country Doctor* argues that human nature is the same everywhere, and that life may be observed and lived to its fullest in a small New England town as well as anywhere else. When Jewett presents this study of how one young woman found her vocation and proved herself worthy of it, she implies that the lessons learned by Nan are relevant beyond the confines of nineteenth century New England. She shows how an individual may be influenced by her environment and biological heritage and yet exert her free will to choose her own path in life.

"Critical Evaluation" by Karen Tracey

Further Reading

Abate, Michelle Ann. "The Tomboy Matures into the New Woman: Sarah Orne Jewett's *A Country Doctor*." In *Tomboys: A Literary and Cultural History*. Philadelphia: Temple University Press, 2008. Abate's examination of the tomboy character in American fiction and film includes an analysis of *A Country Doctor*.

Blanchard, Paula. *Sarah Orne Jewett: Her World and Her Work*. Reading, Mass.: Addison-Wesley, 1994. Discusses *A Country Doctor* as an autobiographical novel. Dr. Leslie resembles Jewett's physician father, and Nan's decision to pursue vocation over marriage is drawn from Jewett's personal experience.

Donovan, Josephine. *Sarah Orne Jewett*. New York: Frederick Ungar, 1980. Analyzes Jewett's fictional themes of city versus country and isolation versus community.

Gale, Robert L. *A Sarah Orne Jewett Companion*. Westport, Conn.: Greenwood Press, 1999. A reference book containing alphabetically arranged entries about Jewett's writings, characters, family members, friends, acquaintances, professional associates, and admirers. The entries on her major works and the most important persons contain brief bibliographies.

Nagel, Gwen L., ed. *Critical Essays on Sarah Orne Jewett*. Boston: G. K. Hall, 1984. Reprints early reviews and contains original critical essays on her works, several of which discuss *A Country Doctor*'s relation to Jewett's other fiction.

Roman, Margaret. *Sarah Orne Jewett: Reconstructing Gender*. Tuscaloosa: University of Alabama Press, 1992. Argues that Jewett creates male and female characters who do not conform to conventions in order to challenge accepted notions about the sexes and to project a world in which any person may live and grow freely.

Westbrook, Perry D. *Acres of Flint: Sarah Orne Jewett and Her Contemporaries*. Rev. ed. Metuchen, N.J.: Scarecrow Press, 1981. Shows how Jewett's work relates to the local-color literary tradition developed by New England women writers after the Civil War.

Wittenberg, Judith Bryant. "Challenge and Compliance: Textual Strategies in *A Country Doctor* and Nineteenth Century American Women's Medical Autobiographies." In *Jewett and Her Contemporaries: Reshaping the Canon*, edited by Karen L. Kilcup and Thomas S. Edwards. Gainesville: University Press of Florida, 1999. This analysis of *A Country Doctor* places the novel within the wider context of nineteenth century women's autobiographical writing.

The Country Girls Trilogy and Epilogue

Author: Edna O'Brien (1930-   )
First published: 1986; includes *The Country Girls*,
    1960; *The Lonely Girl*, 1962; *Girls in Their Married*
    Bliss, 1964
Type of work: Novels
Type of plot: Psychological realism
Time of plot: 1930's-1980's
Locale: Dublin and near Limerick, Ireland; London

Principal characters:
CAITHLEEN "KATE" BRADY, the "good girl"
BRIDGET "BABA" BRENNAN, the "bad girl"
JACQUES "MR. GENTLEMAN" DE MAURIER, Kate's first
    love
EUGENE GAILLARD, Kate's sometime lover, and her first
    husband
CASH GAILLARD, Kate and Eugene's only child
FRANK DURACK, Baba's husband
TRACY DURACK, Baba's daughter

The Story:

The Country Girls. Caithleen "Kate" Brady has an adolescent worldview. Her mother is beautiful but depressed, while Kate's father is a vicious drunk who oppresses and abuses his wife and child. The Bradys own a farm with a beautiful house that they cannot afford. Kate is an only child.

Kate has a schoolgirl crush on Jacques de Maurier, a solicitor in their village who the townspeople have nicknamed Mr. Gentleman for his foreign and gallant ways.

Bridget "Baba" Brennan is Kate's age but is spiteful, unintelligent, and beautiful. Baba frequently bullies and humiliates Kate, but Kate feels helpless to stop it. Somehow, the girls are drawn to one another. Kate envies Baba her kind father while Baba envies Kate her intelligence and quiet demeanor.

Kate earns a scholarship to a convent school, the same day she learns that her house is mortgaged and that Baba is going to the same convent in the fall. While at Baba's house, Kate soon discovers that her mother has drowned while out with another man. Her childhood is over. She remains with the Brennan family over the summer and feels conflicted: She is happy to be safe from the fists of her father, but she is devastated by the loss of her mother.

Mr. Gentleman sees Kate waiting for the bus to Limerick and gives her a lift. At lunch, he flirts with her, and on the way home in the car, he holds her hand. This day becomes a precious memory for Kate.

The convent is a cold, loveless place where the girls band together against the grim atmosphere. Both girls despise it here and eventually are expelled for writing a vulgarity on a holy card. Reveling in their newfound freedom, Kate and Baba are unrepentant when chastised by their respective families over the incident. Caithleen has a distant and uncomfortable relationship with her father but finds a new friend in Mr. Brennan, Baba's father, who protects her from the wrath of her own father. He is kind to her as well.

Baba goes to Dublin for technical school, and Caithleen goes with her because there is nothing left for her at home. She works in a grocery store, and both girls room with a German couple, Joanna and Gustav, in Dublin. Kate becomes more outspoken and does not let Baba bully her. They become close friends, and Baba frequently finds double dates with dull but rich older men. Neither girl is looking for a life partner at this point. Mr. Gentleman finds Kate in Dublin and begins an illicit, albeit chaste, affair with her.

Baba becomes ill with tuberculosis and goes to a sanatorium for six months. Meanwhile, Kate continues her affair with Mr. Gentleman, and they plan a vacation to Vienna to consummate their relationship. Kate waits for Mr. Gentleman to show up, but she receives only a telegram that ends their affair.

The Lonely Girl. Kate has been in Dublin for two years and is still working at the grocery store and living with Baba at Joanna and Gustav's house. The girls date indiscriminately, typically rich older men, and happily remain unattached until Kate meets Eugene Gaillard at a party. Eugene, an older documentary-film director, treats the girls and another man to dinner, and Kate is smitten. She runs into Eugene the next week and is treated to tea. After weeks apart, Kate invites him to tea. They commence a relationship, even though he has reservations.

Eugene starts seeing Kate regularly and buys her a new coat. One evening he comes to tea at Kate's lodging house, where he flirts all evening with Baba. Kate soon learns that Eugene is married, but she still agrees to go with him to his country house. At the country house, Eugene tells Kate the story of his marriage to a woman named Laura. Still, they continue dating. Kate spends Christmas with Eugene, who attempts to seduce her several times over the next few days; Kate is still a virgin and very afraid, so she does not have sex with him. She returns to her old life in Dublin, fearing that all is over with Eugene. He renews their relationship via letter.

Kate soon receives an anonymous letter admonishing her for her relationship with Eugene; her father comes to collect her. She returns home to her father's house for a few days but manages to escape, back to Dublin. Afraid that he will find her at Joanna's home, Kate flees to Eugene's house. Her father and his cronies find her there, barge into the house, and assault Eugene. Kate is hiding under the bed in another room and can hear Eugene's responses to her family's questions. She suddenly realizes that Eugene does not feel the same way about their relationship as she does. This realization fuels her obsession further.

Eugene buys Kate a gold band, and in the evening they consummate their relationship. Kate is twenty-one years old, and Eugene is thirty-five years old.

Baba and her friend, The Body, come to visit, and Baba informs them that Kate's father is coming to the house with the bishop. Kate's father and the bishop show the next day, but Eugene does not let them in. Kate quickly learns that life with Eugene is not bliss. He is often cold and unforgiving, and his friends are pretentious and rude. Kate has frequent spells of moodiness to force emotion from Eugene, but these spells only irritate him.

Baba visits again and reveals that she is pregnant, but she later miscarries. Laura, Eugene's wife, sends a letter threatening Eugene's paternity rights if he marries Kate. Eugene's friends (including an attractive American girl) visit. Eugene flirts outright with the American girl and acts dismissive toward Kate. She leaves Eugene while they are in Dublin for a lunch date, and is left there by him. Baba speaks with Eugene about the situation and informs Kate that her relationship with him is over.

The young women leave for England to start their lives over. Eugene does not see Kate off. In England, Kate enrolls at a university for an English degree and works in a shop, while Baba works as a receptionist at a hotel. The women are still rooming together, and Kate muses about how she is changing.

Girls in Their Married Bliss. Kate and Eugene are finally married and have a child. Baba marries a rich but uneducated Irishman named Frank Durack. Kate, unhappy in her marriage, begins an affair with a married man. After breaking off the affair, Kate is confronted by Eugene, who tells her that their marriage is over. She leaves and asks Baba for shelter, but Baba's husband does not like Kate and forbids her staying there.

Baba willingly goes to dinner with Frank and lets Kate

and Cash (Kate and Eugene's son) stay at her house. When Baba and Frank return, they find an irate Eugene looking to retrieve Cash. Kate cannot find lodgings suitable for both her small son and herself, so she returns Cash to Eugene until she can find something better.

Meanwhile, Baba has an affair with Harvey, a bohemian drummer she had met at Frank's party; she gets pregnant, and Harvey is the father. She never meets Harvey again and attempts to have an abortion, to no avail. She tells Frank the truth, and he accepts the child as his own. Frank adores the child and names her Tracy.

Kate works part time at a cleaner's and lives in a bedsit. Eugene has taken up with Maura, his nanny-housekeeper. Kate tries to use Cash (and concern for him) as a way of getting to Eugene, but it only annoys him and makes her more desperate. She has a nervous breakdown, "accidentally" slashes her wrists, and survives.

Kate sees a psychiatrist. She remembers things about her mother that she had long forgotten and seems to see a connection between her mother's desperate actions, including a need for love, and her own. She finds a house that is suitable for Cash and herself. The first night Cash visits, he begs to go back to his father's house. Kate counts this as a maternal failure and falls deeper into depression.

Six months later, Kate goes to a party and has a less-than-fulfilling sexual encounter that makes her feel lonelier than ever. She attempts to get Cash from school but learns that he has been absent for five days. She later finds out that Eugene and Maura had taken Cash to Fiji to get away from Kate. Kate eventually lets Eugene maintain temporary custody. Baba visits Kate in hospital, who is recuperating from sterilization surgery.

The Epilogue. It is now twenty years later, and Kate drowns. Baba takes her friend's remains back to Ireland and is to meet Cash there for the funeral. Earlier, Baba had been on holiday alone and was about to have an affair when she received news that Frank, her husband, had suffered a stroke. Baba immediately returned home to Frank and felt suffocated by his dependence on her.

Baba remembers that Kate eventually had regained custody of Cash. Kate and Baba had not talked in years because Frank felt intimidated by Kate. About one week before Kate's death, Baba and Kate had finally reunited, and Kate had told Baba about her latest heartbreak.

Baba recalls how she felt touched when she told Cash about his mother's death; his response demonstrated his deep understanding of and affection for his mother. Baba came to realize that it is impossible to understand the choices people make throughout the course of their lives.

Critical Evaluation:

Revolutionary for their honest discussions of sexual situations and Irish societal taboos, Edna O'Brien's *The Country Girls*, *The Lonely Girl*, and *Girls in Their Married Bliss* constitute a body of literature—the Country Girls trilogy—that challenged and changed the landscape of Irish and, arguably, modern fiction. O'Brien was born in Tuamgraney, County Clare, Ireland, in 1930, and did not begin writing until just before she published her first novel in 1960. She has a vast body of work that includes novels, short stories, poetry, drama, translations, and biography.

O'Brien was long deprived of inclusion in the canon for her refusal to follow conformist principles of writing in regard to typical plot contrivances, character portrayals (especially of male characters), and subject matter. She is now embraced with respect and acknowledgment from academia. Indeed, until about the year 2000, a reader may have been hard-pressed to find but few of her short stories anthologized, whereas a few years later, entire academic conferences, as well as academic journal articles and scholarly books, began their studies of her work. Praised as well as panned by critics over the years, O'Brien is a literary luminary who broke the bounds of the expectations set upon women writers in general and Irish women writers specifically.

The Country Girls trilogy was banned in Ireland because of its frank sexual matter and disavowal of cherished Irish societal customs. The novels refuse to lionize the institutions of marriage, marital fidelity, and motherhood, and instead bring to the fore a questioning of those traditions. Kate Brady, a young woman who searches doggedly for romantic love, only to be disappointed time and again, demonstrates the impossibility of a love that denies the self in favor of obsession with the love object. Baba Brennan, the beautiful but abrasive counter to Kate, fares no better when she chooses material security over emotional fulfillment. While some may argue that the stories of Kate and Baba are reminders that progress comes in stages, others argues that their stories serve only as painful reminders that realistic stories of women often end unhappily. O'Brien presents fully developed women who are heavily flawed but always realistic, and they serve to mirror the problems with the prescribed roles allotted to women in Irish society at this time.

O'Brien centers her attention on female characters, some say to the detriment of her male characters. Critics have accused O'Brien of developing only villainous male characters, a contrivance, they argue, that ends up detracting from the verisimilitude of her texts. In terms of *The Country Girls Trilogy and Epilogue*, it is important to note that the points of view are female, and while many of the males fare poorly—

from their assessment—this portrayal is not undeserved. As young girls in a society that demands almost blind obedience from its women in regard to religious observance, familial loyalty, and patriarchal mores, Kate and Baba identify men as untrustworthy, for men and male traditions have consistently refused girls and women agency and voice. In a woman's quest for independence and self-knowledge, men are the means to both happiness and despair. Kate and Baba do not yet understand how to reconcile their own needs with those of a society looking back, and they concentrate their anger at people instead of institutions.

The male characters in the trilogy are the only persons with voice and agency, and they carve very narrow paths for Kate and Baba to follow. Baba has long been considered a lost cause, and her aggressive tendencies have been ignored rather than curtailed. Kate, however, initially the "good girl," finds the sting of recrimination most difficult to bear. Left without a mother to counsel her and a father to guide her, Kate must navigate on her own the treacherous path of adolescence to reach maturity and gain her identity. Feeling adrift, she gravitates toward older men who take advantage of her innocence and naïveté to fulfill their own fantasies of neediness. When Kate denies her father the role in her life as ultimate authority, she faces admonishment and humiliation through the chastisement of and threat of excommunication from the parish priest, as well as physical abuse from her father. Repudiating her father, she looks to the father figures in her life to fill a void that she has not learned how to fill. Therefore, Kate is caught in a self-destructive pattern in which she chooses emotionally unavailable men who make her feel unloved and unwanted.

Baba, Kate's polar opposite, refuses the role of feminine subjectivity and resorts to a type of masculine objectivity to gain happiness. Ultimately, however, this pattern results in misery for Baba, as she marries for money and feels emotionally bankrupt. Both women demonstrate extremes, with Kate showing problems with obsessive neediness and Baba emphasizing the emptiness of graft.

Most striking are the rhetorical aspects of the novels, including issues of voice and plot line. Precisely because O'Brien has her characters speak realistically and openly about the issues in their lives, including abusive and alcoholic fathers, domineering religious figures, emotionally neglectful mothers, manipulative and sexually treacherous older men, and confusing sexual mores, her books are perfect psychological portraits of young women navigating a society in which conformity to authority threatens to undermine their sense of self. Kate and Baba are often infuriating in their self-importance and immaturity, but they also are endearing in their honesty, simplicity, and joie de vivre. Simply put, O'Brien has created two female characters who live and breathe realistically on the page.

Similarly, O'Brien rewrites the narrative for female characters by presenting them with options for escape. Although Kate does not recognize that she has been given the gift of freedom to find her sense of self unrestrained by feelings of sexual obligation—as when Mr. Gentleman ends their relationship in *The Country Girls* and Eugene Gaillard does the same in *The Lonely Girl*—O'Brien does recognize this and refuses to "marry off" Kate in unhappy relationships simply to appease readers' expectations for a "happy" ending. Then, when Kate does "get the guy," this relationship ends, realistically, in misery for both of them. Kate's character cannot sustain fulfilling relationships because she has no idea what she wants and needs for herself.

Similarly, Baba does not find happiness in marriage because to do so would be a betrayal of her character. She does not demonstrate the emotional openness a healthy sexual relationship necessitates, so she cannot, realistically, find a true sense of communion with a man. The closest both women come to happiness is with one another, but they suffer a substantial break in this relationship, too. While disappointing to readers hoping for positive closure for the characters, O'Brien's refusal to write against type and to stay true to character speaks to O'Brien's role as a literary visionary in the evolution of women's literature in the twentieth century.

Valerie Murrenus Pilmaier

Further Reading

Byron, Kristine. "'In the Name of the Mother . . .': The Epilogue of Edna O'Brien's Country Girls Trilogy." *Women's Studies* 31 (July/August, 2002): 447-465. Analyzes the function of O'Brien's epilogue and contrasts it with more traditional literary uses of epilogues in general. Argues that the epilogue does not provide closure to the saga of Kate and Baba, but rather provides disclosure, allowing for a rereading of the entire trilogy.

Colletta, Lisa, and Maureen O'Connor, eds. *Wild Colonial Girl: Essays on Edna O'Brien.* Madison: University of Wisconsin Press, 2006. Any study on O'Brien demands a reading of this book, as it moves O'Brien from the periphery to central in the canon. O'Brien is considered in a multitude of different contexts, from feminist revisionist writer to writer-centered biographer. Central to this volume is Kristine Byron's essay on O'Brien, which piqued the rediscovery of O'Brien in academic circles.

Greenwood, Amanda. *Edna O'Brien.* Tavistock, England: Northcote House/British Council, 2003. This is the first book-length study of O'Brien since 1975, and is a good primer on O'Brien and her work.

Ingman, Heather. "Edna O'Brien: Stretching the Nation's Boundaries." *Irish Studies Review* 10, no. 3 (2002): 253-265. Ingman posits O'Brien as a political writer and silences critics who type O'Brien as unworthy of critical attention.

Laing, Kathryn, Sinead Mooney, and Maureen O'Connor, eds. *Edna O'Brien: New Critical Perspectives.* Dublin: Carysfort Press, 2006. This is another compilation of scholarly essays on Edna O'Brien which helps to demonstrate her mastery of her discipline and her incredible scope of genres. These essays stem from conference papers on O'Brien given at The National University of Ireland, Galway.

O'Connor, Maureen. "Edna O'Brien, Irish Dandy." *Irish Studies Review* 13, no. 4 (2005): 469-477. O'Connor, one of the preeminent O'Brien scholars, speaks to critics who accuse O'Brien of not being Irish enough and not understanding the pulse of modern Ireland because she emigrated so long ago. She locates O'Brien's writing style in the Irish literary tradition of the dandy and firmly establishes O'Brien's "Irishness."

Quintelli-Neary, Margaret. "Retelling the Sorrows in Edna O'Brien's Country Girls Trilogy." *Nua: Studies in Contemporary Irish Writing* 4, nos. 1/2 (2003): 65-76. Examines O'Brien's treatment of female experiences in the Country Girls trilogy in relationship to tragedy.

Schrank, Bernice, ed. "Edna O'Brien Special Issue." *Canadian Journal of Irish Studies* 22, no. 2 (1996). This was the first compendium of scholarly articles on Edna O'Brien and helped to establish her as an author worthy of critical attention. Prior to this time, O'Brien was viewed as a romance writer who dabbled in other genres.

The Country of the Pointed Firs

Author: Sarah Orne Jewett (1849-1909)
First published: 1896
Type of work: Novella
Type of plot: Social realism
Time of plot: Late nineteenth century
Locale: Maine

Principal characters:
THE NARRATOR, a woman writer who is no longer young
ALMIRA TODD, an herbalist
MRS. BLACKETT, her mother
WILLIAM BLACKETT, Almira's younger brother, a
    fisherman and farmer

The Story:

The narrator, a woman writer, comes to Dunnet Landing one summer to escape a too-busy life in Boston. In this Maine coastal town, which impressed her on an earlier visit, she hopes to find a quiet haven in which to complete a long-delayed, important piece of writing. She stays with Mrs. Almira Todd, a widowed herbalist who turns out to be a central person in the village. Almira is a kind of partner both to the doctor and the minister in dealing with physical and emotional ills, especially of the women and children of Dunnet Landing. Almost without realizing it, the narrator finds herself drawn into helping Almira with her work. While Almira gathers herbs in the countryside, the narrator sells remedies and spruce beer at Almira's house on the edge of the village.

When she realizes she is getting little writing done, the narrator resigns her informal sales position and rents the schoolhouse just outside the village as a hermitage for writing during the day. Instead of causing a break between the narrator and Almira, this change brings them closer together. During the early summer evenings, Almira gradually tells the narrator the story of her life, including the fact that she and the man she loves most are prevented by his family from marrying.

In the course of the summer, and with help from Almira, the writer gradually comes to know and treasure the people of Dunnet Landing and to appreciate the richness of lives and characters that at first seemed isolated, insular, and reticent. The aged recluse Captain Littlepage comes to her at the schoolhouse, eager to confide in someone seemingly like himself. He tells her the story of his shipwreck in the northern polar regions and of an account he comes to believe of a mysterious island near the North Pole, the waiting place for dead souls before they move on to the next world. The narrator proves adept at persuading him to converse comfortably, even though she is skeptical of his story and a little impatient at the interruption.

The narrator grows increasingly interested in the people of the region and comes to look forward to meeting and befriending more of them. She meets Almira's brother, William

Blackett, and their mother, Mrs. Blackett, when Almira takes her to Green Island for a visit.

William is a fisherman and farmer who sells bait and raises sheep. Almira is critical of him, thinking that he made too little of his opportunities. He seems shy and reserved, but the narrator meets him while he is digging potatoes for their dinner, and they quickly become friends. Soon after they meet, he shows her his favorite view of the island. In the afternoon, Almira takes the narrator to her favorite place, where the best pennyroyal grows, and confides more about her relationship with her husband, Nathan, and his early death. She thinks him the best of husbands and was sorry to lose him so soon, but she is consoled that he died before discovering that she loved another more.

Before leaving the island, the narrator learns that Mrs. Blackett has a golden gift for making friends that few people possess, "so that they make a part of one's own life that can never be forgotten." In one brief visit, the narrator forms a deep and lasting friendship with Mrs. Blackett. They communicate intimately and silently when Mrs. Blackett shows the narrator her favorite place, the view from her rocking chair.

Soon after the visit to Green Island, Susan Fosdick, a childhood friend who lives to circulate news, comes to stay with Almira. It becomes clear that the two guests will get along well, and the conversation becomes intimate, finally turning to the story of Joanna Todd, Almira's cousin by marriage. "Poor Joanna" came to believe that God would never forgive her for having blamed him when her fiancé deserted her. She isolated herself from the community on Shell-heap Island, a place that is difficult to reach, but the community watched over her. The narrator sees an image of herself in Joanna's chosen isolation. Not long after hearing the story, the narrator visits Joanna's grave on the island.

The high point of the summer is the reunion of the Bowden family, of which Mrs. Blackett is the matriarch. Almira, the narrator, and Mrs. Blackett drive a wagon to the reunion, making short visits at several houses along the way. The reunion brings together many members of the family who see one another no more than once a year, allowing them a short time to express their affection and concern for one another. The reunion includes a grand march of the families across a field and into a grove, where they enjoy a great outdoor feast and a few ceremonies. The narrator succeeds so well during the summer in becoming a part of the community that she is made an honorary Bowden by Almira and Mrs. Blackett. The narrator feels that she becomes a member of a new family and that this family represents all of history's families. As the summer draws to a close, the narrator gets to know another of the reticent old sea captains, Elijah Tilley. Having learned how to relate to these people, the narrator is more at ease with him than with Captain Littlepage as she draws out the story of his persisting grief for his long-dead wife.

When it is time for the narrator to return to the city, Almira's feelings are so strong that she cannot bear to prolong her farewell. She leaves the narrator parting gifts to show those feelings. Among the gifts is the coral pin that Almira's husband brought home for his cousin Joanna, who refused to accept it. Steaming away from Dunnet Landing, the narrator reflects on the rich life of the village as she looks back with love.

Critical Evaluation:

When *The Country of the Pointed Firs* was published, Sarah Orne Jewett's friend Rudyard Kipling said, "I maintain (and will maintain with outcries if necessary) that that is the reallest New England book ever given us." Willa Cather wrote in 1925 that this book, along with Nathaniel Hawthorne's *The Scarlet Letter* (1850) and Mark Twain's *Adventures of Huckleberry Finn* (1884), would stand up to the tests of time.

Jewett wrote four short sequels to this novella: "The Queen's Twin" (1899); "A Dunnet Shepherdess" (1899), in which she introduces William's fiancé, Esther Hight; "The Foreigner" (1900); and "William's Wedding" (1910). In all of these stories, as in the novella, one of Jewett's main themes is the centrality of friendship to a meaningful life. The narrator goes to Dunnet Landing to isolate herself in order to write. She finds that isolation is not really what she needs, although she does need to escape what she characterizes in "William's Wedding" as "the hurry of life in a large town, the constant putting aside of preference to yield to a most unsatisfactory activity." The narrator discovers that what she really needs is to cultivate friendships, to be let into the confidence of the people of Dunnet Landing, and to learn to know them. She is somewhat reluctant at first and a little impatient to get on with her work, but as she gets to know the often ec-

centric but delightful people such as Captain Littlepage, the Blacketts, and Susan Fosdick, she comes to value the treasures in this rich, if sparsely populated, mine of life. Each new acquaintance challenges her in some way to extend and perfect her skills of conversation. By the end of the summer, she has new friends, a new family, and a new home. Her skills of friendship have been honed to a fine edge, so that she can listen with sympathy and warmth to the somewhat ridiculous but touching devotion of Captain Tilley for his dead wife. She learns to open herself to the epiphany of a sudden revelation of spiritual beauty in another and to the communion of sharing such revelations.

Jewett adopted an unusual form for her novella, which gives it the appearance of a collection of superficially related sketches. The narrator's discovery of the richness of the community, her cultivation of friendships, and her development of the skills of conversation give strong thematic unity to these sketches. There is also strong structural unity provided by the gradual integration of the narrator into the community, as well as by the narrator's growth in understanding and appreciation: Chapter 1 brings her to Dunnet Landing; chapters 2-6 show her somewhat reluctantly drawn into intimacy with Almira and earning her trust; chapters 7-11 show her integration into Almira's immediate family; chapters 12-15 develop the contrasting example of Joanna, who left community behind permanently; chapters 15-19 reveal the unity of Almira's immediate family with the larger Bowden family, and that of the Bowden family with all families throughout human history; chapter 20 provides balance and contrast for the narrator's encounter with Captain Littlepage (this time she eagerly and easily pursues the intimacy Captain Tilley offers); and the final chapter takes her away from Dunnet Landing. This organization results in a subtle plot that may seem static to some readers but that inspired later writers to similar experiments. Several major works of twentieth century fiction—among them William Faulkner's *Go Down, Moses* (1942) and Eudora Welty's *The Golden Apples* (1949)—are structurally indebted to Jewett's novella. In the century following its publication, Cather's prophecy proved true. Recognition of the stature of *The Country of the Pointed Firs* increased and the work received more sophisticated attention in scholarship, literary criticism, and literature classrooms.

"Critical Evaluation" by Terry Heller

Further Reading

Blanchard, Paula. *Sarah Orne Jewett: Her World and Her Work*. Reading, Mass.: Addison-Wesley, 1994. In this literary biography, Blanchard devotes one chapter to discussing the novel in the context of Jewett's life and other works. Provides photographs, relevant background and biographical information, and a bibliography.

Cary, Richard, ed. *Appreciation of Sarah Orne Jewett: Twenty-nine Essays.* Waterville, Maine: Colby College Press, 1973. Six of the twenty-nine essays included in this collection deal specifically with *The Country of the Pointed Firs.* Looking at the novel from a historical and sociological perspective, Warner Berthoff argues in "The Art of Sarah Orne Jewett's *Pointed Firs*" that the main story of the book is "the economic disintegration of the coastal towns, the withering away of the enterprise that gave them life." In "An Interpretation of *Pointed Firs*," Francis Fike looks at the major unifying themes of the book.

Church, Joseph. *Transcendent Daughters in Jewett's "Country of the Pointed Firs."* Rutherford, N.J.: Fairleigh Dickinson University Press, 1994. Church provides an excellent examination of Jewett's quasi-autobiographical novel, analyzing the book from a psychoanalytical perspective. Includes notes, bibliographical references, and an index.

Donovan, Josephine. *Sarah Orne Jewett.* New York: Frederick Ungar, 1980. Includes a biographical sketch followed by a discussion of Jewett's artistic principles and main themes. One chapter discusses the novel as a realization of Jewett's themes and purposes. Includes bibliography.

Gale, Robert L. *A Sarah Orne Jewett Companion.* Westport, Conn.: Greenwood Press, 1999. A reference book containing alphabetically arranged entries about Jewett's writings, characters, family members, friends, acquaintances, professional associates and admirers. The entries on her major works and the most important persons contain brief bibliographies.

Howard, June, ed. *New Essays on "The Country of the Pointed Firs."* New York: Cambridge University Press, 1994. A collection of essays interpreting the novel, including discussions of gender, American realism, material culture, empire, regionalism, and nationalism in the book. Includes bibliographical references.

Jewett, Sarah Orne. *An Edited Edition of Sarah Orne Jewett's "The Country of the Pointed Firs."* Lewiston, N.Y.: Edwin Mellen Press, 2003. Reprints the original edition of the novel, published in 1896; subsequent editions added some of Jewett's short stories to the book, destroying the novel's narrative. Includes an introduction and notes by Jewett scholar Jeff Morgan (below).

Joseph, Philip. "The Artist Meets the Rural Community: Hamlin Garland, Sarah Orne Jewett, and the Writing of 1890's Regionalism." In *American Literary Regionalism in a Global Age.* Baton Rouge: Louisiana State University Press, 2007. Joseph analyzes *The Country of the Pointed Firs* and other regional American writing to explain how these works remain relevant to readers living in a twenty-first century global environment.

Morgan, Jeff. *Sarah Orne Jewett's Feminine Pastoral Vision: "The Country of the Pointed Firs."* Lewiston, N.Y.: Edwin Mellen Press, 2002. Detailed analysis of the novel, including an extensive chronicle of its publication history, tracing the many revisions that occurred after its initial publication in 1896. Examines the characters, plot, use of figurative language, and Jewett's creation of the "feminine pastoral" genre.

Nagel, Gwen L., ed. *Critical Essays on Sarah Orne Jewett.* Boston: G. K. Hall, 1984. The introduction to this collection summarizes critical response to all of Jewett's works. Contains contemporary reviews and several later critical essays on the novel and the other Dunnet Landing stories.

Roman, Margaret. *Sarah Orne Jewett: Reconstructing Gender.* Tuscaloosa: University of Alabama Press, 1992. Examines the attitudes toward gender in Jewett's fiction. One chapter shows how *The Country of the Pointed Firs* reflects Jewett's mature ideas about gender identity. Includes bibliography.

Sherman, Sarah Way. *Sarah Orne Jewett: An American Persephone.* Hanover, N.H.: University Press of New England, 1989. Explores the extensive development and use of the myth of Persephone by Jewett and her contemporary writers. Much of the second half of the book shows how Jewett uses the myth in the novel. Includes bibliography.

The Country Wife

Author: William Wycherley (1641?-1715)
First produced: 1675; first published, 1675
Type of work: Drama
Type of plot: Comedy
Time of plot: Seventeenth century
Locale: London

Principal characters:
MR. HORNER, a gallant alleged to be impotent
MR. PINCHWIFE, a jealous husband
MARGERY PINCHWIFE, his dissatisfied wife
ALITHEA, Mr. Pinchwife's sister, a society woman
MR. HARCOURT, a gallant in love with Alithea

The Story:

Mr. Horner, a gallant with a bad reputation for seduction, pretends that he was made impotent through disease and causes word of his misfortune to be spread throughout the town by his quack doctor. Immediately, men who were afraid to let him meet their wives for fear of seduction hasten to assure him that he can visit their homes and escort their women anywhere. Horner's old companions among the town gallants tease him unmercifully, and at first, the women will have nothing to do with him. Among his friends is Jack Pinchwife, who is vastly afraid of being made a cuckold. He does not even let it be known that he is married. His wife is a woman from the country; she, he thinks, does not know enough about fashionable city life to think of taking a lover.

Pinchwife makes the mistake, however, of escorting his wife to a play, where she is seen by Horner and some of his friends. When Pinchwife returns to his lodgings, his wife, tired of being kept locked in the house, asks her husband to let her go walking. A relative, a woman from the town, speaks for her as well. Pinchwife becomes angry with both: at his wife for wanting to go out and at his relative who is, he claims, corrupting her morals. Pinchwife foolishly tells his wife what she is missing in town life—plays, dinners, parties, and dances—and so arouses her interest in all that he is attempting to keep from her for the sake of his honor.

When a party of women come to take his wife to the latest play, Pinchwife refuses to let her go or even to see the visitors. He gives out the excuse that she has smallpox. The excuse fails. At the same time Horner and some other gallants come to call.

The women are urged by their husbands to let Horner take them to the theater, but they, in disgust, refuse, until Horner himself whispers to one of them that the rumor spread about his impotency is untrue. Mrs. Pinchwife is forgotten and left behind.

After some time Mrs. Pinchwife becomes melancholy because she wishes to enjoy the gaiety her husband tells her about but refuses to let her see. At last Pinchwife agrees to take her to a play if she will dress as a man. On the way to the play, accompanied by Pinchwife's sister Alithea, they meet the sister's fiancé, a simpleton who lets his friend, Harcourt, pay court to Alithea. She, realizing that her fiancé is a fool, tries to treat Harcourt coolly, even though her fiancé is angry with her for doing so.

Before they arrive at the theater they meet Horner. Pinchwife, in spite of all he hears about Horner's impotence, is worried lest Horner discover Mrs. Pinchwife's disguise. Horner, recognizing Mrs. Pinchwife, teases the jealous husband by kissing the young "gentleman" and telling "him" the kiss is for his sister, Mrs. Pinchwife. Horner, in addition, tells the "young man" that he is in love with Mrs. Pinchwife.

The following morning Alithea is dressed to marry her fiancé. The bridegroom comes with a parson, actually Harcourt in disguise. Harcourt is still determined to take Alithea for his own, if he can. After some discussion, the marriage is put off for a day.

Meanwhile, Pinchwife tries to force his wife to send a letter calculated to discourage Horner's attentions, but she substitutes a love letter for the one her husband dictated. After taking the letter, Pinchwife locks her in her room and tells her to stay away from the window.

In his own rooms, Horner holds a discussion with his quack doctor and tells him how well his scheme to fool husbands is working. In proof, a well-bred woman comes to his rooms, but the opportunity is lost when her husband follows her. A few moments later two other women arrive, much chagrined when they find Horner entertaining other visitors. Pinchwife, knowing nothing of the substitution, delivers the letter. Upon his return home he finds his wife writing another love letter to Horner. Angered, he draws his sword, but he is interrupted by the entrance of Alithea's fiancé.

Mrs. Pinchwife lies her way out of the situation by saying she is writing the letter for Alithea, who, she says, is in love with Horner. Pinchwife, knowing that Horner is of as good family and as wealthy as his sister's fiancé, thinks that by marrying Alithea to Horner he can keep his wife away from the rake. When he agrees to take Alithea to Horner, his wife disguises herself in Alithea's clothing and presents herself as Alithea to be taken to Horner's lodgings.

Pinchwife unsuspectingly takes his wife to Horner and leaves to get a clergyman to marry the couple. On the way he meets his sister's fiancé, who is puzzled by Pinchwife's tale. When they meet the real Alithea, all are confused. Shortly after Pinchwife leaves, three women appear at Horner's lodgings. During the visit all three discover that Horner enjoyed their favors, while each thinks he is hers alone. After they leave, Horner gets rid of Mrs. Pinchwife after some trouble; she wants to leave her husband and live with Horner.

Pinchwife, Alithea, Harcourt, and the fiancé all arrive to clear up the mystery of the disguised Alithea. The men accuse Horner of double-dealing, and Pinchwife threatens the gallant with his sword. Mrs. Pinchwife, who is loitering nearby, enters the room. To save the honor of all concerned, Alithea's maidservant takes the blame for lying. The doctor comes in unexpectedly and testifies again to the impotency of Horner. His report puts all husbands at their ease again. Only Mrs. Pinchwife, who is unable to leave her husband or to have Horner's favors, is out of sorts.

Critical Evaluation:

This play is the epitome of the spirit of the reign of Charles II. The plot is presented with Restoration boldness, depending as it does on the supposition of Horner's impotence and his amorous adventures with various wives who have been gulled into believing that he is incapable of feelings for the opposite sex. While the main device of the play is frankly indecent, the handling of the theme, particularly in the dialogue, is brilliant. Clever dialogue and the whimsicality of Mrs. Pinchwife's naïveté save the drama from approaching pornography and raise the play to the realm of art. As a result of the play's deftness, readers usually find themselves laughing, along with the characters, at the duplicity of the women and their lover.

William Wycherley's comedies were his contribution to English dramatic literature and in one of them, *The Country Wife*, the Restoration comedy reached its height. Wycherley's first play, *Love in a Wood*, was performed in the spring of 1671 and occasioned the start of a relationship between Wycherley and the duchess of Cleveland, who was mistress to the king. Wycherley was, as a result, brought into the court circle and into the favor of the king. *The Gentleman Dancing-Master*, his second play, apparently opened at Dorset Garden in the fall of 1672. It was not well received by the Restoration audience, perhaps because of its simplicity and lack of vulgarity. *The Plain-Dealer*, first produced in December, 1676, has the distinction of being Wycherley's last play,

his most morally ambiguous, and thus the most discussed of the Restoration comedies, with the exception perhaps of William Congreve's *The Way of the World* (1700). It is from a character in this play that Wycherley received his nickname of Manly from John Dryden.

Wycherley's third play, *The Country Wife*, is considered by most critics to be the best of the Restoration comedies. *The Country Wife* was apparently first produced by the King's Company at the Theatre Royal in Drury Lane on January 12, 1675, and was obviously well received by the audiences of the time, for it immediately became a part of the repertory at the Theatre Royal. Its popularity is still apparent in the fact that it is one of the most often revived of the comedies from its period.

The ethos of the Restoration period presumably had its effect on *The Country Wife*. The theater was being promoted by a libertine, Charles II, who surrounded himself with an equally profligate court. Many aristocrats of the period viewed humanity as depraved and affected a contempt for morality, especially in the form of Puritanism or Republicanism. The bawdiness of *The Country Wife* seems suited to the temper of its times.

The licentious nature of the play, however, brought it criticism during the Restoration, though perhaps it was that some people did not like their mirrored image. As Richard Steele wrote of Horner in *The Tatler* of April 16, 1709, after seeing a production on April 14: He "is a good representation of the age in which that comedy was written; at which time, love and wenching were the business of life, and the gallant manner of pursuing women was the best recommendation at court." Steele also criticized Pinchwife, but again as a representative of the age, "one of those debauchees who run through the vices of the town and believe when they think fit, they can marry and settle at their ease." Steele in his criticism was contributing to the general criticism of the theater that occurred from about 1695 to 1745 and had reached a high point in 1698 with Jeremy Collier's *A Short View of the Immorality and Profaneness of the English Stage*. Collier, unlike Steele, was not generous to Wycherley or his characters, calling Horner "horridly Smutty" and accusing Mrs. Pinchwife, Horner, and Lady Fidget of a "Rankness and Indecency of their Language." Criticism of the play continued into the Victorian period, when perhaps it met its strongest criticism under the pen of Thomas Babington Macaulay in an 1841 essay "The Comic Dramatists of the Restoration." He said of Wycherley's comedies: "In truth Wycherley's indecency is protected against the critic as a skunk is protected against the hunters. It is safe because it is too filthy to handle and too noisome to approach."

Despite the adverse criticism of the play, it was following, perhaps more strongly than some, the satiric method employed by Restoration comedy, which was to present on the stage characterizations that were true to life—some of them to be emulated and some of them to be avoided. The use of laughter in *The Country Wife* closely follows Thomas Hobbes's observation that people laugh because they suddenly recognize their superiority to others. As Hobbes says, "Sudden glory is the passion which maketh those grimaces called laughter; and is caused either by some sudden act of their own that pleaseth them, or by the apprehension of some deformed thing in another, by comparison whereof they suddenly applaud themselves." The fact that Wycherley chose to follow these examples is reinforced by his epigraph to *The Gentleman Dancing-Master*, in which he acknowledges that a great comedy does not merely make the audience laugh; it should say something.

What Wycherley has to say in *The Country Wife* concerns the lack of deep feeling and selfish motives that permeated the sexual morality of his time. Women are not sought after as wives, or even concubines, but rather as mere strumpets. Once the man's sexual desires have been gratified, he will go out looking for another encounter. To make his play instructive as well as illustrative, Wycherley conceived three intrigues in his plot—involving Pinchwife, Horner, and Harcourt—that allow the reader to make a value judgment about how well a character is able to drop his pretense and channel his natural desires into constructive results. Thus, Pinchwife exhibits the least desirably imitative character; despite his selfishly motivated, zealous guarding of his wife, Margery, he is cuckolded. Horner, though admirable in wit and clear in an understanding of himself and others, never drops the role of eunuch and its fringe benefits and thus remains a slave to lust and what he terms the "greatest Monster" in nature—affectation. Harcourt becomes the most admirable as a "rake converted" who is able to translate his desires into true love and respect for the woman Alithea and, at play's end, intends to be a husband to her.

In his concern with the three intrigues of *The Country Wife*, Wycherley introduces a wide variety of Restoration comedy types. There is the jealous man whose jealousy is reproved, the hypocritical ladies of refinement who wish to protect their honor yet are proved lustful wenches, the trusting man whose trust is proved foolish, the rakes whose sole desire is satiating themselves in pleasure, and the fashionable narcissistic Restoration fop. Within this gallery, Horner is perhaps the central character despite the fact that he does not, as previously mentioned, face a totally happy end. In Horner's character Wycherley presents aspects to be applauded

and condemned. His name suggests what he is—a cuckold maker who gains great satisfaction by awarding horns to betrayed husbands. Wycherley's idea for Horner's trick came from *Eunuchus* (161 B.C.E.; *The Eunuch*, 1598) by the Roman playwright Terence. In the play, a young man pretends to be a eunuch so that he can be admitted freely into the company of a young girl. However, unlike Terence's character, Horner does not rape; he uses his disguise only to gain access to willing partners. In this pursuit he is a villain of sorts. Yet in his villainy—cuckolding of husbands and bedding of mistresses—he is to be commended, for he proves that the selfish nature of the foolish men is deplorable, and that the honor of the virtuous ladies is hypocritical. He is also to be pitied, however, because he never rises above base desire. As Horner expresses it, "Ceremony in love is as ridiculous as in fighting; falling on briskly is all should be done on such occasions."

In *The Country Wife* the women characters and their social behavior also meet with varying degrees of censure and praise. With Lady Fidget, Margery Pinchwife, and Alithea, Wycherley presents the differing levels of feminine conduct as he saw them in the Restoration period. These levels ranged from those lustful women who were equal to the men in their desires, to those women of true virtue who sought a love based on more than sexual gratification. Although there are other women of "honor" in the play—Mrs. Dainty Fidget and Mrs. Squeamish—Lady Fidget is the most verbal and active and thus more self-incriminating. In her lustful behavior she is little different from a strumpet except for her hypocrisy, which perhaps makes her more damnable. For instance, at the moment she is about to give herself to Horner her train of thought runs thus: "You must have a great care of your conduct; for my acquaintances are so censorious . . . and detracting, that perhaps they'll talk to the prejudice of my Honour, though you should not let them know the dear secret." So that his dislike of such hypocrisy is made absolutely clear, by the end of the play Wycherley has had Horner partaking of pleasure with all the ladies of virtue. Contrasting Lady Fidget is Margery Pinchwife, lustful but honest about her lust. As Horner says about the love letter she writes him, "'Tis the first love letter that ever was without flames, darts, fates, destinies, lying, and dissembling in it." She is perhaps more admirable for her honesty, yet at the end of the play she is taught to lie by the "virtuous" set. The final female character of note, Alithea, is virtuous in all aspects and is heading for a commendable marriage based on a true love and would seem to be, as the opposite of Lady Fidget, the character for emulation.

One of the comic devices used adeptly by Wycherley in

The Country Wife is the double entendre. This was the apparatus to which Collier took such offense, writing that "when the Sentence has two Handles, the worst is generally turn'd to the Audience. The matter is so contrived that the Smut and Scum of the Thought now rises uppermost; And, like a Picture drawn to *Sight*, looks always upon the Company." Indeed, Wycherley's double entendres are as powerful as Collier describes them (although one may not react to them in the same manner that Collier did), and in act 4, scene 3—the "china scene"—Wycherley is at his best.

The importance of *The Country Wife* lies in the fact that it signals the height, and therefore the beginning of the fall, of Restoration comedy. With its adept social satire, telling visions of selfishness and hypocrisy, and the seldom surpassed farcical china scene, *The Country Wife* stands at the pinnacle of Restoration comedy. However, within the representation of the apparently romantic love of Alithea and Harcourt was the seed of what was to grow within the comedy of that period until it destroyed it. This representation of the ideal in a realistic setting was the chief characteristic of the comedy to come—sentimental or "weeping comedy."

"Critical Evaluation" by Phyllis E. Allran

Further Reading

Harwood, John T. *Critics, Values, and Restoration Comedy.* Carbondale: Southern Illinois University Press, 1982. Provides a lucid account of *The Country Wife* within the context of the history and conventions of Restoration drama.

Holland, Norman N. *The First Modern Comedies: The Significance of Etherege, Wycherley, and Congreve.* Cambridge, Mass.: Harvard University Press, 1967. Perhaps the most influential account of the play. Takes the Harcourt-Alithea relationship as the moral standard by which the actions of the other characters are measured.

Kachur, Barbara A. *Etherege and Wycherley.* New York: Palgrave Macmillan, 2004. Discusses the plays of Wycherley and Sir George Etherege within the context of culture and history in the early years of Charles II's reign. Examines Wycherley's place within the Carolean theater; devotes a chapter to an analysis of love, marriage, and sovereignty in *The Country Wife.*

Marshall, W. Gerald. *A Great Stage of Fools: Theatricality and Madness in the Plays of William Wycherley.* New York: AMS Press, 1993. The chapter on *The Country Wife* is contentious and not entirely convincing, but deserves consideration for its impressive scholarship and insight, especially into the relationship of Margery and Pinchwife.

Milhous, Judith, and Robert D. Hume. *Producible Interpretation: Eight English Plays, 1675-1707.* Carbondale: Southern Illinois University Press, 1985. Highly recommended for anyone interested in Restoration drama. The chapter on *The Country Wife* provides what is one of the best introductions to the play and includes a valuable overview of modern critical approaches. A commendatory blend of wit, exemplary scholarship, and common sense.

Vance, John A. *William Wycherley and the Comedy of Fear.* Newark: University of Delaware Press, 2000. Detailed examination of four of Wycherley's plays, including *The Country Wife.* Argues that Wycherley was not particularly concerned with broad political, social, and moral issues in his plays, but focused instead on the actions and motivations of his insecure and fallible characters.

Young, Douglas M. *The Feminist Voices in Restoration Comedy: The Virtuous Women in the Play-Worlds of Etherege, Wycherley, and Congreve.* Lanham, Md.: University Press of America, 1997. Analyzes *The Country Wife* and three other plays by Wycherley in which a female character demands independence from and equality with her male partner as a condition of marriage or courtship.

Zimbardo, Rose. *Wycherley's Drama: A Link in the Development of English Satire.* New Haven, Conn.: Yale University Press, 1965. Persuasively argues that *The Country Wife* is foremost a satire against "lust that disguises itself."

Couples

Author: John Updike (1932-2009)
First published: 1968
Type of work: Novel
Type of plot: Impressionistic realism
Time of plot: 1962-1964
Locale: Tarbox, Massachusetts

Principal characters:
PIET HANEMA, a builder
ANGELA HANEMA, his wife
FREDDY THORNE, a dentist
GEORGENE THORNE, Freddy's wife and Piet's mistress
FOXY and KEN WHITMAN, newcomers to Tarbox
SEVEN OTHER TARBOX COUPLES

The Story:

As Piet and Angela Hanema undress for the night, they discuss the party they have just attended for the Whitmans, a new couple that has just moved into town. Like most of the other couples in their social group, the Hanemas are middle class, are in their mid-thirties, have several children, and have settled in Tarbox—a quaint village quickly becoming a suburb on the South Shore of Boston—during the previous decade. Brought together by their youth, their recent arrival, their children, and their sense of themselves as representatives of the future rather than the past, these couples became a circle of friends.

Over time, the couples have developed their own social rituals. They gather formally and informally every weekend at planned dinner and cocktail parties, as well as at spontaneous get-togethers after swimming, going to the beach, or playing tennis, basketball, golf, or touch football. They play charades, impressions, and word games; have costume parties and dance to records by Doris Day, Chubby Checker, and Connie Francis; talk about the news, their houses, and their children; drink too much; gossip; and share and hide secrets. According to Freddy Thorne—their unofficial master of revels and resident cynical philosopher—they make a church of one another to hold back the night and replace their parents' religious and political faiths, which most of them have lost.

In 1963, a "post-pill paradise" that seems to offer sex without consequences, adultery has begun to complicate the circle's relationships. The previous year, Marcia little-Smith began an affair with Frank Appleby; when Janet Appleby and Harold little-Smith learned about it, they began one of their own. Before long, the couples stopped hiding their relationships from one another and became a foursome. Rumors circulated, Janet and Marcia shared confidences with their women friends, and the couples soon became known as the "Applesmiths." Piet (pronounced "Pete") is also having an affair—not his first—with Georgene Thorne, while Bea Guerin is making her own desire to be with him perfectly clear.

Foxy and Ken Whitman join the circle. Like most of the men, Ken is a professional, a Harvard-trained biochemist working in Boston; like most of the women, Foxy is attractive, smart, well-educated, and discontented. They have bought the old Robinson house on the shore. Foxy asks Piet to come out to the house to advise them on how to renovate it, and he agrees to take on the job. Foxy is two months pregnant, but they soon begin an affair that continues throughout the summer and her pregnancy. The relationship becomes an obsession for both of them and causes Piet to break off his relationship with Georgene.

While this affair is going on, the couples continue to gather and a variety of other long- and short-term affairs develop within the group. Ben Saltz loses his job, and his wife Irene becomes the first to go to work outside her home. Jon Ong learns he has cancer. Both Janet and Angela begin going to Boston for psychoanalysis. Foxy's son is born in October, and in the weeks immediately following she and Piet do not see each other.

The Thornes plan a pre-Thanksgiving black-tie gala, but it turns out to be on the day that President Kennedy is shot. They decide to go ahead with the party anyway: They have bought all the liquor already, they reason, so it can be a kind of Irish wake. With the television on in the background, the evening begins with some sense of the moment, but it quickly becomes another drunken evening. It ends in farce when Piet, who finds Foxy in a bathroom and begins to make love to her, ends up jumping out of a window to avoid being discovered by Angela. Several days later, Piet goes to see Foxy and the baby and decides that, for him at least, the affair has run its course.

Piet begins seeing Bea Guerin just before Christmas. At a New Year's Eve party, however, he promises to come to see Foxy the following week. They begin sleeping together again, and she becomes pregnant from that encounter. After some hesitation on Foxy's part, they agree that she should have an abortion. Abortion is illegal, however, so they must find someone willing to perform the procedure. Freddy

Thorne knows of a doctor in Boston who will do it, but he has also learned about Piet's affair with Georgene; he refuses to help them unless Piet agrees to convince Angela to sleep with him in order to balance the scales. Piet indignantly refuses but eventually relents. Angela, surprisingly, agrees to sleep with Freddy.

Freddy takes Foxy to Boston for the abortion. Ken learns about the affair and confronts Foxy, who confesses everything, including the abortion. Ken calls the Hanemas and demands they come over to talk. Ken condemns them all, blames the Tarbox couples—including Angela—for the affair, and announces his intention to divorce Foxy. Piet immediately responds that if Ken divorces Foxy, he will "have to" marry her. When the Hanemas return home, Angela asks Piet to leave, and he soon moves into the unfinished attic of a building his firm has been renovating. The Whitmans separate and disappear from town, until Foxy sends Piet a note saying she is coming back to pick up some things from the house and would like to see him. They end up spending a weekend together in his attic bed. She then goes to St. Thomas with her baby to get a divorce.

The Salzes leave town, John Ong dies, and the remaining couples take up bridge. Angela gets a Mexican divorce, stays in Tarbox, and begins to teach at a girls' school. Piet and Foxy marry and move to the Worcester area, where they meet others like themselves and become a couple.

Critical Evaluation:

When he died in January, 2009, at the age of seventy-six, John Updike was generally acknowledged to be the preeminent American man of letters of the second half of the twentieth century. In retrospect, his productivity and versatility were already emerging by the time *Couples* appeared. Between settling with his young family in Ipswich, Massachusetts (the model for his fictional Tarbox), in 1957 and publishing *Couples* in 1968, Updike had already become a frequent contributor to the *New Yorker* and had published eleven books, including *Rabbit, Run* (1960), the National Book Award-winning *The Centaur* (1962), and four collections of short stories. All of these works of fiction received respectful reviews, and one of the central debates that would continue throughout his career had already begun: Some critics embraced the lyrical and impressionistic descriptive style that characterized his fiction as powerful and poetic, while others criticized it as overwrought and distracting.

With *Couples*, Updike became a literary star. He was featured on the cover of *Time* and in *Life*. The novel, published by Alfred A. Knopf, was an instant best seller and remained one for more than a year, selling more than 180,000 hard-

cover and 3 million paperback copies. The book was controversial for its explicit treatment of sexual acts, its detailed descriptions of sexual parts, and its use of four-letter words. It arguably could not have been published by a mainstream American publishing house just a few years earlier, during the Kennedy era in which it was set, because explicit sexuality was then the province of underground and foreign publishers. (In fact, Knopf had agreed to publish *Rabbit, Run* only after Updike cut some of its sexual details.)

Like Philip Roth's best-selling *Portnoy's Complaint* (1969) or Paul Masursky's popular film *Bob and Carol and Ted and Alice* (1969), *Couples* was both a reflection of and a contributor to the new attitudes toward sexuality that emerged in American culture over the course of the 1960's. That these works could both be mainstream successes and be criticized by some as pornographic was evidence of how much things had changed by the end of the decade and of how many people were offended by these changes.

Couples is a novel about more than sex, however. More than a portrait of ten couples, or of their coupling, it is a vivid portrait of a particular time, place, and way of life. The time is the moment of transition between the silent 1950's and the turbulent 1960's, when a vigorous young president's declaration of a new frontier turned out to be the harbinger of changes that led to fundamental transformations in sexual relations, marriage, and the family, as well as civil rights and society as a whole.

To Updike, the personal was the political long before this phrase became a mantra of the feminist movement. His focus was always on the domestic lives of his mainly white, middle-class, Protestant characters. His method was always an impressionistic realism that represented an effort "to give the mundane its beautiful due." He assumed that describing ordinary lives using the conventions of realism would reveal each of those lives to be unique and extraordinary, as well as reflecting how individuals are shaped by, and in turn shape, the currents of their times.

In the four novels that preceded *Couples*, Updike's setting was the Pennsylvania of his youth; with *Couples* and the short stories he was beginning to write at the same time, he began to treat the Massachusetts of his adulthood. "Art hopes to sidestep mortality with feats of attention," he explained in his introduction to *The Early Stories, 1953-1975* (2003). In his description of Tarbox and the way of life of its couples, such feats of attention mark every page. That place at that time is brought to life with absolute authority through detailed descriptions of everything from buildings and furnishings to landscapes and seascapes, from the weathervane at the top of the Congregational Church to a woman's summer tan, from couples doing the Twist to the backyard burial of a hamster, from the gloves women still wore when they dressed up to the Peugeots and Volkswagens that began to appear on country roads, from pick-up basketball games to dinner-party and bedroom conversations.

In giving the mundane its beautiful due, however, Updike did not shy away from showing people and the forces of the world at their worst. He once described his works as moral debates with his readers, asking "what is a good man?" or "what is goodness?" In *Couples*, all of these intentions combine in Piet Hanema. Like Rabbit Angstrom, the protagonist of Updike's Rabbit series, Piet seeks both freedom and security, flight and home. Like Rabbit, he can be incredibly selfish, self-centered, and insensitive, but he is also a man who thinks about morality and God. He is the novel's most fully rounded character and the one with whom a reader becomes most intimate, but he remains an enigma, difficult to like but fascinating to follow. A redheaded sparkplug of a man, he is both a buffoon—doing handstands and cartwheels at parties, pinching women and looking up their dresses—and a seeker after love, faith, and higher meanings.

Neither Piet nor the novel is completely convincing in the religious yearnings Updike wanted to express through them, yet these yearnings remain an essential aspect of the book's character. There are also aspects of the novel that seem dated, even offensive; but these elements do not feel false to the reality of the time. In fact, they seem so accurate a description of the world *Couples* captures that they are among the many reasons that it is still worth reading. Updike's four novels about Rabbit Angstrom remain his greatest achievement as a novelist. *Couples*, though, remains his greatest popular success, a landmark in the culture wars that would continue into the 1990's. The novel provides evidence of its author's decision to follow in the tradition of James Joyce, D. H. Lawrence, and Henry Miller by lavishing his attention on the most intimate moments of his characters' lives.

Bernard F. Rodgers, Jr.

Further Reading

De Bellis, Jack. *A John Updike Encyclopedia.* Westport, Conn.: Greenwood Press, 2000. Includes individual entries on various aspects of the author's life and work.

Detweiler, Robert. *John Updike.* 1972. Rev. ed. New York: Twayne, 1984. An excellent introduction to Updike's concerns and style.

Greiner, Donald J. *Adultery in the American Novel: Updike, James, and Hawthorne.* Columbia: University of South Carolina Press, 1985. Treats *Couples* and makes interesting connections with its predecessor texts by two of the most influential writers of American literature.

Olster, Stacey, ed. *The Cambridge Companion to John Updike.* New York: Cambridge University Press, 2006. A wide-ranging collection of essays on place, realism, religion, women, sex, race, history, popular culture, American myths, and stylistic experiment in Updike's works.

Pritchard, William. *Updike: America's Man of Letters.* South Royalton, Vt.: Steerforth Press, 2000. A sensitive, critically astute, and well-written study of Updike's work that includes a detailed discussion of the genesis of *Couples* and its relationship to other works of the 1960's in which Updike explored sex and adultery.

Tallent, Elizabeth. *Married Men and Magic Tricks: John Updike's Erotic Heroes.* Berkeley, Calif.: Creative Arts, 1982. A study of sexuality in Updike's novels and short stories by a fellow writer.

Updike, John. *Conversations with John Updike.* Edited by James Plath. Jackson: University Press of Mississippi, 1994. A collection of interviews spanning Updike's career that gathers some of his most important comments on *Couples*.

_____. *Picked-Up Pieces.* New York: Alfred A. Knopf, 1975. Updike's second collection of essays; includes "One Big Interview," in which he discusses *Couples*, his other works, and his sense of his vocation.

The Courtesan

Author: Pietro Aretino (1492-1556)
First produced: La cortigiana, 1537; first published, 1534
    (English translation, 1926)
Type of work: Drama
Type of plot: Satire
Time of plot: Early sixteenth century
Locale: Rome

Principal characters:
MESSER MACO, a would-be courtier
MAESTRO ANDREA, a clever charlatan
SIGNOR PARABOLANO, a nobleman
VALERIO, Parabolano's chamberlain
ROSSO, Parabolano's groom, a rogue
ALVIGIA, a procurer
ARCOLANO, a baker
TOGNA, his young wife

The Story:

Messer Maco, a wealthy Sienese fop and a fool, comes to Rome with the intention of becoming a cardinal. Upon his arrival he meets Maestro Andrea, who informs him that he will first have to become a courtier. Maco thereupon announces his desire to become a courtier, and Andrea obligingly promises to transform him into one.

Signor Parabolano, learning that Maco is in town, orders his groom, Rosso, to have all the lampreys he can find sent to Maco as a gift of welcome. When Parabolano leaves, Rosso makes fun of his master's love affairs to the other servants. Valerio, Parabolano's faithful chamberlain, overhears him and runs him off. Rosso swindles a fisherman out of his lampreys by posing as a servant of the pope. When discovered, he convinces the authorities that the fisherman is mad.

Maco receives his first lesson in being a courtier. He is instructed in being, among other things, a blasphemer, a gambler, an adulator, a slanderer, an ingrate, a whore-chaser, an ass, and a nymph.

Next, Rosso visits Alvigia, a procurer. Rosso, overhearing Parabolano talking in his sleep, learns that his master is in love with the matron Livia. If, he tells Alvigia, he can successfully pander to his master's lust, he will secure his position and can also exact revenge on Valerio, Parabolano's chamberlain. Alvigia agrees to help the groom.

Meanwhile, Maco falls in love with Camilla, a courtesan being kept by a Spanish lord. Andrea fears that this new interest will interrupt his fleecing of Maco, but Maco is now all the more determined to become a courtier. He is impatient about Camilla, however, and disguises himself as a groom to gain access to her house. To hinder him, Andrea and Maco's own groom cries out that the sheriff is after him for illegal entry into Rome. Afraid to appear in his own clothes, Maco runs off, still in his disguise as a servant.

Rosso and Alvigia are having their problems, too. Although Parabolano agrees to allow Rosso to secure the services of the procurer for him, Livia proves unapproachable. The two then devise the following plan: Rosso is to tell Parabolano that Livia is willing to meet him, but that, being proper and shy, she will do so only in the profoundest dark; he must promise not to embarrass her with any light whatsoever. Once assured that Parabolano will not be able to see his mistress, Alvigia will substitute the baker's young wife, Togna, for the virtuous Livia. Parabolano, his lust now almost consuming him, is willing to agree to any stipulations. He is willing, even, to believe the calumnies of his groom, and he puts his chamberlain, Valerio, in disgrace.

Maco, hiding in Parabolano's house from the supposed sheriff, finally musters enough courage to emerge for the final courtier-making process. He is placed in a vat that, according to Andrea, is a courtier-mold. There he is thoroughly steamed. Once recovered, he heads for Camilla's house as a full-fledged courtier. Andrea and Maco's groom pretend to be Spaniards storming the house. Maco leaps from the window, terrified, and flees in his underwear.

His embarrassment is followed by that of Parabolano. Togna plans to go to her assignation in her husband's clothes. Suspicious of her design, the old baker feigns drunken sleep while he watches her put on his garments and steal away. He then dresses in her clothes and follows her to the house of the procurer.

Parabolano discovers the ruse once he is alone with Togna. At first he is enraged, but Valerio, embittered and determined to leave Rome and the fickleness of courtiers, arrives in time to calm him down. Admitting that, blinded by lust, he allowed himself to be led around like a fool, Parabolano restores Valerio to favor and begs his forgiveness. Valerio advises him to admit the whole escapade openly and to treat it as a joke so that, by owning up to his own folly, he will be safe from having his enemies use it against him.

As Parabolano is beginning to see the humor in the situation, the baker Arcolano appears, dressed in his wife's clothes. He, too, is enraged, but Parabolano convinces him that he has no designs on his wife. The two, Togna and Arcolano, are forced to kiss and make up. Then, in keeping with the comic ending that Parabolano insists upon, everyone is forgiven—even the conniving Rosso, once he returns a diamond that Parabolano gave him to help seduce Livia. He is a Greek, Parabolano observes, and is only acting according to his nature. Finally Maco appears, seeking help from the "Spaniards." When their true identity is revealed, Maco is shown what a fool he really is. He, in turn, is forced to forgive Andrea.

Critical Evaluation:

By the time of Pietro Aretino, the Italian Renaissance had become overripe. It would be another half-century or more before England's attitudes and culture reached a similar stage of decadence, but the Italians were already experiencing a decline.

With the new concentration upon the world of mortal life, casting aside considerations for the afterlife, it was inevitable that pleasure should come to be regarded as the major purpose of life. Power was important, of course, as Nicolò Machiavelli attested, but, as always, the product of power was pleasure, even if it was only the pleasure of exerting control over one's contemporaries.

Aretino, though he ridicules lechery in this play, is known for his own indulgence in excesses of sensuality. Perhaps that is why he does not excoriate sexual liberties nearly so sharply as he does the inhumanities of court politics. Those who are clever but lacking in wisdom and compassion have always enjoyed clambering over their fellows in their attempts to gain tactical advantage. Aretino seems to have recognized this at an early stage in his life, while discovering also the efficacy of his vituperative pen. The son of a prostitute, he could not rely on kindness or justice from such a world to make his life bearable. It would be difficult to believe that anyone, finding himself living the life of a servant as described by Rosso in act 5, would not seize any available means of moving to a position offering more pleasure and power (as Aretino's writings moved him). Aretino's poison pen is often amusing, sometimes distasteful, occasionally boring, but, given the circumstances, it is always understandable.

Rome, the setting of the play, is as much the butt of Aretino's jokes as are courtly politics. Indeed, Rome and the life at court seem inextricably bound together in the author's mind, perhaps because he was himself nearly murdered once

as a result of court intrigues surrounding the Papacy. He appears to have adopted Venice instead as his home, lavishing his praise upon that city in act 3, and, at tiresome length, upon some of its citizens. The names of those receiving his encomiums did not simply pop into Aretino's head unbidden; aside from those few, like Titian, who seem to have been his friends, he carefully praises those who can be of use to him. He is often quite forthright about this, at one point even going so far as to cause a character to mention his name and his hopes. The fact that such tactics were immensely successful reminds the observer that whereas Aretino's life may have had an offensive odor about it, so did his age.

Although he was neither a great dramatist nor a great poet, Aretino displays great ability to mingle several dialects, assigning different ones to different characters and relishing especially those vigorous speech patterns associated with the illiterate and the poor. At times, the delight his characters show in the scatological can be entertaining.

He seems uninterested in, or incapable of, weaving circumstances of credibility into his characters' entrances and exits or into their shifts in conversational subjects. Often characters simply announce that the subject will change. In many instances the author flings personages on stage and then plucks them off again with no rationale other than the exigencies of his plot.

Only once in the play does he reach the heights of bitter wisdom scaled regularly by the Jacobeans, and that is when Maco catechizes Andrea on life:

MACO: Tell me, how does one come into the world, Maestro?
ANDREA: Through a cave.
. . . .
MACO: But what happens when a man is through living?
ANDREA: He dies in a hole as spiders do.

These lines, with their gothic imagery and cynical accuracy, might easily have excited the envy of John Webster.

One recognizes in *The Courtesan* the topsy-turvy world picture painted so often by other Renaissance dramatists and moralists. Servants here, as elsewhere, are insolent and presumptuous with their masters, and their masters are lustful, foolish, and purblind. When Rosso dupes Parabolano, his deceit being exposed only in the last scene, this bears a similarity to the comedies of Ben Jonson, especially to his *Volpone* (1605). Mosca is a much more fully drawn character, wittier and more alive, but there are definite debts owed by Jonson to just such Italian comedies as this one. If there were nothing else in Aretino to attract Jonson's attention, the Italian's acidic wit would most probably have impressed the Englishman as emanating from a kindred spirit.

Rosso's argument that the way to advancement is through pandering to the lusts of the powerful has echoes in Thomas Middleton's *The Revenger's Tragedy* (pr. 1606-1607, pb. 1607) and in Webster's *The Duchess of Malfi* (pr. 1614, pb. 1623). Perhaps a more revealing, if less definite, parallel lies in Andrea's tutoring of Maco in the art of being a courtier. The tutor-pupil relationship has great dramatic potential for satire on the subject taught, and Aretino makes use of this potential, as does William Shakespeare in *As You Like It* (pr. c. 1599-1600, pb. 1623) when Rosalind, in disguise, instructs Orlando on the many aspects of love. Admittedly, Rosalind is much less harsh in her criticism of lovers and ladies than is Andrea on courtiers and fops, but Andrea's subject is more deserving of acrimony. In addition, Rosalind is the future beneficiary of her precepts; she is dressing a husband, while Andrea is simply plucking a chicken.

Aretino is noted for his realism, sometimes described as "unpleasant." *The Courtesan* contains many examples of realism, among which are the hawking of "histories" in act 1, the selling of lampreys, and the description of meal-taking in the servants' quarters. It is the last that exemplifies the sort of realism that earned the adjective "unpleasant," but it is worth remembering that few realists have escaped the adjective. Aretino, though inconsistent, is in the main a true realist.

"Critical Evaluation" by John J. Brugaletta

Further Reading

Beecher, Donald, ed. *Renaissance Comedy: The Italian Masters*. Vol. 1. Toronto, Ont.: University of Toronto Press, 2008. A full text of *The Courtesan* is one of the plays included in this collection of Italian Renaissance comedies. Beecher's introduction, "Erudite Comedy in Renaissance Italy," describes the characteristics of Italian Renaissance comedy and recounts performance histories of the plays.

Chubb, Thomas C. *Aretino: Scourge of Princes*. New York: Reynal & Hitchcock, 1971. Comprehensive, scholarly life study of the courtier and author. Discusses the composition of Aretino's writings, including *The Courtesan*. Stresses the libertine character of Aretino's life and works.

Cleugh, James. *The Divine Aretino*. New York: Stein and Day, 1966. Highly readable biography of the statesman and writer. Comments on Aretino's prose style in *The Courtesan* and other writings, explaining how he used his experience to vivify his creative works.

Hutton, Edward. *Pietro Aretino: The Scourge of Princes*. London: Constable, 1922. Biographical study of the writer, examining the myths surrounding his licentious lifestyle. A separate chapter discusses his writings, citing examples from *The Courtesan* to highlight Aretino's ability to recreate the life he saw around him.

Roeder, Ralph. *The Man of the Renaissance: Four Lawgivers*. New York: Viking, 1933. Excellent summary of the life and accomplishments of this key figure of the late Renaissance. Highlights the popularity of his writings and examines biographical influences.

Symonds, J. A. *Renaissance in Italy*. Vol. 2. New York: Modern Libraries, 1935. A chapter on Aretino sketches his influence on Italian politics and letters and offers detailed commentary on his contemporaries. Especially helpful for gaining an appreciation of the author's style.

Waddington, Raymond B. *Aretino's Satyr: Sexuality, Satire, and Self-Projection in Sixteenth-Century Literature and Art*. Toronto, Ont.: University of Toronto Press, 2004. Focuses on Aretino's creation and promotion of a public persona through his writing, behavior, and the visual media. Aretino fashioned himself a satyr—a natural being whose satire is a form of truth-telling—and this image eventually eclipsed his reputation as a serious writer.

The Courtship of Miles Standish
And Other Poems

Author: Henry Wadsworth Longfellow (1807-1882)
First published: 1858
Type of work: Poetry
Type of plot: Romantic
Time of plot: 1621
Locale: Massachusetts Bay Colony

Principal characters:
MILES STANDISH, a soldier
JOHN ALDEN, his friend
PRISCILLA, a young woman loved by Standish and Alden

The Poem:

In the colony at Massachusetts Bay, Miles Standish is a gruff captain of pilgrim soldiers whose wife had died after the landing of the *Mayflower* the previous fall. He shares a cabin with John Alden, a young scholar. One night, Standish drops his copy of *Caesar's Commentaries* and turns to Alden, who is writing a letter in which he praises Priscilla, one of the young women of the colony. Standish speaks of his lonely, weary life and of Priscilla, too, living alone; her parents had died during the winter.

Because he is no scholar but only a blunt soldier, Standish asks Alden to convey his proposal of marriage to Priscilla. Taken aback by the request, Alden stammers that it would be wiser for Standish to plead his own case. When the captain asks the favor in the name of friendship, the young man can no longer refuse.

In her cabin, Priscilla is singing the Hundredth Psalm and industriously spinning when Alden arrives at her door. Filled with woe at what he must do, he nevertheless steps resolutely inside. Seizing what seemed an opportune moment, he blurts out the captain's proposal. Priscilla flatly refuses, for she believes that Standish himself should come if she is worth the wooing. She further confuses the young man by asking him why he does not speak for himself. Caught between his own love for Priscilla and his respect for Standish, Alden decides to go back to England when the *Mayflower* sails the next day.

Standish is enraged when he hears the outcome of Alden's wooing, but the captain's tirade is interrupted by news of approaching American Indians. In the colony's council room, he finds an Indian bearing a snakeskin full of arrows—the challenge to battle. Pulling out the arrows, Standish fills the skin with bullets and powder and defiantly hands it back to the Indian. The warrior quickly disappears into the forest. The next morning before anyone else is awake, Standish, his eight men, and their Indian guide leave the village.

Alden does not sail away. Among the people on the beach he sees is Priscilla, who looks so dejected and appealing that he decides to stay and protect her. They walk back to the village together, and Alden describes Standish's reaction to Priscilla's question. He also confides that he had planned to leave the colony but is remaining to look after her.

Standish, marching northward along the coast, broods over his defeat in love but finally decides that he should confine himself to soldiering and forget wooing. When he returns to the village from his attack on the Indian camp, he brings with him the head of one of the Indians and hangs it on the roof of the fort. Priscilla is glad that she did not accept Standish's proposal.

It is now autumn, and the village is at peace with the Indians. Captain Standish is out scouring the countryside. Alden builds his own house and often walks through the forest to see Priscilla. One afternoon, he sits holding a skein of thread as she winds it. As they sit talking, a messenger bursts in with the news that Standish has been killed by a poisoned arrow and that his men have been cut off in ambush.

At last, Alden feels free to make his own declaration. He and Priscilla are married in the village church before the entire congregation. The magistrate reads the service and the elder finishes the blessing when an unexpected guest appears at the door. It is Standish—recovered from his wound—and striding in like a ghost from the grave. Before everyone, the gruff soldier and the bridegroom make up their differences. Then, Standish tenderly wishes Alden and Priscilla joy, and the wedding procession sets off merrily through the forest to Priscilla's new home.

Critical Evaluation:

In *The Courtship of Miles Standish*, Henry Wadsworth Longfellow found inspiration in the American past. Longfellow and other writers of his time wanted to create a common American heritage to bind the nation together and express a uniquely American spirit, as Longfellow had done with *Evangeline* (1847) and *The Song of Hiawatha* (1855). Moreover, the story of John Alden and Priscilla had a special interest for Longfellow because he was one of their descendants. Originally called "Priscilla," the poem reworks family history into American legend.

First and foremost, the tale is a love story, centered in the conflict of love and friendship. With the first scene, Longfellow highlights the contrast between Miles Standish, the tough soldier idolizing Julius Caesar and proud of his many battles and his distinguished ancestry, and the scholar Alden. Standish is short, middle-age, fiery, and decisive; Alden is quiet, young, eloquent, handsome, and shy. Ironically, neither man will openly court the woman they both love.

Between the two men is Priscilla, the poem's calm but firm center, who sees into the hearts of both her wooers. She knows from the beginning what Standish learns only later, namely that romance between the two of them is hopeless, and she sees nobility in Alden, which he initially is not aware of. Outwardly the model of the home-loving Puritan maiden, Priscilla first appears in the poem sitting at the fireside and weaving and singing. Though quiet and demure, she is discerning and, unlike her suitors, willing to speak for herself as she advises Alden to do in the poem's most famous line. She quietly and unobtrusively guides Alden into professing his love. Through her character, Longfellow shows Puritanism turning into the independent American character. Eventually, Alden will follow her example and so proposes, albeit only after he has come to believe that Standish is dead.

Longfellow envelops his love story in early American history. This is a romance among Puritans, who saw the world as a spiritual drama. Thus the conflict between love and friendship in Alden's heart is heightened by his belief that God is testing him. Longfellow admires in the Puritans their courage, strength of character, and endurance. However, he finds more troubling their narrowness, dogmatism, and ferocity, so memorably depicted in the poem by the howitzer affixed to the roof of the colony's church. Though one of the colony's oldest members wants to treat the American Indians with Christian charity, he is drowned out by the louder and more persuasive actions of Standish, who returns the Indian's rattlesnake skin, filled with Puritan gunpowder. The poem ends on a note of reconciliation when the text likens the newlyweds John and Priscilla Alden to the biblical couple Isaac and Rebecca. Both couples are famous lovers who also play a role as founders of a people. Priscilla and John's marriage has become part of the growth of America.

Longfellow and his readers see this poem as a pastoral, but it is pastoral only in its broadest sense—a tender love story set in an uncultivated natural setting. Longfellow shrewdly avoids placing his works in the pastoral's idyllic natural setting, thus avoiding the sentimentality that some

critics have charged him with. His New England, though, is both delightful and frightening, a new promised land and a desert wilderness testing the souls of the righteous. It is a land of killing winters (the plot is initiated by the deaths of Standish's wife and of Priscilla's family during the colony's first winter), disease, hostile Indians, and a soil that only constant labor can cultivate.

Part of this landscape is the American Indian, whose legends Longfellow uses earlier in *The Song of Hiawatha*. In *The Courtship of Miles Standish*, the Indians are the fierce, treacherous enemies of the pilgrims. Though such a portrayal offends many modern readers, Longfellow treats Indians as they were seen by the pilgrims themselves. Modern readers should note that these "savage" natives find their savagery easily matched by that of the pilgrims—represented by the Indian's head Standish places on the roof of Plymouth's fort. While the poem does not ignore the frightening and dark aspects of its tale, these aspects exist at the story's margins. Longfellow had viewed the American past with a scholar's eye, but also with a lover's heart.

Though a traditionalist in poetic theory, Longfellow frequently experimented with verse forms. In this poem, he follows the precedent of *Evangeline* and composes in unrhymed hexameters, a form of six metrical feet for each line of poetry. The meter is dactylic (one accented syllable followed by two accented syllables), but Longfellow frequently substitutes other meters for the dactyl to achieve variety in the poem's rhythm. This variation prevents the dullness that the hexameter in English is often subject to. The long line allows him to create a leisurely and stately, but flowing, rhythm fitted to this love story.

Longfellow enriches his story with biblical allusions that deepen and broaden his simple tale. Moreover, because the Puritans saw themselves as the new Israelites, it is fitting that they regard themselves and their situations in biblical terms. For example, the large Indian warriors are likened to the biblical giant Goliath; Alden sees in Priscilla the virtuous woman spoken of in the book of Proverbs; and Longfellow ends his poem by comparing John and Priscilla to Isaac and Rebecca.

Longfellow enlivens the poem's serious themes with humor and irony. The story is, after all, a comedy, ending with a wedding and a general reconciliation. The poet cunningly deploys irony in his main situation, where Standish gets his friend to plead his case before the woman they both want to marry. Both men come in for their share of fun. Alden's Puritan, overly scrupulous, conscience troubles him almost to the point of madness, while Standish indulges in some classic exaggeration when, in his rage over being rejected by Priscilla, he likens himself to Caesar and Alden as his Brutus.

Like *Evangeline* and *The Song of Hiawatha*, *The Courtship of Miles Standish* had been another popular success for Longfellow, helping him to achieve the position of nineteenth century America's most popular poet. Admirers of Longfellow regard *The Courtship of Miles Standish* as one of his most fully realized works, perhaps his best long narrative poem. The poem offers a tighter plot than his earlier narratives, told briskly and with greater metrical variation. The story offers a satisfying blend of sweet romance, action, and gentle humor, wrapped in a reverent but not idealized view of the American past. The book's popularity helped establish Alden, Priscilla, and Standish in the national imagination, and the story is still part of the Thanksgiving tradition in the United States. The poem also is often reprinted, adapted, and parodied. Its most famous line, "Why don't you speak for yourself, John," has passed into common parlance. Its principal characters stand with Paul Revere, Evangeline, and Hiawatha as part of America's legends.

"Critical Evaluation" by Anthony Bernardo, Jr.

Further Reading

Arvin, Newton. *Longfellow: His Life and Work.* Boston: Little, Brown, 1963. Sees *The Courtship of Miles Standish* as an unpretentious domestic comedy, presented with simple truthfulness, appropriate Puritan coloration, and biblical imagery.

Calhoun, Charles C. *Longfellow: A Rediscovered Life.* Boston: Beacon Press, 2004. A comprehensive and sympathetic biography, in which Calhoun seeks to rehabilitate Longfellow's reputation and document his contributions to American culture and literature.

Ferguson, Robert A. "Longfellow's Political Fears: Civic Authority and the Role of the Artist in *Hiawatha* and *Miles Standish*." *American Literature* 50 (May, 1978): 187-215. Interprets John Alden as representing both the helpless, authority-fearing artist and the personally conflicted Longfellow himself. Interprets Miles Standish's admiration for Julius Caesar as an unpleasant, intended characteristic.

Gale, Robert L. *A Henry Wadsworth Longfellow Companion.* Westport, Conn.: Greenwood Press, 2003. Several hundred alphabetically arranged entries about Longfellow's individual poems, his other writings, his family members and associates, and other aspects of his life and work. Includes an introductory essay and a chronology.

Wagenknecht, Edward. *Henry Wadsworth Longfellow: His Poetry and Prose.* New York: Ungar, 1986. Praises *The Courtship of Miles Standish* for its faultless narrative flow; skillfully evoked atmosphere; unfaltering plot elements; and detailed, realistically presented, and developed characters. Asserts that the work neatly balances comedy and serious drama.

Williams, Alicia Crane. "John and Priscilla, We Hardly Knew Ye." *American History Illustrated* 23 (December, 1988): 40-47. Explains that, although John Alden and Priscilla are elevated by Longfellow to legendary status, biographical information concerning the real pair is sketchy. John, a cooper who became a civil officer, and Priscilla, who inherited considerable money, married about 1623 and by 1650 had eleven children.

Williams, Cecil B. *Henry Wadsworth Longfellow.* New York: Twayne, 1964. Provides a detailed plot summary of *The Courtship of Miles Standish* that includes carefully chosen quotations. Extols the work as part of America's cultural heritage and refers to Longfellow's journals for details about the work's composition.

Youmans, Gilbert. "Longfellow's Long Line." In *Formal Approaches to Poetry: Recent Development in Metrics, Phonology, and Phonetics*, edited by B. Alan Dresher and Nila Friedberg. New York: Mouton de Gruyter, 2006. Youmans analyzes minutely and helpfully Longfellow's use of hexameter in his two major narrative poems written in hexameters, *Evangeline* and *The Courtship of Miles Standish*, showing how Longfellow adapts this difficult form to English verse.

Cousin Bette

Author: Honoré de Balzac (1799-1850)
First published: La Cousine Bette, 1846 (English
    translation, 1888)
Type of work: Novel
Type of plot: Social realism
Time of plot: Early nineteenth century
Locale: Paris

Principal characters:
BARON HULOT
ADELINE, his wife
HORTENSE, their daughter
VICTORIN, their son
LISBETH, Adeline's Cousin Bette
MONSIEUR CREVEL, Baron Hulot's enemy
CÉLESTINE, Victorin's wife and the daughter of Monsieur
    Crevel
COLONEL HULOT, the baron's older brother
MADAME VALÉRIE MARNEFFE, Baron Hulot's mistress
MONSIEUR MARNEFFE, Madame Marneffe's husband
COUNT STEINBOCK, Hortense's husband
BARON MONTÈS, Madame Marneffe's lover

The Story:

One day in the summer of 1838, M. Crevel calls on
Adeline, the Baroness Hulot, to offer to make her his mistress, but she refuses him. M. Crevel swore to be revenged
on Baron Hulot, who stole his former mistress. The baron,
however, spent his fortune in the process and is now unable
to give his daughter Hortense a satisfactory dowry. Hortense
forgets her sorrow over her own marriage prospects by teasing Adeline's cousin Lisbeth, or Cousin Bette, about her
lover. Cousin Bette is the old maid of the family, and her
lover is a sculptor and Polish refugee named Count Steinbock. The attachment between them is that of mother and
son, but Cousin Bette is wildly jealous of his other friends.

That evening, the baron's older brother, Colonel Hulot,
and his son and daughter-in-law, Victorin and Célestine,
come for dinner. Célestine, the daughter of M. Crevel, does
not share her father's dislike of Baron Hulot. After dinner,
the baron escorts Cousin Bette home and then goes to see his
mistress. He finds that she deserted him for a rich duke.

The next morning, Baron Hulot makes plans to seduce
Madame Marneffe, the wife of a clerk who works for him. In
the meantime, Hortense manages to speak to Count Steinbock by buying one of his pieces of sculpture. He calls
shortly afterward. The Hulots feel that the penniless young
nobleman might be a good match for Hortense, but the plan is
kept secret from Cousin Bette.

Baron Hulot arranges to meet Madame Marneffe in Cousin
Bette's rooms. Later, he moves the Marneffes into a more
lavish establishment in the Rue Varennes, and Cousin Bette
goes there to live. Through her new friend, Cousin Bette
learns of the coming marriage between Hortense and Count

Steinbock, for Baron Hulot keeps no secrets from Madame
Marneffe. Cousin Bette was always treated in the family as
the eccentric old maid and the ugly duckling; their stealing
her lover is the final humiliation. She swears vengeance on
the whole Hulot family, and Madame Marneffe agrees to
help her.

As a first step, Cousin Bette introduces M. Crevel to Madame Marneffe. Then she has Count Steinbock imprisoned
for debt, and she tells Hortense that he returned to Poland. No
one suspects that Cousin Bette put him in prison. Once he obtains his release through friends, the wedding plans go ahead.
Baron Hulot manages to raise a dowry for Hortense and plans
to keep himself solvent by sending Adeline's uncle to Algiers. There, Baron Hulot hopes to steal money from the
government through dealings with the army commissary; the
uncle is to be the innocent dupe.

As soon as Hortense is married, Baron Hulot moves
Adeline to a more modest house so that he can spend more
money on Madame Marneffe. She and the baron conduct
their affair quietly and attract little notice. At the same time,
she is also intimate with M. Crevel. M. Marneffe gives little trouble to either of these gentlemen as long as they keep
him supplied with money and a good position at the war office.

When Baron Montès, an old lover of Madame Marneffe,
appears one evening, Baron Hulot and M. Crevel become
worried. That same night, Madame Marneffe refuses to let
Baron Hulot enter her apartment. M. Crevel tells Baron
Hulot that he, too, is Madame Marneffe's lover. The two old
rivals reconcile and go to see Madame Marneffe the next day.

She agrees to consider M. Crevel's offer to marry her after her husband dies, but she tells Baron Hulot that he need not hope to be her lover again. After the two old men leave, she asks Cousin Bette to try to get Count Steinbock to come to her. She always wanted to make a conquest of him, and his downfall will also be Cousin Bette's revenge on Hortense.

Count Steinbock is in need of money, and Cousin Bette slyly suggests borrowing from Madame Marneffe. After the count secretly goes to see her, Madame Marneffe makes a complete conquest of him.

When Madame Marneffe finds herself to be pregnant, she tells each lover separately that he is the father. Hortense believes that Count Steinbock is the father and deserts him to return to her mother. Baron Hulot finds it necessary to visit Adeline to see Hortense and asks her to return to her husband. Hortense refuses and makes a violent scene. Cousin Bette arrives to take Hortense's side. She says that she can no longer stay with Madame Marneffe; she will keep house for old Colonel Hulot. It is her plan to marry the old man and gain control of the only money left in the family.

The baron's affairs are growing desperate. Adeline's uncle in Algiers writes that the plot to steal from the government was discovered and that money is needed to stop an investigation. Madame Marneffe is insisting on money for her child and a better position for her husband. One night, Madame Marneffe leads Baron Hulot into a trap; when M. Marneffe brings the police to the lovers' room, saying he will prosecute unless he is promoted at the war office, the baron agrees.

At last, the Algerian scandal breaks, and the uncle kills himself. Colonel Hulot is crushed by this blow to the family honor. He pays the necessary money from his own savings and dies only a few days later from wounded pride. Cousin Bette has her revenge. Baron Hulot is a ruined man. In his disgrace, he seeks shelter with the mistress who deserted him for the duke. She provides him with some capital and a pretty seamstress to keep him company, and he lives in the slums under an assumed name. Through the efforts of Victorin, now a successful lawyer, the family slowly regains its wealth. Madame Marneffe's child is stillborn, and her husband dies. Victorin is determined to keep his father-in-law from throwing himself away on the woman. He hires an underworld character to inform Baron Montès that Madame Marneffe is having an affair with Count Steinbock and is to marry M. Crevel. Baron Montès takes his revenge on Madame Marneffe and M. Crevel by infecting them with a fatal tropical disease; they both die soon after their marriage.

Adeline begins to do charity work in the slums. On one of her visits, she discovers her husband and brings him back to live with his family. Meanwhile, Cousin Bette retires to her bed with consumption; she dies soon after the return of Baron Hulot, who became a model husband. Soon after his wife hires a new cook, however, Adeline discovers her husband in the servants' quarters with the peasant girl. Adeline dies three days later. Baron Hulot leaves Paris, and as soon as he can, he marries the peasant girl, Agathe. This impropriety causes Victorin to remark that parents can hinder the marriages of their children, but children can do nothing about the actions of their parents in their second childhood.

Critical Evaluation:

Cousin Bette, Honoré de Balzac's final masterpiece, is one of the last novels of his huge, unfinished project, *La Comédie humaine* (1829-1848; *The Human Comedy*, 1885-1893, 1896), and, together with *Le Cousin Pons* (1847; *Cousin Pons*, 1880), belongs to the *Scenes from Parisian Life* segment. The book presents some of Balzac's most somber visions of human depravity but also emphasizes loyalty and devotion. Balzac wrote *Cousin Bette* during the winter of 1846 under the greatest possible pressure from his indebtedness and emotional strain; the strain, coming on top of many years of arduous work, may finally have broken the novelist's strength. It is one of Balzac's longest novels and one of the most perfectly organized and most densely constructed. None of the digressions or the padding that he sometimes used to lengthen stories is present. All the different characters in the tale—the black "angel" Bette, the debauched Hulot, the ambitious Valérie Marneffe, and her scheming husband—interact like the pieces of a vast machine grinding toward the inevitable, ironic conclusion.

Balzac saw society as a unit, a great drama with endless links and relationships. This theme is everywhere evident in *Cousin Bette*. All social levels are portrayed and are interwoven beneath the surface by the threads of human emotions. Hatred ties Bette to the Hulots, passion ties Baron Hulot to Madame Marneffe, ambition connects M. Marneffe to the baron, love ties Hortense to Steinbock, and debt ties Steinbock to Bette. The tangle is at once extremely complicated and entirely plausible. Amazingly enough, Balzac was able to keep not only the threads of this novel in his head but also the threads for the entire series of novels, which included nearly three thousand named characters.

Balzac believed that individuals' antecedents, environment, and upbringing shape their destiny. In this, he anticipated the realist school and such naturalists as Émile Zola. Balzac saw that apparently trivial changes or new conditions had the capacity to bring out latent possibilities in a person and to alter the entire course of that person's life. In his novels and stories, Balzac emphasized the importance of his characters' physical surroundings, the towns and streets and houses in which they lived, the rooms that seemed to trap them, the clothes and gestures that gave them away, and other minutiae of life. In *Cousin Bette*, the descriptions of Paris range from the run-down neighborhood near the Louvre, in which Bette lives, to the shabby elegance of the Hulots' establishment. Everything is vividly detailed, explained, and placed in context. Nothing exists in isolation.

The place of women in society is reflected on many levels in *Cousin Bette*. Bette earns her own way with her needlework and always has. Valérie uses her beauty to further her unscrupulous husband's career and ends up being kept by rich men. Hortense, Bette's cousin, is bred to be a wife and must find a husband or be a burden to her family; she knows this, but she also knows that her father must provide her with a dowry and that she alone is not sufficient to acquire a man's name and place in society. Hortense's mother, Adeline, suffers her husband's indiscretions in silence because there is no socially acceptable recourse. The women must all resort to intrigue and deceit to accomplish anything in the society dominated and controlled by males. Bette is the most independent of the women and the most ruthless, but her efforts—whatever their motivation—are all clandestine. Whatever success she has is possible only because nobody is aware of it. People do not suspect her because she is a woman, plain and no longer young, characteristics that render her almost invisible.

In *Cousin Bette*, as in so many of Balzac's novels, the contrast between the provinces and Paris is an ever-present theme. Bette's peasant shrewdness and her lack of sophistication give the novel its momentum; she is a provincial fighting to make her way in the jungle of Paris. The reader cannot help but feel that Balzac admires her ruthless, astute maneuvering. Balzac was always fascinated by the themes of the individual in conflict with society and of the rebel or criminal personality. His villains often were more vigorous and interesting than his virtuous people, and Cousin Bette is no exception. She is one of Balzac's most intriguing and complex characters, totally unlikable yet hypnotic in her power. Her individuality is symbolized by the way in which she stubbornly reduces her hand-me-down garments from their urban fashion to countrified, colorless rags; she makes the clothes conform to her self-image. Shy and wild, vicious and hard, only her highly developed will keeps Bette from physically attacking her beautiful and resented cousin, Adeline. From the beginning, the reader knows that Bette is capable of anything. Resentment grows within her until it possesses her and changes her into a monster. The countrywoman's

pride will not stop short of complete revenge. Yet, strangely enough, she is content with a secret revenge. It does not matter to her if the Hulots never know that she is the instrument of their ruin. The silent satisfaction is enough for this peasant spinster.

After a long and detailed preparation and exposition in which Balzac establishes the characters and their setting, the pace of the novel increases and the tension mounts to a climax that is as inevitable as that of a classic tragedy. The Hulots and Valérie, Marneffe and Steinbock, all pay the consequences of their sins; all of them let an obsession rule their life. Only Bette emerges triumphant, for she is victorious even after death.

"Critical Evaluation" by Bruce D. Reeves

Further Reading

Bloom, Harold, ed. *Honoré de Balzac*. Philadelphia: Chelsea House, 2003. Collection of essays on some of Balzac's individual novels, including "*Cousin Bette*: Balzac and the Historiography of Difference" by Scott McCracken and "The Feminine Conspiracy in Balzac's *La Cousine Bette*" by James R. McGuire. Other essays discuss the creation of a fictional universe, use of narrative doubling, and allegories of energy in *The Human Comedy*.

Garval, Michael D. "Honoré de Balzac: Writing the Monument." In *"A Dream of Stone": Fame, Vision, and Monumentality in Nineteenth-Century French Literary Culture*. Newark: University of Delaware Press, 2004. Garval describes how France in the nineteenth century developed an ideal image of "great" writers, viewing these authors' work as immortal and portraying their literary successes in monumental terms. He traces the rise and fall of this literary development by focusing on Balzac, George Sand, and Victor Hugo.

Hemmings, F. W. J. *Balzac: An Interpretation of "La Comédie humaine."* New York: Random House, 1967. Chapter 4, "The Cancer," presents a comparative analysis of *Cousin Bette*, *Eugénie Grandet*, and *Père Goriot* as a trilogy of related studies centering on a father whose private obsession jeopardizes his family.

Levin, Harry. *The Gates of Horn: A Study of Five French Realists*. New York: Oxford University Press, 1963. A study of literary realism in France. Chapter 4, an influential overview of Balzac's work, includes several specific references to *Cousin Bette*.

Madden, James. *Weaving Balzac's Web: Spinning Tales and Creating the Whole of "La Comédie humaine."* Birmingham, Ala.: Summa, 2003. Explores how Balzac structured his vast series of novels to create continuity both within and between the individual books. Madden describes how internal narration, in which characters tell each other stories about other characters, enables the recurring characters to provide layers of meaning that are evident throughout the series.

Maurois, André. *Prometheus: The Life of Balzac*. Translated by Norman Denny. Harmondsworth, England: Penguin, 1971. The definitive biography by France's premier literary biographer. A thorough, generally objective, and highly readable account of Balzac's life. Provides detailed context for and some commentary on all of the major works.

Prendergast, Christopher. *Balzac: Fiction and Melodrama.* New York: Holmes & Meier, 1978. Argues for the importance of the conventions and devices of melodrama for the interpretation of Balzac's analyses of French society. Contains a detailed analysis of *Cousin Bette* as well as an overview of previous critical work on the novel.

Robb, Graham. *Balzac: A Life.* New York: W. W. Norton, 1994. A detailed biographical account of Balzac's life and work. Robb describes Balzac's philosophical perspectives and speculates on the psychological motivations underlying his writing.

Stowe, William W. *Balzac, James, and the Realistic Novel.* Princeton, N.J.: Princeton University Press, 1983. Discusses the solutions Balzac and Henry James adopted in solving various problems of realistic fictional representation. Includes a comparative study of the dramatic elements in *Cousin Bette* and James's *The Wings of the Dove*.

Cousin Pons

Author: Honoré de Balzac (1799-1850)
First published: Le Cousin Pons, 1847 (English translation, 1880)
Type of work: Novel
Type of plot: Naturalism
Time of plot: 1840's
Locale: Paris

Principal characters:
SYLVAIN PONS, an elderly musician and amateur art collector
SCHMUCKE, Pons's friend and fellow musician
MADAME CIBOT, a portress at Pons's residence
MONSIEUR DE MARVILLE, Pons's cousin
MADAME DE MARVILLE, Monsieur de Marville's wife and an enemy of Pons
FRAISIER, a rascally attorney
REMONENCQ, a friend and accomplice of Madame Cibot

The Story:

Sylvain Pons is an ugly man who has no family except one cousin, Monsieur de Marville, a rich and influential government official. As a result of his connection, Cousin Pons, as the de Marvilles calls him, is able to dine out at a rich man's home at least once a week. These opportunities satisfy one of Pons's two pleasures in life, a delight in good food well served. Pons's job as conductor of the orchestra at a ballet theater and his series of private music pupils provide him the money to live and to satisfy his other delight in life, collecting works of art.

By the time he is in his sixties, Pons has built up a collection worth more than one million francs, though neither he nor anyone else realizes that it is so valuable. Pons's only friend is a musician in his orchestra, an old German named Schmucke. The two men live together in an apartment filled with Pons's art treasures. Their lives are extremely simple; the portress at the house, Madame Cibot, cooks for them and cleans the apartment, and their work keeps them busy most of the time. The only flaw in their existence, as Schmucke sees it, is the fact that Pons goes out to dinner once a week and sometimes twice.

Even that flaw is remedied when Madame de Marville, the wife of Pons's cousin, grows tired of having the old man in her home and makes her attitude obvious to him. He then begins eating all of his meals at home with Schmucke. Pons, however, is too fond of dining out on rich food to be happy with the arrangement, and he misses the company that he enjoyed for more than forty years. With Schmucke's help, Pons determines to make peace with Madame de Marville by securing a rich husband for Cécile, the de Marvilles' daughter. The attempt is a dismal failure and as a result the de Marvilles' house and those of all their friends become closed to Pons.

The shock of finding that his cousin and all of his cousin's connections regard him as vicious and hateful and will no longer speak to him is too much for Pons. He falls ill, and nothing the doctor can do helps. His friend Schmucke tries to keep their small establishment going with the aid of Madame Cibot, who acts as a nurse, while Schmucke works at the theater or gives music lessons.

It is unfortunate for the two old men that Madame Cibot learns that the art treasures lying about the apartment are extremely valuable. At first she thinks only of having Pons set up an annuity for her at his death, in return for her nursing care, but her avarice eventually leads her to conceive the idea of getting the entire fortune into her own hands. She takes into her confidence a small dealer in bric-a-brac named Remonencq, who in turn enlists the aid of Elie Magus, a Jew with a passion for art. The Jew, with the help of the other two, gains admittance to Pons's apartment and makes an estimate of the collection's value. At the same time, he makes an agreement to pay Madame Cibot more than forty thousand francs if she will get Schmucke, who knows nothing of art, to sell four of his friend's pictures for money to pay Pons's doctor bills.

Poor Schmucke, who thinks only of saving his friend's life, readily agrees to sell four masterpieces, whose value he does not know, for a fraction of their true value. After they are sold, thinking that Pons will never notice, he simply hangs four other pictures in their places. Delighted at her success in fleecing the old men, Madame Cibot decides to try to get all the collection and enlists the aid of the doctor, who is a poor man, and a rascally attorney named Fraisier. Fraisier knows of Pons's influential relatives and points out to Madame Cibot that the relatives will fight any attempt by the portress to get the old man's estate. He also convinces her that they are powerful enough to send her to the guillotine if they can prove her guilt. Feeling that her only chance of success lies with him, Madame Cibot agrees to follow the attorney's advice.

The attorney goes to Madame de Marville, who is also avaricious, and tells her of Pons's wealth and his determination to leave it to Schmucke. Madame de Marville immediately agrees to do anything she can to gain the fortune for herself, for all the family's wealth has gone into her daughter's dowry. She promises to have her husband get good appointments for Fraisier and the doctor, and she consents to set up an annuity for Madame Cibot. When she tells her husband, he agrees.

Fraisier and Madame Cibot then begin to lay plans to find a way into Pons's confidence. Unfortunately, Pons becomes suspicious of Madame Cibot. His suspicions are confirmed when he awakens one afternoon to find Magus, his rival collector, examining the art objects on the walls and tables. Summoning his remaining strength, Pons leaves his sickbed, staggers to the other rooms, and discovers that his paintings are gone. He realizes immediately that someone is fleecing him at poor Schmucke's expense. That night, after Schmucke confesses to selling the paintings, he and Schmucke discuss what they could do. Pons forgives Schmucke, for he knows that the German has no idea of the cash values of the paintings or the more personal value they have for Pons himself.

Pons draws up a will naming Madame Cibot as one of his heirs, in an attempt to deceive her as to his real intentions. He even leaves the will where she will see it. The portress is pleased, although the will does not provide for as much as she wants. Fraisier also sees the document and is pleased because it is a will that can easily be broken in court for the benefit of the de Marville family. Pons hoped that they would react in that way, and the following day he secretly makes a new will that leaves his fortune to the crown, with the stipulation that in return the government will give Schmucke a lifetime annuity.

When Pons dies shortly afterward, his death leaves poor Schmucke in a dreadful state. The German musician knows little of the world, and Pons's death leaves him without judgment or willpower. All he cares about is dying quickly in order to meet his friend in heaven. Because of his state of mind, the plotters believe it will be easy to take the estate away from him.

The de Marvilles, bringing a suit to break the will, hope that Schmucke, to avoid trouble, will accept a small annuity and let them have the bulk of the estate. They are right in their belief, but just as the papers are about to be signed, a messenger brings Schmucke a copy of the charges made in court against the old man, charges that he influenced his friend in an attempt to get the estate. The shock to Schmucke is so great that he dies within a few days, allowing the estate to go unchallenged to the de Marvilles, who denied their cousin and despised him during his last years.

Many people gain by the deaths of Pons and Schmucke. The de Marvilles recoup their fortune; Fraisier, the rascally attorney, receives an office of trust for his part in the affair; the doctor who tended Pons receives a sinecure; Magus, the Jew, has his coveted pictures; and Madame Cibot has her annuity. She also has a new husband, for Remonencq, her fellow conspirator, poisons her husband and then marries her.

Everyone, except Schmucke, the man Pons wanted most to help, benefits from Pons's fortune.

Critical Evaluation:

Honoré de Balzac stood at the dividing line between Romanticism and realism. He was inclined toward the fantastic and supernatural and to the exaggeration of normal human types, but his desire to reproduce concrete fact and to visualize the scene or object made him a superb painter of French society in the first half of the nineteenth century. Both of these aspects of his writing are easily observed in *Cousin Pons*, part of the *Scenes from Parisian Life* segment of Balzac's *La Comédie humaine* (1829-1848; *The Human Comedy*, 1885-1893, 1896).

Balzac's own interest in the supernatural and hereafter is seen in the discussion of fortune-telling and astrology when Madame Cibot calls on the witchlike Madame Fontaine in her den. Balzac devotes several pages to an analysis of the plausibility of the seer's art and the reality of certain types of divination. Human beings do not understand everything that exists in the universe, he says, and should not close their eyes to some possibilities simply because they cannot be explained. This idea leads to a belief that is fundamental in Balzac's philosophy and that played an important part in his writing and in the structure of *The Human Comedy*: predestination. Balzac believed that the fates conspired to lead human beings to their ultimate destinies. Given the circumstances of people's backgrounds and the makeup of their characters and factors of their lives, they have no way of avoiding a particular fate. Balzac considered his job to be that of a recorder setting down the causes and effects of the lives and destinies of his characters, and he believed that his method was scientific and objective.

In *Cousin Pons*, readers see the characters of the old collector Pons and his beloved friend, Schmucke, and how their good and trusting natures are taken advantage of by the avaricious people around them. Given the nature of human beings, it is not surprising that the story works its way to a pathetic and painful conclusion. It would be incorrect to say that Balzac created men and women more horrible than any who lived; Balzac knew very well that people who have been taught that material values are the only important ones will stop at nothing until they have acquired everything they can see within their grasp. The morality or lack of morality in Madame Cibot, Fraisier, Remonencq, and the other characters is the result of many factors, which Balzac draws with his usual skill. None of these people stands outside society; they all are influenced by it and in turn influence it. This is one of the fundamental themes in *The Human Comedy*.

The friendship between Pons and Schmucke is portrayed with a touching humor and sensitivity. The devotion between the two old men provides a counterpoint to the grasping, almost savage, natures of Madame Cibot and the others. Seldom did Balzac portray such a low level of society, but he shows both sides of the coin, the love and generosity possible between human beings as well as the cruelty and hypocrisy. If the negative powers ultimately are victorious, that is merely—Balzac implies—the fates at work. That does not mean, however, that he believes that the negative always wins.

Cousin Pons was intended as a companion volume to *Cousin Bette* (1846). In *Cousin Pons* there is the poor male relation, cruelly treated, but gentle of heart, and in *Cousin Bette* there is the poor female relation, also cruelly treated, but revenging herself. The symmetry pleased Balzac, and, read together, the two novels form a powerful structure and a devastating picture of human nature and its possibilities for good and evil.

The collection of old Pons is one that Balzac, himself an avid collector, would have wanted to own. Pons's passion for antiques was shared by Balzac, as was the old man's terror of other people gazing upon or possibly stealing them. Balzac was always at his best when describing a mania—as in connection with Père Goriot, Eugénie Grandet, and César Birotteau—whether the subject was greed, a passion for collecting, or obsessive parental affection. Balzac did more than sympathize with Pons's mania: He felt with Pons as the old man put together and tried to guard his rooms. The passion for the collection, also shared by the old Jew, Elie Magus, is portrayed with so much intensity that the reader comes to feel some of it as well.

Pons and Schmucke are two of the great characters in Balzac's vast gallery and in all of European literature. They both are extremely funny and very touching. They are "odd" yet never absurd, and they are portrayed with a truth of observation and a subtlety of touch that render them sympathetic despite their quirks of personality. Their strange habits and costumes and their odd passions for collecting, for good food, and for company are not applied by the writer from the outside but emerge from within their living, breathing beings. That is why their ultimate fates are so devastating to the reader; their gentle, unworldly natures soon become objects of concern, and their lives present moral pictures of the most painful kind.

Despite its grim, brutal aspects, *Cousin Pons* is actually a very gentle book. The greater part of the story is devoted to the friendship and the devotion of Schmucke and old Pons. Pons's loyalty for his old friend and his effort to care for

Schmucke even after his own death are touchingly shown. When the grasping natures of Madame Cibot and her allies are held up before this picture of unselfish love, they appear doubly horrible. A tone of quiet melancholy pervades the book, a sadness on the part of Balzac that such a fate should await two such good men. As the chronicler of human nature in all of its forms, however, he cannot flinch. He draws the de Marville household in all of its pettiness and Madame Cibot, a woman who rivals even Cousin Bette when it comes to merciless scheming. Before Balzac, few authors had attempted such an uncompromising look at the varieties of human nature. So honest was his gaze that, even today, readers find themselves flinching at the picture he painted.

"Critical Evaluation" by Bruce D. Reeves

Further Reading

Bertault, Philippe. *Balzac and "The Human Comedy."* Translated by Richard Monges. New York: New York University Press, 1963. A general survey of Balzac's novels that offers little critical analysis of individual works but usefully locates them in relation to Balzac's major themes and interests. Includes a brief biographical sketch.

Bloom, Harold, ed. *Honoré de Balzac.* Philadelphia: Chelsea House, 2003. Collection of essays on some of Balzac's individual novels, including "Discourse, Power, and Necessity: Contextualizing *Le Cousin Pons*" by Jane A. Nicholson. Other essays discuss the creation of a fictional universe, use of narrative doubling, and allegories of energy in *The Human Comedy.*

Garval, Michael D. "Honoré de Balzac: Writing the Monument." In *"A Dream of Stone": Fame, Vision, and Monumentality in Nineteenth-Century French Literary Culture.* Newark: University of Delaware Press, 2004. Garval describes how France in the nineteenth century developed an ideal image of "great" writers, viewing these authors' work as immortal and portraying their literary successes in monumental terms. He traces the rise and fall of this literary development by focusing on Balzac, George Sand, and Victor Hugo.

Hemmings, F. W. J. *Balzac: An Interpretation of "La Comédie humaine."* New York: Random House, 1967. Hemmings's chapter 8, "The Dialectic," presents an analysis of *Cousin Pons*, finding the late novel to be one of Balzac's most pessimistic but also one of his most profound works.

Levin, Harry. *The Gates of Horn: A Study of Five French Realists.* New York: Oxford University Press, 1963. A study of literary realism in France. Levin's chapter 4, an influential overview of Balzac's work, includes several specific references to *Cousin Pons.*

Madden, James. *Weaving Balzac's Web: Spinning Tales and Creating the Whole of "La Comédie humaine."* Birmingham, Ala.: Summa, 2003. Explores how Balzac structured his vast series of novels to create continuity both within and between the individual books. Madden describes how internal narration, in which characters tell each other stories about other characters, enables the recurring characters to provide layers of meaning that are evident throughout the series.

Maurois, André. *Prometheus: The Life of Balzac.* Translated by Norman Denny. Harmondsworth, England: Penguin, 1971. The definitive biography by France's premier literary biographer. A thorough, generally objective, and highly readable account of Balzac's life. Provides detailed context for and some commentary on all of the major works, including *Cousin Pons.*

Robb, Graham. *Balzac: A Life.* New York: W. W. Norton, 1994. A detailed biographical account of Balzac's life and work. Robb describes Balzac's philosophical perspectives and speculates on the psychological motivations underlying his writing.

Crabwalk

Author: Günter Grass (1927-   )
First published: Im Krebsgang: Eine Novelle, 2002
    (English translation, 2003)
Type of work: Novella
Type of plot: Narrative
Time of plot: Early 1930's to the end of the twentieth
    century
Locale: The Baltic and East Germany

Principal characters:
PAUL POKRIEFKE, a journalist
TULLA POKRIEFKE, his mother
KONRAD "WILHELM" POKRIEFKE, Paul's son and a right-
    wing propagandist
WOLFGANG "DAVID" STREMPLIN, critic of right-wing
    propaganda
THE OLD MAN, a former citizen of Danzig, who encourage
    Paul's writing

The Story:

For years, Paul Pokriefke has resisted the urging of his mother, Tulla, to write down the fateful story of the *Wilhelm Gustloff,* an oceanliner whose sinking in the Baltic by a Soviet submarine near the end of World War II almost took Tulla's life. As a journalist, Paul is well qualified for such a writing task. He overcomes his reluctance to delve into the past only when he finds right-wing propaganda on the Web that exploits the maritime disaster.

Pushed along by the old man, an unnamed former citizen of Danzig (now Gdańsk, Poland) with a keen interest in the story, Paul reluctantly begins to research the history of the ship, which was named after Wilhelm Gustloff, a German Nazi Party functionary who, in 1936, had been assassinated by the Jewish student David Frankfurter in Switzerland. Gustloff had become a martyr for the Nazi cause.

Although Tulla barely survived the sinking of the *Wilhelm Gustloff* and even gave birth to Paul during the perilous rescue operation, she still has fond memories of the ship that before World War II was used by the Nazis for recreational purposes to promote their concept of a classless society. Paul, however, comes across a debate on the Web in which a person named Wilhelm (as in Gustloff) and one named David (as in Frankfurter) engage in virtual reincarnations of the two historical characters.

Paul writes a detailed report about the *Wilhelm Gustloff* and its prewar voyages, but he is concerned about the exploitation of the ship's fate by right-leaning circles. He is even more shocked when he discovers that his son, Konrad, uses the pseudonym Wilhelm on his Web site.

In jumping from the past to the present, Paul writes that when World War II broke out in 1939, the *Wilhelm Gustloff* was first converted into a hospital ship and then into floating barracks for sailors in training in a harbor near Danzig. Paul then reports on two meetings among the survivors of the *Wilhelm Gustloff* disaster; at the second of these meetings, which took place after the reunification of Germany, Tulla

extended her efforts to disseminate the legend of the ship by enlisting the services of her grandson, Konrad, who was eager to help.

By January, 1945, Paul writes that the demise of the Third Reich is imminent. The *Wilhelm Gustloff* sails westward, carrying about ten thousand passengers, mostly German refugees from East Prussia and Danzig fleeing from the advancing Soviet Red Army. Among the passengers are more than four thousand babies, children, and adolescents, and also some military personnel. The vast majority perish in the icy waters of the Baltic Sea after the torpedoes of the Soviet submarine under the command of Captain Alexander Marinesko find their target. More than fifty years later, in 1996, Wilhelm and David continue to debate whether the sinking of the ship was a war crime or just retribution for the suffering of the Soviet population and of the victims of the Holocaust.

After Tulla and her newborn are put on dry land by their rescuers, Paul writes that they continue their flight and end up in Schwerin, a city that after World War II became part of the Soviet occupation zone and later the German Democratic Republic, or East Germany. Schwerin also happens to be the birthplace of Gustloff, in whose honor the Nazis erected a monument that was then razed by the Soviets.

Wilhelm and David, writes Paul, continue their debate; the former invites the latter to visit Schwerin to engage in a dialogue. Wilhelm guns down his guest when David contemptuously spits on the remaining traces of the Gustloff monument. Because he is a minor, Konrad is sentenced for manslaughter rather than murder and is sent to a juvenile detention facility. As it turns out, David, whose real name is Wolfgang Stremplin, is not Jewish at all; he identifies with all things Jewish to atone for the sufferings of the Jews in Nazi Germany. The parents of both Konrad and Wolfgang try to determine how they might have contributed to the aberrations of their respective sons.

Konrad appears to have overcome his infatuation with the *Wilhelm Gustloff* when, while in prison, he smashes a model of the ship that he had crafted. However, when Paul comes across a Web site in which his son is declared to be a martyr for a right-wing cause, he realizes that there is no end to neo-Nazi propaganda.

Critical Evaluation:

Günter Grass is a novelist of international stature. He achieved his breakthrough with the publication of his first novel *Die Blechtrommel* (1959; *The Tin Drum* 1961). Hailed by some critics as a stunning success and a promising sign of the rebirth of German letters after a devastating war, others condemned the novel as voyeuristic, obscene, and blasphemous. Despite the initial, fierce criticism, *The Tin Drum* has stood the test of time and is generally acknowledged as Grass's masterpiece; the novel also served as the basis of the screenplay of an Oscar-winning film under the direction of Volker Schlöndorff. When Grass received the Nobel Prize in Literature 1999, *The Tin Drum* was cited as his major literary achievement.

In *The Tin Drum* as well as in subsequent works, Grass's birthplace, the city of Danzig, plays a significant role. In fact, the import of Danzig for Grass's work has been compared to that of Yoknapatawpha County for William Faulkner and Dublin for James Joyce. The irretrievable loss of Danzig as a consequence of World War II, when the former German city became the Polish city Gdańsk, has been a powerful stimulus for Grass's literary imagination. Although especially in the 1970's and 1980's Grass had considerably extended the geographic range of his fiction, he returned to the topic of Danzig and Gdańsk after the felling of the Berlin Wall in November, 1989, and German reunification the following year.

In *Crabwalk*, two of the principal characters—one fictional and one real—hail from Danzig. The first of these characters, the memorable Tulla Pokriefke, appears in two works of fiction in Grass's *Danziger Trilogie*, 1980 (*Danzig Trilogy*, 1987); the second, the old man, is a thinly disguised self-portrait of the author himself. The old man repeatedly professes both his keen interest as well as his competence in all matters related to Danzig, but he is too tired to tackle such a formidable subject as the history of the *Wilhlem Gustloff.*

Hence, the old man hires Paul Pokriefke, a mediocre journalist with an inclination to shirk his responsibility as both a storyteller and a father, who serves as his ghostwriter and whom he advises in literary matters. Thus, the old man opines that the sinking of the *Wilhelm Gustloff* provides the material for a novella, a genre of prose fiction that, according to Johann Wolfgang von Goethe's concise definition, entails a form of narrative that is based on an actual but unheard-of or extraordinary event ("eine sich ereignete, unerhörte Begebenheit"). Indeed, the sinking of the *Wilhelm Gustloff*, which is interwoven with the fictional stories of three generations of Pokriefkes, proves to be a suitable subject for a novella in that it constituted a catastrophe of unimaginable proportions. Only about twelve hundred people survived the sinking, including approximately one hundred infants, young children, and teenagers—a death toll that far exceeded that of the sinking of the *Titanic*, usually considered the epitome of maritime disasters.

Grass follows the conventions of the novella by placing the sinking of the ship at the center of the narrative; however, he deviates from other standard literary techniques associated with the novella, such as a tight, linear, and chronological narrative plot or the prevalence of an objective viewpoint. Rather than sequentially narrating the biographies of the three historical personages—Wilhelm Gustloff, David Frankfurter, and Alexander Marinesko—the narrator opts for the seemingly cumbersome approach of a narrative "crabwalk." Crabs appear to move backward, but they actually scuttle sideways and, hence, move forward rapidly; so, too, does the story of the *Wilhelm Gustloff* unfold.

The novella's reception by critics was mostly positive, in contrast to the reception of Grass's earlier major novel *Ein weites Feld* (1995; *Too Far Afield*, 2000), considered to be highly critical of German reunification. Indeed, Grass had strenuously objected to reunification on the questionable grounds that the legacy of Auschwitz forbade a merger of the two postwar German states. In contrast, *Crabwalk* was widely perceived as an indication of a change in or even reversal of Grass's previous stance because of its clearly drawn lines between perpetrators and victims. At the center of the new "victimization" discourse in Europe in the late 1990's was the flight and expulsion of more than ten million Germans from former German territories such as Pomerania and Silesia, as well as East and West Prussia. Another major topic was the indiscriminate area-bombing of German cities by the Allied Powers during World War II.

Grass's long-time reluctance to address the controversial subject of the expulsions is reflected both in narrator Paul's resistance to writing the story of the sinking of the ship and in the old man blaming himself for not having dealt with the story sooner; the old man calls his avoidance a "regrettable omission" that amounts to a veritable failure. Although the topic of flight and expulsion remained a part of public discourse (and Grass had referred to it in *The Tin Drum*), the normalization of German affairs as a result of reunification in 1990 and the emergence of the Berlin Republic in 1994 provided a more hospitable climate for discussing controversial subjects such as German culpability and suffering. However, there are clear indications that the memorialization of German victimhood in literary texts as well as other media could remain problematic.

The novella ends on a resigned as well as cautionary note when the narrator expresses his dismay about the seemingly unending right-wing propaganda on the Web in which Germans are depicted as victims. Such a problematic perception tends to ignore the lessons of the past.

Siegfried Mews

Further Reading

Braun, Rebecca, and Frank Brunssen, eds. *Changing the Nation: Günter Grass in International Perspective.* Würzburg, Germany: Königshausen & Neumann, 2008. A collection of essays by Grass scholars from various countries who examine his fiction with an emphasis on the international stature of his work.

Hall, Katharina. *Günter Grass's "Danzig Quintet": Explorations in the Memory and History of the Nazi Era from "Die Blechtrommel" to "Im Krebsgang."* New York: Peter Lang, 2007. Presents an interesting examination of Grass's central themes of history and memory through *Crabwalk.* Hall uses the term "quintet" rather than "sextet."

Krimmer, Elizabeth. "'Ein Volk von Opfern?' Germans as Victims in Günter Grass's *Die Blechtrommel* and *Im Krebsgang.*" *Seminar* 44, no. 2 (May, 2008): 272-290. Argues that Grass acknowledges the suffering of Germans without denying their culpability as perpetrators.

Mews, Siegfried. *Günter Grass and His Critics: From "The Tin Drum" to "Crabwalk."* Rochester, N.Y.: Camden House, 2008. Offers a descriptive as well as analytical and evaluative overview of criticism devoted to Grass's fiction. Chapter 15 provides a succinct overview and assessment of the reception of *Crabwalk.*

Moeller, Robert G. "Sinking Ships, the Lost *Heimat*, and Broken Taboos: Günter Grass and the Politics of Memory in Contemporary Germany." *Contemporary European History* 12, no. 2 (2003): 147-182. Takes issue with Grass's implicit and explicit assumptions that victimization discourse had previously been ignored by writers and others.

Veel, Kristin. "Virtual Memory in Günter Grass' *Im Krebsgang.*" *German Life and Letters* 57, no. 2 (2004): 206-218. Analyzes the significance of the Web, which, Veel argues, tends to blur the actual and the imaginary and thus present a type of danger to its users.

Cranford

Author: Elizabeth Gaskell (1810-1865)
First published: 1851-1853
Type of work: Novel
Type of plot: Domestic realism
Time of plot: Early nineteenth century
Locale: England

Principal characters:
MARY SMITH, the narrator
MISS DEBORAH JENKYNS, a genteel spinster
MISS MATILDA "MATTY" JENKYNS, her sister
PETER JENKYNS, their long-lost brother
MRS. JAMIESON, a leader of society
LADY GLENMIRE, Mrs. Jamieson's sister-in-law
MARTHA, Miss Matilda's faithful servant

The Story:

Cranford is a small English village inhabited mostly by ladies. Few gentlemen take up residence there, and most of those who do seem to disappear on various and mysterious errands. The doctor, the shopkeepers, and a few male servants are the only representatives of their sex who cross the ladies' vision with any regularity.

Most of the ladies live in "elegant economy." The spending of money is considered vulgar and showy, and one does not mention being poor unless in private to one's dearest friend. When semiretired Captain Brown moves to Cranford and talks openly about being poor, it is quite an affront to the ladies. The captain is, however, so kind and considerate to everyone, whether they are more or less fortunate than he, that the ladies cannot long resent his vulgar behavior and talk. He has two daughters. The elder, dying of an incurable illness, has a tongue sharpened by pain, but the kind women of

Cranford join the younger daughter in trying to make the dying girl's last days pleasant and comfortable.

The women experience great sorrow when the kind captain is killed while rescuing a small child from an oncoming train. When his elder daughter dies soon after, all of the ladies are hard-pressed to make suitable arrangements for the younger daughter. One day, a former suitor appears and takes her for his wife. The village ladies rest happily in the knowledge that Captain Brown would be pleased with his daughter's security.

Until her death, Miss Deborah Jenkyns was one of the more dominant spinsters in the town. She made all decisions for her younger sister, Miss Matilda, who is fifty-five years old. Miss Matilda, affectionately called Miss Matty by all but her sister, knew that Deborah had the better mind and did not resent her sister's dominance. After Miss Deborah's death, Miss Matty almost has to learn how to live again. Her particular friends are Miss Pole, Mrs. Forrester, and Mrs. Jamieson, who becomes the social leader of Cranford after Miss Deborah's death. Miss Mary Smith also often visits Miss Matty and brings her the good advice of her father, who is Miss Matty's financial adviser. Mary is surprised to learn that Miss Matty long ago had a suitor whom she rejected in order to stay with her mother. Not long after Miss Deborah's death, that gentleman returns to Cranford for a visit. Mary is disappointed that he does not renew his courtship of Miss Matty. Miss Matty grieves, too, but only in secret, for she would never admit to such vulgar sentiments openly. Mary also learns that Miss Deborah and Miss Matty have a brother who disappeared many years before, after being severely punished by their father for playing a practical joke on Miss Deborah. Peter Jenkyns is believed dead, although Miss Matty hears rumors that he is living in India.

The genteel ladies are thrown into a flurry of excitement when they hear that Mrs. Jamieson's sister-in-law, Lady Glenmire, is to settle in Cranford. Since she is the first noblewoman they will encounter, they spend long hours discussing how they should address her. Their worries are for naught, however, for Mrs. Jamieson subtly but firmly informs them that they will not be included in her guest list. At first, the ladies are greatly hurt. Later, Mrs. Jamieson is forced to relent and invites them to call, for most of the country gentility are away or otherwise occupied. Miss Matty, Miss Pole, and Mrs. Forrester first think they will be engaged elsewhere for the fateful night, but their innate kindness and, perhaps, their curiosity prevail, and they accept the invitation. They find Lady Glenmire delightful and no more refined or genteel than they themselves.

Mrs. Jamieson departs from Cranford for a time, leaving Lady Glenmire in charge of her home. Soon after, Lady Glenmire becomes engaged to the doctor of the town, a man whose presence the ladies do not even acknowledge except when his services are needed for bleeding. He is no higher socially than a shopkeeper, but it is exciting that the ladies at last know someone who is to be married. They await Mrs. Jamieson's return with fear and anticipation, and they are not disappointed, for Mrs. Jamieson, deciding to cut Lady Glenmire, states that she always knew her to be of low taste.

The engaged couple are married before Mrs. Jamieson returns. By that time, a great tragedy befalls Miss Matty. The bank in which her estate is deposited closes its doors, and she is left with only thirteen pounds a year. She makes no complaint; her biggest worry is whether Mrs. Jamieson will allow the ladies to continue their friendship with her. Mary Smith sends for her father to see what he can plan for Miss Matty. Careful that she should not know of their gift, Miss Pole, Mrs. Forrester, and another friend give up some of their own small incomes so that they can help their friend. Mary and Mr. Smith persuade Miss Matty to sell tea, but it takes a good deal of convincing to assure her that this will be a genteel way for a lady to supplement her income. Miss Matty's faithful maid, Martha, forces her young man to marry her sooner than he anticipated so that they can rent Miss Matty's house and have her for a lodger. In this way, Martha can continue to look after her old mistress without injuring Miss Matty's pride. Everyone is happy when Mrs. Jamieson returns and says that the ladies can continue to call on Miss Matty because her father was a rector and his daughter, who never married, is entitled to the position he left her.

More good fortune follows. Mary writes to Miss Matty's brother in India. When he receives the letter, Peter Jenkyns sells his property and returns to Cranford to keep his sister in comfort and in some prosperity. Peter also brings about a reconciliation between Mrs. Jamieson and Lady Glenmire, who now calls herself Mrs. instead of Lady. Once more, there is peace in Cranford.

Critical Evaluation:

Elizabeth Gaskell began writing *Cranford* in 1851 when Charles Dickens invited her to send him tales for his new weekly journal, *Household Words*. Dickens and Gaskell were so pleased with the first two *Cranford* stories, which depicted a community of genteel single women in a retired country village, that Gaskell went on to write fourteen more, and what she had initially intended as a lighthearted sketch developed into one of her most subtle fictional creations.

Gaskell's first two novels, *Mary Barton* (1848) and *Ruth* (1853), which she had begun before starting *Cranford*, were both greeted by controversy, *Mary Barton* for what some Victorian readers perceived as an alarming siding with the working class against the employing class, and *Ruth* for its sympathetic treatment of an unwed mother. *Cranford* seemed safer, more distant from such troubling nineteenth century issues. It became particularly popular after Gaskell's death, its biggest sales coming at the turn of the century, and it was praised with such words as "charming," "delightful," "delicate." Well into the twentieth century it continued to be read as a nostalgic portrait of a quaint, old-fashioned, feminine world.

The quaintness and charm are there, and so is some nostalgia, for *Cranford*'s narrator, Mary Smith, writes with a constant awareness that the life she describes is already anachronistic and likely soon to disappear altogether in a rapidly modernizing society. However, the novel is also marked by a clear-sighted probing into the conditions of its female characters' lives in a society that expected the genders to occupy separate spheres.

The opening sentence—"In the first place, Cranford is in possession of the Amazons"—implies that separate spheres might mean immense power for women. Cranford's circle of widows and single ladies pride themselves on their self-sufficiency; they rule their world, and it is one in which men are superfluous.

If, however, the image of Amazons leads readers to expect warrior-women who challenge Victorian orthodoxies about pursuits appropriate for females, Gaskell quickly sets them right in her descriptions of the most conventional of ladies. They may own their own houses—a right denied married Englishwomen until the Married Women's Property Acts passed after 1870—but their economic power is severely curtailed. They glory in their "elegant economy," but such economy is required of them because they live on very small inherited incomes and because they devote themselves to preserving the social rules with which they maintain the class status determined for them by their relation to fathers or husbands. They visit one another and play cards, they fantasize about threats from thieves who turn out not to exist, they read little and are vastly ignorant about the wider world, and in real crises they need help from men.

Gaskell develops the pathos and grotesqueries of the Cranford ladies' lives by focusing on the Jenkyns sisters. The older sister, Deborah, had devoted herself to her authoritarian clergyman father; she never married and was always available to read to him and to help him with correspondence. Gaskell portrays her as something of a social tyrant devoted to preserving the cultural status quo, whether this be a matter of literary style (she scorns any deviation from the formal

eighteenth century sentences of Samuel Johnson, her father's favorite author) or social status (she has prevented her younger sister, Miss Matty, from marrying the farmer Mr. Holbrook, a free spirit who cares nothing about social advancement). After Deborah's death, Miss Matty, who has been allowed no independent will or intellectual development, seems nearly helpless.

The narrative nevertheless leads readers to feel admiration and considerable sympathy for the Cranford ladies. Gaskell's narrator, Mary, contrasts significantly with the women whose lives she describes, for she lives not in Cranford but in Drumble, an industrial city. She is a young woman still residing with her father yet in possession of independent opinions. She responds enthusiastically to modern culture—standing up for Dickens, for example, against Miss Jenkyns' advocacy of Dr. Johnson, and cheering when the visiting Lady Glenmire outrages her status-conscious sister-in-law Mrs. Jamieson by marrying a mere surgeon with the plebeian name of Hoggins. Mary easily sees through the Cranford ladies' snobberies and subterfuges, yet she also loves them. The Jenkyns sisters are her particular friends; she visits them often, and for her the limited lives of the Cranford ladies are full of human interest. Moreover, she sees not only the limitations but the largely good-humored strength with which Cranford's women make the best of these limitations. Above all, she recognizes Miss Matty's sweetness, kindness, and integrity, and she is a perceptive reader of the hidden pain in Miss Matty's life. The novel's climax comes when the women rally around Miss Matty after her livelihood is threatened by the failure of the bank in which Deborah had invested their inheritance. At such points, the narration emphasizes the importance of the kind of mutual support the Cranford ladies, despite their frequent competitiveness, can give one another. The novel's great achievement is the blending of tones with which Mary tells her stories: ironic, satiric, amused, sad, and deeply loving.

That Mary is both an outside observer and an engaged participant also gives her an important role in the novel's action. When Miss Matty loses most of her income, Mary is able to persuade Miss Matty and the other Cranford ladies that she will not lose social status by setting up a shop and earning money. Furthermore, as someone willingly belonging to the wider world, she manages to get a letter to Miss Matty's long-lost brother Peter, who returns from India and, evading suggestions of marriage, establishes a household with his sister. Peter has a particularly interesting relation to the novel's concern with Victorian separations between men and women. He left Cranford in a spirit of rebellion against his father's sternness and his sister Deborah's sexual prudery; he returns as a man comfortably able to express the "feminine" qualities of kindness and loyalty that are Cranford's great strength. In this, he is like male characters who appeared earlier in the novel: Mr. Brown, the proponent of Dickens in the first two chapters; the surgeon Hoggins; and Miss Matty's lost love, Holbrook. If *Cranford* gives something of the impression of a utopian fiction, this is the product not only of its nostalgic love for an older world but also of its proposal that the best human society will cease to insist that men and women construct themselves as different kinds of beings.

"Critical Evaluation" by Anne Howells

Further Reading

Auerbach, Nina. *Communities of Women: An Idea in Fiction.* Cambridge, Mass.: Harvard University Press, 1998. Stresses the virtues of Cranford as a cooperative female community and speculates that the novel may have been influenced by Gaskell's friendship with Charlotte Brontë.

Foster, Shirley. *Elizabeth Gaskell: A Literary Life.* New York: Palgrave, 2002. This accessible introduction to Gaskell relies on the best available biographies. It offers interesting comparisons of Gaskell's novels with others of the period and emphasizes women's issues as addressed by Gaskell.

Hughes, Linda K., and Michael Lund. *Victorian Publishing and Mrs. Gaskell's Work.* Charlottesville: University Press of Virginia, 1999. Places Gaskell's writing in the context of the Victorian era, describing how she negotiated her way through the publishing world by producing work that defied the conventions of her times but was also commercially successful. *Cranford* is discussed in chapter 3.

Keating, Peter, ed. Introduction to *"Cranford" and "Cousin Phillis,"* by Elizabeth Gaskell. Harmondsworth, England: Penguin, 1976. An informative introduction that stresses *Cranford*'s representations of social change.

Nash, Julie. *Servants and Paternalism in the Works of Maria Edgeworth and Elizabeth Gaskell.* Burlington, Vt.: Ashgate, 2007. Examines the servant characters in Gaskell's stories and novels, including *Cranford*, to show how her nostalgia for a traditional ruling class conflicted with her interest in radical new ideas about social equality.

Schor, Hilary M. *Scheherezade in the Marketplace: Elizabeth Gaskell and the Victorian Novel.* New York: Oxford University Press, 1992. Explores *Cranford*'s experimentation with narrative, which is especially interesting for its references to other literary works and for its narrator's attentiveness to Miss Matty's hidden "woman's story."

Stoneman, Patsy. *Elizabeth Gaskell.* 2d ed. New York: Manchester University Press, 2006. Bloomington: Indiana University Press, 1987. A survey of Gaskell's works that stresses *Cranford*'s depiction of women as limited and marginalized by society. Includes a useful bibliography on Gaskell, Victorian women and women writers, and feminist theory and literary criticism.

Uglow, Jennifer. *Elizabeth Gaskell: A Habit of Stories.* New York: Farrar, Straus & Giroux, 1993. An excellent biography that describes Gaskell's writing of *Cranford* and discusses perceptively the novel's themes, characters, and structure. Sees the novel as "an appeal against separate spheres" for men and women.

The Cream of the Jest
A Comedy of Evasions

Author: James Branch Cabell (1879-1958)
First published: 1917
Type of work: Novel
Type of plot: Satire
Time of plot: Twentieth century
Locale: Virginia

Principal characters:
FELIX KENNASTON, an author
KATHLEEN KENNASTON, his wife
RICHARD HARROWBY, his neighbor
ETTARRE, a woman in his novel and his dreams

The Story:

Felix Kennaston tells his neighbor, Richard Harrowby, about his dreams. In writing his novels, Kennaston creates a world much different from the ordinary world of the Virginia countryside, and his dreams contain similar elements of the romantic and the marvelous. To Harrowby, the whole thing seems indecent, for Harrowby is a conventional, unimaginative gentleman farmer who makes his money in soaps and beauty aids.

Kennaston is writing a novel called *The Audit at Storisende*, and in his dreams he identifies himself with a character named Horvendile, who is looking for that elusive and highly improbable creature, the ideal woman. In Ettarre, his heroine, Kennaston feels he finds her. Much of his plot centers on a broken round medallion bearing mysterious symbols, a medallion he calls the sigil of Scoteia.

One afternoon, Kennaston, walking in his garden, stoops to pick up a little piece of shining metal, apparently a broken half of a small disc, and casually drops it into his pocket. Later, while looking over some books in his library, he thinks of the little piece of metal in his pocket. He brings it out and puts it where the light of the lamp falls upon it. At once, he seems to be talking with Ettarre, who explains that he picked up half the broken sigil of Scoteia and that it brings him back to her imagined world of romance and dream. As he reaches out to touch her, she disappears, and Kennaston finds himself sitting again in his library.

Kennaston's novel is published as *The Men Who Loved Allison*, a title that his publisher assures him will bring better sales. When several readers, shocked by what they call indecency in the novel, write indignant letters to the newspapers, the book becomes a best seller. Mrs. Kennaston, who makes it a point never to read her husband's books, enjoys his success. She treats Kennaston with polite boredom.

Strange things happen to Kennaston. One day at a luncheon, a famous man takes him aside and asks him whether he breeds white pigeons. This question puzzles Kennaston, as does the little mirror the man holds in his hand. Another time, he sees an ugly old woman who tells him that there is no price of admission to her world, but that one pays upon leaving. Several times he talks to Ettarre in his dreams.

One day, Kennaston receives an invitation to call on a prelate who comes to Lichfield to attend the bishop's funeral. The prelate praises Kennaston's book. He speaks of pigeons, too, and mentions how useful he finds his little mirror. Kennaston is frankly puzzled. He returns to his dreamland, where, as Horvendile, he experiences almost every passion and emotion known; always, as he reaches out to touch Ettarre, the dream comes to an end.

Kennaston reads widely in philosophy and the classics, and he begins to question the reason for his own existence. He comes to the conclusion that the present moment is all that is real and that the past and future have no part in the reality of today. As a man of letters, he becomes interested in the artistry of creation and decides that God must be happy over his creation of the character of Christ. Probably because of his interest in God as an artist, Kennaston is confirmed in the country church nearby. This act on his part increases his stature among the people of the neighborhood. They even elect him to the vestry.

One day, Kennaston goes to the station to meet his wife's train. While he is waiting, a woman with whom he was once in love comes up to him and starts to talk. She is about to go back to her home in St. Louis. They recall the past, and as she leaves him to get on her train, he has a moment in which he identifies her with Ettarre. His remark to his wife about her, however, is that she is not keeping her good looks as she grows older. What haunts him, however, is that the woman drew from her purse a medallion resembling the sigil of Scoteia.

Kennaston—as Horvendile—dreams of being in many parts of the world in many eras; and one of the mysteries is that he is always a young man approximately twenty-five years of age. He is at Queen Elizabeth's court; he is at Whitehall with Cromwell; he is at the French court of Louis XIV; he is among the aristocrats about to be beheaded during the French Revolution; always beside him is Ettarre, whose contact will bring his dreams to an end.

One afternoon he finds, quite by accident, the missing piece of the sigil of Scoteia in his wife's bathroom. After securing the other piece, he puts them together on his wife's dressing table and begins speculating about the relation of his wife to Ettarre. He hopes that the discovery of the entire sigil will express to her what he is never able to convey. She pays no attention to it, and their life continues its banal rounds. Eleven months later, Mrs. Kennaston dies in her sleep without ever discussing the sigil or its significance with her husband. After her death, he shows Harrowby the two halves of the sigil, by which he almost made his dreams come true. Far from being a magic emblem, the pieces prove to be merely the broken top of a cold cream jar. It is the final disillusionment for Kennaston, who is at last compelled to give up romantic, youthful dreaming for the realities of middle age.

Critical Evaluation:

The Cream of the Jest: A Comedy of Evasions was a pivotal novel in James Branch Cabell's career, marking the change of direction that allowed him to find and perfect a unique literary voice. His earlier novels had made little or no use of the supernatural in their scrupulous investigation of the nature of love and the problems involved in finding and maintaining sexual relationships. His first-published novel, *The Eagle's Shadow: A Comedy of Purse Strings* (1904)— the book that first introduced the character of Felix Kennaston and Kennaston's best-selling novel *The Men Who*

Loved Allison—and his first-written book, *The Line of Love* (1905), were contemporary fictions of a fairly light nature. The collections *Gallantry* (1907) and *Chivalry* (1909), and the novel *The Soul of Melicent* (1913; revised as *Domnei: A Comedy of Woman Worship*, 1920), were romances in a more traditional sense, reexamining the literary roots of the mythology of romantic love. In both types of work, Cabell maintained the strict discipline of decency that was required by the prudish publishers of the day, but he became acutely aware of the ironic folly of attempting to purge the idea of romance of its erotic essence. *The Cream of the Jest* began a merciless satirization of the evasions inherent in prudery. Cabell continued the satirization in an increasingly gaudy and flamboyant fashion, by means of a series of baroque fantasies in which the lofty but anemic ideals of *Gallantry* and *Chivalry* were infused with a dramatic and glorious—but poignantly futile—virility.

In a narrow sense, Kennaston's situation is a fictionalization of Cabell's own; in a broader sense, it embodies and dramatizes a fundamental aspect of the human condition. Every human being has a public and a private self, the former bound and controlled by social rules and conventions, while the latter retains the precious freedom of dreams and daydreams. Everyone, therefore, is acutely aware of the evasions that the public self is forced by politeness to practice. Such evasions are the everyday acts of censorship by which the "indecency" of private desires and fantasies must be carefully hidden. Everyone admits that the wilder impulses of the private self need to be kept in check if civilized social life is to be preserved, but everyone feels that there is something very precious in the emotion-laden dreams whose total suppression would be a terrible tragedy. Everyone, male or female, has a shadowy alter ego like Kennaston's Horvendile and could, if pressed, envision a secret ideal such as Kennaston's Ettarre.

The final movement of the novel's plot is one of deflation, in which it follows the precedent set by all actual erotic adventures. The precious sigil of Scoteia, to whose reunion Kennaston's beloved but excessively dutiful wife remained oblivious, turns out to be nothing more than the broken lid of a jar of cosmetic cream. What the body of the text reminds readers, however, is that people do not live only in reality; people also live in the inner world of the imagination, where the sigil of Scoteia is indeed a sigil, a powerful magical talisman, a symbol of the true heart of human aspiration and human achievement. Richard Harrowby cannot see this, any more than Mrs. Kennaston could, but readers can. Readers can also see the irony in Harrowby's failure; although he is a farmer whose heritage is based in the fecundity of the land

and a businessman whose wealth comes from products whose main purpose is to enhance sexual attractiveness, he maintains the conventional pretense that any public reference to sexual matters, however carefully veiled, is indecent.

The Cream of the Jest proved, ironically, to be prophetic. Kennaston's carefully retitled account of *The Audit at Storisende* is charged with indecency, and the resultant publicity makes it a best-seller. Cabell's next novel—his first full-blown fantasy, heavily spiced with teasing innuendo—was *Jurgen: A Comedy of Justice* (1919), which fell afoul of the courts as well as public opinion, and was made famous by the resultant publicity. In the same way that the Volstead Act, passed in the year of *Jurgen*'s publication, gave birth to speakeasies, so the application of the spirit of Prohibition to U.S. literature gave birth to an opposition. The boldest spokespeople of this opposition were writers who used fantasy, fabulation, and allegory to make fierce fun of their enemies; John Erskine and Thorne Smith played leading roles, but Cabell was the leader, and *The Cream of the Jest* provided the materials for all his later broadsides.

Just as Kennaston followed up *The Men Who Loved Allison* with *The Tinctured Veil* ("that amazing performance which he subsequently gave to a bewildered world"), so Cabell went on to produce further adventures of an uncompromisingly amazing—and, to the reading public, somewhat bewildering—nature. Horvendile and Ettarre were to return time and time again, in slightly different guises, throughout the multistranded complex of works that ultimately came to be known as *The Biography of the Life of Manuel* (1927-1930).

In the eighteen-volume edition of this sprawling masterpiece, *The Cream of the Jest* is the concluding volume, the key to all that has gone before. It is described in the author's afterword as the most potent of all his books. In painstakingly mapped genealogies, Kennaston—Cabell's alter ego within the eighteen-volume series—becomes the ultimate descendant and modern inheritor of the adventurous tradition that descends from Manuel, the legendary hero of *Figures of Earth: A Comedy of Appearances* (1921), whose quest is continued by his followers in *The Silver Stallion: A Comedy of Redemption* (1926). The erotic subtext of *The Cream of the Jest* is elaborated and somewhat revised in the last-written novel of the series, *Something About Eve: A Comedy of Fig-Leaves* (1927), but the jest remained the same throughout, and the sequence deserves to be considered the cream of twentieth century fantasy writing in the United States.

"Critical Evaluation" by Brian Stableford

Further Reading

Davis, Joe Lee. *James Branch Cabell*. New York: Twayne, 1962. Considers all of Cabell's works as confessional pieces and intensely personal romantic flights of fancy. Allots a central role to *The Cream of the Jest*.

Ginés, Montserrat. "James Branch Cabell: Quixotic Love, the Exercise of Self-Deception." In *The Southern Inheritors of Don Quixote*. Baton Rouge: Louisiana State University Press, 2000. Ginés analyzes the work of five Southern writers—Cabell, Mark Twain, William Faulkner, Eudora Welty, and Walker Percy—whose fiction expressed the ideals and spirit of Don Quixote. He describes how the writers were sympathetic to idealistic characters who tilted at windmills, and he points out the similarities between the Spain of Miguel de Cervantes and the social and economic conditions of the American South.

Inge, Thomas M., and Edgar E. MacDonald, eds. *James Branch Cabell: Centennial Essays*. Baton Rouge: Louisiana State University Press, 1983. A compilation of essays that were presented at Virginia Commonwealth University in 1979, in commemoration of the centennial of Cabell's birth. Provides valuable biographical information and criticism.

McDonald, Edgar. "James Branch Cabell." In *Supernatural Fiction Writers: Fantasy and Horror*, edited by Everett F. Bleiler. New York: Charles Scribner's Sons, 1985. A compact commentary on the author's excursions into fantasy.

_____. *James Branch Cabell and Richmond-in-Virginia*. Jackson: University Press of Mississippi, 1993. MacDonald, a senior Cabell scholar at the James Branch Cabell Library at Virginia Commonwealth University, provides a detailed, authoritative biography that focuses on how Cabell was influenced by living in Richmond, Virginia, in the late nineteenth and early twentieth centuries. Includes an excellent bibliography.

Tarrant, Desmond. *James Branch Cabell: The Dream and the Reality*. Norman: University of Oklahoma Press, 1967. A Jungian analysis that considers Horvendile and Ettarre as archetypal images.

Wells, Arvin. *Jesting Moses: A Study in Cabellian Comedy*. Gainesville: University Press of Florida, 1962. Relates Cabell's work to the tradition of French satirical fabulation that descends from François Rabelais to Anatole France.

Crime and Punishment

Author: Fyodor Dostoevski (1821-1881)
First published: Prestupleniye i nakazaniye, 1866 (English translation, 1886)
Type of work: Novel
Type of plot: Psychological realism
Time of plot: Mid-nineteenth century
Locale: Russia

Principal characters:
RASKOLNIKOV, a Russian student
DOUNIA, his sister
SONIA, a prostitute
PORFIRY, the inspector of police
RAZUMIHIN, Raskolnikov's friend

The Story:

Rodion Raskolnikov, an impoverished student in St. Petersburg, dreams of committing the perfect crime. He murders an old widowed pawnbroker and her stepsister with an ax and steals some jewelry from their flat. Back in his room, Raskolnikov receives a summons from the police. Weak from hunger and illness, he prepares to make a full confession. The police, however, call merely to ask him to pay a debt his landlady reported to them. When he discovers what they want, he collapses from relief. Upon being revived, he is questioned; his answers provoke suspicion.

Raskolnikov hides the jewelry under a rock in a courtyard. He returns to his room, where he remains for four days in a high fever. When he recovers, he learns that the authorities visited him while he was delirious and that he said things during his fever that tended to cast further suspicion on him.

Luzhin, betrothed to Raskolnikov's sister Dounia, comes to St. Petersburg from the provinces to prepare for the wedding. Raskolnikov resents Luzhin because he knows his sister is marrying to provide money for Raskolnikov. Luzhin visits the convalescent and leaves in a rage when the young man makes no attempt to hide his dislike for him.

A sudden calm comes upon the young murderer; he goes out and reads the accounts of the murders in the papers. While he is reading, a detective joins him. The student, in a high pitch of excitement caused by his crime and by his sickness, talks too much, revealing to the detective that he might well be the murderer. No evidence, however, can be found that puts direct suspicion on him.

Later, witnessing a suicide attempt in the slums of St. Petersburg, Raskolnikov decides to turn himself over to the police; but he is deterred when his friend, a former clerk named Marmeladov, is struck by a carriage and killed. Raskolnikov gives the widow a small amount of money he received from his mother. Later, he attends a party given by some of his friends and discovers that they, too, suspect him of complicity in the murder of the two women.

Back in his room, Raskolnikov finds his mother and his sister, who are awaiting his return. Unnerved at their appearance and not wanting them to be near him, he places them in the care of his friend, Razumihin, who, upon meeting Dounia, is immediately attracted to her.

In an interview with Porfiry, the chief of the murder investigation, Raskolnikov is mentally tortured by questions and ironic statements until he is ready to believe that he is all but apprehended for the double crime. Partly in his own defense, he expounds his theory that any means justifies the ends of a man of genius and that sometimes he believes himself a man of genius. Raskolnikov proves to his mother and Dounia that Luzhin is a pompous fool, and the angry suitor is dismissed. Razumihin by that time replaces Luzhin in the girl's affections.

Meanwhile, Svidrigailov, who caused Dounia great suffering while she was employed as his governess, arrives in St. Petersburg. His wife died, and he followed Dounia, as he explains, to atone for his sins against her by settling upon her a large amount of money.

Razumihin receives money from a rich uncle and goes into the publishing business with Dounia. They ask Raskolnikov to join them in the venture, but the student, whose mind and heart are full of turmoil, declines; he says good-bye to his friend and to his mother and sister and asks them not to try to see him again.

He goes to Sonia, the prostitute daughter of the dead Marmeladov. They read Sonia's Bible together. Raskolnikov is deeply impressed by the wretched girl's faith. He feels a great sympathy for Sonia and promises to tell her who committed the murders of the old pawnbroker and stepsister. Svidrigailov, who rents the room next to Sonia's, overhears the conversation; he anticipates Raskolnikov's disclosure

with interest. Tortured in his own mind, Raskolnikov goes to the police station, where Porfiry plays another game of cat-and-mouse with him. Raskolnikov's conscience and his paranoia result in immense suffering and torment of mind for him.

At a banquet given by Marmeladov's widow for the friends of her late husband, Luzhin accuses Sonia of stealing money from his room. He observes Raskolnikov's interest in Sonia, and he wishes to hurt the student for having spoken against him to Dounia. The girl is saved by the report of a neighbor who saw Luzhin slipping money into Sonia's pocket. Later, in Sonia's room, Raskolnikov confesses his crime and admits that in killing the two women he actually destroyed himself.

Svidrigailov overhears the confession and discloses his knowledge to Raskolnikov. Believing that Porfiry suspects him of the murder and realizing that Svidrigailov knows the truth, Raskolnikov finds life unbearable. Then Porfiry tells Raskolnikov outright that he is the murderer, at the same time promising Raskolnikov that a plea of temporary insanity will be placed in his behalf and his sentence will be mitigated if he confesses. Raskolnikov delays his confession.

Svidrigailov informs Dounia of the truth concerning her brother, and he now offers to save the student if Dounia will consent to be his wife. He makes this offer to her in his room, which he locks after tricking her into the meeting. He releases her when she attempts unsuccessfully to shoot him with a pistol she brought with her. Convinced at last that Dounia intends to reject him, Svidrigailov gives her a large sum of money and ends his life with the pistol.

Raskolnikov, after being reassured by his mother and his sister of their love for him, and by Sonia of her undying devotion, turns himself over to the police. He is tried and sentenced to serve eight years in Siberia. Dounia and Razumihin, now successful publishers, are married. Sonia follows Raskolnikov to Siberia, where she stays in a village near the prison camp. In her goodness to Raskolnikov and to the other prisoners, she comes to be known as Little Mother Sonia. With her inspiring example, Raskolnikov begins his regeneration.

Critical Evaluation:

Crime and Punishment was Fyodor Mikhailovich Dostoevski's first popularly successful novel after his nine-year imprisonment and exile for alleged political crimes (the charges were of doubtful validity) against the czar. After his release from penal servitude, Dostoevski published novels, short stories, novellas, and journalistic pieces, but none of these brought him the critical and popular acclaim which in

1866 greeted *Crime and Punishment*—possibly his most popular novel. This book is no simple precursor of the detective novel, no simplistic mystery story to challenge the minds of Russian counterparts to Sherlock Holmes's fans. It is a complex story of a man's turbulent inner life and his relationship to others and to society at large. The book must be considered within the context of Dostoevski's convictions at the time he wrote the novel, because Dostoevski's experience with czarist power made a lasting impression on his thinking. Indeed, Dostoevski himself made such an evaluation possible by keeping detailed notebooks on the development of his novels and on his problems with fleshing out plots and characters.

Chastened by his imprisonment and exile, Dostoevski shifted his position from the youthful liberalism (certainly not radicalism) that seemed to have precipitated his incarceration to a mature conservatism that embraced many, perhaps most, of the traditional views of his time. Thus, Dostoevski came to believe that legal punishment was not a deterrent to crime because he was convinced that criminals demanded to be punished; that is, they had a spiritual need to be punished. Today, that compulsion might be called masochistic; but Dostoevski, in his time, related the tendency to mystical concepts of the Eastern Orthodox Church. With a skeptical hostility toward Western religion and culture, born of several years of living abroad, Dostoevski became convinced that the Western soul was bankrupt and that salvation—one of his major preoccupations—was possible only under the influence of the church and an ineffable love for Mother Russia, a devotion to homeland and to the native soil that would brook neither logic nor common sense: a dedication beyond reason or analysis. Thus, expiation for sins was attained through atonement, a rite of purification.

The required expiation, however, is complicated in *Crime and Punishment* by the split personality—a typically Dostoevskian ploy—of the protagonist. The schizophrenia of Raskolnikov is best illustrated by his ambivalent motives for murdering the pawnbroker. At first, Raskolnikov views his heinous crime as an altruistic act that puts the pawnbroker and her sister out of their misery while providing him the necessary financial support to further his education and mitigate his family's poverty, thus relieving unbearable pressures on him. He does intend to atone for his misdeed by subsequently living an upright life dedicated to humanitarian enterprises. Raskolnikov, however, shortly becomes convinced of his own superiority. Indeed, he divides the human race into "losers" and "winners": the former, meek and submissive; the latter, Nietzschean supermen who can violate any law or principle to attain their legitimately innovative and presumably beneficial ends. Raskolnikov allies himself with the "superman" faction. He intends to prove his superiority by committing murder and justifying it on the basis of his own superiority. This psychological configuration is common enough, but, unlike most paranoid schizophrenics, Raskolnikov carries his design through—a signal tribute to the depth of his convictions.

The results are predictably confusing. The reader is as puzzled about Raskolnikov's motives as he is. Is it justifiable to commit an atrocity in the name of improvement of the human condition? This essential question remains unanswered in *Crime and Punishment*; Raskolnikov, egocentrically impelled by pride, cannot decide whether or not he is superior, one of those supermen entitled to violate any law or any principle to serve the cause of ultimate justice, however justice might be construed. Likewise, in his notebooks, Dostoevski implied that he, too, was ambivalent about Raskolnikov's motives. He added, however, that he was not a psychologist but a novelist. He was thus more concerned with consequences than with causality. This carefully planned novel therefore expands upon a philosophical problem embodied in the protagonist.

The philosophical problem in *Crime and Punishment* constitutes the central theme of the novel: the lesson Raskolnikov has to learn, the precept he has to master in order to redeem himself. The protagonist finally has to concede that free will is limited. He has to discover and admit that he cannot control and direct his life solely with his reason and intellect, as he tried to do, for such a plan leads only to emptiness and to sinful intellectual pride. Abstract reason takes the place of a fully lived life and precludes the happiness of a fully lived life; happiness must be earned, and it can be earned only through suffering. Thus, Raskolnikov has to learn that happiness is achieved through suffering—another typically Dostoevskian mystical concept. The climactic moment in the novel, therefore, comes when Raskolnikov confesses his guilt at the police station, for Raskolnikov's confession is tantamount to a request for punishment for the crime and acceptance of his need to suffer. In this way, Raskolnikov demonstrates the basic message of *Crime and Punishment*: that reason does not bring happiness; happiness is earned through suffering.

The epilogue—summarizing the fates of other characters; Raskolnikov's trial, his sentencing, and his prison term; and Sonia's devotion to Raskolnikov during his imprisonment—confirms the novel's central theme. Artistically, however, the epilogue is somewhat less than satisfactory. First, Dostoevski's notes indicate that he had considered and rejected an alternate ending in which Raskolnikov commits suicide. Such a conclusion would have been psychologically sound. The very logicality of Raskolnikov's suicide, however, would have suggested a triumph of reason over the soul. That idea was not consonant with Dostoevski's convictions; thus, he dropped the plan. Second, the ending that Dostoevski finally wrote in the epilogue implies that the meek and submissive side of Raskolnikov's personality emerged completely victorious over the superman. Such an ending contradicts Raskolnikov's persistent duality throughout the novel. Raskolnikov's dramatic conversion thus strains credulity, for it seems too pat a resolution of the plot. For the sophisticated reader, however, it does not greatly detract from the powerful psychological impact of the novel proper or diminish the quality of a genuinely serious attempt to confront simultaneously a crucial social problem and a deeply profound individual, human one.

"Critical Evaluation" by Joanne G. Kashdan

Further Reading

Bloom, Harold, ed. *Fyodor Dostoevsky's "Crime and Punishment."* Philadelphia: Chelsea House, 2004. Collection of essays analyzing the book, including one by the eminent Russian literary critic Mikhail Bakhtin. Some of the other essays discuss the religious themes and the elements of Greek tragedy in the novel.

_____. *Raskolnikov and Svidrigailov.* Philadelphia: Chelsea House, 2004. Collection of essays providing numerous interpretations of two of the novel's central characters.

Jackson, Robert Louis, ed. *Twentieth-Century Interpretations of "Crime and Punishment."* Englewood Cliffs, N.J.: Prentice-Hall, 1974. Includes an essay by Dostoevski on *Crime and Punishment.* The other essays offer many theories on Raskolnikov's personality and consider the metaphysical point of view in the novel.

Johnson, Leslie A. *The Experience of Time in "Crime and Punishment."* Columbus, Ohio: Slavica, 1984. Explains the use of time in the novel as a means for building anxiety and suffering in the characters. Shows how time is manipulated in *Crime and Punishment* and how this treatment of time differs from other works by Dostoevski.

Leatherbarrow, William J. *Fedor Dostoevsky.* Boston: Twayne, 1981. Includes a biographical sketch of Dostoevski, as well as commentary on *Crime and Punishment* and the writer's other work.

_____, ed. *The Cambridge Companion to Dostoevskii.* New York: Cambridge University Press, 2006. Collection of essays that examine the author's life and works, dis-cussing his relationship to Russian folk heritage, money, the intelligentsia, psychology, religion, the family, and science, among other topics. Includes a chronology and bibliography.

McReynolds, Susan. *Redemption and the Merchant God: Dostoevsky's Economy of Salvation and Antisemitism.* Evanston, Ill.: Northwestern University Press, 2008. McReynolds argues that readers cannot fully understand Dostoevski's writings without understanding his obsession with the Jews. She analyzes not only the elements of anti-Semitism in his works but also examines his views of the Crucifixion, Resurrection, morality, and other aspects of Christian doctrine. Chapter 8 focuses on the theme of morality in *Crime and Punishment.*

Miller, Robin Feuer. *Critical Essays on Dostoevsky.* Boston: G. K. Hall, 1986. Contains an essay by Leo Tolstoy and criticism and commentary on Dostoevski. Indicates how perceptions of Dostoevski have changed over time.

_____. *Dostoevsky's Unfinished Journey.* New Haven, Conn.: Yale University Press, 2007. Miller examines Dostoevski's works from numerous perspectives, analyzing the themes of conversion and healing in his fiction, questioning his literary influence, and exploring what happens to *Crime and Punishment* when it is taught in the classroom.

Scanlan, James P. *Dostoevsky the Thinker: A Philosophical Study.* Ithaca, N.Y.: Cornell University Press, 2002. Scanlan analyzes Dostoevski's novels, essays, letters, and notebooks in order to provide a comprehensive account of his philosophy, examining the weakness as well as the strength of Dostoevski's ideas. He concludes that Dostoevski's thought was shaped by anthropocentrism—a struggle to define the very essence of humanity.

Straus, Nina Pelikan. *Dostoevsky and the Woman Question: Rereadings at the End of a Century.* New York: St. Martin's Press, 1994. Straus argues that Dostoevski's compulsion to depict men's cruelties to women is an important part of his vision and his metaphysics. She maintains that Dostoevski attacks masculine notions of autonomy and that his works evolve toward "the death of the patriarchy." Chapter 1 is devoted to a discussion of *Crime and Punishment.*

Williams, Rowan. *Dostoevsky: Language, Faith, and Fiction.* Waco, Tex.: Baylor University Press, 2008. Examines the speech, fiction, metaphor, and iconography in four novels, including *Crime and Punishment.* Williams maintains that the style and goals of Dostoevski's fiction are inseparable from his religious commitments.

Crimes of the Heart

Author: Beth Henley (1952-   )
First produced: 1979; first published, 1982
Type of work: Drama
Type of plot: Comedy
Time of plot: Fall, 1974
Locale: Hazlehurst, Mississippi

Principal characters:
LENNY MAGRATH, thirty, the oldest of three sisters
MEG MAGRATH, twenty-seven, the middle sister
BABE BOTRELLE, twenty-four, the youngest sister
CHICK BOYLE, the sisters' first cousin
DOC PORTER, thirty, Meg's former boyfriend
BARNETTE LLOYD, twenty-six, Babe's lawyer

The Story:

It is Lenny's thirtieth birthday. While trying unsuccessfully to light a small candle on a cookie, she is interrupted by Cousin Chick, who is scandalized by the news that Babe has been charged with shooting her husband Zachery. Doc Porter stops in with some pecans for Lenny and the sad news that her horse Billy Boy was killed by lightning the night before. Meg arrives home, and the two sisters commiserate over all the depressing news—their age, Old Granddaddy being in the hospital, Billy Boy's death, the collapse of Meg's singing career, and Babe's situation.

Chick brings Babe home from jail, annoyed that Babe will not reveal why she shot Zachery. When Chick and Lenny leave, Meg and Babe discuss Lenny's lonely life since breaking up with Charlie from Memphis rather than informing him of her shrunken ovary. They decide to order a huge birthday cake. The Babe's lawyer Barnette arrives, but Babe is reluctant to meet with him and disappears. Barnette reveals to Meg that he has a personal vendetta against Zachery and plans to expose him as a criminal and wife abuser.

After Barnette leaves, Babe confesses to Meg that she has been having an affair with fifteen-year-old Willie Jay, the African American son of her laundry woman. Zachery surprised them and threw Willie Jay out. Babe was so upset that she got Zachery's gun with the plan to kill herself, but the thought of her mother's suicide led her to realize that she wanted to kill Zachery and not herself. Later that evening Babe tells Barnette how she shot Zachery, and he plans a defense, but Zachery wants to show Barnette incriminating evidence he has that will convict Babe.

After visiting Old Granddaddy in the hospital with Meg, Lenny is furious at the lies Meg has told him about her successful career as a singer and film star. She is jealous of Meg because Meg has always got what she wanted, but Babe defends Meg's behavior because Meg had to deal with the shock of finding their mother and the cat dead. They recall the events of Hurricane Camille, when Meg refused to evacuate and told Doc she would marry him if he stayed with her. He stayed; then, the roof fell in and crushed his leg.

When she returns from the hospital, Meg defends her lies to Old Granddaddy, claiming she was just trying to cheer him up. Babe takes out her photo album, and the sisters look at the pictorial record of their past lives. With sisterly affection, they laugh and hug one another and then decide to play cards. The phone rings; Doc is coming over. Lenny reminds Meg that Doc is married. Annoyed, Meg retorts that, while she has had a lot of men, Lenny has not had any—information that Babe has supplied. Lenny turns on Babe, who turns on Meg, who turns on them both. Lenny starts to cry, claiming that no man will ever have her because she can't have children. She exits, with Babe following after.

Doc and Meg catch up on the last five years. She confesses that she does not sing any more and that she had a breakdown and ended up in a psychiatric ward. He invites her for a moonlit ride in his truck. They leave, taking a bottle of bourbon with them.

Zachery's evidence, which Barnette shows Babe, consists of photographs of Babe and Willie Jay together. Babe panics. Lenny relays the news that Old Granddaddy has had another stroke and is comatose.

The following morning, Chick marches in with a list of people to be called when Old Granddaddy passes. Lenny reluctantly agrees to phone half of them. Chick leaves, as Meg exuberantly bursts in, having spent the night with Doc, and ready to confess to Old Granddaddy the truth of her career. Babe and Lenny laugh uncontrollably because Meg is too late, now that Old Granddaddy is in a coma. Out of the hilarity, Meg suggests that Lenny should call Charlie. She agrees, and goes upstairs to do so.

Babe shows Meg the photographs, just as Barnette arrives. Barnette has found compelling evidence of Zachery's corruption, and he feels that Zachery can be convinced to settle the charge against Babe. Barnette leaves with Meg, who is going to pick up Lenny's birthday cake.

Lenny cannot make the call to Charlie. Chick arrives, horrified because she has seen Meg getting out of Doc's truck. Her nasty remarks about Meg infuriate Lenny, who chases

Chick out with a broom. Returning, she feels she has the confidence now to call Charlie. Zachery then calls Babe and informs her that he is going to have her committed.

Zachery's call crystallizes Babe's determination to kill herself, and she looks for some strong cord. Lenny talks to Charlie, who does not care that she cannot have children. Lenny goes off to find Meg, as Babe's first suicide effort fails when the rope breaks. She turns the gas on in the oven, but, while trying to light it, she bumps her head on the oven door. Meg returns with the cake. Babe has had a revelation: Their mother hanged herself with the cat because she did not want to die alone. Meg interprets Zachery's threat as a scare tactic and assures Babe that she is not insane. They admire the cake, and Babe lights the candles. Lenny is thrilled, and her birthday wish is that the three of them have one moment smiling and laughing together. They do.

Critical Evaluation:

Successful as both a playwright and a screenwriter, Beth Henley was born and raised in Jackson, Mississippi, and she drew upon her Southern background for locales and characters in her early plays. *Crimes of the Heart* was first produced at the Actors Theatre of Louisville in Kentucky, where it won an award in the Great American Play Contest. It then traveled to New York, where it won the New York Drama Critics' Circle Award for the Best New American Play and the Pulitzer Prize in drama, as well as receiving a Tony nomination. Henley's 1986 screenplay adaptation of the play was nominated for an Academy Award.

A three-act play confined to one setting and one twenty-four-hour period, *Crimes of the Heart* is a black comedy, with uproarious moments that teeter on the brink of tragedy. Henley stated in an interview that her play is loosely based on Anton Chekhov's *Tri sestry* (pr., pb. 1901; revised pb. 1904; *The Three Sisters*, 1920), a play that she admires. There are analogies to be made between each play's portrayal of three sisters and their discontent, but the works' plots are vastly different. In Henley's play, there are no long scenes and no philosophical discussions of where humanity is headed. Instead, the acts are structured in brief dialogues between two or three characters, with flashes of sibling rivalry as well as of affection. The dialgues recount events of the past and reveal actions of the present. The play's ending is ambiguous: Loose ends are not neatly tied up, and questions remain. There is a final moment of togetherness among the three sisters eating birthday cake, but they seem to recognize that it is only a moment.

The characters are eccentric but, in Henley's skillful hand, believable and charming. The "crimes" of the Magrath sisters are involved partly with their sexual relationships and partly with their history. Lenny is obsessed with her thirtieth birthday, feeling that she is getting old and will never be loved by a man. She is tortured by the knowledge of her shrunken ovary and has been shy and inhibited with men all her life. Her self-hatred has led her to become a nursemaid to her grandparents.

Meg's traumatic discovery of her mother's suicide resulted in her seductive baiting of Doc Porter to stay with her during a hurricane. It also led to her subsequent promiscuity, fictional career, and psychiatric breakdown. Babe, whose actions initiate the play and whose incarceration occasions the reunion of the three sisters, seems at best immature and at worst unbalanced. Still, she is engaging. She has had a sexual relationship with a fifteen-year-old African American boy, violating a serious taboo in the South of the period. After shooting her husband, she casually makes a pitcher of lemonade and offers it to him while he lies bleeding profusely on the floor. She is at her most quixotic in her botched suicide attempts, which could be tragic but instead are hilarious. Despite their individual foibles, the Magraths can find humor and love as sisters.

The three women are portrayed as lonely and unfulfilled; their efforts to find satisfaction are displayed in the consumption of food and drink, a major motif of the play. The first image is of Lenny's attempt to celebrate her own birthday by lighting a candle in a pathetic cookie. Meg devours candy, cigarettes, Coca-Cola, and bourbon, and Babe's thirst is hardly quenched with pitchers of lemonade. The final image of the oversized birthday cake signifies the progress each woman has made toward self-fulfillment and the sisters' strengthened connection with one another.

Old Granddaddy does not appear in the play, but, as a representative of the Southern patriarchy, he has exerted a lifelong power over his granddaughters. He took in the three orphaned girls after their mother's suicide and their father's abandonment, supporting them. However, as an unthinking believer in the stereotype of the submissive, chaste, feminine southern lady, he has encouraged them all to develop in harmful directions. It was Old Grandaddy who told the young Lenny that no man would ever love her because of her shriveled ovary. It was he who flattered and coaxed Meg to pursue a theatrical career that failed, and it was he who apparently encouraged Babe to marry the richest and most powerful man in Hazlehurst—who turned out to be an abuser. He has crippled their progress to adulthood and autonomy, although they are unaware of his corrosive power. Old Granddaddy's passing will open a doorway to freedom for all three sisters. Lenny may now find a life with Charlie, Meg may pursue a more realistic career, and Babe may continue a relationship with Barnette.

At first glance, *Crimes of the Heart* may appear to be simply an offbeat comedy that incorporates a strange mixture of the grotesque and the humorous. On closer examination, however, the power of the southern patriarchy, the depth of the characters, and Henley's insight into women's struggle for identity deserve admiration.

Joyce E. Henry

Further Reading

Fesmire, Julia A., ed. *Beth Henley: A Casebook*. New York: Routledge, 2002. A helpful collection of essays. Examines Henley's works in terms of their themes, structures, and contexts in contemporary literature.

Gupton, Janet R. "'Un-ruling' the Women: Comedy and the Plays of Beth Henley and Rebecca Gilman." In *Southern Women Playwrights*. Tuscaloosa: University of Alabama Press, 2002. A thoughtful comparison of the plays of Henley and Gilman. Argues that they subvert stereotypes of the southern lady.

Henley, Beth. "Expressing 'The Misery and Confusion Truthfully': An Interview with Beth Henley." Interview by Jackson Breyer. *American Drama* 14, no. 1 (2005): 87. A personal introduction to the playwright. Henley speaks of her early life, her education, and her love of the theater and of writing plays.

Laughlin, Karen. "Criminality, Desire, and Community: A Feminist Approach to Beth Henley's *Crimes of the Heart*." In *Contemporary Literary Criticism*. Vol. 235. Detroit, Mich.: Gale, 1986. Analyzes the self-destructive crimes of the Magrath sisters within the context of their dominant patriarchal society.

Paige, Linda Rohrer. "'Off the Porch and Onto the Scene': Southern Women Playwrights Beth Henley, Marsha Norman, Rebecca Gilman, and Jane Martin." In *A Companion to Twentieth Century Drama*. Malden, Mass.: Blackwell, 2005. An interesting comparison of themes and topics shared by the four playwrights. Examines the use of animals in two of Henley's plays.

Plunka, Gene A. "Existential Despair and the Modern Neurosis: Beth Henley's *Crimes of the Heart*." In *Beth Henley: A Casebook*, edited by Julia A. Fesmire. New York: Routledge, 2002. A thorough, insightful Freudian investigation. Sees Meg as narcissistic, Lenny as depressive, and Babe as suffering from existential despair.

Schlueter, June. "Domestic Realism: Is It Still Possible on the American Stage?" *South Atlantic Review* 64, no. 1 (1999): 11-25. Pursues the title question in the plays of Beth Henley, Sam Shepard, Edward Albee, and Arthur Miller. Concludes that Henley has found flexibility in the form, even while subverting it.

The Crisis

Author: Winston Churchill (1871-1947)
First published: 1901
Type of work: Novel
Type of plot: Historical
Time of plot: 1860's
Locale: Missouri and Virginia

Principal characters:
STEPHEN BRICE, a young lawyer from Boston
VIRGINIA CARVEL, his sweetheart
CLARENCE COLFAX, Stephen's rival for Virginia
JUDGE WHIPPLE, Stephen's employer and friend
COLONEL CARVEL, Virginia's father
ABRAHAM LINCOLN, a Republican running for the U.S. Senate

The Story:

Stephen Brice accepts the offer of Judge Whipple, his father's friend, who promises Stephen an opportunity to enter his law firm. In 1858, he moves from Boston to St. Louis with his widowed mother. A personable young man, Stephen finds favor among the people of St. Louis, including Colonel Carvel, and the colonel's daughter, Virginia. Stephen promptly falls in love with Virginia Carvel. He is not encouraged by the young woman at first because he is a New Englander.

One day, Judge Whipple sends Stephen to Springfield, Illinois, with a message for the man who is running for senator against Stephen A. Douglas. When Stephen finally finds his man, Abraham Lincoln, he is in time to hear the famous Freeport debate between Lincoln and Douglas. Lincoln makes a deep impression on Stephen, who goes back to St. Louis a confirmed Republican, as Judge Whipple hoped. Feeling that Stephen will someday be a great politician, the judge had sent him to Lincoln to catch some of Lincoln's idealism and practical politics.

Convinced by Lincoln that no country can exist half slave and half free, Stephen becomes active in Missouri politics on behalf of the Republicans, a dangerous course to take in St. Louis because of the many Southerners living in the city. His antislavery views soon alienate Stephen from the woman he wants to marry, who then promises to marry Stephen's rival, her cousin and fellow Southerner, Clarence Colfax.

Lincoln loses the election for the U.S. Senate, but in doing so he wins the presidency of the United States in 1860. During both campaigns, Stephen works for the Republican Party. An able orator, he becomes known as a rising young lawyer of exceptional abilities.

The guns at Fort Sumter reverberate loudly in St. Louis in 1861. The city is divided into two factions, proslavery Southerners and antislavery Northerners. Friends of long standing no longer speak to one another, and members of the same family find themselves at odds over the question of which side Missouri should favor, the Union or the Confederacy. It is a trying time for Stephen. With a widowed mother and his political activities to look after, he is unable to join the army. Judge Whipple convinces him that, for the time being, he can do more for his country as a civilian. It is hard for the young man to believe the judge when all of Stephen's friends and acquaintances are going about the city in uniform.

When war is declared, Missouri has a little campaign of its own, as the state militia, under the direction of the governor, tries to seize the state. This attempt is defeated by the prompt action of federal forces in capturing the militia training camp without firing a shot. A spectator at that minor engagement, Stephen makes the acquaintance of a former army officer named William T. Sherman and of another shambling man who claims he should be given a regiment. The young officers laugh at him; his name is Ulysses S. Grant.

Among those captured when federal troops overcome the Missouri militia is Clarence, Stephen's rival. Clarence refuses to give his oath and to go on parole, and he soon escapes from prison and disappears into the South. Virginia thinks him more of a hero than ever.

Communications with the South and the Southwest have been cut by the Union armies, and as a result Colonel Carvel goes bankrupt. He and his daughter aid Southern sympathizers attempting to join the Confederate Army. At last, the col-

onel feels that it is his duty to leave St. Louis and take an active part in the hostilities.

The war continues, putting the lie to those optimists who prophesied that hostilities would end in a few months. By the time of the battle at Vicksburg, Stephen becomes a lieutenant in the Union Army. He distinguishes himself in that battle and comes once more to the attention of Sherman. When the city falls, Stephen finds Clarence, now a lieutenant-colonel in the Confederate Army. The Southerner received a severe wound. To save Clarence's life, Stephen arranges for him to be sent to St. Louis on a hospital ship. Stephen knows that he is probably sending his rival back to marry Virginia. Clarence realizes what Stephen did and tells Virginia as much while he is convalescing in St. Louis. The girl vows that she will never marry a Yankee, even if Clarence dies.

Judge Whipple falls ill, and he is nursed by Virginia and by Stephen's mother. While the judge is sinking fast, Colonel Carvel appears. At the risk of his life, he comes through the lines in civilian clothes to see his daughter and his old friend. There is a strange meeting at Judge Whipple's deathbed. Clarence, Colonel Carvel, and Stephen are all there. They all risked their lives, for the Confederates could be arrested as spies, and Stephen, because he is with them, could be convicted of treason. That night, Virginia realizes that she is in love with Stephen.

After the judge's death, Stephen returns to the army. Ordered to General Sherman's staff, he accompanies the general on the march through Georgia. At the battle of Bentonville, Stephen again meets Clarence, who was captured by Union soldiers while in civilian clothes and brought to Sherman's headquarters as a spy. Once again, Stephen intercedes with Sherman and saves the Southerner's life. Soon afterward, Stephen, promoted to the rank of major, is sent by Sherman with some dispatches to General Grant at City Point, Virginia. Stephen recognizes Grant as the man he saw at the engagement of the militia camp back in St. Louis.

During the conference with the general, an officer appears to summon Stephen to meet another old acquaintance, Lincoln. The president, like Grant, wishes to hear Stephen's firsthand account of the march through Georgia to the sea. When Stephen asks for a pardon for Clarence, Lincoln says he will consider the matter. Stephen goes with Lincoln to Richmond for an inspection of that city after it falls to Grant's armies.

Virginia, not knowing of Stephen's intercession on behalf of Clarence, travels to Washington to ask Lincoln for a pardon. She gains an audience with the president, during which she meets Stephen once again. Lincoln grants them the pardon, saying that with the war soon to end, the time to show clemency is come. He leaves Virginia and Stephen alone when he hurries to keep another appointment. The young people realize during their talk with Lincoln that there is much to be forgiven and forgotten by both sides in the struggle that is drawing to a close. The emotion of the moment overcomes their reticence at last, and they declare their love for each other. They are married the following day.

After the wedding, they visit Virginia's ancestral home in Annapolis. A few days later, word comes to them that Lincoln has died from an assassin's bullet.

Critical Evaluation:

America's Winston Churchill—not to be confused with Great Britain's Winston Churchill—was one of the most popular novelists in the early twentieth century. Descended from one of the earliest families of New England, Churchill was born in St. Louis, Missouri, in 1871 and raised there. He received an appointment to the U.S. Naval Academy; although he did well at Annapolis, and in spite of his lack of personal wealth, he chose a literary career. His first novel, *The Celebrity*, was published in 1898, but it was his second, *Richard Carvel* (1899), a historical novel set during the American Revolution, that made Churchill a household name and brought him both popular and critical praise.

The Crisis is something of a sequel to *Richard Carvel*, with Richard's descendants, Virginia Carvel and her father, among the major characters. Churchill initially envisioned *The Crisis* (originally titled *The Third Generation*) as a saga covering the period from the Civil War to the time of its writing, but then restricted the time to the Civil War era alone. The story is set largely in St. Louis, a simple choice since it was Churchill's home until he moved to New Hampshire in 1900. It also gave the author certain advantages in structuring the novel. Missouri was both a slave state and a border state, and Churchill's St. Louis was populated not only by Southerners but also by emigrants from New England who were unsympathetic to the Southern way of life, to its aristocratic values, and to slavery. Churchill explicitly postulates in *The Crisis* that the Civil War was, in many ways, a direct continuation of the struggle between the aristocratic Cavaliers who supported King Charles II during the English Civil War of the 1640's and their opponents, the Parliamentary Puritans. The Puritans migrated to New England, the Cavaliers to Southern states, and in the mid-nineteenth century their descendants met, uneasily, in St. Louis.

Churchill's historical interpretation is not accurate. The Southern aristocracy—and most Southerners were not aristocrats—was a U.S. development with no direct connection to England's Cavaliers, but his reading of the past gives *The Crisis* a dramatic structural conflict of opposites. A more his-

torically accurate choice is Churchill's including as a third community in St. Louis the recent emigrants from Germany, whom he made symbolic representatives of the values of liberty and union.

What made *The Crisis* vastly popular was its Civil War setting. The greatest U.S. tragedy was the stuff of drama. In the early twentieth century, the war's memories, real and imagined, were still fresh and relevant to Churchill's readers. North and South were only recently reconciled, in part because of the recent Spanish-American War of 1898. Feelings were still strong, but enough time had passed that both sides could better understand the position of their opponents.

It is apparent that Churchill agrees with history's verdict: The North's cause was the better cause and deserved to be victorious. Early in the novel, Stephen Brice, a recently arrived upper-class New Englander, views a slave auction and buys a young woman to save her from a worse fate. The South was destined to lose because of its defense of slavery and for its attempt to destroy the Union. Churchill was a man of his times, for whom freedom and liberty for the slaves was necessary and inevitable. Also reflecting his times, Churchill depicts African Americans as free, but not necessarily equal to white Europeans. African Americans in *The Crisis*, as in a later and even more popular novel, Margaret Mitchell's *Gone with the Wind* (1936), are generally presented as being inferior. The recent German emigrants from northern Europe, on the other hand, play an important role in the preservation of the Union. In the early twentieth century, slavery belonged to the past but racism was still deeply entrenched in American society.

The Civil War setting gives *The Crisis* its continuing popularity; it is the only one of Churchill's novels that remained in print after his death in 1947. Fast-paced, full of dramatic incidents and confrontations, and driven by profound moral and philosophical issues that have continued to affect Americans, *The Crisis* seems destined to maintain a broad and lasting readership.

For all of its virtues, *The Crisis* cannot compare with the best American novels of its generation. Churchill's novels were popular among American readers—Theodore Roosevelt wrote words of praise to the author from the White House—but Churchill did not receive the lasting critical recognition accorded to his contemporaries, such as Stephen Crane, Theodore Dreiser, and Frank Norris. Churchill's greatest failure as a novelist is that his major characters are types rather than individuals: Their actions and responses are largely predictable. Stephen and his mother represent the staunch and upright traditional New England Puritans. Virginia and her father, the Colonel, exemplify the Southern aristocracy at its best, while Virginia's admirer and Stephen's rival, Clarence Colfax, epitomizes the Southerner as the cavalier warrior. Eliphalet Hopper is also from New England, but symbolizes the corrupted Puritan: materialistic, opportunistic, and amoral. Judge Whipple is the uncompromising abolitionist who is willing to sunder even old friendships for the cause. Churchill's characters never transcend their two-dimensional construction.

Paradoxically, the best-realized character in *The Crisis* is not one of Churchill's fictional creations but Abraham Lincoln. Churchill took his historical responsibility seriously and did considerable research before writing *The Crisis*, and he successfully captures many of Lincoln's qualities. He is equally successful in his portrayal of William T. Sherman and, to a lesser degree, Ulysses S. Grant, both prominent Civil War generals. The portrayal of Virginia, Stephen, and the other fictional figures, and their resulting predictable actions, however, limit and date *The Crisis*. Still, Churchill tells an exciting and fast-moving story, with the Civil War as the stage, that became and has remained popular.

"Critical Evaluation" by Eugene Larson

Further Reading

Knight, Grant C. *The Strenuous Age in American Literature.* Chapel Hill: University of North Carolina Press, 1954.

Classic study of American literature covering the period 1900 to 1910, largely coinciding with the presidency of Theodore Roosevelt. Successfully integrates the authors, including Churchill, and their works with the times.

Pattee, Fred Lewis. *The New American Literature, 1890-1930.* New York: Century, 1930. Although dated, the work has valuable comments on Churchill's *The Crisis* as being in the Romantic tradition of the Waverley novels of Sir Walter Scott.

Schneider, Robert W. *Five Novelists of the Progressive Era.* New York: Columbia University Press, 1965. Compares Churchill with the other major authors of the period: William Dean Howells, Stephen Crane, Frank Norris, and Theodore Dreiser. Concludes with the argument that Churchill's liberalism was fundamentally affected by the events of World War I.

_____. *Novelist to a Generation: The Life and Thought of Winston Churchill.* Bowling Green, Ohio: Bowling Green State University Popular Press, 1976. This biographical study by an eminent scholar is the most satisfactory work about Churchill. Combines a discussion of his life with an analysis of his novels.

Titus, Warren Irving. *Winston Churchill.* New York: Twayne, 1963. Combines biography and literary analysis. Was the major study of Churchill until the appearance of Schneider's analytical biography.

The Critic
Or, A Tragedy Rehearsed

Author: Richard Brinsley Sheridan (1751-1816)
First produced: 1779; first published, 1781
Type of work: Drama
Type of plot: Satire
Time of plot: Late eighteenth century
Locale: London

Principal characters:
MR. DANGLE, a Londoner with a passion for theatrical affairs
MRS. DANGLE, his wife
MR. SNEER, Mr. Dangle's friend and resident sneer
MR. PUFF, a puff writer and dramatist
SIR FRETFUL PLAGIARY, a dramatist

The Story:

Mr. Dangle, a well-to-do gentleman of London, sits one morning with his wife at breakfast. While Dangle reads the newspapers, Mrs. Dangle complains that her husband's hobby, the theater, is making her house unlivable, with disappointed authors, would-be actors, musicians, and critics

making it their meeting place. Dangle protests vigorously, but as he does so a stream of callers arrives to prove her point.

The first caller is Mr. Sneer. He and Mrs. Dangle get into a discussion on the morality of the stage and the proper material for comedies. Then Sir Fretful Plagiary, a dramatist, is announced. Before he enters, Dangle reports that Plagiary is a close friend but that he cannot accept criticism of his work. Sir Fretful tells how his new play was sent to the Covent Garden theater, rather than to Drury Lane, because of the envy he uncovered there.

Sneer, Dangle, and Sir Fretful Plagiary begin to discuss the last's new play. In the discussion all criticism of his drama is brushed aside in one way or another by the author, who ends up with a diatribe against all who will say anything against his work, including the newspapers. At the end of their talk, a group of musicians enters looking for Dangle's assistance in securing work with the theaters. They are led by an Italian who knows no English and a Frenchman who knows little English but is to act as interpreter.

The Frenchman and the Italian try to make Dangle understand what they want, but with little success. After a trilingual conversation, in which not one of the participants can understand the others, Mrs. Dangle takes the musicians into another room for refreshment and so relieves her husband of their troublesome presence. As the musicians leave Dangle and Sneer alone in the room, Mr. Puff, another dramatist who has a play in rehearsal at the theater, enters. Puff is introduced to Sneer by Dangle as a puffing writer for the newspapers, whose job it is to praise anyone or anything for a price; he is, in short, an eighteenth century press agent. He explains for the benefit of Sneer the various kinds of "puffs" he writes: the direct, the preliminary, the collateral, the collusive, and the oblique. At the end of the conversation, the three agree to meet at the theater to watch a rehearsal of Puff's new play.

Later the three meet, and Puff informs his two friends, Dangle and Sneer, that the time of his play is the days following the defeat of the Spanish Armada during the reign of Elizabeth I. The under-prompter, appearing to notify the author that the rehearsal is ready to begin, says that the play was somewhat shortened. The actors, informed that anything they find unnecessary in the tragedy can be cut, took full liberties with Puff's script.

When the curtain rises, two watchmen are found asleep at four in the morning. Sir Christopher Hatton and Sir Walter Ralegh appear on the stage and begin the exposition of the plot. They are interrupted at intervals by protestations and explanations by the author, who speaks to the actors on the stage and to his two friends observing the rehearsal.

In the second act of the play a love story between the daughter of the fort commander and a captured Spanish prince is introduced, again with continued interruptions by the dramatist, who is enraged at the liberties taken by the actors in cutting his lines and parts of scenes. He and his friends, Sneer and Dangle, discuss dramatic art as the re-

hearsal continues and find various aspects of the play to point up their discussion. Puff is particularly proud of the second sight credited to the heroine, a device by which he is able to describe the defeat of the Spanish Armada without showing the sea fight on the stage.

He is also quite proud of a verbal fencing match between the heroine and the Spanish prince. When Sneer and Dangle find the repartee ambiguous, Puff explains that he wrote the dialogue completely in fencing terms, an explanation that his friends find scarcely more intelligible. Puff irritates the actors by directing them as the rehearsal progresses, and they, in turn, continue to irritate him by cutting out more lines. At their protestations that they cannot act because of his interruptions, he replies heatedly that he has feelings, too, and does not like to see his play shredded by the players.

At the end of the love scene in the play, Puff begins an argument with the under-prompter, who informs him that it is impossible to rehearse the park scene because the carpenters have not built the scenery. Puff angrily announces that they can cut his play as they will; he intends to print it in its entirety.

The next scene in the rehearsal of Puff's play is a sentimental discovery scene not connected with the main story. In reply to his friends' comments, Puff explains that there is no need to have a logical connection between the main plot and the subplot. Then comes what Puff calls the most perfect scene in the play. An actor enters, sits down, shakes his head, arises, and goes off the stage. The shaking of the head, according to Puff, says more than all the words he could write.

In the last scene of the play the Spanish prince is killed in a duel, and his English sweetheart goes mad. After her exit from the stage, a masque procession of all the British rivers and their tributaries passes over the stage, while an orchestra plays George Frideric Handel's *Water Music*. Following the procession, Puff announces to his friends that the rehearsal was good, but that the actors are not yet perfect. To the actors he announces that another rehearsal will be held the next day.

Critical Evaluation:

In Richard Brinsley Sheridan's time *The Critic: Or, A Tragedy Rehearsed* was probably best known for its bitingly satirical portrait of Sheridan's fellow dramatist, Richard Cumberland, who was the model for Sir Fretful Plagiary. Today the play is most important for the light it sheds on what Sheridan thought of the drama prevalent in his own time. By showing the reader the insipidity of the tragedy rehearsed within the play, the laughable defense of trite dramatic devices by its author, and the comments by the actors, Sheridan lets the reader see what he thought of the state of drama during his age.

The principal theme of *The Critic* is the dynamic interplay of illusion and reality. The central focus is on the role language plays in that interplay. Mr. Dangle, Mr. Sneer, and Mr. Puff—the names prepare one for the spirit of the comedy—form the play's comic center, where each character either ridicules or is ridiculed, sometimes both. The play's themes derive from the portrayal of characters who pretend to be better than they are.

Act 1 begins the play's attacks on fakery and moral blindness. Sneer characterizes the age as "luxurious and dissipated," saying it is nevertheless hypocritical enough to produce a drama that ignores "the follies and foibles of society" in favor of dramatizing "the greater vices and blacker crimes of humanity." With the arrival of Sir Fretful Plagiary, the play's attention shifts to a type of individual author. On the pretext of repeating what newspaper reviewers have said, Sneer and Dangle attack Sir Fretful's plagiarism, coarse language, and dullness. The play's main target, however, is Puff and his production of *The Spanish Armada*, a tragedy that illustrates, in comic reversal, the play's plea for elevated standards in the theater and for literary and personal honesty.

The second and third acts present a world within a world and a tragedy within a comedy. Puff's play is a burlesque of the tragic spirit. One of the ways that Sheridan effects his burlesque is to mix the comic outer drama with the highly stylized language and actions of the actors in rehearsal. Puff's understanding of the elevated world of tragedy is satirized by his play's ridiculous actions and by the stilted, hackneyed dialogue of its characters, who bear such names as Whiskerandos and Tilburnia.

Act 1 has alerted the audience to the significance of language in the way people create their own reality and to the potential of language as an instrument of comic ridicule. When introducing Sneer to Mrs. Dangle, for example, Dangle draws attention to the comic resources of language: "My dear, here's Mr. Sneer." Sir Fretful's crime is not only that he steals ideas from others but that he coarsens and dulls what he takes—and is unaware of the fact. Puff boasts an ability to "insinuate obsequious rivulets into visionary groves" and to live off charitable donations by exaggerating his misfortunes.

Such portrayals illustrate the inability of people in general to escape the linguistic prison they erect around themselves, or that is erected around them by others. When Sneer ironically proposes that a statue of Mercury be erected in honor of Puff, a god "of fiction," he offers an apt symbol of Puff, whose nature is expressed in his devotion to artifice, to making a lie seem real. Making illusion seem real, the essence of drama, is one of the play's themes, and Sheridan

seems to be saying that the artifice is morally acceptable as long as the writer keeps clear the line separating truth from fiction. Sir Fretful and Puff are morally reprehensible because they do not keep the line clear, and the irony is that they cannot understand their failure to do so. This failure makes them fools despite their expertise in fakery.

The play argues that people tend to see only what they wish to see—or see only what their natures allow them to see. During the rehearsal of his tragedy, Puff, blinded by vanity, is unable to see how absurd the performance of his tragedy is. When Sneer points out that "the clown seems to talk in as high a style as the first hero," Puff declares he does not make "slavish distinctions." He is incapable of distinguishing good language from bad language, tragedy from farce, or truth from fiction. His failure to achieve this kind of intellectual keenness is the chief lesson of the final two acts. Puff represents a tendency toward vanity and self-delusion in everyone; the play constitutes a moral indictment of human nature.

In Act 1, the duty of drama to inculcate morals is made an issue. Sheridan's play, by implication, offers an example of the principle working as it should, helping the audience to see, through satire and comedy, that people make fools of themselves, and create bad art in the process, when they cannot distinguish fiction from reality. When Sneer says that the theater "in proper hands, might certainly be made the school of morality," Sheridan seems to be inviting the audience to view his play as an exercise in distinguishing right from wrong.

Part of the play's aim is to define good tragedy by showing bad tragedy. In a comic twist, Puff is the guide. Puff's final announcement—"we'll rehearse this piece again tomorrow"—is followed by the stage direction, "Curtain drops/finis." By ending both plays together, Sheridan is suggesting that the worlds of the two plays are interconnected. Puff's tragedy will recycle and so will the world outside the play. By ridiculing the vanity and blindness of Puff, and by suggesting that Puff's world coincides with that of the audience, *The Critic* serves as a warning.

"Critical Evaluation" by Bernard E. Morris

Further Reading

Auburn, Mark S. *Sheridan's Comedies*. Lincoln: University of Nebraska Press, 1977. The first chapter characterizes the nature of comedy between 1748 and 1780, emphasizing Sheridan's role in its development. A separate chapter is devoted to *The Critic*.

Ayling, Stanley. *A Portrait of Sheridan*. London: Constable, 1985. Places *The Critic* in its social and political context. Describes Sheridan's involvement with the theater.

Browne, Kevin Thomas. *Richard Brinsley Sheridan and Britain's School for Scandal: Interpreting His Theater Through Its Eighteenth-Century Social Context*. Lewiston, N.Y.: Edwin Mellen Press, 2006. Refutes criticism that Sheridan's plays are all style and no substance; argues that his plays depict how people from different social classes negotiate issues of British identity, such as money, gender, class, morality, and language. Chapter 5 is devoted to *The Critic*.

Danziger, Marlies K. *Oliver Goldsmith and Richard Brinsley Sheridan*. New York: Frederick Ungar, 1978. The initial chapter places Sheridan's plays in their social and literary context. Another chapter analyzes *The Critic* as a complex study of the relationship of art and life.

Durant, Jack D. *Richard Brinsley Sheridan: A Reference Guide*. Boston: G. K. Hall, 1981. Lists the major editions of Sheridan's work and offers nearly three hundred pages of critical studies dating from 1816 to 1979. Extensive annotations.

Loftis, John. *Sheridan and the Drama of Georgian England*. Oxford, England: Basil Blackwell, 1976. Contains a chronology of Sheridan's life and a bibliography that includes critical studies of Sheridan's plays, background studies, and biographies. Connects *The Critic* to the political climate that influenced the play's satire and to the burlesque tradition.

Morwood, James, and David Crane, eds. *Sheridan Studies*. New York: Cambridge University Press, 1995. Collection of essays about Sheridan's theatrical and political careers, including discussions of "Theatre in the Age of Garrick and Sheridan," Sheridan's use of language, and the challenges of producing his plays. David Crane's essay "Satire and Celebration in *The Critic*" analyzes this play.

O'Toole, Fintan. *A Traitor's Kiss: The Life of Richard Brinsley Sheridan*. London: Granta, 1997. Biography focusing on Sheridan's relationship to his native Ireland. Draws connections between Sheridan's life and his plays, and provides a detailed examination of his political career.

The Critique of Judgment

Author: Immanuel Kant (1724-1804)
First published: Kritik der Urteilskraft, 1790 (English translation, 1892)
Type of work: Philosophy

In *The Critique of Judgment*, Immanuel Kant argues that self-interest is not relevant to making aesthetic judgments; whatever one experiences indifferently is aesthetic. Pleasantness appeals to the senses. The green color of a meadow is a sensation; the pleasurable aspect of the color is a subjective impression. To think of something as good, one must understand the object. To find beauty in something, one needs only the senses. Beyond beauty, the good must have purpose. Only after satisfied interest can one distinguish the person of taste from the person lacking taste. The object of disinterested liking is beautiful. The validation of beauty comes from consensus. In terms of validation, beauty resembles truth.

Taste—noting something as salty, tart, or sweet, for example—is private and individually different. The experience of beauty or taste can be generalized, however, by consensus. Thus, beauty seems part of things. Judgments of taste report emotional states, and beauty connects to the sensations of the experiencing subject. Titillation and emotion are not part of beauty. Kant distinguishes free beauty and dependent beauty: Free beauty does not need conceptualization; dependent beauty requires purpose. Examples of free beauty are colorful birds, colorful fish, colorful wall coverings, or music without theme or lyrics. With these forms of art, one needs no purpose, only taste. Human beings or beasts of burden have purpose. Their beauty relies on one's judging contingent purposes. Beauty can also be a form of a purposive object if a viewer perceives beauty without awareness of purpose. Though the parts of a flower have purpose, the viewer ignorant of botany sees beauty only. Every inflexible routine is contrary to taste and provides boredom. Natural beauty always outweighs artificial routine.

Next, Kant focuses on the sublime. The beautiful and the sublime please directly, but the sublime attracts and repulses: That it, the beauty of the sublime attracts, and its forcefulness repulses. The sublime—an erupting volcano, for example—

exhibits this duality. What is called sublime is that which is great, and such greatness is comparative, not absolute. Consensus validates judgments about greatness.

The truly sublime makes all else seem small. What one sees in a telescope or a microscope is sublime. That is, the sublime transcends measures of sense. Kant uses the example of the pyramids, which one must view from a particular distance to experience their sublimity. If one is too close, the view turns mathematical; if one is too far, the view is unclear. With the right distance, the view is sublime. The noumenon (the thing in itself) is immeasurably vast; it is unimaginable and thus sublime. Aesthetically, numbers become irrelevant or must change. Even war, when orderly and limited by rights of noncombatants, has aspects of the sublime. A thunderstorm is sublime until one understands its nature. The terrors of nature—massive mountains, huge deserts, fathomless gorges, raging streams—are sublime if one contemplates them from a position of safety. Being immersed in these sublime events or places inspires terror.

An object of one's pleasure is an object for comfort, an object of beauty, an object of the sublime, or an object of goodness (*iucundum, pulchrum, sublime, honestum*). Acts inspired by emotion are weak. Novels, tearjerkers, or platitudinous morality plays weaken heart and spirit and distract from moral duties. Beauty is not morality, for outstanding artists may be quite common, arrogant, stubborn, and full of other flaws. Colors have associations with one's moods: White is innocence, and red through violet may be sublime, courageous, giving, friendly, modest, steadfast, or tender. The song of birds is joyous and appreciative of life. All these characteristics are best in nature; imitations are not interesting.

Acting outside rules, genius has originality. Although original nonsense remains nonsense, genius channels nature through hidden sources that science cannot reproduce. Thus, for example, one can learn to become Sir Isaac Newton; one can never learn to be Homer because Homer is a natural force. To judge beauty, one needs taste; to produce beautiful objects, one needs genius. Some artistic works come from genius without taste; others exhibit taste without genius. A genius brings forth institutions of learning for good minds, who learn the rules of what genius has developed. A student going beyond imitation to channeling nature can surpass a master.

Kant divides the arts into the arts of speech, imaging, and sense impressions. Arts of speech are oratorical and poetical arts. Arts of imaging are sense-authentic arts such as architecture or sculpting, or they are sense-deceptive arts such as painting or landscaping. Arts of sense impressions appeal either to hearing (music) or to sight (coloring). These funda-

mental arts combine, so that theatrical spectacle is oratory and sense impressions, song is poetry and music, opera is theatrical spectacle and song, and dance or ballet are sense impressions, music, and spectacle. Tragedy is closest to the sublime because it combines poetry, music, spectacle, and oratory. When the arts do not serve morality, they are purely for diversion. Poetry holds the highest rank because of its honesty. A play of imagination and of forms, poetry is in harmony with reason. Taking second rank is music, for it abstracts the modulations of language and plays with sensations. Painting, for Kant, takes third place.

As oratory, humor is the art of turning suspense into nothing. Kant uses the example of an Indian opening a bottle of ale. Foam escapes voluminously, and the Indian appears surprised. The Englishman asks, "What's so surprising?" The Indian responds, "I'm not surprised at its escape from the bottle; I am surprised at how you got it into the bottle." In another of Kant's examples, a man has invited guests to a funeral. He wants the guests to look mournful. He complains, saying "I gave the guests some money so that they would try to look very sad; however, the more money I gave them, the less sad they appeared." Suspense turns into release—as nothing.

In part 2 of *The Critique of Judgment*, Kant argues that purposiveness is teleological, and that one can recognize purpose in nature as one reflects. Teleology, the study of design and purpose, does not contribute to scientific exploration, for teleology reasons by way of causality. Purpose is relative: For example, detritus, collecting at river deltas, shrinks the ocean; thus, plants receive more land. From the plants' perspective, this process has purpose. From the perspective of marine life, this process is contrary to purpose. Purposiveness depends on perspective. Applying one's sense of purpose to nature makes sense from the human perspective; from a variety of other perspectives, nature is random.

A thing has purpose if it is its own cause and effect. A tree has seeds, which bring forth a tree. The tree is not rationally purposive; it exhibits a reciprocal relationship of cause and effect. Artificial objects cannot have such reciprocity; otherwise, for example, clocks would come from clocks as trees from seeds. Inanimate things are not purposive either; humans merely superimpose an anthropocentric scheme when they reason, for instance, that a glacier "holds" its water "for" humans, animals, and other living things. Reflecting metaphorically that a natural object serves human interests is certainly different from assuming that nature acts on such purpose, which is an unscientific assumption.

One also reasons poorly if one invokes a god for nature's purposiveness and then uses purposiveness to prove that same god's existence. Teleology is a metaphor that helps one to imagine natural phenomena. Such a metaphor cannot reasonably lead to a prime mover. Unifying nature with a primal being, as philosopher Baruch Spinoza suggests, is not helpful either. When all is purposive, then the distinction of purposiveness and nonpurposiveness disappears. Purpose requires rationality. If one speaks of nature's purposes, one turns nature into a rational being. If one assumes that nature follows divine purposiveness, then one cannot understand nature's laws, for these are now divine will, and thus unpredictable. The teleological thread is part of thinking, not part of nature.

Kant distinguishes reason (*Verstand*) as sense and rationality (*Vernunft*) as speculation. Reason's task is to pull rationality back into reality. Reasoning shows nature as made of competing forces; nature is not something that gives character to its parts. An overall purpose in nature would turn nature into technology. Assuming creation and a creator does not help humans understand because the creator's intentions would be unclear. If one goes from the regularities of nature to conclusions about the creator, then one ends up explaining tautologically and trivially what one has already understood in analyzing nature. Teleology applies only to rationality; teleology does not help in the understanding of nature. Teleology is not part of theology because such rationality tries to go beyond nature. Reasoning beyond nature is fanciful imagining (*Schwärmerei*). Teleology does not belong to the natural sciences, for it reflects through explanation without generating knowledge.

Diversity and similarity of natural structures suggest that a single principle underlies natural processes. A primal mother-entity may have led to a step-by-step development of diverse animals and plants and humans. That development might have led from relationship of all to specificity. Kant alludes to philosopher David Hume by pointing out that, if nature required a guiding rationality, then nature's guiding rationality would require another guiding rationality, ad infinitum. Instead of a guiding rationality, one should have to look for nature's autocracy. Such a search would lead to the kind of error that is called pantheism. Purposiveness is solely part of rationality.

One could think that plants are for animals, that animals are for predators, and that humanity is the balancing entity for all—a final purpose. One can also insist that animals exist for the control of plants, that predators exist for the control of animals, and that humans exist for the constraining of predators in cases where humans are not a final purpose. Most probably, nature does not consist of balanced purposes; such a system would have to be paradise. Human purposiveness is

culture. Because nature does not protect humans from disease, pestilence, and hunger, nature, therefore, does not recognize humanity as its purpose. Because people suppress each other, conduct wars, and inflict harm, culture does not govern nature. Only by way of a maturing culture will autonomous humans find a paradiselike happiness on Earth.

Physicotheology is rationality's attempt to draw conclusions from the purposiveness of nature to an overall final purpose of nature. From rationality's purposiveness, one draws conclusions about the prime mover, thus going beyond the facts. Teleological explanations cannot move beyond nature. Ethicotheology attempts something similar with morality, yet only rational beings can be self-governing by moral laws. Drawing conclusions about the character of an eternal, omnipotent, moral being transcends one's facts. Humanity may require gratitude, obedience, and humility; thus, humans imagine a god. Perhaps such an image of fantasy helps humans imagine a stronger morality. Moral law as a condition of freedom lets all rational but finite beings strive toward the highest good by free acts. As warranty of this highest good, some people assume a deity, a redundancy because one has already accepted the moral law. Perhaps assuming a creator helps one commit to moral law. This idea, however, relies on the structure of rationality, not on an existing god.

Kant appears to prefer the notion of rational beings instead of humanity because he does not reject the possibility of animals with rationality. He makes a point of rejecting the Cartesian idea that animals are biological machines. Kant also recognizes that erroneous proofs of a god's existence will not affect common sense; ignoring proofs and errors, people will continue to believe. Kant may have made this last observation after receiving a letter from Emperor William I of Prussia. The letter, signed by someone named Wellner in 1794, tells Kant not to teach atheism, and that if he does, he will lose his job. The third and last edition of Kant's *The Critique of Judgment* was published in 1799, well after he received this letter.

Reinhold Schlieper

Further Reading

DeCaroli, Steven. "A Capacity for Agreement: Hannah Arendt and *The Critique of Judgment.*" *Social Theory and Practice* 33, no. 3 (July, 2007): 361-386. Rightly analyzes relationships between Hannah Arendt's *consensus iuris* and Kant's notions of validity established by consensus in aesthetic judgments.

Murphy, Marguerite. "Pure Art, Pure Desire: Changing Definitions of *l'art pour l'art* from Kant to . . . ." *Studies in Ro-*

manticism 47, no. 2 (Summer, 2008). This journal article focuses on disinterestedness as a principle in the appreciation of the aesthetic and the impact of disinterestedness on literary theory.

Rueger, Alexander. "Kant and the Aesthetics of Nature." *British Journal of Aesthetics* 47, no. 2 (April, 2007): 138-155. This journal article focuses on the aesthetic perception of nature while ignoring purposes of nature.

Stockwell, Cory. "Kant and the Sublime Murmur of the 'We.'" *Mosaic: A Journal for the Interdisciplinary Study*

of Literature 42, no. 1 (March, 2009): 19-33. Kant recognizes that verification in matters of beauty and the sublime is a matter of consensus. This article expands from consensus to community, perhaps in what Kant might refer to as rationality going beyond what reason can sustain.

Zuckert, Rachel. *Kant on Beauty and Biology: An Interpretation of the "Critique of Judgment."* New York: Cambridge University Press, 2007. This book attempts to see Kant's *The Critique of Judgment* as a unified work, the unifying principle being Kant's views of purposiveness.

Critique of Practical Reason

Author: Immanuel Kant (1724-1804)
First published: Kritik der praktischen Vernunft, 1788
    (English translation, 1873)
Type of work: Philosophy

In *The Critique of Practical Reason*, Immanuel Kant argues that principles are subjective (and therefore maxims) if one person considers them; they are objective (and therefore imperatives) if every rational being considers them. Imperatives are either hypothetical or categorical. A hypothetical imperative demands a course of action to achieve a specified result; for example, "If I want to stay dry in the rain, then I should take my umbrella with me." A categorical imperative demands a course of action under all possible circumstances; for example, "Thou shalt not commit murder."

According to Kant, hypothetical imperatives respond to desires, while categorical imperatives constitute rationality. Subjective principles and hypothetical imperatives are empirically oriented; neither can be a fundamental determiner of moral motivation since they serve self-interest. Proper moral motivation cannot follow fleeting pleasures or displeasures; it must follow a noncompromising rationality. Rational beings must imagine their maxims as practical and general laws that fit into a mold of moral rationality. No matter what one plans, the logical form of rationality urges a logical analysis of one's actions. To test one's decisions, one uses an imperative, which is immutable. A basic requirement of morality, autonomous motivation, undergirds this immutable law. Any heteronomy entails random authority (*Willkür*).

Objects inspire pleasure or displeasure; rationality must be free of empirical attractions, having nonsubjective status. Kant provides an example of testing by rationality: Kant is

the recipient of a deposit. The owner has died without leaving a financial record for his heirs. However, Kant cannot deny the existence of the deposit even though no evidence of the deposit exists. If everyone who entered into a contract did so planning to deny the existence of that contract, contracts themselves would cease to exist, rendering the act of falsely contracting itself incoherent.

Kant's example depends upon his formulation of the categorical imperative: "Act such that the maxim of your will can always count also as a principle of general legislation for all." In other words, it should always be logically possible for the maxim behind one's action (for example, "I should only keep promises when it is convenient") to be universalized (for example, "Everyone who finds their promises inconvenient should break them"). The reason this example maxim cannot be generalized is that, if it were, there would no longer be such a thing as a promise. Thus, generalizing the maxim results in logical incoherence, violating the laws of reason.

Kant's practical rule is unconditional; thus, it is a categorical, practical proposition with an a priori truth-value. Even when one follows subjective desires, one must be able to imagine them as tested by moral law. This law is not a derived one; it urges itself upon the mind as part of the structure of rationality as such. Any search for happiness must include the search for the happiness of all who share in one's rationality. The moral community that this concept refers to may vary with changing times and views; Kant does not commit to one ethnic group or even one species.

Selfish expansion of one's happiness makes no sense as a moral ideal. Kant gives the example of an Epicurean reference: If one were to recommend a particular job candidate to maximize the candidate's own pleasures, wealth, or power, a human-resource specialist would reject the recommendation as either mad, mocking, or backstabbing. Furthermore, if one acts wrongly, one must be able to conceive of a punishment for wrongdoing. However, it would be nonsensical to anticipate punishment—that is, a reduction of well-being—in return for reducing one's well-being by not sufficiently seeking happiness. Thus, seeking happiness cannot be a moral virtue. Morality is rooted in rationality, not in Epicurean pleasure.

In the *Kritik der reinen Vernunft* (1781; *Critique of Pure Reason*, 1838), Kant had shown that time and space are mental conditions of how the mind perceives the world. Beyond these phenomena, one can know of a thing-in-itself but cannot experience it. A similar relationship obtains between humans as natural beings and humans as transcendent rational beings. In the evaluation of its perceptions, the mind can rely on the world of phenomena to corroborate its hypotheses with further observations; however, no corroboration is possible with rationality, and moral law is pure rationality. Causation in moral rationality is a given condition of good will. Like geometric figures, the moral law is purely mental.

For Kant, one must ask whether one's plans are possible under the conditions of good will. Morality springs directly from this good will (well-functioning motivation); without that directness, the action does not constitute morality. Self-interest is acceptable, as long as the good will has conditioned it; if so, selfishness is unlikely to become arrogance or outright selfish egoism. The moral law is holy for a perfect being, but, for the will of a finite rational being, the moral law inspires duty and awe. Kant asserts that passionate or emotional commitments to faddishly tearful good-works moralities are on the wrong path: Only a clear moral duty guided by good will produces morality.

Respect focuses on persons, never on things. One may like, love, or fear animals, but one does not respect them. However, persons have a sense of equality. Before a person of high rank, one may bow, but one's spirit never bows. One must have respect for all persons, regardless of social rank. Personhood must be holy to all. Anything can serve as instrument and means, but people are ends in themselves.

"Moral rationality" and "good will" are synonyms for Kant. The highest value, thus, must include the moral law. Epicureans and Stoics obfuscate each other semantically.

For the Epicureans, the highest happiness is virtue; for the Stoics, virtue is the highest happiness. Kant resolves the resulting chicken-or-the-egg question (does worldly happiness cause the maxims of virtue or vice versa?): Since only the maxims of virtue are intrinsically rational, only they can be causative. Nothing in the world can produce moral rationality because it exists independently of the world. Thus, individuals experience themselves independently, outside of time. Conditioned by the moral law, this independent motivation is an operative part of rationality. Cultivating this rationality, one achieves self-contentment (*Selbstzufriedenheit*), a condition similar to happiness.

"Immortal soul" is a required concept in understanding the good will because the will engages in self-improvement endlessly. Only a being that understands itself as eternal could engage in such a process without despairing. A person's infinite identity must be a metaphor of ethics. One assumes the "soul" as one assumes a "god" metaphor, which provides an image of self-perfecting. Rationality works toward a "god" goal in perfecting itself. A "god" metaphor answers a practical need; one cannot have a duty to believe in an existing "god." However, there is a duty to conceptualize the highest good, and doing so is easier when it is imagined in relation to a "god" metaphor.

Christian morality is part neither of the moral law nor of the "god" metaphor, according to Kant. Freedom, immortality, and God are not matters of knowledge; they are transcendent ideas held for logical convenience. One assumes "god," "freedom," and "immortality" for the convenience of moral rationality, although one can never prove them compellingly in the empirical world. One also cannot compel faith; indeed, one benefits by not knowing God and eternity. If one knew those entities, one might act out of fear or hope rather than duty. To do so, however, would annihilate the moral worth of one's actions; it would replace the categorical "I must do this because it is my duty" with the hypothetical and self-interested "I must do this in order to avoid God's wrath and attain His rewards." Motivation from fear or hope would be immaturely mechanical. One must look to the autonomous judge inside, not to heteronomous forces outside. Obedience to human laws is legality, not morality. Legality commonly results in hypocrisy and in doing what advances one's interests under a pretense of lawfulness while one looks for loopholes.

To show that practical rationality is universal, Kant tells of a ten-year-old's reaction to a story about a person who is to bear false witness, such as speaking ill of Ann Boleyn in support of Henry VIII. Bribed by wealth and threatened by pain, loss, and solitude, the person refuses wrong testimony. The ten-year-old clearly recognizes the superior virtue of this person. Further, if one rescues people from a sinking ship and if one loses one's own life in the process, one has practiced a morality that should not be endorsed fully since that person was negligent in his or her duty to him- or herself. Sacrificing oneself to one's country is laudable, yet it suffers the same deficiency of not seeing one's obligations to oneself. Thus, intuition will recognize these moral categories as qualities of behavior universally.

Because morality is a condition of rational beings, such beings follow the good will. Kant sums up lyrically with the following:

> Two thoughts fill me with ever renewing and increasing awe: the starry sky above and the moral law within. The starry sky reminds me of the animal self that has visited the planet for a short while but must return its living matter to the planet. The moral law within places me into a world of transcendent infinity. The former diminishes me; the latter exalts me.

Kant's analysis focuses on how to think morally; it does not explain how to live. His analysis leaves one free to think for oneself. *The Critique of Practical Reason* is powerful precisely because it does not micromanage morality. Kant describes rationality; he does not proscribe behavior. Morality must focus on a wide moral community and not merely on the self, a mainstay of any ethicist's thinking.

Taking responsibility for one's actions is an essential part of ethical thinking. The moral agent within makes all decisions. A moderate measure of expedience can be part of duty ethics. Kant suggests supplications with fingers crossed when one can bow to a person of high rank without bowing with one's inner self; a lie or some measure of hypocrisy seems implicit. Kant does not offer a proof of God, the soul, or free will; he merely suggests that these are good metaphors for thinking about morality. One cannot compel anyone to believe; a metaphor does not require an existing referent.

Kant's thinking is foundational in moral theory. No ethicist today can work without an awareness of Kant's philosophy. At the same time, many thinkers also misunderstand Kant, in part because of his incredibly complicated syntax, which doubtlessly challenges translators.

Reinhold Schlieper

Further Reading

Beck, Lewis W. *A Commentary on Kant's "Critique of Practical Reason."* Chicago: University of Chicago Press, 1960. A useful explication of Kant's moral philosophy.

Freydberg, Bernard. *Imagination in Kant's "Critique of Practical Reason."* Bloomington: Indiana University Press, 2005. Detailed study of the role of the imagination in Kant's philosophy of mind and of its function within his moral system.

Kant, Immanuel. Translated by Werner S. Pluhar and Stephen Engstrom. *Critique of Practical Reason*. Indianapolis, Ind.: Hackett, 2002. This volume contains a review of translations and their difficulties by Pluhar.

Wilson, E. "Kantian Autonomy and the Moral Self. " *Review of Metaphysics* 62, no. 2 (2008): 355-381. Takes Kant to task about some of the concepts that he leaves open. Kant assumed free will, God, and an eternal soul as needed for moral thinking; Wilson presses for answers and clear commitments.

Critique of Pure Reason

Author: Immanuel Kant (1724-1804)
First published: Kritik der reinen Vernunft, 1781
    (English translation, 1838)
Type of work: Philosophy

Immanuel Kant's *Critique of Pure Reason* is a masterpiece in metaphysics designed to explore the possibility of synthetic a priori judgments. A synthetic judgment is one whose predicate is not contained in the subject; an a priori judgment is one whose truth can be known independently of experience.

Kant therefore in effect questioned how it is that statements in which the idea of the subject does not involve the idea of the predicate can nevertheless be true and can also be known to be true without recourse to experience.

To make the question clearer, Kant offered examples of

analytic and synthetic judgments. The statement that "All bodies are extended" is offered as an analytic judgment because it would be impossible to think of a body, that is, a physical object, that was not spread out in space; the statement "All bodies are heavy" is offered as a synthetic judgment, because Kant believed that it is possible to conceive of a body without supposing that it has weight.

The judgment that "All red apples are apples" is analytic because it would be impossible to conceive that something that was red and an apple could possibly not be an apple; the predicate is, in this case, included in the subject. The judgment "All apples are red," however, is synthetic, because it is possible to think of an apple without supposing it to be red; in fact, some apples are green. Synthetic judgments can be false, but analytic judgments are never false.

A priori knowledge is knowledge "absolutely independent of all experience," whereas a posteriori knowledge is empirical knowledge, that is, knowledge possible only through experience. Human beings can know a priori that all red apples are apples (and that they are red), but to know that a particular apple has a worm in it is something that can be known only a posteriori.

The question whether synthetic a priori judgments are possible concerns judgments that must be true—because they are a priori and can be known to be true without reference to experience—even though, being synthetic, their predicates are not conceived in thinking of their subjects. As an example of a synthetic a priori judgment Kant offers the statement "Everything that happens has its cause." He argues that he can think of something happening without considering whether it has a cause; the judgment is, therefore, not analytic. Yet he supposes that it is necessarily the case that everything that happens has a cause, even though his experience is not sufficient to support that claim. The judgment must be a priori. How are such synthetic a priori judgments possible?

One difficulty arises at this point. Critics of Kant have argued that Kant's examples are not satisfactory. The judgment that everything that happens has a cause is regarded either as being an analytic rather than a synthetic a priori judgment (every event being a cause relative to an immediately subsequent event, and an effect relative to an immediately preceding event) or as being a synthetic a posteriori rather than an a priori judgment (which leaves open the possibility that some events may be uncaused). A great many critics have maintained that Kant's examples are bound to be unsatisfactory for the obvious reason that no synthetic a priori judgments are possible. The argument is that unless the predicate is involved in the subject, the truth of the judgment is a matter of fact, to be determined only by reference to experience.

Kant's answer to the problem concerning the possibility of synthetic a priori judgments that pure reason—that is, the faculty of arriving at a priori knowledge—is possible because the human way of knowing determines, to a considerable extent, the character of what is known. Whenever human beings perceive physical objects, they perceive them in time and space; time and space are what Kant calls "modes of intuition," that is, ways of apprehending the objects of sensation. Because human beings must perceive objects in time and space, the judgment that an object is in time must be a priori but, provided the element of time is no part of the conception of the object, the judgment is also synthetic. It is somewhat as if a world were being considered in which all human beings were compelled to wear green glasses. The judgment that everything seen is somewhat green would be a priori (since nothing could be seen except by means of the green glasses), but it would also be synthetic (since being green is no part of the conception of object).

In Kant's terminology, a transcendental philosophy is one concerned not so much with objects as with the mode of a priori knowledge, and a critique of pure reason is the science of the sources and the limits of what contains the principles by which human beings know a priori. Space and time are the forms of pure intuition, that is, modes of sensing objects. The science of all principles of a priori sensibility, that is, of those principles that make a priori intuitions (sensations) possible, Kant calls the transcendental aesthetic.

Human beings do more than merely sense or perceive objects; they also think about them. The study of the existence of a priori concepts, as distinguished from intuitions, is called transcendental logic. This study is divided into transcendental analytic, dealing with the principles of the understanding without which no object can be thought, and transcendental dialectic, showing the error of applying the principles of pure thought to objects considered in themselves.

Using Aristotle's term, Kant calls the pure concepts of the understanding categories. The categories are of quantity (unity, plurality, totality), quality (reality, negation, limitation), relation (substance and accident, cause and effect, reciprocity between agent and patient), and modality (possibility-impossibility, existence-nonexistence, necessity-contingency). According to Kant, everything that is thought is considered according to these categories. It is not a truth about things in themselves that they are one or many, positive or negative, but that all things fall into these categories because the understanding is so constituted that it can think in no other way.

Kant maintained that there are three subjective sources of the knowledge of objects: sense, imagination, and apperception. By its categories, the mind imposes a unity on the manifold of intuition; what would be a mere sequence of appearances, were the mind not involved, makes sense as the appearance of objects.

The principles of pure understanding fall into four classes: axioms of intuition, anticipations of perception, analogies of experience, and postulates of empirical thought in general. The principle of the axioms of intuition is that "All intuitions are extensive magnitudes," proved by reference to the claim that all intuitions are conditioned by the spatial and temporal mode of intuition.

The principle by which all perception is anticipated is that "the real that is an object of sensation has intensive magnitude, that is, a degree." It would not be possible for an object to influence the senses to no degree; hence, various objects have different degrees of influence on the senses. The principle of the analogies of experience is that "Experience is possible only through the representation of a necessary connection of perceptions." Human experience would be meaningless were it not ordered by the supposition that perceptions are of causally related substances that are mutually interacting.

Kant's postulates of empirical thought in general relate the possibility of things to their satisfying the formal conditions of intuition and of concepts, the actuality of things to their satisfying the material conditions of sensation, and the necessity of things to their being determined "in accordance with universal conditions of experience" in their connection with the actual.

A distinction that is central in Kant's philosophy is the distinction between the phenomenal and the noumenal. The phenomenal world is the world of appearances, the manifold of sensation as formed spatially and temporally and understood by use of the categories. The noumenal world is the world beyond appearance, the unknown and unknowable, the world of "things-in-themselves."

In the attempt to unify experience, reason constructs certain ideas—of a soul, of the world, of God. These ideas are, however, transcendental in that they are illegitimately derived from a consideration of the conditions of reason. To rely on them leads to difficulties that Kant's "Transcendental Dialectic" was designed to expose. The "Paralogisms of Pure Reason" are fallacious syllogisms for which the reason has transcendental grounds; that is, the reason makes sense out of its operations by supposing what, on logical grounds, cannot be admitted. The "Antinomies of Pure Reason" are pairs of contradictory propositions, all capable of proof provided the arguments involve illegitimate applications of the forms and concepts of experience to matters beyond experience.

Kant concludes the *Critique of Pure Reason* with the suggestion that the ideas of God, freedom, and immortality arise in the attempt to make moral obligation intelligible. This point was developed at greater length in his *Grundlegung zur Metaphysik der Sitten* (1785; *Foundations of the Metaphysics of Morals*, 1950) and his *Kritik der praktischen Vernunft* (1788; *Critique of Practical Reason*, 1873).

Further Reading

Allison, Henry E. *Idealism and Freedom: Essays on Kant's Theoretical and Practical Philosophy*. New York: Cambridge University Press, 1996. An important interpreter of Immanuel Kant explores relationships between Kant's theory of knowledge and his moral philosophy.

Bohman, James, and Matthias Lutz-Backmann, eds. *Perpetual Peace: Essays on Kant's Cosmopolitan Ideal*. Cambridge, Mass.: MIT Press, 1997. The contributors appraise Kant's theories about and hopes for a universal rationality that would encourage shared moral understanding and reduce political conflict.

Buroker, Jill Vance. *Kant's "Critique of Pure Reason": An Introduction*. New York: Cambridge University Press, 2006. Offers a line-by-line interpretation of the major arguments in the work. Places Kant's philosophy within the context of his predecessors and successive thinkers, explaining how his ideas were a response to the failure of rationalism and the challenge of skepticism.

Cassirer, Ernst. *Kant's Life and Thought*. Translated by James Hayden. New Haven, Conn.: Yale University Press, 1981. Written by an important twentieth century philosopher, this book offers a readable intellectual biography of Kant.

Caygill, Howard. *A Kant Dictionary*. Malden, Mass.: Blackwell, 1995. A reliable reference guide that helps to clarify key concepts and ideas in Kant's philosophy.

Guyer, Paul, ed. *The Cambridge Companion to Kant*. New York: Cambridge University Press, 1992. Helpful essays by contemporary Kant scholars shed light on key aspects of Kant's theory of knowledge, metaphysics, ethics, and religious thought.

Hare, John E. *The Moral Gap: Kantian Ethics, Human Limits, and God's Assistance*. New York: Oxford University Press, 1996. A study of the strengths and weakness of Kant's influential moral philosophy.

Kuehn, Manfred. *Kant: A Biography*. New York: Cambridge University Press, 2001. The first major biography of the philosopher in fifty years. Includes extensive notes and a bibliography.

Luchte, James. *Kant's "Critique of Pure Reason": A Reader's Guide*. London: Continuum, 2007. Aimed at students, this guide provides an overview of the themes in the critique and a detailed interpretation of the work, as well as information about the book's reception and influence. It places the critique within the context of Kant's life and times.

Schönfeld, Martin. *The Philosophy of the Young Kant: The Precritical Project.* New York: Oxford University Press, 2000. A study of the philosopher's work before the *Critique of Pure Reason.*

Schott, Robin May, ed. *Feminist Interpretations of Immanuel Kant.* University Park: Pennsylvania State University Press, 1997. Essayists bring the perspectives of feminist scholarship to bear on Kant's method and thought.

Walker, Ralph. *Kant.* New York: Routledge, 1999. An excellent biographical introduction to the thoughts of the philosopher, clearly presented and requiring no special background. Includes bibliography.

The Crock of Gold

Author: James Stephens (1880/1882-1950)
First published: 1912
Type of work: Novel
Type of plot: Fantasy
Time of plot: Indeterminate
Locale: Irish countryside

Principal characters:
THE PHILOSOPHER
THE THIN WOMAN, his wife
SEUMAS and BRIGID, two children
ANGUS OG, an early Irish god
CAITILIN, his mortal wife

The Story:

In the center of a very dark pinewood lives the two old Philosophers and their wives, the Grey Woman of Dun Gortin and the Thin Woman of Inis Magrath. One couple has a little boy named Seumas, the other a little girl named Brigid. Both are born on the same day. When the children are ten years old, one of the old Philosophers decides that he learned all that he was capable of learning. This conclusion depresses him so much that he decides to die. It is unfortunate, as he points out, that at the time he is in the best of health; however, if the time comes for him to die, then die he must. He takes off his shoes and spins around in the center of the room for fifteen minutes until he falls over dead. So grieved is the Grey Woman that she, too, kills herself, but since she is much tougher than her husband, she spins for forty-five minutes before she dies. The Thin Woman calmly buries the two bodies under the hearthstone.

The people who live on the edge of the pinewood often come to see the Thin Woman's husband when they need advice. One day, Meehawl MacMurrachu comes to the Philosopher to learn who stole his wife's scrubbing board. The Philosopher, after much questioning, finally decides that the fairies took it. He advises Meehawl to go to a certain spot and steal the Crock of Gold that the Leprechauns of Gort na Gloca Mora buried there. For years, the Leprechauns were filling their Crock of Gold by clipping the edges of gold coins that they found in people's houses at night. They need the

gold to ransom any of the little people caught by human beings.

Losing their gold to Meehawl makes the Leprechauns angry, and they try to make Meehawl bring it back by giving him and his wife all kinds of aches and pains. Next, they come stealthily and lure Brigid and Seumas down into a little house in the roots of a tree. However, fear of the Thin Woman is on them, and they set the children free. Then the Great God Pan, the god of the beast that is in every human, lures away Caitilin, Meehawl's daughter, with the music of his pipes. When Meehawl comes with his tale of sorrow, the Philosopher sends Brigid and Seumas to tell Pan to release the girl. Pan, however, refuses to answer their questions. When they tell the Philosopher, he becomes so angry that he orders his wife to bake him some cakes to eat on the way, and he starts off by himself to visit Pan. None of the Philosopher's arguments, however, persuade Pan to free Caitilin, and the Philosopher goes off to get the help of Angus Og of the old gods.

Angus Og goes to see Pan and the girl in their cave and forces the girl to choose between them. Caitilin, who learns the true meaning of hunger and desire with Pan, does not know how to choose. Angus Og explains to her that he is Divine Inspiration, and that if she will come and live with him and be his wife, he will show her peace and happiness. He proves by several signs that he is the favorite of the gods of the earth and has more power than Pan. Caitilin senses that true happiness will be found with Angus Og and that only hunger will be found with Pan; she chooses to leave Pan and go with Angus Og and is saved from the beast in humanity.

The Philosopher, on his way back home, delivers several messages from the god. He gives one message to a young boy, a promise from Angus Og that in time the old gods will return and that before they do, the boy will write a beautiful poem in their praise. Cheered by the news that the gods will soon come back, the Philosopher finally arrives home and greets his wife with such affection that she decides always to be kind to him and never again to say a cross word. Unknown to them, the Leprechauns inform the police in the village that there are two bodies buried under the hearthstone in the Philosopher's house. One day the police break into the house, find the bodies, and accuse the Philosopher of murder. Meanwhile, Brigid and Seumas are playing in the woods, and, quite by chance, they happen to dig a hole and find the Crock of Gold where Meehawl buried it. They give it back to the Leprechauns, but the return of the gold is not enough to set matters right. The police keep the Philosopher in jail. Then the Thin Woman bakes some cakes and sets out to find Angus Og, dragging the children behind her and saying the worst curses there are against the police. The first gods she meets are the Three Absolutes: the Most Beautiful Man, the Strongest Man, and the Ugliest Man. By her wisdom, the Thin Woman is able to answer their questions and save herself and the children from their frightful powers. When they pass these gods, they find the house of Angus Og. He is waiting for someone to come and ask him to aid the Philosopher, for it is impossible for the gods to help anyone unasked.

Calling all the old gods together, Angus Og and his wife lead a great dance across the fields, and then they go down into the town with all the gods following. In the town, their merry laughter brings happiness to all who see them except the most evil of men. The charges against the Philosopher are forgotten, and he is free to go back to his house in the pinewood and dispense wisdom once more. Then the gods return singing to their own country to await the birth of Caitilin and Angus Og's child and the day when the old Irish gods can again leave their hidden caves and hollows and rule over the land with laughter and song.

Critical Evaluation:

On its publication in 1912, *The Crock of Gold* placed James Stephens in the vanguard of writers guiding the Irish Literary Revival of that period. Led by the poet William Butler Yeats, among others, this movement sought to revitalize Irish culture with inspiration derived from ancient Irish myths and legends. The movement placed a strong emphasis on the Irish language and had a mystic reverence for the customs and folklore of poor people, particularly those living off the land. Yeats saw *The Crock of Gold* as an indication that Dublin, the capital of Ireland, was living a deeper spiritual life because the city had nurtured its author, Stephens.

The extravagant praise heaped on *The Crock of Gold* on its publication was matched by its popularity with the reading public. It became a best seller immediately and remains Stephens's most popular work. As a novel, it is impossible to categorize. Part fairy tale, part philosophy, part mythology, part social history with a conscience, it is very comic, tremendously imaginative, and always extravagant in its celebration of language and life.

Stephens's influences in writing the book are marked and in many cases easily traceable. The huge upsurge in writing with native themes and pastoral settings in Ireland in the 1890's and early 1900's gave Stephens the inspiration for much of the plot. Stephens's mentor and one of the leaders of the Irish Literary Revival, Æ (George Russell), believed literally in the existence of spirits, fairies, and gods, and he prophesied their materialization in the Irish countryside and cities. The verbose Philosopher in the novel seems to be at least partly based on Æ, who had a comic tendency to pontificate. On a deeper level Stephens owes a huge and acknowledged debt to the English poet William Blake. Blake saw life as warring extremes—good and evil, intellect and emotion, spirit and matter—that spark the fires of progress. Blake often vilified authority, organized religion, materialism, and the horrors of industrialized society. Stephens touches on all these themes in *The Crock of Gold*, if sometimes in a muted form.

Chief among the protagonists are the Philosopher and Caitilin, the former representing intellectual nature, the latter emotional nature. At the beginning readers see the Philosopher as a rather pedantic, joyless creature with a huge store of information but little knowledge of life's essentials and no capacity for love. His journey to meet the ancient Irish god, Angus Og, transforms him. First the Philosopher meets Pan, representing animal nature, and, despite the Philosopher's anger, he notices that he feels more alive than he did for years after his contact with a pure physicality. Traveling on, he perceives the sadness of some people he meets and their unsureness of how to conduct their affairs. His rendezvous with Angus Og brings him to ecstasy, marrying his intellect with his spirit and awakening a dormant love for his fellow human beings.

Caitilin, whose name suggests she represents the personification of Ireland (Caitilín Ní Houlaháin), also has encounters with these two gods. Meeting Pan entices her sensual nature to blossom and, in imitation of him, she discards her clothes to better express this side of herself. The Philosopher, in this scene representing the repressed domesticated member of civilization, is horrified by this and rails against her and Pan to no avail. Subsequently, Angus Og comes to seek her out and, in a crucial scene of the plot, gets her to leave Pan and come with him. This episode may be interpreted in many ways but probably can best be seen as a suggestion by Stephens that Ireland should gravitate toward what is her own (Pan is a Greek god) and, in Caitilin's terms, foster a union with her spiritual roots that will bear offspring to revitalize Ireland.

Intertwined with these and other journeys (such as the one undertaken by the Thin Woman of Magrath) are Stephens's philosophical discourses, some pages long. Though he seems serious, his manner of dealing with them smacks of whimsicality if not irreverence. Everything is turned upside down in this novel; the momentous and the commonplace exchange places and importance on most every page.

Stephens's theme is straightforward: Imagination, love, joy, and dance need their proper place in modern life. In Ireland, these things should spring from Ireland's own culture. Modern society places too much reliance on reason and the intellect. The result is loneliness and lack of fulfillment. The philosopher's experience in prison, held by uncomprehending policemen obeying the mindless dictates of law, shows Stephens at his most serious. Two fellow prisoners tell wretched stories of society's lack of charity to the old and the sick. At the end, when the Thin Woman asks Angus Og to free her husband, all the gods and spirits of old join him in setting the people free from their bondage, literal and mental.

The Crock of Gold survives as literature because it is funny, profound, elusive, and charming. One could argue that the parts are greater than the whole. Some of the philosophizing, for instance seems half digested, as if Stephens read ideas elsewhere and did not quite make them his own. What works best are the less-deliberate moments: insects talking to cows, children playing with Leprechauns, offhand humor, encounters with peasants. With the beautiful and poetic language, they make this story a classic of fantasy writing.

"Critical Evaluation" by Philip Magnier

Further Reading

Finneran, Richard J. *The Olympian and the Leprechaun: W. B. Yeats and James Stephens*. Dublin, Ireland: Dolmen Press, 1978. Contains many quotes and insights from Yeats on Stephens and his place in Irish literature.

Kiely, Benedict. "Clay and Gods and Men: The Worlds of James Stephens." In *A Raid into Dark Corners, and Other Essays*. Cork, Ireland: Cork University Press, 1999. An insightful analysis of Stephens's work by an Irish writer and literary critic. Describes how Stephens's prose and poetry always "move" and are on "the edge of something more tense and radiant, and more full of movement, than ordinary life."

Kullmann, Thomas. "Irish Mythology, Eastern Philosophy, and Literary Modernism in James Stephens' *The Crock of Gold*." In *Literary Inter-Relations: Ireland, Egypt, and the Far East*, edited by Mary Massoud. Gerrards Cross, England: C. Smythe, 1996. One of the papers delivered at a 1993 conference in which participants examined Ireland's literary relationship to the Middle and Far East. Kullmann's paper examines Irish and Eastern influences, as well as the impact of modernism, on *The Crock of Gold*.

Lennon, Joseph. "Theosophy and the Nation: George Russell (Æ) and James Stephens." In *Irish Orientalism: A Literary and Intellectual History*. Syracuse, N.Y.: Syracuse University Press, 2004. Examines how Stephens combines elements of Irish and Indian folklore to describe the social realities of early twentieth century Ireland. Discusses the influence of Eastern philosophy and Theosophy on Stephens and on other Celtic Revivalists, most notably Æ.

McFate, Patricia. *The Writings of James Stephens: Variations on a Theme of Love*. New York: St. Martin's Press, 1979. Good at placing Stephens in historical and literary context.

Martin, Augustine. *James Stephens: A Critical Study*. Totowa, N.J.: Rowman & Littlefield, 1977. Strong in critical analysis and debating themes.

Pyle, Hilary. *James Stephens: His Work and an Account of His Life*. New York: Barnes & Noble, 1965. Groundbreaking work that separates fact from fiction in Stephens's life. A sympathetic account traces his origins, motivations, and influence.

Quintelli-Neary, Marguerite. "James Stephens: *The Crock of Gold* and *The Demi-Gods*." In *Folklore and the Fantastic in Twelve Modern Irish Novels*. Westport, Conn.: Greenwood Press, 1997. Analyzes how Stephens uses elements of Irish folklore in the two novels.

Crome Yellow

Author: Aldous Huxley (1894-1963)
First published: 1921
Type of work: Novel
Type of plot: Social satire
Time of plot: 1920's
Locale: England

Principal characters:
HENRY WIMBUSH, the owner of Crome
ANNE WIMBUSH, his niece
DENIS STONE, a young poet
MR. SCROGAN, a man of reason
GOMBAULD, an artist
MARY BRACEGIRDLE, a victim of repressions
JENNY MULLION, a deaf but keen-eyed observer

The Story:

Denis Stone, a shy young poet, goes to a house party at Crome, the country home of Henry Wimbush and his wife. He goes because he is in love with Wimbush's niece, Anne. Anne looks down on Denis because he is four years younger than she, and she treats him with scorn when he attempts to speak of love. Mr. Wimbush is interested in little except Crome and the histories of the people who lived in the old house. Mrs. Wimbush is a woman with red hair, probably false, and with an interest in astrology, especially since she recently won a bet on a horse with her star-given information. Other guests at the party include Gombauld, an artist who was invited to paint Anne's picture; the diabolically reasonable Mr. Scrogan; deaf Jenny Mullion; and Mary Bracegirdle, who is worried about her Freudian dreams. Denis and Anne quarrel, this time over their philosophies of life. Denis tries to carry all the cares of the world on his back, but Anne thinks that things should be taken for granted as they come. The quarrel costs Denis his first opportunity to tell Anne that he loves her.

Mary discusses her dreams and repressions with Anne. Having decided to secure either Gombauld or Denis for a husband, she chooses the wrong times to talk with both men. Gombauld is busy painting when Mary comes up to him. Denis is smarting with jealousy over the time Anne and Gombauld spend together.

Ivor Lombard arrives for the party. Ivor, a painter of ghosts and spirits, turns his attentions toward repressed Mary and secretly visits her one night in the tower. He goes away without seeing her again.

At various times, Mr. Wimbush calls the party together while he reads stories of the early history of Crome. These stories are from a history on which Mr. Wimbush worked for thirty years. Denis often wonders if he will ever get a chance to tell Anne that he loves her. Walking in the garden after a talk with Mr. Scrogan, whose cold-blooded ideas about a rationalized world annoy him, he finds a red notebook in which Jenny was writing for the past week. The notebook contains a collection of sharply satirical cartoons of all the people at the house party. Jenny drew him in seven attitudes that illustrate his absurd jealousy, incompetence, and shyness. The cartoons deeply wound his vanity and shatter his self-conception.

He is further discouraged by the fact that there is nothing for him to do at a charity fair held in the park outside Crome a few days later. Mr. Scrogan makes a terrifying and successful fortune-teller; Jenny plays the drums; Mr. Wimbush runs the various races; and Denis is left to walk aimlessly through the fair as an official with nothing to do. Gombauld makes sketches of the people in the crowd, and Anne stays by his side.

The night after the fair, Denis overhears part of a conversation between Gombauld and Anne. Denis is unaware that Anne repulsed Gombauld, for she made up her mind to accept Denis if he ever gets around to asking her; consequently, he spends hours of torture thinking of the uselessness of his life. At last, he decides to commit suicide by jumping from the tower. There he finds Mary grieving, because she received only a brisk postcard from Ivor. She convinces Denis that both their lives are ruined and advises him to flee from Anne. Convinced, Denis arranges a fake telegram calling him back to London on urgent business. When it arrives, Denis realizes with dismay that Anne is miserable to see him go. The telegram is the one decisive action of his life. Ironically, it separates him from Anne.

Critical Evaluation:

Aldous Huxley published this, his first novel, when he was twenty-seven years old. Themes announced in this satirical, loosely knit work were to characterize his future production also: How can people of the modern world find the solutions required by the present to the age-old problems of humanity? What constitutes value? To what extent can historical imperatives be avoided, or, if they still mean something, to what extent can they continue to be implemented? In his justly famous novel of 1932, *Brave New World*, Huxley poses these problems in a way far more integral to the plot. In *Crome Yellow*, such questions—and putative solutions—are put in the mouths of various characters. Since none of these (even Denis Stone, the protagonist and from whose point of view events are seen) is clearly sympathetic, it is not possible to discern in which direction Huxley himself throws his weight. It is more a case of "a plague on all your houses"— nobody escapes Huxley's satirical deconstruction. Romanticism is especially attacked, and such attacks are repeated and developed throughout what might be considered the trilogy formed by his first three novels—*Crome Yellow*, *Antic Hay* (1923), and *Those Barren Leaves* (1925)—and even through the seven-novel series, including *Point Counter Point* (1928), *Brave New World*, *Eyeless in Gaza* (1936), and *After Many a Summer Dies the Swan* (1939), that constitutes Huxley's novelistic output up to 1939. Yet there are many Romantic elements in his writing.

Huxley's work is rife with such contradictions. It well illustrates the poet William Butler Yeats's aphorism that, if rhetoric is what results from one's arguments with others, poetry is the outcome of one's argument with oneself. For example, Huxley knew enough history to deplore the historicism of contemporary thinkers, yet was unable himself to avoid sweeping statements concerning historical tendencies. In *Brave New World*, the vision of the lockstep future is a nightmare, but the few nonconforming characters are not impressive either. *Crome Yellow* might have been a better book had Huxley found an organizing idea—Carl Jung's theory of psychological types comes to mind—to impart a positive spin to the relativism of his people; as it stands, they tend to cancel each other out rather than complement and augment one another.

Huxley's popularity began with the publication of *Crome Yellow* and grew with each successive novel, especially with the people of his own generation, which indicates that Huxley spoke for his peers, that his unresolved contradictions were theirs as well, and that they welcomed such a mirroring— which was, after all, a focusing of their confusions and despair.

Crome Yellow also is an entertaining work, in part because of its setting, an ancient and splendid English country house standing amid sumptuous gardens in a beautiful countryside, at the end of a train ride that passes through stations with such names as Spavin Delawarr, Knipswich for Timpany, and Camlet-on-the-Water. In the grand house itself, there are secret doors, winding staircases, parapets, and towers. As they dine in style or stroll the garden paths, Huxley's characters may articulate radical notions concerning the end of civilization as they know it, and the feeling resulting from the massive destruction and loss of life during World War I may color their behavior, but much proceeds according to traditions that have succeeded through many generations, and a sense of coziness and safety mitigates the dire predictions that are voiced in much of *Crome Yellow*.

The characters are certainly entertaining—or the caricatures, one might almost call them, for Huxley is a gifted cartoonist in prose. The red sketchbook that Jenny Mullion keeps, and at which Denis steals a look, is an emblem of the novel, which is itself a kind of sketchbook filled with uncomfortably accurate lampoons. Like cartoon people, the cast of *Crome Yellow* is composed of static people, of types; no one is changed by his or her experiences in the course of these 150 or so pages. Huxley is interested in human diversity, but not much given to representing its development.

Huxley capably demonstrates throughout *Crome Yellow* his own diverse talents, as satirist, parodist, purveyor of little-known details from history; as poet, versifier, memorizer of—or inventor of—fascinating conversation; as theorist, philosopher, psychologist. At times, these demonstrations amount to nothing more than a half-baked genius strutting his stuff, as certain critics allege; so it must appear to readers, then and now, who are unable to identify with a pert wit fresh out of Eton and Oxford. To many of his contemporaries, who included a number of the brightest intellects as well as the "bright young things," Aldous Huxley, in *Crome Yellow*, was the first to announce the coming of a new sensibility, one that would spurn traditional Great Britain and Europe, and that would not let its own lack of constructive thought deter it from remarking on the wholesale flaws in the thought it was meant to inherit.

As one reviewer at the time wrote, many of Huxley's contemporaries found him "amusing," a word that meant a lot more than "funny." It was their highest term of praise. In an era when the values that had persisted throughout the lengthy Victorian period were now perceived as having failed and led directly to the holocaust of World War I by the more prescient members of the British public, it seemed enough to say so in an engaging and provocative way: Without sounder grounds of value, "amusing" had to suffice. As the grandson of Thomas Henry Huxley, who had championed Darwin, and the relative of Matthew Arnold, who in his famous poem "Dover Beach" (1867) had announced the withdrawal of faith in Christendom, Aldous Huxley inherited a considerable burden of family responsibility for the condition of the present. He was to spend his life seeking solutions, and *Crome Yellow* makes a start by clearing the air of the outdated and the stultifying.

"Critical Evaluation" by David Bromige

Further Reading

Baker, Robert S. *The Dark Historic Page: Social Satire and Historicism in the Novels of Aldous Huxley, 1921-1939.* Madison: University of Wisconsin Press, 1982. Invaluable work, especially the chapter entitled "*Crome Yellow* and the Problem of History."

Barfoot, C. C., ed. *Aldous Huxley: Between East and West.* Amsterdam: Rodopi, 2001. Collection of essays, including analyses of the themes of science and modernity in Huxley's interwar novels, utopian themes in his work, his views of nature, and his use of psychedelic drugs and mescaline. Also includes "White Peacocks in a Waste Land: A Reading of *Crome Yellow*" by Wim Tigges.

Bedford, Sybille. *Aldous Huxley: A Biography.* New York: Alfred A. Knopf, 1974. First-rate, extensive biography that traces Huxley's intellectual and moral development from early childhood on.

Birnbaum, Milton. *Aldous Huxley's Quest for Values.* Knoxville: University of Tennessee Press, 1971. Deals with Huxley's novels by theme rather than by chronology, but the index references to *Crome Yellow* are worth looking up. Birnbaum, a college student in the 1920's, writes in his preface, "In debunking the traditional sources of value he [Huxley] was, in a sense, acting as our surrogate."

Bowering, Peter. *Aldous Huxley: A Study of the Major Novels.* New York: Oxford University Press, 1969. Notes the counterpull, beneath the benign skepticism of its surface, of an underlying gravity in *Crome Yellow*.

Firchow, Peter. *Aldous Huxley: Satirist and Novelist.* Minneapolis: University of Minnesota Press, 1972. Offers sound insights into Huxley's literary technique in *Crome Yellow*.

Meckier, Jerome. *Aldous Huxley: Modern Satirical Novelist of Ideas, a Collection of Essays.* Edited by Peter Firchow and Bernfried Nugel. London: Global, 2006. This collection of Meckier's essays written from 1966 through 2005 includes a discussion of Sir George Sitwell's contributions to *Crome Yellow*.

Murray, Nicholas. *Aldous Huxley: A Biography.* New York: St. Martin's Press, 2003. Murray's 500-plus-page biography and intellectual history is a wide-ranging survey of Huxley's writing and his social, personal, and political life. The book stretches from Huxley's early satirical writing to his peace activism, and from his close relations and friendships with Hollywood filmmakers and other intellectuals to his fascination with spirituality and mysticism. Illustrations, bibliography, and index.

Watt, Donald, ed. *Aldous Huxley: The Critical Heritage.* London: Routledge & Kegan Paul, 1975. Fascinating compendium of reviews, articles, and letters, arranged chronologically. F. Scott Fitzgerald, at that time the author of one published novel, said in his review of *Crome Yellow*, "Huxley . . . is said to know more about French, German, Latin, and medieval Italian literature than any man alive. I refuse to make the fatuous remark that he should know less about books and more about people." Watt's introduction provides further insights into *Crome Yellow*.

Crotchet Castle

Author: Thomas Love Peacock (1785-1866)
First published: 1831
Type of work: Novel
Type of plot: Fiction of manners
Time of plot: Nineteenth century
Locale: England

Principal characters:
EBENEZER MAC CROTCHET, a country squire
YOUNG CROTCHET, his son
LEMMA CROTCHET, his daughter
SUSANNAH TOUCHANDGO, the beloved of young Crotchet
MR. CHAINMAIL, an antiquarian
CAPTAIN FITZCHROME, a young army officer
LADY CLARINDA BOSSNOWL, the beloved of Fitzchrome

The Story:

The squire of Crotchet Castle is descended from Scottish and Jewish ancestors, but he tries to assume the demeanor of a traditional English country squire. He has great ability in making money, and he uses his wealth to buy a manor and a coat of arms. With his wife dead and his son in London, the squire lives with his daughter. Young Crotchet, who inherited his father's love for money, takes his father's gift of a large sum and turns it into enormous profits. His business dealings are shady, however, and many people think his day of reckoning will come. For the present, however, his luck holds. He was engaged to Miss Susannah Touchandgo, the daughter of a great banker, but when that gentleman absconded with the bank's funds, leaving his daughter almost penniless, young Crotchet deserted his love without a backward glance. Susannah went to Wales, where she made her living in simple surroundings, teaching a farmer's children.

Squire Crotchet's daughter Lemma bears some resemblance to her ancestors, a fact that is compensated in the eyes of local swains by the size of her father's fortune. A suitor is not yet selected for her, but there are many who seek her hand and her purse.

Crotchet Castle is a gathering place for philosophers and dilettantes picked at random by Squire Crotchet. These would-be intellectuals engage in long and tiresome disputes on all branches of philosophy and science. One of them, Mr. Chainmail, longs for a return to the customs and morals of the Middle Ages, believing that the present is decidedly inferior to the past. He is violently opposed by other members of the group who worship mammon. None of the philosophers ever changes his views, and each finds much pleasure in expounding his own pet theory.

While strolling through the grounds one day, some of the gentlemen come upon a young army officer, Captain Fitzchrome. Invited to join the group, the captain accepts readily, for he is in love with Lady Clarinda Bossnowl, one of the guests. Lady Clarinda obviously loves the captain, but she is promised to young Crotchet in a match that is purely a business arrangement: his money for her title. The captain pleads with her at every opportunity, but she silences him and her own heart by ridiculing his lack of funds. Lemma, in the meantime, becomes pledged to Lady Clarinda's brother. The four young people spend many hours together, much to Captain Fitzchrome's sorrow.

One day, the squire takes his guests on a river voyage down the Thames. They visit places of learning and culture but see little of either except the buildings supposed to house those attributes. During the trip, the captain finally gives up his hopes of winning Lady Clarinda, and he leaves the party without notifying anyone. He settles in a village inn, where he is later joined by Chainmail, the antiquarian, who left the party to study a ruined castle in the neighborhood. Since the captain knows the way to the castle, he offers to guide Chainmail, but he is called back to London on business before they can undertake their expedition. Chainmail goes on alone.

During his researches, Chainmail catches a glimpse of a nymphlike creature who fascinates him so much that he cannot rest until he makes her acquaintance. When he finally meets her, he learns that she is Susannah. Chainmail finds her perfect in every way but one. He knows she would share the simple, old-fashioned life he loves, but he is determined to marry a lady of gentle birth. Susannah, ashamed of her father's theft, will tell him nothing of her family background. In spite of her reluctance in this respect, Chainmail loves her and spends many happy hours at the farmhouse in which she lives.

When Captain Fitzchrome returns and learns of his friend's plight, he encourages Chainmail to ask for the lady's hand. The antiquarian is, however, unable to change his views. The situation is brought to a climax when they see in the paper an announcement of the approaching marriage of Lady Clarinda and young Crotchet. Susannah is temporarily overcome by the news, and in trying to comfort her, Chainmail inadvertently proposes. Then Susannah tells him of her father's crime. Chainmail, however, can overlook that fact in his joy over the discovery that Susannah is of gentle blood. In a few days, the two are married.

The following Christmas, most of the friends gather again at Crotchet Castle. Lemma married Lord Bossnowl, but Lady Clarinda Bossnowl did not yet marry young Crotchet. The young man is a little dismayed at seeing Susannah married to Chainmail, for he still holds her in affection. Lady Clarinda casts longing glances at the captain, even to the point of singing a song obviously intended for him. She is not sorry, therefore, when young Crotchet disappears. His firm failed, and he is penniless. It is assumed that he crossed the Atlantic to join forces with Susannah's father, who set up business there. Lady Clarinda refuses to be put up for sale again. She gladly accepts Captain Fitzchrome and his smaller but stabler fortune.

Critical Evaluation:

Crotchet Castle is something of a historical novel, not because it attempts to re-create the past but because it reflects so clearly the life and times of its author. Published in 1831, the work was written during the preceding year or two. The setting of the novel extends from the valley of the Thames to Oxford, through a canal to the Severn, and from there to northern Wales. These areas were well known to Thomas Love Peacock, who undertook a walking journey upriver from the Thames valley in 1809 and then wrote a long poem about it, *The Genius of the Thames* (1810). In 1815, accompanied by the poet Percy Bysshe Shelley and some other friends, Peacock made a boat trip up the Thames from Windsor that included visits to Oxford and Lechlade. The same itinerary appears in chapters 9 and 10 of *Crotchet Castle*, except that in the novel the group is able to afford passage through the canal, an economic hurdle that in 1815 forced Shelley and Peacock to change their plans.

Peacock's first trip to northern Wales was in the winter of 1808-1809. During that visit he went on long walks to enjoy the mountain scenery, and he met Jane Gryffydh, the well-educated daughter of a Welsh clergyman, with whom he discussed books. Peacock himself was a prodigious reader, as is apparent in his works, and it is surprising to learn that he attended school only from the age of six to thirteen. However, he read not only English literature but also Greek, Latin, French, and Italian, all in the original languages. Predictably, he was scornful of the university education he never had, an attitude that appears in several of his novels but never more prominently so than in the Oxford portion, chapter 9, of *Crotchet Castle*.

Peacock lacked not only formal education (for which he more than compensated) but also significant vocational experience. Only in 1819 did he apply for and attain a position in the Examiner's Department of the East India Company. Now financially secure and at age thirty-four in want of a wife, he proposed by mail to Jane Gryffydh (whom he did not see for years) and was accepted. Though the marriage was not entirely a success, Jane's knowledge of Wales and of its language and literature influenced several of Peacock's novels. She was almost certainly the original of Susannah Touchandgo, the nymph of Merionethshire. Peacock writes meaningfully in chapter 14 that her favorite author was Jean-Jacques Rousseau, the radical eighteenth century Swiss philosopher and novelist who taught his readers to appreciate the society of children, the beauty of nature, and the pleasure of mountain solitude. Peacock shared these tastes.

Like several of Peacock's other novels, *Crotchet Castle* has a full cast of ideologically committed characters, some of whom reflect actual persons known to the author. These include friends of Shelley, a poet of unconventional ideas whom Peacock knew since the autumn of 1812. (Shelley left England in 1818 but corresponded regularly with Peacock until his death four years later in Italy.) It was largely through his association with Shelley that the more conservative Peacock came to learn of, and sometimes to mock, the various utopian schemes for worldwide reformation. These appear throughout his novels in dialogue, most prominently in chapter 6 ("Theories") of *Crotchet Castle*. As the author declares there, all such reforms are doomed to failure, among other reasons for want of money.

At the time Peacock was writing *Crotchet Castle*, money and reform were issues that aroused extreme public agitation. Though spared the revolutions that swept through Europe in 1848 (and already rocked the French monarchy in 1830), England was wracked in 1831 by riots and incendiary vandalism. Masses of unenfranchised laborers, whose tradi-tional occupations were destroyed by technological advances (weavers put out of work by power looms, for example), had no other means of expressing their discontent than through violence, mob action, and burnings.

Peacock describes such a group in chapter 18 as they attempt to storm Chainmail Hall under their mythical leader, Captain Swing. A preliminary reform bill finally achieved passage through Parliament in 1832. It was followed by other legislation that alleviated the working conditions of women and children in particular, extended the franchise, and eventually established public schools. Peacock, who did not write of such issues in any of his previous novels, deals only briefly with the workers' discontent in *Crotchet Castle*.

Although Peacock may well be charged with being cold or imperceptive toward the social and intellectual changes of his own century—a criticism that is largely valid—in this regard *Crotchet Castle* does not entirely conform to the author's other works. The novel reflects Peacock's awareness of the importance of earned money in achieving and maintaining position not only in British society but in British thought as well. Political and economic power was shifting from the aristocracy to the middle class, which explains the shift to the more concrete taste of mercantilists that dominated the Victorian period.

As the establishment realigned itself to some extent, the position of women within society and within the power structure as a whole remained controversial. Like Shelley, Peacock favored a greater degree of female intellectual freedom than was commonly vouchsafed to women in his time. He expressed his belief in women's intelligence and potential by creating a series of unusually perceptive heroines, of whom Lady Clarinda in *Crotchet Castle* is the most outstanding example. Even so, however, the specter of marriage as a primarily commercial transaction haunts the novel throughout and is not altogether resolved at the end.

The dominant theme of *Crotchet Castle* is money and the fact that all aspects of society and thought ultimately depend upon it. Peacock's awareness of the pound's importance no doubt made him a valuable employee of the East India Company, even as his kind of literary education based on classical and foreign languages slipped into obscurity.

"Critical Evaluation" by Dennis R. Dean

Further Reading

Burns, Bryan. *The Novels of Thomas Love Peacock*. Totowa, N.J.: Barnes & Noble, 1985. Sound criticism, with unsurprising insights. Includes a good discussion of *Crotchet Castle*.

Butler, Marilyn. *Peacock Displayed: A Satirist in His Context.* London: Routledge & Kegan Paul, 1979. An influential book on Peacock, with acute critical discussions of all seven novels, especially *Crotchet Castle.*

Cavaliero, Glen. "Feasts of Reason: Thomas Love Peacock." In *The Alchemy of Laughter: Comedy in English Fiction.* New York: St. Martin's Press, 2000. Peacock's novels are included in this examination of comedy in English fiction, in which Cavaliero discusses how parody, irony, satire, and other types of humor are evident in these works.

Dawson, Carl. *His Fine Wit: A Study of Thomas Love Peacock.* Berkeley: University of California Press, 1970. A comprehensive survey of Peacock's poetry, nonfictional prose, and novels. Good discussions of the Peacockian novel in general and of the individual novels, including *Crotchet Castle.*

Dirda, Michael. "*Crotchet Castle.*" *The Washington Post,* May 18, 2003. Dirda rereads the novel, praising its "kind of fizzy Victorian comedy" and other characteristics of Peacock's writing.

Kjellin, Hakan. *Talkative Banquets: A Study in the Peacockian Novels of Talk.* Stockholm: Almqvist & Wiksell, 1974. An interesting study of Peacock's relations with dialogue and dramatic traditions. Discusses five of his seven novels, including *Crotchet Castle.*

McKay, Margaret. *Peacock's Progress: Aspects of Artistic Development in the Novels of Thomas Love Peacock.* Stockholm: Almqvist & Wiksell, 1992. Traces Peacock's growth as a novelist through his seven novels.

Peacock, Thomas Love. *Novels.* Edited by David Garnett. 2 vols. London: Rupert Hart-Davis, 1963. Discusses *Crotchet Castle* in volume 2. This edition is recommended for its annotations by both Garnett and Peacock himself.

Vidal, Gore. "Thomas Love Peacock: The Novel of Ideas." In *The Essential Gore Vidal,* edited by Fred Kaplan. New York: Random House, 1999. This collection of fiction, essays, and reviews includes Vidal's appraisals of the work of several writers, including an examination of Peacock's novels. Includes chronology and bibliography.

Crow

Author: Ted Hughes (1930-1998)
First published: 1970
Type of work: Poetry

A reader coming upon Ted Hughes's *Crow* for the first time will realize immediately its forceful, almost savage turning away from English poetic tradition. In its harsh treatment of human relations, religious and moral assumptions, and the function of consciousness in the natural world, *Crow* offers page after page of profoundly raucous poetic rebellion.

Hughes's protagonist is Crow—omnivorous, homely, solitary, and ubiquitous. Borrowing from Celtic mythology, the Old Testament, and various aboriginal legends, the poet creates a rich, potent mythology of his own for this figure. "Two Legends" introduces the book's central concerns. It is a litany of enigmatic statements focusing on muscle and on organ, on force as the origin of life: "Black was the without eye/ Black the within tongue/ Black was the heart/ Black the liver, black the lungs." This incantation of the body's tissues ultimately leads to the soul, black also, the sum here of the struggle to overcome or contain the Genesis-like void from which everything springs. Thus in the second legend of the poem, an "egg of blackness" hatches a crow, the figure that will for

the rest of the collection symbolize alternately the life force and the primal element of chaos. He will speak for both intuition and deception and will be a preserver as much as a destroyer. An ambiguous semideity whose hoarse cry celebrates the cyclic processes of birth and death, the crow is "a black rainbow/ Bent in emptiness/ over emptiness/ But flying" that is (in Hughes's final, unpunctuated line of the poem) immutable and free of social, religious, or scientific attempts to organize or to define elemental realities.

These rational or spiritual attempts are alluded to in many of the poems in *Crow* as Hughes turns Crow's baleful stare upon one conventional system of thought after another. Following the biblical "begat" sequence in "Lineage," Hughes offers a trio of poems describing Crow's birth and his paradoxical reliance upon death. "Examination at the Womb-Door" offers a bleak catechism in which the answer to all but two questions is "Death." The interrogator, never identified, reduces Crow—and by implication all creatures, human beings included—to mere anatomical features possessed ultimately by death: "Who owns these scrawny little feet? . . . this bristly scorched-looking face? . . . these unspeakable guts? . . . these questionable brains?" Yet even thus dissected, Crow is only "held pending trial" by this negating power of death. Although death "owns all of space" and is "stronger" than hope, love, and life, Crow is allowed to pass after realizing that he, embodiment of the life force, can paradoxically overcome or outlast death itself. The stark refrain of "death" throughout the poem in fact makes Crow's final response all the more forceful: "But who is stronger than death?/ Me, evidently."

Here, as elsewhere in *Crow*, the tone is equivocal, tentative. Crow is at one level the spirit of inventiveness, of making do. In both "A Kill" and "Crow and Mama" Crow's experiences resemble nothing so much as crash landings after which he must improvise for survival. He smashes into the "rubbish" of the ground in the former poem and crashes on the moon in the latter, only to crawl out and take up the struggle that Hughes sees as the essential reality.

Crow proves resourceful. In "A Childish Prank" he already thrives on malicious humor, as the poem revises the origins of human sexuality into a quintessentially Hughesian myth of pain and misunderstanding. Pondering the problem of how to invest Adam and Eve with souls, God falls asleep, thereby allowing Crow to invest the parents of humanity with the two writhing halves of a bitten worm, which have been dragging man and woman toward each other ever since. The same supplanting of the spiritual or Godly with the physical and naturalistic takes place in "Crow's First Lesson," in which God tries to teach Crow to say—if not to feel or to understand—"love." Every attempt to speak the word results in the creation of something dangerous or grotesque. A final try produces only the sexual grappling of man and woman. God cannot part them, and Crow flies "guiltily off."

The next several poems in the volume involve Crow's sojourns, following his various adventures throughout a blasted world, where civilizations have risen and fallen against the background of an essentially predatory, immutable natural order. "Crow Alights" brings him to mountains, sea, and stars before he comes upon an old shoe, a rusted garbage can, and other refuse of the twentieth century. Though he scrutinizes the evidence, Crow cannot piece it together or explain the motionlessness of the human face and the hand he perceives through a window. The last five lines of the poem—separate, end-stopped one-line stanzas of clipped or fragmented sentences—effectively communicate the sense of wreckage out of which Crow must somehow derive his existence. "That Moment" describes a similar situation. The human race may have just extinguished itself, but the event is merely another opportunity for Crow, who starts searching for his next meal.

On the other hand, when "Crow Hears Fate Knock on the Door" it is a prophecy he feels inside him, more troubling for his being its source, a feeling "like a steel spring/ Slowly rending the vital fibres." It is because of this unease, perhaps, that Crow begins to question his own conduct in the next poem, "Crow Tyrannosaurus." Like the prehistoric Rex, Crow is bound by the most elemental of laws—"the horrible connection," as one critic puts it, "between creature and creature: kill to live." Observing bird and beast and human around him, Crow wonders at all the deaths "gulped" in order to survive. No sooner does he consider the morality of such a natural order than he is compelled by it to kill again. He may wish to change, to refine himself out of the blood and guts of creation, but he cannot escape his design and function. Kill-and-eat mechanism that he is, Crow finds himself stabbing at grubs even as he questions the action. He survives the dinosaur and may outlast humanity, but not through any transcending of his given role.

Nevertheless, Crow does seem to develop something like a conscience. "Conscience" cannot be understood in its religious sense but rather as Crow's coming to terms with the consequences of his actions, both for himself and for others. Even in a poem such as "Crow's Theology" Hughes does not allow the presumably benign realization of God's love to go uncontested. Just as he cannot keep himself from stabbing the grub earlier, Crow must meditate fiercely upon this God and his relationship with the rest of Creation. If God "speaks" Crow's language and Crow's mere existence is somehow a form of divine revelation, as the poem has it, then "what/ Loved the stones and spoke stone?" What, indeed, speaks and loves the silences of creation, including the silence of death? Crow's answer, arrived at through the only philosophy he can know, is that there are two Gods, one much bigger than the other, loving his enemies and having "all the weapons."

As if to test this hypothesis, Crow mounts a challenge in "Crow's Fall," Hughes's rendering of Lucifer's ill-fated aspirations. Here, Crow is described as having once been white, an angelic figure that decides that the sun is "too white" and so tries to attack and defeat it. Crow summons all his powers, but the sun only brightens at this futile assault, leaving Crow so charred that even his voice is left scorched. Like Lucifer, Crow is not killed; also like Lucifer, he manages out of his pride to fashion his own version of events: "Up there . . . Where white is black and black is white, I won." Also like Lucifer, Crow is a "light bringer"; his lessons in endurance and in the rapaciousness of existence are bitter epiphanies.

After his fall, Crow embarks on a series of experiments

with language, testing his powers of perception and creation against the memory of his disastrous try at "love." He discovers in "Crow Goes Hunting" that words bound away like hares, fly off like starlings. He concocts other words to shoot at those escaping him, but none stays within his control. Crow gazes after them "speechless with admiration," beginning to intuit the vexed relation of words to the things they name.

The fablelike "Crow's Elephant Totem Song" dramatizes a similar disquiet. The elephant, originally "delicate and small," is set upon by hyenas maddened with envy and torn into pieces that they carry away into their respective "hells." At the Resurrection—in this tale, not Christ's Second Coming—the elephant reassembles himself: "Deadfall feet," "toothproof body," "bulldozing bones," and "aged eyes, that were wicked and wise." Like Crow's fall from an arrogant purity (whiteness), the elephant's death-and-rebirth into a "wicked and wise" homeliness provides a morality play for Hughes, one based on the law of the jungle or veldt rather than on Judaic or Christian tradition.

From "Crow's Playmates" on, the book rushes to its conclusion, as scene after scene has Crow creating and miscreating. All Crow can do is watch his "works" take on lives of their own and then try to survive the destruction they cause. After he creates gods to keep him company, each tears from him some part of his power until he is but a "remnant, his own leftover, the spat-out scrag." A parallel event occurs in "Crow Blacker Than Ever." Here God and Adam, disgusted with each other, turn toward their respective paradises—heaven and Eve—when Crow mischievously nails together the two realms. The agony this produces, God and humanity unwillingly connected, is what Crow deems his "Creation," victoriously flying "the black flag of himself." The apocalyptic "Crow's Last Stand" begins with a "burning" that Hughes breaks across several lines until reaching what the sun cannot burn any further. The sun "rages and chars" against this last obstacle, obviously an emblem of survival and resilience in the midst of catastrophe: "Crow's eye-pupil, in the tower of its scorched fort." This eye, as pure perception, may be the final, irreducible image of consciousness in Hughes's mythology.

Hughes said his idea in *Crow* was to reduce his style "to the simplest clear cell—then regrow a wholeness and richness organically from that point." The collection's mythic power, brutal diction, and sardonic bleakness of vision make it one of the truly landmark works in post-World War II English poetry. Whether attracted to or repulsed by these qualities, no poet or reader of poetry can claim not to hear the dark echoes of Hughes's *Crow* in the literature of other writers since this collection's appearance.

James Scruton

Further Reading

Feinstein, Elaine. *Ted Hughes: The Life of a Poet*. London: Weidenfeld & Nicolson, 2001. Feinstein's biography recounts the events of Hughes's life, including his marriage to poet Sylvia Plath, providing a generally sympathetic portrait of Hughes.

Gifford, Terry, and Neil Roberts. *Ted Hughes: A Critical Study*. Winchester, Mass.: Faber & Faber, 1981. A thematic approach to the poet's works, with special attention to the relation of humanity to nature in Hughes's "animal" poems.

Hamilton, Ian. *A Poetry Chronicle: Essays and Reviews*. Winchester, Mass.: Faber & Faber, 1973. An example of how widely divergent the critical responses to *Crow* have been. Hamilton points out the "excesses" of the book, such as its "bludgeoning" diction.

Moulin, Joanny, ed. *Ted Hughes: Alternative Horizons*. New York: Routledge, 2004. Published after Hughes's death, this collection of essays seeks to reevaluate the poet's work, with several pieces emphasizing its autobiographical elements. The relationship of Hughes's work to the poetry of his estranged wife, Sylvia Plath, receives special attention.

Sagar, Keith. *The Art of Ted Hughes*. 2d ed. New York: Cambridge University Press, 1980. The chapter on *Crow* is one of the best general introductions to the volume. Provides clear explanations of various mythic sources and helpful extracts from Hughes's essays and interviews.

_____. *The Laughter of Foxes: A Study of Ted Hughes*. Rev. 2d ed. Liverpool, England: Liverpool University Press, 2006. An in-depth examination of Hughes's life and poetry, in which Sagar demonstrates how Hughes's life is revealed in his writings and correspondence. Includes an appendix recounting the background story of *Crow*'s writing and publication.

Scigaj, Leonard M. *The Poetry of Ted Hughes*. Iowa City: University of Iowa Press, 1986. Examines the aesthetic and philosophical purposes behind Hughes's most-criticized elements in *Crow* and in other Hughes volumes, from violent subject matter to awkward structure.

Thwaite, Anthony. *Twentieth-Century English Poetry*. London: Heinemann, 1978. A brief but balanced assessment of *Crow* in terms of its impact on contemporary poetry and its position in the Hughes canon. Thwaite cites the specific shortcomings of several negative critical reactions to the themes and the forms of *Crow*.

The Crucible

Author: Arthur Miller (1915-2005)
First produced: 1953; first published, 1953
Type of work: Drama
Type of plot: Historical
Time of plot: 1692
Locale: Salem, Massachusetts

Principal characters:
THE REVEREND SAMUEL PARRIS, Salem's minister
BETTY PARRIS, his daughter
TITUBA, the Parris family's household slave
JOHN PROCTOR, a respected farmer
ELIZABETH PROCTOR, his wife
MARY WARREN, their servant
ABIGAIL WILLIAMS, Parris's niece and former servant to
   the Proctor family
DEPUTY GOVERNOR DANFORTH, chief magistrate
JUDGE HATHORNE, his assistant
THE REVEREND JOHN HALE, scholar of the supernatural
FRANCIS NURSE, a farmer
REBECCA NURSE, his wife and a beloved matriarch
GILES COREY, an old but vigorous farmer

The Story:

The Reverend Samuel Parris prays over his daughter, who lies stricken with a nameless malady. As he prays, he is angered by the interruption of his Negro slave, Tituba, whom he brought with him from the island of Barbados. Parris is frightened and furious, for he discovered his daughter Betty, Tituba, and some of the village girls dancing in the woods. Now two of the girls, Betty and Ruth Putnam, are ill, and witchcraft is rumored about the village. His daughter Betty and his ward and niece, Abigail Williams, were been participants in a secret and sinful act. Parris feels his position as minister to the community of Salem is threatened. Moreover, he suspects that more than dancing took place.

The frightened Parris sends for the Reverend John Hale, a reputed scholar familiar with the manifestations of witchcraft. While waiting for Hale to arrive, the parishioners reveal the petty grievances and jealousies hidden beneath the veneer of piety of the Puritan community. Parris feels that the community failed to meet its financial obligations to him. He suspects John Proctor, a respected farmer, of undermining his authority. Proctor resents Parris for preaching of nothing but hellfire and the money owed to the parish. Thomas Putnam, a grasping landholder, disputes the boundaries of his neighbors' farms. Ann Putnam lost seven babies at childbirth, and she suspects witchcraft of mothers with large families, most especially Rebecca Nurse, who has eleven healthy children.

Amid this discontent, the learned Hale arrives with his books of weighty wisdom. Under Hale's close questioning concerning the girls' illicit activities in the woods, Abigail

turns the blame away from herself by accusing Tituba of witchcraft. Terrified by the threat of hanging, Tituba confesses to conjuring up the devil. Putnam asks Tituba if she saw the old beggar Sarah Good or Goodwife Osborne with the devil. Sensing her survival at stake, Tituba names both women as companions of the devil. Abigail picks up the accusations and adds the names of other villagers. Soon the rest of the girls begin hysterically chanting out the names of village men and women seen in company with the devil.

At the Proctor farm, Proctor tells Elizabeth that Abigail revealed that the dancing in the woods was only "sport." When Proctor hesitates to go to the authorities with this information, Elizabeth quietly reminds her husband of his past infidelities with Abigail. Their argument is interrupted by the arrival of Hale, who comes to inquire into the sanctity of the Proctor home. Elizabeth suspects that Abigail means to destroy her so that she might become Proctor's wife. Mary Warren, another of the afflicted girls and the Proctors' servant, returns from court where she gave testimony. She gives Elizabeth a rag doll that she made in court.

At this point, officers of the court arrive at the Proctor farm with an arrest warrant for Elizabeth on the charge of witchcraft. They search the house for poppets (dolls) and find the one Mary gave to Elizabeth. They discover a pin in its stomach and take it for proof that Abigail's stomach pains are the result of Elizabeth's witchcraft. Elizabeth is taken away in chains. Proctor confronts Mary, demanding that she tell the court the truth. At the court of Deputy Governor Danforth, Giles Corey, Francis Nurse, and John Proctor present evidence to save their wives from the charge of witchcraft. Danforth confiscates the list of names brought by Francis testifying to Rebecca Nurse's good character and marks the petitioners for arrest. Giles refuses to name the people who back him, so the deputy governor has Corey arrested. When Proctor brings Mary to court to recant, Abigail pretends to be possessed by the evil spirits brought by Mary. Proctor accuses the girls of lying and confesses to committing adultery with Abigail. Danforth refuses to believe that Abigail can be guilty of so great a sin, but Proctor swears that Abigail was dismissed as the Proctors' servant by Elizabeth because she knew of the affair. Danforth brings Elizabeth to the court and questions her regarding Proctor's adultery with Abigail. Elizabeth lies to Danforth to save Proctor's name and ironically condemns him as a perjurer.

In the Salem jail, Parris and Hale beg Rebecca and Proctor to confess to witchcraft in order to save their lives. Hale and Parris realize too late that the accused were victims of the girls' hysteria and the townspeople's private grievances. Rebecca remains firm in her convictions, refusing to confess, but Proctor wavers. Proctor thinks that in lying to the court, he will be only adding a lie to the sin of adultery. Full of self-contempt, Proctor confesses to witchcraft. Having confessed, he refuses to let the court keep his signed confession. He recants his confession and goes to the gallows to save his name.

Critical Evaluation:

Arthur Miller's *The Crucible* was first presented at the Martin Beck Theatre in New York on January 22, 1953, when Senator Joseph McCarthy's House Committee on Un-American Activities was casting a pall over the arts in America. Writers, especially those associated with the theater and the film industry, came under the particular scrutiny of the committee. Those who were blacklisted as Communists were banned from employment. Guilt was a matter of accusation, of being named. The parallels between these two periods of social and political persecution in American history were obvious to playgoers in the 1950's. In both the witch trials and the committee hearings, people were summoned before an unchallengeable authority, interrogated, intimidated, and frequently coerced into the betrayal of others in order to escape being persecuted themselves. Miller's work may also be examined for its intrinsic merit rather than for its status as a political tract. With the passage of time, it becomes clear that *The Crucible* is more than a polemic. It transcends its topical boundaries and speaks of universals common to the human condition. In *The Crucible*, Miller balances the social tragedy of the Salem community against the personal trag-

edy of John Proctor, whose triumph over self restores a sense of moral order in a community torn apart by ignorance, hysteria, and malice. The superstitious ignorance of the Salem villagers transforms a youthful escapade into a diabolic act. Despite Ann Putnam's staunch religious beliefs, she admits to sending her daughter Ruth to Tituba to conjure up the souls of her dead babies so that Ruth, her one remaining daughter, may discover the cause of their seemingly unnatural deaths. Abigail Williams's motives are darker yet. She seeks Tituba's aid to put a curse on Elizabeth Proctor's life so that she can replace her in John Proctor's affections. The villagers' religious beliefs are so suffused with superstition that the villagers readily accept the notion that the girls are bewitched. No one questions the assumption that the girls are under the spell of supernatural forces except Proctor, whose challenge takes the form of oblique dissent, and Rebecca Nurse, who asserts that teenage girls often go through "silly seasons."

When the Reverend Parris discovers the girls cavorting in the forest, it is not surprising that they feign illness as a means of hiding from the accusations of their superstitious elders, for they break terrible taboos. When Abigail seizes upon the device of accusing others to deflect blame away from herself, she sets in motion the forces of envy, greed, and malice. As the hysteria spreads, the townspeople turn on one another, profiting from their neighbors' misfortunes, wreaking vengeance for real or imagined grievances, substituting spite and fear for love and trust.

The court, an extension of the governing theocracy, is meant to ensure stability and social order. It is tragically ironic that as the court grows in power, the community disintegrates. Crops rot in the fields, cows bellow for want of milking, and abandoned children beg in the streets. Having fled England to escape intolerance and persecution, the Puritans establish a community so narrow and closed that deviation from the norm is regarded as sinful and dissent as diabolic. As *The Crucible* so forcefully dramatizes, such a community must implode. Narrow minds cannot be allowed to prevail over the Proctors and Nurses of this world, who are condemned for their generosity of spirit.

Proctor is a reluctant hero. He knows that the court is deceived by Abigail's seeming virtue. He hesitates to expose the fraudulent proceedings, however; to do so means he must reveal his adulterous affair. When he finally bares his heart to the court, his confession is in vain. Unable to believe that he was deceived, Deputy Governor Danforth sends for Elizabeth to discover if she supports Proctor's charge. She knows that her husband is a proud man who values his good name, so she denies her knowledge of the affair, unaware that in telling her first lie she condemns Proctor as a perjurer. It is at this point that Proctor breaks with the community, damning the court's proceedings and all the hypocrites associated with it, not unaware that he includes himself within the compass of his curse.

Faced with hanging, Proctor protests to Elizabeth that for him to "mount the gibbet like a saint" is a pretense. Sainthood is for the likes of Rebecca, not Proctor. Yet Proctor refuses to let the court keep his signed confession, for it is hard evidence of a lie. Like his predecessors, Oedipus and Hamlet, Proctor insists on the truth even if it means his destruction. Rather than sanctify his name on the altar of duplicity, he becomes a martyr for truth, and in doing so he preserves the sanctity of individual freedom.

In *All My Sons* (1947) and *Death of a Salesman* (1949), Miller explored the erosion of family structure in the wake of materialism, and audiences were moved to compassion. In *The Crucible*, his exploration of the destruction of freedom by an ignorant and despotic society moved many viewers to anger. The themes were too close to home and, for Miller, ironically prophetic. In 1956, summoned before the House Committee on Un-American Activities, Miller was cited for contempt of Congress for refusing to name names.

David Sundstrand

Further Reading

Abbotson, Susan C. W. *Critical Companion to Arthur Miller: A Literary Reference to His Life and Work.* New York: Facts On File, 2007. Includes a biography and dictionary-style entries about Miller's works and related subjects, such as the concepts, people, places, and genres in his plays. The entries about his works provide synopses, critical commentary, initial reviews, and performance histories.

Bigsby, Christopher. *Arthur Miller: A Critical Study.* New York: Cambridge University Press, 2005. Bigsby, who has written extensively about Miller, provides in-depth examinations of all of Miller's work, including a chapter on *The Crucible*.

Bloom, Harold, ed. *Arthur Miller's "The Crucible."* New ed. New York: Bloom's Literary Criticism, 2008. Collection of critical essays, including a historian's view of the play's depiction of the Salem witch trials, a feminist interpretation, a comparison of *The Crucible* to Henrik Ibsen's *En folkefiende* (1882; *An Enemy of the People*, 1890), and Miller's own discussion, "*The Crucible* in History."

Carson, Neil. *Arthur Miller.* 2d ed. New York: Palgrave Macmillan, 2008. Provides critical analyses of all of Miller's work, including a chapter on *The Crucible*.

Johnson, Claudia D., and Vernon E. Johnson. *Understanding "The Crucible": A Student Casebook to Issues, Sources, and Historical Documents.* Westport, Conn.: Greenwood Press, 1998. Provides a literary analysis of the play and numerous primary documents describing the religious hysteria in seventeenth century New England, witchcraft in Salem, Massachusetts, and the Communist witch hunts of the 1950's.

Martine, James J. *The Crucible: Politics, Property, and Pretense.* New York: Twayne, 1993. Analyzes the play from a variety of perspectives, viewing it as a response to the 1950's Red Scare, a milestone in the development of Miller's work, an example of the tragic genre, a part of the American theater, and the basis for later adaptations.

Mason, Jeffrey D. *Stone Tower: The Political Theater of Arthur Miller.* Ann Arbor: University of Michigan Press, 2008. Argues that Miller is essentially a political playwright and that *The Crucible* examines personal issues in political terms.

Miller, Arthur. *Conversations with Arthur Miller.* Edited by Matthew C. Roudane. Jackson: University Press of Mississippi, 1987. Miller discusses his work with various interviewers. Includes two useful discussions of *The Crucible*.

Warshow, Robert. "The Liberal Conscience in *The Crucible*." In *The Immediate Experience: Movies, Comics, Theatre, and Other Aspects of Popular Culture.* New York: Doubleday, 1962. Warshow considers the work a wooden political polemic, historically inaccurate, and without a central point.

Cry, the Beloved Country

Author: Alan Paton (1903-1988)
First published: 1948
Type of work: Novel
Type of plot: Social realism
Time of plot: Mid-twentieth century
Locale: South Africa

Principal characters:
THE REVEREND STEPHEN KUMALO, a Zulu clergyman
GERTRUDE, his sister
ABSALOM, his son
MSIMANGU, his friend
MR. JARVIS, his white benefactor

The Story:

The letter brings fear to the hearts of the Reverend Stephen Kumalo and his wife. To a Zulu, letters are rare and frightening. Once opened, they can never be closed again or their contents forgotten. Kumalo waits until he can control his fear before he opens the letter from Johannesburg telling him that his sister is sick and needs his help. The trip will be costly for a poor Zulu clergyman, but he has to go. Perhaps there he can also find their son Absalom, who was not heard from since he left the village. Stephen and his wife know in their hearts that, in Johannesburg, Absalom succumbed to the evil resulting from the white man's breaking up the tribes and compelling black men to work in the mines.

Taking their small savings, Kumalo journeys to the city. He goes first to the mission and meets Msimangu, who wrote the letter. Msimangu is also a clergyman, working for his people in the city as Kumalo works in the country. He sorrowfully tells Kumalo that his sister Gertrude is a prostitute and a dealer in illegal liquor. She and her child are impoverished, even though she once made much money from her trade. Kumalo locates Gertrude, with the help of Msimangu, and finds her willing to go with him to the temporary rooms he found with a good woman. When his business is finished, she and the child will go with him to his home, away from temptation.

Before looking for his son, Kumalo visits his brother John, a successful merchant and a politician who is under surveillance by the police for his ability to stir up the blacks. John is discreet; he takes no chance of being arrested and losing his business. Many of the black leaders sacrifice everything to help their people, but not John. Expediency is his only thought. He left the church and turns a deaf ear to his brother's pleas that he return to a holier life.

Kumalo begins his search for Absalom. With Msimangu, he searches everywhere. Each place they visit adds to his fear, for it becomes clear from their investigation that Absalom is engaged in stealing, drinking, and worse. Often they walk for miles, for the black leaders are urging their people to boycott the buses in order to get the fares reduced. Kumalo learns that Absalom was in the company of John's son, and both of them were in and out of trouble. The trail leads to a reformatory, but Absalom was dismissed shortly before because of his good behavior. The white teacher of the reformatory joins Kumalo in his search, because the boy's behavior reflects on his training. Next, Kumalo finds a girl who, soon to bear Absalom's child, waits to marry him. The old man knows at once that if Absalom is not found, the girl must return to the hills with him and make her home there.

At last, he finds Absalom in prison. Absalom, John's son, and another boy robbed and killed Arthur Jarvis, a white man who befriended the blacks. Brokenhearted, the old man talks with his son. He can tell that Absalom does not truly repent but only says the right things out of fear. His one ray of goodness is his desire to marry the young woman in order to give his unborn child a name. Kumalo weeps for his son, but he weeps also for the wife and children, the father and mother of the slain man.

At the trial, Absalom is defended by a lawyer found by Kumalo's friends. The plea is that the murder was not planned and that the boy shot in fear. The judge, a good man, weighs all the evidence and pronounces a verdict of guilty; the punishment, death by hanging. John's son and the other boy are acquitted for lack of evidence. The verdict is a gross miscarriage of justice, but John is more powerful than Kumalo.

Before Kumalo leaves Johannesburg, he arranges for the marriage between his son and the girl. Then he starts home, taking the girl and Gertrude's child with him. Gertrude disappears the night before they are to leave, but no one knows where she went. She talked of becoming a nun, but Kumalo fears that she went back to her old life; Gertrude likes laughter and fun.

At home, the people welcome their minister, showering love and blessings upon him. The crops are poor that season, and people are starving. Kumalo prays for his people and works for them. He knows that they must learn to use the land wisely, but he is helpless to guide them. He goes to their chief to ask for cooperation, but the chief is concerned only for himself and his family.

Hope comes to the people in the form of a child. He is the grandchild of Mr. Jarvis, the father of the man Absalom murdered. Mr. Jarvis always helped the black people, and, after his son's death, he gave all of his time to the work started by his murdered son. He sends milk for the children and brings in an agricultural demonstrator to help the people restore fertility to the soil. Mr. Jarvis builds a dam and sends for good seed. His grandchild becomes Kumalo's friend; through him, the white man learns of the needs of the people. Kumalo, whose son killed his benefactor's son, is at first ashamed to face Mr. Jarvis. When they meet, few words are exchanged, but each reads the heart of the other and understands the sorrow and grief there.

The bishop comes and tells Kumalo that it would be best for him to leave the hills and the valley, to go where his son's crime is unknown. Kumalo grieves and stands silent. Before the bishop leaves, a letter comes from Mr. Jarvis, thanking Kumalo for his friendship and offering to build his people a new church. The bishop feels ashamed.

When the day comes for Absalom's execution, Kumalo goes into the mountains. He went there before when struggling with fear. Mr. Jarvis, knowing the torment that is in his soul, bids him to go in peace. When the dawn comes, Kumalo cries out for his son. He cries, too, for his land and his people. When will dawn come for them?

Critical Evaluation:

Cry, the Beloved Country is a novel of social protest—a protest against apartheid, the policy of racial segregation that existed in South Africa. When the Reverend Stephen Kumalo travels from his home in Ndotsheni to the capital city of Johannesburg to find his missing family members, he encounters a disintegration of tribal customs and family life. Kumalo learns quickly that the whites, through the policy of apartheid, have disrupted African values and social order. He notes that city life leads to a demoralized lifestyle of poverty and crime for the natives. Even the Reverend Theophilus Msimangu, a priest who offers his assistance to Kumalo, believes that this disintegration of social values cannot be mended. Msimangu does, however, envision hope for "when white men and black men . . . desiring only the good of their country, come together to work for it." The land, in this case, South Africa, is the center of this novel. As the land becomes divided and eroded, so, too, do the people who live on it. Because James Jarvis and Kumalo reach a shared responsibility

for their actions and thoughts as they attempt to understand the loss of their sons, Alan Paton believes that the country of South Africa has hope for restoration of its values and order in its new generation, especially in the sons of Arthur Jarvis and Absalom Kumalo.

Cry, the Beloved Country is structured in three sections. To depict the land as the central focus of this novel, Paton opens chapter 1 with a poetic reverence for "the fairest valleys of Africa." Here the connection between land and people becomes evident. Book 1 points to the erosion of the land as the people leave their native soil. This section focuses on the native soil of the blacks, Kumalo in particular. It is difficult to maintain the beauty and fertility of the land when the tribal natives head for the promises of the city. The land, then, stands desolate. This deterioration is further illustrated in the shantytowns dishearteningly discovered by Kumalo as he enters Johannesburg.

The opening lines are repeated in chapter 18, which begins book 2. The melodic description of the land is now in reference to the whites' partition of South Africa, namely, James Jarvis. The land is not depleted, but well tended. The openness and vitality of the land offer a sheer contrast to the depiction contained in book 1. James Jarvis's farm, the finest one of the countryside, "stands high above Ndotsheni." Paton thus symbolically portrays the destructiveness and divisiveness of apartheid in the ownership of land.

The third section holds a twofold purpose. Chapter 30 brings to light the drought that covers the land of Ndotsheni. Saddened by the land's deterioration, Kumalo knows he must find a way to restore its beauty and fertility. Subsequently, this is assisted by a brewing rainstorm and, most notably, by the generosity of James Jarvis, who hires an agricultural demonstrator to ready plans for tillage. Symbolically, Paton realizes Msimangu's words of hope that only love "has power completely." The reconstruction of the land becomes a joint venture between Kumalo and James Jarvis, between black and white. Taking responsibility for one's actions has brought a new understanding and renewed principles for the good of all humanity.

Stylistically, Paton parallels character to character and action to action to dramatize the social ills of South Africa and its native people, while contrasting these vivid portraits to the lives of the white South Africans. As noted previously, the novel's three sections structurally suggest the two different worlds of Africans and Europeans, then offer a solution and a hope in the third book in the coming together of the two fathers. The safe, calm village life of Kumalo and the farm life of Jarvis parallel the city life in Johannesburg, a city of evil, corruption, and moral inequities for both blacks and whites. The need for truth and justice is paralleled by Kumalo's search for his son Absalom, whom he finds in prison, with Jarvis's news of his son's death. Each father must come to terms with a loss. Although paralleled, it is Jarvis who claims an affinity, "for there is something between" them. Ironically, it is Kumalo's son who shoots and kills Arthur Jarvis. Paton allows this parallel to function in two ways: first, to reflect the suffering of each father; second, to show that both Absalom and Arthur fall victim to apartheid. Paralleling, then, is more than just a structural device, but rather a focus on the issue of race relations in South Africa.

Paton uses unique literary techniques to enhance the poignancy of his themes. He employs intercalary chapters to dramatize the historical setting of the novel. These intercalary chapters serve as Paton's social criticism of the divisive political and social order in South Africa. Paton also uses dashes to indicate dialogue, allowing not only for the realistic portrayal of conversation, but also for the rapid dramatic actions among characters. This simple literary technique generates the movement of plot and points directly to the language. Diction remains simple, yet eloquent in its delivery by the various characters. Kumalo speaks in a mildly solemn language emphasizing his ecclesiastic background; the Reverend Msimangu often speaks in an oratory fashion to proclaim his views. John Kumalo uses the language of violence to demonstrate his anger over apartheid and his love for power as a black leader in Johannesburg. The tribal language brings the novel credence and revelation of a people rooted in tradition and honor.

In 1946, Paton began writing *Cry, the Beloved Country*. Less than four months later, he finished it. Born in South Africa, Paton knew firsthand the tragedy that marked his homeland. He noted that although the story is not true, it is a social record of the truth. *Cry, the Beloved Country* is a classic work of world literature, not only for bringing to light a destructive political system but also for depicting the humanity among people that can be lost in the struggle for justice and power. *Cry, the Beloved Country* is a cry for one's land, a cry for justice, a cry for understanding, and, certainly, a cry for hope. Indeed, this novel speaks for all lost generations who seek direction in a dark world.

"Critical Evaluation" by Carmen Carrillo

Further Reading

Alexander, Peter F. *Alan Paton: A Biography.* New York: Oxford University Press, 1994. A particularly engaging, well-documented, and enormous biography. Provides important background information on the genesis of the novel in chapters 12 and 13.

Bloom, Harold, ed. *Alan Paton's "Cry, the Beloved Country."* Philadelphia: Chelsea House, 2004. A guide designed to help students understand the novel. Includes a biographical sketch of Paton, list of characters, summary and analysis, and essays examining the novel from a variety of perspectives.

Brutus, Dennis. "Protest Against Apartheid." In *Protest and Conflict in African Literature*, edited by Cosmo Pieterse and Donald Munro. New York: Africana, 1969. A notable and substantive critique of *Cry, the Beloved Country* from a black South African perspective. Argues that the novel's simple, direct protest against apartheid is not forceful enough against the monstrosity of racism.

Callan, Edward. *Alan Paton.* Rev. ed. Boston: Twayne, 1982. Contains ten chapters based on Paton's own 1981 volume of autobiography, *Towards the Mountain.* Provides significant general background on Paton's life and times and a critical evaluation of his fiction, drama, biography, and poetry, including a full chapter on *Cry, the Beloved Country.*

_____. *"Cry, the Beloved Country": A Novel of South Africa.* Boston: Twayne, 1991. A supplement to Callan's 1982 study (above), focused on the novel's historical and literary context. Includes an eight-chapter critical reading and interpretation of the novel.

Chiwengo, Ngwarsungu. *Understanding "Cry, the Beloved Country": A Student Casebook to Issues, Sources, and Historical Documents.* Westport, Conn.: Greenwood Press, 2007. A compilation of supplemental materials providing background information about apartheid and social and economic conditions in a segregated South Africa. In addition to essays providing a literary analysis of the book and placing it within its historical context there is a chronology of South African history, as well as numerous primary texts, including excerpts from books, diaries, and articles.

Coetzee, J. M. "South African Liberals: Alan Paton, Helen Suzman." In *Stranger Shores: Literary Essays, 1986-1999.* New York: Viking, 2001. This collection of literary essays by Coetzee, a South African novelist who has won the Nobel Prize in Literature and two Man Booker Prizes, includes a brief discussion of Paton, placing him within the tradition of South African liberalism.

Paton, Jonathan. "Comfort in Desolation." In *International Literature in English: Essays on the Major Writers*, edited by Robert L. Ross. New York: Garland, 1991. Written by his younger son, a general discussion of Alan

Paton's work. Identifies a Christian ethic that calls for comfort in desolation as the most significant element of *Cry, the Beloved Country.*

Van der Vlies, Andrew Edward. "Whose Beloved Country? Alan Paton and the Hypercanonical." In *South African*

Textual Cultures: White, Black, Read All Over. New York: Manchester University Press, 2007. Van der Vlies explores the publication, promotion, and reception of a series of South African writers and their works between 1883 and 2005, including *Cry, the Beloved Country.*

The Crying of Lot 49

Author: Thomas Pynchon (1937-   )
First published: 1966
Type of work: Novel
Type of plot: Dark comedy
Time of plot: One summer between 1963 and 1966
Locale: Northern California

Principal characters:
OEDIPA MAAS, a young woman, and coexecutor of an estate
PIERCE INVERARITY, Oedipa's former lover, a millionaire, now dead
METZGER, a lawyer, and coexecutor of Pierce's will
MIKE FALLOPIAN, a right-wing political extremist
RANDOLPH DRIBLETTE, a stage director
STANLEY KOTEKS, an engineer
JOHN NEFASTIS, an inventor
ZAPF, a bookseller
GENGHIS COHEN, a stamp collector
EMORY BORTZ, a scholar and professor

The Story:

Oedipa Maas receives a letter informing her that she has been named coexecutor of the estate of her former lover, millionaire Pierce Inverarity. She goes to San Narciso to meet Metzger, a lawyer and the estate's coexecutor, and first sees him at the Echo Court Motel. Also at the motel are members of a rock band called the Paranoids. Oedipa is seduced by Metzger after the two watch a television rerun of Metzger playing Baby Igor as a child film star.

Oedipa and Metzger go to an electronic-music bar called the Scope several nights later. She meets Mike Fallopian, an enthusiast for an extreme far-right political group. He explains to her a strange delivery made to the bar by a private mail courier. In the restroom, Oedipa sees a postbox with a post-horn symbol, beginning her discovery of Tristero, a mysterious dark group behind a struggle for private and secret postal delivery in the United States and in Europe.

Next, Oedipa and Metzger go to Fangoso Lagoons, near San Narciso, to see one of Pierce's property developments. The two executors soon meet Manny Di Presso, an attorney for a gangster who had a corrupt business deal with Pierce that involves the bones of former U.S. soldiers and, later, the dumping of some of those bones in the project's la-

goons to attract divers. Later, the Paranoids tell Oedipa of *The Courier's Tragedy,* a Jacobean revenge tragedy by Richard Warfinger that director Randolph Driblette is producing at a little theater (also a part of Pierce's estate). Metzger and Oedipa attend the play, which includes a murder: Men in black murder an Italian Renaissance courier then throw his body in a lake in a scene that uses the name Tristero, a name she remembers from the bar. Oedipa interviews Driblette after the performance, but he refuses to clarify the origin of the idea for the black-clothed Tristero assassins. He does confirm, however, that they are not part of the original text of *The Courier's Tragedy.*

Oedipa attends a Yoyodyne stockholders meeting because Pierce had held stock in the company. Stanley Koteks, a Yoyodyne employee, tells her about John Nefastis, who had invented a perpetual motion machine. Oedipa then tries to locate the edition of Warfinger's plays that could lead to Tristero. She goes to Zapf, a used-books store, to look for the play, but the store owner says he has no copies. She then decides to visit Berkeley to see Nefastis, but before she leaves she visits Mr. Thoth, a ninety-one-year-old man who remembers that his father had told him about mysterious black marauders who murdered Pony Express riders in the American West in the nineteenth century. Thoth, who links this tale to the classic anarchists of Porky Pig cartoons of the 1930's, is wearing his father's old ring, which features the same post-horn symbol that Oedipa had seen at the bar; the ring, she is told, had been cut from the finger of one of the black marauders. Oedipa then consults Genghis Cohen, an eminent stamp collector, about Pierce's own stamp collection. In this collection they find a number of mysterious printed stamps containing black figures, post-horn watermarks, and other ominous marks.

Oedipa, back in Berkeley, buys a copy of the Warfinger text and discovers that it does not contain a reference to Tristero; the text, however, does contain a footnote about a corrupt alternate version of the text (which might contain the reference). She also tries to see the Nefastis machine, but fails. Nefastis instead explains to her the nature of entropy; for example, he tells her that information could become more unclear as it recedes into history. She next wanders through San Francisco at night, mulling over the mystery of Tristero and stumbling over repeated post-horn symbols and mentions of W.A.S.T.E. (We Await Silent Tristero's Empire). She posts a letter via W.A.S.T.E. for a dying old sailor and follows—but to no avail—the courier who picks it up.

Oedipa leaves San Francisco to visit her psychiatrist, Dr. Hilarius, and discovers that he has gone mad. He reveals his Nazi past and fears he is being attacked by Israeli agents. Oedipa helps disarm him and then talks to her husband, Wendell "Mucho" Maas, who is staffing a radio station's mobile unit. Oedipa sees her relationship with her husband slipping away.

Oedipa returns to San Narciso to meet Emory Bortz, the scholar who has edited Warfinger's works. They have long discussions about the mystery of Tristero. She later visits Cohen a second time. He tells her that Pierce's stamp collection (which contains mysterious misprinted stamps) is going to be auctioned off as lot no. 49. Later, Oedipa, at the auction, waits to see a mysterious bidder, possibly an agent of Tristero, who is seeking to buy Pierce's mysterious stamps and to possibly hide or destroy them.

Critical Evaluation:

Thomas Pynchon's short novel *The Crying of Lot 49* puts a comic finger on the tensions that racked modern America in 1964, tensions that continue to be central to the dark comedy that defines America today. On one hand, the novel presents the rich and exotic chaos of the freest country on Earth. On the other hand, the novel probes the psyche of Americans whose longing for meaning extends in the manic directions of over-simplicity, conspiracy, and paranoia in a world that seems to be fragmenting. The story is rendered with a richness of comic invention that creates for the reader a jagged border between laughter and terror.

In form the novel qualifies as a Menippean satire, marked by being loose, digressive, and fairly corrosive. Oedipa Maas wanders through the strangeness of Northern California, and her search for the elusive Tristero and its W.A.S.T.E. postal system is frequently interrupted by vignettes of strange lives and bits of history that may or may not be connected to the central narrative. These vignettes sometimes hang on to the central narrative only by analogies that verge on the surreal; Pynchon often offers these analogies with a scientific tone. For example, Oedipa meets John Nefastis, who has invented a box he claims can separate hot and cold molecules to produce energy via heat differential. This means that information would equal power, but Oedipa cannot make the machine function any more than she can sort out the confusing and uncertain data about the Tristero.

The novel is rich with comic names: Dr. Hilarius, a Nazi psychiatrist; Manny Di Presso, a lawyer; Mike Fallopian, a right-wing believer. It is rich in strange comic moments, such as Oedipa getting caught up in a dance at a Deaf-Mute Society convention where couples dance to their inner music elegantly, and do so without colliding or missing a step.

The novel centers on the struggle to make order and sense of chaos. This struggle is epitomized by Oedipa's attempts to link all the strange hints and indicators that arise during her role as Pierce Inverarity's executor. The story presents all sorts of evidence, but that evidence is fragmentary and uncertain, and it toys with the fringes of paranoia. The fear that this evidence may be nothing more than a sort of revenge on Oedipa leads to her frenzied thoughts about her own abilities to make sense. Much of this frenzy is summed up in a painting she recalls. The painting depicts ethereal blond women in a tower, embroidering vast amounts of clothes that spill out of the tower to become the world. This surrealist image represents many things, but one thing in particular: circularity. That is, the world means what humans make it mean: Subjectivity creates reality.

Oedipa discovers, or seems to discover, that a secret force has been running parallel to known history since the Renaissance. During this era, a private postal carrier had been driven underground by the state-supported and later state-run postal service. Readers of the novel remain unclear about whether her discovery of a secret postal system called W.A.S.T.E. (We Await Silent Tristero's Empire) represents an actual discovery by her. W.A.S.T.E., she finds out, organized the French Revolution, harassed the Pony Express, engineered the American Civil War, and instigated strange and suggestive postage stamp misprints. Even with this uncertainty, Oedipa becomes the model for the ordinary person who begins to suspect conspiracy but has to constantly question her own reasoning. The conclusion of the novel, in which someone representing Tristero appears to Oedipa, is in perfect harmony with the menace and uncertainty that are the book's hallmarks.

Peter Brigg

Further Reading

Colvile, Georgiana. *Beyond and Beneath the Mantle: On Thomas Pynchon's "The Crying of Lot 49."* Amsterdam: Rodopi, 1988. Looks at the challenges Oedipa's puzzle poses for the reader, at the function of the female central character, and at the representation of American society.

Cowart, David. *Thomas Pynchon: The Art of Allusion.* Carbondale: Southern Illinois University Press, 1980. A detailed and fascinating study of how Pynchon creates an intimate web of connections among culture, history, politics, and society, so that even a short novel "spreads out" in its reach.

Grant, J. Kerry. *A Companion to "The Crying of Lot 49."* Athens: University of Georgia Press, 2001. A richly detailed compendium of all the names, places, ideas, and phenomena in *The Crying of Lot 49*. Good for readers new to Pynchon's style of writing.

Mattessich, Stefan. *Lines of Flight: Discursive Time and Countercultural Desire in the Work of Thomas Pynchon.* Durham, N.C.: Duke University Press, 2003. Explores the ways in which Pynchon's critique of late capitalist society describes the emergence of a new conceptualization of time, which Mattessich calls subjective displacement.

O'Donnell, Patrick, ed. *New Essays on "The Crying of Lot 49."* New York: Cambridge University Press, 1991. Contains specific essays on paranoia in the novel and on the way the story is largely constructed of digressions.

Schaub, Thomas, ed. *Approaches to Teaching Pynchon's "The Crying of Lot 49" and Other Works.* New York: Modern Language Association, 2008. Invaluable and long overdue collection of essays features contributions by noted Pynchon scholars. Focuses on techniques for presenting Pynchon's works in the classroom. Also looks at Pynchon's exploration of racial and gender politics. Helpful for students and general readers as well.

Slade, Joseph. *Thomas Pynchon.* 1974. Reprint. New York: Peter Lang, 1990. This book-length study of Pynchon's fiction remains one of the best. Balanced and readable, with especially strong discussion of Pynchon's uses of science.

Smith, Shawn. *Pynchon and History: Metahistorical Rhetoric and Postmodern Narrative Form in the Novels of Thomas Pynchon.* New York: Routledge, 2005. Focuses on Pynchon as a writer of historical fiction and examines his philosophy of history.

Culture and Anarchy

Author: Matthew Arnold (1822-1888)
First published: 1869
Type of work: Social criticism

In *Culture and Anarchy*, Matthew Arnold sought a center of authority by which the anarchy caused by the troubled passage of the Reform Bill of 1867 might be regulated. At its best, his style is clear, flexible, and convincing. He wrote in such a complicated mood of indignation, impatience, and fear, however, that his style and his argumentative method are frequently repetitious and unsystematic. The book is nevertheless a masterpiece of polished prose, in which urbane irony and shifts of ridicule are used to persuade the Victorian

middle class that it must reform itself before it can begin to reform the entire nation.

Writing as a so-called Christian humanist, Arnold primarily directed his criticism against the utilitarianism of the followers of Jeremy Bentham and John Stuart Mill and against the various movements of liberal reform. Disturbed by the social and political confusion, by Fenianism and the Hyde Park Riots of 1866, and by the inability of either the church or the government to cope with the growing unrest both in England and on the Continent, Arnold attempted to describe an objective center of authority that all, regardless of religious or social bias, could follow.

This center of authority is culture, which he defined on the level of the individual as "a pursuit of our total perfection by means of getting to know, on all matters which most concern us, the best which has been thought and said in the world." Because this authority is internal, it is a study of perfection within the individual, a study that should elevate the "best self" through a fresh and free search for beauty and intelligence. By following "right reason," the disinterested intellectual pursuits of the best self, Arnold foresaw a way to overcome the social and political confusion of the 1860's and to prepare for a future in which all could be happy and free. With this basically romantic view of human beings as a means and human perfectibility as the end, Arnold turned to social criticism, carefully showing that no other center of authority was tenable. The ideal of nonconformity, the disestablishment of the church, led to confusion or anarchy because it represented the sacrifice of all other sides of human personality to the religious. The ideal of the liberal reformers, on the other hand, led to anarchy because it regarded the reforms as ends rather than means toward a harmonious totality of human existence.

Arnold clarifies his definition of culture by tracing its origin to curiosity or "scientific passion" (the desire to see things as they really are) and to morality or "social passion" (the desire to do good). Christianity, as he saw it, is like culture in that it also seeks to learn the will of God (human perfection) and make it prevail. Culture goes beyond religion, however, as interpreted by the Nonconformists in that it is a harmonious expansion of all human powers. In even sharper terms, culture is opposed to utilitarianism, which Arnold considered "mechanical" because it worshiped means rather than ends. In fact, anything—materialism, economic greatness, individual wealth, bodily health, Puritanism—that was treated as an end except that of human perfectibility was to Arnold mere "machinery" that led to anarchy. Only culture, the harmonious union of poetry (the ideal of beauty) and religion (the ideal of morality), sees itself as a means that preserves the totality of the individual. Culture looks beyond machinery; it has only one passion—the passion for "sweetness" (beauty) and "light" (intelligence) and the passion to make them prevail. With such a passion it seeks to do away with social classes and religious bias to make the best that has been thought and known in the world (right reason) the core of human endeavor and institutions.

After establishing his definition of culture in terms of the individual, Arnold turned toward the problem of society. He saw the characteristic view of English people toward happiness as the individual freedom, but he also saw that each class had its own opinion as to what it considered freedom to be. In other words, there was a strong belief in freedom but a weak belief in right reason, which should view freedom disinterestedly. This misplacing of belief was to Arnold one of the chief causes of anarchy; it was the mistake of acting before thinking. Ideally, right reason should precede action, and the state should be the disinterested union of all classes, a collective best self. In reality, the state was being led toward anarchy by class interests because the aristocracy, or "Barbarians," was inaccessible to new, fresh ideas; the middle class, or "Philistines," had zeal but not knowledge; and the working class, or "Populace," was raw and untrained. Because culture alone could join the two sides of the individual, culture alone could overcome the narrow views of the three classes. Members of the different classes possessed the same human nature and saw happiness as freedom; also, the best self was common to all classes. Therefore, since authority could be found neither in religion nor in politics, it could be found only in individuals who, by following right reason rather than class bias, could assert their best selves in a harmonious union that sought the best for everyone. The major impediments to such a state were what Arnold called Atheism, the outright denial of such a thing as right reason, and Quietism, the utilitarian belief that reason was the result of habit. These impediments Arnold rejected on the basis of intuition and faith. Ethics can be known intuitively, and by building faith on the individual's intuition the spirit of culture could overcome the present anarchy.

The enlargement of his terms from the individual to the state naturally led Arnold to consider the historical development of the social and political confusion that he confronted. In the famous chapter titled "Hebraism and Hellenism," Arnold accounted for the very ground and cause out of which actual behavior arises, by distinguishing between the energy in human affairs that drives practice, the obligation of duty, self-control, and work (Hebraism) and the energy that drives those ideas that are the basis of right practice (Hellenism). Like the scientific passion, Hellenism's chief function is to see things as they really are, and like the social passion, Hebraism seeks proper conduct and obedience. In other words, what Arnold earlier analyzed as the opposing drives in the individual, he now enlarged to a historical context, all human endeavor in the Western world being associated with either the one or the other drive. Both drives aim at human perfection or salvation, but their means and ideals are sharply different. Hebraism, or "strictness of conscience," inculcates a sense of sin, but Hellenism, the "spontaneity of consciousness," teaches what Arnold called culture.

The rise of Christianity marked the great triumph of Hebraism over Hellenism, but the Renaissance marked the resurgence of Hellenism. Arnold saw the anarchy of the 1860's as the result of Puritanism's reaffirmation of Hebraism in the seventeenth century, a reaffirmation that was against the currents of history. The problem was intensified by the Puritan belief that duty was an end in itself, whereas in reality both great drives are no more than contributions to human development. Thus, in England there was too much Hebraism, so much, in fact, that religion and politics had become mechanical. As a solution, Arnold suggested that Hellenism be imported. In Hellenism, which ultimately is a synonym for culture, the ideals of internal harmony, or the unity of the total human being, and of harmony with things overcome the one-sidedness of Hebraism. The other drive, however, should not be excluded, for Hellenism alone leads to moral relaxation. There should be a harmony of both sides, a union from which would come the awakening of a healthier and less mechanical activity.

After analyzing culture in terms of the individual, the state, and history, Arnold turned to the particular issues before Parliament at the time he wrote. He directed his wit and some of his most vivacious ridicule against the four political reforms that were at the heart of liberalism—the disestablishment of the Irish church, the Real Estate Intestacy Bill, the Deceased Sister's Wife Bill, and free trade—and showed that the liberal reformers lacked disinterestedness, displayed a remarkable absence of reason, and were unconsciously leading to anarchy. By leaving the issues that were uppermost in his mind to the last, he dramatically illustrated that only culture could lead to perfection. For him the four bills were examples of the lack of belief in right reason and the philistine endeavor to act without thought. He warned that without right reason there could be no society and without society there could be no perfection. Only right reason, the disinterested search for the best that has been thought or done regardless of class interests, could defeat anarchy by establishing the way to happiness through harmony.

Culture and Anarchy is one of those works that transcend their generic limitations. Ostensibly an analysis of the contemporary political situation in England and specifically a critique of the growing attitude of liberalism promoted in works such as John Stuart Mill's *On Liberty* (1859), the essays Arnold published originally in the *Cornhill Magazine* under the series title "Anarchy and Authority" have become regarded as the locus classicus of a certain conservative viewpoint that has generated strong reactions for more than one hundred years. The basic premise for Arnold's judgment of contemporary society is that there is an inherent urge toward perfection that resides in every individual. Arnold believed every person capable of being governed by culture. For him, this meant living by the dictates of reason, in such a way that people realize they are not always the touchstone for judgments about either art or conduct; in the estimation of Lionel Trilling, one of his most distinguished critics, the attainment of culture was by Arnold's definition "the conscious effort of each man to come to the realization of his complete humanity." In Arnold's view, self-interest is the major enemy of both individual and social perfection; only when individuals are able to act disinterestedly, putting aside individual and class distinctions to work in harmony for the common good, would they become capable of realizing their best selves.

Although Arnold is eloquent and penetrating in his social criticism, he lacks epistemological sophistication. The question he never addresses is how to determine what is best for individuals and society. He was attacked by contemporaries and criticized by succeeding generations for what many have seen as imperious dogmatism. Arnold claims that right reason can serve as a guide for determining what a person or a society ought to do. He hopes that all will one day be educated to see what is best but argues that until then it is the business of government to restrain individual freedoms when these freedoms allow behavior inconsistent with what is good for society. It is understandable that this view leads to charges that Arnold is actually advocating state control and opting for a kind of approach giving those in authority permission to restrict conduct, perhaps even thought.

In the twentieth century, a time when writing was considered a political act and all conservative writing was subjected to close scrutiny, Arnold became a principal target for literary theorists; their emphasis on the significance of political subtexts negatively affected the reputation of a writer who had considered himself a strong promoter of liberalism and a believer in people's ability to improve their individual and common lots in life.

Revised by Laurence W. Mazzeno

Further Reading

Anderson, Warren D. *Matthew Arnold and the Classical Tradition.* Ann Arbor: University of Michigan Press, 1965. Examines Arnold's lifelong interest in classical literature and civilization. In writing *Culture and Anarchy*, Arnold drew heavily on Greek thought, and he was especially influenced by Plato.

Cockshut, A. O. J. "Matthew Arnold: Conservative Revolutionary." In *Matthew Arnold: A Collection of Critical*

Views, edited by David J. DeLaura. Englewood Cliffs, N.J.: Prentice-Hall, 1973. Looks at *Culture and Anarchy* and four of Arnold's overtly religious works to trace the basic assumptions of his religious position. Arnold's combination of conservatism and skepticism made him seek established religion, but he also sought to change it.

Hamilton, Ian. *A Gift Imprisoned: The Poetic Life of Matthew Arnold*. London: Bloomsbury, 1998. A critical biography that explores the frustrations in Arnold's life, the tension between passion and repression in his poetry, and his decision to abandon poetry for prose writing.

Jump, J. D. *Matthew Arnold*. London: Longmans, 1965. Reassesses the achievement of Arnold the man, the poet, and the critic. Provides an excellent and accessible introduction to *Culture and Anarchy*, tracing the history of composition, political and social contexts, major arguments, and the author's intentions.

McCarthy, Patrick J. *Matthew Arnold and the Three Classes*. New York: Columbia University Press, 1964. A full-length study of *Culture and Anarchy*. Examines Arnold's own relationships with the three classes delineated in his work. Extensive notes, index, and bibliography.

Neiman, Fraser. "Anarchy and Authority." In *Matthew Arnold*. New York: Twayne, 1968. A brief but clear presentation of the major points in *Culture and Anarchy*, with an emphasis on explaining Arnold's terminology. Also includes a chronology, bibliography, and thorough index.

Pratt, Linda Ray. *Matthew Arnold Revisited*. New York: Twayne, 2000. An updated version of Neiman's book (above). Pratt analyzes Arnold's works and concludes with a postmodern interpretation of his writings.

Sterner, Douglas W. *Priests of Culture: A Study of Matthew Arnold and Henry James*. New York: Peter Lang, 1999. Sterner focuses on Arnold's cultural and religious criticism and also examines James's travel literature, demonstrating how the two writers sought an ideal of "culture" as a response to the pressures of change and the crisis of faith in the nineteenth century.

Cupid and Psyche

Author: Unknown
First transcribed: Unknown (English translation, probably 1566)
Type of work: Novel
Type of plot: Mythic
Time of plot: Antiquity
Locale: Greece

Principal characters:
PSYCHE, the daughter of a Greek king
CUPID, the god of love
VENUS, the goddess of love and beauty

The Story:

Psyche, daughter of a Greek king, is as beautiful as Venus and sought after by many princes. Her father, seeking to know what fate the gods might have in store for her, sends some of his men to Apollo's oracle to learn the answer. To the king's horror, the oracle replies that Psyche is to become the mate of a hideous monster, and the king is ordered to leave his daughter to her fate upon a mountaintop, to prevent the destruction of his people. Clad in bridal dress, Psyche is led to a rocky summit and left there alone. The sad and weary young woman soon falls into a swoon.

Venus, jealous of Psyche's beauty, calls her son Cupid and orders him to use his arrows (whoever is struck with one of his arrows falls in love with whomever he or she is looking at) to turn Psyche's heart toward a creature so hideous that mortals will be filled with loathing at the sight of Psyche's mate. Preparing to shoot his arrow, Cupid, seeing his victim, is transfixed by her beauty. He drops his arrow and it strikes him in the leg. He falls in love with Psyche and decides that she should be his forever. While Psyche sleeps, Zephyrus comes at Cupid's bidding and carries her to the valley in which Love's house stands. There she awakens in a grove of trees in which stands a magnificent golden palace. She enters the building and wanders through the sumptuously furnished rooms.

At noon, Psyche finds a table lavishly spread. A voice invites her to eat, assures her that the house is hers, and tells her that the being who is to be her lover will come that night.

As she lies in bed that night, a voice close beside her tells her not to be afraid. The voice speaks so tenderly that Psyche welcomes her unseen suitor and holds out her arms to him. When Psyche awakens the next morning, her lover is gone, but he left behind a gold ring and placed a circlet on her head.

For a time Psyche lives happily in the golden palace, visited each night by the lover whose face she does not see. At last, however, she becomes homesick for her two sisters and her father. One night, she asks her lover to permit her sisters to visit her the next day. He gives his consent, but he warns that she is not to tell them about him.

Zephyrus carries the sisters to the valley. Overjoyed to see them, Psyche shows them the beauties of the palace and gives them many gifts. Jealous of her good fortune, they try to make her suspicious of her unseen lover. They suggest that her lover is a serpent who changes into the form of a youth at night, a monster who will at last devour her. To save herself, they advise her to hide a lamp and a knife by her bed so that she might see him and slay him as he sleeps.

Psyche does as they suggest. That night, as her love lies asleep, she lights the lamp and brings it close so that she might look at him. When she sees the perfectly handsome young man by her side, she is powerless to use her knife. As she turns, sobbing, to extinguish the flame, a drop of burning oil falls on Cupid's shoulder. Awakening with a cry, he looks at her reproachfully. With the warning that love cannot live with suspicion, he leaves the palace. Psyche tries to follow but falls in a swoon at the threshold.

When she awakens, the palace vanishes. Determined to seek her lover, she wanders alone across the countryside and through cities, hunting the god. Meanwhile, Cupid takes his vengeance on her sisters. To each he sends a dream that she will become his bride if she will throw herself from the mountaintop. Both sisters, obeying the summons, find only the arms of Death to welcome them.

No god will give the wandering Psyche shelter or comfort or protect her from the wrath of Venus. At the temples of Ceres and Juno, she is turned away. At last, she comes to the court of Venus herself. Warned by her heart to flee, she is nevertheless drawn before the throne of the goddess. Venus decides that Psyche should be kept as a slave. She is to be given a new task to do each day and is to live until she once more begins to hope.

Psyche's first task is to sort a huge pile of mixed seeds and grain into separate heaps, with the warning that if there is so much as one seed in the wrong pile she will be punished. However, by dusk, she separates only small heaps of grain. Cupid so pities her that he commands myriad ants to complete the task for her.

The next day, Psyche is ordered to gather the golden fleece of Venus's sheep. Obeying the advice of a reed at the edge of the river, she waits until the animals are asleep and then collects the wool that was left clinging to the bushes.

Psyche's third task is to fill a jug with the black water that flows down a steep mountain into the rivers Styx and Cocytus. She is able to complete this task with the aid of a bird that carries the jug to the stream, collects the water, and brings it back to her.

On the fourth day, Psyche is given her most difficult task; she is to go to the land of the dead and there collect some of the beauty of the goddess Proserpine in a golden box. If she succeeds, Venus promises she will treat Psyche kindly thereafter. To visit Proserpine—in the land of the dead—and to return, however, is an impossible achievement. In despair, Psyche determines to cast herself from a tower, but as she is about to kill herself a voice calls to her and tells her how she might fulfill her mission.

Following instructions, Psyche travels to Proserpine's realm. There she might stay on forever if she did not think suddenly of her love. On her way back, she almost reaches the daylight when envy seizes her. She opens the box, thinking she will have whatever it contains for herself, but no sooner does she lift the lid than she falls into a deep sleep filled with nightmares. She would have been there forever had Cupid, going in search of her, not found her. He awakens her with one of his arrows and sends her on to his mother with the box.

Then he flies off and presents himself before Jove with his petition that Psyche be made immortal. Jove, after hearing his pleas, sends Mercury to conduct Psyche into the presence of the gods. There she drinks from the golden cup of ambrosia that Jove hands her and becomes immortal. She and Cupid are at last united for all time.

Critical Evaluation:

Although the story of Cupid's love for Psyche (or at least for a maid) was known by Hellenistic times, the one known literary source for this complete tale is *Metamorphoses* (second century; *The Golden Ass*, 1566) by Lucius Apuleius. This Latin book deals with the transformation of Lucius into an ass, his year-long journey and checkered adventures, his ultimate restoration to human shape, and his devotion to the Egyptian goddess Isis. At the center of this eleven-book work is couched the story of Cupid and Psyche, as told by an old crone to a beautiful young woman. This "pleasant tale and old wives' story," as the crone put it, belongs to the genre of the folktale, and throughout the world variations on this story are known. Apuleius's readers would have immediately recognized the character Psyche as typical of the heroines of Greek "novels" or "romances": She is lovely and in love, but she is also timid, pious, naïve, and curious. This last characteristic, her most serious fault, Apuleius uses to relate Psyche to Lucius, the central figure of the novel. As a result of curiosity, both are violently thrown into a life of suffering and of despair; both overcome their trials and achieve true happiness by devotion to a deity.

Through the years, *Cupid and Psyche* has been recognized for its allegorical possibilities. Cupid ("desire"; Eros in Greek) is one of the oldest allegorical divinities. Psyche, in turn, means "soul." That Apuleius intended symbolic reflection of the larger work is hardly debatable, but that he saw the story as a vehicle of teaching Christian virtue is unfounded. Nevertheless, the universal charm of the story prompted Fulgentius Planciades (sixth century) to allegorize thus: The city is the world, Psyche's father is God, her mother is matter, her sisters represent flesh and the will, Venus is lust, and Cupid is "cupidity"; Fulgentius's allegory, however, does not have satisfactory consistency. Pedro Calderón de la Barca (seventeenth century) saw the three daughters as paganism, Judaism, and the Church, the last of whom was wedded to Christ. The Platonists, who no doubt recognized echoes from Plato's *Phaedros* (*Phaedrus*, 1792), saw the sisters as the tripartite soul: Desire and spirit are overcome by pure reason, and the ultimate acceptance of the rational soul among the gods symbolizes freedom from the Orphic cycle of death and rebirth. Jungians see Psyche as the psychic development of the feminine; Venus symbolizes fertility, and the marriage to Cupid is sexual bondage.

In this story, Cupid is considerably more mature than the familiar Hellenistic winged archer-cherub, and his beauty is emphasized; nevertheless, he is still mischievous and his mother's minion. Venus, however, is an outright burlesque; she seems to have grown more vain with age and motherhood, and her jealousy of the beautiful young virgin Psyche is decidedly un-Christian. Still, such a characterization is necessary if Venus is to be given the role of the folktale witch who sets the apparently impossible tasks, which are also appropriate to Venus's role as mother-in-law, since the wool, grain, water, and beauty are Psyche's symbolic dowry, representing wifely abilities and virtues.

Tasks and journeys are traditional themes in heroic tales, especially when they are punishments for some sacrilege. Psyche's crime, despite her original guilelessness, is twofold: She offends Venus, and she violates her husband's trust. It is interesting to observe how in Apuleius's version Psyche, who is so simple that she cannot even lie to her sisters about her husband, even after being told not to mention him, loses

her innocence as soon as she is persuaded by them to kill the "monster." Thereafter she has a part in the trouble that follows. Psyche, therefore, loses innocence, but she gains knowledge and a chance to regain happiness—eternally. This is the theme of the larger work, the *Metamorphoses*, in which Lucius is initiated into the Isiac mysteries and becomes the priest of Isis, forsaking the evils of a world of asses in human flesh.

In the course of the story, Apuleius has Cupid warn Psyche that if she keeps secret the strange nature of their marriage, the child she bears will remain divine. Apuleius ends his story with the birth of a child who is fittingly called Voluptas, or "Joy." Thus, the eternal union of love and the soul does result in the soul's divine, that is, immortal, joy.

As a product of the classical age, *Cupid and Psyche* is full of familiar classical literary and mythological illusions. The "labors" motif includes the traditional journey to the underworld (such as with Herakles, Orpheus, Odysseus, and Aeneas). The deserted Psyche recalls the despair of Ariadne, Andromeda, and Dido. The theme of the opened container recalls Pandora. Psyche's apotheosis, or deification, finds precedent especially in the myth of Herakles. As for the gods, their portraits become near parodies of Homeric models, in that they act with stereotypical predictability. Later versions of *Cupid and Psyche* are found in Giovanni Boccaccio's *Genealogia deorum gentilium* (c. 1350-1375; genealogies of the Gentile gods) and in Walter Pater's *Marius the Epicurean* (1885). In addition Pedro Calderón de la Barca, Molière, Pierre Corneille, Thomas Heywood, and Joseph Beaumont have told their versions of the Cupid and Psyche fable.

"Critical Evaluation" by E. N. Genovese

Further Reading

Accardo, Pasquale J. *The "Metamorphosis" of Apuleius: Cupid and Psyche, Beauty and the Beast, King Kong.* Madison, N.J.: Fairleigh Dickinson University Press, 2002. Accardo chronicles the history of Cupid and Psyche, from its appearance in *The Golden Ass* to its loss in the Middle Ages, recovery in the Renaissance, and its adaptation in many subsequent versions, including the novel *Till We Have Faces* by C. S. Lewis.

Cavicchioli, Sonia. *The Tale of Cupid and Psyche: An Illustrated History.* Translated by Susan Scott. New York: George Braziller, 2002. Cavicchioli describes how the tale has been represented in art objects, including frescoes, paintings, wedding chests, miniatures, tapestries, stained-glass windows, and sculptures, focusing on images from the fifteenth and sixteenth century Italian Renaissance. The art objects are reproduced in the book's photographs, many of which are in color.

Franz, Marie-Louise von. *The Golden Ass of Apuleius.* Boston: Shambhala, 1992. A psychological interpretation of the Cupid and Psyche myth. An excellent resource for the study and analysis of this myth.

Gollnick, James Timothy. *Love and the Soul: Psychological Interpretations of the Eros and Psyche Myth.* Waterloo, Ont.: Wilfrid Laurier University Press, 1992. A psychological study of the Cupid and Psyche myth. After tracing its origins and literary contexts, Gollnick describes how the tale has been interpreted from both Freudian and Jungian perspectives as well as from other psychological frameworks. Includes select bibliography and index.

Haight, Elizabeth Hazelton. *Apuleius and His Influence.* New York: Longmans, Green, 1927. Although much research has followed in subsequent years, this remains a significant source for comparative studies. Haight traces the tradition of Cupid and Psyche from classical to modern literature; she cites various interpretations of the myth in different historical periods.

Huber, Barbara Weir. *Transforming Psyche.* Montreal: McGill-Queen's University Press, 1999. Huber demonstrates how the myth of Cupid and Psyche can be used to interpret the experiences of women in the modern era, focusing on Psyche's connections to her sisters, her sexuality, her earthbound life, and the birth of her child.

Labouvie-Vief, Gisela. *Psyche and Eros.* New York: Cambridge University Press, 1994. Illustrates theories of the mind and of gender using this myth as foundation. Labouvie-Vief interprets myth as a psychological development to overcome dualistic thinking in terms of gender, and she provides a comprehensive examination of the psychological components of mythmaking.

Neumann, Erich. *Amor and Psyche.* New York: Harper & Row, 1962. Provides detailed commentary that includes classical sources, art illustrations, and occurrences in other literature. Neumann argues that Psyche represents the development of the feminine psyche.

Schlam, Carl C. *The Metamorphoses of Apuleius.* Chapel Hill: University of North Carolina Press, 1992. Schlam offers a detailed commentary on the sources of the myth of Cupid and Psyche and an extensive bibliography. His book also includes theories by a number of other critics who have attempted to explain the myth's origin.

Tatum, James. *Apuleius and "The Golden Ass."* Ithaca, N.Y.: Cornell University Press, 1979. Tatum identifies and compares a number of sources and interpretations of the Cupid and Psyche myth; he also characterizes and analyzes individual parts of the story.

Custer Died for Your Sins
An Indian Manifesto

Author: Vine Deloria, Jr. (1933-2005)
First published: 1969
Type of work: Social criticism

Vine Deloria, Jr., who was one of the most important Native American intellectuals, first achieved prominence with the publication of *Custer Died for Your Sins: An Indian Manifesto*, a collection of eleven essays and an afterword on a variety of topics related to American Indian social, legal, and political issues of the 1960's. Coming at the end of a decade in which the fundamental values of American culture were being rigorously questioned, when American history was being rewritten, and when the younger generation was eagerly searching for alternative lifestyles, Deloria's book quickly became a best seller praised for the wit, the humor, and the energy of its style as well as for its articulate and witty presentation of the Native American point of view and its penetrating critique of mainstream American culture.

Earlier in the 1960's, interest in American Indians was generated by the reissue, in 1962, of *Black Elk Speaks* (1932), the life story of an Oglala Sioux holy man that became a cult classic on college campuses. Then, in 1968, the Pulitzer Prize in fiction was awarded to N. Scott Momaday, the author of *House Made of Dawn* (1968), the first novel written by a Native American to be so honored. Next came *Custer Died for Your Sins* in 1969, quickly followed by Dee

Brown's revisionist presentation of the history of the Indian wars in *Bury My Heart at Wounded Knee* (1970), which also became a national best seller. In their different ways, these four books urged the rejection of the old stereotypes of American Indians and gave a more realistic and more sympathetic view of them than had previously been available in literature that was written almost exclusively from the perspective of white Americans.

Thus, in his opening essay, "Indians Today: The Real and the Unreal," Deloria comments that he intends to discuss the Indian people's feeling of unreality that "has been welling up inside us and threatens to make this decade [the 1970's] the most decisive in history for Indian people." Among the "unreal and ahistorical" beliefs and attitudes that Deloria goes on to enumerate is the claim by many white people to have an Indian ancestor, usually an Indian princess grandmother, and Deloria humorously comments that he "once did a projection backward and discovered that evidently most tribes were entirely female for the first three hundred years of white occupation." Indians, Deloria comments, suffer from misconceptions and stereotyping because white people believe that they are so easy to understand: "Anyone and everyone who knows an Indian or who is *interested*, immediately and thoroughly understands them." Among these "understandings," Deloria lists many myths about Indians, beginning with Christopher Columbus's mistaken belief that the native peoples he met were the inhabitants of India, the later view that they were the ten lost tribes of Israel, and the yet later view that they were little better than wild animals to be "hunted and skinned. Bounties were set and an Indian scalp became more valuable than beaver, otter, marten, and other animal pelts."

However, Deloria argues, not all the harm was done by the Indians' enemies; much of it was done by their "friends," the white do-gooders, missionaries, promoters, scholars, "and every conceivable type of person who believed he could help. White society failed to understand the situation because this conglomerate of assistance blurred the real issues beyond recognition." The essay ends with an enumeration of tribal governments and political organizations as they existed in the 1960's, an analysis of their accomplishments and prospects for the future, and a plea for "fewer and fewer 'experts' on Indians. What we need is a cultural leave-us-alone agreement in spirit and in fact."

The essays that follow take up individually the concerns that are outlined in "Indians Today: The Real and the Unreal." The second essay, titled "Laws and Treaties," begins by pointing out a tragic irony in the history of the United States government's treatment of the Native Americans. President Lyndon Johnson stressed the importance of the United States keeping its commitments in Southeast Asia, and President Richard Nixon pictured the Soviet Union as a menace to world peace because it did not honor its treaties. However, Deloria comments, "Indian people laugh themselves sick when they hear these statements. America has yet to keep one Indian treaty or agreement despite the fact that the United States government signed over four hundred such treaties and agreements with Indian tribes. . . . It is doubtful that any nation will ever exceed the record of the United States for perfidy." Deloria argues, however, that this perfidy is not merely a fact of America's past; more damage is being done to Indian people in the 1960's than was done in the entire nineteenth century. Adding to the Indian people's resentment of their treatment at the hands of a government that daily tramples on Indian treaty rights while insisting on maintaining its commitments in Vietnam is their outrage at the complicity of the Christian churches in the mistreatment of Native Americans. Why, Deloria asks, if the churches actually want justice, do they not speak out about the mistreatment of the Indians?

The essay concludes that America "has always been a militantly imperialistic world power eagerly grasping for economic control over weaker nations," including the Indian nations that were conquered one after another in the United States' march across the North American continent. The war in Vietnam is seen in the essay as only the most recent symptom of the basic lack of integrity of the American government, "a side issue in comparison with the great domestic issues which must be faced—and justly faced—before this society destroys itself."

The next four essays—"The Disastrous Policy of Termination," "Anthropologists and Other Friends," "Missionaries and the Religious Vacuum," and "Government Agencies"—discuss the ways in which those white people who were sympathetic to the Indians have inadvertently caused them more harm than good. Termination was a policy, initiated in the 1950's, intended to end the federally recognized status of Indian tribes, thereby solving the "Indian problem" by assimilating the Indian people into the general population. According to Deloria, however, it was used as another excuse by the government to get its hands on Indian lands.

Anthropologists, no matter how well intentioned, treat Indian people "as objects for observation . . . for experimentation, for manipulation, and for eventual extinction. The anthropologist thus furnishes the justification for treating Indian people like so many chessmen available for anyone to play with." Deloria urges Indian people to reject the anthropologists' "compilation of useless knowledge" and argues that Indians should not cooperate with those who raise no hand to help them. "During the crucial days of 1954, when the Senate was pushing for termination of all Indian rights, not one single scholar, anthropologist, sociologist, historian, or economist came forward to support the tribes against the detrimental policy." According to Deloria, these scholars were not really interested in helping Indian people but merely in exploiting them to further their own academic careers.

Deloria attacks Christian do-gooders and especially Christian denominations that are determined to keep Indian congregations in a mission status and refuse to admit Indians to the ministry for fear that the "purity" of the doctrine will suffer. Thus, Indian people are offended and the "impotence and irrelevancy" of the churches meant a return to traditional religion and the rapid expansion of the Native American Church. Deloria believes that Indian religion, not Christianity, will be the salvation of Indian people, primarily, he says, because Indian religions, regardless of the tribe, view death as a natural occurrence and not a punishment from God. If the Christian missions were really interested in serving the Indians' best interests, they would assist in the creation of a national Indian Christian Church incorporating existing missions and programs into one all-encompassing organization to be put wholly in the hands of the Indian people themselves.

In "Government Agencies," Deloria explains the structure and history of the Bureau of Indian Affairs (BIA), points out its inefficiencies and failures, and offers proposals for changes that need to be made if Indians are to be able to make progress comparable to that of the rest of society. Programming should be based on the size of the tribe, with special consideration for funding given to the thirty-five or so tribes with sufficient population, land, and resources to make large programs feasible. Area BIA offices should be given the bulk of the budgets in discretionary funds in order to maximize flexibility to meet local needs. People employed directly by the tribes should be given civil service status so that they can leave the BIA and work directly for tribal governments without losing time in grade and retirement benefits. The BIA itself should be transferred from the Department of the Interior to the Department of Commerce, where it could be merged with the Economic Development Administration, an agency better able to match tribal projects to available government and private-sector programs.

The best known and most often quoted essay in the collection is the one entitled "Indian Humor." It is based on the premise that one of the best ways to understand a culture is to know what it finds humorous. For too long, Deloria thinks, the stereotype of the humorless, "granite-faced grunting red-

skin has been perpetuated by American mythology." In contrast, Deloria points out that humor was an integral part of traditional Indian cultures. Teasing was used as a method of social control for centuries before the white invasion; it made it possible to correct and mold social behavior while preserving egos and minimizing disputes of a personal nature—an alternative to direct confrontation and public denunciation that preserved the dignity of the accused. In the politically charged atmosphere of the 1960's, humor served as a method of bringing Indian people from various tribes together by focusing on commonalities and creating goodwill, and thus it was an important political tool in the struggle to gain "red power." Satire can circumscribe problems so that possible solutions are suggested, and people are often awakened and "brought to a militant edge" because of jokes.

Among the most politically useful targets of Indian humor are the BIA, where Deloria often counsels Indians to run in case of earthquake because nothing can shake the BIA, and General Custer, who was well dressed for the occasion of his last stand, his body having been found afterward dressed in an Arrow shirt. Humor, according to Deloria, is the cement that holds the Indian movement together: "When a people can laugh at themselves and laugh at others and hold all aspects of life together without letting anybody drive them to extremes, then it seems to me that that people can survive."

The remaining essays are more dated, focusing on what Indian people can do to help themselves in the 1960's. Deloria concludes by reminding Indian people of the great war chief Crazy Horse, who "never drafted anyone to follow him" but was followed because people recognized that what he did was for the people. When he was dying, bayoneted in the back, Crazy Horse said to his father, "Tell the people it is no use to depend on me any more now." Deloria writes, "Until we can once again produce people like Crazy Horse all the money and help in the world will not save us."

Dennis Hoilman

Further Reading

Biolsi, Thomas, and Larry J. Zimmerman, eds. *Indians and Anthropologists: Vine Deloria, Jr., and the Critique of Anthropology.* Tucson: University of Arizona Press, 1997. A collection of essays by Native American and other scholars examining how the relationship between anthropologists and American Indians changed since Deloria criticized anthropologists in *Custer Died for Your Sins.* The concluding essay, "Anthros, Indians, and Planetary Reality," is written by Deloria.

Carriker, Robert C. "The American Indian from the Civil

War to the Present." In *Historians and the American West*, edited by Michael P. Malone. Lincoln: University of Nebraska Press, 1983. This collection of seventeen essays on the historiography of the West is a "critical examination of past and present [literature] while ruminating about the future." Carriker criticizes Deloria for being more political than historical in his writings.

Grounds, Richard A., Grant E. Tinker, and David E. Wilkins, eds. *Native Voices: American Indian Identity and Resistance*. Lawrence: University Press of Kansas, 2003. A collection of essays by Native Americans discussing the issues facing American Indians at the beginning of the twenty-first century. Two essays, "Vine Deloria, Jr., and the Development of a Decolonizing Critique of Indigenous Peoples and International Relations" by Glenn T. Morris and "Contours of Enlightenment: Reflections on Science, Theology, Law, and the Alternative Vision of Vine Deloria, Jr." by Ward Churchill, assess how Deloria's writings have shaped American Indian scholarship and

provide insights into his ideas. Also includes an essay by Deloria, "The Passage of Generations."

Pavlik, Steve, and Daniel R. Wildcat, eds. *Destroying Dogma: Vine Deloria, Jr., and His Influence on American Society*. Golden, Colo.: Fulcrum, 2006. A tribute to Deloria. The essayists measure his influence and discuss his ideas, particularly his belief that dogma is the enemy of critical thinking.

Ruoff, A. Lavonne. *American Indian Literatures: An Introduction, Bibliographic Review, and Selected Bibliography*. New York: Modern Language Association, 1990. Reference has a helpful look at types of life histories and oral literatures to be found in Native American tradition. Comments on Deloria's "keen wit, sharp satire, and political insight."

Steiner, Stan. *The New Indians*. New York: Dell, 1968. Contains comments on Deloria and his place in the Red Power movement, providing a context for the issues raised in *Custer Died for Your Sins*.

The Custom of the Country

Author: Edith Wharton (1862-1937)
First published: 1913
Type of work: Novel
Type of plot: Social realism
Time of plot: Late nineteenth century
Locale: New York and Paris

Principal characters:
UNDINE SPRAGG, a predatory woman
ABNER E. SPRAGG, her father
ELMER MOFFATT, her first husband
RALPH MARVELL, her second husband
PAUL, Undine and Ralph Marvell's son
RAYMOND DE CHELLES, her third husband
PETER VAN DEGEN, her lover

The Story:

Undine Spragg, who moves to New York from Apex City with her parents, is in the city for two years without being accepted into society. Her opportunity comes at last when she is invited to a dinner given by Laura Fairford, whose brother, Ralph Marvell, takes an interest in her. Although his family is socially prominent, Ralph has little money. He is an independent thinker who dislikes the superficiality of such important people as Peter Van Degen, the wealthy husband of Ralph's cousin, Clare Dagonet, with whom Ralph was once in love.

About two months after their meeting, Undine and Ralph become engaged. One night, they go to see a play, where Undine is shocked to find herself sitting next to Elmer Moffatt, someone who knows about her past. She promises to meet

him privately in Central Park the next day. When they meet, Moffatt, a blunt, vulgar man, tells Undine that she must help him in his business deals after she marries Ralph. Moffatt also goes to see Undine's father and, threatening to reveal Undine's past if Mr. Spragg refuses, asks him to join in a business deal.

Mr. Spragg is fortunate in his business deal with Moffatt and is able to give Undine a big wedding. After Ralph and Undine are married, Ralph gradually realizes that Undine cares less for him than for the social world. He also becomes aware of Undine's ruthless desire for money. Her unhappiness and resentment increase when she learns that she is pregnant.

During the next several years, Moffatt becomes a significant financial figure in New York. Ralph, in an attempt to support Undine's extravagance, goes to work in a business to which he is ill-suited. Undine, meanwhile, keeps up a busy schedule of social engagements. She also accepts some expensive gifts from Peter Van Degen, who is interested in her, before Peter leaves to spend the season in Europe. One day, Undine sees Moffatt, who comes to propose a disreputable business deal to Ralph; the deal succeeds and Undine goes to Paris to meet Peter, where soon she spends all the money. She meets the Comte Raymond de Chelles, a French aristocrat, whom she thinks of marrying until Peter tells her that if she stays with him, he will give her everything she wants. At this point, Undine receives a telegram announcing that Ralph is critically ill with pneumonia and asking her to return to New York immediately. Undine decides to stay in Paris.

Ralph recovers. After her uncontested divorce from Ralph, Undine lives with Peter for two months. When he learns that Undine did not go to Ralph while he was ill, Peter is disillusioned and leaves her without getting the promised divorce from his wife Clare. Ralph, meanwhile, returns to the Dagonet household with his son, Paul, for whose sake he begins to work hard at the office. He also resumes work on a novel. Then he learns that Undine is engaged to Comte Raymond de Chelles and badly needs money to have her marriage to Ralph annulled by the church. Undine agrees to waive her rights to her son if Ralph will send her one hundred thousand dollars to pay for her annulment. Ralph borrows half of the needed sum and goes to Moffatt to make another business deal. As Undine's deadline approaches, with the deal not yet concluded, Ralph consults Moffatt, who tells him that the matter is going more slowly than expected and that it will take a year to materialize. Moffatt tells Ralph that he himself was once married to Undine, back in Apex City, but that Undine's parents forced the young couple to get a divorce. After hearing this story, Ralph goes home and commits suicide.

Undine, now in possession of her son, marries Raymond de Chelles. She is very happy in Paris, even though Raymond is strict about her social life. After three months, they move to the family estate at Saint Desert to live quietly and modestly. When Raymond begins to ignore her, Undine becomes bored and resentful of her husband's family for not making allowances for her extravagances, which continue unabated.

One day, she invites a dealer from Paris to appraise some of the priceless Chelles tapestries. When the dealer arrives, the prospective American buyer with him turned out to be Moffatt, now one of the richest men in New York. Over the next several weeks, Undine sees a great deal of her first hus-

band. When the time comes for Moffatt to return to New York, Undine invites him to have an affair with her. Moffatt tells her that he wants marriage or nothing.

Undine goes to Reno, Nevada, where she divorces Raymond and marries Moffatt that same day. Moffatt gives Undine everything she wants, but she realizes that in many personal ways he compares unfavorably with her other husbands. The Moffatts settle in a mansion in Paris to satisfy Undine's social ambitions and her husband's taste for worldly display. When Undine learns that an old society acquaintance, Jim Driscoll, is appointed ambassador to England, she decides that she would like to be the wife of an ambassador. Moffatt tells her bluntly that that is the one thing she can never have because she is a divorced woman. Still dissatisfied, Undine is certain that the one thing she is destined to be is an ambassador's wife.

Critical Evaluation:

The Custom of the Country, one of Edith Wharton's major achievements, was published midway through her productive period between 1905 and 1920, which culminated in a Pulitzer Prize in fiction. As in *The House of Mirth* (1905), Wharton examines with an anthropologist's eye the old New York in which she grew up. As in her masterpiece, *The Age of Innocence* (1920), she shrewdly examines the conventions of society and the men and women who try to break out of them. *The Custom of the Country* reflects not only her concern with American cultural inadequacies and her contempt for the values of the newly moneyed and growing middle class (in this concern she resembles her contemporary, Henry James) but also her interest in the issue of the role of women in society.

Wharton's portrait of Undine is remarkable; nothing quite like it had been attempted in American literature, except perhaps in Theodore Dreiser's *Sister Carrie* (1900). Like Dreiser, Wharton shatters the conventions of the age, which sentimentalized women and consigned them to passive roles in melodramas or staid drawing room comedies and romances. The novel ends with Undine still unsatisfied. Her marriage to Moffatt, financially by far her most successful, is marred by her insatiable desire for more, particularly for anything that might enhance her position in society. From the time she leaves Apex and comes to New York to cut a figure in society, she thrives only when she is noticed and treasured and when her extravagance is indulged. She grows more sophisticated but her character does not change. It is unlikely that she will ever be content, which is why Wharton ends the novel with Undine's longing to be an ambassador's wife.

It would be simplistic merely to see Undine as a villainess—indeed, Wharton does not treat her as such. Rather, Undine represents her times, late nineteenth and early twentieth century America, when the number of business speculators such as Moffatt rose sharply and the old New York of Edith Wharton's childhood gave way to a new class of entrepreneurs. Undine is a kind of robber baron, boosting her stock and conniving at investments in her human capital. She is every bit as ruthless as Moffatt, but since she is a woman she has far less latitude than he does and must depend on pleasing men and on insinuating herself in good society.

Undine is as much a victim as she is a villainess. Neither her father nor the other men in her life tell her the slightest thing about business. Her father has spoiled her with gifts even as he complains that her demands tax his resources. Because she always gets what she wants, she thinks that her father exaggerates his worries about money. To her, money is something men get to please their women, and the men do not disabuse her of that idea. Even Ralph's sad, desperate effort to pay her off with one hundred thousand dollars merely confirms her judgment that men will get her what she wants. It is not surprising that she sees society as rapacious. In this competitive context, she is hardly alone in indulging her appetites.

What does set Undine apart from other self-serving, coldblooded, and unsympathetic fictional women is her almost complete lack of feeling for her son. Moffatt is quite tender with the boy and behaves sensitively as a stepfather, but Undine ignores her son even after she has remarried Moffatt. As Moffatt says, Undine simply cannot help herself. She is so self-obsessed that even her own family will always be ancillary to her.

If Undine remains attractive to Moffatt and to some readers even after the worst is known about her, it is because of her incredible energy. As a woman she has so little room to maneuver or ability to decide on the kind of life she wants. Her life involves constant transitions, yet she never despairs. She is at her finest when she rebels against Raymond de Chelles, her third husband. It is true that she is horribly blind to what home and family mean to him—she proposes to sell the family heirlooms so that she can continue her brilliant seasons in Paris—but she also protests against the stifling double standard that allows Raymond to travel and live his life while she is supposed to sacrifice her wants. Undine refuses to be passive.

Wharton portrays her heroine without so much as a veneer of sentimentality. This has prompted some critics to suggest that she despises Undine, but this view seems untenable given the novel's carefully controlled narrative voice. Undine is not blamed but viewed, rather, in anthropological

terms as a product of her times—as are the other characters. Ralph, for example, elicits much sympathy for his efforts to please Undine and for his acceptance of Undine's behavior. He even tolerates her neglect of their son. Yet Ralph is weak; he does not fight for what he loves, and his suicide is a wasteful, pathetic ending to a life that had some promise. Having begun as a critic of old New York society, he eventually capitulates to its dictates. That he should be so undone demonstrates how ill-prepared he was to contend with life.

Narrow and unimaginative as Undine's parents are, they at least instill in their daughter a will not merely to live but to prevail. What she wants may be vulgar and worthless, yet without energy like hers, social change would be impossible. Without her kind of irreverence, women would be at the mercy of either the Ralphs or the Raymonds. In the context of the dynamic, rapidly changing early twentieth century society, Undine is an appropriate and brilliantly realized creation.

"Critical Evaluation" by Carl Rollyson

Further Reading

Bell, Millicent, ed. *The Cambridge Companion to Edith Wharton*. New York: Cambridge University Press, 1995. Collection of essays, including a critical history of Wharton's work, discussions of Wharton and race and the science of manners, and *"The Custom of the Country*: Spragg and the Art of the Deal" by Elaine Showalter.

Farwell, Tricia M. *Love and Death in Edith Wharton's Fiction*. New York: Peter Lang, 2006. An insightful look at Wharton's beliefs about the nature of love and the way they reflect her philosophical views, namely those of Plato and Charles Darwin. Wharton's own shifting feelings on the role of love in life are revealed in conjunction with the shifting role that love plays for her fictional characters.

Haytock, Jennifer. *Edith Wharton and the Conversations of Literary Modernism*. New York: Palgrave Macmillan, 2008. Although Wharton denied she was a modernist writer, Haytock argues that Wharton's fiction contained elements of modernism, as demonstrated by her writing style and the cultural issues she addresses.

Lee, Hermione. *Edith Wharton*. New York: Knopf, 2007. An exhaustive study of Wharton's life, offering valuable insights and pointing out interesting analogies between her life and her fiction.

Lewis, R. W. B. *Edith Wharton: A Biography*. New York: Harper & Row, 1975. This standard biography provides important background information on the novel and a sensitive critical discussion, placing it in the context of Wharton's other work.

McDowell, Margaret B. *Edith Wharton*. Boston: Twayne, 1976. An introductory study that includes a separate chapter on *The Custom of the Country*, discussing its critical reception, comparing it to other Wharton works, and analyzing its structure, Wharton's use of satire, and her deft treatment of minor characters.

Raphael, Lev. *Edith Wharton's Prisoners of Shame: A New Perspective on Her Neglected Fiction*. New York: St. Mar-

tin's Press, 1991. Compares *The Custom of the Country* with *The House of Mirth* and provides a close analysis of the first novel's structure.

Wolff, Cynthia Griffin. *A Feast of Words: The Triumph of Edith Wharton*. New York: Oxford University Press, 1977. A critical study with significant biographical material that helps illuminate the interpretations of Wharton's novels. Includes a thorough examination of *The Custom of the Country*, emphasizing Wharton's anthropological view of her characters.

Cuttlefish Bones

Author: Eugenio Montale (1896-1981)
First published: Ossi di seppia, 1925 (English translation, 1992)
Type of work: Poetry

Along with Giuseppe Ungaretti and Salvatore Quasimodo, writers of the Hermetic school, Eugenio Montale is one of the most influential poets to shape Italian letters in the twentieth century. Although Montale also wrote literary criticism and about fifteen hundred newspaper and periodical articles, it was his first volume of poetry, *Cuttlefish Bones*, marked by its precision, concision, and concreteness, that gained him public recognition. In its prosody, the collection breaks from traditional Italian poetry in many ways. Most significantly, it marks a final shift from the style of Gabriele D'Annunzio. Montale abandons the linear and rhetorically flourished narrative line and works instead in a highly associative style, in an Italian really spoken, with images as the loci of meaning and abstractions arising from the images. The tone becomes direct and sometimes conversational, and fixed stanzaic patterns modulate to a mix of free verse with varied meters. Montale declared his aesthetic intent: "to rid myself of all waste" in the interest of precision.

Montalean images derive in large part from the world of nature. The imagery of *Cuttlefish Bones* is extremely influenced by the environs of the Cinque Terre area of the Ligurian coast, with its "enchanting arc of rocks and sky," where he went during summers until he was thirty years old. The title refers to fragments of remains of the octopus washed ashore. Indeed, throughout the collection, the sea tosses its "bones" onto the shore and hurls the "sea-wrack starfish cork" "onto the beaches": All of this flotsam is

heaved up, "hurled aside by the torrent of life." The section within *Cuttlefish Bones* with the same title abounds in recurring Ligurian images of the seacoast, the bright sun and the evocation of heat ("that land of searing sun where the air/ goes hazy with mosquitos"), the rocky shoreline, and the cuttlebones. The desolate images of rocks, of "stonebound suffering," are every now and then juxtaposed with messages of inspiration like those of the epiphany of light in the lemon trees, of the re-creation of the winter wonderland of childhood, and of the sunflower, "crazed with light," that can be found where "life evaporates as essence." In contrast, "The Mediterranean" evokes the expansiveness of the sea. Montale apostrophizes: "O immensity, it was you, redeeming/ even the stones in their suffering."

Cuttlefish Bones presages the rest of Montale's work both aesthetically and thematically. The symbol system of the collection is established in "In limine," wherein images of walls, which are representative of boundaries and stasis as well as of the preestablished, are contrasted by the fluidity of the water and the unconfined movement of the wind, which are shown to be emblematic of change, movement, and transformation.

Montale described himself in "The Mediterranean" as "a man intent/ on observing, in himself, and others, the furor/ of fleeting life." He treats this theme and others typical of his times: alienation and anguish in living; isolation and enclosure emblematized by recurrent images of walls and the transgressing of those walls into boundlessness; exile from place, from childhood, from nature; the mixed virtues of being unencumbered by relationships; and the search for the authentic self.

The collection was originally received as a metaphysical statement. The face of a passerby on a crowded street, for instance, shows for a moment "an invisible suffering," but no one notices. Facing the abyss of "nothingness at my back,/ emptiness behind me," the speaker says: "I will feel the terror of the drunken man." After that flash of metaphysical anguish, things of commonplace reality return. Having seen life as void of meaning once, he calls those everyday objects, the "trees, houses and hills," "the usual deception"; he states quietly that he will continue on, "silently," "bearing my secret among the men who do not look back." The "real" world becomes unreal—a motif in his early poetry.

In "The Mediterranean," he describes the sense of futility of a poet trying to say something in the presence of the sea with its "vast language," which contrasts his "moldy dictionary words" and his "clichés/ which student rabble might tomorrow steal in real poetry." Overwhelmed and overawed by the elemental power of the Mediterranean, his consciousness is razed: "My thoughts fail, they leave me." His senses leave him as well, but this has its beneficent side also, in that having no thoughts, and no senses, he is no longer conscious and therefore no longer bound. He has, as he says, "No limit."

Montale's work is not void of the kind of inspiration that can often mount to a statement of faith in the human spirit's drive to endure. In "The Lemon Trees," he describes and defines his poetic, separating it from its predecessors, whom he shows as "the laureled poets" of tradition who walk among "shrubs/ with learned names." He eschews them, the lushness of tradition, and their poetics in favor of those streets that "end in grassy/ ditches" in which boys catch "a few famished eels from drying puddles"—an image that exemplifies Montale's aesthetic decision to create in a language of sparseness, bringing thoughts to meaning through evocative images. In contrast to the images of dryness, paths of water wend their way "into the orchards, among the lemon trees." The smell of the earth "rains its restless sweetness in the heart," and the "smell of the lemon trees" becomes one of the "riches of the world" in which even "we the poor share." These riches, the lemon trees, have the power to melt the "heart's ice," as they transform into "trumpets of gold" which "pour forth/ epiphanies of Light!"

"Don't ask me for words" provided for many the basis on which to term *Cuttlefish Bones* a volume exemplifying Montale's skepticism. The poem confronts with negations. The poet establishes an anti-idealistic situation by telling

readers that he cannot give words that will tell about the soul, and he ends by telling he cannot use language to "open worlds"; all he can tell is a negation, he says: "what we are *not*, what we do *not* want." He cannot, he says, cast what he cannot tell in "letters of fire," emblazoning and illuminating as if it were at once a shining harbinger of hope against a background of emptiness and decay, "lost crocus in a dusty field," and also an emblem of the difficulty of speaking to his generation immediately after World War I. Humanity, he says, confident and "striding," connected with others, is unaware that its impress, its "shadow"—perhaps its soul— might become emblazoned on "a crumbling wall." People are unaware that even their soul, in becoming part of or associated with this crumbling wall, this thing of substance that fades and fails, will not be eternal. Montale the poet speaks directly to the reader, going against Romanticism in saying the poet has only "gnarled syllables," which are "branch-dry," through which he can tell of nothing eternal: not of the soul, and truly not of "formulas" that will help people to see.

"To laze at noon, pale and thoughtful," known to most readers of Italian poetry, almost suspends itself in its lack of action verbs and the repetition of infinitives: "to laze," "to listen," "to gaze," "to peer." The image of the blaze is repeated from the first poem in the series in the image of "a blazing garden wall." In the last sequence of this poem, the action finally moves, and "walking out, dazed with light," the realization dawns on the speaker that life is "trudging along a wall," and that the wall is "spiked/ with jagged shards of broken bottles"—an image typical in rural northern Italy.

"Don't take shelter in the shade" repeats images from "To laze at noon, pale and thoughtful": the shade, the waves, the cliffs, the action of "lazing," and, again, dazzling light, stated to be the "one certainty." The poem "To laze at noon" is transformed: The "lazing" is done by the waves in a time of "distress," and the very material images of earthiness transform into the evanescent; a windhover is like summer lightning, life "powders away," and our passing is done "in a shimmer of dust," the cliffs "fray/ in a webbing of haze," and even the light becomes a "flare of ash." The ash, however, in the last stanza, is illusion burning (or purifying) and vanishing into the certainty of "light"; the movement counters the previous movement in the admonition to another, "let's not throw our strayed lives/ to a bottomless abyss."

Montale acknowledges that one is always part of one's tradition, even when seeming to write against it. In his allusions to such writers as Dante Alighieri and Giacomo Leopardi, he situates himself distinctly in the history of Italian letters as he diverges into new directions. One of the most significant literary artists of the twentieth century, Montale focuses in his poetry upon fragments of objects in order to attempt to transform fragmented vision into a vision of wholeness.

Donna Berliner

Further Reading

Almansi, Guido, and Bruce Merry. *Eugenio Montale: The Private Language of Poetry.* Edinburgh: Edinburgh University Press, 1977. Provides close reading and examination of sources.

Arrowsmith, William, ed. and trans. *Cuttlefish Bones: 1920-1927,* by Eugenio Montale. New York: W. W. Norton, 1992. Arrowsmith's extensive notes and commentary provide invaluable insight into the collection.

Becker, Jared. *Eugenio Montale.* Boston: Twayne, 1986. Introductory overview of Montale's life and work. The chapter on *Cuttlefish Bones* examines themes, images, and characters.

Brook, Clodagh J. *The Expression of the Inexpressible in Eugenio Montale's Poetry: Metaphor, Negation, and Silence.* New York: Oxford University Press, 2002. Examines the struggle with language that Brook defines as a central component of Montale's poetry.

Cambon, Glauco. *Eugenio Montale's Poetry: A Dream in Reason's Presence.* Princeton, N.J.: Princeton University Press, 1982. Cambon's section on *Cuttlefish Bones* treats not only the themes of the book but also the prosody and influences.

Pell, Gregory M. *Memorial Space, Poetic Time: The Triumph of Memory in Eugenio Montale.* Leicester, England: Troubador, 2005. Focuses on the meaning of memory in *Cuttlefish Bones* and other works by Montale. Describes how Montale uses memory as a metaphor for a world "where all has been printed before time" and the poet's task is to "recollect what was already there."

Pipa, Arshi. *Montale and Dante.* Minneapolis: University of Minnesota Press, 1968. First full study in English. Explores Dante's tremendous and formative influence on Montale.

Sica, Paola. *Modernist Forms of Rejuvenation: Eugenio Montale and T. S. Eliot.* Florence, Italy: L. S. Olschki, 2003. Compares the work of the two poets, demonstrating how their nihilism is balanced by a belief in the spiritual, creative, and political power of idealized youth. Describes how both poets sought to rejuvenate what they perceived as a decaying Western culture.

Singh, Ghan Shyam. *Eugenio Montale: A Critical Study of His Poetry, Prose, and Criticism.* New Haven, Conn.: Yale University Press, 1973. An excellent discussion by a translator who received personal commentary from Montale. The introduction effectively places Montale within his tradition.

West, Rebecca J. *Eugenio Montale: Poet on the Edge.* Cambridge, Mass.: Harvard University Press, 1981. An invaluable and detailed study of Montale's themes, style, and poetics.

Cyclops

Author: Euripides (c. 485-406 B.C.E.)
First produced: Kyklōps, c. 421 B.C.E. (English translation, 1782)
Type of work: Drama
Type of plot: Satyr play
Time of plot: Antiquity
Locale: Mount Aetna in Sicily

Principal characters:
ODYSSEUS, king of Ithaca
THE CYCLOPS
SILENUS, aged captive of the Cyclops
CHORUS OF SATYRS
COMPANIONS OF ODYSSEUS

The Story:

As he rakes the ground before the cave of his master, the Cyclops, old Silenus laments the day he was shipwrecked on the rock of Aetna and taken into captivity by the monstrous, one-eyed offspring of Poseidon, god of the sea. About

Silenus gambols his children, the Chorus of Satyrs, who pray with their father to Bacchus for deliverance. Suddenly, Silenus spies a ship and the approach of a group of sailors who are clearly seeking supplies. Odysseus and his companions approach, introduce themselves as the conquerors of Troy, driven from their homeward journey by tempestuous winds and desperately in need of food and water. Silenus warns them of the cannibalistic Cyclops's impending return, urges them to make haste, and then begins to bargain with them over the supplies. Spying a skin of wine, the precious liquid of Bacchus that he did not taste for years, Silenus begs for a drink. After one sip he feels his feet urging him to dance. He offers them all the lambs and cheese they need in exchange for one skin of wine.

As the exchange takes place, the giant Cyclops suddenly returns, ravenously hungry. The wretched Silenus makes himself appear to be terribly beaten and accuses Odysseus and his men of plundering the Cyclops's property. Odysseus denies the false charge, but although he is supported by the leader of the Chorus of Satyrs, the Cyclops seizes two of the sailors, takes them into his cave, and makes a meal of them. Horrified, Odysseus is then urged by the satyrs to employ his famed cleverness, so effective at Troy, in finding some means of escape.

After some discussion, Odysseus hits upon a subtle plan: First they will make the Cyclops drunk with wine; then, while he is in a stupor, they will cut down an olive tree, sharpen it, set it afire, and plunge it into the Cyclops's eye. After that escape will be easy. When the Cyclops emerges from his cave, Odysseus offers him the wine, and the giant and Silenus proceed to get hilariously drunk. So pleased is the monster with the effects of the Bacchic fluid that Silenus without much trouble persuades him not to share it but to drink it all up by himself. The grateful Cyclops asks Odysseus his name (to which the clever warrior replied "No man") and promises that he will be the last to be eaten. Soon the Cyclops finds the earth and sky whirling together and his lusts mounting. He seizes the unhappy Silenus and drags him into the cave to have his pleasure with him.

As the Cyclops lies in a stupor, Odysseus urges the satyrs to help him fulfill the plan they agreed upon, but the cowardly satyrs refuse and Odysseus is forced to use his own men for the task. Soon the agonized Cyclops, shouting that "no man" blinded him, comes bellowing out of the cave. The chorus mocks and jeers at him for this ridiculous charge and gives him false directions for capturing the escaping Greeks. The berserk giant thrashes about and cracks his skull against the rocks. When the escaping Odysseus taunts him with his true name, the Cyclops groans that an oracle predicted that Odysseus would blind him on his way home from Troy, but he foretold also that the clever one would pay for his deed by tossing about on Poseidon's seas for many years. The satyrs hasten to join the escape so that they can once more become the proper servants of Bacchus in a land where grapes grow.

Critical Evaluation:

By purely aesthetic standards, *Cyclops* cannot be considered a valuable or important play, but it otherwise has a twofold interest as the only complete satyr play preserved from ancient Greece and as a dramatization of an episode from Homer's *Odyssey* (c. 800 B.C.E.). Euripides has kept the main line of Homer's tale, but for the sake of enhanced humor has added the character of old Silenus and the Chorus of Satyrs. Furthermore, the exigencies of stage presentation made it necessary for him to change Homer's ingenious escape device to slipping through the rocks past the blind Cyclops. The light tone of the play must have been a welcome relief to the Greek audience, for the play followed three tragedies presented in succession.

The satyr play was traditionally presented at a Greek dramatic festival after three tragedies had been staged. It made fun of tragic characters and themes, deflating tragedy's conceits and devices. As such, it is usually thought to have been designed to provide some comic relief from the prevailing gloom and tension of the three preceding plays. An ancient critic called Demetrius of Phalerum called it "tragedy on holiday," which indicates both its parodic character and its connections with the bawdy celebration of the Dionysian festival. The satyr play may on occasion have had a close connection with the tragedies that preceded it—the satyr play that followed the Oedipus trilogy, for instance, was called *The Sphinx*—but in other cases the link seems more tenuous.

Various opinions have been expressed on the purpose of the satyr play. The notion that it provided light relief after the tragedies is widely held. Others have suggested that it was designed to accompany heavy wine-drinking at the end of the day's celebration of Dionysus. Alternatively, the plays may reflect the incorporation of older, animalistic, agricultural rites involving satyrs into the urban festival of Dionysus in which the dramas were performed. It is known that people dressed up as satyrs, mythical creatures that are humanlike but with elements of horses and goats. Satyrs are described in ancient sources as mischievous, playful, lusty, and hedonistic. They have pointed ears and snub noses and a horse's tail. They represent the unleashed forces of physical desire that normally have to be kept under control. This is why they are closely connected with Dionysus, the god of wine, dancing, and release of pent-up emotions.

Evidence from *Cyclops* and other fragmentary satyr plays suggests some common elements of the genre: the captivity and liberation of the Chorus of Satyrs, the presence of a miraculous invention or substance (wine, fire, the flute), the theme of rebirth or escape from the underworld, and a lively interest in sexual activity. In spite of the similarities with Greek comedy, the satyr play retained its close links with tragedy in meter and language, and in its use of mythological, as opposed to topical, subject matter.

Cyclops is the only complete satyr play that survives. Its moments of slapstick humor—such as the Cyclops's entrance on stage to the strains of a wedding song, the scene of Silenus drinking behind the Cyclops's back, and the final episode with the blinded creature stumbling around the stage—make it an effective burlesque of a well-known Homeric story. Euripides changed Homer's Cyclops from a man-eating savage into a more human personage: He has an intellect, the ability to argue his position, and a sophisticated ideology. He owns cattle as well as sheep and keeps a retinue of slaves. He is even something of a gourmet cook. At the same time, the Cyclops retains his penchant for eating humans. It is this combination of the old and the new, of the barbaric and the civilized, in the Cyclops that makes him such a bizarre character.

The play presents an Odysseus who is a clever and unscrupulous trickster, rather than the noble hero of traditional mythology. Odysseus is the little man fighting against the giant and gets the audience's sympathy as a result. The bullying Cyclops gets the punishment he deserves. The audience nevertheless may feel some sympathy for the Cyclops, who suffers a terrible punishment. The Cyclops in the *Odyssey* is a complex figure, and Polyphemus in this satyr play is more than just a buffoon. The emphasis on the painful effects of the blinding of the Cyclops serves to engage the audience's sympathy. The downfall of the Cyclops, in fact, acquires some tragic coloring.

Cyclops is also the dramatization of the initiation of an individual into the rites of the worship of Dionysus. Polyphemus, for all his knowledge and sophistication, is unfamiliar with wine. He is presented as akin to such figures as Lycurgus or Pentheus, who also have to be converted to Dionysian ways. The liberation of the imprisoned satyrs at the end of the play represents the triumph of the god Bacchus over all obstacles and enemies. Euripides has successfully brought Dionysus into an old Homeric story: Building on the detail of the Cyclops's unfamiliarity with wine, a sign of his savagery and lack of humanity, the playwright has produced a representation of the power of Dionysus.

Cyclops thus offers a fitting end to the tragic trilogy that preceded it. In tragedy, the power of the gods is demonstrated, as well as the inevitability of human fate. The satyr play offers the same basic lesson: Polyphemus takes the place of the tragic hero who is brought low by the god or his agent (in this case, Odysseus is the agent of Dionysus). There may also have been a provocative contemporary reference: The Sicilian setting of the action might well have recalled to the Athenian audience their city's disastrous naval expedition to Sicily a few years before. Such an allusion might point to the fact that the Athenians, like Odysseus and the satyrs, were lucky to get away with their lives; on the other hand, it might suggest that the Athenian populace had acted like a Polyphemus, drunk with ambition and blind to the dangers of arrogance and greed.

"Critical Evaluation" by David H. J. Larmour

Further Reading

Arnott, Peter D., trans. *Three Greek Plays for the Theatre: Euripides, "Medea," "Cyclops"; Aristophanes, "The Frogs."* Bloomington: Indiana University Press, 1961. A fine translation of the play, with an introduction. *Cyclops* is described as a tragedy and a comedy.

Green, Roger L. *Two Satyr Plays: Euripides' "Cyclops" and Sophocles' "Ichneutai."* New York: Penguin Books, 1957. A good translation, with an introduction. Sophocles' *The Searching Satyrs*, an incomplete satyr play, offers a useful opportunity for comparison.

Morwood, James. *The Plays of Euripides*. Bristol, England: Bristol Classical, 2002. Morwood provides a concise overview of all of Euripides' plays, devoting a separate chapter to each one. He demonstrates how Euripides was constantly reinventing himself in his work.

Mossman, Judith, ed. *Euripides*. New York: Oxford University Press, 2003. Collection of essays, some providing a general overview of Euripidean drama, others focusing on specific plays.

Seaford, Richard. Introduction to *Cyclops*, by Euripides. New York: Oxford University Press, 1984. Offers a sixty-page survey of the features of satyric drama in general and of *Cyclops* in particular. The connections of satyr drama with the cult of Dionysus in Athens are emphasized.

Sutton, Dana F. *The Greek Satyr Play*. Meisenheim an Glan, Germany: Hain, 1980. A comprehensive survey of the genre. Traces the history of the satyr play, offers a critical appraisal, and provides a useful bibliography.

Webster, T. B. L. *Monuments Illustrating Tragedy and Satyr Play*. London: Institute of Classical Studies, University of London, 1967. Presents visual evidence from archaeological sources of satyrs and their role in drama. Explores the links between tragedy and the satyr play.

Cymbeline

Author: William Shakespeare (1564-1616)
First produced: c. 1609-1610; first published, 1623
Type of work: Drama
Type of plot: Tragicomedy
Time of plot: First century B.C.E.
Locale: Great Britain and Italy

Principal characters:
CYMBELINE, the king of Britain
THE QUEEN, Cymbeline's wife
CLOTEN, the queen's son by a former husband
IMOGEN, Cymbeline's daughter by a former marriage
POSTHUMUS LEONATUS, Imogen's husband
PISANIO, a servant of Posthumus
IACHIMO, an Italian braggart
BELARIUS, a banished lord
GUIDERIUS and ARVIRAGUS, Cymbeline's sons, reared by
    Belarius
CAIUS LUCIUS, a Roman ambassador

The Story:

Gullible Cymbeline and his conniving queen intend that his daughter Imogen should marry his stepson Cloten. Instead, Imogen chooses the gentle Posthumus and secretly marries him. In a fit of anger, the king banishes Posthumus, who flees to Italy after promising to remain loyal and faithful to his bride. As a token of their vows, Imogen gives Posthumus a diamond ring that belonged to her mother; in turn, Posthumus places a bracelet of rare design on Imogen's arm.

In Rome, Posthumus meets Iachimo, a vain braggart who tries to tempt Posthumus by appealing to his sensuality. Posthumus, not to be tempted into adultery, tells Iachimo of his pact with Imogen and of the ring and bracelet they exchanged. Iachimo scoffingly wagers ten thousand ducats against Posthumus's ring that he can seduce Imogen.

Iachimo goes to Britain with letters to which he forged Posthumus's name, which persuades Imogen to receive him. Using ambiguous implications and innuendo, Iachimo plays on her curiosity about her husband's faithfulness. When that fails to win her favor, he gains access to her bedroom in a trunk which, he tells her, contains a valuable gift he bought in France that is intended for the Roman emperor; he asks that the trunk be placed in her chamber for safekeeping. While Imogen sleeps, he notes the details of the furnishings in the room, takes the bracelet from her arm, and observes a mole on her left breast.

Back in Italy, Iachimo describes Imogen's room to Posthumus and produces the bracelet, which he says Imogen gave him. Incredulous, Posthumus asks Iachimo to describe some aspect of Imogen's body as better proof of his successful seduction. Iachimo's claim that he kissed the mole on Imogen's breast enrages Posthumus. He sends a letter to Pisanio, commanding that the servant kill Imogen, and a let-

ter to Imogen, asking her to meet him in Milford Haven. Pisanio is to kill Imogen as they travel through the Welsh hills.

On the journey Pisanio divulges the real purpose of their trip when he shows Imogen the letter ordering her death. Unable to harm his master's wife, Pisanio instructs her to dress as a boy and join the party of Caius Lucius, who is in Britain to collect tribute to the Emperor Augustus and who is soon to return to Rome. Then Imogen will be near Posthumus and can try to disprove Iachimo's accusations against her. Pisanio also gives Imogen a box containing a restorative, which the queen entrusted to him ostensibly in case Imogen became ill during her trip. The queen actually thinks the box contained a slow-acting poison, which she procured from her physician; he, suspecting chicanery, reduces the drug content so that the substance will do no more than induce a long sleep. Pisanio takes leave of his mistress and returns home.

Dressed in boy's clothing, hungry, and weary, Imogen comes to the mountain cave of Belarius, who was banished from Cymbeline's court twenty years earlier and kidnapped Guiderius and Arviragus, Cymbeline's infant sons. In Wales, the two boys were brought up to look upon Belarius as their father. Calling herself Fidele, Imogen wins the affection of the three men when she asks shelter of them. Left alone when the men go out to hunt food, Imogen, worn out and ill, swallows some of the medicine that Pisanio gave her.

Cymbeline, meanwhile, refuses to pay the tribute demanded by Rome, and the two nations prepare for war. Cloten, who was infuriated by Imogen's coldness to him, tries to learn her whereabouts. Pisanio hopes to trick her pursuer and show him the letter in which Posthumus asks

Imogen to meet him at Milford Haven. Disguised as Posthumus, Cloten sets out to avenge his injured vanity.

In Wales, he comes upon Belarius, Arviragus, and Guiderius while they are hunting. Recognizing him as the queen's son, Belarius assumes that Cloten comes to arrest them as outlaws. He and Arviragus go in search of Cloten's retinue while Guiderius fights with and kills Cloten. Guiderius then cuts off Cloten's head and throws it into the river. Returning to the cave, the three men find Imogen, as they think, dead, and they prepare her for burial. Benevolent Belarius, remembering that Cloten is of royal birth, brings his headless body for burial and lays it near Imogen.

When Imogen awakens from her drugged sleep, she is grief-stricken when she sees lying nearby a body dressed in Posthumus's clothing. Sorrowing, she joins the forces of Caius Lucius as the Roman army marches by on their way to engage the soldiers of Cymbeline.

Posthumus, who is a recruit in the Roman army, now regrets his order for Imogen's death. Throwing away his uniform, he dresses himself as a British peasant. Although he cannot restore Imogen to life, he does not want to take any more British lives. In a battle between the Romans and Britons, Posthumus vanquishes and disarms Iachimo. Cymbeline is taken prisoner and rescued by Belarius and his two foster sons. These three build a fort and, aided by Posthumus, so spurred the morale of the fleeing British soldiers that Cymbeline's army is victorious.

Since he did not die in battle, Posthumus identifies himself as a Roman after Lucius is taken, and he is sent to prison by Cymbeline. In prison, he has a vision in which Jove assures him that he will yet be the lord of the Lady Imogen. Jove orders a tablet placed on Posthumus's chest. When Posthumus awakens and finds the tablet, he reads that a lion's whelp will be embraced by a piece of tender air and that branches lopped from a stately cedar would revive. Shortly before the time set for his execution, he is summoned to appear before Cymbeline.

In Cymbeline's tent, the king confers honors upon Belarius, Guiderius, and Arviragus and bemoans the fact that the fourth valiant soldier, so poorly dressed, is not present to receive his reward. Cornelius, the physician, tells Cymbeline that the queen died after her villainies. Lucius pleads for the life of Imogen, still dressed as a boy, because of the page's youth. Pardoned, Imogen asks Iachimo to explain his possession of the ring he wears. As Iachimo confesses to lying to win the ring from Posthumus, Posthumus enters and identifies himself as the murderer of Imogen. When Imogen protests against his confession, Posthumus strikes her. Pisanio then identifies Imogen to keep Posthumus from striking her

again. The truth disclosed, Belarius understands his foster sons' affinity for Imogen. Posthumus and Imogen, reunited, profess to remain devoted to each other for the rest of their lives.

After Guiderius confesses to the murder of Cloten, Cymbeline orders him bound, but he stays the sentence when Belarius identifies himself and the two young men. Cymbeline then blesses his three children who stand before him. A soothsayer interprets Jove's message on the tablet left on Posthumus's chest. The lion's whelp is Posthumus, the son of Leonatus, and the piece of tender air is Imogen. The lopped branches from the stately cedar are Arviragus and Guiderius, long thought dead, now restored in the king's love. Overjoyed, Cymbeline makes peace with Rome.

Critical Evaluation:

Cymbeline, together with *The Winter's Tale* (pr. c. 1610-1611, pb. 1623) and *The Tempest* (pr. 1611, pb. 1623), belongs to William Shakespeare's final period of writing. These last three plays are marked by their mood of calmness, maturity, and benevolent cheerfulness; a kind of autumnal spirit prevails. This is not to say that *Cymbeline* lacks villains, traumatic events, or scenes of violence—the play contains all these elements—but that the tone is serene in spite of them. *Cymbeline* may be classified as a tragicomedy to distinguish it from such more dazzling predecessors among Shakespeare's comedies as *Love's Labour's Lost* (pr. c. 1594-1595, pb. 1598) and *Twelfth Night: Or, What You Will* (pr. c. 1600-1602, pb. 1623), which have roguish heroes and heroines, dialogues filled with witty and sparkling repartee, and plots abounding in mischievous scheming and complications. The main characters in *Cymbeline*, by contrast, are remarkable for their virtue rather than for their cleverness, wit, or capacity for mischief; Posthumus is a model of earnestness and fidelity, and Imogen is the picture of purity and wifely devotion. The text is memorable not for the brilliance and sparkle of its dialogue, but for its moving poetry. Much of the plot consists of the trials and sufferings of the good characters, brought on by the scheming of the bad ones. However, the play ends as comedy must, with the virtuous rewarded and the wicked punished.

In the plot of *Cymbeline*, Shakespeare combines two lines of action: the political-historical story line of the British king preparing for war with Rome and the love story of Imogen and Posthumus. For the historical background, Shakespeare once again uses Holinshed's *The Chronicles of England* (1577). Finding, however, that Cymbeline, a descendant of King Lear, is too dull to provide for interesting drama, he takes the liberty of assigning to that king the refusal to pay the Roman tribute, which action Holinshed attributes to Cymbeline's son Guiderius. In this way, Shakespeare enlivens the plot with a war, which is resolved in a peace treaty at the end. Imogen's story, however, provides the primary interest in *Cymbeline*, a love story centering on a wager between a cunning villain and a devoted husband regarding the faithfulness of the absent wife; for this story Shakespeare was indebted to one of the tales in Boccaccio's *Decameron* (1349-1351). In addition to the two main story lines, the plot of *Cymbeline* contains many characters traveling in disguise and cases of mistaken identity. In a subplot of Shakespeare's invention, the story is further complicated with the consequences of Belarius abducting and subsequently rearing the king's infant sons in Wales. Such elements lend a certain extravagance to the plot of *Cymbeline*.

Cymbeline bears many resemblances to previous plays of Shakespeare. The figure of the gullible king influenced by his wicked queen reminds one of Shakespeare's *Macbeth* (pr. 1606, pb. 1623), as does the scene of supernatural intervention, the ghosts of Posthumus's family, and the tablet bearing a prophecy. Iachimo does not approach Iago in malignancy, but nevertheless calls to mind Othello's tormentor through his cunning strategies and his manipulation of Posthumus's capacity for jealousy. Likewise, the scenes of Imogen's travels disguised as a boy and her eventual reunion with her lost brothers are reminiscent of Viola's similar adventures in *Twelfth Night*. Perhaps most important, however, is the relation it bears to that final masterpiece, *The Tempest*.

Further Reading

Bergeron, David M. "*Cymbeline*: Shakespeare's Last Roman Play." *Shakespeare Quarterly* 31, no. 1 (Spring, 1980): 31-41. Traces the historical and political factors at work in the play.

Frye, Northrop. *A Natural Perspective: The Development of Shakespearean Comedy and Romance.* New York: Columbia University Press, 1965. Frye puts the play in the context of other late Shakespearean romances. The most interesting commentary available on the role of Imogen and on the visions experienced by Posthumus toward the end of the play.

Hieatt, A. Kent. "*Cymbeline* and the Intrusion of Lyric." In *Unfolded Tales: Essays on Renaissance Romance*, edited by George M. Logan and Gordon Teskey. Ithaca, N.Y.: Cornell University Press, 1989. Hieatt displays *Cymbeline*'s relationship to Edmund Spenser's sonnet sequence "The Ruins of Rome" and other treatments of the theme of historical inheritance in the frame of lyricism. A major reinterpretation of the play and a valuable commentary.

King, Ros. *Cymbeline: Constructions of Britain.* Burlington, Vt.: Ashgate, 2005. Argues that the play is not a romance, as it has often been defined, but a fantastic, black comedy in which Shakespeare easily juggles multiple plots. Places the work in its historical, cultural, and literary contexts and describes how it has been altered in performance to respond to contemporary social pressures.

Lyne, Raphael. *Shakespeare's Late Work.* New York: Oxford University Press, 2007. Provides a detailed reading of *Cymbeline* and other plays written at the end of Shakespeare's career, placing them within the context of his oeuvre. Argues that the late works have a distinct identity, defined as an ironic combination of belief and skepticism regarding faith in God, love of family, reverence for monarchs, and the theatrical depiction of truth.

Mikalachki, Jodi. "*Cymbeline* and the Masculine Romance of Roman Briton." In *The Legacy of Boadicea: Gender and Nation in Early Modern England.* New York: Routledge, 1998. Boadicea, an ancient warrior queen, epitomized the anxiety in early modern England about the excesses and failures of female rule. Mikalachki analyzes how *Cymbeline*'s depiction of ancient Briton reflects this anxiety.

Miola, Robert S. *Shakespeare's Rome.* New York: Cambridge University Press, 1983. Places *Cymbeline* in the context of Shakespeare's Roman plays. Emphasizes how Shakespeare's portrait of Britain has an ambiguous relationship to the Roman imperial legacy.

Parker, Patricia. "Romance and Empire: Anachronistic *Cymbeline*." In *Unfolded Tales: Essays on Renaissance Romance*, edited by George M. Logan and Gordon Teskey. Ithaca, N.Y.: Cornell University Press, 1989. Speculates on what has always been one of the most vexing issues surrounding *Cymbeline*: the fact that half of it seems set in ancient Roman times and the other half in the Italian Renaissance of Shakespeare's lifetime. Parker also traces the influence of Vergil's *Aeneid* (29-19 B.C.E.) on the play, particularly regarding the roles of oracles, prophecy, and kingship.

The Cypresses Believe in God

Author: José María Gironella (1917-2003)
First published: Los cipreses creen en Dios, 1953
   (English translation, 1955)
Type of work: Novel
Type of plot: Historical realism
Time of plot: 1931-1936
Locale: Gerona, Catalonia, northeastern Spain

Principal characters:
MATÍAS ALVEAR, a telegraph operator
CARMEN ELGAZU, his wife
IGNACIO,
CÉSAR, and
PILAR, their children
MOSÉN ALBERTO, a priest
DAVID and OLGA POL, teachers

The Story:

Matías Alvear is transferred by his government employer from Málaga, where his children were born, to Gerona. Though Matías is indifferent to religion, his wife Carmen is very devout and gives her children a strong religious upbringing. Ignacio enters the seminary when he is ten but after a few years decides that he does not want to be a priest. He goes to work in a bank while going to high school at night. In the meantime, César enters another seminary when he is old enough. During this period, Spain becomes a republic in 1931.

After being reproached by Ignacio for being indifferent to the poor, César learns how to be a barber, shaving and cutting the hair of the disabled and the poor. He teaches the slum children reading and arithmetic, but he is forbidden by the railroad workers to teach them the catechism. Ignacio begins studying with David Pol and his wife Olga, a very modern couple. His anarchist cousin José visits from Madrid and gets involved in heckling at conservative political meetings. José and Ignacio are involved in a riot disrupting a dance called to distract attention from a strike.

Ignacio is upset after visiting the insane asylum and finding that the inmates are fed spoiled food. He is expelled from an anarchists' meeting when he objects to destroying the printing press, housed in the local orphanage, on which the conservative paper is printed and which provides the orphanage with much of its income. Doña Amparo, wife of the policeman Julio García, seduces Ignacio.

The anarchists destroy the orphanage's print shop and are arrested, but they are released since no one can prove their guilt. Ignacio passes his examinations and, while vacationing at the seashore with his family, meets Ana María. She is of a higher social class (her father is a businessman) but tired of the *señoritos* (little gentlemen) and finds Ignacio refreshing. After the summer visit, Ignacio does not answer her letters but instead has an affair with the prostitute Candela, from whom he contracts a venereal disease. After his recovery he

reforms, makes a good confession, and is forgiven by his family.

Catalonia declares autonomy from the Spanish central government. A general strike in Gerona called to support this autonomy is countered with martial law. Soldiers storm a meeting of autonomy supporters, and the major is shot by the deputy Santeló. Those at the meeting are imprisoned, among them David, Olga, and Julio García. Mosén Alberto ministers to those imprisoned but most reject his efforts. While the Costa brothers are in jail, their sister Laura institutes reforms in their industries, such as a clinic and a child-care center, under the guidance of Mosén Francisco. Major Martínez de Soria tries those imprisoned and tells Julio that he will be shot if the real culprit is not disclosed. Information from Barcelona implicates Santeló, who is executed. The other prisoners are released, but Julio loses his post as police chief.

Mateo Santos organizes a cell of the Fascist Falange, while Cosme Vila quits his job at the bank to open Communist Party headquarters. Ignacio falls in love with Marta Martínez de Soria, whose brother joins the Falange and is killed in Valladolid. The Popular Front, a merger of all leftist parties, wins a violence-plagued election. Julio returns as chief of police, while David and Olga become commissioners of education and forbid the clergy and nuns to teach while wearing religious habits. The anarchists call a general strike; when it is broken, they set off bombs. To discredit them, the Communists bomb the Diocesan Museum, killing one of Mosén Alberto's maids. At a meeting in the Albéniz theater, the Communists state their demands, including a Workers' Militia and Julio being replaced. The Socialists and liberals demur. After Julio rejects most of the Communist demands, the Communists proclaim a general strike, burn a Christian Brothers church and school, and lynch the sexton. Mateo and his Falangist comrades beat up Dr. Relken, a German archaeologist whom they suspect of being a spy, and go into hiding.

The general strike spreads. The Communists get food for the strikers from the tenant farmers, who withhold the share due their landlords, but give the food only to Party members. The Workers' Militia begins to drill but is sent home by the police (headed by Julio). Cosme Vila is arrested but rescued by the truckers bringing food for the strikers. Gerona becomes polarized between Left and Right. The assassination of the Rightist leader José Calvo Sotelo triggers a civil war in Spain that began with a military insurrection in Africa. Major Martínez de Soria and the Falange occupy Gerona and release the landowners who were imprisoned for owning firearms. When the military in Barcelona is defeated and surrenders, those in Gerona follow orders and yield. Julio and the Loyalist officers arrest Major Martínez while the Communists and Anarchists storm the barracks and get arms. Since Julio will not let them murder the officers who surrender, the militia burns churches, commandeers cars and garages, and arrests suspects.

A revolutionary committee organizes a series of executions. The Alvear family is guarded by a militiaman to whom Ignacio once gave blood, but they are unable to save César, who returns from Collell and is arrested while trying to protect communion wafers from desecration. He and several others are executed; his last view is that of Mosén Francisco, who disguises himself as a militiaman and gives those executed the last rites.

Critical Evaluation:

The Cypresses Believe in God was José María Gironella's third novel and the first to attain widespread success, being translated into several other languages. It is the first part of a trilogy about the Spanish Civil War, the other volumes being *Un millón de muertos* (1961; *One Million Dead*, 1963) and *Ha estallado la paz* (1966; *Peace After War*, 1969). A subsequent volume, *Los hombres lloran solas* (1986; men cry alone), was not as successful. Critics agree that *The Cypresses Believe in God* is the best book in the four-volume chronicle of the Alvear family.

The author wanted to accomplish a threefold task in his study, set in the years preceding the outbreak of the Spanish Civil War and ending with the first incidents of the military insurrection that was eventually victorious under General Francisco Franco. His first concern was a chronicle of the Alvear family, with the coming to maturity of the three children the central feature. His next concern was the portrayal of the small city of Gerona with its population of twenty-five thousand as represented by the characters with whom members of the Alvear family interact: Ignacio's fellow workers at the bank, César's career as a seminarian, Pilar's maturing

and falling in love with Mateo Santos, fellow law student with Ignacio, son of the tobacconist with whom Matías plays dominoes, and organizer of the Falange in Gerona. Finally, as a backdrop there are the incidents of the coming of the civil war, at first distant and then increasingly closer.

Several influences are apparent in Gironella's novel: The family chronicles of Benito Galdós and John Galsworthy are most frequently mentioned, as are the historical novels of Honoré de Balzac and Charles Dickens. Gironella read Leo Tolstoy's monumental *Voyna i mir* (1865-1869; *War and Peace*, 1886) shortly before beginning work on *The Cypresses Believe in God*. Negative influences were the general developments in the early twentieth century novel, which many Spanish critics thought were overly intellectualized. Gironella returned to the techniques of realism and couched his work in a narrative prose style that some critics have considered crude and others factual and direct. His narration contrasts with the linguistic virtuosity, psychologizing, and stream-of-consciousness writing of Gironella's immediate predecessors. The novel is rather slow moving, since the author is seeking to depict the rhythms of a small Spanish city, organized around the seasons and the main religious holidays. However, it is also a novel of action that increases in tempo as the civil war approaches.

There is such a multiplicity of characters in the novel that in the English translation the author placed, at the end, a list of the fictional characters, a list of the historical figures whose names appear in the novel, and an identification of the main political movements in Spain at that time. The reader needs this guidance. The portrayal of the characters is for the most part sympathetic; though the novel is written from the point of view of the insurgents, its protagonists are not saints, and, except at the end, the opponents are not demons. Gironella has various characters state in everyday language the political philosophies that they espouse, thus providing the reader an idea of the complexity of Spanish politics at that time. The destructive aspect of the civil war is revealed in the development of the characters: Mateo Santos, though a good friend of Ignacio and Pilar's sweetheart, organizes and leads the beating of Dr. Relken. Cosme Vila, Ignacio's colleague at the bank, first appears as a character that Dickens might have created and ends as the organizer of executions, including César's. One criticism lodged against the novel is that the coup by the insurgents is portrayed as bloodless, with Dr. Relken's beating their only atrocity, whereas the counter-coup by the anarchists and Communists is characterized by the machine-gunning of praying nuns.

The title of the book comes from the cypress trees that adorn most Spanish cemeteries. As a young seminarian,

César is forbidden by his spiritual advisers to spend too much time visiting cemeteries, and at the end of the novel it is in a cemetery that he is executed. Ignacio's character development parallels that of the author. Both were born at approximately the same time, had initial aspirations toward the priesthood, then worked in a bank. Gironella went on to serve in the insurgent army and, at the time of writing *The Cypresses Believe in God*, was working in a bookstore in Gerona. His novel was enthusiastically received in the United States at the time of its appearance, was a selection of the Catholic Digest Book Club, and was extensively reviewed. It should be read as a counterbalance to novels of the Spanish Civil War that take the Loyalist side, such as Ernest Hemingway's *For Whom the Bell Tolls* (1940) and André Malraux's *L'Espoir* (1937; *Days of Hope*, 1938).

R. M. Longyear

Further Reading

Boyle, John F. "True Fiction." *Commonweal* 130, no. 12 (June 20, 2003). Boyle discusses *The Cypresses Believe in God*, praising the novel for its well-conceived story and its ability to give "shape, color, and substance in understanding the Spanish Civil War."

Ilie, Paul. "Fictive History in Gironella." *Journal of Spanish Studies* 2 (1974): 77-94. Shows that Gironella points out relationships between the novel and historical events of the time. Citations from the novel are all in the original Spanish.

Preston, Paul. *Revolution and War in Spain, 1931-1939*. New York: Methuen, 1984. This set of twelve essays shows that the Spanish Civil War was not one but many wars. Pertinent to the background of *The Cypresses Believe in God* are the essay by Frances Lannon on the responsibilities of the anticlericals and of the Catholic Church in polarizing Spanish society in the 1930's and the chapter by Juan Pablo Pusi on the conflicts between the micronationalism of Catalonia and the Second Republic.

Thomas, Gareth. *The Novel of the Spanish Civil War*. New York: Cambridge University Press, 1990. Gironella's trilogy receives a chapter-length discussion, and the introductory chapters are valuable in providing a context for the novel. The citations from Gironella and his critics are all in the original Spanish or French.

Cyrano de Bergerac

Author: Edmond Rostand (1868-1918)
First produced: 1897; first published, 1898 (English translation, 1898)
Type of work: Drama
Type of plot: Tragicomedy
Time of plot: Seventeenth century
Locale: France

Principal characters:
CYRANO DE BERGERAC, poet and soldier
ROXANE, with whom Cyrano is in love
CHRISTIAN DE NEUVILLETTE, a clumsy young soldier

The Story:

In the theater hall of the Hôtel de Burgundy, a young soldier named Christian de Neuvillette anxiously waits for the beautiful Roxane to appear in her box. Christian fell passionately in love with this woman whom he never met. While he is waiting for her arrival, Christian becomes increasingly upset because he fears that he will never be able to summon sufficient courage to address her, for he believes she is as brilliant and as graceful as he is doltish and clumsy.

In the audience, also waiting for the curtain to go up, is one Ragueneau, a romantic tavern-keeper and tosspot poet, whose friends praise his verses to his face while behind his back they help themselves to the pastries that he makes. Ragueneau inquires of another poet the whereabouts of Cyrano de Bergerac. The actor Montfleury, Cyrano's enemy and one of Roxane's suitors, is to star in the play, and Cyrano threatened him with bodily injury if he appears for the performance. Cyrano, however, did not yet arrive.

At last Roxane appears. The play begins, and Montfleury comes out on the stage to recite his lines. Suddenly a powerful voice orders him to leave the stage. After the voice comes the man, Cyrano de Bergerac, one of the best swordsmen in France. The performance is halted abruptly.

Another of Roxane's suitors tries to provoke a fight with Cyrano by ridiculing his uncommonly big nose. Cyrano, sensitive about his disfiguring nose, becomes the insulter instead of the insulted. Words lead to a duel. To show his contempt for his adversary, Cyrano composes a poem while he is sparring with his opponent, and when he finishes the last word of the last line, Cyrano staggers his man. Le Bret, Cyrano's close friend, cautions the gallant swordsman against making too many enemies by his insults.

Cyrano confesses that he is exceptionally moody lately because he is in love with his lovely cousin Roxane, despite the fact he can never hope to win her because of his ugliness. While Le Bret tries to give Cyrano confidence in himself, Roxane's chaperone appears to give Cyrano a note from his cousin, who wants to see him. Cyrano is overcome with joy. The place selected for the meeting between Cyrano and Roxane is Ragueneau's tavern. Cyrano arrives early, and, while he waits for his beautiful cousin, he composes a love letter, which he leaves unsigned because he intends to deliver it in person. When Roxane appears, she confesses to Cyrano that she is in love. Cyrano thinks for a moment that she is in love with him, but he soon realizes that the lucky fellow is not Cyrano but Christian. Roxane asks Cyrano to take the young soldier under his wing, to protect him in battle. Cyrano sadly consents to do her bidding.

Later, when Christian jests with Cyrano concerning the latter's nose, Cyrano restrains himself for Roxane's sake. When he learns that Cyrano is Roxane's cousin, Christian confesses his love for Roxane and begs Cyrano's help in winning her. Christian is a warrior, not a lover; he needs Cyrano's ability to compose pretty speeches and to write tender, graceful messages. Although his heart is broken, Cyrano gives the young man the letter he wrote in Ragueneau's tavern.

Cyrano visits Roxane to inquire about her love affair with Christian. Roxane, who recently received a letter from Christian, is delighted by his wit. Cyrano does not tell her that he is the writer of the letter.

Shortly afterward Christian tells Cyrano that he now wants to speak for himself in his wooing of Roxane. Under her balcony one evening Christian tries to speak for himself, but he becomes so tongue-tied that he has to ask the aid of Cyrano, who is lurking in the shadows. Cyrano, hidden, tells Christian what to say, and Roxane is so delighted by these dictated protestations that she bestows a kiss on Christian.

A friar appears with a letter from the Count de Guiche, commander of Cyrano's regiment, to Roxane. The count writes that he is coming to see her that night, even though by so doing he is deserting his post. Roxane deliberately mis-

reads the letter, which, she says, orders the friar to marry her to Christian. Roxane asks Cyrano to delay de Guiche until after the ceremony, a request that Cyrano effectively carries out by making the count think that Cyrano is mad. After learning that Roxane and Christian are already married, the duped de Guiche orders Christian to report immediately to his regiment.

In a battle that follows, Cyrano and the other cadets are engaged against the Spanish. During the conflict Cyrano risks his life to send letters to Roxane through the enemy's lines, and Roxane never suspects that the author of these messages is not Christian. Later Roxane joins her husband, and to him she confesses that his masterful letters brought her to his side.

Realizing that Roxane is really in love with the nobility and tenderness of Cyrano's letters, Christian begs Cyrano to tell Roxane the truth. Christian, however, is killed in battle shortly afterward, and Cyrano swears never to reveal Christian's secret. Rallying the cadets, Cyrano charges bravely into the fight, and under his leadership the Spanish are defeated.

Fifteen years pass. Roxane, grieving for Christian, retires to a convent. Each week Cyrano visits Roxane. One day, however, he comes late. When he arrives, he conceals under his hat a mortal wound that one of his enemies inflicted by dropping an object from a building on Cyrano's head. While talking about her dead husband, Roxane recites to Cyrano Christian's last letter, which she keeps next to her heart. With Roxane's permission, Cyrano reads the letter which he himself wrote, even though it has grown so dark that neither he nor Roxane can see the words.

Suddenly Roxane realizes that Cyrano knows the contents of the letter by heart, that he must have written it. With this realization comes her conviction that for fifteen years she unknowingly loved the soul of Cyrano, not Christian. Roxane confesses her love for Cyrano, who dies knowing that at last Roxane is aware of his love and that she shares it with him.

Critical Evaluation:

Edmond Rostand's family was wealthy, and he never seemed to need to be commercial. He worked at a slow and sure pace and chose his themes as they came to him. His canon includes one volume of poetry, *Les Musardises* (1890), and the dramas *Les Romanesques* (1894; *The Romantics*, 1899), *La Princesse lointaine* (1895; *The Far Princess*, 1899), *La Samaritaine* (1897; *The Woman of Samaria*, 1921), *Cyrano de Bergerac* (1897), *L'Aiglon* (1900; *The Eaglet*, 1898), and *Chantecler* (1910; *Chanticleer*, 1910).

Dramatic invention, the use of splendid and spectacular settings, the presence of an eloquent, witty, and adventuresome hero, the conflict of love versus honor, the recklessness and self-sacrifices of the characters, and the point of honor upon which the whole play turns—all are elements of the romance tradition and are present in *Cyrano de Bergerac*. *Cyrano de Bergerac* is a perennial favorite with theater audiences. Cyrano is more than a hot-tempered swordsman who gets into trouble because he resents people who make fun of his nose. Cyrano de Bergerac symbolizes magnanimity, unselfishness, and beauty of soul. Motion picture and television adaptations as well as several successful stage revivals of *Cyrano de Bergerac* over the years demonstrate that Rostand's popular turn-of-the-century verse play is a classic. Written shortly before the beginning of the twentieth century, *Cyrano de Bergerac* reflects the themes and symbols of late nineteenth century romanticism, with its emphasis on the heroic individual who feels he has failed. In its story of ill-fated lovers and wasted lives, and in its symbolic moon as mother-and-home of the hero, and in its historical context, *Cyrano de Bergerac* is the culmination of a romantic revival in French literature.

In tone the play charts a drastically different course from the "decadent" products that filled the theaters during the same period. In creating Cyrano, Rostand reached into the seventeenth century for his character. The real Cyrano was a little-known writer who lived in France from 1619 until his death in 1655. The bearer of an unusually large nose, he wrote about it in his books—books that may be described as the early ancestors of the science fiction genre.

It is tempting to speculate that Rostand also found his proper tone in the seventeenth century, for *Cyrano de Bergerac* is a play based on certain Renaissance-like assumptions, such as the reality of honor and the drama it can create when confronted with a passion such as love. The theme of the play—"the making of a style out of despair"—also has affinities with seventeenth century values. People in Europe during the Renaissance were still experiencing the example as well as the ideal of the heroic individual: the exhilarating belief that one can, with courage, strength, and intellectual ability, will into being—create—the world as one chooses. It remained for Rostand's age to turn the coin from "man is everything" to "man is nothing." An underlying assumption of *Cyrano de Bergerac* is the presence of despair, but Rostand handles it lightly, and it is the style which one can create within this framework of despair that interests him. Rostand's word for style becomes "panache"—literally "white plume" but a word with broad symbolic connotations in the play. The word signifies something of a swashbuckling

quality. It conveys a sense of superiority, courage, pride. A man with "panache" would swagger, and, like Cyrano, he is almost bound to have enemies.

In spite of its evident stage popularity, *Cyrano de Bergerac* has taken its share of critical abuse from reviewers, who have panned it as insincere, as shallow and bustling physical activity, and as a study in useless sacrifice. The extravagance of the play, in terms of setting, language, and action, and its improbabilities also clash with the expectation of critics more accustomed to realism. Cyrano, however, is a poet, like his author; Rostand uses this play, as he does all of his works, as a vehicle for his own lyric voice.

This important point brings up a related problem the play offers to those who cannot read it in the original French. Those unfamiliar with French must depend upon translations, and although there are several English ones from which to choose, all suffer to some extent because of linguistic and cultural differences that accompany language barriers. Rostand uses the Alexandrine couplet, which gives the language of the play a weighty balance of rhyme and rhythm. Rhyming couplets in French are simply easier on the ear than they are in English. French has more rhyming endings and more acceptable combinations of its rhyming words than have proved possible in English. Out of five readily accessible English translations, three attempt to retain the poetic tone by using blank verse or rhymed verse. The other two avoid the restrictive nature of Rostand's preferred rhyme scheme. One is unrhymed but a close literal translation; the other uses various rhyme schemes freely and attempts to find English or American parallels for Rostand's witty references to French life and history, providing a lengthy introduction to explain why the changes were made. Regardless of what translation is used, the high lyrical style of the play is evident. One translation focuses on the concept of "panache" by using the French term in different contexts throughout the play. It helps to define this last word of Cyrano, which serves as a key to the play's meaning. For example, early in the play at the Pont Nesle battle, Cyrano declares that he came alone except for his triple-waving plume, this "proud panache." Later, in the debate with de Guiche over whether it is honorable for the latter to throw off his white scarf to escape, Cyrano argues that the white plume is a man's panache, a manifestation of his very soul, not to be bartered or squandered but to be preserved as a sign of contempt for his enemies.

Finally, at the end of the play and the end of his life, Cyrano describes the leaves as falling with a certain panache: They float down like trailing plumes of fading beauty, masking their fear of returning to the inevitable ashes and dust of biblical prophecy; they fall gracefully, with style, as though they are flying. Truly, *Cyrano de Bergerac* is about style created out of despair.

"Critical Evaluation" by Jean G. Marlowe

Further Reading

Amoia, Alba della Fazia. *Edmond Rostand*. Boston: G. K. Hall, 1978. One of the few English-language monographs about Rostand's life and work. Provides a valuable introductory overview.

Chandler, Frank Wadleigh. *The Contemporary Drama of France*. Boston: Little, Brown, 1920. Rostand is depicted as "an idealist endowed with a sense of humor." Ranks *Chantecler*, however, at a slightly higher level than *Cyrano de Bergerac* for "the scintillating wit, the brilliant extemporization, the profusion of words and images that make us dizzy." Good for comparing the tone of *Cyrano de Bergerac* with the rest of Rostand's canon.

Chweh, Crystal R., ed. *Readings on Cyrano de Bergerac*. San Diego, Calif.: Greenhaven Press, 2001. A companion to the play, examining its structure, style, themes, and characters.

Clark, Barrett Harper. *Contemporary French Dramatists*. Cincinnati, Ohio: Stewart & Kidd, 1915. A short but informative essay on Rostand, his work habits, and his thin but excellent canon. Helps put *Cyrano de Bergerac* in perspective and explains why subsequent dramas did not measure up to the masterpiece. Discusses the "nose" monologue in some detail.

Freeman, Edward. *Edmond Rostand, Cyrano de Bergerac*. Glasgow: University of Glasgow, French and German Publications, 1995. An overview and analysis of the play, designed for students.

Lloyd, Susan M. *The Man Who Was Cyrano: A Life of Edmond Rostand, Creator of "Cyrano de Bergerac."* Bloomington, Ind.: Unlimited, 2002. Provides information on the origins of Rostand's most famous play. Describes how he expressed his own character and ideals through his fictional characters, most notably Cyrano de Bergerac.

Rostand, Edmond. *Cyrano de Bergerac: A Heroic Comedy in Five Acts*. Translated and edited by Louis Untermeyer. New York: Heritage Press, 1954. This deluxe edition, with color illustrations by Pierre Brissard, features a foreword introducing the person on whom the stage figure is based. Includes brief biographical notes and a performance history to 1947.

Smith, Hugh Allison. *Main Currents of Modern French Drama*. New York: Henry Holt, 1925. Acknowledges *Cyrano de Bergerac* as definitive in evaluating the qualities and worth of Rostand's poetic drama. Summarizes articles that appeared after the first production. Finds the play's "freshness and salubrity" the main source of its popularity. Argues that the play was not the beginning of a new school but rather an indication of "the survival and culmination of Romanticism."

Cyropaedia

Author: Xenophon (c. 431-c. 354 B.C.E.)
First transcribed: Kyrou paideia, after 371 B.C.E.?
    (English translation, 1560-1567)
Type of work: Long fiction

Among the surviving authors of ancient Greek literature, Xenophon has the distinction of being the first who wrote in a variety of prose genres, forms that in turn deal with an even greater variety of subject matter. Most of the early prose writers of Greece devoted themselves with notable single-mindedness to history, the philosophic or scientific treatise of a given sort, dialogue, or rhetoric. Xenophon, however, wrote in nearly all of these forms. What is more, one of his latest works is a composition that even now is essentially sui generis. *Cyropaedia* has been called a historical romance. The name may be convenient, but there is no adequate classification for the work. "Didactic-romantic-political-fictional-biography" might come closer.

Xenophon incorporated into *Cyropaedia* some treatment of nearly all the topics that he developed separately in his more restricted works. Of his historical interests, despite the title and ostensible subject, there is only a slight trace: The historical and geographical reliability of Xenophon's tale is minimal. The *Ellēnika* (411-362 B.C.E.; *History of the Affairs of Greece*, 1685), covering Greek history from the point where Thucydides left off in 411 B.C.E. to the death of Epaminondas in 362 B.C.E., and *Kyrou anabasis* (between 394 and 371 B.C.E.; *Anabasis*, 1623) remain his only strictly historical creations. The latter, a famous account of the author's participation as a young man in a Greek mercenary army expedition deep into the Persian Empire, is probably his best work. *Cyropaedia* resumes some of the *Anabasis*'s telling of expert generalship in exotic terrain. The extensive discussions of Cyrus's wise arrangements in military, political, social, and economic order recall the concerns reflected in Xenophon's *Lakedaimoniōn politeia* (n.d.; *Constitution of Sparta*, 1832), *Logos eis Agēsilaon Basilea* (wr. c. 361/360 B.C.E.; *Agesilaus*, 1832) on the Spartan king, here treated as a model leader, *Hierōn ē tyrannikos* (date unknown; *Hiero*, 1832), and *Oikonomikos* (c. 362-361 B.C.E.; *Xenophon's Treatise of Household*, 1532), all written in the fourth century B.C.E. The account of Cyrus's education and the portrait of his personal virtues and world-wisdom, which culminates in his deathbed discourse to his sons on the soul, continue in their way the philosophical writings of Xenophon that are centered on Socrates, chiefly in the *Apomnēmoneumata* (c. 381-355 B.C.E.; *Memorabilia of Socrates*, 1712). The attentions devoted to horsemanship, hunting, and conviviality ("Cyrus at Banquet," for example) are vestiges of still other works of his. As a final seasoning for the whole, Xenophon includes the first love romance in Western literature, the story of Pantheia and Abradatas.

This topical cross section presents a complex of matters from which a writer of genius might well have woven an absorbing tapestry comprising an intellectual and cultural summary of the age, an encyclopedic bildungsroman, such as Johann Wolfgang von Goethe's *Wilhelm Meisters Lehrjahre* (1795-1796; *Wilhelm Meister's Apprenticeship*, 1824) or Thomas Mann's *Der Zauberberg* (1924; *The Magic Mountain*, 1927). Xenophon failed to do so. The quality of the product can be assessed after the following summary.

In book 1, Cyrus the Great is born of Cambyses, king of Persia, and Mandane, the daughter of Astyages, king of Media. Reared until his twelfth year in Persian simplicity and discipline, he then visits Media for five years. There, he learns to ride a horse and hunt, and he wins the friendship and admiration of the Medes by his virtues. He returns home and completes his training under his father's guidance. When Media is threatened by an Assyrian invasion, Cyaxares, the son of the now-deceased Astyages, asks aid of the Persians. Cyrus is sent in command of the Persian forces.

In book 2, which begins in Media, Cyrus reorganizes his army and prepares it physically and psychologically for combat. The king of Armenia, a vassal to Cyaxares, revolts.

In book 3, Cyrus reconquers the king of Armenia by brilliant strategy and recovers his allegiance to Cyaxares by equally brilliant diplomacy. He executes a similar feat with the Chaldeans, the neighbors of the Armenians. Cyaxares and Cyrus then advance together to meet the Assyrians, and, thanks largely to Cyrus's generalship, the Assyrians are defeated in a first engagement at the border.

In book 4, Cyaxares becomes jealous of Cyrus's reputation and decides to stay behind with his own army, allowing Cyrus to move ahead as he pleases. Cyrus, however, persuades most of the Median army to accompany him as well. He wins over to his side the Hyrcanians, a subject people of the Assyrians. After a second defeat of the Assyrians, he provides the Persians with a cavalry force of their own. In growing vexation, Cyaxares orders that the Median "volunteers" with Cyrus be sent home. Cyrus sends a message in justification of his noncompliance. Gobryas, a vassal of the Assyrian king, defects to Cyrus.

In book 5, Cyrus advances to the walls of Babylon, but he postpones an assault on the city. Three more subject peoples accede to the Persians. Cyrus returns to the border of Media and there confronts the spleen and chagrin of Cyaxares with such dexterity that his uncle is publicly reconciled to him.

In book 6, further military preparations are carried on in winter quarters. Pantheia, the wife of a noble subject of the Assyrian king, was captured earlier and given to the keeping of Araspas, a Median officer in Cyrus's entourage. Araspas attempts to seduce her, but she appeals to Cyrus and is protected. In consequence, her husband, Abradatas, is won over to Cyrus.

In book 7, a massive army of Assyrians and allies under the command of Croesus, king of Lydia, is defeated. Before the battle, Pantheia takes leave of Abradatas, who dies a hero's death in the fighting. Pantheia kills herself over his body. Croesus, captured after the siege of Sardis, is generously treated by Cyrus. After several other campaigns, Babylon is taken by stratagem, and victory is complete.

In book 8, Cyrus organizes his empire, marries the daughter of Cyaxares, and after a long reign holds a final edifying discourse on his deathbed. A surprising postscript sarcastically details the degeneration of the Persians since the time of Cyrus.

On the very face of it the arrangement is unpromising. The action advances without complication except for such essentially irrelevant episodes as those involving Pantheia. Xenophon's political and moral concerns, to be sure, are worked in by series of dialogues and speeches, devices that Thucydides employed with brilliant effect. (Mann's *The Magic Mountain* again provides some parallels.) For Thucydides, however, the issues and personalities of the Peloponnesian War were problematic and many-sided. Xenophon's Cyrus, by contrast, is so idealized that no counterforce can provide tension. The nearest thing to confrontation lies in the theme of the growing jealousy of Cyaxares. Thucydides would have presented in Cyaxares a distillate of everything vital in Spartan and Athenian culture that opposed the composite of Athenian-Spartan ideals read by Xenophon into the figure of Cyrus. Xenophon's Cyaxares, however, is no such foil; he is a pathetic individual manipulated by his hero-gentleman nephew.

The didactic material is not simply embedded in the framework of successive events without human complication; a degree of attention to context could still have made the segments memorable. For the most part, however, when Xenophon settles into a discourse or dialogue, he produces repetitious, platitudinous elegance. Skill in specious conversation was clearly part of the Greek ideal of the gentleman. In this fashion, Xenophon manages to flesh out his stick-figure design to some four hundred pages.

One moral to be drawn, then, is that *Cyropaedia* should never be read straight through except in Greek, where style gives some spice to many dull pages. In justice, it should also be admitted that a wisely condensed English version is worth its reading time. Anecdotes possessed of point and humor, moments with some vividness of situation and character, do occur. For example, some country bumpkin rookies in training are told that they must march behind their lieutenant. When the lieutenant is by chance sent on a postal errand, the entire platoon obediently runs off behind him. At times, the practical wisdom has its interest. Cambyses Cyrus tells how to manage his men: When encouraging them with hopes that are not certain to be fulfilled, one should not personally suggest these doubtful hopes; get someone else to act as a mouthpiece.

More important, however, some acquaintance with the text of *Cyropaedia* will always be worthwhile because of the position this book occupies in the development of the ancient political imagination. Both Xenophon and another Socratic enthusiast gave their minds to the problem of the inadequacy of existing Greek political systems. In its artistry and profundity, Plato's *Politeia* (388-366 B.C.E.; *Republic*, 1701) may transcend Xenophon. Plato, however, never conceived of a satisfactory political order larger than the city-state, and the times were leaving him behind.

Further Reading

Due, Bodil. *The "Cyropaedia": Xenophon's Aims and Methods*. Aarhus, Denmark: Aarhus University Press, 1989. Provides a concise and general summary of the characters, themes, and structures of the work. Recommended for those with some knowledge of ancient Greek.

Gera, Deborah Levine. *Xenophon's "Cyropaedia": Style, Genre, and Literary Technique*. New York: Oxford University Press, 1993. A rigorously argued close reading that also gives attention to questions of the work's sources in the Greek and Persian traditions.

Hirsch, Steven. *The Friendship of the Barbarians*. Hanover, N.H.: University Press of New England, 1985. Uses Xenophon's work to explore the Greeks' views of other peoples. Argues that far from being ethnocentric, the Greeks admired many aspects of their Persian adversaries' culture. Addresses anthropological and historical, as well as literary, concerns.

Nadon, Christopher. *Xenophon's Prince: Republic and Empire in the "Cyropaedia."* Berkeley: University of California Press, 2001. Detailed analysis of the work, including an examination of its depiction of republican and imperial politics. Many critics have wondered why *Cyropaedia*, which generally idealizes Cyrus, switches tone in its conclusion, describing the swift degeneration of Cyrus's empire and raising questions about his achievements. Nadon maintains that the work is unified and coherent, pointing out Xenophon's critiques of Cyrus throughout the text.

Tatum, James. *Xenophon's Imperial Fiction: On "The Education of Cyrus."* Princeton, N.J.: Princeton University Press, 1989. One of the best treatments of *Cyropaedia* available for the general reader. Illuminates rhetoric, political leadership, literary history, and the canon of ancient classics.

_____, ed. *The Search for the Ancient Novel*. Baltimore: Johns Hopkins University Press, 1994. Indispensable reference for studying the narrative form of the Hellenistic romance, of which *Cyropaedia* is the earliest available example.

Waterfield, Robin. *Xenophon's Retreat: Greece, Persia, and the End of the Golden Age*. Cambridge, Mass.: Harvard University Press, 2006. Attempts to round out Xenophon's account of Cyrus's Persian campaign by providing additional details of military logistics, the lives of Greek and Persian soldiers, motivations for the war, and other aspects of the battle. Compares Cyrus's experiences in Persia with present-day developments in the Middle East.

D

Daisy Miller
A Study

Author: Henry James (1843-1916)
First published: 1878
Type of work: Novella
Type of plot: Psychological realism
Time of plot: Mid-nineteenth century
Locale: Vevey, Switzerland; Rome

Principal characters:
DAISY MILLER, an American tourist
WINTERBOURNE, an American expatriate
GIOVANELLI, Daisy's Italian suitor

The Story:

Winterbourne is a young American who has lived in Europe for quite a while. He spends a great deal of time at Vevey, which is a favorite spot of his aunt, Mrs. Costello. One day, while he is loitering outside the hotel, he is attracted by a young woman who appears to be related to Randolph Miller, a young American boy with whom he was talking. After a while, the young woman exchanges a few words with him. Her name is Daisy Miller. The boy is her brother, and they are in Vevey with their mother. They came from Schenectady, Winterbourne learns, and they intend to go next to Italy. Randolph insists that he wants to go home. Winterbourne learns that Daisy hopes to visit the Castle of Chillon. He promises to take her there, for he is quite familiar with the old castle.

Winterbourne asks his aunt, Mrs. Costello, to meet Daisy. Mrs. Costello, however, will not agree because she thinks the Millers are common. That evening, Daisy and Winterbourne plan to go out on the lake, much to the horror of Eugenio, the Millers' traveling companion, who is more like a member of the family than a courier. At the last moment, Daisy changes her mind about the night excursion. A few days later, Winterbourne and Daisy visit the Castle of Chillon. The outing confirms Mrs. Costello's opinion that Daisy is uncultured and unsophisticated.

Winterbourne makes plans to go to Italy. When he arrives, he goes directly to the home of Mrs. Walker, an American whom he met in Geneva. There he meets Daisy and Randolph. Daisy reproves him for not having called to see her. Winterbourne replies that she is unkind, as he just arrived on the train. Daisy asks Mrs. Walker's permission to bring an Italian friend, Mr. Giovanelli, to a party that Mrs. Walker is about to give. Mrs. Walker agrees. Then Daisy says that she and the Italian are going for a walk. Mrs. Walker is shocked, as young unmarried women do not walk the streets of Rome with Italians. Daisy suggests that there would be no objection if Winterbourne would go with her to the spot where she is to meet the Italian and then walk with them.

Winterbourne and Daisy set out and eventually find Giovanelli. They walk together for a while. Then Mrs. Walker's carriage draws alongside the strollers. She beckons to Winterbourne and implores him to persuade Daisy to enter her carriage. She tells him that Daisy is ruining her reputation by such behavior; she becomes familiar with Italians and is quite heedless of the scandal she is causing. Mrs. Walker says she will never speak to Winterbourne again if he does not ask Daisy to get into the carriage at once. Daisy, refusing the requests of Mrs. Walker and Winterbourne, continues her walk with the Italian.

Mrs. Walker is determined to snub Daisy at the party. Winterbourne arrives, but Daisy has not yet make her appearance. Mrs. Miller arrives more than an hour before Daisy appears with Giovanelli. Mrs. Walker has a moment of weakness and greets them politely; but, as Daisy comes to say goodnight, Mrs. Walker turns her back upon her. From that time on, Daisy and Giovanelli find all doors shut to them. Winterbourne sees her occasionally, but she is always with the Italian. Everyone thinks they are having an affair. When Winterbourne asks her if she is engaged, Daisy says that she is not.

One night, despite the danger from malarial fever, Giovanelli takes Daisy to the Colosseum. Winterbourne, encountering them in the ancient arena, reproaches the Italian for his thoughtlessness. Giovanelli says that Daisy insisted upon viewing the ruins by moonlight. Within a few days, Daisy is dangerously ill. During her illness, she sends word to Winterbourne that she was never engaged to Giovanelli. A week later, she is dead.

As they stand beside Daisy's grave in the Protestant cemetery in Rome, Giovanelli tells Winterbourne that Daisy would never have married her Italian suitor, even if she had lived. Then Winterbourne realizes that he himself loved Daisy without knowing his own feelings and that he could have married her had he acted differently. He reasons, too, late, that he has lived in Europe too long and that he has forgotten the freedom of American manners and the complexity of the American character.

Critical Evaluation:

Henry James's *Daisy Miller*, which explores the social expectations placed upon Americans traveling in Europe, reveals the hypocrisy inherent in judging other people. Throughout the novella, the reader is provided with numerous clues that the Miller family is not particularly sophisticated, although clearly wealthy. Winterbourne, for example, observes that Daisy Miller has beautiful clothing, but that her appearance suffers from "a want of finish." Daisy's mother, Mrs. Miller, who makes little attempt to control her children, has a habit of saying the wrong thing at the wrong time and is unaware that her daughter's behavior is unacceptable. Eugenio, the Millers' courier, acts shocked and disapproving when Daisy displays her inappropriate social conduct. He simply expects the Millers to know better.

Daisy, a young woman who knows her mind in a time when women were considered incapable of complex thought, confounds characters such as Mrs. Walker, who represents European standards of social conduct. Daisy, through her innocent, logical assessment of the social restrictions to which she is expected to adhere, reveals the hypocrisy of these expectations. When Winterbourne tells her, for example, that flirting is considered inappropriate behavior for young, unmarried women, Daisy retorts that flirting would seem more proper in unmarried women than in married women. Her logic is irrefutable; ironically, as Winterbourne discloses, there are married women with whom flirting might take a serious turn. Daisy flirts fearlessly, in public, but she is the most exemplary among her peers. She is the most honest.

In contrast, Winterbourne is reputed to have spent a great deal of time in Geneva in the company of an older woman whom no other character in the novel has seen. Moreover, the text implies that this woman may be married. In light of this possibility, Winterbourne's hypocrisy is clear. Daisy, too, spends a great deal of time with an attractive, unmarried Italian who dotes on her, but her relationship with him is chaste. The sexist double standard that ruled Victorian morality made Winterbourne's behavior acceptable and Daisy's not.

Daisy's behavior, in fact, is a refreshing deviation from the standard presentation of women of her time in art and literature as weak, fragile creatures. Winterbourne's aunt, Mrs. Costello, suffers from numerous headaches and hence spends a lot of time resting, for example. Even Mrs. Miller, who adheres to so few social rules, manages to be ill most of the time; she rarely sees the beautiful artifacts of the countries she visits and is virtually unable even to go for short walks. When Winterbourne arrives in Italy, he hopes to find a Daisy who fits his own image of ideal femininity, one who gazes out the window of an antediluvian Roman dwelling, longing for his arrival. Winterbourne finds no such creature. Daisy is vivacious, strong-minded, and refreshingly assertive. She asserts to Winterbourne, for example, that she has "never allowed a gentleman to interfere with anything" that she does. In a time when women were the property of men, this sentiment is refreshing, even to Winterbourne.

Winterbourne, for all of his supposed sophistication, cannot shake his attraction to Daisy. He continually attempts to make her behavior conform to his dualistic expectations for women. As far as Winterbourne is concerned, Daisy is either good or bad. She cannot simply be who she is. Ironically, when Winterbourne finds, upon his arrival in Italy, that Daisy is spending a great deal of time with Mr. Giovanelli, he believes that she should have instinctively known that Giovanelli is inappropriate company. The irony lies in his own inability to recognize that perhaps he is inappropriate company for Daisy, or she for him. The hypocrisy of his thinking is thus continually revealed.

Throughout the novella, Daisy confounds other Americans who are traveling abroad, as was the custom of well-to-do Americans of the late nineteenth century. Yet, sadly, as the novella reaches its conclusion, Daisy Miller, who catches a fever after recklessly going out late in the evening, loses her life. Her death is not dramatized in an overt attempt to impart a moralistic message about prudence to the reader. Rather, her death provides her with a level of social acceptance that she never attained in life. She is buried in a small Protestant cemetery; the burial in consecrated ground professes her innocence and morality. Her funeral is well attended, another clear indication of her virtue. As if these indications are not enough, Giovanelli tells Winterbourne outright that Daisy was innocent. Another subtle irony emerges in that although Winterbourne may think himself socially superior to Giovanelli, he is clearly Giovanelli's inferior, as Winterbourne is uncouth enough to insult Giovanelli at Daisy's funeral. Furthermore, Giovanelli never questions Daisy's innocence, while Winterbourne continually wavers in his judgment of Daisy's character, even telling her at one point that she should not flirt with anyone except him.

One of the greatest tragedies of the novella is not that Daisy is continually misjudged by her hypocritical peers for her nonconformist behavior, but that she eventually conforms. The beautiful virgin dies in the prime of her life. In so doing, she conforms to another common portrayal of ideal femininity in art and literature. Winterbourne learns the gravity of his misjudgment of Daisy not only through Giovanelli but also through Mrs. Miller, who informs Winterbourne that Daisy spoke of him on her deathbed. Daisy's greatest concern was that Winterbourne know that she was not engaged to Giovanelli. The novella then makes clear that Daisy might very well have been in love with Winterbourne, although she refused to adhere to the social standards of what was considered appropriate behavior toward him or toward Giovanelli. The novella ends with a reference to Winterbourne's possible relations with a foreign woman in whom he is much interested, implying that his own adherence to the hypocritical double standard continues. Daisy, after all, was also much interested in a foreign man, yet her behavior cost her her life.

"Critical Evaluation" by Dana Reece Baylard

Further Reading

Freedman, Jonathan, ed. *The Cambridge Companion to Henry James.* New York: Cambridge University Press, 1998. A collection of essays that provides extensive information on James's life and literary influences and describes his works and the characters in them.

Graham, George Kenneth. *Henry James: The Drama of Fulfilment.* New York: Oxford University Press, 1975. Concentrates on the tragicomedy of Winterbourne's attempt to understand Daisy. Examines the interplay between the social and the personal, and the rational and the emotional.

Hoffmann, Charles G. *The Short Novels of Henry James.* New York: Bookman, 1957. Examines how *Daisy Miller* presents European social codes as constraints on evil— and Daisy's defiance as foolish American innocence of evil. Looks at the theme of appearance (Daisy's corruption) versus reality (Daisy's innocence).

Pollak, Vivian R., ed. *New Essays on "Daisy Miller" and "The Turn of the Screw."* New York: Cambridge University Press, 1993. Contains feminist and psychological interpretations of the two novels, as well as a study of the books within the context of the Victorian period. Includes an introduction and bibliography.

Reed, Kimberly C., and Peter G. Beidler, eds. *Approaches to Teaching Henry James's "Daisy Miller" and "The Turn of the Screw."* New York: Modern Language Association of America, 2005. Includes essays analyzing the two novels from a variety of perspectives.

Samuels, Charles Thomas. *The Ambiguity of Henry James.* Champaign: University of Illinois Press, 1971. Shows how *Daisy Miller* fits into James's view of the guilt of innocence. Daisy is culpable, as are her persecutors—especially the fastidious Winterbourne, yearning for American purity in a fallen world.

Tintner, Adeline R. *The Museum World of Henry James.* Ann Arbor: University of Michigan Press, 1986. Concentrates on James's use of the portrait of Pope Innocent X as analogy and contrast to Daisy's innocence in the work. Points out the ironic ending: that Winterbourne will be subject to the gossip he sought to avoid.

Wagenknecht, Edward. *Eve and Henry James: Portraits of Women and Girls in His Fiction.* Norman: University of Oklahoma Press, 1978. Looks at the origins of *Daisy Miller*, the controversy it aroused, and its literary counterparts. Considers Daisy's character, her refusal to conform, and her ignorance of corruption.

Dame Care

Author: Hermann Sudermann (1857-1928)
First published: *Frau Sorge*, 1887 (English translation, 1891)
Type of work: Novel
Type of plot: Domestic realism
Time of plot: Nineteenth century
Locale: Germany

Principal characters:
PAUL MEYERHOFER, a simple farmer
MAX MEYERHOFER, his father
ELSBETH MEYERHOFER, his mother
ELSBETH DOUGLAS, a neighbor girl

The Story:

About the time their third son, Paul, is born, the Meyerhofers lose their country estate, Helenenthal, through forced sale. Meyerhofer tries to keep his wife, Elsbeth, in ignorance of what is going on, but she is so uneasy that at last he tells her that a family named Douglas bought his property.

Meyerhofer is a violent man, given to grandiose schemes to gain wealth and endowed with a martyr complex. It suits him to move his family to a humble farm, within sight of Helenenthal, where they will be constantly reminded of their lost prosperity. Elsbeth, a docile woman, shudders at the prospect.

Mrs. Douglas, a kindhearted woman, comes to see the mother and her baby. She assures Elsbeth that she can stay on at Helenenthal as long as the family wishes. The two women become good friends. Mrs. Douglas acts as godmother for Paul, and Mrs. Meyerhofer is godmother for Elsbeth, a daughter born to the Douglases a short time later. In spite of their friendship, however, Meyerhofer takes offense at a fancied slight and moves his family in bleak November to a farm on the moor.

In those poor surroundings, Paul has a secluded childhood. His mother, sensing his retiring disposition, is kind to him, but his father is brutal. He continually ridicules his son by comparing him unfavorably with his two lively older brothers. He often beats Paul, and after the beatings his mother comforts him. She often tells him stories; the one he remembers best is a frightening tale about Dame Care, a gray woman who put great burdens on poor people. Some years after they move, Elsbeth has twin daughters, Katie and Greta.

About the time Paul is learning to whistle, bad times come to the farm. The mortgage is due, and there is no money to pay it. Day after day, Meyerhofer drives into town and comes back very late, usually drunk. Despite her fear of her husband, Elsbeth determines to seek help. She takes Paul with her to Helenenthal on a memorable visit. There she explains her husband's dislike for the Douglas family and asks for

their help. The amiable Mr. Douglas gives her the money to pay the mortgage. Paul plays with Elsbeth Douglas while the grown-ups visit.

Paul does not succeed easily at school. He has to study a long time to get his work done, and he has to memorize all the answers to problems. His handwriting, however, is very good. The Erdmann brothers, wild-eyed and saucy, make his life miserable for years. They often beat him, steal his lunch, and throw his clothes into the river.

The Meyerhofer property is surrounded by a peat bog. Always too busy to pay attention to his farm, Meyerhofer buys a used steam engine to harvest peat. He gives half his harvest as down payment to Levy, a sharp trader, and hires an engineer whom Levy recommends. The old engine, however, will never run, and Meyerhofer learns that the supposed engineer is only a tramp hired by Levy for a few days' imposture. That winter, when Levy comes to collect the other half of the harvest, the duped Meyerhofer drives him off with a whip. Levy, a shrewd man of business, goes to a lawyer. Meyerhofer is compelled to give up his harvest and, in addition, to pay a heavy fine.

After the older brothers are sent away to school, there is no money to educate Paul, who is sent to confirmation classes. He sees Elsbeth Douglas there, and he even sits near her. She is kind to the boy and goes out of her way to speak to him. The Erdmann brothers tease them about the friendship and say that Paul is sweethearting. Hating ridicule, Paul seldom speaks to Elsbeth Douglas after that.

Paul toils on the farm for five years and gets little help from his father. Once, when he is out seeding a distant field, Paul sees Elsbeth Douglas. Delighted to see him again, she gives him a book of Heinrich Heine's poetry; she is impressed with Paul's ability to whistle whole symphonies. Once after she was abroad for a long time, a party is given on her return, to which Paul and his family are invited. The rest of the Meyerhofers go early in the day, but Paul goes after dark so that no one will see his shabby clothes. He watches his two sisters having a merry time, and he sees his father talking grandly with Mr. Douglas.

Out of sympathy for Paul, Mr. Douglas agrees to go in with Meyerhofer on one of his schemes. On the strength of Mr. Douglas's endorsement, Meyerhofer borrows money recklessly. When he hears what is going on, Mr. Douglas comes to the farm and tells Meyerhofer to stop. Meyerhofer sets the dog on him, but Mr. Douglas, though bitten, chokes the savage beast. While Paul is apologizing to his neighbor, Meyerhofer attacks a servant, Michel, who had watched the scene. Michel picks up an ax. Paul takes it away from him and throws it down a well. Then he carries his struggling father into the house. From that day on, Paul is master in the household.

While Paul is wandering late one night near Helenenthal, he sees brilliant flames shooting from his farm buildings. Michel had fired the barn. Paul is able to save the house, the livestock, and the old steam engine, but everything else is lost.

Beaten in spirit, Elsbeth dies a lingering death. At the funeral, Paul sees Elsbeth Douglas again. Since her own mother is incurably ill, she feels a strong bond of sympathy for Paul. Later Paul, with the aid of books on mechanics sent by his remote brothers, begins to rebuild the steam engine that was his father's folly. He works so hard that he has little time to look after his sisters. One night he overhears them in the meadow with the Erdmann boys and learns that his sisters' honor was smirched by his old enemies. Waiting in a deserted road for them at night, he forces them at pistol point to swear they will marry Katie and Greta.

Paul finally gets the old steam engine operating, and he begins to cut and market peat. As his trade increases, he becomes a man of substance and travels about Germany. He hears of Elsbeth Douglas from time to time and knows that she plans to marry her cousin.

One night, eight years after their barn burned, Paul suspects that his father is planning to burn the Douglas barn. To divert him from his mad deed, he sets fire to his own house and barn and is seriously burned in the flames.

Paul is taken to Helenenthal. The searchers find Meyerhofer dead of a stroke near the Douglas barn, a broken pot of petroleum by his side. Although it is Elsbeth Douglas's wedding day, she insists on staying by Paul's bed. The vicar is sent away, and her cousin leaves. For many weary days, Elsbeth Douglas watches over Paul.

After his recovery, Paul is tried for the deliberate burning of his own house. Admitting his guilt, he blames himself for always being so timid and withdrawn. Now that he has lost everything, he feels free at last. Dame Care, who was his

nemesis all of his life, is routed. Paul is sentenced to two years in prison. On his release, Elsbeth Douglas and Mr. Douglas meet him to take him home. Both Helenenthal and Elsbeth Douglas will be his.

Critical Evaluation:

Dame Care is an outstanding example of German Romanticism, a style colored by a kind of world-sadness, completely rural settings, and a sentimental tone. *Dame Care* covers a wide span of years in its action, but it is gracefully concise without being abrupt. Hermann Sudermann exhibits a paternal sympathy for his characters; perhaps his greatest gift is his understanding of all classes of people.

The novel is an extraordinary study of a human being who becomes trapped by circumstances into sacrificing his life to his family. With great subtlety and psychological penetration, Sudermann portrays the gradual development of Paul's conviction that his life must be the way it is. Paul longs to be selfish but can never bear to shirk responsibility. He knows that people take advantage of him, but he cannot deny help to those who need him. Sudermann poignantly describes the plight of this conscientious young man, carefully avoiding sentimentality or falseness of tone. He captures the right sympathetic note as he writes about Paul, and the novel's style is even and restrained throughout, allowing the events to produce the emotional reaction.

Fairy tales form a background for the story of Paul's growing up and subsequent bondage. They are the only frame of reference young Paul has, as he tries to comprehend the dark and mysterious world. It is natural that he should think of Elsbeth Douglas in the white house as a fairy princess far above him. The subtle, tender, slowly maturing relationship between Paul and Elsbeth is related by the author with a mastery of nuance and suggestion; the mutual pain that the two young people experience is never made melodramatic or false, although their situation might seem to be that of a romantic melodrama.

The power of selfishness is hauntingly dramatized in the book, as Paul's family convinces him that he must live apart from the joys of ordinary mortals. All he can do, he tells Elsbeth, is watch over the happiness of others and make them as happy as possible. After the final catastrophe, however, he realizes that nobody has appreciated his sacrifices, nobody has noticed that he has given away his own happiness. People who take do so without concerning themselves about those who must do the giving.

Sudermann shows as much skill with scenes of action as he does with psychological analysis. The dramatic moment when Paul saves his father's life and establishes himself as master of the farm is brilliantly rendered; the two fires that destroy the farm are described with vivid, vigorous prose. The countryside around the farms and village is pictured clearly, with concise, yet poetic, descriptions.

Sudermann is as successful at bringing to life the minor characters as he is the major ones; Paul's selfish and self-centered brothers and sisters and guilt-tormented, half-mad father are particularly well done. Elsbeth Meyerhofer, Paul's mother, might have become a cliché figure, the long-suffering wife, but she is portrayed with a sensitive and subtle understanding that makes her a genuine human being; her suffering is completely understandable and therefore pitiable. Many of the characters are unlikable, and often the story is painful to read, but it is, thanks to the author's great skill, completely engrossing from beginning to end. *Dame Care* presents a stark but realistic view of human nature, alleviated only by the decency of a few rare individuals.

Further Reading

Bithell, Jethro. *Modern German Literature, 1880-1950*. London: Methuen, 1959. Brief sketch of Sudermann's career that concentrates on his dramas. Points out connections between *Dame Care* and Sudermann's later works; concludes that the novel is a bildungsroman that praises the value of hard work.

Dukes, Ashley. *Modern Dramatists*. 1912. Reprint. Freeport, N.Y.: Books for Libraries Press, 1967. Brief sketch of Sudermann's accomplishments as a dramatist. Useful for understanding the author's concerns about social conditions, which influenced both his dramas and his fiction, including *Dame Care*.

Mainland, W. F. "Hermann Sudermann." In *German Men of Letters*, edited by Alex Natan. Vol. 2. London: Oswald Wolff, 1963. Surveys Sudermann's accomplishments and notes how his popularity as a dramatist led to a revival of interest in his novels, which were written during the early years of his career. Briefly comments on the themes in *Dame Care*.

Phelps, William Lyon. *Essays on Modern Novelists*. New York: Macmillan, 1918. Includes a chapter on Sudermann's novels. Uses his works as examples for highlighting strengths and weaknesses of late nineteenth century German fiction. Praises *Dame Care* for its structural unity and its qualities of realism, calling it "an anatomy of melancholy."

Stroinigg, Cordelia. *Sudermann's "Frau Sorge": Jugendstil, Archetype, Fairy Tale*. New York: Peter Lang, 1995. Analyzes *Dame Care* in relationship to the *Jugendstil* art movement, which was at its peak popularity in Germany from 1890 to 1905. Discusses the novel's characters, symbolism, fairy tale motifs, and structures, arguing that they predate many of the *Jugendstil* conventions and characteristics.

The Damnation of Theron Ware

Author: Harold Frederic (1856-1898)
First published: 1896
Type of work: Novel
Type of plot: Social realism
Time of plot: 1890's
Locale: New York State

Principal characters:
THERON WARE, a young Methodist minister
ALICE WARE, his wife
FATHER FORBES, a Catholic priest
CELIA MADDEN, a rich, young Irish-Catholic woman
DR. LEDSMAR, Father Forbes's friend
MR. GORRINGE, a trustee of Theron's church

The Story:

Theron Ware goes to the annual statewide meeting of the Methodist Episcopal Church with great expectation of being appointed to the large church in Tecumseh. He is greatly disappointed, therefore, when he is sent to Octavius, a small rural community. To the minister and his wife, the town and its citizens do not appear formidable at first, but a hint of what is to come occurs the first morning after their arrival. A boy who delivers milk to Mrs. Ware informs her that he cannot deliver milk on Sunday because the trustees of the church will object. Shortly afterward, the trustees tell the new minister that his sermons are too dignified and that Mrs. Ware's Sunday bonnet is far too elaborate for a minister's wife.

Theron and his wife are depressed. Unhappy in his new charge, Theron decides to write a book about Abraham.

One day, Theron assists an injured Irish-Catholic workman and goes home with him to see what help he might give. At the man's deathbed, Theron observes the parish priest and a pretty young redhead, Celia Madden, who assists him. Upon their acquaintance, the minister is surprised to find that his earlier hostility to Catholics and the Irish is foolish. These people are more cultured than he, as he learns a few evenings later when he goes to the priest for some advice in connection with his proposed book.

At the priest's home, he meets Dr. Ledsmar, a retired physician interested in biblical research. The priest and the doctor know a great deal about the culture of Abraham and his people. They try to be tactful, but the young minister quickly sees how wrong he has been to think himself ready to write a religious book on any topic; all he knows is the little he was taught at his Methodist seminary.

Upon leaving Father Forbes and the doctor, Theron walks past the Catholic church. Hearing music within, he enters to find Celia at the organ. Later, he walks home with her and discovers that she is interested in literature and art as well as music. Once again that evening, Theron is made to realize how little he actually knows. He goes home with the feeling that his own small world is not a very cultured one.

Three months later, there is a revival at Theron's church. Mr. and Mrs. Soulsby, two professional exhorters, arrive to lead a week of meetings that are designed to pay off the church debt and to put fervor into its members. The Wares, who entertain the Soulsbys, are surprised to find that the revival leaders are very much like insurance salespeople, employing similar tactics. During the revival week, Theron is nonplussed to discover what he thinks are the beginnings of an affair between his wife and one of the trustees of his church, Mr. Gorringe.

In a long talk with Mrs. Soulsby, Theron tells her that he almost decided to give up the Methodist ministry because of the shallowness he discovered in his congregation and in his church. Mrs. Soulsby points out to him that Methodists are no worse than anyone else in the way of hypocrisy and that all they lack is an external discipline. She also reminds him that he is incapable of making a living because he lacks any worldly training.

Theron's life is further complicated when he realizes that he is beginning to fall in love with Celia. As a result of her interest in music, he asks her advice in buying a piano for his home, and she, unknown to him, pays part of the bill for the instrument. He also finds time to call on Dr. Ledsmar, whose peculiar views on the early church interest him. He disgusts the old doctor, however, with his insinuations of an affair between Father Forbes and Celia.

In September, the Methodists of Octavius have a camp meeting. Its fervor does not appeal to Theron, after his more intellectual religious reading and his discussions with Celia and Father Forbes, and he goes off quietly by himself. In the woods, he comes upon a picnic given by Father Forbes's church. At the picnic, he meets Celia and has a long talk with her, kisses her, and tells her of his unhappiness in his double bondage to church and to wife.

Soon afterward, he alienates Celia by telling her that he is afraid of scandal if he is seen talking with her. He also offends Father Forbes by reports that Dr. Ledsmar speaks slightingly of Celia. The priest tells his housekeeper that he is no longer at home to Theron.

One day, Theron openly confronts his wife with his suspicions about her and Mr. Gorringe. She denies the charges, but her very denial seems to speak against her in her husband's mind. In his unhappiness, he goes to see Celia. She is not at home, but her brother, who is dying slowly of tuberculosis, sees him. With the license of the dying, he says that when Theron arrived in Octavius he had the face of an angel, full of innocence, but that in the eight months the minister spent in the little town, his face took on a look of deceit and cunning. Celia's brother continues by warning the minister that he should stay among his own people, that it is bad for him to tear himself from the support that Methodism gave him.

Leaving the Madden home, Theron learns that Celia is going to New York City. It occurs to him that Father Forbes is also going to the city that evening and perhaps they are traveling together. He goes home and tells his wife that urgent business calls him to Albany; then he goes to the station and boards the train unseen. In New York, he sees the priest and Celia meet, and he follows them to a hotel. After the priest leaves the hotel, Theron goes upstairs and knocks at Celia's door. She tells him that she is busy and does not wish to see him, adding that she noticed him following her earlier in the journey. While he pleads with her, Father Forbes comes in with some other gentlemen and informs Theron that they came to New York to get another brother of Celia out of a bad scrape.

Dismissed, Theron stumbles down the stairs. A few days later, he arrives at the Soulsby house at dawn. He tells an incoherent story of trying to commit suicide, of stealing money from the church at Octavius, and of wandering alone about the city for hours while he tried to drink himself to death.

The Soulsbys take him in and send for his wife. He is ill for months. After his recovery, both he and his wife realize that he was never meant for the ministry. Through the Soulsbys,

Theron is finally able to make a new start in a real estate office in Seattle. Theron knows he will make a successful real estate agent; or, if that fails, he can try politics. There is still time enough for him to be in Congress before he is forty.

Critical Evaluation:

The often controversial and always turbulent course of Harold Frederic's life centered on his struggle to be recognized as a novelist. Born the son of a freight conductor in Utica, New York, in 1856, Frederic rose from relatively humble beginnings. His father died before Frederic was two, and lacking substantial resources, Frederic got little education beyond high school. Like so many of the noted American writers of his time, Frederic began writing as a journalist. His strong political views almost immediately led him into a series of controversies, and he changed papers frequently, eventually landing at *The New York Times*, where he received acclaim for his work as London correspondent. Life was never smooth, however, for Frederic. Late in life, he endured constant criticism for his extramarital affair with a woman who bore him three children. Even his death inspired scandal. Bedridden in 1898 with a stroke, Frederic requested a doctor, but his Christian Scientist mistress summoned a faith healer who proved ineffective in preventing Frederic's death. The mistress and faith healer were acquitted of manslaughter, but not before their highly publicized trial received international notoriety.

Throughout his life, Frederic sought artistic recognition. Although he published several novels, few received any acclaim. *The Damnation of Theron Ware* nevertheless enjoyed commercial success and earned critical recognition during the author's lifetime. Its stature continued growing after his death, and by the middle of the twentieth century, the novel had come to be seen as a literary masterpiece. A fine example of literary realism with strong elements of naturalism, *The Damnation of Theron Ware* creates a biting portrait of life in post-Civil War America, as drawn from the author's varied experiences and acquaintances. Read superficially, *The Damnation of Theron Ware* offers an excellent story, but this often delightful surface rests on a complicated web of elements that supports multiple interpretations. For example, the novel can be read as a representation of the intellectual and theological turmoil of the late nineteenth century and as a sophisticated psychological study of a flawed individual.

The characters of the novel can symbolize conflicting social and ideological forces in post-Civil War America. For example, Theron's congregation at Octavius, and the Methodist establishment in general, represent a middle America which, in Frederic's view, has stubbornly maintained the tra-

ditional forms of Protestantism but has lost touch with its moral and spiritual underpinnings. Consequently, Theron's society plods unreflectingly on as an intellectually narrow, prudish, and blatantly hypocritical mob easily susceptible to emotional appeals. On the other hand, Dr. Ledsmar, an atheist researcher who performs medical experiments on unwitting subjects, reflects new scientific thought. Ledsmar's Darwinian view of humanity and its institutions, along with his callous indifference to individual rights and dignity, depicts the amoral objectivity of science carried to an extreme. At the same time, the Catholic Father Forbes, who should exemplify spiritual devotion, follows a philosophical trend similarly lacking in moral integrity. Father Forbes sees different religions as simply various results of humanity's need for ritual and security; for the priest, Christianity is simply another useful myth. Ledsmar sees people as objects for study, whereas Forbes sees them as childlike savages who alternately interrupt his hedonistic pleasures or serve as subjects for his intellectual amusements. Father Forbes views his priestly functions as a necessary service for the benefit of the ignorant masses.

The two women who act as catalysts for Theron, Celia Madden and Sister Soulsby, also represent particular ideologies. Celia may be seen as the true Emersonian romantic, the artistic individualist who creates her own rules. As an Irish Catholic, Celia may be interpreted as a stereotype of her unusual background; however, her differences seem more likely designed to distinguish her from the Protestant mainstream. Celia differs from Father Forbes in that she appears to have a strong sense of morality; nevertheless, her high moral tone does not prevent her from amusing herself with Theron's discomfort. Celia's professed Hellenism and her disdain of propriety blatantly announce her nonconformity; Sister Soulsby readily conforms with any ideology that is useful. She represents a pragmatism inherent in American culture since the Puritans. Her pragmatism, however, lacks moral purpose. Although Sister Soulsby works for the Methodists, she has just as readily plied her talents for less savory causes. Soulsby differs from the Methodist establishment in having no illusions about her hypocritical actions. As she indicates to Theron, she assumes that the ends justify the means and believes, as does Father Forbes, that values are relative.

Theron seems to represent the struggle to find some moral center among the turbulent social and intellectual landscape of his time, but his flawed character dooms this quest. Seen from a psychological perspective, much of Theron's plight seems his own fault. Theron suffers from great pride and ambition. He sees his assignment to the provincial Octavius as a slight by people incapable of appreciating him, so he is predisposed to scorn the members of his new parish as backward and unworthy. However, the naïve and inexperienced minister greatly overestimates his knowledge and intellect, thereby opening himself to disaster when he ventures outside the familiar environment of Methodism. By emphasizing Theron's perspective of events, Frederic highlights Theron's many self-serving misperceptions. Dazzled by Celia's attention and by her risqué behavior, Theron mistakenly assumes that she finds him romantically desirable. Impressed by Father Forbes's casual derision of religion, Theron foolishly tries to emulate the priest's intellectual approach and incorrectly assumes that Father Forbes will appreciate derogatory remarks about Methodists. When Theron must finally confront his misplaced optimism and inflated self-image (the British version of the novel was titled *Illumination*), he tries to kill himself. Theron's illumination does not last long. He ends the novel engrossed in new delusions of his own greatness.

Frederic ensures that his readers share Theron's dilemma. By undermining all the sources of moral and intellectual value in the novel, the author leaves blind stupidity as the only path by which Theron can avoid being disillusioned, at best. As a result, Frederic masterfully captures the anxiety and confusion brought about by the rapid changes of the late nineteenth century. Not surprisingly, despite all of his weaknesses, Theron is typically seen as one of the more sympathetic characters of American fiction.

"Critical Evaluation" by Thomas Hockersmith

Further Reading

Bennett, Bridget. *The Damnation of Harold Frederic: His Lives and Works.* Syracuse, N.Y.: Syracuse University Press, 1997. A scholarly biography with a separate chapter on *The Damnation of Theron Ware.* Includes a chronology, detailed notes, and extensive bibliography.

Briggs, Austin, Jr. *The Novels of Harold Frederic.* Ithaca, N.Y.: Cornell University Press, 1969. A starting point for any discussion of the novel. While considering Frederic's work as a whole, it considers sources for, influences on, and critical reactions to *The Damnation of Theron Ware.*

Filetti, Jean S. *An Examination of Political Pessimism in the Works of American Novelist Harold Frederic, 1856-1898.* Lewiston, N.Y.: E. Mellen Press, 1998. Filetti concludes that Frederic's fiction expressed his pessimism and skepticism about the popular conceptions of grassroots democracy, agrarian America, and the West as a democratic frontier in the late nineteenth century.

Foote, Stephanie. "The Region of the Repressed and the Return of the Region: Hamlin Garland and Harold Frederic." In *Regional Fictions: Culture and Identity in Nineteenth-Century American Literature.* Madison: University of Wisconsin Press, 2001. This chapter includes a lengthy analysis of *The Damnation of Theron Ware,* comparing it to other works of American regionalism. Foote argues that the novel is a critique of the "cultural economy" of regionalism because "regionalism is predicated on the uneven development of capitalism, which produces a radically unbalanced cultural landscape."

MacFarlane, Lisa Watt. "Resurrecting Man: Desire and *The Damnation of Theron Ware.*" *Studies in American Fiction* 20, no. 2 (Fall, 1992): 127-143. Focuses on "the convergence of gender and religion" in the novel and argues that Frederic uses Theron as a transitional or mediating figure for the evolving roles of women in society.

Michelson, Bruce. "Theron Ware in the Wilderness of Ideas." *American Literary Realism, 1870-1910* 25, no. 1 (Fall, 1992): 54-73. Focuses on the place and especially the time in which the action takes place. Argues that the novel uses Theron's character to express the particular difficulties of maintaining identity in the turmoil of the age.

Myers, Robert M. *Reluctant Expatriate: The Life of Harold Frederic.* Westport, Conn.: Greenwood Press, 1995. Examines how Frederic was shaped by his culture and describes how his relationship with his publishers affected his career and fiction. The preface provides a succinct overview of the state of Frederic's reputation. Includes very useful notes and a bibliography.

O'Donnell, Thomas F., and Hoyt C. Franchere. "The Damnation of Theron Ware." In *Harold Frederic.* New York: Twayne, 1961. A chapter in a standard biography of Frederic, this study places the novel in the context of the author's life and offers a general critical analysis.

Oehlschlaeger, Fritz. "Passion, Authority, and Faith in *The Damnation of Theron Ware.*" *American Literature* 58, no. 2 (May, 1986): 238-255. While emphasizing the sociological and gender themes of the novel, Oehlschlaeger argues that the novel focuses on the breakdown of traditional authorities in the late nineteenth century.

The Dance of Death

Author: August Strindberg (1849-1912)

First produced: Dödsdansen, första delen and
  Dödsdansen, andra delen, 1905; first published, 1901
  (English translation, 1912, as *The Dance of Death I* and
  The Dance of Death II)

Type of work: Drama

Type of plot: Psychological realism

Time of plot: Late nineteenth century

Locale: Sweden

Principal characters:

EDGAR, a captain in the Swedish coast artillery

ALICE, his wife

JUDITH, their daughter

CURT, Alice's cousin

ALLAN, Curt's son, in love with Judith

The Story:

For twenty-five years Edgar, a captain in the Swedish coast artillery, and his wife, Alice, live an unhappy existence. Their unhappiness is caused by Edgar's contempt for everyone else in the world; he thinks of himself as a better being than others, even his wife, and he makes their marriage a tyranny. They live on an island off the coast, where Edgar is the commanding officer of the artillery detachment. Living in an old prison, they avoid the other people of the island as well as officers of the post and their wives. Indeed, Alice is virtually a prisoner in her home. The only means of communication she has with the mainland is through a telegraph key, which she teaches herself to operate. She keeps her skill with the telegraph a secret, for her husband does not want her to have any means of communication with the outside world.

Alice's only hope of release from her husband's tyranny lies in the fact that he is ill and might die at any time. On their silver wedding anniversary, Curt, Alice's cousin, arrives on the island to officiate as the quarantine officer. On his first visit to Edgar and Alice he learns about the life that they lead, when Edgar suffers an attack and Alice gloats over her husband's illness. Curt, who was divorced by his wife, also learns that Edgar caused the divorce and persuaded the court to award the custody of the children to Curt's wife.

During the two days that Edgar is ill, grave changes take place in the three people. Alice turns gray-haired. Feeling that the time has come when she should admit her age, she stops tinting her hair. She also becomes an object of distrust to Curt, for she tries to make love to her cousin while her husband is ill. Curt, unable to understand her actions, cannot fully realize how much she hates her husband and how much she suffered during the past twenty-five years. Edgar himself resembles a corpse after his illness, but he immediately tries, upon his recovery, to dominate the others.

On the third day after his attack the captain tells his wife he is going to divorce her. In retaliation, she tries to have him convicted of the embezzlement of government funds, of which he is innocent. She also embraces her cousin Curt in her husband's presence, at which time Edgar tries to kill her with his saber. After that incident, both husband and wife become calm, admitting they tortured each other enough. They both say they hope that they can get along with each other peaceably, if not happily.

A few months later Curt's son Allan, a cadet stationed with Edgar's artillery company, falls in love with Judith, the daughter of Alice and Edgar. The parents, failing to realize the youngsters are serious in their affair, think that Judith is making game of Allan at her father's request, for Edgar hates Allan because he is Curt's son. At the time Edgar is trying to arrange a marriage for Judith with a major in the regiment, a man older than Edgar. The lovers' quarrels of the two young people only serve to heighten the illusion under which the three grownups labor.

Edgar, meanwhile, is also busy undermining Curt's position as quarantine officer. After gleaning information from Curt, he publishes articles about quarantine management in periodicals and thus gains a reputation for himself in a field in which he is ignorant. After his retirement, the result of his illness, he plans to run for the national legislature, in opposition to Curt, who expects to try for an office. Edgar completely discredits Curt with the voters by taking up a subscription for his rival, who, acting on Edgar's advice, lost a great deal of money in an unwise investment. With deliberate malice, Edgar does everything he can to discredit Curt in the eyes of the world and to reduce him to abject poverty and dependence.

After Curt loses his money, Edgar buys his house and its furnishings and then leaves the house exactly as it was, in order to make the loss more poignant to Curt. Then Edgar is made an inspector of quarantine stations, an appointment that makes him Curt's superior in employment. Curt, accepting his reverses calmly and stoically, refuses to lose his head, although Alice tries to make him seek revenge. Alice still hopes that her ailing husband might die, before he can completely ruin the lives of Curt, his son Allan, Judith, and Alice herself.

In the meantime the captain continues his plan to marry Judith to a man who can help to fulfill Edgar's ambitions. Instead of marrying her to the major, he arranges a marriage to the colonel of his old regiment, notwithstanding the fact that the colonel is more than forty years older than Judith. As far as anyone can suppose, the marriage is to take place; Judith seems to be agreeable to the match. Alice makes one last attempt to spoil the plan, but a letter she writes is intercepted by Edgar and returned by him to his wife.

Judith herself ruins Edgar's scheme by revealing her true love to Allan. To prevent the marriage, she calls the colonel on the telephone, insults him, and breaks off the engagement. Then, with her mother's aid, she arranges to go to Allan at the military post to which Edgar sent him. The failure of his plan is too much for Edgar. He suffers an apoplectic stroke, much to the delight of his wife, who sees revenge at last for all that she and the other members of the family suffered at the sick man's hands. Unable to control her delight at Edgar's approaching death, she taunts him on his deathbed with the fact that he is hated and that his evil plans are finally going awry. His only answer, since he lost the power of speech, is to spit in her face.

After Edgar's death, which occurs within a few hours, both his wife and her cousin admit that death changes their attitudes toward the dead man. Alice says she loved him as well as hated him, and she hopes that peace will rest with his soul.

Critical Evaluation:

This particular play was written in two parts, in a way that is comparable to the two parts of William Shakespeare's *Henry IV* (c. 1597-1598) in that *Henry IV* is two plays for the most part because it is too long to be one. The first part of *The Dance of Death* deals with the parents and the second with their children.

August Strindberg's specialty in his plays was the stripping bare of "that yawning abyss which is called the human heart," as one of his characters calls it. Perhaps only Fyodor Dostoevski in modern literature has penetrated equally to the depths of psychological torment. His characters say things that most people feel at times, but which they restrain themselves from expressing or even admitting to themselves. Strindberg was obsessed with the dual nature of the human brain, with the contrast between inner feelings and their outer expression. The power and horror of *The Dance of Death* comes from this expression of the normally suppressed thoughts of the characters. This startling honesty seems to shatter moral and social conventions and to leave both characters and audience vulnerable and exposed. "It's horrible," says one of the characters in one of Strindberg's later plays, "don't you find life horrible?" The reply is, "Yes, horrible beyond all description." The endurance of the characters in the face of madness and violence suggests that they see, in spite of everything, that there is no acceptable alternative.

From the first lines of *The Dance of Death*, one is struck by the intensity of the speeches. Alice and Edgar are caught in the midst of a duel, or, rather, in the last and brutally final stages of a duel. When the play opens, the conflict is only verbal, but it soon becomes more passionate and more violent. At times, the dialogue seems to be on the verge of becoming no more than an insane ranting, and yet there are moments when Strindberg rises above his fury and sums up the tragedy of life in a few sentences.

It is vital to understand the intimate relationship between Strindberg's life and work to comprehend fully his dramas, particularly *The Dance of Death*. Essentially pessimistic, Strindberg lived a tortured existence, from a childhood of poverty and insecurity to years as a minister and then a medical student to a period as a journalist. His first major play, a historical drama, was rejected by the Swedish Royal Theatre. He became famous with the publication of his first novel, *Röda rummet* (1879; *The Red Room*, 1913) but he continued writing plays. The conflict between the sexes inspired some of his most intense dramas, including *Fadren* (1887; *The Father*, 1899) and *Fröken Julie* (1888; *Miss Julie*, 1912), and, ultimately, *The Dance of Death*. Although Strindberg was married three times, the central relationship of his life was his violent and tormented first marriage. Like D. H. Lawrence, Strindberg was obsessed with the idea of the lower-class male, himself, marrying the aristocratic lady and then bringing her down to his own level. This obsession is reflected in *Miss Julie* and in the relationship between Alice and Edgar in *The Dance of Death*. The disaster of his marriage and the loss of his four children drove him into alcoholism, and, despite his growing fame as a writer, he became a lonely and unhappy man, unable to find steady employment.

In his later plays, Strindberg combined the techniques of naturalism with his unique vision of psychology. These bold dramas, with realistic dialogue, highly wrought symbols (such as the wedding ring, the fortress, the wreaths, and the piano in *The Dance of Death*), and stark settings, brought about a revolution in European drama. One of his last and greatest plays, *The Dance of Death* reflects his first marriage and the collapse of his life afterward. All of his work possesses extraordinary vitality, but in *The Dance of Death*, Strindberg transforms essentially autobiographical material into a drama of exceptional power. His work influenced later playwrights such as Elmer Rice, Eugene O'Neill, Luigi Pirandello, and Edward Albee.

Strindberg has been accused of hating his female characters, and no character has prompted this statement more than Alice in *The Dance of Death*. Were Strindberg's greatest plays the product of a dangerous and intense misogyny? Is this what gives his brilliant psychological dramas their peculiarly perverse power? No doubt he did suffer from paranoia, brought on by his many personal problems, and his writing suggests, in places, paranoiac tendencies. The women in the plays, such as Julie and Alice, tend to be strong and vengeful creatures, who deliberately try to lead men to destruction. The power of *The Dance of Death* and other dramas of this late period must be due, also, to a deep introspective analysis of his sufferings, for, between his bouts of madness, Strindberg was able to examine his mental disturbance and to make use of the knowledge he gained from such examinations. From a reckless, Bohemian existence, he emerged, in his last years, into a guilt-ridden form of Christianity, Swedenborgian mysticism, and a Schopenhauerian pessimism according to which the real world exists outside human understanding. His third marriage, to the young actress Harriet Bosse, dissolved after less than three years, and he discovered that he had inoperable cancer. Then, suddenly, the Swedish people recognized his greatness and began speaking of a Nobel Prize for him. "The anti-Nobel Prize is the only one I would accept," he retorted. When his first wife died in 1912, he collapsed, although he had not seen her for twenty years. Three weeks later, he was dead.

Some critics have said that both Edgar and Alice are monsters battling to the death, like a pair of dinosaurs clashing in some ancient swamp, but the fact is that they are not monsters any more than are the characters of *The Father* or *Miss Julie* or any other of his plays. They are two trapped individuals struggling desperately to survive, but not knowing what to do; every frantic gesture that they make only wounds them more. They are, perhaps, two of the most pitiful characters in modern literature. The scenes in which Alice plays the Hungarian dance on the piano and Edgar performs the violent jig with his jangling spurs and in which Alice hurls her wedding ring at Edgar are excruciatingly painful, cutting beneath the layers usually left by more conventional playwrights. Alice and Edgar are bound together by a love-hate relationship that neither can escape, except into death. As Strindberg knew,

distance and time cannot release a man or woman from certain types of bondage. At the end of the first part of the play, Edgar realizes how hopelessly he and his wife are bound, and laughs that they might as well celebrate their silver wedding anniversary. "Let us pass on," he cries. Somehow, they endure, and that, perhaps, is the message of the play. Alice, when Edgar dies at the end of the second part, finally understands that she loved Edgar, as well as hated him, and she prays for peace for him. By implication, she also prays for herself.

"Critical Evaluation" by Bruce D. Reeves

Further Reading

Hildeman, Karl-Ivan. "Strindberg, *The Dance of Death*, and Revenge." *Scandinavian Studies* 35, no. 4 (November, 1963): 267-294. Asserts that character sketches and events in *The Dance of Death* are based on Strindberg's sister and brother-in-law. Concludes that Strindberg created these characters as punishment or revenge for real or imagined injury.

House, Poul, Sven Hakon Rossel, and Göran Stockenström, eds. *August Strindberg and the Other: New Critical Approaches*. Amsterdam: Rodopi, 2002. Collection of papers delivered at a 2000 conference, "Strindberg at the Millennium—Strindberg and the Other," interpreting the motif of "the other" and "otherness" in Strindberg's work.

Johnson, Walter. "Strindberg and the *Danse Macabre*." In *Strindberg: A Collection of Critical Essays*, edited by Otto Reinert. Englewood Cliffs, N.J.: Prentice-Hall, 1971. Discusses Strindberg's use of the medieval image of Death characterized by the *danse macabre* (the dance of death) as a symbol in parts 1 and 2. Contends that the dance symbolizes life as an evil dream, while death becomes a release from the horrors of hell/life. Includes a detailed bibliography.

Meyer, Michael. *Strindberg: A Biography*. New York: Random House, 1985. Includes relevant biographical information on many of Strindberg's major plays, including *The Dance of Death*. Meyer has translated eighteen of Strindberg's plays into English and is knowledgeable about the playwright. His biography is concerned primarily with Strindberg's influence on modern theater. Includes subject index.

Robinson, Michael. "Prisoners at Play: Form and Meaning in Strindberg's *The Dance of Death* and Beckett's *Endgame*." In *Studies in Strindberg*. Norwich, England: Norvik Press, 1998. Traces the relationship of theatrical naturalism and absurdist modernism by pointing out similarities in the plots, language, structure, dramatic method, and underlying themes of *The Dance of Death* and Samuel Beckett's *Endgame*.

_____, ed. *The Cambridge Companion to August Strindberg*. New York: Cambridge University Press, 2009. Collection of essays analyzing Strindberg's work, placing it within the context of his life and times. Eszter Salczer's essay, "A Modernist Dramaturgy: *A Dream Play* and *The Dance of Death*," analyzes these two plays.

Shideler, Ross. "Strindberg's Struggle." In *Questioning the Father: From Darwin to Zola, Ibsen, Strindberg, and Hardy*. Stanford, Calif.: Stanford University Press, 1999. Examines how Strindberg adapted late nineteenth century Darwinian ideas and the women's rights movement to create family dramas and novels in which he questioned the role of the father. Maintains *The Dance of Death* exemplifies Strindberg's lifelong preoccupation with husbands and fathers who resist the charms of liberated women.

Valency, Maurice. *The Flower and the Castle: An Introduction to Modern Drama*. New York: Macmillan, 1963. Comprehensive discussion of all of Strindberg's major plays and his contribution to modern theater. Includes subject index and selected bibliography.

A Dance to the Music of Time

Author: Anthony Powell (1905-2000)

First published: 1976; includes *A Question of Upbringing*, 1951; *A Buyer's Market*, 1952; *The Acceptance World*, 1955; *At Lady Molly's*, 1957; *Casanova's Chinese Restaurant*, 1960; *The Kindly Ones*, 1962; *The Valley of Bones*, 1964; *The Soldier's Art*, 1966; *The Military Philosophers*, 1968; *Books Do Furnish a Room*, 1971; *Temporary Kings*, 1973; *Hearing Secret Harmonies*, 1975

Type of work: Novels

Type of plot: Tragicomedy and social realism

Time of plot: 1914-1971

Locale: London and Venice

Principal characters:

NICHOLAS JENKINS, a novelist

KENNETH WIDMERPOOL, a school acquaintance

PETER TEMPLER, a school acquaintance

JEAN TEMPLER, his lover before his marriage

CHARLES STRINGHAM, his school friend

J. G. QUIGGIN, a fellow student, and later a left-wing critic

MARK MEMBERS, a fellow student, and a poet

GILES JENKINS, his raffish uncle

SIR MAGNUS DONNERS, an industrialist

MYRA ERDLEIGH, a friend of Uncle Giles, and a clairvoyant

CHIPS LOVELL, a friend of Jenkins and a fellow scriptwriter

LADY MOLLY JEAVONS, Lovell's aunt by a former marriage

LADY PRISCILLA TOLLAND, a debutante, later married to Lovell

LADY ISOBEL TOLLAND, her older sister, who marries Jenkins

ERRIDGE, their eldest brother, later Lord Warminster

HUGH MORELAND, a composer and one of Jenkins's closest friends

MATILDA WILSON, an actor, who later marries Moreland

MACLINTICK, a music critic and admirer of Moreland

DR. TRELAWNEY, a cult leader and magus

ROWLAND GWATKIN, Jenkins's company commander at the outset of World War II

PAMELA FLITTON, Stringham's niece who marries Widmerpool

X TRAPNEL, a novelist and short-story writer

RUSSELL GWINNETT, an American professor who writes a biography of Trapnel

The Story:

Nicholas Jenkins is in school at Eton College along with three other youth, Charles Stringham, Peter Templer, and Kenneth Widmerpool. Jenkins uses his friendship with the other young men to cement his acquaintance with various areas of life: Widmerpool's ambition, Stringham's aristocratic connections, and Templer's social ease and familiarity with sex. A visit from Jenkins's scapegrace uncle, Giles, forecasts unstable elements in the adult world.

On a visit to Templer's family, Jenkins meets Templer's sister Jean, for whom he develops a crush. He then goes to France to practice the language in a French home, only to encounter Widmerpool, who is the object of jest and abuse on the part of the French people who know him. Jenkins also falls in love with the daughter of his host. Returning to England, he enters Oxford, where he becomes initiated into literary circles, meeting two young writers, Mark Members and J. G. Quiggin, who seem to have an odd love-hate relationship with each other.

Jenkins moves to London and works for a publisher of art books. He encounters a bizarre array of people ranging from the artist Edgar Deacon to the industrialist Sir Magnus Donners. He attends a whirl of parties and initiates several unsuccessful love affairs, encountering Widmerpool several times along the way. He spends a weekend at Peter Templer's country house, where he once again meets Jean and begins a serious relationship with her. Jenkins decides on a career as a writer of fiction, even as Members and Quiggin vie for the patronage of a prominent novelist. Stringham, meanwhile, begins his descent into drunkenness and depression. Jean abruptly leaves Jenkins and returns to her husband, accompanying him to South America.

Jenkins begins encountering various members of the large, aristocratic, and quite eccentric Tolland family. Through the offices of Quiggin, he meets the family's head, the left-wing gadfly Lord Erridge and, eventually, Erridge's sister Isobel. Jenkins knows as soon as he sees Isobel that he will marry her, and indeed the two do marry some months later. Widmerpool also gets engaged, to an older widow, but the outcome is disastrous. Widmerpool emerges humiliated and chastened, causing amused comment on the part of Jenkins's family friend, the octogenarian General Aylmer Conyers.

Composer Hugh Moreland is probably Jenkins's best friend. Moreland's wife, Matilda, is the former mistress of Donners, and she helps Moreland secure patronage in the aristocracy. Stringham's mother holds a party for Moreland, at which Stringham momentarily shows some of his old vigor. The darker side of the Bohemian world, however, is revealed when Moreland's friend, music critic Maclintick, commits suicide.

It is the late 1930's, and war clouds are gathering. Jenkins thinks back to the beginning of World War I in 1914, when a disturbance in the domestic staff of his parents' household mystically heralded the instigation of the war, announced dramatically by Uncle Giles. Another element of the 1914 tableau, the mystical cult leader Dr. Trelawney, reappears mysteriously at the seaside in 1939, months after Jenkins has sensed the coming of the war in a masque of the seven deadly sins held at Donners's castle in Stourwater. Widmerpool assists Jenkins in obtaining a commission in the army, and Moreland is shocked to find Matilda has gone back to Donners.

Jenkins is appointed a subaltern (second lieutenant) in a Welsh regiment stationed in Northern Ireland. He develops a close bond with the regiment's ambitious but melancholy captain, Rowland Gwatkin, and generally adapts well, if unevenly, to army life. Isobel gives birth to a son just as Jenkins must end a leave and return to duty. Gwatkin compromises his army career by silliness over a woman, and the inattention to duties resulting therefrom. Jenkins is transferred to divisional headquarters, where, to his tremendous surprise, he finds his immediate superior is Widmerpool.

In a late night literary discussion with the divisional commander, General Liddament, Jenkins fears he has blotted his army copybook when he rashly finds fault with the work of the general's favorite Victorian novelist. The case is quite the opposite, however; their talk will eventually result in a more satisfying posting. Widmerpool is not Jenkins's only surprise from his past, as he discovers Stringham is a waiter in the division's mess unit. Although his circumstances are reduced, Stringham has conquered his alcoholism and has regained his integrity. Jenkins goes back to London only to experience the height of the Blitz, in which several of his relatives and old friends are killed. On the same trip, Jenkins attempts to transfer into a liaison unit that works with the Allied Powers.

Jenkins meets Pamela Flitton, Stringham's hostile and sexually aggressive niece. Pamela begins to cut a wide swath through Jenkins's network of friends and acquaintances, having an affair with Templer, among others. Jenkins finds out that Stringham, eager to go to the front lines, has been sent to Singapore, where he is tortured and killed during the Japanese occupation. Templer dies while attempting to aid the Yugoslav resistance. Moreland lingers on, but is never the same and dies some years after the end of the war. The war ends, and Jenkins attends the victory celebration at St. Paul's

Cathedral. After the service, he meets Jean Templer, now the wife of a Latin American military attaché. Widmerpool, who has risen rapidly through the ranks during the war, amazes everyone by marrying Flitton.

The war changes Jenkins's social landscape forever. Most of his close friends are dead. His literary career, however, continues, and he becomes involved with editing the periodical *Fission*. Through this post he encounters Quiggin and Members again, as well as meeting the prominent cultural opinion-maker Lindsay "Books-do-furnish-a-room" Bagshaw. Jenkins becomes friendly with the younger novelist X Trapnel. Trapnel is a tragic figure whose artistic talents are never matched by stability in life. He falls in love with Pamela Widmerpool, whose husband has been named a life peer. Pamela leaves Widmerpool for Trapnel, but then spurns Trapnel as well, leading him to suicide.

Widmerpool is found to have intrigued with a communist puppet government in Eastern Europe, and is disgraced. Pamela becomes involved with American academic Russell Gwinnett, who is writing a biography of Trapnel; she kills herself in the course of pursuing a relationship with Gwinnett. Gwinnett's biography of Trapnel is eventually awarded the Sir Magnus Donners Prize (the financier had died some years previously). At the prize banquet, Jenkins encounters Widmerpool, who has become an enthusiast for the 1960's youth counterculture.

Widmerpool eventually joins a cult led by the insidious and charismatic Scorpio Murtlock, a spiritual disciple of Trelawney. Murtlock abuses Widmerpool and finally causes his death. One of Murtlock's disciples, however, escapes from the cult and rescues a painting by Stringham that came to Widmerpool through his marriage to Pamela. As this painting is exhibited at an art gallery, Jenkins encounters Jean and has a final meeting with his first love. Jenkins contemplates the course of his life and meditates on the nature of the seasons and the patterns that govern the music of time.

"The Story" by Margaret Boe Birns

Critical Evaluation:

Anthony Powell's *A Dance to the Music of Time* is a *roman-fleuve*, a long sequence of novels that together make up a single unified work. Other examples of the *roman-fleuve* in English fiction include C. P. Snow's eleven-volume *Strangers and Brothers* (1940-1970) and Henry Williamson's fifteen-volume *A Chronicle of Ancient Sunlight* (1951-1969). In French, examples of the *roman-fleuve* include Romain Rolland's *Jean Christophe* (1904-1912, 10 vols.), Jules Romains's *Men of Good Will* (1932-1946, 27 vols.), Roger

du Gard's *Les Thibaults* (1922-1940, 8 vols.), and Marcel Proust's *Remembrance of Things Past* (1913-1927, 7 vols.), to which Jenkins sometimes refers in his narration. Powell's sequence also is reminiscent of the work of nineteenth century novelists such as Leo Tolstoy (1828-1910), whose books, though much longer, have huge casts of characters.

Powell's work, in its Englishness, is like that of Charles Dickens (1812-1870) as well, as it teems with delightful native eccentrics. Perhaps Powell would not have welcomed this comparison, however, because the novelist Nicholas Jenkins, Powell's alter ego, on more than one occasion, voices his lack of admiration for the Victorian novelists.

The length of the *roman-fleuve* allows the novelist to develop characters over time, to convey something of the density and complexity of life itself. Powell memorably achieves these effects; at the same time, he is virtually unique among practitioners of the *roman-fleuve* in that his viewpoint is essentially comic. His narrative is not stylized or experimental in form, nor is it naturalistic, wherein the narrator purports to allow the characters and events to speak solely for themselves. In these novels, everything related is filtered through the intelligence and the temperament of the narrator, Jenkins. He has a ready eye for life's ironies and absurdities. Thus, a sequence of novels featuring broken marriages, mental breakdowns, failures in business, the military, and the arts; deaths in battle, and suicides—because of the perspective and personality of the narrator—can be read as comedy.

A Dance to the Music of Time draws its title from a painting by Nicolas Poussin. At the beginning of the novel, Jenkins watches some workers gathered around a fire and is reminded of Poussin's painting, the one in which the seasons, hand in hand and facing outward, tread in rhythm to the notes of the lyre that the winged and naked greybeard plays. The image of time brings thoughts of mortality, of human beings, facing outward like the seasons, moving hand in hand in intricate measure and stepping slowly, methodically, sometimes a trifle awkwardly, in evolutions that take recognizable shape. This image of "the music of time," to the tune of which "partners disappear only to reappear again, once more giving pattern to the spectacle," governs the entire sequence. This structure, therefore, supports the many apparently coincidental appearances and reappearances of characters (again, as in Dickens). Perhaps these coincidental encounters are made more plausible because of the relative closeness of the upper middle-class, aristocratic, and artistic circles within which Jenkins moves.

The twelve novels of the cycle are grouped in four subsections, or movements. The first movement, which includes *A*

Question of Upbringing, *A Buyer's Market*, and *The Acceptance World*, traces the progress of Jenkins from youth to experience. Powell's treatment of this passage is highly unsentimental; for Jenkins, youth is something to be endured and overcome, and the prevailing mood of the opening novels is one of waiting for life to begin in earnest. This mood is not Jenkins's alone; indeed, throughout the cycle, Jenkins himself is rarely the focus of attention. He is, rather, a participant-observer whose experience enables the reader to meet an extraordinary diversity of characters. Jenkins is all that can be desired in a narrator. He is curious, temperate, and—when not in love—sensible. Because he is a writer, the behavior of characters and the events of their lives often strike within him a literary chord. These observations may provoke analogies—from classical writings, from poetry, even from hymns sung during church services. He is literary but not pedantic.

A Question of Upbringing begins in December, 1921, and although Powell does not always supply exact dates for the action, they usually can be reconstructed with reasonable accuracy following the internal chronology of the cycle, and with reference to historical events mentioned in each respective text. The location in this volume is an exclusive English public school. (This is one of the first biographical details linking Jenkins with his creator: Powell attended Eton College from 1919 to 1923.) Among Jenkins's schoolmates are three characters destined to play an important role in the cycle. Of these, the most important is Kenneth Widmerpool, the only character other than the narrator to figure in all twelve volumes of the sequence. A disagreeable youth and, ultimately, a despicable man, Widmerpool appears at intervals through Jenkins's life; their relationship embodies the metaphor of the dance, according to which one is bound to one's "partners" by an inscrutable design. More sympathetic characters are Jenkins's friends Charles Stringham and Peter Templer. Stringham is appealing yet self-destructive; Templer is smooth, confident, and mature beyond his years.

The first section of *A Question of Upbringing* introduces these characters in the school setting. In the summer following his graduation, Jenkins visits the Templers and meets Peter's younger sister, Jean, then about sixteen or seventeen years old, to whom he is greatly attracted. In the fall of 1923, following a farcical interlude in France, Jenkins enters the university (unnamed, but presumably Oxford, where Powell attended Balliol College from 1923 to 1926). A long comic scene set several months later in the rooms of a power-hungry don, Sillery, introduces two of Jenkins's fellow students who become recurring characters in the cycle: J. G. Quiggin, later to attain celebrity as a Marxist critic and all-

around man of letters (although he leaves the university without a degree), and Mark Members, who makes his reputation as a poet and then, like Quiggin, branches out into the role of man of letters.

A Buyer's Market, the second novel in the sequence, opens in the summer of 1928 or 1929 and concludes in October of the same year. Jenkins, having graduated from the university, has found employment in London, where he works for a publisher that specializes in art books but issues other sorts of books as well. After his own graduation, Powell had joined the publishing house of Duckworth.

Stringham and Widmerpool, in a coincidence typical of the entire sequence, both find themselves working for Sir Magnus Donners, a prominent industrialist. In structure, this volume follows the pattern established in the first volume. It consists of four chapters, each of which centers on a comic episode or set piece. With some variation, this is the method that Powell follows throughout.

A Buyer's Market introduces the first of many artists and artists manqué who populate the cycle: Edgar Deacon, a seedy, egotistical, untalented painter with an attraction to young men (he dies in the course of the novel after a drunken fall), and Ralph Barnby, a far better painter but one whose art is very much tied to the Zeitgeist of the 1920's; he is also a notorious womanizer. The central scene of the novel is a party at the home of Milly Andriadis, a socialite in her mid-thirties who has a brief affair with Stringham before his marriage, which takes place near the end of the volume. This party continues Jenkins's initiation into the world of experience: "I was . . . more than half aware," he reflects, "that such latitudes are entered by a door through which there is, in a sense, no return."

A second set piece features Donners giving a tour of the dungeons at Stourwater Castle, his home, which occasions comment on his voyeuristic and otherwise perverse sexual proclivities. Among the party is the former Jean Templer, now Jean Duport; her loutish husband, Bob Duport, several years older than Jenkins and his contemporaries, is an aggressive entrepreneur who makes and loses great sums of money.

The Acceptance World (the title is British financial jargon for what is known in the United States as trading in futures) completes Jenkins's initiation. In the course of this volume, which spans the period from autumn, 1931, to summer, 1933, Jenkins publishes his first novel (Powell published his first novel, *Afternoon Men*, in 1931) and carries on an intense affair with Jean, still going as the book ends but showing signs of ending. Later, Jenkins learns that while their affair was still going, Jean had already been with the man for whom she eventually leaves Jenkins, Jimmy Brent, an odious character whose appeal to Jean is incomprehensible to Jenkins.

An important figure in this volume is the novelist St. John Clarke, introduced briefly in *A Buyer's Market*. Clarke, an Edwardian writer who in his time attains both popular and critical success, becomes a kind of litmus test: Referred to in various ways by various characters in the sequence, he represents for Jenkins all that is artistically cheap and meretricious. Also introduced here is the clairvoyant Myra Erdleigh, whom Jenkins meets in the hotel rooms of his uncle, Giles. This scene, the opening scene of *The Acceptance World*, is one of the most important in the entire twelve volumes. The sequence features many references to occult phenomena, in addition to the often uncanny coincidences that are the very texture of the action. Powell's attitude toward such phenomena is neither credulous nor debunking. He clearly believes that some experiences of occult phenomena—second sight, telepathy (at least of a low-grade variety), and so on—are valid. Their recurring presence in the cycle (along with instances of obvious charlatanry) has a larger import as well, for they point to the mystery of human existence—a mystery not confined to realms designated "occult."

When Erdleigh reads the cards and tells Jenkins his future, he is immediately startled by her perspicacity, but he quickly discounts that effect, observing that "such trivial comment, mixed with a few home truths of a personal nature, provide, I had already learnt, the commonplaces of fortune-telling." Still, Erdleigh's insights into Jenkins's character are genuinely perspicacious and, as the reader gradually appreciates, her specific predictions concerning his future are all, in time, fulfilled—genuinely fulfilled, not merely finding the loose "confirmation" of a fortune-cookie oracle.

The first movement of the cycle, then, concludes with Jenkins and his contemporaries firmly established in the "acceptance world," the world in which the essential element—happiness, for example—is drawn from an engagement to meet a bill. Sometimes the goods are delivered, even a small profit made; sometimes the goods are not delivered, and disaster follows; sometimes the goods are delivered, but the value of the currency is changed.

The second movement includes *At Lady Molly's*, *Casanova's Chinese Restaurant*, and *The Kindly Ones*. It is 1934 as *At Lady Molly's* begins, and Jenkins has moved from his publishing job to work as a scriptwriter for a British studio, having meanwhile published his second novel. (Powell had left publishing for journalism in 1936.) A fellow scriptwriter, Chips Lovell, is a nephew by marriage to Molly Jeavons. Early in the novel, he takes Jenkins to a party at the Jeavonses, where he hopes to meet Priscilla Tolland, a young

woman whom he is pursuing. Later, at the country cottage of J. G. Quiggin (currently domiciled with Peter Templer's former wife, Mona, a former model), Jenkins meets Priscilla's older sister, Isobel. They are but two of the ten children of Lord Warminster; the eldest, Erridge, is Quiggin's landlord and patron, sharing his Marxist views. In his understated way, Jenkins reports that he knew at first sight that Isobel would be his wife.

The novel begins by introducing, via Jenkins's reminiscences of long family friendship, General Aylmer Conyers, one of the most delightful and most warmly portrayed figures in the entire sequence. Retired, nearing the age of eighty, Conyers is still formidable: He trains dogs, plays the cello, and discusses the works of psychoanalyst Carl Jung, which he has recently discovered and absorbed with great interest. This volume also follows the fates of Widmerpool, whose fiancé breaks their engagement when he cannot perform as a lover, and Stringham, whose alcoholism and alienation are severe.

Casanova's Chinese Restaurant begins with a flashback to 1928-1929 that introduces Hugh Moreland, a composer who is one of Jenkins's closest friends and who becomes an important recurring character. The first section of this novel, discounting the flashback, is set in 1933 and 1934 and overlaps in time some of the action of *At Lady Molly's*. By this stage, the fifth novel in the sequence, the special effects of the *roman-fleuve* begin to come into play. The texture is denser; much can be accomplished simply by mentioning the name of a familiar character in a new (and often surprising) context.

Much of *Casanova's Chinese Restaurant* is concerned with marriage and marriages. Jenkins marries Isobel; Moreland marries actor Matilda Wilson (to whom Jenkins is introduced by Moreland), a former mistress of Donners. There is also the bitterly—indeed, pathologically—unhappy marriage of the Maclinticks; Maclintick, a music critic who worships Moreland, in his own words, "with the proper respect of the poor interpretive hack for the true creative artist," ends by committing suicide after his wife, Audrey, leaves him. His suicide dissuades Moreland from pursuing his affair with Priscilla Tolland; a week later, her engagement to Chips Lovell is announced.

The movement concludes with *The Kindly Ones*, which begins with a long flashback to 1914. Jenkins recalls his governess's lesson, that the Greeks so greatly feared the Furies that they renamed them the Eumenides—the Kindly Ones—hoping thus to placate them. The flashback evokes the mood of imminent disaster, the sense that the Furies are about to strike again, yet it does so in an oblique fashion, for much of the action is broad comedy involving the Jenkins family servants. Introduced in this section is the cult leader and magus Dr. Trelawney. After another brief flashback, to 1928 or 1929, and sections set in 1938 and 1939, the novel concludes in the fall of 1939, several weeks after the outbreak of World War II, with the brother of Ted Jeavons (Lady Molly's husband) promising Jenkins to expedite his call-up by the army.

The third movement, which includes *The Valley of Bones*, *The Soldier's Art*, and *The Military Philosophers*, spans the war years, during which, like his protagonist, Powell had served. It could be argued that the war novels act as the fulcrum for the series. They serve as the bridge between the first six novels and the final three. They chronicle the years that change British society utterly and, therefore, the lives of Jenkins and everyone he knows.

Most novelists of Powell's generation mined their World War II experiences for material. The third movement of *A Dance to the Music of Time* and the war trilogy of Evelyn Waugh are perhaps the most successful. Waugh's *Men at Arms* (1952), *Officers and Gentlemen* (1955), and *Unconditional Surrender* (1961; also known as *The End of the Battle*) feature a protagonist who is similar to Jenkins in age and background and who, like him, ends his military career working with Balkan allies (as Powell and Waugh themselves did). For a vivid picture of the English at war, these two trilogies can be read with profit.

As *The Valley of Bones* opens early in 1940, Jenkins has been commissioned as a second lieutenant in a Welsh regiment, soon to be stationed at a school for chemical warfare quartered on a decaying estate in Northern Ireland. The title comes from a biblical passage in the book of Ezekiel that refers to a valley filled with bones. The text is chosen by the chaplain, Popkiss, for his sermon: The Lord breathes life into the bones, and they become a great army. Much of the action of this volume centers on the tragicomic fate of Jenkins's immediate superior, Rowland Gwatkin (in civilian life an employee of a small bank), whose romanticism proves his downfall. When, at the end of the volume, Jenkins is transferred and then told to report to the deputy assistant adjutant-general at divisional headquarters in Northern Ireland, it is no surprise that the officer to whom he reports turns out to be Widmerpool.

Widmerpool's machinations and running battles with fellow officers figure prominently in the next volume, *The Soldier's Art*. Jenkins, on the other hand, fears that he is sometimes too straightforward for the good of his military career. In chapter 1, he has a talk with his commanding officer and, when asked about his taste in books, mentions with admiration Honoré de Balzac's massive *La Comédie humaine* (1829-1848; 17 volumes; *The Comedy of Human Life*, 1885-

1893, 1896 [40 volumes]; also known as *The Human Comedy*, 1895-1896, 1911 [53 volumes]), treating every aspect of French society. General Liddament reads Anthony Trollope. Jenkins's praise of Balzac and negative critique of Trollope, reckless under the circumstances, is an insight into what the author considers to be literary success. Stringham makes an unexpected reappearance as a waiter in the mess where Jenkins regularly eats. In fact, Stringham gives the book its title. In chapter 3, he quotes a passage from Robert Browning that refers to the soldier's art.

Literary allusions continually play a role within Powell's literature. Widmerpool not only rejects Jenkins's suggestion that they help Stringham in some way but also arranges for his transfer to a mobile laundry unit due to be sent to the Far East—an eventuality of which Stringham maintains indifference ("Awfully chic to be killed").

On leave in London, Jenkins meets Lovell, currently estranged from Priscilla (who is carrying on an affair) but hopeful of getting her back. Later, after Lovell has left the restaurant where he and Jenkins had met, Jenkins sees Priscilla and her lover. That night, both Lovell and Priscilla (and Lady Molly, at whose house Priscilla is staying) are killed in air raids at different locations. Jenkins has a final conversation with Widmerpool before leaving divisional headquarters. When his old schoolmate asks about the subject of his conversation with General Liddament, Jenkins replies that they talked about Trollope and Balzac. Widmerpool seems momentarily confused as to whether he means the writers or two generals by those names.

In the final volume of the third movement, *The Military Philosophers*, Jenkins has a new posting, working in the War Office in Whitehall in allied liaison, eventually with special responsibility for Belgian and Czech forces. Widmerpool, who has been promoted, is also working in Whitehall, with access to policy makers at the highest levels. Early in the volume, Jenkins meets his old school friend Peter Templer and is struck by his air of detachment and fatalism. Templer has recently had an affair with Stringham's niece, Pamela Flitton, a beautiful but malicious femme fatale who inexplicably turns her attention to Widmerpool, to whom she is soon engaged. Later in the volume, when Templer is sent to the Balkans on a secret mission and is killed by communist partisans, Pamela accuses Widmerpool of complicity in Templer's death. There is also word, confirmed by Widmerpool, that Stringham had been captured by the Japanese at the fall of Singapore and died in a prisoner-of-war camp. Finally, this volume features the reappearance of Jean Duport, at first unrecognizable to Jenkins as the wife of a Latin American attaché, Colonel Flores, some years her junior.

Until the third movement, Jenkins has lived among the well born, the well educated, or both. Only when he joins the army does he associate intimately with people of other ranks (enlisted men) and—because England lacks sufficient Oxford and Cambridge graduates to fill out its officer corps—with junior officers from a civilian background of minor white-collar employment. Among the best drawn of these are stoic Sergeant Pendry, who dies mysteriously during a training exercise; Sayce, the company's whining slacker; Corporal Gwylt, the company's ladies' man; Bithel, a tippling junior officer, who led a marginal, if not disreputable, civilian life; Warrant Officer Diplock, who embezzles company funds, then deserts to Ireland; Blackhead, a civil servant and master of bureaucracy, who sees it as his duty to stop every initiative in its tracks; and Vavassor, the indispensable porter in Jenkins's building in Whitehall, who is uniformed like a hotel doorman. Women like Maureen, the barmaid who is Gwatkin's undoing, play their parts as well. These working-class and lower middle-class characters join the *comédie humaine* of Powell's England.

The deaths of Templer and Stringham are symbolic of the end of a period and, indeed, a way of life. The postwar world presents a strange new landscape. Such is the mood of the final movement, comprising *Books Do Furnish a Room*, *Temporary Kings*, and *Hearing Secret Harmonies*. In *Books Do Furnish a Room*, which begins in the winter of 1945-1946 and concludes in the fall of 1947, Jenkins, who was unable to write during the war and finds that he is still not ready to attempt a novel, undertakes a study of Robert Burton, entitled *Borage and Hellebore*.

Much of this volume is concerned with the postwar literary scene, especially with the antics of J. G. Quiggin and the crowd associated with his magazine *Fission*, edited by the disreputable journalist Lindsay "Books-do-furnish-a-room" Bagshaw. Also introduced in this context is one of the most interesting characters in the cycle, X Trapnel (based on Powell's acquaintance with writer Julian MacLaren-Ross). Trapnel is a novelist and short-story writer of enormous gifts and idiosyncratic manner whose immediate postwar success is not followed up; his decline to a premature death is hastened by an affair with Pamela Widmerpool.

Between the time of *Books Do Furnish a Room* and that of *Temporary Kings*, there is an interval of more than ten years—the first such substantial gap in the sequence. *Temporary Kings* begins in the summer of 1958 at an international writers' conference in Venice. The arrival of an American professor, Russell Gwinnett, who is at work on a biography of X Trapnel, prompts memories of Trapnel's death. After a leisurely and blackly comic account of the conference and its

attendant intrigues, the scene shifts back to England, where Widmerpool is about to be charged with espionage on behalf of the Soviets. (Later, the case is dropped, presumably in exchange for information from Widmerpool.) Pamela pursues Gwinnett and dies in bed with him in a hotel, having taken an overdose of drugs; there are rumors of necrophilia, consistent with Gwinnett's past. Hugh Moreland, long in ill health and living in reduced circumstances with Maclintick's widow, Audrey, dies at the end of this volume.

There is another ten-year interval between the conclusion of *Temporary Kings* and the opening of the final volume of the sequence, *Hearing Secret Harmonies*, in the spring of 1968. Several new characters are introduced, including the cult leader Scorpio Murtlock (who claims to be a reincarnation of Dr. Trelawney) and the niece of Jenkins, Fiona Cutts, who is one of Murtlock's disciples. (The time of the action is the same as that of the infamous Charles Manson "family" and similar phenomena of the 1960's.) Familiar figures appear as well: Widmerpool, after a stint in California, has returned to England in a new guise, as a champion of the counterculture; Gwinnett's book on Trapnel, *Death's-Head Swordsman*, thought to have been abandoned, is published and wins the Sir Magnus Donners Prize. New and old characters come together when Widmerpool joins Murtlock's cult (which he tries to take over) and Gwinnett, in England to receive the prize and pursue research for his new book, later titled *The Gothic Symbolism of Mortality in the Texture of Jacobean Stagecraft*, attends the cult's rites and witnesses Murtlock's assertion of supremacy over Widmerpool. A year or so later, Widmerpool dies on a dawn run with fellow cultists; meanwhile, Gwinnett has married Fiona.

The final volume concludes with Jenkins lighting an autumn bonfire, the smoke of which reminds him of the worker's fire that he contemplated at the beginning of the first volume. In turn, the memory brings to mind a long passage from Robert Burton's *The Anatomy of Melancholy* (1621), asserting with a kind of biblical eloquence the cyclical order of human life ("one purchaseth, another breaketh; he thrives, his neighbor turns bankrupt; now plenty, then again dearth and famine"). When in the concluding scene of volume twelve, Jenkins is reminded of Poussin's painting (as he was in the opening scene of volume one), the reader is reminded of the many times during the course of the sequence when a painting or a musical composition has stirred the memory of the narrator.

A Dance to the Music of Time is a remarkable achievement for many reasons, but above all it is distinguished by its richly varied cast of characters. It is a mistake to claim, as some critics have, that Powell has documented the British experience in the middle decades of the twentieth century. Certainly, his novels give the flavor of the period as it was experienced by a certain class, but his interest is always in his characters as individuals, not as types.

Indeed, insofar as it is possible to summarize the message of a twelve-volume sequence of novels, that message may be found in Powell's approach to his characters. Powell himself has observed that if one writes about people as they are, one will inevitably write comedy. His characters are unpredictable and frequently contradictory in their twists and turns; yet for this reason they are extremely lifelike. They are wonderfully rendered as much through the tact and tolerance as by the perceptiveness of a thoroughly admirable narrator. *A Dance to the Music of Time* suggests that at the heart of human experience, as of every individual life, there is an irreducible mystery.

"Critical Evaluation" revised by Patrick Adcock

Further Reading

Barber, Michael. *Anthony Powell: A Life*. Woodstock, N.Y.: Overlook Press, 2004. Barber chronicles Powell's career and places him within the context of literary life in twentieth century England. Although Barber was not Powell's official biographer, he was able to conduct several interviews with his subject. Includes photographs.

Berberich, Christine. "Dancing to the Music of Widmerpool: The Gentleman in Anthony Powell's *A Dance to the Music of Time*." In *The Image of the English Gentleman in Twentieth-Century Literature: Englishness and Nostalgia*. Burlington, Vt.: Ashgate, 2007. Berberich's discussion of Kenneth Widmerpool is included in her study of how the English gentleman has been portrayed in twentieth century literature. She demonstrates how writers use the gentleman character as a means to critique society and to represent changing concepts of gender, class, and nationality.

Birns, Margaret Boe. "Anthony Powell's Secret Harmonies: Music in a Jungian Key." *Literary Review* 27 (Fall, 1981): 80-92. Analyzes the psychological and discursive elements in Powell's novel from the perspective of Carl Jung's archetypal theories, focusing especially on the Jenkins-Widmerpool relationship.

Birns, Nicholas. *Understanding Anthony Powell*. Columbia: University of South Carolina Press, 2004. Chapter 3 provides an almost two-hundred-page examination of *A Dance to the Music of Time*, emphasizing the role that both world wars and the Cold War played in Powell's life and writing. Provides an extensive analysis of Widmerpool and his relations to the minor characters and the narrator, demonstrating how Powell did not create a single champion against evil.

Brennan, Neil. *Anthony Powell*. Rev. ed. New York: Twayne, 1995. One-third of this introductory overview of Powell's life and work is devoted to *A Dance to the Music of Time*. Contains a chronology of Powell that includes his family ancestry.

Joyau, Isabelle. *Understanding Powell's "A Dance to the Music of Time."* New York: St. Martin's Press, 1994. Wide-ranging and full of provocative observations. Especially good on the minor characters, whose significance is often missed. Convincingly establishes Powell as a major modern novelist.

Russell, John. *Anthony Powell: A Quintet, Sextet, and War*. Bloomington: Indiana State University Press, 1970. This pioneering study of Powell remains surprisingly relevant, even though it was written when the series was only three-fourths complete. Good on the psychology of Jenkins and the moral significance of Charles Stringham.

Selig, Robert L. *Time and Anthony Powell*. Madison, N.J.: Fairleigh Dickinson University Press, 1991. A skillful and comprehensive work, in which Selig artfully explores the novel's relevance to contemporary narrative theory.

Spurling, Hilary. *Invitation to the Dance: A Guide to Anthony Powell's "Dance to the Music of Time."* Boston: Little, Brown, 1977. This useful guide helps readers to navigate the complexities of Powell's series. Contains a synopsis of each volume, by chapter and time sequence, and an extensive character index.

Dancing at Lughnasa

Author: Brian Friel (1929-   )
First produced: 1990; first published, 1990
Type of work: Drama
Type of plot: Psychological realism
Time of plot: Summer, 1936
Locale: County Donegal, Ireland

Principal characters:

MICHAEL MUNDY, the narrator, a young man, looking back
on the summer when he was seven years old
KATE, Michael's schoolteacher aunt
MAGGIE, Michael's aunt, who keeps house for the family
AGNES, Michael's aunt, who works at home as a knitter
ROSE, Michael's aunt, also a knitter
CHRIS, Michael's unmarried mother
GERRY EVANS, Michael's father
JACK, Michael's uncle, a missionary priest just returned
from Uganda

The Story:

The adult Michael reflects aloud on the summer of 1936, when he was seven years old and lived in rural County Donegal. His mother Chris, his father Gerry, his uncle Father Jack, and his four aunts form a silent, motionless tableau as the backdrop for his monologue. That was the summer they got their first radio and had their first contact with Dublin music. It was also the summer in which Father Jack, sick, came home to die after twenty-five years of missionary work in Uganda, uninterrupted except for a brief stint as a chaplain in the British army, which explains the ornate officer's uniform he wore.

The adult Michael, Kate, Gerry, and Father Jack then leave the stage. It is a warm summer afternoon. The domestic routines of a loving family in the kitchen of a remote, rural cottage proceed. Maggie is preparing food for the hens; Agnes is knitting gloves to meet her assigned quota of two dozen per week; Rose is replenishing the supply of turf (peat) for the fire; Chris is ironing; the sisters make amiable small talk. Rose, unexpectedly, breaks into a bawdy music-hall song and dance; Maggie joins her. The simple Rose, the others are chagrined to learn, has a date planned with a local married man, Danny Bradley.

The young Michael (invisible to the spectator, his lines spoken by the adult Michael) works on his two kites in the garden. While he does this, his aunt Maggie asks him the first of five riddles she has for him. The child recounts his and their disappointment over the recent return of the missionary priest, Jack, broken in health and mind.

Kate, the grade-school teacher, returns from Ballybeg, where she was shopping for all of them, quinine for Father Jack included. Rose teases her about her crush on old Austin Morgan. All the talk in Ballybeg, Kate reports, is of the upcoming harvest festival; the sisters agree in a verbal rush of

enthusiasm to go to it. Rose spontaneously throws herself into a mad dance, following which Kate vetoes the whole scheme as inappropriate.

Out in the yard, Maggie, miming a bird, pays back young Michael for frightening her earlier by pretending to see a rat. She comes inside and receives her cigarettes, sharing the gossip from Kate's shopping expedition. When they learn of a village boy badly burned at the pagan Lughnasa Festival in the hills, it is Rose who supplies the details. Maggie learns of a former girlfriend of hers visiting from London with her children and remembers a dance they attended in a foursome years ago. While the women talk, Father Jack wanders in and out, his memory disturbed. In the background, the radio plays Irish dance music. Maggie launches into a wild solo dance, joined soon by the others; only Kate dances alone. They all continue, rapt, even after the very unreliable radio stops working.

The sisters are squabbling about their division of domestic labor when they are disturbed by the approach of Gerry, the Welsh father of Michael, Chris's child. Kate relents sufficiently to allow Chris to invite Gerry inside; she has not seen him in more than a year. At the front door, Chris learns that he was teaching dancing in Dublin but is now selling gramophones door-to-door. She tells him young Michael is now in school. It is his intention, he tells her, to fight with the International Brigade in Spain. When the radio spontaneously starts inside the house, the couple responds to "Dancing in the Dark" by dancing down the lane, while Kate watches from inside the house. Even though Gerry promises to be back in two weeks before he leaves for Spain, Chris will not agree to marry him.

The lives of the other family members are also not going well. Kate feels her world is collapsing; the local parish priest is threatening her with the loss of her job. Father Jack's mind continues to be disturbed. Befuddled by his African experiences and having trouble with the English language, he wanders into the kitchen. He saw a white bird on his windowsill that morning. When Agnes tells him that it was Rose's pet rooster, it causes him to reminisce about the African rituals and native dances he knew.

The narrator, the adult Michael, concludes act 1 with an omniscient, informative monologue. Father Jack was indeed sent home in disgrace after giving up his faith and joining the native culture. Kate was fired from her teaching position. Rose was romantically involved with a married man, and both she and her mentor Agnes's knitting contracts were canceled. Michael saw his mother and father dancing again, in harmony despite the lack of music, but there was to be no marriage. The family community was rapidly disintegrating.

The final act opens three weeks later. Maggie sings a romantic song and talks to young Michael, who is expecting a bicycle from his father, a bicycle that will never arrive. She poses riddles to him, only the last of which—Why is a gramophone like a parrot?—is not answered. It is becoming increasingly clear that Father Jack's religious context is no longer Christian. After he seems to be getting healthier, he dies suddenly, within a year of his coming home. Rose disappears, returning later to confess that she was with Danny Bradley up in the hills where the Lughnasa Festival was held. She and Agnes secretly leave for England, where, the narrator reports, they eventually die miserable deaths: Agnes of exposure on the Thames Embankment, Rose in a hospice.

Michael's parents carry on with their separate lives. Gerry, who also danced with Agnes and Maggie before he left, is injured in Spain in a fall from his motorcycle. Eventually, he marries another woman and starts a new family in Wales. Chris goes to work in the new knitting factory for the rest of her life. Michael finally closes the Lughnasa time in his memory; he sees dancing everywhere as the stage lights, wordlessly, are brought down.

Critical Evaluation:

Brian Friel is one of Ireland's most prolific and successful contemporary dramatists. *Dancing at Lughnasa* won both London's Olivier Award and New York's Tony Award for Best Play. Though successful in New York with *Philadelphia Here I Come* (1964), Friel is better known in Dublin and London for dramatic triumphs such as *Faith Healer* (1979), the more political *Translations* (1980), and *Molly Sweeney* (1994).

Friel was educated for the priesthood at Maynooth Seminary, Ireland, but, instead of taking Holy Orders, he became a teacher like his father. Following the success of his very elegant short stories, available in two collected editions, *The Saucer Full of Larks* (1969) and *The Gold in the Sea* (1966), he gave up teaching and devoted himself to the theater, working in 1963 at the Guthrie Theater in Minneapolis.

Dancing at Lughnasa (pronounced LOO-na-sah) represents Friel's utilization in his writing of the regional life he knows so well. Young artists are often advised to write about what they know, and Friel demonstrates just how satisfying this course can be for a much wider audience than simply the people of his home, the northern counties of Ireland, the locale in which he situates *Dancing at Lughnasa* and much of his writing. This geographic area and this family life become metaphors for a wider audience by far. Friel's concern here is to show the fragility of any community and his keen awareness of the slippery quality of language as a means of communication.

The dominant metaphor in this play is the dance, a claim that becomes much clearer in a theatrical production than in a simple reading of the text. Ironically, for a wordsmith as skilled, careful, and responsible as Friel, it is the dancing in the play, as opposed to the frozen immobility of the tableaux that open and close the drama, which most makes his point about the necessity of honest communication, or connection, between and among people in any context.

Behind the action, never appearing on stage, is the pagan dancing of the Lughnasa Festival in the hills. Lugh (pronounced "Loo") is an ancient pre-Christian, Celtic god of fertility and harvest, still honored by some of the "Christians" in Ballybeg (Gaelic for "small town"). Father Jack's beating of rhythms with young Michael's kite sticks supplies yet another pre-Christian art form to the mix. The radio the sisters enjoy so much is their intermittent link to the traditional Irish folk music and dance; it is also their link to the popular dance music of the time in which the play is set. Chris and Gerry dance together beautifully, though marriage is out of the question because of Gerry's lack of reliability as a provider.

This play suggests that communities, including family communities, are under a severe threat. Many writers have extolled the virtues of local communities while failing to offer a clearer solution to prevent their erosion. Here, Friel shows the reader the doomed cottage industry of knitting and the corrosive religious prejudice from religious orthodoxy that leads to Kate's dismissal from her teaching post because of her link to the lapsed Catholic, Father Jack. Political engagement, a thorny issue for Irish writers such as Friel, is evidently not Friel's answer to these problems. Gerry's involvement in the Spanish Civil War is bathetic and ridiculous; he gets his war wound from falling off his motorcycle.

For Friel, communication is evidently an important key to community at all levels. Words came dangerously close to failing in the Irish politics of the time of the play including a litany of broken treaties. What might work better, Friel suggests in this play, is the necessary trust and harmony needed to dance. Everyone in this family does dance, with the exception of Michael. As the lights are brought down finally on the stage, the tableau moves ever so slightly to the music, the mysterious source of which is not the radio: "Dancing . . . because words were no longer necessary."

Archibald E. Irwin

Further Reading

Boltwood, Scott. *Brian Friel, Ireland, and the North*. New York: Cambridge University Press, 2007. Traces the evolution of Friel's career through a chronological analysis of his plays, including *Dancing at Lughnasa*. Examines Friel's opinions about the partition of Ireland and the Irish Republic and discusses how these views affect his work.

Corbett, Tony. *Brian Friel: Decoding the Language of the Tribe*. Dublin: Liffey Press, 2002. Focuses on the political and social aspects of Friel's plays, placing them within the context of the developing Irish state. Examines themes of nationality, community, language, communication, and "otherness" in the plays.

Coult, Tony. *About Friel: The Playwright and the Work*. London: Faber & Faber, 2003. Collection of interviews in which Friel and others discusses his plays and the experience of staging them.

Dantanus, Ulf. *Brian Friel: The Growth of an Irish Drama- tist*. London: Faber, 1987. A thorough appraisal of Friel's work and themes through 1986.

Lahr, John. "Brian Friel's Blind Faith." *The New Yorker*, October 17, 1994. Explores Friel's work up to 1994 and sympathetically fits *Dancing at Lughnasa* into its context: Dancing becomes "a means of approaching the nonsectarian religions."

McGrath, Niall. *Spiritual Ciphers: Priest and Shaman Characters in Selected Drama by Brian Friel*. Ballyclare, Ireland: Black Mountain Press, 2005. Focuses on the spiritual themes and the characters of priests and shamans in *Dancing at Lughnasa* and six other plays.

MacNeil, Maire. *The Festival of Lughnasa*. Dublin: University College Dublin Press, 1982. Situates the pagan harvest festival in its European context, surviving as it did in Ireland at least until 1962.

Peacock, Alan, ed. *The Achievement of Brian Friel*. Gerrard's Cross, England: Colin Smythe, 1994. A broad collection of sixteen essays from scholars and theater professionals on Friel's breadth and sympathy of interest and on his plays, including *Dancing at Lughnasa*.

Pine, Richard. *The Diviner: The Art of Brian Friel*. Dublin: University College Dublin Press, 1999. Pine provides a postcolonial analysis of Friel's plays.

Roche, Anthony, ed. *The Cambridge Companion to Brian Friel*. New York: Cambridge University Press, 2006. Collection of essays analyzing specific plays, as well as common elements of Friel's work, such as the visual dimension of his dramaturgy, gender issues in his plays, and Friel as a postcolonial playwright. Helen Lojek's essay "*Dancing at Lughnasa* and the Unfinished Revolution" focuses on this play.

Dangerous Acquaintances

Author: Pierre Choderlos de Laclos (1741-1803)
First published: Les Liaisons dangereuses, 1782
(English translation, 1784)
Type of work: Novel
Type of plot: Psychological realism
Time of plot: Mid-eighteenth century
Locale: Paris and environs

Principal characters:
CÉCILE DE VOLANGES, a young girl of good family
MADAME DE VOLANGES, her mother
THE COMTE DE GERCOURT, Cécile's fiancé
THE CHEVALIER DANCENY, Cécile's admirer
THE MARQUISE DE MERTEUIL, a fashionable matron and Gercourt's former mistress
THE VICOMTE DE VALMONT, a libertine
MADAME DE TOURVEL, the wife of a judge
SOPHIE CARNAY, Cécile's confidant
MADAME DE ROSEMONDE, Valmont's aunt

The Story:

When Cécile de Volanges is fifteen years old, her mother removes her from a convent in preparation for the girl's marriage to the Comte de Gercourt. The match is arranged by Madame de Volanges without her daughter's knowledge. Shortly after her departure from the convent, Cécile begins an exchange of letters with Sophie Carnay, her close friend. Cécile has few contacts with her fashionable mother except for trips they make together to shops to purchase an elaborate wardrobe. The little she knows about the plans for her future she learns from her maid.

The unscrupulous Marquise de Merteuil sees in the proposed marriage an opportunity to get revenge on Gercourt, who some time before deserted her for a woman of greater virtue. In her wounded vanity, she schemes to have the Vicomte de Valmont, a libertine as unscrupulous as herself, effect a liaison between Cécile and the Chevalier Danceny. Such an affair, circulated by gossip after Cécile and Gercourt are married, will make the husband a laughingstock of the fashionable world. To complete her plan for revenge, the marquise also wants Valmont to seduce Madame de Tourvel, the woman for whom Gercourt abandoned her. Madame de Tourvel is the wife of a judge. As a reward for carrying out these malicious schemes, the Marquise de Merteuil promises to reinstate Valmont as her own lover.

Valmont is able to arrange a meeting between Cécile and Danceny. Although she is attracted to the young man, Cécile hesitates at first to reply to his letters. She conceals her eventual consent to write him, even to speak of love, from her mother. Valmont meanwhile turns his attention to Madame de Tourvel, who is a virtuous woman and, aware of the vicomte's sinister reputation, tries to reject his suit. Nevertheless, she finds herself attracted to him, and in time she agrees to write to him but not to see him. She also stipulates that Valmont is not to mention the subject of love or to suggest intimacy. Eventually Valmont and Madame de Tourvel become friends. Aware of her indiscretion even in friendship, she finally tells Valmont that he must go away, and he accepts her decision.

In the meantime, although she writes him letters in which she passionately declares her love, Cécile is steadfast in her refusal to see Danceny. Cécile grows more mature. She still writes to Sophie, but not as frankly as before. Instead, she turns for advice to the Marquise de Merteuil, whom she sees as a more experienced woman. The marquise, impatient with the slow progress of the affair between Cécile and Danceny, informs Madame de Volanges of the matter, with the result that the mother, in an angry interview with her daughter, demands that Cécile forfeit Danceny's letters. The marquise's plan produces the effect she anticipates; Cécile and Danceny declare themselves more in love than ever.

Hoping to end her daughter's attachment to Danceny, Madame de Volanges takes Cécile to the country to visit Madame de Rosemonde, Valmont's ailing aunt. Valmont soon follows, on the Marquise de Merteuil's instructions, to keep the affair alive between Cécile and the young chevalier and to arrange for Danceny's secret arrival. Valmont, bored with rustic life, decides to take Cécile for himself. Under the pretext of making it safer for him to deliver Danceny's letters, he persuades her to give him the key to her room. At the first opportunity, Valmont seduces her. At first the girl is angered and shocked; before long, however, she surrenders herself to him willingly. Valmont is at the same time continuing his attentions to Madame de Tourvel. Deciding that persistence accomplishes nothing, he tries ignoring her, whereupon Madame de Tourvel writes to offer her friendship.

Cécile, deeply involved with Valmont, writes the Marquise de Merteuil, asking for her advice on how to treat Danceny. Madame de Volanges, who is unaware of the situation, also writes the marquise, telling her that she is considering breaking off the match with Gercourt; her daughter's happiness, she declares, is perhaps worth more than an advantageous marriage. In reply, the marquise earnestly cautions Madame de Volanges on a mother's duty to guide a daughter and to provide for her future.

Madame de Tourvel also becomes a guest of Valmont's aunt, giving Valmont the opportunity to seduce her. He is tempted but takes greater pleasure in seeing her virtue humbled. After his rejection and her own moral scruples force Madame de Tourvel to flee in shame, she writes Madame de Rosemonde a letter in which she apologizes for her abrupt departure and explains her emotional straits. Madame de Rosemonde's reply is filled with noble sentiments and encouragement.

Valmont is surprised to find himself deflated by Madame de Tourvel's departure. His ego suffers another blow when Cécile locks him out of her room. The marquise is more impatient than ever with Valmont's slow progress, and she decides to work her revenge through Danceny. Her first step is to captivate the young chevalier. He succumbs to her but nevertheless continues to write impassioned letters to Cécile.

Valmont decides to possess Madame de Tourvel. Afterward, he describes her initial hesitation, surrender, and complete abandon in a triumphant letter to the Marquise de Merteuil, closing his account with the announcement that he is coming at once to claim the promised reward. The marquise manages to put off his claim, however, by reproving him for his handling of his affair with Madame de Tourvel. The difference between this and his other affairs, she says, is that he has become emotionally involved; his previous conquests were smoothly and successfully accomplished because he regarded them only as arrangements of convenience, not relationships of feeling. The irony underlying her attitude is that she is still in love with Valmont and did not count on losing him, even for a short time. She loses control of the strings by which she dangled Valmont to satisfy her desire for vengeance.

Valmont tries to free himself of his emotional involvement with Cécile and Danceny. Cécile miscarries his child; Danceny's devotion no longer amuses him. Although Valmont makes every effort to win the favor of the marquise, she holds him off and, after a quarrel, capriciously turns from him to Danceny and makes that young man a slave to her charms and will.

Both Valmont and the marquise are eventually defeated in this duel of egotistic and sexual rivalry. Danceny, having learned of Valmont's dealings with Cécile, challenges the vicomte to a duel and mortally wounds him. As he is dying, Valmont gives the chevalier his entire correspondence with the marquise. Once her malice is exposed, she is ruined socially. When an attack of smallpox leaves her disfigured for life, she flees to Holland. Madame de Tourvel, already distressed because of the treatment she received from Valmont, dies of grief at his death. Cécile enters a convent. Danceny gives the incriminating letters to Madame de Rosemonde and, vowing celibacy, enters the order of the Knights of Malta. Madame de Rosemonde seals the letters that brought disaster or death to everyone who was involved with so dangerous an acquaintance as the Marquise de Merteuil.

Critical Evaluation:

Dangerous Acquaintances, the only novel by the French artillery officer Pierre Choderlos de Laclos, is a slow-paced but fascinating story, in which Laclos proved himself a master of the epistolary form popularized by Samuel Richardson and other novelists of the eighteenth century. The letters are so skillfully arranged, and the characterizations so scrupulously presented, that the reader willingly accepts the letters as real and the characters as people rather than as devices for telling a story. The illusion is furthered by Laclos's use of frequent footnotes to explain details in the letters.

Frequently in the history of Western literature, certain works that were initially castigated as indecent, immoral, or blasphemous later came to be acknowledged not only as artistic triumphs but as powerful moral statements. Such is the case with Laclos's *Dangerous Acquaintances*. Enormously

popular, yet roundly condemned, the novel was seen as outright scandalous. The real hostility toward the book, however, may have stemmed not from its immoral themes but from Laclos's ruthless honesty in portraying the social, intellectual, and erotic climate of mid-eighteenth century French society, unmitigated by stylistic indirection or sentimental distortion. Moreover, it seems curious to call a book corrupt in which the transgressors are so thoroughly punished for their machinations. Indeed, to later readers, the ending seems too easy and perhaps melodramatic. Valmont's deathbed conversion is almost sentimental, and Madame de Merteuil's smallpox seems gratuitous.

There is in the work a chilling quality in the manner in which Valmont and Madame de Merteuil manipulate and destroy the lives of others as players would move pieces around a chessboard. Although called an erotic novel, there is, in fact, little sexual passion and no emotional involvement in these intrigues. Love is an almost entirely intellectual activity, and this is Laclos's primary moral point. Valmont and Madame de Merteuil represent the final product of eighteenth century rationalism; they have reasoned their feelings out of existence.

A closer look at the "game" suggests yet deeper and more complex motivations than the simple pleasures of manipulation and petty spite. Although Valmont and Madame de Merteuil for the most part maintain a tone of light, elegant bantering between themselves, comparing notes as friendly rivals, their competition is in deadly earnest, yet their ultimate opponents are not their various victims but they themselves. Cécile de Volanges, Chevalier Danceny, and Madame de Tourvel are merely surrogates that Valmont and Madame de Merteuil use to get at each other. *Dangerous Acquaintances* is truly one of the most brilliant, elegant, and brutal "battle-of-the-sexes" works ever written.

Valmont and Madame de Merteuil are at once products and victims of their society. They have absorbed and accepted its rationalistic basis. They have subjugated their emotional impulses to it, and they are both suppressed by its social norms and rituals. Valmont is a soldier without a war. Predisposed by training to military command, Valmont is bored and restless in the stagnant, aimless, ritualized society in which he finds himself. He uses amatory combat as a weak substitute for the real thing.

Madame de Merteuil's situation and psychology are somewhat more complicated. As an aristocratic woman, her freedom of action is severely circumscribed. She has the potential to be passionate but is forced into an arranged marriage with a dull old man. She is brilliant and resourceful but faces a lifetime of meaningless social activity that will eventually stultify her capacities. She is free-spirited and experimental but bound by behavioral norms and a rigid double standard that threatens to ostracize her for the slightest dereliction. Madame de Merteuil has refused to accept these limitations for herself; she has, in fact, determined to use them to her own advantage. "Ought you not to have concluded," she writes Valmont, "that, since I was born to avenge my sex and to dominate yours, I must have created methods unknown to anybody but myself?" Thus, although Madame de Merteuil impresses readers as a "moral monster," Laclos does raise the question as to how she came to be that way. In many ways, she seems to be an earlier version of Henrik Ibsen's Hedda Gabler, whose frustrated passions and abilities also turned to viciousness and eventually to self-destruction.

Madame de Merteuil destroys herself, because both her suppressed passion for Valmont and her need to dominate him are too strong to remain in equilibrium. For his part, Valmont, too, feels the need to dominate, as is clear when he presents his ultimatum to Madame de Merteuil—"from this day on I shall be either your lover or your enemy." To that, she responds "Very well—War!" and rationalistic erotic intrigue becomes mutual self-destruction. Because the emotions cannot remain suppressed, rational self-control gives way to vindictive impulse, and love is replaced by self-defeating hate.

Further Reading

Conroy, Peter V. *Intimate, Intrusive, and Triumphant: Readers in the "Liaisons dangereuses."* Amsterdam: Benjamins, 1987. Concludes that the fictional reader is the most powerful character "in" the book, more powerful than the narrator. Discusses form and technique from the perception of the reader.

Free, Lloyd R., ed. *Laclos: Critical Approaches to "Les Liaisons dangereuses."* Madrid: Studia Humanitas, 1978. Eleven essays by critics discussing evil, characterization, suspense structures, language, and contemporary consciousness.

Koehler, Martha J. *Models of Reading: Paragons and Parasites in Richardson, Burney, and Laclos.* Lewisburg, Pa.: Bucknell University Presses, 2005. While focusing on the depiction of women in novels by Samuel Richardson, Koehler also compares these works to *Dangerous Acquaintances.*

Meltzer, Françoise. "Laclos' Purloined Letters." *Critical Inquiry* 8, no. 3 (Spring, 1982): 515-529. Points out that in the epistolary novel, it is the fictional reader who most clearly creates the text. Discussion, which is informed by the work of Jacques Derrida and Jacques Lacan, argues ironically that a purloined letter always arrives at its destination.

Miller, Nancy K. "Rereading as a Woman: The Body in Practice." *Poetics Today* 6, nos. 1-2 (1985): 291-299. Examines the scene in which the Vicomte de Valmont writes a letter to Madame de Tourval literally on the Marquise's body, and gives a feminist reading of male production of reading and its "rules."

Roulston, Christine. *Virtue, Gender, and the Authentic Self in Eighteenth-Century Fiction: Richardson, Rousseau, and Laclos.* Gainesville: University Press of Florida, 1998. Examines *Dangerous Acquaintances* and other eighteenth century sentimental fiction which presented a new type of protagonist—a character who was authentic, virtuous, and usually a woman.

Roussel, Roy. "The Project of Seduction and the Equality of the Sexes in *Les Liaisons dangereuses.*" *Modern Language Notes* 96, no. 4 (May, 1981): 725-745. Presents an argument that seduction almost wishes not to succeed, since the process itself is enjoyable. Seducers seek to define themselves against traditional codes that demonstrate their arbitrary nature.

Wolfgang, Aurora. *Gender and Voice in the French Novel, 1730-1782.* Burlington, Vt.: Ashgate, 2004. An analysis of *Dangerous Acquaintances* and three other eighteenth century French novels whose narrators are women. Explains how the emergence of women-centered salon culture and new feminine styles of poetry spurred the creation of a new type of French literature with a more modern sensibility and more innovative forms and techniques.

Daniel Deronda

Author: George Eliot (1819-1880)
First published: 1876
Type of work: Novel
Type of plot: Social realism
Time of plot: Mid-nineteenth century
Locale: Rural England, London, and the Continent

Principal characters:
DANIEL DERONDA
MIRAH LAPIDOTH, a girl he saves from drowning
SIR HUGO MALLINGER, Daniel's guardian
LADY MALLINGER, his wife
GWENDOLEN HARLETH, a beautiful young lady
MRS. DAVILOW, her mother
MRS. GASCOIGNE, Mrs. Davilow's sister
MR. GASCOIGNE, her husband
REX, their son
ANNA, their daughter
MALLINGER GRANDCOURT, Gwendolen's husband and
    Sir Hugo's heir
LUSH, his follower
HERR KLESMER, a musician
CATHERINE ARROWPOINT, his wife and an heiress
HANS MEYRICK, one of Deronda's friends
MRS. MEYRICK, his mother
EZRA COHEN, a shopkeeper in the East End
MORDECAI, a boarder with the Cohens and Mirah's brother
MRS. LYDIA GLASHER, Grandcourt's former mistress

The Story:

Gwendolen Harleth, a strikingly beautiful young woman, is gambling at Leubronn. Playing with a cold, emotionless style, she wins consistently. Her attention is suddenly caught by the stare of a dark, handsome gentleman whom she does not know and who seems to be reproving her. When her luck changes and she loses all her money, she returns to her room to find a letter from her mother requesting her immediate return to England. Before she leaves, Gwendolen decides that she will have one more fling at the gaming tables. She sells her turquoise necklace for the money to play roulette, but before she can get to the tables, the necklace is repurchased and returned to her with an anonymous note. Certain that the unknown man is her benefactor, she feels that she cannot very well return to the roulette table. She goes back to England as soon as she can. Her mother recalls her because the family lost all their money through unwise business speculations.

A high-spirited, willful, accomplished, and intelligent young woman, Gwendolen is Mrs. Davilow's only child by her first marriage and her favorite of all her children. From her second marriage to Mr. Davilow, who is now dead, she has four colorless, spiritless daughters. About one year earlier, she moved to Offendene to be near her sister and brother-in-law, the prosperous, socially acceptable Gascoignes and

because she wished to arrange a profitable marriage for her oldest daughter. Gwendolen's beauty and manner impressed all the surrounding gentry. Her first victim was her affable cousin Rex Gascoigne, who was willing to give up his career at Oxford for Gwendolen. His family refused to sanction this unwise move, however, and Rex, broken in spirit, was sent away for the time being. Gwendolen remained unmoved by the whole affair.

Soon afterward, the county became excited over the visit of Mallinger Grandcourt, the somewhat aloof, unmarried heir to Diplow and to several other large properties owned by Sir Hugo Mallinger. All the young ladies were eager to get Grandcourt to notice them, but it was Gwendolen, apparently indifferent and coy in her conversation, whom the well-mannered but monosyllabic Grandcourt courted for several weeks. Gwendolen's mother, uncle, and aunt urged her to try to secure Grandcourt, and just when it seemed that Grandcourt would propose and Gwendolen accept, Mrs. Lydia Glasher appeared. Grandcourt's scheming companion, Lush, brought Mrs. Glasher to tell Gwendolen that she left her husband to live with Grandcourt and is now the mother of four of his illegitimate children. She begged Gwendolen not to accept Grandcourt so that she might have the chance to secure him as the rightful father of her children. Gwendolen, promising not to stand in Mrs. Glasher's way, went immediately to join friends at Leubronn.

Before he came to Leubronn, Daniel Deronda, the man whom Gwendolen encountered in the gambling casino, was Sir Hugo Mallinger's ward. He did not know his parents, but Sir Hugo always treated him well. Sir Hugo, who married late in life, had only daughters. Although he lavished a great deal of expense and affection on Deronda, his property was to go to his nephew, Mallinger Grandcourt. At Cambridge, Deronda was extremely popular. There, he earned the undying gratitude of a poor student named Hans Meyrick, whom Deronda helped to win a scholarship at the expense of his own studies. One day after leaving Cambridge while in a boat on the river, Deronda saved a pale and frightened young woman, Mirah Lapidoth, from committing suicide. She told him that she was a Jewess who returned after years of wandering with a brutal and blasphemous father to look for her lost and fondly remembered mother and brother in London. Deronda took her to Mrs. Meyrick's home, where Mrs. Meyrick and her daughters nursed the penniless Mirah back to health.

When Gwendolen returns to Offendene, she learns that her family will be forced to move to a small cottage and that she will have to become a governess. The idea oppresses her so strongly that when she sees Grandcourt, who was pursuing her on the Continent, she agrees at once to marry him in spite of her promise to Mrs. Glasher. Her mother, aunt, and uncle know nothing of Mrs. Glasher; Grandcourt knows only that she spoke to Gwendolen, knowledge that he keeps to himself.

After their marriage, Grandcourt is revealed to be a mean, domineering, and demanding man. He sets out to break Gwendolen's spirit. In the meantime, at several house parties, Gwendolen meets Deronda and finds herself much attracted to him. At a New Year's party at Sir Hugo Mallinger's, Gwendolen, despite her husband's disapproval and biting reprisals, speaks to Deronda frequently. When she tells him her whole story and confesses breaking her promise to Mrs. Glasher, Deronda suggests that she show her repentance by living a less selfish life and by caring for and helping those less fortunate than she. Gwendolen, realizing the folly of her marriage to Grandcourt and wishing to find some measure of happiness and peace, decides to follow the course Deronda proposes.

Meanwhile, Deronda is attempting to secure Mirah's future and, if possible, to find her family. Mirah is an actress and has some talent for singing. Deronda arranges an interview for her with Herr Klesmer, a German-Jewish musician with many connections, who can get Mirah started on a ca-

reer. Herr Klesmer is very much impressed with Mirah's singing. He knew Gwendolen at Offendene and refused to help her when she asked for singing engagements because he thought her without sufficient talent; that was the first blow to Gwendolen's ego. Herr Klesmer married Miss Arrowpoint, next to Gwendolen the most talented and attractive girl in Offendene.

Still trying to find Mirah's family, Deronda wanders in the London East End. There he becomes friendly with the family of Ezra Cohen, a crafty but generous shopkeeper. On the basis of some slight evidence, Deronda for a time believes that the man might be Mirah's brother. Through Ezra's family, he also meets Mordecai, a feeble and learned man, with whom he immediately feels a great kinship. Mordecai takes Deronda to a meeting of his club, a group of men who discuss scholarly, political, and theological topics.

Deronda is delighted when he learns that Mordecai is really Mirah's brother. This discovery helps Deronda to acknowledge and accept his own spiritual and literal kinship with the Jews. The boy of unknown origin, able to move successfully in the high society of England, finds his real home in London's East End.

Critical Evaluation:

George Eliot published her last novel, *Daniel Deronda*, in 1876, shortly after the highly successful *Middlemarch* (1871-1872). The novel chronicles the growth in consciousness of a self-conscious and self-seeking young man, Daniel Deronda, whose moral perception broadens as he becomes aware of his own identity and his mission as a Jew. His growth is encouraged by Mordecai, who is the incarnation of what unifies the Jews and who reflects Eliot's sympathetic understanding.

Deronda's growth in consciousness and sympathetic understanding are mirrored in and facilitated by Gwendolen Harleth's parallel growth from utter selfishness to a broader and deeper sense of herself and her fellows. Deronda's growing ability to communicate with her and to experience mutual understanding prepares him for the deeper affinity that he comes to feel for Mordecai and his dreams of Jewish nationalism.

As of the very first reviews, many critics saw the novel as being divided into two parts: the Deronda or Jewish part, which includes Mirah and Mordecai, and the Gwendolen or English part, which includes Grandcourt. Almost everyone found fault with the character and mission of Deronda and described him as being effeminate, wooden, lifeless, helpless, pedantic, clumsy, unsatisfying, analytical, vague, and tentative; he was described as lacking vitality and as being too theorizing, melodramatic, and dull. At the same time the English part was highly praised, and Gwendolen was judged to be one of the most successful heroines Eliot had created. Critics found Gwendolen to be charming, interesting, and psychologically realistic. Indeed, among George Eliot's women, Gwendolen is the most rebellious against patriarchal traditions, and her struggle to overcome her egoism and learn submission is totally believable.

Even the style and philosophy of the two parts of the novel have been compared for their differences. The Deronda part is idealistic and deals in allegorical and epic terms with the history and the heritage of the Jewish people; the Gwendolen part is realistic in every sense.

Deronda's Jewish heritage is effectively used to symbolize the principles of solidarity that underline Eliot's moral message. Many readers have responded positively and with appreciation to Eliot's extensive knowledge of Jewish culture, the depth of her Talmudic studies, and her sympathetic treatment of the plight of the Jews in Britain (the character Deronda was thought to be patterned after Benjamin Disraeli and Deronda's mother after Disraeli's mother).

The unifying element for both plots is found in the use of imagery and other artistic devices that incorporate both plots into the major theme and demonstrate the growth in sympathetic understanding that Deronda and Gwendolen exhibit. Both characters are in the crisis of alienation and acquisition of self until they gradually learn to recognize their own identities and intended purposes; in the course of that, each learns submission. Their heritage is revealed in relation to their mothers and in their growing sexual awareness. Patterns of imagery involving vision, light, eyesight, and reflecting pools and glasses define and chronicle their growing self-perception and insight into the hearts of others.

As the characters experience the inner conflict between sympathy and selfishness, references to and experiences with theater and music help enlarge their sympathies. River imagery is used in many ways. At first the characters are merely drifting with a lack of purpose, but as they mature, they begin to row energetically. Bridges of understanding develop in meetings that take place on actual bridges. Other significant patterns of images that delineate the growth of sympathy involve specific reactions to gems and precious stones and the interpretation of writing, texts, and language. Dreams chronicle crises in spiritual growth, and sensuous relationships provide opportunities to analyze morality within complex social networks.

Deronda grows as he becomes Gwendolen's moral leader and helps her to outgrow her narrow egoism; being directed by his nobler nature and seeing him assume his cosmic role

shocks her into an awareness of self. She learns to accept her own limitations, to fulfill her obligations to her mother and others, to outgrow her dependence on Deronda, and to stand alone. She is released from the bondage of her marriage to the sinister Grandcourt. Deronda's involvement with Gwendolen serves as a catalyst to bring him to admit that Mirah is the woman he loves and to usher him into his public role. Both Deronda and Gwendolen learn that to lose one's life is to find it.

As a young man, Deronda believed he was the illegitimate child of Sir Hugo Mallinger, who has raised him as his son. By the time Deronda goes to Genoa to learn the truth about his birth, he has been prepared in every possible way to receive the knowledge that his mother, Madame Alcharisi, imparts to him. Even though she has neglected her duty to her race and to her family, her son is mature enough to be glad that he is a Jew. He is ready to learn more of her personal and national heritage from the manuscripts and family records in the trunk that her grandfather had preserved for him, and he allows Mordecai to interpret the documents to him and instruct him in the meaning of her inheritance.

Eliot's last novel is a powerful and in some ways inspired work, as fascinating for its defects as for its successes, since both reflect not only the author's established strengths as a novelist but also her inventiveness and willingness to explore new areas and strive for greater depth and breadth in her fiction. *Daniel Deronda* shares with its predecessors a penetrating insight into human relationships, a sensitive portrayal of individual moral and emotional growth, an astute and critical analysis of Victorian values, and a unifying moral vision of life.

"Critical Evaluation" by Constance M. Fulmer

Further Reading

Armstrong, Heather V. *Character and Ethical Development in Three Novels of George Eliot: "Middlemarch," "Romola," "Daniel Deronda."* Lewiston, N.Y.: Edwin Mellen Press, 2001. Focuses on the encounters between characters in the three novels, applying philosophical concepts to an analysis of these works. Examines Eliot's ideas about morality, duty, sympathy, and imagination.

Caron, James. "The Rhetoric of Magic in *Daniel Deronda*." In *The Critical Response to George Eliot*, edited by Karen L. Pangallo. Westport, Conn.: Greenwood Press, 1994. Argues that Eliot's techniques and rhetoric support her theme of characters moving toward ideal humanity, and that she uses such elements from romance as evil, witches, sorcery, and divination to fuse ideas and actions.

Hardy, Barbara. *George Eliot: A Critic's Biography.* London: Continuum, 2006. An examination of Eliot's life combined with an analysis of her works, which will prove useful to readers with some prior knowledge of her writings. Includes an outline of her works and the events in her life.

_____, ed. *Critical Essays on George Eliot.* New York: Barnes & Noble, 1970. This collection, edited by a pioneer in Eliot studies, helped interest critics in feminist analyses of her work. One of the essays is devoted to an analysis of *Daniel Deronda.*

Karl, Fred. *George Eliot: Voice of a Century.* New York: Norton, 1995. Karl's biography draws on valuable new archival material and feminist criticism, depicting Eliot as an author whose work symbolized "the ambiguities, the anguish, and divisiveness of the Victorian era."

Levine, George, ed. *The Cambridge Companion to George Eliot.* New York: Cambridge University Press, 2001. Collection of essays analyzing Eliot's work from various perspectives, including discussions of her early and late novels and of Eliot and realism, philosophy, science, politics, religion, and gender.

Paris, Bernard J. *Rereading George Eliot: Changing Responses to Her Experiments in Life.* Albany: State University of New York Press, 2003. Paris reconsiders Eliot's fiction and decides her greatest strength lies in the "psychological intuition" that is evident in her portrayal of characters and relationships. He demonstrates her skill by closely analyzing the major characters in *Daniel Deronda* and *Middlemarch.*

Rignall, John, ed. *Oxford Reader's Companion to George Eliot.* New York: Oxford University Press, 2000. An encyclopedic volume with entries that cover everything about the novelist, including her pets and homes, as well as her themes and various contexts in which to place her works.

Thompson, Andrew. *George Eliot and Italy: Literary, Cultural, and Political Influences from Dante to the Risorgimento.* New York: St. Martin's Press, 1998. Examines the influence of Dante and the Risorgimento, or the nineteenth century Italian nationalist movement, on Eliot's novels. Chapters 8-10 focus on the influence of Dante, Italian poetry, music, and prophecy in *Daniel Deronda.*

Zimmerman, Bonnie. "Gwendolen Harleth and 'The Girl of the Period.'" In *George Eliot: Centenary Essays and an Unpublished Fragment,* edited by Anne Smith. Totowa, N.J.: Barnes & Noble, 1980. This analysis of Gwendolen's role describes her as the culmination of Eliot's theory on women: She is Eliot's most rebellious and egoistic heroine and receives the most dreadful punishment.

Danton's Death

Author: Georg Büchner (1813-1837)
First produced: Dantons Tod, 1902; first published, 1835 (English translation, 1927)
Type of work: Drama
Type of plot: Tragedy
Time of plot: Spring, 1794
Locale: Paris

Principal characters:
GEORGES DANTON and CAMILLE DESMOULINS, deputies of the National Convention
ROBESPIERRE and SAINT-JUST, members of the Committee of Public Safety
JULIE, Danton's wife
LUCILLE, Desmoulins's wife
MARION, a prostitute

The Story:

The action occurs between March 24 and April 5, 1794, during the French Revolution's Reign of Terror. Georges Danton, who raised armies that had saved the Republic, becomes indifferent to politics, yet he retains sufficient popularity to pose a threat to the extremist Revolutionary leader Robespierre, who gains and keeps power by executing leaders of his opposition.

Danton, several friends, and their ladies exchange witticisms as they play cards through most of a night. At the same time, Camille Desmoulins tries to bring Danton back into the political arena to lead the attack against Robespierre's totalitarian faction. Meanwhile Robespierre invites citizens to follow him to the Jacobin Club, where he dominates the Committee of Public Safety. At the club, Robespierre proclaims in a long tirade that he is an incorruptible leader and that his government was forced to proceed despotically against the villainy of Royalists, foreigners, and other enemies. To punish such oppressors of humankind is mercy, he insists; to forgive them would be stupid and even barbaric. He maintains that the French Republic needs to deploy weapons of terror to save its ideals, and he asks his listeners to trust his policies.

Instead of opposing Robespierre, Danton prefers to flirt with the prostitute Marion, who rhapsodizes about the joys of the body in a monologue in which she compares herself to a sea that swallows all men. Danton's moderate friends, who heard Robespierre's impassioned oratory, warn him of the latter's enmity, but Danton only shrugs off their advice, certain that Robespierre's people will not dare arrest him. When the two leaders meet in debate, Danton urges Robespierre to stop his massive slaughter of alleged conspirators, while the latter counters that a Revolution that is only half-finished is digging its own grave. After Danton leaves the room, Robespierre, in an extended soliloquy, convinces himself that even though some people might accuse him of acting out of personal jealousy, Danton is a threat to the Republic and has to be eliminated.

The Committee of Public Safety orders the arrests of the Dantonists. Instead of fleeing or fighting, Danton remains passive and introspective, brooding remorsefully about the bloodshed of the September, 1793, massacres of Royalists, for which he takes responsibility. His wife, Julie, reminds him that he thereby saved the nation, but he remains unconvinced that those massive executions were necessary. At the National Convention, Robespierre seeks to justify his decision to move against Danton's group. He compares himself to Moses leading his people into the desert on their way to the promised land.

Danton and a number of his associates are now imprisoned, joining friends and acquaintances who previously were arrested. Formally arraigned by Robespierre's subordinates, Danton demands that his accusers appear before him. The session of the Revolutionary Tribunal adjourns without granting his demand. Robespierre's leading deputy, Saint-Just, then "discovers" a plot by the Dantonists to blow up the National Convention. The Dantonists are thereupon condemned to the guillotine, even though Danton publicly accuses Robespierre's Committee of Public Safety of high treason.

Awaiting execution, Danton meditates extensively on death and bids farewell to his beloved body, about to become a "broken fiddle." He prophesies that Robespierre's violent death will follow his within six months, a historically accurate forecast. As the Dantonists are taken by cart to the execu-

tion square, they banter among themselves and forgive one another's sins. After the guillotine does its grisly work, Desmoulins's wife, Lucille, deliberately shouts, "Long live the King!" She is immediately arrested as a Royalist, sure to share her husband's fatal fate.

Critical Evaluation:

Georg Büchner's life was brief but intense, and his extraordinary talents merit no less than the word genius. Before he died of typhoid fever at the age of twenty-three, he had obtained a doctorate in philosophy, taught comparative anatomy at the University of Zurich, been formidably active as a political revolutionary, composed scientific papers, translated two dramas by Victor Hugo into his native German, and outlined a course of lectures on the history of German philosophy. Above all, he had written three plays and one story that mark him as one of Germany's, indeed Europe's, most brilliant authors.

Büchner's impact was felt, directly or indirectly, by virtually every important playwright after him. He can be studied as a forerunner of naturalism, social realism, psychological irrationalism, expressionism, existentialism, and the theater of the absurd. In the search for the taproot of twentieth century drama, one need dig no further than his texts.

Danton's Death may well be the best first play ever written. It is profound, relentless, passionate, eloquent, complex, and tragic. Above all, it is remarkably original, even though Büchner was influenced by earlier German dramatists and by William Shakespeare. Like Johann Wolfgang Von Goethe's *Götz von Berlichingen, mit der eisernen Hand* (1773; *Goetz of Berlichingen, with the Iron Hand*, 1799), *Danton's Death* presents a vast historical panorama composed of short, episodic, loosely connected scenes, and with broad strokes it achieves a fullness and earthiness of detail and creates a multitude of characters. Goethe's Götz, however, is an idealized robber baron, and his play demonstrates the possibility of heroic action; Büchner's Danton is an antihero and this work shows extreme skepticism about the feasibility of heroism.

The playwright who most clearly commanded Büchner's admiration is Shakespeare. Danton's self-communing soliloquies go straight back to Hamlet's. Like Hamlet, Danton is passive, introspective, melancholy, bored, witty, morbid, and prone to subject the assumptions of others to ironic analysis. Büchner's Lucille, when she gives way to hysteria, recapitulates Ophelia's mad scene. In addition, Büchner casts the French Revolution in the Roman world of such Shakespearean texts as *Julius Caesar* (pr. 1599-1600, pb. 1623), *Antony and Cleopatra* (pr. c. 1606-1607, pb. 1623), and *Coriolanus* (pr. c. 1607-1608, pb. 1623); each of these features, as

Danton's Death does, a recklessly blind protagonist and coarse, obscene, easily swayed mobs.

Büchner is faithful to respected scholarly sources for the struggle between Danton and Robespierre that occurred in France during the early 1790's. His primary historic debt is to F. A. Mignet's *Histoire de la Révolution française* (1826) and L. A. Thiers's *Histoire de la Révolution française* (1825-1827). He derived many of the external events in *Danton's Death* from these sources and sometimes reproduces verbatim whole speeches by the historic Danton. His portrait is historically accurate in featuring Danton's joviality, generosity, passionate temperament, hedonism, and carelessness in courting danger. His stress on Danton's laziness, fatalism, sensuality, and disillusionment has aspects that are both traditional and contemporary.

Büchner is highly original, however, in presenting Danton as an unheroic hero who, even when capable of stirring action, chooses not to engage in it. Because of his disillusionment with politics and human nature, his only desire is for death. Unlike such classic, developing heroes as Oedipus or Lear, the static Danton fails to experience any moments of insight or recognition, and he does not begin in an initial state of innocence or ignorance from which, as a result of the dramatic action, he enters the world of experience and increased knowledge. Without choosing to wrestle with his fate, Danton indicates repeatedly that he has come to regard all human behavior as ultimately futile, doomed to destruction, without hope or reason. Each man, he declares, is isolated in his impenetrable shell, unable to come to know his fellow, adrift on a sea of anguish and desolation.

The play's first scene illustrates this pessimism and Büchner's adroit juggling of dramatic styles. The initial conversation, ostensibly about love, is loaded with wit and bawdry. Julie, Danton's devoted wife, is concerned about his cynicism. "Don't you believe in me?" she asks him. He replies:

> How should I know! We know little enough about one another. We're thick-skinned creatures who reach out our hands toward one another, but it means nothing—leather rubbing against leather—we're very lonely.

The apprehensive Julie tries to obtain emotional reassurance from her husband, but he refuses to comfort her, instead asserting that for people to know one another, it would be necessary to crack open their skulls and draw forth their thoughts one by one from their brain fissures. Danton will restate the same idea several times in the play.

Büchner's plot is anti-Aristotelian, in that the central emotional crisis of the drama is not released through the contrivances of plot structure. Instead of being clearly organized with a beginning, middle, and end, the text begins at the end of the middle and continues as one extended end. Robespierre organizes the accusations against the Dantonists, followed by their arrest, trial, and execution. Danton, by contrast, refuses to offer any resistance and thereby resigns himself to his fate. What the play amounts to is a slow dance of death, with Danton invoking life's nullity in richly metaphoric imagery as he prepares himself for extinction.

The pervasive dramatic confrontation is in the opposed temperaments of Robespierre and Danton. Büchner shows the former as a damaged psychopath who projects his vengeful, aggressive impulses on others and sees himself as a divinely appointed instrument of justice who can do no wrong. His language reflects the rhetoric of totalitarianism: It is loaded with absolute assertions and dogmatic clichés, devoid of humor, and dominated by abstractions such as "virtue," "immorality," and "the healthy strength of the people." While Robespierre is prepared to sacrifice any number of people to what he is convinced is his absolutely necessary program, Danton refuses to set in motion any further acts of political violence, resigned instead to the futility of politics and history.

Although he is the passive antihero, Danton is mentally and morally superior to his opponent. He jibes at Robespierre's pomposity, jokes with the mob, eschews self-pity, and contrives an endless succession of striking metaphors to express his stoic resignation. He uses wit as an alternative to anger and dilutes his despair in affectionate teasing of his friends. In the conflict between these leaders, Büchner achieves a timeless, universal polarity between the impatient zealot filled with self-righteous fervor and the weary humanist who can no longer believe in a better life to come.

Gerhard Brand

Further Reading

Hamburger, Michael. "Georg Büchner." In *Contraries: Studies in German Literature*. New York: Dutton, 1970. Hamburger is a distinguished critic and translator of German literature. His essay focuses on the profound boredom that saps the willpower of Büchner's heroes.

Hilton, Julian. *Georg Büchner*. New York: Grove Press, 1982. Hilton pays special attention to the scenic structure of *Danton's Death* and to Büchner's influence on such contemporary playwrights as Bertolt Brecht, John Arden, and David Storey.

Holmes, T. M. *The Rehearsal for Revolution: Georg Büchner's Politics and His Drama "Dantons Tod."* New York:

Peter Lang, 1995. *Danton's Death* is often interpreted as Büchner's expression of political disillusionment over the collapse of the French Revolution. Holmes describes how French communist-oriented republicans in the 1830's—a group of people with whom Büchner was associated—shared this sense of disappointment about the failure of the revolution.

Knight, A. H. F. *Georg Büchner.* Oxford, England: Basil Blackwell, 1951. This is the first full-length study of Büchner in English. It examines all of Büchner's writings thoroughly, including his letters. In the discussion of *Danton's Death*, Knight examines at length Büchner's use of historic sources.

Lindenberger, Herbert. *Georg Büchner.* Carbondale: Southern Illinois University Press, 1964. Lindenberger writes gracefully and perceptively, with particular sensitivity to Büchner's uses of rhetoric and dramatic form. His chapter on Büchner's forebears and descendants is illuminating.

Lyon, John B. "Violence and the Tenacity of the Self: 'I Am Something, That's the Misery of It!'—Georg Büchner's *Danton's Death.*" In *Crafting Flesh, Crafting the Self: Violence and Identity in Early Nineteenth-Century German Literature.* Lewisburg, Pa.: Bucknell University Press, 2006. Lyon examines images of wounded bodies in works of German literature, including *Danton's Death*, describing how these images are linked to changing philosophical conceptions of the self.

Reddick, John. *Georg Büchner: The Shattered Whole.* New York: Oxford University Press, 1994. Seeks to offer new interpretations of *Danton's Death* and Büchner's other works and discusses the playwright's values, ideas, and politics. Reddick argues that Buchner was aesthetically way ahead of his time primarily because his idealistic assumptions and aspirations were far behind the times.

Schwartz, Alfred. *From Büchner to Beckett: Dramatic Theory and the Modes of Tragic Drama.* Athens: Ohio University Press, 1978. Schwartz distinguishes and traces various patterns of tragedy. He examines Büchner's kaleidoscopic art of composition, in which each scene expresses the violent assaults of history on people's lives.

Daphnis and Chloë

Author: Longus (fl. second or third century)
First transcribed: Poimenika ta kata Daphnin kai Chloen, third century C.E. (English translation, 1587)
Type of work: Novel
Type of plot: Pastoral
Time of plot: Indeterminate
Locale: Island of Lesbos

Principal characters:
DAPHNIS, a young shepherd
CHLOË, a shepherdess

The Story:

On the Greek island of Lesbos, a goatherd named Lamo one day finds a richly dressed infant boy being suckled by one of his goats. Lamo and his wife, Myrtale, hide the purple cloak and ivory dagger the boy wore and pretend he is their own son. They name him Daphnis. Two years later, a shepherd named Dryas discovers an infant girl being nursed by one of his sheep in a cave of the nymphs. This child also is richly dressed. Dryas and his wife, Nape, keep the girl as their own, giving her the name Chloë.

When the two children are fifteen and thirteen years old, they are given flocks to tend. Daphnis and Chloë play happily together, amusing themselves in many ways. One day, while chasing a goat, Daphnis falls into a wolf pit, from which he is rescued unharmed by Chloë and a herdsman she summoned to help her. Daphnis begins to experience delightful but disturbing feelings about Chloë. Dorco, a herdsman, asks permission to marry Chloë but is refused by Dryas. Disguising himself in a wolf skin, Dorco shortly afterward attempts to seize Chloë. Attacked by the flock dogs, he is rescued by Daphnis and Chloë, who innocently think he was merely playing a prank. Love, little understood by either, grows between Daphnis and Chloë.

In the autumn some Tyrian pirates wound Dorco, steal some of his oxen and cows, and take Daphnis away with them. Chloë, who hears Daphnis calling to her from the pirate ship, runs to aid the mortally wounded Dorco. Dorco gives her his herdsman's pipe, telling her to blow upon it. When she blows, the cattle jump into the sea and overturn the ship. The pirates drown, but Daphnis, catching on to the horns of two swimming cows, comes safely to shore.

After the celebration of the autumn vintage, Daphnis and Chloë return to their flocks. They attempt in their innocence to practice the art of love, but they are not successful. Some young men of Methymne come to the fields of Mitylene to hunt. When a withe used as a cable to hold their small ship is gnawed in two by a goat, the Methymneans blame Daphnis and set upon him. In a trial over the affair, Daphnis is judged innocent. The angry Methymneans later carry away Chloë. The god Pan warns the Methymnean captain in a dream that he should bring back Chloë, and she is returned. Daphnis and Chloë joyfully celebrate holidays in honor of Pan.

The two lovers are sad at being parted by winter weather, which keeps the flocks in their folds. In the spring the lovers happily drive their flocks again to the fields. When a woman named Lycaenium becomes enamored of the boy, Daphnis finally learns how to ease the pains he feels for Chloë, but Lycaenium warns him that Chloë will be hurt the first time she experiences the ecstasy of love. Through fear of doing physical harm to his sweetheart, the tender Daphnis will not deflower his Chloë. Meanwhile, many suitors, Lampis among them, ask for the hand of Chloë, and Dryas almost consents. Daphnis bewails his inability to compete successfully with the suitors because of his poverty. With the aid of the nymphs he then finds a purse of silver, which he gives Dryas in order to become contracted to Chloë. In return, Dryas asks Lamo to consent to the marriage of his son, but Lamo answers that first he must consult his master, Dionysophanes.

Lamo, Daphnis, and Chloë prepare to entertain Dionysophanes, but Lampis ravages the garden they prepared because he was denied Chloë's hand. Fearing the wrath of his master, Lamo laments his ill fortune. Eudromus, a page, helps to explain the trouble to Lamo's young master Astylus, who promises to intercede with his father and blame the wanton destruction on some horses in the neighborhood. Astylus's parasite, Gnatho, falls in love with Daphnis but is repulsed. Finally, the depraved Gnatho receives Astylus's permission to take Daphnis with him to the city. Just in time, Lamo reveals the story of the finding of Daphnis, who is discovered to be Dionysophanes' son. Meanwhile, Lampis steals Chloë, who is later rescued by Gnatho. After Dryas tells how Chloë was found as a child, it is learned that she is the daughter of Megacles of Mitylene. Thus the supposed son and daughter of Lamo and Dryas are revealed as the children of wealthy parents who are happy to consent to their marriage. The wedding is celebrated amid the rural scenes dear to both bride and groom. Daphnis becomes Philopoemen, and Chloë is named Agele. On her wedding night Chloë at last learns from Daphnis how the delights of love are obtained.

Critical Evaluation:

Daphnis and Chloë (the work has also been translated as *The Pastoral Loves of Daphnis and Chloë*, 1924, and as *The Story of Daphnis and Chloë*, 1908) first appeared in English in a version by Richard Waldegrave in 1587, but the translation made by George Thornley in 1657 is more familiar. More recent translations by George Moore and Jack Lindsay are considerably more readable but have not enjoyed wide circulation. *Daphnis and Chloë* was an influential work throughout Renaissance Europe, its subject matter and style being respectfully recapitulated in pastoral romances produced in the vernacular throughout Europe. Like many late classical works, however—the most notorious examples are credited to Petronius and Lucian—*Daphnis and Chloë* came to be considered an indecent work because of its relative frankness about sex. For this reason the English text retired for a while in the nineteenth and early twentieth centuries into the shady realm of privately printed editions. Unlike the satires of Petronius and Lucian, however, *Daphnis and Chloë* contains nothing deliberately coarse or obscene; its allegory of the growth and maturation of sexual love is handled with scrupulous delicacy that seems intended to avoid giving offense.

Although the labored and archaic style of the Thornley translation obscures the fact, *Daphnis and Chloë* is in several ways a strikingly modern work. It has better claims to be considered the first protonovel than any other work of classical literature. Its plot—comprising an event-crowded obstacle course that continually parts the two lovers but finally delivers them to a marriage blessed with unexpected wealth and status—foreshadows the formula that has by far been the most successful in the popular fiction of more than a century. It is also one of the earliest works to take for granted that the life of rural folk needs to be tactfully explained and sentimentally glorified for the benefit of a thoroughly "civilized" (in its literal sense of city-bred) audience. The nostalgic reverence for the pastoral in *Daphnis and Chloë* is identical in spirit to that which infects a great deal of nineteenth, twentieth, and twenty-first century fiction; even its disapproval of Gnatho's homosexuality is far more reminiscent of modern attitudes than of what are usually thought of as the attitudes of ancient Greece.

What remains classical about *Daphnis and Chloë* is its careful use of allegory, particularly in its use of the Greek pantheon. Its invocation of Pan is, however, self-consciously metaphorical and artificial. Unlike the dramas of several centuries earlier, in which the gods are treated with reverent awe as overlords of human destiny, the attitude of *Daphnis and Chloë* is conspicuously casual. This offhandedness is a natural partner of the somewhat anecdotal style of early prose fiction, but it is as much a cause as an effect. The author can refer to the gods without excessive stylization because he is fully conscious of the fact that they are, for him, symbolic. His account of the myth of Echo and the tale of Pan and Syrinx assumes that the audience knows them as fables or amusing stories. When Pan afflicts the Methymneans with the panic named after him, he acts as a friend doing a favor, not as a loftily offended god wreaking havoc upon human playthings.

It is not merely Pan's name that is carefully diminished by the author of the romance; the names "Daphnis" and "Chloë" have their own significance. One attribute of the name Chloë is "Blooming," and it has been used as a surname of the goddess Demeter, protectress of the green fields. The original Daphnis was the alleged son of Hermes and a nymph, who was brought up by the nymphs and taught by Pan to play the flute; he became a shepherd and the inventor of bucolic poetry. Pan symbolizes nature; the names allotted to the hero and heroine of the story symbolize agriculture and animal husbandry. As the plot finally emphasizes, these are essentially technologies, but they are products of civilization that must work within the framework of nature. Necessity rules that they must be harmonized, at least to some extent, with nature's wildness and seasonally patterned fecundity. The nostalgic manner of the tale is a gentle reminder to a civilized audience that all their triumphs of artifice and manners remain rooted in the soil and the pastures.

There remains in all this a certain honest reverence, but it is a buoyant politeness rather than the somber and fatalistic reverence of Greek tragedy. The name that Daphnis takes after his marriage, Philopoemen, would also have been well known to the original hearers of the tale, being that of the last great military leader Greece produced before losing its political independence. Having come into his proper heritage, Daphnis is transformed from herdsman to hero. This indicates nostalgia for an era when Greece was the fountainhead of civilization rather than a mere handmaiden of Rome.

Few people today would read *Daphnis and Chloë* for pleasure; the text is too cluttered and too discursive, the prose irredeemably primitive even in more sensitive and less florid translations than Thornley's. Those who read the tale for instructive purposes, however, cannot help but notice that in almost everything that is currently read for pleasure some echo of *Daphnis and Chloë* sounds. The message that it puts across is still being broadcast. To say that it stands as the remote ancestor of all modern romance stories is not to insult it but rather to confirm that it contains the seeds of a vast and flourishing literary growth, and is—in its assiduously modest fashion—a great work.

"Critical Evaluation" by Brian Stableford

Further Reading

Barber, Giles. *Daphnis and Chloë: The Markets and Metamorphoses of an Unknown Bestseller.* London: The British Library, 1989. A fascinating study of the bibliographic history of the work and its reception by various audiences.

Fekete, David J. "Two Vast Antagonists: Longus and Plato." In *A Rhapsody of Love and Spirituality.* New York: Algora, 2003. Contrasts Longus's depiction of interpersonal love in *Daphnis and Chloë* with Plato's ideas of transcendent love, arguing that these conflicting views are the origin of modern confusion about love.

Hardin, Richard F. *Love in a Green Shade: Idyllic Romances Ancient to Modern.* Lincoln: University of Nebraska Press, 2000. Examines the idyllic romance tradition in literature, with special emphasis on *Daphnis and Chloë*. Surveys the work's reception from its rediscovery in the Renaissance through its various adaptations in English, French, Spanish, and other languages.

Longus. *Daphnis and Chloë.* Translated by George Thornley and with an introduction by J. M. Edwards. New York: Putnam, 1924. Reprint. Cambridge, Mass.: Harvard University Press, 1989. The Thornley translation is revised and augmented by J. M. Edwards, whose introduction details the various manuscript sources. Includes a useful appendix on the origins of the work.

_____. *The Story of Daphnis and Chloë.* Translated, annotated, and edited by W. D. Lowe. Cambridge, England: Deighton Bell, 1908. Reprint. New York: Arno Press, 1979. Perhaps the most useful edition for academic purposes because of its elaborate annotations.

Morgan, J. R. "Longus." In *Time in Ancient Greek Literature,* edited by Irene J. F. de Jong and René Nünlist. Boston: Brill, 2007. Studies the narration of *Daphnis and Chloë,* focusing on the order in which events are presented and other aspects of time in the work.

The Dark Journey

Author: Julien Green (1900-1998)
First published: Léviathan, 1929 (English translation, 1929)
Type of work: Novel
Type of plot: Psychological realism
Time of plot: Early twentieth century
Locale: France

Principal characters:
PAUL GUÉRET, a neurotic tutor
ANGÈLE, a young woman who works in a laundry
MADAME LONDE, a restaurant proprietor
MONSIEUR GROSGEORGE, Guéret's employer
MADAME GROSGEORGE, his wife
FERNANDE, a young girl

The Story:

Paul Guéret is an incompetent, prematurely aged tutor hired to instruct the sickly, unintelligent son of a prosperous provincial family named Grosgeorge. Knowing himself to be a failure and tired of his wife, whom he no longer loves, Guéret had hoped that life would be better in Chanteilles; within a month, however, he is just as wretched there as he had been in Paris, where his feelings of self-pity and frustration had often driven him into sordid love affairs. In Chanteilles, bored by his dreary surroundings, he soon finds himself infatuated with Angèle, a young woman who works in a laundry. Hoping to become her lover, he begins to write her letters asking her to meet him. Sometimes he follows her at a distance when she delivers clean laundry to her customers.

One night, Guéret accosts Angèle at a footbridge on the outskirts of the town. Hating himself for his shabby clothes and stammering speech, he offers her a cheap ring stolen from his wife. Although she accepts the ring, Angèle does not encourage his attentions. His abrupt yet furtive ardor both attracts and repels her.

That same night, Guéret goes by chance to the Restaurant Londe in nearby Lorges. There Madame Londe, the proprietor, presides majestically behind her cashier's desk. A sly woman whose days are given over to spying and gossip, she delights in alternately cajoling and bullying her patrons, who seem to hold her resentfully in awe. When Guéret enters, she is disturbed because he is a stranger and she knows nothing about him. She refuses to let him pay for his dinner and has him write his name in her account book. Her desire is to add him to her regular clientele.

Madame Londe's hold over her patrons is a sinister one, maintained through her niece, Angèle. Because the young woman is indebted to her for food and a room, Madame Londe is able to force Angèle to sell her favors to the regular customers of the restaurant. With knowledge thus gained of the guilt and secret vices of her patrons, Madame Londe is able to dictate to them as she pleases. Her own position as a

procurer gives her no worry—her only concern is her lust for power over others.

Upset by his desire for Angèle, Guéret pays little attention to his duties as a tutor. André Grosgeorge is a poor student, but his mother shrewdly blames Guéret for her son's slow progress. Madame Grosgeorge is a woman in whom the starved passions of her girlhood have turned to a tortured kind of love that finds its outlet in cruelty and treachery. Because her husband, whom she despises, ignores her nagging tirades, she takes special pleasure in beating her son and in humiliating Guéret.

Monsieur Grosgeorge feels sorry for the browbeaten tutor. Having guessed that Guéret is unhappily married, Grosgeorge bluntly advises him to find a mistress before he wastes his years in moping dullness, saying that is the course he himself has followed. One day, Monsieur Grosgeorge boastingly shows Guéret a note he has received in which the writer asks Grosgeorge to meet her the next night. Guéret, staring at the letter, shakes with suppressed rage when he recognizes Angèle's handwriting.

After several meetings with Guéret, Angèle becomes more independent in her attitude toward Madame Londe. Because Guéret's conduct is quite different from that of other men who seek her favors, she no longer wishes to sell herself and act as her aunt's informant. During a quarrel she has with Madame Londe when she refuses to keep an assignation the old woman has arranged, Angèle threatens to leave. Madame Londe becomes worried. Afraid that she will lose her hold over her patrons, she begins to train Fernande, a twelve-year-old girl, to take Angèle's place.

Guéret returns to the Restaurant Londe. As he eats his meal, he learns from the talk of the other diners that Angèle is Madame Londe's niece and that she has sold herself to most of the men there. That night, driven to desperation by his knowledge, he breaks into Angèle's bedroom. It is empty. When Madame Londe, awakened by his entry, screams for help, he runs away and hides in the woods. On his way back to Chanteilles, he meets Angèle. In a sudden, brutal fury, he picks up a branch and strikes her until her face and head are covered in blood.

All that day Guéret skulks beside the river. As he is sneaking back into town after dark, he meets a feeble old man. Fearing capture, he seizes the old man's stick and beats him to death. Filled with blind terror, he flees across the yards of unknown houses and through back streets of the town.

The neighborhood is shocked by the brutality of the crimes that have been committed, and for weeks the townspeople refuse to venture into the streets at night. Angèle, disfigured for life, refuses to give the name of her assailant and remains shut up in her room above the restaurant. Only Madame Grosgeorge scoffs at those who bolt their doors at dusk. Indeed, she seems to relish the idea that the shabby, blundering tutor has scarred the face of her husband's mistress and violently disrupted the monotony of her own existence.

Eventually the outcry diminishes, and Guéret, unable to stay away from Angèle, returns to the district. Madame Grosgeorge sees him near the footbridge and calls out to him that she will meet him there the next evening. She returns the next night, but Guéret does not appear, although she waits impatiently for more than an hour. Later, he comes to her villa, and she, unknown to her husband, hides the fugitive in her private sitting room. She promises that she will give him money and some of her husband's clothing before she sends him away in the morning.

His presence in the house, however, gives her such strange satisfaction that she refuses to let him go as she had promised. The next morning, she goes to her sitting room and tries to talk to him about his crimes. When his answers show only that he is still in love with Angèle, Madame Grosgeorge feels cheated. She had admired Guéret for his violence, but now she despises him for his foolish passion. Again, she locks him in the room while she tries to decide what to do. Little Fernande arrives to deliver some laundry, and, on impulse, Madame Grosgeorge writes a note for Fernande to take to Angèle, telling her that Guéret is in her house and asking that the police be called.

Madame Londe, always on the alert, intercepts the message and hurries to give the alarm. Angèle, learning what has happened, sends Fernande to warn the fugitive that he must escape at once. Meanwhile, Madame Grosgeorge has returned to Guéret. When he insists that she let him go, she locks both of them in the sitting room and throws the key out the window. Then she tells him that Angèle knows his whereabouts and that if he is betrayed, Angèle will be to blame. Madame Grosgeorge takes a revolver from her desk, puts it in her belt, and calmly prepares to write a letter. Fernande runs into the

garden, and Guéret, leaning out the window, asks her to pick up the key and unlock the door. He then hears the sound of a shot behind him—Madame Grosgeorge has shot herself.

Critical Evaluation:

Writing always somewhat outside the mainstream of French (and American) fiction, Julien Green managed literally to survive most of his contemporaries, remaining active as a writer and granting frequent interviews well into his nineties. In Green's case, the happy accidents of longevity and sustained productivity assured a continued interest in his work, including those novels published near the start of his career. *The Dark Journey* was the third of Green's novels to be published while the author was still in his twenties. His early novels are marked by a sureness of touch rare for an author of that age, especially in the creation and delineation of his characters. Green's characters impose themselves on the reader, drawing him or her deeply into a threatening reality that lurks just beneath the surface of everyday life. Thus do Guéret's yearnings, harmless enough at the start, pass quickly into obsession, violence, and murder.

Using shifting viewpoints, although always narrating in the third person, Green shows society as a potential danger zone of conflicting preoccupations and obsessions. Like some of the most memorable characters in Honoré de Balzac's multivolume *La Comédie humaine* (1829-1848; *The Human Comedy*, 1895-1896, 1911), written a century earlier, many of Green's characters tend to be monomaniacs, motivated by a single overriding passion. Unlike Balzac, however, Green presents his characters in inevitable conflict rather than in isolation, showing the society portrayed to be more menacing than entertaining. As Glenn S. Burne points out in his major survey of Green's work, of all the characters' preoccupations, Guéret's obsession with sex and love is, in a sense, the most normal. Like many of Green's featured characters, however, Guéret proves hopelessly inarticulate, unable to communicate with Angèle or anyone else, perhaps because his lack of attractiveness, even if only self-perceived, has hampered his social development.

In the hands of another writer, a character such as Guéret might prove comic or even sympathetic; as portrayed by Green, however, Guéret becomes and remains a danger both to himself and to others. Likewise, Madame Londe, whose peculiar lust for power might emerge as laughable in another context, poses dangers of which she herself might well be unaware. As Burne observes, the traditional concept of fate looms large in *The Dark Journey*, often invoked or blamed by the characters themselves as they proceed to their doom. No doubt the characters' extreme self-centeredness has much to do with their fates; were any of them less self-absorbed, they might well find time to understand one another.

Although it precedes by at least a decade the more religious and mystical phases of Green's career as a novelist, *The Dark Journey* in many ways invites comparison with certain novels of François Mauriac, a frankly religious and Roman Catholic novelist in whose dark narratives God is most often revealed by his absence; in other words, the misadventures of Mauriac's characters, in the author's view, might well prepare them for the revelation or discovery of God. For the haunted, driven characters of *The Dark Journey*, however, no such revelation seems possible or even imaginable. The unrelieved bleakness of the moral and emotional landscape invites the reader to consider other options.

"Critical Evaluation" by David B. Parsell

Further Reading

Armbrecht, Thomas J. D. *At the Periphery of the Center: Sexuality and Literary Genre in the Works of Marguerite Yourcenar and Julien Green*. Atlanta: Rodopi, 2007. Comparative study of the two twentieth century writers focuses on the depictions of homosexuality in their novels and plays.

Burne, Glenn S. *Julian Green*. New York: Twayne, 1972. Offers a comprehensive overview of the first forty-five years of Green's career, culminating in his induction into the Académie Française in 1971. Provides a good interpretation of *The Dark Journey*.

Dunaway, John M. *The Metamorphoses of the Self: The Mystic, the Sensualist, and the Artist in the Works of Julien Green*. Lexington: University Press of Kentucky, 1978. Traces the sources and evolution of Green's narrative art. Includes brief discussion of *The Dark Journey*, relating it to the prevalence of violence in Green's early fiction.

O'Dwyer, Michael. *Julien Green: A Critical Study*. Portland, Oreg.: Four Courts Press, 1997. Provides a biographical introduction and a critical assessment of Green's novels, short stories, plays, autobiography, journals, and other writings. Highlights the importance of understanding Green's American background in order to gain a full appreciation of his work. Includes a foreword by Green.

_____. "Julien Green: Expatrie et Sudiste." In *Exiles and Migrants: Crossing Thresholds in European Culture and Society*, edited by Anthony Coulson. Portland, Oreg.: Sussex Academic Press, 1997. Examines how Green's experience as an expatriate American southerner in France affected his work.

Peyre, Henri. *French Novelists of Today*. New York: Oxford University Press, 1967. Provides a good overview of Green's career, presenting him as standing outside both the French and the American traditions from which his work derives. Includes informative readings of Green's early and midcareer fiction.

Stokes, Samuel. *Julian Green and the Thorn of Puritanism*. 1955. Reprint. Westport, Conn.: Greenwood Press, 1972. First full-length study of Green's novels published in English remains a good source of information. Focuses on the various intellectual influences that help explain the spiritual background of Green's work.

Dark Laughter

Author: Sherwood Anderson (1876-1941)
First published: 1925
Type of work: Novel
Type of plot: Psychological realism
Time of plot: 1920's
Locale: Old Harbor, Indiana

Principal characters:
BRUCE DUDLEY, formerly John Stockton, a Chicago reporter
SPONGE MARTIN, a workman close to the grass roots
FRED GREY, owner of an automobile wheel factory
ALINE, his wife

The Story:

Bruce Dudley's name is really John Stockton. He grows tired of being John Stockton, reporter on a Chicago paper and married to Bernice. His wife, who works on the same paper and writes magazine stories on the side, thinks him flighty, and he admits it. He wants adventure, and he wants to go back to Old Harbor, the river town in Indiana where he spent his childhood. With less than three hundred dollars, he leaves Chicago, Bernice, and his job on the paper. He picks up the name Bruce Dudley from two store signs in an Illinois town. After a trip down the Mississippi River to New Orleans, he goes to Old Harbor and gets a job varnishing automobile wheels in the Grey Wheel Company, which is owned by Fred Grey.

Working in the same room with Bruce is Sponge Martin, a wiry old fellow with a black mustache who lives a simple, elemental life. That is the reason, perhaps, why Bruce likes him so much. Sometimes when the nights are fair and the fish are biting, Sponge and his wife pack up sandwiches and moonshine whiskey and go down to the river. They fish for a while and get drunk, and then Sponge's wife makes him feel like a young man again. Bruce wishes he could be as happy and carefree as Sponge.

When Bruce was making his way down the Mississippi, he stayed for five months in an old house in New Orleans, where he watched African Americans and listened to their songs and laughter. It seemed to him, listening to their dark laughter, that they lived as simply as children and were happy.

Aline, the wife of Fred, sees Bruce walking out the factory door one evening as she sits in her car waiting for her husband. She does not know who he is, but she remembers another man to whom she felt attracted in the same way. In Paris, after the war, she saw a man at Rose Frank's apartment whom she desired. Then she married Fred, who was recovering from the shock of the war, even though he was not the man for whom she wished.

One evening, Bruce passes by the Grey home as Aline stands in the yard. He stops and looks first at the house and then at Aline. Neither speaks, but something passes between them. They find each other.

Aline, who advertised for a gardener, hires Bruce after turning down several other applicants. Bruce quit his job at the factory shortly before seeing her advertisement. When he first begins to work for Aline, they both maintain some reserve, but each of them carries on many imaginary conversations with the other. Fred seems to resent Bruce's presence on the grounds, but he says nothing to the man, and when he questions his wife, he learns that she knows nothing of Bruce except that he is a good worker.

Aline watches her husband leave for the factory each morning and wonders how much he knows or guesses. She thinks a great deal about her own life and about life in general. Her husband is no lover. Few women nowadays have true lovers. Modern civilization tells people what they cannot have, and people belittle what they cannot possess. Because people do not have love, they make fun of it, are skeptical of it, and besmirch it. The play between Aline and the two men continues silently. Two black women who work in Aline's house watch the proceedings. From time to time, they

are heard laughing, and their dark laughter sounds mocking. White folks are strange, making life so complicated, whereas black people take what they want simply, openly, happily.

One day in June, after Fred went to march in a veterans' parade and the servants went to watch the parade, Aline and Bruce remain on the property alone. She sits and watches him work in the garden. Finally, when he looks at her, he follows her into the house through a door she purposely leaves open. Bruce leaves the house before Fred returns, and he disappears from Old Harbor. Two months later, Aline tells Fred she is expecting a child.

When Fred comes home one evening in the early fall, he sees his wife and Bruce together in the garden. Aline calmly calls to him and announces that the child she is expecting is not his. She and Bruce waited, she goes on, to let him know they are leaving. Fred pleads with her to stay, knowing she is hurting herself, but they walk away; Bruce carries her two heavy bags.

Fred stands with his revolver in his hand a few minutes later, telling himself that he cannot dispassionately let another man walk away with his wife. His mind is filled with confused anger, and for a moment he thinks of killing himself. Then he follows the pair along the river road. He is determined to kill Bruce, but he loses sight of the two in the darkness. In a blind fury, he shoots at the river. On the way back to his house, he stops to sit on a log. The revolver falls to the ground, and for a long time he sits crying like a child.

After Fred returns to his home and goes to bed, he tries to laugh at what has happened, but he cannot. Outside in the road, he hears a sudden burst of laughter. It is the younger of the two black servants who work in the Grey home. She cries out loudly that she knew all the time, and again there comes a burst of dark laughter.

Critical Evaluation:

Sherwood Anderson's *Dark Laughter* is a serious novel that emerged from the aftermath of World War I and reflects the literary and stylistic devices pioneered in that era. For writers, artists, and thinkers, World War I represented the end of intellectual, scientific, political, moral, and psychological certainties. Before the war, intellectuals considered Western culture to be the finest flowering and the highest expression of human civilization. In its barbarism and in the duration and intensity of its savagery, unprecedented in human history, the war shattered that belief. Scientific discoveries shook hitherto unquestioned assumptions about the Newtonian universe. Karl Marx's theories and the Russian Revolution undermined confidence in social classes and political systems. Sigmund Freud, by elaborating a theory of an active unconscious and an unconscious life, destroyed the idea that human beings were a given, known quantity.

All of these developments form the context for the movement in literature in which accepted patterns of characterization, sequence, and symbols were radically altered. It is in this context that Anderson's *Dark Laughter* can be understood best. In the novel. Anderson tries both to formulate a criticism of the old values made disreputable by the war and to set forth new values by which people could live.

Anderson establishes two dramatic poles in the novel: One embodies a natural, honest, sincere relationship to life; the other (embodying the old, prewar values) represents an artificial, mechanical, and dishonest approach. Fred Grey and Bernice Stockton are characters who lead superficial and distant lives. Fred imagines himself to be sensitive, cultured, and generous, but he is actually morally coarse, suspicious, and tightfisted. Above all, he is separated from the realities of life by his economic position and inner sterility.

Bernice, the wife from whom Bruce Dudley fled, is a variation of the same type. Her specialty is literature, but from hints of the story she is writing—a precious, unreal thing—it becomes clear that her characters and plot reflect her own superficial romanticism rather than the actual conditions of life. She is a member of an "in group" of writers and intellectuals, and Anderson indicates that this membership is more important to her than infusing her art with truth.

In contrast to these characters are Bruce Dudley, Sponge Martin, and, to some extent, Aline Grey. Anderson casts these people as representatives of the new, hopeful values that have come to life after the trauma of war. Sponge and his wife, for example, have a genuine connection to real life. Their sexual life is natural and unaffected, they have few pretensions; and they are generous and simple. Bruce, the central character in the novel, is a writer more interested in the truth than in "word slinging." Leaving Bernice is a rejection of her literary pretensions. In falling in love with Aline and fathering her child, he is answering the deeper, underlying currents in life.

For Aline, who vacillates between these poles, the marriage to Fred represents a confused surrender to the conventional life. Running away with Bruce means coming to terms with life as it is, not as it exists in the decadent literary circles of postwar France, in the romantic fantasies of her adolescence, or in the expected routines of upper-middle-class life in the United States.

It is clear that, just as Anderson is criticizing an outworn and mechanical value system, he is also criticizing an earlier literary tradition, which did not come to terms with the natural, primitive side of life or seek out and explore the unconscious. If literary tradition discusses only the superficial and agree-able aspects of life, then Anderson heartily disapproved of it. He hoped that *Dark Laughter* would support and represent a new literary tradition to correspond to the new postwar values.

Anderson admitted that *Dark Laughter* was influenced by James Joyce, for he used such modernist techniques as breaking sections of narrative into fragments, scattering parts of poems throughout the text, using subjective, semi-stream-of-consciousness narration, and switching points of view. As a matter of fact, the techniques employed in *Dark Laughter* probably reflect more generally the literary climate of the 1920's rather than a specifically Joycean influence.

Dark Laughter also displays certain negative features of the American literary climate of the 1920's, perhaps most visible among them a racist component in many passages. With his title *Dark Laughter*, Anderson refers to the natural, honest pole of human behavior that he espouses. Associated with this naturalness are "primitive," "uncivilized," and "amoral" qualities that Anderson links to black people. In fact, *Dark Laughter* refers to the laughter of black maids in the Grey household when they learn of Aline's adultery. Such prejudices, commonplace in the era in which *Dark Laughter* was written, need not overshadow the major intent of the book. *Dark Laughter* expresses an important opposition of ideas in mid-twentieth century literary terms: The reader is asked to choose between real life and superficial life; and, in that sense, Anderson has presented the reader with a profound moral choice.

"Critical Evaluation" by Howard Lee Hertz

Further Reading

Anderson, David D. "Anderson and Myth (1976)." In *Critical Essays on Sherwood Anderson*, edited by David D. Anderson. Boston: G. K. Hall, 1981. Connects content to Anderson's effort to define the myth underlying his own life. Concludes that in *Dark Laughter* Anderson is pleading for individualism in a materialistic America and that the novel is the rejection of rejection.

Bassett, John Earl. "Novels of Midlife Crisis." In *Sherwood Anderson: An American Career*. Selinsgrove, Pa.: Susquehanna University Press, 2006. An interpretive overview of Anderson's life and literary career. The chapter "Novels of Midlife Crisis" devotes several pages to a plot summary and analysis of *Dark Laughter*.

Burbank, Rex. *Sherwood Anderson*. New York: Twayne, 1964. An accessible text with a chapter-long consideration of *Dark Laughter* that gives a historical context for the novel. Provides an effective interpretive plot summary and critical analysis of the work. Includes a preface and chronology, minimal notes and references, a selected bibliography, and an adequate index.

Flanagan, John T. "The Permanence of Sherwood Anderson." In *Critical Essays on Sherwood Anderson*, edited by David D. Anderson. Boston: G. K. Hall, 1981. Emphasizes the autobiographical nature of Anderson's fiction, connects his lifestyle to that of characters such as Bruce Dudley, and addresses his writing style. Flanagan presents *Dark Laughter* in a positive light.

Rideout, Walter B. *Sherwood Anderson: A Writer in America*. 2 vols. Madison: University of Wisconsin Press, 2006-2007. The most extensive and, according to some critics, the definitive biography of Anderson.

Townsend, Kim. *Sherwood Anderson*. Boston: Houghton Mifflin, 1987. An excellent literary view of the novel, describing the influence of various writers. Sees Anderson as seeking complete identification with the black characters of his novel. Townsend evaluates the work as a failure, despite the fact that it captures the rhythms of life in the 1920's.

White, Ray Lewis. *Sherwood Anderson's Memoirs: A Critical Edition*. Chapel Hill: University of North Carolina Press, 1969. Offers a good selection of the writer's reflections on *Dark Laughter*. Includes an account of how the family maid, Kate, inspired the novel. Also includes a selected bibliography and index.

Darkness at Noon

Author: Arthur Koestler (1905-1983)
First published: 1940
Type of work: Novel
Type of plot: Social realism
Time of plot: 1930's
Locale: Russia

Principal characters:
NICHOLAS RUBASHOV, a political prisoner
IVANOV, a prison official
GLETKIN, another official
MICHAEL BOGROV, another prisoner
KIEFFER (HARE-LIP), an informer
NUMBER 1, the supreme leader of the party

The Story:

Nicholas Rubashov, former commissar of the people and once a power in the party, is in prison. Arrested at his lodgings in the middle of the night, he is taken secretly to cell 404, which bears his name on a card just above the spy hole. His cell is located in an isolation block for political suspects.

At seven o'clock in the morning, Rubashov is awakened by a bugle, but he does not get up. Soon he hears sounds in the corridor. He imagines that someone is to be tortured, and he dreads hearing the first screams of pain. When the footsteps reach his own section, he sees through the eye hole that guards are serving breakfast. Rubashov does not receive any breakfast because he reported himself ill. He begins to pace up and down the cell, six and a half steps to the window, six and a half steps back.

Soon he hears a quiet knocking from the wall of the adjoining cell, 402. In communicating with one another, prisoners use the "quadratic alphabet," a square of twenty-five letters, five horizontal rows of five letters each. The first series of taps represents the number of the row; the second series the number of the letter in the row. Thus, words can be spelled. From the communications Rubashov has with his

neighbor, Rubashov pictures him as a military man, one not in sympathy with the methods of the great leader or with the views of Rubashov himself. From his window he sees prisoners walking in the courtyard for exercise. One of these, a man with a harelip, looks repeatedly up at Rubashov's window. From his neighbor in cell 402, Rubashov learns that Hare-Lip is a political prisoner who was tortured in a steam bath the day before. A little later Hare-Lip, in cell 400, sends Rubashov his greetings, via the inmate of 402, but he will not give his name.

Three days later, Rubashov is brought up for his first examination. The examiner is Ivanov, Rubashov's old college friend and former battalion commander. During the interview the prisoner learns that he is accused of belonging to the opposition to the party and that he is suspected of an attempt on the party leader's life. Ivanov promises a twenty-year prison term instead of the death penalty if Rubashov confesses. The prisoner is given a fortnight to arrive at a decision.

After the hearing, Rubashov is given paper and pencil. He uses them to formulate his ideas on the party, society, and his own predicament. As he does so, he remembers a German called Richard whom he expelled from the party, thereby ensuring Richard's certain death at the hands of the Gestapo. Three weeks later, Rubashov himself was arrested by the German police but resisted giving any information despite hideous torture. Pacing his cell, he also casts his mind back on Little Loewy, a tireless advocate for the party in the Belgian ports. Rubashov expelled him, too, for deviating from the party line, and Loewy hanged himself. In a somber mood, Rubashov finally remembers Arlova, his secretary and mistress, whose cries for Rubashov's help he totally ignored.

The night before the time set by Ivanov expires, Rubashov feels a tension in the atmosphere. His friend in 402 communicates to him that one of the prisoners is to be shot. This prisoner is Michael Bogrov, who is Rubashov's close friend. As the condemned man is brought through the corridors, the prisoners tap his progress from one cell to another and drum on the doors of their cells as he passes. The beaten, whimpering figure of Bogrov comes by Rubashov's cell. Rubashov hears his friend shout to him as his friend is dragged down the stairs.

Rubashov's second hearing takes place late at night. Ivanov comes to Rubashov's cell with a bottle of brandy and persuades him that to keep faith with the living is better than betrayal of the dead. Accordingly, Rubashov writes a letter to the Public Prosecutor renouncing his own oppositional attitude and acknowledging his errors. The third night after delivering the letter to the warder, Rubashov is awakened and taken to the office of Gletkin, another official of the prison. Under blinding lights in Gletkin's office, he is questioned day and night for an interminable period of time. He learns that Ivanov was liquidated for conducting Rubashov's case negligently. Gletkin calls in Hare-Lip as a witness against Rubashov. It is only with great difficulty that Rubashov recognizes in that broken, cringing man the son of his former friend and associate, Kieffer. The bright spotlight, the lack of sleep, the constant questionings—these factors combine to make Rubashov sign a trumped-up charge that he plotted to take the life of the party leader.

Rubashov committed none of these crimes. He is merely the victim of Number 1's megalomania. One night he hears the sound of drumming along the corridor. The guards are taking Hare-Lip to be executed. When the drumming starts again, Rubashov knows that his time has come. He is led into the cellar. Another party incident is closed.

Critical Evaluation:

When Arthur Koestler began writing *Darkness at Noon* in 1938, much of Europe squirmed under the heel of totalitarian forces. The threat of fascism was very apparent to many intellectuals, but that of communism not nearly so much. Many naïve and prominent figures looked to the Soviet Union for leadership in the long march to a distant utopia. Koestler, a Communist Party activist for most of the 1930's, knew the reality at first hand. He had seen countless numbers of friends censored and executed by the Communist Party. He had traveled extensively in the Soviet Union and seen its economic backwardness and widespread famine. Against this historical background, *Darkness at Noon* may be viewed first of all as a factually accurate account that uses the techniques of fiction. Koestler writes in a spare, straightforward fashion without stylistic flights. The understatement of the horrors and madness of the prison conveys its sordidness without adornment. The characters are not the anguished superhumans of Greek tragedy but small gray figures in a bureaucratic nightmare. They ride along in a train of destiny over which they not only have no control but also have no understanding.

Koestler focuses on the show trials as the particular manifestation of the Communist suppression. These trials took place throughout the 1930's and represented the bloodthirsty, paranoid effort of Joseph Stalin (who is represented as Number 1 in the novel) to consolidate his position as dictator by liquidating all opposition, including his own former comrades in the Russian Revolution. The protagonist of the novel, Rubashov, is fictional, but he represents many Communist Party leaders who did exist and met their deaths through trumped-up charges brought against them by the Soviet police. Much of the narrative takes place inside the mind of Rubashov and presents a brilliant psychology study. Rubashov is a man trying to reconcile his present dilemma with the beliefs and actions of his earlier years. More specifically, Koestler addresses an issue that puzzled political analysts of his day: Why did those accused in the show trials plead guilty in open court to crimes that they did not commit? In answering this question, Koestler leads the reader through many dark labyrinths of Rubashov's logical mind. The book on one hand sheds light on Rubashov's conviction in the ultimate rightness of all the Communist Party's actions and on the other shows his cynicism about the economic and political realities of the time. Koestler describes Rubashov's sad mistreatment in the prison and then demonstrates with flashbacks that the high-ranking Communist is no innocent. Previously he has thrown people to the wolves for political reasons and once merely to save himself. Ultimately Koestler seems to suggest that Rubashov confesses because of exhaustion and his reasoned conviction that in doing so he will render the Party one last service. Rubashov had previously resisted torture successfully in a fascist prison. While in the service of the Communist Party, he had shown great moral and physical courage.

Koestler's theme is means and ends. To Rubashov, the push to an honorable and humanitarian goal justifies unsavory actions to achieve that goal. In this case the goal is a utopian Communist society in which no one wants economically, in which the upper class withers away, and in which people rule themselves spontaneously and fairly. The means to this end are best determined by the utterly ruthless "militant philosophers"—the leaders of the Communist Party. Koestler also wrote on this theme in his first novel, *The Gladiators* (1939), concerning a revolution by slaves against the Roman Empire. The hero, Spartacus, has great success at first, but his unwillingness to quell disorder among his own troops and followers causes his downfall. Spartacus's revolution failed whereas the Russian Revolution succeeded. Koestler implies that the difference was that the Communist leaders stopped at nothing to achieve their ends. In so doing they negated their highest aspirations and, in a sense, therefore also failed in their revolution to bring a classless perfect world. All through the book Rubashov wrestles with this problem of means and ends. Rubashov hopes, faintly, that the Communist Party will be proven right by history. He abases himself publicly to this end, gambling his only remaining card, his logic, that the Party will ultimately be proven to be on the true path.

Except for remembered incidents, the novel takes place almost entirely inside a prison. It could be argued that Koestler loses some breadth of vision with this setting. Some critics have pointed out that the novel has no middle ground, no ordinary lives lived by Russians who are not in prison and who are not members of the Communist Party. This observation misses the point of Koestler's writing the book, which is to examine and expose the Communist Party's mentality. The suffocating prison, with its dark corridors, closed off from the outside world and operating under its own logic, is a concretization of the Communist dystopia and a metaphor for the Communist rationale. *Darkness at Noon* has a place as one of the great political novels of the twentieth century and puts Koestler in the forefront of political writers such as George Orwell and Aleksandr Solzhenitsyn. On its publication in France after World War II, *Darkness at Noon* influenced public opinion against the Communist Party and possibly prevented it from gaining power. With the end of the Cold War in the 1980's, the historical events it depicts became less relevant but, as an allegory of the fallacy of using pure logic as a guide to human affairs and of the dangers of justifying immoral behavior with political expediency, it remains as potent as ever.

"Critical Evaluation" by Philip Magnier

Further Reading

Bloom, Harold, ed. *Arthur Koestler's "Darkness at Noon."* Philadelphia: Chelsea House, 2004. Collection of essays providing various interpretations of the novel, including a comparison of the novel with George Orwell's *Nineteen Eighty-Four*, discussions of *Darkness at Noon* as a political novel, the function of Rubashov's toothache, and reaction to the novel in postwar France.

Cesarani, David. *Arthur Koestler: The Homeless Mind.* New York: Free Press, 1999. A thorough reassessment of Koestler's life, ideas, and writings, which explores, among other subjects, his Jewish background, relationships with women, and political activities. Includes bibliography and index.

Judt, Tony. "Arthur Koestler, the Exemplary Intellectual." In *Reappraisals: Reflections on the Forgotten Twentieth Century.* New York: Penguin Books, 2008. Judt includes a discussion of Koestler in his book, which seeks to inform twenty-first century readers about the social thought and socially motivated activism of the twentieth century.

Koestler, Arthur. *The Invisible Writing: The Second Volume of an Autobiography, 1932-1940.* London: Hutchinson, 1969. Koestler discusses his activism in the Communist Party, his travels to the Soviet Union, his imprisonment in fascist Spain, and his denunciation of communism in *Darkness at Noon.*

Levene, Mark. *Arthur Koestler.* New York: Frederick Ungar, 1984. Overview of Koestler's political writing, including a chapter on *Darkness at Noon.*

Pearson, Sidney A. *Arthur Koestler.* Boston: Twayne, 1978. Includes a chapter on *Darkness at Noon.*

Rothkopf, Carol Z. *"Darkness at Noon": A Critical Commentary.* New York: American R. D. M., 1963. Scholarly, complete, and well-written discussion of the novel.

Sperber, Murray A., ed. *Arthur Koestler: A Collection of Critical Essays.* Englewood Cliffs, N.J.: Prentice-Hall, 1977. Includes essays by George Orwell and Saul Bellow, as well as an intellectually tortuous attack on *Darkness at Noon* by a French Marxist.

Sterne, Richard Clark. *Dark Mirror: The Sense of Injustice in Modern European and American Literature.* New York: Fordham University Press, 1994. A substantial discussion of *Darkness at Noon* is included in this book, which analyzes literature that treats the conflict between natural, ethical law and more "realistic" concepts of justice.

Das Kapital

Author: Karl Marx (1818-1883)
First published: Volume 1, 1867; volumes 2 and 3,
    edited by Friedrich Engels, 1885, 1894 (English
    translation, 1886, 1907, 1909)
Type of work: Politics and economics

Karl Marx's writings, especially *Das Kapital*, initiated the worldwide growth of communism as a dynamic political force. Economic imbalance prompted a revolutionary uprising of the proletariat, but its form was immensely influenced by this book. Certainly Marx exposed the roots of the Russian Revolution, which occurred decades after his death.

Many of Marx's revolutionary ideas had already been expressed in his *Manifest der Kommunistischen Partei* (1848; with Friedrich Engels; *The Communist Manifesto*, 1850), which he wrote with Friedrich Engels. *Das Kapital* was, however, more than another call to arms; it was an attempt to base communism on a theory of political economy that was scientifically and dialectically defensible. Whereas the *Communist Manifesto* is a passionate document, an outline of a political philosophy, and something of a prophecy, *Das Kapital* is a scholar's treatise, the product of years of research and reflection, and a work of economic theory that continues to challenge professional economists. This contrast is illuminating, for the communist movement has always been characterized by contrast: the intellectual leads the laborers; the reasoned defense is supplemented by violence and murder; and the scholar's program comes alive in revolution and the threat of war.

In the *Communist Manifesto*, Marx and Engels argue that the history of all societies is a history of class struggles and that the struggle became one between the bourgeois class and the proletariat. They state that because all the injustices of society result from the economic advantage the bourgeoisie have over the proletariat, the proletariat will finally rebel and take over the means of production, forming a classless society and a dictatorship of the proletariat. In *Das Kapital*, Marx uses a dialectic method that was inspired by Georg Wilhelm Friedrich Hegel, though it is put to a different use. Marx claimed that his dialectic method was the "direct opposite" of Hegel's, that with Hegel the dialectic "is standing on its head" and "must be turned right side up again, if you would discover the rational kernel within the mystical shell." The method is not mysterious; it involves attending to the conflicting aspects of matters under consideration in order to be able to attain a better idea of the whole. Thus Marx describes

his "rational" dialectic as including "in its comprehension and affirmative recognition of the existing state of things, at the same time, also, the recognition of the negation of that state, of its inevitable breaking up." He goes on to maintain that his account regarded "every historically developed social form to be in fluid movement, and therefore takes into account its transient nature not less than its momentary existence." Marx's dialectic method led to what became known as dialectical materialism, the theory that history is the record of class struggles and the conflict of economic opposites.

Das Kapital begins with a study of commodities and money. Marx distinguishes between use value and value, the latter being understood in terms of exchange value but involving essentially the amount of labor that goes into the production of the commodity; "that which determines the magnitude of the value of any article is the amount of labour socially necessary, or the labour-time socially necessary for its production."

Money results from the use of some special commodity as a means of exchange to equate different products of labor. Money serves as "a universal measure of value." According to Marx, it is not money that makes commodities commensurable; rather, it is the fact that commodities are commensurable in terms of human labor that makes money possible as a measure of value. Money begets money through the circulation of commodities: This is Marx's general formula for capital. Money is the first form in which capital appears, precisely because it is the end product of a circulatory process that begins with the use of money to purchase commodities for sale at higher than the purchase price.

Capital would not be possible without a change of value. If money were used to purchase a commodity sold at the initial price, no profit would be made, no capital made possible. To explain the surplus value that emerges in the process, Marx reminds the reader that the capitalist buys labor power and uses it. The material of production belongs to the capitalists; therefore, the product of the productive process also belongs to them. The product has a use value, but capitalists do not intend to use the product; their interest is in selling it for a price greater than the sum of the costs of its production, including the cost of labor. The realization of surplus value is possible, finally, only by some sort of exploitation of the laborer: The capitalists must manage to make the cost of labor less than the value of labor.

One way of increasing surplus value is by increasing the productiveness of labor without decreasing the workday. The problem that then arises is the problem of keeping the price of commodities up. One solution takes the form of using large numbers of laborers and dividing them for special tasks. Capitalists take advantage of lower prices of commodities by paying labor less and purchasing materials more cheaply. At the same time, through a division of labor, they achieve greater productiveness without a corresponding rise in labor cost. In other words, capitalists hire individuals and put them to work in cooperation with others; they pay for the labor power of those individuals, but they gain the value that comes from using that power cooperatively.

Marx rejects the idea that machinery is introduced to make work easier. He argues that "like every other increase in the productiveness of labour, machinery is intended to cheapen commodities, and, by shortening that portion of the working day, in which the labourer works for himself, to lengthen the other portion that he gives, without an equivalent, to the capitalist. In short, it is a means for producing surplus value." Marx concludes that the possibility of the growth of capital depends on using labor in such a way as to free the capitalist from the need to pay for the use of labor power. He decides that capital is "the command over unpaid labour. All surplus value . . . is in substance the materialisation of unpaid labour."

Capitalist production, according to Marx, "reproduces and perpetuates the condition for exploiting the labourer. It incessantly forces labourers to sell their labour-power in order to live, and enables the capitalist to purchase labour-power in order that he may enrich himself." Accordingly, the division between people described in terms of classes is inevitable in a capitalistic society.

Marx explains the self-destruction of the capitalistic society by arguing that from the exploitation of laborers the capitalists, if they have the economic power, pass to the exploitation of other capitalists and, finally, to their expropriation. "One capitalist always kills many." When, therefore, the monopolistic tendencies of capitalists begin to hinder the modes of production and the mass exploitation of workers reaches a peak of misery and oppression, an uprising of the proletariat will destroy the capitalist state. "Capitalist production begets, with the inexorability of a law of Nature, its own negation." The transformation into the socialized state is much quicker and easier than the transformation of the private

property of the workers into capitalist private property, for it is easier for the mass of workers to expropriate the property of a few capitalists than for the capitalists to expropriate the property of the laborers.

Das Kapital has often been criticized as an economic study written in the style of German metaphysics. It is generally regarded, particularly by those who have never read it, as an extremely difficult book, in both content and style. By its nature it is a complex, scholarly work, but it clearly and directly expounds Marx's ideas, and its theory is lightened by many hypothetical cases with which Marx vividly illustrates his points. In considering the work of other scholars, he is respectful if not acquiescent. Perhaps the primary fault of this momentous work is not that it is too difficult but that it is too simple. To argue that capital is made possible by exploitation of labor may be to ignore the ways in which profit can be realized and labor paid to the satisfaction of both the capitalist and the laborer. Nevertheless, impartial criticism of such a thesis is impossible. Whether a capitalist economic system gives cause for revolution is something that can only be shown by history.

Further Reading

Bidet, Jacques. *Exploring Marx's "Capital": Philosophical, Economic, and Political Dimensions.* Translated by David Fernbach. Boston: Brill, 2007. Examines the theoretical development of *Das Kapital*, analyzing its various drafts. Argues that both the novelty and endurance of Marx's ideas can be attributed to his formulation of concepts with inseparable economic and political aspects.

Carver, Terrell, ed. *The Cambridge Companion to Marx.* New York: Cambridge University Press, 1991. The essays in this volume focus on Marx the philosopher and attempt to draw a distinction between Marxism and Soviet communism.

Gouverneur, Jacques. *Contemporary Capitalism and Marxist Economics.* Translated by Richard LeFanu. Totowa, N.J.: Barnes & Noble, 1983. Provides a nonmathematical account of the socioeconomic bases of Marxist theory. The first part focuses on the Marxist concepts of value and surplus value, and the second consists of a Marxist analysis of Western European capitalism.

Hollander, Samuel. *The Economics of Karl Marx: Analysis and Application.* New York: Cambridge University Press, 2008. An account and technical assessment of Marx's economic theories set forth in *Das Kapital* and his other publications. Focuses on the criticism Marx might have encountered in his time. Chronicles the evolution of Marx's economic analysis from the 1840's through 1863.

Kernig, Claus D., ed. *Marxism, Communism, and Western Society: A Comparative Encyclopedia.* 8 vols. New York: Herder and Herder, 1972. The stated purpose of this comprehensive work was to provide a compatible system of thought to enhance communications between the capitalist West and the then-communist East. Provides a snapshot of Marxist thought at a time when the communist world appeared to be at the height of its power.

Sowell, Thomas. *Marxism: Philosophy and Economics.* New York: Morrow, 1985. An excellent jargon-free introduction to the foundations of *Das Kapital.* Ideal for the general reader who has had no prior exposure to Marxism.

Suchting, Wallis A. *Marx: An Introduction.* New York: New York University Press, 1983. Places the complicated philosophical and economic questions raised in *Das Kapital* against the background of the Revolution of 1848, the First International, the uprising of the Paris Commune, and other major historical events.

Wheen, Francis. *Marx's "Das Kapital": A Biography.* New York: Atlantic Monthly Press, 2007. Chronicles the twenty years Marx spent writing *Das Kapital.* Examines the book's influence on philosophers, writers, and revolutionaries and its impact on twentieth century history.

Daughter of Fortune

Author: Isabel Allende (1942-   )
First published: Hija de la fortuna, 1999 (English translation, 1999)
Type of work: Novel
Type of plot: Historical
Time of plot: 1800-1853
Locale: Chile, England, California, and China

Principal characters:
ELIZA SOMMERS, a Chilean English girl who is raised by three British siblings
MAMA FRESIA, a Chilean of the Mapuche tribe who is a servant in the Sommers household
JOAQUIN ANDIETA, a young and poor Chilean revolutionary with whom Eliza falls in love
JOHN SOMMERS, a sailor
ROSE SOMMERS, his sister
JEREMY SOMMERS, his brother
TAO CHI'EN, a Chinese doctor who helps Eliza as she travels to California as a stowaway
JOAQUIN MURIETA, a famous bandit
JACOB TODD (JACOB FREEMONT), a reporter and Rose's former boyfriend

The Story:

A baby in a wicker basket is left on the doorstep of the British Import and Export Company in Valparaiso, Chile, on March 15, 1832. Rose Sommers—an unmarried sibling of Jeremy Sommers, a prominent member of the company—decides to adopt the baby, whom she finds irresistible. With the consent and support of her brother, Rose names the baby Eliza and raises her in the austere British tradition, with all the privileges and strict discipline common to a nineteenth century, upper-class British family.

As part of her Victorian upbringing, Eliza is taught the English language and learns to play the piano, two skills that will benefit her greatly in the future. Eliza's upbringing is also very much influenced by Mama Fresia, the Native Chil-

ean servant and cook in the Sommers household. Mama Fresia teaches Eliza the native art of cooking and exposes her to the traditions and practices of the Mapuche tribe, thereby allowing Eliza to experience both worlds and both cultures. This bicultural upbringing is advantageous to her as she grows from childhood to adolescence and as she begins her travels to a different world.

Blessed from birth with an almost photographic memory and a keen sense of smell, Eliza becomes an accomplished cook, skillfully blending the gastronomic practices of the Indian and British cultures. Eliza's memory is prolific and almost magical: She is able to remember, with utmost clarity, lying as a baby inside the discarded box of Marseilles soap that served as her first crib. She remembers Miss Rose bending over her cradle and even recalls the color of the dress that Miss Rose was wearing at the time.

Eliza's adolescent years are punctuated by ambivalence toward the circumstances of her birth: On one hand, Miss Rose tells her that she must have been left by wealthy British colonists because the basket in which she was found was constructed of the finest wicker and adorned by a mink coverlet, both outward signs of lavishness theretofore unimaginable in Chile. On the other hand, Mama Fresia informs her that she was found in a crate, wrapped in a man's sweater and without a diaper. She further tells the child that had Eliza not been blessed with blond hair at her birth, Miss Rose and her brother Jeremy would not have adopted her. Eliza quickly realizes that the topic of her birth is not to be discussed in the Sommers household, and she rapidly becomes accustomed to the almost mystical and mythical nature of her origin.

As Eliza matures, her acute sense of smell is sharpened, as is her extraordinary ability to remember even the most obscure items and occurrences in her life. Eliza's life is uncomplicated and normal, and she enjoys the process of maturation and growth, although even at this early stage her independent personality and character become apparent. At the age of sixteen, she falls desperately in love with Joaquin Andieta, a modest clerk who works for Jeremy in the British Import and Export Company. Andieta lives with his mother in abject poverty and expresses anxiety for her well-being. Eliza's family is shocked by Eliza's love for Andieta, whom they consider uncouth and unsuitable for her. Her independent streak is demonstrated when she has an affair with Andieta and becomes pregnant by him.

In 1849, news of the discovery of gold in California reaches South America, prompting many Chileans to migrate to California to seek their fortune. Andieta decides to join the California gold rush, hoping to make his fortune and to free himself and his mother from the cycle of poverty. A few months after his departure, Eliza, who is very much in love with him, decides to follow him to California so they can be together. She stows away on a ship and is helped in this adventurous and difficult voyage by a Chinese doctor named Tao Chi'en who befriends her and is sympathetic to her plight. For the duration of the very arduous voyage, Eliza lives hidden in the bowels of the ship and, as a consequence of this hardship, becomes ill and weak. Her frailness results in a painful miscarriage, which she survives with the help and meticulous attention of Chi'en. The doctor relates to Eliza details about his past life in China, including his brief but happy marriage to Lin. According to him, Lin was sickly and feeble and died soon after they were married. This exchange of information between Chi'en and Eliza during the voyage forms the basis for their future relationship in California.

When they arrive in San Francisco, Eliza notes that the majority of the people there are men. To adapt to her new surroundings, she pretends to be a man, dressing herself in a man's attire. At first, she supports herself by selling homemade Chilean snacks in the streets, while Chi'en earns money by practicing his profession. Chi'en quickly becomes disillusioned with America when he observes the greed of the people and the proliferation of prostitutes in the streets of San Francisco. Having earned some money by selling food, Eliza dresses herself as a cowboy, changes her name to Elias Andieta, and, claiming to be Joaquin's brother, sets out to find him. As she begins this odyssey, Rose and Jeremy back in Chile are stunned by her disappearance. When their brother John arrives home, Rose informs him that Eliza is in actuality his daughter from a previous random affair with a Chilean woman. Sensing that his daughter left for California, John leaves for San Francisco to find her.

Unable to locate Joaquin, Eliza decides to travel through California, relating to Tao Chi'en what she observes by means of occasional letters. She realizes that she no longer loves Joaquin and that she needs to find some means to support herself, as she is almost penniless. In a small town, she encounters a traveling band of prostitutes led by Joe Bonecrusher, and they employ her as a piano player and a cook. Since she is dressed in men's clothing, the members of Bonecrusher's retinue mistakenly assume that she is homosexual.

Chi'en, meanwhile, settles in San Francisco, determined to return to China as soon he has saved enough money to realize the journey. He expresses pleasure at receiving random letters from Eliza, whose company he now misses. John Sommers arrives in San Francisco and searches for his daughter. He accidentally meets Jacob Todd, Rose's former boyfriend, who now goes by the name of Jacob Freemont and is a journalist. Freemont promises to help John find Eliza. Freemont writes and publishes newspaper articles about Joaquin Murieta, a notorious bandit whose description bears a striking resemblance to that of Joaquin Andieta.

Because he misses Eliza's company, Chi'en decides to go look for her at Bonecrusher's. He finds her and takes her back with him to San Francisco, where the two of them organize an association dedicated to helping and rehabilitating young Chinese prostitutes. Chi'en and Eliza's friendship develops into a stronger bond, and they fall in love. The novel ends with the shooting death of Murieta, whose head is exhibited in San Francisco. Chi'en and Eliza go to see the bandit's head to find out whether Murieta and Andieta are indeed the same person.

Critical Evaluation:

Born in Peru in 1942 and raised in Chile, Isabel Allende became one of Latin America's foremost writers. Allende studied in private schools in Chile and was an avid reader of the works of William Shakespeare. In addition to *Daughter of Fortune*, she has written many novels, short stories, and memoirs, including *La suma de los días* (2007; *The Sum of Our Days*, 2008), *Inés del alma mía* (2006; *Inés of My Soul*, 2006), and *La casa de los espíritus* (1982; *The House of the Spirits*, 1985).

In *Daughter of Fortune*, Allende provides panoramic and historical perspectives on the California gold rush, U.S. and Chinese history, and the familial dynamics operating in nineteenth century Chile. The novel offers a broad panorama of violence, death, love, and compassion as depicted through both the major and the minor protagonists of this epic tale. Eliza personalizes the courageous, unconventional, and extraordinarily self-sufficient nineteenth century heroine who independently embarks on an adventure in a foreign country to find her lover.

Although she is true to her original romantic purpose, Eliza soon discovers that her quest is for freedom and personal identity. In the end, she realizes that she is not in love with Joaquin and that she needs to forge her own future in America. These realizations eventually change her outlook, as she begins to see California as a gateway to independence and as a means of freeing herself from the chains of accepted and traditional feminine roles. With painfully detailed paragraphs, Allende portrays Eliza as an authentic figure who, contrary to nineteenth century standards, epitomizes the feminist spirit of independence and freedom. At the end of the novel, through the omniscient narrative style of the writer, Eliza is able to look at herself objectively as she realizes that true freedom comes with being able to make choices, including the choice of whom to love and where to live.

Allende describes every character, including minor ones, in great detail, as through them she explores the major themes of love, exploitation of minorities, the role of women in nineteenth century California, and the searches for identity and freedom. Through the detailed prism of *Daughter of Fortune*, the author provides a historical view of life in nineteenth century America, China, and Valparaiso, Chile, and examines in compelling and abundant detail the exploitation of women and minorities through accurate portrayals of both the minor and the major protagonists of the novel. Allende achieves this in great part by meticulously demonstrating her characters' reactions to their observed environment: Eliza

becomes more independent as she has to reinvent herself and refocuses her priorities; Tao Chi'en becomes disillusioned by what he sees in America; Mama Fresia scoffs at the wealthy in Chile and disappears after helping Eliza escape; the Sommers family clings to its Victorian upbringing as a means of visibly separating itself from the lower class in Chile; as Joaquin Murieta, Andieta becomes a Robin Hood-type bandit in California until he is captured and killed. Allende sometimes utilizes the magical and the mystical to dramatize the lives of the protagonists and to record, in convincing narrative style, the history of an era. *Daughter of Fortune* is an elaborate and exhaustive novel that solidly situates Allende as one of the foremost contemporary Latin American writers of fiction.

Víctor Manuel Durán

Further Reading

Bloom, Harold, ed. *Isabel Allende*. Philadelphia: Chelsea House, 2003. A comprehensive compilation of essays examining magical realism, female imagination, and other areas of Allende's writing.

Cox Castellucci, Karen. *Isabel Allende: A Critical Companion*. Westport, Conn.: Greenwood Press, 2003. A detailed analysis of the characters, plot, historical context, and style of *Daughter of Fortune*.

Feal, Rosemary G., and Yvette E. Miller. *Isabel Allende Today: An Anthology of Essays*. Pittsburgh, Pa.: Latin American Literary Review Press, 2002. A collection of essays examining Allende's skills as a storyteller.

Oboler, Suzanne, and Deena J. González, eds. *The Oxford Encyclopedia of Latinos and Latinas in the USA*. New York: Oxford University Press, 2005. An informative source for people beginning to study Isabel Allende and her works; discusses the author's biography and its influences on her writings.

Rambaldo-Minero, María de la Cinta. *Isabel Allende's Writing of the Self: Trespassing the Boundaries of Fiction and Autobiography*. Lewiston, N.Y.: E. Mellen Press, 2003. A thorough and critical examination of the autobiographical elements in Allende's fiction, focusing on her construction of individuality in her novels.

Zayas, Celina Correas. *Isabel Allende: Life and Spirits*. Translated by Margaret Sayers Peden. Houston, Tex.: Arte Público Press, 2002. An informative discussion of Allende's life, focusing on literary traditions, such as Magical Realism, that have influenced her writings.

David Copperfield

Author: Charles Dickens (1812-1870)
First published: 1849-1850, serial; 1850, book
Type of work: Novel
Type of plot: Bildungsroman
Time of plot: Early nineteenth century
Locale: England

Principal characters:
DAVID COPPERFIELD, the narrator
CLARA, his mother
MISS BETSEY TROTWOOD, David's grandaunt
CLARA PEGGOTTY, a nurse
MR. DANIEL PEGGOTTY, her brother
EMILY, his orphan niece
HAM, his orphan nephew
MR. MURDSTONE, David's stepfather
MISS JANE MURDSTONE, his sister
MR. CREAKLE, the master of Salem House
JAMES STEERFORTH, David's schoolmate
TOMMY TRADDLES, a student at Salem House
MR. WILKINS MICAWBER, a man of pecuniary difficulties
MR. WICKFIELD, Miss Trotwood's solicitor
AGNES WICKFIELD, his daughter
URIAH HEEP, a clerk
MR. SPENLOW, the man under whom David studied law
DORA SPENLOW, his daughter and later David's wife
MR. DICK, Miss Betsey's protegé

The Story:

David Copperfield is born at Blunderstone, in Suffolk, six months after his father's death. Miss Betsey Trotwood, an eccentric grandaunt, is present on the night of his birth, but she leaves the house abruptly and indignantly when she learns that the child is a boy, since only a girl can be named after her. David spends his early years with his pretty young mother and a devoted servant named Peggotty.

The youthful widow is soon courted by Mr. Murdstone. Soon after she marries him, she discovers that he is stingy and cruel. David is packed off with Peggotty to visit her relatives at Yarmouth. Her brother converted an old boat into a home by the sea, where he lives with his niece, who is called Little Em'ly, and his sturdy young nephew, Ham. Little Em'ly and Ham are David's first real playmates, and his visit to Yarmouth remains one of the few happy memories of his lonely childhood. After Mr. Murdstone's sister, Jane, arrives to take charge of her brother's household, David and his mother never again feel free from the dark atmosphere of suspicion and gloom the Murdstones create about them.

One day, in a fit of childish terror, David bites his stepfather on the hand. He is immediately sent off to Salem House, a wretched school near London, where his life is more miserable than ever under a brutal headmaster named Mr. Creakle. In spite of Mr. Creakle's harsh treatment and bullying, how-

ever, David's life is endurable because of his friendship with two boys, the lovable Tommy Traddles and the handsome, lordly James Steerforth.

David's school days end suddenly with the death of his mother and her newborn infant. When he returns home, he discovers that Mr. Murdstone dismissed Peggotty. Barkis, the stage driver, whose courtship was meager but earnest, took Peggotty away to become Mrs. Barkis, and David finds himself friendless in his former home. Soon he is put to work in an export warehouse in London, in which Murdstone has an interest. As a ten-year-old worker in the dilapidated establishment of the wine merchants Murdstone and Grinby, David is overworked and half-starved, and he loathes his job and the people with whom he has to associate. He does meet the Micawber family, however, in whose house David lodges. The impecunious Mr. Micawber is sent to debtor's prison shortly afterward and decides, on his release, to move with his family to Plymouth. After he loses these good friends, David decides to run away.

The only relative he knows is his father's aunt, Miss Betsey Trotwood, of whom he knows only that she lives in Dover and was indignant at his birth. He nevertheless sets out, full of hope; on the way he is robbed of the few things he possesses and consequently arrives at Miss Betsey's home in a wretched state. At first, his reception is not encouraging, but Miss Betsey takes the advice of Mr. Dick, a feebleminded distant kinsman who lives with her, and lets David into the house. While she deliberates about what to do with her bedraggled nephew, she writes to inform Mr. Murdstone, who thereupon comes with his sister to Dover. Miss Betsey, disliking both Murdstones intensely at first sight, again takes Mr. Dick's advice and keeps David.

Much to the boy's joy, Miss Betsey almost immediately sends him to a school in Canterbury run by Mr. Strong, a headmaster quite unlike Mr. Creakle. During his stay at school, David lodges with Miss Betsey's lawyer, Mr. Wickfield, and his daughter, Agnes, with whom he is very happy. He also meets Uriah Heep, Mr. Wickfield's cringing, hypocritical clerk with the clammy handclasp.

When David finishes school at the age of seventeen, Miss Betsey suggests that he take some time before deciding on a profession. On his way to visit his old nurse Peggotty, David meets Steerforth again and goes home with his former schoolmate. There he meets Steerforth's mother and Rosa Dartle, a young woman who is passionately in love with Steerforth. Years before, the quick-tempered Steerforth struck Rosa, who still carries the scar.

David persuades Steerforth to come with him to see Peggotty and her family. At Yarmouth, Steerforth meets Little Em'ly, who is by this time engaged to Ham. She and Steerforth are immediately attracted to each other.

David finally decides that he wishes to study law. Accordingly, he is articled to the law firm of Spenlow and Jorkins in London. When he says good-bye to Agnes, she tells him she distrusts Steerforth's influence over him; she also expresses uneasiness about Heep, who is on the point of entering into partnership with her father, who is showing signs of feebleness. As he leaves the house, David encounters Heep, who tells him that he wants to marry Agnes, which outrages David.

After his new life begins in London, David is invited to the home of his employer, where he meets and instantly falls in love with Mr. Spenlow's pretty daughter, Dora. Soon they become secretly engaged. About the same time, however, David hears the distressing news that Little Em'ly ran away with Steerforth. Shortly after he becomes engaged to Dora, Miss Betsey comes to London to tell David that she lost all of her money. After failing in his attempt to recover some of the money for his articles with Spenlow and Jorkins, David takes a part-time job as secretary to Mr. Strong, his former headmaster. Because that job pays very little, David also begins to study to be a reporter of parliamentary debates.

Mr. Spenlow's sudden death dissolves the partnership of Spenlow and Jorkins, and David learns to his dismay that his former employer died almost penniless. After studying hard, David becomes a reporter, and at the age of twenty-one he marries Dora. While these events are happening, David keeps in touch with Mr. Micawber, who now becomes Heep's confidential secretary. Though something finally turns up for Mr. Micawber, his relations with David and even with his own family become somewhat mysterious, but Mr. Micawber's conscience soon gets the better of him and at a meeting he arranges at Mr. Wickfield's home, he reveals Heep's criminal perfidy. Heep for years robbed and cheated Mr. Wickfield, and Miss Betsey discovers that it is he who is responsible for her own financial losses.

Mr. Micawber, clearing his conscience, decides to take his family to Australia, where he is sure something will turn up. By that time Emily, whom Steerforth deserts, returns to her uncle Peggotty and they, too, go to Australia. As David watches their ship put out to sea, it seems to him that the sunset is a bright promise for their new life.

The great cloud in David's life now becomes his wife's delicate health. Day after day she fails, and in spite of his tenderest care, he sees her grow more feeble and wan. Agnes, like the true friend she always was, is with him on the night of Dora's death. As in his earlier troubles, he turns to Agnes in the days that follow and finds comfort in her sympathy and understanding. Upon her advice, he decides to go abroad for a while. First, however, he goes to Yarmouth to put a last letter from Emily into Ham's hands. While he is there, a storm causes a ship to founder off the coast. Ham dies in a courageous attempt to rescue a survivor clinging to a broken mast. Later that day, the waves wash his body ashore and that of the false Steerforth.

David lives in Europe for three years. One day, soon after his return, Miss Betsey slyly suggests that Agnes might soon be married. Heavyhearted, David goes to offer her his good wishes. When she bursts into tears, he realizes that what he hopes is true—her heart is his. To the great delight of matchmaking Miss Betsey, Agnes and David are married, and David settles down to begin his career as a successful novelist.

Critical Evaluation:

"But, like many fond parents, I have in my heart of hearts a favorite child. And his name is David Copperfield." This is Charles Dickens's final, affectionate judgment of the work that stands exactly in the middle of his novelistic career, with seven novels preceding and seven following it (excluding the unfinished *The Mystery of Edwin Drood*, 1870). When he began the novel, he was in his mid-thirties, secure in the continuing success that had begun with *Sketches by Boz* (1836) and *Pickwick Papers* (1836-1837). It was a good time to take stock of his life and to make use of the autobiographical manuscript he had put by earlier; he did not try to conceal the personal element from his public, who eagerly awaited each of the nineteen numbers of the serialized first publication of *David Copperfield* between May, 1849, and November, 1850. Dickens is readily identified with David Copperfield, and as Dickens phrased it, he viewed his life through the "long Copperfieldian perspective."

Although much in the life of the first-person narrator corresponds to Dickens's own life, the author altered a number of details. Unlike David, Dickens was not a genteel orphan but the eldest son of living and improvident parents; his own father served as the model for Micawber. Dickens's childhood stint in a shoeblacking factory seems to have been somewhat shorter than David's drudgery in the warehouse of the wine distributors Murdstone and Grinby, but the shame and suffering he felt were identical. Whereas young Dickens failed in his romance with a pretty young girl, David is permitted to win his first love, Dora, but Dickens then imparts to Dora's character the faults of his own wife, Kate.

However fascinating the autobiographical details, *David Copperfield* stands primarily on its merits as a novel endowed with the bustling life of Dickens's earlier works but controlled by his maturing sense of design. In addition to the compelling characterization of the protagonist, the novel abounds with memorable portrayals. The square face and black beard of Mr. Murdstone, always viewed in conjunction with that "metallic lady," Miss Murdstone, evoke the horror of dehumanized humanity. Uriah Heep's writhing body, clammy skin, and peculiarly lidless eyes suggest a subhuman form more terrifying than the revolting nature of his "umbleness." Above all the figures that crowd the lonely world of the orphan rises the bald head of Mr. Micawber, flourishing his command of the English language and his quizzing glass with equal impressiveness.

These vivid characters notwithstanding, David is very definitely the hero of his own story. This is a novel of initiation, organized around the two major segments of the hero's development, childhood and early manhood. The plot focuses steadily on the testing he receives that is to qualify him for full manhood. He makes his own choices, but each important stage of his moral progress is marked by the intervention and aid of his aunt.

Initially, David is weak simply because he is a child, the hapless victim of adult exploitation; but he is also heir to the moral weakness of his childish mother and his dead father, who was an inept, impractical man. Portentously, David's birth is the occasion of a conflict between his mother's Copperfieldian softness and Miss Betsey's firmness, dis-

played in her rigidity of figure and countenance. From a state of childish freedom, David falls into the Murdstone world. The clanking chains of Miss Murdstone's steel purse symbolize the metaphorical prison that replaces his innocently happy home. Indeed, for David, the world becomes a prison. After his five days of solitary confinement at Blunderstone, he enters the jail-like Salem House School, and after his mother's death, he is placed in the warehouse, apparently for life. His involvement with the Micawbers offers no escape either, for he is burdened with their problems in addition to his own.

Although David repudiates the tyrannical firmness of which he is for a time a victim, he does not actively rebel except once, when he bites Mr. Murdstone. Instead, like his mother, he submits—fearfully to the Murdstones and Creakle and worshipfully to the arrogant Steerforth. He also escapes into the freedom of fantasy through books and stories and through the lives of others, which he invests with an enchantment that conceals from him whatever is potentially tragic or sordid.

David's pliant nature, nevertheless, shares something of the resolute spirit of his aunt, Miss Betsey. Looking back on his wretched boyhood, David recalls that he kept his own counsel and did his work. From having suffered in secret, he moves to the decision to escape by his own act. The heroic flight is rewarded when Miss Betsey relents and takes him in. In accordance with her character, she trusses up the small boy in adult clothes and announces her goal of making him a "fine fellow, with a will of your own," with a "strength of character that is not to be influenced, except on good reason, by anybody, or by anything." The first cycle of testing is complete.

The conventionally happy years in Dover and Canterbury mark an interlude before the second major cycle of the novel, which commences with David's reentry into the world as a young man. Significantly, he at first resumes the docile patterns of childhood. Reunited with Steerforth, he once again takes pride in his friend's overbearing attitude, and he allows himself to be bullied by various people, above all servants. He evades the obligation to choose his own career by entering into a profession that affects him like an opiate. In Dora's childlike charms, he recaptures the girlish image of his mother. At this point, however, the firm Miss Betsey, having cut short his childhood trials, deliberately sets in motion his adult testing with her apparent bankruptcy.

Responding to his new challenges, David falls back upon his childhood resources. At first, in unconscious imitation of Murdstone, he tries to mold Dora, but then consciously rejects tyranny and chooses instead resignation and understanding for the fact that she can be no more than his "child-wife." He responds with full sympathy to the tragedy of Emily's affair with Steerforth, but he needed that proof to be finally disenchanted with the willfulness that had captivated his boyish heart. Most important, he recovers the saving virtue of his childhood, his ability to suffer in secrecy, to keep his own counsel, and to do his work. As his trials pile up—poverty, overwork, disappointment in marriage, his wife's death, and the tribulations of the friends to whom his tender heart is wholly committed—he learns to conquer his own undisciplined heart.

The mature David who emerges from his trials has profited from his experiences and heritage. His capacity for secret suffering is, for him as for Miss Betsey, a source of strength, but his, unlike hers, is joined to the tenderheartedness inherited from his parents. Her distrust of humans has made her an eccentric. His trusting disposition, on the other hand, though rendering him vulnerable, binds him to humankind.

Although Miss Betsey sets a goal of maturity before David, Agnes is the symbol of the hard-won self-discipline that he finally achieves. She is from the beginning his "better angel." Like him, she is tenderhearted and compliant, yet far from being submissive; she is in control of herself in even the most difficult human relationships. Since it is never distorted by distrust of humankind, her firmness of character is the only influence David should accept in his pursuit of the moral goal Miss Betsey has set before him.

By the time David has recognized his love for Agnes, he has also attained a strength of character similar to hers. The appropriate conclusion to his quest for maturity is his union with Agnes—who is from the beginning a model of the self-disciplined person in whom gentleness and strength are perfectly balanced. Furthermore, the home he builds with her is the proper journey's end for the orphaned child who has grasped at many versions of father, mother, family, and home: "Long miles of road then opened out before my mind, and toiling on, I saw a ragged way-worn boy forsaken and neglected, who should come to call even the heart now beating against him, his own." He has outgrown the child-mother, the child-wife, the childhood idols, even the childhood terrors, and he is a mature man ready to accept love "founded on a rock." In the context of a successful, completed quest, the novel ends with a glimpse of the complete man, who writes far into the night to erase the shadows of his past but whose control of the realities is sufficient in the presence of the woman who is always symbolically "near me, pointing upward!"

"Critical Evaluation" by Catherine E. Moore

Further Reading

Bloom, Harold, ed. *Charles Dickens' "David Copperfield."* New York: Chelsea House, 1987. Bloom's introduction considers the novel as the original portrait of the artist as a young man. Eight other essays, all written after 1969, include examinations of the novel's moral unity and mirror imagery.

Cain, Lynn. *Dickens, Family, Authorship: Psychoanalytic Perspectives on Kinship and Creativity.* Burlington, Vt.: Ashgate, 2008. Focuses on *David Copperfield* and three other novels that Dickens wrote during the decade beginning in 1843, a period of feverish personal and professional activity. Cain argues that his representation of the family in these novels is a paradigm for his development as an author.

Collins, Philip. *Charles Dickens: "David Copperfield."* London: Edward Arnold, 1977. Brief study that focuses on the work itself rather than on Dickens or his methods. Discusses the novel's specific strengths and weaknesses and examines how the novel's serial publication affected its structure. Most useful for the student who has read some of Dickens's contemporaries.

Dunn, Richard J., ed. *Approaches to Teaching Dickens' "David Copperfield."* New York: Modern Language Association of America, 1984. Intended for teachers but fascinating and helpful for students. Includes descriptions of other books and materials useful for understanding the novel and for determining discussion topics and approaches for classroom use.

_____. *A Routledge Literary Sourcebook on Charles Dickens's "David Copperfield."* New York: Routledge, 2004. Includes numerous materials to supplement the novel, including a contextual overview, chronology, other writings by Dickens and other nineteenth century authors, selected nineteenth century reviews of the novel, modern interpretations published between 1958 and 2001, and a discussion of key passages in the novel.

Hardy, Barbara. *Dickens and Creativity.* London: Continuum, 2008. Focuses on the workings of Dickens's creativity and imagination, which Hardy argues is at the heart of his self-awareness, subject matter, and narrative. *David Copperfield* is discussed in chapter 4, "The Artist as Narrator in *Doctor Marigold, David Copperfield, Bleak House,* and *Great Expectations,*" and in chapter 9, "Shakespeare in Dickens: *David Cooperfield* and *Great Expectations.*"

Jordan, John O., ed. *The Cambridge Companion to Charles Dickens.* New York: Cambridge University Press, 2001. Collection of essays with information about Dickens's life and times, analyses of his novels, and discussions of

Dickens and language, gender, family, domestic ideology, the form of the novel, illustration, theater, and film.

Paroissien, David, ed. *A Companion to Charles Dickens.* Malden, Mass.: Blackwell, 2008. Collection of essays providing information about Dickens's life and work, including Dickens as a reformer, Christian, and journalist, Dickens and gender, technology, America, and the uses of history. Also includes the essay *"David Copperfield"* by Gareth Cordery.

Storey, Graham. *"David Copperfield": Interweaving Truth and Fiction.* Boston: Twayne, 1991. A very accessible study. After three chapters that discuss the novel's autobiographical elements and critical reception, Storey presents an extended reading focusing on children and childhood. Includes a bibliography and chronology.

Vogel, Jane. *Allegory in Dickens.* Tuscaloosa: University of Alabama Press, 1977. In the chapters about *David Copperfield*, which make up a great deal of the book, the author proposes that the novel can be read—and was written—as a Christian allegory of the spiritual journey from Creation to Heaven. Thought-provoking, though not always convincing.

The Day of the Locust

Author: Nathanael West (1903-1940)
First published: 1939
Type of work: Novel
Type of plot: Social realism
Time of plot: 1930's
Locale: Hollywood, California

Principal characters:
TOD HACKETT, novice costume and set designer
CLAUDE ESTEE, a successful screenwriter
FAYE GREENER, a would-be actress
HARRY GREENER, a has-been vaudeville clown
HOMER SIMPSON, a retired bookkeeper

The Story:

Tod Hackett, a set and costume designer, arrives in Hollywood, still idealistic from Yale. He works on his painting, *The Burning of Los Angeles*, to fulfill his dream of becoming a successful artist. As he watches people from his movie studio window, he sees soldiers moving like a mob, with a fat man cursing at them through a megaphone. Tod observes how people masquerade by dressing in roles and how houses reflect odd mixtures of architectural styles. He recalls the day when Abe Kusich showed him his seedy hotel, and Tod immediately became obsessed with Faye Greener.

At Claude Estee's party, Tod is initiated into Hollywood's perverse pleasures. To amuse guests, Estee decorates his pool with a life-size rubber reproduction of a grotesque dead horse, its stiff legs straight up, distended belly enormous, and black tongue hanging out. Joining the partygoers at Audrey Jennings's brothel, Tod watches part of a pornographic film; then seeing Faye's best friend, Mary Dove, he tries to engage Faye's services.

Failing to do so, he ingratiates himself, keeping Faye and her sickly father, Harry, company. One day, after Homer Simpson appears with flowers and wine to court Faye, Tod learns that while selling homemade polish, Harry collapsed at Homer's house. Then Tod meets another rival for Faye's attention, Earle Shoop. The three go to the hillside camp of Miguel, a Mexican who raises fighting gamecocks. After they eat, they drink tequila. Unable to stand Faye's seductive dancing with Miguel, Earle cracks him in the head. Tod, caught up in the frenzy, grabs at Faye as she runs past him. Until his passion and anger are exhausted, Tod envisions his artistic depiction of violence: Los Angeles burning amid a gala holiday crowd.

Although Faye abandons him, the following evening (while Faye goes to the movies with Homer), Tod gets trapped into hearing her sick father reminisce about his vaudeville career. The next day Harry dies. To pay for funeral expenses, Faye works at Mrs. Jennings's brothel. Harry's funeral resembles a theatrical performance, with arguments about the cheap casket, dramatic hymns pleading for Christ's coming, and curious onlookers being urged to view the corpse. Tod convinces Faye that venereal disease from prostitution will destroy her beauty.

Instead of relying on Tod for support, Faye moves in with Homer, who pays her expenses (a business arrangement, she will become a star and will pay him back with interest) and does the housework. Their daily routine consists of shopping, dinner out, movies, and ice cream sodas. Homer's neighbor is Maybelle Loomis, a stage mother desperately trying to make a child star of Adore, her eight-year-old, who dresses like a man, with plucked and shaped eyebrows. He performs upon command a sexually suggestive song, complete with erotic gestures. Adore and Faye deserve to be in pictures, agree Tod and Homer.

No longer wanting to be sexually aroused but rejected by Faye, Tod avoids her for several months. He goes to bizarre Hollywood churches and sketches worshipers. In one church he observes people whipped into religious fervor by a man preaching messianic rage with threats of the Tiger of Wrath and the Jackal of Lust.

Against his better judgment late one night, Tod joins Homer and Faye at a nightclub featuring female impersonators. While Faye dances with a stranger, Homer admits that to please Faye, he let Earle and Miguel live in his garage, despite Miguel's disgusting gamecocks. When Tod and Claude attend a cockfight there, they witness this brutal sport that ends with the losing cock's death. Homer invites them in for drinks, and the erotic Faye, whom Tod calls a whore, takes center stage. She drunkenly dances with Miguel and Earle. A scuffle breaks out. Later, after Homer and Earle find Faye in bed with Miguel, she moves out, leaving Homer distraught.

Tod returns to Homer's the next morning to comfort Homer. Faye will survive because of her sexual opportunism, Tod realizes. Although he imagines raping her, he cannot complete his violent fantasy. Leaving a restaurant, he sees that Kahn's Persian Palace Theatre attracts thousands for a world movie premiere. A radio announcer describes the frenzied crowd, like a revival preacher moving an audience to hysteria. Tod fights his way through the surging crowd, getting kicked and swept away. Then he spots Homer walking dazed, in a catatonic stupor, with his suitcases and with his pants over his night clothes. He says he is going back to Iowa. While sitting on a bench to wait for a taxi, Homer is hit in the face with a stone thrown by Adore. Homer goes berserk, stomping Adore despite Tod's attempts to pull him off. Suddenly, the crazed mob tears Tod away from Homer and engulfs the child-attacker. Another part of the wild mob surges, and Tod feels his ribs cracking and his leg throbbing. People in the mob enjoy the riotous free-for-all that started with a sighting of actor Gary Cooper. Desperately clinging to a fence, Tod envisions his painting, with Faye, Harry, Homer, Claude, and himself fleeing a mob. After a police officer rescues him, Tod asks to be taken to Claude's. Tod in his hysteria, imitates the police car siren in a loud scream.

Critical Evaluation:

Nathanael West (born Nathan Weinstein) worked in Hollywood in 1933 on the film script for his novel *Miss Lonelyhearts* (1933) but was disillusioned when his suggestions were ignored and his book twisted beyond recognition; it was retitled in its script form as *Advice to the Lovelorn*. In 1935, he returned to Hollywood to gather material for his fourth and last novel, *The Day of the Locust*. He lived in poverty for many months, supported by his brother-in-law, humorist S. J. Perelman, until he found work as a scriptwriter. His first produced film was, ironically enough, *Ticket to Paradise* (1936). For most of the next five years, he worked for several major studios until his death in 1940 in a car accident. He was fascinated by and cynical about Hollywood, knowing that screenwriters had their writing revised or rejected. They could not write anything really good, but they could make good money if they were lucky. West preferred mechanical work on lesser quality, formulaic films so he could save his creative energies for his own fiction. Writing movie scripts came easily, and West was considered a competent craftsman at his trade. West's screenwriter friends F. Scott Fitzgerald and William Faulkner also considered screenwriting to be mere hack work for Hollywood's dream factory. Fitzgerald (who, coincidentally, died the day before West died in 1940) left unfinished a Hollywood novel, *The Last Tycoon* (1941). Along with Fitzgerald's novel, West's *The Day of the Locust* is considered among the finest in the Hollywood novel genre.

Structured into twenty-seven chapters like movie scenes, the book presents an insider's perspective of Hollywood's dream factory and underworld society. West achieves a sense of reality with his richly detailed, accurate settings of the Hollywood landscape—movie lots, hotels, churches, restaurants, bars, brothels, streets, and canyons. In fact, this realistic detail merges with grotesquely exaggerated images to create a sense of surrealism. Comedy is juxtaposed with tragedy, and as a result the plot's pace seems somewhat uneven. The disjointed feeling conveys exactly the dual nature of Hollywood's reality and fantasy. Being familiar with his father's construction business, West uses architectural images—of houses, theaters, and churches—to depict Hollywood as home of the grotesque, the gaudy, the materialistic. Tod comments on the comic artificiality of the houses: "It is hard to laugh at the need for beauty and romance, no matter how tasteless, even horrible. . . . Few things are sadder than the truly monstrous." This third-person limited omniscient viewpoint (through Tod's consciousness) often reflects West's views. Tod fears that in selling out to Hollywood, he is prostituting his talents to a lesser art. The fascination-repulsion is at the emotional heart of the novel, which West began in 1935 while he lived in Hollywood, then a seedy section of Los Angeles. Earlier in the thirties he managed two New York City hotels catering to low-life clientele;

he was well acquainted with writers, artists, prostitutes, vaudeville comics, and dwarfs, so he knew from experience how the desperate, the unemployed, and the poverty-stricken stood on breadlines during the Great Depression. They obsessively attended movies and read magazines to get their vicarious thrills of glamour and wealth.

The studio lot's dream-dump becomes a central metaphor for Hollywood's chaos and shoddiness. Movies promised paradise, the South Seas dream of escape. They became instead a dream-dump, like the studio's pile of discarded props and sets. Tod's seedy hotel is a microcosm of the world of dreamers. The movie lot is a microcosm of dream makers. The collapse of the Waterloo set is only one of many images of total chaos and destruction in this surrealistic world of grotesquerie.

The portrayal of Hollywood's artificiality directly relates to the dream-become-nightmare theme. Claude's home, a reproduction of a Southern antebellum mansion, well exemplifies the grotesquely comic impulse to startle and amuse. Images of phony structures in "Caliphonia" parallel the phony people, not only in their various costumes that represent their make-believe roles but also in their physical descriptions: West's characters are degenerate—for example, Homer's weird hands, Harry's mechanical laugh, Earle's two-dimensional face like a mechanical drawing. Moreover, a sense of unreality exists in the decadence of Faye, Earle, Abe, and Miguel. No healthy sexual relationships are depicted—only violent erotic fantasies, prostitution, sadism and masochism, female impersonators, impotence, and promiscuity. By satiric reduction, love becomes a vending machine. For many who come to the land of "sunshine and oranges," Hollywood's artificiality is a cheat. Tod captures people's despair in his series called *The Dancers*; he draws people (based on his friends) as they "spin crazily and leap into the air with twisted backs like hooked trout." Betrayed and cheated after years of slaving away for nothing, people become victims or they resort to violence.

The fury of the living dead, with their anarchic power, epitomizes both Tod's vision in *The Burning of Los Angeles* and West's prophecy in *The Day of the Locust*. West had seen at movie premieres how people worshipped glamorous stars with such insane jealousy, almost like hatred, that they could have shredded the stars' flesh as much as their clothes. Through violence, the cheated and betrayed ultimately take revenge. West's vision of the apocalypse, when locusts ravage the land, turns the American Dream into the Hollywood nightmare.

"Critical Evaluation" by Laura M. Zaidman

Further Reading

Bombaci, Nancy. "Nathanael West's Aspiring Freakish Flâneurs." In *Freaks in Late Modernist American Culture: Nathanael West, Djuna Barnes, Tod Browning, and Carson McCullers*. New York: Peter Lang, 2006. Focuses on West's fascination with genetically maimed and distorted people, examining how his representation of these marginalized characters challenges modernist aesthetics and social values.

Comerchero, Victor. *Nathanael West: The Ironic Prophet*. Syracuse, N.Y.: Syracuse University Press, 1964. Argues that the novel should be read as a satire of a declining Western culture. Provides a perceptive analysis of West's apocalyptic vision.

Dunne, Michael. "Nathanael West: 'Gloriously Funny.'" In *Calvinist Humor in American Literature*. Baton Rouge: Louisiana State University Press, 2007. Calvinist humor, in Dunne's definition, is the perception of humankind's imperfection. He demonstrates how this humor is used in works by West and other American writers whose fiction is populated with flawed characters.

Madden, David, ed. *Nathanael West: The Cheaters and the Cheated*. De Land, Fla.: Everett/Edwards, 1973. Contains five assessments of *The Day of the Locust*, as well as several general essays on West's work.

Malin, Irving. *Nathanael West's Novels*. Carbondale: Southern Illinois University Press, 1972. Offers a close textual analysis of West's images, metaphors, and symbols as clues to the novel's themes and characterization.

Martin, Jay. *Nathanael West: The Art of His Life*. New York: Farrar, Straus & Giroux, 1970. The first full-length biography and critical study. Analyzes the novels in the context of West's Hollywood years; also includes twenty pages of photographs and a detailed listing of his film writing.

_____, ed. *Nathanael West: A Collection of Critical Essays*. Englewood Cliffs, N.J.: Prentice-Hall, 1971. Includes short essays by West's contemporaries William Carlos Williams and W. H. Auden.

Rhodes, Chip. "Nathanael West: Desire, Art, and Cynicism." In *Politics, Desire, and the Hollywood Novel*. Iowa City: University of Iowa Press, 2008. Examines *The Day of the Locust* and other novels that depict the influence of the film industry upon American politics and ideas of romance.

Veitch, Jonathan. *American Superrealism: Nathanael West and the Politics of Representation in the 1930's*. Madison: University of Wisconsin Press, 1997. Contains separate chapters on each novel, as well as an introduction discussing the "crisis of representation in the 1930's."

De Profundis

Author: Oscar Wilde (1854-1900)
First published: 1905
Type of work: Epistolary literature

The eighty-page manuscript of this letter rests in the British Museum. It was written in Reading Gaol on prison paper during the last months, from January to March, of Oscar Wilde's two-year sentence for "unnatural practices," or homosexuality. It was addressed to Lord Alfred Douglas, but when Wilde was not allowed to send it from prison he handed it to his friend Robert Ross the day after he was released on May 19, 1897, with instructions to type a copy and send the original to Lord Alfred, who always claimed he never received it. Part of the work was first published under Ross's title, *De Profundis*, in 1905 and again in 1908. A typescript was given by Ross to Vyvyn Holland, Wilde's younger son, who published it in 1949. Rupert Hart-Davis demonstrated that this first complete edition contained hundreds of errors, and he published the manuscript after it was released by the British Museum from the fifty-year restriction Ross placed on it when he deposited the manuscript in 1909. As a letter, it becomes the center of the definitive edition of Wilde's letters; in the shorter form edited by Ross it is both an apologia and a literary essay. Nevertheless, in its entirety it has a unity and a unique value as Wilde's testament to his life as an artist.

Since it is cast in the form of an epistle, the work needs some contextual reference to Wilde's life and works before and after his imprisonment and the composition of the letter. The prison sentence marked the end of his marriage, his income, and his life in England; thereafter he lived in exile as Sebastian Melmoth. One link with the past, however, was not broken: the association with Lord Alfred Douglas. Wilde's return to the young man, the cause of his imprisonment, divorce, and bankruptcy, and to the kind of associates whose evidence had convicted him, seems to invalidate the promise to lead a new life with which *De Profundis* closes. Wilde claimed, however, that while, on one hand, the conditions of exile, disgrace, and penury drove him to those acquaintances, on the other, they were the creations of his art and not the conditions of his life. Wilde's one conviction was that he was an artist, and he doggedly transposed the terms of life and art. His term for the new life was Dante's *La vita nuova* (c. 1292). Similarly, Wilde's *The Picture of Dorian Gray* (1890) was to be the parable of his life; it was more true to his life because of its artistry than was his biography. The strain of maintaining this paradox ended his life three years after his release and finished his writing career shortly after the composition of *De Profundis*. The resolution of the paradox is the intention of the long letter.

This epistle is therefore connected both with Wilde's biography (in which sense it is autobiography) and with his literary canon. In the letter, he suggests that his sentence and fate are "prefigured" in works such as *The Picture of Dorian Gray*. The immediate artistic fruits of the "new life" are the two letters to the *Morning Chronicle* and *The Ballad of Reading Gaol* (1898), his only writing after *De Profundis*; parts of the last amount to a prose poem falling somewhere between the prose of the two letters and poetry of the ballad, Wilde's longest and most effective poem. The two letters are included in Ross's 1908 edition and show plainly the real conditions under which *De Profundis* was written. Wilde sums them up as constant hunger, diarrhea from the rotten food, and insomnia from the diarrhea and the plank bed in his cell. His description of prison life is vivid and awful; out of his experience, immediately after his release, he showed courage in writing letters to defend a discharged warder and to plead for decent treatment of child prisoners. Perhaps he could have played a prominent role in prison reform had not exile intervened; yet it is difficult to see Wilde in that role unless he really meant what he said in *De Profundis*. As it was, events showed that this epistle belonged to the realm of art and not to life.

Wilde's request to have the letter copied by Ross showed that he thought of it as art, his "letter to the world." The covering letter to Ross described his three intentions: He would explain, not defend, his past; describe his spiritual and mental crisis in prison; and outline his future plans. The aptness of Ross's title from Psalm 130 is obvious, but the work is not so much the salvation of a lost soul as it is Wilde's artistic equivalent of this, the groping toward an artistic resolution of the paradox that the pursuit of beauty leads to the ugliness of Reading Gaol. The past is covered mostly in the longer first half of the letter, in reproaches to Lord Alfred Douglas, which were at least somewhat merited but relevant only if Wilde recognized Lord Alfred as the alter ego of that past and not of the future. This failure to interpret his past life as a work of art indicates the failure of the remaining portion of the letter, printed in Ross's edition of 1908.

This general section of *De Profundis* is in two related parts. The first states Wilde's reliance on the paradox that art is life, life art; his problem is to see the art in his present situation, which he sums up in the word "sorrow." If he really feels sorrow, then sorrow must be artistic or of artistic value; he decides that his art (that is, life) lacked the dimension of shadow (that is, sorrow), and his present sorrow must have been intended for the purpose of improving his art. If Wilde can transpose his prison sentence into an aspect of art, then his paradox holds good. There is evidence in the letters of his friends that he did just this soon after his release, when he wittily described Reading Gaol as an enchanted castle, complete with ogres, dungeons, and devices of torture.

The second part of this section then plays with an artistic creation or symbol of sorrow: the Man of Sorrows, by which Wilde indicated himself, Christ, and all people to the limited extent that he could be interested in anyone but himself. He pursues the Christian analogy daringly to argue not that he is Christ but that Christ (like Wilde) was the supreme artist of life. He had the imagination to feel the sufferings of a leper without being that leper, while at the same time Christ preserved his individuality. Similarly, his sympathetic imagination and artistry compelled him to turn himself into an artistic symbol of the truth about life: the Man of Sorrows. Wilde is thus not serving a prison sentence; as an artist, he is creating an artistic (that is, symbolic) statement about life. In this way he is able to absorb the most "sorrowful" experience of his life, the half-hour he stood on the center platform at Clapham Junction on his way to Reading Gaol and endured the mockery of the populace.

Having accomplished this artistic stroke (and advised Lord Alfred as a fellow poet to do likewise), Wilde proposes the two subjects on which he would like now to write. The first, the presentation of Christ as the forerunner of the Romantic movement in life, was largely covered in his previous outrageous analogy; its extension here leads him to the proposition that the sinner is as near a perfect human as humans can know because, in repenting, he can actually alter his past; thus he is the artist of the present and of the past.

The second subject, the life of art considered in relation to conduct of life, is much more the nub of Wilde's attitude to his past and his future. As he admits, everybody will simply point to Reading Gaol as the logical conclusion of the artistic life as Wilde practiced it. He dodges the logic by three lofty assertions. He is now so much the repentant sinner that he can even pity those who mocked him at Clapham Junction; that it was reliance on the Philistines (that is, the original legal ac-

tion he instituted against Queensbury) that brought him to Reading Gaol; that the supreme concern of the artist is what he says of himself, not what others say. His own statements, Wilde asserts, must be the truth because what he says will be an artistic creation.

Thus Wilde's perverse reading of the obvious analogies in the Christian story made him miss its whole point of sacrifice (though he considers he was sacrificed for Lord Alfred) and confirms his original paradox, absolves him from all blame, and nullifies the whole meaning of Reading Gaol. The artist has triumphed over his real situation but only at the cost of life itself.

Further Reading

Bashford, Bruce. "Fathoming the Soul in *De Profundis*." In *Oscar Wilde: The Critic as Humanist*. Madison, N.J.: Fairleigh Dickinson University Press, 1999. Examines how Wilde attempts to create a theory of self-realization in this work.

Buckton, Oliver. "'Desire Without Limit': Dissident Confession in Oscar Wilde's *De Profundis*." In *Victorian Sexual Dissidence*, edited by Richard Dellamora. Chicago: University of Chicago Press, 1999. Describes how Wilde in *De Profundis* sought to challenge the public's view of him as a sexual pervert by projecting onto Lord Alfred Douglas the characteristics that ultimately were responsible for his imprisonment.

Ellman, Richard, ed. *The Artist as Critic: Critical Writings of Oscar Wilde*. Chicago: University of Chicago Press, 1968. Explores Wilde's theory that suffering could be important for an artist; Wilde believed in "the realization of man through suffering." Examines Wilde's mentality when writing *De Profundis*.

_____, ed. *Oscar Wilde: A Collection of Critical Essays*. Englewood Cliffs, N.J.: Prentice-Hall, 1969. Discusses Lord Alfred Douglas's obligation to answer Wilde's letter to him. Looks at Wilde's attitude toward Christ as the supreme artist and forgiver.

Kileen, Jarlath. *The Faiths of Oscar Wilde: Catholicism, Folklore, and Ireland*. New York: Palgrave Macmillan, 2005. Examines Wilde's work, focusing on his lifelong attraction to Catholicism. Explores the influence of his Protestant background, and his antagonism toward it, on his writings.

McKenna, Neil. *The Secret Life of Oscar Wilde*. London: Century, 2003. Controversial and groundbreaking biography focusing on the influence of Wilde's sexuality, and of homosexuality in the Victorian era, on his life and work. Includes illustrations, bibliography, and index.

Nassaar, Christopher S. *Into the Demon Universe: A Literary Exploration of Oscar Wilde.* New Haven, Conn.: Yale University Press, 1974. Deeply analyzes *De Profundis*. Compares it to the "demon universe," since Wilde had warned that a balance must be maintained in the "demon universe of life"; in *De Profundis*, Wilde loses this perspective. Argues that Wilde creates a personal myth in which he views his own life and in which Christ becomes an important symbol.

Pearce, Joseph. *The Unmasking of Oscar Wilde.* London: HarperCollins, 2000. Focuses on Wilde's emotional and spiritual searching, including his fascination with Catholicism. The numerous references to *De Profundis* are listed in the index.

Dead Souls

Author: Nikolai Gogol (1809-1852)
First published: Myortvye dushi, part 1, 1842; part 2, 1855 (English translation, 1887)
Type of work: Novel
Type of plot: Social satire
Time of plot: Early nineteenth century
Locale: Russia

Principal characters:
PAVEL IVANOVITCH TCHITCHIKOFF, an adventurer
MANILOFF, the man from whom he buys souls
TENTETNIKOFF, the bachelor whom he tries to marry off
PLATONOFF, Tchitchikoff's later traveling companion
KLOBUEFF, a spendthrift whose estate he buys
KONSTANTIN SKUDRONZHOGLO, a wealthy landholder who lends him money
ALEXEI IVANOVITCH LYENITZEN, the official who throws him into jail

The Story:

Pavel Ivanovitch Tchitchikoff arrives in the town accompanied by his coachman, Selifan, and his valet, Petrushka. He is entertained gloriously and meets numerous interesting people, many of whom insist on his visiting them in their own homes. Nothing suits Tchitchikoff better. After several days of celebration in the town, he takes Selifan and begins a round of visits to the various estates in the surrounding country.

His first host is Maniloff, a genial man who wines and dines him in a manner fit for a prince. When the time is ripe, Tchitchikoff begins to question his host about his estate. To his satisfaction, he learns that many of Maniloff's souls, as the serfs are called, died since the last census and that Maniloff is still paying taxes on them and will continue to do so until the next census. Tchitchikoff offers to buy these dead souls from Maniloff and so relieve him of his extra tax burden. The contract is signed, and Tchitchikoff sets out for the next estate.

Selifan gets lost and in the middle of the night draws up to a house that belongs to Madame Korobotchkina, from whom Tchitchikoff also buys dead souls. When he leaves his host, he finds his way to an inn in the neighborhood. There he meets Nozdreff, a notorious gambler and liar. Nozdreff recently lost a great deal of money at gambling, and

Tchitchikoff thinks he will be a likely seller of dead souls. When he broaches the subject, Nozdreff asks him the reason for his interest in dead souls. For every reason Tchitchikoff gives, Nozdreff calls him a liar. Then Nozdreff wants to play at cards for the souls, but Tchitchikoff refuses. They are arguing when a police captain comes in and arrests Nozdreff for assault on a man while drunk. Tchitchikoff thinks himself well rid of the annoying Nozdreff.

Tchitchikoff's next host is Sobakevitch, who at first demands the unreasonable sum of one hundred rubles for each name of a dead soul. Tchitchikoff finally persuades him to accept two and a half rubles apiece, a higher price than he planned to pay.

Pliushkin, with whom he negotiates next, is a miser. He buys one hundred twenty dead souls and seventy-eight fugitives after considerable haggling. Pliushkin gives him a letter to Ivan Grigorievitch, the town president.

Back in town, Tchitchikoff persuades the town president to make his recent purchases legal. Since the law requires that souls, when purchased, be transferred to another estate, Tchitchikoff tells the officials that he has land in the Kherson province. He has no trouble in making himself sound plausible. Some bribes to minor officials help.

Tchitchikoff proves to be such a delightful guest that the people of the town insist that he stay on and on. He is the center of attraction at many social functions, including a ball at which he is especially interested in the governor's daughter. Soon, however, rumors spread that Tchitchikoff is using the dead souls as a screen, that he is really planning to elope with the governor's daughter. The men, in consultation at the police master's house, speculate variously. Some say he is a forger; others think he might be an officer in the governor-general's office; one man puts forth the fantastic suggestion that he is really the legendary Captain Kopeykin in disguise. They question Nozdreff, who was the first to report the story of the purchase of dead souls. At their interrogation, Nozdreff confirms their opinions that Tchitchikoff is a spy and a forger who is trying to elope with the governor's daughter.

Meanwhile, Tchitchikoff catches a cold and is confined to his bed. When at last he recovers sufficiently to go out, he finds himself no longer welcome at the houses of his former friends. He is, in fact, turned away by servants at the door. Tchitchikoff realizes it will be best for him to leave town.

The truth of the matter is that Tchitchikoff began his career as a humble clerk. His father died leaving no legacy for his son, who served in various capacities, passing from customs officer to smuggler to pauper to legal agent. When he learned that the Trustee Committee would mortgage souls, he hit upon the scheme of acquiring funds by mortgaging dead souls that were still on the census lists. It was this purpose that sent him on his current tour.

He turns up next on the estate of Andrei Ivanovitch Tentetnikoff, a thirty-three-year-old bachelor who retired from public life to vegetate in the country. Learning that Tentetnikoff is in love with the daughter of his neighbor, General Betrishtcheff, Tchitchikoff goes to see the general and wins his consent to Tentetnikoff's suit. He brings the conversation around to a point where he can offer to buy dead souls from the general. He gives as his reason the story that his old uncle will not leave him an estate unless he himself already owns some property. The scheme so delights the general that he gladly makes the transaction.

Tchitchikoff's next stop is with Pyetukh, a generous glutton whose table he enjoys. There he meets a young man named Platonoff, whom Tchitchikoff persuades to travel with him and see Russia. The two stop to see Platonoff's sister and brother-in-law, Konstantin Skudronzhoglo, a prosperous landholder. Tchitchikoff so impresses his host that Skudronzhoglo agrees to lend him ten thousand rubles to buy the estate of a neighboring spendthrift named Klobueff.

Klobueff says he has a rich old aunt who will give great gifts to churches and monasteries but will not help her destitute relatives. Tchitchikoff proceeds to the town where the old woman resides and forges a will to his own advantage, but he forgets to insert a clause canceling all previous wills. On her death, he goes to interview His Excellency, Alexei Ivanovitch Lyenitzen, who tells him that two wills were discovered, each contradicting the other. Tchitchikoff is accused of forging the second will and is thrown into prison. In the interpretation of this mix-up, Tchitchikoff learns a valuable lesson in deception from the crafty lawyer he consults. The lawyer manages to confuse the affair with every public and private scandal in the province, so that the officials are soon willing to drop the whole matter if Tchitchikoff will leave town immediately. The ruined adventurer is only too glad to comply.

Critical Evaluation:

When Nikolai Gogol began work on *Dead Souls* in the 1830's, he developed a picaresque anecdote, initially suggested by poet Alexander Pushkin, that was crudely satiric. Eventually the concept grew into a "poema," or an epic, signaling its broad scope, patriotic flavor, and symbolic content. Although the censors forced him to alter the "Tale of Captain Kopeykin" in the tenth chapter of the novel and to change the title "Dead Souls," with its blasphemous and politically charged implications, to "The Adventures of Tchitchikoff," the work drew universal admiration. By the time the work was published in 1842, Gogol anticipated two more volumes describing the moral rebirth of Tchitchikoff and the ideal state of the Russian nation. Gogol's consistent dissatisfaction with the draft prevented him from publishing the continuation. The five chapters of volume 2 did not appear until three years after his death in 1852.

Gogol's contemporaries emphasized the accuracy of his portraits of Russian life, his realism. Some critics viewed Gogol's Russia as a faithful copy or justified the negative portrayals as necessary for a balanced depiction of Russia, while others objected to his cruel depiction of Russian life. The novel was interpreted variously from purely satiric to morally uplifting. Although Gogol's work was frequently discussed as a commentary on the unjust institution of serfdom, *Dead Souls* instead emphasizes the imperfections of government bureaucracy and satirizes officials working within that system. Gogol focuses his attention primarily on the middle class, rather than the high nobility, noble landowners, urban bureaucrats, or the peasantry. The provincial setting allows, however, for ample presentation of varied social groups. *Dead Souls* develops generalizations about Russian manners, speech, characters, and spirit within episodes of comic and lyric digression.

The first six chapters of the novel establish Tchitchikoff's mirrorlike amiability as he visits a series of Russian landowners: the vapid and obliging Maniloff, the suspicious Madame Korobotchkina, the misanthropic Sobakevitch, the hyperbolic Nozdreff, and the miserly Pliushkin. In order to buy the legal titles to recently deceased serfs, he mimics the dominant obsession of each. Gogol manages to sustain the enigma of Tchitchikoff through these shifts of behavior. Only near the end of the novel does Gogol flesh out his hero by supplying his biography and preparing him for the next stage on the road. The late inclusion of the biography makes it apparent that the Tchitchikoff mirroring has been mutual. Maniloff now appears as a parody of Tchitchikoff decorum; Korobotchkina's bargaining emerges as a variant of his cunning; Nozdreff represents his prevarication; Sobakevitch manifests his calculating maneuvers; Pliushkin figures as his acquisitional passion.

In the first half of the novel, Gogol delineates a gallery of portraits by outlining each landowner's physical appearance, home, family, hospitality, and reaction to Tchitchikoff's proposal. Gogol's methods of characterization exhibit a tension between the general and the particular, between typical traits and idiosyncratic detail. Although all the main characters belong to the same social class, they represent distinct personality types: Maniloff's sentimental inertia, Nozdreff's wild prevaricating, Sobakevitch's bearlike bluster, and Pliushkin's disfiguring thrift acquire significance as typifying generalities. Even when drawing the abundant minor figures, Gogol emphasizes the generalized nature of certain looks or behavior and yet gives them unique and comic names. At the same time, the traits of Gogol's characters, particularly Tchitchikoff's acquisitiveness, are features of the times.

The metaphysical implications of the title, denying of the soul's immortality, drew controversy. The title seems to describe the characters, all of whom represent varying degrees of spiritual or intellectual deadness. Throughout the text, categories of living and dead commingle. The deceased serfs are sometimes treated as if they were alive, while minor figures appear in great detail only to disappear without further mention. The fragmentary second part of the novel begins to trace the spiritual rebirth of Russia as well as that of Tchitchikoff.

The road embodies the dominant structural principle of the work. The novel begins with Tchitchikoff's arrival and ends with the continuation of his journey. The celebrated closing paragraph likening Russia to a speeding troika establishes the connection between Russia and Tchitchikoff, whose destinies are both unresolved. As the instrument of Tchitchikoff's quest, the road represents experience, movement, and change. The dynamic of the road balances the inertia of the landowners. Finally, the road describes the narrative itself. Since the concept of a journey loosely structures the novel, digressions, random events, and episodic characters seem natural. In his lyric asides, the narrator compares his enterprise to a journey where unexpected turns create significant developments. Gogol takes his cue from the picaresque novel, with its wandering heroes, outlandish adventures, and digressive narrators.

The first volume is characteristic in its lack of plot or resolution. From the opening paragraph, essentials are blurred and irrelevancies are sharply etched. Gogol is particularly fond of suspending the action while he develops a simile at such length that it functions as a tale in its own right. While the epic simile generates beauty out of mundane details or broadens the significance of events, Gogol's extended similes often become comic digressions. Similes emerge to mock conventions of epic narration and to make fun of the characters and events of Gogol's own tale. Gogol combines comedy of situation and slapstick physical humor with verbal humor, including witty puns, absurd neologisms, purposefully vague dialogue, and exaggerated formulaic expressions. The plot is consistently overwhelmed by comic details and lyric digressions.

Dead Souls is largely a book written about how it is written. The authorial interruptions are confessions, admonishments, pleas for sympathy, and complaints about probable misunderstandings. Throughout the text, the narrator anticipates objections to his "low" language, his use of a scoundrel as a hero, the lack of love intrigue, and other differences from conventional novels. The interpolated "Tale of Captain Kopeykin" in the tenth chapter is a masterpiece of *skaz*, or mannered narration in which the speaker unwittingly vies with his story for attention using a vivid manner that overshadows the content of the story. Ultimately, the entire narrative exists as a performance, a colloquial stylization replete with outlandish words and irrelevancies balanced by a desire for lofty lyricism and moral uplift. *Dead Souls* finally emerges as an enigmatic work that continues to fluctuate between the comic and the tragic, the epic and the picaresque.

"Critical Evaluation" by Pamela Pavliscak

Further Reading

Bojanowska, Edyta M. *Nikolai Gogol: Between Ukrainian and Russian Nationalism*. Cambridge, Mass.: Harvard

University Press, 2007. Bojanowska analyzes Gogol's life and works in terms of his conflicted national identity. Gogol was born in Ukraine when it was a part of the Russian empire; Bojanowska describes how he was engaged with questions of Ukrainian nationalism and how his works presented a bleak and ironic portrayal of Russia and Russian themes.

Fanger, Donald. *The Creation of Nikolai Gogol.* Cambridge, Mass.: Harvard University Press, 1979. An interesting consideration of the relationship between Gogol and his readers. Evaluates Gogol's commentary on literature within his texts and explores the road as the dominant metaphor of *Dead Souls.*

Gippius, V. V. *Gogol.* Edited and translated by Robert Maguire. Durham, N.C.: Duke Univeristy Press, 1989. This classic treatment of Gogol's life and works is enhanced by glosses on contemporary figures. The book treats Gogol's literary influences in detail. The chapter on *Dead Souls* considers the structure of the novel as a gallery of caricatures and explores Gogol's reformulation of the picaresque novel.

Griffiths, Frederick, and Stanley Rabinowitz. *Gogol, Dostoevsky, and National Narrative.* Evanston, Ill.: Northwestern University Press, 1990. Places Gogol's work within the framework of the epic tradition. Evaluates stylistic aspects of the text, such as Homeric similes and hyperbole, that create the mock-heroic mood of *Dead Souls.*

Maguire, Robert, ed. and trans. *Gogol from the Twentieth Century.* Princeton, N.J.: Princeton University Press, 1976. A collection of well-known Russian essays. These varied approaches to Gogol's work include a consideration of Gogol as a realist depicting provincial life, a psychoanalytic evaluation of his prose, and a stylistic analysis of his wordplay. The introduction provides a thorough overview of the criticism.

Nabokov, Vladimir. *Nikolai Gogol.* Norfolk, Conn.: New Directions, 1944. The clever tone of Nabokov's book mirrors that of Gogol's prose. While the stylistic analysis is eclectic and brilliant, the primary focus is on banality: Nabokov maintains that Gogol's genius is his attention to the absurd in everyday life.

Spieker, Sven, ed. *Gogol: Exploring Absence—Negativity in Nineteenth Century Russian Literature.* Bloomington, Ind.: Slavica, 1999. A collection of essays on Gogol focusing on the negativity in *Dead Souls* and his other works and in the works of other Russian writers. Bibliography and index.

Weiner, Adam. "The Evils of *Dead Souls.*" In *By Authors Possessed: The Demonic Novel in Russia.* Evanston, Ill.: Northwestern University Press, 1998. Weiner analyzes *Dead Souls* and other nineteenth and twentieth century Russian "demonic novels," which he defines as novels in which the protagonists are incarnated with the evil presence of the Devil.

Death and the King's Horseman

Author: Wole Soyinka (1934-　　　)
First produced: 1976; first published, 1975
Type of work: Drama
Type of plot: Tragedy
Time of plot: 1944
Locale: Oyo, Nigeria

Principal characters:
ELESIN OBA, the king's horseman
PRAISE-SINGER, leader of Elesin's retinue
IYALOJA, a senior woman of the Oyo market
SIMON PILKINGS, a colonial district officer
JANE PILKINGS, his wife
SERGEANT AMUSA, a colonial police officer
JOSEPH, the Pilkingses' houseboy
BRIDE, a young woman
OLUNDE, Elesin's oldest son

The Story:

The alafin (king) dies. It is time for his chief lieutenant, Elesin Oba, to will his own death, so that he might accompany the alafin on his passage to the next life. As Elesin enters the market, the Praise-Singer pleads with him to tarry a while, to enjoy the last fruits of life in this world. Elesin, a man of enormous courage, rejects this plea and boasts of his readiness to meet death without fear. He talks of the Not-I bird that sounds at the approach of death, echoed by people from all levels of society who seek to flee death—all but he, the king's horseman, who was born and lived for this moment.

The women of the marketplace, led by Iyaloja, also ask whether he is truly ready to face death, praising him all the while for his strength of will. On this night, nothing can be denied him: rich clothing, fine food, beautiful women, all are at his pleasure. A beautiful young woman, the Bride, catches his eye. He determines that he will have her, even though she is already promised as a bride to Iyaloja's son. Tactfully, Iyaloja suggests that he should not claim the Bride, just as an honorable man will leave food at a feast for the children. The insistence of the king's horseman at this moment cannot be denied, however, and Elesin and the woman retire to the bridal chamber.

At the district officer's house, the Pilkingses prepare to attend a costume ball in honor of the visiting British prince. They are modeling their disguises, ritual masks of the Yoruba dead cult, when Sergeant Amusa arrives to report a disturbance in the marketplace caused by Elesin's preparations for death. A Muslim, Amusa is flustered by the Pilkingses' blasphemous use of the death masks in a nonreligious context and cannot express himself clearly. The Pilkingses' servant, Joseph, a convert to Christianity, explains what is happening, whereupon Simon Pilkings decides to halt the ritual suicide, upholding Western ideals of the sanctity of life. Pilkings orders Amusa to make the arrest while he and his wife go to meet the Prince.

Back in the marketplace, Amusa's attempt to enter the bridal chamber and arrest Elesin is blocked by Iyaloja and the young women, who mock the policeman as a eunuch neutered by the white colonial authorities. Defeated by the women, Amusa retreats to seek reinforcement. Then Elesin emerges from the bridal chamber bearing bloodstained bedclothes, evidence of the Bride's virginity and his success in impregnating her, creating a union of life and the passage to death. Filled with vitality and sexual satisfaction, he momentarily loses his will to die, but recovers and falls gradually into a trance. As his spirit moves away from this world, his body begins a heavy dance accompanied by the Praise-Singer's ritual pronouncements.

Amusa arrives at the ball in tattered clothing to report his failure to arrest Elesin. Pilkings, admonished by his supervisor to maintain control, takes matters into his own hands, going off to arrest Elesin. While he is gone, Elesin's son Olunde, whom the Pilkingses befriended and sent to England to study medicine, arrives, expecting to bury his father after hearing in England of the alafin's death. As Jane Pilkings and Olunde speak of England, Olunde shows that he does not accept British values, despite his Western education.

Seeking a topic on which they might agree, Olunde and Jane discuss the progress of the war. Jane tells him of an English naval captain who died while destroying his ship, thereby saving the city. She finds his self-sacrifice difficult to understand, convinced there must have been another way. Olunde finds the self-sacrifice life-affirming, being death in the cause of life. Jane then informs him that her husband is en route to prevent Elesin's suicide. Olunde explains that Pilkings's success would be catastrophic because of the ritual importance of the horseman's death. Pilkings returns and becomes nervous and distracted on hearing Olunde's words. The mood is explained when a heavily chained Elesin arrives on the scene; Pilkings has succeeded. Olunde first ignores his father's presence and then rejects him, calling him, like Amusa, an eater of leftovers.

In his prison cell beneath the resident's palace, Elesin first blames Pilkings for arresting him. The moment at which Elesin should have joined the alafin on his journey to heaven passed with the arrest, and it is too late to restore the cosmic order. Elesin claims to have regained his sense of purpose after experiencing the contempt of his son, but Elesin is no longer able to carry out his own death. When Pilkings is called away, Elesin shifts blame to the Bride for tempting him away from his destiny. In truth, the white man only provided an excuse for him to succumb to his desire to remain in the world, enjoying its pleasures.

The Pilkingses return to the cell to announce a visitor, Iyaloja, who castigates Elesin for his loss of will and the betrayal of his people. She also announces that a volunteer is found to carry Elesin's last message: that he will not come to the waiting alafin. When the body of this messenger is carried into the prison area, Pilkings and Elesin are both horrified to recognize Olunde, who takes his father's place. In a final affront to Elesin's lost honor, Pilkings refuses to allow Elesin to whisper the ritual message in his son's ear, thus—from the Yoruba perspective—completing the destruction of the cosmic order. Left with nothing to salvage, Elesin strangles himself with his own chains before the colonial authorities can react. His death, however, comes too late to fulfill his hereditary function. What hopes remain lie with the unborn child the Bride carries, the only fruit of the night's events.

Critical Evaluation:

When Wole Soyinka became the first African to win the Nobel Prize in Literature in 1986, his work was cited for its strongly mythic blending of African—specifically Yoruban—ritual with Western dramatic forms, a blending that is particularly evident in *Death and the King's Horse-*

man. The play is based on an actual event in Nigerian colonial history. In 1946, British officials intervened to prevent a ritual suicide such as Elesin Oba attempts in the play. In the traditional Yoruba cosmology, which by the 1940's was already eroded by the introduction of Christianity, the dead king must be joined by his courier, who acts as a mediator between the living and the dead. Insofar as the continuity of living and dead is central to Yoruba concepts of community, Elesin's failure to carry out his suicide threatens the social order.

The play begins with an evocation of African ritual. The scene in the marketplace appears completely out of time: There are no white people, no mention whatever of the colonial circumstances, and the ritual suicide being undertaken is one that has occurred repeatedly in Yoruba history. It is into this world that the first intimations of Elesin's lack of will are introduced. The audience witnesses his desire for the young woman, who represents life. Despite Elesin's protestations, his fear of death is evident. Only after this theme has been established does the play shift, in act 2, to a more familiar Western pattern of realistic drama, when it moves to the topic of the colonial powers.

The British colonial officer and his wife demonstrate their inability to comprehend spiritual values not only by their profaning of profoundly religious symbols for use as costumes at a masked ball but also by Simon Pilkings's blasphemous references to Christianity before his devout servant Joseph. It is their obliviousness to the sacred that enables them to bring about Elesin's failure. His understanding of his spiritual role makes his failure tragic. The role of the colonial district officer, Pilkings, in stopping the suicide, tempts the audience to see the play as enacting the cultural conflict between African traditions and the usurping colonial power. Soyinka warned against such a reductive reading and in fact altered events to make the colonial intervention less significant than it was in the historical antecedent. Further, by moving events from the postwar period to 1944, he creates parallels between sacrifices undertaken by the British and the sacrifice that Elesin fails to make.

Soyinka complicates matters by presenting two models of sacrifice among the British: the naval captain who destroys his damaged munitions ship to preserve the city and the prince who risks his life to bolster morale among the colonists. Matters are further complicated by Olunde's decision to substitute for his father, despite his manifest lack of belief in the tradition that calls for this sacrifice. At the beginning of the play, the Western-educated Olunde expects, after the burial of his father, to resume his medical studies rather than to inherit his father's ritual role.

Instead of a limited political tract on the colonial suppression of Yoruba customs, then, Soyinka presents a more complex metaphysical conflict within the soul of his protagonist. Much of the play's first act is given to Elesin's song about the "Not-I bird," the desire to deny death that, he claims, afflicts all human beings but himself. At the moment of truth, however, Elesin proves as vulnerable to fear as the rest of humanity; called upon to die for the sake of his community, he chooses to live for himself.

The play's merging of Western and traditional motifs and its tendency to complicate apparently clear lines of division reflect Soyinka's conviction that there is no pure literature, that all art reflects the combination and complication of various traditions. The inability to cast the play into a simple cultural category marks its continuity with other great works of modernist art. In *Death and the King's Horseman*, Soyinka appropriates Western forms to speak for Africans.

A. Waller Hastings

Further Reading

Gates, Henry Louis, Jr., ed. *In the House of Oshugbo: Critical Essays on Wole Soyinka*. New York: Oxford University Press, 2002. Twenty-six writers provide analyses of individual plays, biographical information, comparisons of Soyinka's work with that of Bertolt Brecht and James Joyce, and discussions of literary theory, the art of writing, and Yoruba culture.

Jeyifo, Biodun. *Wole Soyinka: Politics, Poetics, and Postcolonialism*. New York: Cambridge University Press, 2004. Focuses on the connection of Soyinka's works to his involvement in radical political activity, describing how he uses literature and the theater for political purposes. References to *Death and the King's Horseman* are listed in the index.

_____, ed. *Conversations with Wole Soyinka*. Jackson: University Press of Mississippi, 2001. A collection of Soyinka's interviews with Henry Louis Gates, Jr., Anthony Appiah, Biodun Jeyifo, and others. These interviews help clarify many aspects of Soyinka's work.

_____, ed. *Perspectives on Wole Soyinka: Freedom and Complexity*. Jackson: University Press of Mississippi, 2001. A collection of critical essays written during three decades. Its major contribution is its analysis of Soyinka's work using several schools of critical theory, from feminism to phenomenology. The essays also discuss Soyinka's postcolonial politics and aestheticism. The numerous references to *Death and the King's Horseman* are listed in the index.

Katrak, Ketu H. *Wole Soyinka and Modern Tragedy: A Study of Dramatic Theory and Practice.* Westport, Conn.: Greenwood Press, 1986. Extended study of the roots of Soyinka's art in Yoruba ritual and Western dramatic traditions. Argues that *Death and the King's Horseman* dramatizes the common fear of death that can be allayed only with ritual suicide, while criticizing the tradition itself and seeking a mythic revision suitable for the modern world.

Ogundele, Wole. "*Death and the King's Horseman*: A Poet's Quarrel with His Culture." *Research in African Literatures* 25, no. 1 (Spring, 1994): 47-60. Treats the play from a social and political perspective, focusing on the social conditions influencing Elesin's moral position.

Ralph-Bowman, Mark. "'Leaders and Left-Overs': A Reading of Soyinka's *Death and the King's Horseman.*" *Research in African Literatures* 14, no. 1 (February, 1983): 81-97. Emphasizes the spiritual aspects of the play, portraying Elesin as a failed Christ figure whose actions constitute blasphemy and Olunde as a redemptive figure, upholding his culture despite exposure to the West.

Soyinka, Wole. *Death and the King's Horseman: Authoritative Text, Backgrounds and Contexts, Criticism.* Edited by Simon Gikandi. New York: Norton, 2003. In addition to the text of the play, this edition provides information about Yoruba culture and religious beliefs, a map of Yorubaland, a discussion of the role of theater in traditional African culture, and several critical essays providing various interpretations of the play.

Whitaker, Thomas R. "Wole Soyinka." In *Post-Colonial English Drama*, edited by Bruce King. New York: St. Martin's Press, 1992. Describes *Death and the King's Horseman* as a revision of Yoruba folk opera, under the influence of Western tragedy and Ibsen-like realism. Argues that all moral positions in the play are made problematic by the mingling of Western and African traditions.

Death Comes for the Archbishop

Author: Willa Cather (1873-1947)
First published: 1927
Type of work: Novel
Type of plot: Historical realism
Time of plot: Last half of the nineteenth century
Locale: New Mexico and Arizona

Principal characters:
BISHOP JEAN MARIE LATOUR, Vicar Apostolic of New Mexico
FATHER JOSEPH VAILLANT, his friend and a missionary priest
KIT CARSON, a frontier scout
JACINTO, an Indian guide

The Story:

In 1851, Father Jean Marie Latour reaches Santa Fé, where he is to become Vicar Apostolic of New Mexico. His journey from the shores of Lake Ontario is long and arduous. He loses his belongings in a shipwreck at Galveston and suffers painful injury in a wagon accident at San Antonio. When he arrives, accompanied by his good friend Father Joseph Vaillant, the Mexican priests refuse to recognize his authority. He has no choice but to ride hundreds of miles into Mexico to secure the necessary papers from the bishop of Durango.

On the road, he loses his way in an arid landscape of red hills and gaunt junipers. His thirst becomes a vertigo of mind and senses, and he can blot out his own agony only by repeating the cry of the Savior on the Cross. As he is about to give up all hope, he sees a tree growing in the shape of a cross. A short time later, he arrives in a Mexican settlement called Agua Secreta (hidden water). Stopping at the home of Benito, Father Latour first performs marriage ceremonies and then baptizes all the children.

At Durango, he receives the necessary documents and starts the long trip back to Santa Fé. Father Vaillant in the meantime wins over the inhabitants of Santa Fé and sets up the episcopal residence in an old adobe house. On the first morning after his return, Father Latour, now officially bishop, hears the unexpected sound of a bell ringing the Angelus. Father Vaillant tells him that he found the bell, bearing the date 1356, in the basement of old San Miguel Church.

On a missionary journey to Albuquerque in March, Father Vaillant acquires a handsome cream-colored mule as a gift and another just like it for Bishop Latour. These mules, Contento and Angelica, faithfully serve the men for many years. On another trip, as the two priests are riding together on their mules, they are caught in a sleet storm and stop at the rude shack of the American Buck Scales. His Mexican wife warns the travelers by gestures that their lives are in danger, so they ride on to Mora without spending the night. The next morning, the Mexican woman appears in town and tells them that her husband murdered and robbed four travelers and that he killed her three babies. As a result, Scales is brought to justice and his wife, Magdalena, is sent to the home of Kit Carson, the famous frontier scout. From that time on, Carson is a valuable friend of the two priests. Magdalena later becomes the housekeeper and manager for the kitchens of the Sisters of Loretto.

During his first year at Santa Fé, Bishop Latour is called to a meeting of the Plenary Council in Baltimore. On the return journey, he brings back with him five nuns sent to establish the school of Our Lady of Light. Attended by Jacinto, an American Indian who serves as his guide, Latour spends some time visiting his own vicariate. Padre Gallegos, whom he visits at Albuquerque, acts more like a professional gambler than a priest, but because he is very popular with the natives, Latour does not remove him at that time. At last, he arrives at the end of his long journey, the top of the mesa at Acoma. On that trip, he hears the legend of Fray Baltazar, killed during an uprising of the Acoma Indians.

A month after his visit, he suspends Padre Gallegos and puts Father Vaillant in charge of the parish at Albuquerque. On a trip to the Pecos Mountains, Vaillant falls ill with an attack of the black measles. Bishop Latour, hearing of his illness, sets out to nurse his friend. Jacinto again serves as guide on the cold, snowy trip. When Latour reaches his friend's bedside, he finds that Carson has arrived before him. As soon as the sick man can sit in the saddle, his friends take him back to Santa Fé.

Bishop Latour decides to investigate the parish of Taos, where the powerful old priest Antonio José Martinez is the ruler of both spiritual and temporal matters. The following year, the bishop is called to Rome. When he returns, he brings with him four young priests from the Seminary of Montferrand and a Spanish priest to replace Padre Martinez at Taos.

Bishop Latour has one great ambition: to build a cathedral in Santa Fé. He is assisted by the rich Mexican rancheros but above all by his good friend Don Antonio Olivares. When Don Antonio dies, it is found that he left his estate to his wife and daughter during their lives, after which it is to go to the church. Don Antonio's brothers contest the will on the grounds that the daughter, Señorita Inez, is too old to be Doña Isabella's daughter. The bishop and his vicar have to

persuade the vain, coquettish widow to swear to her true age of fifty-three, rather than the forty-two years she claims. Thus the estate eventually goes to the church.

Father Vaillant is sent to Tucson, but after several years, Bishop Latour decides to recall him to Santa Fé. When he arrives, the bishop shows him the stone for building the cathedral. About that time, Bishop Latour receives a letter from the bishop of Leavenworth. Because of the discovery of gold near Pike's Peak, he asks to have a priest sent there from Bishop Latour's diocese. Father Vaillant, the obvious choice, spends the rest of his life in Colorado, though he returns to Santa Fé with the papal emissary when Bishop Latour is made an archbishop. Father Vaillant later becomes the first bishop of Colorado, and he dies there after years of service. Archbishop Latour attends his impressive funeral services.

After the death of his friend, Father Latour retires to a modest country estate near Santa Fé. He dreamed during all his missionary years of the time when he could retire to his own fertile green Auvergne in France, but in the end he decides that he cannot leave the land of his labors. He spends his last years with memories of the journeys he and Father Vaillant made over thousands of miles of desert country. Bernard Ducrot, a young seminarian from France, becomes like a son to him during those last years.

When Father Latour knows that his time has come to die, he asks to be taken into town to spend his last days near the cathedral. On the last day of his life, the church is filled with people who come to pray for him, as word that he is dying spreads through the town. He dies in the still twilight, and the cathedral bell, tolling in the early darkness, carries the news to the waiting countryside that death comes for Father Latour.

Critical Evaluation:

When writing of her great predecessor and teacher, Sarah Orne Jewett, Willa Cather expressed her belief that the quality that gives a work of literature greatness is the "voice" of the author, the sincere, unadorned, and unique vision of a writer coming to grips with the material chosen. If any one characteristic can be said to dominate the writings of Cather, it is that of a true and moving sincerity. She never tried to twist her subject matter to suit a preconceived purpose, and she resisted the temptation to dress up homely material. She gave herself absolutely to her chosen material, and the result was a series of books both truthful and rich with intimations of the destiny of the American continent. By digging into the roots of her material, she exposed deeper meanings, which she expressed with a deceptive simplicity. Her vision and craftsmanship were seldom more successful than in *Death*

Comes for the Archbishop. Cather merged her voice with her material so completely that some critics have said that the book is almost too polished and lacks the sense of struggle necessary in a truly great novel. This, in fact, indicated the magnitude of the author's achievement and the brilliance of her technical skill. *Death Comes for the Archbishop* resonates with the unspoken beliefs of the author and the resolved conflicts that went into its construction. On the surface, it is cleanly wrought and simple, but it is a more complicated and profound book than it appears at first reading. Cather learned well from Sarah Orne Jewett the secrets of artless art and of sophisticated craftsmanship that disarms by its simplicity.

Death Comes for the Archbishop is a novel that reaffirms part of the American past, the history of the Catholic Southwest beautifully told through the re-creation of the lives of Bishop Lamy and Father Macheboeuf, two devout and noble missionary priests in the Vicariate of New Mexico during the second half of the nineteenth century. The novel combines the narrative with bright glimpses into the past in stories that cut backward into time. Tales and legends that extend beyond the period of American occupation into three centuries of Spanish colonial history and back to the primitive tribal life of the Hopi, the Navajo, and the vanished cliff-dwellers break the chronicle at many points, giving it density and variety and allowing the work to recapture completely the spirit and movement of the pioneer West. It is true that this novel is an epic and a regional history, but much more than either, it is a tale of personal isolation, of one man's life reduced to the painful weariness of his own sensitivities. Father Latour is a hero in the most profound sense of the word, displaying virtues of courage and determination, but he is also a very human protagonist, with doubts and inner conflicts. His personality is held up in startling contrast to that of his friend, Father Vaillant, a simpler, though no less good, individual. Cather's austere style perfectly captures the scholarly, urbane, religious devotion that characterizes Father Latour, and the reader is always aware of a sense of the dignity of human life, as exemplified in the person of one individual. Cather is not afraid to draw a good man, a man who could stand above others because of his deeds and innate quality.

Although based on a true sequence of events, the book focuses less on plot than on character and, perhaps more specifically, the interplay of environment and character. Throughout the book, the reader is aware of the human reaction to the land, and that of one man to the land he has chosen. Subtly and deeply, the author suggests that the soul of the man is profoundly altered by the soul of the land. Cather never doubts that the land, too, possesses a soul and that this soul can transform a human being in complex and important

ways. She is fascinated by the way the landscape of the Southwest, when reduced to its essences, seems to reduce human beings to their essences. Cather abandons traditional realism in this book and turns toward the directness of symbolism. With stark pictures and vivid styles, she creates an imaginary world rooted in but transcending realism. The rigid economy with which the book is written gives it unusual power in the reader's mind long after the reading. The greatest symbol is provided by the personality of Bishop Latour, who stands like a windswept crag in the vast New Mexico landscape and represents the nobility of the human spirit despite the inner conflicts against which all must struggle.

The descriptions of place set the emotional tone of the novel. The quality of life is intimately related to the landscape, and the accounts of the journeys and the efforts to survive in the barren land help to create an odd warmth and almost surreal passion in the narrative. Bishop Latour and Father Vaillant establish a definite emotional relationship with the country; if the other characters in the book are less vividly realized as individuals, it is perhaps because they do not seem to have the same relationship with the land. Certainly none of them is involved in the intense love-hate relationship with the land with which the two main characters struggle for so many years.

Although the narrative encompasses many years, the novel is essentially static and built of a series of rich images and thoughtful movements highlighted and captured as by a camera. This quality of the narrative is a characteristic of Cather's style: The frozen moments of contemplation and glimpses into Father Latour's inner world and spiritual loneliness are the moments that give the book its greatness. Despite the presence of Kit Carson, the novel is not an adventure story any more than it is merely the account of a pair of churchmen attempting to establish their church in a difficult new terrain. The cathedral becomes the most important symbol in the final part of the book, representing the earthly successes of a man dedicated to unworldly ambitions. This conflict between the earthly and the spiritual is at the heart of Bishop Latour's personality and at the heart of the book. The reader understands, at the end, when the bell tolls for Father Latour, that the man's victory is greater than he ever knew.

"Critical Evaluation" by Bruce D. Reeves

Further Reading

De Roche, Linda. *Student Companion to Willa Cather.* Westport, Conn.: Greenwood Press, 2006. An introductory overview of Cather's life and work aimed at high school and college students and the general reader, with discussion of character development, themes and plots of six novels. Chapter 8 focuses on *Death Comes for the Archbishop*.

Fryer, Judith. *Felicitous Space: The Imaginative Structures of Edith Wharton and Willa Cather*. Chapel Hill: University of North Carolina Press, 1986. An important inquiry into the meaning of actual and imagined spaces in the works of the two writers. Explores Cather's unfurnished rooms and landscapes and gives particular attention to her use of color and light in *Death Comes for the Archbishop*.

Gerber, Philip. *Willa Cather*. Boston: Twayne, 1975. A brief but solid introduction to Cather's life and literary career. *Death Comes for the Archbishop* is seen as a retreat into the past and as an implicit comparison to an inferior present, which accounts for its elegiac tone. Contains a select annotated bibliography of criticism.

Lee, Hermione. *Willa Cather: A Life Saved Up*. London: Virago, 1989. A feminist analysis of Cather as a writer of split identities, sexual conflicts, and stoical fatalism.

Lindermann, Marilee. *The Cambridge Companion to Willa Cather*. New York: Cambridge University Press, 2005. Thirteen essays, including some that examine Cather's politics, sexuality, and modernism. One of the essays focuses on *Death Comes for the Archbishop*.

March, John. *A Reader's Companion to the Fiction of Willa Cather*. Westport, Conn.: Greenwood Press, 1993. An excellent source for any reader of Cather. Contains, alphabetically listed, often lengthy explanations of place names, proper names, and other objects of importance in Cather's fiction.

Nelson, Robert J. *Willa Cather and France: In Search of the Lost Language*. Urbana: University of Illinois Press, 1988. Places aspects of *Death Comes for the Archbishop* in the tradition of French Catholicism.

O'Brien, Sharon. *Willa Cather: The Emerging Voice*. New York: Oxford University Press, 1987. A feminist reinterpretation of Cather's life, relationships with family and female friends, and works.

Skaggs, Merrill Maguire. *After the World Broke in Two: The Later Novels of Willa Cather*. Charlottesville: University Press of Virginia, 1990. Provides an intellectual history that focuses on the works of Cather's artistic maturity. Sees *Death Comes for the Archbishop* as Cather's greatest achievement because of its ability to ask and provide answers to questions of faith, art, and the continuity of life.

Stout, Janis P., ed. *Willa Cather and Material Culture: Real-World Writing, Writing the Real World*. Tuscaloosa: University of Alabama Press, 2005. Collection of essays examining the importance of material culture in Cather's life and work, including discussions of the objects among which she lived and about which she wrote, the symbolism of quilts in her work, and "Material Objects as Sites of Cultural Mediation in *Death Comes for the Archbishop*" by Sarah Wilson.

Wagenknecht, Edward. *Willa Cather*. New York: Continuum, 1994. A deep and wide-ranging survey of Cather's entire production, including an excellent critical analysis of *Death Comes for the Archbishop*.

Woodress, James. *Willa Cather: A Literary Life*. Lincoln: University of Nebraska Press, 1987. A superb general treatment of Cather's life and literary production.

Death in the Afternoon

Author: Ernest Hemingway (1899-1961)
First published: 1932
Type of work: Autobiography

Ernest Hemingway's *Death in the Afternoon* is a personal examination of bullfighting in Spain during the 1920's and 1930's. Hemingway began visiting Spain in the summer of 1923 and quickly became involved in the world of bullfighting. He stayed in the same hotels, ate in the same restaurants, and drank in the same bars as the matadors. He followed them as they performed in different cities. Eventually, he began making annual trips to Pamplona, where bullfights were held in connection with the religious festival of San Fermín. Pamplona became the setting for the climactic scenes of *The Sun Also Rises* (1926).

Drawing on this background, Hemingway attempts in *Death in the Afternoon* to celebrate "the modern Spanish bullfight" and to explain it "both emotionally and practically" for an audience of Americans. Hemingway assumes that his readers may be disgusted by the idea of bullfighting, but he wants them to give him the opportunity to show them what it is all about before they arrive at a judgment.

Death in the Afternoon is more than a book about bullfighting, however. The book is as much a book about Hemingway as it is a book about bullfighting. It is filled with his perceptions, his experiences, and his way of looking at life. So much of the information given in the book is autobiographical that it must be read in order to understand the life of Hemingway.

Chapter 1 begins with a narration of Hemingway's own early experience with bullfighting. He reports that he first went to the bullfights because of the influence of Gertrude Stein. Before going, Hemingway says that he expected to be horrified by the killing of the horses in the ring during the bullfight. He went, however, because it served a goal of his writing. He was trying to learn how to "put down what really happened in action; what the actual things were which produced the emotion you experienced."

With this goal in mind, Hemingway went to Spain to study the bullfights, but once there he found them to be so complicated and so compelling that he began to study bullfighting for its own sake.

The rest of chapter 1 is an interesting mixture of essay and personal observation. Hemingway deals with the question of the morality of bullfighting by writing on the difference between people who identify psychologically with animals (and thus who think the bullfights are barbaric because bulls and frequently horses are killed) and people who identify with humans (and become upset only when the matador performs poorly or is injured). He deals with the question of the aesthetics of bullfighting by writing about how the enjoyment of the art of bullfighting increases in the same way that a person develops an ear for music or a sensitive palate for wine. The basic thread of the narrative is always bullfighting, but Hemingway cannot keep himself from engaging in asides, telling anecdotes, and making lengthy commentaries on other subjects. In this book on bullfighting, Hemingway is creating a persona that developed over the years into the voice of "Papa" Hemingway. In letters that Hemingway wrote before *Death in the Afternoon* he often apologizes for the advice that he gives to family and friends, calling himself a Dutch uncle. At the time of the writing of *Death in the Afternoon*, he begins to stop apologizing. His tone throughout the book is one of a kindly, knowledgeable guide who knows what is best for the reader.

Hemingway was not an old man when he wrote *Death in the Afternoon*. He was relatively young. The arrogance that cost Hemingway many friends over the years is, in this book, beginning to show. There are passages in the book in which Hemingway sounds more like a bully than a kindly guide, and

the overall impression that he gives of himself is that of a much older and much more experienced man. This arrogance is seen in an extreme degree in his attacks on other authors, which are sprinkled throughout the book. Hemingway suggests that some writers write the way they do because they are sexually frustrated; if they would take care of this problem, their writing would improve greatly. The book contains vicious asides about fellow writers such as William Faulkner, Aldous Huxley, André Gide, and Jean Cocteau. The book was widely condemned by critics for this meanness when it first appeared.

Hemingway also shows his fascination with technical trivia in *Death in the Afternoon*. Hemingway loved any type of activity that involved the complicated use of equipment. With bullfighting Hemingway was able to indulge this fascination to an extreme degree. His discussion of the various pieces of equipment and the techniques used in bullfighting takes up four chapters. Hemingway also demonstrates an almost encyclopedic knowledge of the bulls that are specifically bred for bullfights. He devotes another four chapters to a discussion of the size, weight, power, and mating habits of the bulls.

Another example of Hemingway's love for technical trivia is the book's series of appendices. One appendix contains sixty-four pages of black and white photos of bulls, bullfighters, fight techniques, and even of a horn wound on a matador's leg as it is being operated on. Hemingway includes detailed captions that explain the significance of each photo. Another appendix defines the meaning of hundreds of Spanish bullfighting terms, but also has whimsical entries on pickpockets, sodomites, and "tarts about town."

When *Death in the Afternoon* was first published, some critics accused Hemingway of padding the book with appendixes that were of little use to the reader. Certainly, many of the appendixes are very useful to the student of bullfighting, but some of them probably are padding. One appendix, for example, is nothing more than a series of notebook entries from Hemingway's Paris years about the reactions of his friends and family members (whom he does not identify by name) to their first bullfight.

In addition to Hemingway's evolving persona and his obsession with details, *Death in the Afternoon* also demonstrates the author's recurrent fascination with death. One of the book's major themes is the decadence of modern bullfighting, as opposed to the purity of bullfighting's earlier years. Decadence in bullfighting involves the matador's using tricks to appear to be a lot closer to the bull (and thus to danger and death) than he really is. The decadent matador causes the crowd of onlookers to feel an emotion that is false because he is really in no great danger.

True bullfighting, according to Hemingway, is something else. Bullfighting is not really a sport, since it is not an equal contest between man and bull. The drawing power of the fight is tragedy. The odds of the matador being killed are small. However, the competent matador can "increase the amount of danger of death that he runs" to the precise degree that he wishes. It is to the matador's credit if he deliberately attempts something that is extremely dangerous. It is to his dishonor if he does something dangerous through ignorance or torpidity. To Hemingway, that a man hazards death, while working at the limits of his skill to avoid it, makes a bullfight worth seeing.

Hemingway evaluates a number of bullfighters against the standard of their genuineness in hazarding death. He discusses great matadors of the past, such as Joselito and Belmonte, and bullfighters of his time, such as Sidney Franklin, the "pride of Brooklyn," an American who was trying to earn a living in Spain as a matador in the 1930's.

There are passages in the book in which Hemingway also seems intent on shocking his readers. He graphically describes the goring of bullfighters in the ring and the subsequent operations in hospitals. He includes one of his short stories, "A Natural History of the Dead," at the end of chapter 12.

The reader of *Death in the Afternoon* can learn a great deal of technical information about bullfighting. The greater appeal of this book is not what it teaches about bullfighting but rather what it teaches about a man who loved bulls, bullfights, matadors, and Spain: Hemingway.

In *Death in the Afternoon* Hemingway is encountered as a human being, without the veil of fiction. He is a writer at the height of his creative powers and at the height of his own arrogance. Hemingway shows his readers a clear picture of who he is by describing the things he loves and the things he hates. This picture is not always a flattering one. It contains his greatness, his pettiness, and his cruelty. The picture is, however, an extraordinarily accurate one. *Death in the Afternoon* must be read by anyone who wants to understand Hemingway.

Howard Cox

Further Reading

Bloom, Harold, ed. *Ernest Hemingway*. Philadelphia: Chelsea House, 2005. Contains articles analyzing Hemingway's work by a variety of writers, including such eminent literary critics as Edmund Wilson, Robert Penn Warren, and Carlos Baker. Features Edward F. Stanton's essay, "Of Bulls and Men."

Castillo Puche, José. *Hemingway in Spain*. Translated by Helen R. Lane. Garden City, N.Y.: Doubleday, 1974. Enlightening account of the time that Hemingway spent in Spain during the last years of his life.

Eastman, Max. "Bull in the Afternoon." In *Art and the Life of Action*. New York: Alfred A. Knopf, 1934. Scathing review of *Death in the Afternoon* that describes Hemingway's literary style as one of "wearing false hair on his chest." Hemingway and Eastman came to blows over this review.

Fantina, Richard. *Ernest Hemingway: Machismo and Masochism*. New York: Palgrave Macmillan, 2005. Focuses on Hemingway's heroes. Fantina argues that Hemingway's male protagonists are "profoundly submissive" and display a "masochistic posture toward women." References to *Death in the Afternoon* are listed in the index.

Griffin, Peter. *Along with Youth*. New York: Oxford University Press, 1985. Chapter 1 discusses early influences on Hemingway's writing and argues that *Death in the Afternoon* is Hemingway's version of Mark Twain's *Life on the Mississippi*.

Hotchner, A. E. *Hemingway and His World*. New York: Vendome Press, 1989. Recounts all of the events in Hemingway's life that went into the making of *Death in the Afternoon* and gives a sampling of the critical reaction to the book. Lavishly illustrated with photographs of the places in Spain that Hemingway visited and of Hemingway as a young man.

Mandel, Miriam B. *Hemingway's "Death in the Afternoon": The Complete Annotations*. Lanham, Md.: Scarecrow Press, 2002. Contains several hundred alphabetically arranged entries about people, animals, and cultural artifacts mentioned in the book. The introduction provides background information about bullfighting.

_____, ed. *A Companion to Hemingway's "Death in the Afternoon."* Rochester, N.Y.: Camden House, 2004. Collection of twelve essays, including discussions of the composition, publication, reception, literary background, depiction of Spain and bullfighting, and the legacy of *Death in the Afternoon*.

Trogdon, Robert W., ed. *Ernest Hemingway: A Literary Reference*. New York: Carroll & Graf, 2002. A compendium of information about Hemingway, including photographs, letters, interviews, essays, speeches, book reviews, copies of some of his manuscripts-in-process, and his comments about his own work and the work of other writers.

Wagner-Martin, Linda. *Ernest Hemingway: A Literary Life*. New York: Palgrave Macmillan, 2007. Examines Hemingway's life, especially his troubled relationship with his parents. Wagner-Martin makes insightful connections between his personal life, his emotions, and his writing.

A Death in the Family

Author: James Agee (1909-1955)
First published: 1957
Type of work: Novel
Type of plot: Domestic realism
Time of plot: Summer, 1915; May 15-20, 1916
Locale: Knoxville, Tennessee

Principal characters:
RUFUS FOLLET, a six-year-old boy
JAY, Rufus's father
MARY, Jay's wife and Rufus's mother
CATHERINE, Rufus's younger sister
FRANK and RALPH, Jay's brothers
ANDREW, Mary's brother
HANNAH LYNCH, Jay and Mary's friend and helper

The Story:

Part 1 of the novel's three parts opens with Rufus (James Agee's real, and detested, nickname) being taken, joyously, by Jay, his father, to see a slapstick Charlie Chaplin movie, one that is all the funnier for being slightly risqué. Afterward, deciding to "hoist a couple," Jay takes Rufus into a bar, where Jay brags about his boy's reading ability, which Rufus, somewhat dismayed, realizes is his father's way of not embarrassing him about his inability to fight off other boys. Balance is soon restored, the bonding tightens, and the contract between them reaffirms, as Rufus is offered a Life Saver—man-to-man—as Jay uses another to cloak his breath and Rufus grasps that when his father sets out on a slow, contented pace homeward it is because Jay genuinely savors time spent with his son. That gentle night, as Rufus drifts into sleep, he hears his father telling his mother that he will return before the kids are awake and then the grinding sounds of the family Ford being cranked. In the morning, Mary explains why Jay is not at breakfast.

His parents were awakened by a phone call from Jay's younger brother, Ralph. Ralph and Jay's ill father lives on a farm miles out of Knoxville, and the message was that their father is dying. Jay decided, chancing that his brother was right, to make the trip. Mary prepared Jay for his journey while Rufus and his younger sister, Catherine, slept.

Rufus imagines his father's thoughts as he drove to the farm: Jay's thoughts of home, encounters at the ferry, and the pleasant feel of Jay moving into his home country. Rufus imagines Mary, too, strict and religious, lying in bed, reviewing her marriage: its flaws, her dislike of Jay's rural background, his lack of religion, her unconcern for his father, her resentment that others forgive Jay his weaknesses because of his generous ways, and her deep anger over the burdens he imposes upon her. She thinks of the gulf that widens between them, but she grimly sees her duty to put the future in the children and to raise them Catholic.

Rufus meanwhile dreams of his father exorcising his childish fears during a nightmare by joking and singing to

him and of his mother's different comforting and songs. He recalls both parents' discussing the imminent birth of his sister, Catherine. Together, these are Rufus's filtered remembrances of the varieties of love he receives and of the loves he perceives between others.

Part 2 deals with the accidental death that shatters the sense that Rufus and his family made of their world: the phone call conveying the ominous news of the accident, the family's trying to cushion Mary's shock with confirmation of Jay's instantaneous death, Mary's efforts to shield the children, and the full realization of the tragic event rippling through the family. Rufus, meanwhile, reflects on visits with relatives that bared to him the network of familial relationships. He contrasts his family life with the torture and tensions he suffers at the hands of other boys.

Mary, in part 3, explains Jay's death to Rufus and Catherine, answering their questions as best she can but not quite clarifying the meaning of death. A priest is called. Relatives and friends arrive in preparation for the funeral. Finally Mary allows her children a last view of their father before his interment, Rufus all the while trying to comfort a bewildered Catherine. Afterward, placed in others' charge, Rufus glimpses his father's coffin and is proud Jay is so heavy and that it takes several men to handle it. When the graveyard ceremony concludes, Uncle Andrew confides a miracle to Rufus: Andrew saw a beautiful butterfly land on Jay's coffin, a sign of Jay's ascent to heaven. Andrew then bitterly denounces the priest, the funeral's religious claptrap, and those who prayed, leaving Rufus baffled and full of unasked questions before he is taken home.

Critical Evaluation:

The novel's nostalgic evocation of an earlier, quiet time is set by "Knoxville: Summer 1915," a poetic reminiscence James Agee wrote in 1936. It was selected by an editor to be a preface to the novel, which was not quite complete when Agee died. The preface re-creates childhood memories of the peaceful summer evenings of Agee's middle-class Knoxville home as the women finish their kitchen work and the men, collars open and in shirtsleeves, watched by their children and older relatives, turned out to water their lawns. Such evenings are filled with shapes formed by spraying hoses, the sounds of nozzles being adjusted, and the recollections of the family, its work set aside momentarily, sitting outside on a quilt making small talk, watching the sky, waiting for the night to come. The preface closes with a life-affirming benediction: "May God bless my people, my uncle, my aunt, my mother, my good father, oh, remember them kindly in their time of trouble; and in the hour of their taking away."

Cast as a novel, *A Death in the Family* is Agee's long-planned autobiographical memorial to his father. The event that inspired the memorial was a simple one, though its consequences were not. Hugh James (Jay) Agee died in an automobile accident outside Knoxville, Tennessee, on May 18, 1916. Jay had been responding to an emergency call from a brother that their father was dying. The brother had been drinking and, ironically, there was no emergency, a situation made more poignant by the reader's foreknowledge of what is to happen. Six-year-old Rufus, Jay's son, whose childhood memories, dreams, and reconstructions inform the story, idolizes his father (rather than his mother, Mary) as the nurturing parent, the model around whom he senses his place in the world and the beginning of his own identity. His father's death shatters the delicate balance and tranquillity of Rufus's childhood, and, in fact, marked Agee for the remainder of his own rather brief life.

A 1958 Pulitzer Prize winner, Agee's *A Death in the Family* is a touching and lyrical novel of domestic love. Combining strains that are romantic and modernist, it works at different levels around a number of important themes. Agee's—Rufus's—childhood love of his father, delicate and balanced but prone to damage by a wrong word or look on the part of those who compose Rufus's world, provides the novel's main theme. Agee's story, however, goes beyond this theme.

Agee was a southern writer who could be associated with a particular southern locale and era. Within that framework he was also in many ways a southern traditionalist, although the novel's abundant detail includes the depiction of sentiments and situations that are universal. Agee carefully documents the erosion of rural values among people like his father by Knoxville's growing industrialization during the years of his childhood. The harsh noises of passing streetcars that make his little sister Catherine cry and the grinding, whirring metallic sounds of Jay cranking his Ford, a disturbance to family and neighborhood alike, are only two of many examples of this erosion that Agee sought to evoke.

The clash of rural and urban values is likewise played out within his parents' mutual love. Jay remains countrified at heart while Mary, quite consciously, is an urban Catholic. Socially, Mary and her relatives look down on Jay. To be sure, Jay dominates his household, but he is oblivious to the price Mary pays in chagrin at his ways. Gentle enough, patient in his way, generous, hardworking, practical, devoted, and deeply attached to his country roots, he nonetheless is sometimes an embarrassment. While he accedes to Mary's wish to raise the children as Catholics, he is personally unreligious and unbaptized, a sore point with Mary's priest as well as occasion for her brother Andrew's outrage at the funeral. Jay's humor, in addition, runs to the vulgar, or so it seems in his day; he swears, spits, enjoys bending the elbow, and lapses into rural idioms and songs. His death by a prime symbol of modernization, the Ford automobile, and his father's wasting away are metaphors for the decline of the old rural South.

In addition to the evocations of tensions between Rufus's parents and within the extended family (some of them healthy tensions that stitch together the framework of family loves), Agee laces the novel with concerns about the forces that are pulling those networks asunder. Those forces manifest themselves in physical separations and in those fragmentations that attend urban living. In this light, Jay is "a victim of progress," but so, too, are Rufus, Mary, and Catherine; no one can say how the family might have developed differently had Jay lived.

A Death in the Family is like a photograph, sharp in its details of a family in a moment in time, during an age in passage, never to be experienced again, and all the more precious in recognition of the photograph's ephemeral qualities. Enduring qualities remain, evoked by the photograph: Jay and Mary singing their son through his nightmares, Rufus feeling his father's hands stroking his head, Rufus smelling Jay's leather and tobacco, kids on their bellies reading comics, parental admonitions to Rufus about respecting differences (those of black people, of relatives, and of old folks): all archetypal memories, recognizable to everyone, and timeless.

Clifton K. Yearley

Further Reading

Agee, James. *"A Death in the Family": A Restoration of the Author's Text*. Edited by Michael A. Lofaro. Knoxville: University of Tennessee Press, 2007. The version of the novel that was published in 1957 was heavily edited; this version, published fifty years later, is the restored, unedited text. Among the differences between the two, the unedited version contains forty-five chapters instead of twenty, is chronological and has no flashback chapters, and uses real names of people and places and more regional speech patterns. The unedited version also contains an introductory essay, describes how to read the 1957 version in comparison to the latter edition, and includes a draft of Agee's memories of his father's death.

Barson, Alfred T. *A Way of Seeing: A Critical Study of James Agee.* Amherst: University of Massachusetts Press, 1972. A revisionist view of Agee, whose earliest critics thought that his talents were dissipated by his diverse interests but who judged him to have been improving at the time of his death. Barson inverts this thesis, stating that Agee's finished work should not be so slighted and that his powers were declining when he died.

Bergreen, Laurence. *James Agee: A Life.* New York: E. P. Dutton, 1984. A thorough and well-researched biography that discusses *A Death in the Family.* Includes many fine photographs.

Doty, Mark A. *Tell Me Who I Am: James Agee's Search for Selfhood.* Baton Rouge: Louisiana State University Press, 1981. An interesting study of Agee's search for selfhood, in which the remembrances in *A Death in the Family* play a major role.

Folks, Jeffrey J. "Art and Anarchy in James Agee's *A Death in the Family.*" In *In Time of Disorder: Form and Meaning in Southern Fiction from Poe to O'Connor.* New York: Peter Lang, 2003. Folks's collection of essays examines how Agee and other southern writers sought to create a sense of social order in their work in response to perceptions that society was unjust, chaotic, and governed by random chance

Kramer, Victor A. *Agee and Actuality: Artistic Vision in His Work.* Troy, N.Y.: Whitston, 1991. Kramer explores the aesthetics of Agee's writing, and he provides a valuable resource for identifying the controlling themes that pervade the author's work.

_____. *James Agee.* Boston: Twayne, 1975. A lifelong Agee scholar, Kramer has invaluable insights on the novel.

_____. "Mood and Music: Landscape and Artistry in *A Death in the Family.*" In *James Agee: Reconsiderations,* edited by Michael A. Lofaro. Knoxville: University of Tennessee Press, 1992. Kramer's analysis of the novel is one of thirteen essays detailing the full range of Agee's writings.

Madden, David, ed. *Remembering James Agee.* Baton Rouge: Louisiana State University Press, 1974. Includes essays and recollections by Agee's friends, which provide human dimensions to the novel.

Moreau, Geneviève. *The Restless Journey of James Agee.* Translated by Miriam Kleiger. New York: William Morrow, 1977. A sensitive portrayal of Agee and his work.

Death in Venice

Author: Thomas Mann (1875-1955)
First published: Der Tod in Venedig, 1912 (English translation, 1925)
Type of work: Novella
Type of plot: Symbolic realism
Time of plot: Early twentieth century
Locale: Italy

Principal characters:
GUSTAV VON ASCHENBACH, a middle-aged German writer
TADZIO, a young Polish boy

The Story:

Gustav von Aschenbach is a distinguished German writer whose work brings him world fame and a patina of nobility from a grateful government. His career is honorable and dignified. A man of ambitious nature, unmarried, he lives a life of personal discipline and dedication to his art. In portraying heroes who combine the forcefulness of a Frederick the Great with the selfless striving of a Saint Sebastian, he believes that he speaks for his race as well as for the deathless human spirit. However, his devotion to the ideals of duty and achievement bring him close to physical collapse.

One day, after a morning spent at his desk, he leaves his house in Munich and goes for a walk. His stroll takes him as far as a cemetery on the outskirts of the city. While he waits for a streetcar to take him back to town, he suddenly becomes aware of a man who stands watching him from the doorway of the mortuary chapel. The stranger, who has a rucksack on his back and a walking staff in his hand, is evidently a traveler. Although no word passes between watcher and watched, Aschenbach feels a sudden desire to take a trip, to leave the cold, wet German spring for the warmer climate of the Mediterranean lands. His impulse is strengthened by the fact that he encountered a problem of technique that he is unable to solve in his writing. He decides to take a holiday and leave his work for a time, hoping to find relaxation for mind and body in Italy.

He goes first to an island resort in the Adriatic but becomes bored with his surroundings before too long and books passage for Venice. On the ship, he encounters a party of lively young clerks from Pola. With them is an old man whose dyed hair and rouged cheeks make him a ridiculous but sinister caricature of youth. In his disgust, Aschenbach fails to notice that the raddled old man bears a vague resemblance to the traveler he saw at the cemetery in Munich.

Aschenbach's destination is the Lido. At the dock in Venice, he transfers to a gondola that takes him by the water route to his Lido hotel. The gondolier speaks and acts so strangely that Aschenbach becomes disturbed. Because of his agitation, he never notices that the man looks something like the drunk old scarecrow on the ship and the silent stranger at the cemetery. After taking his passenger to the landing stage, the gondolier, without waiting for his money, hastily rows away. Other boatmen suggest that he might have been afraid of the law because he has no license.

Aschenbach stays at the Hotel des Bains. That night, shortly before dinner, his attention is drawn to a Polish family, which consists of a beautiful mother, three daughters, and a handsome boy of about fourteen. Aschenbach is unaccountably attracted to the youngster, so much so that he continues to watch the family throughout his meal. The next morning, he sees the boy playing with some companions on the beach. His name, as Aschenbach learns while watching their games, is Tadzio.

Disturbed by the appeal the boy has for him, the writer decides to return home. On his arrival at the railroad station in Venice, however, he discovers that his trunks were misdirected to Como. There is nothing for him to do but wait for his missing luggage to turn up, so he goes back to the hotel. Although he despises himself for his vacillation, he realizes that his true desire is to be near Tadzio. For Aschenbach there begins a period of happiness in watching the boy and anguish in knowing they must remain strangers. One day, he almost

summons up enough courage to speak to the boy. A moment later, he becomes panic-stricken for fear that Tadzio might be alarmed by an older man's interest. The time Aschenbach set for his holiday passes, but the writer almost forgets his home and his work. One evening, Tadzio smiles at him as they pass each other. Aschenbach trembles with pleasure.

Guests begin to leave the hotel; there are rumors that a plague is breaking out in nearby cities. While loitering one day on the Piazza, Aschenbach detects the sweetish odor of disinfectant in the air, for the authorities are beginning to take precautions against an outbreak of the plague in Venice. Aschenbach stubbornly decides to stay on despite the dangers of infection.

A band of entertainers comes to the hotel to serenade the guests. In the troupe is an impudent, disreputable-looking street singer whose antics and ballads are insulting and obscene. As he passes among the guests to collect money for the performance, Aschenbach detects on his clothing the almost overpowering smell of disinfectant, an odor suggesting the sweetly corruptive taints of lust and death. The ribald comedian also bears a strange similarity to the gondolier, the rouged old rake, and the silent traveler whose disturbing presence gave Aschenbach the idea for his holiday. Aschenbach is torn between fear and desire. The next day, he goes to a tourist agency where a young clerk tells him that people are dying of the plague in Venice. Even that confirmation of his fears fails to speed Aschenbach's departure from the city. That night, he dreams that in a fetid jungle, surrounded by naked orgiasts, he is taking part in horrible, Priapean rites.

By that time his deterioration is almost complete. Even though he allows a barber to dye his hair and tint his cheeks, he still refuses to see the likeness between himself and the raddled old fop whose appearance disgusted him on shipboard. His behavior becomes more reckless. One afternoon, he follows the Polish family into Venice and trails them through the city streets. Hungry and thirsty after his exercise, he buys some overripe strawberries at an open stall and eats them. The odor of disinfectant is strong on the sultry breeze.

Several days later, Aschenbach goes down to the beach where Tadzio is playing with three or four other boys. They begin to fight, and one of the boys throws Tadzio to the ground and presses his face into the sand. As Aschenbach is about to interfere, the other boy releases his victim. Humiliated and hurt, Tadzio walks down to the water. He stands facing seaward for a time, as remote and isolated as a young Saint Sebastian, then he turns and looks with a somber, secret gaze at Aschenbach, who is watching from his beach chair. To the writer, it seems as though the boy is summoning him.

He starts to rise but becomes so giddy that he falls back into his chair. Attendants carry him to his room. That night, the world learns that the great Gustav von Aschenbach died suddenly of the plague in Venice.

Critical Evaluation:

Together with James Joyce and Marcel Proust, Thomas Mann is often considered one of the great writers of the early twentieth century. Mann, who was awarded the Nobel Prize in Literature in 1919, was born into an upper-middle-class German family and left his country in 1933 because of his opposition to Adolf Hitler and the Nazi regime. He later came to the United States, where he taught and lectured. A scholar as well as an artist, Mann shows in his works the influence of such diverse thinkers as Friedrich Nietzsche, Arthur Schopenhauer, Richard Wagner, and Sigmund Freud. The problem of the artist's role in a decadent, industrialized society is a recurring theme in many of his works, including *Buddenbrooks* (1901), *Tonio Kröger* (1903), *Death in Venice*, and *Der Zauberberg* (1924; *The Magic Mountain*, 1927).

Death in Venice, Mann's best-known novella, is a complex, beautifully wrought tale dealing with the eternal conflict between the forces of death and decay and the human attempts to achieve permanence through art. Mann portrays the final triumph of death and decay, but not before the hero, Gustav von Aschenbach, has experienced an escape into the eternal beauty created by the imagination of the artist. The escape of the famous writer is accomplished, however, not by his own writings but by the art of his creator, Mann. Form and order do finally impose themselves on the chaos of his life; corruption and death are transformed into the purity of artistic beauty.

The characterization of a literary hero of his age is subtle and complex. Author of prose epics, philosophical novels, novels of moral resolution, and aesthetics, Aschenbach has created the hero for his generation. He is aware that his success and talent rely on a basis of physical stamina as well as of moral and mental discipline, and his work is a product of strain, endurance, intellectual tenacity, and spasms of will. He recognizes, however, that his writing has been to some degree a "pursuit of fame" at the expense of turning his back on a full search for truth. As the novella opens, Aschenbach is exhausted and no longer finding joy in his craft; he has become aware of approaching old age and death and is faced with the fear of not having time to finish everything he desires to write. Restlessly walking in the beauty of the English Garden of Munich, Aschenbach is inspired to leave his relatively rootless life on a pilgrimage for artistic renewal in Venice, the perfect symbol of human art imposed on nature's chaos. This journey motif begins with his glimpse of a stranger in a cemetery, a foreigner with a skull-like face and a certain animal ruthlessness.

Arriving at the port of Venice, he discovers that his gondolier is taking him out to sea rather than into the city; the gondolier's physical description ominously echoes that of the stranger of the cemetery. The gondola itself is specifically compared to a black coffin. The trip becomes the archetypal journey of life to death and of a man into the depths of himself. Aschenbach discovers Venice, the symbol of perfect art in his memory, to be dirty, infected, corrupt, and permeated by the odor of the human disease and pollution spread in the natural swamp on which the artifice is built. Aschenbach's own transformation to a "foreigner," one who belongs in Venice, is accomplished at an increasingly mad tempo after the moment when, turning his back on the possibility of escaping Venice by train, he collapses at a fountain in the heart of the city. His death becomes almost self-willed; he dies not because of the plague, not because of his love of Tadzio, but because of his will to live and to create atrophy.

The exterior events of the story, which are minimal, can be properly explained only in terms of the inner conflict of the artist. To produce art, Aschenbach believes he must practice absolute self-denial, affirming the dignity and moral capacity of the individual in the face of a world of self-indulgence that leads to personal abasement. However, he is also a man and, as such, has drives connecting him to the chaos of the formless elements of nature. This inner conflict is objectified in the boy Tadzio, who embodies all that Aschenbach has rejected in fifty long years of dedication to Apollonian art. As his desire for Tadzio becomes obsessive and drives him to neglect his body and dignity, disintegration sets in and death becomes irrevocable. Subconsciously, Aschenbach is choosing to pursue the basic sensual, Dionysian side of himself that he has always denied.

Mann uses dream visions to underline and clarify Aschenbach's subconscious conflicts. His first hallucination of the crouching beast in the jungle is evoked by the glimpse of the stranger at the Byzantine chapel in Munich. This vision literally foreshadows the trip to Venice and metaphorically foreshadows the inner journey during which Aschenbach discovers the jungle and beast within himself. The second vision on the beach in Venice, in the form of a Platonic dialogue, explores the interrelatedness of art, love, and beauty with human bestiality. In a third major dream hallucination, Aschenbach is initiated into the worship of the Dionysian rite and finally glimpses "the stranger god" of sensual experience, formless chaotic joy, and excesses of emotion. The most striking vision occurs at the end of the novella, when Aschenbach, viewing the amoral beauty of perfection of form in Tadzio silhouetted against the amoral, formless beauty of the sea, accepts the promise inherent in the sea's chaos as the equivalent of the beauty produced by order and moral discipline. Readers assume the vision to be objective reality until brought sharply and suddenly into the present reality of Aschenbach's dead body. Ernest Hemingway used this same technique later in his own novella-length study of death and art, "The Snows of Kilimanjaro" (1961).

Mann's use of natural, geographical symbols also underlines the central conflicts of the novella. Aschenbach identifies the discipline of his art with Munich, a city of northern Europe, and with the snowy mountains. These places are associated with health, energy, reason, will, and Apollonian creative power. Against them, Mann juxtaposes the tropical marshes, the jungle animal and plant life, the Indian plague, the sun and the sea, which are associated with Dionysian excesses of emotion and ecstasy in art. The beast, the jungle, the plague, chaos lie within the nature of humanity and art just as clearly as do mountains, self-denial, will, and reason, qualities that enable human beings to construct artifice upon the chaos of nature. Great art, Nietzsche says in *Die Geburt der Tragödie aus dem Geiste der Musik* (1872; *The Birth of Tragedy out of the Spirit of Music*, 1909), is a product of the fusion rather than the separation of the calm, ordered, contemplative spirit of Apollo and the savage, sensual ecstasy of Dionysus. This is what both Aschenbach and the reader discover in Mann's *Death in Venice*.

"Critical Evaluation" by Ann E. Reynolds

Further Reading

Cohn, Dorrit. "The Second Author in *Der Tod in Venedig*." In *Critical Essays on Thomas Mann*, compiled by Inta M. Ezergailis. Boston: G. K. Hall, 1988. An examination of the highly ironic relationship between the narrator of the story and his protagonist, Gustav von Aschenbach. An excellent example of close textual analysis of one specific aspect of the novella.

Heller, Erich. "The Embarrassed Muse." In *Thomas Mann: The Ironic German*. 1958. Reprint. South Bend, Ind.: Regnery/Gateway, 1979. Places the novella in the context of Mann's other works before embarking on a detailed discussion of the irony Mann employs in the narrative. Heller pays special attention to the story's focus on art and the artist.

Kurzke, Hermann. *Thomas Mann: Life as a Work of Art, a Biography*. Translated by Leslie Willson. Princeton, N.J.: Princeton University Press, 2002. An English translation of a work that was celebrated upon its publication in Germany. Kurzke provides a balanced approach to Mann's life and work, and he addresses Mann's homosexuality and relationship to Judaism.

Lehnert, Herbert, and Eva Wessell, eds. *A Companion to the Works of Thomas Mann*. Rochester, N.Y.: Camden House, 2004. A collection of essays about the range of Mann's work, including discussions of his late politics, female identities and autobiographical impulses in his writings, and an analysis of *Death in Venice*.

Mundt, Hannelore. *Understanding Thomas Mann*. Columbia: University of South Carolina Press, 2004. Mundt discusses the themes, concerns, presentation, and meanings of many of Mann's works, using his later published diaries as one of the sources for her analysis. Chapter 6 is devoted to *Death in Venice*.

Reed, T. J. *"Death in Venice": Making and Unmaking a Master*. New York: Twayne, 1994. One of the best general overviews of the story with sections on literary and historical context, good close readings, and a look at the story's genesis and its relationship to Mann and German history. Includes an annotated bibliography.

Robertson, Ritchie, ed. *The Cambridge Companion to Thomas Mann*. New York: Cambridge University Press, 2002. A collection of essays, some analyzing individual works and others discussing Mann's intellectual world, Mann and history, his literary techniques, and his representation of gender and sexuality. *Death in Venice* is analyzed in chapter 6.

Shookman, Ellis. *Thomas Mann's Death in Venice: A Novella and Its Critics*. Rochester, N.Y.: Camden House, 2003. Shookman chronologically chronicles the literary reception of Mann's novella from its initial publication in 1912 to criticism appearing from 1996 through 2001. Some of the critics included are authors D. H. Lawrence, Mario Vargas Llosa, and Mann himself.

_____. *Thomas Mann's "Death in Venice": A Reference Guide*. Westport, Conn.: Greenwood Press, 2004. Aimed at students and general readers, the guide provides a plot summary and discusses the novella's context, ideas, narrative art, and reception.

Weiner, Marc A. "Music and Repression: *Death in Venice*." In *Undertones of Insurrection: Music, Politics, and the Social Sphere in the Modern German Narrative*. Lincoln: University of Nebraska Press, 1993. A brief but thorough analysis of musical tropes and meanings in the novella. Focuses on interpretation and provides an excellent discussion of the musical aspects of *Death in Venice*.

Death of a Hero

Author: Richard Aldington (1892-1962)
First published: 1929
Type of work: Novel
Type of plot: Political
Time of plot: World War I
Locale: England

Principal characters:
GEORGE WINTERBOURNE, the protagonist
MR. GEORGE WINTERBOURNE, his father
MRS. GEORGE WINTERBOURNE, his mother
ELIZABETH, his wife
FANNY WELFORD, his mistress

The Story:

When word comes that George Winterbourne was killed in the war, his friend tries to reconstruct the life of the dead man to see what forces caused his death. The friend served with George at various times during the war, and it is his belief that George deliberately exposed himself to German fire because he no longer wanted to live.

George's father is a sentimental fool and his mother a depraved wanton. The elder Winterbourne married primarily to spite his dominating mother, and his bride married him under the mistaken notion that he was rich. They resigned themselves to mutual hatred, and the mother showered her thwarted love on young George. She imagined herself young and desirable and was proud of her twenty-two lovers. Her husband went to a hotel when she was entertaining, but he prayed for her soul. They were the most depressing parents to whom a child could be exposed, and they caused young George to hate them both. Soon after receiving word of their son's death, the elder Winterbourne is killed in an accident. After thoroughly enjoying her role as a bereft mother and widow, Mrs. Winterbourne marries her twenty-second lover and moves to Australia.

By the time he reached young manhood, George mingled with all sorts of unusual people. He dabbled in writing and painting, and sexual freedom was his goal, even though he experienced little of it. At the home of some pseudointellectual friends, he first met Elizabeth. They were immediately compatible: Both hated their parents, and both sought freedom. At first, Elizabeth was shocked by George's attacks on Christianity, morals, the class system, and all other established institutions, but she decided that he was a truly "free" man. In fact, it was not long before she adopted his ideas; soon free love was the only thing she would talk or think about.

George and Elizabeth considered themselves extremely sensible. They did not talk of love, only sex, and they saw no reason why they should marry to experience sex as long as they were careful not to have a baby. They decided that there would be no sordidness to cloud their affair, and that they

were both free to take all the other lovers they pleased. That was freedom in an intelligent way. Elizabeth was even more insistent of that than George.

When, however, Elizabeth mistakenly thought that she was pregnant, her progressive ideas disappeared and she insisted that George marry her at once for the sake of her honor and reputation. They were married, much to the horror of their families. When Elizabeth learned that she was not pregnant—in fact, the doctor told her that she could not possibly have a child without an operation—her old ideas returned. She became an evangelist for sex, even though she detested the word. Marriage made no difference in George's and Elizabeth's lives. They continued to live separately and to meet as lovers.

When Elizabeth made a trip home, George became the lover of her best friend, Fanny Welford, another enlightened woman. He was sure that Elizabeth would not mind, for she had become the mistress of Fanny's lover, but to his surprise Elizabeth created a scene over Fanny. On the surface, the young women remained friends, each unwilling to admit a bourgeois dislike of the situation.

When war broke out, George was drafted and immediately sent to France. The war and the killing horrified George, and obsessively he began to think about his own death. He was brave, but not from any desire to be a hero; rather, the monotony of his existence seemed to demand that he keep going even though he was ready to drop from fatigue. The knowledge of the ill-concealed dislike between Fanny and Elizabeth began to prey on his mind. There seemed to be only two solutions: To drift along and accept whatever happened or to get himself killed in the war. It seemed to make little difference to him or anyone else which course he chose. His letters to his two women depressed each of them. He could have spared himself his anxiety, for each took other lovers and gave little thought to George.

George's depression increased. He felt that he was degenerating mentally as well as physically and that he was wasting what should have been his best years. He knew that he would be terribly handicapped if he did live through the war, that those not serving would pass him by.

George was made an officer and sent back to England for training. There he lived again with Elizabeth, but she left him frequently to go out with other men. Fanny, too, seemed to care little whether she saw him or not. Talk of the war and his experiences obviously bored them, and they made only a small pretense of interest. He spent his last night in England with Fanny while Elizabeth was off with someone else. Fanny did not bother to get up with him the morning he left. She awoke lazily and went back to sleep again before he even left the flat.

Back at the front, George found that he was ill-suited to command a company. Although he did his best, he was constantly censured by his colonel, who blamed George for all the faults of his untrained and cowardly troops. George could think of little but death. During a particularly heavy German shelling, he simply stood up and let the bullets smash into his chest.

Critical Evaluation:

Although two-thirds of *Death of a Hero* is concerned with the life of George Winterbourne before World War I, the novel presents the prewar era as a prelude to the great catastrophe that followed. Richard Aldington leaves no doubt about the ultimate target of his satire, vociferously denouncing the hypocritical Victorian platitudes that held killing to be chivalrous and erotic love to be shameful: "It was the regime of Cant before the War which made the Cant during the War so damnably possible and easy." Although Aldington blames the war on the older generation, he finds the younger generation, including the supposedly enlightened intelligentsia, almost equally guilty. Not only was the conduct of the war itself dishonest, he claims, but it was also the expression of a pervasive dishonesty in English society.

Death of a Hero is more than simply a war novel, for it treats the experience of the whole generation of men who fought in the war and makes an urgent appeal for a less repressive society. The events of the book are closely based on Aldington's personal experiences both as a member of the avant-garde in prewar England and as a runner and officer during the war, yet the novel presents George Winterbourne's experience as representative. His death is ambiguous: Although his final act is clearly suicidal, the implication is that he has been driven to it by the tragic fate of the young men of his time whom society had denied such basic necessities as love and truth.

George's death takes place on the same day as that of Wilfred Owen (1893-1918), the preeminent poet of "the pity

of war," on November 4, 1918, just one week before the armistice. Owen's poems, like *Death of a Hero*, gave expression to the camaraderie between fighting men and the great psychological abyss that the war experience opened between soldiers and civilians.

In his section headings Aldington suggests that his novel is constructed like a symphony, with four movements (a prologue and three parts) in progressively slower tempos: allegretto, vivace, andante cantabile, and adagio. In the prefatory letter to Halcott Glover, however, Aldington also describes it as a jazz novel, constructed on principles such as those he had used for his long poem *A Fool i' the Forest* (1924). Although certain musical motifs are brilliantly used in the descriptions of bombardment in part 3, it is difficult to see how the musical analogy functions continuously to give the novel its form, and the tempo indications seem superfluous to the reading experience.

In part 1, it is clear that Aldington wants to make his characters, especially George's contemptible parents, stand for all of society. To have drawn them three-dimensionally might have detracted from that purpose, but his presenting them as caricatures makes it difficult for the reader to find them interesting or significant, especially as the war episode (which gives point to Aldington's satire) is yet to come. The reader feels that these "grotesques," as Aldington describes them, are made of straw—targets too trivial to warrant such lurid invective.

Part 2 further shows how George is betrayed by those who profess to care about him. Although George's love interests, Elizabeth and Fanny, at first appear to be more sympathetic and human than his parents, they, too, eventually betray George and come to stand in contrast to the comparatively guileless, trusting protagonist. Several of Aldington's famous literary friends appear in this section as amusing, absurdly self-absorbed, and pretentious characters in George's London bohemian set—the poet Ezra Pound as the sculptor Upjohn, the novelist D. H. Lawrence as Comrade Bobbe, and the poet T. S. Eliot as Waldo Tubbe.

Only when George enters the army does he find companions whose simple courage is admirable and inspiring. His commanding officer, Evans, is honest and hardworking, yet he would certainly have been an object of scorn had he appeared in parts 1 or 2. Here, however, he is a sympathetic character, suggesting that the war somehow humanizes men and enables them to transcend cant. The war section, which includes vivid descriptions of the horror of the trenches, has generally been considered to be the most effective and praiseworthy of the novel's three parts. Aldington's skill as a poet, even as an Imagist poet devoted to precise description and fresh cadences, has been perceived in his magnificent accounts of bombardment and combat.

Aldington was well known in literary circles as a poet, but his first novel made him famous on both sides of the Atlantic, for although it received mixed reviews in the press, it was an immediate best-seller. (An unexpurgated edition was published in France in 1930 though most of the phrases that the original publishers had censored were far from offensive.) *Death of a Hero* was in the vanguard of a great wave of literature about World War I that began to appear in 1929, after a decade in which there had been little interest in war writing. The work remains one of the more distinguished contributions to this body of work, although it has received only modest critical attention. In retrospect, it is clear that it gave early expression to the major themes of World War I prose and shows unusual insight into such frequently neglected questions as the relationship between the war and changing attitudes toward women and sexuality. Some writers were, however, able to find more satisfactory solutions to the problem of expressing protest against the war than the fierce invective that often interrupts the narrative in *Death of a Hero*.

Most commentary on Aldington's work tends to concentrate either on his notorious biographical works or on his role in the Imagist movement. Both the novel's admirers and its detractors tend to react to the same quality: its relentless ferocity. The narrator at times almost browbeats the reader, and Bernard Bergonzi compares the novel unfavorably with more patient denunciations of the war such as Robert Graves's *Goodbye to All That* (1929) and Edmund Blunden's *Undertones of War* (1928). For its admirers, however, it is precisely as a novel whose flaws are owing to its overwhelming bitterness that it gives a voice to the "lost generation."

"Critical Evaluation" by Matthew Parfitt

Further Reading

Ayers, David. "Proto-Fascism of Richard Aldington's *Death of a Hero*." In *English Literature of the 1920's*. Edinburgh: Edinburgh University Press, 1999. Ayers's examination of *Death of a Hero* focuses on the novel's relationship to fascism and its treatment of war, women, and male-male relations.

Bergonzi, Bernard. *Heroes' Twilight: A Study of the Literature of the Great War*. New York: Coward, McCann, 1966.

Bergonzi devotes several pages of this readable and wide-ranging study to *Death of a Hero*, arguing that the novel suffers from the author's lack of detachment from his subject.

Doyle, Charles. "Port-Cros and After, 1928-1929." In *Richard Aldington: A Biography*. Carbondale: Southern Illinois University Press, 1989. Includes a substantial, balanced discussion of *Death of a Hero*, with critical commentary on its principal themes and literary merits. Acknowledges the stylistic flaws but argues that the novel played an essential role in the "imaginative reconstruction" of the war.

McGreevy, Thomas. *Richard Aldington: An Englishman*. London: Chatto & Windus, 1931. McGreevy, a personal friend of Aldington, includes an extensive, if rather subjective, study of *Death of a Hero*. Focuses on the novel's formal characteristics.

Morris, John. "Richard Aldington and *Death of a Hero*—or Life of an Anti-Hero?" In *The First World War in Fiction: A Collection of Critical Essays*, edited by Holger Klein. New York: Barnes & Noble, 1977. Judicious and attentive critique of the novel, with a particular focus on the problems of satiric tone.

Smith, Richard Eugene. *Richard Aldington*. Boston: Twayne, 1977. An accessible introduction to Aldington's life and works. Includes a chapter on *Death of a Hero* and a useful bibliography of criticism to 1976.

Willis, J. H., Jr. "The Censored Language of War: Richard Aldington's *Death of a Hero* and Three Other War Novels of 1929." *Twentieth Century Literature* 45, no. 4 (Winter, 1999): 467. Critiques four novels written after World War I—Aldington's *Death of a Hero*, Ernest Hemingway's *A Farewell to Arms*, Erich Maria Remarque's *All Quiet on the Western Front*, and Frederick Manning's *The Middle Parts of Fortune*—to demonstrate how these authors responded to the obscenity laws of the 1920's, which made it difficult for writers to portray the bitter experiences of modern warfare realistically.

Zilboorg, Caroline. "'What Part Have I Now That You Have Come Together?': Richard Aldington on War, Gender, and Textual Representation." In *Gender and Warfare in the Twentieth Century: Textual Representations*, edited by Angela K. Smith. New York: Manchester University Press, 2004. Analysis of *Death of a Hero*, focusing on its treatment of World War I and the relationships between men and women during the war.

Death of a Salesman

Author: Arthur Miller (1915-2005)
First produced: 1949; first published, 1949
Type of work: Drama
Type of plot: Tragedy
Time of plot: 1940's
Locale: New York and Boston

Principal characters:
WILLY LOMAN, a traveling salesman
LINDA, his wife
BIFF, their older son
HAPPY, their younger son
CHARLEY, their neighbor
BERNARD, Charley's son
UNCLE BEN, Willy's successful brother
HOWARD WAGNER, Willy's boss

The Story:

Very late one night, having that morning set out on a sales trip to Portland, Maine, Willy Loman returns to his Brooklyn home because he repeatedly drove his car off the side of the road. Now sixty-three years old, Willy has worked as a traveling salesman for the Wagner Company for more than thirty years. Of late, his sales have declined because his old customers are dying or retiring. The company takes away his salary to make him work on straight commission. His wife, Linda, comforts Willy when he returns and encourages him to ask Howard Wagner for a position in the New York office, where he will not have to travel and can once again earn a guaranteed salary.

Upstairs in their old bedroom, Willy's sons, Biff and Happy, reminisce about their happier times as adolescents and talk about how disappointing their lives are. At thirty-four years of age, Biff has held many different kinds of jobs since leaving high school, and he feels that he is not progressing toward anything. He was a high school football star but did not win a college scholarship because he failed a mathematics course and refused to make up the credits to graduate at summer school. Biff has just returned home from working on a farm in Texas, and that morning Willy already begins criticizing him about his failure to make money and to find a prestigious profession. Biff's younger brother, Happy, remains in New York City, working in a low-level sales position and spending most of his time seducing women. As they talk, Biff and Happy decide they can be successful and much happier if they go into business together.

While Biff and Happy talk upstairs, Willy sits in the kitchen and talks loudly to himself, reliving moments from his past: Biff preparing for an important football game, Biff and Happy cleaning the family car, Willy's own joy in working with his hands on projects around the house, and his afternoons in a hotel room with a woman on one of his sales trips to Boston. Eventually, Willy's neighbor, Charley,

comes over from next door. As Charley and Willy talk and play cards, Willy imagines that he is talking to his older brother, Ben, who once invited Willy to join him in Alaska to make his fortune. After Charley returns home, Willy moves outside, still caught up in his imagined conversation. Linda comes back downstairs and tells Biff and Happy of her fear that Willy is planning to kill himself; she had discovered a piece of rubber hose connected to a gas pipe in the basement. When Willy comes back into the house, the conversation turns to the dreams Willy has of Biff becoming a successful salesman and an entrepreneur. At Willy's urging, the family agrees that the next morning Biff should see Bill Oliver, one of his former bosses, and ask for a loan to start a sporting goods business.

The next morning, Willy goes to his own boss, Wagner, to ask for a position in the New York office. Instead of getting a new position, however, he is fired from his job. Willy leaves Wagner's office and goes to Charley's office to ask for a loan to pay his bills. There he encounters Charley's son, Bernard, a boyhood friend of Biff and Happy and now a successful lawyer arguing cases in front of the Supreme Court. Willy asks how Bernard managed to succeed when Biff and Happy failed, but Bernard asks why Biff, after flunking mathematics, never went to summer school so as to graduate from high school.

Happy goes to a local restaurant to arrange a dinner to celebrate Biff's successful meeting with Mr. Oliver, but when Biff arrives he reports that Mr. Oliver did not remember him and that, in his anger, Biff impulsively stole Mr. Oliver's fountain pen. When, however, he hears his father's news that he was fired, Biff lies about his meeting with Mr. Oliver and, to console his father, describes it as a success. Happy arranges for two women to join them at the restaurant. When Willy goes to the washroom, Biff and Happy leave the restaurant with the two women and abandon their father. In the washroom, Willy has a flashback and remembers the time, right after Biff flunked his mathematics course, when Biff came to Boston on a surprise visit and caught Willy with another woman in his hotel room. It was this discovery that kept Biff from going to summer school and from graduating from high school.

After leaving the restaurant, Willy decides on the way home that the best way he can provide for his wife and sons is to commit suicide, so that the life insurance settlement of twenty thousand dollars would come to them after his death. Happy and Biff return home from their dates with the two women and are greeted by Linda's reprimand for abandoning Willy at the restaurant. Biff responds angrily, accusing Willy and Happy of not facing the reality of their ordinary lives. He claims that he finally understands himself and will go back to farming and working with his hands, outdoors, where he is genuinely happy. This emotional confrontation ends with Biff crying on his father's shoulder. Moved by his son's display of affection, Willy leaves the house and drives the car to his death. In the play's last scene, in the cemetery after Willy's funeral, Linda talks to Willy over his grave and reflects on the irony that he killed himself just as they finished paying for their house.

Critical Evaluation:

Following in the tradition of the classic Norwegian playwright Henrik Ibsen, Arthur Miller is concerned above all with the relationship between the individual and society. His investigations range from his portrait of the industrialist Joe Keller in *All My Sons* (1947), who sacrifices the safety of World War II fighter pilots and ruins his business partner to satisfy his desire for financial success, to examining the connection between the dysfunctional marriage of Sylvia and Phillip Gellburg and the rise of Nazism in *Broken Glass* (1994). In *Death of a Salesman*, Miller focuses on the relationship between society and the individual's concept of self. As a consequence of living in a capitalistic society that emphasizes materialistic values, Willy Loman has a defective sense of self. He is obsessed not only with financial success but also, more specifically, with appearances and impressions and with being considered important and "well-liked" by others. Willy passes these superficial values on to his two sons, Biff and Happy. In the course of the play, Biff becomes more aware of his real needs and feelings and frees himself from this destructive concept of self. Only then is Biff able to care more deeply for his father, and he breaks down and cries in his arms. Willy is moved by his son's love, but his understanding is incomplete, as becomes clear when he commits suicide under the impression that this is the only way to give

Biff financial prosperity. At the play's end it is clear that Biff will heal himself and go back out West to find work that suits his genuine concept of self, while Happy will probably repeat the misdirected life of his father.

Miller's plays often mix his characteristically realistic style with expressionistic techniques. In *Death of a Salesman*, he enhances the theme of self-awareness by using techniques to distort time and space and to represent the working of Willy's mind. While playing cards with his neighbor Charlie, for example, Willy imagines that he sees his brother Ben, who appears on the stage as if he were a real person. By allowing the past and the present to intermingle freely, Miller represents the confusion and distress in Willy's mind. In fact, Miller's working title for the play was "The Inside of His Head" and his original concept for the stage set was a model of an enormous face, inside of which the action was to take place. In having the action follow and portray Willy's meandering mind, Miller creates a psychological quality that reflects Willy's confusion about identity. As Willy's mind wanders in his past, talking to his brother Ben or remembering building projects around the house, Willy's true self is revealed. He is a man who loves to work outdoors with his hands, the kind of man that Biff finally comes to accept as his true self. As Biff says over Willy's grave, "there's more of him in that front stoop than in all the sales he ever made."

Death of a Salesman is of crucial importance to literature because it once again raises the question whether tragedy is possible with a common hero. The Aristotelian concept of tragedy, which dominated dramatic literature until the nineteenth century, insists that only characters of noble birth or soul can be tragic heroes. In the eighteenth and nineteenth centuries, however, an increasing number of plays with tragic endings were written about common people. In 1949, concurrent with his play's appearance on Broadway, Miller published a defense of the play as a genuine tragedy in the essay "Tragedy and the Common Man," in which he argued that all that is required for tragic stature is a hero willing to "lay down his life" to secure "his 'rightful' position in his society."

Miller won a Pulitzer Prize in drama in 1949 for *Death of a Salesman*, and for many years thereafter he was considered, alongside Eugene O'Neill and Tennessee Williams, one of America's greatest playwrights. Of his many subsequent plays, perhaps only *The Crucible* (1953) and *After the Fall* (1964) had comparable popular and critical impacts. Undoubtedly his masterpiece, *Death of a Salesman* remains Miller's most enduring work.

Terry Nienhuis

Further Reading

Abbotson, Susan C. W. *Critical Companion to Arthur Miller: A Literary Reference to His Life and Work.* New York: Facts On File, 2007. Includes a biography and dictionary-style entries about Miller's works and related subjects, such as the concepts, people, places, and genres in his plays. The entries about his works provide synopses, critical commentary, initial reviews, and performance histories.

Bigsby, Christopher. *Arthur Miller: A Critical Study.* New York: Cambridge University Press, 2005. Bigsby, who has written extensively about Miller, provides in-depth examinations of all of Miller's work, including a chapter on *Death of a Salesman.*

Bloom, Harold, ed. *Arthur Miller's "Death of a Salesman."* Updated ed. New York: Chelsea House, 2007. Collection of critical essays about *Death of a Salesman*, including discussions of family values, Miller's poetic use of demotic English, and shame, guilt, empathy, and the search for identity in the play. Includes an essay with Miller on the occasion of the play's fiftieth anniversary.

_____. *Willy Loman.* New York: Chelsea House, 1991. A collection of sixteen extracts from books and articles, with ten complete essays providing an excellent selection of criticism focusing on Willy as a literary character. Includes a provocative introduction by Bloom in which he discusses Willy as a tragic hero.

Carson, Neil. *Arthur Miller.* 2d ed. New York: Palgrave Macmillan, 2008. Provides critical analyses of all of Miller's work, including a chapter on *Death of a Salesman.*

Dukore, Bernard F. *"Death of a Salesman" and "The Crucible."* Atlantic Highlands, N.J.: Humanities Press International, 1989. An excellent introduction for beginning students. Analyzes the text from both literary and theatrical perspectives and examines selected productions of the play to demonstrate the rich embodiment of literary ideas.

Hays, Peter L., and Kent Nicholson. *Arthur Miller's "Death of a Salesman."* London: Continuum, 2008. An introduction to the play, designed for students. Provides information about the play's background, context, structure, style, characters, and production history.

Koon, Helene Wickham, ed. *Twentieth Century Interpretations of "Death of a Salesman."* Englewood Cliffs, N.J.: Prentice Hall, 1983. An anthology of ten essays that provides a wide variety of critical approaches to the play. A standard source.

Mason, Jeffrey D. *Stone Tower: The Political Theater of Arthur Miller.* Ann Arbor: University of Michigan Press, 2008. Argues that Miller is essentially a political playwright and that *Death of a Salesman* examines political issues in personal terms

Miller, Arthur. *"Salesman" in Beijing.* New York: Viking Press, 1984. Miller's fascinating and highly readable diary account of the famous production he directed of *Death of a Salesman* in Beijing, China, in 1983, where the universality of the play became most evident. Includes photographs by his wife, Inge Morath.

Murphy, Brenda. *Miller: "Death of a Salesman."* New York: Cambridge University Press, 1995. Chronicles the history of significant productions of the play in English and in other languages, discussing film, radio, and television adaptations as well as stage presentations.

Roudané, Matthew C., ed. *Conversations with Arthur Miller.* Jackson: University Press of Mississippi, 1987. Transcriptions of thirty-nine interviews with Miller conducted between 1947 and 1986. Notable for personal insights into Miller and the productions of his plays. The interviews persistently return to questions concerning *Death of a Salesman* and Miller's theories on tragedy.

The Death of Artemio Cruz

Author: Carlos Fuentes (1928-   )
First published: La muerte de Artemio Cruz, 1962
   (English translation, 1964)
Type of work: Novel
Type of plot: Social realism
Time of plot: 1889-1959
Locale: Mexico

Principal characters:
ARTEMIO CRUZ, a dying tycoon
CATALINA, his wife
LORENZO, his son, who is killed in the Spanish Civil War
TERESA, his daughter
GLORIA, his granddaughter
GERARDO, his son-in-law
DON GAMALIEL BERNAL, his father-in-law
GONZALO BERNAL, a young lawyer executed by Villistas
FATHER PAEZ, a priest
REGINA, a dead woman Artemio had loved
LILIA and LAURA, Artemio's mistresses
PADILLA, Artemio's secretary
LUNERO, a mulatto peon

The Story:

Artemio Cruz is on his deathbed, stricken by a gastric attack upon his return from a business trip to Hermosillo on April 9, 1959. As he lies in his mansion in a fashionable section of Mexico City, the stench in his nostrils is as much from the moral corruption of his life as from the processes of decay already at work in his body. Disregarding Cruz's protests, who abandoned the church years before, an officious priest tries to administer the last sacrament. Doctors subject him to indignities with their instruments as they examine his body. In the background stands his estranged wife and the daughter who despises him. Although they pretend concern for the dying man, their greatest anxiety concerns his will, and he refuses to tell them where he put it. His only hold on reality is a tape recording with an account of business deals and proposed transactions, which his secretary, Padilla, plays for him. While the people jostle about in his room, Artemio drifts between past and present in a series of flashbacks tracing the events that brought him to his present state.

In 1919, he was an ambitious young veteran of the revolution arriving at the home of the Bernal family in Perales. Ostensibly he was there to bring to a bereaved father and sister an account of Gonzalo Bernal's death before a Villista firing squad. In reality, he meant to insinuate himself into the confidence of the old *hacendado*, marry his daughter, Catalina, and get possession of the Bernal estates. After he married Catalina, however, his wife never realized that Artemio really fell in love with her; influenced by Father Paez, the family priest, she believed that she paid with her soul for her father's security, and she hated herself for the passion to which Artemio could move her at night. Husband and wife ended up despising each other, and she blamed him when their son, whom he removed from her control, was killed while fighting in the Spanish Civil War. Before Catalina, Cruz loved Regina, a camp follower who was taken hostage by Villa's troops and hanged. After her death, there were other women, including Lilia, the young mistress he took on a holiday in Acapulco and who betrayed him there, and Laura, who later married someone else.

In addition to his adventures with women, Artemio recalls ruining his neighbors at Perales and getting possession of their lands, using bribery and blackmail to buy his first election as a deputy, giving lavish parties, negotiating business deals, ruining competitors, and all the while preparing himself for the loneliness and desolation he would feel when his time came to die.

Two episodes throw light on the later years of Artemio's career. One is the story of his capture by a Villista troop. Sentenced to death, he decided to give information to the enemy. Although he later killed the officer to whom he promised betrayal, he was guilty by intent. Some justification for his deed came from Gonzalo Bernal, the disillusioned idealist who nevertheless went bravely to his death, who declared that once a revolution is corrupted by those who act only to live well and to rise in the world, battles may still be fought and won but the uncompromising revolution is lost.

In the last episode, Artemio returns to his beginnings. He was born on the petate, the mat symbolic of the peon's condition, son of a decayed landowner and a half-caste girl. His only friend during his early years was Lunero, a mulatto who served the needs of Artemio's half-crazed old grandmother and his lazy, drunken uncle. After the boy accidentally shot his uncle, he ran away to Veracruz. There, a schoolmaster tutored Artemio and prepared him for the part he would play in the revolution before he lost his ideals and chose betrayal and the rejection that ultimately led him to the corrupting use of power over other men's lives and the spiritual ruin of his own.

Critical Evaluation:

To many Mexicans, the Revolution of 1910 is the great and inescapable fact in their country's destiny and their own personal identity. A second conquest of the land and the past, it was the climax of four centuries of turbulent history and the adumbration of all that had happened since. The revolution did more than topple the paternal dictatorship of Porfirio Díaz: It tore a nation apart with fratricidal strife and put it together again in a strange new way that continued to disturb and puzzle its citizens. The war swept away lingering remnants of colonialism, brought a long-lived oligarchy into being, created a new middle class, moved Mexico into the twentieth century, and helped to shape a literature both ancestral and prophetic in its depictions of a sad and violent land.

In some ways, the situation can be compared to the aftermath of the Civil War in the United States, where for decades Americans tried to see their fraternal conflict in perspectives of cause and consequence. Among American Southerners, especially, there remained a sense of the uniqueness of the experience, a sense of national tragedy. A somewhat similar spirit prevails in some aspects of Mexican life, but on a greater scale and complicated by a growing belief that the revolution failed and the real revolution was still to come. In fact, Mexican intellectuals in the late twentieth century were often self-conscious in much the same manner that William Faulkner and writers of his generation were self-conscious, obsessed with feeling for place, burdened by the past, uneasy in the new society and with what had been lost in the process of change, and seeking to reclaim old values in their stories and poems. Feeling that history had isolated them in their own particular moment in time—the parochialism of the revolution—Mexican writers often turned inward to create a literature veering between fury and outrage and the poetry of nocturnal silence. They lived, to borrow a phrase from the poet Octavio Paz, in a "labyrinth of solitude." It was José Luis Cuevas, the avant-garde painter, who first used the term "Cactus Curtain" in protest against the isolation of the Mexican artist. In an earlier novel, *La región más transparente* (1958; *Where the Air Is Clear*, 1960), Carlos Fuentes said that it is impossible to explain Mexico but only to believe in

it with anger, a feeling of outrage, passion, and a sense of alienation.

This statement makes clear that the author rejects Mexican life of his time but at the same time uses it in his novels to test his sensuous powers and dramatic vigor. The country he writes about is not the land that tourists see or a land of tradition; it is the country of art, a place and people transformed by compelling imagination into something rich, strange, and meaningful. This is one explanation for his restless technical experiments with broken narrative structures, shifting points of view, solemn hymns to landscapes and time, and the interior monologues by which he tries to probe the conscience and consciousness of his people. If he has not yet assimilated in his own writing the influences he has absorbed from such varied figures as Marcel Proust, James Joyce, Faulkner, John Dos Passos, and Thomas Wolfe, he has nevertheless put his borrowings to brilliant use in catching the tempo of Mexican life in its present stage of uncertainty and indirection.

Although his methods may vary in his discontinuity of form and the labyrinthine turnings of his style, his theme remains constant. His novels are studies in the responsibility that power, knowingly or unknowingly, brings and the corruption that almost necessarily accompanies power. He began with *Where the Air Is Clear*, a novel set against the background of Mexico City, where the extremes of poverty and wealth allowed a study in breadth of what had happened on all levels of society after the revolution failed to fulfill its promises. Central to Fuentes's theme is Federico Robles, once an ardent revolutionary but now a driving power in the country's political and financial life. His rise in the world through treachery, bribery, ruthless exploitation and his corruption of better men have made him many enemies. The novel presents the story of more than one man's ruin, however. Underlying the events of the story are the long shadows the failed revolution has thrown into the present, the realization of wasted effort, of lives lost to no purpose, of high aims given over to meaningless deeds of sensuality, folly, and outrage. As can be seen at the end, Robles is what he is because others in their selfishness and pride have assisted in his rise. Now they hate him because they see in him an enlarged image of themselves. *Where the Air Is Clear* is saved from becoming an ideological polemic by the underlying consideration of much that is flawed and gross in the human condition.

Fuentes tells a similar story in *Las buenas conciencias* (1959; *The Good Conscience*, 1961), although in that novel his concern is with a family, grandfather, father, and son rather than with a single individual. The setting is Guanajuato, where the oldest of the Ceballos, a dry-goods merchant, laid the foundation of a family fortune. Representative of the new middle class, the materialistic, ambitious Ceballos men marry for position, play cynical political games for security, and carry on shady business deals for gain. Society accepts them, the state protects them, and the Church sustains them. The writer's picture of chicanery and corruption is magnificent, but the book breaks abruptly in the middle to present in Jaime Ceballo, the youngest of the family, a story of adolescent confusion and rebellion. Torn between the self-seeking practices of his family and the teachings of the Church, he attempts to follow the example of Christ, fails, and falls back on radicalism as the only alternative to the greed, lust for power, and hypocrisy of his class. The ending, unconvincing after the ironical, somber overtones orchestrated through the earlier sections of the novel, suggests that it was dictated more by the writer's Marxist beliefs than the logic of character and experience.

The Death of Artemio Cruz is more limited in its presentation of this theme than Fuentes's previous work. The book is somewhat flawed by a bewildering cross-chronology, in which the points of view constantly shift and intermingle, and by the varied stylistic effects. In the end, however, the novel rises above its faults in its compelling picture of one man's life and the relation of that life to the years of disorder and change that had conditioned the course of twentieth century Mexican history. The central figure is again a force in the land, a millionaire who has climbed to his position of wealth and power by violence, blackmail, bribery, and brutal exploitation of the workers. Like Federico Robles, he is a former revolutionist who stands for the Mexican past and its present. (The robber bands who represented the extreme of the revolutionary effort, Fuentes seems to say, have now been replaced by the robber barons of modern finance and politics.) On the wall of his office, a map shows the extent of his holdings: a newspaper, mines, timber, hotels, and foreign stocks and bonds; not shown are sums of money on deposit in English, Swiss, and United States banks.

Fuentes handles the character of Artemio Cruz with considerable subtlety and skill. He does not gloss over his character's cynicism, opportunism, or brutal ruthlessness, but he saves him from being presented as a monster of calculation by showing his relationships with the three people who mean most in his life: Lunero, the devoted mulatto for whose sake he committed a murder; Regina, the girl killed by Villistas; and his son, Lorenzo. Through the novel, like a refrain, runs a reference to the time just before Lorenzo went off to fight in the Spanish war when father and son took a morning ride toward the sea. By the end of the novel, Artemio's story fulfills all that it promised to a young boy, one man's journey with no real beginning or end in time, marked by love, solitude, violence, power, friendship, disillusionment, corruption, forgetfulness, innocence, and delight. There is also in this story the depiction of how a man's death is joined to his beginning.

Fuentes employs three voices in the narrative. The first is the third person, used to present in dramatic form the events of Artemio's life as they are pieced together in past time. The second is the "I" of the present, as the old man lies dying, shrinking from the decay of his body, and taking fitful account of what is going on around him. The third is a vatic presence never identified that addresses Artemio as "you." This, perhaps, is the unrealized Artemio, the man he might have been. He is a lover of the land that the real Artemio robbed and raped, the product of history, or the re-created moral conscience of the revolution. He speaks in metaphors, poetry, and prophecy about history and time, and places and people, because they belong to the beautiful but sad and tragic land of his birth.

The Death of Artemio Cruz is a divided book, terse, chaotic, passionate, and ironic. Too much has been made, undoubtedly, of Fuentes as one of Mexico's angry young men. In spite of his Marxist beliefs, he is essentially a romantic, and he possesses an exuberant, powerful talent. Aside from the surface effects of undisciplined but compelling style, Fuentes's writing is strikingly clear and unhackneyed, even in translation.

Further Reading

Bloom, Harold, ed. *Carlos Fuentes' "The Death of Artemio Cruz."* New York: Chelsea House, 2006. Collection of essays that analyzes various aspects of the novel, including its structure, theme, point of view, and depiction of fathers, sons, memory, and time.

Boldy, Steven. *The Narrative of Carlos Fuentes: Family, Text, Nation.* Durham, England: University of Durham Press, 2002. Analyzes *The Death of Artemio Cruz*, describing how this book and Fuentes's other early novels used the genre of the family drama to address broader issues of Mexican identity, history, and intellectual traditions.

Faris, Wendy B. *Carlos Fuentes.* New York: Frederick Ungar, 1983. Fine overview of Fuentes's works with considerable detailed analysis. Includes a twenty-two-page chapter that focuses solely on *The Death of Artemio Cruz*, discussing the novel's plot, theme, and presentation.

Guzmän, Daniel de. *Carlos Fuentes.* New York: Twayne, 1972. Excellent overview of Fuentes's life and career through the 1960's. Discusses initial critical reception of *The Death of Artemio Cruz*, presents a description of the narrative and a plot summary, and considers the significance of the novel in Fuentes's evolution as a writer.

Gyurko, Lanin A. *Lifting the Obsidian Mask: The Artistic Vision of Carlos Fuentes.* Potomac, Md.: Scripta Humanistica, 2007. Designed as a guidebook for students of Latin American literature, this book provides analysis of all of Fuentes's work.

Harss, Luis, and Barbara Dohmann. *Into the Mainstream: Conversations with Latin American Writers.* New York: Harper & Row, 1967. Includes a chapter entitled "Carlos Fuentes, or the New Heresy," which provides an interview-based discussion of Fuentes and his works and includes considerable background on post-revolutionary Mexican society and literature.

Sommers, Joseph. *After the Storm: Landmarks of the Modern Mexican Novel.* Albuquerque: University of New Mexico Press, 1968. A twelve-page discussion of *The Death of Artemio Cruz* treats the novel's tone, structure, point of view, and treatment of time, followed by more detailed consideration of the work's theme and its literary quality. Includes some comparison to Fuentes's earlier novel *Where the Air Is Clear.*

Vázquez Amaral, José. *The Contemporary Latin American Narrative.* New York: Las Américas, 1970. A brief chapter on *The Death of Artemio Cruz*, part overview and part review, compares Fuentes's novel and Mariano Azuela's *The Underdogs* (1915, serial; 1916, book) as novels of the Mexican Revolution.

The Death of Empedocles

Author: Friedrich Hölderlin (1770-1843)
First published: Der Tod de Empedokles, 1826 (English translation, 1966)
Type of work: Drama
Type of plot: Tragedy
Time of plot: Fifth century B.C.E.
Locale: Agrigentum and Mount Etna

Principal characters:
EMPEDOCLES, a prophet and healer
KRITIAS or MECADES, the ruler of Agrigentum
MANES, Empedocles' former teacher
MECADES,
HEMOCRATES,
PAUSANIAS,
PANTHEA, and
DELIA, observers and commentators

The Death of Empedocles is a verse drama of Friedrich Hölderlin's middle period (1793-1799), when his worldview of idealistic pantheism—that the human being is part of a cosmos in which all things express the nature of divinity—was called into question by issues raised in his intense study of the philosophical works of Johann Gottlieb Fichte. Fichte asserts in his philosophy that it is the individual consciousness alone that gives meaning to the world. Such a view challenges the holistic aspect of pantheism. While in many respects *The Death of Empedocles* has been seen as Hölderlin's dramatization of his inner conflict, it is also a representative work of the movement of many Romantics away from an interest in classical themes toward their struggle to express innovative perceptions of the relationship between humanity and nature and between humanity and divinity. *The Death of Empedocles* is one of the works that marks this transformation.

Like his contemporaries and immediate predecessors, Hölderlin considered the problem of what is proper to humankind and what is not: some abilities and some knowledge are not appropriate for the mortal state because, being primarily of the flesh and not solely of the spirit, people do not have the powers of perception to understand. Ironically, humanity desires to understand those very things that it cannot. Empedocles attempts to expose the secrets of the soul and of the workings of the universe to a humanity that cannot have the capacity to understand them.

The Death of Empedocles, which takes place at Agrigentum and at the foot of Mount Etna, is a version of the legend of the Greek philosopher, poet, and statesman, Empedocles. Empedocles, who lived c. 490 to 430 B.C.E., threw himself, according to legend, into the crater of Mount Etna to prove that he was a god. Empedocles was reputed to know many of the secrets of the gods, of the universe, and of life and death.

In the play, Empedocles' problem is that he aspires to be more than a man but will always be less than the gods. Critics have noted the similarity between Hölderlin's Empedocles and Christ in many respects, the most significant being that they are both figures of matter and of spirit who overcame their states through death and transformation to another state—deification for Christ, reunion with elemental nature for Empedocles. Empedocles' tragedy is that he becomes one with the divine spirit of the universe and thereby alienates the ruling powers of Agrigentum. He chooses to share his visions with the people, undermining the authority of the religious establishment. According to Hölderlin's plan for his final version, Empedocles is a redeemer figure who must die in order for his civilization to flourish. Hölderlin's vision of the universe is Romantic and cyclical; for him, death and life become part of the same process, harmony is broken and reestablished, and things form, decay, and reassemble themselves—even civilization is subject to decay and restoration.

The drama remains in three fragments, none of which Hölderlin finished. Versions 1 and 2 show Empedocles as a prophet with the tragic flaw of pride. Half tragic hero and half Christ figure, Empedocles has the powers of the magician to heal and to move the elements, but his desire to be reunited with the gods causes him to disregard the pleas of his followers that he return to them from his exile. In the second version, before the action of the play begins, Empedocles, "That tender soul . . . run to waste," wishes to share his understanding with his people, but in this version, he is insolent and despotic. This tragic hero of the second version is a Romantic who not only falls but also bemoans his own fall. His first speech shows him imploring the gods and the forces of nature to consider him in his solitariness. His vision of the universe contributes to his fall; ultimately, he understands that his own powers of perception and his ability to control the elemental forces condemn him to solitude. By the third version, Hölderlin transcends his own self-imposed strictures of classical tragedy to create, in fragmentary form, a work in which Empedocles' personal motive for suicide, that of reuniting with the gods, takes on the universal significance of the redemption of civilization.

In the first version, Kritias, the archon or ruler in Agrigentum, who represents government, remarks that Empedocles' teachings so affect the people that they, in their belief that he ascended into heaven, are disaffected against the laws of the state. Hermocrates, who represents religion, counsels that Empedocles is abandoned by the gods, who formerly so favored him, because he comes to be on such familiar terms with them that he actually forgets that he can never be one

of them, and forgets the "difference" between them. It is Hermocrates who will curse him and who plans to show the people that Empedocles, rather than having risen, is actually in his garden in a state of abject depression.

The second version omits this scene and opens instead with the interchange between the priest and the archon, Kritias, who is renamed in this version Mecades. As in the first version, in discussing the stature of Empedocles among the citizenry of Agrigentum, Mecades and Hermocrates say that Empedocles overreaches his own boundaries: Because of his familiarity with the gods, the people adulate him excessively, honoring him for stealing the "fire of life" from heaven, and cease honoring their laws and customs. Hermocrates describes the downfall of the noble-minded Empedocles, how he became like the "superstitious rabble with no soul," which causes the loss of his power.

Empedocles' meditative soliloquy, which in version 1 is the third scene, opens version 2. Empedocles reflects on his fallen state, on his previous state as a powerful seer to whom people applied for renovation of their spirits, and on the necessity of his being punished for his pride in presuming to be too much of the world of the gods. He calls out to the divinities of the earth and sky.

In dialogue with Pausanias, he reveals his pantheism: He recalls having heard the melodies of the powers of nature and her "ancient harmony," and he regrets that nature's powers deserted him, claiming that the greater one's good fortune, the worse one's downfall. Pausanias then asks of Empedocles one of the key questions of the drama: Can one control one's own feelings, or can the forces of darkness reach even into the human heart? Another way to phrase the question: Do people have free will, or are they ruled by fate? He implores Empedocles to remember that he was and still is a person. Empedocles counters with the Romantic statement, "You do not know me, nor yourself, nor life, nor death." In his bitterness, he says that the world is a "dead stringed instrument" without him to animate it with "a language and a soul"; nature is his serving girl, and the gods live for the people only insofar as he proclaims them. He informs Pausanias that the things for which Pausanias admires him are those things that destroy him: the vast extent of his powers of understanding the universe and his abilities to control the elements, often for the good of humanity. This scene breaks off as Empedocles begins a disquisition on the transformative power of the word.

In versions 1 and 2, Empedocles explains to Pausanias that his fall from grace is due to being too blessed by the gods, that ultimately he became too insolent in his pride. In the fragmentary conclusions to act 2 of the second version, there follows an interchange between Panthea and Delia. In the second version, in contrast to the first, the question of the morality of Empedocles' contemplated suicide is emphasized through the discussion of Panthea, Delia, and Pausanias. Panthea is supportive of Empedocles, and Pausanias rather glorifies him in his decision, but Delia objects.

Panthea expresses the dichotomy between the gods and nature, proclaiming that it is nature rather than the gods who gave Empedocles his lofty soul. Delia comments on the death of Empedocles in lines that bemoan the transitory nature of existence. Panthea remarks upon the fact that living things fade, that "the best,/ Even they seek out their destroyers," which are the "gods of death." In anguish, she implores, "O Nature, why do you/ Make it so easy?/ For your hero to die?" With his death, Panthea moans, the hearts of humanity draw away from nature and from "the holy All": She closes with the comment, "For we who are blind?/ Needed a miracle once." The real problem is not only that Empedocles suffers a tragic fall through pride but also that in so doing, he creates a state of disharmony with nature, losing sight of the holiness of all living things. In Hölderlin's Romantic philosophy, the drawing of human hearts away from "the holy All" constitutes communal spiritual cataclysm. It is in his third version that he tries dramatically to redeem this act through Empedocles.

Version 1 continues with the visit to Empedocles in his garden by several people, including Kritias and Hermocrates, who curses Empedocles in his wish to commit suicide and who spurs the crowd on to drive Empedocles into exile. The action builds to a turning point when, on Mount Etna, Empedocles and Pausanias see the crowd coming up the mountainside. Hermocrates declares to the people that Empedocles is forgiven, but Pausanias tells them that Empedocles intends to commit suicide. The people threaten to kill Hermocrates and proclaim their desire to make Empedocles their king. Empedocles, however, remarks that the era of democracy is arrived, and that although he will not go home with them, he will give them a message, that message being the holiest thing he has to give. He then speaks to them of death and life and of the transformative nature of civilization. He implores them to defy the old ways and to engage in a worship of nature, for only then will humanity attain true peace, the "life of the world."

Critics have noted the Christological allusions. Empedocles becomes aware that the time of his own purification and transformation is at hand; he is one lent to life for only a short time; he fulfills his purpose to the people. Becoming too aware of the divine in the world, he knows he must pass on, and he bids Pausanias to arrange things, including a last sup-

per. Version 2 concludes as, invoking Jupiter, Empedocles passes out of this state in an overwhelming cognizance of the divinity of the universe.

Although the third version consists of only three finished scenes, Hölderlin's notes give a fairly good notion of the direction in which he intended to take the work. He intended to expand the first act and to include four more acts, in which the bewildered crowd comes to understand the implications of the death of Empedocles. While in versions 1 and 2 Empedocles' fall from grace is a central issue, in version 3 the thematic focus shifts to the moral questions, including those that attend the contemplation of suicide by a leader who is a poet, prophet, magician, and healer.

Version 3 opens with Empedocles in exile, awakening, describing his position between "Father Etna and his close relative, the Thunderer." High up in a place where he sings "natural songs" with the eagles, he is in harmony with nature as well as in proximity to the gods. Dramatic tension in this version is significantly heightened with the introduction of a new character, Strato, as king of Agrigentum, and brother of Empedocles. In soliloquy, Empedocles says that his brother exiled him, but that he nevertheless makes a new life for himself; he knows he sinned against humanity by serving them blindly as the elements like "fire or water" serve, but not as a human being with a human heart would serve. He therefore deserves to be driven out by his people, and it is this forced exile that reestablishes the bond between him and nature. He pronounces that "death is what I seek. It is my right," and that his need for the human heart ends.

In the third scene of the third version, Hölderlin departs in a radically different direction, one that lifts this work out of the realm of imitative tragic classicism and into innovative Romanticism. In it, Manes, Empedocles' former teacher, admonishes Empedocles for his decision to commit suicide and causes him to come to terms with this decision. Manes admits to Empedocles, however, that there is one situation in which suicide may be allowed, and that concerns a very specific individual in a very specific situation. While remaining doubtful throughout, he describes Empedocles as this kind of individual: one who partakes of both the human and the divine realms in a time of transformative social and political upheaval. This would be a person who can so absorb the conflicts in the world into himself that he serves as an example to humanity of what is possible: of the strength of the peace that is within their power to create. He must die, then, because he would himself be worshiped, and people would forget that their objective is not for them to worship him but to do as he does. Cosmically, his death heralds a new order, a new civilization. Hölderlin's notes make clear that this is the direction the story would take. In the projected conclusion, Manes believes that Empedocles is actually the "historical redeemer," "the chosen one who kills and gives life, in and through whom a world is at once dissolved and renewed." Manes gives to the people the great secret of Empedocles, his last will, as the basis for the new civilization.

The historical Empedocles presumably attracted Hölderlin: Fundamentally a pantheist, Empedocles was adept at manipulating the forces of nature; essentially an idealist, he believed in political democracy. Empedocles' theory of the cyclic nature of the universe may have attracted Hölderlin as well. Ultimately, however, *The Death of Empedocles* represents the influences of the German Romantics who preceded Hölderlin. Hölderlin was acutely aware that people are of the world of matter as well as of the world of spirit, and so people cannot really ever become part of the realm of pure spirit. In other words, people may strive for perfection, but human perfection is paradoxically imperfect: It can be only a shadow of true spiritual perfection. Not to recognize the vast difference between the ideal state and the real state is cosmically disastrous. Empedocles' pride postpones his recognition of this difference.

It is unfortunate that Hölderlin never finished this play. Even as it stands, it is a major document in the history of European Romanticism. There is the curious circumstance of three versions, which, read together (and with Hölderlin's notes) as one work, provide a substantial view of the progress of a poet's mind in a time of artistic as well as social and political transformation.

Donna Berliner

Further Reading

Fioretos, Aris, ed. *The Solid Letter: Readings of Friedrich Hölderlin*. Stanford, Calif.: Stanford University Press, 1999. Collection of essays, including analyses of Hölderlin's poetry, a discussion of his philosophy of poetry, and two pieces relating to *The Death of Empedocles*: "Figures of Duality: Hölderlin and Greek Tragedy" by Arnaud Villani and "Disowning Contingencies in Hölderlin's *Empedocles*" by Stanley Corngold.

Fóti, Véronique M. *Hölderlin's Philosophy of Tragedy*. Albany: State University of New York Press, 2006. Focuses on Hölderlin's conception of tragedy within the broader context of German philosophy, including the ideas of Georg Wilhelm Friedrich Hegel and Friedrich Nietzsche. Fóti analyses three fragmentary versions of *The Death of Empedocles* and demonstrates how they reflect Hölderlin's philosophy.

George, Emery E., ed. *Friedrich Hölderlin: An Early Modern*. Ann Arbor: University of Michigan Press, 1972. Shows how Hölderlin's work presages treatments and techniques that developed later in the nineteenth century.

Hamburger, Michael. "Hölderlin." In *Contraries: Studies in German Literature*. New York: E. P. Dutton, 1970. Contains a significant discussion of Hölderlin's interpretation of the notion of the poet as seer and of the place of *The Death of Empedocles* in this tradition.

Hölderlin, Friedrich. "The Ground for Empedocles." In *Friedrich Hölderlin: Essays and Letters on Theory*. Translated and edited by Thomas Pfau. Albany: State University of New York Press, 1988. Discusses *The Death of Empedocles* and the nature of drama as well as the opposing principles of the rational consciousness and the irrational forces of nature.

Stahl, E. L. "Hölderlin's Idea of Poetry." In *The Era of Goethe: Essays Presented to James Boyd*. Oxford, England: Basil Blackwell, 1959. Discusses Hölderlin's aesthetic notions in the context of those of his contemporaries.

Unger, Richard. *Friedrich Hölderlin*. Boston: Twayne, 1984. An accessible chapter on *The Death of Empedocles* examines the changes from version to version.

_____. *Hölderlin's Major Poetry: The Dialectics of Unity*. Bloomington: Indiana University Press, 1975. Places Hölderlin's work in the framework of his notion of the oneness of the universe.

The Death of Ivan Ilyich

Author: Leo Tolstoy (1828-1910)
First published: Smert Ivana Ilicha, 1886 (English
    translation, 1887)
Type of work: Novella
Type of plot: Psychological realism
Time of plot: 1880's
Locale: St. Petersburg and nearby provinces

Principal characters:
IVAN ILYICH GOLOVIN, a prominent Russian judge
PRASKOVYA FEDOROVNA GOLOVINA, his wife
PETER IVANOVITCH, his colleague
GERASIM, his servant boy

The Story:

During a break in a hearing, a group of lawyers gathers informally. One, Peter Ivanovitch, interrupts the good-natured arguing of the others with the news that Ivan Ilyich, a colleague they greatly respect, is dead. Unwittingly, each thinks first of what this death means to his own chances of promotion, and each cannot help feeling relief that it is Ivan Ilyich and not himself who died.

That afternoon, Peter Ivanovitch visits the dead man's home, where the funeral is to be held. Although he meets a playful colleague, Schwartz, he attempts to behave as correctly as possible under such sorrowful circumstances, as if by observing the proper protocol he can persuade himself into the proper feelings. He looks respectfully at the corpse and talks with Ivan's widow, Praskovya Fedorovna, but he is continually distracted during his talk by an unruly spring in the hassock on which he sits. While he struggles to keep his decorum, Praskovya speaks only of her own exhaustion and suffering. Peter, suddenly terrified by their mutual hypocrisy, longs to leave; once the widow pumps him for information about her pension, she, too, is glad to end the conversation. At the funeral, Peter sees Ivan's daughter and her fiancé, who are angrily glum, and Ivan's little son, who is tear-stained but naughty. Only the servant boy, Gerasim, speaks cheerfully, for he is the only one who can accept death as natural. Peter leaves and hurries to his nightly card game.

Ivan Ilyich was the second and most successful of the three sons of a superfluous bureaucrat. An intelligent and popular boy, he seemed able to mold his life into a perfect pattern. As secretary to a provincial governor after completing law school, and later as an examining magistrate, he was the very model of conscientiousness mingled with good humor. He managed the decorum of his official position as well as the ease of his social one. Only marriage, although socially correct, did not conform to his ideas of decorum; his wife, not content to fulfill the role he chose for her, became demanding and quarrelsome. As a result, he increasingly shut himself off from his family (which grew with two chil-

dren) and found the order and peace he needed in his judiciary affairs.

In 1880, however, he was shattered by the loss of two promotions. In desperation, he went to St. Petersburg, where a chance meeting led to his obtaining a miraculously good appointment. In the city, he found precisely the house he always wanted, and he worked to furnish it to his taste. Even a fall and a resulting bruise on his side did not dampen his enthusiasm. He and his wife were delighted with their new home, which they thought was aristocratic, although it looked like the homes of all those who wished to appear well-bred. To Ivan, life was at last as it should be: smooth, pleasant, and ordered according to an unwavering routine. His life was properly divided into the official and the personal, and he kept the two halves dexterously apart.

Ivan began to notice an increasing discomfort in his left side. He finally consulted a specialist, but the examination left him frightened and helpless, for although he understood the doctor's objective attitude as akin to his own official one, he felt that it gave his pain a terrible significance. For a time, he felt that he was recovering by following prescriptions and learning all he could about his illness, but renewed attacks terrified him. Gradually Ivan found his whole life to be colored by the pain. Card games became trivial; friends seemed to do nothing but speculate on how long he would live. When Ivan's brother-in-law came for a visit, his shocked look told Ivan how much illness changed him, and he suddenly realized that he faced not only illness but also death. Through deepening terror and despair Ivan shrank from this truth. Other men died, not he. Desperately, he erected screens against the pain and the knowledge of death it brought, but it lurked behind court duties and quarrels with his family. The knowledge that it began with the bruise on his side only made his condition harder to bear.

As Ivan grew steadily worse, drugs failed to help him, but the clean strength and honesty of the peasant boy, Gerasim, nourished him, for Ivan felt that his family members were hypocrites who chose to pretend that he was not dying. Death to them was not part of that same decorum he, too, once revered and was therefore hidden as unpleasant and shameful. Only Gerasim could understand his pain because only he admitted that death was real and natural.

Ivan retreated increasingly into his private anguish. He hated his knowing doctors, his plump, chiding wife, his daughter and her new fiancé. Lamenting, he longed to have his old, happy life again, but only memories of childhood revealed true happiness. Unwillingly he returned again and again to this knowledge as he continued questioning the reasons for his torment. If he always lived correctly, why was this happening to him? What if he was wrong? Suddenly, he knew that the faint urges he consciously stilled in order to do as people thought proper were the true urges. Since he did not know the truth about life, he also did not know the truth about death. His anguish increased as he thought of the irrevocable choice he made.

His wife brought the priest, whose sacrament eased him until her presence reminded him of his deceptive life. He screamed at her to leave him, and he continued screaming as he struggled against death, unable to relinquish the illusion that his life was good. Then the struggle ceased, and he knew that although his life was not right, it no longer mattered. Opening his eyes, he saw his wife and son weeping by his bedside. Aware of them for the first time, he felt sorry for them. As he tried to ask their forgiveness, everything became clear to him. He must not hurt them; he must set them free and free himself from his sufferings. The pain and fear of death were no longer there. Instead, there was only light and joy.

Critical Evaluation:

The Death of Ivan Ilyich is quite short, but it is one of the greatest pieces of fiction in any language. In it, Leo Tolstoy examines the hollowness of bourgeois existence. Ivan Ilyich is a successful member of the state bureaucracy. Throughout his life he has carefully adjusted his conduct so as to please his superiors and to arrange a life that runs smoothly and without complication. He is the perfect example of the conforming, "other-directed" man. Only shortly before his death does he discover the horror that lies behind his seemingly successful life.

The story opens in an unusual but significant way. Rather than tell the reader of Ivan's early years, Tolstoy presents the dead Ivan stretched out at home, attended by his wife and closest friend, Peter Ivanovitch. The behavior of the mourners indicates more about Ivan's life than any chronicle could. Rather than grieve over his death, they are worried about their own affairs. His wife asks Peter Ivanovitch about her

pension, hoping to persuade him to help her arrange for an increase, while he frets about missing the bridge game he had planned. They both pretend to feelings of grief they do not feel. The work proceeds to answer the question what was it about Ivan's life that could have resulted in so little concern for him after his death. This portion of the novella dramatizes the statement that opens the second section: "Ivan Ilyich's life had been most simple and most ordinary and therefore most terrible."

Ivan's progress from law school to the position of examining magistrate is marked by careful obedience to authority both in legal matters and in matters of taste and style of life. His early pangs of conscience at youthful actions are overcome when he sees people of good position doing the same thing without qualms. Still, he never becomes a rake or hellraiser; he is, rather, anxiously correct and proper. He makes a proper marriage—one that serves to advance him—and then gradually proceeds to alienate his wife and children by avoiding domestic complications in the name of his job. In this separation between his private life, with its potential for affection, and his public duties, he furthers the process of fragmentation within himself. He becomes punctilious at home as well as at work. All of his life takes on an official and artificial character, from which only the natural process of dying can release him as it educates him. In the opening scene, readers are told that "his face was handsomer and above all more dignified than when he was alive." His death is a form of rescue.

His job is a game that he had played with great seriousness—like the bridge games he hurries to after work. He never abuses his power as a magistrate but always conducts himself "by the book." Most of all, he is careful never to become personally involved in the carrying out of justice. He is a perfect arm of the state, a perfect product of its bureaucratic machinery. Naturally, he never questions the system of justice he is paid to administer. It is significant that he rises no higher than the middle rank of officialdom. Those above him have perceived that he is essentially mediocre.

Nevertheless, his life seems to flow along easily, pleasantly, and correctly. He decorates his new home, supervising much of the work closely. He imagines that the result is very special, but Tolstoy states that Ivan's home, characteristically, looks exactly like the homes of other people of his class and station. Underneath the smooth surface of this life something is wrong, and it refuses to stay concealed. Instead, it manifests itself in the form of an illness, probably cancer, which gradually consumes Ivan's vitality. When he goes to the doctor he feels guilty and desperately uncertain. For the first time, he learns what it is like to be the recipient of the games those in authority play—like a criminal dragged to the bar. The doctor cannot or will not tell him what is wrong (he probably does not know). Gradually, Ivan declines until he is bedridden. His disintegrating flesh begins to give off a strange and unpleasant odor. He becomes hateful to himself and to his wife, who up to now has pursued a life of idle and superficial pleasure. Even more than physical pain, Ivan suffers from spiritual torment. His prior habits of life have given him no resources with which to face death. Moreover, he is perpetually troubled by the question of why he is suffering when he took such pains to lead a correct life. What if he has been wrong all along? In the grip of despair, he searches for hope at any hand, but no hope presents itself until he finds it possible to accept the kind attentions of his servant Gerasim.

Gerasim is the opposite of Ivan. A healthy, simple peasant, he has never known the artificial life of a bureaucrat and social climber. He does not fear death and, thus, does not mind being in the presence of the dying Ivan. He is in tune with the natural. Ivan is able to accept him because he feels that there is no deception in Gerasim's attitude toward him, whereas he sees nothing but deception in the kind and cheerful attitudes of his wife and friends (a reaction, in part, to the falseness of his former life). When Gerasim sits for hours with his master's legs propped up on his shoulders, Ivan feels unaccountable relief. Still, Gerasim's presence only partially modifies Ivan's agony. Essentially, he must go through the process of dying by himself. Perhaps Gerasim's naturalness does bring Ivan to the conviction of the worthlessness of his former life, but death is Ivan's best educator. It gradually and painfully strips away the artificial and the vain. It reduces Ivan to the elemental position of an organism dependent on the natural processes of life. Interestingly, Ivan thinks most of all of his early youth at this time. He recalls when he was still an innocent, uncorrupted by the false system he slavishly aspired to enter. In a sense, he is yearning to recapture the natural instincts represented by Gerasim. Death offers him the chance. In the final hours of his interminable decline, Ivan grows still. He has a vision of light and freedom. Death becomes for him a door to a larger and purer existence.

"Critical Evaluation" by Benjamin Nyce

Further Reading

Christian, R. F. *Tolstoy: A Critical Introduction*. New York: Cambridge University Press, 1969. Discusses *The Death of Ivan Ilyich* and compares the novella with Franz Kafka's *The Trial* (1925). Relates the plot and structure of *The Death of Ivan Ilyich* to the works of later writers whom it may have influenced.

Courcel, Martine de. *Tolstoy: The Ultimate Reconciliation*. Translated by Peter Levi. New York: Charles Scribner's Sons, 1988. A thorough discussion of Tolstoy. Explains the social and political atmosphere at the time of *The Death of Ivan Ilyich*. Finds many parallels between this novella and Tolstoy's life.

Jahn, Gary R. *"The Death of Ivan Ilich": An Interpretation*. New York: Twayne, 1993. Includes an extensive chronology of Tolstoy and the literary and historical context of the work. Presents information about critical reception and social, psychological, and philosophical issues; contains a section on structure and style. Gives an extensive reading of the plot.

_____, ed. *"The Death of Ivan Il'ich": A Critical Companion*. Evanston, Ill.: Northwestern University Press, 1998. Collection of original and reprinted essays analyzing the style, symbolism, and thematic concerns of the novella and providing psychological commentary. In addition, Jahn provides an introduction and factual and interpretative annotations to the text of the novella, with information about its settings, artistic devices, organizational schemes, and other aspects of the work.

McLean, Hugh. *In Quest of Tolstoy*. Boston: Academic Studies Press, 2008. McLean, a professor emeritus of Russian at the University of California, Berkeley, and longtime Tolstoy scholar, compiled this collection of essays that examine Tolstoy's writings and ideas and assess his influence on other writers and thinkers. Includes discussions of the young Tolstoy and women and Tolstoy and Jesus, Charles Darwin, Ernest Hemingway, and Maxim Gorky.

Noyes, George Rapall. *Tolstoy*. New York: Dover, 1968. Discusses the interconnection of Tolstoy's many works and refers to biographical information pertinent to understanding his writings. Finds *The Death of Ivan Ilyich* to be more intense and focused than other works by the author.

Orwin, Donna Tussig, ed. *The Cambridge Companion to Tolstoy*. New York: Cambridge University Press, 2002. Collection of essays, including discussions of Tolstoy as a writer of popular literature, the development of his style and themes, his aesthetics, and Tolstoy in the twentieth century. References to *The Death of Ivan Ilyich* are listed in the index.

Rowe, William W. *Leo Tolstoy*. Boston: Twayne, 1986. An excellent companion for readers of Tolstoy. Chapters provide biographical information and analyses of several novels and stories, including a discussion of the structure and main character of *The Death of Ivan Ilyich*. Contains a chronology of Tolstoy's life, a bibliography, and an index.

The Death of the Heart

Author: Elizabeth Bowen (1899-1973)
First published: 1938
Type of work: Novel
Type of plot: Psychological realism
Time of plot: After World War I
Locale: London and Seale, England

Principal characters:
THOMAS QUAYNE, the owner of Quayne and Merrett, an
  advertising agency
ANNA QUAYNE, his wife
PORTIA QUAYNE, his sixteen-year-old half sister
ST. QUENTIN MILLER, an author and a friend of the
  Quaynes
EDDIE, an employee of Quayne and Merrett
MAJOR BRUTT, a retired officer
MRS. HECCOMB, Anna's former governess

The Story:

Anna Quayne's pique demands an outlet—she can no longer contain it all within herself; therefore, while St. Quentin Miller shivers with cold, she marches him around the frozen park, delivering herself of her discontent. The trouble, of course, started with Portia, for the Quayne household was not the same after the arrival of Tom's sixteen-year-old half sister. Not that Portia is all to blame; the business began with a deathbed wish. Who could have expected dying old Mr. Quayne to ask Tom to take a half sister he hardly knew, keep her for at least a year, and give her a graceful start in life? As she explains to St. Quentin, Anna herself hardly knows how to cope with the arrangement, although she tries to accept it with outward tranquillity. Now she stumbled across the girl's diary, glimpsed her own name, and was tempted to read. It is obvious that Portia is less than happy and that she is scanning the atmosphere of her brother's house with an unflattering eye.

While Anna is thus unburdening herself, the subject of her discussion returns home quietly from Miss Paullie's lessons. She is vaguely disturbed to learn from Matchett, the housekeeper, that Anna commented upon the clutter in Portia's bedroom. Later, she shares tea with Anna and St. Quentin when they come in, tingling with cold; but the atmosphere seems a bit stiff, and Portia readily agrees with Anna's suggestion that she join her brother in his study. Portia feels more at ease with Tom, even though he clearly finds conversation with her awkward.

By now, Portia knows that there is no one in whom she can readily confide. At 2 Windsor Terrace, Matchett offers a certain possessive friendship; at school, only the inquisitive Lilian takes notice of her. Major Brutt is better than either of these; in her presence, his eyes show a fatherly gleam, and she likes the picture puzzle he sent. Anna tolerates the Ma-

jor—he is her only link with an old friend, Pidgeon—but Major Brutt seldom ventures to call, and Portia sees him mostly in the company of others.

Another of Anna's friends whom Portia sometimes sees is Eddie. Eddie, however, is seemingly beyond the range of Portia's clumsy probing for companionship. He is twenty-three years of age and brightly self-assured. Anna finds it amusing to have him around, although she often rebukes his conceit and presumption; she goes so far as to find him a job with Quayne and Merrett. One day, Portia hands Eddie his hat as he takes leave of Anna; the next day he writes to her. Before long, they are meeting regularly and secretly.

Having no wish to alienate Anna, Eddie cautions Portia not to mention him in her diary, but he revels in Portia's uncritical adoration. They go to the zoo, to tea, and ultimately to his apartment. Matchett, who finds Eddie's letter under Portia's pillow, soon becomes coldly jealous of his influence. Even Anna and Tom become slightly restive as they realize the situation. Meanwhile, Portia is falling deeper and deeper in love. When Eddie lightly declares that it is a pity they are too young to marry, Portia innocently takes his remarks as a tentative proposal. Although he carefully refrains from real lovemaking, Portia feels sure he returns her love.

With the approach of spring, Anna and Tom reveal their intention to spend a few weeks in Capri. Since Matchett will houseclean while they are gone, they decide to send Portia to Mrs. Heccomb, Anna's former governess, who lives in a seaside house at Seale. Portia, dismayed by the prospect of separation from Eddie, is only partially consoled by his promise to write.

Eddie does write promptly; so does Major Brutt, with the promise of another picture puzzle; and Seale, happily, turns out better than Portia expected. Having none of Anna's remoteness, Mrs. Heccomb deluges her guest with care-free chatter. Her two grown-up stepchildren react somewhat more cautiously, because they were prepared to find Portia a highbrow. When they realize she is only shy, they quickly relax; the radio blares while they vigorously shout over it about roller skating, hockey games, and Saturday-night parties. Portia gradually withdraws from her shell of loneliness. Within a few days, she feels enough at home to ask Daphne Heccomb if Eddie might spend a weekend at Seale. Daphne consents to relay the request to her mother, and Mrs. Heccomb affably approves.

Eddie's visit is not a success. His efforts to be the life of the party soon have Mrs. Heccomb wondering about the wisdom of her invitation. At the cinema, his good fellowship extends to holding hands enthusiastically with Daphne. When a distressed Portia utters mild reproaches, he intimates that she is a naïve child. Walking together in the woods on their final afternoon, Portia learns that Eddie has no use for her love unless it can remain uncritical and undemanding. Her vision of an idyllic reunion shatters as she begins to see his instability. Two weeks later, her stay at Seale ends. Back in London, Matchett triumphantly informs her that Eddie left word that he will be out of town a few days.

Walking home from school not long afterward, Portia encounters St. Quentin, who inadvertently reveals Anna's perusal of the diary. Upset, she seeks comfort from Eddie once more. No longer gratified by her devotion, he makes her feel even more unwanted; and the sight of a letter from Anna, lying on Eddie's table, convinces Portia that they are allied against her. As she leaves his apartment, it seems unthinkable that she can ever return to Windsor Terrace; her only possible refuge now is Major Brutt. She goes, therefore, to the Karachi Hotel, surprising the worthy major as he finishes his dinner. Surprise changes to alarm as she pleads her case: Will he take her away, will he marry her? She could relieve his loneliness, she could care for him, she could polish his shoes. With as much serenity as he can muster, the major affirms that polishing shoes is a job with which women have little success; with a little time and patience, her position will soon appear less desperate. He wishes very much to call the Quaynes, for it is getting late and they will be worried. Portia believes that she is defeated, but she can still choose ground on which to make a final stand. Very well, she finally agrees, he might call them, but he is not to tell them she is coming. That will depend, she finishes enigmatically but firmly, on whether they choose to do the right thing.

The major is right; the Quaynes are worried. After the telephone rang, their momentary relief is succeeded by real confusion. What, after all, would Portia consider the right thing for them to do? It would have to be simple. With help from St. Quentin, they finally decide, and Matchett is sent in a taxi to fetch her.

Critical Evaluation:

Elizabeth Bowen is most often at her best as a writer when she is writing from the perspective of the marginalized—in *Eva Trout* (1968), Bowen writes from the margins of madness. In *The House in Paris* (1935) and *The Death of the Heart*, the marginalized experience is depicted through the eyes of a commonly peripheral period of experience, through the perspective of the child and the adolescent. Portia Quayne is the observing consciousness through which the adult world is revealed for the hypocrisy and shallowness that marks the relationship between Thomas and Anna Quayne.

Portia, the half sister of Thomas, is brought to live in the Quayne household after being orphaned. Her presence in the house brings to a head the many tensions that were brewing there before her arrival. Bowen's use of the child's consciousness gives perspective to the adult world. This emphasis on the "fallenness" of adult perspective is reinforced in the titles of the three sections of the novel, "The World," "The Flesh," and "The Devil." These three section titles relate to the baptismal rites of the Anglican Book of Common Prayer, and, more generally, signify the three obvious sources of spiritual temptation that mark the Quaynes' dispirited lifestyle and Portia's own falling into the world of the adult.

The title of the story has a double resonance: It relates to the condition of the Quaynes in their marriage, and, perhaps more important, it serves as a caveat for Portia, whose heart, or center of feeling, is being systematically worn down throughout the novel.

Bowen's writing often captures the fading era of the stout British character and the passing of the world of manners that attends the era's demise. The novel's title thus also relates in a general way to the fatal end of an entire empire's place in the world. The death of the heart of British character is at stake throughout the novel, as it is seen to reside at last in the type of people that the Quaynes represent. The world of British manners about which Bowen wrote so clearly had suffered a double blow as a result of the two world wars. In *The Death of the Heart*, all the characters suffer under a cultural malaise that not even the introduction of the young can surmount. Bowen shows the British upper middle class as being too self-involved to give any clear direction to the young, especially young women.

Bowen's decision to make her central character an orphan serves various dramatic purposes. First, Portia's status as an orphan works to exonerate her from the situation into which she is forced. She does not do anything to create the tensions between Anna and Thomas, and, as a parentless child, she is placed in the position of observing the adult world, while only being indirectly related to what takes place within it. Second, Portia's status as an orphan gives her the privilege of serving as a somewhat distanced narrative consciousness. Her interactions with Anna are not fraught with the same tensions that one could expect from a typical parent-child relationship. Portia, being parentless, can double as Anna's own not yet fully developed self. Portia learns from the Quaynes that emergence into the adult world, at the threshold of which she stands, brings with it a certain "death" or loss of innocence. Portia's surrogate position with regard to Anna's own maternal sense, however, teaches Anna that, contrary to the way she is living, the heart does not have to die completely to develop to its greatest extent.

Bowen's narrative style combines the use of the third-person narrator with interpolations from Portia's diary, thus giving the reader a firsthand look at what Portia is thinking and how events are registering with her. Significantly, Portia's diary excerpts are found in the section "The Flesh," underscoring that even processes of reflection must take place through the senses. In this way, Bowen plays with the notion that the flesh, or the world of bodily sensation and gratification, is also humankind's foundation for building a more intuitive and spiritual understanding of the world around it.

Bowen manipulates her narrative technique according to the section headings; through indirection, the primary means in the novel by which the characters understand one another; and by showing Portia's growth over a period of time. Bowen aims for a psychological realism throughout the story by limited use of the techniques of the bildungsroman, or novel of personal development. Portia is a personality in the making. Because the central character is a young woman at a formative stage in her life, the reader can interpret the story as a coming-of-age novel, in which both the adults and the child reach a point of perception about themselves and one another.

Finally, the novel must be understood within the context of the novel of manners. Bowen excels at writing about the manners and mores of the British upper middle class. *The Death of the Heart* is generally considered one of her finest achievements in the genre. Although it explores the darker side of human relations, it is not without humor and the ability to entertain.

"Critical Evaluation" by Susan M. Rochette-Crawley

Further Reading

Austin, Allan E. *Elizabeth Bowen*. Rev. ed. Boston: Twayne, 1989. A good introduction to Bowen. Discusses her style, syntax, use of narrator, and evocative settings. Analyzes careful blending of the two themes—the loss of innocence and the revival of a stagnant relationship. Praises her narrative voice for awareness, perception, humor, and compassion. Includes an annotated bibliography.

Blodgett, Harriet. *Patterns of Reality: Elizabeth Bowen's Novels*. The Hague, the Netherlands: Mouton, 1975. Explores religious imagery in the novel, stressing the heroine's status as a Christ-like victim. Includes a bibliography of works by and about Bowen.

Bloom, Harold, ed. *Elizabeth Bowen*. New York: Chelsea House, 1987. Offers an introduction and previously published criticism. The article by poet and fiction writer Mona Van Duyn examines *The Death of the Heart*'s fictional techniques.

Coles, Robert. *Irony in the Mind's Life*. Charlottesville: University Press of Virginia, 1974. Clear, insightful analysis of setting, theme, and character, especially the adolescent Portia's innocent capacity for malevolence as she struggles with the seven deadly sins. Discusses the importance of Lilian and Eddie.

Corcoran, Neil. *Elizabeth Bowen: The Enforced Return*. New York: Oxford University Press, 2004. Corcoran analyzes several of Bowen's novels, demonstrating how these and other works focus on three themes that are central to Bowen's writing: Ireland, children, and war. Chapter 5, "Motherless Child: *The Death of the Heart*," focuses on this novel.

Ellmann, Maud. *Elizabeth Bowen: The Shadow Across the Page*. Edinburgh: Edinburgh University Press, 2003. Introduction to Bowen's life and writings, using historical, psychoanalytical, and deconstructivist approaches to interpret her works. *The Death of the Heart* is discussed in chapter 5.

Glendinning, Victoria. *Elizabeth Bowen: Portrait of a Writer*. London: Weidenfeld & Nicolson, 1977. Presents Bowen as the last of the Anglo-Irish writers, discussing incidents and individuals in Bowen's life that are reflected in *The Death of the Heart*. Evaluates innovative authorial voice over technique.

Heath, William. *Elizabeth Bowen: An Introduction to Her Novels*. Madison: University of Wisconsin Press, 1961. Discusses the novel's structure, including transitions between its three sections. Analyzes character and theme, finding Matchett the moral authority of the novel. Compares Bowen with Henry James, Jane Austen, and T. S.

Eliot. Includes an extremely helpful introduction and annotated bibliography.

Kenney, Edwin, Jr. *Elizabeth Bowen*. Cranbury, N.J.: Bucknell University Press, 1975. Presents *The Death of the Heart* as a culmination of Bowen's themes of youthful innocence confronting a world of unsympathetic fallen adults. Describes Bowen's contrasting the child with the adult, innocence with experience, and the past with the present, including detailed analysis of the relationship between Portia and Anna.

Lassner, Phyllis. *Elizabeth Bowen*. Basingstoke, England: Macmillan, 1990. A timely, sophisticated evaluation with a feminist approach. The primary and secondary bibliographies include lists of pertinent readings in feminist theory, myth, and psychology.

Lee, Hermione. *Elizabeth Bowen: An Estimation*. London: Vision Press, 1981. Includes an excellent chapter emphasizing the moral viewpoint of *The Death of the Heart* and its depiction of social values.

The Death of Virgil

Author: Hermann Broch (1886-1951)
First published: Der Tod des Vergil, 1945 (English translation, 1945)
Type of work: Novel
Type of plot: Philosophical
Time of plot: 19 B.C.E.
Locale: Brundisium (Brindisi, Italy)

Principal characters:
PUBLIUS VIRGILIUS (VIRGIL) MARO, the chief poet of Rome
AUGUSTUS CAESAR, the emperor of Rome
PLOTIA HIERIA, a woman Virgil had once loved
LYSANIAS, a young boy
A SLAVE

The Story:

The imperial fleet returns from Greece to Brundisium, bearing with it Emperor Augustus and his poet, Virgil, who is dying. Augustus sought Virgil and brought him back from the peace and calm in Athens to the shouting Roman throngs—to the mob with its frightening latent capacity for brutality, its fickle adoration of its leaders. These are, however, the Romans whom Virgil glorified; the nobles he saw on ship greedily eating and gaming are their leaders. Dapper, sham-majestic Augustus is their emperor.

Fever-ridden, the poet hears a boy's song as the ship enters the harbor. Later, as he is carried from the ship, a beautiful boy appears from nowhere to lead his litter away from the tumult surrounding the emperor, through narrow streets crowded with garbage ripening into decay and full of the miseries of the flesh where women jeer at him for being rich and weak. The women's insults make him aware of his own sham-divinity and of the futility of his life. Dying, he at last sees clearly the hypocrisy of his life, like the shining, hollow emperor whom he serves.

At the palace, he is taken to his chambers. The boy, Lysanias, remains with him as night falls. In the depths of a violent seizure, Virgil recognizes his own lack of love. Conscious of his dying body and the infested night, he knows

that, like the Augustus-worshiping masses, he followed the wrong gods; that in his devotion to poetry he from the beginning gave up the service of life for that of death; that it is too late for him to be fulfilled, for even his *Aeneid* remains unperfected. Some recurrence of vigor drives him to the window. Looking into the night, he knows that not only his poem remains to be fulfilled; some knowledge still lies ahead for him to achieve. The necessity of the soul is to discover itself, since through self-discovery it finds the universe: The landscape of the soul is that of all creation. Human beings must learn, not through the stars but through other human beings.

Two men and a woman interrupt his thoughts when they come through the streets quarreling and shouting good-natured obscenities, guffawing their bawdiness with that male laughter whose matter-of-factness annihilates rather than derides. This laughter in the beautiful night reveals something of the nature of beauty itself. Beauty is the opponent of knowledge; because it is remote, infinite, and therefore seemingly eternal, it is pursued wrongly for its own sake. The same nonhuman laughter is hidden in it. The artist who pursues beauty plunges into loneliness and self-idolatry; because he chooses beauty rather than life, his work becomes adornment rather than revelation. This path Virgil chose: Beauty's cold egotism instead of love's warm life, which is true creativity. Thus he died long before, even before his renunciation of the lovely Plotia, whom he now remembers.

The need for contrition because of his refusal of love—a refusal of the pledge given to all—overwhelms him. The fever rises within him, bringing strangely prophetic visions of Rome in ruins with wolves howling, of giant birds droning. As reality returns, he knows that for his own salvation he has to burn the *Aeneid*.

Lysanias reads to him as he drifts into a calm dream, shining with a knowledge of all past earthly happenings and a vision of something to come. Not yet, but soon, will come one in whom creation, love, and immortality will be united, one who will bear salvation like a single star, whose voice he seems to hear bidding him open his eyes to love, for he is called to enter the creation. As the fever leaves him and dawn breaks, he momentarily doubts the voice. Then comes the vision of an angel and, at last, undisturbed sleep.

Virgil awakens to find two old friends who come to cheer him. Their bluff reassurances change to incredulity when they hear that he plans to burn the *Aeneid*. Their arguments against his own conviction that his book lacks reality because he lacks love are blurred by his fevered perception. Lysanias, whose existence seems questionable to his friends, appears with a Near Eastern slave to reaffirm that Virgil is the guide, although not the savior. Plotia comes and calls him to an exchange of mutual love and the destruction of his work, the renunciation of beauty for love. Suddenly he and Plotia are exposed, and power thunders around him.

Augustus comes to ask Virgil not to burn the *Aeneid*. In the ensuing interview, Virgil's rising delirium makes him not only supernaturally aware of truth but also confused as to reality: The invisible Plotia guards the manuscript; the invisible Lysanias lurks nearby; the room sometimes becomes a landscape. Augustus insists that the poem is the property of the Romans, for whom it was written. Virgil tries to explain that poetry is the knowledge of death, for only through death can one understand life; unlike Aeschylus, whose knowledge forced him to poetry, he, Virgil, sought knowledge through writing poetry and therefore found nothing.

Augustus and the slave seem to be talking, and Augustus is the symbol of the state he created, which is order and sobriety and humanity's supreme eternal reality. The slave, awaiting the birth of the supreme ancestor's son, is steadfastness and the freedom of community. The truth of the state must be united to the metaphysical by an individual act of truth, must be made human to realize perfection. Such a savior will come, whose sacrificial death will be the supreme symbol of humility and charity. Virgil still insists that he must sacrifice his work because he did not sacrifice his life, that destroying a thing that lacks perception will redeem both himself and the Romans.

Augustus, growing angry, accuses Virgil of envy. In a moment of love, Virgil gives him the poem, agreeing not to destroy it. He asks, however, that his slaves might go free after his death. As he talks of his will to his friends, renewed attacks of fever bring him ever stranger hallucinations. He calls for help and finds he can at last say the word for his own salvation.

After he finishes dictating his will, it seems to him that he is once more on a boat, one smaller than the one that brought him into the harbor the day before, rowed by his friend Plotius and guided by Lysanias. About him are many people he knows. Gradually, all disappear as he floats into the night; the boy becomes first a seraph whose ring glows like a star, then Plotia, who leads him into the day again. Reaching shore, they enter a garden where, somehow, he knows that she becomes the boy and the slave and that he becomes all of them; then he is also the animals and plants, then the mountains, and finally the universe, contained in a small white core of unity—and nothing. He is commanded to turn around, and the nothing becomes everything again, created by the word in the circle of time. Finally, he is received into the word itself.

Critical Evaluation:

In 1938, Hermann Broch had to flee his native Austria because he was Jewish. It was only through the intervention of sympathetic friends and acquaintances, among them James Joyce, that Broch succeeded in leaving Europe. Once in America, he set to work finishing the novel *The Death of Virgil*.

At the heart of this novel lies the question whether or not to destroy Virgil's last great creation, the epic poem the *Aeneid* (29-19 B.C.E.). A dying artist contemplates the value of his art and confronts the hard reality of politics, trying to come to grips with the fact that his work, the *Aeneid*, celebrates the Roman state and its new ruler, Augustus Caesar (first Roman emperor, also called Octavian when younger, 27 B.C.E.-14 C.E.).

During approximately the first half of the book, Virgil contemplates the imperfection of the world and the resulting fallibility of art. He concludes that art, even his own art, is incapable of rectifying the state of imperfection and that the artist is doomed to failure. Thus the *Aeneid* becomes the ultimate symbol of all that is wrong with the world and of art's inability to impose perfection.

Beauty has come to frighten Virgil. In a fever, he makes his way to the window to witness a vulgar, disgusting scene on the street between two men and a woman. As they teeter off, however, they blend into the night and become part of a greater beauty. He, the poet, who has dedicated his life to beauty, must face beauty's indifferent incorporation of the vile. He wonders what his own responsibility is to the world around him, thus reflecting Broch's thoughts at a time when most of Europe had succumbed to fascism.

Virgil arrives at his decision to burn his work through an inner monologue, in isolation. Once he discloses his intent to burn the *Aeneid*, those around him raise their voices in protest. It is, however, not until Augustus enters the room that the protests begin to carry weight for Virgil. In the long debate between the two, which consumes about one-fifth of the novel, Virgil manages to parry Augustus's many attempts at persuasion. It is not Virgil's debt to himself, to art, or to the Roman people that sways Virgil from his resolve to burn his epic poem. It is a flash of Augustus's anger, which penetrates Virgil's protective façade. When Augustus questions Virgil's fidelity toward him, his longtime patron and now leader of the Roman world, Virgil realizes that the ultimate sacrifice would be not to destroy his work but to give it to Augustus. Virgil's act, one of love, proclaims a new, Christian era.

In Broch's novel, an essential element of Virgil's dissatisfaction with the *Aeneid* is that it glorifies a worldly age that he senses is passing. Although he had been raised in the Jewish faith, Broch, like so many of his generation, had converted to Christianity as an adult. The "Christian Virgil" is an essential element of Broch's image of Virgil. In the novel, the Roman poet has a vision adumbrating the coming of Christ. Indeed, for Broch, Virgil is the ideal figure symbolizing the passing of one age to another.

In the early part of the twentieth century, it was commonly thought that many parallels existed between those times and the Roman age. Thinkers such as the German historian Oswald Spengler and the British historian Arnold Toynbee used Rome—particularly Rome's disintegration—as a model with which to analyze twentieth century culture. This attitude generally prevailed when the Virgil bimillennial celebration took place in 1930, and it was reflected in Theodor Haecker's 1931 book *Virgil, Father of the West*. Broch read the book and especially liked Haecker's interpretation of Virgil as proto-Christian. In 1936, Broch wrote a first, much shorter version of his Virgil story for a radio broadcast in March, 1937. Eventually, there were five versions, each successively building into the final, grand, lyrical narrative.

Broch had no formal training in classics, and he gleaned almost everything he knew about Virgil's life from Haecker's book. In the first versions of Broch's novel, he focused on the death of the poet and his crisis of art. Only later did he introduce what became the central theme of the book: the destruction of the *Aeneid*. He learned about the legend through a friend's translation of the preface to an old edition of Virgil. From early versions of his novel, it is clear that Broch knew Virgil's *Eclogues* (43-37 B.C.E.), but reference to the *Aeneid* is curiously absent. Since the *Eclogues* provide the main focus of Christian attention to the Roman poet, this is another indication that Broch's interest in the Roman poet was driven by the image of the Christian Virgil.

Although *The Death of Virgil* is usually referred to as a novel, Broch tried to avoid any particular genre. He himself referred to the work as a poem extending over more than five hundred pages. The German language lends itself to long, convoluted constructions, but Broch pushed even German conventions to the limit, with some sentences going on for page after page. The book is separated into four sections—Water, the Arrival; Fire, the Descent; Earth, the Expectation; and Ether, the Homecoming—which Broch conceived of in musical terms. (The American conductor Leonard Bernstein once made plans to write a symphony based on Broch's novel, envisioning four movements to correspond to the four sections, and the French composer Jean Barraqué actually did base parts of a symphony on the work.) Much of the novel is cast in a stream-of-consciousness style, which represents Virgil's inner universe. This gives way in part three to the external world of conversation. Here, the utterances, as in the dialogue between Virgil and Augustus, resemble the brief thrusts and parries of a fencing duel.

"Critical Evaluation" by Scott G. Williams

Further Reading

Bartram, Graham, and Philip Payne. "Apocalypse and Utopia in the Austrian Novel of the 1930's: Hermann Broch and Robert Musil." In *The Cambridge Companion to the Modern German Novel*, edited by Bartram. New York: Cambridge University Press, 2004. *The Death of Virgil* and *Sleepwalkers* are analyzed and placed within the wider context of 1930's Austrian literature in this essay about novelists Broch and Robert Musil.

Broch de Rothermann, H. F. *Dear Mrs. Strigl: A Memoir of Hermann Broch*. Translated by John Hargraves. New Haven, Conn.: Beinecke Rare Book & Manuscript Library, 2001. Broch's son recalls his father, focusing on the personal rather than on Broch's writing. Describes Broch's relationship with his father, his exile in the United States, and other aspects of his often difficult life. In both English and German.

Dowden, Stephen D., ed. *Hermann Broch: Literature, Philosophy, Politics (The Yale Broch Symposium 1986)*. Columbia, S.C.: Camden House, 1988. Includes articles by Luciano Zagari ("'Poetry Is Anticipation': Broch and Virgil") and Vasily Rudich ("Mythical and Mystical in *The Death of Vergil*: A Response to Luciano Zagari"), which deal directly with *The Death of Virgil*, as well as other essays from the 1986 Yale Broch Symposium, which offer insights into all of Broch's work.

Halsall, Robert. *The Problem of Autonomy in the Works of Hermann Broch*. New York: Peter Lang, 2000. Halsall argues that concerns about autonomy are central to understanding Broch's literature and philosophy and demonstrates how these concerns are evident in his major novels.

Hargraves, John A. *Music in the Works of Broch, Mann, and Kafka*. Rochester, N.Y.: Camden House, 2001. Although Hargraves examines music as an element in the work of three German writers, this study concentrates on Broch because Hargraves maintains that of the three, Broch was the most interested in expressing the primacy of music in his work. Includes essays discussing Broch's discursive writings on music and the musical elements in several of his novels.

Lützeler, Paul Michael. *Hermann Broch: A Biography*. Translated by Janice Furness. London: Quartet Books, 1987. A thorough and interesting study, which helps to illuminate the circumstances surrounding the creation of *The Death of Virgil*.

_____, ed. *Hermann Broch, Visionary in Exile: The 2001 Yale Symposium*. Rochester, N.Y.: Camden House, 2003. Contains papers delivered at an international symposium that present a wide range of interpretations of Broch's work. Several papers analyze various elements of *The Death of Virgil* and *The Sleepwalkers*.

Untermeyer, Jean Starr. "Midwife to a Masterpiece." In *Private Collection*. New York: Alfred A. Knopf, 1965. The personal account of the translator of *The Death of Virgil*, who worked closely with Broch on the translation during his time at Princeton.

Ziolkowski, Theodore. *Virgil and the Moderns*. Princeton, N.J.: Princeton University Press, 1993. Particularly valuable for its discussion of Broch's use of Virgil in relation to other twentieth century writers.

The Death Ship
The Story of an American Sailor

Author: B. Traven (1890?-1969)
First published: Das Totenschiff, 1926 (English translation, 1934)
Type of work: Novel
Type of plot: Social realism and picaresque
Time of plot: 1920's
Locale: Belgium, the Netherlands, France, Spain, the Mediterranean Sea, and the Atlantic Ocean

Principal characters:
GERARD GALES, an American sailor
STANISLAV KOSLOVSKI, an experienced Polish sailor and his shipmate and friend

The Story:

It is a few years after World War I when experienced American sailor Gerard Gales sails as a deck hand aboard the cargo ship *Tuscaloosa* from New Orleans, Louisiana, to Western Europe. In Antwerp, Belgium, Gales leaves the ship for a night on the town. After carousing, he returns to the docks to find that the *Tuscaloosa* had left on its return voyage earlier than scheduled. He is stranded penniless in the foreign port. Worse, he had left his seaman's card and other proof of identity aboard the ship. Picked up by local police, he is brought before a magistrate, who orders Gales to be deported under penalty of life imprisonment. In the dead of night, he is escorted to the border with the Netherlands, given food, and told to cross the border.

In Rotterdam, Gales approaches the American consul for assistance. However, without proper documentation—such as a passport, birth certificate, or sailor's identification—he cannot prove he is a U.S. citizen, thus the counsel cannot do anything except provide Gales food and lodging for a few days. Once again, local police become aware of his presence. Threatened with imprisonment at hard labor for vagrancy, he is given enough food and money to return to Antwerp. Unwilling to do so, Gales hitchhikes around the Netherlands, surviving on the generosity of strangers.

When his money runs out, Gales begs passage on a British ship, which carries him as far as Boulogne, France. Traveling to Paris via train, he is discovered without a ticket and sentenced to ten days in prison. Upon his release, he is given fifteen days to leave the country, or suffer a long term behind bars. Gales again sees the American consul, who can do nothing for the sailor without documentation. Caught in Toulouse, Gales on a lark claims to be German rather than an American. He is imprisoned for a short time and again ordered to leave France. He drifts south toward Spain, sleeping in barns and living on handouts from peasants. Stumbling upon a French fortress, he is suspected of being a German spy; he is to be shot at sunrise. However, the French relent, and he will be pardoned if he goes to Spain.

In his guise as a German, Gales is welcomed to Spain. He is fed and clothed, and the authorities, indifferent to such things as formal identification, allow him to travel the country freely. He journeys from Seville to Cadiz to Barcelona, living by begging, and is accepted as one more among the rootless millions unable to find work in the global recession following the Great War. One day, fishing off a pier and feeling purposeless, he is offered work on an ancient, decaying freighter called the *Yorrike*. Gales accepts the job, although he realizes the vessel is a death ship: overinsured, flagless, near-derelict, and staffed by men like himself, who are without documentation. The ship limps aimlessly from port to port carrying random cargo, including smuggled munitions to war-torn nations, until the owners decide when it is most profitable to sink it.

Aboard the *Yorrike*, Gales—hiding his identity by calling himself Pippip and claiming to be Egyptian—is made drag man, the worst job on a ship of horrors. He is required to shovel tons of coal for the ship's voracious, temperamental boilers and perform other dangerous tasks that burn and scar his body. Working conditions are deplorable. Passageways are unlighted and hazardous. Lifejackets are absent, and lifeboats are riddled with holes. There are no mattresses or blankets for the narrow bunks, and food is monotonously awful. No soap is provided to wash off coal residue. Petty officers are martinets who throw troublemakers into a hold to be devoured by rats. Pay is at best uncertain.

Gales soon becomes friends with a Polish sailor, Stanislav Koslovski, who helps him learn the ropes and teaches him how to survive day-to-day. Despite the hellish conditions, Gales adapts. After four months, he comes to accept his lot, and his fire-gang crew mates have become comrades. What choice does he have? Without documents, his only options are to exchange the *Yorrike* for another death ship, or to leap over the rail and drown himself.

Having made peace with his circumstances, Gales goes ashore one day with Stanislav in an African port. Walking along the docks, they admire other ships, in particular a new British vessel called the *Empress of Madagascar*. Invited to dine aboard a neighboring Danish ship, Gales and Stanislav learn about the *Empress of Madagascar* from a friendly sailor. Despite many amenities that the crew of the *Yorrike* can only imagine, the *Empress of Madagascar* is also a death ship: A flawed engine design makes it too slow and impractical to haul freight, so it is doomed to be sunk.

Returning to the familiar, now comfortable *Yorrike*, Gales and Stanislav are shanghaied. When they awake, they find to their dismay they are aboard the *Empress of Madagascar* and are pressed into service as firemen to keep the boilers stoked and the engines turning. Though the pay is union standard, meals are plentiful and cabins are spacious. Gales and Stanislav know the ship will be scuttled soon, probably while they are tending to the boilers; they will be unable to escape death if this is the case. They search for the best route to the deck, and settle down to wait.

The destruction of the ship occurs within days, somewhere off the west coast of Africa, away from usual sea lanes. Crewmen drill holes in the hull to flood the ship and cause the boilers to explode. However, the unexpected happens: Instead of rolling over on its side, the *Empress of Madagascar* goes down by the bow, smothering the boiler fires and drowning most officers and able-bodied seamen. Prepared for the sinking, Gales and Stanislav are among the few survivors. Two lifeboats, with the captain aboard, manage to launch, but both are smashed by waves. Only Gales and Stanislav are left alive. The ship, meanwhile, has not sunk, but is wedged half-submerged, stern-up on a reef. Gales and Stanislav clamber aboard, and for a few days live like kings, gorging on fine foods and swilling expensive liquors.

Inevitably, a storm brews and heavy seas dislodge the ship, forcing Gales and Stanislav into the water. They lash themselves onto a piece of wooden wreckage to await rescue. During the next several days, they hallucinate, seeing the lights of cities and believing fondly that their former vessel is steaming to pick them up. Stanislav, after swallowing salt water, goes insane, unties his bindings, and plunges beneath the waves, leaving Gales, too weak to undo his own knots, to his fate.

Critical Evaluation:

Written in a naturalistic style with plain, unadorned language, and peppered with mild epithets and profanity, B. Traven's novel *The Death Ship* is part picaresque novel, part character study, and part proletarian lament. The story is told from the perspective of an ordinary person, a particular and unique representative of the faceless sea of humanity. The story proceeds from one apparently random incident to the next, and then to an inevitable conclusion.

The Death Ship, a symbol for the voyage toward oblivion that every living thing must make, is an important introduction to the themes and fatalistic tone that prevail in the bulk of Traven's other long fiction. *The Death Ship*, Traven's first published novel, is a work of imagination in the literary tradition of earlier sea-story adventures written by writers such as Herman Melville and Joseph Conrad (in the novel, Traven alludes to Conrad, who had died in 1924). The novel is likewise based on the author's own real-life experiences. He had earned his passage from a Europe in political, social, and economic upheaval to postrevolutionary Mexico, where he would live the rest of his life. Though the conclusion of *The Death Ship* seems to tell of the end of character Gerard Gales, he lives to appear again in two of Traven's subsequent novels: *Der Wobbly* (1926; *The Cotton-Pickers*, 1956) and *Die Brücke im Dschungel* (1929; *The Bridge in the Jungle*, 1938).

A central issue of the novel is the matter of identity. National governments—in Traven's time or now—define a person upon the strength of his or her documentation, even, one could say, upon the thickness of his or her wallet. Without proper credentials (certificates, passports, visas, written records) or without money to bribe officials, a person does not exist and therefore has no rights; also, without a solid past supported by papers, a person has no future. This is an entirely appropriate subject for Traven, because the question of his own mysterious identity has been a topic of interest for scholars and researchers for many years. Evidence suggests that Traven was either a German named Otto Feige or an anarchist named Ret Marut, escaping persecution in Europe. Others argue that he was Chicago-born Traven Torsvan, or the reclusive author's supposed Mexican agent and translator Hal Croves, or perhaps all of these at various times. More creative theories propose that Traven was really writer Jack London in disguise, or the illegitimate son of Wilhelm II, or satirist Ambrose Bierce, who had disappeared in Mexico

about ten years before Traven surfaced there. Complicating the problem is the large number of pseudonyms under which the author is known to have written. Speculation about why Traven chose to hide his true identity—in contrast to most serious writers, who depend upon appearances and public relations to sell books—runs rampant.

Closely allied to the concept of identity in *The Death Ship* is the topic of bureaucracy. Gales, like the protagonist in Franz Kafka's novel *Der Prozess* (1925; *The Trial*, 1937), moves through frustrating, labyrinthine governmental systems at the mercy of petty, self-important officials employed by the state (and, thus, relatively immune to the vagaries of economics). These officials are empowered to dispense passports, certificates, sailor's cards, licenses, and similar documents. Without such documents, Traven maintains, a person can survive in the modern world only on a lawless, subsistence level.

Labor versus management also comes under close scrutiny in *The Death Ship*. Gales, typical of ordinary workers everywhere, is in opposition to his immediate superiors, who represent the owners. (The character's name may been an homage to Linn Gale, editor of the monthly publication of the Industrial Workers of the World, also known as the Wobblies—a union organization the author frequently wrote about.) Traven, a constant defender of the downtrodden and dispossessed, establishes a theme in *The Death Ship* that reappears in his later fiction: the dichotomy of those who actually provide the labor—often at great bodily risk—to keep an enterprise going and those who profit from the sweat of the workers and who ultimately have no real concern for their employees' welfare. To the owners, those desperate to earn a living can always be found to replace those who become injured or sick, or who die on the job. To Gales, and to Traven, such a state of affairs is reprehensible, akin to slavery. However, both the author and his characters realize that little can be done to change their situation.

As in the author's later novels, mundane events in *The Death Ship* serve as catalysts to discuss issues of greater import. The simple words of Traven's unsophisticated, uneducated characters, like Gales, encompass cosmic ideas: the meaning of existence, life and death, bravery and cowardice, appearance and reality, freedom and slavery, the religious and the supernatural. Such concerns, the author contends, are—regardless of time, place, race, creed, gender, social status, or other distinctions—universal. This commonality of experience makes *The Death Ship* as worthy of consideration today as it was when originally published in 1926.

Revised by Jack Ewing

Further Reading

Baumann, Michael L. *B. Traven: An Introduction*. Albuquerque: University of New Mexico Press, 1976. Discusses Traven as a proletarian writer, focusing on his attitudes toward nationalism and capitalism. Compares language and subject matter in the 1926 German original of *The Death Ship* with the 1934 English translation.

Chankin, Donald O. *Anonymity and Death: The Fiction of B. Traven*. University Park: Pennsylvania State University Press, 1975. A clear, insightful psychoanalytic analysis of character and theme in *The Death Ship*. Provides historical and geopolitical background. Discusses literary parallels in the works of Joseph Conrad, Herman Melville, and others.

Guthke, Karl S. *B. Traven: The Life Behind the Legends*. Translated by Robert C. Sprung. Chicago: Lawrence Hill Books, 1987. Guthke was the first biographer to have access to Traven's archives. He tries to untangle the details of Traven's puzzling biography, separating the many myths and inaccuracies from the realities of his life.

_____. "In 'A Far-Off Land': B. Traven." In *German Novelists of the Weimar Republic: Intersections of Literature and Politics*, edited by Karl Leydecker. Rochester, N.Y.: Camden House, 2006. Traven is one of the twelve German writers whose work is analyzed in this study of Weimar Republic literature and the political, social, and economic instability of the era. Essay on Traven discusses *The Death Ship*.

Mezo, Richard E. *A Study of B. Traven's Fiction: The Journey to Solipaz*. San Francisco: Mellon Research University Press, 1993. A comprehensive critical analysis of theme, character, style, and structure in Traven's fiction. Discusses the development of the persona of character Gerard Gales in *The Death Ship* and later works. A good introduction to Traven and his fiction.

Pateman, Roy. *The Man Nobody Knows: The Life and Legacy of B. Traven*. Lanham, Md.: University Press of America, 2005. Attempts to discover the major influences on Traven's life and work by considering his alternative biographies. Examines his politics and his humanist anarchism and analyzes *The Death Ship* and his other works.

Raskin, Jonah. *My Search for B. Traven*. New York: Methuen, 1980. An interesting account of the many mysteries surrounding Traven's multiple identities. Compares manuscript, typescript, and various print editions of *The Death Ship*, tracing the development of Gales, the introduction of Stanislav Koslovski, and the symbolic importance of the ships of the novel.

Stone, Judy. *The Mystery of B. Traven*. Bloomington, Ind.: iUniverse, 2007. A new edition of a well-received 1977 work. Includes excerpts from the only extended series of interviews with Traven, incorporates a discussion of the theme of *The Death Ship*, and reveals Traven's complex social philosophy—all important factors in analyzing the author's fiction.

Treverton, Edward. *B. Traven*. Lanham, Md.: Scarecrow Press, 1999. This book explores the author's career through his work. Features an extensive illustrated bibliography covering first and subsequent editions of his books published around the world.

The Decameron

Author: Giovanni Boccaccio (1313-1375)
First published: 1349-1351 (English translation, 1620)
Type of work: Short fiction
Type of plot: Frame story
Time of plot: Antiquity and the Middle Ages
Locale: Italy

Principal characters:
THE THREE TEDALDO SONS, three gentlemen of Florence
ALESSANDRO, their nephew
THE DAUGHTER OF THE KING OF ENGLAND
TANCRED, prince of Salerno
GHISMONDA, his daughter
GUISCARDO, her lover
ISABETTA, a young woman of Messina
LORENZO, her lover
GALESO, a stupid young man of Cyprus, known as Cimone
EFIGENIA, his love
LISIMACO, a young man of Rhodes
FEDERIGO DEGLI ALBERIGHI, a young man of Florence
MONNA GIOVANNA, his love
PERONELLA, a wool comber of Naples
PERONELLA'S HUSBAND
STRIGNARIO, her lover
NATHAN, a rich man of Cathay
MITRIDANES, a rich man envious of Nathan
SALADIN, Sultan of Babylon
MESSER TORELLO, a wealthy countryman of Pavia
GUALTIERI, the son of the Marquess of Saluzzo
GRISELDA, his wife

The Story:

A terrible plague is ravaging Florence, Italy. To flee from it, a group of seven young women and three young men, who meet by chance in a church, decide to go to a villa out of town. There they set up a working arrangement whereby each will be king or queen for a day. During the ten days they stay in the country, each tells a story, following certain stipulations laid down by the daily ruler. The stories range from romance to farce, from comedy to tragedy.

Pampinea's Tale About the Three Tedaldo Young Men. When Messer Tedaldo dies, he leaves all of his goods and chattels to his three sons. With no thought for the future, they live so extravagantly that they soon have little left. The oldest son suggests that they sell what they can, leave Florence, and go to London, where they are unknown.

In London, they lend money at a high rate of interest, and in a few years, they have a small fortune. Then they return to Florence. There they marry and begin to live extravagantly again, while depending on the moneys still coming to them from England.

A nephew named Alessandro takes care of their business in England. At that time, there are such differences between the king and a son that Alessandro's business is ruined. He stays in England, however, in the hope that peace will come and his business will recover. Finally, he returns to Italy with a group of monks who are taking their young abbot to the pope to get a dispensation for him and a confirmation of the youthful cleric's election.

On the way, Alessandro discovers that the abbot is a woman, and he marries her in the sight of God. In Rome, the woman has an audience with the pope. Her father, the king of England, wishes the pope's blessing on her marriage to the old king of Scotland, but she asks the pope's blessing on her marriage to Alessandro instead.

After the wedding, Alessandro and his bride go to Florence, where she pays his uncles' debts. Two knights precede the couple to England and urge the king to forgive his daughter. After the king knights Alessandro, the new knight reconciles the king and his rebellious son.

Fiammetta's Tale of Tancred and the Golden Cup. Tancred, prince of Salerno, loves his daughter Ghismonda so much that, when she is widowed soon after her marriage, he does not think to provide her with a second husband, and she is too modest to ask him to do so. Being a lively woman, however, she decides to have as her lover the most valiant man in her father's court. His name is Guiscardo. His only fault is that he is of humble birth.

Ghismonda notices that Guiscardo returns her interest, and they meet secretly in a cave, one entrance to which is through a door in the young widow's bedroom. Soon she is taking her lover into her bedroom, where they enjoy each other frequently.

Tancred is in the habit of visiting his daughter's room at odd times. One day, when he goes to visit, she is not there. He sits down to wait in a place where he is, by accident, hidden by the bed curtains from his daughter and her lover, who soon come in to use the bed.

Tancred remains hidden, but that night he has Guiscardo arrested. When he berates his daughter for picking so humble a lover, she scolds him for letting so brave a man remain poor in his court. She begs nothing from Tancred except that he kill her and her lover with the same stroke.

The prince does not believe Ghismonda will be as resolute as she sounds. When her lover is killed, Tancred has his heart cut from his body and sent to her in a golden cup. Ghismonda thanks her father for his noble gift. After repeatedly kissing the heart, she pours poison into the cup and drinks it. Then she lies down upon her bed with Guiscardo's heart upon her own. Tancred's own heart is touched when he sees her cold in death, and he obeys her last request that she and Guiscardo be buried together.

Filomena's Tale of the Pot of Basil. Isabetta lives in Messina with her three merchant brothers and a young man named Lorenzo, who attends to their business affairs. Isabetta and Lorenzo fall in love. One night, as she goes to Lorenzo's room, her oldest brother sees her. He says nothing until the next morning, when the three brothers confer to see how they could settle the matter so that no shame should fall upon them or upon Isabetta.

Not long afterward, the three brothers set out with Lorenzo, claiming that they are going part way with him on a journey. Secretly, however, they kill and bury the young man.

After their return home, the brothers answer none of Isabetta's questions about Lorenzo. She weeps and refuses to be consoled in her grief. One night Lorenzo comes to her in a dream and tells her what happened and where he is buried. Without telling her brothers, she goes to the spot indicated in her dream and finds her lover's body there. She cuts off his head and wraps it in a cloth to take home. She buries the head in dirt in a large flowerpot and plants basil over it. The basil flourishes, watered by her tears.

She weeps so much over the plant that her brothers take away the pot of basil and hide it. She asks about it often, so the brothers grow curious. At last they investigate and find Lorenzo's head. Abashed, they leave the city. Isabetta dies of a broken heart.

Pamfilo's Tale of Cimone, Who Becomes Civilized Through Love. Galeso is the tallest and handsomest of Aristippo's children, but he is so stupid that the people of Cyprus call him Cimone, which means "Brute." Cimone's stupidity so embarrasses his father that the old man sends the boy to the country to live. There Cimone is content, until one day he comes upon Efigenia, whose beauty completely changes him.

He tells his father that he intends to live in town. The news worries his father for a while, but Cimone buys fine clothes and associates only with worthy young men. In four years, he is the most accomplished and virtuous young man on the island.

Although he knows she is promised to Pasimunda of Rhodes, Cimone asks Efigenia's father for her hand in marriage. He is refused. When Pasimunda sends for his bride, Cimone and his friends pursue the ship and take Efigenia off the vessel, after which they let the ship's crew go free to return to Rhodes. In the night, a storm arises and blows Cimone's ship to the very harbor in Rhodes where Efigenia is supposed to go. Cimone and his men are arrested.

Pasimunda has a brother who is promised a wife, but this woman is loved by Lisimaco, a youth of Rhodes, as Efigenia is loved by Cimone. The brothers plan a double wedding.

Lisimaco makes plans with Cimone. At the double wedding feast, Lisimaco, Cimone, and many of their friends snatch the brides away from their prospective husbands. The young men carry their beloved ones to Crete, where they live happily in exile for a time, until their fathers intercede for them. Then Cimone takes Efigenia home to Cyprus, and Lisimaco takes his wife back to Rhodes.

Fiammetta's Tale of Federigo and His Falcon. Federigo degli Alberighi is famed in Florence for his courtesy and his prowess in arms. He falls in love with Monna Giovanna, a woman who cares nothing for him, though he spends his fortune trying to please her. Finally he is so poor that he goes to the country to live on his farm. There he entertains himself only by flying his falcon, which is considered the best in the world.

Monna's husband dies, leaving her to enjoy his vast estates with one young son. The son strikes up an acquaintance with Federigo and particularly admires the falcon. When the boy becomes sick, he thinks he might get well if he can own Federigo's bird.

Monna, as a last resort, swallows her pride and calls upon Federigo. She tells him she will stay for supper, but Federigo, desperately poor as he is, has nothing to serve his love except the falcon, which he promptly kills and roasts for her.

After the meal, with many apologies, Monna tells her host that her son, thinking he will get well if he has the falcon, desires Federigo's bird. Federigo weeps to think that Monna asks for the one thing he cannot give her.

The boy dies soon after, and Monna is bereft. When her brothers urge her to remarry, she finally agrees to do so, but she will marry no one but the generous Federigo, who killed his pet falcon to do her honor. Federigo marries into great riches.

Filostrato's Tale of Peronella, Who Hid Her Lover in a Butt. Peronella is a Neapolitan wool comber married to a poor bricklayer. Together they make enough to live comfortably. Peronella has a lover named Strignario, who comes to the house each day after the husband goes to work.

One day, when the husband returns unexpectedly, Peronella hides Strignario in a butt (large keg or barrel). Her husband brings home a man to buy the butt for five florins. Thinking quickly, Peronella tells her husband that she already has a buyer who offered seven florins for the butt and that he is at that moment inside the butt inspecting it.

Strignario comes out, complaining that the butt is dirty. The husband offers to clean it. While the husband is inside scraping, Strignario cuckolds him again, pays for the butt, and goes away.

Filostrato's Tale of Nathan's Generosity. In Cathay lives a rich and generous old man named Nathan. He has a splendid palace and many servants, and he entertains lavishly anyone who comes his way.

In a country nearby lives Mitridanes, who is not nearly so old as Nathan but just as rich. Since he is jealous of Nathan's fame, he builds a palace and entertains handsomely everyone who visits. One day, a woman comes thirteen times asking alms. Furious when Mitridanes calls her to task, she tells him that she once asked alms of Nathan forty-two times in one day without reproof. Mitridanes decides that he will have to kill Nathan before his own fame will grow.

Riding near Nathan's palace, Mitridanes discovers Nathan walking alone. When he asks to be directed secretly to Nathan's palace, Nathan cheerfully takes him there and establishes him in a fine apartment. Still not realizing Nathan's identity, Mitridanes reveals his plan to kill his rival. Nathan arranges matters so that Mitridanes comes upon him alone in the woods.

Mitridanes, curious to see Nathan, catches hold of him before piercing him with a sword. When he discovers that Nathan is the old man who first directed him to the palace, made him comfortable, and then arranged the meeting in the woods, Mitridanes realizes that he can never match Nathan's generosity, and he is greatly ashamed.

Nathan offers to go to Mitridanes' home and become known as Mitridanes, while Mitridanes will remain to be known as Nathan. By that time, however, Mitridanes thinks his own actions will tarnish Nathan's fame, and he goes home humbled.

Pamfilo's Tale of Saladin and Messer Torello. In the time of Emperor Frederick the First, all Christendom unites in a crusade for the recovery of the Holy Land. To see how the Christians are preparing themselves and to learn to protect himself against them, Saladin, the Sultan of Babylon, takes two of his best knights and makes a tour through Italy to Paris. The travelers are disguised as merchants.

Outside the little town of Pavia, they come upon Messer Torello, who is on his way to his country estate. When they ask him how far they are from Pavia, he tells them quickly that the town is too far to be reached that night and sends his servants with them to an inn. Messer Torello senses that the three men are foreign gentlemen and wants to honor them; he has the servants take them by a roundabout way to his own estate. Meanwhile, he rides directly home. The travelers are surprised when they see him in his own place, but, realizing that he means only to honor them, they graciously consent to spend the night.

The next day, Messer Torello sends word to his wife in town to prepare a banquet. The preparations are made, and both Torellos honor the merchants that day. Before they leave, the wife gives them handsome suits of clothes like those her husband wears.

When Messer Torello becomes one of the Crusaders, he asks his wife to wait a year and a month before remarrying if she hears nothing from him. She gives him a ring with which to remember her. Soon afterward, a great plague breaks out among the Christians at Acre and kills many men. Most of the survivors are imprisoned by the sultan. Messer Torello is taken to Alexandria, where he trains hawks for Saladin and is called Saladin's Christian. Neither man recognizes the other for a long time, until at last Saladin recognizes a facial gesture in Torello and makes himself known as one of the traveling merchants. Torello is freed and lives happily as Saladin's guest. He expects daily to hear from his wife, to whom he sends word of his adventures. His messenger is shipwrecked, however, and the day approaches when his wife will be free to remarry.

At last Torello tells Saladin of the arrangement he and his wife made. The sultan takes pity on him and has Torello put to sleep on a couch heaped with jewels and gold. Then the couch, whisked off to Italy by magic, is set down in the church of which his uncle is abbot. Torello and the abbot go to the marriage feast prepared for Torello's wife and her new husband. No one recognizes Torello because of his strange beard and "oriental" clothing, until he displays the ring his wife gave him. Then with great rejoicing they are reunited, a reward for their earlier generosity.

Dioneo's Tale of the Patient Griselda. Gualtieri, eldest son of the Marquess of Saluzzo, is a bachelor whose subjects beg him to marry. Although he is not anxious to take a wife, he decides to wed poor Griselda, who lives in a nearby hamlet. When he goes with his friends to bring Griselda home, he asks her if she will always be obedient and try to please him and never be angry. Upon her word that she will do so, Gualtieri has her stripped of her poor gown and dressed in finery becoming her new station.

With her new clothes, Griselda changes so much in appearance that she seems to be a true noblewoman, and Gualtieri's subjects are pleased. She bears him a daughter and a son, both of whom Gualtieri take from her. In order to test her devotion, he pretends to have the children put to death, but Griselda sends them off cheerfully since that is her husband's wish.

When their daughter is in her early teens, Gualtieri sends Griselda home, clad only in a shift, after telling her that he intends to take a new wife. His subjects are sad, but Griselda remains composed. A short time later, he calls Griselda back to his house and orders her to prepare it for his wedding, saying that no one else knows so well how to arrange it. In her ragged dress, she prepares everything for the wedding feast. Welcoming the guests, she is particularly thoughtful of the new bride.

By that time Gualtieri thinks he tested Griselda in every possible way. He introduces the supposed bride as her daughter and the little boy who accompanies the girl as her son. Then he has Griselda dressed in her best clothes, and everyone rejoices.

Critical Evaluation:

Giovanni Boccaccio, Dante Alighieri, and Francesco Petrarch were the leading lights in a century that is considered the beginning of the Italian Renaissance. Dante died while Boccaccio was a child, but Petrarch was a friend during his middle and later life. Dante's work was essentially of the spirit; Petrarch's was that of the literary man; Boccaccio's broke free of all tradition and created a living literature about ordinary people. *The Decameron* is his most famous work. Since its composition, readers and critics have made much of its hundred entertaining and worldly tales, comic and tragic, bawdy and courteous, satiric and serious, that compose this work. Unfortunately, much early criticism was moralistic, and Boccaccio was faulted for devoting his mature artistic skill to a collection of "immoral" stories.

The Decameron has fared better in the twentieth and twenty-first centuries, with more solid critical inquiries into the work's literary significance and style. Boccaccio's collection has been considered representative of the Middle Ages; it has also been viewed as a product of the Renaissance. The work is both. *The Decameron* not only encompasses literary legacies of the medieval world but also goes far beyond Boccaccio's own time, transcending, in tone and style, artistic works of both previous and later periods.

The structure, with its frame characters, has many analogues in medieval literature; the frame story—a group of tales within an enclosing narrative—was a device known previously, in Europe and in the East. The material for many of Boccaccio's stories was gleaned from Indian, Arabic, Byzantine, French, Hebrew, and Spanish tales.

Although *The Decameron* is not escapist literature, the idea and nature of the framework have much in common with medieval romance. There is the idealistic, pastoral quality of withdrawal into the pleasant place or garden, away from the ugly, harsh reality of the surrounding world. The ten young people who leave Florence—a dying, corrupt city that Boccaccio describes plainly in all of its horrors—find only momentary respite from the charnel house of reality; but their existence for ten days is that of the enchanted medieval dreamworld: a paradise of flowers, ever-flowing fountains, shade trees, soft breezes, where all luxuries of food and drink abound. Virtue and decorum reign. There is no cynicism or lust in the various garden settings, where the pastimes are strolling, weaving garlands, or playing chess. Even Dioneo, who tells the most salacious stories, is as chaste in his conduct as Pampinea, Filomena, Filostrato, and the others. One critic has even seen in these frame characters a progression of virtues and described their stories as groups of exempla praising such qualities as wisdom, prudence, or generosity.

Against this refined and idealized medieval framework are the stories themselves, the majority marked by realism. The locale of each story is usually an actual place; the Italian cities of Pisa, Siena, and especially Florence figure largely as settings. The entire Mediterranean is represented, with its islands of Sicily, Corfu, Rhodes, Cyprus, and Ischia. France, England, and Spain also serve as backgrounds. In one story, the seventh tale on the second day, beautiful Altiel, the Sultan of Babylon's daughter, after being kidnapped, travels in the space of four years over most of the Mediterranean, the islands, Greece, Turkey, and Alexandria. Boccaccio is also concerned with restricted spatial reality, and he sketches, in close detail, internal settings of abbeys, bedrooms, churches, marketplaces, castles, and inns. Different social classes have their own language and clothing. Many characters—such as Ciappelletto, living in profanation of the world; Rinaldo abandoned in nakedness and cold by his fellow men; Peronella, the deceitful Neapolitan wool comber cuckolding her husband; the whole convent of nuns eagerly lying with the youth Masetto—these Boccaccio describes in believable, human situations.

Although he draws upon the entire arsenal of medieval rhetoric, the author of these one hundred stories goes beyond figures of speech and linguistic tools in his modern paradoxical style and cynical tone. Although his satire often bites deeply, his comic mood generally embraces evil and holiness alike with sympathy and tolerance. His treatment of themes, situation, and character is never didactic. Like Geoffrey Chaucer, Boccaccio is indulgent, exposing moral and social corruption but leaving guilty characters to condemn themselves.

A novella such as the comic tale of Chichibio, told on the sixth day, is pure comic farce, moving rapidly by question and answer, playfully rollicking to a surprise ending brought about by this impulsive, foolish cook. The story of Rossiglione and Guardastagno, ninth tale of the fourth day, has a tragic plot, but the narrators draw no moral in either case. The interaction of character, scene, and plot brings into relief forces that motivate the world of humanity and allows the readers to judge if they must. Again and again, characters in the tales are relieved from moral responsibility by the control of fortune.

Throughout *The Decameron*, Boccaccio concerns himself primarily with presenting a human world as he observed and understood it. In this presentation, there is no pedantry or reticence; he paints men and women in all of their rascality, faithlessness, nobility, and suffering, changing his Italian prose to suit the exigency of purpose, whether that results in a serious or comic, refined or coarse, descriptive or analytical style. Boccaccio has command of many styles and changes easily from one to another.

In utilizing fables and anecdotes from many medieval sources, in employing figurative and rhythmical devices from books on medieval rhetoric, and in structuring his framework according to the chivalric world of valor and courtesy, among other things, Boccaccio's work is a product of the Middle Ages. In its frank, open-minded treatment of worldly pleasures, in its use of paradox and cynicism, and in its realistic handling of character, however, *The Decameron* transcends the medieval period and establishes a literary pattern for the Renaissance and after.

"Critical Evaluation" by Muriel B. Ingham

Further Reading

Branca, Vittore. *Boccaccio: The Man and His Work.* Translated by Richard Monges and Dennis J. McAuliffe. Edited by McAuliffe. New York: New York University Press, 1976. A biography of Boccaccio and a critical analysis of *The Decameron.* Details of Boccaccio's life and culture are chronologically correlated to his body of work; the analysis emphasizes literary traditions.

Deligiorgis, Stavros. *Narrative Intellection in "The Decameron."* Iowa City: University of Iowa Press, 1975. Organized by day, treating each successive story in its turn. Provides a comprehensive view of the work's themes and its narrative framework.

De Sanctis, Francesco. "Boccaccio's Human Comedy." In *Critical Perspectives on "The Decameron,"* edited by Robert S. Dombroski. 1972. Reprint. New York: Barnes & Noble, 1976. Analyzes the purpose, tone, and focus of *The Decameron.* Includes an incidental comparison of Boccaccio's style and emphasis in *The Decameron* to Dante's.

Gittes, Tobias Foster. *Boccaccio's Naked Muse: Eros, Culture, and the Mythopoeic Imagination.* Toronto, Ont.: University of Toronto Press, 2008. Examines all of Boccaccio's works, including *The Decameron*, to demonstrate how he used an innovative and coherent system of mythology in order to express his cultural experience and address the needs of his readers.

Koff, Leonard Michael, and Brenda Deen Schildgen, eds. *"The Decameron" and "The Canterbury Tales": New Essays on an Old Question.* Madison, N.J.: Fairleigh Dickinson University Press, 2000. Collection of essays assessing how Boccaccio's work influenced *The Canterbury Tales*, comparing common characteristics and some of the individual tales in both works.

Lee, A. C. *"The Decameron": Its Sources and Analogues.* New York: Haskell House, 1966. An annotated list of possible and probable sources for the individual tales told by the characters in *The Decameron*, plus parallels where the same stories are told by different writers of other ages and cultures. A careful collation and synthesis, containing a helpful index.

McGregor, James H., ed. *Approaches to Teaching Boccaccio's "Decameron."* New York: Modern Language Association of America, 2000. Guide designed to assist undergraduate instructors. Includes essays advising how to teach the work in various settings and providing information about the book's religious and historical contexts, critical reception, representation of women, and influence upon European literature.

Mazotta, Giuseppe. "*The Decameron*: The Marginality of Literature." In *Critical Perspectives on "The Decameron,"* edited by Robert S. Dombroski. 1972. Reprint. New York: Barnes & Noble, 1976. Discusses *The Decameron* as a vehicle for interpreting history, as well as for using secular literature as a means of coping with mutability and death.

Migiel, Marilyn. *A Rhetoric of "The Decameron."* Toronto, Ont.: University of Toronto Press, 2003. Migiel interprets the representation of gender in the work, focusing on the relationship between the male and female storytellers and the male author and his imagined female readers.

Decline and Fall
An Illustrated Novelette

Author: Evelyn Waugh (1903-1966)
First published: 1928
Type of work: Novel
Type of plot: Social satire
Time of plot: Twentieth century
Locale: England and Wales

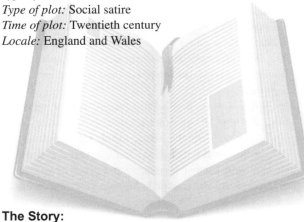

Principal characters:
PAUL PENNYFEATHER, a serious-minded young Oxonian
SIR ALASTAIR DIGBY-VAINE-TRUMPINGTON, a young aristocrat
ARTHUR POTTS, a noble-minded young man
DR. AUGUSTUS FAGAN, the head of Llanabba Castle School
FLOSSIE and DIANA, his daughters
MR. PRENDERGAST, a former clergyman
CAPTAIN GRIMES, a public-school man
PETER BESTE-CHETWYNDE, one of Paul's pupils
MARGOT BESTE-CHETWYNDE, his mother
SOLOMON PHILBRICK, a confidence man
SIR HUMPHREY MALTRAVERS, later Lord Metroland, a British politician

The Story:

At Scone College in Oxford, the annual dinner of the Bollinger Club ends with the breaking of glass. Reeling out of Sir Alastair Digby-Vaine-Trumpington's rooms, the drunken aristocrats run to earth the inoffensive divinity student Paul Pennyfeather and forcibly leave him trouserless before they go roaring off into the night. Bollinger members can be fined, but the college authorities feel that Paul deserves more severe punishment for running across the quadrangle in his shorts. As a result, he is sent down for indecent behavior. After informing him that under his father's will his legacy could be withheld for unsatisfactory behavior, his unsympathetic guardian virtuously announces his intention to cut off Paul's allowance.

Through a shoddy firm of scholastic agents, Paul becomes a junior assistant master at Llanabba Castle, Wales. Llanabba is not a good school. Its head is Dr. Augustus Fagan, whose lectures on service are intended to cover up the inadequacies of his institution. He has two daughters: Flossie, a vulgar young woman with matrimonial ambitions, and Diana, who economizes on sugar and soap. One of the masters is Mr. Prendergast, a former clergyman who suffers from doubts. The other is Captain Grimes, who wears a false leg and is, as he frankly admits, periodically in the soup. A bounder and a scoundrel, he puts his faith in the public-school system, which may kick a man out but never lets him down. Grimes thinks he was put on his feet more often than any public-school man alive. His reluctant engagement to Flossie is his protection against the next time he finds himself in trouble.

Paul is in charge of the fifth form. When he meets his class for the first time, most of the boys claim that their name is Tangent. An uproar arises between the would-be Tangents and a few non-Tangents, but Paul puts an end to the situation by announcing that the writer of the longest essay will receive half a crown. After that, he has no more trouble. Mr. Prendergast, whose own students behave outrageously and make fun of his wig, wonders why Paul's classes are always so quiet. Paul considers young Peter Beste-Chetwynde the most interesting of his pupils.

Arthur Potts is one of the few men Paul knew at Scone; he writes that Alastair Trumpington regrets Paul's dismissal and wants to send him twenty pounds. Hearing of the offer, Grimes wires for the money in Paul's name.

When several parents expressed their intention to visit Llanabba Castle, Dr. Fagan decides to honor their visit with the annual field sports meet. Philbrick, the butler, objects to his extra duties. He confides to Paul that he is a crook who took the post in order to kidnap little Lord Tangent, but that he reformed after falling in love with Diana. He tells Mr. Prendergast that he is really Sir Solomon Philbrick, a millionaire shipowner, and he leaves Grimes under the impression that he is a novelist collecting material for a book.

The sports meet is not a success. Lady Circumference, Lord Tangent's mother, is rude to everyone when she distributes the prizes. The Llanabba Silver Band plays. Margot Beste-Chetwynde creates a social flurry when she arrives with a black man. In carrying out his function as the starter, Mr. Prendergast accidentally shoots Lord Tangent in the heel and later becomes drunk and abusive. Paul falls in love at first sight with Peter Beste-Chetwynde's beautiful widowed mother.

The term drags to a close. Lord Tangent's foot becomes infected, and he dies. Grimes, landing in the soup once more, announces his engagement to Flossie, but the marriage turns out as badly as he expected. When detectives arrive to arrest Philbrick on charges of false pretense, he flees. A few days later, Grimes's clothing and a suicide note are discovered on the beach.

Engaged to tutor Peter during the vacation, Paul goes to his home, King's Thursday. At the time Margot Beste-Chetwynde bought the place from her impoverished bachelor brother-in-law, Lord Pastmaster, it was the finest example of Tudor domestic architecture in England. Bored with it, however, she commissioned Otto Silenus, an eccentric designer, to build a modernistic house in its place. Silenus builds a structure of concrete, glass, and aluminum. It is a house for dynamos, not people, but people come there anyway for an endless round of house parties.

When Paul finally finds enough courage to propose to Margot, she accepts him because Peter thinks the young Oxonian will make a better stepfather than Margot's rival suitor, Sir Humphrey Maltravers, the minister of transport. During preparations for the wedding, Paul learns that Margot still carries on her father's business, a syndicate vaguely connected with amusement enterprises in South America. Grimes turns up mysteriously in her employ. Potts, now working for the League of Nations, also takes an unexplained interest in Margot's business affairs.

A few days before the wedding, Margot asks Paul to fly to Marseilles and arrange for the passage of several cabaret entertainers to Rio de Janeiro. He does so without realizing that he is bribing the officials he interviews. On his wedding morning, Paul is having a final drink with Alastair when a Scotland Yard inspector appears and arrests him on charges of engaging in international white-slave trafficking.

Margot flees to her villa at Corfu and does not appear at the trial. Potts, a special investigator for the League of Nations, is the chief witness for the prosecution. Convicted of Margot's crimes, Paul is sentenced to seven years' penal servitude. He serves the first part of his sentence at Blackstone Gaol, where he finds Philbrick a trustee and Mr. Prendergast the chaplain. Shortly after, Prendergast is killed by a crazed inmate, and Paul is removed to Egdon Health Penal Settlement. Grimes is briefly one of his fellow prisoners, but one day, while serving on a work gang, he walks off into the fog. Everyone but Paul assumes that he perishes in a swamp. Grimes, whose roguery is timeless, can never die. Margot comes to visit Paul. She announces her intention to marry Maltravers, now Lord Metroland and the Home Secretary.

Paul's escape from Egdon Heath is carefully contrived. On orders from the Home Secretary, he is removed for an appendicitis operation in a nursing home owned by Dr. Fagan, who forsook education for medicine. After a drunken doctor signs a death certificate stating that Paul died under the anesthetic, Alastair, who becomes Margot's young man, puts him on a yacht that carries him to Margot's villa at Corfu. Officially dead, Paul enjoys the rest he thinks he deserves. Wearing a heavy mustache, he returns to Scone some months later to continue his reading for the church. When the chaplain mentions another Pennyfeather, a wild undergraduate sent down for misconduct, Paul says that the young man is a distant cousin.

At Scone, the annual dinner of the Bollinger Club ends with the breaking of glass. Paul is reading in his room when

Peter Beste-Chetwynde, Lord Pastmaster since his uncle's death, comes in; he is very drunk. Paul's great mistake, Peter says, is that he became involved with people like Margot and himself. After his departure, Paul settles down to read another chapter in a book on early church heresies.

Critical Evaluation:

Decline and Fall mingles farce with grim tragedy. Episodic in form, with many of its scenes no more than a page or so in length, it is a penetrating yet hilarious study of disordered English society in the period between the wars. Evelyn Waugh insisted that his books were not intended as satires, since the satirical spirit presupposes a stable and homogeneous society against which to project its critical exposure of folly and vice. For all that, the writer demonstrates in this novel a tremendous talent for comic satire. Paul Pennyfeather's misadventures reflect one phase of the contemporary mood of disillusionment. The character of Grimes, on the other hand, who is a bounder and a cad, is timeless—a figure who would have been as much at home in the days of the Caesars as he was in the reign of King George V. Waugh's distortions and exaggerations have also the quality of fantasy, for in his pages the impossible and the believable exist simultaneously on the same plane.

Decline and Fall is the first and possibly the best work of Waugh, a luminary of the English satirists. The novel is notable for its economy of time and space. The action extends over one year, and the protagonist's circumstances at the beginning and end are virtually identical, which neatly rounds off the story. Waugh's prose is sparse, his epigrams unlabored, as in, for example, Paul Pennyfeather's quip that the English public school is a perfect conditioner for life in prison. Waugh lays low individuals and whole classes of society with a flick of a proper name: Digby-Vaine-Trumpington for a vain, trumpeting young aristocrat; Maltravers for a secretary of transportation; Prendergast for a clergyman aghast at his apprehension of divine indifference; Grimes for an earthy rascal; Pennyfeather for an impecunious, half-fledged scholar.

The tone is persistently cheerful. No amazement is expressed, even by the innocent and beleaguered protagonist, at anything that befalls him. Tragedies occur offstage. The death of Prendergast, for example, is revealed in a hymn. Lord Tangent's demise is recorded as follows: In chapter 8, he is shown crying because he has been wounded in the foot by a bullet from the starter's pistol; in chapter 12, Peter Beste-Chetwynde reports in an aside that Tangent's foot is gangrenous; in chapter 13, the news comes that the foot is being amputated; finally in chapter 19, it is reported in an offhand way that he has died.

The list of groups and institutions that excite the author's scorn is extensive; his opprobrium falls on the aristocracy, the newly rich, the universities, the public schools, old-school penology, newfangled penology, the House of Lords, the House of Commons, the Church of England, historical landmarks, modern architecture, and the League of Nations, to name a few. Although the novel manages to be hilarious at the expense of practically everybody, it has a serious side, or rather a serious center, namely, the schoolboy virtue of Pennyfeather contrasted with the cheery rascality of Grimes.

It is evident from the start that Paul is a right thinker and a square shooter. He owes his educational opportunities as much to his own industry, intelligence, and moderation as to the legacy left by his parents. He is earnest, diffident, and idealistic; in short, he is the very model of a middle-class English divinity student. The incredible things that happen to him seem at first reading to represent repeated assaults of a corrupt society on a genuinely decent character. Captain Grimes, on the other hand, shows up as a bounder of the very worst kind, a poseur who relies on public-school connections to rescue him from his frequent immersions in "the soup." He milks the fellowship of honor and duty for all it is worth and does not hesitate to abandon ship at the first sign of bad weather—women, children, and gentlemanly behavior notwithstanding.

For all his roguery, however, Grimes is not a villain. He is instead the most sympathetic character in the novel. The chief element of his personality is common sense; it is he, and not Paul, who is the author's persona, who embodies the impulses of sanity as opposed to the precepts of class and culture. During the war, for example, when faced with court-martial or honorable suicide, he relies on drink and old school ties to see him through alive, and they do. Trapped into marriage, he simply bolts, once into the public schools, once into the sea. Imprisoned, he makes his escape by sinking into a quicksand from which, Paul and the reader are confident, he will rise to drink his pint in new guise but with the old elemental verve. He is self-indulgent, brave, resourceful, and not to be humbugged.

Although self-disciplined, Paul is meek, credulous, and fundamentally passive by contrast. Everything that happens to him, good or bad, simply happens. His rather mild passion for Margot Beste-Chetwynde strikes him like lightning; his actual proposal of marriage is all Margot's doing. He acquiesces alike to expulsion from college and rescue from prison with the same spongy plasticity cloaked beneath the ethical pose of being a good sport. In fact, it may be argued that believers in this schoolboy code of ethics suffer from a profound moral laziness and invite the outrages perpetrated on them in its name by those who do not believe in it. Paul's explanation of why he does not outface Potts and take money from Trumpington is illustrative. He defines a gentleman as someone who declines to accept benefits that are not his by right or to profit from windfall advantage. Implicit in this stance is a kind of flabby ethical neutrality disguised as self-respect, a certain pride in taking no action. Grimes's judgment is sounder and more vigorous, for he recognizes Potts as a stinker in prosecuting Paul for a crime he committed inadvertently.

The author remarks at one stage that Paul does not have the makings of a hero. No more has he the makings of a villain, for villainy requires the kind of enterprise exemplified by Margot. It is not Paul's decline and fall that are recorded here but the degeneration of a society in which custom and privilege combine to nurture all manner of waste and wickedness. Paul is merely part of the problem. Grimes, the voice of blackguardism and good sense, is part of the solution. Paul toasts the stability of ideals, Grimes the passing moment.

Despite Grimes, however, *Decline and Fall* ends on a rather grim note, with Peter a wastrel and Paul embracing a pinched orthodoxy. The underlying sense is of honorable old forms giving way to a new and nastier regime, a theme that Waugh also pursued in later works. Indeed, he espoused it in his own life to the extent of rejecting the new order altogether. As a result, he was virtually a hermit at the time of his death.

"Critical Evaluation" by Jan Kennedy Foster

Further Reading

Beaty, Frederick L. *The Ironic World of Evelyn Waugh: A Study of Eight Novels*. DeKalb: Northern Illinois University Press, 1992. Argues that Waugh is more an ironist than a satirist and examines his various uses of irony. Chapter 2 is a study of *Decline and Fall*.

Carens, James F. *The Satiric Art of Evelyn Waugh*. Seattle: University of Washington Press, 1966. Published in the year of Waugh's death, this study of all his major works concentrates on specific satiric effects and the way in which the author achieved them. *Decline and Fall* is discussed in chapters 1 through 7.

Cowley, Malcolm. "*Decline and Fall.*" In *Critical Essays on Evelyn Waugh*, edited by James F. Carens. Boston: G. K. Hall, 1987. Initially published only three years after the appearance of *Decline and Fall*, this essay compares that novel with *Vile Bodies* and concludes that the first is greatly superior. An interesting early evaluation of Waugh.

Crabbe, Katharyn W. *Evelyn Waugh*. New York: Continuum, 1988. Following a brief biography in chapter 1, Crabbe devotes the six remaining chapters to the novels; *Decline and Fall* is analyzed in chapter 2.

Patey, Douglas Lane. *The Life of Evelyn Waugh: A Critical Biography*. Malden, Mass.: Blackwell, 1998. Examines Waugh's life within the context of his work, providing critical assessments of his novels and other writings. Chapter 2 includes a discussion of *Decline and Fall*.

Stopp, Frederick J. *Evelyn Waugh: Portrait of an Artist*. Boston: Little, Brown, 1958. A standard work, which suffers only from having been published before Waugh completed his World War II trilogy. All the other novels, including *Decline and Fall*, are discussed in detail.

Villa Flor, Carlos, and Robert Murray Davis, eds. *Waugh Without End: New Trends in Evelyn Waugh Studies*. New York: Peter Lang, 2005. Collection of papers presented at a 2003 symposium during the centenary of Waugh's birth. Includes discussions of Waugh and Catholicism, his depiction of the English gentleman, and homosexual themes in works by Waugh and E. M. Forester.

Waugh, Alexander. *Fathers and Sons: The Autobiography of a Family*. London: Headline, 2004. Alexander Waugh, the grandson of Evelyn, chronicles four generations of his family, focusing on its father-son conflicts and its literary achievements. Includes illustrations, bibliography, and index.

The Decline of the West

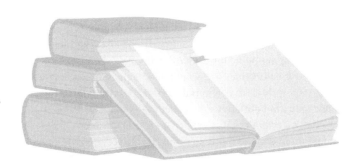

Author: Oswald Spengler (1880-1936)
First published: Der Untergang des Abendlandes, 1918,
   in one volume; 1922, in two volumes (English
   translation, 1926, 1928)
Type of work: Philosophy and history

In *The Decline of the West*, German philosopher and mathematician Oswald Spengler urges a new understanding of the world. In this work of historical philosophy, which was written mostly before World War I, Spengler names eight "high cultures" (the term he prefers), or civilizations, of human history: Babylonian, Egyptian, Chinese, Indian, Classical (Greek and Roman), Arabian, Western, and Mexican (Aztec/Mayan). Five of these cultures he uses as examples, but he discusses in more detail the Classical, Arabian, and Western cultures.

Spengler considers his work to be a morphology of history, meaning that he treats every culture separately, as a living organism, and tries to identify each culture's birth, growth, decline, and death. Furthermore, to Spengler, no culture is superior. He uses the term "culture" to describe the growth and living stage, or soul, of an organism, and the term "civilization" to identify an organism's declining stage, in which human creativity vanishes. A culture's soul is held together by a bond of blood, and civilization actually destroys culture; with this destruction, the soul begins to die. A culture's civilization stage could last hundreds of years in a petrified state. Because cultures are constantly changing, history is an endless series of formations and transformations. The one part of the formation that Spengler does not clearly describe is that of birth.

Three concepts are vital to understanding Spengler's morphology of history: the unity of development in the life of each separate culture; each stage in the life cycle of all cultures lasts for about the same length of time; and every stage is contemporaneous with those of other cultures. The general pattern is that all cultures begin in a nonurban setting and then gradually move into urban developments, in which growth and materialism eventually lead to its decline.

In *The Decline of the West*, Spengler compares European conditions with the later years of Hellenistic Greece and the Roman Republic, ending about the time of the Roman emperor Julius Caesar. Spengler recognizes the paradox of Western culture first honoring its Classical foundation then reaching out to other cultures. Classical humans had been

static, but Western humans became dynamic, always looking for ways to expand their cultures.

Spengler follows the cyclical philosophy of history, in which all cultures go through a cycle of life similar to human life—birth, youth, maturity, decline, and death. The cycles follow a basic two-hundred-year pattern, although a major culture like the West might include several such cycles, one after the other. Spengler rejects the linear view of history and the use of the ancient-medieval-modern approach to the study of history. He says that every culture should be studied on its own. With this interpretation, he became an early advocate of historical relativism, the view that truth is relative to each historical period; truth for one culture might not be truth for another culture. Spengler, however, does not realize the self-contradiction inherent in this philosophy. He does not deny that cultures can have ideals, but he does deny the unlimited potential to reach those ideals. The end of a culture would be determined not by choice but by destiny, an end not unlike fate, an idea derived from the ancient Greeks.

Spengler's coverage of religion, especially Judaism and Christianity, is confusing. He includes the beginning of Christianity in chapter 14, which covers Arabian culture—what he calls Magian—and classifies Christianity as one of the mystery religions of that region. To Spengler, religion is metaphysical, provable not by knowledge but by experience.

In *The Decline of the West*, Spengler defines the West as comprising western Europe and the United States. He makes no distinction between the two regions because, he argues, they both grew out of the same basic culture. He pinpoints the birth of the West to c. 1000 and to historical events such as the Norman Conquest of England. For his native Germany, the rise of the Holy Roman Empire is most significant. After minicycles such as the Renaissance, the Reformation, the Enlightenment, and the French Revolution, Western culture reached its climax in the nineteenth century. Then, as a result of the tensions that led to World War I, the soul of the West began to die. The end, he believes, will be an unavoidable, protracted fall, not a single catastrophic event. A new culture, ruled by a modern-day Caesar, will arise from the ashes. Individualism, materialism, and democracy will disappear, but the masses will soon accept the new order.

Spengler does not oppose the principle of democracy, but he feels, somewhat like Plato, that people lack the will to fulfill their democratic responsibilities. He also believes that democracy will be subverted by the role of the press and by money in politics. In ascribing the word "Faustian" to Western culture, Spengler is arguing that Western ideals and goals are unattainable; in effect, he is arguing that the spiritual values of the West are being sacrificed for material gain.

With the takeover of Germany by Adolf Hitler and the Nazis in 1933, Spengler's work was seen in a new light. He initially believed that he would be exiled because of the pessimism of his works. However, a meeting with Hitler saved him from exile; his writings, though, were suppressed by the Third Reich.

The best commentary on *The Decline of the West* comes from Spengler himself. About two years before his death in 1936, Spengler had written in a letter to a friend that,

I can see more clearly ahead, but I feel more lonely than ever, not as if I were among the blind, but among people with their eyes bandaged so that they cannot see their house falling down.

A short time later, Spengler accurately predicts a global war:

We are standing perhaps on the threshold of the Second World War, in which the alignment of nations is unknown. . . . If we do not see our relation to the world as the most important problem which faces us, destiny—and what a destiny—will pass us by without pity.

Spengler died in 1936, so he did not witness another "gigantic conflict," as he had termed World War I, which he had experienced first hand. This new gigantic conflict was World War II, and further decline.

Glenn L. Swygart

Further Reading

Delacampagne, Christian. *A History of Philosophy in the Twentieth Century*. Translated by M. D. DeBevoise. Baltimore: Johns Hopkins University Press, 1999. Includes a discussion of Spengler in chapter 2, "Philosophies of the End," because of the pessimistic nature of his work. Emphasizes his doctrine of Prussian socialism, which he had considered the answer to the deterioration of European civilization.

Farrenkopf, John. *Prophet of Decline: Spengler on World History and Politics*. Baton Rouge: Louisiana State University Press, 2001. A detailed analysis of *The Decline of the West*, its background, and its influence on interpretations of European history. Introduces the reader to the Spengler archive in Munich, Germany.

Fennelly, John F. *Twilight of the Evening Lands: Oswald Spengler—A Half Century Later*. New York: Brookdale Press, 1972. Gives a good definition of Spengler's theory of cultural growth and decline. Includes an appendix, "Origins and Rationale of Twentieth Century Liberalism," which discusses Spengler's role in the creation of that movement.

Helps, Arthur, trans. and ed. *Letters of Oswald Spengler*. New York: Alfred A. Knopf, 1966. Features many letters written by Spengler between 1913 and his death in 1936. Gives clear insight into his thoughts, especially during his last years after Adolf Hitler had come to power in Germany, when his own writings were being censored.

Hughes, H. Stuart. *Oswald Spengler: A Critical Estimate*. New York: Charles Scribner's Sons, 1952. An early post-World War II critique of Spengler in light of the Third Reich. Covers the influences on Spengler that led to his theories. Includes those persons Hughes calls new-Spenglerians, Arnold Toynbee and Pitirim Sorokin.

Spengler, Oswald. *The Hour of Decision—Part One: Germany and World-Historical Revolution*. Translated by Charles Francis Atkinson. 1933. Reprint. Honolulu: University Press of the Pacific, 2001. This last major work of Spengler, after many years of defending and trying to explain *The Decline of the West*, does much to clarify his theory, as well as to express his fears in an increasingly dangerous Europe being dominated by Hitler. Provides a valuable sequel to *The Decline of the West*.

The Deerslayer
Or, The First War-Path, a Tale

Author: James Fenimore Cooper (1789-1851)
First published: 1841
Type of work: Novel
Type of plot: Historical
Time of plot: 1740
Locale: Northern New York State

Principal characters:
NATTY BUMPPO, a woodsman called Deerslayer by the Delawares
HURRY HARRY, a frontier scout
CHINGACHGOOK, Deerslayer's Delaware friend
THOMAS HUTTER, owner of the lake
JUDITH HUTTER, a young woman Thomas Hutter claims as his daughter
HETTY HUTTER, Judith's sister
WAH-TA!-WAH, Chingachgook's beloved

The Story:

Natty Bumppo, a young woodsman known as Deerslayer, and Hurry Harry travel to the shores of Lake Glimmerglass together. It is a dangerous journey, for the French and their Iroquois allies are on the warpath. Deerslayer is planning to meet his friend Chingachgook, the young Delaware chief, so that they might go against the Iroquois. Hurry Harry is on his way to the lake to warn Thomas Hutter and his daughters that hostile Indians are raiding along the frontier. Harry is accustomed to hunt and trap with Hutter during the summer, and he is an admirer of Hutter's elder daughter, the spirited Judith.

Hutter and his daughters live in a cabin built on piles in the middle of the lake. Hutter also builds a great, scowlike vessel, known among frontiersmen as the ark, on which he travels from one shore of the lake to the other on his hunting and trapping expeditions. On their arrival at the lake, the two find a hidden canoe. Having paddled out to the cabin and found it deserted, they proceed down the lake and come upon the ark anchored in a secluded outlet. Hutter already learned of the Indian raiders. The party decides to take refuge in the cabin, where they can be attacked only over the water. The men manage to maneuver the ark out of the narrow outlet and sail it to the cabin. They have one narrow escape, for as the ark clears the outlet, six Indians try to board the boat by dropping from the overhanging limbs of a tree. Each misses and falls into the water.

Under cover of darkness, Hutter, Deerslayer, and Hurry Harry take the canoe and paddle to shore to get Hutter's two remaining canoes hidden there. They find the canoes and, on their way back to the ark, sight a party of Indians camped under some trees. While Deerslayer waits in a canoe offshore, the other two men attack the Iroquois camp in an attempt to obtain scalps, for which they can receive bounties. They are captured. Deerslayer, knowing that he is powerless to help them, goes to sleep in the canoe until morning.

When Deerslayer awakens, he sees that one of the canoes drifted close to shore. To rescue it, he is forced to shoot an Indian, the first man he ever kills. Returning to the fort with his prizes, Deerslayer tells the girls of their father's fate. It is agreed that they will delay any attempt at rescue until the arrival of Chingachgook, whom Deerslayer is to meet that night.

The party goes in the ark and meets Chingachgook at the spot where the river joins the lake. Back in the cabin, Deerslayer explains that the Delaware came to the lake to rescue his sweetheart, Wah-ta!-Wah, who was stolen by the Iroquois. Suddenly, they discover that Hetty Hutter disappeared. The girl, somewhat feebleminded, casts off in one of the canoes with the intention of going to the Indian camp to rescue her father and Hurry Harry.

The next morning, Wah-ta!-Wah comes upon Hetty wandering in the forest. She takes the white girl to the Iroquois camp. Because the Indians believe deranged persons are protected by the Great Spirit, she suffers no harm.

It is Deerslayer's idea to ransom the prisoners with some rich brocades and carved ivory that he and Judith found in Tom Hutter's chest. Its contents were known only to Hutter and Hetty, but in this emergency, Judith does not hesitate to open the coffer. Meanwhile, a young Iroquois rows Hetty back to the cabin on a raft. Deerslayer tells him that the party in the cabin will give two ivory chessmen for the release of the captives. He is unable to drive quite the bargain he planned. In the end, four chessmen are exchanged for the men, who are returned that night.

Hetty brings a message from Wah-ta!-Wah. Chingachgook is to meet the Indian girl at a particular place on the shore when the evening star rises above the hemlocks that night. Hurry Harry and Tom Hutter are still determined to obtain scalps. When night closes in, Hurry Harry, Hutter, and Chingachgook reconnoiter the camp. To their disappointment, they find it deserted and the Indians camped on the beach, at the spot where Wah-ta!-Wah is to wait for Chingachgook.

While Hutter and Harry sleep, the Delaware and Deerslayer attempt to keep the rendezvous, but the girl is under such close watch that it is impossible for her to leave the camp. The two men enter the camp and boldly rescue her from her captors. Deerslayer, who remains to cover their escape, is taken prisoner.

When Judith hears from Chingachgook of Deerslayer's capture, she rows Hetty ashore to learn what became of the woodsman. Once more, Hetty walks unharmed among the superstitious savages. Deerslayer assures her there is nothing she can do to help and that he must await the Iroquois' pleasure. She returns to Judith.

As the girls paddle about, trying to find the ark in the darkness, they hear the report of a gun. Torches on shore show them that an Indian girl was mortally wounded by a shot from the ark. Soon the lights got out. Paddling to the center of the lake, they try to get what rest they can before morning comes.

When daylight returns, Hutter heads the ark toward the cabin once more. Missing his daughters, he concludes that the cabin would be the most likely meeting place. Hutter and Harry are the first to leave the ark to go into the cabin. There the Iroquois, who came aboard in rafts under cover of darkness, were waiting in ambush. Harry manages to escape into the water, where he is saved by Chingachgook. Judith and Hetty came to the ark in their canoe. After the Indians go ashore, those on the ark go to the cabin. They find Hutter lying dead. That evening, he is buried in the lake. Hurry Harry takes advantage of the occasion to propose to Judith, but she refuses him.

Shortly afterward, they are surprised to see Deerslayer paddling toward the ark. He was given temporary liberty in order to bargain with the fugitives. The Iroquois send word that Chingachgook will be allowed to return to his own people if Wah-ta!-Wah and Judith became brides of Iroquois warriors. Hetty, they promise, will go unharmed because of her mental condition. Although Deerslayer's life is to be the penalty for refusal, these terms are declined.

Deerslayer does not have to return to his captors until the next day, and that evening he and Judith examine carefully the contents of her father's chest. To the girl's wonder, she finds letters indicating that Hutter was not her real father but a former buccaneer whom her mother married when her first

husband deserted her. Saddened by this knowledge, Judith no longer wishes to live at the lake. She intimates to Deerslayer that she loves him, only to find that he considers her above him in education and in intelligence.

When Deerslayer returns to the Iroquois the next day, he is put to torture with hatchets. Hetty, Judith, and Wah-ta!-Wah come to the camp and attempt to intercede for him, but to no avail. Suddenly, Chingachgook bounds in and cuts his friend's bonds. Deerslayer's release is the signal for the regiment from the nearest fort to attack, for Hurry Harry went to summon help during the night.

The Iroquois are routed. Hetty is mortally wounded during the battle. The next day, she is buried in the lake beside her parents. Judith joins the soldiers returning to the fort. Deerslayer departs for the Delaware camp with Chingachgook and his bride.

Fifteen years later, Deerslayer, Chingachgook, and the latter's young son, Uncas, revisit the lake. Wah-ta!-Wah is long since dead, and, though the hunter inquires at the fort about Judith, he can find no one who knows her. There is a rumor that a former member of the garrison, then living in England on his paternal estates, was influenced by a woman of rare beauty who was not his wife. The ark and the cabin in the lake are falling into decay.

Critical Evaluation:

The fifth and final volume of James Fenimore Cooper's Leatherstocking Tales, *The Deerslayer* portrays Natty Bumppo as an idealistic youth raised among American Indians. Bumppo, in this novel nicknamed Deerslayer, is somewhere between twenty-two and twenty-four years old. Despite his daring and resourcefulness, he must rise to adulthood by meeting the challenge of human conflict when he is faced with the realities of tribal warfare and is forced to kill his first foe. Deerslayer not only discovers the ruthlessness of civilized men but also encounters a different kind of danger in the will of a woman. Cooper's novel is a bildungsroman, the story of a young man's gaining the courage of his convictions and a moral certainty. In *The Deerslayer*, Cooper creates an idyllic view of the early American frontier, when the western boundary was New York's Lake Ostego (renamed Lake Glimmerglass in the novel). Cooper also includes such themes as the concept of gifts, the conflict between the Native American code of behavior and that of the Europeans, and the distinction between natural law and moral law.

In the novel, Deerslayer kills his first Indian, rejects the proposal of a beautiful young woman, fends off the missionary efforts of the woman's feebleminded sister, and worries about the appropriateness of Indian customs for a white man. He often reflects on the beauties of the wilderness.

The dominant mood of the novel is peaceful and serene. Cooper digresses to stress the peace and quiet of the forest at early morning, high noon, and evening. What breaks the peace and solitude of the forest are the sounds of gunshots and passionate, invading white men. Deerslayer talks to Hetty Hutter about his reverence and awe for the forest, God's creation. He learns more from studying "the hand of God as it is seen in the hills and the valleys, the mountaintops, the streams, the forests, and the springs" than the invading white people in the novel learn from studying the Bible. The invaders, rather than finding the beauty in nature, seldom give it a second thought while they destroy it, especially when it serves their economic purposes.

Two alien objects invade the primal scene of Lake Glimmerglass: Hurry Harry's large boat, called the ark, and Thomas Hutter's "castle," a house built on piles over the water. Both Hutter and Hurry Harry are at the bottom of the moral scale. Hurry Harry, as his name implies, is restless. He considers members of other races to be animals and prides himself on his good looks, physical strength, and capability to rationalize his wants. Both he and Hutter are economically motivated, and they value and respect only money. They will do anything to get it, even killing American Indian women and children for their scalps. Hutter's values are shared by his daughter Judith, who worships the physical in both her own beauty and in the handsomeness of the British soldiers. These three characters represent the more unpleasant aspects of human nature. Their notion of gifts is one of materialistic acquisition.

In opposition to the views of Hutter, Judith, and Hurry Harry, Deerslayer, his Delaware friend, and Hetty live close to nature. The Delawares and Deerslayer follow their own gifts to lead a satisfactory life. They kill only what they eat. When they scalp, it is for glory. Since they are uneducated in the ways of the white people, they know no better; when they scalp they remain blameless.

Although both Hetty and Deerslayer affirm a higher good, both are relatively unthinking, Deerslayer being uneducated and Hetty being born simpleminded. Cooper frequently describes them in childlike terms. Both are removed from the sophisticated temptations of civilized life and try to live in accordance with Christian morality. Their notion of gifts, like that of the American Indians, is to take what is necessary from nature to survive.

Hetty affirms a Christian life that is impossible in a fallen world. Cooper makes the point that the totally un-Christian life is complete chaos when he sends Hetty to the Huron camp to plead for the lives of her father and Hurry Harry. She is confounded when the Huron chief, Rivenoak, asks her why the white people do not follow the injunctions of Christ to forgive one's enemies and turn the other cheek.

Deerslayer straddles his two worlds. He follows what he calls the law of nature: "to do, lest you should be done by." Deerslayer is first a hunter, becoming a warrior when he takes his first victim's life. He graciously offers his enemy another chance at life, but it is refused. When Deerslayer shoots quickly, the American Indian notices his quick eye and renames him Hawkeye. Even in killing his second enemy, Deerslayer is not the aggressor. His actions are less than Christ-like—he does not turn the other cheek—but they are practical, invoking the universal injunction of self-defense. Deerslayer is a compromise between the best and the worst human traits. He shows that virtue does not depend on education but may be corrupted by it. Physically unattractive, he shows that a beautiful soul may reside behind an ugly exterior.

The Deerslayer does not end on an optimistic note. Lake Glimmerglass returns to its natural state, and the selfish characters move to the fort; Deerslayer and his Indian compatriots disappear into the wilderness. The reader, however, knows that settlers will use axes to clear the forests and guns to kill the animals and the American Indians. As Deerslayer, Chingachgook, and Uncas slip into the wilderness, they are overcome with a sense of what might have been, but the reader knows that what might have been never comes to pass.

"Critical Evaluation" by Thomas D. Petitjean, Jr.

Further Reading

Barnett, Louise K. "Speech in the Wilderness: The Ideal Discourse of *The Deerslayer*." In *Desert, Garden, Margin, Range: Literature of the American Frontier*, edited by Eric Heyne. New York: Twayne, 1992. A well-balanced essay that deals with the differing levels of diction in the characters' voices in *The Deerslayer* and how such speech patterns work in the evolution of the frontier mythos.

Cooper, James Fenimore. *The Deerslayer: Or, The First War-Path*. New York: Modern Library, 2002. In addition to the text of the novel, this edition has explanatory notes on the text by James Franklin Beard, a leading Cooper scholar, and an introduction by eminent American literary critic Leslie A. Fiedler.

Krauthammer, Anna. *The Representation of the Savage in James Fenimore Cooper and Herman Melville*. New York: Peter Lang, 2008. Focuses on Cooper's and Melville's creation of Native American, African American, and other non-European characters, including the characters of Natty Bumppo and Chingachgook who appear in *The Deerslayer.* Discusses how these characters were perceived as "savages," both noble and ignoble, by American readers.

Person, Leland S., ed. *A Historical Guide to James Fenimore Cooper.* New York: Oxford University Press, 2007. Collection of essays, including a brief biography by Cooper biographer Wayne Franklin and a survey of Cooper scholarship and criticism. *The Deerslayer* is discussed in "Cooper's Leatherstocking Conversations: Identity, Friendship, and Democracy in the New Nation" by Dana D. Nelson. Also features an illustrated chronology of Cooper's life and important nineteenth century historical events.

Ringe, Donald A. *James Fenimore Cooper.* New York: Twayne, 1962. Excellent general overview of the works of Cooper, including *The Deerslayer.* Places the works in the construction of the myth of the American frontier.

Schachterle, Lance. "Fenimore Cooper's Literary Defenses: Twain and the Text of *The Deerslayer.*" *Studies in the American Renaissance* (1988): 401-417. Schachterle takes to task Mark Twain, who criticized Cooper's prose style and *The Deerslayer* in his essay "Fenimore Cooper's Literary Offenses."

Selley, April. "'I Have Been, and Ever Shall Be, Your Friend': *Star Trek, The Deerslayer,* and the American Romance." *Journal of Popular Culture* 20, no. 1 (Summer, 1986): 89-104. Asserts that *The Deerslayer* is a romantic novel that constructs the mythos of the American frontier, and that this mythos is carried on in late twentieth century popular culture through television's *Star Trek* series.

Verhoeven, W. M., ed. *James Fenimore Cooper: New Historical and Literary Contexts.* Atlanta: Rodopi, 1993. An interesting collection of essays, including such topics as the American romance tradition; property, marriage and women; and frontier myth and anti-myth. Includes bibliographical references

The Defence of Guenevere, and Other Poems

Author: William Morris (1834-1896)
First published: 1858
Type of work: Poetry

The Defence of Guenevere, and Other Poems, the first collection of poems published by William Morris, is one of the three or four principal expressions of Pre-Raphaelitism in poetry. Although Morris had only just turned twenty-four when the volume appeared, it epitomizes his poetic qualities and foreshadows his artistic attainment. Algernon Charles Swinburne, his contemporary, wrote concerning it: "Such things as are in this book are taught and learned in no school but that of instinct." It was Swinburne's opinion that no other literary work had ever shown more distinctly the mark of native character and that the poetry was entirely original. He saw Morris as "not yet a master," but "assuredly no longer a pupil." Not unmindful of certain technical faults and an occasional hint of confusion in the work, Swinburne nevertheless went on to say that Morris's volume was incomparable in its time for "perception and experience of tragic truth" and that no other contemporary poet had a "touch of passion at once so broad and so sure."

Swinburne may have overstated the case for the originality of the poems; Morris shows strong influences of Sir Thomas Malory and Jean Froissart, though more in regard to selection of subject matter than in its presentation. His Arthurian poems reveal a genuine passion and exceptional beauty, especially in passages such as the vibrant, breathtaking narrative description that opens the title poem. Despite their freshness and strong feeling, these poems are in what may be designated the tapestry tradition—there is a hint of the decorative about them. Those poems derived more clearly from Froissart than from Malory, however (among them "Sir Peter Harpdon's End," "Concerning Geoffrey Teste Noir," and the grim "Haystack in the Floods") attest Morris's realization that, even in the Middle Ages, the tourney was not the only aspect of war.

Although Morris had a lifelong passion for beauty, he also had a need for certain harsh or stark elements, and these are present in these poems. The touches of this power are evident in this first volume of his poems. An example of such stark description may be found in these lines from "Concerning Geoffrey Teste Noire":

> I think 'twas Geoffrey smote him on the brow
> With some spiked axe; and while he totter'd, dim
> About the eyes, the spear of Alleyne Roux
> Slipped through his camaille and his throat; well, well!

When Sir Peter Harpdon's wife Alice, upon hearing of her husband's death, cries: "I am much too young to live,/ Fair God, so let me die," readers recognize in the cry a kind of Shakespearean poignancy. Among the many other qualities of this first book of poems is the apparent simplicity of a lyric such as "Golden Wings," which attains deep sincerity as it smoothly reflects early memories in a manner distinctly Morris's own. There is also the plain perfection of the little poem, "Summer Dawn," in which, departing momentarily from the dreams and histories of long-past lives and battles, Morris speaks simply in his own voice of his desire for communion.

Morris, while studying medieval romances and admiring them for their curious intrinsic beauty, became convinced that if people could move backward through time to the age of the sea kings, they should find the essential characteristics of the race to be exactly like those of today. Admittedly, he found the Middle Ages much more ignorant, cruel, and savage than the ages preceding or following; nevertheless, he concluded that people of those times must have had feelings, desires, and thoughts quite like those of people of his time. His society had much in common, then, with that of the Middle Ages; one should, therefore, study the terrible times of the Middle Ages in order to understand them and to understand better one's own time.

Morris gives readers some brief, sudden, and flashing pictures of that far-off time. The title poem presents a queen about to be burned at the stake; then, at the sound of a horse's hooves, she knows that her lover is coming to her rescue. One of the most powerful of these pictures is presented in "The Haystack in the Floods." Not revealing either how the tragedy began or how it ended, the poem opens with the haunting questions:

> Had she come all the way for this
> To part at last without a kiss?
> Yea, had she borne the dirt and rain
> That her own eyes might see him slain
> Beside the haystack in the floods?

Readers are at first told only enough about the woman Jehane to make them wonder about her character and to know that as she rides along she is miserable. Her lover Robert, who rides some distance ahead of her with a few armed men, is confronted by his adversary Godmar and numerous armed men. At first she fears for her own safety rather than Robert's:

> My God! my God! I have to tread
> The long way back without you; then
> The court at Paris; those six men;
> The gratings of the Chatelet;
> The swift Seine on some rainy day
> Like this, and people standing by,
> And laughing, while my weak hands try
> To recollect how strong men swim.

In her despair she contemplates accepting Godmar, the man whom she hates. Robert, whose men refuse to fight against the heavy odds, charges the enemy and is captured, disarmed, and bound. When after long hesitation Jehane refuses to come willingly to his castle, Godmar and his men murder Robert before her eyes. The poem ends with an uncertainty about her fate. Does she go mad? Will she be taken back and burned at the castle from which she has escaped? The reader may even suspect that she is feigning madness and that before the castle is reached she will yield to Godmar, who may then retain her until he tires of her. Having given the reader this glimpse of medieval passion, selfishness, suffering, and cruelty, Morris ends the poem, after Godmar's men have beaten Robert's brains out, on this note:

> Then Godmar turned again and said:
> So, Jehane, the first fitte is read!
> Take note, my lady, that your way
> Lies backward to the Chatelet!
> She shook her head and gazed awhile
> At her cold hands with a rueful smile,
> As though this thing had made her mad.
> This was the parting that they had
> Beside the haystack in the floods.

Another grim, moving poem, a Browningesque monologue called "The Judgement of God," supplies a second example of the same device.

Other noteworthy poems in the book are "The Little Tower," "The Wind," "The Eve of Crecy," "In Prison," and "The Blue Closet." All extremely original, they display a wide range in idea and theme. In their ability to make readers understand the feelings of pain, terror, or heroic effort at particular moments in the lives of people, they all have great psychological insight. For example, Guenevere's horrible soliloquy, revealing that she has wondered how the fire would quiver yards above her head, in its startlingly true psychology, improves upon the narrative of the original story. Especially in his use of monologue and dialogue, Morris successfully demonstrates that the poet can best revive the past not by detailed description of things but by faithful expression of the feelings of persons who lived long ago.

Without exaggeration, Morris's *The Defence of Guenevere, and Other Poems* may be called an outstanding first volume of poetry. However, like the early volumes of most poets, it did not make any particular impact upon the reading public when it appeared in 1858. This lack of acclaim for the volume may have been a factor in Morris's withdrawing for some time from the writing of poetry. Another factor was his feeling that writing poetry was neither particularly notable nor difficult and that it had no precedence over the new and exciting experiments in tapestry weaving and dyeing in which he was already engaged. Morris was content with the appreciation accorded the volume by a few of his friends, among them Dante Gabriel Rossetti, to whom it was dedicated.

Further Reading

Clutton-Brock, Arthur. *William Morris*. New York: Parkstone Press, 2007. Biography chronicling Morris's multifaceted career, including his work as a poet and prose writer.

Helsinger, Elizabeth K. *Poetry and the Pre-Raphaelite Arts: Dante Gabriel Rossetti and William Morris*. New Haven, Conn.: Yale University Press, 2008. Examines the works of the two poet-artists in order to describe the aesthetics of the Pre-Raphaelite movement and its expression in both literature and art. Chapter 3, "Lyric Color and *The Defence of Guenevere*," focuses on this work.

Kirchhoff, Frederick. *William Morris*. Boston: Twayne, 1979. Literary biography of Morris. Places *The Defence of Guenevere, and Other Poems* within the larger context of Morris's life and creative accomplishments, especially his writings.

Le Bourgeois, John Y. *Art and Forbidden Fruit: Hidden Passion in the Life of William Morris*. Cambridge, England: Lutterworth Press, 2006. An analysis of Morris's life and poetry, describing his attachment to his sister Emma, who was a source of inspiration for his work.

Morris, William. *The Defence of Guenevere, and Other Poems*. Edited by Margaret A. Lourie. New York: Garland, 1981. A scholarly edition of the poems with extensive notes that explain passages in the poetry. A critical introduction with a full bibliography places this work in its setting of Victorian poetry.

Oberg, Charlotte. *A Pagan Prophet, William Morris*. Charlottesville: University Press of Virginia, 1978. A study of Morris's writings as the sum of a "living unity" of his creative vision. The poems in *The Defence of Guenevere, and Other Poems* are discussed last, out of chronological order, to demonstrate their relationship to the themes of Morris's other work.

Silver, Carole. *The Romance of William Morris*. Athens: Ohio University Press, 1982. Examines the idea of romance, in its broadest literary and artistic sense, as revealed in Morris's works. A chapter is devoted to how *The Defence of Guenevere, and Other Poems* exemplifies Morris's concept of the genre of romance.

Tompkins, J. M. S. *William Morris: An Approach to the Poetry*. London: Cecil Woolf, 1988. A study of Morris's poetry, which is defined not only as verse but also as prose romances. The opening chapter analyzes the poems in *The Defence of Guenevere, and Other Poems* with particular emphasis on explaining the sources in medieval literature that inspired Morris to compose these works.

Defence of Poesie

Author: Sir Philip Sidney (1554-1586)
First published: 1595
Type of work: Literary criticism

Sir Philip Sidney's *Defence of Poesie* is an attempt to raise poetry above the criticism that had been directed at it by contemporary critics and to establish it as the highest of the arts, best fitted both to please and to instruct, the two aims stated by Horace in his *Ars poetica* (c. 17 B.C.E.). The first part of *Defence of Poesie* is primarily theoretical; Sidney weighs the respective merits of philosophy, history, and poetry as teachers of virtue. In the final section, he surveys the state of English literature soon after 1580.

The importance of Sidney's *Defence of Poesie* can best be appreciated by understanding the political climate of the late sixteenth century. A growing number of religious leaders were condemning the production of imaginative literature; lyric and dramatic works were viewed as little more than tools for corruption. Furthermore, much of the writing being produced in England was hackneyed and trite. Nevertheless, Sidney, a student of the classics and a poet himself, believed there was both aesthetic and moral value in poetry, which he defined broadly to include all imaginative literature. Well versed in Greek and Roman literature, familiar with both classical and Renaissance defenses of the arts, the courtier-artist took it upon himself to champion the practice of writing. The task proved formidable, since no earlier justification seemed to be able to counter the charges that imaginative literature was simply a vile distraction that promoted idleness at best, immorality at worst. Sidney found that the only way to defend the practice of poetry was to redefine its function and assign it a more significant aesthetic role. Modeling his work on both classical and Renaissance predecessors, Sidney constructs in the *Defence of Poesie* a formal argument, in a style reminiscent of the Roman orator Cicero and his followers in the practice of rhetoric, to explain the value of poetry and to delineate those qualities that make the poet a valuable teacher.

Sidney's first argument for the supremacy of poetry is that it was the "first light-giver to ignorance"; the first great works of science, philosophy, history, and even law were poems. Both the Italian and English languages were polished and perfected by their poets, Dante Alighieri, Giovanni Boccaccio, and Petrarch on the one hand, Geoffrey Chaucer and John Gower on the other. Even Plato illuminated his philosophy with myths and dramatic scenes.

Both the Hebrews and the Romans gave high distinction to poets, considering them prophets, messengers of God or the gods. The Greeks called their writers "makers," creators, who alone could rise above this world to make a golden one. Sidney writes of the poet: "So as he goeth hand in hand with Nature, not enclosed within the narrow warrant of her gifts, but freely ranging only within the zodiac of his own wit."

The aim of poetry, of all earthly knowledge, is "to lead and draw us to as high a perfection as our degenerate souls, made worse by their clayey lodgings, can be capable of." The moral philosopher feels himself the best teacher, for he can define and discuss virtue and vice and their causes; the historian argues that his examples from the past are far more effective instructors than the abstractions of the philosopher. Sidney finds the virtues of both combined in the poet, who can give precept and example. He cites Homer's demonstration of wisdom personified in Ulysses; of valor, in Achilles; of anger, in Ajax. The poet is free to portray the ideal, while the historian must be faithful to his subjects, and they, being human, mingle faults with their virtues. The poet may show evil punished and good rewarded; the historian must record the vagaries of fortune, which allows the innocent to suffer and the vicious to prosper.

The poet has other advantages over the philosopher; however true the philosopher's statements may be, they are hard to follow. The poet "doth not only show the way, but giveth so sweet prospect into the way as will entice any man to enter into it." People will willingly listen to stories of Aeneas or Achilles, unaware of the lessons they are learning. Having established the superiority of poetry to his own satisfaction, Sidney analyzes both the pleasing and the instructive aspects of the various literary genres, trying to determine what faults may have brought poetry into disrepute. The pastoral can arouse sympathy for the wretchedness of the poor or illustrate civil wrongs in fables about sheep and wolves; satire makes one laugh at folly and thus reform. Comedy, which has been disgraced by "naughty play-makers and stage-keepers," is valuable for the ridicule it casts upon people's faults, which people scorn as they laugh. Tragedy, stirring up feelings of wonder and pity, "teacheth the uncertainty of this world, and upon how weak foundations gilden roofs are builded."

Sidney finds nothing to criticize in the work of the lyric poet, who lauds virtuous acts, gives moral precepts, and sometimes praises God, and he defends epic poetry as the greatest of all the genres: "For, as the image of each action stirreth and instructeth the mind, so the lofty image of such worthies most inflameth the mind with desire to be worthy, and informs with counsel how to be worthy."

Concluding his defense, Sidney takes up the most frequently repeated criticisms of poetry: that it is merely rhyming and versifying; that there are other kinds of knowledge that are worthier of one's time; that poetry is "the mother of lies"; that it inspires evil lusts; and that Plato banished it from his commonwealth. Against the first objection Sidney reiterates his statement that poetry is not exclusively that which is written in verse, although he defends the use of verse on the grounds that it is a great aid to the memory and that it is "the only fit speech for music."

The second argument has already been answered; if poetry be the greatest of teachers and inspirations to virtue, it must be worthy of the greatest share of people's attention. To the contention that poets are liars, Sidney replies that since they never affirm their subjects to be literally true or real, they cannot lie. Although they do not reproduce details of life from specific incidents, neither do they attempt to prove the false true. They call upon the imagination for the "willing suspension of disbelief" and tell not "what is or is not, but what should or should not be."

Sidney confesses that there is some justice in the condemnation of poetry for its scurrility, but he imputes the fault to bad poets who abuse their art, rather than to poetry itself. He suggests that Plato, in banishing poets from his Republic, was barring those bad writers who corrupted youth with false pictures of the gods, not the art of poetry itself.

Satisfied with these answers, Sidney then turns to the specific problems of literature in England in his own day. He sees no reason for poetry to flourish in Italy, France, and Scotland, and not in his own nation, except the laziness of the poets themselves. They will neither study to acquire ideas nor practice to perfect a style for conveying these ideas. A few English writers and works are, however, worthy of a place in world literature. Sidney praises Chaucer and the lyrics of the Earl of Surrey, and he finds that Edmund Spenser's *The Shepheardes Calender* (1579) "hath much poetry in his eclogues," although he objects to Spenser's use of rustic language, on the grounds that neither Theocritus nor Virgil, the most famous classical writers of pastoral, employed it. For the rest of English poetry, Sidney has only scorn, for it seemed to him meaningless: "One verse did but beget another, without ordering at the first what should be at the last;

which becomes a confused mass of words, with a tinkling sound of rime, barely accompanied with reason."

The public criticism of drama seems to him justified, with a very few exceptions. He commends *Gorboduc* (1561), a melodramatic Seneca-type tragedy by Thomas Norton and Thomas Sackville, for its "stately speeches," "well-sounding phrases," and "notable morality," but he is disturbed by the authors' failure to observe the unities of time and place. The rest of the tragedies of the age seem absurd in their broad leaps in space and time, spanning continents and decades in two hours. A true Aristotelian in his views on drama, Sidney is convinced that stage action should be confined to one episode; other events may be reported in the dialogue to provide necessary background for the central events. He objects, too, to the presence of scurrilous comic scenes, chiefly designed to evoke loud laughter from the audience, in the tragedies.

Sidney's last target is the affected artificial diction of lyric poetry, especially of love poetry. He believes that the wildly imaginative conceits of the Euphuists are tedious, and he praises, in contrast, the sense of decorum, of fitting diction and imagery, of the great classical orators.

After a few comments on the relative merits of qualitative and quantitative verse and on types of rhyme, Sidney addresses his readers, promising fame and blessings to those who will appreciate the values of poetry and laying this curse on those who will not: "While you live you live in love, and never get favor, for lacking skill of a sonnet; and when you die, your memory die from the earth, for want of an epitaph."

Readers familiar with classical conceptions of poetry may find a disturbing dissonance in *Defence of Poesie*; at times, Sidney seems to speak in theoretical terms borrowed from Plato (who questioned the value of poetry); at other times he seems to focus, as did Aristotle, on the task of defining the elements of imaginative literature and championing poetry's moral value. In actuality, Sidney is attempting to synthesize the Platonic and Aristotelian conceptions of poetry and to integrate them with the new neoclassical concept of criticism as a practical endeavor intended to assess the worth of individual works. Like Aristotle, Sidney stresses the importance of the poem as a made object. Significantly, however, he also emphasizes the importance of the imagination in the creation of art; poets rely not simply on what they see around them, but also on that inner quality that gives them the capacity to create people, places, situations, and emotions much like those of the everyday world, but in some ways better or worse, to serve as models for human behavior.

The *Defence of Poesie* presents principles generally accepted by the critics throughout the Renaissance: The author leans heavily upon the dicta of the most-noted classical critics, Aristotle, Plato, and Horace, and his standards are echoed by the major English critics of the seventeenth and eighteenth centuries, John Dryden, Alexander Pope, and Samuel Johnson. The notion that the poet is somehow an agent for good inspired not only the writers of Sidney's own day, but also those of succeeding generations; the great English Romantics—among them William Wordsworth, Samuel Taylor Coleridge, Percy Bysshe Shelley, and John Keats—are the inheritors of Sidney's belief that poetry has the power of moving people to do good. It is but one small step to move from Sidney's assertion in *Defence of Poesie* that the final end of poetry is "to lead and draw us to as high a perfection . . . as our degenerate soules" can reach, to Shelley's pronouncement in his own *Defence of Poetry* that "poets are the unacknowledged legislators of the world."

Sidney's essay is one of the most polished and interesting pieces of Elizabethan prose, and his comments on the writing of his own time have been borne out by the judgment of the centuries. Although this work is the first major piece of English literary criticism, it has seldom been surpassed in the centuries since Sidney's death.

Revised by Laurence W. Mazzeno

Further Reading

Berry, Edward. *The Making of Sir Philip Sidney*. Toronto, Ont.: University of Toronto Press, 1998. A combination of biography, literary criticism, and social history, in which Berry describes how Sidney created himself as a poet by creating depictions of himself in some of his characters, including the intrusive persona of *Defence of Poesie*.

Lawry, Jon S. *Sidney's Two Arcadias: Pattern and Proceeding*. Ithaca, N.Y.: Cornell University Press, 1972. The introduction examines *Defence of Poesie* as an expression of Sidney's ideas regarding the heroic poem and the classical idea of the poet. It is seen as a commentary on and preface to Sidney's *Arcadia* (1590).

Myrick, Kenneth. *Sir Philip Sidney as a Literary Craftsman.* 2d ed. Lincoln: University of Nebraska Press, 1965. Surveys Sidney's literary career as a humanist, courtier, and poet; studies *Defence of Poesie* as a classical oration. Useful notes connect the work to other studies of the text.

Sidney, Sir Philip. *"An Apology for Poetry" or "The Defence of Poesy."* Edited by Geoffrey Shepherd. London: Thomas Nelson and Sons, 1967. The introduction analyzes the classical form of *Defence of Poesie* and its intellectual context and background. Almost a hundred pages of notes add further interpretation and contextual connections.

_____. *Defence of Poesy*. Edited by Lewis Soens. Lincoln: University of Nebraska Press, 1970. A substantial introduction analyzes and interprets Sidney's text. Further explanation is provided by extensive notes and a bibliography that lists pertinent texts.

Spingarn, J. E. *A History of Literary Criticism in the Renaissance*. 2d ed. Westport, Conn.: Greenwood Press, 1976. This major study of the history of literary criticism argues that modern criticism began in the sixteenth century. Assigns Sidney a major role in that history and credits him with introducing the principles of classical criticism into England through *Defence of Poesie*.

Stewart, Alan. *Philip Sidney: A Double Life*. London: Chatto & Windus, 2000. The title of this biography refers to the fact that the handsome, well-born, and talented Sidney was belittled in England by Elizabeth I, while he was acclaimed for his writing and statesmanship on the Continent.

Stillman, Robert E. *Philip Sidney and the Poetics of Renaissance Cosmopolitanism*. Burlington, Vt.: Ashgate, 2008. Argues that *Defence of Poesie* was influenced by the Philippists, an elite intellectual community associated with Philip Melancthon, one of the leaders of the German Reformation. Demonstrates how Sidney's education by this continental community led him to dignify fiction-making as a compelling form of public discourse which could promote new concepts of reading, writing, ecumenicalism, and freedom from political tyranny.

A Defence of Poetry

Author: Percy Bysshe Shelley (1792-1822)
First published: 1840
Type of work: Essay

Readers familiar with other great "defenses" of poetry may find Percy Bysshe Shelley's *A Defence of Poetry* unusual, even confusing. There is little practical analysis of the elements of good literary work. There is no methodical history of poetry, as one reads in Sir Philip Sidney's *Defence of Poesie* (1595). There are no pronouncements about rules of composition. Instead, Shelley offers a philosophical analysis of the role of the poet as a special kind of person, one who can see the essential harmonies of the world beneath the discordant images people find in their everyday lives. Whereas Aristotle, Sidney, or John Dryden see the poet as a superb craftsman capable of delighting readers through the masterful blending of form and content, Shelley assigns the poet a higher calling: the revelation of truth about life and the promotion of universal betterment.

These high claims are justified by Shelley's insistence that the production of poetry is not simply a craft. Rather, the true poet is a visionary who is inspired to create art as a means of revealing something about the nature of the world. The poem itself is merely an attempt to reproduce that vision. Such claims have been misinterpreted, and Shelley has been accused of promoting automatic writing or of devaluing the importance of craftsmanship. On the contrary: Shelley sees the imagination as a shaping power that gives form to the poet's vision, and only those who master form can hope to convey their vision to readers. Similarly, claims that Shelley is a promoter of emotional poetry are wrongheaded; he is insistent that the practice of poetry involves the intellect as well as the heart. He believes that great poets have a special gift that allows them to use the materials of their own time (the forms and subjects that might appeal to their contemporary readers), but transcend the limits of time and place to speak to people of all ages.

In this essay Shelley is defending poetry—"my mistress, Urania"—against the attack by Thomas Love Peacock in "The Four Ages of Poetry," published in the first and only issue of the *Literary Miscellany* in 1820. The polemical exchange came to nothing, for *A Defence of Poetry* remained unpublished until 1840. In his essay, Peacock had elaborated the familiar figure of the Golden and Silver Ages of classical poetry into four (Iron, Gold, Silver, and Brass), skipped over "the dark ages," and repeated the succession in English po-

etry. Peacock's point was that poetry never amounts to much in civilized society; Shelley's defense is that poetry is essential. Their views were antithetical and neither made contact with the other: Peacock's attack is a boisterous satire, Shelley's defense is an elevated prose poem.

Nevertheless, Peacock's article is still a necessary preface to Shelley's arguments, not because one prompted the other or because Shelley adopted Peacock's historical method in the middle section of his essay, but because, as a pair, they show the opposing preferences of the older public for eighteenth century wit and of the younger for enthusiasm. Peacock's "The Four Ages of Poetry" has also the merit of being amusing; Shelley is never amusing. Peacock's argument is that poetry belongs properly to primitive societies, that as they become civilized they become rational and nonpoetical; hence it was not until the late seventeenth century that England equaled, in the work of William Shakespeare and John Milton, the Golden Age of Homeric Greece. Early nineteenth century England seemed, to him, to have reached the Age of Brass in poetry but a kind of Golden Age in science; therefore, poetry should be left to the primitive societies where it belongs. Peacock is most amusing in his picture of the first Age of Iron, in which the bard of the tribal chief "is always ready to celebrate the strength of his arm, being first duly inspired by that of his liquor." Apart from Homer, Peacock respects no poet, not even Shakespeare, who mixed his unities and thought nothing of "deposing a Roman Emperor by an Italian Count, and sending him off in the disguise of a French pilgrim to be shot with a blunderbuss by an English archer." Peacock's jest turns sour as he tires of his figure, and his strictures on contemporary poetry become a diatribe of which the gist is that "a poet of our times is a semibarbarian in a civilized community." Shelley, to whom Peacock sent a copy of his essay, was stirred to write his only prose statement on his craft. In it he came to the memorable conclusion that "Poets are the unacknowledged legislators of the world."

A Defence of Poetry falls into three parts. First, Shelley presents an argument that all people are poets in some degree, for poetry is an innate human faculty; hence, it is seen in all societies at all times and to eternity. In the second part, he attempts the historical proof, which he abandons in the third to make a subjective and poetic affirmation of the perpetual presence and ennobling virtue of poetry. In presenting his beliefs, Shelley uses the ideas that inspire his poems and attempts to codify them from the base Peacock had given him. Peacock could begin at once with his first age, however; Shelley found it necessary to begin by defining his notion of poetry. Two major ideas run through this first section and are reflected in the rest of the essay: the Platonic idea of mimesis, in which the imagination responds to the eternal verities it glimpses behind the material form, and the eighteenth century idea of the "sympathetic imagination" that, of its own initiative, extends itself and assumes an empathy with external objects and beings. The first idea leads Shelley to assert the superiority of the poet as the most active in using the glimpses of truth and conveying them to lesser beings for their uplifting; for this reason, the poet is the most powerful influence on humankind, a "legislator." The second idea gives the poet an insight into the ills of humankind which, once understood, can be corrected; here is the second meaning of "legislator."

The first part presented is in two sections, dealing first with the mimetic, then with the expressive powers of poetry, which powers are part of the definition of poetry; the other two parts of the definition are contained in four paragraphs on the form of poetry, especially on its use of language, the medium that makes it superior to other art media and which is called "measured" in contradistinction to "unmeasured" language or prose. The whole essay is prefaced by four paragraphs that define poetry in the largest or organic sense, not by its mechanics. These paragraphs go to the heart of the difference between Peacock and Shelley.

Shelley begins with a distinction between reason and imagination, leaving to the former the work of numbering, analyzing, and relating objects; the imagination perceives the similitude of objects in their innate values, not in their appearance, and synthesizes these values, presumably, into a valid and Platonic One or Truth. The synthetic principle of the imagination is poetry; the individual is compared to "an Aeolian lyre," subject to impressions external and internal but possessing an inner principle (poetry) that produces not simply melody but harmony. Poetry is thus both the name of a form of language (measured) and of the power of producing it and benefiting from the poem. Shelley asserts that poets are "the institutors of laws, and the founders of civil society" because they discover the laws of harmony and become "legislators" by giving these laws the form of a poem. The poetic product or poem may be an act of mimesis, but the act proceeds from the poetic faculty highly developed in the poet and contained in all people: "A poem is the very image of life expressed in its eternal truth."

The argument in the second section of the first part, devoted to the effects of poetry on society, has been anticipated in the foregoing analysis. *A Defence of Poetry*, as an "apologia," could well end at that point, but Shelley wanted to convince Peacock that his theory has external evidence. This he offers in the second part of the essay.

The historical method had already been touched on in Shelley's example of the propensity of the savage or child to imitate the impressions it receives, as a lyre produces melody only. Shelley's reading of history is as willful as Peacock's in his assertion that the morality of an age corresponds to the goodness or badness of its poetry; he adduces Greek classical drama as an evidence of a healthy society and Hellenic bucolic poetry as a sign of decay when the poets ceased to be the acknowledged legislators of the Alexandrian Hellenes. In order to cope with the same progression of health and decay in the literature of Rome, which would seem to prove Peacock's scheme, Shelley shifts the whole cycle into "episodes of that cyclic poem written by time upon the memories of men." He encounters further difficulty in coping with Christianity, for, by Shelley's theory, Jesus must be a great poet: "The scattered fragments preserved to us by the biographers of this extraordinary person, are all instinct with the most vivid poetry." Something went wrong in the Dark Ages, which brought "the extinction of the poetic principle . . . from causes too intricate to be here discussed." Shelley feels safer with Dante Alighieri and John Milton: "But let us not be betrayed from a defence into a critical history of poetry."

After abandoning the historical method which, had he followed Peacock step by step, would have brought him up to his contemporaries, Shelley returns to his defence by attacking "the promoters of utility" and, by implication, Peacock. To the utilitarian objection that poetry simply produces pleasure and that pleasure is profitless, Shelley asserts that the pleasure of poetry lies not in its superficial melody but in its innate harmony, alone capable of checking "the calculating faculty" that has already produced "more scientific and economical knowledge than can be accommodated to the just distribution of the produce which it multiplies." Shelley follows this with a paragraph that summarizes the duality of the "poetic faculty"; by synthesis it "creates new materials of knowledge and power and pleasure," and by its expressive powers it reproduces those materials "according to a certain rhythm and order which may be called the beautiful and the good."

Shelley's peroration, his personal and poetic justification for poetry, opens with three paragraphs beginning: "Poetry is indeed something divine"; "Poetry is the record of the best and happiest moments of the happiest and best minds"; "Poetry turns all things to loveliness." This is the moving genius of *Adonais*. Searching for the best proof to defend poetry from the rationalizations of Peacock, Shelley follows the prompting of his own "poetic principle" in concluding *A Defence of Poetry* with a sustained lyric in prose that Peacock could never match. The power of this essay is still inspiring. It constitutes Shelley's best claim outside his verse to be a "legislator" to the world.

Further Reading

Clark, David Lee, ed. *Shelley's Prose: Or, The Trumpet of a Prophecy*. 3d ed. London: Fourth Estate, 1988. The introduction examines Shelley's theory of poetry within the broader context of his ideas about religion and other aspects of his philosophy. Contains an annotated text of *A Defence of Poetry* and an annotated bibliography.

Clark, Timothy. *The Theory of Inspiration: Composition as a Crisis of Subjectivity in Romantic and Post-Romantic Writing*. New York: Manchester University Press, 1997. Examines theories of inspiration in Western poetics since the Enlightenment. Analyzes *A Defence of Poetry* to describe how Shelley depicted the process of composition as a state of subjective crisis and transformation.

Daiches, David. *Critical Approaches to Literature*. 2d ed. New York: Longman, 1987. Discusses the Platonic idealism of *A Defence of Poetry* in terms of poetry and social morality, language and imagination. Relates the essay's ideas to those of Sir Philip Sidney, William Wordsworth, and Samuel Taylor Coleridge.

Duffy, Cian. *Shelley and the Revolutionary Sublime*. New York: Cambridge University Press, 2005. Focuses on Shelley's fascination with sublime natural phenomena and how this interest influenced his writing and ideas about political and social reform.

Fry, Paul H. *The Reach of Criticism: Method and Perception in Literary Theory*. New Haven, Conn.: Yale University Press, 1983. A chapter discusses the relation of *A Defence of Poetry* to the tenets of Longinus, John Dryden, and others. Closely analyzes the language, ideas, and theoretical basis of the essay; considers the essay one of the best works on the debate between poetry and science.

Jordan, John E., ed. *A Defence of Poetry*, by Percy Bysshe Shelley, and *The Four Ages of Poetry*, by Thomas Love Peacock. Indianapolis, Ind.: Bobbs-Merrill, 1965. Introduction interprets the significance of Shelley's essay. Copious notes explain the text and connect it to the works of previous writers.

Morton, Timothy, ed. *The Cambridge Companion to Shelley*. New York: Cambridge University Press, 2006. Ten essays on various aspects of Shelley's life and work, including Shelley as a lyricist, dramatist, storyteller, political poet, and translator, and the literary reception of his writings. The references to *A Defence of Poetry* are listed in the index.

Defender of the Faith

Author: Philip Roth (1933-   )
First published: 1959
Type of work: Short fiction
Type of plot: Social realism
Time of plot: May-August, 1945
Locale: Camp Crowder, Missouri

Principal characters:
NATHAN MARX, the narrator, a Jewish U.S. Army sergeant recently returned from combat in Europe
PAUL BARRETT, a captain, Marx's bigoted and abusive commanding officer
SHELDON GROSSBART, a conniving Jewish trainee
LARRY FISHBEIN, a secular Jewish trainee
MICKEY HALPERN, an observant Jewish trainee
ROBERT LAHILL, the unsophisticated corporal in charge of the barracks
LEO BEN EZRA, a major, the Jewish chaplain at Camp Crowder

The Story:

Nathan Marx recounts his experiences shortly after his posting to Camp Crowder, Missouri. An infantry sergeant, Marx has spent two years in heavy combat in the European theater of World War II. In May, 1945, he is reassigned to the United States, tasked with helping train fresh recruits before they are sent abroad. Soon after Captain Paul Barrett, his gruff and abusive new commanding officer, introduces him to the troops, Marx is approached by one of the camp's trainees, a private named Sheldon Grossbart. Grossbart asks whether Marx will continue his predecessor's practice of ordering the men to clean their barracks every Friday night. He complains that it forces Jewish soldiers like himself to choose between religious worship and their military duties. Jews are a rarity at Camp Crowder, and he notes that attendance at Friday night services arouses resentment among the other soldiers. Grossbart suspects that Marx, too, is Jewish and hints that he should be sympathetic toward the plight of a coreligionist. However, denying any tie to Grossbart, Marx is curt and formal and insists that he will not make unusual accommodations for him. It is only when he uses the Yiddish word *shul* to refer to the site of sabbath services that Marx reveals his own Jewish identity.

Marx later informs Captain Barrett about Grossbart's request. The officer is disdainful of Grossbart as a Jew who seeks special privileges, and he praises Marx for not allowing his own Jewishness to interfere with his military responsibilities. However, Marx asks Corporal Robert LaHill to announce to the soldiers that they are free to attend religious services whenever they are held. On Friday night, just before going off to synagogue, Grossbart and two other Jewish recruits, Larry Fishbein and Mickey Halpern, try to thank Marx for being supportive of their situation. Marx remains frosty, refusing to acknowledge anything binding him to these Jews who seem too inexperienced to know not to salute a sergeant or call him "sir." After the three privates march off to *shul*, however, Marx summons up fond memories, long repressed, of his childhood in a Jewish neighborhood in the Bronx.

Marx finds himself following Grossbart, Fishbein, and Halpern to sabbath services. Although the company's Jewish chaplain, Major Leo Ben Ezra, tells the soldiers that they must try to make do with the nonkosher food they are served, Grossbart complains to Marx that Halpern has gotten sick trying to eat ham and other items forbidden by the Jewish dietary code. Marx advises them not to call attention to themselves, but Grossbart replies that he intends to assert his religious rights and protest that they are forced to consume *trafe*, or nonkosher food.

A week later, a furious Captain Barrett summons Marx to account for Grossbart's behavior. The private's father had written to his congressional representative to complain that the meals the Army makes him eat violate his religious principles, and the captain is under pressure from his superiors to deal with the matter. When Barrett and Marx go together to speak with Grossbart, Barrett is furious and Grossbart defiant, while Marx resists aligning himself with his fellow Jewish soldier. After Barrett leaves, Grossbart admits that he forged the letter from his father to the congressman and that he does not in truth keep kosher.

Some time later, Grossbart, appealing to the sergeant's sympathy for a fellow Jew, prevails on Marx to provide passes for Grossbart, Fishbein, and Halpern to spend Passover at a relative's home in St. Louis. He does so, but he is then furious to learn that the three used their precious leave from basic training not to celebrate Passover at a seder but rather to dine at a Chinese restaurant. Marx refuses Grossbart's plea that the sergeant intercede to block the imminent assignment of the three Jewish trainees to the Pacific. Soon after this refusal, Marx learns that Grossbart has managed to finagle for himself a safe posting to Fort Monmouth, New Jersey instead. Marx proceeds to alter the assignment, ensuring that Grossbart, like Fishbein and Halpern, whose interests he claims to be defending, will also soon be shipping out to the Pacific, where heavy fighting still rages. The story concludes with Grossbart and Marx each resigned to accept the complexities of his fate.

Critical Evaluation:

"Defender of the Faith" was published in 1959 in Philip Roth's first book, *Goodbye, Columbus, and Five Short Stories*. The four other short stories accompanying the book's title novella were "The Conversion of the Jews," "Epstein," "You Can't Tell a Man by the Song He Sings," and "Eli, the Fanatic." The volume was honored with the National Book Award and launched Roth's career with more attention than is normally accorded a literary debut. Each of the pieces explores the tensions between Jewish particularism and assimilation to a universalist American identity, a theme already attracting wide interest through the works of Saul Bellow and Bernard Malamud. Roth was soon being considered the junior member of a brilliant triumvirate that included himself and these two other authors as the leading figures in the newly fashionable category of "American Jewish literature." Together with Bellow and Malamud (with whom he did not otherwise have a great deal in common), Roth resisted the label "Jewish author," but his very resistance became an important theme in his work.

Despite the accolades it received, Roth's first book in general and "Defender of the Faith" in particular were also denounced by some Jewish commentators as anti-Semitic. The story was attacked, by rabbis and others, for its portrayal in Nathan Marx of a self-hating Jew and in Sheldon Grossbart of an unctuous Jewish finagler, a con artist who manipulates tribal loyalties to advance his personal agenda. Roth was accused of defaming his own people by perpetuating negative stereotypes of Jews. The early burden of justifying his art and identity shaped the rest of Roth's long, productive career. Refusing the role of ethnic cheerleader, he countered the criticism with two essays, "Some New Jewish Stereotypes" (1961) and "Writing About Jews" (1963), as well as with several works of fiction in which a fictional novelist, most often Nathan Zuckerman, is condemned for writing books that are not "good for the Jews." Roth has not denied his Jewishness or the fact that he is drawn again and again to depicting Jewish characters, but he has insisted on the freedom to pursue his art without sectarian obligations. There is a bit of Nathan Marx in Roth's reluctance to be a defender of the Jews.

In 1945, when the enormity of the Holocaust had not yet registered fully, casual anti-Semitism was still common in American society, and the paradigm of the melting pot required that members of minority groups conform to the values and customs of the white Christian majority. Captain Barrett probably does not consider himself a bigot when he disparages the overtly Jewish Grossbart, observing that his pushiness is typical of his people. Although he respects Marx as a war hero, he expects the sergeant to keep his Jewishness to himself. Having blocked out family memories to contend with the grim realities of combat, Marx seems eager to oblige. However, when Grossbart, Fishbein, and Halpern call upon him to affirm his solidarity with them and protect their interests, he is asked to become a "defender of the Jews." It is comically ironic that Marx, who aspires to abandon his Jewish identity and be simply an American soldier, is placed in the position of advocating for the special interests of an assertive Jew. Grossbart puts him on the defensive by accusing him of being a self-hating Jew. The irony is compounded if the title "Defender of the Faith" is taken as applying also to Grossbart, whose pretense of being a pious Jew standing up for the rights of his beleaguered people is merely a cover for advancing selfish interests.

"Defender of the Faith" proceeds as a battle of wits between two cunning antagonists, Marx and Grossbart. The private employs several rhetorical gambits in his strategy to win the sergeant over to his devious purposes. He draws on Marx's nostalgia for a Jewish childhood and on the lure of ethnic solidarity. In addition, Marx has only recently re-

turned—unscathed, at least physically—from war against a nation that committed genocide against his own people, and hostility toward Jews persists even at home. The combat veteran is vulnerable not only to survivor's guilt but also to a belief that Jews continue to require defenders. Though Grossbart recognizes that Marx sees through him, he is able to manipulate that very awareness—until the final coup de grâce, when Marx hoists Grossbart on his own petard, reversing the private's sneaky ploy and dispatching him to combat in the Pacific. The master conniver is outwitted, as Marx ends up defender of an American faith in honesty and justice.

Throughout the story, language serves as both an instrument and an indicator of character development. To get through the war intact, Marx has had to stifle any private feelings, and at Camp Crowder he tries to speak in the impersonal manner of a military functionary. Grossbart complains that he talks like a goy, or gentile. By contrast, whenever he is in Marx's presence, Grossbart peppers his speech with Yiddishisms, words like *liebschen*, *ballabusta*, and *gefilte fish* that signal his Jewishness and set him apart from most of the other military personnel. However, they also serve as shibboleths, code words that affirm a kinship with Marx and lure him into alliance with the three Jewish trainees. As Grossbart succeeds in breaking through Marx's emotional armor, Yiddish words such as *shul* and *tsimas* seep into the sergeant's vocabulary. Nevertheless, it is with a Yiddish-inflected inversion of word order ("For each other we have to learn to watch out, Sheldon") that Marx finally rejects Grossbart's tribal calls and teaches a lesson in wider ethical obligations. At the conclusion of a memoir that he shapes with fluent, lucid English, Marx embraces the ambiguous fate of being American.

Steven G. Kellman

Further Reading

Baumgarten, Murray, and Barbara Gottfried. *Understanding Philip Roth*. Columbia: University of South Carolina Press, 1990. A thematically organized examination of Roth's oeuvre to 1990.

Cooper, Alan. *Philip Roth and the Jews*. Albany: State University of New York Press, 1996. Presents Roth as the leading chronicler of Jewish experience in the United States.

DaCrema, Joseph. "Roth's 'Defender of the Faith.'" *Explicator* 39, no. 1 (1980): 19-20. Concentrating on Nathan Marx's use of language, DaCrema traces the sergeant's evolution into a mature, self-aware Jew.

Halio, Jay L. *Philip Roth Revisited*. New York: Twayne,

1992. An overview of Roth's work that emphasizes the role of truth-telling humor.

Parrish, Timothy, ed. *The Cambridge Companion to Philip Roth*. New York: Cambridge University Press, 2007. Eleven essays provide an overview of Roth's career. The first, by Victoria Aarons, focuses on American-Jewish identity in Roth's short fiction.

Pinsker, Sanford. *The Comedy That "Hoits": An Essay on the Fiction of Philip Roth*. Columbia: University of Mis-

souri Press, 1975. A study of the bittersweet humor in Roth's early work.

Royal, Derek Parker, ed. *Philip Roth: New Perspectives on an American Author*. Westport, Conn.: Praeger, 2005. Collects seventeen essays that track Roth's writings chronologically. The first essay, by Jessica G. Rabin, focuses on the early short stories. Contains a dozen essays examining such topics as the novel's chronology, language, and narrative design.

Deirdre

Author: James Stephens (1880/1882-1950)
First published: 1923
Type of work: Novel
Type of plot: Folklore
Time of plot: Heroic Age
Locale: Ireland

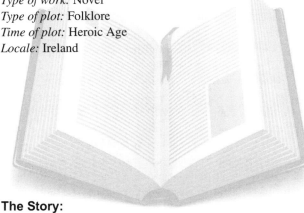

Principal characters:
CONACHÚR MAC NESSA, king of Ulster
CLOTHRU, his first wife
MAEVE, his second wife
CATHFA, his father and a magician
LAVARCHAM, his conversation-woman
FERGUS MAC ROY, his stepfather
NESSA, his mother
FELIMID MAC DALL, his storyteller
DEIRDRE, Felimid's daughter and the ward of Conachúr
UISNEAC, Conachúr's brother-in-law
NAOISE,
AINNLE, and
ARDAN, Uisneac's sons

The Story:

The king of Ulster has a daughter called Assa, the Gentle. She loves knowledge and has many tutors. One day, returning from a visit to her father and finding her tutors killed, she buckles on her armor and sets out to find the murderer. Henceforth her name is Nessa, the Ungentle. While she is bathing in the forest, Cathfa, the magician, sees and loves her. He offers to spare her life only if she will marry him. Their son is Conachúr mac Nessa. After a while, Nessa leaves Cathfa, taking her son with her.

When Conachúr is sixteen years old, Nessa is still the most beautiful woman in the land. Fergus mac Roy, the new king of Ulster, is only eighteen years old, but he falls in love with Nessa as soon as he sees her. She promises to marry him only if Conachúr can be king for a year while she and Fergus live away from court. Fergus agrees, but after the year is up, Conachúr keeps the throne, and Fergus becomes one of his most trusted followers.

Nessa arranges a marriage between Conachúr and Clothru, daughter of the high king of Connacht. On a visit to her father, Clothru is killed by her sister Maeve. Conachúr's first son is born just before she dies. Bent on vengeance, Conachúr goes to Connacht. There he sees Maeve and, changing his mind, he marries her against her wishes. When she goes to Ulster with him, she takes along great riches and also a guard of one thousand men.

During one of his journeys at a time when Maeve refuses to accompany him, he stops at the house of Felimid mac Dall, his storyteller. That night, Conachúr sends a servant to say that Felimid's wife should sleep with him. The servant returns to say that Felimid's wife cannot accommodate him as she is expecting a child. Soon the men hear the wail of the newborn infant. Conachúr asks his father to interpret the wail and other evil omens that the men saw recently. Cathfa prophesies that the child then born, a girl, will be called The

Troubler and that she will bring evil and destruction in Ulster. When one of his followers suggests that Conachúr have the child killed immediately, he sends for the infant; but he decides it is not becoming for a prince to evade fate, and he lets the child live. Deirdre is her name.

Conachúr has Deirdre brought up at Emania by Lavarcham, his conversation-woman, who lets the girl see no one but women servants and a guard of the oldest and ugliest swordsmen in Ulster. Lavarcham can adapt herself to any situation or group of people; while acting as a spy for Conachúr, she also learns everything that has to be taught to Deirdre to prepare her for the place Lavarcham decides she should have in the kingdom.

Lavarcham reports regularly to Conachúr so that, while he never sees Deirdre, the king knows how she progresses month by month. He refuses to believe Lavarcham's glowing reports; besides, at that time, he is well satisfied with Maeve. On the other hand, Lavarcham reports at length to Deirdre about Conachúr until the child knows all his whims, his boldness, and his majesty.

Maeve, who never forgives Conachúr for marrying her against her will, finally decides to leave him. She is so unforgiving that she refuses to leave behind one thread of her clothes or one bit of her riches. Since some of the riches include great herds of cattle, flocks of sheep, heaps of silver and jewelry, and pieces of furniture, she makes careful plans to get everything away when Conachúr is not looking. She trusts no one entirely, but she has a spy, mac Roth, who is even more diligent than Conachúr's Lavarcham. He discovers that Conachúr is to take a trip to Leinster; he even follows Conachúr's company for two full days until he feels the group is far enough away to be unable to get back in time; then he returns to help Maeve in her flight. Only Lavarcham guesses that something might happen, but her messengers do not reach Conachúr before Maeve flees.

Conachúr grieves for Maeve, but he is unable to bring her back to Ulster. In the meantime, Lavarcham begins to brood about the matter. The whole kingdom wants the king to remarry, and Deirdre is sixteen years old. Lavarcham persuades the king to come to see Deirdre.

Although Lavarcham teaches Deirdre all that she needs to know about Conachúr, she does not realize that the child thinks of the king as ancient and fears him a little. Nor does Lavarcham know that Deirdre, longing for people of her own age, learns how to escape the guards around Emania.

Deirdre is first tempted to go beyond the walls by a campfire that she wants to investigate. Around it she sees three boys: Naoise, who is nineteen, Ainnle, who is seventeen, and Ardan, who is fourteen. They are the sons of Uisneac, who

married Conachúr's sister. Deirdre startles them when she first appears in the light of the fire, but they all laugh and tell so many good stories that she knows she will go back again. The younger boys insist that Naoise will soon be the champion of Ulster, and Deirdre does not doubt it.

When Conachúr goes to see Deirdre, he finds her the most beautiful girl in Ulster, and he intends to marry her immediately. Lavarcham, however, makes him wait a week, after which he will have a three-month feast. In love with Naoise, Deirdre is horrified at the idea of marrying a man who is so old and huge, but several nights pass before she can make her way to the campfire again. At her pleading, the brothers take her out of the country.

Six years later, Conachúr decides that Deirdre and the sons of Uisneac should be brought back from Scotland, their place of refuge, but the boys will not return except under the protection of one of Conachúr's trusted men. Fergus and his sons are sent to Scotland with assurances of safety. Deirdre has a dream and begs Naoise not to leave, but he declares that Fergus is honorable.

When the travelers reach the coast of Ulster, Fergus is detained by one of Conachúr's men, and Fergus's sons take Deirdre and the sons of Uisneac under their protection. Arriving at Conachúr's court at night, they are lodged in the fortress called the Red Branch. Then Deirdre knows there will be trouble, because Conachúr does not receive them under his own roof.

Conachúr sends his men to batter down the doors and to bring Deirdre to him. The sons of Uisneac and Fergus make quick sallies, dashing out one door and in another, and kill so many of Conachúr's warriors that at last the king orders the fortress to be set on fire. As Deirdre and the boys flee, Conachúr asks Cathfa to stop them. Cathfa casts a spell that makes the boys drop their arms, and they are captured. Conachúr has the sons of Fergus and Uisneac killed. When Deirdre kneels over Naoise's dead body, she sips his blood and falls lifeless.

Critical Evaluation:

One of the primary features of the Irish literary renaissance was the discovery, regeneration, and translation of ancient Irish myths into modern forms. Among the great Celtic legends, perhaps the most popular was the tragic love story of Deirdre, The Troubler, and her lover, Naoise. Probably the greatest artistic representations of this fable of fate, love, betrayal, and death are the dramatic versions by William Butler Yeats (*Deirdre*, 1906) and John Millington Synge (*Deirdre of the Sorrows*, 1910). However, although James Stephens's prose interpretation of the myth may lack the austere poetic grandeur of Yeats's play or the tragic intensity of Synge's, it has a psychological penetration and lively narrative thrust that makes it not unworthy of mention alongside those great predecessors.

In many ways, Stephens's version is the most modern one of the Deirdre legend. Although very different from each other, both Yeats and Synge sought to capture the atmosphere of the romantic Irish past of legend and folklore in their plays. Stephens, however, is more interested in a modern psychological analysis of the characters and their actions. At the same time, he does not ignore the flavor of archaic Celtic myth; in developing his story, he takes great pains to present the medieval culture and background as authentically and thoroughly as he could. *Deirdre*, therefore, contains that mixture of the lyrical and the realistic, the ancient and the modern, and the solemn and the irreverent that characterizes Stephens's best work in all genres.

Stephens was a brilliant Irish writer of poetry and prose whose best work was grounded in the early literature of his own country. Just as he attempted to bring Irish folklore to life in *The Crock of Gold* (1912), so he tried to revitalize ancient Gaelic legend in *Deirdre*. In this novel, he writes of the beautiful and mystical Deirdre, of brave and handsome Naoise, and of strong and willful Conachúr, who is loved by all his people and who is almost great. It is not only the people in the story that are remembered afterward; there are also many memorable scenes. *Deirdre* is a novel of legend and fantasy with a core of realism.

It has been claimed—with some justice—that Stephens's emphasis on detailed psychological analysis and explanation slows down the action in the first book and that he fails in the crucial scene—the flight of the lovers—by having it reported secondhand. If the first book is uneven, however, the second is delightful and occasionally powerful. Their personalities and motivations having been carefully delineated in the first book, the characters, and their decisions and actions, are thoroughly believable in the second one. All of the second book is excellent, and several moments—such as the suppressed tragedy evident in the gaiety of Naoise's younger brothers, Deirdre's realization of Conachúr's treachery, and especially Deirdre's death on the body of her dead lover—approach greatness.

It was not Stephens's purpose to idolize the old Irish myths but to make them alive and familiar for his own times. In spite of a setting eight centuries in the past, readers of *Deirdre* have little difficulty in believing in and relating to a gallery of vivid, passionate characters: the gentle, aristocratic King Fergus, too casual and perhaps lazy to avert tragedy; Conachúr, brave yet insecure, whose sense of honor and

duty cannot overcome his passionate nature; the sons of Uisneac, united yet individualized, apparently carefree yet serious and heroic; and finally, Deirdre herself, intense, intuitive, innocent yet wise, who passionately and courageously strives for a happiness that she knows from the beginning will never be granted to her.

Further Reading

Fackler, Herbert V. *That Tragic Queen: The Deirdre Legend in Anglo-Irish Literature*. Salzburg, Austria: Institut für Englische Sprache und Literatur, Universität Salzburg, 1978. Explores various nineteenth century versions of the Deirdre story and their influence on subsequent treatments of the legend. Analyzes the distinctive character of Stephens's imaginative reinvention of the bardic material. Places Stephens's work in its various contexts.

Foster, John Wilson. *Fictions of the Irish Literary Revival*. Syracuse, N.Y.: Syracuse University Press, 1987. A critically sophisticated overview of the context in which Stephens's work was created. The relationship between *Deirdre* and works of other contemporary fabulists is evaluated, providing a significant sense of the novel's genre. Assesses the originality of Stephens's rhetorical strategies and modernizing emphases in *Deirdre*.

Kiely, Benedict. "Clay and Gods and Men: The Worlds of James Stephens." In *A Raid into Dark Corners, and Other Essays*. Cork, Ireland: Cork University Press, 1999. An insightful analysis of Stephens's work by an Irish writer and literary critic. Describes how Stephens's prose and poetry always "move" and are on "the edge of something more tense and radiant, and more full of movement, than ordinary life."

Lennon, Joseph. "Theosophy and the Nation: George Russell (Æ) and James Stephens." In *Irish Orientalism: A Literary and Intellectual History*. Syracuse, N.Y.: Syracuse University Press, 2004. Examines how Stephens combines elements of Irish and Indian folklore to describe the social realities of early twentieth century Ireland. Discusses the influence of Eastern philosophy and Theosophy on Stephens and other Celtic Revivalists, most notably Æ.

McFate, Patricia. *The Writings of James Stephens*. London: Macmillan, 1979. A thematic survey of Stephens's prose, plays, and poems. The discussion of *Deirdre* focuses on the story's origins in Irish myth, highlighting Stephens's adaptation of this legend. Includes a chronology and a comprehensive bibliography.

Martin, Augustine. *James Stephens: A Critical Study*. Dublin: Gill and Macmillan, 1977. A comprehensive analysis of all of Stephens's writings. A discussion of *Deirdre* is included in the account of Stephens's artistic involvement with Irish myth, folktale, and saga. The analysis of the novel concentrates on the significance of jealousy in its plot.

Pyle, Hilary. *James Stephens: His Work and an Account of His Life*. London: Routledge & Kegan Paul, 1965. Remains the most accessible source of biographical information about Stephens. Provides detailed discussion of the influences on his work, such as the poetry of William Blake and Eastern philosophy. The full range of Stephens's writings is also considered in the light of an intimate knowledge of the contexts in which they were produced.

Deirdre

Author: William Butler Yeats (1865-1939)
First produced: 1906; first published, 1907
Type of work: Drama
Type of plot: Tragedy
Time of plot: Antiquity
Locale: Ireland

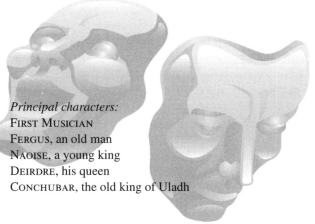

Principal characters:
FIRST MUSICIAN
FERGUS, an old man
NAOISE, a young king
DEIRDRE, his queen
CONCHUBAR, the old king of Uladh

The Story:

Two musicians converse in a woodland house. The First Musician rehearses the background of the play: King Conchubar finds Deirdre as a young child in the wood, hires a nurse to care for her, and, as she attains womanhood, falls in love with her. Just before Conchubar is to wed Deirdre, Naoise, a young man, climbs the hill to the woodland house where Deirdre is sequestered and abducts her.

Fergus, an old man, enters the house and informs the musicians that Deirdre and Naoise are to arrive momentarily. They have been in self-exile, hiding from Conchubar's jealous wrath. Having softened, the old king invites them to return. Fergus insists that King Conchubar has overcome his jealousy and forgives the young lovers. When the musicians express skepticism, Fergus grows angry. Although he insists that he will dance for pure joy at the change in King Conchubar, the First Musician notices forbidding-looking men moving around outside.

Upon entering the house, Deirdre and Fergus express apprehension that King Conchubar did not arrange to welcome them. Fergus conjectures that Conchubar will appear to welcome his guests himself, and he observes to Naoise that Deirdre's uneasiness is understandable: Having been reared outside polite society, she does not understand the inviolability of the king's vow. Surrendering his own uneasiness to Fergus's assurance of safety, Naoise tells Deirdre that it is ungrateful of them to doubt their host. Fergus remarks that he believes the best of everyone, and that such belief is capable of influencing people to behave well.

Deirdre speaks quickly to the First Musician, and from his veiled remarks she divines that Conchubar intends to kill Naoise and force her to become his unwilling queen. Deirdre's sudden anguished cry attracts Naoise, who admonishes her not to criticize the king. Reminding her of Conchubar's oath, he instructs Deirdre that, "when we give a word and take a word/ Sorrow is put away, past wrong forgotten." Fergus pragmatically reminds the lovers that the house stands in the stronghold of King Conchubar's power and flight is impossible. Realizing that she and Naoise are trapped, Deirdre exclaims that she will buy their freedom by mutilating herself, to "spoil this beauty that brought misery/ And houseless wandering on the man I love."

Naoise urges her to do nothing, for, indeed, their fate is unalterable. As if to punctuate Naoise's fatalism, a messenger arrives and announces that Conchubar has prepared supper and awaits the company of his guests. The faithful Fergus gushingly confesses that he, too, had suspected Conchubar's intentions, but that all is well again. Naoise gently chides himself for doubting Conchubar. Deirdre, who knows better, calmly notes that the messenger did not finish delivering his message.

Only Deirdre and Fergus are being invited to supper, the messenger concludes; Naoise, "the traitor that bore off the queen," is unwelcome. The trap is sprung and Conchubar's treachery revealed. Naoise quickly discovers that the woods around the house swarm with Conchubar's soldiers: Flight and fight are equally futile. In a defiant gesture of self-control, he and Deirdre join in a game of chess.

Conchubar appears at the window, then slips back into the night. Naoise chases him, presuming that Conchubar flees from fear, but Deirdre snatches a knife from the First Musician, pretending that she will help Naoise in his flight. When Conchubar makes his appearance in the room, he gloats that Naoise is entangled in the net set to trap him. Conchubar first sternly warns Deirdre that he will kill Naoise unless she consents to walk into his house, in full public view, and as of her own free will. Deirdre beseeches Conchubar to allow her and Naoise to go free, emphasizing, naïvely, that his subjects will praise and extol him for his forgiveness. Realizing that Conchubar is adamant in his refusal to let her go, Deirdre then poignantly instructs Naoise to depart. "I will not live long, Naoise," she says, urging him to leave and forget her. Deirdre begs Conchubar to accept that she is to blame for the wrong he suffered. Naoise's strength and fighting skill could prove useful to the kingdom. Even while Deirdre is begging for Naoise's life, he is taken outside to be slaughtered by the impassive and vindictive king.

When Deirdre is confronted with the bloody evidence of Naoise's death, she staggers, trembling, over to the musicians. Conchubar brutally commands her to come to his room: "The traitor who has carried off my wife/ No longer lives./ For he that called himself your husband is dead." At the peak of her grief, Deirdre feigns consent to Conchubar's command, ambiguously asserting, "It is but wisdom to do willingly/ What has to be done." Conchubar, for all his craftiness, imagines that Deirdre is weary of opposing him and will surrender to him. Deirdre then appeals to the king's vanity, asking to be allowed to gaze one last time upon Naoise's body in private. As she slips behind the curtain, where she takes her life, Conchubar boasts to Fergus, "Deirdre is mine." Conchubar's delight turns to outrage, however, when he sees that she killed herself. Bitterly, he declares that he acted wisely in choosing Deirdre for his queen and correctly in preventing a boy lover from taking her from him.

Critical Evaluation:

William Butler Yeats, who is remembered primarily as one of the most celebrated and influential lyric poets of the twentieth century, produced eleven short plays based upon the heroic literature of Ireland and concerned chiefly with the exploits of the Ulster hero Cuchulain. Yeats based *Deirdre*, his second play, on a section of the translation of the Gaelic tale of *Cuchulain of Muirthemne* (1902), done by his friend, Lady Gregory, changing it slightly to suit his artistic needs. Although Padraic Colum found that the language of the play "has high excellence," he complained that the character-

izations were exasperating, the result, according to A. S. Knowland of a "mixture of naturalism and lyricism," a mixture he agreed was uneasy. Lennox Robinson, however, called it "the most supremely satisfactory of Yeats's one-act verse-plays."

Yeats's dramatic method was to pit strong characterizations in opposition, juxtaposing poetic diction and rhythms with what he called "speech close to that of daily life." In his dialogue of 1915, *The Poet and the Actress*, he wrote "In every great play . . . you will find a group of characters . . . who express the dream, and another group who express its antagonist." The aim of drama is to pit these forces against one another in battle. "Those who try to create beautiful things without this battle in the soul, are merely imitators," he believed.

In *Deirdre*, Yeats presents the conflict of the otherworldly Deirdre with the powerful and crafty King Conchubar. The play proceeds in a series of oppositions. At first, Conchubar remains a foreboding presence, the dark shadow of Deirdre's hope. Deirdre's act of faith in returning to Conchubar's kingdom anticipates the faithlessness of Conchubar's vow to welcome and protect her and her lover, Naoise. Yeats emphasizes the vow, both to highlight its social significance and to contrast it with the stronger vow of love that Deirdre has pledged to Naoise. Later, Conchubar deceitfully offers to spare Naoise's life if Deirdre will pretend to the kingdom that she has returned of her own volition. Deirdre matches this double deceit with double fidelity, at first appealing as a loyal subject to Conchubar's honor as a king, then sacrificing herself to keep her pledge of love to Naoise.

A. Norman Jeffares has noted that Yeats's concern with drama was with the heroic, and the final contrast in *Deirdre* evokes the most distinctive trait of heroic literature, full belief in the unrivaled importance of enduring renown. Whereas Conchubar shrinks from the sacrifice that would ensure the regeneration of his honor, Deirdre unhesitatingly embraces it, directing the musicians to celebrate the felicity of her marriage, "knowing that all is happy, and that you know/ Within what bride-bed I shall lie this night,/ And by what man, and lie close up to him,/ For the bed's narrow, and there outsleep the cockcrow." Deirdre's last few thoughts include how she should rightfully be remembered, but Conchubar sinks into self-justification and paranoia.

Deirdre's act of heroism is an example of Yeats's notion of the dream, what Richard Ellman terms "the highest, most vigorous imaginative exercise." Whereas she has surrendered herself to a transcendent value, Conchubar, the dream's antagonist, has not. Yeats implies that Deirdre's ill-starred passion and the implacable demands of kingship are both extraordinary and irresistible and that both exact a total sacrifice of the self, a gift of one's individuality and character. Conchubar reneges on the obligations of kingship, recognizing only its prerogatives and powers. His selfishness, or his position within what Ellman categorizes as "the chaos of circumstances," overcomes him. Deirdre rises above it.

Yeats has written that in tragic art "one distinguishes devices to exclude or lessen character." By contrast, individuality belongs only to comedy. Conchubar makes a comical king only. It is a final flourish of *Deirdre*'s artfulness that in King Conchubar's acid insistence upon the appropriateness of his behavior, the audience can comprehend the scope of Deirdre's achievement in transcending hers by an act of selflessness and imagination.

Michael Scott Joseph

Further Reading

Bushrui, S. B. *Yeats's Verse-Plays: The Revisions, 1900-1910*. Oxford, England: Clarendon Press, 1965. An exhaustive treatment of *Deirdre*, covering all aspects of its composition and production. Bushrui's examination of Yeats's revisions strongly underscores the influence *Deirdre* continued to exert upon Yeats's imagination.

Doggett, Rob. "Setting Ireland's House in Order: Performances of Gender and Nationhood in *Cathleen ni Houlihan* and *Deirdre*." In *Deep-Rooted Things: Empire and Nation in the Poetry and Drama of William Butler Yeats*. Notre Dame, Ind.: University of Notre Dame Press, 2006. Focuses on selected plays and poems which reflect Yeats's ambivalence toward Irish nationalism in the years when Ireland was making the transition from British colony to partially independent nation. Argues that nationalism for Yeats is a series of masks that he adapts, rejects, and re-creates.

Howes, Marjorie, and John Kelly, eds. *The Cambridge Companion to W. B. Yeats*. New York: Cambridge University Press, 2006. Collection of essays providing an overview of Yeats's work in all genres, including a discussion of Yeats and the drama.

Jeffares, A. Norman, and A. S. Knowland. *A Commentary on the Collected Plays of W. B. Yeats*. New York: Macmillan, 1975. Provides detailed production information, including names of various casts of actors, performance dates, and a bibliography of printings of the play. Includes useful literary background to the characters taken from analyses of traditional texts.

Knowland, A. S. *W. B. Yeats, Dramatist of Vision*. New York: Barnes & Noble, 1983. An inclusive study of Yeats's plays, in which one chapter offers an extended textual analysis. Readers might disagree with some of Knowland's dogmatic judgments, but his steady analysis is generally illuminating.

Richman, David. *Passionate Action: Yeats's Mastery of Drama*. Newark: University of Delaware Press, 2000. Draws on Yeats's correspondence and the many drafts of his plays to chronicle his work as a playwright and theatrical producer.

Taylor, Richard. *A Reader's Guide to the Plays of W. B. Yeats*. New York: Macmillan, 1984. Introductory essay that glosses the plot, characterization, construction, language, and stage imagery of *Deirdre*. Analyses of Yeats's other plays add to a broader knowledge of his aesthetic.

Yeats, W. B. *Deirdre: Manuscript Materials*. Edited by Virginia Bartholome Rohan. Ithaca, N.Y.: Cornell University Press, 2004. Contains manuscripts of three substantially different versions of the play that were written through its first performance, as well as subsequent revisions that reflect what Yeats learned over the years about stage production.

Deirdre of the Sorrows

Author: John Millington Synge (1871-1909)
First produced: 1910; first published, 1910
Type of work: Drama
Type of plot: Tragedy
Time of plot: The past
Locale: Ireland

Principal characters:
DEIRDRE, a heroine of Gaelic legend
NAISI, Deirdre's lover
CONCHUBOR, high king of Ulster
FERGUS, Conchubor's friend
LAVARCHAM, Deirdre's nurse
AINNLE and ARDAN, Naisi's brothers
OWEN, Conchubor's attendant and spy

The Story:

King Conchubor keeps Deirdre, the beautiful young woman he resolves to make his bride, at the home of Lavarcham, the old nurse, on Slieve Fuadh. One rainy evening, Conchubor and his friend Fergus arrive to find that Deirdre, to the king's displeasure, is still out gathering nuts and sticks in the woods. Lavarcham warns the king that Deirdre will not be anxious to see him, and she repeats the old prophecy that Deirdre was born to bring destruction into the world. When Deirdre comes in, the king presents her with rings and jewels and remonstrates with her for staying out in the woods. Deirdre defends her behavior and says that she has no desire to go to Emain to become queen.

Conchubor pleads with her, talking of his loneliness, his love for her, and the rooms he prepared for her in his castle at Emain. Deirdre insists that in spite of the fact that she is pledged to Conchubor she would prefer to remain in the simple cottage with Lavarcham as long as possible. Conchubor, growing impatient, insists that she be ready to go to Emain and become his queen within a few days.

After he leaves, Lavarcham urges Deirdre to be sensible and bend to Conchubor's wishes, but Deirdre keeps talking about other defiant legendary heroines and about Naisi and his brothers, the bravest men in the woods. Deirdre goes to dress elegantly for one of the last nights of her freedom.

In the meantime Naisi and his brothers arrive at the cottage to take refuge from the storm. Lavarcham is not eager to let them in, but they claim that a beautiful lady whom they met in the woods promised them refuge from the storm. They enter, but Lavarcham, sensing trouble, tries unsuccessfully to get rid of them. They are still in the room when Deirdre returns. Deirdre provides food for Ainnle and Ardan. When they leave the cottage she asks Lavarcham to leave also. Alone with Naisi, she tells him of Conchubor's imminent suit. Deeply in love by this time, they decide to marry and run away in spite of their knowledge of the troubles foretold. They ask Ainnle, who returns to the cottage, to marry them before they flee into the night.

Seven years pass during which Deirdre and Naisi, with Ainnle and Ardan, live happily beside the sea in Alban. One day Lavarcham arrives to announce that Fergus is on his way with peace offerings from King Conchubor and to plead with Deirdre to accept the king's offer. Deirdre insists on her loyalty to Naisi. Owen, Conchubor's trusted man, arrives with word that Naisi and Fergus are already talking on the path below; he rudely advises Deirdre to leave Naisi and return to the king. Owen thinks that seven years of love are more than enough and that Deirdre will one day be old and yearn for the comfort of the royal palace. Owen also reveals that he is jealous of Naisi and hates him because he killed Owen's father some time before.

Fergus, on his arrival, says that Conchubor in his peace offering invites Naisi and Deirdre back to Emain in peace. Naisi and Deirdre wonder if they should accept the offer. They talk of age, the possible death of love, and the happiness of their seven years, despite some difficult times, at Alban. They experienced such perfect years, they decide to accept Conchubor's offer and return to Emain; they feel they will never know such complete happiness at Alban again. Owen returns, screaming that it is all a plot, and then runs out and splits his head against a stone. Believing Owen mad, Naisi and Deirdre accept Fergus's promise that no trick is involved, and they set out for Emain to meet Conchubor again.

Lavarcham, arriving first to speak with Conchubor, finds him a lonely old man. After assuring the king that he can never gain Deirdre's love, she reports that Owen, despairing of ever gaining Deirdre, ran mad and destroyed himself. Conchubor's warriors arrive and report that they separated Naisi and Deirdre from Naisi's brothers. When Naisi and Deirdre arrive, they find themselves in a tent. A freshly dug grave is concealed by curtains next to the tent. They speak mournfully, for they strongly suspect a plot against them. Conchubor returns, welcomes them, and seems, in spite of the evidence of the tent, the grave, and warriors lurking nearby, to mean his offer of peace seriously. Then, as he and

Naisi are about to clasp hands of friendship, Naisi hears his brothers cry for help. Naisi starts to leave, although Deirdre pleads with him to stay. Naisi curses the softness of women and runs out. The king's warriors kill Naisi as they killed his brothers.

Conchubor urges Deirdre to end her mourning for Naisi and become his queen. Deirdre continues to lament and will have nothing to do with Conchubor. Fergus appears and announces that he burned Emain because the king went back on his pledge not to harm Naisi. Fergus, who acted in good faith, tries to protect Deirdre, but Deirdre uses Naisi's knife to commit suicide and join him in another world without defiling their love. After Deirdre's death, all mourn. Conchubor, old and broken, is led away by Lavarcham.

Critical Evaluation:

Deirdre of the Sorrows, John Millington Synge's last play, was not performed until after his death. The play deals with Irish legend, dramatizing an account of the beautiful Irish heroine who preferred death along with her lover to life as the wife of the king. The play is full of this romantic dedication, fully developed in Synge's rich Irish idiom. The language of the Irish peasant is given power and dignity as it is shaped into the tragic movement of the play. The play is also not without touches of humane characterization. The king is not simply a cruel ruler; he is also a sad and lonely man who deeply regrets the deaths he has caused. Naisi is not simply a martyred hero but also the husband who rants that his wife has caused him to be a softer man and allowed him to desert the ways of his brothers and his companions in arms. The play contains the rich warmth of Synge's local and distinctively Irish characterizations and the romantic quality of the legendary.

In spite of his relatively small output—four full-length plays and two one-acts—Synge is justly considered one of the finest dramatists of the modern stage and the Abbey Theatre's most important playwright prior to Sean O'Casey. Completed shortly before his death, but never revised to the author's complete satisfaction, *Deirdre of the Sorrows* can be seen as Synge's final statement on the joys of life, the possibilities, both good and bad, of love, and the inscrutability of human destiny.

The real strength of the play, and the thing that probably sets it apart from the many other dramatic versions of this famous Irish myth, comes from the way Synge combines an austere mood of classic, almost Grecian tragedy with characterizations that are immediate, human, and sympathetic. Deirdre first impresses the audience as a flighty young woman who chases in the woods gathering twigs and nuts with little concern for her future queenly role. Her initial re-

action to King Conchubor's demand for immediate marriage is to beg, like a petulant child, for more time. Almost immediately, however, her mature, defiant, inner strength asserts itself. Faced with Conchubor's implacability, she grows into maturity almost instantly: "From this day," she tells her old nurse Lavarcham, "I will turn the men of Ireland like a wind blowing on the heath." She then dons her royal regalia, assuming the status of a queen, and, by giving herself without hesitation to Naisi, unflinchingly accepts the doom foretold for her. Yet, for all of her tragic grandeur, the girlish element in her character remains evident throughout.

Likewise, the other principal characters contain aspects of both the tragic and the mundane. Naisi is heroic and passionate, willing to risk exile and death for the love of Deirdre. He is also irritable, impulsive, and occasionally inconsistent. Toward the end of the play he admits to Fergus: "I've had dreams of getting old and weary, and losing my delight in Deirdre."

Conchubor is also pictured as a mixture of the grand and the petty. On one hand he establishes himself as a ferocious king, given to extremes of heroism and violence. His desire for Deirdre is intense, and his plans for her are grandiose. The strength of his feelings is evidenced by the lengths to which he is willing to go to secure her, including the destruction of his own kingdom, and by the vengeful rage that is aroused against those who stand in his way, especially Naisi and his brothers. At the same time he is a pitiful old man desperately denying the effects of time and clinging to an image of himself as virile by taking a young and beautiful wife. "There's one sorrow has no end surely," he tells Deirdre, "that's being old and lonesome."

This powerful merging of the heroic and the human reaches its dramatic peak in the scene in which the lovers separate forever. Deirdre believes that the only way they can escape inevitable disillusionment and acrimony in their passion is to give themselves up to Conchubor's vengeance, thereby avoiding the slower, but more painful ravages of time. Naisi agrees because he, too, sees that their passion has spent itself, their youth is fading, and the price of their destiny must be paid. "It should be a poor thing to see great lovers and they sleepy and old." At the moment of parting, however, they have a bitter, petty squabble. Thus, their deaths represent not a victory of passion over fate, but a concession to human imperfection, even in the most noble of characters.

Deirdre of the Sorrows represented a change in direction for Synge. He had previously avoided Irish myth on purpose, feeling it to be unrealistic and irrelevant. What further directions he would have taken had he lived can only be left to conjecture.

Further Reading

Castle, Gregory. *Modernism and the Celtic Revival.* New York: Cambridge University Press, 2001. Analyzes how Synge and other Irish Revivalists employed techniques of anthropology to translate, reassemble, and edit material from Irish folk culture, using this material to combat British imperialism.

Gonzalez, Alexander G., ed. *Assessing the Achievement of J. M. Synge.* Westport, Conn.: Greenwood Press, 1996. Collection of fourteen original essays interpreting Synge's drama. "Synge's *Deirdre of the Sorrows*: Defamiliarizing the Myth" by Eileen J. Doll focuses on this play.

Kopper, Edward A., Jr., ed. *A J. M. Synge Literary Companion.* Westport, Conn.: Greenwood Press, 1988. A valuable collection of sixteen chapters by leading scholars, covering all aspects of Synge's life and work. An excellent introduction to the critical literature; good bibliographies.

McDonald, Ronan. *Tragedy and Irish Literature: Synge, O'Casey, Beckett.* New York: Palgrave, 2002. Examines the work of Synge and two other Irish playwrights, describing how the culture of suffering, loss, and guilt shapes their ideas of tragedy. Defines a peculiarly Irish form of tragedy by locating common themes and techniques in the playwrights' work.

Price, Alan. *Synge and Anglo-Irish Drama.* London: Methuen, 1961. Extensive discussion of this play as a transformation of Irish legend and as the embodiment of

Synge's persistent themes. Contrasts the play favorably with those of Synge's contemporaries, calling it "perhaps the finest thing Synge ever wrote."

Ritschel, Nelson O'Ceallaigh. *Synge and Irish Nationalism: The Precursor to Revolution.* Westport, Conn.: Greenwood Press, 2002. Argues that Synge's plays are deeply rooted in ancient Irish literature, describing how his use of this material reflects his nationalist agenda.

Saddlemyer, Ann. "*Deirdre of the Sorrows*: Literature First . . . Drama Afterwards." In *J. M. Synge: Centenary Papers 1971*, edited by Maurice Harmon. Dublin: Dolmen, 1972. Focuses on Synge's blend of myth and characterization within his theory of art and drama. Traces the roots of this play to Synge's interest in music, Jean Racine, and life on the Aran Islands.

Synge, J. M. *J. M. Synge: Collected Works.* Vol. 2, edited by Alan Price. New York: Oxford University Press, 1968. Scholarly edition, providing the biographical context of Synge's last two years, when this play was being written. Contains a transcription of his worksheets, draft manuscripts, and related notebook entries.

Thornton, Weldon. *J. M. Synge and the Western Mind.* New York: Barnes & Noble, 1979. Argues that this play is resistant to heroic stereotypes of Celtic myth and presents Deirdre and Naisi as motivated by common needs and fears. Thus, the play is more psychologically complex than the mythic plays of his contemporaries.

Dejection
An Ode

Author: Samuel Taylor Coleridge (1772-1834)
First published: 1802; collected in *Sibylline Leaves*, 1817
Type of work: Poetry

"Dejection: An Ode" is generally considered the last of Samuel Taylor Coleridge's major poems. Coleridge wrote a draft of the poem on April 4, 1802, and published a significantly revised and shortened version in December of 1802 in *The Morning Post.* As its subtitle indicates, "Dejection" is an ode. The English ode from at least the time of Abraham Cowley in the mid-seventeenth century was an irregular form that generally served as a way for a poet to address interior states of

mind and turns of cognitive reflection in an overall lyric frame.

Coleridge begins his poem by quoting from the medieval English ballad of Sir Patrick Spens, citing the image of the new moon rising as the last vestiges of the old moon are disappearing. This optical effect is seen by the ballad, and sailors' lore generally, as presaging a dire storm. Coleridge's opening thus recalls the interest in oral and popular tradition that the poet and his sometime friend, sometime rival William Wordsworth produced in their coauthored *Lyrical Ballads* (1798) and that, in Coleridge's own case, influenced his best-known poem, "The Rime of the Ancient Mariner" (1798). However, even as he calls on the sonorous orality of the ballad to begin his ode, Coleridge makes clear the distance of his own poem from that form.

Whereas the ballad uses simple, resonant language, Coleridge tends to use more abstract or discursive words. Indeed, the gap between the palpable density of the ballad and the cerebral ruminations of the rest of the poem epitomizes the very distance from primal inspiration that preoccupies the poet throughout the course of the ode. Coleridge uses rhyme in his ode, much like his English predecessors and unlike the ancients, but the rhyme scheme is not in successive pairs of couplets it had been in previous English odes. The rhyme scheme is complex and inconsistent. The first stanza has ten separate rhymes, alternating three times between direct and interspersed rhymes. Formally, it could not be more different from the straightforward rhyme scheme of the ballad. The poem, however, is not blank verse, which Wordsworth certainly found a fitting vehicle for similar poems. The decision to use any rhyme, albeit idiosyncratic rhyme, gives "Dejection" formal ballast that lends a steady beat to its often agonized and contorted line of exposition. Rhyme is used often in the poem—at one point in stanza 5, four end-lines rhyme in a row, "power," "hour," "shower," and "dower"— but the argumentation is so strong that the rhyme is never obtrusive and often barely noticeable.

Ironically, the ballad of Sir Patrick Spens became part of the canon of Englsih literature almost wholly as a result of the attention Coleridge called to it. The intellectual meditation of Coleridge was needed to bring the oral ballad into scholarly focus. Coleridge himself may have had some wisdom about even such primal forces as the sea and weather that the ballad did not, yet this percipience is virtually annulled by the poem's sense of severance from feeling. The poem's combination of turbulence and malaise is quite unusual: Turmoil usually carries intense emotion with it, but the poem feels innoculated from the intensities of both joy and pain.

"Dejection" is often seen as Coleridge's own commentary on his declining poetic powers or as presaging the shift in his intellectual attention from the writing of poetry to the formulation of the vast and intricately organized system of criticism unfolded in his *Biographia Literaria* (1817). The quandary of the poem is explicitly raised at the end of the second stanza. The poem has earlier complained of a "dull pain," a grief that is not even cathartic in its emotional release but "stifled, drowsy, unimpassioned." Coleridge recounts to the poem's addressee, Sara Hutchinson, his experience of gazing on the beauty of the woods, the sky, the moon, and the stars, registering them mentally without, however, being convulsed by their emotional force as presumably he once had been. The stanza concludes: "I see, not feel, how beautiful they are."

This deficiency of inner feeling is the quandary addressed in the remainder of the poem. Given that "Dejection" was Coleridge's last major poem and given that he turned increasingly to criticism after writing it, critics have often read the ode as expressing the problems of affect and creativity that it diagnoses, problems the poem is unable to resolve. There is no ideal meld of ego and other. The poet says he "may not hope from outward forms" to win the spirit of true nature, whose aspiration is epitomized by an image of a green light that lingers in the west.

The frustrations of the poem's speaker raise questions. When one sees but does not feel beauty, can one adequately grasp that beauty? How can one be a poet without feeling "inspired"? Can one's mind navigate an act of poetic perception without affect? Coleridge chastises himself for not feeling enough, yet the poem itself is not a failure, even as it seems to chronicle the imaginative shortcomings of the poet. The thematic affirmation of wisdom and persistence at the end is augmented by the imaginative achievement of the poem. "Dejection" shows the poet's mind contesting the problem, not just contemplating it. It is out of this activity that "Dejection" ends up conjuring "the natural man," even if that quality of naturalness is stolen "by abstruse research." Coleridge's optimism may have been manufactured; the resolution at the end may have been willed or premeditated. That does not necessarily mean it is false. Coleridge, who later, in his criticism, so powerfully wrote of how the imagination weaves and knits together disparate phenomena, asserts in "Dejection" that imagination takes effort. Imagination must negotiate both the internal pitfalls of dejection and the outward perils of turbulence. It cannot afford to be naïve or to dispense with the intellect. What on one level is inauthentic is on another level a voluntary exercise. The mind can make experience that does not come naturally.

The Eolian lute, which comes to the fore in the poem's sixth stanza, is an unusual instrument, built in order for the wind to play upon it. The poet uses this device to intensify the moods of nature, but he prefers the exclusively natural "music" of the wind playing on mountains and trees. The Eolian lute is a trope for the poet's own will. It represents the sense of something in addition to nature that is concomitant with his mental exertions. It is not a shaping force; it can, in the terms of the poem's lexicon, "receive" but not "give." It is more a meteorological than a musical instrument. The poem has earlier said, in effect, that nature does not really matter unless people make it matter, that humans are the ones who supply nature's "wedding garment" and her "shroud." Coleridge had, seven years earlier, written a poem called "The Eolian Harp" (1795) that pictured the instrument as an accompaniment to domestic happiness amid natural bliss. In "Dejection," the mood has darkened, and Coleridge no longer apostrophizes Sara Fricker—his wife at the time, the "pensive Sara" of the original poem—but rather Sara Hutchinson, his extramarital love interest in 1802.

In the original *Morning Post* version of the ode, Sara Hutchinson is named. In the final version, she is merely addressed as "Lady," possibly to avoid confusing eventual readers of the collected poems by including two poems addressed to different Saras. Not only did Fricker and Hutchinson share the same Christian name, but they were also both sisters of wives of Coleridge's friends and fellow poets. The first Sara's sister Edith had married Robert Southey; the second Sara's sister Mary had married Wordsworth. This repetition of name and circumstance emphasizes the more agitated, less tranquil 1802 revision of the harp-apostrophe combination, yet many critics would argue that Coleridge's agonized address to the second Sara is less a wish-fulfillment of domestic bliss and more a revelation of the poet's troubled state of mind. Thus, "Dejection," wrangles honestly with the affective complexity of its tableau, thereby generating an unfettered joy that rebukes the delights of "the sensual and the proud" because it has required more struggle to achieve it.

Nicholas Birns

Further Reading

Brice, Benjamin. *Coleridge and Skepticism.* New York: Oxford University Press, 2007. Interesting on the poem's compositional process and Coleridge's poetic relationship to Wordsworth.

Christie, Will. *Samuel Taylor Coleridge: A Literary Life.* New York: Palgrave, 2006. The most authoritative and incisive biography of Coleridge; sheds light on the state of mind and circumstances of Coleridge at the time he wrote the poem.

Mellor, Anne K. *English Romantic Irony.* Cambridge, Mass.: Harvard University Press, 1980. Insightful analysis of the poem as, in different moments, both happy and sad. An important counterpoint to readings of the poem that emphasize the poet's incapacity and paralysis.

Roe, Nicholas. *Samuel Taylor Coleridge and the Sciences of Life.* New York: Oxford University Press, 2001. Places the poem in the context of what Roe terms Coleridge's "dejection years" and deftly explicates both its physical and its metaphysical aspects.

Schulz, Max. *The Poetic Voices of Coleridge.* Detroit, Mich.: Wayne State University Press, 1963. Schulz's dual emphasis on arrangement and instability is especially sensitive to the dialectic of these qualities evident in the poem.

West, Sally. *Coleridge and Shelley: A Textual Engagement.* Aldershot, England: Ashgate, 2007. Especially good on the music and weather imagery on the poem, as well as its simultaneous conjuring of both emotion and detachment.

Delia

Author: Samuel Daniel (1562?-1619)
First published: 1592
Type of work: Poetry

The evidently unauthorized publication of a portion of Samuel Daniel's sonnet sequence *Delia* in 1591, as part of Sir Philip Sidney's *Astrophel and Stella*, marked the introduction of the perfected version of a major poetic form that, within a few years, had become one of the dominant methods of expression in English poetry. While Daniel may be relatively unknown in comparison to Sidney, Edmund Spenser, or William Shakespeare, with *Delia*, first published in complete form in 1592, he became one of the important contributors to the development and growth of English poetry, and he remains a central figure in Elizabethan intellectual life.

One of the most notable features about the English Renaissance is the extremely rapid intellectual, cultural, and artistic development of the period. Two of the major cultural and artistic accomplishments of the English Renaissance, the blank verse play and the sonnet sequence, were innovations that were introduced relatively suddenly and perfected rapidly. The forms, once available, were utilized by artists ranging across the full intellectual spectrum, and, within a single generation, often within a period of a few years, English authors produced enduring masterpieces in both forms.

For example, *Gorboduc* (1561), by Thomas Sackville and Thomas Norton, is credited with being the first English play written in blank verse; it also served as the prototype for the five-act, multiple-scene play. *Gorboduc* spurred other writers to present a variety of plays ranging from tragedy to comedy to history. English literature reached a peak in its development by being exposed to a new and powerful method of presenting dramatic action.

Fairly soon after its initial production, *Gorboduc* was accorded mainly historical interest and its style and stagecraft considered rudimentary and crude; still, it was an important step forward, and within thirty years the genre had developed to the point that Christopher Marlowe and Shakespeare could write their masterpieces. The relatively crude beginning present in *Gorboduc* was rapidly explored and exploited.

A similarly rapid development and fruition took place with the sonnet sequence. The sonnet originally developed on the continent of Europe, with writers such as Petrarch and his followers fixing the major themes, forms, and poetic devices. Spreading throughout Europe, the sonnet convention added refinements from French poets such as Joachim du Bellay before gaining English attention in the early part of the sixteenth century, when Sir Thomas Wyatt introduced the form into English literature. Achieving limited circulation in manuscript form during Wyatt's life (although Wyatt seems to have planned to publish), his sonnets first saw wide distribution when they were printed in 1557 in a volume known as Tottel's *Miscellany*. Tottel's *Miscellany*, a collection of more than 250 poems by various writers, was to become one of the most significant contributions to English literature; its value was not so much in its own excellence, but in the development that it inspired in other writers.

Between 1580 and 1583, the Elizabethan courtier and soldier Sir Philip Sidney turned to the sonnet form and produced *Astrophel and Stella*, the first of the great Elizabethan sonnet sequences. Purposefully unpublished during Sidney's brief lifetime, *Astrophel and Stella* was first printed in 1591 in an unauthorized edition by the printer and publisher Thomas Newman. In addition to Sidney's sonnet sequence, the volume Newman published included twenty-eight additional sonnets by Samuel Daniel; these sonnets were the core of

Daniel's own sonnet cycle, *Delia*. In this fashion, two of the most influential works of this particular genre were made public. This was appropriate, for Daniel was an admirer of Sidney's poetic style and was associated with Sidney's sister, Mary, Countess of Pembroke.

Unlike Sidney, who had adhered to the older custom of being reluctant to publish his work, once Newman had issued the pirated edition, Daniel was ready to provide the reading public with the authentic version of *Delia*. In 1592, Daniel published *Delia* as an independent volume, adding four additional poems and revising others. He continued to revise and republish the work throughout the 1590's, adding new sonnets, removing older poems, and revising others. The 1594 edition of *Delia* had fifty-five sonnets, twenty-three of them from Newman's earlier edition. In 1601, Daniel produced his most thoroughgoing revision, which left the work in substantially the form in which it is best known. Significantly, as proof of the enduring relationship between Daniel and the Sidney circle, the book was dedicated to the Countess of Pembroke.

While *Astrophel and Stella* is undoubtedly the greater of the two sonnet cycles, *Delia* is itself an outstanding example of the genre, and one of the finest and most influential produced during the Elizabethan period. In its story, themes, imagery, structure, and language it follows the particular and often quite rigorous conventions that governed how the Elizabethans believed sonnet sequences should be written.

The story of *Delia*, as with so many other sonnet sequences dating back to Petrarch, is that of unrequited love. The author of the sonnets, who need not be closely or literally identified with Daniel himself, is in despair; his beloved scorns him, preferring another suitor. The lover has tried every means he can conceive of to win the beloved's heart, but she remains as adamant as she is indifferent. In the end, there is little hope except that his poems will endure as testimony to her cruelty and his faithful love.

Some critics and scholars have sought to read into this generic setting a real situation in which Daniel himself loved and was rejected. There is a reason, or perhaps rather an excuse, for such an interpretation because Sidney's sequence in *Astrophel and Stella* alludes to his love for Penelope, Lady Rich. In Daniel's case, there is little evidence to support a real-life counterpart to his poetic misery; it would seem, instead, to be a case of the poet's following the conceits of the genre, nothing more.

In *Delia*, Daniel helps to establish the themes and imagery that rapidly came to dominate the majority of Elizabethan and sonnet sequences. His sonnets contain numerous references to classical mythology; insistent appeals to natural history as a source of moral lessons; and frequent reminders of the transitory quality of beauty, in particular the beauty of Delia, which, along with all mortal things, however lovely, is doomed to decay. This last theme was to become a central motif in later sonnet sequences, including Shakespeare's.

Daniel was a talented and conscientious craftsman, and *Delia* is structured in such a way that the individual sonnets flow from one to the other, giving a sense of organic unity and progress; the story, such as it is, is made to have sense and coherence and seems to be moving forward, even if that motion is toward an unhappy ending. Daniel frequently uses the device of sharing themes, images, and words between sonnets, thereby linking them together.

An example of this is found in sonnets 32 through 35, in which Daniel concentrates on the transitory nature of beauty, using the imagery of flowers, spring, and summer, all of which fade and give way to weeds and winter. The words "winter" and "flowers" are found throughout this particular section of the sequence.

In some cases, Daniel repeats words and phrases from one sonnet to the next. Sonnet 24, for example, ends with the line, "Reign in my thoughts, my love and life are thine," and sonnet 25 opens: "Reign in my thoughts, fair hand, sweet eye, rare voice." Sonnet 42 finishes with the thought that "women grieve to think they must be old," while the next poem opens with the poet reminding himself, "I must not grieve my Love."

Daniel's use of language is fluent and dignified, avoiding the feigned antique language of Spenser and the vigorously colloquial style of Thomas Nashe. Perhaps because of his association with the Sidney circle, Daniel was highly conscious of the ideal of poetic decorum, especially in language, which was greatly esteemed in the earlier years of the Elizabethan Renaissance. His word choice is restrained, and his images are carefully chosen. His images are often based on mythological sources. The opening lines of his most famous sonnet from the sequence displays both qualities:

> Care-charmer sleep, son of the sable night,
> Brother to death, in silent darkness borne:
> Relieve my languish, and restore the light,
> With dark forgetting of my care's return.

This verse, fluent and flowing, shows Daniel's work in *Delia* at its best and helps explain how and why this sequence played such an important role in the development of English literature. The ability to use the sonnet form to comment on complex emotional feelings and intellectual concepts became a recognized possibility with the publication of Sidney's *Astrophel and Stella* and Daniel's *Delia*. Daniel's sonnets helped to establish the Elizabethan sonnet as a versatile and powerful instrument of English poetry.

Daniel's impact on the literature of his time was important and undeniable. The numerous editions of *Delia* that came in rapid succession clearly indicate a considerable popularity for the sequence; this popularity helps to explain the vogue for the sonnet sequence, which rapidly exerted great power over the English literary scene. Daniel was one of the first to produce, in perfect form, a genre in which English writers could write in a new and sophisticated fashion. The emotional, rhetorical, and intellectual versatility of the sonnet form provided English literature with a vehicle that it subsequently used to express some of its most profound and moving thoughts.

Michael Witkoski

Further Reading

Klein, Lisa M. "*Delia*, the Countess of Pembroke, and the Literary Career of Samuel Daniel." In *The Exemplary Sidney and the Elizabethan Sonneteer*. Newark: University of Delaware Press, 1998. Daniel is one of the sixteenth century English sonneteers whose work is examined in this study of the genre.

Lewis, C. S. *English Literature in the Sixteenth Century, Excluding Drama*. New York: Oxford University Press, 1954. Still one of the best surveys of English Renaissance literature. Lewis's comments on Daniel are informative and enlightening.

Pilcher, John. "Essays, Works, and Small Poems: Divulging, Publishing, and Augmenting the Elizabethan Poet, Samuel Daniel." In *The Renaissance Text: Theory, Editing, Textuality*, edited by Andrew Murphy. New York: Manchester University Press, 2000. Pilcher examines the texts of Daniel's published works to describe how he wrote his poetry, drama, and prose histories, how they were presented to friends and patrons, and how they were sold in English bookshops. Includes a literary analysis of Daniel's writings.

Rees, Joan. *Samuel Daniel: A Critical and Biographical Study*. Liverpool, England: Liverpool University Press, 1964. The standard biography of Daniel. Provides insight into Daniel's sonnets, especially those in *Delia*.

Ryding, Erik S. *In Harmony Framed: Musical Humanism, Thomas Campion, and the Two Daniels*. Kirksville: Sixteenth Century Journal Publishers, Northeast Missouri State University, 1993. Describes how Samuel Daniel and two other English Renaissance poets modeled their work on ancient Greek and Roman verse, seeking to recapture the marriage of words and music that is found in these classical poems. The analysis of selected poems reprints the words as well as musical inscriptions for these works.

Seronsy, Cecil. *Samuel Daniel.* New York: Twayne, 1967. An introductory volume on Daniel, providing an overview of his life and works. Excellent background discussions on the period, including the political and intellectual currents of the time.

Spiller, Michael R. G. *Early Modern Sonneteers: From Wyatt to Milton.* Plymouth, England: Northcote House/

British Council, 2001. This study of the development of the English sonnet in the sixteenth and seventeenth centuries includes a chapter on Daniel, providing a critical assessment of his poetry. Designed for students and general readers.

Ure, Peter. "Two Elizabethan Poets: Daniel and Ralegh." In *The Age of Shakespeare*, edited by Boris Ford. Rev. ed. New York: Penguin Books, 1982. An excellent comparison of two highly accomplished poets of the period, which introduces the reader to a sense of the social, intellectual, and artistic standards of the period.

A Delicate Balance

Author: Edward Albee (1928-   )
First produced: 1966; first published, 1966
Type of work: Drama
Type of plot: Absurdist
Time of plot: October, in the mid-1960's
Locale: The living room of a large and well-appointed suburban house

Principal characters:
AGNES, a handsome woman in her late fifties
TOBIAS, her husband, a few years older
CLAIRE, Agnes's sister, several years younger
JULIA, Agnes and Tobias's daughter, thirty-six years old
EDNA and HARRY, friends of Agnes and Tobias, very much like them

The Story:

Agnes and Tobias, an affluent elderly couple married for about forty years, sip after-dinner drinks in their living room one autumnal Friday evening. They chat pleasantly about Agnes's persistent belief that she might one day easily go mad. Agnes's younger sister Claire comes down from her room to apologize for an embarrassing incident she caused during dinner and is severely rebuked by Agnes for her drunkenness. Agnes then goes to telephone her daughter Julia, who lives some distance away. Left alone with Claire, Tobias inquires about her previous experiences with Alcoholics Anonymous. She explains that she felt alienated at those meetings and, after relating a bitter anecdote about herself, insisted that she was not an alcoholic because she drank willfully. Agnes returns, informing them that Julia is leaving her husband and will come home immediately. She reproaches Tobias for failing to admonish his daughter appropriately following her three previous divorces, and he responds by telling a story about a cat he once owned that stopped liking him for no apparent reason; when his efforts to regain his pet's affection failed, he had it euthanized.

While Agnes and Claire comfort him, unexpected guests

arrive. Harry and Edna, close friends for forty years, felt uneasy and distressed at home alone. Pressed to explain, they relate that after dinner they suddenly became strangely frightened, for no particular reason. They could no longer endure remaining alone in their house. Agnes offers them Julia's room for the night, and they retire. Claire suggests that she knows exactly what happened.

Saturday evening before dinner, Agnes tries to calm Julia, who is angry about the intruders who remained locked in her former bedroom all day. Agnes casually describes a psychoanalytical study she is reading about the reversal of sex roles in American society. Feigning the attitude of a father when Tobias enters, Agnes leaves Julia to be counseled by Tobias. Father and daughter merely quibble and argue about her three previous marriages until Claire interrupts them to tell about her unsuccessful attempt to buy a topless bathing suit at a local department store. An antagonistic conversation ensues among the three. It continues until Agnes joins them for cocktails and reports that Harry and Edna earlier requested sandwiches to be brought to their room. Julia explains that she left her husband because of his insupportable negative attitudes. Harry and Edna come down, announcing that they are going home to get their things and will return after dinner.

Julia upbraids her mother for prohibiting any discussion of serious matters during dinner. Agnes claims merely to have been keeping the family "in shape" on uneven ground by maintaining a reasonable balance among all the elements. Claire comes in with an accordion but is persuaded not to play it. After the sisters exchange sarcastic remarks concerning their sexual histories, they all discuss whether to permit the unwelcome guests to remain any longer. While Agnes and Tobias greet their returning friends, Claire and Julia discuss this awkward situation. When Edna enters the room, Julia expresses her hostility quite openly, but Edna insists that she has some rights. Julia then blocks access to the sideboard, preventing Harry from mixing drinks. Growing hysterical at the persistence of their demands, she runs screaming from the room. Tobias returns and is giving an account of Julia's continuing fit of hysteria upstairs when Julia enters with a pistol and orders her father to expel the unwanted guests immediately. Tobias disarms her, and, while Edna is explaining that long-term friendship gives them the right to live there, Agnes leads her daughter up to bed. Harry and Edna retire, along with Claire, leaving Tobias alone in the living room.

Early Sunday morning, as Tobias sits awake, Agnes comes down. They discuss the changes their marriage has undergone over the years. Tobias explains that he thought through their present dilemma during the night but, when pressed by his wife for his decision, he begs her advice. She refuses, insisting that he, firmly supported by his family, should assert his authority. She reminds him of past occasions when he failed to do so. Claire and Julia serve coffee and orange juice, and Claire openly spikes her juice with vodka. They discuss their situation, Agnes pointing out that their guests brought a disease, a plague of sorts, with them. She leaves it to Tobias to decide whether to permit the guests to remain.

Harry and Edna come down. Left alone by the women, Tobias and Harry have drinks. Harry explains that, were their positions reversed, he would not let unwanted guests stay in his house. Tobias, becoming emotional and eventually hysterical, insists that Harry and Edna remain, though he confesses that he does not honestly want them to.

The women return. Overhearing Tobias imploring Harry to stay, Edna requests that their bags be brought down so that they might leave. Julia joins Claire in a drink as the couples say good-bye. After Harry and Edna's departure, the three women praise Tobias for handling the situation effectively. Agnes pleasantly notes the possible danger of having three early-morning drinkers in the house.

Critical Evaluation:

The success of Edward Albee's first play, *The Zoo Story* (1959), was followed by that of *The American Dream* (1961) and the controversial *Who's Afraid of Virginia Woolf?* (1962). *A Delicate Balance* (1966), a more restrained work, was awarded a Pulitzer Prize in drama in 1967, a distinction also bestowed upon *Seascape* (1975) in 1976 and *Three Tall Women* (1991) in 1994. Disliking literary labels, Albee reluctantly identifies himself as an eclectic, with dramatic roots extending as deeply into the plays of Anton Chekhov and Eugene O'Neill as into those of Samuel Beckett and Tennessee Williams. His plays generally deal with people's attempts to make sense for themselves of their senseless positions in a senseless world. The plays work effectively, largely through their rich verbal texture. Albee possesses an extraordinary ear for the inflections and rhythms of speech and writes lines that are essentially musical in their flow: Voices echo and answer themselves and one another like instruments of different timbres playing a chamber composition. This highly complex counterpoint of convoluted sentences set against robust American colloquialisms is filled with black humor, comic irony, and tragic sarcasm.

A Delicate Balance concerns the failure of relationships among family members and their closest friends. Albee's theme is that people often thoughtlessly espouse superficial values that later trap them into maintaining insincere relationships. Adjusting to appearances rather than to reality, they suffer through serious failures in communication and eventually lose any possibility of finding any gratifying emotional fulfillment. Evasions in the guise of "making do" and "making it work" enable the four principal characters in the play to pretend to themselves and to one another that their family is a happy one, or at least quite average, because their relationships appear similar to those prevailing in many other families around them. When forced eventually to examine their fantasy worlds honestly, they discover them to be empty and meaningless, and they are left alone, deprived of their illusions, with some new and difficult truths to face and ponder—or to reject.

Agnes establishes and controls a smooth surface of routine and habit in order to cover the web of interlocking illusions and self-deceptions that prevail in the minds of the other family members. This routine excludes honest self-awareness in the characters as well as sincere emotional responses in their interactions with others. Agnes tolerates the presence of her alcoholic sister in her home but never tries to understand her; Tobias gently chides his daughter for her failed marriages but ignores her unhappiness; and Agnes and Tobias live amicably together but lack deep emotional bonds. Julia tells her father that her indifference to him appeared during her adolescence, when she first perceived his withdrawal of affection from her. Claire, who alone sees reality clearly, drowns her perceptive insights in alcohol because she finds them too distressing to endure, but she sometimes blurts them out in lightning-quick flashes of sarcastic or sardonic wit. These humorous remarks provide comic relief while at the same time supply an outsider's view of the activities of the other characters.

Harry and Edna, a couple "very much like Agnes and Tobias," have similarly devised a workable routine to fill the spiritual void hidden at the heart of their existence. When, becoming old, they perceive the imminent approach of death, they are struck with terror by the emptiness of lives based on appearances alone, without any deeply rooted values or sincere feelings to sustain them. This is the "plague" they bring with them to their friends' home—an awareness of their failure to become the persons they might have been, to have loved as they might have loved had they dared to commit themselves to the arduous quest for reality, accepting the pain and sorrow that truth brings with it as the price to be paid for spiritual progress.

The sudden awareness of emptiness that shatters the habitual, comfortable complacency prevailing in the lives of Harry and Edna could well prove contagious to the mirror couple with whom they seek refuge, because the same void fills the house of Agnes and Tobias, although they do not yet acknowledge its presence. When Tobias must decide whether to allow these friends to reside in his house, he confronts the dilemma of illusion versus reality in his own life: To reject them would be to admit that they wasted forty years in maintaining a pseudofriendship based primarily on proximity rather than on affection. Because he cannot bring himself to face this terrible reality, he implores them to stay. Harry, who already looked deeply into the void, now knows better and rejects Tobias's insincere plea.

The play ends with no definitive resolution, though alternative possible endings are suggested. The pain of failure in a relationship is hard for Tobias to bear. It is something he always avoided; failing years before, for example, to regain the affection of his cat, he had her killed. He now endures an ordeal by fire and could emerge from it purified. He might yet advance to become a truly loving husband and father. Julia joins Claire for a drink, which suggests that she may adopt her aunt's solution of seeking oblivion to escape her problems. Agnes greets the morning sun ambiguously: A new era may now begin for them all, or the sunlight may illuminate merely a repetition of the routine that governed them in the past. The outcome appears unfavorable. Agnes observes pessimistically near the end of the last act, "[Y]ou wait; and time

happens. When you *do* go, sword . . . shield . . . finally . . . there's nothing there . . . save rust; bones; and the wind."

Raymond M. Archer

Further Reading

Amacher, Richard E. *Edward Albee*. Rev. ed. Boston: Twayne, 1982. A fine overview of Albee's plays and career. Considers the influence of the Theater of the Absurd on Albee's work.

Bigsby, C. W. E. *Albee*. Edinburgh: Oliver & Boyd, 1969. Identifies Albee's liberal humanistic and existential concerns. An excellent analysis of Albee's thought, with a perceptive discussion of *A Delicate Balance*.

Clum, John M. "'Withered Age and Stale Custom': Marriage, Diminution, and Sex in *Tiny Alice, A Delicate Balance*, and *Finding the Sun*." In *The Cambridge Companion to Edward Albee*, edited by Stephen Bottoms. New York: Cambridge University Press, 2005. Clum's analysis of the three plays is included in this collection of essays designed to enhance readers' and viewers' understanding of Albee's work.

Gross, Robert F. "Like Father, Like Son: The Ciphermale in *A Delicate Balance* and *Malcolm*." In *Edward Albee: A Casebook*, edited by Bruce J. Mann. New York: Routledge, 2003. This study of male characters in the two plays is included in a collection of essays analyzing Albee's innovations in theatrical form and content.

Kolin, Philip C., and J. Madison Davis, eds. *Critical Essays on Edward Albee*. Boston: G. K. Hall, 1986. Includes two essays focusing on *A Delicate Balance*: "Only Time Really Happens to People [*A Delicate Balance*]" by Walter Kerr and "Toby's Last Stand: The Evanescence of Commitment in *A Delicate Balance*" by M. Gilbert Porter.

Paolucci, Anne. *From Tension to Tonic: The Plays of Edward Albee*. 1972. Reprint. Wilmington, Del.: Griffon House Press, 2000. One of the most insightful studies available. Focuses on Albee's use of language, especially metaphor and irony. Contains a chapter on *A Delicate Balance*.

Perry, Virginia I. "Disturbing Our Sense of Well-Being: The 'Uninvited' in *A Delicate Balance*." In *Edward Albee: An Interview and Essays*, edited by Julian N. Wasserman. Houston: University of St. Thomas Press, 1983. *A Delicate Balance* is one of the plays analyzed in this collection of essays.

Roudané, Matthew. *Understanding Edward Albee*. Columbia: University of South Carolina Press, 1987. An excellent starting point for the study of Albee's work. Traces the development of his affirmative existential vision.

Rutenberg, Michael E. *Edward Albee: Playwright in Protest*. New York: DBS, 1969. Written with Albee's cooperation. Concentrates on political and social dimensions of Albee's work. Contains two interviews and an interesting analysis of *A Delicate Balance* from a sociological point of view.

Zinman, Toby. "*A Delicate Balance*." In *Edward Albee*. Ann Arbor: University of Michigan Press, 2008. Zinman, an English professor and a drama critic for the *Philadelphia Inquirer*, analyzes the themes in this and other plays by Albee.

Deliverance

Author: James Dickey (1923-1997)
First published: 1970
Type of work: Novel
Type of plot: Bildungsroman
Time of plot: Late twentieth century
Locale: Georgia

Principal characters:
ED GENTRY, a bored suburbanite
LEWIS MEDLOCK, Ed's best friend, a survivalist
DREW BALLINGER, an executive for a soft-drink company
BOBBY TRIPPE, an insurance salesman
TWO MOUNTAIN MEN

The Story:

Lewis Medlock, Ed Gentry, Drew Ballinger, and Bobby Trippe decide to canoe a river in north Georgia before it is dammed. Lewis promises them an enjoyable time away from the pressures and routines of the city. The four men spend September 14 on the river and have the type of day that Lewis promised. The next morning Ed agrees to take Bobby in his canoe because Lewis is frustrated with Bobby's ineptness and weakness.

Ed and Bobby stop to rest on the bank since they are tired and, ironically, are well ahead of Lewis and Drew. Two men step out of the woods, one of them trailing a shotgun by the barrel. The taller man seems to be toothless, and the shorter man has white stubble on his face and a stomach that falls through his overalls. In an attempt to pacify these mountain men, Ed tells them that he and Bobby are not government agents looking for a still and would even be interested in buying some moonshine from them if they have it. This comment seems to set something in motion for the mountain men, and they take Ed and Bobby at gunpoint deeper into the woods. The tall, lean man ties Ed to a tree with Ed's own belt and then turns to Bobby. While the tall man holds the gun, the white-bearded man sodomizes Bobby. They turn then to Ed and decide that he will perform oral sex on the tall man. As they exchange the gun an arrow appears in the middle of the tall man's chest. Lewis and Drew arrived upon the scene quietly, hearing Bobby's screams, and Lewis had drawn his bow on the tall man and waited for an opportunity to let the arrow fly. The tall man dies, and the white-bearded man runs off into the woods and disappears. Drew wants to take the body to the sheriff, but Lewis wants to bury it in the woods because the area will be covered with water soon. The men vote with Ed because they think his way is the least complicated for their present and future lives. They bury the man and the shotgun deep in the woods and go back on the river to go home.

Drew and Ed are paddling together in the first canoe when Drew falls out. This spill causes the other canoe to turn over in the rapids, and everyone swims for safety. The wooden canoe is broken in half, leaving only the aluminum canoe. Lewis's leg is broken as well, and Drew cannot be found. Lewis tells Ed and Bobby that Drew was shot from the top of the cliff. Ed understands then that the white-bearded man is on top of the cliff waiting for them to head out in the canoe so that he can kill them. Ed realizes that, in order for them to survive, he has to climb the cliff and kill the mountain man. He spends a good part of the night of September 15 climbing the cliff with his bow and arrow. He hides in a tree at the top, and, when the white-bearded man appears at the top of the cliff, Ed shoots him with an arrow. He falls out of the tree after the shot and his other arrow pierces his side. He lowers the mountain man's body down the cliff and buries it in the river.

That morning, September 16, Ed, Bobby, and Lewis start back down the river in the aluminum canoe. Before long, they see Drew's body backed up against the rocks. He apparently was shot. They bury his body in the river, also as a way of avoiding legal complications, and continue toward the town of Aintry.

Once they return, they have the problem of explaining to the authorities what happened. They tell the police that they spilled from their canoes farther down the river than they actually did, hoping the police will not find the bodies. They also say that Drew drowned in that spill. One deputy does not believe them and thinks that they came upon his brother-in-law, who is missing. The police drag the river where Ed told them to and come up with nothing. Ed and Bobby drive home while Lewis stays in the hospital because of his broken leg.

Ed lies to Drew's wife, telling her the same story he told the police. He never tells his wife anything, and he lives in fear, for a while, of headlights in the night. Lewis and Ed eventually buy cabins on another lake and practice their archery there, keeping secret the fact that they buried three men in two days.

Critical Evaluation:

After the publication of *Deliverance* in 1970 and the release of the film in 1972, public response and critical response took opposite turns. If best-seller status and box-office records are any indication of how a public appreciates a work of literary or cinematic art, then *Deliverance* was a huge success. The initial critical response, however, was less than kind. Most critics compared James Dickey's novel with his earlier poetry and found the novel severely lacking. The film suffered a similar fate at the hands of reviewers who, predictably enough, often compared it to the novel and found the film superficial and lacking in psychological depth. Time has shown, however, that the critics might have been premature in shelving this novel under "popular fiction" or some other rubric that denotes literature offered to the masses and not worth taking seriously. In fact, this novel is one of the most profound examples of bridging popular fiction with a literary tradition, which in this case is Romanticism and mythology.

Most of the readings of *Deliverance* see traditional mythological elements at work, whether it be Romantic appropriations of nature or Jungian archetypes and images of rebirth. Dickey has stated that the literary and mythological precedent for the novel comes from a review of books on mythology that he read in college. He remarks that he was especially interested in the concepts of rites of passage, in which initiates undergo a separation from their everyday world. Initiates enter a special source of power in another world, and then a life-enhancing return to that everyday world. One book that Dickey knew of was Joseph Campbell's *The Hero with a Thousand Faces* (1949), and Campbell understands the three stages of normal world, the special world, and return as elements of all hero myths.

Ed is the main character and the hero who undergoes trials and tests, ultimately facing his own death, in order to bring meaning back to his world. Ed's everyday world is meaningless, full of the bad art that he produces for money as a graphic artist and empty of anything worthy of painting. Ed is bored, and this boredom pervades every part of his life, from his work to his archery to his home life. The world that Ed inhabits is filled with artificiality, like the paper deer he shoots at the archery range. Lewis's call to run the river offers Ed the opportunity to get out of his routine, if only for a weekend, and to experience something different, something that would soon be lost.

The nature of Ed's transformation is heroic and thus sexual, psychological, and mythological. He encounters the earth goddess in the form of a sheer cliff that he climbs in the middle of the night. This particular example of the earth presents two contradictory attributes to him. At times she seems to want to throw him off the cliff; at other times she offers him handholds from what seems to be a flat surface. As he climbs the wall, Ed's feeling of intimacy toward it grows. He describes his movements as more sensual than any sexual experience he has had.

Following an Oedipal theme, the meeting with the figure of mother earth is followed by confrontation with the father, who is represented by the man on top of the cliff. The father figure is a particularly violent one. In fact, the father is the archetypal enemy, symbolizing to the unconscious all of life's enemies. The hero must engage the father in battle, which will result in the shattering of the hero's ego and perhaps the loss of his life. Ed reflects on his unity with the mountain man, thinking so long and hard about the man on the cliff that he believes that their minds fuse in the moonlight. When Ed's arrow finds its mark and the man on the cliff dies, the mythological process is at its climactic point. The two men are one, and the world is one. All dualities are transcended; therefore, as Ed's arrow of death hits its target, his other arrow pierces Ed's flesh, "the flesh that age and inactivity were beginning to load on me." This is Ed's symbolic death. He has killed the part of him that civilization has created. Pierced by his own arrow, Ed is now complete. His limited ego-vision has been replaced by a mystical realization and experience of the one.

What Ed brings back to the everyday world from this journey is personal; what he brings back brings no boon to the world at large. Rather, his experience exists as a trace, a meaning that is never fully present but exists as a line where the unconscious once made its mark. All that is left in Ed's world are such traces of the mythical. He maintains this trace, for example, in his art, which after his return has rivers running through it. Overall, Ed's experience of return is that his life returns to something like normal. Once the river is dammed (the pun is clearly intended) he can "sleep as deeply as Drew was sleeping." Ed's experience has indeed been life-changing, but the change continues to be buried further and further under the pressure of the artificiality of everyday life. This pressure continually forces Ed's experience deeper and threatens to eliminate it altogether. Rather than resolve this tension between the influence of the mythical journey and the pressure of the everyday world to force it out of existence, Dickey leaves it unresolved. The reader is left doubting not only that Ed will be experiencing any more adventures, but also whether or not there will be space left for the taking of such adventures. Sacred space is disappearing, and, as Lewis might say, one ought to get up there and see it before it is gone.

Gregory Salyer

Further Reading

Calhoun, Richard J., and Robert W. Hill. *James Dickey.* Boston: Twayne, 1983. The first book-length study of Dickey's work, this study attempts to analyze virtually everything Dickey wrote during a twenty-two-year period, so that at times the discussions are rather sketchy. Still, this book provides a solid introduction to Dickey.

Clabough, Casey Howard. *Elements: The Novels of James Dickey.* Macon, Ga.: Mercer University Press, 2002. Full-length study of Dickey's novels, with Clabough tracing the common elements in *Deliverance,* and *To the White*

Sea (1993). In addition to examining these published works, Clabough discusses Dickey's unpublished fiction, including a novel manuscript and five screenplay prospectuses.

Dickey, Christopher. *Summer of Deliverance: A Memoir of Father and Son.* New York: Simon & Schuster, 1998. Dickey's son, Christopher, recalls the corrosive effects of fame upon his father, recalling how his father's drinking and his destructive relationship with his family intensified after the release of the film adaptation of *Deliverance.*

Hart, Henry. *James Dickey: The World as a Lie.* New York: Picador, 2000. A narrative biography detailing the rise and self-destruction of a literary reputation. Hart argues that lying was a central theme in Dickey's art and life; while the book contains little literary analysis, it describes how Dickey lied in order to dramatize his personality and embellish the events of his life.

Kirschten, Robert, ed. *Critical Essays on James Dickey.* New York: Maxwell Macmillan International, 1994. Provides early reviews and a selection of more modern scholarship, with essays by Robert Bly, Paul Carroll, James Wright, Wendell Berry, among other writers. Includes two essays about *Deliverance.*

_____. *Struggling for Wings: The Art of James Dickey.* Columbia: University of South Carolina Press, 1997. A compilation of reviews and essays about Dickey's work, as well as interviews with the author. Although most of the reviews and essays focus on his poetry, there are several that discuss *Deliverance.*

Delphine

Author: Madame de Staël (1766-1817)
First published: 1802 (English translation, 1803)
Type of work: Novel
Type of plot: Epistolary
Time of plot: Late eighteenth century
Locale: France

Principal characters:
DELPHINE D'ALBEMAR, a rich, talented young widow
MATILDA DE VERNON, her kinswoman and daughter of Madame de Vernon
MADAME DE VERNON, Delphine's close friend and confidant
LÉONCE MONDEVILLE, Matilda de Vernon's fiancé
MADAME D'ERVIN, a friend of Delphine
MONSIEUR DE SERBELLANE, Madame d'Ervin's lover
MONSIEUR DE VALORBE, Delphine's beloved

The Story:

Delphine d'Albemar is a rich young widow who marries her guardian after her father's death. Her husband, who was her tutor in childhood, instills in her the best of sentiments and virtues. As a result of her education, however, she does not wish to submit to the dogmas of society or church. Although she is a member of the French nobility, she is a believer in revolutionary doctrine, a dangerous way of thinking in France during the years immediately preceding the French Revolution. In addition, she, unlike most women of her time and position, refuses to let men do her thinking for her. After her husband's death, which occurs when she is twenty years old, Delphine is emotionally, intellectually, and financially independent.

Shortly after her husband's death, Delphine proposes giving away a large part of her fortune to Matilda, a relative of her husband and the daughter of Delphine's close friend, Madame de Vernon. Despite the warnings of Mademoiselle d'Albemar, Delphine's sister-in-law, that Madame de Vernon is a very treacherous person, the gift is made so that Matilda can marry Léonce Mondeville, a Spanish nobleman. No one met Léonce Mondeville, for the marriage was arranged by Matilda's mother, a longtime friend of the proposed bridegroom's mother.

When Mondeville arrives in Paris, he meets his future wife and Delphine. Much to Delphine's dismay, she falls in love with him and he with her. To Delphine, who bestowed on Matilda the fortune that is making the marriage possible, it seems that fate plays its worst trick of irony. For a time, it seems as if the two lovers might find a way out of the difficulty. As her confidant in the problem, Delphine takes Matilda's own mother, Madame de Vernon. Matilda's mother has no intention of allowing so advantageous a match to slip through her and her daughter's fingers, and she plots to turn Mondeville against Delphine.

Meanwhile, Delphine is aiding Madame d'Ervin in a love affair with Monsieur de Serbellane. Because de Serbellane is seen going into Delphine's house late at night, scandal links her name with his, although he went there to see Madame d'Ervin. A short time later, Madame d'Ervin's husband surprises the two lovers in Delphine's home. When de Serbellane kills the husband in a duel, scandal names Delphine as the woman in the case. Delphine, desiring to maintain her friend's honor, does not relate the true cause of the quarrel that precipitates the duel. Anxious to clear herself with Mondeville, however, Delphine asks Madame de Vernon to act as her friend. Instead of telling what really happened, the older woman tells him that Delphine and de Serbellane are lovers and that Delphine is about to leave France to join de Serbellane in Italy.

Mondeville prepares to marry Matilda, although he does not love her. Although Delphine realizes that someone misrepresented her to her lover, she can find no way to prevent the marriage. Only after the marriage takes place does Delphine learn that Madame de Vernon's duplicity caused the rift between herself and Mondeville. At that time, anxious not to hurt Matilda, Delphine promises herself not to see Mondeville and to try to forget her passion for him. Unfortunately, they continue to love each other greatly. A few months later, Madame de Vernon, on her deathbed, confesses her guilt.

Feeling themselves cheated, the lovers decide to continue seeing each other, although their course is dangerous to their honor and unfair to Matilda. Society is soon whispering that Delphine and Mondeville are lovers. Actually, there is nothing immoral in their affair, but society assumes the worst. De Valorbe, a friend of Delphine's late husband, learns of the state of affairs and resolves to marry her in order to remove her from a compromising situation. His intention arouses Mondeville's jealousy, although Delphine protests that she does not love de Valorbe and will never marry him. One night, de Valorbe goes to Delphine's house in the hope that she will hide him from the police. Mondeville sees him there and challenges him to a duel. De Valorbe, hoping to escape from the country before he is imprisoned on political charges, refuses to fight. A witness stirs up the scandal once again. Soon everyone believes that the two men accidentally met while both going to assignations with Delphine, and her name is publicly dishonored. In addition, de Valorbe's refusal to meet Mondeville places him in disgrace.

Learning at last that her husband and Delphine are in love, Matilda goes to Delphine and reveals that she is to have a child. Moved by Matilda's pleas, Delphine decides to leave France. She goes to Switzerland and becomes a pensionary at a convent that is under the direction of Mondeville's aunt. De Valorbe follows her there and causes her name to become common gossip. When he offers to clear her name by marriage, Delphine refuses his proposal and decides to remain in the convent. De Valorbe, moved to distraction, commits suicide, but before he dies he clears Delphine's reputation with Mondeville.

Word comes to Mondeville's aunt that Matilda is dying. She is in league with Mondeville's mother and persuades Delphine to become a nun. They are able to have the pope waive the required year's novitiate. By the time Mondeville goes to the convent to claim Delphine, she has already taken her vows.

Meanwhile the republican government takes over in France and disallows the vows of religious orders. Friends persuade Delphine that she should renounce the vows and return to France to marry her lover. She leaves the convent, only to discover that public opinion condemns her action. Rather than make her lover live a life of misery, she refuses to marry him.

Mondeville goes to join the Royalist forces fighting against the republican French government, but before he can join them he is captured and sentenced to death as a traitor. Delphine tries unsuccessfully to secure his pardon. When she fails, she takes poison and then joins him when he goes to the execution ground. She dies on the spot where he is to be executed. At first, the soldiers refuse to shoot Mondeville. Having no desire to live, he taunts them until they pick up their muskets and kill him. Friends take the bodies of Delphine and her lover and bury them side by side, so that they, kept apart in life, might be close in death.

Critical Evaluation:

Delphine appears in the form of letters, the epistolary form, which was almost outmoded by the time of Madame de Staël. In addition, the tone of the novel is in the sentimental vein of many French and British novels of the first rank in the first half of the eighteenth century. The origin of the sentiment was undoubtedly Jean-Jacques Rousseau, for whom Madame de Staël had a very high regard. In *Delphine*, there is constant reflection of the ideas of Rousseau and other advanced political thinkers and philosophers of the late eighteenth century, for such doctrines as the education of women, political equality, freedom of religious conscience, anticlericalism, and devotion to reason appear constantly in the letters written by Delphine to the other characters in the novel. The novel is, therefore, an index to the temper of Madame de Staël's circle at the time.

Delphine is in many ways a *roman à clef*. It describes a strong, independent woman who is brilliant and desirable, and who lives her life in many different contexts: In the space of one novel, Delphine is a respected and financially independent widow who then becomes a destitute pensionary (almost a nun), but only after becoming a notorious figure in the eyes of her society. Madame de Staël was a woman much like Delphine. She never became a nun, but Staël had such a forceful character and brilliant literary and social career that it was difficult for some to regard her as a woman because she resisted common definitions and paradigms for a female of that time. In fact, Prince Talleyrand, French statesman and Napoleon's most trusted adviser, once said of *Delphine*, "I understand that Madame de Staël, in her novel, has disguised both herself and me as women." This not only shows that her novel has strong autobiographical elements but also shows

that she resisted, in life and in her fiction, many social norms and barriers, including those of gender. Such was the power of her charisma that it became a standard joke among polite company that after Napoleon's fall, only three major powers remained: England, Russia, and Staël.

There are many similarities between Delphine and her creator. Both lived amid the French Revolution, and both were involved in sexual and political intrigues of the day. Delphine's journey to Switzerland and back to France echoes Staël's life; her father, the brilliant financier and politician Jacques Necker, had residences in both countries. Staël had affairs with many notables, including Friedreich Schlegel and Talleyrand. Finally, note how the changing political times radically affect Delphine's fortunes: At first, she is considered a dangerous woman for resisting the mores and traditions of the time. Then, after the Revolution, things have changed so much that she is now in a convent, and it takes the state to free her because it has made such vows illegal.

Staël had similar reversals and changes of fortune, for she and her father had to worry about the latest political change in France: With the slightest change of a minister or bureaucrat, one's head could be lost, and it is to Necker and Staël's credit that such a thing never happened to them. *Delphine* contains some of the most penetrating examples of how individual life is altered, hemmed in, and contained by the state. However, it also shows how the mind and spirit can overcome such limitations; Delphine always remains outside the norm, and the tension between what is expected of Delphine by state and society, and what Delphine actually does, makes the novel a classic.

Delphine is not the only character who confronts state and societal tyranny. Mondeville dies at the hands of the state. He becomes somewhat heroic at the end when he invites the guards to kill him. Through this act, he wrests power away from his executors and shows that in the face of death he is able to form a self outside the limits of the tyranny that is killing him. Both lovers take their own lives and in death are united outside the hypocritical moral strictures of their day.

Delphine is an epistolary novel, meaning that it is written in the form of letters to and from various characters. Though much has been made about the fragmented and incomplete nature of epistolary novels, it is important to understand that in an epistolary novel the author intends to represent the whole story, and that writing in epistolary form enables an author to relate a story without the confinement and sentiment of an omniscient narrator. *Delphine* ranks as one of the great Romantic novels. One of the many favorable contemporary reviews of the book commented that there were so many Parisians staying home to read *Delphine* that the streets were empty at night, and that no one was attending the theaters. Staël, with books such as *Delphine* and her masterly essay "On Literature," helped to establish Romanticism as a great movement.

Delphine agitates against the submission of women and strives to represent how liberty is always ruined by society and its structures. However, the novel shows that in one case a social convention can be tyrannical, and in another that same convention can bring a measure of freedom. This is what makes *Delphine* so interesting as a novel. Delphine is able, at times, to change her subordinate position into one of authority and power. Normally, being a widow in her society would be a great handicap, but Delphine is able to forge an independence at least partly of her own making. She understands that she can break through the frame of the normal petit-bourgeois existence. Her time in the convent, then, can be seen as an attempt at a form of liberty, though the meddling of her relations foils this attempt. At other times, what would normally be a gesture that brings power actually mires Delphine into a social web of deceit and heartbreak: When she gives money to Matilda, all her troubles begin. Hence, Staël certainly understood the changeableness of one's fortunes in social and political contexts.

The ironic situations that ensue from the intrigues and loves in *Delphine* are frightening as well as eminently entertaining. *Delphine*'s use of irony, in fact, helps to mark the novel as a great Romantic text. Her ironic treatment of death as a bringer of life makes this novel break away from the sentiment of many novels of its time. Although it has great similarities to other lesser novels, it refrains from open moralizing and allows the characters and situations to speak in relation to themselves, rather than in a slavish relation to existing cultural constructs.

"Critical Evaluation" by James Aaron Stanger

Further Reading

Goodden, Angelica. *Madame de Staël: The Dangerous Exile*. New York: Oxford University Press, 2008. A biography of Staël that focuses on her exile from France, describing how her residence outside the country gave her the freedom to be an active dissident. The chapter "*Delphine* and Its Aftermath" examines the circumstances under which Staël wrote this novel, analyzes the work, and discusses Napoleon I's negative reaction to it.

_____. *Madame de Staël: "Delphine" and "Corinne."* London: Grant & Cutler, 2000. Provides a summary of critical literature about the two novels.

Gutwirth, Madelyn. *Madame de Staël, Novelist: The Emergence of the Artist as Woman*. Champaign: University of Illinois Press, 1978. Gutwirth, one of the most respected authorities on Staël, depicts her as a woman able to redefine the relation between art and gender. Demonstrates how Staël was able to deploy her art in order to emerge as a strong subject. A groundbreaking work for discussing gender issues in Staël.

Gutwirth, Madelyn, Avriel Goldberger, and Karyna Szmurlo, eds. *Germaine de Staël: Crossing the Borders*. New Brunswick, N.J.: Rutgers University Press, 1991. Illuminating reading for those interested in reading Delphine as a transgressor of the social fabric of late eighteenth century Europe.

Herold, J. Christopher. *Mistress to an Age: A Life of Madame de Staël*. Indianapolis, Ind.: Bobbs-Merrill, 1958. Available in many libraries and by far the most informative and entertaining biography of Staël. Relates stories and facts about her liaisons, contacts, and famous meetings with legendary cultural and literary figures. Gives complexion to Staël, and therefore to *Delphine*.

Hogsett, Charlotte. *The Literary Existence of Germaine de Staël*. Carbondale: Southern Illinois University Press, 1987. Examines the complex relationships between Staël's life and her female characters. Includes an informative foreword by Madelyn Gutwirth.

Marso, Lori Jo. *(Un)Manly Citizens: Jean-Jacques Rousseau's and Germaine de Staël's Subversive Women*. Baltimore: Johns Hopkins University Press, 1999. Analyzes fictional works by the two French Enlightenment writers in order to examine their concepts of the self, citizenship, and democratic politics. Chapter 4, "The Loving Citizen: Staël's *Delphine*," examines alternative visions of citizenship in this novel.

Staël, Madame de. *An Extraordinary Woman: Selected Writings of Germaine de Staël*. Translated and with an introduction by Vivian Folkenflik. New York: Columbia University Press, 1987. A collection of de Staël's most memorable statements, quips, and pieces of fiction.

Delta Wedding

Author: Eudora Welty (1909-2001)
First published: 1946
Type of work: Novel
Type of plot: Regional
Time of plot: Early 1920's
Locale: Mississippi

Principal characters:
LAURA MCRAVEN, a cousin to the Fairchilds
DABNEY FAIRCHILD, a bride-to-be
ELLEN, her mother
BATTLE, her father
SHELLEY, her sister
GEORGE FAIRCHILD, her uncle
ROBBIE, George's wife
TROY FLAVIN, a plantation manager

The Story:

Nine-year-old Laura McRaven makes her first journey alone from Jackson to the Delta to visit her dead mother's people, the Fairchilds. One of her cousins, Dabney Fairchild, is to be married, and Laura's chief regret is that she cannot be in the wedding party because of her mother's recent death. She remembers Shellmound, the Fairchild plantation, and knows that she will have a wonderful time with her exciting cousins and aunts. The Fairchilds are people to whom things happen, exciting, unforgettable things.

At Shellmound, Laura finds most of the family assembled for the wedding. Although children her age are her companions, she is also aware of the doings of the grownups. It is obvious that the family is not happy about Dabney's marriage. Her husband-to-be is Troy Flavin, the manager of the plantation, whose inferior social position is the main mark against him. Uncle Battle, Dabney's father, is most of all reluctant to let one of his family go from him, but he cannot bring himself to say anything to Dabney, not even that he will miss her. Laura finds this behavior to be very strange. They seldom talk as a united family, but they always act as one. There are so many members of the family that it is hard for Laura to keep them straight. Uncle Battle's wife is Aunt Ellen, and their oldest daughter is Shelley, who is going to be a nun. Again the whole family disapproves of her plan, but there is seldom any attempt to get her to change her mind. The obvious favorite is Uncle George, Battle's brother. Uncle George also married beneath him. He and his wife, Robbie, live in Memphis, where everyone knows poor Uncle George can never be happy.

When George arrives for the wedding festivities, he is alone and miserable. Robbie left him, and he came down alone to see his family. Not wanting to make Dabney unhappy, they do not tell her of Robbie's desertion. The children and the aunts and grand-aunts are not told either, although one by one they begin to suspect that something is wrong. Ellen could kill Robbie for making George unhappy, but she keeps her feelings to herself except when she is alone with Battle, her husband.

Robbie's anger at her husband began on the afternoon of a family outing. George risked his life to save one of the cousins, a feebleminded child caught in the path of a train as they crossed a railroad trestle. After that incident, Robbie was never the same with George. She seemed to want him to prove that he loves her more than he loves his family.

Probably Shelley understands the family best. She knows that they built a wall against the outside world, but she suspects that they are more lonely than self-sufficient. Most people take the family as a group, loving or hating them all together. Only Uncle George seems to take them one by one, loving and understanding each as an individual. Shelley thinks that this is why they all love Uncle George so much.

Dabney seems to wish for more than she has in her love for Troy. Sometimes she feels left out, as if she were trying to find a lighted window but finds only darkness. She loves Troy, but she wants to feel even more a part of him. She also wishes that her family will try to keep her with them; she wants to make certain of their love.

Preparations for the wedding create a flurry. The dresses were ordered from Memphis, and when some of the gowns fail to arrive, there is the usual hubbub among the women, a concern that the men cannot appreciate. One of the children falls sick at the last minute, so that Laura is made one of the wedding party after all. Troy's mother sends some beautiful handmade quilts from her mountain shack. Troy feels proud, but the Fairchilds are even more self-consciously and unwillingly ashamed of his background.

After their wedding, Dabney and Troy will live at Marmion, an estate owned by the family. Dabney rides over to see the house. Looking at the stately buildings and the beautiful old trees, she knows that best of all she would love being inside it, looking out on the rest of the world. That is what she wants the most, to be inside where she is a part of the light and warmth. That is what marriage must give her.

All the time, unknown to any of the family but Shelley, Robbie is not far away. She is coming after George in hopes that he is looking for her. What almost defeats Robbie is the fear that she did not marry George but the whole Fairchild family. It is that fear that made her angry at the affair on the railroad trestle. Wanting desperately to come first with George, she knows instinctively that he can never set her apart or above the family. Contrite and humble, she goes to Shellmound. The fact that George is not even there at the moment hurts her even more, for she wants very much for him to be miserable without her. He is, but it is not the Fairchild way to let anyone see his true feelings.

Robbie probably understands the secret of the family when she says that the Fairchilds love each other because, in so doing, they are really loving themselves. That fact is not quite true in George's case. He is the different one. Because of his gentleness and his ability to love people as individuals, he lets Robbie see his love for her without ever saying the words she longs to hear.

The wedding is almost an anticlimax, a calm scene following gusty storms of feeling. Troy and Dabney take only a short trip, for Troy is needed to superintend the plantation. While they are gone, Battle works the field hands hard to get Marmion ready for them. Dabney is anxious to move in, but the move is not so necessary after her marriage as it seemed before; she no longer feels left out of Troy's life. She thinks her life before was like seeing a beautiful river between high banks, with no way to get down. Now she finds the way, and she is at peace. Indeed, the whole family seems to have righted itself.

When Aunt Ellen asks Laura to live with them at Shellmound, her being wanted by the Fairchilds seems too wonderful to believe. Laura knows that she will go back to her father, but still feeling that she really belongs to the Fairchilds seems like a beautiful dream. She clings briefly to Aunt Ellen, as if to hold close that wonderful moment of belonging.

Critical Evaluation:

Eudora Welty has created in Shellmound, the home of the Fairchild family in *Delta Wedding*, a world set apart from the rest of southern plantation society of the 1920's. Shellmound is a haven, isolated from the mainstream of southern life and unaffected by extremes of grief and suffering: There is no racial tension, no poverty, no war or natural catastrophe, no sense of alienation and instability generated by contact with modern urban society, and no severe moral deficiencies in

the characters that would preclude natural human happiness. The Fairchild estate is thus the perfect stage upon which to play out a drama about the growth of every type of love, from romantic to filial to platonic.

The main focus of the book, therefore, is on the nature of the numerous members of the Fairchild clan and on their relationships. Welty shows how the men are different from the women, how the "insiders" are different from those who have married into the family, how each person relates to the others, and how each person grows individually and privately. In order to explore these various aspects, the author utilizes different narrative voices, thus enabling the reader to view the characters from different perspectives. Aunt Tempe, for example, provides the older generation's point of view; she believes that Delta women have inherited traits that cannot be learned by outsiders, traits that enable them subtly to control their men and the plantations. At the young end of the spectrum is nine-year-old Laura, who comes to live at Shellmound temporarily after her mother's death; she provides the child's viewpoint of events during the hectic wedding preparations. The most objective, wise, and clear-sighted outlook, however, is provided by Aunt Ellen. As an "outsider" (she married Battle Fairchild), she not only sees the situation more accurately than her more involved and subjective relatives but also brings to her judgment insights from the world beyond the plantation.

What distinguishes the Fairchilds most is their simultaneous independence from and reliance upon one another; each person is at once intensely caught up in family concerns and fiercely private and separate. The only member who transcends the insular closeness of the circle to achieve a more universal outlook on life is Uncle George; able to feel and see beyond the limitations of life at Shellmound, he is nevertheless tied to the Fairchilds in his heart. Through the family's constant attempts to study and understand George, and through George's emotional involvement in events at the estate, Welty reveals a group of people at once selfishly exclusive and warmly affectionate, tender, loving, and devoted.

Further Reading

Bloom, Harold, ed. *Eudora Welty*. Updated ed. New York: Chelsea House, 2007. Collection of essays analyzing Welty's work, including pieces by writers Robert Penn Warren and Elizabeth Bowen. Includes discussions of Welty's sense of place; her transformation of the public, the private, and the political; and "'The Treasure Most Dearly Regarded': Memory and Imagination in *Delta Wedding*" by Welty biographer Suzanne Marrs.

Carson, Barbara Harrell. *Eudora Welty: Two Pictures at Once in Her Frame.* Troy, N.Y.: Whitston, 1992. Though intended for academics, Carson's work is clearly written and generally accessible. One chapter is devoted to *Delta Wedding*, and the introduction sets forth her thesis that Welty's fiction includes opposed perspectives without reconciling them. Contains an extensive bibliography and index.

Kreyling, Michael. *Eudora Welty's Achievement of Order.* Baton Rouge: Louisiana State University Press, 1980. One of the best book-length studies of Welty. Focuses on the development of her fictional technique and the growth of her aesthetic sensibility and unique voice.

_____. *Understanding Eudora Welty.* Columbia: University of South Carolina Press, 1999. Examines Welty's work and summarizes its critical reception, including the opinions of the New Critics and feminist reviewers. Chapter 4 is devoted to an analysis of *Delta Wedding.*

Marrs, Suzanne. *Eudora Welty: A Biography.* Orlando, Fla.: Harcourt, 2005. Literary biography provides insight into Welty's life and writing and serves to refute some popular conceptions of the writer. Marrs, a friend of Welty, maintains the writer was not the perfect southern lady described by other biographers.

Prenshaw, Peggy W., ed. *Eudora Welty: Thirteen Essays.* Jackson: University Press of Mississippi, 1983. Reprint of selections from *Eudora Welty: Critical Essays,* 1979. An excellent collection of essays, this compilation, unlike most, includes substantial work by significant writers. These essays deal more with Welty than with *Delta Wedding,* but they do map out major directions for the reader.

Thornton, Naoko Fuwa. "*Delta Wedding*: A Celebration of a Horrible World." In *Strange Felicity: Eudora Welty's Subtexts on Fiction and Society.* Westport, Conn.: Praeger, 2003. Examines two kinds of metafiction in Welty's major works: literary issues, such as language, readership, and authorship, and the social subtexts below the surface of the works.

Turner, Craig W., and Lee Emling Harding, eds. *Critical Essays on Eudora Welty.* Boston: G. K. Hall, 1989. Includes three landmark essays on *Delta Wedding:* "Delta Fiction" places Welty's novel in the tradition of the old South. "*Delta Wedding* as Region and Symbol" analyzes the novel's formal structure. "Meeting the World in *Delta Wedding*" explores its mature artistry and lyricism.

Vande Kieft, Ruth M. *Eudora Welty.* Rev. ed. Boston: Twayne, 1987. A classic guide to reading Welty; one of the best beginning sources, despite later scholarship. Analyzes the structures, messages, and characters in her works, focusing on the mystery and duality at the heart of her fiction.

Westling, Louise. *Sacred Groves and Ravaged Gardens: The Fiction of Eudora Welty, Carson McCullers, and Flannery O'Connor.* Athens: University of Georgia Press, 1985. Explores the impact of the southern conception of womanhood on *Delta Wedding* and two other Welty novels. Discusses Welty's fiction in relation to McCullers and O'Connor.

Demian

Author: Hermann Hesse (1877-1962)
First published: 1919 (English translation, 1923)
Type of work: Novel
Type of plot: Bildungsroman
Time of plot: Early twentieth century
Locale: Germany

Principal characters:
EMIL SINCLAIR, a seeking youth
MAX DEMIAN, his friend and mentor
BEATRICE, a beautiful young girl whom Sinclair idolizes
FRANZ KROMER, a brutal bully
PISTORIUS, an organist
KNAUER, a suicidal young man
FRAU EVA, Demian's mother

The Story:

Emil Sinclair, an innocent ten-year-old child of strict, pious German parents, lives in a world of kindness, good behavior, and love. Desperately wanting to be liked, he relates a boastful tale among a group of friends. The tale is about the time he and a friend stole a sackful of apples. Realizing the story to be a lie, bully Franz Kromer approaches Sinclair, claiming nevertheless to know the person from whom the apples were stolen, and demands money to keep quiet. Sinclair gives Kromer the few pfennigs he has, but Kromer renews his blackmail threat and extends his power over Sinclair. Terrified, Sinclair steals from his mother to pay Kromer.

Soon, a new boy in school, Max Demian, perceives the nature of Sinclair's problem and somehow removes him from Kromer's influence. Almost immediately, Sinclair, despite having recurring nightmares—the worst being his murderous assault upon his own father—regains his place in the security of his family's sphere. In confirmation class, his automatic acceptance of the traditional view of the story of Cain and Abel is challenged by Demian, who sees Cain as a marked man of genius and, therefore, the target of jealous individuals. In another confirmation class, Demian impugns the story of Jesus' crucifixion between two thieves by paying tribute to the unrepentant thief as a man of character and labeling the repentant thief as a "sniveling coward." Demian's insistence that, inasmuch as God belongs to his godly followers, a God for the world's other half—the evil half—is necessary for balance, strikes a chord with Sinclair, whose memory of Kromer's introduction into a world opposite that of Sinclair's family is still painful.

Sinclair goes away to boarding school in Stuttgart and becomes friends with an older student, with whom he begins visiting bars and drinking wine. While his friend speaks of older women and sex, Sinclair gains fame as a youthful boozer apparently bent upon self-destruction. Threatened with expulsion from school, Sinclair remains unmoved, even after two visits from his father. Once in a park, Sinclair sees a tall, slender, young woman, who impresses him profoundly. He gives her the name Beatrice and, without saying a word to her, begins to worship her image. As darkness and evil disappear from him, he begins to seek purity and spirituality in his life. His behavior changes, becoming serious and dignified. He takes up painting. Attempting to produce a likeness of Beatrice, he idly paints a face that he later recognizes as that of Demian.

Sinclair remembers various conversations he had had with Demian, particularly one about the barely visible coat of arms on the entrance to Sinclair's house. That night, Sinclair dreams of being encouraged by Demian to eat the decorative bird on the house and is horrified to feel the heraldic bird coming to life inside him. During the days that follow, Sinclair paints the bird, and it becomes a sparrow hawk that resembles the ancient coat of arms. Sinclair mails the painting to Demian.

Some days later in school, Sinclair finds a note from Demian directing him to the God, Abraxas. Strangely, a lecture being given at that moment by his professor identifies Abraxas as a god for "uniting the godly and the devilish ele-

ments," meaning that Abraxas is both god and devil. Sinclair, who on his walks hears organ music, follows the music to a small church, where he frequently sits on the curb and listens. Once, afterward, he follows the organist to a bar and becomes acquainted with the eccentric musician Pistorius. They have long talks together. During this time, Sinclair meets a schoolmate, Knauer, who, tortured by the sexual turmoil of adolescence, has come to see suicide as the only answer. He seeks help from Sinclair, who is unable to provide much help.

Sinclair becomes eighteen years old and attends the university. At last, he meets Demian's mother, Frau Eva, who invites him into her house with a number of good friends who are joined together by their belief in individual development. Sinclair looks upon Frau Eva as the Universal Mother. Sinclair lives at her house for some time.

At the end of one year, World War I breaks out, and Sinclair and Demian join the military. Several months later, Sinclair is wounded. Waking up in a shelter, he discovers Demian on the bed next to him. Demian dies after giving Sinclair a farewell kiss from his mother and himself. Sinclair understands he is now on his own.

Critical Evaluation

Hermann Hesse's novel *Demian* appeared in 1919 under the pseudonym Emil Sinclair. It was perceived immediately as an important work and was awarded the Fontane Prize for new writers, which required Hesse to reveal himself as the novel's creator. The book had emanated from a series of seventy-two psychoanalytic sessions between J. B. Lang, an allegiant of noted Swiss psychologist Carl Jung, and Hesse, following a series of setbacks for Hesse that included ostracism from Germany for his antiwar stance, the long critical illness of his son, his father's death, and his wife's mental deterioration. The book details Hesse's inner development, depicted through the progress of Emil Sinclair, in his quest to know himself.

The novel follows the bildungsroman pattern, predominant in German novels from the era of German Romanticism, beginning in the late eighteenth century and continuing until the twentieth century. Typical of the goals of Romanticism, it explores the growth and development of the individual who is searching for a meaningful existence. Hesse includes autobiographical material that depicts family and environmental influences as well as intense psychological development. In Hesse's bildungsroman, the innocent youth, Sinclair, has been wrenched from the peace and security of his childhood by Franz Kromer, whose vile behavior plunges Sinclair into a dark, alien side of existence.

When Sinclair's mentor, Max Demian, rids him of

Kromer, Sinclair retreats to family bliss and purity, only to experience subtle pangs of longing to escape from his family, too. His infrequent talks with Demian severely challenge his conventional thinking with regard to religious beliefs. Although Sinclair cringes at Demian's pronouncements at the time, he thinks about them later and comes to consider their merits.

The biblical Cain's "mark" was one of distinction, signifying those persons who resist traditional beliefs and seek earnestly to become themselves. Sinclair speaks of the "two worlds" he has recently experienced, to which Demian responds that Sinclair's youth prevents his understanding of what is "forbidden." Demian adds that if Sinclair continues the path he is on, he will be able to make his own laws. Obviously, Hesse's book leads away from all conventional beliefs, including Christianity, and toward self-realization.

The long, arduous path of development for Sinclair takes stranger turns when he goes away to boarding school at the age of fourteen. Having given up the beliefs of his pietist family and finding nothing to replace those beliefs, Sinclair becomes a wastrel, sinking into drunkenness. Infatuated with a beautiful girl, whom he names Beatrice and who saves him from dissipation, he attempts to paint her likeness as an object of adoration; but the painting increasingly resembles Demian. Sinclair realizes that his salvation is connected with Demian and that his sexuality and the torment it has engendered have been transformed into the spirituality and purity of sainthood.

While the stages of guilt and knowledge of good and evil through which Sinclair passes follow the traditional bildungsroman's progress in personal development, Hesse extends his path into a penetration of Sinclair's psychological world. At the point in the confirmation class, when a note to Sinclair from Demian directs him to the professor's lecture on Abraxas, it becomes apparent that Sinclair's external reality is in the process of fading, as increasing emphasis is being placed upon his inner reality. Also, readers begin to question whether Demian, Beatrice, and Frau Eva even exist outside Sinclair's unconsciousness.

Inasmuch as Hesse recovered from his breakdown by following the ideas of Jung through Lang—as expressed in Jung's *Wandlungen und Symbole der Libido* (1912; *The Psychology of the Unconscious*, 1915)—it becomes prudent to examine Hesse's *Demian* for evidence of Jungian symbols that, along with the bildungsroman pattern, denote levels of individual development. Some symbols, defined by Jung as expressions with many meanings that indicate things not easily identified, are associated with concepts that reflect the beginning of self-knowledge early in the novel.

Sinclair's early discovery of the polarity of the world as "light" and "dark," which initially exposes him to the evils of the outside world, is actually the initial step in his freedom from his childhood. Clinging to the refuge of childhood produces dreams and fantasies, which suggests the inhibition of independence and the eventual ability to know for oneself what is forbidden. Sinclair's drunken stage at boarding school, whether true in the literal sense or the psychological one, leads to the vision of the beautiful girl (Beatrice), for whom he transfers his psychic energy or libido into worshipful adoration.

The symbols of awakening for Sinclair continue through his painting of the bird that Demian, in a dream, forces him to eat. The painting depicts the bird, traditional symbol for the soul, fighting its way out of its shell or destroying its accustomed existence to be born again. At this point, Sinclair, a reborn soul on his way to discovering his own personal God, meets Pistorius, the organist who represents Lang to Hesse.

Breaking free of Pistorius to continue alone on his path, Sinclair's inner struggle causes him to become aware of the mark of Cain on his brow—a perhaps barely perceptible image on his face that strikes fear in weaker mortals. His meeting with Frau Eva, who also wears the mark of Cain and seems to be the mother of all beings, completes the absorption of his outside world by his inner world. Demian, Sinclair's friend or demon, has been absorbed entirely within Sinclair, and Frau Eva, as a symbol of his inner psyche, attempts to lead Sinclair deeper within himself. After Demian's death, Sinclair realizes he has all answers within himself. Sinclair's absorption of all the psychic projections he encounters on his journey makes him an enlightened being who, according to the beliefs of German philosopher Friedrich Nietzsche, exists in isolation.

Demian spoke mostly to German youths returning home from World War I, largely demoralized by the war and in need of being reminded of the value of the human spirit by one of their own writers. Hesse's success in the United States was delayed until the 1960's and 1970's, when the hippie generation claimed him as a guide to psychedelic experiences and proceeded to polarize responses to his work into extreme, untenable positions.

Mary Hurd

Further Reading

Bloom, Harold, ed. *Hermann Hesse*. Philadelphia: Chelsea House, 2003. Collection of essays provides interpretations of Hesse's works, including the novel *Demian*. Novelist Thomas Mann's classic introduction to *Demian* is also reprinted in this volume.

Casebeer, Edwin F. *Herman Hesse.* New York: Thomas Y. Crowell, 1972. Part of the Writers from the Seventies series, critical appreciations of writers whose works were influenced by war. Hesse, a pacifist, produced his major novels between World War I and II, which were catalysts for the personal upheaval he endured.

Field, George Wallis. *Herman Hesse.* New York: Twayne, 1970. A succinct account of Hesse's life and a study of various phases of his work and the genres in which he wrote. Examines Hesse's major novels and provides critical evaluations.

Hesse, Hermann. *The Fairy Tales of Hermann Hesse.* New York: Bantam Books, 1995. A collection of Hesse's imaginative tales that promote understanding of his early artistic development. Stories depict individuals who forsake human society to become loners or poets and who search for meaning in their lives.

Richards, David G. *The Hero's Quest for the Self: An Archetypal Approach to Hesse's "Demian" and Other Novels.* Lanham, Md.: University Press of America, 1987. Applies the theories of Carl Jung to a discussion of Hesse's novel, including *Demian.* Asserts that Hesse anticipated

Jung and that his works serve as "poeticized" models of Jungian concepts.

Robertson, Ritchie. "Gender Anxiety and the Shaping of the Self in Some Modernist Writers: Musil, Hesse, Hoffmannsthal, Jahnn." In *The Cambridge Companion to the Modern German Novel,* edited by Graham Bartram. New York: Cambridge University Press, 2004. Hesse's novels are among the works examined in this introductory survey of German-language novels from the late nineteenth and early twentieth centuries. Includes a chronology and a bibliography.

Serrano, Miguel. *C. G. Jung and Hermann Hesse: A Record of Two Friendships.* 1966. Reprint. Einsiedeln, Switzerland: Daimon, 1998. Serrano, a late, close friend of Jung and Hesse, recounts meetings with Hesse and Jung and discusses correspondence between himself and the two men.

Ziolkowski, Theodore, ed. *Hesse: A Collection of Critical Essays.* Englewood Cliffs, N.J.: Prentice-Hall, 1973. Essays survey Hesse's work. Includes an introduction that discusses the phenomenon of "Hessemania," the cultlike response to Hesse, and the crossing-over of his icons to popular culture. Includes ten essays by renowned writers such as Martin Buber and Thomas Mann.

Democracy
An American Novel

Author: Henry Adams (1838-1918)
First published: 1880
Type of work: Novel
Type of plot: Political realism
Time of plot: Late nineteenth century
Locale: Washington, D.C.

Principal characters:
MADELEINE LEE, a wealthy young widow
SYBIL ROSS, Lee's younger sister
JOHN CARRINGTON, a lawyer, in love with Lee
SILAS P. RATCLIFFE, a corrupt U.S. senator, who wants to marry Lee

The Story:

Madeleine Lee, also known as Mrs. Lightfoot Lee, a wealthy New York widow, decides to spend the winter in Washington, D.C. Since the death of her husband, Lee has lost interest in New York society and has tried to find meaning in the study of philosophy and in philanthropy. She wants to go to Washington, the center of American political life, to see what the world of power can offer.

On a December 1 in the latter half of the nineteenth century, Lee and her younger sister, Sybil Ross, move into their rented house on Lafayette Square in Washington. Lee is intellectually inclined, artistic, and skeptical, and Sybil is sociable, straightforward, and religious. Lee takes up the practice of sitting in on sessions of the U.S. Congress, and during her visits there she meets John Carrington, a lawyer from Virginia. Carrington, about forty years old, is a former Confederate soldier whose formerly wealthy plantation family became impoverished in the American Civil War.

Carrington invites Lee to attend what he says may be the

last speech of Illinois senator Silas P. Ratcliffe, known as the Prairie Giant of Peoria. After narrowly missing his party's nomination for the U.S. presidency, Ratcliffe is, according to Carrington, expected to be appointed U.S. secretary of state or secretary of the Treasury by the new president. Lee later meets Ratcliffe at a senatorial dinner, to which she is invited by her friend, Schuyler Clinton, the senator from New York. At the dinner she also meets Lord Skye, the British minister to the United States.

Ratcliffe begins visiting Lee at the Sunday evening gatherings at her home. Her social gatherings are popular with other Washington figures, such as Baron Jacobi, an elderly and cynical Bulgarian minister; the secretary of the Russian Legation, Count Popoff; Connecticut congressman C. C. French; the wealthy Philadelphian, Hartbeest Schneidecoupon; and historian Nathan Gore, whose specialty is the history of Spain in America (Gore hopes that the new president will name him minister to Spain). Gore is particularly interested in cultivating the acquaintance of Ratcliffe because he believes the senator may help him win the desired ministry.

Ratcliffe quickly becomes enamored of Lee, in part because he is genuinely attracted to her and in part because he sees marriage with her as an asset in his quest for the presidency. Carrington falls in love with her as well. For her part, Lee values Carrington's friendship and character, but she also is drawn to the possibility of being a positive influence on the openly corrupt Ratcliffe and on American politics through Ratcliffe.

The weather is becoming warmer, and Carrington serves as a guide on a trip to George Washington's Mount Vernon. On the trip are Lee, Sybil, Gore, Lord Skye, the flirtatious Victoria Dare, and Lord Dunbeg, an Irish aristocrat and friend of Lord Skye. Mrs. Samuel Baker, the widow of a recently deceased lobbyist who has worked with Carrington, goes on the trip as well. The courtship of Dare and Lord Dunbeg, begins with the Mount Vernon trip. The trip also gives everyone a chance to discuss George Washington, and to contrast the politics of the first president with those of Ratcliffe.

Back in Washington, D.C., the newly elected president, who is from Indiana, is advised by his associates to try to sideline the powerful and dangerous Ratcliffe. They devise a plan to have the president appoint Ratcliffe as secretary of the Treasury in a cabinet in which the new secretary will have no allies. The plan is to then dismiss Ratcliffe when he proves to be unable to operate effectively in this setting. In the meanwhile, Ratcliffe attempts to court Lee by presenting himself as needing her help and advice, playing on her sense of duty. The wily politician also starts creating alliances so that the Treasury job will actually turn out to his own advantage.

Sybil and Carrington take another outing to Virginia, where Sybil learns of Carrington's tragic experiences in the Civil War, and Carrington talks to her about his love for her sister. The two agree to enter into an alliance to prevent a marriage between Lee and Ratcliffe. At about the same time, Ratcliffe learns that Carrington is executor for the estate of lobbyist Baker, with whom the Illinois senator had some extremely corrupt dealings. Ratcliffe begins his own maneuvering to sideline Carrington with a job appointment that will remove Carrington as a barrier to the pursuit of Lee. The senator begins by offering Carrington a job in the Treasury Department through Lee, both to test Carrington's enmity and to portray himself to the widow as a person of good will. When Carrington refuses the job, the politician arranges to have the secretary of state appoint the attorney to a highly desirable position in Mexico.

Before leaving the country, Carrington meets again with Sybil and reminds her of their earlier conversation. He leaves a sealed letter with her, which she is to give Lee if it seems a wedding with Ratcliffe cannot be avoided. Only Lee and Ratcliffe are to read the letter. The historian, Nathan Gore, disappointed in his ambitions for the Spanish ministry, also attempts to warn Lee about the new Treasury secretary.

The grand duke and duchess of Saxe-Baden-Hombourg, Germany, visit Washington. Because the duchess is also an English princess, Lord Skye is obliged to give the couple a ball. The duchess develops an intense dislike for the vulgarities of the new president. Also, because there has been friction between the First Lady and Lee, the visiting noblewoman insists on keeping Lee at her side throughout the ball. At the end of the party, Ratcliffe proposes to Lee.

Lee is on the verge of accepting the proposal when Sybil gives her Carrington's letter. The letter discloses a substantial payoff that the late Baker's company had made to Senator Ratcliffe to get a bill passed to subsidize Baker's company. Lee is so disturbed by this new evidence of Ratcliffe's extreme corruption that she refuses the proposal and shows the letter to the politician, just as Carrington requested. In a fit of anger, he pushes the elderly Baron Jacobi out of his way on leaving Lee's house and the old man responds by hitting him in the face with a walking cane.

Back in New York, Sybil writes to Carrington and tells him about Ratcliffe's failed proposal and about her sister's plans to go abroad. In an extra note, Sybil encourages Carrington to again try his courtship with Lee.

Critical Evaluation:

In *Democracy*, Madeleine Lee represents Henry Adams's own efforts to influence American politics, and her ultimate rejection of Ratcliffe represents Adams's frustrations with the U.S. political system. As the great-grandson of U.S. president John Adams and the grandson of U.S. president John Quincy Adams, the younger Adams had a strong sense of the ideals inherited from the time of the nation's beginnings.

In his autobiography, *The Education of Henry Adams* (1907), Adams describes his childhood, which was spent in the atmosphere of the late eighteenth century, a mood still surrounding family homes in Boston and nearby Quincy. He also describes his early relationship with his grandfather, the former president. This sense of the past kept him from ever completely accepting the raucous and rapidly industrializing society of his own day. Like Lee, Adams was a member of the elite, and despite his ties to the founding leaders of the nation, he remained an outsider and a spectator rather than an actor, as he describes himself in the autobiography.

From the time of his graduation from Harvard in 1858 until 1860, Adams traveled and studied in Europe. Soon after his return, the new U.S. president, Abraham Lincoln, appointed his father, Charles Francis Adams, minister to the United Kingdom. Henry accompanied his father as private secretary. During this time as a close spectator of political events, Henry developed the idea that he could best influence American democracy through journalism. Character Lee's disenchantment with the philosophical study of Herbert Spencer and other fashionable thinkers reflects Adams's own decision to turn from intellectual activities to active involvement in politics through journalism.

Also like Lee, Adams was disappointed and frustrated with his efforts at political reform. He took up journalism in Washington, D.C., in 1868, at the beginning of the administration of President Ulysses S. Grant, an honest man unfamiliar with the devious politics of the late nineteenth century who presided over a period of notorious corruption.

It is unclear exactly when Adams wrote *Democracy*. It was published anonymously in early April, 1880, and only in 1918 did the publisher reveal Adams as the author. However, the political schemes of Ratcliffe and his associates could easily be drawn from activities Adams witnessed in Washington.

One of the great strengths of *Democracy* as a political novel is that it is the view of an outsider with an insider's understanding of the workings of American politics. Among later writers, Gore Vidal—also the scion of a political family—comes closest to Adams as an observer of government through fiction. Adams also is a master of prose style, and his writing is incisive and witty. However, his greatest works are probably his histories and his autobiography. The scenes in *Democracy*, although vivid portrayals of Washington life,

tend to give the impression of staged sets. The characters in the novel are interesting, but they are not completely three-dimensional and lifelike.

Despite its limitations, *Democracy* is an important work of American literature not only because it is an early example of the political novel but also because it illustrates so many of the trends of the second half of the nineteenth century. The novel is a study of the growing collusion of business and government, the conflicting cultural attitudes of Americans toward Europe, the increasing sympathy with the defeated South, and the rise of new classes of individuals to power, among other topics.

Carl L. Bankston III

Further Reading

Brookhiser, Richard. *America's First Dynasty: The Adamses, 1735-1918*. New York: Free Press, 2002. A history of the politically important Adams family. This book discusses Henry Adams's privileged insight into American politics.

Chalfant, Edward. *Better in Darkness: A Biography of Henry Adams—His Second Life, 1862-1891*. Hamden, Conn.: Archon Books, 1994. The second volume of Chalfant's comprehensive three-volume biography of Henry Adams, this work covers the period of Adams's efforts at political reform and his career as a muckraking journalist during the period that saw the publication of *Democracy*.

Dawidoff, Robert. *The Genteel Tradition and the Sacred Rage: High Culture versus Democracy in Adams, James, and Santayana*. Chapel Hill: University of North Carolina Press, 1992. A discussion of the influence of the French political theorist Alexis de Tocqueville, author of *Democracy in America*, on Adams as well as on novelist Henry James and philosopher George Santayana. Chapter 2 considers *Democracy* a critical reflection on the limitations and problems of the democratic system.

O'Brien, Michael. *Henry Adams and the Southern Question*. Athens: University of Georgia Press, 2005. A study of Adams's perspective on the American South. O'Brien's work provides background for the character John Carrington in *Democracy*.

Simpson, Brooks D. *The Political Education of Henry Adams*. Columbia: University of South Carolina Press, 1996. An examination of Adams's political career that will help readers understand the frustrations with democracy expressed by Adams in the novel. Simpson argues that Adams wanted to reform American politics through his journalism and lobbying, but that he undermined himself by offending the people he sought to influence.

Democracy

Author: Joan Didion (1934-   )
First published: 1984
Type of work: Novel
Type of plot: Political
Time of plot: 1950's-1970's
Locale: Honolulu; Seattle; Jakarta, Indonesia; Kuala Lumpur, Malaysia

Principal characters:
JOAN DIDION, narrator
HARRY VICTOR, a U.S. politician
INEZ CHRISTIAN VICTOR, his wife
JACK LOVETT, a secret intelligence operative
BILLY DILLON, Harry's campaign strategist
JANET CHRISTIAN ZIGLER, Inez's sister
PAUL CHRISTIAN, Inez and Janet's father
CAROL CHRISTIAN, their mother
JESSIE and ADLAI VICTOR, Inez and Victor's children

The Story:

Inez Victor and Jack Lovett sit talking in a bar outside Honolulu, Hawaii, in the spring of 1975; on the television they watch the evacuations of South Vietnam. Lovett recalls certain memories: the pink sky at dawn and the smell of the air after the rain during the Pacific nuclear tests of 1952-1953, and an image of Inez, a seventeen-year-old girl, flowers pinned in her hair, and their encounter in Jakarta, Indonesia, during Harry Victor's political campaign in 1969.

Joan Didion, an author, admits to have been thinking of Inez and Jack, and of the events that led up to and transpired during 1975. She confesses that the story of Inez and Jack was not the tale she had intended to tell, for her initial interest was in Inez's family history: its rise to fortune as one of the most prominent families in Hawaii, in certain events that led to the family's failure and collapse, and in the events surrounding Carol Christian's desertion of the island and her teenage daughters, Inez and Janet. Didion chooses instead to center on one image, that of Jack waiting for Inez. In a nonlinear narrative, Didion arranges moments from Inez's history, including how Inez finally came to Kuala Lumpur, how she first met Jack at the age of seventeen and began their enduring yet intermittent love affair, how they came to meet in Jakarta in 1969, and finally, how tragic occurrences brought them back to each other in 1975.

Didion relates certain details about Inez's life. In 1955, a few years after Jack and Inez's first meeting, Inez marries Harry Victor, who hopes to become an elected politician. At the time of her marriage, Inez is two months pregnant; she miscarries, however. With Harry's career as a U.S. representative underway, she dons the role of supportive politician's wife, adopting, too, the pressures and responsibilities of public life. As a result, Inez later admits to retaining little memory of her own history, expressing now that she is losing track, yet she had remained a loyal supporter of her husband's career. She and Jack continued to meet, here and there, on occasion.

Inez and Harry have two children, twins Adlai and Jessie. Adlai is an arrogant young man responsible for crashing two automobiles, in one case seriously injuring his female passenger yet exhibiting little remorse. Daughter Jessie is a heroin addict who had attempted suicide and was later admitted to a rehabilitation program in Seattle, Washington.

In the spring of 1975, Inez learns of the shooting death of Hawaiian representative Wendell Omura and the mortal wounding of her sister, Janet. Her father, Paul Christian, later confesses to the crime: revenge for an alleged financial betrayal that is never fully disclosed. Harry's campaign strategist, Billy Dillon, works quickly to soften the potential media reaction. As a result, Paul is found unfit to stand trial and is sentenced to a mental facility instead. Inez, back on the island to make arrangements for Janet's funeral, finds Jack waiting for her.

Before the funeral, Inez hears word that her daughter, Jessie, has left Seattle and has boarded a plane for Saigon in pursuit of work. Inez leaves her husband, while she and Jack go to search for her daughter. Jack uses his contacts for information regarding the girl's whereabouts, and Inez waits in a hotel in Hong Kong. Jack soon finds Jessie working as a waitress at an American Legion Club in Saigon and arranges for her return to the United States.

Months later, after meeting Inez, Didion learns of Jack's death; he had died of a heart attack in a swimming pool in Jakarta. Inez sees to his quick and secret burial in Honolulu, after which she leaves for Kuala Lumpur, where she now resides helping refugees. Didion relates that Harry's political campaign has since faded; Dillon has found a new representative to groom. Harry now lives in Brussels, Belgium, and works as an envoy to the European Common Market. Adlai clerks for a federal judge in San Francisco, and Jessie is doing well in Mexico City, where she is writing a novel. Didion admits that she believes Inez will stay on in Kuala Lumpur, until the last refugee is dispatched.

Critical Evaluation:

Democracy received critical attention for its unique narrative style—a fragmented narrative in which writer Joan Didion is herself a character in the novel. She acts as author, narrator, and reporter of this story, assembling images, recollections, and historical events relating to protagonist Inez Victor's life in an attempt to gain meaning from them. Didion introduces herself as the author at the start of the second chapter, and from this point remains a presence, consistently disrupting the narrative and rearranging and revisiting events outside logical chronology. These are actions that ultimately disturb the novel's coherence, and so too the reader's ability to easily comprehend meaning.

Critics remain divided regarding the effectiveness of this strategy. Some argue that her intrusions undermine the novel's affect, while others maintain that this destabilization of certainty and meaning was perhaps Didion's intent: to relate her belief that the political world is one in which meaning is not certain or stable, and perhaps unknowable.

An underlying feeling of uncertainty indeed pervades the novel; as author and character, Didion herself admits that the images and recollections she holds may be problematic to the composition of a story, but she further states that one must "go with what you have." In addition to the fragmented nature of the memories, reality and fiction are further blurred by Didion's place in her own novel as both character and author. She recalls, for example, the moment she had first met Jack Lovett—while working with Inez at *Vogue*; she tells about her conversations with Harry Victor and how she had dined with Billy Dillon; she recounts article clippings and photographs depicting Paul Christian's arrest. She details these relationships as memories, and yet the reader must also never forget that she, as the author, also is consciously constructing a fictive narrative.

This current of uncertainty applies not only to the narrative structure of the novel but also to its political implications. Throughout *Democracy*, Didion draws attention to the idea that individuals are reduced to mere actors on the stage of American politics, regardless of what "side" they are on or how transparently they seem to play their roles. The novel, set during the beginnings of the Vietnam War in the 1950's through the withdrawal of U.S. troops from Southeast Asia in 1975, creates a dichotomy between "state actors," and "non-state actors"—that is, between public, seemingly legitimate political actors and shadowy, ill-defined ones.

U.S. Congressman turned senator Harry Victor is a state actor, a role Jack equates to "a radio actor," a mouthpiece for his campaign manager, a disembodied voice. Harry is a man concerned most with constructing the right image, that is, with giving speeches, arranging press meetings, and lecturing about ideals. In reality, he has little grasp of the tumultuous events transpiring around him. This is evident, for example, in his bringing his family to vacation in Jakarta in 1969, a dangerous time in Indonesia, filled with civil and political unrest. In this case, Harry is merely a puppet bowing to the commands of his political strategist, Billy Dillon. In this world, reality is a concept constructed by the media and consumed by the American public; reality is consciously created and manipulated by those with power.

Jack, in contrast to Harry, is a nonstate actor, a secret operative whose business dealings are never fully known but are assumed to be less than legitimate. Like Inez, a woman without memory, Jack is a man who maintains no knowable past; neither seem to belong to any place, except, as Didion remarks, with each other. It is perhaps for this reason their romance endures. Unlike Harry, who relies on orchestrated speeches and ideals, Jack relies on action and understands global events, having experienced firsthand the brutal reality of politics in his business; he has seen the ugly trickling down of policy where the wheel hits the road—where that wheel hits human lives. While Harry remains consumed with his agenda, insulated except to his political aspirations, it is Jack who escorts Inez and the children to safety after the bombing of the embassy in Jakarta, and it is Jack who safely recovers Jesse in Saigon and sees to her return home.

Inez, and to some extent her children, must occupy a role on the sidelines as Harry's loyal supporter; she becomes a casualty of this scripted world of actors; she loses track of events and has difficulty differentiating among versions of her life as she watches them unfold in the media; she loses track of the real story and the spin. Indeed, as Inez remarks, she lives a life "in which the major cost [is] memory." Although Inez attempts to assert an independent self at times—for example, when she expresses desire to aid the refugees—she is paralyzed by Harry's agenda.

Ultimately, after Jack's death, Inez leaves Harry and her children and settles in Kuala Lumpur to help the refugees, vowing to stay on until the last is dispatched; she herself has become a kind of refugee from political life. The visions of Harry's campaigns have dissipated, as have the connections among the family members themselves. All have relocated to different sectors of the globe. In the end, Didion leaves readers with a less than optimistic view of democracy; for all its best intentions, its motivations and machinations are as human and fallible as any social construction.

Danielle A. DeFoe

Further Reading

Brady, Jennifer. "Points West, Then and Now: The Fiction of Joan Didion." *Contemporary Literature* 20, no. 4 (Autumn, 1979): 452-470. Contextualizes aspects of Didion's work in relation to the closing of the American frontier, or the American West.

Ching, Stuart. "A Hard Story to Tell: The Vietnam War in Joan Didion's *Democracy*." In *Fourteen Landing Zones: Approaches to Vietnam War Literature*, edited by Jeffrey W. Hunter. Detroit, Mich.: Gale Group, 2000. Drawing thematic comparisons between William Butler Yeats's "Second Coming" and Didion's *Democracy*, Ching remarks upon the cyclical narrative patterns that, placed against the historical backdrop of the Vietnam War, signify society's collapse into chaos and disorder.

Felton, Sharon, ed. *The Critical Response to Didion*. Westport, Conn.: Greenwood Press, 1993. This study provides extensive criticism and evaluation of Didion's work. Includes a bibliography and an index.

Jarvis, Stephen. "Didion's *Democracy*: Dated in a Deconstructing Universe." *Journal of the Theoretical Humanities* 5, no. 3 (December, 2000): 93-104. This journal article offers a theoretical, yet accessible, approach to interpreting Didion's narrative style in *Democracy*.

Nadel, Alan. "Failed Cultural Narratives: America in the Postwar Era and the Story of *Democracy*." *Boundary 2* 19, no. 1 (Spring, 1992): 95-120. Using Didion's novel *Democracy* as a model, Nadel explores democracy as a concept inviting contradictory interpretations, thus failing as a unifying cultural narrative.

Parish, Tim. "After Henry Adams: Rewriting History in Joan Didion's *Democracy*." *Critique* 47, no. 2 (Winter, 2006): 167-184. Argues Didion's novel retells Henry Adams' *Democracy* and *Education* by exploring the political corruption that Adams's work predicts.

Tager, Michael. "The Political Vision of Joan Didion's *Democracy*." *Critique* 31, no. 3 (Spring, 1990): 173-184. Examines the "bleak political vision" *Democracy* predicts as a result of three factors: the maintenance of national security, media influence, and loss of historical connection.

Democracy in America

Author: Alexis de Tocqueville (1805-1859)
First published: De la démocratie en Amérique:
  volume 1, 1835; volume 2, 1840
  (English translation, 1835/1840)
Type of work: Politics

Alexis de Tocqueville lived in a time of enormous political change, when every conceivable variety of political theory flourished. He was born shortly after the French Revolution had turned France into the empire; in his lifetime occurred those further changes that transformed France, at least nominally, into a republic. His object in writing *Democracy in America* was twofold: to write about the new nation that he so much admired and to establish a new way of examining ideas of politics. Instead of proceeding from ideas of right and responsibility, Tocqueville preferred to begin by analyzing social institutions as they functioned in reality. Instead of working, as Jean-Jacques Rousseau had worked, from an arbitrary picture of the beginnings of humanity in a natural condition,

Tocqueville preferred to work from what was statistically observable. Thus, *Democracy in America* begins with a picture of the geography of the new continent, its weather, its indigenous tribes, its economy, and its natural resources. In this respect, *Democracy in America* is the forerunner of the scientific spirit in the investigation of social structures.

Much of *Democracy in America* is concerned with institutions, and the first institution described by Tocqueville is that of the partition of property. He points out that it is customary in the nations of Europe to divide property by the laws of primogeniture. The result is that property remains fixed in extent and in possession; the family, no matter how changed in each generation, is linked to the wealth and political power of landed property. The family represents the estate, the estate the family, and naturally a strong inequality is carried from one generation to another. The foundations of American culture are to be found, Tocqueville points out, in the equal partition of land and fortune. Land is continually broken up into parcels, sold, developed, and transformed. The accompanying wealth and power are much more fluid than in societies in which descent really dominates fortune. The subsidiary effect of equal partition is that people have access to careers from which they might be blocked in another system.

Tocqueville was fascinated by the practice of equality, a phenomenon rarely encountered in France during his lifetime. Several chapters concern political equality; he is one of the first great commentators on the democracy of U.S. townships and corporations in the early nineteenth century. He emphasizes that it is fundamental to understand the nature of the township, particularly in its New England tradition. The key to the nature of the United States, he asserts, is the wide and responsible nature of freedom at the level of municipal government. This gives the citizen a direct voice in the government and trains the citizen for the representative democracy of the federal government. Tocqueville points out that, under this form of government, power is concentrated in the hands of the voter; the legislative and executive branches have no power of their own, but merely represent those who appoint them. To us, this fact is commonplace, but it was a new idea for the citizens of Europe in the nineteenth century.

Although much of this work is in praise of democracy in the United States, Tocqueville makes some important qualifications. His first principle is that abuse in government occurs when one special interest is served to the exclusion of all others. This kind of abuse, he remarks, formerly occurred when the upper classes imposed their will on the lower, or when military, feudal, financial, or even religious values operated to the exclusion of all others. His great qualification of democracy is that it makes possible a tyranny of the majority. He states that it is conceivable that the free institutions of the United States may be destroyed by forcing all minorities to give up their freedoms for what is supposedly the good of the majority. In that case, he concludes, democracy will give way first to despotism and then to anarchy. Above all things, Tocqueville is taken with equality, and that principle, regardless of the greatest good for the greatest number, is what animates his opinion.

Democracy in America is principally about its great subject, but there are in it many reminders of a larger view that its author has. One constant theme of the book is that the Old World must learn from the New World; in fact, the book func-

tions not so much as an independent study of a unique phenomenon as a study of comparative political science. The French will not succeed, the author remarks, if they do not introduce democratic institutions. There will be independence for none, he adds, unless, like the republic of the United States, the French grant independence for all. With uncommon prescience, he predicts the totalitarian potentialities of the twentieth century, in which unlimited power restricted itself not to a class, but first to a party, and then to a single man. The famous ending of the first volume carries this insight to a more elaborate and specific culmination. There are two nations, Tocqueville asserts, that probably will dominate the next century, Russia and the United States. One, he says, is driven by the desire for power and war, the other by the desire to increase domestic prosperity. He predicts that there will be no peace until the aggressiveness of Russia is checked by the peacefulness of the United States: He looks to a future in which the principle of servitude will encounter that of freedom.

The second volume of *Democracy in America* was published five years after the first. The first volume had established its author as one of the best political thinkers in Europe. It won for him not only the esteem of the best minds of the Continent but also financial and political rewards, so that from the time of its publication Tocqueville was to take an active part as a member of the French government. The second volume is concerned not with the basic economic and social characteristics of the United States but with subsidiary questions about the nature of American culture. Tocqueville asks, for example, how Americans cultivate the arts and whether or not eloquence is to be encountered in the rhetoric of Congress. He covers the progress of science as well as that of poetry, the position of religious minorities, even the meaning of public monuments in a democracy. His general conclusion on the arts in the United States is that they do not flourish as they do in other political climates, for the arts require an atmosphere of privilege and an amount of money that a tax-conscious public is quite unlikely to spend. The useful, he says, is much preferred in a democracy to the beautiful. The artist becomes an artisan and, the author remarks with some delicacy, tends to produce imperfect commodities rather than lasting works of art.

If these qualifications are admitted, they are also weighted; Tocqueville believes that a lowering of some standards is amply compensated by a heightening of others. Particularly in the matter of foreign policy, he admires the republican sense as well as form of government. Toward the end of *Democracy in America*, he ruminates on the inclinations toward war and peace of different forms of government.

The democratic form, he judges, is predisposed to peace because of various influences: the rapid growth of personal wealth; the stake in property; the less material but equally important gentleness of heart that allows the citizens of a democracy a more humane view of life. Yet, when the democratic government is involved in war, the same application of ambition and energy that is so marked in commercial life results often in military success as well. Tocqueville's last thoughts about the democracy and its army deal with the danger to any society from its own standing army, and he covers substantially the same ground on this matter as do the authors of the Federalist Papers.

Democracy in America ends with the restatement that despotism may be encountered even in republics. The author admits that democracies can, on occasion, be violent and unjust, but he believes these occasions are exceptional. They will be more and more frequent, however, in the proportion that equality is allowed to lapse. Among the last of Tocqueville's animated descriptions is that of the "flock of timid and industrious animals" who have given up their individuality to a strong central government. He urges a balance between central and decentralized power, the constant consciousness of equality for all members of the polity.

Further Reading

Commager, Henry Steele. *Commager on Tocqueville.* Columbia: University of Missouri Press, 1993. Lucid essays, written by a distinguished American historian, on Tocqueville's democratic visions. The conclusion discusses the contemporary relevance of Tocqueville's ideas for politics in the United States.

Epstein, Joseph. *Alexis de Tocqueville: Democracy's Guide.* New York: HarperCollins/Atlas, 2006. A portrait of Tocqueville, focusing on his contributions to political science. Chronicles the development of his ideas and assesses the accuracy of his prophecies about the future of American democracy.

Janara, Laura. *Democracy Growing Up: Authority, Autonomy, and Passion in Tocqueville's "Democracy in America."* Albany: State University of New York Press, 2002. Feminist analysis of *Democracy in America*, examining the gendered and familial foundations of Western democracy and Tocqueville's ideas of democratic maturity.

Locke, Jill, and Eileen Hunt Botting, eds. *Feminist Interpretations of Alexis de Tocqueville.* University Park: Pennsylvania State University Press, 2009. Twelve essays examining the relationship of Tocqueville's life and work to modern feminism, including discussions of gender, sexuality, race, class, nationality, ethnicity, and colonialism in his works.

Mancini, Matthew. *Alexis de Tocqueville.* New York: Twayne, 1994. Accessible, comprehensive survey concentrates on *Democracy in America* and introduces the major themes in Tocqueville's works. Contains a worthwhile bibliography for students new to Tocqueville's writings.

Martineau, Harriet. *How to Observe Morals and Manners.* New Brunswick, N.J.: Transaction, 1989. Published originally in 1838, this book was the first methods text in the social sciences. It clearly explicates patriarchal, classist, racist, and other biases that plague the undisciplined observations which Tocqueville employed as the empirical foundation for *Democracy in America*.

Pope, Whitney, in collaboration with Lucetta Pope. *Alexis de Tocqueville: His Social and Political Theory.* Beverly Hills, Calif.: Sage, 1986. Critiques Tocqueville's pertinence for modern social theory and compares his ideas with those of Karl Marx, Emile Durkheim, and other social theorists. Includes a useful bibliography.

Schleifer, James T. *The Making of Tocqueville's "Democracy in America."* Chapel Hill: University of North Carolina Press, 1980. A detailed, archivally based appreciation of *Democracy in America*. Rewarding analysis of Tocqueville's definitions of democracy.

Swedberg, Richard. *Tocqueville's Political Economy.* Princeton, N.J.: Princeton University Press, 2009. Examines *Democracy in America* and Tocqueville's other works to analyze his ideas about economics and the relationship of the economy to the rest of society.

Welch, Cheryl B., ed. *The Cambridge Companion to Tocqueville.* New York: Cambridge University Press, 2006. Collection of essays providing numerous interpretations of Tocqueville's works, including discussions of Tocqueville in the twenty-first century, his views on threats to liberty in democracies and on the democratic religious experience, and his new political science. James T. Schleifer provides a reconsideration of *Democracy in America*, and Oliver Zunz describes how this book was read in nineteenth century America.

Democratic Vistas

Author: Walt Whitman (1819-1892)
First published: 1871
Type of work: Social criticism

Written when Walt Whitman was in his early fifties, *Democratic Vistas* demonstrates the author's discouragement at what he saw in America. The sobering effects of the Civil War, the death of Abraham Lincoln, and the overwhelming change resulting from the Industrial Revolution are quite evident as Whitman attempts to introduce a plan for the development of a golden age in the New World.

Like Whitman's poetry, the work has no substantial organization; it tends to ramble and to be repetitious. Nevertheless, in its portrait of Whitman's philosophy, and in its analysis of the potentiality of the American society, *Democratic Vistas* is extremely significant. Its criticism of American politics, culture, and values in general was partly the result of the disillusionment that existed after the Civil War, but the considerations are still quite applicable to American society.

Simply stated, the thesis of *Democratic Vistas* is that, while America is surpassing all other nations industrially and has the material facilities to continue its advancement, it lacks a distinct culture or spiritual identity. According to Whitman, such an identity could only come about through works of literature written in new literary styles by new artists. In effect, he is stating that the United States has the human resources, the material resources, and the sound political structure to make itself the most nearly ideal society that has ever existed. As Whitman views the American scene, however, he sees no unique values, no real expression of these new concepts, but only a materialistic society relying on old ideas and traditional expressions. Thus, the overall result of the work is a plea for great literary works that would serve as a foundation for a new society.

Though the work has no organization other than the repetition of this same theme, Whitman's approach follows four general divisions: a portrait of the American society and its values, a statement of the basic principles and ideals that represent the goals of the "mass, or lump character" of America, the principle of the individual as the focal point for the ideal society, and great literature as the force that will bring about this society.

Whitman begins by stating his central theme—that the United States will never be great unless it is able to separate itself from the Old World tradition:

> I say that democracy can never prove itself beyond cavil, until it founds and luxuriantly grows its own forms of art, poems, schools, theology, displacing all that exists, or that has been produced anywhere in the past, under opposite influences.

Whitman further states that the United States is a new experiment founded on new principles and cannot rely on old ideas. While some might argue that the "republic is, in performance, really enacting today the grandest arts, poems, etc., by beating up the wilderness into fertile farms, and in her railroads, ships, machinery, etc.," Whitman responds that "society, in these States, is canker'd, crude, superstitious and rotten":

> The official services of America, national, state, and municipal, in all their branches and departments, except the judiciary, are saturated in corruption, bribery, falsehood, maladministration; and the judiciary is tainted.

After dwelling on the "lamentable conditions" that exist in the United States, Whitman states that the answer to such problems is a "new-founded literature" that would be "consistent with science, handling the elements and forces with competent power, teaching and training men."

Having thus established the tone of his essay, Whitman proceeds to the first main consideration, an analysis of the present American society. His portrait of the "lump character" shows that the artist has, in the past, had to struggle against the masses. He also shows that the reverse has been true, for literature "has never recognized the People." It is Whitman's belief that the United States is experiencing the birth of a new sort of mass personality that is courageous, all-inclusive, and potentially great. To deny cultural identity to this mass would be to destroy this potentiality.

> We believe the ulterior object of political and all other government (having, of course, provided for the police, the safety of life, property, and for the basic statute and common law, and their administration, always first in order), to be among the rest, not merely to rule, to repress disorder, etc., but to develop, to open up to cultivation, to

encourage the possibilities of all beneficent and manly outcroppage, and of that aspiration for independence, and the pride and self-respect latent in all characters.

In other words, Whitman believed that physical freedom is only part of America's goal. The society as a whole can progress only when it possesses a cultural freedom and a set of ideals that will enable the people to attain a transcendent spirituality. Still, the law and the political form are important to Whitman, for it is only in this governmental structure that people of all races and backgrounds can be brought together. Whitman even sees in the future a greater prosperity of the masses and a tremendous growth of society: "The true gravitation-hold of liberalism in the United States will be a more universal ownership of property, general homesteads, general comfort—a vast, intertwining reticulation of wealth."

According to Whitman, this wealth, plus a genuine solidarity of mass spirit and integrity, will make this system survive. Two examples that he gives to prove this point are that "the land which could raise such as the late rebellion, could also put it down," and that the fervor of the Americans is also evident in the interest that they show in the election of their leaders: "I know nothing grander, better exercise, better digestion, more positive proof of the past, the triumphant result of faith in human kind, than a well-contested American national election."

Having discussed the quality of the United States' political system and the character of the mass of its people, Whitman then turns to the individual, for "rich, luxuriant, varied personalism," argues Whitman, is the key to civilization. All else, such as literature or government, is important only insofar as it assists in the "production of perfect characters among the people." It was Whitman's belief that this principle is the basis for the United States' future.

Whitman defines individuality as creativity, that independent thought by which each person is able to transcend the mass, and he states that it is precisely this quality that Americans lack. He attributes this failure to an attachment to "Culture," or traditional learning. The scholar, for example, is taught what to believe, and consequently believes in nothing. Rather than serving to motivate creativity, this type of culture only systematizes and stagnates individuality.

It is not that Whitman objects to culture; he argued earlier for the necessity of a unique culture if the United States was to rise above materialism. He simply believes that, instead of being limited to the "parlors or lecture rooms," culture should be distributed among all people of all classes. In short, the masses should be given the opportunity to achieve iden-

tity. The nation has indeed developed people who are physically strong and educated, says Whitman, but the "gloomiest consequences" will result if people are left with an "unsophisticated Conscience."

The third and final section of the essay is devoted to the concept of a great American literature, the power that Whitman believes will enable the development of the "primary moral element" necessary for an enhanced American culture:

A boundless field to fill! A new creation, with needed orbic works launch'd forth, to revolve in free and lawful circuits—to move, self-poised, through the ether, and shine like heaven's own suns! With such, and nothing less, we suggest that New World Literature, fit to rise upon, cohere, and finalize in time, these States.

By "New World Literature" Whitman does not mean quantity; this nation has, he states, more publications than any other country. Rather, he is referring to literary forms that would represent the United States as the Bible, the works of Homer, Plato, and Aeschylus represent their respective civilizations. Nor should Americans resort to the achievements of the past, for these works were written for remote times and problems: "Ye powerful and resplendent ones! ye were, in your atmospheres, grown not for America, but rather for her foes, the feudal and the old—while our genius is democratic and modern." Whitman summarizes what has thus far been accomplished by describing the stages of development in American writing. He states that America has gone through two stages in preparation for a third and final stage, without which the first two become useless: "The First stage was the planning and putting on record the political foundation rights of immense masses of people. . . . The Second stage relates to material prosperity, wealth, produce. . . ." The third and final stage will be "a native expression-spirit," "a sublime and serious Religious Democracy sternly taking command." This spirit of impetus can come from no other land, because the foundations for this literature exist only in the United States.

The artist who will produce this literature will be a student of nature. "Part of the test of a great literatus," says Whitman, "shall be the absence in him of the idea of the covert, the lurid, the maleficent, the devil . . . hell, natural depravity, and the like." More important, however, will be his faith, his simplicity of statement, and his "adherence to natural standards."

Whitman is no less explicit in his description of the themes of these great works. He says, "Nature, true Nature, and the true idea of Nature, long absent, must, above all, become fully restored, enlarged, and must furnish the pervading atmosphere to poems, and the test of all high literary and aesthetic compositions."

Here Whitman is not referring to the "posyes and nightingales of the English poets," but to the spiritual significance, symbolic and implicit, in the unity of all created matter. By means of this expression all men will be able to understand the essential harmony in the universe and thus regain their faith which has been "scared away by science."

Exactly how the artist will go about this process is not really made clear; but Whitman does say that a whole new idea of composition must be the means. In any case, he assures the reader that the nation cannot rest on what has already been accomplished; the hope of the nation is in the future.

The final tone of Whitman's essay is one that pervades the whole work; he is desperate and is trying to convince the reader that he or she should also be concerned. Earlier in his career, Whitman had thought that great American literature was on the verge of being created. At the writing of *Democratic Vistas*, he sees that that of which he has dreamed has not occurred, and he attempts to motivate the potential philosopher-artists through this essay. The result is that, when he has not obscured his message with too many words, he has given an excellent critique of American society that is as significant now as it was in Whitman's day.

Further Reading

Aspiz, Harold. *Walt Whitman and the Body Beautiful*. Urbana: University of Illinois Press, 1980. Considers *Democratic Vistas* a mature reflection of Whitman's feminism: his belief in women's potential, their maternal and physical capabilities, and the need for female influence on society.

Erkkila, Betsy. *Whitman the Political Poet*. New York: Oxford University Press, 1989. Examines Whitman's politics. Argues that *Democratic Vistas* moves toward socialism and affirms a more feminized, cooperative society.

Holloway, Emory. *Whitman: An Interpretation in Narrative*. New York: Biblo and Tannen, 1969. Considers *Democratic Vistas* a transitional work moving the poet from despair to hope, from physicality to spirituality, and from individuality to nationality in his writing.

Kummings, Donald D., ed. *A Companion to Walt Whitman*. Malden, Mass.: Blackwell, 2006. Provides information on Whitman's life, the cultural and historical contexts of his works, his use of language, his writing style, and the reception and legacy of his writings. An essay by Robert Leigh Davis provides an analysis of *Democratic Vistas*.

Mancuso, Luke. "Reconstruction Is Still in Abeyance: Walt Whitman's *Democratic Vistas* and the Federalizing of National Identity." In *The Strange Sad War Revolving: Walt Whitman, Reconstruction, and the Emergence of Black Citizenship, 1865-1876*. Columbia, S.C.: Camden House, 1997. Argues that the essay is "symptomatic of the larger cultural debate" in post-Civil War America about granting voting rights to African Americans.

Rosenblatt, Louise. "Whitman's *Democratic Vistas* and the 'New Ethnicity.'" In *Making Meaning with Texts: Selected Essays*. Portsmouth, N.H.: Heinemann, 2005. Examines the work from the perspective of reader-response theory, arguing that Whitman shows his readers how men and women can accept themselves and others for their own uniqueness.

Scholnick, Robert J. "The American Context of *Democratic Vistas*." In *Walt Whitman: Here and Now*, edited by Joann P. Krieg. Westport, Conn.: Greenwood Press, 1985. Considers the response of *Democratic Vistas* to the publication of Thomas Carlyle's *Shooting Niagra: And After* (1867), other period reactions to Carlyle, and the pessimistic essays on similar themes by painter Eugene Benson.

Snyder, John. *The Dear Love of Man: Tragic and Lyric Communion in Walt Whitman*. Paris: Mouton, 1975. Argues that *Democratic Vistas* offers literature as a means of giving spiritual meaning to America's corrupt and materialistic society. Whitman's vision is both tragic concerning the present and idealistic about the future.

The Demon

Author: Mikhail Lermontov (1814-1841)
First published: 1855 (English translation, 1875)
Type of work: Poetry

Principal characters:
THE DEMON
PRINCE GOUDAL, heir to a Caucasian robber chief
TAMARA, his daughter, a beautiful Caucasian princess
THE YOUNG BRIDEGROOM, her betrothed
THE GUARDIAN ANGEL
THE AGED GUARDIAN

The Poem:

The Demon, banished from Heaven, soars over the earth despondent about the memories of his once glorious past, when he knew both faith and love. No force challenges him as he spreads evil and strife around the world, but it has all been too easy and he has become bored and indifferent, even to the magnificent beauty of the Caucasus. The created universe leaves him cold and disdainful. Even the lush valleys of Georgia leave him feeling bitter and contemptuous.

Meanwhile, the aged Prince Goudal plans for the marriage of his only daughter, the beautiful Tamara. Outwardly she appears pleased, and she dances and smiles, but within her heart she has misgivings about leaving her home and becoming subservient to her new relatives. The Demon flies past her, sees her dancing, and immediately falls in love with her. His empty and lonely soul is aroused by her beauty and innocence, and he feels confused.

The Demon then espies the young bridegroom excitedly riding toward the wedding, and he distracts the young man from visiting a shrine along the way. The bridegroom pursues a pair of Ossetian robbers, but after a brief chase, he is mortally wounded and his horse shows up at Goudal's castle in the mountains bearing his corpse. Tamara is anguished, but the Demon's strange voice calls out to comfort her and to advise her to wait. The words inflame her passions, but when he enters her bedroom as if in a shadowy dream, looking "unearthly handsome" and forlorn in his love, she detects no radiance from his head.

A fearful and suspicious Tamara begs her father to turn the other suitors away and allow her to enter a convent as a nun. Even in a remote convent, however, secluded among the mountains and forests, she continues to sense the Demon's presence in forbidden dreams and to feel attracted by his unearthly beauty.

Tamara cannot meditate or pray properly, unable to stop thinking about the Demon. She becomes indifferent to the beauties of nature. When she attempts to pray to icons of the Virgin Mary, she ends up thinking about the Demon of her troubled dreams, and she fantasizes passionate embraces with him. She prays to the saints, but her heart yearns for the Demon.

At first, the Demon does not dare approach the convent, but finally he enters the garden and serenades Tamara with such tender, ethereal music that he is himself overwhelmed to the point of dropping a single tear, perhaps the first since his exile from Heaven. The Demon enters her room with love and joy, where he is confronted by Tamara's Guardian Angel. Their standoff is brief, for the Demon turns aside the angel with a malicious grin, claiming Tamara as his prize because she has already sinned in her heart.

When Tamara asks the Demon what he wants from her, he tells her it is her beauty, and he confesses all of his malice and evil, telling her, "I only kill and never save." He promises to repent if she will yield to him. When she asks him why he pursued her, the Demon is only able to tell her that he felt as if he had desired her since the beginning of Creation. He professes to regret his loneliness and he expresses some sense of hope, perhaps even for reconciliation with God. He claims his great freedom and his power over puny mortals have come to mean nothing to him.

Tamara attempts to resist his seduction, but she thinks if she could persuade him to renounce his evil ways and to take a solemn oath, she could accept his love. The Demon swears an elaborate and apparently sincere oath rejecting his demonic life and insisting he desires only her love and his reconciliation with God. Holding out the promise of a life of pleasure and power beyond the transitory joys of Earth, the Demon appeals to her for her love, but when Tamara succumbs and allows him to kiss her, she gives out a single shriek and dies instantly.

The Aged Guardian, the cloister's old watchman, feels a premonition after midnight. He may be unconsciously aware both of the kiss and of Tamara's dying cry and moan, but when he listens he cannot actually hear anything but the wind. He crosses himself, prays silently, and continues on his dark rounds.

Tamara's beauty remains even in death. She is more richly attired at her elaborate funeral than she had ever been in life, and her lips retain a strange smile. Her grieving father builds a church high in the mountains as a memorial to her. When an angel begins to fly away with Tamara's sinful human soul, the Demon attempts to claim her for himself. Only then does Tamara's soul see the anger and hatred in the Demon, and she prays for protection. The angel informs the Demon that Tamara's soul has been severely tried and will be granted salvation. The arrogant but defeated Demon is left alone and hopeless, cursing love, humankind, and the world itself.

Thereafter, villagers claim that Prince Goudal's castle is haunted by a tragic ghost, but in the village life goes on as usual and nothing is left to tell succeeding generations of the old tragedy. Goudal's castle falls into disarray and becomes the haunt of spiders and serpents. High on a nearby mountain the church remains, but it is deserted and often beset by snowstorms. No pilgrims go that way, and the names of Goudal and Tamara are forgotten.

"The Story" by Ron McFarland

Critical Evaluation:

Critics and scholars who comment on Mikhail Lermontov's *The Demon* generally regard it as his best or most famous narrative poem, and they agree that it has been his most influential. It served as the source for Anton Rubinstein's opera, which premiered in 1875; as the inspiration for a series of paintings by Mikhail Vrubel; and as a model for several poems by Symbolist poet Aleksander Blok. Lermontov's demonic protagonist may have influenced as well such novels as Fyodor Dostoevski's *Idiot* (1868; *The Idiot*, 1887).

Commentators have focused considerable attention on precursors whose works might have influenced Lermontov's conception of the plot and themes of the poem and of the Demon as its main character. Among these influences, Romantic poet Lord Byron appears to have been the most important, as Lermontov had learned to read English to fully to appreciate his work. Moreover, his own biographers generally agree that Lermontov might have modeled his own behavior after the popular Byronic paradigm that features an alienated or socially outcast wanderer or exile who is inclined to be moody and temperamental, passionate, arrogant or aloof, disdainful of social convention, destructive (even self-destructive), and, despite these tempestuous psychological characteristics, deeply bored.

Alexander Pushkin established the so-called Byronic hero in Russian literature, particularly in the long-verse novel *Evgeny Onegin* (1825-1832, serial; 1833, book; *Eu-*

gene Onegin, 1881). Lermontov greatly admired Pushkin's work and wrote a poem critical of Czar Nicholas I's court after Pushkin was killed in a duel. Lermontov's provocative poem was widely praised, but the czar had him arrested and assigned to active duty in the Caucasus, where Russia was involved with ongoing warfare against the Muslim Georgians, Chechens, and Ossetians. Lermontov subsequently chose Caucasian settings for both *The Demon* and his renowned short novel, *Geroy nashego vremeni* (1839, serial; 1840, book; *A Hero of Our Time*, 1854).

Some commentators detect characteristics of Onegin in the Demon, but others perceive his origins in characters from Johann Wolfgang von Goethe's *Faust: Ein Fragment* (1790; *Faust: A Fragment*, 1980), Byron's *Cain: A Mystery* (pb. 1821) or some of his exotic Asian verse tales, Thomas Moore's *The Loves of the Angels* (1823), Alfred de Vigny's narrative poem *Eloa* (1824), and Charles Robert Maturin's gothic novel *Melmoth the Wanderer* (1820). Lermontov is known to have been familiar with all of these texts, but he appears to have had no direct knowledge of John Milton's *Paradise Lost* (1667, 1674). Some readers propose Milton's Satan as either a parallel or an antitypical character.

All of these approaches to *The Demon* might be described as extrinsic in nature; that is, they require some knowledge beyond the poem itself to explicate or interpret it. The same may be said of textual criticism, which has drawn considerable attention because the poem was drafted no fewer than eight times over a ten-year period (1829-1839), beginning when Lermontov was only fourteen or fifteen years old and ending just two years before his death at age twenty-seven in a duel in Pyatigorsk, a fashionable spa in the Caucasus. The final version of the poem circulated widely in manuscript form after Lermontov's death in 1841, but it was not published until 1855 (in Germany); it first appeared in Russia in 1859.

Interpretations of the poem tend to focus on the mysteriously ambiguous and elusive character of the protagonist. Why, for example, does the presumably evil Demon, who claims to be indifferent to the beauty of the natural world, believe he might be redeemed by the love of a beautiful, mortal woman? What, specifically, did he do to cause his exile from Heaven? Does the Demon know that his kiss will be fatal to Tamara? (In early versions of the poem the Demon intends to murder Tamara with his fatal kiss.) Readings that respond to such questions, and studies of Lermontov's imagery and other poetic techniques, regard such questions as "intrinsic"; that is, they deal primarily with aspects of the text itself, such as character, plot, structure, setting, and style (diction, syntax, meter, and use of imagery and figurative language).

What is the relationship, for example, between the narrator, who offers vivid images of the setting in the mountains of the Caucasus, and the Demon, who professes only scorn for the striking landscape, presumably because God had created it?

While Lermontov was working on an early draft of *The Demon*, he also wrote a short lyric called "My Demon" in response to a verse by Pushkin with the same title. Instead of denouncing the spirit of negation as Pushkin does in his work, Lermontov expresses his attraction to what he calls the sinister collection of evils. His Demon, as he first describes him, is a fierce being: "He scorns pure love; he rejects all prayers; he beholds blood indifferently." In a version of the poem written two years later, the Demon is less forbidding and violent. He has become more intimately bound to life, and in a sense he is a more direct representation of Lermontov himself: "The proud demon will not depart, as long as I live, from me." The dark side of the poet's personality taunts him with images of bliss and purity, but he presents these qualities as being wholly unattainable.

An autobiographical critic might see in the Demon of both the lyric and the long narrative poem some of Lermontov's personal demons: his rejection by various women; his rebellion against social convention, both political and religious; his struggle to assert personal freedom or selfhood (autonomy); his pessimistic and self-destructive disposition. Such a critic might also suggest that in portraying himself as the Demon, Lermontov wishes either to draw his readers' sympathy or to castigate himself for his own misdeeds and failures. Perhaps, also, Tamara's tragic death, even though it leads to her redemption and salvation, constitutes some form of retaliation against a would-be love. Such a reading might connect the doomed bridegroom, identified in some versions as Sinodal, with a romantic rival. Various critics have drawn a line of descent from the Demon to Pechorin, the protagonist of Lermontov's *A Hero of Our Time*; Pechorin is widely regarded as Lermontov's alter ego.

From a different interpretive perspective, however, such an approach to the poem misses the point entirely. Especially since the end of the twentieth century, scholars and critics have approached *The Demon* as a sort of metaphysical or ethical meditation or discourse on the problem of evil in the world and the relationship between God and humans. One critic argued that

> The question of the Demon's sincerity is crucial. If he is sincere in his desire to renounce evil but incapable of doing so, he is a tragic, even an heroic figure; if he perjured himself to win [Tamara], then he fully deserves the reconfirmation of God's sentence on him.

Another critic finds that the Demon "falls far short of any attempt to construct a truly evil being. Once an angel himself, and exiled for no stated reason, he is not a whole-hearted malefactor." Still another critic suggests the Demon is a post-Romantic character whose "morally amorphous" nature reflects a modern perception whereby the very uncertainty and ambiguity of his evil leaves it "more insidious and treacherous" than is the case when the nature of evil is codified by conventional religious traditions or ethical standards. One intriguing reading of the poem holds that Tamara is "knowingly" seduced and that "the poem's ethical center" shifts to her and, thereby, "to the reader, who is encouraged to identify with her" as she becomes "a full-fledged ethical agent who freely chooses love over doubt." Most commentators agree that her role had evolved considerably between the early and late manuscript versions of the poem.

Rejecting the premise that the poem centrally concerns ethical or metaphysical issues, some critics argue that *The Demon* focuses primarily on an "inner psychological conflict" particularly as it pertains to the themes of alienation and loss. With his protagonist, Lermontov "explores the universal human desire to find a place in the universe, to regain paradise lost"; specifically, the Demon, like Pechorin and perhaps like Lermontov himself, seeks to fill his feeling of emptiness with "the promise of erotic bliss," but in this effort he fails miserably, perhaps tragically.

Further Reading

Allen, Elizabeth Cheresh. *A Fallen Idol Is Still a God: Lermontov and the Quandaries of Cultural Transition.* Stanford, Calif.: Stanford University Press, 2006. A critical examination of Lermontov's writing, placing it within the context of his time and culture. Argues that he is a writer who defies categorization, straddling the line between Romanticism and realism, and sees the Demon as representing no clear idea of evil.

Davidson, Pamela. "The Muse and the Demon in the Poetry of Pushkin, Lermontov, and Blok." In *Russian Literature and Its Demons*, edited by Davidson. New York: Berghahn Books, 2000. Suggests that Lermontov explores "the demonic potential inherent in the creative process" in the poem; the Demon's seduction of Tamara "becomes a mirror image of the act of artistic creation," but ultimately demonic efforts at creation lead not to salvation or divine union, but to destruction.

Eikhenbaum, B. M. *Lermontov.* Translated by Ray Parrott and Harry Weber. Ann Arbor, Mich.: Ardis, 1981. Considers *The Demon* to be the last example of the "Russian lyrico-epic narrative poem." Offers a concise stylistic commentary on the poem's emotional-phonic qualities.

Garrard, John. *Mikhail Lermontov*. Boston: Twayne, 1982. Argues that in *The Demon*, Lermontov handles an important and complex topic "in an intellectually impoverished context" and, unlike other commentators, that the poem lacks a philosophy. Sees the characters, including the Demon, as insufficiently motivated and under-realized.

Golstein, Vladimir. *Lermontov's Narratives of Heroism*. Evanston, Ill.: Northwestern University Press, 1998. Focuses on the theme of heroism and the individual in Lermontov's works, including *The Demon*. Argues that the Demon, whose dominant feature is not so much "malice" as "indifference" or "boredom," attempts to deal with his alienation and loss of paradise through his erotic love for Tamara. One of the most perceptive commentaries on the poem.

Kelly, Laurence. *Lermontov: Tragedy in the Caucasus*. New York: George Braziller, 1977. Reprint. London: Tauris Parke, 2003. An autobiographical reading of the poem, seeing *The Demon* as embodying Lermontov's unhappy experiences with romantic love. Salvation through love is impossible for the Demon, as for other fictional Lermontov characters and for the author himself.

Powelstock, David. *Becoming Mikhail Lermontov: The Ironies of Romantic Individualism in Nicholas I's Russia*. Evanston, Ill.: Northwestern University Press, 2005. Posits that Lermontov had a coherent worldview, which Powelstock defines as "Romantic individualism," and demonstrates how this philosophy explains contradictions in the writer's life and works. Suggests that later revisions of the poem shifted the poem's ethical center from the Demon to Tamara and the poem's readers.

Pyman, Avril. "The Demon: The Mythopoetic World Model in the Art of Lermontov, Vrubel, Blok." In *Russian Literature and Its Demons*, edited by Pamela Davidson. New York: Berghahn Books, 2000. Comments on the relationships between Lermontov's poem and Mikhail Vrubel's sketches and paintings and Aleksander Blok's Symbolist poems. Some reference to Anton Rubenstein's opera.

Reid, Robert. "Lermontov's *Demon*: A Question of Identity." *Slavonic and East European Review* 60, no. 2 (1982): 189-210. Considers the polarization between humanistic and metaphysical readings. Notes that Tamara's beauty attracts the Demon because he confuses it with moral goodness; argues that natural beauty can persuade but not save or redeem. One of the most important approaches to the poem.

_____. "Lermontov's *The Demon*: Identity and Axiology." In *Russian Literature and Its Demons*, edited by Pamela Davidson. New York: Berghahn Books, 2000. Examines the philosophical (ontological and aesthetic) and ethical dimensions of the Demon and finds him "not a whole-hearted malefactor."

The Deptford Trilogy

Author: Robertson Davies (1913-1995)
First published: 1983: includes *Fifth Business*, 1970; *The Manticore*, 1972; *World of Wonders*, 1975
Type of work: Novels
Type of plot: Moral
Time of plot: 1908-1971
Locale: Canada, England, and Switzerland

Principal characters:
LEOLA CRUICKSHANK, a small-town beauty
MARY DEMPSTER, a minister's wife
PAUL DEMPSTER, her son, a magician with the stage name Magnus Eisengrim
LIESL NAEGELI, Eisengrim's lover and assistant
DUNSTAN RAMSAY, a schoolmaster
PERCY BOYD "BOY" STAUNTON, a wealthy lawyer
DAVID STAUNTON, Boy's son, a criminal lawyer
DR. JOHANNA VON HALLER, a Jungian analyst
WILLARD, a circus magician

The Story:

Fifth Business. Even as a child, Boy Staunton plays dirty. He puts a stone in the snowball he lobs at Dunstan Ramsay's back. His friend ducks, and the snowball hits Mary Dempster's head, throwing the minister's wife into premature labor. Paul Dempster weighs only three pounds at birth. He lives, but his mother is "soft in the head" ever after. The ten-year-old Dunstan knows that his fate is inextricably linked to that of Boy and the Dempsters. The snowball was aimed at him, and he feels guilty for having ducked it. He saves the stone as a reminder.

As he reaches puberty, Dunstan is tormented by desire for the town beauty, Leola. Ridden by guilt, he seeks escape in books on magic and fancies himself a magician. He performs tricks for young Paul, but he lacks dexterity. Dunstan's parents forbid him to visit the Dempsters after the young wife is caught in the arms of a tramp, on whom she says she took pity. On another occasion, Dunstan is severely reprimanded for bringing her home in a moment of panic when he should instead have called the doctor. He is, however, convinced that she worked a miracle when his brother came back to life.

Dunstan comes to think of Mrs. Dempster as a saint when he fights in France during World War I. He is hit by shrapnel and crawls to a ruined chapel, certain that he is dying. A bomb explodes nearby, lighting up the statue of a saint. It is Mrs. Dempster's face. The vision stays with him while he convalesces in England and returns to Canada. Back in Deptford, he learns that Mrs. Dempster has left town; her husband died in the swine flu epidemic, and her son ran away with a circus. Dunstan's parents are dead; his brother died in the war; and Boy, back from private school and a desk job in the army, has won Leola.

Dunstan leaves Deptford, takes a degree in history, and begins teaching at the private school Boy attended. One day, he meets the tramp who got Mrs. Dempster in trouble; the tramp, who became a minister to the homeless, credited Mrs. Dempster with having saved him. Dunstan takes summer vacations in Europe, where he studies saints' lives and writes books on saints and myths. At a circus one evening, he sees Paul, who becomes a great stage magician.

Boy and Leola raise two children, Caroline and David. Boy is egotistical and Leola, unhappy, attempts suicide. When she loses her will to live and dies, Boy remarries. Dunstan makes a small fortune on investments, thanks to Boy's advice, so he is able to maintain the aging and demented Mrs. Dempster in a nursing home and to continue his studies and travels. In Mexico, he again meets Paul, who is now performing under the name Magnus Eisengrim. Dunstan writes Eisengrim's "autobiography," a total fiction. Together with Eisengrim's lover, Liesl, he devises a fortune-telling act to be performed by the "brazen head of Friar Bacon" as the finale of Eisengrim's show on his first Canadian tour.

During the Toronto engagement, Dunstan arranges a dinner with Boy and Eisengrim. He reveals the fateful connection among the three of them and produces the stone that Boy

threw sixty years before. Boy and Eisengrim leave together. Later that night, Boy's car is fished out of Lake Ontario, with Boy at the steering wheel and the stone in his mouth. "Who killed Boy Staunton?" someone cries out during the "brazen head" act on the closing night. Everyone, the answer seemed to say.

The Manticore. It is David Staunton, Boy's son, who shouts the question. The occasion makes him realize that he is uncontrollably angry and needs psychological counseling. He flies to Zurich the next day and begins therapy with a Jungian analyst. He recounts the events that followed his father's death: his quarreling with his stepmother; his drinking too much; his fuming about the will. He cries for the first time in years. Despite an initial resistance to self-revelation, he launches an exploration of his personal history over the past forty years and recounts his childhood in Deptford and Toronto. He remembers his parents' estrangement; his first night of drinking after his mother's death; his one true love, which was broken off by his overly protective parents; his one sexual encounter, which his father arranged for him behind his back. He tells of his legal studies in Oxford, his practice of criminal law, his father's remarriage, their growing separation. The analysis continues three times a week for the next year, and Dr. von Haller plays many roles as David projects one archetypal image after another onto her. She becomes the Shadow, the Friend, the Anima, and he begins to understand his inner cast of characters. Before the Christmas holiday, she says he is ready for the second stage of analysis, which will move into the transpersonal realm.

When David shouted the question, Dunstan had a heart attack. Liesl took him to a hospital, then disappeared. When Dunstan hears from her next, she is at her castle in Switzerland, where she invites him to join her and Eisengrim. He quits his teaching job and sorts out his thoughts in a long letter to his former headmaster. He becomes a permanent guest at the castle. When David joins them for Christmas, they are able to cast light on the words that the "brazen head" spoke in answer to his question. Liesl takes David to an ancient cave where bears were once worshiped. David knows he will continue his quest, whether in analysis or on his own.

World of Wonders. Liesl's castle becomes the scene for a television documentary on a nineteenth century magician, whose show Eisengrim is to re-create. During the filming, Eisengrim agrees to tell his real life story as the subtext for the documentary. He tells of Dunstan's first lessons in magic, of his abduction by a magician named Willard, and of his work in a traveling circus called the World of Wonders. He reveals the backstage life of a circus troupe and tells of Willard's sad decline into drug addiction and total dependence.

He tells of his first magic shows, his work in the theater in England and Canada, and his liaison with Liesl.

The film crew moves to London for final shots, and the three friends gather in Eisengrim's bed at the Savoy for a final discussion. Dunstan still wants to understand the answer that Liesl spoke through the "brazen head" after David shouted his question. Eisengrim explains to Dunstan, more fully than he did to David, exactly what happened on the last night of Boy's life. Boy confessed that he dreaded the political office that he long sought and finally won. Eisengrim remarked that he could always resign, not realizing that Boy's great hero was the prince who became Edward VIII and was forced to abdicate in 1936. He recognized the suicidal thoughts that crossed Boy's mind and did not try to stop them.

Critical Evaluation:

With *The Deptford Trilogy*, Robertson Davies went from being a respected essayist and playwright in his native Canada to an internationally acclaimed writer of moral fiction. In an earlier trilogy of novels, *The Salterton Trilogy* (1951-1958), Davies demonstrated a talent for social satire. After *The Deptford Trilogy*, which is generally considered his masterpiece, he went on to write *The Cornish Trilogy* (1981-1988).

The first novel in *The Deptford Trilogy*, *Fifth Business*, is Dunstan's long letter to his former headmaster, in which he explains how he came to understand his role in life. *The Manticore* is David's story of how he came into analysis, followed by his journal during analysis and his diary entries during the holiday at Liesl's castle. *World of Wonders* is Eisengrim's life story as told to the film director and recorded in Dunstan's notes. Each novel stands on its own. Indeed, Davies remarked that he did not plan the second novel until the first was in print, or the third novel until the second was finished. Nevertheless, each adds to the others and, taken together, the novels show three sides of a story begun with the spiteful throw of a snowball.

Each narrator has a story he needs to tell. Dunstan needs to establish that he is a serious scholar and not an old duffer; David, that he is a skilled lawyer and a family leader, not just an alcoholic; and Eisengrim, that he is a consummate artist as well as a dexterous deceiver. Each man is an egotist, and each has a grievance against that great egotist Boy Staunton: He was a village bully who caused a woman to go into labor and robbed her son of eighty paradisiacal days in the womb; a faithless friend; and an overbearing father. Boy also has a story to tell, but he tells his to only one person in the hour before his abdication from life.

"Fifth business" is a theater term for the character who is neither hero nor heroine, confidant nor villain, but nevertheless essential to the resolution of the dramatic plot. Late in life, Dunstan discovers that the term describes him, and he comes to realize that his accusations propelled Boy toward suicide. However, his professional studies of history and myth prepare him to recognize his own myth.

The manticore is a mythological beast with the head of a man, the body of a lion, and the tail of a scorpion. David dreams of a manticore held on leash by a Sibyl. The manticore has his face and realizes that he needs a female guide. He first thinks that Dr. von Haller will be the guide, but it is with Liesl as his guide that he descends to the depths of human consciousness. David learned to cross-examine witnesses before he met the archetypal figures within himself, but depth psychology balances his legal reasoning with a better understanding of himself.

The World of Wonders is not only the circus that Paul ran off with but also the phantasmagoria that he creates. His stage name, which Liesl suggests, means "Great Iron Hard One"; it shows his psychological affinity with the wolf in the Grimm Brothers' fairy tales, who is often called *Eisengrim*. When he takes on the name, he ceases to be the circus performer or theatrical stuntman and becomes his real self.

Like David, Dunstan and Liesl are interested in Jungian psychology. Jung's typology of personality functions helps to explain the dynamics of character interactions in the trilogy. David learns that he is primarily a thinking type, whereas Dunstan, the scholar, discovers that he is driven by feeling, including a lifelong feeling of resentment toward Boy. Eisengrim is a sensing type, very aware of the external world, and Liesl is deeply intuitive. These are their dominant functions, but all of them become more balanced as they come to understand their life stories. It is Boy who is always a boy in some sense, always attached to a romantic dream and never quite able to accept what he becomes. He abdicates; the others find new life.

Dunstan says he is "reborn" when he survives his war wounds under the watchful eye of his saint. Similarly, David is reborn when he emerges from the cave in the Alps, and Paul is reborn when he becomes Eisengrim. Those who are reborn have a sense of time outside time, which is one way of defining the mythic time of depth psychology. The "brazen head" begins by evoking time present and time past, and suggesting that its pronouncements are timeless and belong to a world when "Time is past." This is another way of defining mythic time.

The three novels have a total of twelve chapters. Such classical epics as Vergil's *Aeneid* (c. 29-19 B.C.E.) were also written in twelve books or in multiples of twelve. This may not be a complete coincidence, for Liesl and the other characters insist that a life of epic heroism is still possible. The classical epic has a mythic pattern that Dunstan finds in the saints' lives he studies and in the history he teaches. The sixth book of the *Aeneid* is a descent into the underworld in search of oracular knowledge. Similarly, the sixth chapter in Davies' trilogy concerns Boy's death, David's desperate question, and Liesl's Sibylline answer through the "brazen head." The great work of the epic hero is to return from the underworld and to act on the oracular knowledge. Dunstan does this when he returns from war, Eisengrim when he emerges from hard work inside an automaton, and David when he breaks out of his long neurosis.

Davies' first readers in Canada recognized thinly disguised places and thought they recognized people, too. Readers who know of the author's colorful life story may be tempted to see autobiographical touches in the trilogy, for each of the three narrators bears a resemblance to some aspect of Davies. Dunstan Ramsay has the same initials as Robertson Davies, though in reverse, and shares Davies' teaching profession and his connection to a wealthy family. David Staunton, who is known to his friends as Davey, comes to share Davies' interest in Jungian psychology. Magnus Eisengrim, whose initials spell "me," shares Davies' interest in theater and illusion. *Fifth Business* appeared after the death of the author's father, and all the novels are concerned with fathers and sons. Readers would do well, however, to remember what Eisengrim says to David about his autobiography: It does not give the facts of his life, but it comes close to the spiritual reality. Always the master of illusion, Davies would point out that his true story is in his fiction.

Thomas Willard

Further Reading

Cameron, Elspeth, ed. *Robertson Davies: An Appreciation.* Peterborough, Ont.: Broadview Press, 1991. Provides an interview with Davies and seventeen essays, some by such Canadian authors as John Kenneth Galbraith and Joyce Carol Oates.

Chorney, Tatjana Takseva. "The Myth and Magic of a Textual Truth and/or a Metaphorical Reading of *The Deptford Trilogy*." In *Robertson Davies: A Mingling of Contrarieties*, edited by Camille R. La Bossière and Linda Morra. Ottawa, Ont.: University of Ottawa Press, 2001. An in-depth interpretation, in which Chorney applies Davies' ideas about the structure and themes of his novels, about his readers, and about magic and text to examine the trilogy.

Davis, J. Madison, ed. *Conversations with Robertson Davies.* Jackson: University Press of Mississippi, 1989. More than two dozen interviews with Davies, originally published in newspapers and magazines or broadcast on radio and television. Includes some reference to all the Deptford novels. Also provides a general introduction, a list of Davies' books, a chronology of his life, and a helpful index.

Grant, Judith Skelton. *Robertson Davies: Man of Myth.* New York: Viking, 1994. The authorized biography, covering all but the last year of Davies' life. Provides critical commentary on Davies' novels as well as information on his dealings with publishers.

Lawrence, Robert G., and Samuel L. Macey, eds. *Studies in Robertson Davies' "Deptford Trilogy."* Victoria, B.C.: English Literary Studies, University of Victoria, 1980. Eight essays on Davies' craft that discuss the author's interest in folklore, psychology, and theater. Davies' introductory essay, "*The Deptford Trilogy* in Retrospect," gives a valuable account of the trilogy's genesis.

Monk, Patricia. *The Smaller Infinity: The Jungian Self in the Novels of Robertson Davies.* Toronto, Ont.: University of Toronto Press, 1982. Discusses Davies' knowledge of psychology, specifically that of Carl Jung. Contains a separate chapter on each novel in the trilogy, a bibliography, and an index.

Peterman, Michael. *Robertson Davies.* Boston: Twayne, 1986. The first book-length study of Davies' life and work. Includes a long chapter on the trilogy.

Ross, Val. *Robertson Davies: A Portrait in Mosaic.* Toronto, Ont.: McClelland & Stewart, 2008. Ross compiled recollections of Davies from about one hundred people, including family members, academic colleagues, other writers, Hollywood directors, and his barber. Their combined comments create a portrait of Davies the man and the writer.

Descent into Hell

Author: Charles Williams (1886-1945)
First published: 1937
Type of work: Novel
Type of plot: Moral
Time of plot: June and July in the 1930's
Locale: Battle Hill, near London

Principal characters:
PAULINE ANSTRUTHER, an orphaned woman in her twenties
MARGARET ANSTRUTHER, her grandmother
PETER STANHOPE, an eminent poet
LAWRENCE WENTWORTH, a military historian
ADELA HUNT, an aspiring actress
HUGH PRESCOTT, her suitor
MRS. LILY SAMMILE, a neighbor
MRS. PARRY, a civic leader engaged in directing a play

The Story:

In the suburb of Battle Hill, Peter Stanhope is involved in the production of his verse drama. He is an eminent poet and inhabitant of the Manor House, which belonged to his family before the housing estate was built. Under the leadership of the capable Mrs. Parry, a group of his neighbors has the privilege of performing his new play in his garden, but only one of them, Pauline Anstruther, even remotely grasps the spiritual significance of his pastoral fantasy. Pauline's sensibility is so quickened by the nuances of his verse that she confides to him the terror that haunted her for years: the recurrent appearance of her doppelgänger.

Stanhope explains to her the principle of substitution: One person, through love, can assume the burden of another so that the sufferer is relieved. When Pauline becomes willing to accept his offer to bear her burden, she discovers that she is no longer tortured by her own problem. Instead, she is given the opportunity to bear someone else's burden of fear. Her growth in grace influences everything around her.

As the rehearsals for the play proceed, Pauline's role as leader of the chorus is paralleled by her role in the supernatural drama that is taking place concurrently in Battle Hill. The spiritual energy released through the play sets in motion a series of events that transcends ordinary time, affecting a number of other inhabitants of the suburb. The housing estate, built in the 1920's, took its name from the hill, which was a site for battles from the time of the ancient Britons to the period of the Tudors. While the estate was being built, the timeless "magnetism of death," still powerful on the Hill (as the suburb was usually called), touched a despairing unskilled laborer, who hanged himself on the scaffolding of an unfinished house. His restless spirit still inhabits the area, unrecognized by the occupant of the finished house, Lawrence Wentworth, a noted military historian and adviser to the producer of the play. A middle-aged bachelor, Wentworth develops a secret passion for pretty, conceited Adela Hunt, who is the heroine in the play and the girlfriend of the leading man, Hugh Prescott. Wentworth's jealousy is so consuming that he is destroying himself as surely as the suicide did. Pauline's grandmother, Mrs. Anstruther, is dying, but her death is the natural fulfillment of a well-spent life. Shortly before she dies, she is visited by an unpleasantly ingratiating and vaguely sinister neighbor, Mrs. Lily Sammile, who appears unexpectedly at several crises in the novel.

Pauline's love for her grandmother is dutiful but detached during the years since her parents' death. She lives in Mrs. Anstruther's house as a dependent and companion. It is not until Stanhope relieves her of her fear that Pauline can talk to her grandmother about it and appreciate the depth of the old woman's love. Mrs. Anstruther initiates Pauline further into the doctrine of substituted love by explaining that she can be called upon to bear the pain of their ancestor, John Struther, whose martyrdom by fire is well-known family history.

As Mrs. Anstruther approaches the limits of mortality, she can see the face of the suicide as he looks into her window during his ceaseless wandering. Soon she tells Pauline that Pauline has to go out in the middle of the night because someone needs her near Wentworth's. Pauline thinks that Mrs. Anstruther's mind is wandering, but somehow Pauline also knows that she has to go. She discovers she no longer fears the dark, and she sees the dead man in ordinary mortal form. He asks the way to London, gently refuses her offer to pay his fare, and sets off to walk to the city. As she watches him, his form is transmuted into the agonized body of her ancestor, and she is given the opportunity of bearing his burden by enduring the fire in a mystical experience of real pain. This happens during the night between the dress rehearsal and the first performance of the play. Mrs. Anstruther dies five minutes after Pauline gets home, but the death does not keep Pauline from acting in the play, as the producer feared. Love gives Pauline a new perspective on time and mortality.

As a counterpoint to Pauline's experience throughout the novel, Wentworth's love operates negatively because it focuses on himself. His passion is for his idea of Adela rather than for the real person, and his jealousy of Prescott is so powerful that it creates a tangible image of the woman who, he imagines, visits him with increasing frequency and becomes his mistress. In the bedroom where the suicide hangs himself, Wentworth's reason is destroyed by his fantasies of false love. The crisis of his descent into hell is reached on the day of the dress rehearsal, when Mrs. Parry consults him, as a military historian, on a detail in the costumes of the guards. Wentworth knows that they are wrong and that he can arrange for them to be altered. He is so preoccupied with his erotic experience, however, that he cannot be bothered and tells an expedient lie instead of the truth. This sacrifice of the historian's integrity confirms the loss of his soul. The next day his seat at the play is empty. On the afternoon of the performance, there is an unnatural stillness in the atmosphere, like the calm before a storm. Some of the cast complains of the heat, but the play proceeds successfully, and the only disturbance is Mrs. Sammile's fainting at the end. After that, a number of residents of the Hill feel unwell, but life proceeds normally. Mrs. Anstruther is buried. Pauline makes plans to move into London and take a job.

A few days after the funeral, Adela and Prescott walk and carry on a mild argument that reveals the difference between them. Prescott's love for Adela is consistent with his habit of seeing life clearly, while Adela's love for him is an aspect of her desire to manipulate others. As their walk takes them near the cemetery, they meet Mrs. Sammile. While they talk to her, they become transfixed by the sight of the graves opening. Mrs. Sammile shrieks and disappears into a small shed at the edge of the cemetery. Adela screams and starts running, pursued by Prescott, shouting that the illusion is caused by the wind blowing up loose earth on the graves. His mind clears rapidly, and, as it does his love fades, so that he gives up the pursuit.

Adela's wild flight leads her to the house of the man who she knows idolizes her. When she looks through the window, she sees the image of herself that his diseased imagination creates, and she collapses in terror. Found by a policeman and taken home, she awakens delirious with the impression that she forgot her part in the play, a key passage about perception and love. When Pauline calls to see her, Adela insists that Pauline has to find Mrs. Sammile in the shed by the cemetery, to give her Adela's part and thus make her well. Pauline, sensing that Mrs. Sammile is, in fact, Lilith, the image of

false love, tries to offer Adela her own help in recovering her part, but she finds that only by promising to look for the old woman can she ease Adela's tortured spirit.

The climax of love's triumph over death in the novel comes when Pauline goes, as she had previously gone out into the night at the request of her dying grandmother, to confront Mrs. Sammile in the cemetery shed. Recognizing her as the illusion rather than the reality of love, Pauline rejects her promises of rewards with a laugh of pure contented joy. Lilith dissolves into the dust and rubble of the old unused shed, which collapses from Pauline's push on the door. In attempting to bear Adela's burden, Pauline thus finds the completion of her own part in the drama of Battle Hill and is ready to leave for London. Seen off on the train by Stanhope, who says his own role is to comfort the many people in the community who are ill, she looks forward with joy to her new life in the city. Wentworth travels on the same train but refuses her company and goes in a daze to a historian's dinner at which his lifelong rival is honored. Wentworth sinks into complete insensibility.

Critical Evaluation:

The surrealistic effect of supernatural events taking place in a natural setting is the keynote of Charles Williams's narrative treatment of spiritual experience. Ordinary life is revealed as an image of a deeper reality. The play in which all the characters are involved becomes an image of life itself in which each person must perfect his or her own role in harmony with others. The setting of Battle Hill suggests the hill of Golgotha, and Lily Sammile's lair is revealed to Pauline as an aspect of Gomorrah. For Lawrence Wentworth, the journey into the city becomes the way to Gomorrah; but Pauline's destination is the Eternal City. She tells Peter Stanhope that it seems funny to be discussing the times of trains to the new Jerusalem, but for the poet the interdependence of the temporal and the eternal is fully assimilated fact.

The characterization, like the plot, is determined by the theme. Only Pauline Anstruther and Wentworth, who experience salvation and damnation respectively, are fully delineated. The other characters are sketched with only enough detail to give them substance as examples of different aspects of love. Stanhope and Mrs. Anstruther are seen only in relation to Pauline, Adela Hunt primarily in contrast to Pauline, and Hugh Prescott in contrast to Wentworth. Williams never falls into the error often attributed to John Milton and other authors of making his diabolical characters more attractive than the good ones. Mrs. Sammile is described with a few telling details that make her seem real, slightly pathetic, and obscurely repulsive. Stanhope, in contrast, expresses his sanctity through an easy kindliness and sense of humor. The essence of goodness is seen as a quality of joy that permeates the lives of those who accept it in love. This joy is reflected not only in the characters but in the style, taking the form of wry humor in the descriptions of the play rehearsals and almost poetic rhapsody in the passages of mystical experience. The great variety in style and mood emphasizes Williams's conviction, exemplified in the plot, that reality in human life exists in multiple planes of time and space.

Of Williams's eight novels, his *Descent into Hell* contains his most humane dramatization of his vision of life and the best artistic integration of fictional elements. His indebtedness to visionary poets such as Dante Alighieri, William Wordsworth, Coventry Patmore, and his Christian colleagues (including C. S. Lewis and J. R. R. Tolkien) among the literary group called the Inklings cannot be overstated. As Williams explained it, his novels are sequels, each building upon themes established early in his writing career. The purpose of his fiction is to communicate his uniquely personal Christian vision of the good life. One may investigate, then, the extent to which *Descent into Hell* achieves Williams's purpose, and the extent to which the novel achieves his purpose without the reader having to refer to Williams's influences.

The difficulty of such an assessment is reflected in the frustration sometimes expressed about the genre of Williams's novels. His vision is so personal that his novels may be considered a genre unto themselves, without relatives within the literary tradition. A hybrid genre—supernatural horror/thriller—has been suggested for Williams's work and has gained some acceptance. Williams is generally classified as a fantasy fiction writer, but no doubt he considered his supernatural characters and settings the least fictional aspect of his work. The suburban ordinariness of the characters of *Descent into Hell* seems to exclude this work from the horror/thriller category into which Williams's other novels may be placed. A solution to the problem of how to categorize *Descent into Hell* may lie in Williams's devotion to Arthurian legend and to medieval literary forms, among which the exemplum, or story illustrative of a point in a sermon, acts as a model for *Descent into Hell*. Williams wrote in order to convey his main theme of "co-inherence"—mutual Christian charity. His primary symbol for this theme is the City.

In his earlier novels, fictional elements of plot and character are subordinate, sacrificed to theological and thematic considerations and a sometimes undisciplined plethora of supportive images. Over time and with practice, Williams improved his control over the complex narrative form of the novel. The artistic flaws of his early novels (melodramatic and oversimplified plots and flat, stereotypical characterizations), all the result of his eagerness to present his vision, are less apparent. In *Descent into Hell* and subsequent works, plot and theme merge and complement each other, and the characters, still recognizable as Williams's types, are more fully realized and empathetic—including even the diabolical ones such as Lily Sammile.

What is central in all of Williams's work, and comes to a convincing narrative unity in *Descent into Hell*, is his fundamental theme, Christian co-inherence. Co-inherence is the interdependent relation of believers who care for and willingly help one another; these constitute the Body of Christ, the major image of which is the City—the natural city, London, and the supernatural City of God. Pauline's choice of city life is that of Christian life, present in *Descent into Hell* as "the doctrine of substituted love," based on the Gospel command, "Bear ye one another's burdens." The puzzlement that readers may experience when confronted by such terms is further complicated by Williams's repeated theme, the theology of romantic love. For Williams, this means that marriage is the primary mode of co-inherence. To Williams, sexual love stands for divine love, a doctrine that appears, from the point of view of Augustinian Christianity, eccentric at best. Christian life is traditionally a matter not of sexual joy, which is short-lived even in marriage, but of restraint over bodily claims. In *Descent into Hell*, Pauline is not concerned with eros but with caritas, or affection between teacher and student—Stanhope and herself. Ironically, Williams's treatment of marriage is a reason for the success and credibility of *Descent into Hell*—Williams succeeds when he departs from his typical plot.

The poet T. S. Eliot considered Williams's novels entertaining reading even if a person did not want to explore deep significance in them. The characters of *Descent into Hell* are believable enough so that Eliot's observation holds true. It is informative to consult Williams's nonfiction work, such as *The Figure of Beatrice* (1943), for definition of the visionary experience of love, or *The Descent of the Dove* (1939), a history of the Holy Spirit in the Church, for clarification of Williams's doctrine of co-inherence. Pauline's journey of enlightenment and her involvement with the other characters in Stanhope's play-within-the-novel, the spectators and actors, and the author Stanhope himself, are, however, interesting and enjoyable by themselves, without investigation of the ideas behind them. The lessons about true and false goals are thought-provoking, but Williams is never preachy in presenting his Christian vision. He allows it to speak for itself, as it can through the characters, who are involved in ordinary activities that are nevertheless suspenseful and engaging.

Not all Christians agree that Williams's main themes are correct or orthodox. Some traditionalists say that eros and agape are irreconcilable, but if present investigations into the role of the body in redemption proceed as it now seems they will for some decades to come, Williams's identification of physical and divine love in the setting of Christian marriage, or perhaps even in friendship, may be prophetic. In any case, Williams's reputation in the future will hinge on the relevance of his themes, which in turn depend on the progress and direction of Christianity more than on the greatness of his fiction. Williams's greatest strengths are the force of his imagination and the clarity of his vision. His fiction meets the needs of his themes, and that is all it needs to do.

"Critical Evaluation" by Diane Brotemarkle

Further Reading

Ashenden, Gavin. *Charles Williams: Alchemy and Integration*. Kent, Ohio: Kent State University Press, 2008. Examines the influence of Williams's interest in neo-Rosicrucianism on his novels and poetry.

Bleiler, Everett F. *The Guide to Supernatural Fiction*. Kent, Ohio: Kent State University Press, 1983. The treatment of Williams's novels is brief (pages 532 to 534), but it places them in the context of the fantasy genre.

Cavaliero, Glen. *Charles Williams: Poet of Theology*. New York: Macmillan, 1983. Explains influences on Williams and contains excellent descriptions of Williams's originality. Pages 78 to 90 provide interpretative commentary on *Descent into Hell*.

Dunning, Stephen M. *The Crisis and the Quest: A Kierkegaardian Reading of Charles Williams*. Carlisle, Cumbria, England: Paternoster Press, 2000. Uses the philosophy of Søren Kierkegaard to analyze the crisis between Christianity and hermiticism in Williams's work and to chronicle his attempts at resolution.

Fredrick, Candice, and Sam McBride. "Women as Mythic Icons: Williams and Tolkien." In *Women Among the Inklings: Gender, C. S. Lewis, J. R. R. Tolkien, and Charles Williams*. Westport, Conn.: Greenwood Press, 2001. Williams and the other two authors were members of the Inklings, a group of male intellectuals that met at Oxford during the 1930's and 1940's. This book examines the role of women in the three authors' lives, their attitudes toward women, and the depiction of women in their work.

Hadfield, Alice Mary. *Charles Williams: An Exploration of His Life and Work*. New York: Oxford University Press, 1983. A critical biography by Williams's colleague at Oxford University Press. Hadfield understood Williams's creative intentions and was a trusted confidant in his circle of family and friends.

Reilly, R. J. *Romantic Religion: A Study of Barfield, Lewis, Williams, and Tolkien*. Athens: University of Georgia Press, 1971. Reprint. Great Barrington, Mass.: Lindisfarne, 2007. Examines the theological and philosophical ideas of a group of writers and intellectuals now known as the Oxford Christians. Devotes a chapter to Williams.

Shideler, Mary McDermott. *The Theology of Romantic Love: A Study in the Writings of Charles Williams*. Grand Rapids, Mich.: Wm. B. Eerdmans, 1966. An indispensable study of Williams's central theological ideas and recurring symbolism.

The Descent of Man

Author: Charles Darwin (1809-1882)
First published: 1871
Type of work: Science

The firestorm of controversy that followed the publication of *On the Origin of Species by Means of Natural Selection* (1859) had died down considerably by the time Darwin decided to publish his book about the origin of the human species. Consistent with his meticulously detailed analysis of the origin of species within the animal kingdom, Darwin explains in *The Descent of Man* how the human animal, too, evolved from lower forms. The impact of his pronouncement was somewhat blunted on his contemporaries because many assumed these conclusions after reading the *On the Origin of the Species*; the famous argument between Thomas Huxley and Bishop Wilberforce, in which the latter vehemently denied that his family tree included any apes or monkeys, took place a decade before Darwin dared to publish his findings about human genealogy. Nevertheless, until Darwin spoke, lesser luminaries could be dismissed; once the great biologist made it clear that he held no privileged place for humankind in the evolutionary process, the rift between scientific and religious explanations for the creation was complete.

The chief scientific significance of Darwin's work lies in his insistence on the prominence of sexual selection in determining human evolution. Important for the history of ideas, however, is Darwin's insistence that no special privilege should be accorded to humanity's "moral sense." He insists that the development of moral qualities in human beings is simply a part of the normal process of evolution. In his system, there is no need for a God who creates the human soul or speaks directly to humankind to explain how to live. In the twentieth and twenty-first centuries, the implications of *The Descent of Man* proved to be more troubling for theologians than for scientists.

Problems beset Darwin when he turned from his brilliant biological study of 1859 to the more particular analysis of the relation of humanity to the natural world. These problems are immediately seen in the organization of Darwin's argument: More than two-thirds of the book is an exhaustive discussion of sexual selection. The book may lack the inspiration of *On the Origin of Species*, but in its summary and evaluation of the anthropological thought after the publication of that earlier masterpiece, *The Descent of Man* is one of the most important books of the nineteenth century.

In his introduction Darwin says that he plans to consider three things: whether people descended from some preexisting form, how they developed if indeed they did so descend, and what value the differences between races have to such a development. He draws evidence of the descent of the human species from his vast knowledge of medicine and biology. That people share bodily structure, embryonic development, and rudimentary organs with other mammals seems to him to be evidence enough for asserting a common ancestry. Since anthropologists and paleontologists had not at that time discovered significant relics of prehistoric human life, Darwin's affirmation of the descent of humanity is based on logic; thus he amasses an almost overwhelming number of analogies to strengthen his case. These analogies enable him to trace the development of humanity from lower animals, but in order to do so he must assume a definition of humanity. Darwin maintains that humanity's uniqueness is not due to any one characteristic but to a combination of many: upright position, acquisition of language and tools, a delicate and free hand, and superior mental powers. In the possession of these traits humanity is different only in degree. In fact, Darwin musters evidence to show that animals have curiosity, imagination,

attention, and reason, attributes that earlier philosophers thought set people apart from the rest of the animal world.

Writing as a biologist, not as a moral philosopher or as a theologian, Darwin does not try to consider the implications that his theory has for the various religious and philosophical explanations for the origin of the human race—be they that man was made from clay and woman from a rib, or that the human form sprang from God's forehead. The single attribute that separates humanity from the rest of the animal world, Darwin thinks, is moral sense. Moral sense, the offspring of conscience, is the result of an evolutionary process; conscience came to the human race from a struggle between duty (sympathy and the social instincts) and desire (the urge for complete freedom). The belief in God also evolved, originating in dreams and developing through "spiritual agencies" into gods. It is this application, a logical outcome of Darwin's theories, that horrified both conservative Christians and idealistic philosophers, for the theory completely eliminated the validity of revelation or of supramundane enlightenment.

Darwin concentrates on the rise of civilization from savagery. Natural selection and the struggle for survival advanced the intellectual powers so that the history of human institutions is the history of the evolution of the intelligence. As tribes grew stronger, the members learned to perceive the consequences of their actions, thereby developing moral sense. Then, as people became more and more aware of their moral sense, advanced civilizations with sophisticated religions and technologies were able to develop.

This discussion of the rise of civilization brings Darwin to the differences between races. Because individual members of different races can be mated so as to form fertile offspring and because the similarities between races far outnumber the differences, Darwin assumes that races are subsets of the one species. Furthermore, Darwin discards the hypotheses that each race descended from a primal pair, that the racial differences were caused by the conditions of life, and that the races evolved independently. The only theory that can explain the differences between races is sexual selection. The question of sexual selection, necessary to prove his assumption about race, leads Darwin into the argument that fills two-thirds of his book.

In *On the Origin of Species*, Darwin bases his theory of evolution primarily on natural selection or the struggle for survival. In other words, a slight modification in an animal's structure might allow it to survive whereas another animal that lacked this modification would die. Existence, then, is a continual warfare in which the animal with the slight advantage wins. In *The Descent of Man* Darwin considerably modifies his view of nature by analyzing sexual selection, a different kind of biological warfare. When animals have their sexes separated, the male and female organs of reproduction differ; these are primary sexual characteristics. There are other differences, however, not directly connected with the act of reproduction, and these are secondary sexual characteristics. Usually the males have the most pronounced secondary sexual characteristics (for example, the brilliant plumage of many male birds); the males acquire these characteristics not from being better fitted for existence (natural selection) but from having gained advantage over other males and having transmitted their advantages to male offspring. There are usually more males than females, so that there is a struggle among males for the possession of the female; hence the female has the opportunity of selecting one out of several males. The strongest females have first choice among the males; therefore, the secondary sexual characteristics that pass through the strongest male and female have the most chance of outnumbering those characteristics that pass through weaker partners. In this way, the dominant characteristics are also the strongest. The more active the rivalry among the males, the more pronounced will be the variations between male and female.

Basing his analysis of the animal world upon these principles, Darwin begins with the lower classes of the animal kingdom. In the lowest classes these characteristics are absent because most often the sexes are joined in the same individual, but in the subkingdom of the Arthropoda undoubtable examples of secondary sexual characteristics appear. Darwin presents his most convincing case, however, in his long discussions on insects and birds. In both of these subkingdoms the characteristics are so clearly noticeable that Darwin accumulates material until he overwhelms his readers. Readers are presented with so much detailed information that they are willing to accept the evidence submitted, and the conclusions the evidence indicates, before Darwin applies his conclusions to humanity.

The secondary sexual characteristics of humanity are more complex than those of birds or of insects because humanity is more complex, but this is a difference only in degree. The adult male, for example, has a beard and hairiness of the body (although there is wide variation among tribes or races); he loves to fight and has greater endurance and strength than the female. As a result of his love of battle, the male delights in competition and develops his intellect more than woman, who is less selfish. Having noted a few of these characteristics, Darwin asks how they came to be. Because men vied with one another for the woman, the choice of the woman led to certain secondary sexual characteristics. For example, racial differences, he theorizes, are the result of ancient concepts of beauty; the remote ancestors of the African race preferred women who were dark-skinned and flat-nosed. Thus, Darwin is able to describe the differences among races without violating his basic theory of the descent of humanity from lower forms of life.

Darwin anxiously awaited the reaction to the publication of *The Descent of Man* and was surprised when he discovered that people were interested but not shocked. In fact, the book was anticlimactic. The disturbance caused by *On the Origin of Species* was calmed and was not stirred up again, and *The Descent of Man* became a book primarily for biologists.

Further Reading

Clark, Ronald W. *The Survival of Charles Darwin: A Biography of a Man and an Idea.* New York: Random House, 1984. Comprehensive and very readable biography that gives background on the conception, composition, and publication of *The Descent of Man.* Includes notes, bibliography, and index.

Dawson, Gowan. *Darwin, Literature, and Victorian Respectability.* New York: Cambridge University Press, 2007. Despite Darwin's adherence to Victorian standards of respectability, his works were condemned as obscene and he was accused of encouraging sexual impropriety and unrespectable free-thinking. Dawson's book describes the controversy over his ideas, making numerous references to *The Descent of Man,* which are listed in the index.

Desmond, Adrian, and James Moore. *Darwin: The Life of a Tormented Evolutionist.* New York: Warner Books, 1991. Chronicles Darwin's controversial life; focuses on the critical reception of *The Descent of Man* within his circle of friends and colleagues and on the business concerns of publishing the book.

_____. *Darwin's Sacred Cause: How a Hatred of Slavery Shaped Darwin's Views on Human Evolution.* Boston: Houghton Mifflin Harcourt, 2009. Describes how Darwin's abolitionism was the inspiration for his theories of evolution. Chronicles his family's antislavery activism and the genesis of his belief in a common human heritage.

Francis, Keith A. *Charles Darwin and "The Origin of Species."* Westport, Conn.: Greenwood Press, 2007. The book's title is misleading because *On the Origin of Species* is not the sole focus of Francis's narrative. He also describes how Darwin reached the conclusions set forth in *The Descent of Man,* tracing Darwin's early years at Cambridge University, his voyage on the *Beagle,* and his subsequent research about natural and sexual selection.

Ghiselin, Michael T. *The Triumph of the Darwinian Method.* Berkeley: University of California Press, 1969. Explores the centrality of *The Descent of Man* to Darwin's thought and, in turn, the centrality of the book's chief theory, sexual selection, to the theory of evolution. Also examines Darwin's methodology.

Gruber, Howard E. *Darwin on Man: A Psychological Study of Scientific Creativity.* 2d ed. Chicago: University of Chicago Press, 1981. Gruber traces the development of Darwin's thinking and his intentionally delayed application of his theories to humanity. Analyzes the central ideas of *The Descent of Man.*

Hull, David L. *Darwin and His Critics: The Reception of Darwin's Theory of Evolution by the Scientific Community.* Cambridge, Mass.: Harvard University Press, 1973. Introductory discussion of Darwin's inductive methods and such arcane topics as teleology and the empiricist-rationalist dichotomy. Hull includes letters and reviews from Darwin's contemporaries.

Desert

Author: J. M. G. Le Clézio (1940-   )
First published: Désert, 1980 (English translation, 2009)
Type of work: Novel
Type of plot: Epic realism
Time of plot: 1909-1912 and 1970's
Locale: Western Sahara and France

Principal characters:
NOUR, a boy from the desert
MA AL-AÏNINE, a sheik
LALLA, a contemporary girl
AAMMA, her adoptive mother
HARTANI, a shepherd
A PHOTOGRAPHER

The Story:

During the winter of 1909-1910, a long caravan moves along a harsh valley in the Western Sahara Desert. It comprises people from the south, who seek to escape the war brought by the soldiers—colonial powers engaged in the conquest of Africa. These refugees converge on Smara to seek the protection of Sheik Ma al-Aïnine, Water of the Eyes, founder of the holy city. As more and more tribes join them, their campsites multiply. A boy named Nour, descendant of the legendary al-Azraq, the Blue Man, is among the travelers. The sheik distinguishes Nour in the crowd, intensely gazes upon him, and tells the boy of the spiritual teachings that the sheik once received from the Blue Man.

In the 1970's, a girl named Lalla lives in a shack outside a city of the Moroccan littoral. She likes to run in the dunes and to observe the creatures that she discovers in the sand, the water, and the sky, as well as the variations of the light, the color of the water, and the direction of the wind. Aamma, the woman who has adopted her, has told Lalla the story of her birth: Her mother, Hawa, came from the country of the Blue warriors to the south. When the time for Lalla's birth arrived, Hawa leaned against a tree with her arms hanging from a branch. The child was born at dawn.

Aamma's response is not as explicit when Lalla asks about al-Azraq, the Blue Man of her ancestors, but the girl thinks about him during her solitary walks. She calls him al-Ser, the Secret, and feels his intense gaze upon her. Lalla's best friend is a young shepherd, Hartani, who lives on the edge of the desert. Hartani knows about scorpions, secret paths in the desert, and light in the caverns. He sees "with his body," knowing with all his senses. He does not speak the language of humans, but Lalla understands his signs, the expressions on his face, and the shine in his eyes.

Lalla grows up. Aamma pressures her to marry a rich man from the city. The girl chooses freedom; she joins Hartani on the plateau of stones and soon calls him her husband.

The caravan continues its march. Women and children, beaten by the sun, slow down. The weak drag along at the back of the column. Nour no longer remembers a time when he was not on the move.

From the railing of a ship, Lalla discovers Marseille. It is not the shining city of her dreams. She sleeps in an apartment as dilapidated as most houses in the Panier neighborhood. The size of the city amazes her, and she walks endlessly through its streets. There are people, mainly poor people, from all over the world. Lalla, who is pregnant with Hartani's child, feels dizzy when surrounded by the crowd. She works in a squalid hotel, cleaning the rooms of immigrant workers. She meets a photographer who is stricken by her beauty. Images of her face appear on the covers of magazines, first in Marseille, then in Paris. As a fashion star, Lalla uses her mother's name, Hawa. Since she cannot read or write, she signs autographs with the sign of her tribe.

The red city of Taroudant will not open its doors to the caravan. The travelers continue toward the north and Marrakech. They are weak and hopeless, leaving behind corpses by the hundreds. At night, they tell stories about the glorious past, when Sheik Ma al-Aïnine was a hero.

Two columns of soldiers from the French army march to close in on Ma al-Aïnine rebels. Their leaders are anxious to put an end to the adventures of the sheik, whom they see as a fanatic determined to drive the Christians from the desert. The soldiers fighting for the Europeans have powerful arms. The colonizers' banks hold sufficient money to buy allies and exploit Africa's mines.

The first encounter takes place in June, 1910. Afterward, the foreigners advance from city to city, while the portion of the caravan that escaped the June massacre stops in Tiznit. Nour, heartbroken, watches the death of Ma al-Aïnine.

Lalla gets up at dawn to return home. She travels for days before reaching the shantytown where she grew up. She walks to the dunes and finds a familiar tree. The pains of childbirth come in waves, as rhythmic as the sound of the sea; they crash through her body as though they will tear it apart. At dawn, Lalla, following the tradition of her tribe, hangs from a branch and gives birth to Hawa.

In March, 1912, countless tribes gather around Agadir. The sheik's son arrives with his warriors. Colonel Mangin's cannons and machine guns sweep over the riverbed. After burying their dead, Nour and the survivors start walking on the southern trail. They have nothing left. They are the last free men of the desert.

Critical Evaluation:

Desert was first published in 1980. With its publication, J. M. G. Le Clézio abandoned the avant-garde literature of his beginnings. Instead of directly critiquing Western culture and its rationality, he chose in this novel to celebrate a non-Western culture that provides its people with a grasp on the universe and their place in it. He also continued to defend the oppressed. *Desert* is considered, together with *Le Chercheur d'or* (1985; *The Prospector*, 1993), one of the best works by Le Clézio. He was awarded the Nobel Prize in Literature in 2008.

Desert is composed of two different narratives: a historical one about the colonial war of the French army and its African allies against the tribes of the desert, and the contemporary story of Lalla. These narratives, distinct by their contents, are also presented on the pages of *Desert* in different ways: the first one is printed in a column narrower than the column used for the second one.

The historical narrative is precise: readers can follow the march of the caravan on a map, from Smara to Agadir; the decisive events are dated. It is not a chapter in a history book, however. The narrative provides a vivid description, rich in detail, of the travelers, their surroundings, their origins, and their activities. It also has a spiritual content: the legends, values, and beliefs of the desert tribes, especially the Berik Allah ("those who are blessed by God").

The figure of al-Azraq, the ancestor, the Blue Man, serves as an example for the warriors of the caravan. His teachings are an inspiration for all. On Earth, the leader of the travelers is the formidable Sheik Ma al-Aïnine, whose gaze moves young Nour and can relieve a blind soldier. The caravan travelers are part of a tradition; they are also part of the world that surrounds them—the stones, the sand, the rivers, and the night. Their daily activities are shaped by these spiritual realities, which account also for the epic tone that permeates their narrative. This epic style is achieved through the use of stylistic elements, such as long lists of names, places, or tribes, which are repeated as if they were incantations. Nour, the boy who witnesses and survives the destruction of his people, adds a human dimension to the collective drama. In the vision presented here, the people of the desert have a tradition and spiritual guidance. The Christians, by contrast, have weapons and businessmen waiting to exploit the region's natural resources. They are said to have only one god: money.

The description of the long march serves as a background for the main narrative, Lalla's story. Numerous elements link the two narratives: Nour's mother and Lalla's mother are both descendants of the Blue Man; Nour and Lalla share the same belief in transcendence represented by the intensity of a gaze or the light of the desert; the verses sung by Lalla are also heard during the march.

Lalla's story takes place, in the long section titled "Happiness," in a positive context. The emphasis here is on the natural world. The anecdote concerning Lalla's origins on one hand, and her departure to the north on the other hand, frame central chapters dedicated to the elements—wind, light, fire, air, and water—and their influence on the girl and other human beings. Hartani, the boy without human language, is her master as far as the knowledge of the desert is concerned. For Lalla, human life is part of nature and even part of the cosmos, as indicated by the symbolic value of the sky, the light, and the flight of a white gull, as well as her own emotions when she feels the gaze of al-Azraq upon her.

In the novel's second part, "Life with the Slaves," Lalla is isolated from her world and struggles to survive in Marseille. She is not any poorer than she was in her shantytown, and she has a friend, but she is deprived of the light that represented transcendence in Africa. The desert world is permeated by the history, the legends, and the values and beliefs of its people. The Western one, especially for immigrants, is empty. The riches with which her success as a model provides her have no value for Lalla. One morning, she carves the sign of her tribe on a piece of soap for the photographer and returns to the desert. She carries Hartani's child in her womb and gives birth in the dunes of her childhood, under the fig tree where Haman, the fisherman, used to tell her stories. Hanging from the tree, Lalla instinctively repeats the motions made by her own mother and by all the women of her tribe before her. Her pain spreads out "over the whole expanse of the sea, the whole expanse of the dune, all the way out to the pale sky." The birth of "Hawa, daughter of Hawa" is represented as a cosmic event.

In his book on Le Clézio, Masao Suzuki rightfully compares the long march of the caravan toward the north with Lalla's journey to the northern cities of Marseille and Paris. He writes that the two geographical itineraries are similar but their results are opposed. The nomads' values are powerless when faced with the materialistic ambitions of the north; the people of the desert return to the south, defeated and stripped of everything. On the contrary, Lalla's return is, in the critic's words, the triumph of the desert and its values. It could be added that a new life is born and the survivors of the Agadir massacre, the free men of the desert, are assured of a future by the girl born at the feet of the old tree.

According to Raymond Mbassi Atéba, in *Desert*, Le Clézio "lets Africa reveal itself" instead of revealing it through a Eurocentrist vision. The novel displays an intimate knowledge of the region that it describes, a formidable insight into the soul of its inhabitants, and a flow of words as powerful as the natural forces that govern life in the desert. Since 1985, Le Clézio, in search of his own identity, has introduced biographical elements into his writings. He continues tirelessly on his literary and extraliterary travels.

Gisèle C. Feal

Further Reading

Amoi, Alba, and Bettina Knapp, eds. *Multicultural Writers Since 1945*. Westport, Conn.: Greenwood Press, 2004. Includes a five-page introduction to Le Clézio. A basic but useful introduction because little has been written in English on this author.

Le Clézio, Jean-Marie Gustave. *Onitsha*. Translated by Alison Anderson. Lincoln: University of Nebraska Press, 1997. A semiautobiographical novel that describes the writer's experiences in Africa as a child.

Moser, Keith A. "Privileged Moments." In *The Novels and Short Stories of J. M. G. Le Clézio: His Contemporary Development of a Traditional French Literary Device*. Lewiston, N.Y.: Edwin Mellen Press, 2008. A study of lyrical experiences in Le Clézio's fiction and their relationship to and intervention within traditional French representations of such experiences.

Desire in Language
A Semiotic Approach to Literature and Art

Author: Julia Kristeva (1941-   )
First published: Séméiotiké: Recherches pour une sémanalyse, 1969; *Polylogue*, 1970 (English translation, 1980)
Type of work: Literary criticism

Julia Kristeva, in *Desire in Language*, contends that the relationship between language and society is crucial to understanding the construction of meaning through literary narratives. She argues that the metaphysical premises upon which language rests are essential in exposing the signifying process—the subject matter of semiotics.

Kristeva's own version of semiotics (theory of signs), however, significantly diverges from the traditional discipline developed by linguists Ferdinand de Saussure and Charles S. Peirce, to the extent that she focuses less on the abstract structure of language than on the speaking human subject (the subject). Following psychoanalyst Sigmund Freud, Kristeva claims that the speaking subject is split between the unconscious and conscious levels. She names her approach "semanalysis," which analyzes a signifying phenomenon, such as a novel, drama, music, or painting, at its unconscious, preverbal, and preoedipal levels. Semanalysis seeks to uncover the split within the speaking subject whose narrative signifies something other than what is overtly expressed. Thus, the analysis subverts the narrative's underlying metaphysical and epistemological constructs.

Desire in Language comprises ten essays written in a period of about ten years. The essays were first published in *Séméiotiké* (1969) and *Polylogue* (1977), reflecting the literary and social theories prevalent in France in the 1960's and 1970's, including poststructuralism, structural Marxism, and feminism. In the essays, Kristeva draws on the insights of thinkers as diverse as Karl Marx, Friedrich Engels, Georg Lukács, Jacques Lacan, Roman Jakobson, and Mikhail Bakhtin. The book relies heavily on psychoanalytic approaches in interpreting literary texts and artworks as expressions of repressed and forbidden sexuality.

In the book's opening chapter, "The Ethics of Linguistics," Kristeva argues that the ethical rules of discourse developed by traditional linguists, semioticians, and grammarians separate language from its speaker, concerned as they are with, mainly, internal coherence of meaning and metalinguistic considerations. In contrast, Kristeva urges a shift in the semiotic rules of ethics from objective meaning structures to the speaking subject. She points to poetry as offering an opening for this shift. In poetry, the dialectics of the subject is revealed at its subverbal levels. She next illustrates the kind of semiotic rules of ethics she envisions with a discussion of Jakobson's contributions to linguistic studies, such as his interpretive readings of Russian poets Vladimir Mayakovsky and Velimir Khlebnikov.

Kristeva, who moves from the semiotics of poetry to the semiotics of the novel in the second chapter, "The Bounded Text," introduces the concept of the ideologeme. An ideologeme is an overarching epistemic complex of ideas and themes that form the intersection of textual arrangements and utterances. Because ideologemes are embedded at the structural level of a text, reflecting its sociohistorical context, their identification and analyses are crucial to understanding what is being signified. Kristeva distinguishes between the ideologeme of the sign and the ideologeme of the symbol. The ideologeme of the sign on which a novel as a

modern form of writing is based differs from the ideologeme of the symbol that characterizes medieval writings. She believes that the novel marks an epistemological break from medieval semiotic practices, in that it resolves conceptual dualisms, such as that between the alethic (what is necessary) and the deontic (what is obligatory), through a nondisjunction of oppositional dyads. Furthermore, from a semiotic viewpoint, a novel represents a narrative with a structural finitude, often indicated by the death or murder of the "speaker."

In the third chapter, "Word, Dialogue, and Novel," Kristeva relies on Bakhtin to advance the thesis that writing contains a dialogical structure—unrecognized by traditional semiotics. This dialogue occurs at the intersection of a horizontal axis, consisting of a speaker in relation to an addressee, and a vertical axis, consisting of words. Thus understood, each word within a text intersects with numerous other words, making the text an actual "mosaic of quotations" that continuously absorbs and transforms other words from other texts. Every text is thus a dialogue that enjoins semiotics with the task of uncovering multiple modalities and forms of writing within writings, a task that is accomplished through procedures that are intended to expose their unconscious and preverbal levels.

A text's dialogical character also demands that the text be read as part of, and as a response to, other texts that have preceded it. Thus understood, semiotics is also carnivalesque in nature; it is subversive and rebellious, shrinking the distance between the author and audience, self and the other. Kristeva notes that the spirit of carnivalesque discourse was present in ancient Greece, as evidenced by Socratic dialogues and Menippean satires. Furthermore, Kristeva recognizes her mentor, Roland Barthes, as the "precursor and founder of modern literary studies," arguing that he placed writing at the intersection of the subject and history. She asserts that writing, according to Barthes, is a "negative operation" because it highlights "contestation, rupture, flight, and irony."

In the fourth chapter, "How Does One Speak to Literature?" Kristeva returns to one of the central themes of the book and argues that the nature of the speaking subject is often ignored. She notes that Edmund Husserl's elevation of the subject as transcendental ego (above empiricist and psychological fragmentations) is intended to establish, unlike the Cartesian ego, that the subject is constituted in the act of constituting the object. Any signifying practice is thus predicated on the unity of the operating consciousness. At the same time, such a subject must be aligned with its instinctual heterogeneity, which is apprehended through the methods opened up by Freud and Lacan.

The final chapters apply the insights of psychoanalysis to signifying practices. In chapter 6, "The Father, Love, and Banishment," Kristeva subjects Samuel Beckett's dramatic monologue *Not I* (pr. 1972) and his short story *First Love, and Other Shorts* (1974) to a Freudian analysis to support the thesis that the overcoming of the superego symbolized by the father's death is necessary to experience sexual love. Kristeva further argues that writing also reveals the existence of the other, going beyond subjectivism and psychologism, and speech finds its meaning in the love for the father's death, or murder. Beckett's writings often signify acts of patricide and tell tales of mother-son incest. The same themes also are said to underlie the paintings of Leonardo da Vinci and Michelangelo during the Renaissance, a period of cultural history in which Christianity, the religion of the father (patriarchy), was recast as a form of Humanism that celebrated sexuality, pleasure, and acquisitiveness.

Turning to music as a form of signifying practice, Kristeva examines in chapter 7, "The Novel as Polylogue," Philippe Sollers's writings on vocalization. Through intonation and rhythm, music leads to a silent place within the subject, observes Kristeva. In a Freudian turn, she describes singing as a structural signifier of erotic instincts, asserting that music emerges from that domain within the subject that is controlled by the "phallic mother." For a language to be expressed in music it must confront this mother, the first other whom the son meets. Singing is a different sort of incest, a liberating one, because in singing Oedipus turns into Orpheus and the mother's control is broken.

Kristeva goes on to unveil the underlying sexual signifiers contained in the Renaissance paintings of Giotto and Giovanni Bellini, focusing on color as a signifier. In chapter 8, "Giotto's Joy," Kristeva theorizes that color represents an excess of meaning to be interpreted psychoanalytically. The choice of color signifies the speaking subject's internal conflicts, sexual in origin, and the ideological values of the age. Renaissance paintings, while professing to serve Catholic theology, in effect betrayed this theology by valorizing Humanism and sexuality. In chapter 9, "Motherhood According to Giovanni Bellini," Kristeva contends that Bellini's portrayal of motherhood exemplifies this betrayal, as his paintings refer to the sublimated expressions of father-daughter incest and the "homosexual facet" of motherhood. The pictorial art of motherhood, such as the Madonna and child Jesus, had been a favorite theme of Renaissance artists, also betraying repressed instincts.

Desire in Language concludes with the chapter "Place Names," which is devoted to the Freudian discovery of infantile sexuality, its implications for understanding the parent-child relationship, and its significance for psychoanalysis. Implied is the notion that since Freud's discovery of the Oedipus complex and infantile sexuality, academic and other discourse on neurosis and motherhood involves a semiotics of the repressed and its signifying structures.

Mathew J. Kanjirathinkal

Further Reading

Becker-Leckrone, Megan. *Julia Kristeva and Literary Theory*. New York: Palgrave Macmillan, 2005. A comprehensive treatment of Kristeva's broad, multidisciplinary, and distinctive approach to literary theory, covering many of the concepts and perspectives discussed in *Desire in Language*.

Doane, Janice L., and Devon Hodges. *From Klein to Kristeva: Psychoanalytic Feminism*. Ann Arbor: University of Michigan Press, 1996. The authors discuss the shifting focus on motherhood within the context of object-relations theory and its link to feminist interpretations of psychoanalysis. Chapter 3, "Kristeva's Death-Bearing Mother," offers an interesting discussion of Kristeva's views on psychoanalytic feminism.

Gambaudo, Sylvie. *Kristeva, Psychoanalysis, and Culture: Subjectivity in Crisis*. London: Ashgate, 2007. Kristeva explains that psychoanalysis is the unifying thread that links the differing themes that appear in her works.

McAffee, Nöelle. *Julia Kristeva*. New York: Routledge, 2004. Part of the Routledge Critical Thinkers series, this highly readable introduction to Kristeva's key concepts and theories includes examinations of the notion of subjectivity and of how the speaking subject is influenced by internal and external forces.

Oliver, Kelly, and S. K. Keltner, eds. *Psychoanalysis, Aesthetics, and Politics in the Work of Julia Kristeva*. Albany: State University of New York Press, 2009. While this collection of essays covers the whole of Kristeva's work, it offers valuable insights into the trajectory of her thought. Part of the series Insinuations: Philosophy, Psychoanalysis, Literature.

Desire Under the Elms

Author: Eugene O'Neill (1888-1953)
First produced: 1924; first published, 1925
Type of work: Drama
Type of plot: Tragedy
Time of plot: 1850
Locale: A farmhouse in New England

Principal characters:
EPHRAIM CABOT, a farmer
SIMEON,
PETER, and
EBEN, his sons
ABBIE, his third wife

The Story:

When the news of gold discoveries in California reaches New England, Simeon and Peter Cabot, who have spent their lives piling up stones to fence their father's farm, become restless. In the summer of 1850 they are ready to tear down the fences that seem to hem them in, to rebel against their close-fisted old father, and for once in their lives to be free. One day, Ephraim Cabot hitches up his rig and drives off, leaving the farm in charge of his three sons, Simeon, Peter, and their younger half brother, Eben, all three of whom hate their father and see him for what he is: a greedy, self-righteous hypocrite. The older brothers hate Ephraim for what he did to them, but Eben hates his father because he stole the land that belonged to his mother and then worked her to death on the farm. Eben feels that the farm belongs to him, and he means to have it. He inherits some of old Ephraim's stony implacability as well as his sensuality, and he gives expression to the latter on his trips down the road to visit Minnie, the local prostitute, who earlier belonged to his father.

Realizing that Simeon and Peter want to go to California, yet have no money to take them there, Eben thinks up a plan to get rid of them once and for all. While Ephraim is away, he offers them three hundred dollars each in gold if they will sign a paper renouncing all claims to the farm. Eben found the money, which belonged to his mother, buried beneath the floorboards of the kitchen. The brothers accept Eben's offer and set off for California.

Shortly afterward, old Ephraim arrives home with Abbie Putnam. He is seventy-six, she thirty-five, but she has decided that she wants a home of her own. When old Ephraim offers to marry her, she accepts him at once, and by the time she moves into the Cabot homestead she is determined that whatever happens the farm will be hers someday. She tries unsuccessfully to make friends with Eben, who at first hates her as he would hate any other woman coming to take his mother's place and the farm that rightfully belongs to him. After a time, though, Eben begins to notice that life on the farm is easier since his stepmother arrived. However, the realization that Abbie can influence his father as she desires only strengthens Eben's determination to resist her attempts to conciliate him. Some of his taunts become so pointed that Abbie complains to Ephraim, falsely hinting that Eben made advances toward her. When the old man thereupon threatens to kill his son, she realizes that she went too far and must take a different approach. After that, Abbie subtly instills in Ephraim's mind the idea that a son and heir who would inherit the farm after his death would be a better way of getting back at Eben than killing him outright. The old man, flattered at the thought that at the age of seventy-six he might have a son, agrees to leave Eben alone.

One night, after Ephraim goes out to sleep in the barn, Abbie sees her opportunity to secure her hold on the farm. She lures Eben into his mother's parlor, a room that has not been opened since her death, and seduces him, breaking down his scruples with the suggestion that by cuckolding his father he can get revenge for Ephraim's treatment of his mother.

The result is the son Abbie hopes for. To celebrate the child's birth, Ephraim invites all the neighbors to a dance in the kitchen of the farmhouse. Many of the guests suspect the true circumstances and say so as openly as they dare. Ephraim pays no attention to the insinuations, and outdances them all, until even the fiddler drops from sheer exhaustion.

While the revelry still is going on the old man steps outside to cool off. There he and Eben, who was sulking outside, quarrel over the possession of the farm. Spitefully, Ephraim taunts his son with his knowledge of how Abbie tricked him out of his inheritance. Furious, Eben turns on Abbie, threatening to kill her and telling her he hates her and the child he fathered when she tricked him. By this time, however, Abbie is genuinely in love with Eben, and, thinking the child is the obstacle keeping them apart, she smothers it in an effort to prove to her lover that it is he and not the child she wants. When he discovers what happened, Eben is enraged and shocked, and he sets off to get the sheriff for Abbie's arrest.

When Ephraim discovers that Abbie killed the child that was not his, he, too, is shocked, but his heart fills with contempt at his son's cowardice in giving Abbie over to the law. On his return to the farm, Eben begins to realize how much he loves Abbie and how great her love for him must be to induce her to take the child's life. When the sheriff comes to take Abbie away, he confesses that he is an accomplice in the crime. The two are taken off together, both destined for punishment but happy in their love. Ephraim is left alone with his farm, the best farm in the county. It is, the sheriff tells him, a place anybody would want to own.

Critical Evaluation:

Desire Under the Elms was the last of Eugene O'Neill's naturalistic plays and one of his most effective. The structural set, showing the entire farmhouse with one wall removed, was an innovation in its day. In this play, O'Neill's daring reduction of human motives to the simple impulses of love, hate, lust, and greed gives an impression of human nature as convincing and complete as the more complex studies of his later plays.

One of O'Neill's most admired and frequently performed plays, *Desire Under the Elms* provoked enormous controversy during its first stagings. Some audiences were scandalized by what one critic called "distresses" that "range from unholy lust to infanticide, and include drinking, cursing, vengeance, and something approaching incest." In Los Angeles, the cast was arrested for having presented a lewd, obscene, and immoral play. A bizarre trial followed, in which at one point the entire court witnessed a special private performance. The jury was finally dismissed when they could not resolve their deadlock, eight members voting for conviction and four for acquittal.

It gradually became apparent that O'Neill was aiming at something more than a shocking revelation of unconscious drives and primordial fears, elements that were clearly subordinate to his larger purpose of reintroducing authentic tragic vision to American theater. O'Neill's supporters could point out that the Greek and biblical sources that had inspired the play were replete with the very "immoralities" he depicted.

Euripides' *Hippolytos* (428 B.C.E.; *Hippolytus*, 1781) and Jean Racine's *Phèdre* (1677; *Phaedra*, 1701) served as O'Neill's principal models. These works both draw on the archetypal plot in which a father returns from a journey with a wife, who falls in love with her new stepson. This attachment, at first resisted or concealed, results in a struggle between father and son, in which the father achieves a Pyrrhic victory that costs him both son and spouse. The situation is tragic in that all participants are forced to make conscious choices of evil for the sake of a higher good. It is fate that so

structures events as to necessitate the downfall of essentially noble characters. O'Neill complicates the classic plot by introducing Old Testament motifs: the hardness and vengeance of God; the superiority of justice over mercy; and the battle among sons for birthrights and fatherly favor. He also relies on Freudian psychology in his treatment of sexual relationships.

It is questionable whether O'Neill does finally succeed in giving true tragic stature to his characters. There can be no doubt that his drama possesses genuinely tragic aspects, but that the whole deserves the term "tragedy" is doubtful. Three considerations sustain this judgment. First, Eben's basic motivation remains unclear throughout the play, as does the central question whether he is the rightful heir to the farm. Second, in being as preoccupied as they are with struggles for possession and revenge, Abbie and Eben lack that nobility of purpose that the reader associates with truly tragic characters. Third, Eben is made to seem totally a victim of psychological drives, and he does not arrive at his choices freely. This element in particular makes pathos, not tragedy, the dominant quality in *Desire Under the Elms*.

At least one critic has persuasively argued that O'Neill designed his play around a single moral fact: Ephraim Cabot ruined the life of Eben's mother—"murdered her with his hardness," as Eben says—and this sin now cries out for retribution. O'Neill's opening stage directions call for two enormous, expressionistically rendered elms that bend over the farmhouse; they should suggest suffering women and dominate the entire scene with "a sinister maternity." From the beginning, Eben proclaims his monomaniacal desire to take "her vengeance on him—so's she kin rest quiet in her grave." When Abbie enters the parlor, her scheming and erotic tendencies are momentarily subdued by the felt presence of the dead woman's spirit. Eben does not allow himself to be seduced until he is assured that he is doing his mother's will.

The structure of the action reinforces this central theme. In part 1, Eben solidifies his claim to the farm by inducing his half brothers to leave. He uses his mother's money to do this, thus depriving Ephraim of both the fortune and the assistance of his older sons. In part 2, Eben takes Ephraim's wife from him, begets a son, and sets in motion the process whereby Ephraim is humiliated in the eyes of the community. In part 3, Abbie's killing of the child prevents Ephraim from naming a new heir, and Abbie and Eben's departure dooms Ephraim to that condition of isolation that he has always feared most. He becomes in effect an exile, living on a farm that has become a curse to him. With that, the pattern of crime and justified punishment has been completed.

Tragic in outline, *Desire Under the Elms* is less than tragic in substance. O'Neill lets the issue of Ephraim's persecution of Eben's mother become clouded. This information comes only from Eben, who is a somewhat unreliable source, given his overwhelming Oedipus complex and his deep desire to inherit the farm. That Eben stands to benefit economically by his revenge tends to tarnish his motivation and undermine his credibility. O'Neill intensifies the economic theme by showing how deeply Peter and Simeon covet the farm, and by casting doubt on Eben's claim that he has a clear legal right of ownership. Ephraim, who has worked the farm for years, discounts the claim completely.

Ironically, the fact that *Desire Under the Elms* is not a fully realized tragedy probably accounts partially for its appeal, as does O'Neill's choice of a pastoral, precivilized setting that helps convey the workings of unconscious forces with astonishing power. Although outraged protests such as the sensational Los Angeles court case came from irate middle-class theatergoers, it was actually the literate American middle class that formed O'Neill's most avid audience. O'Neill was an iconoclast whose attacks, likened in one of his early poems to torpedoes fired from the submarine of his soul, were directed against middle-class complacency. Much to its credit, however, the audience whose values were under fire responded to plays such as *Desire Under the Elms* with that respect and enthusiasm that springs from recognition of the truth, however disconcerting or uncomfortable that truth may be.

"Critical Evaluation" by Leslie E. Gerber

Further Reading

Alexander, Doris. *Eugene O'Neill's Creative Struggle: The Decisive Decade, 1924-1933.* University Park: Pennsylvania State University Press, 1992. Attempts to trace the plays to probable sources. Sees O'Neill's playwriting as an opportunity "to confront and solve" problems in his own life. Analyzes the composition and final text of *Desire Under the Elms* in relationship to O'Neill's death wish after his mother died.

Bloom, Steven F. *Student Companion to Eugene O'Neill.* Westport, Conn.: Greenwood Press, 2007. Includes a brief biographical sketch, a discussion of O'Neill's literary heritage, and a chapter providing critical analysis of *Desire Under the Elms.*

Bogard, Travis. *Contour in Time: The Plays of Eugene O'Neill.* Rev. ed. New York: Oxford University Press, 1988. Recognizes O'Neill's plays as efforts at self-understanding. Attempts to analyze the plays in relation to events in O'Neill's life. Especially effective at developing the psychological and mythic elements in *Desire Under the Elms.*

Carpenter, Frederic I. *Eugene O'Neill.* Rev. ed. Boston: Twayne, 1979. An effective, short introduction to O'Neill's life and plays, emphasizing the tragic dimensions of the dramas. Sees "the spirit of nature" as the "final hero" of *Desire Under the Elms,* since the play emphasizes that human attempts at ownership and possession result in pain and inevitable loss.

Manheim, Michael, ed. *The Cambridge Companion to Eugene O'Neill.* New York: Cambridge University Press, 1998. Collection of essays about O'Neill's life and works, including discussions of the theater in his time; notable stage productions of his work; his depiction of female, African, and Irish American characters; and analyses of his plays written in his early, middle, and late periods.

Shaughnessy, Edward L. *Down the Nights and down the Days: Eugene O'Neill's Catholic Sensibility.* Notre Dame, Ind.: University of Notre Dame Press, 1996. Although O'Neill renounced Catholicism when he was fifteen, Shaughnessy finds evidence that he retained some of his Catholic upbringing and brought this moral sensibility to his plays, including *Desire Under the Elms.*

Sheaffer, Louis. *O'Neill: Son and Artist.* Boston: Little, Brown, 1973. An authoritative biography of O'Neill. Includes helpful details about the incidents in O'Neill's life related to *Desire Under the Elms,* as well as about the play's composition and immediate reception.

Törnqvist, Egil. *Eugene O'Neill: A Playwright's Theatre.* Jefferson, N.C.: McFarland, 2004. Demonstrates how O'Neill was a controlling personality in the texts and performances of his plays. Describes his working conditions and the multiple audiences for his works. Examines the titles, settings in time and place, names and addresses, language, and allusions to other works in his dramas.

Voglino, Barbara. "'Devout' Admirers of the Sunrise: Theatricality in *Desire Under the Elms.*" In *"Perverse Mind: Eugene O'Neill's Struggle with Closure."* Madison, N.J.: Fairleigh Dickinson University Press, 1999. Focuses on nine plays written at different periods of O'Neill's career in order to demonstrate how the failed endings of the early works developed into the successful closures of his later plays.

The Devil upon Two Sticks

Author: Alain-René Lesage (1668-1747)
First published: Le Diable boiteux, 1707; revised, 1720,
    1726 (English translation, 1708)
Type of work: Novel
Type of plot: Picaresque
Time of plot: Early eighteenth century
Locale: Madrid

Principal characters:
DON CLEOPHAS LEANDRO PEREZ ZAMBULLO, a student
ASMODEUS, the demon in the bottle
DON PEDRO DE ESCOLANO, a Spanish nobleman
DONNA SERAPHINA, his daughter

The Story:

On a dark October night in Madrid, Don Cleophas Leandro Perez Zambullo, a student of Alcala, is in dreadful trouble. While visiting Donna Thomasa, his beloved, three or four hired bravos set upon him in her apartment, and when he loses his sword in the struggle, he is forced to take flight over the rooftops of the neighboring houses. Spying a light in a garret, he enters through a window and discovers an empty room furnished with the strange gear of a magician. As he is taking stock of the place, he hears a sigh and soon realizes that he is being addressed by a demon in a bottle. To the student's questionings, the spirit replies that he is not Lucifer, Uriel, Beelzebub, Leviathan, Belphegor, or Ashtaroth, but Asmodeus, the Devil on Two Sticks, who always befriends hapless lovers. Cleophas thereupon breaks the vial and out tumbles a monstrous dwarf, with the legs of a goat, a stature of less than three feet, and a grotesque and grimacing face. Half concealed by extraordinary clothing and a curiously embroidered white satin cloak are the two crutches on which the dwarf hobbles about.

Because Cleophas is eager to escape his pursuers and Asmodeus wishes to avoid his captor, the magician, the two do not linger in the attic. Cleophas grasps the edge of the demon's cloak, and off they fly into the sky over Madrid. For the remainder of their association together, Asmodeus entertains his companion with views of all that is happening in the city, explaining the circumstances and characteristics of those into whose houses they look.

At first, they peer into the houses immediately beneath them. Asmodeus shows Cleophas some ridiculous views of a coquette, a nobleman, a poet, and an alchemist. At last, they come to a mansion where cavaliers and their ladies are celebrating a wedding. The demon proceeds to tell the story of the count de Belflor and Leonora de Cespedes.

The count de Belflor, a gallant young man of the court, fell in love with Leonora de Cespedes and wished to make her his mistress. By guile, the gift of a well-filled purse, and the promise of another thousand pistoles when he accom-

plished his scheme, he secured the aid of her duenna, Marcella, who prevailed on the young woman to admit the nobleman to her chamber at night. One morning, as the count was making a hasty departure, for dawn was breaking, he slipped and fell while descending the silken ladder lowered from Leonora's bedchamber. The noise awakened Don Luis de Cespedes, her father, who slept in the room above. Uncovering the truth and enraged by this stain on the family honor, the old don confronted his daughter's lover. The count offered to provide for Don Pedro, Leonora's brother, who was a student, but he refused to marry the daughter, giving as his false excuse a marriage that the king supposedly already arranged for the young courtier.

Later, after reading a reproachful letter written by Leonora, the count was moved to repentance. About the same time, Leonora's brother, Don Pedro, played truant from his studies at Alcala to pay court to an unknown young beauty whom he was secretly meeting. In a street brawl, his life was saved by the count, who happened to be passing by. The count asked the young man to go with him to act as guard while he had an interview with Leonora. The truth was revealed when Don Luis confronted his son, and the count asked for the hand of Leonora and bestowed that of his sister, Donna Eugenia, on his new friend and brother. Don Pedro was overjoyed when he discovered that his secret love was the sister of the count de Belflor. The two couples are married, and Cleophas, guided by the demon, witnesses the festivities of their double wedding. Only Marcella, the treacherous duenna, has no part in the mirth; Don Luis sends her to a nunnery to spend her ill-gotten pistoles and prayers to win pardon for her wickedness.

Directing Cleophas's attention to other homes in the city, Asmodeus shows him the plight of an impoverished marquis, a plagiarizing author, a procurer of young men for rich widows, and a printer of antireligious books. At Cleophas's request, the dwarf secures revenge for his mortal companion on the faithless Donna Thomasa. While she is entertaining the assassins she hires to attack Cleophas, Asmodeus puts the men into a jealous rage over her and sets them to fighting. So great is the disturbance they cause that neighbors summon the police, who on their arrival find two of the men slain. The assassins are thrown into the city dungeon, and Donna Thomasa is eventually sentenced to be transported to the colonies. Thus proud Cleophas has his revenge.

Next, Asmodeus reveals the circumstances of the wretches in the nearby prison and madhouse. Poisoners, assassins, servants falsely accused and servants deserving imprisonment, a dishonest surgeon, and others are all displayed in their cells. At the madhouse, Cleophas sees political and religious fanatics, as well as those maddened by jealousy, grief, and the ingratitude of their relatives. Asmodeus also takes the opportunity to show Cleophas other people who should be confined in an insane asylum, for their brains are addled by avarice, egotism, and the uncontrollable pangs of love.

Suddenly, from their vantage point above the city, the two glimpse a raging fire in a house beneath them. To everyone's horror, the beautiful Donna Seraphina, daughter of Don Pedro de Escolano, is trapped in an upstairs room. Asmodeus, at the entreaties of Cleophas, assumes the shape and appearance of the young student and brings the girl out of the burning building safely. After the rescue, Asmodeus tells Cleophas that he suddenly decided on a grand design: The young man will ultimately marry the lovely Donna Seraphina, for her noble father already believes himself deeply indebted to the handsome young cavalier.

Asmodeus continues the strange tour of Madrid with portrayals of the unrevealed secrets of those buried in the tombs of a churchyard and with glimpses of bedside death scenes of true grief, avarice, jealousy, and self-seeking. By way of contrast, he then tells Cleophas a long and circumstantial tale of true friendship and love.

Don Juan de Zarata, a gallant of Toledo, murdered his false wife's lover and fled to Valencia. Near the outskirts of that city, he stopped a duel between Don Alvaro Ponzo and Don Fabricio de Mendoza, rivals for the hand of the beautiful young widow, Donna Theodora de Cifuentes. On the advice of Don Juan, the lady was allowed to choose between her suitors; her choice was Don Fabricio. Through that meeting, the young Toledan and Don Fabricio became inseparable companions. Don Fabricio, however, could not understand his friend's seeming indifference to the charms of Donna Theodora. What he did not suspect was that the Toledan was greatly attracted to the lady and she to him, but that out of regard for friendship Don Juan made every effort to repress his passion. Unhappy in her own unrealized love for Don Juan,

the lady finally decided to return to her estate at Villareal. When the Toledan confessed the truth to Don Fabricio, that gentleman was so moved by Don Juan's delicacy of feeling that he vowed no rivalry in love could ever part them.

Meanwhile, Donna Theodora was kidnapped by Don Alvaro's ruffians and put on a vessel bound for Sardinia. Don Fabricio and Don Juan set out in pursuit, but the ship on which they sailed was overtaken by Tunisian pirates, and the two were made prisoners. Separated in their captivity, they were in despair. Don Juan, sold to the dey of Algiers, was made a gardener. At length the dey, impressed by the bearing and courtesy of his Christian slave, made him his confidant. The dey had in his harem a Spanish lady whose grief appeared inconsolable; he asked Don Juan to speak to her as a countryman and assure her of her master's tender regard. To Don Juan's surprise, the lady proved to be Donna Theodora, also taken captive when her abductors were killed by Algerian pirates.

From that time on, Don Juan planned to deliver Donna Theodora from her captivity; at last, aided by an unknown accomplice, they made their escape. Their unknown benefactor turned out to be Don Fabricio, who was rescued by a French privateer. Mistaking Don Juan for the false Don Alvaro, Don Fabricio stabbed his friend and then, discovering his error, plunged his sword into his own breast. The condition of Don Fabricio grew worse, and he died soon after the arrival of the fugitives in Spain. Torn between their mutual love and grief for their friend, Donna Theodora and Don Juan were at last free to marry. A short time later, Don Juan was mortally injured in a fall from his horse. Half mad with grief, Donna Theodora soon followed him to the grave.

At length, the sleeping city awakens. Protesting that he is not weary, Cleophas urges the little demon to let him see more. Asmodeus directs his glance to the activities in the streets of beggars, artisans, a miser, and a philosopher. Then they come upon the throngs of people gathering for the king's levee: Faithless and forgetful noblemen, those seeking their own good fortune, gamblers, an honest magistrate, and others await their turn to appear before the king. Cleophas, however, cannot be shown into the king's presence since the royal cabinet, as Asmodeus explains, is under the exclusive control of other devils.

For diversion, Asmodeus takes Cleophas to see the arrival of ransomed slaves at the Monastery of Mercy. Each captive has his own fears and hopes, and Asmodeus recounts the past and future of scores of these wretches. A few slaves meet with happy circumstances upon gaining their freedom, but most of them meet with grief, loneliness, and disappointment.

At that point, Asmodeus becomes aware that his master, the magician, misses him, and he departs swiftly after making the student promise that he will never reveal to mortal ears all that he saw and overheard that night. Cleophas returns to his own apartment and sinks into a deep slumber that lasts a day and a night. When he awakens, he goes to call on Donna Seraphina, where he is welcomed by the grateful Don Pedro, her father. During a later visit in the house where he is now an honored guest, Cleophas confesses that it was not he who rescued the girl from the flames. Although overcome by astonishment, Don Pedro waves the explanation aside. After all, it was at Cleophas's insistence that Donna Seraphina was brought from the blazing house unharmed. A few weeks later, the wedding of Donna Seraphina and Cleophas is celebrated with much magnificence, and the happy bridegroom never has occasion to regret the night of freedom he provided for the Devil on Two Sticks.

Critical Evaluation:

Alain-René Lesage is chiefly remembered for his long picaresque novel, *Histoire de Gil Blas de Santillane* (1715-1735; *Gil Blas*, 1749, 1962), but his early publication of *The Devil upon Two Sticks*, with its extensive revision and enlargement in 1726, created far more excitement in his own day and is still an interesting example of the early realistic novel of manners. As he did in most of his prose fiction, Lesage worked from a Spanish original, borrowing his title and some of the early incidents from *El Diablo Cojuelo* (1641), by Luis Vélez de Guevara. Once started, however, the novel drew further and further away from its Spanish model and entertained Lesage's contemporaries by introducing a wealth of anecdotes and reminiscences, portraits and sketches of some of the most prominent of Parisian personages, under the guise of Spanish names. Lesage's satire is trenchant and ironical, though never gross or vulgar. Lesage sees humanity with a sharp and critical eye, and he is particularly successful in his witty portrayals of authors, actors, lawyers, the social world, and "persons of quality." Like most picaresque fiction, the novel is loosely plotted; within a central narrative concerning the fortunes of Don Cleophas, a young Spanish cavalier, Lesage introduces scores of other tales, ranging from brief summaries of a few sentences to short stories running for several pages or chapters. The major plot remains in evidence throughout the book, however, and the author concludes his tale with a suitably romantic ending.

Although a satire on human nature, *The Devil upon Two Sticks* is an amiable, almost lighthearted work; the author attacks his victims with wit and grace, his high spirits and good humor balancing the grotesqueness inherent in the story.

Asmodeus, the lame devil, helps Cleophas to see through the false fronts, both physical and moral, assumed by most people. The devil and his young rescuer thereby provide a framework for the stories that compose most of the narrative; Asmodeus shows Cleophas a man or woman and then exposes the person, telling his or her story with merciless truth. If there is any consistent message in *The Devil upon Two Sticks*, it is always to doubt first impressions and to seek to penetrate beneath the façades that individuals show the world.

Asmodeus is a unique character, a grotesque vision comparable to Caliban or John Milton's fallen angels. Without possessing the dark powers of the greater demons, he presides over the vices and follies of humankind rather than over the crimes. He is malicious, but not cruel, and prefers teasing and ridiculing humanity to torturing it. He possesses so much wit and playful malice and is so vividly portrayed that he almost walks away with the book, making the reader forget that he is not intended to be anything more than a momentarily friendly fiend.

Cleophas, the fiery young Spaniard, is the perfect foil for Asmodeus. He is lacking enough in discretion to be glad of the opportunity to peek behind closed doors and barred windows and to discover the shocking truths about apparently respectable people. The other characters, who come and go in the secondary tales, are described with precision and amazing dexterity; few authors can summarize human nature, in its many shades and phases, in so few words. Lesage's satire is never heavy-handed, and his humor is never blunted by anticipation. In many respects, *The Devil upon Two Sticks* is surer of touch and wittier than the author's more famous *Gil Blas*; certainly, the skill he shows in drawing the scenes and completing the characterizations is reason enough for the book to be at least as well known. At times, the author reaches heights in this book that he never does in *Gil Blas*, such as in his personification of death. Even here, his humor breaks through to add still another dimension to his vision, when, having described one of the terrific phantom's wings painted with war, pestilence, famine, and shipwreck, he adorns the other with the picture of young physicians taking their degrees. The narratives that make up the book are of differing lengths and of varying interest, but all of them are entertaining and executed with wit and style.

Further Reading

Bjornson, Richard. "The Picaresque Hero Arrives." *The Picaresque Hero in European Fiction*. Madison: University of Wisconsin Press, 1977. Comments on Lesage's adaptation of Vélez de Guevara's story and notes the dramatic significance of changes, including the transformation of the devil into a spirit presiding over the foolish as well as the evil.

Green, Frederick C. *French Novelists, Manners, and Ideas from the Renaissance to the Revolution*. New York: Frederick Ungar, 1964. Describes *The Devil upon Two Sticks* as a preparatory work for Lesage's greater novel, *Gil Blas*. Explains why the novel was popular with Lesage's contemporaries.

Gutiérrez, Ellen Turner. *The Reception of the Picaresque in the French, English, and German Traditions*. New York: Peter Lang, 1995. Traces the development of the picaresque novel from its origins in Spain through its adaptation as a genre in France, England, and Germany. Includes a discussion of Lesage and his novel *Gil Blas*.

Mylne, Vivienne. *The Eighteenth Century French Novel: Techniques of Illusion*. New York: Manchester University Press, 1965. A chapter on Lesage provides insight into the novelist's creative process and principal themes. Notes his use of stock situations and local color to vivify the narrative of *The Devil upon Two Sticks*.

Rivers, Kenneth T., ed. *A Survey of French Literature*: Vol. 3, *The Eighteenth Century*. New rev. 3d ed. Newburyport, Mass.: Focus/R. Pullins, 2005. This is a French-language anthology, but it contains an English-language introduction discussing trends in eighteenth century French literature and a short biography of Lesage in English, as well as an abridged excerpt of *Gil Blas* in French.

Showalter, English. *The Evolution of the French Novel, 1641-1782*. Princeton, N.J.: Princeton University Press, 1972. Comments on characterization, the role of the narrator, and influences that shaped Lesage's novel. Notes the author's success in using this improbable story as a means of illuminating a "moral truth."

Spencer, Samia I., ed. *Writers of the French Enlightenment*. Vols. 313-314 in *Dictionary of Literary Biography*. Detroit, Mich.: Thomson Gale, 2005. Volume 1 of this two-volume survey of French literature includes an essay on Lesage, featuring biographical information, a discussion of his writings and critical reception, and a bibliography.

Symons, Arthur. Introduction to *The Devil upon Two Sticks*. London: Navarre Society, 1927. Discusses the literary background upon which Lesage draws for his story. Highlights the novelist's use of his tale as a satire on the supposed progress of civilization.

The Devil's Elixirs
From the Posthumous Papers of Brother Medardus, a Capuchin Friar

Author: E. T. A. Hoffmann (1776-1822)
First published: Die Elixiere des Teufels: Nachgelassene Papiere des Bruders Medardus, eines Kapuziners, 1815-1816 (English translation, 1824)
Type of work: Novel
Type of plot: Fantasy
Time of plot: Eighteenth century
Locale: Germany and Italy

Principal characters:
MEDARDUS, a monk
AURELIA, a young noblewoman
FRANCESCO, a painter
PRINCE VON ROSENTHURM
COUNT VICTORIN, Medardus's brother
LEONARDUS, a prior
AN ABBESS
PIETRO BELCAMPO, a hairdresser

The Story:

Francis is born at the Convent of the Holy Lime-Tree in Prussia, at the moment that his father is dying. At Kreuzberg, the abbess of the Cistercian convent makes him her pupil. When he is sixteen years old, he becomes a monk at the Capuchin convent in Konigswald and takes the name of Medardus. Medardus is put in charge of the relics of the convent. Among them is a strange elixir. Legend says that all who drink of the potion will belong to the devil, and that if two persons drink of it, they will share the same thoughts and desires but secretly wish to destroy each other.

On St. Anthony's Day, Medardus preaches a sermon about the elixir. While he is talking, he sees in the audience a painter he saw once at the Convent of the Holy Lime-Tree. The sight disturbs him so much that he begins to rave like a madman. Later, in an attempt to regain his full senses, he drinks some of the elixir.

One day during the confessional, a beautiful woman, in appearance exactly like a painting of St. Rosalia, tells Medardus that she loves him and then leaves. Medardus determines to run away to find her. Before he can escape from the convent, however, Prior Leonardus sends him on an errand to Rome. On the way to Rome Medardus sees an officer leaning over a precipice. When Medardus tries to save him, the officer falls over the ledge. At that moment a page appears and tells Medardus that his disguise is very good. Medardus goes to the nearby castle, where he meets an old man, Reinhold, who seems to be expecting him. Reinhold tells him that Baron von F——, the owner of the castle, has a son, Hermogen, and a daughter, Aurelia, by an Italian wife who later died. The baron then married Euphemia, a sinister woman who is carrying on an affair with Count Victorin, a former suitor. The count is in the habit of disguising himself in order to gain entrance to the castle.

Medardus becomes convinced that he is Victorin. When he sees that Aurelia is the mysterious lady who looks like St. Rosalia, he feels that fate is guiding him. He tries to approach Aurelia, but she runs away. Hermogen witnesses the incident, so Medardus kills him. As Medardus flees from the castle, he hears that Euphemia is dying of a poison she intended for him. Taking refuge in the woods, Medardus cuts off his beard and changes into clothes that Victorin's page brings him.

When Medardus arrives in Frankenburg, he recognizes the painter who disturbed his sermon on St. Anthony's Day. After he tries to kill the man with a stiletto, Medardus is rescued from an angry mob by Pietro Belcampo, an odd hairdresser. At the forest house of the Prince von Rosenthurm, Medardus meets a monk who looks like him and who drinks some of his elixir. Medardus later goes to the castle, where the court physician shows him a picture of a person who again looks just like him. The man is Francesco, who, together with a strange painter, was brought to the court by the prince's brother, the duke of Neuenburg. The duke was engaged to an Italian countess and had married her, but on their wedding night, the duke was found murdered by a stiletto wound. The bride claims, however, that the groom came to the bridal chamber without a light, consummated the marriage, and left. The painter, accused of the murder, escapes, and the countess goes to live in a distant castle.

Francesco is engaged to the sister of a princess. During the marriage ceremony, the painter reappears. Francesco faints while trying to kill the painter with a stiletto. The next day he leaves, still unwed. It is later learned that the Italian countess gave birth to a son named Victorin. Francesco's intended bride leaves to become the abbess at Kreuzberg.

Hearing these tales, Medardus realizes that Francesco must be his father. At a party that night, Medardus is astonished to see that the princess is accompanied by Aurelia. When Aurelia recognizes him, he is charged with the murder of Hermogen and imprisoned. Later, he is released because his double, a mad monk who greatly resembles him, confessed to the crime. Medardus also learns that he and Victorin are stepbrothers.

Medardus becomes engaged to Aurelia. On the day that he is to marry her, he sees the mad monk being taken to the scaffold. Suddenly Medardus begins to rave. In his frenzy he stabs Aurelia, rescues the monk from the cart, and escapes into the woods. When he regains consciousness, he finds himself dressed as a monk in an Italian madhouse. He was taken there by Belcampo, the hairdresser, who says that he found Medardus in the woods, naked, with a monk's robe lying beside him.

Medardus goes next to a Capuchin convent near Rome. While there, he learns that Aurelia is alive. He also sees a strange book that a mysterious painter left at the convent. It contains sketches of paintings Medardus saw at the Convent of the Holy Lime-Tree and the history of the artist. He is Francesco, a painter who drank of St. Anthony's elixir.

Among his works, according to the account, is a painting of the martyrdom of St. Rosalia. One day he met a woman who looked just like the painting. They married, but his wife died soon after their son was born. Then Francesco, accused of sorcery, fled with his child, whom he nourished on the elixir. From Francesco's son the family branched out and included the Princess von Rosenthurm, the abbess, the first Baroness von F——, Euphemia, and Victorin.

Medardus, now repenting his past, punishes himself so much that he becomes known to the pope, who speaks of making the monk his confessor. Having incurred the antagonism of the papal confessor in this manner, Medardus, realizing that his life is in danger, leaves Rome.

He returns to the Cistercian monastery and sees Prior Leonardus, who says that Victorin came there, claimed to be Medardus, and then disappeared. By piecing together the strange sequences of events, Medardus and Leonardus realize that Medardus and Victorin, two brothers who drank of the elixir, tried to destroy each other. Leonardus also tells Medardus that Aurelia is to become a nun that day, taking the name of Rosalia. This news so disturbs Medardus that while Aurelia is taking her vows he has an impulse to stab her, but after an inward struggle, he conquers his demon and has peace in his soul. Suddenly there is a disturbance in the church. Medardus's double, dressed in rags, runs to the altar, shouts that Aurelia is his intended bride, stabs her in the heart, and escapes. Medardus rushes to Aurelia's side. Close by he sees the mysterious painter, who says that Medardus's trials will soon end. Aurelia regains consciousness, tells Medardus that he and she are destined to expiate the guilt of their family, and then dies. The people in the church, seeing the painter emerge from a picture over the altar, believe that a miracle occurred; they regard Aurelia, now called Rosalia, as a saint.

Medardus, fully recovered, can clearly tell truth from falsehood, and from Leonardus and the abbess he receives forgiveness for his past deeds. Leonardus then asks him to commit his life story to writing. Completing this task, he awaits the time when he will join Aurelia in heaven.

Father Spiridion, the librarian of the Capuchin monastery at Konigswald, appends a note to Medardus's manuscript. He writes that one night, hearing strange sounds from Medardus's cell, he investigates and sees a tall man who says that the hour of fulfillment will come soon. Then Medardus dies, one year to the minute from the time of Aurelia's death. Father Spiridion adds that the painting of St. Rosalia, which the monastery acquired, bore, on the day of Medardus's funeral, a wreath of roses. The wreath was put there by Pietro Belcampo, who later joins the order and becomes Brother Peter.

Critical Evaluation:

The Devil's Elixirs is modeled on Matthew Gregory Lewis's classic gothic novel *The Monk* (1796), which the character Aurelia reads. Like Lewis, E. T. A. Hoffmann employs a monk as a central character in order to emphasize the sharp difference that might exist between the image that one presents to the world, in speech and public behavior, and the inner self of one's fantasies, desires, and impulses. Lewis's Ambrosio is, however, a monster of calculated hypocrisy whose embarkation upon a career of sin, although doubtless unwise, is the result of a conscious decision; the situation of Hoffmann's Medardus is more confused.

Medardus's confusion is communicated to the text that tells his story, which becomes inordinately convoluted. Attempts to say what happens in the story are bound to fail. The linear plot of *The Monk* is much easier to follow—Ambrosio is drawn inexorably to his damnation. The plot might be deemed unsatisfactory on precisely that account. When one becomes aware of the conflicts that exist between one's social self and one's inner self, those conflicts are often confused, and it really is not clear exactly how much control one's powers of conscious reason have over the anarchic thrust of one's appetites and emotions. It never is clear, even to those who commit horrible crimes, to what extent they

were driven by forces outside their control. In admitting that the business of submitting to temptation is dreadfully confused, Hoffmann offers the reader an account of an inner life that, however luridly it may be supernaturalized, is psychologically accurate. It is possible to pity Medardus.

The double is a central motif in gothic fiction, particularly that of Germany. The German word frequently applied to the motif, doppelgänger, figures in a popular saying whose literal translation is: "He who sees his going double must go himself," that is, die. The double of gothic fiction carries an implicit threat of impending death. In most stories involving doubles—of which the most famous American example is Edgar Allan Poe's "William Wilson"—the double becomes an externalized projection of the inner self, and takes into the social arena all the impulses and designs that must be eliminated from the social self in order to preserve the harmony of social relationships. Such "escapes" of the inner self inevitably cause embarrassment to the social self, whose falsity stands revealed.

Medardus's double is the libertine aristocrat Victorin, the man Medardus might have become had he not been led by the ridicule of a gaggle of teasing girls to suppress his sexuality and take holy orders. Medardus thinks that Victorin has been destroyed, but he has not; he is merely submerged within Medardus's personality, ready to resurface when the conditions are right. What Medardus tries to construe as an altogether proper regard for an image of St. Rosalia eventually reveals itself as sexual attraction. St. Anthony might have been able to rise above such temptations—as symbolized by the Satanic elixir—but Medardus is not. He tries to find a way back from his commitment to celibacy, following St. Paul's advice that it is "better to marry than to burn." Alas, his secret desires are no more tolerant of the prospect of monogamy than they are of the prospect of celibacy; instead of being the instrument of his salvation, Aurelia becomes one more aspect of his confusion.

In the end, Aurelia's removal by the angry double permits Medardus a brief interval of peace. He is reassured by her dead body that he—that is, his social self—will be able to enjoy an untroubled union with her in heaven (a place from which unruly inner selves are banned). His own account of his tribulations, given in a written confession that is of necessity the product of his conscious, rational self, ends on a very hopeful note. The appendix added by Father Spiridion seems to tell a different tale, although Spiridion does not realize it: The reader will almost certainly conclude that the "horrible voice" that summons Medardus to his fate is that of the devil.

In concluding the story thus, Hoffmann perhaps sides

with those who think that if a Last Judgment occurs, then people must answer for their secret thoughts and desires as well as their public speeches and actions. On the other hand, Hoffmann has piled layers of confusion so thickly upon his plot by making Spiridion as unreliable a narrator as Medardus that one hesitates to accept this idea as final. Perhaps the ending is to be read as a calculated ambiguity, signifying a genuine uncertainty as to where the limits of personal responsibility lie—or ought to lie.

"Critical Evaluation" by Brian Stableford

Further Reading

Brown, Marshall. *The Gothic Text*. Stanford, Calif.: Stanford University Press, 2005. This examination of Gothic novels includes a chapter in which Brown analyzes *The Devil's Elixirs*.

Daemmrich, Horst S. *The Shattered Self: E. T. A. Hoffmann's Tragic Vision*. Detroit, Mich.: Wayne State University Press, 1973. Explores the divisions of the self in *The Devil's Elixirs* and Hoffmann's shorter works.

Herdman, John. *The Double in Nineteenth-Century Fiction*. New York: St. Martin's Press, 1991. Chapter 4, subsection 2, is a detailed analysis of *The Devil's Elixirs*.

McGlathery, James M. *E. T. A. Hoffmann*. New York: Twayne, 1997. A critical introduction to Hoffmann's life and work, focusing on critical reception to his work, his own critical writings, and an analysis of his major works of fiction.

Negus, Kenneth. *E. T. A. Hoffmann's Other World*. Philadelphia: University of Pennsylvania Press, 1965. A study of Hoffmann's use of the supernatural.

Passage, Charles E. "E. T. A. Hoffmann's *The Devil's Elixirs*: A Flawed Masterpiece." *Journal of English and Germanic Philology* 75, no. 4 (October, 1976): 531-545. A detailed account of the novel.

Riou, Jeanne. *Imagination in German Romanticism: Re-Thinking the Self and Its Environment*. New York: Peter Lang, 2004. Riou studies the works of Hoffmann and other German writers and philosophers to examine the Romantic concept of the imagination and the imagination's critique of reason.

The Devotion of the Cross

Author: Pedro Calderón de la Barca (1600-1681)
First produced: La devoción de la cruz, 1643; first published, 1634 (English translation, 1832)
Type of work: Drama
Type of plot: Tragedy
Time of plot: Seventeenth century
Locale: Siena, Italy

Principal characters:
EUSEBIO, a foundling
JULIA, his sister
LISARDO, his brother
CURCIO, their father
GIL, a peasant
MENGA, a peasant woman
ALBERTO, a priest

The Story:

Two rustics, Gil and Menga, are looking for a lost donkey when they spy two men preparing to fight a duel. Lisardo, one of the men, is angry that anyone as low-born as Eusebio, the other, should aspire to marry Julia, Lisardo's sister.

Eusebio explains by telling a miraculous story. He was one of two infants abandoned beneath a wayside cross. Taken home by a shepherd, the famished baby bit the breast of his foster mother, who threw the child into a well, where his rescuers found him floating safely with arms crossed. Later the house in which he was living burned, but the fire broke out on

the Day of the Cross, and once more he survived unharmed. More recently, in a shipwreck, he floated to safety on a raft of two crossed planks. He explains that since he obviously acquired nobility by devotion to the cross, he deserves Julia. Lisardo denies the claim and they fight. As happened before in Eusebio's life, no harm comes to him in a dangerous situation. As Lisardo lies dying of his wound, he begs in the name of the cross for Eusebio to save him. The amazed peasants report that they saw Eusebio pick up his dying enemy and carry him to a convent.

Back in Siena, Julia is fearful of her father's discovery of letters she received from Eusebio. When her lover appears, wanting to take her away with him before she learns about her brother's death, her father's arrival forces him to hide and to listen to Curcio as he voices his long-held suspicions of his wife's infidelity. Curcio is interrupted by the arrival of four peasants carrying the body of Lisardo. Julia, grieving, orders the killer out of her life forever.

Eusebio, brokenhearted, turns bandit and through his cruelty rises to command a troop of outlaws. Only captives mentioning the cross escape death at his hands. One day a bullet-creased prisoner is brought in carrying a volume titled *Miracles of the Cross*. He is Father Alberto, and in gratitude for having his life spared the priest promises Eusebio that he will be on hand to hear the bandit's last confession.

News arrives that Lisardo's father, having put Julia into a convent, is pursuing Eusebio with soldiers. Scorning danger, Eusebio lets his passion for Julia take him to the convent, where he finds her in bed. Before he can take her, he sees on her breast the same sign of the cross that is on his own skin. The mark tells him that she was the other child left beside the cross, his sister, and so he runs away. Julia, who tried to fight him off in her cell, begins to pursue him in masculine attire. She does not know why he refused to love her.

When the soldiers overtake him, Curcio wounds Eusebio fatally. Then the cross on the young man's body reveals to Curcio that he slew his own son, abandoned with his twin sister because of the father's baseless suspicions of his wife's unfaithfulness.

With his dying breath, Eusebio calls for Father Alberto. Four shepherds arrive to bury his body. The priest also appears as he promised. He explains that because of God's pleasure in Eusebio's devotion to the cross, his soul was left in his body long enough for him to make his confession and to be redeemed.

Critical Evaluation:

To understand a religious play such as *The Devotion of the Cross*, one must keep in mind that Spain was a deeply religious nation, and that Pedro Calderón de la Barca truly expressed its feelings and ideas in the seventeenth century. The most popular of Spanish playwrights after the death of Lope de Vega in 1635, Calderón wrote secular and religious dramas until he took holy orders in 1651. From that time until his death he wrote only religious plays. *The Devotion of the Cross* is one of his early works. Since the characters and the setting are Italian, some critics assign it to the period when he was a soldier in Italy. The plot is less complicated than is usual in Calderón's work.

The Devotion of the Cross was one of the most controversial of the Baroque dramatist's works. First there was the problem of authorship; only in the latter part of the twentieth century was the play universally accepted as Calderón's. Then there were the critics whose analyses, at times oriented more toward the political and the religious than toward the literary, had more to do with Catholic Spain and Protestant England than the subject matter of the text itself.

Eighteenth and nineteenth century critics were outraged at the extravagance of the plot and the fetishism of what they claimed was the play's underlying philosophy, namely that salvation was possible through the obsessive veneration of an inanimate object. Even some of Calderón's admirers admitted that the mature Calderón himself probably was scandalized by this early work. Most chronologies give the date of composition as 1633, one that would place it close to that of Calderón's masterpiece *Life Is a Dream* (1635).

Criticism of *The Devotion of the Cross*, however, has now come full circle. Far from the derision of Protestant critics, or a mere mention in a footnote by Hispanic scholars, the play is now praised for its allegorical nature and is viewed as representative of Calderón's thematic and dramatic craftsmanship.

Curcio is the character in whom the Caldernian imprint is most evident. A tyrannical father, one of a long line of the dramatist's dysfunctional male parents, he is also afflicted by the fatal Calderonian disease, a blind self-aggrandizement that is outwardly manifested in violent spasms of honor. One such outbreak leads him to commit the deed, the murder of his wife, that has poisoned his life and that eventually causes the destruction of his entire family. Rosmira dies but not before giving birth to twins. Julia, one of the twins, is saved, however, the other twin, Eusebio, is lost. Even though Curcio secretly believes in his wife's innocence, and no one else has even doubted her, his pride forces him to kill her. Exterior appearances, even admitted self-delusions, are what matter to him. They are his identity. This concept of self has robbed his son of his identity, a confusion that is given dramatic irony in the scene in which Eusebio and Julia, unknown brother and sister, but also lovers, confront each other over the dead body of their brother Lisardo, who is killed because he ridicules Eusebio's lack of family and position. (Some students of seventeenth century staging have asserted that in the performance, Lisardo would have been lying crosswise between Eusebio and Julia with the corpse's hands also placed in a position similar to a cross.)

Far from being just an effective stage device or a dramatic motif, the symbol of the cross represents true identity. On an individual level, it is Eusebio's only link with his past. Found at the foot of a cross and possessed of a mysterious birthmark in the shape of a cross, Eusebio's life history has been marked by this sign. Nevertheless, his veneration of the cross is not a blind devotion to the object, the superstitious fetishism seen by early critics, but, instead, it is an authentic perception, although dimly glimpsed at times, of what the symbol can reveal to him about his life. It is a hope that Eusebio does not lose, even after he descends into a life of violence and crime. In fact, fetishism is explicitly derided in the scene in which the comic figure Gil cynically covers himself with imitation crosses and is captured anyway.

The cross is not just the personal symbol of identity for Eusebio, but in the larger Christian worldview of this drama, it is the symbol of truth for all humanity. Some readings of *The Devotion of the Cross* have focused on the heavy allegorical content of the work. Eusebio, therefore, is marked with the sign of the cross, as are all Christians. Eusebio's fall from grace is representative of Adam's fall from paradise, and his salvation, even after death, symbolizes the powerful redemptive gift of Christ's mercy. Eusebio's life, also like that of all Christians, is colored by the original sin of the father—in a religious context again, that of Adam's fall, but in Eusebio's life, first by the decision of his father to murder his mother and, second, by his father's vengeance after Lisardo's death; his father's vengeance deprives him of his lands and possessions and forces him into a life of flight and crime.

Curcio, therefore, has twice stripped his son of his identity, and Curcio's vindictive pursuit leads to Eusebio's death. Curcio is, after all, the one who committed murder at the foot of a cross, and every evil consequence in the play can be traced to the consequences of his actions. He is the puppet master pulling the strings, and this sense of a malevolent presence controlling their lives makes the protagonists desperate. They seem driven to lash out at anyone or anything. They lack self-control, and their lives seem predestined.

This repudiation of free will on one hand and the emphasis on an uncritical, all-forgiving grace—no matter what the crimes of the sinner—on the other hand have bothered some students of Calderonian drama and have possibly contributed to the initial hesitation in attributing the play to Calderón, who has been seen as the foremost champion of free will and has repeatedly been cited as one of the precursors of Existentialism. Calderón did write several works with strong fatalistic undertones, most of which were set in pre-Christian—therefore, unredeemed—times. The mood of these works is similar to that of *The Devotion of the Cross*. In *The Great Cenobia* (1625), for example, characters such as Cenobia either accept their fate with stoic fortitude, or they rage against it. In either case, there is no thought of changing

destiny. In *The Devotion of the Cross*, Eusebio and Julia are portrayed as innocent victims of their father's crime and pride, and they are branded by his follies, just as surely as by their cross birthmark. A miracle is necessary to save them, and only Christ's grace triumphs over blindness and egotism and the oppression of society's rigid codes. Interpreted in this light, the dual theme of the play is Calderónian, a search for self-identity filtered through a protest at a tyrannical honor code and a vindication of free will, with the difference that here the free will belongs to God.

"Critical Evaluation" by Charlene E. Suscavage

Further Reading

Benabu, Isaac. *Reading for the Stage: Calderón and His Contemporaries*. Rochester, N.Y.: Tamesis, 2003. Analyzes playtexts for works by Calderón and contemporary playwrights. A playtext is usually read by the theater company at the beginning of a play's production and provides the playwright's directions for staging his or her work. Benabu's examination of playtexts discusses the religiosity of Spanish theater in the Golden Age, Calderón's devotional comedies, and the character of Pedro Crespo in *The Mayor of Zalamea*.

Heigl, Michaela. *Theorizing Gender, Sexuality, and the Body in Calderonian Theater*. New Orleans, La.: University Press of the South, 2001. Focuses on the transvestites, scolds, sodomites, monsters, and other "deviant" characters in Calderón's plays, demonstrating how they embody the idea of excess and subvert the boundaries between the sexes and between different social classes. Heigl maintains that these characters represent the inherent corruption and perversion in society.

Honig, Edwin. *Calderón and the Seizures of Honor*. Cambridge, Mass.: Harvard University Press, 1972. Detailed analysis of the often debated theme of honor in Calderón's plays. Selected quotes from the plays are in English, but the Spanish is provided in an appendix.

McKendrick, Melveena. "The *Bandolera* of Golden Age Drama: A Symbol of Feminist Revolt." *Bulletin of Hispanic Studies* 46 (1969): 1-20. Discusses the *bandolera*, a popular figure of the age. Also discusses Calderón's portrayal of Julia.

Parker, A. A. "The Father and Son Conflict in the Drama of Calderón." *Forum for Modern Language Studies* 2 (1966): 99-133. Critically acclaimed study of one of the pivotal themes in Calderonian drama. An excellent starting point for further study.

_____. "Towards a Definition of Calderonian Tragedy."

Bulletin of Hispanic Studies 39 (1962): 223-237. One of the seminal essays of modern Calderonian criticism. Discusses Parker's famous theory of shared responsibility. His analysis of *The Devotion of the Cross* is the most widely accepted.

Rodríguez Cuadros, Evangelina. "Pedro Calderón de la Barca." In *The Cambridge History of Spanish Literature*, edited by David T. Gies. New York: Cambridge University Press, 2004. An overview of Calderón's life and work, placing it within the broader context of Spanish literature.

Thacker, Jonathan. *A Companion to Golden Age Theatre.* Rochester, N.Y.: Tamesis, 2007. An introductory overview of Spanish Golden Age theater. In addition to a chapter on Calderón, the book examines the work of other playwrights, describes the different types of plays produced in this era, and traces the growth and maturation of Spanish theater.

Dhalgren

Author: Samuel R. Delany (1942-   )
First published: 1975
Type of work: Novel
Type of plot: Science fiction
Time of plot: 1975
Locale: Bellona, in the American Midwest

Principal characters:
THE KID, a drifter and poet
LANYA and DENNY, his lovers
ROGER CALKINS, a newspaper editor

The Story:

A drifter and former inmate of a mental hospital who cannot even remember his own name meets a strange naked woman in a wood. After they make love, she directs him to a cave where he climbs a rock face and discovers a chain festooned with mirrors, prisms, and lenses. Obeying some barely understood whim, he wraps the chain around his body. Drifting on, he travels to the midwestern city of Bellona where an apocalypse of some kind has occurred. As he enters the city, the drifter encounters a group of women who are leaving it. They give him a weapon known as an orchid, an arrangement of blades worn on a strap around the wrist.

On his first night in Bellona, the drifter meets Tak, a former engineer, who takes to calling him "kid" (during the course of the novel, he will be variously known as Kidd, the kid, or the Kid; readers never learn his real name). Tak introduces the Kid to a community of hippies living rough in the park. One of them, a harmonica-playing and independent-minded woman named Lanya, will become his lover. Lanya hands the Kid a notebook, the first words of which are the first words of *Dhalgren*. Whoever kept the notebook previously wrote on only one side of each page, so the Kid decides to keep the book and write his own poems on the facing pages.

For a while, the Kid has a job helping a family called Richards move their apartment. In the midst of the chaos and confusion that characterize the vastly depopulated Bellona, Mrs. Richards is desperately trying to hold onto her safe, middle-class lifestyle, but the cracks are clearly showing. The family becomes the first appreciative audience for the Kid's poems.

The Richardses' daughter, June, was the victim of what was either a rape or a consensual but violent sexual encounter with a large black man, George Harrison, on the very night of the apocalypse (there is a suggestion that the two events may have been in some way linked). June is now obsessed with George, who has become a celebrity in the city, but she is too nervous to approach him. When the Kid gives June a poster of a naked George, her younger brother Bobby threatens to reveal her secret, and she kills him by arranging for him to fall down an open elevator shaft. Trying to recover the body, the Kid is helped by a group of young squatters who belong to a gang called the Scorpions. The Scorpions, whose violent reputation is not entirely unjustified, take their name from the projectors they wear; the devices cast huge, multicolored images of various beasts about them as they roam the streets.

Bellona is a place cut off from the rest of the world, where the normal rules of behavior no longer apply. It is shrouded under permanent dense clouds, though once the clouds part to reveal two moons in the sky. On another occasion, the Sun rises so close that it fills half the sky. No radio or television signal reaches the city, the power supply is intermittent, and people scavenge for food, but there seems to be no shortage of drink. Time, in particular, is out of joint: The Kid meets a number of people who were born in the same year as he was but who are different ages. The city's newspaper, published by the powerful but mysteriously elusive Roger Calkins, bears dates chosen more or less at random. Visitors come to stay with Calkins. One, an eminent poet named Newboy, reads the Kid's poems, and, although his response to them is ambiguous, he arranges for Calkins to publish them in a book to be called *Brass Orchids*.

The Kid coincidentally meets up with the Scorpions as they raid a department store where the former staff have taken to firing pot shots at people from the store windows. His calmness under fire, taking a rifle away from one person and saving the life of one of the Scorpions, gives him a reputation as a hero. When he decides to join the Scorpions, he is automatically made the leader of the gang. He and Lanya form a sexual threesome with a Scorpion named Denny.

Further exploits, including spotting white snipers at a black church service and rescuing five children from a fire, cement the Kid's reputation as a hero. His book is published to general acclaim. A book-launch party staged by Calkins is filled with sexual and threatening encounters. However, a series of meetings—with former astronaut Captain Kamp, with Calkins in a monastery garden, and with former psychoanalyst Madame Brown—cause the Kid to question the reality of his experiences, suggesting that the encounter that opened the book was just a dream. Finally, another cataclysm rends the city, causing him to lose touch with Denny and Lanya and forcing him to flee Bellona with nothing resolved.

Critical Evaluation:

Samuel R. Delany is one of the most powerful and distinctive writers to have emerged in American science fiction in the 1960's. Both African American and gay, he gave a voice to two groups that had rarely been heard in the genre before, often including echoes of his own autobiographical experiences in his fiction. More than that, Delany, who held the Butler Chair of English at the State University of New York at the time *Dhalgren* was published and who has since held a number of distinguished academic positions, has long been one of the most challenging critics of the genre. He had already experimented with the structure and narrative voice of his fiction, notably in the self-referentiality of his previous novel, *Nova* (1968). It was hardly surprising, therefore, that *Dhalgren* should have been the first significant work of science fiction to have employed the techniques of postmodernism.

The novel famously opens in mid-sentence and ends partway through a sentence, the two linking together so that the novel forms an endless loop. This type of device was employed by James Joyce in *Finnegans Wake* (1939), which ends with the word "the." A more appropriate comparison, however, might be between *Dhalgren* and Joyce's *Ulysses* (1922). Like *Ulysses*, Delany's novel tells of a central character's odyssey through a city that is symbolically imbued with scenes from mythology. While *Ulysses* is cast within the dramatic harmony of a single day, *Dhalgren* is outside time. No temporal references in the book ever make sense (at various points, the Kid experiences events that seem to him to occur within a single day, although others inform him that several days have passed). Where *Ulysses* ends with Molly Bloom's long, unpunctuated monologue, *Dhalgren* ends with a long extract from the Kid's notebook, complete with misspellings, insertions, strikethroughs, and marginalia.

The mythic quality of Bellona and its inhabitants is wild and various, as Delany draws on many different sources. The episode called "House of the Ax," for instance, largely set in the Labrys Apartments, echoes elements of Greek myth. The final, belated appearance of Roger Calkins behind a screen in a monastery garden calls to mind the wizard from the 1939 film adaptation of *The Wonderful Wizard of Oz* (1900), a small man behind a large screen. The novel's major mythological reference seems to be the one obliquely suggested by its title.

Dhalgren's title is mysterious. The name William Dhalgren appears in a list of names that the Kid finds in his notebook; the list is given in full twice, and there are two further references to parts of the list, both including the name Dhalgren. For a while, it seems that this might be the Kid's own name, though in the end it is suggested (though, like much else in the novel, never explicitly stated) that it is the name of a minor character, a reporter on Calkins's newspaper who appears only in two brief scenes. There is only one other occasion on which the word appears in the novel, but this episode is significant: During an extended sex scene, the Kid finds the word running endlessly through his mind, until it starts to change shape and Dhalgren becomes Grendel, the monster in the Old English saga *Beowulf* (eighth to eleventh century). This is the only time that Delany makes even an oblique reference to Grendel and hence to *Beowulf*, even though that poem clearly provides much of the mythic underpinning for the novel.

It is equally possible to read the Kid as Beowulf, the warrior leader with his band of men gathered around him in the mead hall (the Scorpions in their nest), and as the monster, the dark underside of a city become myth. The Kid can also be identified with the legendary King Arthur and with the Arthurian figure the Fisher King: The Kid always has one foot bare, causing him to walk with a slight limp. This limp, which is referred to several times throughout the text, becomes a symbolic equivalent of the Fisher King's lameness. In fact, so profuse are the mythic resonances throughout *Dhalgren* that it becomes almost too easy to make such identifications. Perhaps it is better simply to recognize such echoes without making them too specific.

The novel also serves as an extended metaphor for an outsider trying to succeed in the literary world during the long tail of the 1960's. The novel effectively starts with the Kid beginning to write his poems in the notebook. Each incident is accompanied by the Kid writing it down, agonizing over choice of words, crossing words out, and rewriting them. He begins to find an audience when he reads his poems to the Richards family then goes on to receive advice and help from a more established poet, Newboy. His poems are accepted by a publisher, he reads proofs, the book is published, and the climax of the main body of the novel is the launch party.

The story of the Kid's book is broken up by scenes of violence and social decay, by long and explicit sex scenes, and by scenes that establish the Kid as an outsider striving for acceptance within the literary world. Once the launch party closes the story of the book, the character of *Dhalgren* itself changes: The (relatively) coherent third-person narration is replaced by the deliberately incoherent first-person narration of the notebook, in which the Kid feels increasingly distanced from his own work even as he sees more people reading it. Toward the end, he begins to doubt that he even wrote the book at the same time that he doubts whether any of the events depicted within the novel is anything more than a dream.

For all his importance within the science-fiction genre, Delany is not always an easy writer to read. Some parts of *Dhalgren* are overwritten, some parts are deliberately obscure, and some of the sex scenes are uncomfortably direct (Delany has written a number of works of pornography). Nevertheless, *Dhalgren* is a compelling and challenging work that had a profound effect upon the science fiction of the 1970's and continues to be one of the key texts within the genre.

Paul Kincaid

Further Reading

Adair, W. Gilbert. *The American Epic Novel in the Late Twentieth Century: The Super-Genre of the Imperial State*. Lewiston, N.Y.: E. Mellen Press, 2008. Compares *Dhalgren* to three other American epic novels: *Centennial* (1974), *The Executioner's Song* (1979), and *Gravity's Rainbow* (1973). Reads each text in terms of its representation of and response to American empire.

Delany, Samuel R. *Heavenly Breakfast*. New York: Bantam, 1979. One of a number of autobiographical works by Delany, this book deals specifically with his experiments in communal living that fed directly into the situations explored in *Dhalgren*.

Fox, Robert E. *Conscientious Sorcerers*. Westport, Conn.: Greenwood Press, 1987. Places Delany in the context of other black postmodern writers, including LeRoi Jones (Amiri Baraka) and Ismael Reed.

McEvoy, Seth. *Samuel R. Delany*. New York: Frederick Ungar, 1984. The chapter on *Dhalgren* that concludes this work examines it as a series of puzzles relating to being a writer.

Sallis, James, ed. *Ash of Stars: On the Writing of Samuel R. Delany*. Jackson: University Press of Mississippi, 1996. This collection contains two key essays on *Dhalgren*, and there are references to the novel throughout the book.

Tucker, Jeffrey A. *A Sense of Wonder: Samuel R. Delany, Race, Identity, and Difference*. Middletown, Conn.: Wesleyan University Press, 2004. Includes a chapter on the contentious interplay between racial and sexual identity in *Dhalgren*.

The Dialogic Imagination

Author: Mikhail Bakhtin (1895-1975)
First published: Voprosy literatury i estetiki, 1975
    (English translation, 1981)
Type of work: Essays and literary criticism

The Dialogic Imagination by Russian theorist Mikhail Bakhtin comprises four essays that examine the novel as a living genre, one that resists classification in terms of its form, function, and placement in literary history. The word "dialogic" in the title distinguishes between dialogue (two or more people communicating interactively through language) and monologue (one person speaking, thinking, or writing in solitude). Bakhtin views language as a duality; it is both an established structure of meaning that exists prior to a language user and a unique production of meaning made immediate by a language user. Meaning is constantly created and recreated through dialogic processes. Bakhtin believes that the novel is uniquely dialogic in contrast to other genres that tend to be monologic. Imaginatively and practically, novels engage in conversations with other works of literature, those that predate them and those yet to be written. Additionally, a dialogic relationship exists between author and reader.

The four essays in *The Dialogic Imagination* are works of literary theory unified by their focus on the novel as a distinct and developing genre. Bakhtin concerns himself with the unique nature of the novel, its relationship to other genres, and its origins and development. Compared with other genres whose patterns are established and fixed, such as the epic, the novel according to Bakhtin is a fluid, developing form, one that resists generic categorization. Frequently in these essays, Bakhtin uses the novel as a vehicle for his exploration of ideas about the nature of language and its relationship to social structures.

The first essay in the volume, "Epic and Novel," compares these two genres. While previous critics believed that the novel evolved from the epic, Bakhtin finds the two forms antithetical. The epic lauds a complete and irrecoverable past, while the novel, fond of inconclusiveness and multiplicity, predicts a vital future. For Bakhtin, the epic has unalterable characteristics, including ties to a national past that serves as both its subject and its source. He argues that, because its origins predate written language and are memory-based, the epic is separated by a chasm from contemporary reality. Bound as it is to an unrecoverable past—a monologic past that cannot engage with the present—the epic is a dino-

saur, a lifeless genre. The epic is connected to an idealized past with no connection to the present. The dead speak, but the living cannot reply.

In contrast to the static epic, Bakhtin notes, the novel resists containment. Attempts to define the novel, he observes, are always accompanied by caveats: The novel is multilayered and plot-based, except when it is not; the novel is a love story, except when it is not; the novel is written as prose, except when it is not. While scholars traditionally date the emergence of the novel to Miguel de Cervantes' *Don Quixote de la Mancha* (1605, 1615), Bakhtin traces its roots further back to folktales that disrupt authoritative texts by their elicitation of laughter. He recognizes novelistic tendencies as early as Plato's Socratic dialogues (c. fourth century B.C.E.). Plato's use of blended dialects, his penchant for irony, and the connections he draws to a living reality—a reference to people expressing ideas active in their own time—allows these works to engage in dialogue with readers in the future. Bakhtin suggests that the novel defies classification and remains a living genre because of its tendency to borrow from nonfiction forms of writing such as the epistle, memoir, and history. Bakhtin predicts that the novel, unlike the epic, will remain dialogically connected to the present as it continues to evolve.

The second essay, "From the Prehistory of Novelistic Discourse," provides an account of two elements in ancient and medieval literature that were essential to the emergence of the modern novel. Focusing on humor and polyglossia (the presence of several languages in the same geographic region), Bakhtin examines certain texts from past eras that he believes were precursors to the novel. He observes that the standard genres of epic, lyric, and tragedy in Ancient Greek and Roman texts were always accompanied by parodic doubles that were outside the genre of the works they parodied. Bakhtin notes that a parodic poem is not a poem; it is a distinct and separate category of discourse that incorporates both the lyric language of traditional poetry and numerous opposing discourses, including regional dialects. Encounters with other cultures and languages (ancient Rome was trilingual) led to an expanded conception of language and its uses.

The myth of one unifying language was dispelled through parodic works that employed many types and levels of discourse.

Bakhtin notes a similar occurrence in medieval literature in the popular parodies of sacred texts. Religious rituals and observances had comic doubles in carnival games and plays in which peasants could portray foolish bishops and prattling kings, thus dissolving established hierarchies, at least temporarily, in the name of entertainment. These parodies broke through the monologic nature of established and condoned texts and reveled in dialogic possibilities. Secular festivals, like parodic literature, provided opportunities for common people to talk back to and poke fun at their social superiors. Bakhtin concludes "that every parody is an intentional dialogized hybrid. Within it, languages and styles actively and mutually illuminate one another." Bakhtin rejects the notion that competition between modes of literature led to the development of the novel; rather, he believes that centuries of interaction between diverse cultures, languages, and levels of society allowed the novel to emerge.

"Forms of Time and of the Chronotope in the Novel" appears third in the volume, and it is perhaps the most rigorous of the four essays in terms of its subject matter. "Chronotope" is a Bakhtinian coinage that merges "chronology" with "topography"; the term refers to the time-space variables that Bakhtin believes organize every act of writing. While chronotopes are present in other genres, chronotopes are most various in the novel. Bakhtin follows developmental changes in the novel by examining how time and space function as units of organization in works by authors as diverse as Aristophanes (c. 446-386 B.C.E.), François Rabelais (1494-1553), and Leo Tolstoy (1828-1910). By focusing on how chronotopes function uniquely in the novel, Bakhtin is able to further prove the novel's distinctness from other genres.

The volume concludes with "Discourse in the Novel," an essay in which Bakhtin presents his philosophy of language. He writes about the self-conscious nature of discourse—that is, its awareness of other consciousnesses. This idea of self-consciousness is exemplified by "heteroglossia," a term Bakhtin uses to convey the multiplicity and diversity of voices present in any discourse. Observing that poetry has been the favored genre within the institution of literature and that prose has been held in lesser esteem, Bakhtin traces this assessment back to the privileging of poetics over rhetoric by ancient philosophers. Poetry, because of its stylistics, is esteemed for its aesthetic appeal, while prose, which is closer to rhetoric, is regarded for its utility, its ability to instruct or to persuade. Bakhtin questions why useful language, such as the common modes of rhetoric employed by the masses, is considered inferior to poetry, when the latter is employed by only a select few.

Additionally, Bakhtin identifies two forces present in language that help explain his observed disparity between poetry and prose. Borrowing terminology from scientific discourse, he argues that centripetal force governs monologic language and compels elements of language toward a codified center, while centrifugal force governs dialogic language and disperses those same rhetorical elements outward in various directions. Bakhtin proposes that poetic language is centripetal and prose language centrifugal. Poetry is object-focused and inwardly directed, while prose is subject-focused and outwardly directed. Furthermore, Bakhtin notes that the novel is both heteroglossic (multivocal) and dialogic (engaged in conversation). Ideas communicated by novels are not anchored to a safe and official site of meaning; on the contrary, they are dispersed into the world of readers who engage with authors in their own making of meaning.

Bakhtin's contributions to literary theory and criticism are significant. By emphasizing the heteroglossic nature of discourse, he reshapes critical views on the relationship of literature and language to society. By revealing that all language is dialogic, and emphasizing the explicitly dialogic nature of the novel, he argues implicitly that the novel is the most authentic form of literature, since it embraces rather than denies its dialogic character. In *The Dialogic Imagination*, Bakhtin recognizes that the novel, distinct among all other genres, is a vital, developing literary form still in its nascent state and one that holds the greatest potential for future developments in literature. The novel may even resurrect dead genres. As other forms of writing become more novelized—that is, as they assume the open-ended characteristics of the novel, Bakhtin sees the possibility for their revitalization.

Dorothy Dodge Robbins

Further Reading

Bostad, Finn, et al., eds. *Bakhtinian Perspectives on Language and Culture: Meaning in Language, Art, and New Media.* New York: Macmillan, 2005. Collection of essays that apply Bakhtinian theory to various media.

Clark, Katarina, and Michael Holquist. *Mikhail Bakhtin.* Cambridge, Mass.: Harvard University Press, 1984. This biography traces the development of Bakhtin's ideas against the backdrop of Stalin's repressive regime.

Dentith, Simon. *Bakhtinian Thought: An Introductory Reader.* New York: Routledge, 1994. Presents major concepts in Bakhtinian theory with helpful examples.

Hirschkop, Ken, and David G. Shepherd, eds. *Bakhtin and Cultural Theory.* 2d ed. New York: Manchester University Press, 2002. Collection of scholarly essays that examine the relevance of Bakhtin's ideas to cultural theory.

Morson, Gary, and Caryl Emerson. *Mikhail Bakhtin: Creation of a Prosaics.* Stanford, Calif.: Stanford University Press, 1990. Provides a comprehensive examination of

Bakhtin's work as a whole. Focuses on terminology, authorship, and theories.

Vice, Sue. *Introducing Bakhtin.* New York: Manchester University Press, 1997. Employs examples from popular culture, in particular cinema, to bring clarity to Bakhtinian terms such as carnival, the dialogic, chronotope, and heteroglossia.

The Dialogues of Plato

Author: Plato (c. 427-347 B.C.E.)
First transcribed: 399-347 B.C.E. (English translation, 1804)
Type of work: Philosophy

Principal personages:
SOCRATES, the Athenian philosopher
GORGIAS, a Sophist
PROTAGORAS, a Sophist
CRITO, Socrates' contemporary, an aged friend
PHAEDRUS, a defender of rhetoric
ARISTOPHANES, a poet and playwright
THEAETETUS, a hero of the battle of Corinth
PARMENIDES, the philosopher from Elea
PHILEBUS, a hedonist
TIMAEUS, a philosopher and statesman
PLATO, Socrates' pupil

The Dialogues of Plato rank with the extant works of Aristotle as among the most important philosophical works of Western culture. The extent of Plato's influence is partly due to the survival of his works, unlike those of earlier Greek philosophers, as well as to the fact that at various times in the history of the Christian church his ideas were used in the process of constructing a Christian theology (though in this respect Aristotle's influence was greater). The principal cause of his past and continuing effect on human thought, however, is the quality of his work.

The distinctive character of Platonic thought finds adequate expression in the dialogue form. Although Plato, like all philosophers, had his favored perspectives from which he interpreted and, consequently, saw the world, he realized better than most philosophers that philosophy is more an activity of the mind than the product of an investigation. This is not to say that philosophy does not, in some legitimate sense, illuminate the world. In the process of making sense out of experience, the philosopher is restless: No single way of clarifying an idea or a view is entirely satisfactory, and there is always much to be said for an alternative mode of explanation.

When distinctive Platonic conceptions finally become clear, they do so against a background of penetrating discussion by means of which alternative ideas are explored for their own values and made to complement the conception that Plato finally endorses. As an instrument for presenting the critical point-counterpoint of ideas, the dialogue is ideal, and as a character in control of the general course and quality of the discussion, Socrates is unsurpassed.

Socrates was Plato's teacher, and it was probably out of respect for Socrates the man and the philosopher that Plato first considered using him as the central disputant in his dialogues. Reflection must have reinforced his decision, for Socrates was important more for his method than for his fixed ideas, more for his value as a philosophical irritant than as a source of enduring wisdom. The Socratic method is often described as being designed to bring out the contradictions and omissions in the philosophical views of others; better yet, it can be understood as a clever technique for playing on the ambiguities of claims so as to lead others into changing their use of terms and, hence, into apparent inconsistency.

The extent to which Plato uses the dialogues to record Socrates' ideas and to which he uses Socrates as a proponent of his own ideas will probably never be conclusively answered. The question is historical, but in the philosophical sense it makes no difference whose ideas found their way into the dialogues. A fairly safe assumption is that it was Socrates who emphasized the importance of philosophical problems of value, knowledge, and philosophy itself. He probably argued that it is important to know oneself, that the admission of one's own ignorance is a kind of wisdom possessed by few individuals, and that virtue is knowledge.

Certainly Socrates must have had a devotion to his calling as philosopher and critic: No one who regarded philosophy as a game would have remained in Athens to face the charge that by philosophy he had corrupted the youth of Athens, nor would he have refused a chance to escape after having been condemned to death. Socrates' courage and integrity are recorded with poignant power in the *Apology*, the dialogue in which Socrates defends himself and philosophy against the charges brought against him; the *Crito*, in which Socrates refuses to escape from prison; and the *Phaedo*, in which Socrates discusses the immortality of the soul before he drinks the hemlock poison and dies.

Of the ideas presented in the dialogues, perhaps none is more important than Plato's theory of Ideas or Forms. This theory is most clearly expressed in the *Republic*, the dialogue in which the problem of discovering the nature of human justice is resolved by considering the nature of justice in the state. Plato distinguishes between particular things, the objects experienced in daily living, and the characters that things have, or could have. Goodness, truth, beauty, and other universal characters—properties that can affect a number of individual objects—are eternal, changeless, beautiful, and the source of all knowledge. Although some critics claimed that Plato is speaking metaphorically when he talks, through Socrates, about the reality of the Forms, the dialogues leave the impression that Plato considers the Forms to exist, in some sense peculiar to themselves, as universals or prototypes that things may or may not exemplify.

A survey, however brief, of the range of questions and tentative answers to be found in the dialogues provides no more than a bare inkling of Plato's power as a philosopher. Only a careful reading leads to a true appreciation of the depth of Plato's speculative mind and the skill of his dialectic. Only a reading, moreover, can convey Plato's charm, wit, and range of sympathy. Whether the final result may be in good part attributed to Socrates as Plato's inspiring teacher is unimportant. Socrates as the subject and Plato as the writer (and philosopher—in all probability more creative than Socrates) combine to create an unforgettable image of the Hellenistic mind.

Although many of the dialogues concern themselves with more than one question, and although definitive answers are infrequent so that discussions centering on a certain subject may crop up in a number of different dialogues, certain central problems and conclusions can be isolated in the *Dialogues*.

Charmides centers on the question "What is temperance?" After criticizing a number of answers, and without finally answering the question, Socrates emphasizes the point that temperance involves knowledge. *Lysis* and *Laches* consider, respectively, the questions "What is friendship?" and "What is courage?" The first discussion brings out the difficulty of the question and of resolving conflicts of values; the second one distinguishes courage from a mere facing of danger and makes the point that courage, as one of the virtues, is a knowledge that involves willingness to act for the good. The *Ion* exhibits Socratic irony at work on a rhapsodist who is proud of his skill in the recitation of poetry. Socrates argues that poetry is the result of inspiration, a divine madness. In the *Protagoras*, Socrates identifies virtue and knowledge, insisting that no one chooses evil except through ignorance. One of a number of attacks of the Sophistical art of fighting with words is contained in the *Euthydemus*.

In the *Meno*, the philosopher Socrates and his companions wonder whether virtue can be taught. The doctrine that ideas are implanted in the soul before birth is demonstrated by leading a slave boy into making the correct answers to some problems in geometry. At first it seems that since virtue is a good and goodness is knowledge, virtue can be taught. Because, however, there are no teachers of virtue, it cannot be taught; in any case, because virtue involves right opinion, it is not teachable. In the *Euthyphro*, the idea that piety is whatever is pleasing to the gods is shown to be inadequate.

The *Apology* is the most effective portrait of Socrates in a practical situation. No moment in his life had graver consequences than the trial resulting from the charge that he corrupted the youth of Athens by his teachings, yet Socrates continued to be himself, to argue dialectically, and to reaffirm his love of wisdom and virtue. He pictured himself as a gadfly, stinging the Athenians out of their intellectual arrogance. He argued that he would not corrupt anyone voluntarily, for to corrupt those about him would be to create evil that might harm him.

Socrates is shown as a respecter of the law in the *Crito*; he refuses to escape after having been pronounced guilty. In the *Phaedo* he argues that the philosopher seeks death because his whole aim in life is to separate the soul from the body. He argues for the immortality of the soul by saying that opposites are generated from opposites; therefore, life is generated from death. The soul is by its very nature the principle of life; hence, it cannot itself die.

The dialogue *Greater hippias* does not settle the question "What is beauty?" but it does show, as Socrates points out, that "All that is beautiful is difficult." The subject of love is considered from various philosophic perspectives in the *Symposium*, culminating in the conception of the highest love as the love of the good, the beautiful, and the true. *Gorgias* begins with a discussion of the art of rhetoric and proceeds to the development of the familiar Socratic ideas that it is better to suffer evil than to do it, and that it is better to be punished for evildoing than to escape punishment.

The *Parmenides* is a fascinating technical argument concerning various logical puzzles about the one and the many. It contains some criticism of Plato's theory of Ideas. Plato's increasing interest in problems of philosophic method is shown by the *Cratylus*, which contains a discussion of language beginning with the question whether there are true and false names. Socrates is not dogmatic about the implications of using names, but he does insist that any theory of language allow people to continue to speak of their knowledge of realities.

The *Phaedrus* is another discourse on love. It contains the famous myth of the soul conceived as a charioteer and winged steeds. In the *Theaetetus*, Socrates examines the proposal by Theaetetus that knowledge is sense perception. He rejects this idea as well as the notion that knowledge is true opinion.

The *Sophist* is a careful study of sophistical method with emphasis on the problem of being and non-being. In the *Statesman*, Plato continues the study of the state he initiated in the *Republic*, introducing the idea—later stressed by Aristotle—that virtue is a mean.

Socrates argues in the *Philebus* that neither pleasure nor wisdom is in itself the higher good, since pleasure that is not known is worthless and wisdom that is not pleasant is not worth having; only a combination is wholly satisfactory. A rare excursion into physics and a philosophical consideration of the nature of the universe are found in the *Timaeus*. Here Plato writes of God, Creation, the elements, the soul, gravitation, and many other matters.

The *Critias*, an unfinished dialogue, presents the story of an ancient and mythical war between Athens and Atlantis; and with the *Laws*, the longest of the dialogues, Plato ranges over most of the areas touched on in his other dialogues, but with an added religious content: Soul is the source of life,

motion, and moral action; there is an evil soul in the universe with which God must deal.

Further Reading

Benson, Hugh H., ed. *A Companion to Plato*. Malden, Mass.: Blackwell, 2006. The book's twenty-nine essays include an overview of Plato's life; discussions of his use of the dialogue form and his method of dialectics; and examinations of his philosophical ideas about epistemology, metaphysics, psychology, ethics, politics, and aesthetics.

Blondell, Ruby. *The Play of Character in Plato's Dialogues*. New York: Cambridge University Press, 2002. Focuses on the characterization in Plato's dialogues, viewing it as both a literary form and as fundamental to his philosophical concern with moral character. Argues that the dialogues should be read as drama and analyzes the use of character in *Hippias Minor, Republic, Theaetetus, Sophist*, and *Statesman*.

Corlett, J. Angelo. *Interpreting Plato's Dialogues*. Las Vegas, Nev.: Parmenides, 2005. Discusses various approaches to understanding Plato's writings. Argues that the dialogues were influenced by Plato's respect for his teacher, Socrates, and for the way Socrates engaged others in philosophical conversations.

Cormack, Michael. *Plato's Stepping Stones: Degrees of Moral Virtue*. New York: Continuum, 2006. Analyzes the Platonic claim that "virtue is knowledge" by examining the role of knowledge in dialogues from Plato's early and middle period. Compares and contrasts concepts of "craft knowledge" and "moral knowledge."

Grube, G. M. A. *Plato's Thought*. Indianapolis, Ind.: Hackett, 1980. A good exposition of Plato's thought designed for both specialists and nonspecialists. Focuses on broad themes, such as the Ideas, Eros, the soul, the gods, and education, rather than on individual dialogues. Includes a valuable bibliographic essay.

Guthrie, W. K. C. *Plato, the Man and His Dialogues: Earlier Period* and *The Later Plato and the Academy*. Vols. 4 and 5 in *A History of Greek Philosophy*. New York: Cambridge University Press, 1975, 1978. Contains a lucid summary and substantial discussions of each dialogue. Scholarly and authoritative, yet fully accessible to the general reader.

Kahn, Charles H. *Plato and the Socratic Dialogue: The Philosophical Use of a Literary Form*. New York: Cambridge University Press, 1996. A study of Plato's use of the dialogue form as a means for exploring and developing key philosophical positions and dispositions.

Raven, J. E. *Plato's Thought in the Making: A Study of the*

Development of His Metaphysics. New York: Cambridge University Press, 1965. Investigates the relative contributions of Socrates and Plato. Treats primarily the *Protagoras*, *Gorgias*, *Meno*, *Phaedo*, *Symposium*, *Republic*, *Phaedrus*, *Parmenides*, *Sophist*, and *Timaeus*. Appropriate for the general reader.

Rhees, Rush. *Plato and Dialectic*. Vol. 2 in *In Dialogue with the Greeks*. Edited by D. Z. Phillips. Burlington, Vt.: Ashgate, 2004. Uses the philosophical concepts of Lud-

wig Wittgenstein to analyze eight of the dialogues, including *Gorgias*, *Symposium*, *Sophist*, and *Phaedo*.

Warnek, Peter A. *Descent of Socrates: Self-Knowledge and Cryptic Nature in the Platonic Dialogues*. Bloomington: Indiana University Press, 2005. Interprets the dialogues as an inquiry into Socrates' nature, depicting the ancient Greek philosopher as a demonic and tragic figure whose obsession with self-knowledge transformed the course of philosophy.

Diana of the Crossways

Author: George Meredith (1828-1909)
First published: 1885
Type of work: Novel
Type of plot: Psychological realism
Time of plot: Nineteenth century
Locale: England

Principal characters:
DIANA MERION WARWICK, a young woman of beauty and charm
AUGUSTUS WARWICK, her husband
LADY EMMA DUNSTANE, Diana's friend
THOMAS REDWORTH, Diana's friend and admirer
LORD DANNISBURGH, another friend
SIR PERCY DACIER, a young politician in love with Diana

The Story:

All of fashionable London is amazed and shocked when the beautiful and charming Diana Warwick suddenly leaves her husband's house. The marriage was ill-fated from the start, for Augustus Warwick, a calculating, ambitious politician, considered the marriage to Diana as largely one of convenience. Diana, for her part, accepted his proposal as a refuge from the unwelcome attentions to which her position as an orphan exposed her.

Diana Merion first appears in society at a state ball in Dublin, where her unspoiled charm and beauty attract many admirers. Lady Emma Dunstane introduces Diana to Thomas Redworth, a friend of her husband, Sir Lukin Dunstane. Redworth's attentions so enrage Mr. Sullivan Smith, a hot-tempered Irishman, that he attempts to provoke the Englishman to a duel. Redworth pacifies the Irishman, however, to avoid compromising Diana by a duel fought on her account.

Later, while visiting Lady Emma at Copsley, the Dunstane country home in England, Diana is forced to rebuff Sir Lukin when he attempts to make love to her. Leaving Copsley, she goes to visit the Warwicks. Thomas tells Lady Emma that he loves Diana, but by then it is too late. Diana has already agreed to marry Augustus Warwick.

In London, the Warwicks live in a large house and enter-

tain lavishly. Among their intimates is Lord Dannisburgh, an elderly peer who becomes Diana's friend and adviser. While Warwick is away on a government mission, the two are often seen together, and Diana is so indiscreet as to let Lord Dannisburgh accompany her when she goes to visit Lady Emma, which gives rise to unkind gossip. On his return, Warwick, who is incapable of understanding that his wife is innocent, serves Diana with a divorce suit in which he accuses her of infidelity and names Lord Dannisburgh as correspondent. Diana disappears from Warwick's house and from London. In a letter, she tells Lady Emma that she intends to leave England. Her friend, realizing that flight will be tantamount to confession, feels sure that before she leaves the country, Diana will go to Crossways, her father's old home. Determined that Diana should remain and boldly defend herself, Lady Emma sends Redworth to Crossways with instructions to detain Diana and persuade her to stay with the Dunstanes at Copsley.

Lady Emma guesses correctly; Diana is at Crossways with her maid. At first, she is unwilling to see Lady Emma's point of view, for she thinks of her flight as a disdainful stepping aside from Warwick's sordid accusations; finally, however, she gives in to Redworth's arguments and returns with him to Copsley.

Although the court returns a verdict of not guilty to the charge Warwick brings against her, Diana feels that her honor is ruined and that in the eyes of the world she is guilty. For a time, she is able to forget her own distress by nursing her friend, Lady Emma, who is seriously ill. Later, she leaves England to go on a Mediterranean cruise. Before her departure, she writes a book entitled *The Princess Egeria*.

In Egypt, she meets Redworth, now a brilliant member of Parliament. He is accompanied by Sir Percy Dacier, Lord Dannisburgh's nephew and a rising young politician, who falls in love with her and follows her to the Continent. He is recalled to London by the illness of his uncle. Diana follows a short time later and learns on her arrival in London that Redworth is active in making her book a literary triumph. He arouses interest among the critics because he knows that Diana is in need of money.

Lord Dannisburgh dies, with Diana at his bedside during his last illness. He is her friend, and she pays him that last tribute of friendship and respect regardless of the storm of criticism it elicits. When Lord Dannisburgh's will is read, it is learned that he left a sum of money to Diana.

In the meantime, Diana inadvertently makes an enemy of the socially ambitious Mrs. Wathin, who thinks it her social duty to tear Diana's reputation to shreds. In part, her dislike is motivated by jealousy that Diana should be accepted by people who would not tolerate her. Her actions are also inspired by Warwick, Mrs. Wathin's friend, who, once he loses his suit against Diana, tries to force his wife to return to him.

Sir Percy's attentions are distressing to Diana. She is half in love with him but is still legally bound to Warwick. She faces a crisis when Mrs. Wathin calls to announce that Warwick, now ill, wants Diana to return and act as his nurse. Diana refuses, whereupon Warwick threatens to exercise his legal rights as her husband. Sir Percy, who informs her of Warwick's intention, asks her to elope with him to Paris. She agrees but is saved from that folly by Redworth, who arrives to tell her that Lady Emma is ill and about to undergo a serious operation at Copsley. Diana goes with him to be at her friend's side.

Lady Emma nearly dies, and the gravity of her condition restores Diana's own sense of responsibility. She orders Sir Percy to forget her. He continues to pursue her, however. One day, he confides the tremendous political secret that the prime minister is about to call on Parliament to pass some revolutionary reform measures. Then he attempts to resume his former courtship, but Diana refuses to listen to him; she feels that if she cannot not have Sir Percy as a lover, she cannot keep him as a friend.

Because Diana is in desperate need of money—she was forced to sell Crossways to pay her debts, and her later novels did not bring her any money—she goes to the editor of a paper that opposes the government party and sells him the information Sir Percy gave to her.

When the paper appears with a full disclosure of the prime minister's plan, Sir Percy accuses her of having betrayed him and discontinues his friendship with her. A short time later, he proposes to a young lady of fortune. About the same time, Warwick is struck down by a cab in the street and killed. Diana has her freedom at last, but she is not happy, knowing she is in public disgrace. Although she burns the check in payment for the information she disclosed, it is common knowledge that she betrayed Sir Percy and that he retaliated by marrying Constance Asper, an heiress. When Sullivan Smith proposes marriage, Diana refuses him and seeks refuge in the company of her old friend, Lady Emma. Her stay at Copsley frees her of her memories of Sir Percy, so much so that on her return to London she is able to greet him and his bride with dignity and charm. Her wit is as sharp as ever, and she takes pleasure in revenging herself upon those cross who attempted to destroy her reputation with their gossip and slander.

On another visit to Copsley, she meets Redworth again, who is now a railroad promoter and still a distinguished member of Parliament. When he invites her and Lady Emma to visit Crossways, Diana learns that Redworth bought her old home and furnished it with the London possessions she was forced to sell. He bluntly tells Diana that he bought the house and furnished it for her because he expects her to become his wife. Not wishing to involve him in the scandals that circulated about her for so long, she at first pretends indifference to his abrupt wooing. Lady Emma urges her to marry Redworth, however, since he has loved her for many years. At last, aware that she brings no real disgrace to Redworth's name, she consents to become his wife.

Critical Evaluation:

Any novel by George Meredith requires attention not only to the actual work but also to the wider aspects of the technique of fiction. Meredith was an original writer of deep concentration and mature force. His Diana is a character who is head and shoulders above most nineteenth century fictional English heroines, offering the charm of femininity as well as the portrait of one perplexed by convention and yet aware of its force. Her predicament involves errors in judgment but becomes a glory to her, and her career compels the reader's belief that a life that will not let go its harvest of errors until they are thoroughly winnowed is a human drama of deepest interest. Diana, beautiful, witty, and skeptical of social convention and moral expediency, is the embodiment of

Meredith's philosophy and art, and she shows that an individual can extract wisdom from life's experiences.

Diana of the Crossways is the most emphatically feminist of Meredith's novels, but a woman too intelligent and spirited to accept willingly her "place," as defined by Victorian society, figures prominently in virtually all of his fiction. Some, such as Diana's friend Emma Dunstane or Lady Blandish of *The Ordeal of Richard Feverel* (1859), manage to confine their protest to witty commentary while playing their assigned roles; others, like Diana, are forced by circumstances into active rebellion.

It is generally agreed that Meredith's chief model for his beautiful, brilliant, hard-beset heroines was his own first wife. In the fine poem sequence *Modern Love* (1862), he traces, thinly disguised, the course of their marriage from its happy and passionate beginnings through the conflicts that led to his wife's running off with an artist friend of Meredith. Although bitter at first, Meredith learned much from the experience of his first marriage and came to accept major responsibility for its failure. His novels repeatedly depict a loving and loyal woman virtually driven into the arms of another man by the blind egoism of her husband or lover. Asked by Robert Louis Stevenson on whom the protagonist of *The Egoist* (1879) was modeled, Meredith replied that his fatuous hero was drawn "from all of us but principally from myself."

Meredith believed that his society was dominated by egotism, chiefly that of men, and was both fearful and suspicious of anything bright and beautiful because of the threat that it posed to complacency. He shared the Victorian belief in progress, but he defined progress in terms of intelligence and sensibility. Choosing the comedy of wit as his preferred mode, he attacked the dull and smug and called for "brain, more brain." He recognized the tragedy of life but ascribed it to human failure. As he wrote in *Modern Love*, "no villain need be. We are betrayed by what is false within." The falseness may spring from self-deception or from unquestioning acceptance of what "the world" proclaims. What can save people is the ability to be honest with themselves and to see the world as it is, as well as the courage to act on their perceptions even in defiance of social norms.

Many of Meredith's contemporaries shared his belief in a continuing evolution of human beings' spiritual and intellectual capacities, but few besides Robert Browning were as ardent in affirming also "the value and significance of flesh." For Meredith, the goal of life was to realize one's full potentialities in a vital balance: "The spirit must brand the flesh that it may live."

Meredith's Diana fully exemplifies his philosophy of life. The central metaphor of the novel is the "dog-world" in hot pursuit of its quarry, a beautiful woman too intelligent and sensitive to play the role society demands of her, that either of "parasite" or of "chalice." Diana is, however, no spotless, perfect victim of malign persecutors. In precept and practice, Meredith scorned sentimental melodrama. Young and inexperienced, Diana brings much of her trouble on herself. She marries for protection and position, a prudent move by worldly standards but disastrous in its consequences. Achieving a measure of independence, she endangers it by her extravagance, and she is finally almost destroyed by an impulsive, desperate act. Although elements of the "dog-world" are moved by envy and malice, most of Diana's adversaries act "honorably" in their own eyes; it is the conventions of honor, of respectability, and—most important—of the place of women in Victorian society that nearly overpower her.

The resolution of the plot would seem to be a compromise if the novel were the feminist tract it has been called: Diana does not finally triumph as a fully independent person, accepted by society on her own terms and admired for her wit and nerve. Only rescued from despair by her friend Emma, she proves herself capable of standing alone but chooses instead to marry again. As Meredith presents her choice, however, it is not compromise but fulfillment. Her marriage to Redworth, who truly understands and values her, represents the ideal wedding of flesh and spirit, achieved not by good luck but after a process of striving, blundering, learning from mistakes, and finally seeing and accepting life as it is.

Diana of the Crossways was an immediate success upon publication, probably because its theme had been taken from a recent scandal involving a brilliant and beautiful Irishwoman, Mrs. Caroline Norton, who had been accused (as it proved, falsely) of selling an important government secret. Critics have generally tended to rate the work high among Meredith's works, often second only to his masterpiece *The Egoist*, and its themes are of perhaps even broader interest in the twenty-first century than they were in 1885. However, later readers have experienced some difficulty with Meredith's famous style, the joy and the despair of his admirers.

From his first work of fiction, *The Shaving of Shagpat* (1855), to his last, the prose of this admirable writer became progressively more poetic in its richness, precision, compactness, and indirection. In the earlier novels, it is a beautiful addition to plot and characterization; in the later, it sometimes detracts from or even obscures them. Oscar Wilde may not have been entirely fair in claiming that as a novelist Meredith could do everything but tell a story, yet in *Diana of the Crossways* and other later novels he often seems fastidiously averse to saying anything directly. The texture of his prose makes demands that not all readers are willing to meet, but the attentive reader is richly rewarded in beauty, wit, and subtlety of thought and expression. The very dazzle and density of Meredith's style, embodying as it does his vigorous and invigorating vision of life, continues to delight new generations of readers.

"Critical Evaluation" by Katharine Bail Hoskins

Further Reading

Conrow, Margaret. "Meredith's Ideal of Purity." *Essays in Literature* 10, no. 2 (Fall, 1983): 199-207. Explores Meredith's definition of the ideal of sexual purity and his double standard. Examines the Lugano scene in *Diana of the Crossways.*

Daniels, Elizabeth A. "A Meredithian Glance at Gwendolen Harleth." In *George Eliot: A Centenary Tribute*, edited by Gordon S. Haight. Totowa, N.J.: Barnes & Noble, 1982. Like George Eliot, Meredith did not wish to overturn Victorian marriage, but he was sharply critical of the callous nature of the male ego and believed that society needed women with fuller psychological development.

Deis, Elizabeth J. "Marriage as Crossways: George Meredith's Victorian-Modern Compromise." In *Portraits of Marriage in Literature*, edited by Anne C. Hargrove and Maurine Magliocco. Macomb: Western Illinois University Press, 1984. Discusses Meredith's position on marriage as a transitional one.

Elam, Diane. "'We Pray to Be Defended from Her Cleverness': Conjugating Romance in George Meredith's *Diana of the Crossways.*" *Genre* 21, no. 2 (Summer, 1988): 179-201. Argues that Meredith's text self-consciously thematizes romance, employing it not only as a process of structuring the novel but also as a subject of the narrative. Shows that reality outside the novel is also a narrative construction.

Fraser, Robert. "Nineteenth-Century Adventure and Fantasy: James Morier, George Meredith, Lewis Carroll, and Robert Louis Stevenson." In *A Companion to Romance: From Classical to Contemporary*, edited by Corinne Saunders. Malden, Mass.: Blackwell, 2004. Fraser's essay about Meredith and three other British writers is included in this study of romance literature, which charts the genre from its beginnings through the twenty-first century.

Harris, Margaret. "George Meredith at the Crossways." In *A Companion to the Victorian Novel*, edited by William Baker and Kenneth Womack. Westport, Conn.: Greenwood Press, 2002. An introductory overview of the Victorian novel. Contains essays about Meredith and other authors and discussions of the historical and social context of the Victorian novel, the growth of serialization, and the different genres of Victorian fiction.

Jones, Mervyn. *The Amazing Victorian: A Life of George Meredith*. London: Constable, 1999. Jones's biography aims to recover Meredith from obscurity and introduce the author to a new generation of readers. He links Meredith's life to his writing and includes a forty-page appendix recounting the plot summaries of all of Meredith's novels.

McGlamery, Gayla. "In His Beginning, His Ends: The 'Preface' to Meredith's *Diana of the Crossways.*" *Studies in the Novel* 23, no. 4 (Winter, 1991): 470-489. A close reading of the difficult opening chapters, with their contorted style and philosophical pronouncements, as a demonstration of all that Meredith hopes to achieve in the rest of the novel. Notes the new direction in his handling of identity and in his relationship to the reader.

Roberts, Neil. *Meredith and the Novel*. New York: St. Martin's Press, 1997. Roberts employs twentieth century literary criticism, especially the ideas of literary critic Mikhail Bakhtin, to analyze all of Meredith's novels. Includes bibliographical references and an index.

Diary

Author: Samuel Pepys (1633-1703)
First published: 1825, as *The Diary of Samuel Pepys*; enlarged editions, 1848-1849, 1875-1879, 1893-1899, 1970-1983
Type of work: Diary

The *Diary* of Samuel Pepys is a unique document in the annals of English literature, perhaps of all literature. There are other fascinating day-to-day accounts of interesting and momentous times, and some of these were written by people of genius, but there is only one other autobiographical collection—the recently discovered journals of James Boswell—that combines fascinating subject matter and genius of composition with the intriguing story that is associated with the *Diary* of Pepys.

There is an important difference between Boswell and Pepys. Boswell, as his editors admit, was writing for posterity; Pepys was not. Pepys's *Diary* was written for himself only, apparently for the sole purpose of allowing its author to savor once more, at the end of each day, the experiences of the preceding twenty-four hours. There is no evidence of revision of any kind, and the book was written in a shorthand that protected it from posterity for more than a hundred years after its author's failing eyesight forced him to give up keeping his diary.

Pepys's method of composition gives the *Diary* an immediacy that makes Boswell's *Journals* appear sedulously organized. The coded shorthand allows for admissions of personal animosities and revelations of scandalous behavior that otherwise would not be found in the writings of a responsible public official. That Pepys was a responsible, high-ranking public official is the last factor that contributes to the importance of his work. Boswell was the scion of an important Scottish family and a member of the Scottish bar, but (aside from his Corsican experience) the only history in which he was involved was literary history. Pepys was involved with the history of a nation at a very important time.

The *Diary* is important in a number of ways. First, it is of great value as a document of the Restoration period. No writer of a historical novel based on the history of the time could possibly create a character familiar with as many important events as was the opportunistic busybody, Pepys. One of the most influential figures in bringing about the return of the Stuarts in 1660 was the former Cromwellian, Sir Edward Montague, who was assisted by his able cousin and protégé, Pepys. It was Sir Edward who commanded the fleet that sailed from Holland and returned triumphantly with the king. On board the flagship, kissing the king's hand, firing a cannon to salute the new monarch (and burning an eye in the process), commenting on the plainness of the queen, taking charge of the king's dog in the landing at Dover was, again, Pepys.

Later, made Clerk of the Acts of the Navy Board because of his assistance to the Stuarts (Sir Edward was made Earl of Sandwich), he remained at his post in London and wrote down his observations of the terrible plague from which most members of his class fled in panic. It was Pepys, again, who did his best to keep the English Navy afloat during the Dutch Wars, and Pepys who defended the Navy in a brilliant speech before Parliament in the investigation that followed (1668). Earlier (September 2, 1666), when the great fire of London broke out, it was Pepys who rushed to the king to inform him of the catastrophe and to suggest the blowing up of houses to prevent the spread of the fire. Pepys, who had a part in all these events, tells of them in a straightforward, unselfconscious account unvarnished by fear of what his contemporaries would think or of what posterity would think.

Along with vivid pictures of the major events of Restoration history are day-to-day accounts of the less earthshaking but equally revealing activities in the life of the London that Pepys shared, accounts that make the *Diary* a document of social, cultural, and artistic history as well. Here Pepys's concern with—his actual delight in—detail brings a particular world of the past to life. Readers see the crowded, unsanitary, and often impassable London streets. At times, during trips to Pepys's father's house in Brampton or during excursions to the country, the reader catches glimpses of rural existence in the days of Charles II. Readers see life in the houses of the well-to-do and the noble and, occasionally, at court. On a more mundane scale, there is Pepys's concern with clothes (his father was a tailor and he reflects a professional knowledge) and his greater concern with managing his own household. Unfortunately for revelations on this score, Pepys had no children, but his problems in household management included his handling of the affairs of his rather shiftless parents, brothers, and sister, the maintenance of a staff of servants that grew as his own wealth increased, and domestic supervision of his beautiful but erratic—sometimes docile, sometimes temperamental—young wife. In regard to the arts, there is a wealth of material on the theater and on music. Pepys was an inveterate playgoer. Though his frequent attendance bothered his basically Puritan conscience and though he made intermittent vows to refrain, it is seldom that many entries go by in which some play that he saw is not commented on. These comments are so frequent that, in fact, the *Diary* is an invaluable source of information to the student of Restoration drama. It is equally valuable to the specialist in the history of music: Pepys was not only an accomplished musician but also a composer, and the delight in music that he expresses gives insight into a particularly musical age.

Artistic beauty was not the only kind that captivated the practical and mercenary Pepys. Since he was equally attracted to beauty in its carnal manifestations, his pursuit of beauty in feminine form and his diligent (but finally unsuccessful) attempts to hide these pursuits from his wife provide insight into the mores of the Restoration period. These accounts of the diarist's philanderings—honest, but hidden by the elaborate code—are a part of the personal revelation that the work provides.

In spite of its importance as a historical and a social document, the *Diary* is, on its most intriguing level, the self-portrait of a man, drawn in strong and certain lines with no detail, however uncomplimentary, however compromising, omitted. That it is the portrait of a man active in the affairs of his day adds to its interest; but the main value comes from its unstinting wealth of circumstantial detail. However, the detail and the man cannot be separated: The love of detail and the love of life that inspired the keeper of the *Diary* make up the essence of the man himself. The *Diary* is a celebration of the things of this world and a portrait of the man who praised them.

Further Reading

Coote, Stephen. *Samuel Pepys: A Life.* New York: Palgrave, 2001. Sympathetic and colorful account of Pepys's life, including the ten years Pepys chronicled in his own diary. Portrays Pepys as a convivial, ambitious, and curious individual.

Morshead, O. F. Introduction to *The Diary of Samuel Pepys: Selections*, edited by O. F. Morshead. New York: Harper & Row, 1960. Offers a brief biography of Pepys and his family, a publishing history of the diaries, and commentary on the diaries' content. Notes Pepys's energy, his artless style, and his surprising frankness.

Sutherland, James. *English Literature of the Late Seventeenth Century.* New York: Oxford University Press, 1969. Examines the subjects of Pepys's diary and notes his self-analysis and his remarkable honesty.

Taylor, Ivan E. *Samuel Pepys.* New York: Twayne, 1967. This general introduction to Pepys and his diaries organizes its chapters around the themes of Pepys's work, including his politics, family life, theatergoing, and womanizing.

Tomalin, Claire. *Samuel Pepys: The Unequalled Self.* New York: Vintage Books, 2003. Biographer Tomalin reconstructs Pepys's life based on his own diary, as well as numerous other resources, creating a portrait of the famed diarist as intelligent, energetic, and a savvy politician.

Willy, Margaret. *English Diarists: Evelyn and Pepys.* London: Published for the British Council and the National Book League by Longmans, Green, 1963. Includes a brief sketch of Pepys's life and a discussion of the scope of his diaries with reference both to what they reveal about his personality and to the historical events they record.

The Diary of a Country Priest

Author: Georges Bernanos (1888-1948)
First published: Journal d'un curé de campagne, 1936
   (English translation, 1937)
Type of work: Novel
Type of plot: Psychological realism
Time of plot: 1920's
Locale: France

Principal characters:
A PARISH PRIEST, the diarist
THE CURÉ DE TORCY, a superior of the narrator
DOCTOR MAXENCE DELBENDE, the narrator's friend
SERAPHITA DUMOUCHEL, a young parishioner
MONSIEUR DUFRETY, a former classmate of the narrator
THE COUNT, a wealthy resident of the parish
THE COUNTESS, his wife
MADEMOISELLE CHANTAL, their daughter
MADEMOISELLE LOUISE, the governess at the chateau

The Story:

A thirty-year-old priest who is in charge of the Ambricourt Parish in France records in his diary his impressions and activities over a period of one year. His purpose in keeping the diary is to maintain frankness with himself in his relationships with his parishioners and in his service to God.

The priest is a man of marked humility, sympathy, simplicity, and great loneliness. Son of a poor family in which there was much suffering and hardship, he plans to raise the scale of living in his parish. His plans for a village savings bank and for cooperative farming are discussed at his first monthly meeting with the curates, but his plans are disapproved because of their pretentious scope and his lack of personal influence in the parish. This blow, which causes him to question whether God is prepared to use his services as he did the services of others, is intensified by the words of his superior and ideal, the Curé de Torcy, and of his friend, Dr. Maxence Delbende, who soon afterward commits suicide because of his disappointment at not receiving a legacy he expected.

These two men thwart the young priest's ambition with their belief that the poor cannot be raised for religious and social reasons. God gives the poor a dignity, the Curé de Torcy says, which they do not wish to lose in his sight. According to the doctor, poverty serves as a social bond and a mark of prestige among the poor. In the eyes of the Church, the curate believes, the rich are on the earth to protect the poor.

Undaunted, the priest accepts an invitation to the chateau, where he hopes to get financial help for his parish projects from the count. He is unsuccessful in this, but he devotes himself with all his physical energy, which is limited because of insomnia and a chronic stomach disorder, to the spiritual advancement of his parish. Even here, however, his efforts are ill-spent. He questions his success in teaching a cate-

chism class when the children do not respond as he hopes, and he is tormented by the attentions of Seraphita Dumouchel, a young student in the class, who discomfits him by her suggestive questions and remarks to the other children and by the scribbled notes she leaves about for the young priest to find.

Seraphita later befriends him when on a parish visit he suffers a seizure and falls unconscious in the mud. A few days later, however, bribed by sweets, she tells Mademoiselle Chantal, the count's strong-willed, jealous daughter, that the priest fell in drunkenness. The story is believed because it is known among the parishioners that the priest drinks cheap wine and because his physical condition is growing progressively worse.

The priest's spiritual strength shows itself in his theological dealings with the count's family. In conversation and in confession, Mademoiselle Chantal tells him that her father is having an affair with Mademoiselle Louise. The daughter, believing that she is to be sent to England to live with her mother's cousin, declares that she hates everyone in her household—her father and the governess for their conduct and her mother for her blindness to the situation. After asserting that she will kill Mademoiselle Louise or herself and that the priest will have to explain her conduct to God, she gets his promise that he will discuss the girl's problems with her mother.

The priest goes to the chateau to confer with the countess regarding her daughter's spiritual state. There he finds the mother in an even more atheistic frame of mind than that of her daughter. Her spiritual depression results from the death of her baby son, twelve years earlier. During a prolonged philosophical discussion, in which she ridicules the priest for his theological idealism and his lack of vanity and ambition, the countess describes with bitterness the hateful selfishness of her daughter and relates with indifference the count's many infidelities.

Before he leaves the chateau, the priest senses a spiritual change in his wealthy parishioner when she throws into the fire a medallion containing a lock of her son's hair. The priest, always humble, tries to retrieve the locket. In a letter delivered to him at the presbytery later in the day, the countess tells him that he gave her peace and escape from a horrible solitude with the memory of her dead child. The countess dies that night.

The priest's success in helping to redeem her soul leaves him with an uncertain feeling. He does not know whether he is happy or not. If his reaction is happiness, it is short-lived. When the details of his session with the countess become known as a result of Mademoiselle Chantal's eavesdropping, criticism and derision are heaped on him. The canon reprimands him because he assumed the role of her confessor, and the Curé de Torcy ridicules his approach in dealing with the countess. Members of the family, unstable as they are in their relationships, accuse him of subversive tactics.

His lack of social grace, his personal inadequacies, and his professional ineptitude seem to increase as his physical condition grows worse. Because his hemorrhages continue, he decides to consult Dr. Lavigne in Lille. His last major bungle is in connection with this medical aid. Forgetting the name of the doctor recommended to him in Lille, he turns to the directory and mistakenly chooses the name of Dr. Laville. The physician, a drug addict, bluntly diagnoses the priest's ailment as cancer of the stomach. From the doctor's office, the priest goes to the address of his old schoolmate at the seminary, Monsieur Dufrety, who long urged his friend to visit him. There he dies that night.

In a letter from Monsieur Dufrety to the Curé de Torcy, details of the priest's death are described. In great suffering and anguish following a violent hemorrhage, the priest held his rosary to his breast. When he asked his old friend for absolution, his request was granted and the ritual performed in a manner, Monsieur Dufrety writes, that could leave no one with any possible misgivings. The priest's last words affirmed his great faith in the whole scheme of things because of God's existence.

Critical Evaluation:

A Catholic novelist in the manner of Julien Green and François Mauriac, Georges Bernanos was a visionary for whom the forces of good and evil were genuine presences. He shows a fierce integrity in his writing, although his views are sometimes oversimplified or inconsistent. His charac-

ters, while representing extremes of human behavior ranging from saintliness to depravity, are battlegrounds for good and evil, and their souls are the prize. These priests and other individuals who devote their lives to God are powerfully imagined and realistically drawn.

The Diary of a Country Priest has a meager plot because Bernanos is more interested in showing a man's thoughts and basic principles than in describing general human behavior; this novel is a fictional presentation of priestly attitudes, functions, and tribulations. Through this philosophical and realistic treatment of life in a small French parish, readers recognize Bernanos's high regard for Joan of Arc as the symbol of France. In the simplicity of her peasantry and saintliness, the maid is not unlike the diarist. Compassion and tenderness characterize the writing, which in translation sustains the poetic charm and fluency of the original. Humankind's holiness is Bernanos's keynote.

One of the themes of *The Diary of a Country Priest* is that of the conflict between individual religious ecstasy and the day-to-day "housekeeping" of the church. The young priest's aspirations, at once naïve and noble, are touching, but his failure to live up to them causes him increasing unhappiness. He wants more than anything else to be of use to God and to his parishioners, but he feels thwarted at every step and is not sure why. The picture of the hard, narrow villagers, with their materialistic and shallow ways, their stubbornness and malice, is vivid and complete; the reader soon understands the pain of the youthful priest's frustration when he is unable to elevate them spiritually.

Boredom, Bernanos suggests, is the beginning of evil, or at least the ground in which it grows. The young priest sees that life for his parishioners is nothing but boredom. The nature of injustice worries him as does the nature of true poverty. Everyone constantly gives him advice, warning him of intolerance, excessive dedication, or pride, but none of them can see into his heart and mind and understand what really troubles him. The naïve and unworldly qualities of the young priest give him an innocent charm.

Despite his inexperience, the priest knows that "each creature is alone in his distress." His growing wisdom is a growing realization of the loneliness of the individual. From the beginning, he is beset by ailments and becomes obsessed by them; soon, illness dominates his physical existence, but his spiritual life grows richer and more intense.

At the end, the priest learns that true humility does not lie in self-hatred, but rather that the supreme grace is to "love oneself in all simplicity." His death, revealed in a moving letter from his friend to his superior, expresses his ultimate sense of peace.

Further Reading

Blumenthal, Gerda. *The Poetic Imagination of Georges Bernanos: An Essay in Interpretation*. Baltimore: Johns Hopkins University Press, 1965. An analysis of the poetic imagination at work in the novel. Associates this poetic vision with Bernanos's mystical explication of human behavior.

Brée, Germaine, and Margaret Guiton. "Private Worlds." In *An Age of Fiction: The French Novel from Gide to Camus*. New Brunswick, N.J.: Rutgers University Press, 1957. Interprets the country priest as a figure tormented by private and public incompatibilities. His diary is therefore a reflection of what the priest cannot, perhaps dares not, communicate to his parish or to church authorities.

Bush, William. *Georges Bernanos*. Boston: Twayne, 1969. Bush discusses Bernanos's contention that evil in modern society is connected with conservative social forces and that humans secretly covet totalitarian order. Examines *The Diary of a Country Priest* as a vehicle of private thoughts that sustain the dying priest; chief among these thoughts is the possibility that self-realization comes only with death.

Curran, Beth Kathryn. *Touching God: The Novels of Georges Bernanos in the Films of Robert Bresson*. New York: Peter Lang, 2006. French filmmaker Bresson adapted *The Diary of a Country Priest* for a film. Curran explains how both Bernanos and Bresson articulate grace and redemption through the suffering and death of their protagonists.

Field, Frank. "Georges Bernanos and the Kingdom of God." In *Three French Writers and the Great War: Studies in the Rise of Fascism*. New York: Columbia University Press, 1975. Field overestimates the effect of World War I on Bernanos's pessimism but he offers insights into the political and social underpinning of *The Diary of a Country Priest*. Although impressionistic, this study links Bernanos to larger trends in 1920's ideology.

Hebblethwaite, Peter. *Bernanos: An Introduction*. New York: Hillary House, 1965. This work emphasizes the importance of childhood events as the psychological determinant of adult behavior. Offers a close reading of *The Diary of a Country Priest* with a detailed analysis of Bernanos's innovative techniques. The priest is presented as an exemplar of spiritual tenacity.

Tobin, Michael R. *Georges Bernanos: The Theological Source of His Art*. Montreal: McGill-Queen's University Press, 2007. A biography and literary critique of Bernanos's work. Tobin analyzes the themes of Bernanos's works to demonstrate how the incarnation of God in Jesus Christ was the fundamental theological truth common to all of his writings.

Whitehouse, J. C. *Vertical Man: The Human Being in the Catholic Novels of Graham Greene, Sigrid Undset, and Georges Bernanos*. London: Saint Austin Press, 1999. Whitehouse analyzes and compares the works of the three novelists, concentrating on how they depict the relationship of the individual human being with his or her God.

The Diary of a Young Girl

Author: Anne Frank (1929-1945)
First published: Het Achterhuis, 1947 (English translation, 1952; revised, 1995)
Type of work: Autobiography
Time of plot: June 12, 1942-August 1, 1944
Locale: Amsterdam

Principal personages:
ANNE FRANK, a teenage Jewish girl
MARGOT FRANK, her older sister
OTTO FRANK, their father
EDITH FRANK-HOLLÄNDER, their mother
MR. VAN DAAN, Otto's business associate
MRS. VAN DAAN, Van Daan's wife
PETER VAN DAAN, their son
ALBERT DUSSEL, a dentist

The Story:

On June 12, 1942, at the height of World War II in Europe, Anne Frank celebrates her thirteenth birthday in hiding from the Nazis. Two days later, she makes her first entry in her new diary. She writes about her birthday celebration and about her gifts, which include the diary. She continues to make regular entries until August 1, 1944, three days before her Jewish family and four other Jews are discovered by German security police in a hiding place—called the Secret Annex—above Anne's father's former office at Prinsengracht 263 in Amsterdam. Someone had tipped off the police.

On July 13, 1942, one week after the Franks move into their hiding place, they are joined in the Secret Annex by the van Daans and their son, Peter. On November 16, Albert Dussel, a dentist, joins them in hiding.

Anne writes to an imaginary friend named Kitty about how she is maturing as she adapts to living in tense confinement. The Secret Annex is on the top floor of Otto Frank's former office with the Travis Company. The still-in-business company rents the office space and is staffed by people who are loyal to Otto and his family and who are committed to helping him and the others who are hiding upstairs. The entrance to the Secret Annex is behind a bookcase that can be pulled out to reveal the staircase it hides.

With a perception that belies her youth, Anne records the dynamics and interrelationships of the people who live in this cramped space. Anne has a close relationship with her father, Otto, an intelligent, practical man, but her relationship with her mother, Edith Frank-Holländer, is strained, mostly by the confinement in which the two, and the others, are forced to exist.

The confinement is intensified because the exiles have to keep utterly silent during office hours, lest a visitor hear them moving about. Even though Anne and the others in hiding can move about more freely at night, they must do so in the dark. Any flicker of light detected by passersby might lead to their discovery.

Anne is beginning to feel the stirrings of adolescent sexuality, but she has no one to help her deal with them, except Peter, two years her senior. Anne, who had initially disliked Peter, gradually grows to love him. Within the confining Secret Annex, the two must act with restraint. Peter's mother is a controlling woman who is often at odds with Anne, frequently ending her stinging criticisms of her with the words "If Anne were my daughter," to which Anne responds with "Thank heavens I'm not!"

Although Anne is keenly aware of the hazards under which she and the others live, she retains an optimistic attitude and, above all, still believes in the inherent goodness of people. This remarkable adolescent refuses to be overcome by her hatred for her oppressors, the Nazis and their collaborators. She accepts her life with extraordinary courage. On April 11, 1944, Anne writes one of the longest and most exciting entries in the diary: "I know that I'm a woman, a woman with inward strength and plenty of courage."

Critical Evaluation:

The Diary of a Young Girl chronicles the coming of age of a sensitive and highly talented Jewish teenager named Anne Frank. At the time she made her first entries into her now-famous diary, she was pampered and immature. Former American first lady Eleanor Roosevelt, in her introduction to the book's first edition in English, comments on the diary's remarkable veracity, noting that a writer as young as Frank could be counted on to write truthfully.

Roosevelt, too, contends that the greatest evil of the Holocaust and the war that it had spawned was the degradation of the human spirit. Frank is not oblivious to this degradation, but she is somehow able to distance herself from it. With her life in danger every day, she still looks ahead optimistically. She fantasizes about what she and those sequestered with her—her mother, father, and sister, and four others—will do when their exile ends.

The diary essentially falls into two portions, the first year and the second year of Anne's confinement in the Secret Annex. In the course of the consecutive entries in the diary, Anne develops from a bright but somewhat spoiled young girl into a mature person whose psychological insights are impressively keen. Although she sometimes shows her annoyance at the people with whom she is hiding, she reveals no hatred for the Nazi oppressors who are out to annihilate all European Jews (and who, ultimately, kill two-thirds of the world's Jewish population). She realizes that she may be caught up in the net of anti-Semitism that pervades much of Europe, but she does not permit herself to dwell on this threat.

After their arrest on August 4, 1944, the eight people who had been in hiding for more than two years in the Secret Annex were transported to the Westerbork transit camp, then to Auschwitz. Later, Anne and her sister, Margot, were sent to the Bergen-Belsen concentration camp in Germany. Both of them died at the camp in March, 1945, just one month before Bergen-Belsen was liberated by British forces. Only Otto Frank, Anne's father, survived. He returned to Amsterdam, found that his daughter's writings had been saved, and became instrumental in the publication of Anne's diary.

The Diary of a Young Girl has been translated into more foreign languages than any other book written in the twentieth century. It has been adapted for film and stage, and its influence remains enormous.

R. Baird Shuman

Further Reading

Barnouw, David, and Gerrold van der Stroom, eds. *The Diary of Anne Frank: The Revised Critical Edition.* Translated by Arnold J. Pomerans et al. New York: Doubleday, 2003. This is the most accurate version of Anne Frank's diary. The editors use handwriting analysis and other sophisticated techniques to verify the authenticity of various portions of the manuscript.

Brenner, Rachael F. *Writing as Resistance: Four Women Confronting the Holocaust—Edith Stein, Simone Weil, Anne Frank, and Etty Hillesum.* University Park: Pennsylvania State University Press, 1997. Brenner includes Frank in a significant group of women who resisted Nazi incursions into their countries by recording, in writing, the effects of these incursions.

DeCosta, Denise. *Anne Frank and Etty Hillesum: Inscribing Spirituality and Sexuality.* Translated by Mischa F. C. Hoynick and Robert E. Chesal. New Brunswick, N.J.: Rutgers University Press, 1998. An interesting study of two contemporary young Jews who had been in hiding during the Nazi occupation of the Netherlands in World War II.

Frank, Anne. *Anne Frank's Tales from the Secret Annex.* Translated by Susan Massotty. Edited by Gerrold van der Stroom and Massotty. New York: Bantam Books, 2003. A collection of Frank's other writings, including her short stories, fables, personal reminiscences, and an unfinished novel, *Cady's Life.* A revealing look into a little-known side of Frank the writer.

Hillesum, Etty. *"An Interrupted Life" and "Letters from Westerbork."* Translated by Arnold J. Pomerans. New York: Henry Holt, 1996. Hillesum, a Jewish woman who, like Frank, had been in hiding in the Netherlands during World War II, writes about her experiences as an exile and at the Westerbork camp. Like Frank, she did not survive.

Lindwer, Willy. *The Last Seven Months of Anne Frank.* Translated by Alison Meersschaert. New York: Pantheon Books, 1991. This resource considers the increasing maturity of Frank during her exile in the Secret Annex for more than two years.

Rittner, Carol, ed. *Anne Frank in the World: Essays and Reflections.* Armonk, N.Y.: M. E. Sharpe, 1998. Twelve essays by recognized scholars examine Frank's life and diary. Includes a useful section listing videos and teaching resources on Frank and the Holocaust.

Van Galen Last, Dick, and Rolf Wolfswinkel. *Anne Frank and After: Dutch Holocaust Literature in Historical Perspective.* Amsterdam: Amsterdam University Press, 1996. A valuable resource that considers Frank's writing in relation to Dutch postwar literature on the Holocaust.

The Diary of Anaïs Nin
1931-1934

Author: Anaïs Nin (1903-1977)
First published: 1966
Type of work: Diary

From the age of eleven until her death at the age of seventy-four, Anaïs Nin kept a series of diaries. Her father, a well-known composer and musician, had abandoned her, her mother, and her two brothers, forcing the family to move from France, where Nin was born, to New York City. Nin began her diary on the long journey to the United States.

The main diary, dating from the early 1930's, grew to seven published volumes. After Nin's death, another four volumes were published as *The Early Diary of Anaïs Nin* (1982, 1983, 1985). Rupert Pole, her second husband and the executor of her estate, published another four volumes beginning in 1986 that are based on her original diary, which became known as the unexpurgated diary to distinguish it from the original. These unexpurgated versions are known individually as *Henry and June* (1986), *Incest* (1992), *Fire* (1995), and *Nearer the Moon* (1996). The original *Diary of Anaïs Nin* is the earliest volume of those published in 1966. The first volume, which covers 1931 to 1934, is widely considered the best and most important of the original works.

Although a novelist, poet, and literary critic of considerable talent and reputation, Nin is best remembered as a diarist and for her considerable influence on other artists, including her lover Henry Miller. His *Tropic of Cancer* (1934) and *Tropic of Capricorn* (1938), two novels steeped in sex and violence, were banned in the United States until the 1960's. Nin wrote the preface to *Tropic of Cancer* and financed its initial printing.

Although she quit school at the age of sixteen, Nin was attracted to avant-garde writers, artists, and musicians and developed her personal style and her writing style while sitting in the cafés of Paris, listening and observing and then capturing it all in her diary. For a time, Nin worked as an artist's model and also studied Spanish dance. While in Cuba in 1923, she married Hugh Parker Guiler, a banker, and later a filmmaker known as Ian Hugo. He also was an illustrator of Nin's books. After Guiler was transferred to a bank in Paris, he and Nin lived in Louveciennes, in the western suburbs of Paris. Nin and Guiler agreed that he would never be mentioned in her diaries. In fact, Nin was reluctant to admit that she was married and never discussed her marriage during interviews. By any measure, their marriage was open. Nin had several affairs during her years married to Guiler, including with Miller, psychoanalyst Otto Rank, and playwright-poet Antonin Artaud.

In contrast to Miller's work, *The Diary of Anaïs Nin* is sexually implicit. Nin keeps sex in the background, obscured by opaque references and cloying allusions. The diary is often unilluminating in its descriptions of events and its depictions of persons. Indeed, the diary makes for an unreliable witness to history. However, Nin's prose is lyrical and flowing, a lovely stream of phrases sacrificed to the author's unquenchable thirst for introspection and self-knowledge.

In her first diary volume, Nin submits her psyche to the examination of two psychoanalysts, Rank and René Allendy. As one might suspect from an addicted diarist, comparing her need to document her life to a drug addict's need for a fix, Nin is keen for analysis, to have a professional explore the depths of her mind much as she has done her entire life. Nin later becomes a practicing psychoanalyst for some time with Rank, who was at one time a devoted follower of Sigmund Freud, but later was ostracized from Freud's circle for calling into question some of his mentor's work.

Volume one of *The Diary of Anaïs Nin* opens with the publication of Nin's first book, the nonfiction work *D. H. Lawrence: An Unprofessional Study* (1932). The attorney Nin had hired to represent her to the publisher of her book introduced Nin to an American writer living in Paris, Miller. Over the course of their years spent together in Paris, Miller and Nin read and critiqued each other's works, edited each other's manuscripts, and spent many hours talking about Miller's second wife, June. June is Miller's literary muse, the inspiration and central character in his most important novels. June profoundly affected Nin as well, and June became the inspiration for a portion of Nin's second novel, *Winter of Artifice* (1939).

Nin's first novel, *House of Incest* (1936), worried her family because of its title. As is made abundantly clear in the second unexpurgated volume of her diary, *Incest*, Nin had an incestuous relationship with her father. What began as child sexual abuse became a consensual sexual affair in the 1930's and was reportedly precipitated by psychoanalysis, in which it was suggested that Nin undertake the affair and then abandon her father, as he had abandoned her and her mother and brothers. Her family need not have worried; *House of Incest* is not an account of Nin's personal experience, at least not in any recognizable fashion. The work is a prose poem, presented in metaphorical terms—incest here refers more to self-seeking, an understanding of one's own psychological motivations. In volume one of the diary, Nin's father appears and seeks a nonsexual relationship with his daughter, one befitting an aging man who has ostensibly given up sexual conquests for a more chaste familial relationship. Nin refers to him as The Double in volume one, perhaps alluding to his role as both father and lover.

In Henry and June, Nin thought she saw people who were more alive than she. Married and struggling to write poetry and literary criticism, Nin turned to her diary to find herself, not always her true self but the self she wished she were. The diary is a distorted reflection of its author, a mirror that is more flattering than critical. When volume one opens, Nin is transitioning. She changes her clothes, her friends, her interests. She is a work in progress, a laboratory experiment in metamorphosis; her diary is her lab book. She records her progress, triumphs, and losses in a way that shows the influence of surrealism on her life. She is her own palette.

Nin's lasting reputation is a salacious one. Much of her reputation comes from the popularity of two small books: *Delta of Venus: Erotica* (1977) and *Little Birds: Erotica* (1979). As with everything else she learned, Nin was self-taught when it came to sex. She gained her education through French books of erotica that she found hidden in the back of a closet in a house her family had rented. According to Nin, she was an innocent when she had found the books; after reading them, there was nothing she did not know about sex. While struggling as writers in Paris, she and Miller, to make money, wrote erotica for a private collector who paid them one dollar per page. It was this work that paved the way for the two small volumes of erotica, which were published posthumously.

A citizen of the United States, Nin lived much of her life in New York and on the West Coast. Although she never divorced Hugh Guiler, she moved back to the United States with him, and they lived independently of each other. Their independence was such that Nin married Rupert Pole, a man nearly twenty years younger, whom she had met in New York in 1947. The couple married in Arizona in 1955, making Nin a bigamist. For eleven years, Nin balanced two marriages, flying from coast to coast to be with Pole and with Guiler, who learned of Nin's second marriage only after her death. Nin had her marriage to Pole annulled in 1966.

Randy L. Abbott

Further Reading

Bair, Deirdre. *Anaïs Nin: A Biography*. New York: Putnam, 1995. A massive biography by a scholar steeped in the literature of the period and the author of biographies of Samuel Beckett and Simone de Beauvoir.

Bloshteyn, Maria R. *The Making of a Counter-culture Icon: Henry Miller's Dostoevsky*. Toronto, Ont.: University of Toronto Press, 2007. Describes how Fyodor Dostoevski was a model for Nin, Henry Miller, and Lawrence Durrell, all of whom strove to emulate the Russian writer's psychological characterizations and narrative style in their own work.

Bobbitt, Joan. "Truth and Artistry in *The Diary of Anaïs Nin*." *Journal of Modern Literature* 9, no. 2 (May, 1982): 267-276. This is an examination of the style, literary quality, and artistic truthfulness of *The Diary of Anaïs Nin*.

Felber, Lynette. "The Three Faces of June: Anaïs Nin's Appropriation of Feminine Writing." *Tulsa Studies in Women's Literature* 14, no. 2 (Autumn, 1995): 309-324. This article explores feminism in Nin's writings and her efforts to capture the essence of June Miller, Henry Miller's wife, as a way to introduce feminine discourse.

Fitch, Noel Riley. *Anaïs: The Erotic Life of Anaïs Nin*. Boston: Little, Brown, 1993. This book makes use of interviews, archives, and unpublished works to explore the woman behind the diary and the life experiences that influenced Nin's direction as an artist.

Franklin, Benjamin, V. *Anaïs Nin Character Dictionary and Index to Diary Excerpts*. Troy, Mich.: Sky Blue Press, 2009. A detailed resource that features an index of all persons, places, and works from Nin's unpublished diary excerpts. Also includes descriptions of every character in her published fiction.

Knapp, Bettina L. *Anaïs Nin*. New York: Ungar, 1979. This work examines surrealism and its impact on Nin's fiction, especially *House of Incest*.

Pierpont, Claudia Roth. *Passionate Minds: Women Rewriting the World*. New York: Alfred A. Knopf, 2000. Evocative interpretive essays on the life paths and works of twelve women, including Nin, connecting the circumstances of their lives with the shapes, styles, subjects, and situations of their art.

Tookey, Helen. *Anaïs Nin, Fictionality and Femininity: Playing a Thousand Roles*. New York: Oxford University Press, 2003. Examines Nin's work within historical and cultural contexts, focusing on her representations of identity and femininity and her concept of self-creation through various kinds of narratives and performances.

_____. "I Am the Other Face of You: Anaïs Nin, Fantasies, and Femininity." *Women: A Cultural Review* 12, no. 3 (Winter, 2001): 306-324. Explores Nin's duality, the reality her critics accuse her of omitting, and the artistic, fully alive woman Nin wishes to portray.

The Dining Room

Author: A. R. Gurney, Jr. (1930-   )
First produced: 1982; first published, 1982
Type of work: Drama
Type of plot: Comedy
Time of plot: Approximately 1930 to 1980
Locale: Northeastern United States

Principal characters:
FATHER, a conservative autocrat
MOTHER, his wife
GIRL, his daughter
BOY, his son
GRACE, a conservative matron
CAROLYN, her daughter
ARCHITECT, a practical designer
PEGGY, a philandering wife
GRANDFATHER, a wealthy patriarch
NICK, his grandson
OLD LADY, an anile matriarch
AUNT HARRIET, a grande dame
TONY, her nephew, a student
JIM, a beleaguered father
MEG, his married daughter
STANDISH, a guardian of family honor
HARVEY, an orderly man of affairs
RUTH, a host
ANNIE, a servant
A DINING ROOM TABLE, a venerable family heirloom

The Story:

An unnamed real estate agent and her client discuss the possible uses of the dining room in an old house available for sale. Although the client expresses some sentimental interest in the room, he declines to make an offer on the home, and the two plan to look elsewhere.

At a different time and place, the siblings Arthur and Sally argue over which of them will get the dining room table left behind by their widowed mother, who moved to Florida. The issue remains unresolved, and the Father, a precise, finicky man, starts complaining to Annie, the servant, that on the previous day he found a seed in his orange juice. He begins instructing his son and daughter in breakfast-table deportment and criticizes the deficiencies of his son's teacher, Miss Kelly. The Father is joined by his wife, the Mother, while another husband, Howard, expresses irritation with his wife, Ellie, because she starts to do schoolwork on the dining room table. He complains that the table and its place mats, his family's heirlooms, are very valuable, and he tries to persuade her to work elsewhere. When she resists he storms out and Ellie, unfazed, returns to her work on the table.

Carolyn, a young teenager, next explains to her unreceptive mother, Grace, why she wants to go to the theater with her aunt Martha. Grace, who believes that the eccentric,

mildly bohemian Martha will be a bad influence on Carolyn, tries to make her daughter stay home to fulfill other obligations while insisting that Carolyn is free to make up her own mind. To Grace's chagrin, Carolyn decides to go with her aunt.

A young boy, Michael, who is sick and at home from school, tries to talk a servant, Aggie, into staying on in the family service. At the same time, an Architect and Psychiatrist begin to discuss plans for remodeling the house so that it can be used both as a home and as an office. The Architect recalls his past in such a room and his unwilling participation in agonizing family-dinner rituals. To the hesitant Psychiatrist, he proposes that the dining room, a relic, be sacrificed for office and reception space.

A children's birthday party for a boy named Brewster follows, hosted by Peggy, Brewster's mother. Ted, the father of one of the children, arrives to pick him up, and as the party progresses, Ted and Peggy, sotto voce, discuss their deteriorating adulterous liaison. When the children go off to play party games, the Grandfather, an elderly man of about eighty, enters and sits at the head of the dining table. He is approached by Nick, his grandson, who is sent to ask him for financial support for his education at a private, exclusive preparatory school. After remarking wistfully that things were different when he was young and that times are not so easy, the Grandfather agrees to help. Toward the end of the Grandfather's litany, Paul begins examining the table, checking to see why it developed a wobble, which worries its owner, Margery. After crawling under the table with Paul, Margery discovers, to her dismay, that the table, made in 1898, is an American replica of an earlier English piece. The two plan to repair the table together and leave for the kitchen to seal their partnership with a drink.

In the wake of their departure, celebrants gather in the dining room for a Thanksgiving dinner. Two of them, Stuart and Nancy, try to explain the situation to the Old Lady, Stuart's mother, but she is completely disoriented and fails to understand what is happening. The men at the dinner sing for her, and for a moment it appears that she might come around, but when they finish, the Old Lady, lost in her youth, asks them to call for her carriage, noting that her mother expects her home for tea. Stuart and his brothers escort her out, leaving the women behind to commiserate about the situation over stiff drinks.

Two girls, Helen and Sarah, released from school, enter next and discuss raiding the pantry liquor supply. In the absence of Sarah's mother, they plan to invite some boys for a party. Kate and Gordon, illicit lovers, appear, fresh from a guilty tryst. They attempt to regain their composure over tea but are taken aback by the unexpected arrival of Kate's son, Chris, whose coldness toward Gordon reveals his suspicions about the relationship between Gordon and his mother. Aunt Harriet, an aristocratic host, lectures her nephew, Tony, a student at Amherst, on good manners and the proper use of the elegant table pieces she shows him. After taking notes and pictures, he explains that he is going to use the material in an anthropology class presentation on the WASP culture of the northeastern states. Irate over the disclosure, Aunt Harriet orders him to leave.

Jim and his mature, married daughter, Meg, file into the room. As Jim fortifies himself with Scotch, Meg subjects him to a recital of her problems, which involve the breakdown of her marriage and her affairs with a married man and another woman. She hopes to renew herself with a visit at home, but Jim will only agree to letting her stay for a brief, temporary visit.

Standish, defending family honor, explains to his wife and children why he has to go to his club to try to force an apology from Binky Byers, who while in the steam bath publicly alluded to the homosexuality of Standish's brother, Uncle Henry. An old man, Harvey, then begins to explain to his son, Dick, that he wants him to comply with the funeral ar-

rangements he made for himself. He confides that he has already written his own obituary and planned his funeral service, including very specific written directions. He also explains that he is leaving his best legacy, the dining room, to Dick.

At the end, Annie, the servant, explains to Ruth, her employer, that she is retiring and will no longer be available for service to the family. After Annie leaves, Ruth speaks wistfully of a recurrent dream she has, a dream of a perfect party, to which all her family and friends are invited. The Host then comes in, and, as the guests gather, raises a glass of wine and proposes a toast to everyone.

Critical Evaluation:

The Dining Room resembles some of A. R. Gurney's other plays, like the earlier *Scenes from American Life* (1970), in that it develops as a series of interlocking vignettes or minidramas that only loosely relate to one another. The individual scenes are all built around the play's central stage property, the large dining room table that dominates the set and plays a role in the lives of the characters who use it.

There are fifty-seven distinct characters in the two-act comedy, none of them central. All appear only once, except Annie, a servant, who appears near the beginning of the play and at the end. The characters are not related to anyone outside their own vignette, but most share a common heritage and culture: They are upper-middle-class WASPs living someplace in the northeastern United States sometime between the Great Depression of the 1930's and the early 1980's.

The play clearly shows that their way of life is changing. In fact, a major theme of *The Dining Room*, developed through generational contrasts, is that the WASP version of American culture has become outmoded and, to the younger generation, increasingly irrelevant. The central, archetypal symbol of that culture is the dining room and the large dining table, reminders of a day when families sat down together for long formal dinners, during which children, seen but not heard, learned about their heritage, against which, to some degree, they all finally rebel.

In some of the vignettes, the generational gulf seems deep and permanent, as in the second-act episode with Tony and Aunt Harriet. To Tony, the WASPs of the northeastern United States are "a vanishing culture," like the Cree Indians of Saskatchewan and the Kikuyus of Northern Kenya, and he, one of its scions, is determined to learn about it from studying the eating habits of the culture, as if it were a long-extinct society with only fossilized artifacts remaining to bear witness to its identity. That suggestion outrages Aunt Harriet, who threatens to drive to Amherst and castrate Tony's anthropology professor with one of her pistol-handled butter knives.

Although Gurney's intent is to evoke laughter, his humor is gentle and sympathetic. His characters are mostly decent people, even when they cling to reactionary beliefs and biases or commit immoral acts. Standish's sense of honor seems a bit ludicrous, for example, but it is honor nevertheless. Nick's grandfather, in another vignette, airs his grumpy intolerances, but in the end he proves kind and generous, almost despite himself. Clearly, in Gurney's world, most of the characters at least try to do the right thing.

Gurney's comic collage is not constructed in a chronological order. Events are only occasionally given hints as to the intended time frame through references to related events, issues, and public figures. Nor is there any logical relationship between juxtaposed vignettes. They only interlock, like cinematic lap dissolves, with one minidrama beginning while another is still ending. At the openings and endings of vignettes, characters from two distinct vignettes are briefly on stage together but totally unaware of one another. The episodes are like distinct pearls strung on a delicate thread of a common ethos.

As notes to the play explain, *The Dining Room* is designed for an ensemble cast of six performers, with each actor playing several parts. The play therefore has greater continuity in performance than when read, for while characters do not reappear, the actors do. Furthermore, much of the play's comic appeal is bolstered by the fact that performers must play parts ranging from exuberant, excited children at a birthday party to octogenarians who are losing touch with reality. Because the players are transparently actors mimicking characters, the whole is given an improvisational quality that helps keep the tone light even when such serious issues as marital infidelity and dying are broached. However, the wistful recollection of what many of the older characters consider to have been a better time and place also elicits real nostalgia in the audience. In chronicling the passing of old ways, Gurney evokes a sense of bittersweet respect that infuses his humor with warmth and wisdom.

John W. Fiero

Further Reading

Gilman, Richard. Review of *The Dining Room* and *The Middle Ages*, by A. R. Gurney, Jr. *The Nation*, April 30, 1983. Identifies Gurney as "the poet laureate of middle-consciousness" and discusses *The Dining Room* as a typical work.

Gurney, A. R., Jr. "Pushing the Walls of Dramatic Form." *The New York Times*, July 27, 1986. Gurney provides analysis of his own work, his methods of coping with restrictions on artistic freedom, and his new themes and experimentation in structure.

Levett, Karl. "A. R. Gurney, Jr., American Original." *Drama* 147 (Autumn, 1983): 6-7. A good survey of Gurney's work up to and including *The Dining Room*, which is identified as the play that "consolidated Gurney's reputation." Also identifies influences on Gurney using some of the playwright's own observations.

Simon, John. "Malle de Guare." *New York*, March 8, 1982. Argues that the play is derived from Thornton Wilder's *The Long Christmas Dinner* (1931) and discusses its "trickiness," its use of ingenious structural devices.

Sponberg, Arvid F., ed. *A. R. Gurney: A Casebook*. New York: Routledge, 2004. A collection of materials about Gurney. Contains an interview in which Gurney discusses his life and creative process, discussions with actors and a director who have worked with Gurney, and reprints of selected newspaper and journal articles written by Gurney. Also features essays analyzing his work, including examinations of race, class, gender, sexual orientation, and the dynamics of anger in his plays and "*The Dining Room*: A Tocquevillian Take on the Decline of WASP Culture."

Sternlicht, Sanford V. *A Reader's Guide to Modern American Drama*. Syracuse, N.Y.: Syracuse University Press, 2002. An overview of twentieth century American drama, with several chapters summarizing theater history and discussions of seventy playwrights. Gurney is one of the playwrights whose work is examined.

Weales, Gerald. "American Theatre Watch, 1981-1982." *Georgia Review* 36 (Fall, 1982): 517-526. Places *The Dining Room* in a group of ethnic-conscious plays successfully produced in commercial theater over two Broadway seasons.

Dinner at Antoine's

Author: Frances Parkinson Keyes (1885-1970)
First published: 1948
Type of work: Novel
Type of plot: Detective and mystery
Time of plot: 1948
Locale: New Orleans, Louisiana

Principal characters:
ORSON FOXWORTH, president of the Great Blue Fleet
    Company
RUTH AVERY, his niece
RUSSELL ALDRIDGE, her suitor, an archeologist
AMÉLIE LALANDE, a widow and potential lover of
    Foxworth
CARESSE LALANDE, her younger daughter
ODILE LALANDE ST. AMANT, her older, married daughter
LÉONCE ST. AMANT, Odile's husband
DOCTOR VANCE PERRAULT, the Lalande's family doctor
JOE RACINA, a writer
TOSSIE PRIDE, Odile's maid
SABIN DUPLESSIS, Odile's former suitor
DETECTIVE-CAPTAIN THEOPHILE "TOE" MURPHY, New
    Orleans police investigator

The Story:

A private party is being held at Antoine's, a New Orleans restaurant that has been a landmark since 1840. The purpose of the party, hosted by wealthy businessman Orson Foxworth, is to introduce his niece Ruth, who is visiting for the Mardi Gras season, to a circle of his friends. Ruth soon notes tensions between Odile St. Amant, her husband Léonce, and her sister Caresse. Odile is suffering from a nervous disorder, and her husband is openly flirting with Caresse. Foxworth, who has been in Central America for some years on business, is renewing his affection for Amélie Lalande and seriously considering marriage. During dinner, Ruth begins a friendship with Russell Aldridge. Following dinner, the party adjourns to the Blue Room for dancing, but Odile is forced to leave early by symptoms of what is later diagnosed as Parkinson's disease.

The next day, Doctor Perrault tells Odile she will become completely helpless and dependent yet might live for many years. Despondent, Odile meets with Sabin Duplessis, an old friend with whom she once was in love. When he had been mistakenly declared killed in action during World War II, Odile had become attracted to St. Amant and subsequently married him. However, Sabin still loves Odile, and when she asks him for a war souvenir, a German pistol, he gives it to her.

While Odile and Sabin are rediscovering their love for each other, Caresse and Léonce are about to begin an affair. However, an automobile accident brings Caresse to her senses. Hours later, Odile, having left a suicide note, is dead

from a gunshot. The police come, and the questions begin. Although Odile's death looks like a suicide, police detective "Toe" Murphy is not sure that Odile shot herself, because there are no powder burns on the body. During the course of his investigation, Toe discovers that several people might have benefited by Odile's death. Tossie Pride, who has loved and cared for Odile all her life, is arrested for murder because her fingerprints are found on the gun. Toe knows that Tossie did not kill Odile, however: Tossie is illiterate, so she could not have written the suicide note, which has disappeared.

While Toe searches for the real murderer, other characters make their own discoveries. Foxworth discovers the shallowness of Amélie and retracts his offer of marriage; Caresse is completely over her infatuation with Léonce and receives a job offer that will require her to move to New York City; and Ruth and Russell fall in love. With the aid of Joe Racina, Caresse clears her name with Toe, and Foxworth, who was at one point a suspect, is also cleared of murder. The murderer turns out to be Doctor Perrault, who had initially thought to help Odile by facilitating her suicide with access to an overdose of morphine. The doctor had realized that Odile should not commit the mortal sin of suicide, so when he saw that she had already overdosed and was beyond his help, he shot her to prevent her from dying by her own hand. Perrault provides this information in a letter, delivered to Caresse, at a final dinner at Antoine's. An envoi concludes the novel, wrapping up the stories of the principal characters and solving the final mystery of what happened to the suicide note.

Critical Evaluation:

Frances Parkinson Keyes was born in Virginia, the daughter of John Henry Wheeler and Louise Fuller Wheeler. She decided to be an author when she was seven years old; her mother did not approve and wished for a more conventional life for her daughter. As a child, Keyes traveled throughout Europe and became proficient in languages. At age eighteen, she married Henry Wilder Keyes, who was twenty-two years older than she was. Henry was elected governor of New Hampshire and later served three terms in the United States Senate. Frances learned a great deal about politics while living in Washington, D.C., and that knowledge is evident in her writing. What prompted her to return to her love of writing was money. Neither she nor her husband had a great fortune, and she started writing to help pay household bills. After her husband died, Keyes began to write full time. She wrote more than fifty books and is best known for her popular fiction. Her novels sold more than twenty million copies, and seven made the *New York Times* best-seller list, including *Dinner at Antoine's*.

Most of Keyes's novels are historical romances, but in *Dinner at Antoine's* she tried something different: a murder mystery. The main plot of the novel is typical of a mystery. It unfolds chronologically and is moved forward by the search for Odile's murderer. Keyes begins the novel with the dinner that not only introduces a number of characters but also provides information on relationships between the characters. As a mystery, the pace of the novel is slow. This slowness is due in part to a subplot involving the political situation between the United States and Central American countries that echoes actual events that followed World War II. Keyes's knowledge of Washington, D.C. and past unethical activities to promote U.S. business interests in small Latin American countries is illustrated as Foxworth secretly works to merge his upstart Great Blue Fleet Company with the long-established Trans-Caribbean Company, his main business competitor. The plot's movement is also slowed by Keyes's characteristic descriptions not only of people but also of events, such as the Twelfth Night Revels. In determining the identity of the murderer, Keyes uses the "least likely person" format, which provides a final twist to the plot.

The novel has a large cast of characters; eight are introduced at the first of three dinners at Antoine's, which is a real New Orleans restaurant. Generally, the characters are wealthy, upper-class individuals who are members of New Orleans's "high society." With some exceptions, the characters are somewhat stereotyped. Léonce St. Amant, the philandering husband of Odile, is a cardboard rake with such an overused "come on" line that his new love begins to rethink

having an affair with him. Amélie Lalande is a beautiful, selfish, mindless woman given to having hysterics or airs, depending on the situation. There are also some admirable minor characters, such as Joe Racina's wife, a former nurse injured in the war.

Caresse Lalande is a major character who changes for the better over the course of the novel, going beyond the traditional roles of obedient daughter, loyal wife, loving mother, and the belle of Creole society. When first seen, Caresse, wearing a too-revealing dress, is flirting with Léonce. She is beautiful and a debutant, but she also has a job, a radio program where she talks about styles, old recipes, and society in general. Although Caresse plans to begin an affair with Léonce, she changes her mind, and after her sister's death she no longer has any interest in Léonce. Caresse comes to realize the shallowness of her mother and her own comparatively empty lifestyle and seizes the opportunity to leave New Orleans to take a job in New York City. There, Caresse becomes not only a successful radio personality but also the focus of a line of cosmetics. In this character, Keyes shows how a woman can go beyond the traditional role society has prescribed for her. Caresse embraces a career and breaks from her family and home environment to achieve success as a working woman. The character resembles Keyes herself, who had a career despite the disapproval of her family and her husband.

As is typical of some older novels, each chapter includes a brief description of what will happen in the chapter. This description appears on a separate page that also includes the chapter number and a drawing by Joseph Donaldson. As she does in many of her novels, Keyes begins the book with a foreword. Her readers came to expect these forewords, but they were condemned by her critics with "scathing remarks," as Keyes notes.

Although critics generally disparage Keyes's novels, decrying her predictable plotting, stereotyped characters, excessive use of detail, and lack of insight into the human condition, her novels were extremely popular. People read Keyes's books to discover exotic places, be introduced to generally interesting characters, and learn something about a specific time and place. Keyes thoroughly researched the background information included in her novels and, when possible, took up residence in the city where a novel was to be set. While writing *Dinner at Antoine's*, Keyes lived at Beauregard House in New Orleans. Part of Keyes's appeal is to be found in her detailed descriptions of places, events, and even flowers. In this novel, for example, she provides specific information about growing a particular type of camellia.

The strength of *Dinner at Antoine's* is that the setting, the events, and the behavior of the characters in social situations all provide a snapshot of a specific time and place. Keyes creates the texture of the place, including local lore, dialects, and traditions. A reader who has never visited Metairie Cemetery, described by Keyes as the "great city of the dead," can see and experience the place through her words. To read *Dinner at Antoine's* is to take a look at social history. The novel makes specific references to World War II and its effects on the people of New Orleans. These references range from characters reestablishing themselves after the war to the end of rationing and the return of luxury items in stores. Also of interest are the characters' manners, which shape their interactions with one another according to a specific set of social customs. Much as Jane Austen paid close attention to the rules of a specific society, Keyes proves in her writing to be a miniaturist. Unlike Austen, however, Keyes portrayed characters and a world that have not continued to intrigue generations of readers. Literary criticism of Keyes is sparse and not current, and she receives scant attention in schools. She wrote not to enlighten but to entertain, and that she did, as attested by the millions of readers who enjoyed her books.

Marcia B. Dinneen

Further Reading

Bond, Barbara. "Romances with Tension." *The New York Times Book Review*, November 21, 1948, p. 43. Review of *Dinner at Antoine's* that describes it as a "high-society" mystery that will be predictable for mystery fans but entertaining for Keyes's loyal readers.

Bonin, Jane F. "Frances Parkinson Keyes: Mining the Mother Lode." *Louisiana Literature* 5, no. 1 (Spring, 1988): 71-77. Focuses on Keyes's ability to evoke place and her skill in describing both the look and the manners of New Orleans's Creole aristocracy.

Ehlers, Leigh A. "'An Environment Remembered': Setting in the Novels of Frances Parkinson Keyes." *Southern Quarterly* 20, no. 3 (Spring, 1982): 54-65. Analyzes Keyes's use of setting to underline events in her plots.

Hamner, Earl. *Generous Women: An Appreciation*. Nashville, Tenn.: Cumberland House, 2006. Includes a chapter discussing Keyes's representation of New Orleans as a "gift" to her readers.

Keyes, Frances Parkinson. "Self-Portrait." In *The Book of Catholic Authors*, edited by Walter Romig. 5th ser. Grosse Pointe, Mich.: Walter Romig, n.d. Keyes provides background on her career as a writer.

Kirkus, Virginia. "The Value of the Best Seller: An Appraisal of Frances Parkinson Keyes." *English Journal* 40, no. 6 (June, 1951): 303-307. Kirkus defends Keyes as an author, refuting her critics and pointing out her sound scholarship, as well as her skill at writing entertaining fiction.

Wernick, Robert. "The Queens of Fiction: Keyes, Caldwell, Ferber Reign Perennially over Best-Sellerdom." *Life*, April 6, 1959, p. 139. Discusses Keyes's habits as a researcher and as a writer. Notes that her novels are not long on plot but are full of atmosphere.

Dinner at the Homesick Restaurant

Author: Anne Tyler (1941-   )
First published: 1982
Type of work: Novel
Type of plot: Comic realism
Time of plot: 1925-1979
Locale: Baltimore, Virginia, and Pennsylvania

Principal characters:
PEARL CODY TULL, a dying woman
BECK TULL, Pearl's husband
CODY,
EZRA, and
JENNY, their children
LUKE, Cody's son
HARLEY BAINES, Jenny's first husband
SAM WILEY, Jenny's second husband
JOE ST. AMBROSE, Jenny's third husband
RUTH SPIVEY TULL, Cody's wife
MRS. SCARLATTI, restaurant owner

The Story:

Pearl Tull is dying. She is eighty-five years old. Her son Ezra stays with her. One of her dying wishes is that Ezra invite all the people in her address book to her funeral. One of those people is Beck Tull, Ezra's father, whom he hasn't seen since 1944, when Beck got tired of being married and left his wife and children never to return, he said, even to visit the children.

In 1944, Pearl pretends that Beck has not abandoned her. She raises her children herself, working part-time at the Sweeney Brothers grocery store. When her only friend visits her, she pretends that Beck is away on a business trip. Although at times she abuses her children, calling them names and hitting them, all of them seem on the surface to turn out fine. One day, Beck comes back to town and stands in front of the house, watching. Cody comes out. When Beck sees that Cody is getting along well without him, Beck goes on his way without letting the family know he was there.

Cody, the oldest sibling, has a love-hate relationship with his brother Ezra. He feels jealousy for Ezra that colors everything he does. He feels that he and Ezra are always in a contest and that each time they compete Ezra either wins or, as in a game of Monopoly, quits without a struggle. Cody is so determined to win games he and his family members play that he cheats. Ezra, however, seems unaware of any contest between himself and Cody. When Ezra becomes engaged to Ruth Spivey, Cody determines to win her away from Ezra. He succeeds, marrying Ruth.

Cody becomes employed as an efficiency expert. He moves his family from place to place, helping make companies more efficient. He hardly ever visits his family in Baltimore. When he does, the visits are always short, sometimes cut even shorter by his perception that Ezra is trying to win Ruth back. He and Ruth have a son, Luke, who hardly ever sees his grandmother but loves her dearly. When Luke is thirteen, the family moves temporarily to Virginia, where his father has a serious accident. While recuperating, Cody gets angry and says to Ruth in front of Luke that Luke is really Ezra's child. Luke then hitchhikes to Baltimore to Ezra's restaurant. After this event, the relationship between Luke and Cody improves significantly. They are goose hunting when Pearl dies.

Ezra is the most easygoing of the Tulls. He seems passionate about two things: the restaurant business and Ruth. Ezra works for for Mrs. Scarlatti at her restaurant, and they become close friends. Much to Pearl's dismay, Mrs. Scarlatti sells part interest in the restaurant to Ezra for one dollar. When Mrs. Scarlatti is in the hospital, Ezra redesigns the inside of the restaurant and renames it the Homesick Restaurant. Mrs. Scarlatti dies, and he becomes the owner. Ezra lives at home and cares for his mother. He is with Pearl when she dies.

Jenny becomes a pediatrician in Pennsylvania. She has two unsuccessful marriages, the first to a genius named Harley Baines and the second to Sam Wiley. She thinks of Sam as the husband she loved the most. Sam and Jenny have a daughter, Becky. Both Jenny and Becky at times suffer from anorexia. When Becky is a baby, Jenny is alone, serving her residency in pediatrics. Jenny finds herself on the verge of a breakdown. She mistreats her baby in ways similar to the ones in which Pearl mistreated her. When Pearl discovers how sick Jenny is, she comes to Pennsylvania to help. She arranges for Jenny to take leave from her work. She treats Becky and Jenny extremely well and, with Cody's help, arranges for Becky to have caregivers when Jenny returns to her residency. Jenny then becomes much more relaxed. Jenny goes into pediatric practice in Baltimore and marries Joe St. Ambrose, who has six children. They have one child together. Jenny becomes so relaxed that when one of her stepsons repeatedly gets into trouble, she makes jokes about it, not taking it seriously.

Ezra is the most family-centered of the Tull children. He repeatedly plans family dinners at Mrs. Scarlatti's restaurant and then at his own. The dinners usually end in disaster, with family members fighting and leaving before the meal is finished. Sometimes, the dinners break up before the family starts to eat.

After Pearl's funeral, Ezra wants to have a family dinner at the Homesick Restaurant. Beck attends the funeral, and Ezra invites him to the dinner. Cody is upset because he does not consider Beck part of the family. He and Beck argue at the dinner, and when Sam and Jenny's baby begins to choke, Beck runs off. Cody wants to let him go, but Ezra insists that everyone try to find him and bring him back. Cody eventually joins in the hunt. He hopes to run into Luke. He sees someone that he thinks is Luke sitting on a curb, but it turns out to be Beck. The others find Cody and Beck and bring them both back to the restaurant. Finally, the family may finish a dinner at the Homesick Restaurant.

Critical Evaluation:

When *Dinner at the Homesick Restaurant* was published in 1982, reviewers welcomed it as the best book Anne Tyler had written thus far. Critics were especially delighted at Tyler's realist portrayal of family life, including many of the ways in which she portrayed the Tull family as dysfunctional, and the depth of her character portrayals in general.

Some, however, objected to the book's happy ending, in which it seems that the Tull family may finally get through an entire meal. The book was nominated in 1983 for a Pulitzer Prize and for the National Book Critics Circle award, and it won a Pen/Faulkner Award for Fiction.

Many critics discuss the multiple meanings of the word "homesick," especially focusing on its meanings of longing for home and being sick of home. Pearl, as a single parent, tries to make a home for her family. At the same time, however, she is too closely connected to home. She has no friends in the Baltimore neighborhood in which she lives. She refuses to make friends with any of the other women there. She wears a hat when she works at Sweeney Brothers to discourage any of the women shopping there from being friendly with her and to imply that she is just there temporarily, even though she works there for many years. She has only one friend, who visits her only once. When her son Cody buys Pearl a bus ticket so she can visit her friend, she refuses it because, she says, the visit would require her to miss Ezra's birthday.

Cody leaves home and hardly ever visits. He buys a house and some land outside Baltimore, intending to live there and have many children, but, when he does get married, he lets the house fall into ruin. Instead, he moves his family from place to place, depending on where he is working. He repeatedly asserts that his mother treated him terribly, insisting that she was always angry. Nonetheless, he buys her the house she lives in and sees that she is cared for. When Pearl dies, Cody becomes very defensive with Beck for leaving her. His homesickness involves both love and hate for his home. He ironically spends most of his life trying to win his mother's love, something he has all along.

Jenny leaves home to go to college and medical school in Pennsylvania, but she ends up practicing medicine in Baltimore and living not too far from her mother. Her feelings for her mother change when her mother cares for her during her breakdown. The woman she remembers as being so vicious turns out to be gentle and caring. Jenny eventually learns that, although there are some terrible things about Pearl and she does some unforgiveable things, Pearl did a fairly good job of raising her children.

Ezra remains at home with Pearl. In his recollections, Pearl is a good, loving mother. He cares for her in her old age. He names his restaurant Homesick because he wants to provide people with a place where they can enjoy the comforts of home as they dine. His homesickness is of a different sort from that of his siblings. In a way, he is emotionally crippled by home, unable to stand up for himself, unable to observe people and their motives carefully, and unable to have any

adventure in his life. When he is drafted during the Korean War, he avoids service by sleepwalking. He claims that he knows he is sleepwalking but does it anyway so he can go home. In a sense, Ezra sleepwalks through life. When Cody wins Ruth's love, Ezra is bewildered. He had not known that the two of them were interested in each other. Ezra is a gentle soul who dreams of a united family living in harmony. Thus, he keeps planning family dinners even though they usually end in disaster and always involve hard feelings.

The shape of the novel is a circle, beginning as Pearl is dying and ending with her death. Toward the end of her life, she goes blind. She asks Ezra to read to her from her diary. To Ezra, it seems that she is hunting for some particular passage. He is right. She finally finds it and is content, saying he need not read her any more diary entries. The passage, from 1910, describes a time when Pearl was about sixteen years old. In it, she kneels in the garden weeding. A neighbor plays the piano. A fly buzzes around. In recounting the experience, Pearl wrote that she was "on such a beautiful green little planet. I don't care what else might come about, I have had this moment. It belongs to me." Hearing about this episode provides Pearl with the peace she needs so that she can die easily. Her vision of a universe in harmony with all of its parts is one she carries with her all her life and revisits on her deathbed. By having Ezra invite Beck to the funeral, Pearl hopes to reunite her family and make this kind of harmony available to her children.

Many critics point out the importance of time in Tyler's novel. Cody tells his son that he loves time. The time Cody talks about is linear. He discovers circular time when he searches for Beck after the funeral dinner falls apart. This kind of time, represented in Pearl's diary entry, is that in which things repeat themselves but not in exactly the same way; it is the time that unites the seasons into a year, that knits the episodes in human lives into a cyclical whole, that makes unity not just of families but of all things. In her moment in the garden, Pearl pierced to the center of this kind of time. As Jenny seems to recognize, even her abuse of Becky illustrates this kind of time, with Jenny repeating the actions of her mother. Both Pearl and Cody, it seems, forget circular time until Pearl is ready to die and, in Cody's case, until after Pearl dies. The circle of time also matches the circular structure of the book.

Richard Tuerk

Further Reading
Adamson, Lynda G. *Thematic Guide to the American Novel.*
    Westport, Conn.: Greenwood Press, 2002. Includes a sec-

tion discussing the representation of marriage in *Dinner at the Homesick Restaurant*.

Croft, Robert W. *Anne Tyler: A Bio-Bibliography*. Westport, Conn.: Greenwood Press, 1995. Treats both primary and secondary works, including dissertations and theses and many book reviews.

_____. *An Anne Tyler Companion*. Westport, Conn.: Greenwood Press, 1998. Contains overviews of Tyler's life and the themes of her works, as well as an alphabetical listing of specific works, characters, themes, and motifs. Briefly analyzes *Dinner at the Homesick Restaurant* and provides a list of works about the novel.

Evans, Elizabeth. *Anne Tyler*. New York: Twayne, 1993. An easily accessible introduction to Tyler and her works through *Saint Maybe* (1991). Treats, among other things, the child abuse in *Dinner at the Homesick Restaurant*.

Petry, Alice Hall. *Understanding Anne Tyler*. Columbia: University of South Carolina Press, 1990. This book, one of a series from the University of South Carolina Press devoted to the complete works of individual authors, is a good introduction to Tyler and her works. Chapter 8 treats *Dinner at the Homesick Restaurant*, assessing its place in modern American literature. It emphasizes family relations in the book.

Voelker, Joseph C. *Art and the Accidental in Anne Tyler*. Columbia: University of Missouri Press, 1989. Chapter 7 treats *Dinner at the Homesick Restaurant*, investigating the book's unity and its use of symbols.

The Dinner Party

Author: Claude Mauriac (1914-1996)
First published: Le Dîner en ville, 1959 (English translation, 1960)
Type of work: Novel
Type of plot: Experimental
Time of plot: 1950's
Locale: Paris

Principal characters:
BERTRAND CARNÉJOUX, the host, an editor and a novelist
MARTINE (PILOU) CARNÉJOUX, his wife
EUGÉNIE PRIEUR, an aging belle of Parisian society
GILLES BELLECROIX, a scenarist and an aspiring novelist
LUCIENNE OSBORN, the egocentric wife of an American film producer
ROLAND SOULAIRES, a rich but frustrated bachelor
MARIE-ANGE (MARIETTA) VASGNE, an actress and Bertrand's mistress
JÉRÔME AYGULF, a childhood friend of Martine and a substitute guest

The Dinner Party is an experimental novel. There is no narrator, and speakers are not identified except by subject matter, leitmotif, or an occasional self-apostrophe. The text is a fusion of conversation and soliloquy. There are crosscurrents of two or three different subjects, stichomythic or protracted, and Claude Mauriac creates the illusion of simultaneity in the varied mental associations evoked by some passing remark. The difficulties of following such a presentation of multiple experiences are only initial; they are resolved in the development of character patterns that emerge despite the loss in translation of the uniqueness of language assigned to individual characters.

In the mid-twentieth century, the experimental novel was a subspecies of the traditional novel. Examples of experi-

mental novels such as *The Dinner Party* must nevertheless be assessed as is any work of art in an established medium. What Mauriac accomplished in *The Dinner Party* is impressive. To treat at book length the incidental chatter and random musing of eight people during a dining period of perhaps two hours is an undertaking vulnerable to arousing boredom in the reader. Not a single character in the book emerges as a great or memorable one; the relations of the characters to one another are rather trivial and in fact represent clichés of the beau monde. Nevertheless, without telling a significant story or symbolizing any extensive meaning, Mauriac sustains his kaleidoscope of sophisticated sensibilities with remarkable intensity.

There is no perceptibly dominant theme, simply a dinner

party experience observed and recorded by means of the dramatic method and the interior monologue. The characters, nevertheless, are thoroughly interesting people. Their talk—about history, aristocratic genealogy, literature (Marcel Proust, Maurice Barrès, Anatole France, Graham Greene, and Gerard Manley Hopkins), astrology, travel, God, and even intellectual parlor games—is generally absorbing, occasionally informative, and often amusing. Their thoughts about one another, about themselves, and about the matters that happen to arise are compounded of vanity, lust, boredom, jealousy, creative perceptivity, intelligence, insight, and hopeful intentions, all projected with a psychological subtlety and effectiveness that impart true unity to the book. Other characters, in the persons of the seductive servant Armande or members of fashionable society who are talked about or recalled in memory, add to the dimensions of the emanating reality. Details of the courses served, descriptions of spots on the tablecloth or crumbs on a chair, and appraisals of the quality of the champagne being consumed are brilliantly integrated into the vibrant texture of the writing.

The situation that Mauriac creates out of his assemblage of characters is reminiscent of Proust. The atmosphere Mauriac's characters breathe is rarefied. His people are elegant, aristocratic (or socially pretentious), artistic, and sensual. They are aware of social stratification, youth fading into age, their desire for one another, the interplay of their sensibilities, and the projection of their personae. Henri Bergson hovers over the table: The diners indulge in flights of memory stimulated by simple words or sensations; they consider their future, but everything is focused on the present moment of consciousness.

There is no head of the table as such, but the host sits as nearly opposite his wife as a round table seating four men and four women will allow. He is Bertrand Carnéjoux, the forty-six-year-old editor of the magazine *Ring* and author of a successful novel entitled *Sober Pleasures* (the original manuscript bore the more revealing title "Metaphysics of Physical Passion"). Preeminent in Carnéjoux's mind is the desire to write another novel of even greater artistic integrity, formulated in a new way that will bring the words and thoughts of his characters into immediate juxtaposition. More than once, as he notes his conversation at the table, he regrets that he does not find it possible to achieve the same brilliance, the same eloquence when he is at work over a manuscript in his study. Meanwhile, he presides over the party, secure in his knowledge of amorous success with every woman present except one. His conversation is mainly about literature, his thoughts divided between love affairs and plans for writing.

His wife, Martine, is twenty-six years old, intimately

known as Pilou, and the wealthy and innocent daughter of Irene, one of Bertrand's former mistresses. Throughout the party, her thoughts are mainly radiant expressions of love for her two children, Rachel and Jean-Paul, but she is also tempted to respond to the attentions of Gilles Bellecroix.

Bellecroix is a forty-nine-year-old screenwriter who attained greater fame than Bertrand but who is not satisfied inwardly with his achievement. He is obsessed with the idea that he must produce a good novel to realize himself. Meanwhile, he observes the dinner guests with a cinematic eye, visualizing meaningful scenes in flickers of pose or behavior. Between him and Bertrand is a latent rivalry that carries over into Gilles's flirtation with Martine, whose dancing on an earlier occasion is unforgettable to him. Gilles finds his real center of being, however, in his wife Bénédicte; he knows that for him true happiness lies in love, fidelity, monogamy.

Eugénie Prieur, still, at sixty-seven, called "Gigi" by young blades of Paris, is the oldest guest (too old to have been one of Bertrand's conquests), full of rich nostalgic memories, the wisdom of long experience, and an intimate knowledge of social machinations. The perspective with which she endows her world is further documented by her conversations about historic family connections.

Roland Soulaires, forty-five, is temperamentally a J. Alfred Prufrock who hides his fears and his insecurity behind his idle dreams and his clever talk with Eugénie about social identification. Extremely wealthy, but fat and bald, he fails to interest the beautiful guest at his left, the twenty-four-year-old Marie-Ange Vasgne. Formerly a Canadian farm girl named Marietta but now a sultry blonde model and aspiring actress, Marie-Ange is Bertrand's current mistress who dares near the end of the party to tease him by inquiring after Marie-Plum, another mistress whom Bertrand is never able to forget. Everyone's knowledge of these affairs, admitted or not, is the measure of civilization for these people. Marie-Ange toys with the numbers one through six, as though seeking a pattern of sense in the world.

Lucienne Osborn, forty-two, is married to an American film producer, not present at the dinner. Her mind vapid, her body faded, she is preoccupied with thoughts of television sets, suntans, her dog Zig, and her lover, Léon-Pierre.

Jérôme Aygulf, who is twenty, finds himself out of his element. A childhood friend of Martine, he is invited only at the last moment after another guest sends regrets. Jérôme, aspiring but naïve, is at the opposite end of the scale from Eugénie. He finds himself longing for the attention and patronage of Bertrand more than for anything else. Insecure and a little awkward in this society, he nonetheless attracts the attention of Marie-Ange.

The Dinner Party belongs in that class of novels, including also Henry James's *The Sacred Fount* (1901) and André Gide's *Les Faux-monnayeurs* (1925; *The Counterfeiters*, 1927), in which a novelist as a character thinks interchangeably about experience and the novel. The center of interest in Mauriac's book really lies in the thoughts and comments expressed by Bertrand and Gilles about the novel form. Referring to his novel, Bertrand speaks of a new kind of fiction, one in which on some common occasion, such as the present dinner party, time and space would be suspended. Contemplating his next work, which will fuse thought and speech, Bertrand responds to Paul Claudel's definition of the simplicity of truth along the line of Denis Diderot's Proustian statement that "Everything we have ever known . . . exists within us without our knowing it." The book is studded with criticism of novelists and theories of the novel, ideas that reveal character but also illuminate the practice of Mauriac in this particular novel. In one way or another, *The Dinner Party* raises a host of interesting questions about fiction.

Further Reading

Mauriac, Claude. *The New Literature.* Translated by Samuel I. Stone. New York: George Braziller, 1959. Critical study of twentieth century French literature by the author of *The Dinner Party.* Especially useful for gaining appreciation of Mauriac's theory of fiction; explains his concept of aliterature, which he used in creating *The Dinner Party* and other novels.

Mayhew, Alice. "All Things at Once." *Commonweal* 81 (September 25, 1964): 20. Assesses the "suite of four novels" in which Mauriac explores problems of communication in the twentieth century. Discusses the role of Bertrand Carnéjoux in *The Dinner Party* and other works in Mauriac's sequence.

Mercier, Vivian. *The New Novel from Queneau to Pinget.* New York: Farrar, Straus and Giroux, 1971. Lengthy chapter on Mauriac. Contains an extensive analysis of *The Dinner Party*; attempts to aid readers in understanding Mauriac's complex method of narration. Claims that his presentation of characters borders on stereotype and caricature.

Moore, Harry T. *Twentieth Century French Literature Since World War II.* Carbondale: Southern Illinois University Press, 1966. Brief review of Mauriac's work as a novelist. Classifies him with others writing "antinovels" after World War II. Sketches his aims in *The Dinner Party* and notes his use of readers' aids to assist in interpreting the work.

Roudiez, Leon. *French Fictions Today.* New Brunswick, N.J.: Rutgers University Press, 1972. A chapter on Mauriac includes commentary on *The Dinner Party* that focuses on the author's techniques of narration and highlights his preoccupation in the book with sex and death.

The Disciple

Author: Paul Bourget (1852-1935)
First published: Le Disciple, 1889 (English translation, 1898)
Type of work: Novel
Type of plot: Psychological realism
Time of plot: Late nineteenth century
Locale: Paris and Riom, France

Principal characters:
ADRIEN SIXTE, a philosopher
ROBERT GRESLOU, his disciple, and later a private tutor
MARQUIS DE JUSSAT, a hypochondriac, and employer of Greslou
CHARLOTTE, his daughter
LUCIEN, her younger brother
ANDRÉ, her older brother

The Story:

Adrien Sixte grows up in a peculiar way. His hardworking father wants him to study for one of the professions. However, despite the boy's early promise in school, he never studies at a university. His indulgent parents allow him to spend ten lonely years in study. In 1868, at the age of twenty-nine, Adrien publishes a five-hundred-page work called *The Psychology of God.* By the outbreak of the Franco-Prussian War, Adrien has become the most discussed philosopher in France. He follows his first study with two more books, *The Anatomy of the Will* and *The Theory of the Passions*, which are even more provocative than his first.

Soon after the death of his parents, Adrien settles into a regular routine in Paris. So faithful is he to his schedule that the inhabitants of the quarter can set their watches by his movements. He spends eight hours of every twenty-four hours in work, takes two walks each day, receives callers (chiefly students) on one afternoon in the week, and on another afternoon makes calls on other scholars. By patient labor and brilliant insight, he develops to his complete satisfaction his deterministic theory that each effect comes from a cause, and that if all causes are known, results can be predicted accurately. He applies his theory to all forms of human activity, to vices as well as to virtues.

One day, neighbors are startled to see Adrien leave his apartment hurriedly at an unusual hour. To his great consternation, he has received a notice to appear before a magistrate in the affair of Robert Greslou, one of his students, and he also has a letter from Robert's mother saying that she will visit him that very day at four o'clock on an urgent matter.

The sophisticated judge is incredulous when he learns that Adrien never reads the newspapers. The celebrated savant had not heard of Greslou's imprisonment after being charged with the murder of Charlotte de Jussat. Adrien soon learns that the suspect has been arrested on purely circumstantial evidence, that the proof of his guilt or innocence may well be only psychological. Hence, Adrien, the master, must testify as to his disciple's ideas on psychological experience. Adrien explains that if a chemist can analyze water into hydrogen and oxygen, he can synthesize hydrogen and oxygen into water. Similarly, if a psychological result can be analyzed into its causes, the result can be reproduced by those same causes; that is, by the scientific method, one can predict human behavior. The judge is interested and inquires if his theory applies to vices. Adrien says that it does, for, psychologically, vices are forms of behavior that are as interesting and valid as social virtues.

When he returns home, Adrien finds Robert's mother waiting for him. She protests her son's innocence and begs Adrien to save her boy. Adrien remembers Robert as a precocious student of philosophy, but he really knows little of him as a person. The mother begs Adrien to help and gives him a manuscript written by Robert while in jail. The manuscript includes a note of instruction: If Adrien reads the document, he must agree to not try to save Robert; if the condition is unacceptable, he must burn the manuscript immediately. With many misgivings, Adrien takes the document and reads it. It is a minute and detailed account of Robert's upbringing, his studies, and his experiences in the Jussat home.

Robert's story is as follows: Always brilliant, Robert does outstanding work in school, and early in his studies shows a pronounced talent in psychology. Most of his time is devoted to study, but a developing sensuality shows itself sporadically. Since he has grown up at Clermont, he lacks some of the polish imparted at Paris; in consequence, he fails an examination. While awaiting another opportunity to enter the university, Robert accepts a year's appointment as tutor to Lucien de Jussat.

At the Jussat country home, Robert finds an interesting household. Lucien, his pupil, is a simple thirteen-year-old boy. André, the older brother, is an army officer fond of hunting and riding. The father is a hypochondriac. Charlotte, the daughter of the family, is a beautiful nineteen-year-old woman.

Robert soon begins the studied seduction of Charlotte. He has three reasons for such a step. First, he conceives a distaste for André and wants to put him in his place. Second, his developed sexuality makes the project attractive. Finally, and probably most important, he wants to test his theory that if he can determine the causes leading to love and sexual desire, he can produce desire by providing the causes. Robert keeps careful notes on procedures and results.

Robert knows that pity is close to love. Consequently, he arouses the pity of Charlotte by mysterious allusions to his painful past. Then, by carefully selecting a list of novels for her to read, he sets about inflaming her desire for passionate, romantic love. Robert, however, is too hasty. He makes an impassioned avowal to Charlotte and frightens her into leaving for Paris. Just as Robert begins to despair of accomplishing his purpose, the illness of Lucien recalls Charlotte. Robert writes her a note telling her of his intention to commit suicide. He prepares the strychnine and waits. When Charlotte comes, he shows her the poison and proposes a suicide pact. Charlotte accepts, provided she can be the first to die. They spend the night together. Robert has triumphed.

Next morning, Robert repudiates the pact, prompted in part by a real love for Charlotte. The next day, she threatens to call her brother if Robert attempts to stop her own attempt at suicide, for she has read Robert's notes and knows she is simply the object of an experiment. After writing a letter to her brother André, telling him of her intended suicide, she drinks the strychnine. Robert is arrested soon afterward on suspicion of murder.

Adrien comes to the end of the manuscript and begins to feel a moral responsibility for his disciple's act. Disregarding the pledge implicit in his reading, he sends an anonymous note to André asking him if he intends to let Robert be convicted of murder by concealing Charlotte's letter. André resolves to tell the truth and, in a painful courtroom scene, Robert is acquitted.

Immediately after the trial, André goes to look for Robert. Scarcely able to resist, since he has been ready to die with Charlotte's secret safe, Robert meets André willingly. On the street, André pulls out a gun and shoots Robert in the head. Robert's mother mourns beside the coffin; Adrien also mourns because he accepts moral responsibility for the teachings that have prompted his disciple's deed.

Critical Evaluation:

Paul Bourget's most famous novel had a profound effect on the world of French letters. Its author had begun publishing as a poet in 1872; he had turned out perceptive novels beginning in 1885. His *Essais de psychologie contemporaine* (1883; essays in contemporary psychology), followed by *Nouveaux Essais de psychologie contemporaine* (1885; new essays on contemporary psychology) proved most influential. He was scarcely an obscure writer.

Until *The Disciple*, however, Bourget was known mostly for his social criticism (the *Essais*, describing the literary environment in which he matured, were considered a landmark) and for his highly passionate novels. Indeed, conservatives thought his work almost pornographic. With *The Disciple*, he broke unexpected ground, exploring the responsibility of those whose teachings and writings influence our actions. Adrien Sixte, in his story, is the most moral of scholars, but, however unintentionally, his doctrines lead young Robert Greslou to commit a heinous crime. Bourget blames Greslou's teacher, Adrien. In so doing, Bourget is also peering into the mirror of his own soul, because Adrien is a thinly disguised portrait of the French nineteenth century historian, philosopher, and literary critic Hippolyte Taine. He was Bourget's own mentor and role model, who argued that if one knows all the causes for a given action, one can inevitably predict it.

The literary doctrines then in vogue, as practiced by such French novelists as Émile Zola, followed deterministic criteria, depicting characters as lacking free will and thus not responsible for their actions; heredity and environment held them in thrall. Bourget was not so much repudiating determinism as demanding religious responsibility for what he viewed as human, not inanimate, causes.

Taine was sorely wounded by his old disciple Bourget's stand, even writing the author to deny any resemblance between Adrien and himself, adding that he never would have counseled Robert to act as Adrien did. Interestingly enough, Bourget had based his plot on two real cases, the latter, involving a writer Bourget actually knew, occurring only a few months before *The Disciple* was published. His book owed some of its popularity to its unusual mixture of psychological analysis and sensational murder mystery, not to speak of the formerly objective psychologist's new role as an antipositivist, antiskeptic, Christian moralist.

For the rest of his long life, Bourget continued to compose essays and novels deploring anti-Christian, especially anti-Catholic, behavior, rigging his plots to show the tragedies that befall his heedless characters. As in the work of so many Victorian writers (compare the plots of his good friend, novelist Henry James), his heroes and heroines are faced with heroic dilemmas. How they deal with them reflects their character strengths and weaknesses. Such thesis literature rapidly becomes obsolete, once the social problems besetting any given age are solved. At worst, it is scarcely readable, the plots transparently contrived, the puppet characters plainly made of cloth. Bourget, however, wrote well and, more to the point, always remained a keen psychologist. From time to time, he even reverted to his former, determinist point of view.

To understand the excitement generated by *The Disciple*, it may help to state that the French take literary and social doctrines very seriously indeed. Since Honoré de Balzac, French literature, especially novels, had been moving away from what many critics have seen as its roots, a naturalism emphasizing exact depictions of milieu—businesses, shops, factories, farms, the salons of the rich, the hovels of the poor, city and country, entrepreneur and peasant. As Balzac would announce, the surroundings explain the individual, even as individuals explain their milieu. The writer aims for accuracy of description, psychology being of secondary importance. The job of art, then, is to reveal truth, without concern for its effect on its audience. Bourget, in challenging this concept, was reverting to the older notion that the duty of art is to instruct while pleasing.

Bourget also was returning to the tradition of psychological realism with which the French have always felt comfortable. Arguably the first French novel, though in verse, is the anonymously written *Châtelaine de Vergy*, a thirteenth century French psychological masterpiece. Madame de Lafayette's *La Princesse de Clèves* (1678; *The Princess of Clèves*, 1679) is universally recognized as an almost perfect gem of psychological realism. The works of Denis Diderot and of Pierre Choderlos de Laclos (*Les Liaisons dangereuses*, 1782; *Dangerous Liaisons*, 1784) carry the tradition into the next century, followed by the works of Alfred de Musset and Benjamin Constant a few generations later.

The tradition persists into the present. Psychologically probing the love life of the French adolescent, mature beyond his or her years, has, even recently, remained a staple of the French novel. It is seen in the novels of Raymond Radiguet and Françoise Sagan. Bourget was quite simply acknowledging the roots of French literature. His *Essais* had revealed a perspicacious observer, his novels confirmed the diagnosis, and *The Disciple* justified his reputation.

However, thematically the novel is a response to a crisis in the European spirit and a reaction against the practices of a previous generation of French writers. *The Disciple* is the product of a continent-wide awareness that scientific progress had questioned the validity of traditional religious faith, especially that faith's role as the source of a transcendentally sanctioned morality that guides behavior in this world and offers immortality to believers in the next. *The Disciple* addresses the same themes as Ivan Turgenev's *Ottsy i deti* (1862; *Fathers and Sons*, 1867), whose central character, Bazarov, rejects all faiths and adopts rationalism. *The Disciple* also addresses the same themes as Fyodor Dostoevski's *Prestupleniye i nakazaniye* (1866; *Crime and Punishment*, 1886), in which Raskolnikov kills two people to illustrate his superiority to conventional morality.

For Adrien, vice and virtue are socially constructed in a godless universe, as he explains to the judge who calls him into his office in an attempt to identify the role of Adrien's teachings on Robert's actions. Later, Robert himself will be possessed by a desolating vision of the inevitable death of the planet, "only a ball without air and without water, from which man has disappeared, as well as plants and animals." Terrified, he decides that as the here and now is all humans will ever experience, then humans must "exalt it by increasing its intensity." He longs for the transient youthful presence of the woman he has coldly decided to seduce.

Robert is an arresting portrayal of intellectual arrogance worthy of comparison with Godwin Peak of George Gissing's *Born in Exile* (1892), another atheistic hypocrite who sees no world beyond the present world. The reader simultaneously respects Robert's intellectual honesty while deploring his emotional coldness and sympathizing with his later acquisition of lacerating self-knowledge.

The Disciple's tripartite structure cleverly presents the same events from different perspectives, thus taking advantage of the human pleasure in finding oneself mystified, then enabled to understand—that is, catered to by—popular murder mysteries. First, the judge presents what he assumes to be the facts of the murder of Charlotte de Jussat. Then Robert's account, which makes up most of the novel, narrates the true course of events. Third, Adrien and André each reacts to the revelation of the truth; the two then provide between them a morally satisfying denouement.

Bourget's reputation as an exponent of the psychological novel is buttressed by his elaboration in *The Disciple* of the idea of the multiple personality, a sophisticated perception that humans do not possess a stable ego but rather are each made up of the cumulative effects of conscious and unconscious mental operations and responses.

Finally, *The Disciple* is notable for the beauty of its depictions of the gentle Auvergne landscapes, which Bourget knew and loved from the days of his youth spent hiking in the countryside. He always possessed a strong sense of place and subscribed to the doctrines of his friend Maurice Barrès, whose novel *Les Déracinés* (1897) depicts the dangers of forcing people to abandon the land of their birth.

Some readers dislike Bourget's moralizing, Christian slant, but few can deny his persuasive intensity. Many of the French youth of his day (to whom the novel is dedicated) had agreed with him. He continued to exert a strong influence on France's social conscience well into the twentieth century, though after World War I, his hold was destined to weaken. *The Disciple*, in any case, may still be read for its superb depiction of the need for moral responsibility.

"Critical Evaluation" by Armand E. Singer;
revised by M. D. Allen

Further Reading

Auchincloss, Louis. "James and Bourget: The Artist and the Crank." In *Reflections of a Jacobite*. 1961. Reprint. Clifton, N.J.: Kelley, 1973. Auchincloss chides Bourget for assuming the role of France's social and moral guide. Useful as an alternative perspective on Bourget.

Chaitin, Gilbert D. *The Enemy Within: Culture Wars and Political Identity in Novels of the French Third Republic*. Columbus: Ohio State University Press, 2009. A thorough, scholarly account of the culture wars of the French Third Republic. Examines the formation of a French national identity in the context of new educational laws advocating secular instead of Christian morality. Explores the "intimate relations among literature, education, philosophy, morality, and political order" and the novels that were written and published in response to the debates, including *The Disciple*.

Goetz, T. H. "Paul Bourget's *Le Disciple* and the Text-Reader Relationship." *French Review* 52 (October, 1978): 56-61. Discusses the author's concerns over the influence of the authority figure (that is, the writer) upon his or her audience, especially the nation's youth.

Lee, David C. J. "Bourget's Debt to Herbert Spencer: *Le Disciple* and the Self-Adjusting Watch." *Modern Language Review* 95, no. 3 (July, 2000): 653. Examines how Spencer's concepts of evolution influenced Bourget's novel, focusing on the book's central themes of clocks and living by the clock.

Discipline and Punish
The Birth of the Prison

Author: Michel Foucault (1926-1984)
*First published: Surveiller et punir: Naissance de la
    prison,* 1975 (English translation, 1977)
Type of work: History, philosophy, and social criticism

Michel Foucault's *Discipline and Punish* is a critical philo-sophical history of the modern prison and its attendant in-stitutions. Foucault considered the work to be more than the reporting of history; he believed it to be an archaeology of history, the uncovering of social forces and relations that shaped history. The book comprises ten chapters divided into four main parts that examine torture, punishment, discipline, and the prison.

Chapter 1, "The Body of the Condemned," opens with an account of a public execution in France in 1757. Foucault then cites a mundane prison timetable from 1837 to show how quickly the attitudes toward punishment changed. By beginning his work with a depiction of death, Foucault im-mediately subverts the title of the book, which contains the word "birth." In addition, the unspeakably gruesome and horrifying narrative of the execution shocks the reader into opposing physical torture as a mode of criminal punishment. Foucault, however, is teasing the reader. Although he op-poses torture, he quickly reveals that his purpose in *Disci-pline and Punish* is not to argue against torture in favor of prison as a better method of dealing with criminals; rather, his purpose is to critique the modern penal system and its un-derlying philosophy. This penal philosophy, he argues, per-vades society outside the prison.

Foucault argues that the move from torture to incarcera-tion has not made punishment more humane; it only trans-ferred the locus of the punishment from the body to the soul. Punishment no longer addresses a criminal act; instead, it addresses criminal motives and abnormality, aspects of the soul that are judged by mental-health experts. Delinquents are now a class of individuals who are created by the penal system.

The first chapter also introduces Foucault's methodology. His work is a "correlative history of the modern soul and of a new power to judge" that proceeds according to four rules: Situate the study of punishment within the larger social sys-tem, view punishment as the exercise of political power, dis-cover the underlying epistemological processes that inform both the penal system and the human sciences, and try to un-cover a system of power relations that accounts for the changes in the penal system and the inclusion of scientific evaluation. According to Foucault, power is a characteristic of the entire social system, and it unconsciously affects ev-eryone. Power is not an abstraction; it always exists in the context of power relations. Also, power is not under the con-trol of the individual; power controls the individual within the complex society.

The "truth of the crime" is the focus of chapter 2, "The Spectacle of the Scaffold." Foucault argues that the ancient practices of inquisition, torture, and execution functioned in society to establish in the body of the accused the truth of the crime. The execution reestablished order in the power struc-ture. The public nature of the execution was an important part of the punishment because execution was a ritual and a ceremony, and ceremonies require observers who, in observ-ing, become participants. The public, however, sometimes resisted this top-down exercise of power by intervening in the process. The public itself often killed, or released, the criminal.

Part 2, "Punishment," includes two chapters: "General-ized Punishment" and "The Gentle Art of Punishment." Here, Foucault turns his attention to the reform movements that arose in the eighteenth century. Reformers objected to the excessive and inhumane punishments of criminals. Foucault, however, argues that the reformers were acting not out of concern for the criminal but out of economic interest. As the Industrial Revolution increased the production of goods, crime centered more on property than on persons. Crimes against property were crimes against society rather than crimes against the king. Punishment, then, no longer served to protect the interests of the king; instead, it served to protect the interests and rights of society. Punishment was no longer a ritual; it became a deterrent to subsequent crimes.

Foucault shows how society began to notice that to deter crime, punishment must match the crime, and that more serious crimes must be matched with harsher penalties. In France, however, the prison was not yet acceptable as a place for criminal punishment because the prison was a place for debtors and others who were confined at the whim of the king. The prison did not become an acceptable and primary vehicle for punishment until it offered a way for the rehabilitation of criminals; it began to subject the criminal to complete control. The prisoner was formed into an obedient citizen. This total control over the prisoner also required secrecy. The beginning of the prison, Foucault argues, marks the beginning of coercive institutions in modern society.

In part 3, "Discipline," Foucault argues that although the body is no longer subjected to torture, it is still the object of control. The chapter "Docile Bodies" demonstrates how the soldier embodies the ideology of total control and coercion. Military discipline operates on the principle of rank, place, rules, and control of time. The body of the soldier becomes part of a larger machine that registers a new technology of power. Discipline aims at training.

The next chapter, "The Means of Correct Training," presents training as a threefold process: hierarchical observation, normalizing judgment, and the examination. In a disciplinary environment (for example, schools, factories, and prisons) everyone is under observation. Discipline operates by rules of normalcy, and judgment functions to normalize behavior. It divides individuals into categories and ranks based upon their adherence to the rules; thus, normalcy becomes the desired state of being. The examination is the means by which the observing hierarchy can judge, quantify, classify, reward, and punish. The examining machine is manifested in the hospital and the school, where the individual becomes documented, fixed, and analyzed. For Foucault, the forcing of normalcy upon the individual is an oppressive evil of modern society that silences the voice of those outside the norm.

Observation reaches its pinnacle in "Panopticism," the title of the next chapter, in which Foucault uses the quarantine of plague victims and the Panopticon as models for disciplinary observation. The Panopticon, designed by social philosopher Jeremy Bentham in the eighteenth century, is a circular prison with a central tower, from which an observer can see into every cell without being seen. Prisoners have no privacy and never know when they are being watched, or not. The Panopticon is the perfect operation of power, the most efficient method of control. It is an expression of unhindered and unending examination. For Foucault, the Panopticon is a paradigm for the functioning of power in modern society, and it symbolizes his thesis. Although modern society is based upon individual freedom, the state controls disciplinary institutions and operates panoptic systems that observe, examine, classify, and coerce everyone into conformity with the norm.

Three final chapters are grouped under the heading "Prison." The prison is a necessary outgrowth of the pro-

cesses that have been detailed up to this point in the book. Prisons are "complete and austere institutions" that exercise complete control over inmates. The prison isolates the individual, regulates activities, and observes behavior. The integration of prison, hospital, and workshop creates a penitentiary in which the soul of the prisoner is disciplined. The criminal sciences examine and judge the prisoners, classifying them as delinquents.

The two concluding chapters, "Illegalities and Delinquency" and "The Carceral," argue that the prison has been subject to a cyclical process of failure and reform. However, this process cannot be eliminated because it fulfills a role in the overall matrix of power relations in society. The prison has failed to reduce offenses, but it has succeeded in separating forms of illegality into classifications that can be managed and observed.

Foucault does not seek to eliminate the prison, but he hopes to uncover the social forces that lie behind the origination, development, and continuance of the prison. He suggests that progress in the human sciences may provide hope for the future.

Lee Roy Martin

Further Reading

Danaher, Geoff, Tony Schirato, and Jen Webb. *Understanding Foucault.* 2000. Reprint. Thousand Oaks, Calif.: Sage, 2007. A good general introduction to Foucault's thought written in a clear and accessible style. *Discipline and Punish* is discussed throughout the work. Includes a useful glossary of terms.

Deleuze, Gilles. *Foucault.* Translated and edited by Seán Hand. 1988. Reprint. New York: Continuum, 2006. Deleuze, a well-known critical philosopher in his own right, offers an advanced insightful study, interpretation, and critique of Foucault's principle ideologies.

Downing, Lisa. *The Cambridge Introduction to Michel Foucault.* New York: Cambridge University Press, 2008. Written with students in mind, this comprehensive introduction explains Foucault's themes, examines his broad impact, and addresses the influence of his writings on later movements, such as feminism.

Dreyfus, Hubert L., and Paul Rabinow. *Michel Foucault: Beyond Structuralism and Hermeneutics.* Chicago: University of Chicago Press, 1982. Analyzes Foucault's ideas and argues that Foucault essentially proposes a new method for interpreting reality. Also argues that Foucault attempts to integrate objective scientific method with subjective hermeneutics.

Eribon, Didier. *Michel Foucault.* Translated by Betsy Wing. Cambridge, Mass.: Harvard University Press, 1991. This readable biography emphasizes Foucault's intellectual development, literary career, and professional context while providing a sketch of his personal life. Includes Foucault's opinions of his contemporaries.

Macey, David. *Michel Foucault.* London: Reaktion Books, 2004. A comprehensive biography that addresses every aspect of Foucault's influential and controversial life. Macey analyzes Foucault's contributions to philosophy and history, recounts his political activism, and investigates his death from AIDS-related complications in 1984.

O'Leary, Timothy, and Christopher Falzon, eds. *Foucault and Philosophy.* Malden, Mass.: Wiley-Blackwell, 2010. This thorough collection on Foucault's ideas includes a discussion of *Discipline and Punish* and of related concepts in his other works.

Discourse on Method

Author: René Descartes (1596-1650)
First published: Discours de la méthode, 1637 (English translation, 1649)
Type of work: Philosophy

To the French philosopher René Descartes, the act of doubting seemed clearly to mark the proper starting point for all philosophical inquiries. The methodology that flows from this approach, many of Descartes's successors have insisted, laid the foundations of modern philosophy. The beginning of *Discourse on Method* is a systematic tearing down of learning and education; understanding does not rest, Descartes implies, on received information.

Although usually identified simply as the *Discourse on Method,* the full title Descartes gave to his brief, five-part essay more accurately reveals the nature of his subject. The full title is *Discours de la méthode pour bien conduire sa raison & chercher la vérité dans les sciences* (*Discourse on the Method of Rightly Conducting the Reason and Seeking for Truth in the Sciences*). The *Discourse on Method* appeared along with three other essays that augment Descartes's fundamental propositions with details. They were all incorporated in his *Philosophical Essays.* Descartes believed that all people possess good sense and the unique ability to reason, so the *Discourse on Method* was written in French in an era when Latin was the language of Europe's academic, intellectual, and religious elites. It was Descartes's intention to reach a relatively large audience.

Descartes completed this essay well before 1637. When he was twenty-three, in fact, he recorded a series of dreams that inspired him to establish a new philosophical and scientific system. Moreover, his basic ideas and methodology were shared among his friends and correspondents for years before the book was published. Several things had dissuaded him from publishing. He was aware, first of all, of Galileo Galilei's condemnation by the Catholic Church for having defended the theory of Nicolaus Copernicus (published in 1512) that Earth and the other planets revolved about the Sun. Rigorously trained by Jesuits at La Flèche College and a sincere Catholic, Descartes accordingly suppressed his own cosmological ideas until he had gotten them to conform to those of his church. He also deeply valued time for meditation, thought, and reflection: time, that is, for leisure. Consequently, to publish his views was to invite the time-consuming bothers caused by approving adherents and by angry critics alike. Furthermore, since to his own satisfaction he had largely resolved many of the intellectual problems he examined, he lacked incentive to publish. The urgings of friends, a sense of social obligation, and some vanity persuaded him, at the then-advanced age of forty-one, finally to publish.

In the *Discourse on Method* Descartes approached the ancient philosophical questions of What is true? and What is certain? He employed a novel method. He styled his exposition modestly. He was not interested, he wrote, in pedantically laying down precepts for others to follow. They, after all, would respond to the dictates of their own reason. He was concerned also about the possibility of being in error, so much so that he offered his "Tract . . . merely as a history, or . . .

as a tale" that might yield examples worthy of emulation. Read in this light, the *Discourse on Method* recounts the steps of his intellectual adventure, the progress made en route, and the conclusions drawn when he reached his destination.

To launch himself anew Descartes describes how, figuratively, he divested himself of intellectual baggage and of prejudices acquired from his worldly experience. As one born of a seminoble class, for instance, he had engaged in the diversions of aristocrats, had served with the armies of Maurice of Nassau and Johann Tzerclaes, Count Tilly, during his early twenties, and had spent several years in Paris studying science, prior to embarking upon two decades of solitude and immersion in his work in Holland, later in Sweden. The experiences and the conventional authorities that once had nourished his mind had ceased to sustain him. The insights and methods of languages, history, theology, morals, ethics, eloquence, poetry, jurisprudence, medicine, and scholastic philosophy—in each of which he was well versed—he discarded as too obscure and too imprecise to afford him a pathway to truth and certainty.

What Descartes sought to discover was a body of self-evident truth. He sought certainties that, with the common endowments of good sense, humanity could accept. Descartes also wrote the *Discourse on Method* with another purpose in mind. What he sought to effect, in addition, was the reconciliation of the mechanical explanation of everything in nature (the assumptions of the new science of his day) with the cherished spiritual doctrines and values of Christianity.

Descartes chose mathematics as the exemplar of the precise and logical reasoning that could be applied to the resolution of philosophical problems. The rigorous rules and axioms of mathematics, it seemed evident to him, showed the way to certainties. Certain it was and always would be, for example, that three and three were six. A young child and a mathematical genius eternally arrive at the same result. Descartes had a profound interest in mathematics, and he made an indelible impact on its advancement. He has been recognized universally for his seminal contributions to algebra and, among other achievements, he is generally credited with founding analytical geometry. Important mathematical concepts continue to bear his name.

It was as a mathematician, then, that Descartes turned to rectifying philosophy, doubting everything, and reducing everything to what he alone, not authority, could establish as certain. Such reductionism established a single fact: Doubt itself could not be doubted. For, logically, to doubt was to think, and to think was to exist. From this reasoning comes the famous affirmation: *Cogito, ergo sum* (I think, therefore I am). This Descartes described as "the first and most certain knowledge that occurs to one who philosophizes in an orderly manner." Acknowledging his famous phrase to be a clear and self-evident axiom, a test of truth that provides a distinctly perceived certainty, Descartes proposed as a general rule that everything clearly perceived as its corollary is true.

Having found a starting point of self-evident truth, the next step for Descartes was to resolve another problem: What if there were no God, or if there were, what if God were a deceiver who surrounds people with illusions? To unravel these questions, he began by positing his idea that God, the Creator of all things, a perfect, infinite being, preexisted within him. The idea of God had to be innate. Nothing comes from nothing, and since there is something, God exists. Descartes had not created himself and thereby was imperfect and mortal. The conception of God had to have been received from a perfect, omnipotent, omniscient, and infinite being, therefore making it manifest that God exists. Descartes's knowledge of God implied the existence of a being greater than Descartes himself.

With God established as a certainty, Descartes then deals with the ancient philosophical problem of body and mind. It was essential for Descartes to reconcile the new science, to which he was devoted, to his religion, which claimed an equal measure of his devotion. Mounting evidence from science, most of it based upon mathematical inquiries and solutions, demonstrated that the entire physical world could be explained in mechanical terms (with God as the prime mover of the universe). God designed these mechanics, setting the physical bodies of the universe in motion in unalterable conformity with unchanging laws. For Descartes, natural laws were laws of motion, and differences between physical bodies were explicable as differences between their various parts. Having created the world as chaos, God, according to Descartes, thereafter enabled it "to act as it is wont to do": evolve in obedience to those laws.

Using medical analogies, Descartes assigned human functions to the realm of nature; they operate in accordance with its mechanical laws. He declared, however, that humanity's rational and spiritual qualities were entirely separate from bodily functions and could not be "educed from the power of nature." Humanity's "Reasonable Soul," that is, its rational and spiritual attributes, had been created by God. Occasionally, mind and body interact, which accounts for human comprehension of sensations and appetites. Descartes's notion of such "occasionalism" still left mind and body substantially separate. The mechanical and passive body that operates in accord with the laws of nature eventually dies, but the soul continues on as immortal.

The *Discourse on Method* is a master sketch. Descartes deploys the details of his theory of mathematical methodology and ways to discover scientific truth in the three essays printed along with the *Discourse on Method* as well as in his *Meditationes de prima philosophia* (1641; *Meditations on First Philosophy*, 1680) and his *Principia philosophiae* (1644; *Principles of Philosophy*, 1983). Collectively, neither these nor other of Descartes's writings represent a systematic theory of knowledge. His interests were never pointed in that direction. Rather, the *Discourse on Method* and his other essays expound a method of identifying truth or self-evident certainties. Alone, one's sensory experiences, he believed, can never yield either self-evident truths or certainties. Certainties result from individuals' reasoning deductively from basic principles that were inherent in the mind. Such principles are innate, fixing in the mind the standards that guide it to truth.

The *Discourse on Method*, however, leaves unexplained how innate ideas enter the mind in the first place, though the implication is that God places them there. Descartes also remains vague about how one's faculty of reason comes to possess natural canons for assessing truth. The meaning imparted to innate ideas is likewise confused. Sometimes Descartes implies that innate ideas impress themselves on the mind. Sometimes, he calls innate ideas principles discovered in the soul. Elsewhere he suggests the soul has the power to generate the knowledge from experience. He is unclear, too, about how, if God is pure spirit, he could lay down the rules governing a mechanical universe or could impart motion to matter.

Critics swiftly pointed to the deficiencies of Descartes's rationalism and use of a priori reasoning. They readily comprehended that his errors stem from his attempts at reconciling a mechanistic science with Catholic theology. Before long, philosophers Gottfried Leibniz, Immanuel Kant, Nicolas Malebranche, Pierre Bayle, Baruch Spinoza, and Thomas Hobbes, among others, tried rectifying, or avoiding, Descartes's difficulties. Other philosophers such as John Locke simply rejected Descartes's entire concept of innate ideas, or the way he separated the material and the spiritual. For their part, Jesuits denounced the message of the *Discourse on Method* and officially banned it in 1663. Dutch Calvinists likewise opposed it, and many French and German universities prohibited students from reading it.

The *Discourse on Method* nevertheless won Descartes an international reputation. Cartesian philosophy soon garnered a host of disciples, drew attention to vital questions,

and expounded the philosophical values of an orderly, logical mathematical method.

Clifton K. Yearley

Further Reading
Beck, L. J. *The Method of Descartes*. New York: Garland, 1987. Provides a clear exposition of the *Discourse on Method* which, though scholarly, is easily understandable.

Cottingham, John. *Descartes*. New York: Routledge, 1999. An excellent biographical introduction to the thoughts of the philosopher, clearly presented and requiring no special background. Includes bibliography.

_____, ed. *The Cambridge Companion to Descartes*. New York: Cambridge University Press, 1992. A helpful collection of essays focusing on a variety of topics in Descartes's thought.

Foley, Richard. *Working Without a Net: A Study of Egocentric Epistemology*. New York: Oxford University Press, 1993. A careful exposition of Descartes's analysis of skepticism and the prospects human beings have for obtaining knowledge.

Gaukroger, Stephen. *Descartes: An Intellectual Biography*. New York: Oxford University Press, 1995. A veteran interpreter of Descartes offers an important account of Descartes's intellectual development and the times and places in which it took place.

Kreeft, Peter. *Socrates Meets Descartes: The Father of Philosophy Analyzes the Father of Modern Philosophy's "Discourse on Method."* San Francisco: Ignatius Press, 2007. Imagines a meeting in which Socrates cross-examines Descartes about his *Discourse on Method*. Kreeft maintains that Socrates and Descartes are the two most important philosophers who have ever lived; he enumerates seven features of their thought that unite them and distinguish them from other philosophers.

Schouls, Peter A. *Descartes and the Possibility of Science*. Ithaca, N.Y.: Cornell University Press, 2000. An examination of the role of imagination in Cartesian philosophy.

Sepper, Dennis. *Descartes's Imagination: Proportion, Images, and the Activity of Thinking*. Berkeley: University of California Press, 1996. Explores Descartes's views about the nature of human experience and its prospects for obtaining knowledge about reality.

Strathern, Paul. *Descartes in Ninety Minutes*. Chicago: Ivan Dee, 1996. A quick but helpful introductory overview to key points in Descartes's thought.

Vinci, Thomas C. *Cartesian Truth*. New York: Oxford University Press, 1998. An evaluation of the strengths, weaknesses, and implications of Cartesian approaches to questions about knowledge and truth.

Williams, Bernard. *Descartes: The Project of Pure Enquiry.* Harmondsworth, England: Penguin Books, 1978. A detailed, analytic dissection of the careful structure of Descartes's most important philosophical arguments.

Yolton, John W. *Perception and Reality: A History from Descartes to Kant.* Ithaca, N.Y.: Cornell University Press, 1996. Yolton appraises the significance of Descartes's attempts to show how it is possible for human beings to obtain knowledge in spite of skepticism.

Disgrace

Author: J. M. Coetzee (1940-   )
First published: 1999
Type of work: Novel
Type of plot: Social realism
Time of plot: Late 1990's
Locale: Cape Town and the Eastern Cape of South Africa

Principal characters:
DAVID LURIE, a professor in his fifties
MELANIE ISAACS, a student with whom Lurie has an affair
LUCY, Lurie's daughter

The Story:

David Lurie was once a professor of classics and modern languages at Cape Town Technical University, but, in the changing climate toward pragmatics and rationality in post-apartheid South Africa, he has been relegated to teaching "communications skills," which serves to strengthen his feelings of obsolescence in a rapidly changing culture. Lurie is further alienated from social relations by two divorces and his recent estrangement from his child, Lucy, who lives on the Eastern Cape. Lurie's social aloofness has led him to satisfy his sexual urges with a prostitute named Soraya, until he destroys the arrangement by attempting to contact her outside their normal meetings. Lurie soon attempts to fill the resulting void with a twenty-year-old student in his Romantic poetry class named Melanie Isaacs.

Lurie successfully seduces Melanie after a couple of missteps, but she is reticent during the few sexual encounters they have; Lurie is conscious that at least one of these encounters is only barely consensual and is tantamount to rape. Melanie's attendance in Lurie's class becomes sporadic, and it is clear that Lurie is losing control of the situation; Melanie's boyfriend harasses him, and his car is vandalized. Lurie grows increasingly certain that his students know about his affair, and soon his fears are confirmed by a visit from Melanie's father.

Lurie evades Mr. Isaacs, who has come to discuss the affair Lurie is having with his daughter; he is not, however, able to evade the sexual harassment case filed against him by the university. Lurie has no patience for the proceedings; he is given ample opportunity to express remorse, enter counseling, and save his job, but he steadfastly refuses. It seems to his colleagues as if he purposefully wishes to destroy himself. He succeeds; Lurie resigns and moves from Cape Town to his daughter's smallholding in the town of Salem on the Eastern Cape.

Lucy lives alone on her small farm, raising and selling crops and running a small kennel. Lurie has difficulty adjusting to the life of the farm but soon occupies himself volunteering at a local animal shelter, as well as helping Lucy on the farm.

The alien but peaceful routine of the farm lasts until Lurie and Lucy are attacked by three black men they invite inside to use the phone. The men quickly take Lucy into the house and lock the door, and Lurie is knocked unconscious while the men take Lucy to another room and rape her. Lurie awakes to find himself being doused with a chemical and set afire; he loses his hair and suffers severe burns to his scalp. The men have killed all but one of the dogs in the kennel and stolen everything of value, leaving the house a shambles. Lucy reports the attack and the burglary but refuses to report the rape, much to Lurie's chagrin.

After the attack, it becomes clear that Lucy's neighbor and business partner Petrus was somehow involved, but Lucy refuses to change anything about her living situation, which further enrages Lurie. Soon, at a celebration with Petrus in honor of acquiring more land, Lucy sees one of the men that attacked her, a disturbed youth named Pollux. Still, she refuses to press charges.

As their disagreements cause the distance between Lurie and his daughter to grow, Lurie spends increasing amounts of time at the shelter with Bev and even has a brief affair with her. Lurie's duties consist mainly of assisting in the euthanasia of the dogs and disposing of their bodies. Lurie is becoming increasingly affected by his involvement with the animals, and he eventually takes over the cremation duties to ensure that the dogs' bodies are treated respectfully.

During this time, Lurie repeatedly argues with Lucy and entreats her to move, but she refuses; Lurie eventually returns to Cape Town. In Cape Town, Lurie seeks an audience with Mr. Isaacs and finally apologizes during an uncomfortable dinner; when Lurie finally takes up residence in his house again, he finds it has been robbed and vandalized. He eventually visits Lucy again at her home, and discovers she is pregnant from the rape and determined to keep the child. Lucy decides to sell her land to Petrus in exchange for permission to stay in the house, and for his protection—an arrangement that amounts to a civil marriage. The novel ends with Lurie renting a room in Grahamstown, helping Lucy at the market on weekends, and again volunteering at the animal shelter.

Critical Evaluation:

When *Disgrace* was awarded the Booker Prize for fiction in 1999, J. M. Coetzee became the only author thus far to receive that award more than once. (Coetzee had also won for his novel *Life and Times of Michael K* in 1983.) Coetzee was awarded the Nobel Prize in Literature in 2003 for his morally and ethically charged examinations of South African culture, especially of the implications and effects of apartheid (state-mandated racial segregation and oppression).

Disgrace marked a stylistic departure for Coetzee, ushering in an era critics have dubbed his "recent" fiction. Up until *Disgrace*, with the exception of *Age of Iron* (1990), Coetzee's novels were classifiable at least in part as allegories of political conditions in South Africa, as a result of their displaced treatments of politics, race, location, and time. *Disgrace*, however, was clearly "of the times" in which it was written: postapartheid South Africa in the late 1990's. Legislation passed in 1990 and 1991 repealed the majority of the apartheid laws, but segregation and discrimination were still largely in effect until free elections in 1994 produced a black-majority government, marking the end of state-sanctioned apartheid though not its embedded economic and social aftereffects.

Disgrace is set in a rapidly changing and evolving South Africa. The novel has been criticized by South African commentators for painting a bleak picture of the cultural rebuilding process underway. Although this portrait of South Africa is a pivotal backdrop for *Disgrace*, the narrative is tightly centered on David Lurie's point of view and his ethical journey, not on politics.

David Lurie realizes he is a relic, and he lives uncomfortably in the culture of the new South Africa. Though he does not articulate it, he identifies strongly with the colonial oppressors—the white ruling class that held power in South Africa from the time it was first colonized by the Dutch in the 1600's until the elections of 1994. As an academic, Lurie occupies a station in life that was formerly one of the seats of colonial power, but power is shifting away from the classical Western disciplines of the humanities. As his role in life is failing him, so do traditional connections: He is twice divorced, is not close to his daughter, and resorts to a prostitute for intimacy.

Lurie's choice of sexual partners—first Soraya and later Melanie Isaacs, both of black or "colored" racial ancestry (under the legal categories of apartheid)—speak to Lurie's identification with the power structure; Lurie is attracted to the exotic "other"—that which is forbidden and radically outside himself—in a fashion described by Palestinian cultural critic Edward Said in his critique of Orientalism. Additionally, Lurie is extremely selfish, egotistical, and self-serving, attitudes associated with oppressors. The seduction of Melanie Isaacs is unjustifiable by any moral standards, though Lurie at times tries to rationalize his motives.

In a novel that presents a character such as David Lurie, readers might expect some kind of conscious attempt on his part to seek redemption; however, as is typical of Coetzee's work, the movement of Lurie's character is subtle and often ambiguous. One critic describes *Disgrace* as an antibildungsroman; instead of describing the creation of Lurie's sense of self, it describes the complete loss of it.

Because of his affair with Melanie Isaacs and his stubborn refusal to express remorse, Lurie moves from a relatively secure position of power and selfhood to an insecure position where the normal rules of society as he understands them do not apply. He moves from tacit and literal victimizer to victim. Lurie cannot accept that power in the new South Africa is no longer born of racial difference; he is both a figurative victim of the new times who cannot find a way to live and a literal victim, as he is imprisoned and burned in the attack on Lucy's farm. This literal victimization is the catalyst for Lurie's growth toward what one critic terms "a sympathetic consciousness" and what another critic describes as a state of "grace," meaning a receptivity to religious types of experience. This state contrasts with the "disgrace" of the novel's title, referring in one sense to Lurie's willful separation from anything outside himself.

Lurie's development of a "sympathetic imagination" at the close of the novel offsets his nearly complete self-absorption at the beginning of the novel. One way his consciousness develops is by identifying with the female victims of rape—he has been a rapist himself, although he can scarcely realize it, and he must learn to see his crime from the victim's point of view. His actions with Melanie are parallel to Lucy's rape at the farm. He begins to understand through Lucy that her rape happened because of history: Since Lucy is a white woman, she is implicitly implicated by history as one of the colonial oppressors of black people. There is no logic to the rape except as an effect of the political landscape, which Lucy accepts and Lurie cannot.

While changes in Lurie's perspective signal some of his growth, the largest actions he takes toward developing a less selfish consciousness are apparent when he is working at the animal shelter. Although Lurie thought he would get used to euthanizing the dogs, the more he does it, the more it affects him—and inexplicably so, to his mind. Eventually, he is so appalled by the treatment of the dogs by the workers at the crematorium that he takes over the task himself to see that the dogs are treated with "dignity and respect," ideas that are profoundly human moral constructs. Lurie is at first skeptical of the rationale of animal rights advocates, but he comes deeply to value animal rights, a theme often found in Coetzee's fiction and essays.

Although Lurie moves toward a compassion beyond selfishness when working at the shelter, he frustrates readers and critics alike when he does not take the logical next step in his sympathies: He does not transmit his new understanding to humans or take any larger action. As is typical of Coetzee's protagonists, Lurie's revelations are only for himself and of questionable value to society at large. At face value, *Disgrace* offers few answers for the questions it asks and solves few of the moral dilemmas it presents.

Alan C. Haslam

Further Reading

Attridge, Derek. "Age of Bronze, State of Grace: *Disgrace*." In *J. M. Coetzee and the Ethics of Reading*. Chicago: University of Chicago Press, 2004. Examines the relationship of *Disgrace* to the political and cultural landscape of South Africa in the late 1990's.

Attwell, David. "Contexts: Literary, Historical, Intellectual." In *J. M. Coetzee and the Politics of Writing*. Berkeley: University of California Press, 1993. A thorough introduction to the complex themes of Coetzee's work and the relation of that work to South Africa.

Barnard, Rita. "J. M. Coetzee's *Disgrace* and the South African Pastoral." *Contemporary Literature* 44, no. 2 (2003): 199-224. Examines *Disgrace* as depicting the erosion of the myth and reality of the pastoral ideal in South Africa.

Beard, Margot. "Lessons from the Dead Masters: Wordsworth and Byron in J. M. Coetzee's *Disgrace*." *English in Africa* 34, no. 1 (May, 2007): 59-77. An in-depth examination of the role of the Romantic poets William Wordsworth and Lord Byron in *Disgrace*, which moves beyond a reflection of Lurie's Eurocentrism toward larger issues.

Cooper, Pamela. "Metamorphosis and Sexuality: Reading the Strange Passions of *Disgrace*." *Research in African Literatures* 36, no. 4 (2005): 22-39. Investigates the processes of Lurie's evolution in *Disgrace* as related to social and political shifts in sexuality in postapartheid South Africa.

Cornwell, Gareth. "Realism, Rape, and J. M. Coetzee's *Disgrace*." *Critique* 43, no. 4 (2002): 307-322. Examines *Disgrace* as a realist text in the context of Coetzee's relationship to and critiques of realism.

Donovan, Josephine. "'Miracles of Creation': Animals in J. M. Coetzee's Work." *Michigan Quarterly Review* 43, no. 1 (2004): 78-93. Explores the relationship of themes in *Disgrace* and other Coetzee works to the author's animal rights advocacy.

Herron, Tom. "The Dog Man: Becoming Animal in Coetzee's *Disgrace*." *Twentieth Century Literature* 51, no. 4 (2005): 467-490. Elaborates on the function of animals in *Disgrace* to address issues of race and language.

Kossew, Sue. "The Politics of Shame and Redemption in J. M. Coetzee's *Disgrace*." *Research in African Literatures* 34, no. 2 (2003): 155-162. Explores the influence of postapartheid South African politics on the relationship between the private and public worlds in *Disgrace*.

Marais, Mike. "J. M. Coetzee's *Disgrace* and the Task of Imagination." *Journal of Modern Literature* 29, no. 2 (2006): 75-93. Makes a detailed case describing Lurie's redemption in terms of his development of a "sympathetic imagination."

The Dispossessed
An Ambiguous Utopia

Author: Ursula K. Le Guin (1929-   )
First published: 1974
Type of work: Novel
Type of plot: Science fiction
Time of plot: Several hundred years in the future
Locale: Urras and its moon, Annares, in the Tau Ceti
    solar system

Principal characters:
SHEVEK, a physicist
TAKVER, Shevek's sworn life partner
SABUL, a physicist who is Shevek's mentor and later rival
BEDAP, Shevek's childhood friend
LAIA ASIEO ODO, a revolutionary
DR. ATRO, a physicist
DR. SAIO PAE, a physicist
EFOR, Shevek's manservant

The Story:

Urras and Annares are twin planets orbiting Tau Ceti, a star eleven light years from Earth. Roughly a million years ago, Urras, Earth, and a number of other planets were colonized by Hain. The Hainish abandoned their colonies, which subsequently evolved in different directions. The nation of A Io has become the most powerful on Urras. A highly class stratified society, it experiences an uprising by anarchists led by the revolutionary Laia Odo. The anarchists fail to bring about revolution, but they are permitted to colonize Annares, Urras's barely habitable desert moon, where they are free to order their colony as they see fit. Once the colony is founded, the people of Annares and Urras have minimal contact. Eighty years later, the Hainish reestablish contact with Urras.

Seventy years after the Hainish contact Urras, an Annarean physicist named Shevek is invited to A Io to receive a coveted scientific prize and continue his work on the simultaneity principle, which his hosts believe holds the key to faster-than-light space travel. Shevek accepts the invitation, becoming the first person from either society to travel between the moon and the planet since Annares was colonized. Shevek sees himself as an emissary of reconciliation between Annares and Urras. Some of his fellow Annaresti consider him a traitor and attempt, unsuccessfully, to prevent his departure.

Shevek's childhood has been spent in an "ambiguous utopia," a society in which private property is virtually nonexistent and no individual has official power to coerce another. When he is two, his engineer mother abandons him to work in a distant city, and he spends most of his childhood in dormitories. The communal ethic, lack of family ties, and constant peer pressure to conform work tolerably well for the average child. However, others require a level of autonomy and individual expression that the regimented society theoreti-

cally allows but in practice discourages. These Annaresti include Shevek, whose mathematical genius is evident at an early age; Bedap, a profound social thinker; and other friends with artistic talents. Gazing up at the "moon" (Urras), the friends wonder whether what they have been told about the evil society their forebears rejected still holds true.

Despite the spartan communal existence and long hours spent performing menial labor, Shevek establishes himself, by age twenty, as a rising star in physics. He leaves the provincial community in which he grew up to work under Sabul, Annares's leading physicist, at the National Institute of Sciences in Abbenay. There, he discovers that the institute's scientists enjoy privileges that others on Annares do not: Shevek feels vaguely guilty, slightly tainted by the sin of being "propertarian," when he is assigned his own sleeping room and allowed seconds on dessert at the institute cafeteria. Under Sabul, he learns Iotic to read the works of Atro, the leading Urrasti physicist, from whom Sabul has plagiarized most of his own work. At first, Shevek has free rein to correspond with Atro and produces important papers based on the collaboration. Sabul becomes increasingly jealous of Shevek, however, and he places barriers in the way of his publishing. The magnum opus of his early career, *Principles of Simultaneity*, sits on the shelf for four years, only to appear in an abridged version.

Their conflicts with Sabul and the difficulties they experience communicating with counterparts on Urras lead Shevek, Bedap, and their friends to open an unauthorized publishing and telecommunications network and to step up efforts to reestablish ties with Urras. These efforts, while not technically forbidden, meet with much hostility and opposition.

Annaresti customs are permissive with respect to sex. Shevek has ample opportunities for sexual encounters as a teenager, but he finds casual sex unsatisfactory and has become virtually celibate when he meets Takver, a fish geneticist from his hometown. The two quickly decide they are meant for each other and that they want to be permanent partners, a status their society allows but does not support. While Takver is pregnant with their daughter, a severe prolonged drought strikes Annares. The Division of Labor ships Shevek to a remote region to do manual labor. When he returns to Abbenay, he discovers that Takver has been reassigned to a distant laboratory and his position at the institute has disappeared. For four years, he labors under conditions of extreme privation. When the couple is at last reunited, they are determined to do anything it takes to allow Shevek to realize his full potential as a physicist. It is this resolve that leads to the foundation of the publishing venture to circumvent Sabul. This venture, in turn, leads to Shevek's invitation to travel to A Io.

Shevek arrives on Urras empty-handed. He has not yet formed a coherent theory, and he has learned not to commit preliminary versions of a theory to paper where they can be plagiarized and coopted. For his first few months on Urras, Shevek is in a state of awe at the society's opulence. His hosts install him in a faculty residence at A Io University and carefully shield him from the poverty and oppression that are still very much a part of Urrasti life. He learns for the first time of the existence of the Hainish and their plan for a federation of worlds. Atro introduces him to the works of the Terran physicist "Ainstain," upon whose theory of General Relativity Atro has drawn heavily, though with more originality than Sabul has exhibited.

Despite being allowed to work under seemingly optimal conditions, Shevek makes no progress. The outbreak of a war between A Io and the nation of Thu leads him to suspect that, if he were to solve the problem of simultaneous transmission of matter, A Io would use the knowledge to coerce other nations and planets rather than to cooperate with them. The attitudes of A Ioan physicists seem to support this suspicion: Atro's judgment on social issues is clouded by his aristocratic heritage and blind patriotism, and the current head of the Physics Institute, Saio Pae, is a political manipulator.

Shevek becomes aware that there is an undercurrent of support for the revolutionary principles of Odonianism among A Io's working classes. Their revolutionary fervor fanned by opposition to the war, the Odonians have been trying to contact Shevek, because he is a citizen of an Odonian society. His first attempt to respond ends in a drunken spree. The tension revives his scientific inspiration, but he falls ill. During his illness, Shevek is tended by his manservant Efor, who tells him what life is like for the poor. Efor advises him on

how to escape from surveillance at the university and puts him in contact with the revolutionaries.

Shevek, now close to solving the simultaneity problem, agrees to address a massive demonstration of workers. While he is speaking, police helicopters descend on the crowd, machine-gunning demonstrators. Shevek and a badly injured man take refuge in a warehouse basement. While they cower there, the man dies, and Shevek puts the final touches on the theory behind a practical simultaneous communication device called an ansible. His theory cannot enable faster-than-light travel for physical objects, but it will make it possible for people on different planets to communicate instantaneously, rather than waiting long weeks or months for messages to travel between worlds.

Revolutionaries smuggle Shevek out of the capital city and deposit him at the Terran embassy in Rodarred, where he is granted asylum. There, he presents the Hainish with his plans for an ansible, as a gift. They realize the device's profound significance to forging an interplanetary federation based on voluntary cooperation for the sake of mutual benefit.

His gift received, Shevek returns to Annares on a Hainish starship, accompanied by a Hainish individual. This person is traveling as an unofficial ambassador to learn what else the unique communitarian anarchy of Annares has to offer the fledgling Federation of Known Worlds.

Critical Evaluation:

Ursula K. Le Guin's *The Dispossessed* is a complex novel that can be approached either as a work of literature or as a statement of social philosophy couched as fiction. It occupies a position somewhat intermediate between a work of pure science fiction—such as Isaac Asimov's *Foundation* series (1951-1993), which is set in the distant future, involves a plethora of inventions critical to the plot, and is populated by characters who think and behave like American men—and a philosophical work such as Thomas More's *De Optimo Reipublicae Statu, deque Nova Insula Utopia* (1516; *Utopia*, 1551), which is couched as fiction but has minimal action and characterization and is mainly a vehicle for ideas.

The Dispossessed is as much about the process by which new ideas develop as about the ideas themselves. The narrative framework of the novel consists of pairs of chapters, the first describing Shevek's upbringing and scientific career on Annares, the second his life during the time (roughly a year) he spends on Urras. The chapter pairs portray Shevek undergoing parallel odysseys of discovery, thwarted aspirations, and finally a personal breakthrough under extremely adverse conditions that translates into scientific revolution.

Much critical analysis of the novel focuses on the details of the social structure represented by Annares, arguing whether the author intended to provide a sort of blueprint for an ideal society, or, alternatively, a warning about how egalitarianism stifles individual creativity. Such critiques sometimes overlook the facts that the novel is about two different societies, each one unlike actual Earth societies in different ways, and that it portrays the relationship between these societies as much as it portrays each society in itself. Le Guin herself downplays the importance of specific ideas. In a somewhat tongue-in-cheek response to Laurence Davis and Peter Stillman's scholarly *The New Utopian Politics of Ursula Le Guin's "The Dispossessed"* (2005), "a response, by ansible, from Tau Ceti," she writes

I've spent a good deal of vehemence objecting to the reduction of fiction to ideas. . . . When treated—even with much praise—as a methodical ax grinder, I'm driven to deny that there's any didactic intention at all in my fiction. . . . Of course there is. I'm dead set against preaching, but the teaching impulse is often stronger than I am.

Le Guin's approach to human similarities and differences, whether in the science fiction context of the Hainish cycle, the fantasy world of Earthsea, or the imaginary but plausibly Slavic country of Orsinia, is strongly influenced by her upbringing. Le Guin is the daughter of noted anthropologist Alfred Kroeber, best known for his work with Native Americans in California. Her childhood exposed her to a cosmopolitan community of scholars who shared a common respect for the value of cultures very different from those of middle-class America. She has said that, whereas the science in most works of science fiction is physics, the science in her works is often anthropology.

A common thread throughout the Hainish cycle is that of intercultural journeys and returns that open channels of communication and stimulate socio-spiritual growth in both cultures. *The Dispossessed* differs from most utopian fiction in that it involves a citizen of a utopia journeying to and interacting with a culture more closely resembling real-world cultures. In that respect, it more closely resembles Samuel Johnson's *Rasselas, Prince of Abyssinia: A Tale by S. Johnson* (1759) than it does More's *Utopia* (1516). Shevek's journey opens the way for communication not only between two planets but also among all the known worlds.

As one of a small number of women science fiction and fantasy writers considered to be writing enduring literature, Le Guin has been criticized for not presenting a sufficiently feminist point of view, particularly in *The Dispossessed* and

The Left Hand of Darkness (1969), which is set on a planet all of whose inhabitants are hermaphroditic. In both novels the principal protagonist is male or masculine. While Annares's ambiguous utopia was designed by a woman and theoretically allows equality of the sexes, Takver's struggles to find love, create beauty, and raise children reveal that it is not a woman-friendly environment. One is left wondering whether some melding of the cultures will produce a better alternative, but this is never stated explicitly.

The balance achieved by the union of opposites, epitomized by the yin-yang symbol, also forms a subtext in several of Le Guin's works. In *The Dispossessed*, the contrast is between the two worlds: one lush, the other barren, one egalitarian and poor, the other stratified and rich. As a single interconnected unit, they achieve what neither could on its own.

Martha A. Sherwood

Further Reading

Bittner, James W. *Approaches to the Fiction of Ursula K. Le Guin.* Ann Arbor: University of Michigan Research Press, 1984. Compares Le Guin's works to Asimov's *Foundation* series and provides many quotations from Le Guin's own writings on her art.

Bloom, Harold, ed. *Modern Critical Views: Ursula Le Guin.* Philadelphia: Chelsea House, 1986. A multiauthored volume incorporating many different perspectives. A chapter on *The Dispossessed* analyzes the novel in terms of anarchist political theory.

Cummins, Elizabeth. *Understanding Ursula Le Guin.* Columbia: University of South Carolina Press, 1990. Chapter 3 treats the Hainish cycle. Emphasizes utopian themes in its analysis of *The Dispossessed*.

Davis, Laurence, and Peter Stillman, eds. *The New Utopian Politics of Ursula Le Guin's "The Dispossessed."* New York: Lexington Books, 2005. Mainly an analysis of the novel as political theory; contains Le Guin's "A Response, by Ansible, from Tau Ceti."

DeBolt, Joe, ed. *Ursula Le Guin: Voyager to Inner Lands and to Outer Space.* Port Washington, N.Y.: Kennikat Press, 1979. Collection of essays on Le Guin's life and work. An essay on *The Dispossessed* sees it as a critique of Western sociology.

Ferns, Chris. *Narrating Utopia: Ideology, Gender, Form in Utopian Literature.* Liverpool, England: University of Liverpool Press, 1999. Compares Le Guin to other utopian writers and addresses her handling (or lack thereof) of the topic from a feminist perspective.

District and Circle

Author: Seamus Heaney (1939-   )
First published: 2006
Type of work: Poetry

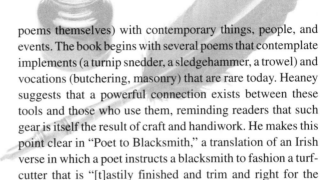

Seamus Heaney's *District and Circle* consists primarily of lyric verse composed in a variety of forms. Most notably, Heaney returns to and elaborates upon many themes that have remained central to his poetic vision. Some poems in this volume—including "Anahorish 1944," "The Tollund Man In Springtime," and "The Blackbird of Glanmore"— directly reference earlier works. Other poems in *District and Circle* contain more subtle resonances with earlier poems. *District and Circle*'s "The Harrow-Pin," with the lines "Horses' collars lined with sweat-veined ticking,/ Old cobwebbed reins and hames and eye-patched winkers,/ The tackle of the mighty, simple dead," calls to mind the opening lines of "Gone" from the 1969 collection *Door Into the Dark*: "Green froth that lathered each end/ Of the shining bit/ Is a cobweb of grass-dust."

In 2007, the book won the Poetry Book Society's T. S. Eliot Prize for Poetry and the *Irish Times* Poetry Now Award. Reviewers and readers have hailed the book as a touchstone volume.

The book's title words, "district" and "circle," function both as nouns and verbs. On the one hand, a district can refer to a particular place or area, a space with clear parameters or unique jurisdictions. A circle is a distinctive shape as well as a group of acquaintances or intimates (for example, a family circle or a circle of friends). Read another way, the terms also convey a sense of action. "District" describes the act of dividing or organizing an area or space into discrete parts, while "circle" evokes a move to return, encompass, surround, or gather around. Taken as verbs, "district" and "circle" are expressed in the present tense, conveying the idea that these acts occur perpetually, without ceasing. "District" and "circle" also refer to lines on the Tube, London's subway. Significantly, the title poem takes place in London, and others, such as "To George Sefaris in the Underworld" and "Out of This World," allude to nether realms for which the Tube stations and subway platforms serve merely as earthly imitations.

Parsing the title yields some insight into Heaney's organization of the volume as a whole and illuminates some of the paradoxes he often describes or suggests in most of the poems, many of which center on a specific memory or the act of remembering. Another device Heaney uses is the juxtaposition of old, sometimes ancient, objects (including words and poems themselves) with contemporary things, people, and events. The book begins with several poems that contemplate implements (a turnip snedder, a sledgehammer, a trowel) and vocations (butchering, masonry) that are rare today. Heaney suggests that a powerful connection exists between these tools and those who use them, reminding readers that such gear is itself the result of craft and handiwork. He makes this point clear in "Poet to Blacksmith," a translation of an Irish verse in which a poet instructs a blacksmith to fashion a turfcutter that is "[t]astily finished and trim and right for the hand." As a result, technology and practiced skill inherently affirm ingenuity and creativity, both of which also serve as equipment for the poet.

Heaney ironically elaborates on the connections between craft, muscle-memory, and poetic work as the volume progresses. In "Anahorish 1944," for example, the poet describes Irish hog butchers and children watching U.S. soldiers marching on the roads of Northern Ireland en route to their Normandy deployment during World War II. The sight of them with their mass-produced gear, "guns on their shoulders" and accompanied by "[a]rmoured cars and tanks and open jeers," provides a curious if not jarring contrast to the slaughterhouse awash in "sunlight and gutter-blood" and men in "gloves and aprons coming down the hill." Heaney juxtaposes the quotidian barbarity of skilled meat cutters coming upon the orderly display of armed soldiers advancing to what will be one of the bloodiest, most chaotic, and decisive events of World War II.

In other poems, Heaney further explores the ambivalent powers of technology both to preserve and destroy, a theme associated with the poet since the publication of "Digging" in the 1966 volume *Death of a Naturalist*. In that famous early poem, Heaney first compares the pen in his hand to a gun and then resolves by poem's end to use the pen as a spade to dig through experience, memory, and language to craft his art. In *District and Circle*'s "Helmet," the poet marvels at the functional details fashioned onto an Irish American firefighter's headgear. The inspired yet practical design of the individual helmet ultimately serves as a synecdochic emblem of the firefighter's heroism, which the poet imagines as a defiant Anglo-Saxon shield-wall attempting to quell all-consuming flames.

"Anything Can Happen," a version of a Horatian ode, provides one of the most dramatic instances of Heaney's reimaginings. Ostensibly Horace's description of the capricious powers of Jupiter, Heaney's variation mentions how the Roman god's uncontrollable lightning is so powerful that it can clog "the Atlantic shore itself," overturn "the tallest towers," and daunt "those in high places." Though not explicitly, Heaney's language evokes the September 11, 2001, terrorist attacks. Horace's original ode, then, serves as the tool or technology Heaney uses to reveal a conceptual parallel that resonates beyond both poets' respective time and place. Also, like the turnip-snedder introduced in the volume's opening pages, or like the firefighter's helmet, a reader can conceive of Horace's poem as an artifact, something Heaney has found, which awakens memories of shared human experience transcending the particulars of an individual's existence.

Heaney further explores this empathetic imagination in several of the elegiac works in *District and Circle*. In "Stern" and "Out of This World," respectively, Heaney recalls moments shared in life with the poets Ted Hughes and Czesław Miłosz that have become transformative utterances over time. Likewise, in the short sequence "Home Fires," Heaney offers readers imaginary recollections of Dorothy Wordsworth and W. H. Auden as informal tributes to people he did not personally know but whose lives nonetheless remain exemplary.

Several critics have commented that in *District and Circle*, Heaney introduces a tone of concern in his career-long celebration of the natural world's resilience and the ineffability, or indescribability, of its cycles. Even though readers can discern Heaney's worry, poems appearing later in its pages sound this note most definitively. Beginning with "In Iowa," in which a speaker conceives with terrifying clarity a prophecy of "[n]ot parted but . . . of rising waters," through the poem "Moyulla," which describes a river degraded by industrial exploitation, Heaney most directly explores green, or ecological, themes in these poems.

Ultimately, *District and Circle* asserts Heaney's characteristically confident resolve. "Planting the Alder" concludes with a mantralike imperative that reaffirms the curative powers of nature: "Plant it, plant it,/ Steel-head in the rain." For Heaney, this affirmation closely corresponds to a sense of belonging, and the last few poems in the volume expand on this notion by collectively gravitating toward references to home and returning to familiar environments.

"The Blackbird of Glanmore" closes the volume. This poem brilliantly redresses many of the devices and themes Heaney presents in *District and Circle* by revisiting yet another early work, "Mid-Term Break," in which Heaney recollects the funeral of his brother who died in youth. Here, Heaney associates the long-deceased boy with a blackbird who resides on the grounds of the poet's cottage in Glanmore. Heaney's identification with the blackbird as the genius of his home is so complete that the poet achieves "a bird's eye view" of himself as a "shadow on raked gravel/ In front of my house of life." The low-roofed house of death evoked earlier in the poem is transformed by the blackbird's lively activity, quickening the poet's memories and in so doing invigorating confidence in his own creativity.

J. Greg Matthews

Further Reading

Bloom, Harold, ed. *Seamus Heaney*. Philadelphia: Chelsea House, 2002. An introductory analysis containing a biography, extracts from critical essays, thematic and structural analyses of Heaney's work, and an index of themes and ideas.

Crowder, Ashby Bland, and Jason David Hall, eds. *Seamus Heaney: Poet, Critic, Translator*. New York: Palgrave Macmillan, 2007. The contents in this collection broadly survey Heaney's works. Includes essays on Heaney's reading, his use of allusions, and his interests in non-English-language poetry.

Desmond, John F. *Gravity and Grace: Seamus Heaney and the Force of Light*. Studies in Christianity and Literature 2. Waco, Tex.: Baylor University Press, 2009. Though he does not directly address *District and Circle*, Desmond offers a compelling reading of a transcendent religious vision evident in Heaney's poetry.

Garratt, Robert, ed. *Critical Essays on Seamus Heaney*. New York: G. K. Hall, 1995. A collection of essays analyzing Heaney's poetry and the feminine principle in his work, and comparing his poetry to the poetry of Dante, William Butler Yeats, William Wordsworth, and James Joyce.

Heaney, Seamus. *Stepping Stones: Interviews with Seamus Heaney*. Edited by Dennis O'Driscoll. New York: Farrar, Straus and Giroux, 2008. Heaney articulates his views on art, politics, religion, and many other themes relevant to his life and works. Chapter 13, "'So Deeper into It," specifically addresses *District and Circle*.

Jones, Chris. "Old English Escape Routes: Seamus Heaney, the Caedmon of the North." In *Strange Likeness: The Use of Old English in Twentieth Century Poetry*. New York: Oxford University Press, 2006. Examines how and why Heaney uses Old English language in his poetry.

Maloney, Karen Marguerite. *Seamus Heaney and the Emblems of Hope.* Columbia: University of Missouri Press, 2007. The author concentrates on Heaney's use of Irish and other mythologies in his work, as well as his abiding interest in European prehistory and archaeology. Poetry predating *District and Circle* receives primary coverage.

O'Donoghue, Bernard, ed. *The Cambridge Companion to Seamus Heaney.* New York: Cambridge University Press, 2009. This volume collects high-quality essays assessing Heaney's entire career. Topics include Heaney's popular reception and his responses to feminism.

Zamorano Llena, Carmen. "Postnationalist Identity and Sites of Memory in the Latest Work of Seamus Heaney, Derek Mahon, and Paul Durcan." *Études Irlandaises* 32, no. 2 (Autumn, 2007): 155-171. This essay compares Heaney's treatment of identity and memory in *District and Circle* with the works of two notable contemporaries. The author focuses on Heaney's evolving view of Ireland and his response to globalization.

The Divan

Author: Hafiz (c. 1320-c. 1389/1390)
First transcribed: Dīvān, c. 1368 (English translation, 1891)
Type of work: Poetry

The Divan of Hafiz is one of the glories of Persian literature in its golden age and a classic of Eastern literature. Hafiz was the pen name of Shams al-Din Muhammed, a Persian who, early in his life, turned to the serious study of philosophy, poetry, and theology. The pen name he adopted means "a man who remembers," a title normally bestowed upon persons who commit the Qur᾿ān to memory. In Hafiz's case, the title was not unwarranted, for he was a dervish who taught the Qur᾿ān in an academy founded by his patron.

While *The Divan* is the best known of Hafiz's works, he also wrote in various other patterns common to Persian poetry. The *Divan* itself is a collection of short poems, lyric in quality, in the form known as *ghazals*. In the original Persian, these poems consist of from five to sixteen couplets (called *baits*). The particular poetic form has been compared to the ode and the sonnet in English-language poetry because of the lyric qualities, the length, and the subject matter. One curious feature of Hafiz's *ghazals* is that the last two lines normally contain the poet's name. The first line of each *ghazal* introduces the rhyme, which is repeated in every other succeeding line within the poem.

Although relatively little known in the Western world, Hafiz's *Divan* has remained the most popular poetry ever written in his native land. It has even been considered oracular, and Persians sometimes consult it by opening the book and placing a finger on a chance passage, hoping to have an answer thereby to whatever question has arisen. Such a procedure, or a variation of it, was supposedly done at the death of the poet. Because of exception taken to some of his poems, his corpse was at first denied the usual burial rites. To settle the question, some of his *ghazals* were written on slips of paper and placed in an urn, one to be drawn out by a child. According to legend, the verse drawn by chance from the urn said that Hafiz should be given appropriate funeral rites, as he would enter Paradise; thus the question was settled.

Through the centuries there has been debate over whether his poetry should be taken literally or symbolically, with those who see in *The Divan* a serious work by a great Persian philosopher and student of the Qur᾿ān taking one side of the question, and those who see it as a fine expression of a warmly alive human being taking the other. Western readers who cannot see anything religious in these superficially hedonistic poems should call to mind the religious expression, veiled in sensual imagery, in the poetry of John Donne and Richard Crashaw in England, Saint John of the Cross in Spain, and Edward Taylor in the United States.

Literal or symbolic, the imagery of Hafiz's poetry is warm, human, even passionate. There is no escaping, even in translation, the sincerity of the poet. Like most Eastern poetry, the imagery may even seem lush to Western readers, as in the following example:

The east wind at the dawn of day brought a perfume from the tresses of my beloved, which immediately cast my foolish heart into fresh agitation.

I imagined that I had uprooted that flower from the garden of my heart, for every blossom which sprang up from its suffering bore only the fruits of pain.

From fear of the attacks of her love, I set my heart free with bloody strife; my heart dropped gouts of blood which marked my footsteps.

I beheld from her terrace how the glory of the moon veiled itself in confusion, before the face of that dazzling sun.

In his poems, Hafiz lauds the love between man and woman, and he praises the beauty of women, their eyes, their lips, their hair, their features, their forms. He also sings of wine and men, as in these lines:

O Cupbearer! bring the joy of youth; bring cup after cup of red wine.

Bring medicine for the disease of love; bring wine, which is the balm of old and young.

Do not grieve for the revolution of time, that it wheeled thus and not thus. Touch the lute in peace.

Wisdom is very wearisome; bring for its neck the noose of wine. When the rose goes, say, "Go gladly," and drink wine, red like the rose.

If the moan of the turtle does not remain, what matter? Bring music in the jug of wine.

Whether one can interpret this praise of wine as symbolic of spiritual substance is open to question. That there is passion, grace, and charm in the lines is, however, undeniable. The same is true of the following, also typical of Hafiz:

O interpreter of dreams! give good tidings because last night the sun seemed to be my ally in the joy of the morning sleep.

At the hour when Hafiz was writing this troubled verse, the bird of his heart had fallen into the snare of love.

An interesting legend about one of Hafiz's poems in *The Divan* has come down through the ages. In the poem, he offered willingly to exchange both the rich cities of Bokhara and Samarkand for the mole on the cheek of his beloved. When the great conqueror Tamerlane learned of the poem and had an opportunity, he sent for the poet and rebuked him, saying that Hafiz should not have offered to give away what did not lay in his power to bestow. Not entirely subdued, even in the presence of the great Tamerlane, Hafiz supposedly re-plied that it was through such generosity that he came to the attention of the mighty conqueror. Over and over again in *The Divan*, another city is mentioned, his own native city of Shiraz, which he loved greatly. ("Hail, Shiraz! incomparable site! O Lord, preserve it from every disaster!") From the fame of Hafiz and his poems, Shiraz came to be a symbol of poetic inspiration among poets who followed him.

The reader of *The Divan* may make comparisons between Hafiz's lyrics and those of Omar Khayyám, an earlier Persian poet and one whose work is more widely known among English-speaking readers through the adaptation by Edward FitzGerald (published 1859). The works of the two poets have much in common. The apparent hedonism, the similar imagery, and the same flowing mellifluousness are found in the work of both men. The obvious difference is the superficial one of form: Omar Khayyám wrote in quatrains, as the word "Rubáiyat" indicates, and Hafiz wrote in the form of the *ghazal*. A more important difference lies in the attitudes expressed in the poems. Hafiz is the more serious, despite an apparent hedonism. There is a greater inclination on the part of Hafiz to be religious, to place his faith in Allah and his wisdom, inscrutable as the poet may find it.

Further Reading

Arberry, Arthur J. *Classical Persian Literature*. London: George Allen & Unwin, 1958. An account by one of the most accessible translators of Hafiz, with a discussion of Hafiz in English.

Browne, E. G. *The Tartar Dominion, 1265-1502*. Vol. 3 in *Literary History of Persia*. Bethesda, Md.: Iranbooks, 1997. A new edition of the four-volume history of Iranian literature originally published in 1902. Chapter 4 in the third volume devotes more than forty pages to Hafiz's poetry, and there are many other references to the poet listed in the index.

Hafiz. *The Collected Lyrics of Hafiz of Shiraz*. Translated by Peter Avery. Cambridge, England: Archetype, 2007. Avery, a scholar of Persian literature, has translated all 486 poems in *The Divan*, and his translations are published here with extensive annotations.

_____. *The Divan-i-Hafiz*. Translated by H. Wilberforce Clarke. Bethesda, Md.: Ibex, 1998. A new edition of Clarke's English translation of *The Divan*, including extensive annotations to the poems, a biography of Hafiz, and an index of the figures of speech in the work. This edition features a new introduction by Hafiz scholar Michael C. Hillmann, who provides information about Hafiz's life and the historical and literary characteristics of the *ghazal*.

Hillmann, Michael C. *Iranian Culture: A Persianist View.* Lanham, Md.: University Press of America, 1990. An assessment of Hafiz and his place in the Persian literary tradition.

Meisami, Julie Scott. *Medieval Persian Court Poetry.* Princeton, N.J.: Princeton University Press, 1987. Discusses Hafiz within the tradition of Persian court poetry and patronage.

Rypka, Jan. *History of Iranian Literature.* Dordrecht, the Netherlands: D. Reidel, 1968. Incorporates scholarship to 1968, especially by Iranian scholars. Emphasizes the social setting of the poems.

Schimmel, Annemarie. "The Genius of Shiraz: Sa'di and Hāfez." In *Persian Literature*, edited by Ehsan Yarshater. Albany, N.Y.: Bibliotheca Persica, 1988. The perspective of a distinguished scholar of Persian mysticism.

The Divine Comedy

Author: Dante (1265-1321)

First transcribed: La divina commedia, c. 1320 (English translation, 1802)

Type of work: Poetry

Type of plot: Allegory

Time of plot: One week beginning on Thursday night before Easter, 1300

Locale: Hell, Purgatory, and Heaven

Principal characters:

DANTE, poet from Florence who journeys through the afterlife

VIRGIL, the pilgrim's guide through Hell and Purgatory

BEATRICE, the pilgrim's beloved and guide through Heaven

The Poem:

Dante finds himself lost in a dark, frightening wood. To regain his path, he tries to climb a mountain, but a leopard, a lion, and a wolf block his way. The Roman poet Virgil approaches him and offers to conduct him through Hell and Purgatory as the only way back to the right path. Virgil comes at the request of a lady from Heaven, Beatrice (a woman whom Dante once loved), who will guide the pilgrim through Heaven once he reaches it.

When the travelers arrive at Hell's entrance, Virgil explains that the large group of souls outside the gates lived their lives without committing to good or evil, so neither Heaven nor Hell will accept them. At the River Acheron, where they find the ferryman Charon, Dante is seized with terror and falls unconscious. Aroused by a loud clap of thunder, he finds himself across the river and follows his guide through Limbo, the first of the nine circles of the funnel-shaped Hell. The souls in Limbo, most of whom lived in ancient times, lived virtuous lives but were not baptized (since Christ had not yet come to Earth when they lived). Unlike the other souls in Hell, they are not undergoing any torments.

The next four circles Dante and Virgil visit are reserved for those who committed sins of incontinence. In the second circle, they meet Minos, the infernal judge, who appoints newly arrived sinners to their appropriate circle for punishment. Dante is overcome by pity as he witnesses the souls who are guilty of sexual sin being eternally buffeted by a stormy wind. He speaks to two souls and faints when he hears their story. The third circle houses gluttons, who are forced to lie in muck under a constant rain of filthy hail, snow, and stagnant water and are guarded by the terrifying three-headed dog Cerberus. In the next circle, guarded by Plutus, Dante witnesses the prodigal and the avaricious in two semicircles rolling heavy boulders and clashing up against each other. Dante and Virgil reach the muddy river Styx, in which the wrathful are submerged and are tearing at one another. Dante meets someone he knows, as he does in many circles, but for the first time he feels no pity for the sinners as he begins to understand the justice of Hell's torments. At Virgil's signal, the ferryman Phlegyas transports them across Styx to the city of Dis.

The city of Dis, or lower Hell, encompasses the last four circles of Hell. When Dante and Virgil are denied admittance by the fallen angels who guard the city's walls and gates, a terrified Dante wants to retrace his steps and return the way he came. However, an angel arrives from Heaven and commands the rebellious spirits to allow the two travelers passage. Once inside Dis, they discover fiery tombs that house the souls of heretics, and Dante speaks to two of the tormented. During a pause in their journey made necessary by the increasing stench from below, Virgil explains the philosophical rationale for the moral ordering of Hell's nine circles and describes the next three.

The Minotaur—the raging half-man, half-bull—guards the seventh circle of souls who committed violence against others, against themselves, and against God. Dante and Virgil see a red river of boiling blood, in which murderers are submerged. Dante is transported by a centaur across this river to a forest and discovers that the gnarled trees there contain the souls of those who committed suicide. Next, they come to a plain of burning sand, where they find those who sinned against God (blasphemers) or nature (homosexuals and usurers). Flakes of fire rain down on all three groups. Among the homosexuals, Dante is astounded to find a former mentor, and he speaks with three souls from Florence. The two poets then come to a precipice.

To reach the eighth circle far below, Virgil summons Geryon, a frightful flying monster with a scorpion's tail, to transport them. When they reach the bottom, they see ten moat-like ditches in descending sequence, connected by rocky bridges. Each ditch houses sinners who committed a type of fraud. Dante finds here, for instance, seducers, flatterers, diviners, sellers of political offices and favors, hypocrites, and thieves. The ten separate torments endured by frauds range from sitting in dung (flatterers) to wearing leaden coats that appear golden on the outside (hypocrites). In this circle, Dante speaks to many people and Virgil speaks to Ulysses.

Hearing a horn blow, the travelers see a group of giants buried up to their waists who surround the ninth circle, in which traitors are encased in ice. After being lowered into this final circle by the giant Antaeus, Dante converses with some of the souls there and learns the nature of their particular betrayals. At the center of this lowest circle, they see the monstrous figure of Satan, with three faces and six wings, frozen up to his waist. Climbing down his leg, they reverse direction and journey up to the earth's surface in the opposite direction of Hell.

Dante and Virgil emerge on Easter Sunday morning from Hell's foul air to the pure atmosphere of the Island of Purgatory, located in the unexplored Southern Hemisphere of Earth. A grassy plain surrounds a conical mountain with seven circular ledges that has an insurmountable wall around its base. They soon see a boat propelled by an angel transporting souls of recently deceased people who are destined for Heaven but who must first undergo purification. Dante recognizes a musician friend among them. As Virgil and Dante stroll through the plain, they encounter many souls who explain that they are kept in this area, ante-purgatory, because they delayed their repentance. They plead with Dante, as do many souls in this realm, to ask their families to pray for them when he returns to the Northern Hemisphere. While sleeping, Dante is transported up to the gate of Mount Purgatory by Lucia, a lady from Heaven. The angel guarding the gate inscribes seven marks with the tip of his sword on Dante's forehead, one for each of the seven capital sins common to human beings.

Once past the gate, the two poets ascend a narrow winding path and arrive at the first ledge. They see souls bent over, carrying heavy stones on their backs. Here and on every ledge, the souls meditate on examples of the vice of which they are being cleansed and of its opposite virtue—in this case, pride and humility. As Dante climbs to the next ledge, the angel guarding the connecting stair removes the first mark on his forehead—a procedure that will be repeated from ledge to ledge. On the second ledge, the souls wear sackcloth and have their eyelids sewn shut with wire while they listen to examples of envy and generosity. The wrathful, on the next ledge, are enveloped in blinding smoke, and on the fourth ledge, Dante and Virgil witness the purging of sloth when they see souls forced to run continuously. One of the souls here asserts that human beings have free will and choose their ultimate destinies.

Virgil discusses the nature of love and the moral order of the mountain, explaining that the sinful dispositions on this mountain can be categorized as examples of misdirected, defective, or excessive love. On the fifth ledge, where avarice and prodigality are purged, the prostrate souls face the ground. Virgil and Dante are joined by the Roman poet Statius, who has completed his cleansing here and who accompanies them to the sixth ledge, where gluttony is purged by fasting. The souls on the seventh and final ledge are being cleansed of lust by fire. Afraid of being burned, Dante refuses to enter the fire until Virgil informs him that he will see his beloved Beatrice only if he walks through it.

An angel now directs the poets to a path that leads to the original Garden of Eden. As they stroll through a lovely forest, Dante comes to a stream; on the other side, a beautiful woman is gathering flowers. She tells him that this stream, Lethe, will remove his memory of sin and that another stream in the garden, Eunoe, will restore memories of good deeds. After Dante sees a procession that includes personages representing the books of the Bible, Beatrice arrives with heavenly attendants and Virgil disappears, returning to Limbo. Beatrice reproaches Dante for his unfaithfulness to her after she died, but, convinced of his sincere repentance, she agrees to lead him through Heaven.

After witnessing symbolic reenactments of church history in the garden, Beatrice and Dante rise effortlessly and instantly through the nine heavenly spheres, which are characterized by ever-increasing light and joy. Beatrice tells Dante that although the true dwelling place of all blessed souls is the Empyrean, which is outside space and time, souls appear as lights in each sphere to indicate to him their different degrees of blessedness. On the sphere of the Moon, Dante finds those who were forced to break their vows of chastity in religious life. Here, as elsewhere in Heaven, Dante asks many questions, and Beatrice or another blessed soul answers him. Beatrice then leads him to Mercury, where he sees the souls of those who were interested in their own glory and hears Justinian narrate a survey of the history of the Roman Empire. From there, they rise to Venus, where Dante converses with souls whose lives were marked by excessive passions.

Arriving at the fourth sphere, the Sun, Dante and Beatrice are encircled by a group of lights representing the great theologians. As spokesman, Thomas Aquinas, a Dominican friar, names and comments on each of the souls and narrates the life of Saint Francis of Assisi. A second circle of lights surrounds the first, and a new spokesman, Bonaventure, a Franciscan friar, narrates the life of Saint Dominic and then names the souls in that second circle.

When Beatrice and Dante rise to Mars, the fifth sphere, they see crusaders and martyrs, who appear as sparks in the shape of a cross. Dante meets his ancestor Cacciaguida, who commissions him to report all that he has seen when he returns to Earth and warns him that he will be driven into exile in the future. Next, on Jupiter, Dante sees the souls of those who administered justice faithfully, such as King David and Charlemagne, who appear in the shape of an eagle's head and neck. In the seventh sphere, Saturn, Dante finds the great contemplatives such as Saint Benedict.

When they arrive at the sphere of fixed stars, Dante looks down on the earth and is astonished by its insignificance with respect to the cosmos. He undergoes examinations by the apostles Peter, James, and John on faith, hope, and love to see if he is properly prepared to enter the Empyrean. Adam approaches the group and tells Dante about his brief time in the Garden of Eden. Peter bitterly laments the corruption in the Church and commissions Dante to repeat what he has just heard when he returns to Earth.

In the ninth sphere, Dante sees God as a point of light encircled by the nine orders of angels who rotate all the lower spheres. Beatrice then leads him into the Empyrean, where he first sees symbolic visions of Heaven's assembly and is strengthened thereby to see it in its true form, which he compares to a white rose. After realizing that Beatrice has returned to her heavenly seat, Dante sees an old man at his side,

Bernard of Clairvaux, a medieval mystic, who prays for his final vision of God. Dante sees God first as light, then as three rainbow-colored rings, representing the Trinity; his culminating vision is of humanity's union with God in Christ.

Critical Evaluation:

Dante was born of a poor but noble Florentine family. Unusually well educated for his time and social class, he was knowledgeable in science, theology, and philosophy and was a well-known man of letters. He lived in politically tumultuous times and was active in his city's government. During an absence from Florence in 1301, his party was overthrown and he was sentenced to exile in 1302. For a time, he tried to clear his name, but he was never allowed to return to his beloved Florence upon the threat of being burned. Dante wrote *The Divine Comedy* in exile and died in Ravenna.

Dante chose to write the masterpiece *The Divine Comedy* in Italian, although the language of scholarship at that time was Latin. Dante's major writings in Latin include his political essay *De monarchia* (c. 1313; English translation, 1890; also known as *Monarchy*, 1954; better known as *On World Government*, 1957) and his compelling defense of the written vernacular as an appropriate medium of expression, *De vulgari eloquentia* (c. 1306; English translation, 1890). Although Dante used Latin for a number of very important letters and for a few poems, his language of choice was his native Tuscan dialect, which became the basis of modern Italian. His earliest major work—*La vita nuova* (c. 1292; *Vita Nuova*, 1861; better known as *The New Life*), a mystical-spiritual account of his love for Beatrice that combines prose and poetry—was written in Italian, as were *Il convivio* (c. 1307; *The Banquet*, 1887), a philosophical commentary on four of his poems, and a number of lyric poems. The greatest tribute to the eloquence of written Italian is, however, *The Divine Comedy*.

The work that Dante first titled *La commedia* (the adjective "divina" was added by others and first appeared in the 1555 edition) is an intentionally complex work. It is divided into three sections, or canticles: *Inferno* (Hell), *Purgatorio* (Purgatory), and *Paradiso* (Heaven). The poem is subdivided into one hundred cantos: one for the prologue and thirty-three for each of the main sections. Each canto consists of three-verse units, *terzine*; each verse is composed of eleven syllables, for a total of thirty-three syllables in each *terzina*. The rhyme scheme that Dante invented for the poem, called *terza rima*, consists of each rhyme (except the first) occurring three times: *aba; bcb; cdc, ded,* and so forth. This scheme creates an interlocking pattern that produces a very closely knit poem.

Number symbolism plays an important part in *The Divine Comedy*. As a typical medieval poem, it relies heavily on mystical associations with numbers. It is not difficult to discern, for example, the relationship between one poem in three canticles and one God in the three form of the Trinity. The number two reflects the duality of nature as seen in the pairing of opposites such as corporeal and spiritual, active and contemplative, Church and State, Old Testament and New Testament, and the (inverted) mountain-shaped Hell and the purgatorial mountain.

Three signifies Father, Son, and Holy Ghost; the three theological virtues of faith, hope, and charity; and other combinations. Dante's *terzine* and *terza rima* are significant in this regard and are meant to honor the Trinity. Among multiple examples in the poem, the pilgrim is initially blocked on his path by three beasts, has three guides, spends three nights in Purgatory, and has three dreams there. The number four—the number of the seasons, elements, humors, directions, and cardinal virtues—combines with three to make the mystical seven: the number of days of creation, days of the week, days of Dante's journey, virtues and vices (embodied in the structure of Mount Purgatory), and planets, among many other instances. Nine, the multiple of three times three, becomes the basis for the overall structure for each of the realms of the afterlife: There are nine circles of Hell, nine areas of Purgatory (ante-purgatory, seven ledges, and the garden), and nine spheres of Heaven.

In his famous "Epistle to Cangrande," in which he dedicates the *Paradiso* to that Veronese nobleman, Dante sheds light on many aspects of his poem. He explains his poem's title by indicating that a comedy begins with a difficult situation but has a happy ending and is written in a humble style that is accessible to all (as opposed to the dire ending and high style of tragedy). He claims that his poem, like Scripture, has various levels of meaning: Although the literal subject of the poem is the state of souls after death, its allegorical subject is the exercise of free will by men and women and the moral consequences of their choices resulting in torment or reward in the next world. He affirms that his poem's purpose is practical, not speculative: to help lead readers from misery to happiness, which consists in the knowledge of God.

The journey of Dante's pilgrim, which constitutes the poem's plot, is an explicitly Christian journey, initiated by grace, through the world of an afterlife that is based on Christian teachings and principles. As such, Dante's main source for the poem is the Bible, which is referred to directly or indirectly more than 570 times. Dante quotes, paraphrases, and alludes to many biblical verses; more than forty biblical personages appear in the poem; Christian dogma is explained;

and biblical events are symbolically reenacted. The literal events of the poem signify corresponding spiritual realities. The pilgrim's loss of the right path, for example, is also the loss of his path to salvation; the dark wood reflects his sinful state. The journey of Dante's pilgrim from the dark wood of sin and error to the light and truth of Heaven is meant as a reenactment, on an individual level, of the spiritual significance of the Exodus. The removal of the seven marks from the pilgrim's forehead as he climbs each ledge of Purgatory indicates his cleansing and healing from the stains and wounds of sin. His pilgrim's descent into Hell on Good Friday, his emergence from it on Easter Sunday morning, and his rising into the heavens is an imitation of Christ's death, resurrection, and ascension.

Although there is direct exposition of Christian truth, primarily in the *Paradiso*, many of Dante's teaching points are not directly stated but, rather, are embedded in the things his pilgrim witnesses. The geographical layout of each realm of the afterlife, for instance, is an implicit running commentary on the spiritual conditions of souls. The sinners in Hell—in its traditional location under the earth—are cut off from the Sun. Since the Sun represents light, truth, and God, the very location of these sinners reflects the fact that they are cut off from God. Each successive circle is farther down in the earth and thus farther from the Sun, indicating Dante's evaluation of the increasing seriousness of any given sin. On Mount Purgatory, as the souls climb upward, they are moving closer to the Sun and thus closer to God, signifying their growth in virtue as well. The gravity of each vice purged is reflected in the physical structure of the mountain, where the most serious sinful inclination (pride) is purged on its lowest ledge, and the least serious (lust) is cleansed on its highest ledge. In the *Paradiso*, the degree of blessedness for redeemed souls is indicated by the distance from or closeness to the Empyrean of the sphere in which they appear to the pilgrim. Dante's topography, then, carries a nonverbal message.

Another indirect commentary can be found in the torments in Hell and the purifications of Purgatory. They are not merely innovative, interesting, or random; they are designed to provoke thought about the nature of each sin and vice. In Hell, each particular type of suffering, which Dante calls a *contrapasso* (counter-suffering), does not stem from God's eye-for-an-eye retribution but rather reflects the essence of the sin the soul has committed, which now becomes its own punishment. Sinful lovers are whirled around by a tempestuous wind because they allowed themselves to be carried away by their passions. Murderers are submerged in a boiling river of blood because they chose to shed the blood of human beings; the degree to which they shed blood determines the degree to which they are submerged in the river. Those who betrayed others are encased in ice because they chose to be cold-hearted. Souls in Hell, then, experience an infernal version of the disordered condition of the sin to which they clung and that now constitutes their essential being for all eternity.

Unlike the torments in Hell, in Purgatory the souls' sufferings are curative, not punitive: Souls do penance by practicing the opposite of their vice. The proud, with their haughty looks, are now bent over and have their eyes cast down. The envious, who looked greedily upon what others had, now have their eyelids sewn shut. The lustful, who burned with fiery passion, are now purged by a cleansing fire. Dante almost never spells out the connection between a sin and its punishment or a vice and its cleansing, leaving that connection for readers to ponder and to discover.

Just as the literal events in the poem have underlying significance, so too do the characters. The characters in Dante's afterlife are, necessarily, all the people who have ever lived and died, beginning with Adam and ending on Good Friday of 1300. The more than six hundred characters specifically named in the poem are historical and classical figures, including personages from the Old and New Testaments, emperors and other rulers, artists and poets, popes and other clergy, and noble men and women. Since no group enjoys a favored status in the afterlife, people from each category can be found in all three realms. Although Dante's characters can represent theological, political, philosophical, or moral realities, their historical reality and their complexity as human beings remain intact.

Dante shapes his characters according to the typological or figural approach to history, in which human beings continue to be themselves but carry other meanings as well. Dante's Virgil is the historical Roman poet who wrote the *Aeneid* (c. 29-19 B.C.E.; English translation, 1553), but he also signifies natural philosophy, reason, poetry, and the Roman Empire (which Dante felt was divinely ordained to establish earthly peace and order). Beatrice ("blessed" in Italian) retains her identity as the young Florentine woman whom Dante loved since his youth and who died in 1290, but she often functions in the poem as the personified character of Wisdom in the Old Testament and thus also signifies revelation, grace, and theology.

The underlying significance of each of these two guides often dictates what they can or cannot do in the poem. For example, Virgil, as embodying natural philosophy and reason, can guide the pilgrim through Hell and Purgatory because the tools he embodies can discover that sin is a disordered state to be rejected (Hell) and that moral virtues are desirable (Purgatory). However, Virgil cannot go any farther because

natural philosophy and reason have limits to the truths they can discover. In order for the pilgrim to understand the heavenly realities of God's nature and salvation history, revelation and theology are needed. This is why Virgil is replaced by Beatrice as the guide through Heaven. As with other aspects of his poem, Dante does not explain these points for his readers, expecting them to arrive at an understanding of these things on their own.

Although he is writing a Christian poem with reliance on the Bible and theologians such as Augustine and Thomas Aquinas, Dante incorporates classical and mythological elements into his poem in a wide variety of ways. His references at the very beginning of the poem to Aeneas's journey to the underworld and St. Paul's journey to the heavens indicate that he intends his poem to syncretize classical and Christian traditions. Believing that ancient authors and myths attained some elements of truth—even if they did so imperfectly at times—he draws on Virgil's and Ovid's writings as poetic models, and he bases part of the moral order of Hell on the division between incontinence and malice found in Aristotelian ethics. On all the ledges of Mount Purgatory, the examples of virtue that the souls meditate on come not just from the Bible and history but from myth as well.

At times, Dante synthesizes and adapts classical elements to align with Christian truth for his own purposes. The guardians of the nine circles, for instance, are mythological or classical creatures that Dante chooses as embodiments of the sin of a given circle. Three-headed Cerberus—traditionally the classical guardian of Hades—has three mouths, so he now guards the gluttonous; Plutus—traditionally the Roman god of Hades—is also the god of wealth, so he now guards the avaricious and the prodigal, who misused wealth in different ways. Throughout the poem—even in the *Paradiso*, where the emphasis is on direct Christian teaching—classical stories, gods, and characters are referred to and used in similes, metaphors, and allusions to help describe the pilgrim's inner experience and the things he sees.

No brief explanation can do justice to the majesty and depth of this monumental achievement in the history of Western poetry, and no sweeping generalization can adequately account for its complexity of ideas or the intricacy of its structure. Its epic scope and encyclopedic nature make *The Divine Comedy* a key to the study of medieval civilization. However, its focus on the ultimate issues of life and death, the Creator's relationship to all of creation, and the moral consequences of human behavior transcend time, making Dante's poem perennially relevant.

Joanne G. Kashdan; revised by Marsha Daigle-Williamson

Further Reading

Bernardo, Aldo S., and Anthony L. Pellegrine. *Companion to Dante's "Divine Comedy": A Comprehensive Guide for the Student and General Reader.* Binghamton, N.Y.: Global Academic, 2006. A wealth of information to enhance understanding of the work. Includes a biography of Dante; a chronology; essays placing *The Divine Comedy* within the context of medieval philosophy and literature; capsule summaries of the *Inferno*, *Purgatory*, and *Paradise*; and several essays providing critical analysis of the evolution of the work, Dante's objectivity, and his writing style. Also contains a character analysis, study questions, select bibliographies, a glossary, and an index.

Freccero, John. *Dante: The Poetics of Conversion.* Edited by Rachel Jacoff. Cambridge, Mass.: Harvard University Press, 1986. A collection of seventeen essays by a leading critic of Dante. Demonstrating the centrality of Saint Augustine's thought for Dante, Freccero builds on the writings of Charles Singleton while refining many of his ideas.

Havely, Nick. *Dante.* Malden, Mass.: Blackwell, 2007. Good introduction that places Dante's life and work within the context of literary and cultural traditions. Examines key themes and passages in his writings, especially in *The Divine Comedy*, and recounts the critical reception of *The Divine Comedy* from the fourteenth through the early twenty-first centuries. Contains illustrations and explanatory diagrams of Dante's "other worlds."

Hawkins, Peter S. *Dante: A Brief History.* Malden, Mass.: Blackwell, 2006. An introductory overview primarily to Dante's work, focusing on *The Divine Comedy*. Discusses Dante's journey to God in each of the three parts of *The Divine Comedy*, as well as Beatrice, religion, and the afterlife.

Hede, Jesper. *Reading Dante: The Pursuit of Meaning.* Lanham, Md.: Lexington Books, 2007. Unlike many scholars who maintain that *The Divine Comedy* is unified by its account of a journey through the afterworld, Hede argues that the poem's three parts are unified by a coherent vision of divine order.

Jacoff, Rachel, ed. *The Cambridge Companion to Dante.* 2d ed. New York: Cambridge University Press, 2007. Collects fifteen essays by distinguished scholars that provide essential background to and critical evaluations of Dante's life and work. Includes key studies by historians and literary scholars.

Scott, John A. *Understanding Dante.* Notre Dame, Ind.: University of Notre Dame Press, 2004. A critical overview of Dante's work. Chapters 6 through 10 on *The Divine Comedy* discuss its structure and worldview and analyze the poetic aspects of the work, including its versification, language, rhyme scheme, and use of metaphors and similes.

Singleton, Charles Southward. *Dante Studies.* 2 vols. Cambridge, Mass.: Harvard University Press, 1954-1958. Often regarded as among the most influential studies published by an American Dante scholar, this classic two-volume work interprets Dante's poem using a fourfold allegorical model. Singleton's approach remains a point of departure for much American Dante scholarship.

Sowell, Madison U., ed. *Dante and Ovid: Essays in Intertextuality.* Binghamton, N.Y.: Medieval and Renaissance Texts and Studies, 1991. Collection of essays addressing the crucial question of how the Christian poet Dante made use of the classical poet's texts; offers perspicacious commentary on the Ovidian presence throughout Dante's masterpiece.

The Divine Fire

Author: May Sinclair (1863-1946)
First published: 1904
Type of work: Novel
Type of plot: Psychological
Time of plot: 1890's
Locale: England

Principal characters:
SAVAGE KEITH RICKMAN, a young writer
HORACE JEWDWINE, a literary editor
LUCIA HARDEN, Rickman's inspiration
FLOSSIE WALKER, Rickman's fiancé
MR. PILKINGTON, a financier

The Story:

Horace Jewdwine, a literary editor, thinks he discovered a genius in Savage Keith Rickman, a young and unknown poet who earns his living by making catalogs for his father, a bookseller. Jewdwine hesitates, however, to declare openly that Rickman is a genius, for his reputation could suffer if the young man then proves otherwise. He encourages Rickman privately but fails to give him the public recognition that would mean so much to the young writer.

Rickman himself cares little for fame or money. He knows that he is a genius, that is, that part of him is a genius. He is also a student, a young man about town, a journalist, a seeker after simple pleasures, and sometimes a drunk. He finds it difficult to have so many facets to his nature. One part wars constantly with the others; but no matter in what form he finds himself, honor never leaves him. Even when drunk, he continues to be honorable.

Rickman's intelligence and his ability to judge books are the foundations upon which the elder Rickman built his financial success as a book dealer, yet father and son never understand each other. Money is the father's god; the muse is Rickman's. The father is backed by and supported by Mr. Pilkington, a financier of questionable ethics but a great success. When Pilkington informs him that the Harden library might soon be on the market, the old man sends his son to evaluate it. At the same time, Miss Lucia Harden, daughter of the owner of the library, asks for someone to catalog it for her. Rickman is chosen because his knowledge of old books is infallible.

Rickman is awed by Lucia. She is the daughter of a baronet and far above him in station, but from the first, he knows that she is destined to be his inspiration. Lucia is Jewdwine's cousin, and he is unhappy when he learns of her association with Rickman. He knows Rickman is beneath her, but he also knows that his cousin is moved by poetry. Jewdwine thinks that he himself will one day marry Lucia and inherit the library and the country estate, but he cannot bring himself to ask for her hand; making decisions is almost impossible for Jewdwine.

While working for Lucia, Rickman learns that his father and Pilkington are planning to pay a ridiculously low price for the Harden library. In order to help the girl, he writes to Jewdwine and asks him to buy the library at a fair figure. Jewdwine fails to answer the letter. When Lucia's father dies suddenly, leaving her indebted to Pilkington, Rickman goes to his father and tries to persuade him to change the offer. The old man refuses, and Rickman leaves the bookshop forever, refusing to compromise his honor in return for the partnership his father offers him if he will stay. Not wanting to hurt Lucia, he tells her little of what happened. He even tries to excuse Jewdwine's failure to buy the library and so salvage some of her father's estate.

Pilkington takes the Harden house and furniture and Rickman's father the library. After Rickman leaves him, the old man's business begins to fail, and he is forced to mortgage the library to Pilkington. The books are stored, pending redemption. Rickman does not see Lucia again for five years.

Back in London, Rickman continues to write for various journals. Jewdwine gives him a junior editorship on the journal he edits, and the job allows Rickman to live fairly comfortably. He puts his serious writing away in a drawer. Although the product of his genius, it will bring no money. Eventually, he is trapped into a proposal of marriage by Flossie Walker, a fellow boarder. Flossie will never understand the ways of genius; her world is a house in the suburbs decorated with hideous furniture. Rickman finds himself with the house bought and the wedding date set.

Chance saves him. After five years, Lucia visits a friend in Rickman's boardinghouse, and the two meet again. No word of love is spoken, for Lucia, even without her fortune, is still above him, and Rickman has no desire to hurt Flossie, who waited two years for him to accumulate enough money for their marriage. He and Lucia, however, find inspiration and comfort in their renewed acquaintance. The real blow to Flossie's dreams comes when Rickman's father dies, leaving him a small inheritance. With it, Rickman will be able to redeem the mortgaged Harden library from Pilkington and return it to Lucia. If he does so, he will not be able to marry for at least two more years. Flossie cannot understand Rickman's belief that a debt of honor can be just as binding as a legal debt. Rickman is greatly relieved to learn that Flossie refuses to wait. She quickly marries another boarder and finds her house in the suburbs, complete with nursery.

Rickman lives through years of grinding labor. He works all night, starves himself, and lives in an unheated attic to redeem the complete library. He gets extensions from Pilkington, who enjoys the sight of genius chasing an impossible goal. His friends lose track of him. He loses his job with Jewdwine because he will not compromise his honor even in his desperate need to help Lucia. At last, he seems doomed to fail, for his lack of food and his feverish work have made him desperately ill. Friends find him and take him, unconscious, to a hospital. Later, they find the work of his genius while going through his belongings. When it is published, Rickman's fame is assured. Poor Jewdwine! How he wishes now that he had the courage to claim Rickman in time. By that time, however, Jewdwine sacrificed his own principles, and success is beyond hope for him.

When he recovers, Rickman goes to Lucia. He finds her ill and unable to walk. When she learns that his illness was caused by his having worked for her, the gift is almost more than she can bear. With his aid, she arises from her bed. Cured of the malady that she knows now is only heartbreak, she sees Rickman whole, the genius and the man fused at last.

Critical Evaluation:

May Sinclair's *The Divine Fire* deals with the frustrations of a young poet of exceptional talent whose valuable energies are wasted in the struggle to make a living and to fulfill an enormous, self-imposed financial obligation. Sinclair shows a wide variety in her work, but there are techniques in *The Divine Fire* that are characteristic of her general style; the novel also contains many of the same attitudes and psychological concerns frequently found in her fiction.

Stylistically, Sinclair is somewhat of a naturalist. In comparison with her other works, *The Divine Fire* is relatively long and leisurely paced, but it shares with them an acute attention to detail and an objectivity of observation. Through her skillful and unobtrusive selection of details to present, Sinclair creates a powerful impression of realism that carries its own meaning without need of comment by the author. Sinclair was influenced by H. G. Wells and thus interested in exposing the mediocrity of middle-class values and their deadening effect on the spirit. Her intent was to dramatize the way an individual life—whether an unusual one such as Keith Rickman's or a quite ordinary one such as Flossie Walker's—is molded by external forces. Rickman's career, therefore, illustrates to some extent the dictum found in Sinclair's earlier novel *Audrey Craven* (1897): "In our modern mythology, Custom, Circumstance, and Heredity are the three Fates that weave the web of human life." Sinclair, nevertheless, does not approach the pessimism of Thomas Hardy or Theodore Dreiser, and she is often unwilling to accept the naturalist solution. In *The Divine Fire*, Rickman, after all of his suffering, is finally recognized as a genius and united with Lucia.

Although Sinclair was not a Freudian, she was certainly aware of the important psychological assumptions beginning to be made in her generation and of their implications. The reader discovers in all of her work that same sensitivity and insight into emotions and motivations that inspire *The Divine Fire*. She is particularly aware of the various kinds of oppression that produce frustration; one type that appears frequently—and reminds readers of Sinclair's similarities to Henry James—is the oppressiveness parents exert over their children. Also reminiscent of James are her portraits of seemingly nice people who are in reality self-serving and unscrupulous—portraits that reflect not only her interest in the discrepancy between appearance and reality but also her desire to expose hypocrisy and false values.

Further Reading

Bloom, Harold, ed. *May Sinclair.* New York: Chelsea House, 1986. Excerpts from several sources summarizing Sinclair's accomplishments as a novelist. Includes excellent reviews of *The Divine Fire* from the time of the novel's first publication.

Boll, Theophilus. *Miss May Sinclair, Novelist: A Biographical and Critical Introduction.* Rutherford, N.J.: Fairleigh Dickinson University Press, 1973. Detailed though somewhat favorably biased study of Sinclair's life and career. Comments on the significance of *The Divine Fire* to her reputation, and offers brief analyses of plot and narrative techniques.

Brown, Penny. "May Sinclair: The Conquered Will." In *Poison at the Source: The Female Novel of Self-Development in the Early Twentieth Century.* New York: St. Martin's Press, 1992. Discusses Sinclair's work as exemplifying the way twentieth century female novelists portray the difficulties faced by women who try to develop a sense of identity. Links *The Divine Fire* with other early Sinclair works that share affinities with Victorian fiction.

Kaplan, Sydney J. *Feminine Consciousness in the Modern British Novel.* Urbana: University of Illinois Press, 1975. A chapter on Sinclair is included in this study of five female British novelists whose works focus on the tensions between the ideal of sexual equality and the realities of female subordination. Comments on the use of psychological techniques in Sinclair's fiction.

Kunka, Andrew J., and Michele K. Troy, eds. *May Sinclair: Moving Towards the Modern.* Burlington, Vt.: Ashgate, 2006. Collection of essays examining Sinclair's literary career and individual works. Includes discussions of Sinclair's early reception in Europe and her supernatural fiction, as well as comparisons of her work to that of Virginia Woolf and the Brontë sisters. "A Sort of Genius: Love, Art, and Classicism in May Sinclair's *The Divine Fire*" by Diana Wallace analyzes this novel.

Miracky, James J. "The Sexing of Genius: May Sinclair's Experimental Novels." In *Regenerating the Novel: Gender and Genre in Woolf, Forster, Sinclair, and Lawrence.* New York: Routledge, 2003. Focuses on Sinclair's depiction of the strife encountered by both male and female artistic geniuses.

Raitt, Suzanne. *May Sinclair: A Modern Victorian.* New York: Oxford University Press, 2000. An account of Sinclair's life and work, based in part on newly discovered manuscripts. Describes how Sinclair's life reflects the struggles of women in her generation to attain intellectual and social freedom.

Zegger, Hrisey. *May Sinclair.* Boston: Twayne, 1976. A good general introduction to the novelist's career. Classifies *The Divine Fire* as an idealistic novel, calling it an allegory of the individual's journey through life. Considers it one of Sinclair's least successful artistic productions, despite its popularity.

Divine Love and Wisdom

Author: Emanuel Swedenborg (1688-1772)
First published: Sapientia angelica de divino amore et de divina sapientia, 1763 (English translation, 1788)
Type of work: Religious philosophy

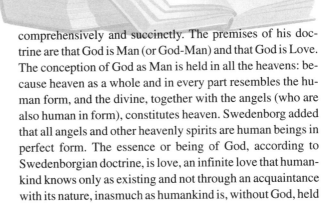

Early in his life, Emanuel Swedenborg established a lasting reputation as a scientist in many scientific fields, including physics, astronomy, mathematics, engineering, and human anatomy. His research in several of these fields culminated in important publications that showed him well in advance of his time. His work in anatomy, for example, anticipated some of the later theories of physiology, including those involving the functions of the ductless glands.

With respect to his later writings in religion and theosophy, Swedenborg's reputation is a mixed one. Between 1743 and 1745 he suffered a mental and religious crisis that changed his life and his work. During the crisis, according to his own report, he underwent mystical experiences in which he believed he was given access to the spiritual world. He saw visions of that world, heard and took part in celestial conversations, and received divine instruction. In 1745, during a third great spiritual experience, Swedenborg reported having witnessed the second advent of Christ and having been instructed to establish a "New Church." From his visions and the instructions he purportedly received grew Swedenborg's theosophical writings, for which he used Latin. Although he wrote voluminously on his doctrines, Swedenborg did not found a sect, for he believed that members of any church could follow his doctrines. Later his followers did constitute the Church of the New Jerusalem, or New Church.

Like all theosophical writings, those of Swedenborg depend for their importance on how seriously readers are willing to take the author's reports of divine inspiration and revelation. If this is accepted, the writings assume tremendous, even cosmic, significance, for Swedenborg did not attempt to disguise or conceal the supernatural source of his doctrines. He stated as fact that his doctrines were the results of visions granted to him by God, and he calmly and routinely noted certain facts and points either overheard in conversations among the angels or witnessed during the times he was transported spiritually to heaven. He regarded his mission seriously, sincerely believing that he had been commanded to interpret the spiritual world and explicate the Bible's true spiritual intent to humankind.

Swedenborg's most important theosophical work is *Divine Love and Wisdom*, in which he stated his system most comprehensively and succinctly. The premises of his doctrine are that God is Man (or God-Man) and that God is Love. The conception of God as Man is held in all the heavens: because heaven as a whole and in every part resembles the human form, and the divine, together with the angels (who are also human in form), constitutes heaven. Swedenborg added that all angels and other heavenly spirits are human beings in perfect form. The essence or being of God, according to Swedenborgian doctrine, is love, an infinite love that humankind knows only as existing and not through an acquaintance with its nature, inasmuch as humankind is, without God, held to the natural world.

For Swedenborg, the manifestation of God and his infinite love is a living sun. That spiritual sun corresponds in heaven to the "dead" sun of the natural world and is the source of spiritual life. The sun of the natural world, according to Swedenborg, is the source of life in nature, which is but a receptacle of life, not a source. Just as the spiritual sun and the natural sun are distinct but analogous in part and whole, so are heaven and earth distinct but analogous. Swedenborg warned, however, that space and time are concepts only of the natural world and are not to be found in the structure of the infinite and perfect realm of heaven. In heaven, according to the cosmology expounded in *Divine Love and Wisdom*, are three uncreated, distinct, and eternal degrees, corresponding to which in the natural world there are three finite degrees. Swedenborg did not describe in *Divine Love and Wisdom* how these degrees exist, but only stated that they are love, wisdom, and use, or, to put it another way, end, cause, and effect. The three degrees exist, declared Swedenborg, in every human being at birth, although as a creature of the natural world the human being is unaware of them. As the degrees are opened successively to the individual, so is God in people and people in God, according to the doctrine. Light from the spiritual sun flows into human beings as they shun evil, meaning that they can gain in wisdom; but the "heat" of the spiritual sun, or love, cannot be received. The natural mind of the lowest degree, said Swedenborg, is a hell in itself, while the mind that is spiritualized becomes a heaven. In other words, by love and the opening of each of the successive degrees human beings can rise toward God. According to *Di-*

vine Love and Wisdom, the end of creation, both spiritual and natural, is to become perfectly the image of God-Man.

Swedenborg undertook to answer the question of creation that has bothered countless numbers of theologically minded persons in every generation: Did God create the universe out of nothing, or did he form a cosmos from the stuff of chaos? According to Swedenborg:

> Every one of enlightened judgment sees that the universe was not created out of nothing, because it is impossible to make anything out of nothing; for nothing is nothing, and to suppose anything to be made out of nothing is absurd and therefore contrary to the light of truth, which comes from the divine Wisdom . . . . Everyone of enlightened judgment also sees that all beings were created out of self-existent substance, the very BEING out of which all things that exist come forth: and as God is the only self-existent Substance, and thus is essential BEING, it is plain that this is the source of all things that exist.

Swedenborg suggests that there are pairs in all parts of the body in order that everyone may achieve the love and wisdom of divinity. He notes that the eyes, ears, nostrils, hands, loins, and feet exist in pairs, and that the heart, brain, and lungs are divided into two parts. The right-hand parts, according to his views, have a relation to love and the left-hand parts a relation to wisdom.

The doctrine propounded in *Divine Love and Wisdom* grants to all human beings the means of achieving the spiritual heaven, for in the Swedenborgian view it is a false doctrine that the Lord arbitrarily excludes any members of the human race from salvation.

Further Reading

Bergquist, Lars. *Swedenborg's Secret: The Meaning and Significance of the Word of God, the Life of the Angels, and Service to God, a Biography*. London: Swedenborg Society, 2005. Comprehensive biography, placing Swedenborg's life and work within the context of Sweden's declining power in the eighteenth century. Explains Swedenborg's core ideas, defining him as a founding father of modern spirituality and Western philosophy.

Dole, George F., ed. *A View from Within: A Compendium of Swedenborg's Theological Thought*. New York: Swedenborg Foundation, 1985. A discursive and thorough survey of Swedenborg's theology by a respected scholar. Well-organized and helpful to any serious student. For a more concise rendition of his biography and key concepts see *A Scientist Explores Spirit: A Compact Biography of Emanuel Swedenborg, with Key Concepts of Swedenborg's Theology*. West Chester, Pa.: Swedenborg Foundation, 1992.

James, Henry. *The Secret of Swedenborg: Being an Elucidation of His Doctrine of the Divine Natural Humanity*. 1869. Reprint. New York: AMS Press, 1983. Still an essential guide to Swedenborg's understanding of the multifold symbolic and allegorical relations between God's love and human nature.

Lachman, Gary. *Into the Interior: Discovering Swedenborg*. London: Swedenborg Society, 2006. Examines Swedenborg's ideas about mysticism, sexuality, and radicalism and their relationship to modern philosophy.

Morris, Herbert Newall. *Flaxman, Blake, Coleridge, and Other Men of Genius Influenced by Swedenborg*. Norwood, Pa.: Norwood, 1975. Aids in understanding various literary and cultural figures who were influenced by Swedenborg's philosophy.

Swedenborg, Emanuel. *Angelic Wisdom About Divine Love and About Divine Wisdom: Angelic Wisdom About Divine Providence*. Translated by George F. Dole. West Chester, Pa.: Swedenborg Foundation, 2003. In addition to the text of Swedenborg's book, this edition contains an introduction and extensive annotations. Like many of the editions published by the Swedenborg Foundation and the Swedenborg Society, this one is authoritative.

Trobridge, George. *Swedenborg: Life and Teaching*. 5th ed., rev. New York: Swedenborg Foundation, 1992. Important biography of Swedenborg, with a lucid discussion of his belief system.

Diving into the Wreck

Author: Adrienne Rich (1929-   )
First published: 1973
Type of work: Poetry

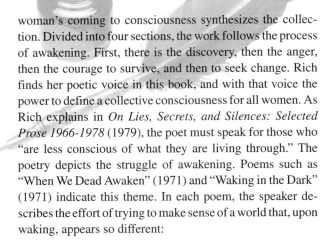

In 1974, Adrienne Rich received the National Book Award for *Diving into the Wreck*. In a statement written with Audre Lorde and Alice Walker, who also were nominated, she rejected the award as an individual but accepted it on behalf of women, dedicating the occasion "to the struggle for self-determination of all women." This vision of herself as writing for and in the presence of women has guided her work. Feminism provides Rich with the framework for her vision of transformation for herself and for other women.

Her seventh book of poetry, the collection is, in part, a clarification of her identity as a member of the women's movement of the previous decade. Receiving critical acclaim from the onset of her career, including being chosen by W. H. Auden for the Yale Younger Poets Award for her first collection, *A Change of World* (1951), Rich has sought a position in the male-dominated literary world. In the late 1960's and early 1970's she became politically active in antiwar protests and the feminist movement. Rich saw her poetic power and political ideology merge, creating a powerful poetic vision that informs *Diving into the Wreck*. Rich, one of America's foremost poets, has explored, analyzed, and depicted her own physical, psychic, and intellectual rebirth in her prose and poetry. Although her later works, including her prose text *Of Woman Born: Motherhood as Experience and Institution* (1976) and her poetry collection *The Dream of a Common Language* (1978), dramatize the theme of rebirth in detail, the initial exploration of this theme takes place in the collection *Diving into the Wreck*. In this work, the poet embraces an individual and a collective consciousness that provides for her transformation.

Rich identifies the world of the fathers as an oppressive patriarchal one that restricts a woman's existence in every way, psychologically and physically, individually and collectively. In *Of Woman Born: Motherhood as Experience and Institution*, she asserts that "the kingdom of the fathers" denies women their power, permeating every institution and experience, determining and defining women and their roles politically and socially. Further, she concedes that patriarchal assumptions have shaped both women's moral and intellectual history. For women to move from being powerless to powerful, they must confront their past and redefine themselves in the present and for the future. The central theme of a

woman's coming to consciousness synthesizes the collection. Divided into four sections, the work follows the process of awakening. First, there is the discovery, then the anger, then the courage to survive, and then to seek change. Rich finds her poetic voice in this book, and with that voice the power to define a collective consciousness for all women. As Rich explains in *On Lies, Secrets, and Silences: Selected Prose 1966-1978* (1979), the poet must speak for those who "are less conscious of what they are living through." The poetry depicts the struggle of awakening. Poems such as "When We Dead Awaken" (1971) and "Waking in the Dark" (1971) indicate this theme. In each poem, the speaker describes the effort of trying to make sense of a world that, upon waking, appears so different:

> working like me to pick apart
> working with me to remake
> this trailing knitted thing, this cloth of darkness
> this woman's garment, trying to save the skein.

The poet describes the struggle to survive in a world in which she is the stranger. Her existence is questioned because the "dead language" does not describe the altered state that she has upon waking. Although the speaker knows she is awake, "yet never have we been closer to the truth," the doubt and disbelief still linger and only "the words," such as those written in "your diaries," are what keep her sane. In the poem "Waking in the Dark," the speaker characterizes the waking as almost unnatural. She sees herself as being the only one who is awake in an "unconscious forest."

The process of awakening brings anger, as illustrated in the poems "From the Prison House" (1971) and "The Phenomenology of Anger" (1972). In the first poem, the speaker paints "the world of pain" as being imminent even when she sleeps. For her, the vision "must be unblurred" and clear for her to describe in detail a better place. The poet is the one who must remember every detail, to forget nothing about the world of violence and pain that has held her prisoner. In her essay "When We Dead Awaken: Writing as Revision" (1971), Rich describes women as "sleepwalkers" who in coming awake find that they are not alone. Essentially, she envisions that in the awakening, each woman forms a "collective reality" that is critical for her survival. This concept is emphasized in both poems. Further, the persona in "The Phenomenology of Anger" reiterates Rich's view that victimization and anger are real experiences for women. In one stanza the speaker muses that the world is no longer viable as she rejects the "fantasies of murder" and resolves to hate so as to rid herself of the lies of a world that she has decided to reject. Her hate turns into fire as she ritualistically burns up the old life, cleansing herself for the new one in which she is powerful.

The process of awakening is painful and lonely. The speaker of "Merced" (1972) describes herself as crying "without knowing which thought/ forced water to my eyes." In "Song" (1971) the loneliness is defined as being the first one awake "in a house wrapped in sleep." The loneliness is necessary, however, to find one's personal strength and truth. The speaker relates that if she is lonely it is like the loneliness of one taking the first breath of a new dawn. The tone of hope, not despair, however, characterizes the process, for it is one that will produce a clearer vision of the self.

"Diving into the Wreck" (1972) is the centerpiece of the collection. "The wreck" is the history of women. Rich begins to comprehend the damage that has been done to all women by the "book of myths." In the first stanza, she readies herself by loading the camera, checking her knife, putting on her rubber suit and "the awkward mask." All of these symbolize that she must be prepared for what she may find and must remain in control. In this stage of reawakening, she has gone beyond her individual consciousness into the "hold" where other women sleep "with drowned face" and "open eyes." She clarifies her reason for the exploration:

> I came to explore the wreck.
> The words are purposes
> The words are maps.
> I came to see the damage that was done
> and the treasures that prevail.

Her tone is somber and decisive. She knows that without words, she is without meaning, yet she must go underwater, where words cannot be spoken, to gain understanding. As she circles the wreck, she becomes an androgyne, "I am she; I am he." She dives into the hold of the wreck. There she discovers the half-destroyed instruments; they represent the state of the history of women. Although they have been left to rot, there is hope because they are only half destroyed. The hope lies not in the book of myths "in which our names do not appear" but in the instrument of the poet who, "by cowardice or courage," finds her and women's way back to the surface. In the final stanza, she enacts the final step: moving from the

individual's awakening to the collective state of consciousness: "We are, I am, you are."

To classify *Diving into the Wreck* as merely a collection of political poetry would be a mistake. It is poetry because of its feminism. Rich's feminism is a natural extension of her poetry; for Rich, feminism is about empathy. Rich describes conflicts on the individual and the collective levels; she discovers the living connection between the political and the personal. Her poetry chronicles an individual's transformation into a strong, artistic, powerful voice, one that attempts to articulate her own change as it mirrors the collective reality of her time.

The poet creates a powerful language capable of describing this new vision. Rich accomplishes this in *Diving into the Wreck*. The poetry in this collection heralds that of her later collections, including *The Dream of a Common Language* (1978), in which she gives birth to "a whole new poetry." To have arrived at such a point in the artist's journey, Rich had to be the explorer of the past, as she is in the poem "Diving into the Wreck." To acquire this expertise, this vital knowledge, it is necessary to "re-vision," a process she defines in an essay as that of looking back and reperceiving an old text from a new perspective. The poet revises the past history of women, the one written by men, and then guides the reader back to the present with a clearer view of both the past and the present. Rich has a transformative power and exhibits it in *Diving into the Wreck*.

Cynthia S. Becerra

Further Reading

Flynn, Gale. "The Radicalization of Adrienne Rich." *Hollins Critic* 11 (1974): 1-15. Describes the complex evolution of Rich through her poetry, including *Diving into the Wreck*. Examines her political ideology and its impact on her works.

Jackaman, Rob. "Adrienne Rich *Diving into the Wreck*." In *Broken English/Breaking English: A Study of Contemporary Poetries in English*. Madison, N.J.: Fairleigh Dickinson University Press, 2003. Focuses on Rich's use of language, describing how she seeks to speak in an "undamaged" and "uncompromised" voice.

Jong, Erica. "Visionary Anger." *Ms.* 2, no. 1 (July, 1973): 30-34. Thoughtfully examines *Diving into the Wreck* in the context of Rich's philosophy and past work. Assesses her impact on feminist thought.

Langdell, Cheri Colby. *Adrienne Rich: The Moment of Change*. Westport, Conn.: Praeger, 2004. Examination of Rich's life and career, tracing the evolution of her poetry.

Discusses the concepts of nation, the female body, power, and women's sexuality expressed in her work.

Rich, Adrienne. *Adrienne Rich's Poetry: Texts of the Poems, the Poet on Her Work, Reviews, and Criticism.* Edited by Barbara Charesworth Gelphi and Albert Gelphi. New York: W. W. Norton, 1975. A thoughtful study of the author's work.

_____. *On Lies, Secrets, and Silence: Selected Prose, 1966-1978.* 1979. Reprint. New York: W. W. Norton, 1995. Presents a detailed account of Rich's intellectual rebirth through her prose. Identifies the literary works and figures who have influenced her.

Sickels, Amy. *Adrienne Rich.* Philadelphia: Chelsea House, 2005. Concise biography and overview of Rich's life and work.

Templeton, Alice. *The Dream and the Dialogue: Adrienne Rich's Feminist Poetics.* Knoxville: University of Tennessee Press, 1994. Examines how Rich's poetry was influenced by feminist ideas and, conversely, how her poetic technique shaped her idea of feminism. Begins by analyzing *Diving into the Wreck*, describing the tension between epic, eulogistic, and lyric poetry in that collection.

Waddell, William S., ed. *"Catch If You Can Your Country's Moment": Recovery and Regeneration in the Poetry of Adrienne Rich.* Newcastle, England: Cambridge Scholars, 2007. Eight essays interpret Rich's poetry, beginning with her passionate poems about feminist awakening from the mid-1960's through the early 1980's and advancing to her later, more political verse.

Do Androids Dream of Electric Sheep?

Author: Philip K. Dick (1928-1995)
First published: 1968
Type of work: Novel
Type of plot: Science fiction
Time of plot: 1992
Locale: San Francisco

Principal characters:
RICK DECKARD, a bounty hunter
IRAN DECKARD, his wife
JOHN ISIDORE, a chickenhead
RACHAEL ROSEN, an android
BUSTER FRIENDLY, an android
PRIS, an android

The Story:

World War Terminus has left the Earth a radioactive wreck. Most survivors have emigrated to Mars, where the authorities promise them an easy life with android servants. Only those too poor to emigrate, or who have been genetically damaged by radiation (the chickenheads), remain on Earth. They huddle in scattered population groups; use mood organs that allow them to predetermine how they will feel each day; follow Buster Friendly, who is on television and radio twenty-three hours a day; and practice Mercerism, a universal religion that teaches empathy and community-feeling through repeated images of an old man struggling to climb a barren hillside. Animal life has been more severely affected by the war than has humankind, so social status in this bleak postapocalyptic world is determined by keeping an animal; those who cannot afford an animal keep a robot simulation.

Rick Deckard is a bounty hunter whose job is to retire (kill) androids who attempt to escape their servitude on Mars. He and his wife, Iran, have an electric sheep, but they dream of being able to afford a real animal. Deckard gets his

chance when six Nexus-6 androids escape to San Francisco. The Nexus-6 is the most advanced android to date, indistinguishable from humans, and it is not at all clear that the standard Voigt-Kampff Empathy Test for identifying androids will work on them. So Deckard must first visit the manufacturers. The first individual on whom he tries the test, Rachael Rosen, seems to come out as human, but Deckard is suspicious and asks her one last question. Her answer reveals that she is indeed an android. Rachael then offers to help him hunt down the escaped androids, but he rejects her offer.

The first android is masquerading as a Russian police officer, but Deckard sees through the deception and kills him. The second is a singer with the San Francisco Opera, but before he is able to administer the Voigt-Kampff test, she has him arrested. Though himself a police officer, Deckard is taken to a station he does not know, which is staffed by police he does not know and who do not know him. When he tries to phone out, he cannot contact anyone who recognizes him. It turns out that the entire happening is an elaborate front set up by the third of the androids. With the help of another bounty hunter who is not sure whether he himself is an android or a human, Deckard is able to kill the android and escape from the fake station. The two bounty hunters then return to the opera and shoot the other android. The bounty from the three androids he retired gives Deckard enough money to buy a real goat.

John Isidore is a chickenhead who does not meet the minimum intelligence standards for emigration. He works as a driver for an electric-animal repair center and lives alone in an abandoned apartment block. He soon finds someone else living in the same building, a young woman called Pris who seems scared of everything. Isidore tries to befriend her, though she treats him with disdain. Later, two of her associates, Roy and Irmgard Baty, show up; Pris, Roy, and Irmgard Baty are the three remaining Nexus-6 androids, though Isidore does not recognize them as such. The three use Isidore to fetch and carry for them as they take over his apartment as a hideout, but though he recognizes that he is being exploited he still relishes the companionship. Then Isidore discovers a live spider, and Pris tortures it by cutting its legs off one by one, and at last Isidore loses his faith in his new friends.

Meanwhile, Deckard has discovered where the remaining androids are hiding. Uncertain of his ability to take them all on, he decides to take up Rachael's offer of help. They meet in a hotel and make love, but when he realizes she is trying to distract him from his quest, he abandons her. At the same time, Buster Friendly, now revealed to be an android, announces that Mercerism is based on a fake. Buster Friendly's denouncement—an attempt to undermine human reliance on empathy—backfires, and Mercerism instead becomes stronger. Mercer himself appears to Deckard and helps him dispose of the first of the androids at Isidore's building. After this, it becomes quite easy for Deckard to deal with the last two androids.

Back home, Deckard's wife reveals that a woman (Rachael) had killed their goat. Deckard sets off after Rachael, but he has many doubts. He stops in a desert landscape surprisingly like the one in which Mercer is seen. Deckard then discovers a toad, which was thought to be extinct, and takes it home. His wife discovers that the toad is artificial, but still orders electric flies for it to eat.

Critical Evaluation:

Do Androids Dream of Electric Sheep? is best known as the source material for the Ridley Scott film *Blade Runner* (1982), but the novel is actually a far richer story than even the film, which has become a cult classic. The novel encapsu-

lates many of the recurring themes and images in Philip K. Dick's work.

Although Dick persistently tried to achieve mainstream success, only one of his numerous "nongenre" novels would be published in his lifetime. As a science-fiction writer, however, Dick enjoyed almost immediate success, and by the time of his death he was acclaimed as arguably the best science-fiction writer in the world. Part of this acclaim is based on the quality of his writing: witty, sparse, yet able to handle the most complex ontological ideas with complete clarity. Another part of this acclaim, however, is his ability to wrest the many variations, both comic and disturbing, from the narrow set of concerns he pursues obsessively.

In *Do Androids Dream of Electric Sheep?*, Dick covers, for example, wide-ranging themes such as the instability of reality, the disturbing likeness between nature and artifact, and addiction and religious belief. He handles these weighty themes with an unfailing lightness of touch, but also with a firm grip of the drama of his story.

Dick's work is full of ordinary people doing routine and generally low-paying work. They are often married, though their marriages are more likely to be companionable than entirely satisfying. The people are restless, filled with a usually ill-defined sense that they should be doing something better with their lives. His characters are humdrum and distinctly unheroic; Rick Deckard is certainly not the action hero portrayed in *Blade Runner*. When longings for change are answered, therefore, his characters are ill-equipped to deal with the disruptions, and their individual response is likely to be an obstinate muddling through rather than a decisive action.

In *Do Androids Dream of Electric Sheep?*, the disruption to Deckard's reality comes in two ways; literally, when he is assigned to retire the unprecedented number of six androids in one day, not only promising relative wealth but also promising great danger; and figuratively, when he is taken to the unfamiliar police station. For a while it seems that he has been transported into a different reality, one he does not know and one that does not know him (a consistent trope in Dick's work). These occurrences force him to be more suspicious of the world around him.

Parallel to this uncertainty about ontological reality are questions about the nature of humanity. Dick's novels are filled with simulacra, whose resemblance to humans casts doubt upon human notions of self. The Nexus-6 androids in *Do Androids Dream of Electric Sheep?* are a perfect representation of this characteristic. They are indistinguishable from humans except for their lack of empathy (though it should be noted that the servitude forced upon them by their human creators also shows little in the way of empathy). At one point in the story, Deckard must rely on another bounty hunter, Phil Resch, who is himself so lacking in empathy that both Deckard and Resch himself have doubts whether he is actually human.

Deckard is capable of loving the android Rachael, but she reveals that she is the same model as—and physically identical to—android Pris, whom Deckard must kill. In the end, when Deckard has gone through so much self-doubt it is questionable whether he will continue working as a bounty hunter, he finds that he can feel as much empathy for an artificial creature—the toad he finds in the desert—as he can for a live creature. Readers, however, have to ask whether the chickenhead, Isidore, who unquestioningly accepts everyone he meets, whether human or android, is not the better person.

Humanity, though, is determined not only by likeness to androids. The mood organs, which can predetermine any person's sense of well-being, represent Dick's view of humanity; even worse is watching television. Dick often introduces drugs in his fiction as a way of changing reality, but when he wants to portray addiction, he chooses television rather than drugs. The characters in *Do Androids Dream of Electric Sheep?* are clearly addicted to the near-inescapable Buster Friendly Show, though it presents a repetitive and corrosive diet of trivia.

For Dick, television is a pabulum for the masses, but so is religion. Soon after *Do Androids Dream of Electric Sheep?* was published, Dick had a mystical experience of his own that affected everything he wrote thereafter. At this time, though, his views on religion had been decidedly ambiguous. The novel's religion, Mercerism, is typical for Dick: Devotees, or adherents, watch a loop of film that shows an old man struggling to get up a hill in a bleak, featureless landscape, all the while being assailed by unseen enemies. Whenever the old man is struck and wounded by a rock thrown by these unseen enemies, watchers suffer the same wound. No sense of triumph, however, comes with the old man's ascent of the hill, for he is instantly translated to the depths once more to begin his upward journey again. Mercerism does little but instill a sense of community and consolation in an adverse world. Nevertheless, it is considered by the androids to be the center of the human cult of empathy, and so they seek to undermine the religion through their agent Buster Friendly. Curiously, it is only after Mercerism is revealed to be a fake that it starts to have a real-world effect: Mercer appears to Deckard and aids him in his confrontation with the last three androids.

Near the story's end, Deckard finds a toad, a creature thought to be extinct and one particularly sacred to Mercer, in a landscape curiously similar to the scene of Mercer's ascent. When Deckard discovers that the toad is a fake, his empathy for the creature is not diminished. In a novel so filled with simulacra, the message in the end seems to be to love the fake as much as the real.

Paul Kincaid

Further Reading

Calvin, Rich, et al. "Approaching Philip K. Dick's *Do Androids Dream of Electric Sheep?* and Ridley Scott's *Blade Runner.*" *SFRA Review*, no. 240 (June, 1999). This journal article presents a series of study guides to Dick's novel and to Ridley Scott's film that is based on the novel.

Carrère, Emmanuel. *I Am Alive and You Are Dead: A Journey into the Mind of Philip K. Dick*. New York: Henry Holt, 2004. Carrère seeks to recapture Dick's spirit, taking an often painful but well-examined journey into the writer's mind. This biography describes how Dick transformed the conventions of science fiction to create novels reflecting the anxiety of America in the 1950's and 1960's.

Mckee, Gabriel. *Pink Beams of Light from the God in the Gutter: The Science-Fictional Religion of Philip K. Dick*. Lanham, Md.: University Press of America, 2004. Examines Dick's religious experiences and demonstrates how he communicates these experiences in his fiction. Includes a bibliography and an index.

Palmer, Christopher. *Philip K. Dick: Exhilaration and Terror of the Postmodern*. Liverpool, England: Liverpool University Press, 2003. Provides a postmodern interpretation of Dick's work. Explores Dick's reactions to postmodern ideas about humanism and his use of images related to movement and stasis. Includes analysis of many of his novels.

Robinson, Kim Stanley. *The Novels of Philip K. Dick*. Ann Arbor, Mich.: UMI Research Press, 1984. A survey of Dick's narrative structures and fictional techniques by a highly respected science-fiction writer.

Sutin, Lawrence. *Divine Invasions: A Life of Philip K. Dick*. New York: Harmony Books, 1989. The definitive biography of Dick, which places his novels in the context of his life.

Warrick, Patricia S. "The Labyrinthian Process of the Artificial: Philip K. Dick's Androids and Mechanical Constructs." In *Philip K. Dick*, edited by Joseph D. Olander and Martin Harry Greenberg. New York, Taplinger, 1983. An early but still essential essay on Dick's portrayal of mechanical beings.

_____. *Mind in Motion: The Fiction of Philip K. Dick*. Carbondale: Southern Illinois University Press, 1987. Excellent studies of eight of Dick's novels that Warrick believes are representative of his best work, including *Do Androids Dream of Electric Sheep?*

Doctor Faustus
The Life of the German Composer Adrian Leverkühn, as Told by a Friend

Author: Thomas Mann (1875-1955)
First published: Doktor Faustus: Das Leben des deutschen Tonsetzers Adrian Leverkühn, erzählt von einem Freunde, 1947 (English translation, 1948)
Type of work: Novel
Type of plot: Philosophical
Time of plot: 1885-1945
Locale: Germany

Principal characters:
ADRIAN LEVERKÜHN, an arrogant, sickly musical genius
SERENUS ZEITBLOM, his lifelong friend and the narrator
WENDELL KRETSCHMAR, Adrian's music teacher
EHRENFRIED KUMPF and EBERHARD SCHLEPPFUSS, teachers of theology
RÜDIGER SCHILDKNAPP, a poet and Adrian's friend
RUDOLF SCHWERDTFEGER, a violinist befriended by Adrian
INEZ INSTITORIS, a woman in love with Schwerdtfeger
CLARISSA RODDE, her sister
MARIE GODEAU, a woman whom Adrian loves
NEPOMUK SCHNEIDEWEIN, Adrian's young nephew

The Story:

At the outset, Serenus Zeitblom doubts his ability to narrate understandably the life story of his friend Adrian Leverkühn. His friend is a musical genius whose strange, doomed career shows many parallels with the course of German history in the twentieth century. A former professor of philology, living in retirement and out of sympathy with the Adolf Hitler regime and greatly concerned for the future of his country, Zeitblom hesitantly begins his task in May, 1943.

Adrian Leverkühn was born in 1885 on a farm near Kaiseraschern, in Thuringia. His family was of superior yeoman stock, and his father, a man interested in curious natural phenomena, did everything in his power to stimulate his son's intellectual curiosity. Adrian's boyhood friend, Zeitblom, was a frequent visitor in the Leverkühn household. Years later Zeitblom can remember his friend's absorbed interest in a book filled with pictures of exotic lepidoptera. One in particular, *Heroera Esmeralda*, fascinated the boy because of its unusual beauty and protective coloring. Adrian was introduced to music by a hired girl who taught him old folk songs.

Because the farm was to go to an older brother, the family intended that Adrian, a boy of brilliant mind and arrogant disposition, would become a scholar. When he was ten years old, he entered the school in Kaiseraschern. Living in the house of his uncle, a dealer in musical instruments, he had the run of the shop and began to play chords on an old harmonium. When his uncle overheard his efforts, he decided that the boy ought to have piano lessons. Adrian began to study under Wendell Kretschmar, the organist at the cathedral. Adrian's chief interest at that time, however, was theology,

and he entered the University of Halle with the intention of preparing himself for the clergy. Zeitblom, certain that his friend's choice was dictated by the arrogance of purity, went with Adrian to his theological lectures. One of the teachers was Ehrenfried Kumpf, a forthright theologian who enlivened his classes by insulting the devil with epithets that Martin Luther might have used. Another instructor was Eberhard Schleppfuss, whose lectures were filled with anecdotes and sly undertones of demonism and witchcraft.

Given the range of his talents, Adrian could have chosen a career in scholarship, theology, or music. At last, unable to reconcile his interest in philosophy and science with theological precepts, he turned to music and began, still under Kretschmar's training, experiments in theory and technique that were to determine the highly original nature of his art. Before long, the pupil surpassed the instructor. When Zeitblom was drafted for a year of compulsory military duty, Adrian was exempted because of his frail constitution and went to Leipzig for further study. With Kretschmar's encouragement, he began to compose. A new friend of his, Rüdiger Schildknapp, was an Anglophile poet whose enthusiasm for William Shakespeare led to Adrian's decision to plan an opera based on *Love's Labour's Lost* (pr. c. 1594-1595, pb. 1598). A sinister guide, somewhat like Schleppfuss in appearance, lured Adrian to a brothel one night. When a girl in the house—an Esmeralda, he called her—approached him, he ran from the place. Later he tried to see the girl again, but she went to Pressburg. Adrian followed her and there voluntarily contracted the venereal infection that led to the strange flowering of his genius and the eventual wreckage of his life.

Several years afterward, during a holiday in Italy, he imagined a medievalistic encounter with the devil, who in return for his soul promised him twenty-four years in which to fulfill his powers as an artist.

Before his Italian journey, Adrian lived for a time in Munich. There his friends were artists and young intellectuals, among them Rüdiger Schildknapp, a novelist named Jeanette Scheurl, the young violinist Rudolf Schwerdtfeger, several actors, and the daughters of his landlady, Inez and Clarissa Rodde. Zeitblom met these people through Adrian and became interested in them. In 1912, Zeitblom married. A short time later, on his return from Italy, Adrian retired to a Bavarian farm presided over by motherly Frau Else Schweigestill. In this retreat, during the next twenty years, he composed the music that established his fame, and Zeitblom taught in Freising, not far away. During that entire time, the friends saw each other frequently. Zeitblom wrote the libretto for Adrian's opera on *Love's Labour's Lost*.

When war broke out in 1914, Zeitblom went into the army and served until he was discharged with typhus. Adrian wrote *Marvels of the Universe* and a composition based on the *Gesta Romanorum*. During the war, Inez married Dr. Helmut Institoris, but she was secretly in love with Schwerdtfeger and maintained an adulterous relationship with the violinist for years. Adrian's health began to improve after the war. His great work of that period was an oratorio entitled *Apocalypse*. As his fame grew, he acquired a patroness, Madame de Tolna, a wealthy Hungarian widow whom Zeitblom never met. In the meantime, Schwerdtfeger broke off his love affair with Inez. Their first meeting after their separation was at the funeral of Inez's sister, Clarissa, an actress who was driven to suicide by a blackmailing lover.

Adrian yielded at last to Schwerdtfeger's urging and composed a violin concerto for the musician. About that time Adrian met the attractive Marie Godeau. Hoping to marry her, he sent Schwerdtfeger to act as his emissary in his courtship, but the violinist fell in love with the young woman and wooed her for himself. Shortly after the engagement was announced, Inez boarded a streetcar in which her former lover was riding and shot him. Adrian blamed himself for his friend's death.

Fate had one more blow in store for the composer. Adrian's nephew, Nepomuk Schneidewein, of whom he was paternally fond, came to stay with Adrian at the Schweigestill farm while convalescing from an illness. There little Echo, as his uncle called him, suddenly contracted cerebrospinal meningitis and died. It seemed to Adrian that he lost the child he himself might have had. He never completely recovered from his grief.

He continued to work on his masterpiece, a symphonic cantata called *The Lamentation of Doctor Faustus*. In the early summer of 1930, he invited a number of his friends and some critics to hear excerpts from the work, but his explanation of his composition was so disordered and blasphemous that many of the guests left before he sat down to play the score. As he struck the first chords, he fell senseless to the floor.

Adrian lived in madness for the next ten years, and he died, tenderly cared for by his aged mother, at his Thuringian birthplace in 1940. Zeitblom was among the few old friends present at the funeral. It seemed to him then, and the certainty grows upon him as he writes the story of Adrian's life, that his friend somehow reflects the progress of the German nation, a land that was arrogant, isolated, and dehumanized and is now—as the old philologist penned his final pages in April, 1945—reeling toward its final destruction.

Critical Evaluation:

Doctor Faustus, like other novels by Thomas Mann, particularly his monumental *Der Zauberberg* (1924; *The Magic Mountain*, 1927), is enormously complex and built up of layer upon layer of interlocking references not only to the present but to the entire history of European civilization. However, it is constructed on a very simple premise, that of inversion. Throughout the book, things are turned upside-down, and readers again and again encounter, as in a magic mirror, their expectations being stood on their heads. Where hell is expected to be hot, it is instead described as freezing cold. The devil is no burning presence; instead, a chill emanates from him. Music, far from being the result of passionate inspiration, turns out to be the result of a highly cerebral, invented system of composition. Adrian Leverkühn's art is the result not of a special blessing but of a common curse, syphilis. Finally, the narrator of this novel, which attempts to encapsulate the history of the German people while telling the tale of a heroic (or antiheroic) figure, turns out to be an insignificant professor in a provincial town.

No doubt the paradoxical nature of the plot of *Doctor Faustus* owes something to Mann's own situation. He wrote this most German of books in Los Angeles, where he lived in exile, having been forced to leave his homeland after Adolf Hitler came to power. His home and possessions had been impounded, his honorary doctorate canceled, and his citizenship revoked. While his character Serenus Zeitblom (a name that roughly translates to "serene flower-of-the-time") is tracing the progress of World War II from within Germany, Mann was following it from eight thousand miles away.

Certainly Mann composed his novel's inversions quite deliberately and down to the smallest detail. Adrian's final work, *The Lamentation of Doctor Faustus*, is modeled in part on Ludwig van Beethoven's Symphony No. 9 (it even takes an hour and a quarter to perform, as does Beethoven's symphony), but where the choral passages in Beethoven's symphony are based on Friedrich Schiller's "Ode to Joy," Adrian's last work is referred to as an "Ode to Sorrow." Mann even has Adrian say that his *Lamentation* is a retraction of Beethoven's Symphony No. 9.

Through Adrian, Mann challenges a number of ideas stemming back to the nineteenth century when Beethoven wrote his symphony. What Mann wants to question, he has Adrian deny: That a nation-state is good, that music is a force for good, that great artists are agents of good, that history teaches that humanity is moving upward into the light and that this progression in inevitable and must succeed. Long before the end of this novel, all such assumptions have become extremely dubious.

However, Romanticism always had within itself this darker, despairing strain, the essential doubt that existence is worthwhile. *Doctor Faustus*, to be truly anti- or un-Romantic, would have had to dispense with its tragic hero, its vast battlefields, its deal with the devil, and its focus on individual suffering and joy, which confers value and meaning on life even though Adrian might wish to deny that life offers these. A truer opposite to the Romantic spirit in literature would be writing that de-emphasized the role of the individual in shaping history and ignored the significance of nations and of liberty, equality, and fraternity as human rights.

It is precisely because Mann's beliefs are those Romantic ideals that he was impelled to write this novel, for he saw these ideals endangered on every side during the 1930's and 1940's. The enemy of human beings is everywhere present in Mann's world, not least in the movement in art known as modernism. Mann's description of Adrian's system of composition was based on information Mann received from a mutual acquaintance about Arnold Schoenberg's so-called method of composing with twelve tones related only to one another. Mann considered this method to be highly constructivist and to a considerable extent anti-inspirational and repressive of certain elements in art that he believed essentially human. Upon this basis, Mann drew connections from fascism to modernism and from both of these to disease and to the devil.

The strength of the novel derives from the interest Mann gives to these questions. Ultimately, evil may be simply more interesting than good, because it raises more forcefully the questions of free will and determinism, choice and fate.

Faustian pacts with the devil, a child dying in agony from meningitis, a great composer deliberately contracting a venereal disease from a prostitute—these can make compelling literature. Mann has scruples, moral misgivings, and a very real terror of the world gone mad, but he satirizes these in the hypocritical mealy-mouthed figure of the narrator. The readers' sympathies go rather with the man who has lost his soul to accomplish something indestructible, no matter what that something, than to the ordinary narrator. Adrian is a highly cultured, civilized man committed to the symbolic rather than the actual acting-out of his destructive impulses. Compared to Zeitblom, however, he is a monster, a vehicle for forces both natural and supernatural, and as such, a riveting subject for a book.

"Critical Evaluation" by David Bromige

Further Reading

Bergsten, Gunilla. *Thomas Mann's "Doctor Faustus": The Sources and Structure of the Novel*. Translated by Krishna Winston. Chicago: University of Chicago Press, 1969. Still one of the best detailed treatments of the novel's background and construction. Includes a useful appendix of Mann's source materials and a thorough, though now dated, bibliography.

Grimstad, Kirsten J. *The Modern Revival of Gnosticism and Thomas Mann's "Doktor Faustus."* Rochester, N.Y.: Camden House, 2002. Gnosticism, with origins in the early Christian era, is a religion that balances a pessimistic view of life with an optimistic belief in the divinity of the human spirit. Grimstad applies Gnostic ideas to analyze Mann's novel.

Heller, Erich. "Parody, Tragic and Comic." In *Thomas Mann: The Ironic German*. 1958. Reprint. South Bend, Ind.: Regnery/Gateway, 1979. A careful and approachable reading of *Doctor Faustus* as tragic parody of art and artists, history, religion, and humankind's ability to create meaning.

Kurzke, Hermann. *Thomas Mann: Life as a Work of Art, a Biography*. Translated by Leslie Willson. Princeton, N.J.: Princeton University Press, 2002. An English translation of a work that was celebrated upon its publication in Germany. Kurzke provides a balanced approach to Mann's life and work, and he addresses Mann's homosexuality and relationship to Judaism.

Lee, Frances. *Overturning "Dr. Faustus": Rereading Thomas Mann's Novel in Light of "Observations of a Non-Political Man."* Rochester, N.Y.: Camden House, 2007. Lee looks at the views contained in Mann's collection of political essays, *Reflections of a Non-Political Man* (1918) to analyze *Doctor Faustus*'s depiction of German fascism.

Lehnert, Herbert, and Peter C. Pfeiffer, eds. *Thomas Mann's "Doctor Faustus": A Novel at the Margin of Modernism.* Columbia, S.C.: Camden House, 1991. Originally presented at a symposium on *Doctor Faustus*, the essays in this volume concentrate on several central aspects of the novel: women, Jews, questions of modernism in history, music, philosophy, narcissism, love, and death. A general introductory essay situates the novel historically.

Lehnert, Herbert, and Eva Wessell, eds. *A Companion to the Works of Thomas Mann.* Rochester, N.Y.: Camden House, 2004. A collection of essays about the range of Mann's work, including discussions of his late politics, female identities, and autobiographical impulses in his writings, and "'German' Music and German Catastrophe: A Re-Reading of *Doktor Faustus*" by Hans Vaget.

Mann, Thomas. *The Story of a Novel: The Genesis of "Doctor Faustus."* Translated by Richard and Clara Winston. New York: Alfred A. Knopf, 1961. A fascinating and enlightening account of how Mann came to write the novel. A delightful counterpart to more traditional scholarly criticism. Provides biographical connections and interesting information on the problems of writing in exile.

Mundt, Hannelore. *Understanding Thomas Mann.* Columbia: University of South Carolina Press, 2004. Mundt discusses the themes, concerns, presentation, and meanings of many of Mann's works, using Mann's later published diaries as one of the sources for her analysis. Chapter 11 is devoted to *Doctor Faustus*.

Robertson, Ritchie, ed. *The Cambridge Companion to Thomas Mann.* New York: Cambridge University Press, 2002. A collection of essays, some analyzing individual works and others discussing Mann's intellectual world, Mann and history, his literary techniques, and his representation of gender and sexuality. Chapter 11 provides an analysis of *Doctor Faustus*.

Doctor Faustus

Author: Christopher Marlowe (1564-1593)
First produced: c. 1588; first published, 1604
Type of work: Drama
Type of plot: Tragedy
Time of plot: Sixteenth century
Locale: Germany

Principal characters:
FAUSTUS, master of all knowledge
WAGNER, his servant
LUCIFER, the fallen angel
MEPHOSTOPHILIS, a devil
GOOD ANGEL
EVIL ANGEL

The Story:

Faustus is born to a common family in Rhodes, Germany. In his maturity, while living with relatives in Wittenberg, he studies theology and becomes a doctor as well. However, Faustus is so swollen with conceit that, like Daedalus, the ancient Greek inventor, he strives too far, becoming glutted with learning. He conspires with the Devil and falls, accursed to Hell.

At the outset of his downward path, Doctor Faustus finds himself complete master of three fields of knowledge—medicine, law, and theology. As a medical doctor, he achieves huge success and great renown. After obtaining good health for his patients, he faces no challenge except achieving immortality for them. He concludes that law is nothing but an elaborate moneymaking scheme. He thinks that only theology remains, but that it leads to a blind alley. He knows that the reward of sin is death and that no one can say that he or she is without sin; all people, guilty of sin, consequently die.

Necromancy, or black magic, greatly attracts Faustus. Universal power would be within his reach, the whole world would be at his command, and emperors would lie at his feet, if he could become a magician. Summoning his servant, Wagner, Faustus orders him to contact Valdes and Cornelius, believing they could teach him their black arts.

The Good Angel and the Evil Angel each try to persuade Faustus. Faustus is in no mood to listen to the Good Angel. He exults over the prospects of his forthcoming adventures. He will get gold from India, pearls from the oceans, tasty delicacies from faraway places; he will read strange philosophies, cull from foreign kings their secrets, control Germany with his power, reform public schools, and perform many other fabulous deeds. Eager to acquire knowledge of the black arts, he departs to study with Valdes and Cornelius. Before long the scholars of Wittenberg begin to notice the doctor's prolonged absence. Learning from Wagner of his master's unhallowed pursuits, the scholars lament the fate of the famous doctor.

Faustus's first act of magic is to summon Mephostophilis. At the sight of the ugly Devil, he orders Mephostophilis to assume the shape of a Franciscan friar. The docile obedience of Mephostophilis elates Faustus the magician, but Mephostophilis explains that magic has limits in the Devil's kingdom. Mephostophilis claims that he does not actually appear at Faustus's behest but comes, as he will to any other person, because Faustus curses Christ and abjures the Scriptures. Whenever someone is on the verge of being damned, the Devil will appear.

Interested in the nature of Lucifer, Faustus questions Mephostophilis about his master, the fallen angel, and about Hell, Lucifer's domain. Mephostophilis is cagey. He claims that the fallen spirits, being deprived of the glories of Heaven, find the whole world to be Hell. Even Mephostophilis urges Faustus to give up his scheme. Faustus, however, scorns the warning, saying that he will surrender his soul to Lucifer if the fallen angel will give to Faustus twenty-four years of voluptuous ease, with Mephostophilis attending him.

While Faustus indulges in an intellectual dispute concerning the relative merits of God and the Devil, the Good Angel and the Evil Angel, symbolic of Faustus's inner conflict, appear once again, each attempting to persuade him. The result is that Faustus is more determined than ever to continue his course.

Mephostophilis returns to assure Faustus that Lucifer is agreeable to the bargain, which must be sealed in Faustus's blood. When Faustus tries to sign his name, however, his blood congeals, and Mephostophilis has to warm the liquid by fire. Significantly, the words "Fly, man" appear in Latin on Faustus's arm. When Faustus questions Mephostophilis about the nature of Hell, the Devil claims that Hell has no limits for the damned. Intoxicated by his new status, Faustus disclaims any belief in an afterlife. In this way, he assures himself that his contract with Lucifer will never be fulfilled, in spite of Mephostophilis's own warning that he himself is living proof of Hell's existence.

Faustus, eager to enjoy the promise of the Devil's offerings, demands books that will contain varied information regarding the Devil's regime. When the Good Angel and the Evil Angel come to him again, he thinks that he is beyond repentance. Again, the opposing angels incorporate themselves into Faustus's mind, until he calls on Christ to save him. Nevertheless, as he speaks, wrathful Lucifer descends upon his victim to admonish him never to call to God. As an appeasing gesture, Lucifer conjures up a vision of the Seven Deadly Sins—Pride, Covetousness, Envy, Wrath, Gluttony, Sloth, and Lechery.

Faustus travels extensively throughout the world, and Wagner marvels at his master's rapid progress. In Rome, at the palace of the pope, Faustus, becoming invisible as a result of his black arts, astounds the Roman Catholic pope by snatching items from the holy man's hands. Like a gleeful child, Faustus asks Mephostophilis to create more mischief. When Faustus returns home, the scholars eagerly question him about many things unknown to them. As Faustus's fame spreads, Charles V, emperor of Germany, asks him to conjure up the spirit of Alexander the Great. A skeptical knight scoffs at such a preposterous idea, so Faustus, after fulfilling the emperor's request, spitefully places horns on the head of the knight.

Foreseeing that his time of merriment is drawing to a close, Faustus returns to Wittenberg. Wagner senses that his master is about to die because Faustus is giving him all of his worldly goods. As death draws near, Faustus speaks with his conscience, which, taking the form of an old man, begs him to repent before he dies. When Faustus declares that he will repent, Mephostophilis cautions him not to offend Lucifer. Faustus asks Mephostophilis to bring him Helen of Troy as a lover to amuse him during the final days of his life.

In his remaining hours, Faustus converses with scholars who love him, and the fallen theologian reveals to them his bargain with Lucifer. Alone, he utters a final despairing plea that he be saved from impending eternal misery, but in the end he is borne off by a company of devils.

Critical Evaluation:

Doctor Faustus is probably Christopher Marlowe's most famous work. A contemporary of William Shakespeare, and author of nondramatic poetry as well, Marlowe wrote only seven plays. If Shakespeare had died at an equally young age—twenty-nine rather than fifty-two—Marlowe might be the more famous of the pair. Marlowe was one of the first English writers to perfect black verse—unrhymed iambic pentameter—and to use it with flexibility and poetic effect in drama. He was killed in a tavern brawl.

The manuscripts of *Doctor Faustus*, surviving in different versions, were revised by theatrical companies after Marlowe's death in 1593. Printed versions of the play, one in 1604 and another in 1616, indicate further editorial adjustments, particularly involving the comic scenes. Scholars do not agree about which version is more authentic. They agree that Marlowe wrote the tragic scenes, but disagree about the authorship of the comic scenes. Moreover, they question whether the comic scenes comment on or detract from the main plot.

The comic scenes of *Doctor Faustus*, however, follow the medieval practice of the farce or interlude—humorous, clownish, or boisterous amusement that entails variations on or exaggerations of Faustus's dealings with Mephostophilis. For instance, the servants and the clowns try to conjure devils, and Faustus's sale of a horse to a horse-courser, who returns to pull off Faustus's leg after the horse proves to be a creation of black magic, parody Faustus's own more serious deviltry. The episode involving Faustus's pulled-off leg, actually a bundle of hay that dissolves, suggests Faustus's own bodily disintegration at the end of the play and the disintegration of his chances for salvation. Faustus remains giddy with hollow, short-lived successes. He never experiences the somber reflection that usually grips the living in the presence of mortal decay. Overall, the comic elements present thematic reminders of how evil lures by deceit and blunts or vulgarizes sensibility.

Marlowe based *Doctor Faustus* on the early sixteenth century German doctor Johann Faust, a practitioner of magic, who was thought to have sold his soul to the Devil in exchange for knowledge and magical power. Marlowe dramatizes tales that gathered around Faustus's name, those typically involving the conflict between human aspiration and human limitation. His version of the life of Faustus greatly enriches and extends its scope. He incorporates many literary, philosophical, and religious contexts.

In particular, Marlowe structures *Doctor Faustus* as a morality play combining religious instruction with vivid entertainment. The morality play, a medieval poetic drama, mingles tragic and comic aspects of ordinary life with Christian liturgical services and the homily. Its concern is humanity's earthly existence and spiritual state, but especially humanity's well-being in the afterlife. Death stands as preoccupation, as in the play itself, because it ought to bring every moment of life into sharp focus. The present should be viewed as a preparation for eternal life; the struggle for salvation calls for faith, endurance, repentance, and constant alertness. Furthermore, the morality play is allegorical; it personifies virtues and vices. Good and bad forces in a person's heart and mind are presented in the likeness of living men and women, and they act in accord with their names or natures. For example, in the morality play, the main character, representing all, encounters characters such as Faith, Hope, and Charity as well as Pride, Lust, and Envy. The ensuing struggle demonstrates life's trials and the soul's particular relation to God,

and Christ's blood is shed for its salvation. Medieval culture had emphasized that believers should detach themselves as much as possible from things of this world.

Through elements of the morality play, Marlowe makes Doctor Faustus's situation expressive of the lives of all believers. For example, he presents the conflicting dialogues of the Good and Evil angels and Faustus's response to them as a form of spiritual decision-making in slow motion that is intended to teach through contrasts. These dramatic encounters, as with those involving Faustus and Mephostophilis, and the varying comic ones, illustrate that acts of choice and their motivations have temporal and eternal consequences.

In addition, Marlowe sets the morality-play framework of *Doctor Faustus* within the wider context of Renaissance Christian humanism, in which intellectual and cultural currents greatly differ from the medieval period. He makes Doctor Faustus represent the new learning that highlights the importance of individual thought, expression, and worldly experience. Christian humanism seeks to extend boundaries of knowledge beyond the religious sphere, with a revival of classical learning. It stresses all knowledge of human and physical nature, the arts, and sciences together. It values and appreciates the present life—the good things of the here and now and the almost unlimited potential of humans to be, have, or do what they would. For example, the discovery of the New World had greatly broadened physical, intellectual, and imaginative horizons. Human beings, having wondrous capabilities and possibilities, should realize them through generalized curiosity about all things. Struggles to understand how the world works and to discover how its parts are connected makes humans more than they already are.

Initially, Faustus exemplifies the new humanistic learning and its open-ended possibilities; he is a person at the height of human knowledge and is the greatest theologian in Europe, despite humble origins. Although typifying the high aspiration of the Renaissance, he grows discontent, unhappy with the constraints of his learning and his life, unable even to approximate his personal ambitions. He wants, for example, observable proof of answers to ultimate or cosmic questions and increasingly seeks fame or worldly renown and sensual gratification, epitomized in Helen of Troy. He turns to forbidden, occult things, acting against his better knowledge.

Like some other humanists, Marlowe's Faustus retains the superstitious belief that black magic or diabolism, though unholy, is achievable and would raise him to the superhuman heights he seeks. He thinks the fact of death and the dread of it, as well as the existence of evil and its depth, renders orthodox forms of knowledge inadequate. He might make the tragic quality of life more manageable or tolerable by means of magical or demoniac practices. He knows that these practices involve yielding his soul to the Devil or to one of the Devil's surrogates; the personal appearance of a devil in this world was accepted as proof that black magic works. Faustus, in return for his soul, receives use of supernatural knowledge or power for twenty-four years, the parallel with hours of the day indicating the brief time in comparison with eternity. His supposed supernatural ability is a mystery operating outside the laws of God and nature. He thinks it attainable by select intellectuals only. It was thought to bring worldly gratification and a sense of self-sufficiency, or independence from faith. It would momentarily compensate for the destruction that haunts life and provide demonstrable answers to life's final questions, goals otherwise unreachable.

Still, Faustus realizes, though sporadically, that attempts to remedy somehow the brevity of human life—the toil and trouble inherent in it—by means of a power other than God are sinful and false, bringing damnation. Also, he wavers in convincing himself that the soul dies with the body, that he will accordingly escape damnation, his contract with Lucifer voided. His indecision, a delirium of self-deception, demonstrates the perversion or deformity that is the actual nature of evil, something he sees in the parade of the Seven Deadly Sins but fails to understand. In addition, because of his pride, the root of the Seven Deadly Sins, Faustus never recognizes Mephostophilis, Lucifer, and Beelzebub as sly, worldly-wise tempters and tricksters, temptation always and everywhere being present in life; nor does he recognize the devils as unwilling servants of God, a means of divine justice.

Furthermore, Marlowe adds another source of tension and conflict to his play, the doctrine of predestination. Formulated by John Calvin, the sixteenth century reformer and theologian, the doctrine declared that Christ's redeeming death extended to the elect souls alone, those predetermined by God for salvation; others, for whom it is denied, human nature being inherently sinful, will be damned. The English church, making concessions to Calvinists within it, taught a form of the doctrine, that some souls are predestined to be saved, remaining silent about the others. As Marlowe suggests through Faustus, the church, existing to draw people to Christ, may, through its Calvinistic teaching, push them away.

In his opening soliloquy, Faustus reflects upon his life and the patterns of his thought and feeling, which had been shaped by the morality play, Christian humanism, and predestination. Apparently, he develops a pessimistic fatalism, a layer upon layer of inability or helplessness, a combination of perverse reasoning, foolishness, delusion, and madness.

He thinks that whatever he chooses the result is the same—death in this life and damnation in the next. He cites Saint Paul's Epistle to the Romans—"The wages of sin is death"—but he omits the rest of the verse—"But the gift of God is eternal life through Jesus Christ, our Lord." His refusal of that "gift"—something Christ has already done for him—is eventually revealed for the arrogance and blindness it is. As the play unfolds, Faustus reaffirms his belief that his condemnation cannot be transcended through an appeal to God's grace, his pact with the Devil strengthening his certainty that his sins are too great to be forgiven and that his destiny is predetermined. He ignores that a sincere prayer to Christ, however briefly or humbly said, will be answered; that God's mercy, without limit, open to all who ask, and so easily acquired, will make whatever happens work for his good. Christ's "free gift" will do for him what he cannot and need not do for himself. Nevertheless, Faustus makes his assurance of doom a self-fulfilling prophecy, rejecting the goodness of good—Christ's redeeming sacrifice.

Faustus's disappointment in his pact with Lucifer begins immediately, as he learns what he already knows: that God made the universe, that Hell is wherever God is not, and that his choices will lead him to Hell for eternity. His dissatisfaction continues, his desire for power and fame reducing him to diversionary trifles: mocking the pope, conjuring up grapes in winter, pursuing images of beautiful women; all are devils disguised to fulfill his wishes. The comic subplot also illustrates the futility of his pact. For example, the least-educated clown summons a demon; magic is shown to be nonexistent; and a demon appears whenever anyone disavows Christ. Faustus surrenders true power—the power of faith, choice, and intellect—for empty gestures that perish with occurrence.

The final scene of the play summarizes the tragic irony of Faustus's life; the clock counts the minutes left in the life of a person who, having determined life's length, remains incapable of calling upon Christ when there is no unpardonable sin. Faustus will not accept that divine mercy predominates over divine justice, and he wants to hide from God. Hell, shadowing him throughout the play, completes its objective because the terms of his contract have been fulfilled. Isolated, alienated from God, and screaming in futility that he will burn his books, Faustus is confronted by devils, who tear him apart limb by limb; only his soul remains intact, taken to Hell.

"Critical Evaluation" by Sandra K. Fischer;
revised by Timothy C. Miller

Further Reading

Brooke, Nicholas. "The Moral Tragedy of *Dr. Faustus*." *Cambridge Journal* 5 (1952): 663-687. Focuses on the moral choices presented to Faustus. Attempts to incorporate the comic subplots of *Doctor Faustus* in a unified reading of Renaissance dualism, which would render the play an aesthetic whole and thus a dramatic success.

Cheney, Patrick, ed. *The Cambridge Companion to Christopher Marlowe*. New York: Cambridge University Press, 2004. A collection of essays that includes discussion of Marlowe's life, his modern relevance, his literary style, the use of gender and sexuality in his work, and his reception and influence. Thomas Healy provides an analysis of *Doctor Faustus*.

Deats, Sara Munson, and Robert A. Logan, eds. *Placing the Plays of Christopher Marlowe: Fresh Cultural Contexts*. Burlington, Vt.: Ashgate, 2008. Features several essays on *Doctor Faustus*, including discussions of magic and the play's early modern language of addiction. Also looks at the play's imprint upon William Shakespeare's *The Tempest*.

Hopkins, Lisa. *Christopher Marlowe: A Literary Life*. New York: Palgrave, 2000. A study of Marlowe's career and what is known of his life. Hopkins focuses on Marlowe's skepticism toward colonialism, family, and religion.

_____. *Christopher Marlowe, Renaissance Dramatist*. Edinburgh: Edinburgh University Press, 2008. An introduction to Marlowe's plays, discussing their themes, theatrical contexts, and performance histories from 1587 through 2007. Also examines Marlowe's relationship to William Shakespeare and his theatrical achievements. References to *Doctor Faustus* are listed in the index.

Levin, Harry. *The Overreacher: A Study of Christopher Marlowe*. Boston: Beacon Press, 1964. Examines the sources of the Faust legend and places them in the context of the fall of Lucifer from Heaven. Examines the comic scenes to find in them a burlesque of the main plot.

Oz, Avraham, ed. *Marlowe*. New York: Palgrave Macmillan, 2003. Collection of essays about Marlowe's plays, including "*Doctor Faustus*: Subversion through Transgression" by Jonathan Dollimore, "*Doctor Faustus* and Knowledge in Conflict" by Catherine Belsey, and "Reading Faustus's God" by Alan Sinfield.

Doctor Pascal

Author: Émile Zola (1840-1902)
First published: Le Docteur Pascal, 1893 (English translation, 1893)
Type of work: Novel
Type of plot: Naturalism
Time of plot: Late nineteenth century
Locale: Southern France

Principal characters:
DR. PASCAL, a doctor interested in heredity
CLOTILDE, his niece
MARTINE, their devoted old servant
MADAME FÉLICITÉ ROUGON, Dr. Pascal's mother
DR. RAMOND, a friend of Dr. Pascal and Clotilde
MAXIME, Clotilde's brother

The Story:

The July afternoon is extremely hot, but the room is well protected from the heat by heavy wooden shutters. In front of a huge carved oak armoire, Dr. Pascal patiently looks for a particular sheet of paper. The search is not easy. For about thirty years, the doctor was amassing manuscripts for his work on heredity. A smile comes over his face when he finds the paper, and he hands it to his niece and asks her to copy it for their friend, Dr. Ramond. Clotilde takes it without interrupting her work on a pastel drawing of flowers that is intended for an illustration plate in the doctor's book.

Martine, the housekeeper, comes in to repair the tapestry on an armchair. She has been with the doctor for thirty years, ever since he came to Plassans as a young doctor. Thirteen years later, following the death of his wife, Dr. Pascal's brother sent Clotilde, then seven years old, to live with him. Martine cared for the child according to her own zealous religious convictions.

Dr. Pascal completes Clotilde's instruction by trying to give her clear and healthy ideas on everything. The three live in peaceful happiness, although a certain uneasiness is now beginning to grow out of their religious conflicts. Martine considers it a pity that such a kind man as her master refuses to go to church; the two women agree that they will force him to attend services.

Later that afternoon, old Madame Rougon comes by, ostensibly for a visit but actually to inspect everything. Hearing her son in the next room, she expresses displeasure that he is again doing what she calls his "devilish cooking." She tells Clotilde of the unpleasant rumors about the doctor's new drug. If only he could try spectacular cures on the famous people of the town, she declares, instead of always treating the poor. She wants him to be a success, like his two brothers, but Dr. Pascal is most unlike the rest of his family. He practiced medicine for only twelve years; after that, he invested his money with a private broker and now lives on its returns. Martine receives the money every three months and uses it to the best advantage. When his patients pay him, Dr. Pascal throws the money in a drawer. When he visits a poor patient, he often leaves money there instead of receiving payment. He is completely absorbed in his research and his fight against suffering.

Madame Rougon is upset most by the fact that the big oak armoire contains detailed information on each member of the family. Afraid that the doctor's papers might fall into the hands of a stranger, she asks Clotilde to give her the key. She opens the cupboard, but as she reaches for the files, Dr. Pascal enters; she leaves demurely as if nothing happened. It is Clotilde who receives the brunt of the doctor's anger. From that time on, Dr. Pascal feels that he is being betrayed by the two human beings who are dearest to him, and to whom he is dearest. He keeps all the drawers of his desk tightly locked.

One day, Maxime comes for a visit. Still young, he is already worn out by his dissolute way of life. Having ascertained that his sister is not planning to get married, he asks her to come to Paris with him. Clotilde is frightened at the idea of leaving Dr. Pascal's home, but she promises to go to her brother if someday he really needs her.

After Maxime's visit, the house returns to its state of subdued tension until a Capuchin comes to Plassans to preach. Clotilde, deeply shaken by his preaching, asks Dr. Pascal to burn all of his papers. He refuses. He also has another fruitless discussion with his mother, who is constantly begging the young girl to destroy the files.

One night, Dr. Pascal finds Clotilde trying to steal his papers. While she helps to replace them, he makes a last attempt to convince her of the value of his work. He shows her the files and explains the use he is making of them. Clotilde is almost persuaded but asks for time to think about the matter.

One day, the doctor returns to the house in great agitation.

A patient died of a heart attack while he was giving him an injection. Dr. Pascal refuses Clotilde's attempted comfort, and when his mother hints that he might be going insane, he nearly believes the suggestion. He feels he may be suffering from the same condition as his grandmother, who was never well-balanced and is now, at the age of one hundred and four, living in a sanatorium. Anxious and helpless, Clotilde and Martine watch over him.

Dr. Ramond comes and asks Clotilde to marry him, but she says that she needs time to consider his proposal and that she will answer him soon. In the meantime, she asks him what he thinks of her uncle's condition. Dr. Pascal overhears the conversation, and from that time on his health becomes worse. Although he allows Clotilde to take care of him, he will not let her come into his room when he is in bed. She finally persuades him to try some of his own injections, as Dr. Ramond suggests. As he begins to show improvement, she tries to restore his faith in his research. He is overjoyed when she finds the key to the armoire and brings it to him.

At last, Dr. Pascal declares that he feels greatly improved, and he tells Clotilde that she should begin to think about a date for her marriage. Clotilde does not seem concerned. One day, as they are coming back from a walk, she asks him to help untie her hat. Suddenly, as he bends close to her, he realizes how greatly he desires her. Disturbed by the strength of his feelings, he insists that she give Dr. Ramond a definite date for the wedding. A short time later, he buys her an extravagant present of lace, which he puts on her bed. That night, Clotilde comes running to his door and tells him that if her marriage is the occasion for the gift, she is not going to marry Dr. Ramond. He, Pascal, is the man she loves. That night she becomes his.

A period of extreme happiness follows for both Clotilde and Dr. Pascal. Martine, after disappearing for a full day to show her disapproval, continues her faithful service. One day, Martine returns with the news that the broker embezzled the doctor's funds and fled. She performs miracles in preparing meals, using the money accumulated in the drawer, but at last their situation becomes really desperate. Dr. Pascal and Clotilde seem quite unconcerned and wait patiently for the matter to be settled in court.

Madame Rougon keeps busy. She produces a letter from Maxime, now disabled, in which he asks for his sister, and she heaps contempt on Dr. Pascal for keeping the young woman without marrying her and for not being able to feed her properly. Dr. Pascal is happy when Clotilde refuses to go to her brother, but, feeling guilty, he pretends that he needs time to devote himself to his research and insists that she should go. Deeply hurt, Clotilde nevertheless obeys.

Dr. Pascal goes on working, waiting, meanwhile, for the painful joy of Clotilde's letters. His health suffers, and he has two heart attacks. Dr. Ramond brings him the news that some of his money is recovered. About the same time, he receives a letter from Clotilde, telling him that she is pregnant. He immediately wires her to return. She leaves at once, but he dies two hours before she arrives. He did, however, muster enough strength to complete his files concerning himself, Clotilde, and their unborn child.

While Clotilde is in Dr. Pascal's room, Madame Rougon, with the help of Martine, burns all his papers. Clotilde later uses the shelves to store her baby's clothes.

Critical Evaluation:

Doctor Pascal, the twentieth and final novel in Émile Zola's Rougon-Macquart series, is significant both as a reflection of Zola's personal life and as the culmination of his vast, ambitious history of the second empire. If *Doctor Pascal* does not possess the literary energy of some of the other novels in the Rougon-Macquart series, it nevertheless reveals many of Zola's characteristic interests and obsessions.

Doctor Pascal centers on the love between an older doctor and a young woman, his niece. This relationship mirrors Zola's love for Jeanne Rozerot, a beautiful, modest twenty-year-old seamstress whom Zola's wife had employed. Rozerot became his mistress in 1888 (he was near fifty at the time), and for her sake he went on two extreme diets to lose weight. He seems to have loved her very much, and he eventually had two children by her (although he had none with his wife, Alexandrine). He was not, however, willing to divorce his wife, despite the fact that he disapproved of extramarital affairs. Alexandrine had been his loyal companion through very hard times, and he could not bring himself to desert her now. Alexandrine was unhappy about the affair, but after Zola died, she behaved most humanely; she agreed to meet his children, treated them kindly, and even made it possible for them to bear their father's name legally.

Doctor Pascal is thus a very personal novel and reflects much about the life of the novelist. It is also personal in the sense that Dr. Pascal, as much as any other character in Zola's fiction, embodies the author's own intellectual interests and commitments. Dr. Pascal the scientist is devoted to curing nervous disorders and to keeping a record of his family. Zola, too, often viewed himself and his work as "scientific." In opposition to what he considered to be the unreality of the Romantics, Zola was determined to place his work on a firm scientific basis; in fact, he often saw his own fiction as a form of "experimentation." Dr. Pascal's record of the Rougon-

Macquart family permits Zola to review the chronicle of the figures and incidents in this "history" and, at the same time, to express his views on the significance of heredity in the affairs of men and families. Dr. Pascal—and, by inference, Zola—takes the genetic material of the Rougon-Macquarts extremely seriously. Although the laws of heredity may not be completely understood, and although Dr. Pascal's injections are not medically successful, Dr. Pascal's belief in the power and explanatory force of science remains unshaken.

In fact, Dr. Pascal's belief in science—and the opposition to that belief from those closest to him—forms the chief intellectual concern of the novel. The objections to the doctor's scientific approach are religious and social, whereby the former, although virulent, is ultimately less threatening to Zola than the latter. Dr. Pascal's treasured servant, Martine, objects to Pascal's tampering with God's plan, but she takes action to help destroy the doctor's valued historical files only after being incited by Madame Rougon, Dr. Pascal's mother.

Madame Rougon's motives are entirely selfish. She does not want the honor of the family stained by an exposure of defects. Her only pride is her family, and she cannot tolerate the prospect of family shame. Taking advantage of Martine's simplicity, Madame Rougon finally succeeds in destroying all of Dr. Pascal's meticulously recorded chronicle. In a sense, this destruction of the family records is a logical conclusion of the degeneration of the Rougon-Macquarts, a family that, despite a few branches still growing, has degenerated and become self-destructive.

If the parallel between Dr. Pascal and Zola holds, the question arises whether Zola's literary work is also metaphorically destroyed as the Rougon-Macquart series comes to an end. Perhaps Zola believed that life would take its revenge on literature, that the truth he sought to express could not be borne. The forces of reaction, both social and religious, would stifle and burn his work.

That fate was not in store for Zola's literary work, although it was, in a sense, in store for Zola himself. Shortly after the publication of *Doctor Pascal*, Zola intervened in the notorious Dreyfus affair. Alfred Dreyfus, a Jewish officer, was convicted of treason by the French authorities, and the conviction was upheld despite another officer's having confessed to the crime and fled the country. When Zola thereupon attacked the authorities for anti-Semitism, hypocrisy, and lies, he was forced into temporary exile in England.

Zola's courageous action in behalf of Dreyfus and his opposition to anti-Semitism are particularly important in evaluating Zola's naturalist theory, which occupies a central role in *Doctor Pascal*. Because of Zola's emphasis on genetic determinism, his work might be open to accusations of racialism. Because of the stress he places on forces that mold men's lives, over which they have no control, he also could be accused of fatalism. The critic Georg Lukács, for example, refuses even to include Zola in the literary tradition of progressive realism. Nevertheless, in his literary output as in his life, Zola affirmed his confidence in the forces of science, progress, and, above all, life. Despite the destruction of the doctor's files, the reader is left with the impression at the end of the novel that Dr. Pascal's work will continue after him.

The emotional interest of the narrative, the center of gravity of the fiction, lies in the love of an older man for a young woman. Zola explores their feelings with extreme delicacy and insight, and the child resulting from their love is meant to signify the rebirth of hope and humanity. The child more than compensates for the destruction of the files. If that destruction is seen as revenge against scholarship, science, and art, then the birth of the child signals the victory of the positive forces of life over the forces of despair and negativism.

Although the novel holds significant intellectual content as well as relevance to Zola's life and career, there is a certain weariness in Zola's telling that may be the result of Zola's already having written an enormous number of pages in his vast chronicle. Like his character Dr. Pascal, Zola was no longer a young man. The narrative may be judged to lack the intensity of his earlier works, but it nevertheless glows with compassion and loving faith.

"Critical Evaluation" by Howard Lee Hertz

Further Reading

Berg, William J., and Laurey K. Martin. *Émile Zola Revisited.* New York: Twayne, 1992. Focuses on the Rougon-Macquart series, using textual analysis and Zola's literary-scientific principles to analyze each of the twenty novels.

Brooks, Peter. "Zola's Combustion Chamber." In *Realist Vision.* New Haven, Conn.: Yale University Press, 2005. Zola's novels are among the works of literature and art that are examined in this study of the realist tradition in France and England during the nineteenth and twentieth centuries.

Brown, Frederick. *Zola: A Life.* New York: Farrar, Straus and Giroux, 1995. A detailed and extensive biography of Zola that discusses his fiction and the intellectual life of France, of which he was an important part. Shows how Zola's naturalism was developed out of the intellectual and political ferment of his time; argues that this naturalism was a highly studied and artificial approach to reality.

Gallois, William. *Zola: The History of Capitalism.* New York: Peter Lang, 2000. Interprets the Rougon-Macquart novels as a history of capitalism, drawing connections between Zola's novels and the work of economists and sociologists Karl Marx, Max Weber, and Émile Durkheim. Includes bibliography and index.

Grant, Elliott M. *Émile Zola.* New York: Twayne, 1966. Detailed analyses of Zola's works, as well as his theories, plans, and methods. Includes a discussion of *Doctor Pascal,* the final volume of the Rougon-Macquart cycle and a pivotal work in Zola's oeuvre.

Haavik, Kristof Haakon. "*Le Docteur Pasqual*: The Triumph of Life." In *In Mortal Combat: The Conflict of Life and Death in Zola's "Rougon-Macquart."* Birmingham, Ala.: Summa, 2000. Argues that life and death "are bitterly opposed forces" in the Rougon-Macquart, and the "epic struggle" between them is the "central unifying thread" of the series.

Hemmings, F. W. J. *Émile Zola.* Oxford, England: Clarendon Press, 1966. Discusses *Doctor Pascal* as the summation of the Rougon-Macquart cycle. The birth of a male child at the end illustrates the theme of rebirth and rejuvenation. The character of Dr. Pascal is interpreted as incorporating Zola's own ideas and philosophy of life.

Nelson, Brian. *Zola and the Bourgeoisie: A Study of Themes and Techniques in "Les Rougon-Macquart."* Totowa, N.J.: Barnes & Noble, 1983. *Doctor Pascal* is included in a discussion of utopia and sex in the bourgeois world. Concludes that the novel illustrates themes of decadence and renewal. Links Zola's utopian vision of progress to the value of work.

_____, ed. *The Cambridge Companion to Émile Zola.* New York: Cambridge University Press, 2007. Collection of essays, including discussions of Zola and the nineteenth century, his depiction of society, sex, and gender, and Zola's utopias. Includes a summary of Zola's novels, a family tree of the Rougon-Macquarts, a bibliography, and an index.

Doctor Thorne

Author: Anthony Trollope (1815-1882)
First published: 1858
Type of work: Novel
Type of plot: Domestic realism
Time of plot: Mid-nineteenth century
Locale: Barsetshire, England

Principal characters:
DOCTOR THORNE, a country doctor
MARY THORNE, his niece
SQUIRE GRESHAM, the owner of Greshamsbury Park
LADY ARABELLA, his wife
FRANK GRESHAM, their son
ROGER SCATCHERD, a stonemason and later a baronet
LOUIS PHILIPPE, his son
MISS DUNSTABLE, an heiress

The Story:

Greshamsbury Park, in the county of Barsetshire, dominates the life of the surrounding countryside. Unfortunately, Greshamsbury's lord, Squire Gresham, is rapidly spending himself into poverty. Most of his financial troubles result from the desire of his wife, Lady Arabella De Courcy Gresham, to get him into politics. The squire inherited his father's seat in Parliament but lost it because of his Whig leanings. Barsetshire is overwhelmingly Tory and does not approve of Gresham's Whig friends or the fact that his wife's aristocratic family, the De Courcys, are aggressively Whig in sentiment. Gresham twice tries to regain his seat in the Parliamentary elections because his wife fancies being the wife of a member of Parliament, but he is unsuccessful and loses a great deal of money in financing his campaigns.

Therefore, when his son Frank came of age, Squire Gresham has not much to offer him in the way of financial security. Lady Arabella sees as their only hope the possibility of Frank's marriage to a wealthy heiress. That he might do such a thing, however, seems rather doubtful, for, much to the distress of his mother and her family, Frank is in love with Mary Thorne, niece of the local doctor. Frank and Mary knew each other all their lives, and Mary was educated along with the young Greshams at Greshamsbury Park.

Mary was brought to live with her uncle, Doctor Thorne, when she was a mere infant. The real circumstances of her birth—that she is the illegitimate child of Doctor Thorne's brother and Mary Scatcherd, a village girl—are known only to the doctor. Even Mary's brother Roger, who killed his sister's betrayer, did not know that Doctor Thorne adopted the child. Roger, a poor stonemason, was sentenced to six months in prison for his crime. When his term was up, he was told that the child had died. Since the doctor stood in high favor with Squire Gresham and regularly cared for Lady Arabella, his niece, an attractive child and near the age of the Gresham children, took her lessons with them. By the time

Frank was of age, Mary seemed part of the family. Lady Arabella, however, is determined that this is not to be the literal state of affairs, for Mary has no money.

One of Squire Gresham's greatest misfortunes is the forced sale of a particularly choice part of his estate to pay off his most pressing debts. Doctor Thorne, acting as agent for the squire, finds a buyer in Sir Roger Scatcherd, the former stonemason, who now possesses a title, a seat in Parliament, and a large fortune. Although he knows nothing of the existence of his sister's illegitimate child, Sir Roger is in close contact with Doctor Thorne because he is a chronic alcoholic, and Doctor Thorne is often called on to attend to him after his drinking bouts.

The loss of the property greatly diminishes the value and extent of the estate Frank will someday inherit. Fortunately, one of the Gresham daughters is engaged to marry money, a politician who wants the Gresham and De Courcy family connections. A second daughter is to marry the local vicar and is thus assured of a respectable position, although one without much money. Frank is his mother's real hope, and to save him from his unfortunate entanglement with Mary, Lady Arabella's family invites Frank to De Courcy Castle for a visit.

The Countess De Courcy hopes to make a match between Frank and Miss Dunstable, a family friend and a woman considered the wealthiest heiress in England. Miss Dunstable, ten years older than Frank and much more worldly wise, is clever and sharp-tongued. When, mostly to humor his aunt, Frank pretends to woo her, he finds her good company. She sees through his pretended amorous interest immediately, and they become the best of friends, after which she becomes Frank's confidant and adviser.

Sir Roger is in such poor health from excessive drinking that he decides to make his will, leaving everything to Louis Philippe, his equally alcoholic son. When Doctor Thorne learns the terms of the will, he tells Sir Roger that Mary's child is still living, whereupon Sir Roger makes her his heir in the event of his son's death.

Lady Arabella, finding Frank's attachment for Mary unchanged, will not allow the girl to visit Greshamsbury. When Frank arrives home and is made aware of this, he is furious. The family insists, however, that he has to marry wealth, particularly because the sister who was to have made an advantageous marriage was jilted.

Sir Roger is also in difficulties. Having discovered a fraud in his election, the committee unseats him, and the shock is too great for the old man. He goes on another drinking bout and dies from the effects. Louis Philippe, who inherits the estate, meanwhile also forms an attachment for Mary, but she remains true to Frank. The only hope for the happiness of Mary and Frank seems to lie in the death of Louis Philippe, who is well on his way to following his father to the grave. Having paid a visit to the squire for the purpose of foreclosing on some debts, Louis Philippe goes on a drinking spree that leaves him weak and very ill.

In a stormy interview soon afterward, Lady Arabella demands that Mary end her engagement to Frank. Mary refuses to be the one to break her promise, but she does ask the young man to release her because of the hopelessness of the situation in which they find themselves. Frank refuses, insisting that they love each other. Then Louis Philippe dies. When Doctor Thorne jubilantly tells Mary the news of her inheritance, her marriage to Frank becomes possible. With Mary now an heiress, not even the proud De Courcys can object to so excellent a match. For the first time in years, an atmosphere of rejoicing hangs over Greshamsbury Park.

Critical Evaluation:

Doctor Thorne is the third novel in Anthony Trollope's Barsetshire series, succeeding *The Warden* (1855) and *Barchester Towers* (1857). As in the first two novels, Trollope describes the social realities of his mythical county, providing extraordinary insight into the English class structure and the social realities of the nineteenth century. Unlike the first two works, which were concerned with the insular ecclesiastical world of a cathedral town, Trollope turns his attention in this novel to the landed wealth of Barsetshire. The gentry, represented by the Greshams, are in decline because of the political imprudence of the squire, who aligns himself with his wife's family, the De Courcys, notoriously aristocratic and notoriously Whig. Having lost his Tory constituency and his money, Squire Gresham attempts to save the estate for his son.

It is at this point that Doctor Thorne, one of Trollope's ideal gentlemen, enters the story. The squire's only confi-

dant, he serves not only as the family physician but also as its moral and spiritual counselor. Rigorous in his ethics, proud of his social station, and in no way awed by the upper classes, Doctor Thorne supports the squire in his attempt to restore the estate to its former vigor. Despising snobbish and pretentious aristocrats such as the De Courcys, who have no loyalty to the life of the land, he seeks to help his friend by advising various economies and suggesting judicious loans.

If the moral strength that saves Greshamsbury Park comes from the doctor, it is the money of Sir Roger Scatcherd that enables Gresham to recoup and permits Frank and Mary to wed. Scatcherd, who represents the new industrial wealth, unwittingly saves the agriculture of the area from the moneylenders of London. It is in this alignment that Trollope reveals his political sympathies with the English upper middle class and his antagonism to the aristocracy and their morality.

Doctor Thorne surpasses both of its predecessors in its range of characters and situations. It relies very heavily on melodrama, and the ending is distinctly reminiscent of a fairy tale, yet the scene setting and dialogue are as good as anything Trollope ever wrote. "Frank must marry money" is the refrain that integrates the novel. Lady Arabella is quite willing to sacrifice everything—her son's happiness, Mary Thorne's reputation, Doctor Thorne's medical care of her—if only her son will attach himself to a rich woman. Lady Arabella's husband, Squire Gresham, supports her, even though in his heart he approves of Mary and wants to honor his son's love for her. Scatcherd thinks the power of his money will secure Mary for his dissolute son, Louis Philippe, who thinks the same. Doctor Thorne, who is neither intimidated nor awed by the aristocratic Gresham and De Courcy families, realizes the difficulty of Mary's situation. If she does not inherit her uncle's money, the prospects for her and Frank are bleak. Even Mary, although she never disavows her love for Frank, is willing (at Lady Arabella's urging) to write him a letter releasing him from his promise to marry her.

The only character besides Frank who steadfastly refuses to concede to the power of money is Miss Dunstable. An heiress in her thirties who is tired of the many men who have courted her for her money, she tells Frank that if he sticks by his first love, his determination to marry for love will eventually provide him with a living as well. Her advice would seem sentimental if she were not presented as such a worldly character. She is one of Trollope's finest creations, a shrewd and sophisticated woman who insists that Frank act on his own feelings and principles. To marry money, Miss Dunstable implies, will be not his salvation but his ruin, for he will have lost his real self.

Through the sensible Miss Dunstable Trollope sounds his theme that it is not blood or money that makes the man or woman but rather strength of character. Miss Dunstable seems a happy and well-adjusted person precisely because she knows herself and her society so well. Unlike so many of the other characters, she is not hypocritical, self-deceiving, or self-serving.

Trollope's other admirable characters have similar traits. Doctor Thorne, though less polished than Miss Dunstable and considerably more abrupt in his social intercourse, exhibits the same trueness of spirit. He is quite willing to offend Lady Arabella in the defense of his niece, Mary, whose excellent character, he realizes, is her only possession. For a similar reason, Doctor Thorne admires Scatcherd, a violent man and a drunkard, for his plain speaking and hard-working life.

Of course, Doctor Thorne and the other honest characters suffer for their plain speaking and their refusal to submit to money interests or the aristocracy. Trollope allows them to survive, however, and even thrive because their fierce defense of self is combined with sensitivity to the power of social norms and authorities. Thus Doctor Thorne continues to treat Lady Arabella professionally as a doctor, even while he takes exception to her treatment of his niece; for one thing, he needs the income from ministering to the Gresham family. Frank Gresham, too, shows respect for his family's values by agreeing to go away for a year to test their view that his separation from Mary will destroy his love for her. Trollope's most mature characters, in other words, assert themselves without repudiating societal standards. They have firm but flexible personalities, and in due course they are rewarded with success.

Trollope's management of plot and dialogue is enthralling. He delays the announcement of Mary's inheritance of Scatcherd's fortune until the end of the novel. He ingeniously takes Lady Arabella and Doctor Thorne through several confrontation scenes that gradually intensify the differences between them. Through his description of Louis Philippe's pathetic decline and death from too much drink and self-indulgence, he shows someone without any inner resources dying in a surfeit of wealth.

Trollope mitigates the melodramatic and fairy-tale aspects of his story with his narrative voice. The narrator often acknowledges that he is telling a story and even apologizes for faults such as the excessive length of the novel's first two chapters; he considers them necessary to explain the social and historical background of Frank and Mary's story, but he regrets that he has to introduce so much material so early in his novel. These confessions are disarming. The reader seems to be taken into the novelist's confidence. Indeed, Trollope invites the reader to feel superior to the narrator and at the same time indulgent toward his loquacious asides and digressions.

Because Trollope's theme is the nature of society and the power of money, because he draws characters with such precision and allows them to speak for themselves, his narrator is free to embark on many asides and subplots, for each digression from the main story enriches the background. As historian and novelist, Trollope resembles in tone the Henry Fielding of *The History of Tom Jones, a Foundling* (1749). Both novelists fully immerse readers in their characters' lives and yet retain a vivid consciousness of themselves as writing literature. Trollope does not go as far as the earlier Fielding in discoursing on the conventions of storytelling; on the contrary, his voluble narrator assumes an awareness of the tradition of novel writing and confines his comments only to the shape of his own story. The relaxed, casual tone and leisurely narrative are an extension of Trollope's supple moral insights.

"Critical Evaluation" by Carl Rollyson

Further Reading

Booth, Bradford. *Anthony Trollope: Aspects of His Life and Art.* Bloomington: Indiana University Press, 1958. Considers *Doctor Thorne* inferior to the two earlier Barsetshire novels because of Trollope's reliance on melodrama, which detracts from the novel's realism, but concedes the enormous appeal of Trollope's storytelling. Analyzes what Booth describes as Trollope's "conservative-liberalism."

Bridgham, Elizabeth A. *Spaces of the Sacred and Profane: Dickens, Trollope, and the Victorian Cathedral Town.* New York: Routledge, 2008. Describes how Trollope and Charles Dickens use the setting of Victorian cathedral towns to critique religious attitudes, business practices, aesthetic ideas, and other aspects of nineteenth century English life.

Bury, Laurent. *Seductive Strategies in the Novels of Anthony Trollope, 1815-1882.* Lewiston, N.Y.: Edwin Mellen Press, 2004. A study of seduction in all of Trollope's novels. Argues that seduction was a survival skill for both men and women in the Victorian era and demonstrates how Trollope depicted the era's sexual politics.

Hall, N. John. *Trollope: A Biography.* New York: Oxford University Press, 1991. Comments on the origins of *Doctor Thorne*'s plot, its popularity in spite of the critics' reservations, the engaging narrative mode, and Doctor Thorne as a typical Trollope hero.

MacDonald, Susan Peck. *Anthony Trollope.* Boston: Twayne, 1987. Concise discussion of the narrator of *Doctor Thorne*, showing how his interventions intensify the story's thematic and ethical complexity and enhance the novel's realism.

Markwick, Margaret. *New Men in Trollope's Novels: Rewriting the Victorian Male.* Burlington, Vt.: Ashgate, 2007. Examines Trollope's novels, tracing the development of his ideas about masculinity. Argues that Trollope's male characters are not the conventional Victorian patriarchs and demonstrates how his works promoted a "startlingly modern model of manhood."

_____. *Trollope and Women.* London: Hambledon Press, 1997. Examines how Trollope could simultaneously accept the conventional Victorian ideas about women while also sympathizing with women's difficult situations. Demonstrates the individuality of his female characters. Discusses his depiction of both happy and unhappy marriages, male-female relationships, bigamy, and scandal.

Mullen, Richard, and James Munson. *The Penguin Companion to Trollope.* New York: Penguin, 1996. A comprehensive guide, describing all of Trollope's novels, short stories, travel books, and other works; discusses plot, characters, background, tone, allusions, and contemporary references and places the works in their historical context.

Overton, Bill. *The Unofficial Trollope.* Totowa, N.J.: Barnes & Noble, 1982. Extensive analysis of *Doctor Thorne,* emphasizing Trollope's vision of contemporary history and his handling of the complex plot.

Super, R. H. *The Chronicler of Barsetshire: A Life of Anthony Trollope.* Ann Arbor: University of Michigan Press, 1988. Explains the biographical origins of *Doctor Thorne,* its relationship with the Barsetshire series, and its critical reception. Discusses how Trollope handles the theme of marriage in this novel and others.

Doctor Zhivago

Author: Boris Pasternak (1890-1960)
First published: Doktor Zhivago, 1957 (English translation, 1958)
Type of work: Novel
Type of plot: Social realism
Time of plot: 1903-1943
Locale: Moscow, the eastern front, and Siberia, Russia

Principal characters:
YURII ANDREIEVICH ZHIVAGO, a physician, poet, and man of goodwill
EVGRAF ANDREIEVICH ZHIVAGO, his half-brother
NIKOLAI NIKOLAIEVICH VEDENIAPIN (UNCLE KOLIA), his maternal uncle
ANTONINA ALEXANDROVNA GROMEKA (TONIA), his wife
LARISA FEODOROVNA GUISHAR (LARA), the wife of Pavel Antipov
PAVEL PAVLOVICH ANTIPOV (PASHA) (also known as STRELNIKOV), a Red commissar
INNOKENTII DUDOROV (NIKA), the son of a revolutionary terrorist
MISHA GORDON, the son of a Jewish lawyer, a friend of Yurii Zhivago
VICTOR IPPOLITOVICH KOMAROVSKY, a shady lawyer and the seducer of Lara
LIBERIUS AVERKIEVICH MIKULITSYN, a Red partisan leader
TANIA, the daughter of Yurii Zhivago and Lara

The Story:

Yurii Zhivago, a ten-year-old boy, attends his mother's funeral. His uncle, Nikolai Nikolaievich Vedeniapin, consoles him. After the funeral, Yurii spends the night in a monastery room. He does not know that his father has deserted his family. His father's business was once extensive; then, suddenly,

all was gone. Yurii is very fond of his uncle, a former priest who later becomes a famous writer, university professor, and scholar of the revolution and who believes in strong individuals.

Three years later, Yurii experiences spells of unconsciousness while grieving and praying for his mother's soul—indicative of an early inclination to mysticism. His father, Andrei Zhivago, commits suicide while traveling on a train. His lawyer, Victor Komarovsky, who was traveling with him at the time, maintains that Zhivago was an alcoholic and killed himself in a fit of alcoholic withdrawal.

As Yurii is growing up, his uncle places him to live with the Gromeko family and their daughter, Tonia. Some young men around them are revolutionaries, including Pasha Antipov. Amalia Guischar, the French widow of a Russian general, opens a dressmaking shop in Moscow. She is supported by Komarovsky, who succeeds in seducing her sixteen-year-old daughter Lara. Pasha Antipov falls in love with Lara. Amalia attempts suicide because of Komarovsky. Yurii, now a medical student, accompanies the doctor who treats her. As a result, Yurii sees Lara for the first time.

Although Lara is flattered by her affair with Komarovsky, she is also perturbed by it and is trying to break it off, but Komarovsky persists. When her brother Rodia needs money he has gambled away, Komarovsky offers to give Lara the money Rodia needs but only if she asks for it. Realizing that he will likely keep blackmailing her forever, Lara attempts to kill Komarovsky at a Christmas party, where Yurii is also present. She is placed with a helpful family and she manages to finish a school for teachers. She marries Pasha, but not before she tells him everything, which changes his life decisively. They decide to go to Yuriatin, in the Urals. Yurii is fascinated by mingling with people from the lower levels of society. He has also begun to write poetry. He marries Tonia Gromeko and their first child is born shortly before World War I.

After the war erupts, Yurii, who has become a doctor, joins the army. The Antipovs and their daughter Katenka are doing well in Yuriatin, but their marriage is not without problems. Each tries to behave more nobly, but Pasha is having second thoughts, thinking of divorce, yet he loves Lara more than ever. After many sleepless nights, he decides to join the army, thus solving the dilemma. When he stops writing, Lara sets out to look for him, having joined the army as a nurse.

Yurii is wounded by an artillery shell and meets Lara again in the hospital. She does not have favorable impressions of him. Yurii's friends have published his book of poetry without his permission. The news about the revolution in Petersburg reaches him. He and Lara are often brought together in the hospital. He writes to Tonia about Lara, making his wife jealous, but he tells her he does not even know where her room is. Yurii observes the disintegration and anarchy in the growing chaos of the country. This reinforces his early fa-

vorable attitude toward the revolution and his hopes for a solution and a better life. He also shows the first inklings of his infatuation with Lara, but she soon leaves. So does Yurii. On the train to Moscow, he muses about Tonia, his sympathy for the seemingly inevitable revolution by the Bolsheviks, Lara, and the future of Russia.

Back in Moscow in the fall of 1917, Yurii's son slaps him, frightened by his beard, showing how estranged they have become. Life is much harsher and full of scarcities. People are taking sides, and Yurii feels alone. He still hopes for betterment, but he is no longer sure. The revolution gathers momentum. Dealing with patients, Yurii contracts typhus. Suddenly, his half-brother Evgraf appears and helps the family, suggesting they go to the family estate Varikino, near Yuriatin, which they do in April, 1918. On the long train journey to Varikino, the Zhivagos experience many inconveniences and meet many interesting people. In conversations with them, Yurii declares that history has not consulted him, indicating the beginning of a change in his views on revolution. Another train rumbles by, and people think it is Comissar Strelnikov. On a stroll, Yurii is taken to see "the boss," who seems to recall vaguely the name Zhivago. Yurii tells him that he is going to Varikino in search of seclusion and obscurity. Strelnikov tells him that he might drop by to see his wife and daughter, although they belong to another life now. They part without Yurii realizing that Strelnikov is Pasha Antipov.

At Varikino, the Zhivagos are met coldly by a family of Social Democrats, the Mikulitsyns, who support the Bolshevik Revolution, but Yurii tells them that Marxism as a science is too self-centered and removed from the facts and that politics does not appeal to him. He does not like people who do not care about the truth. Yurii confesses that he used to be very revolutionary but now thinks that nothing can be gained by brute force and that people must be drawn to good by goodness. He also believes that man is born to live, not to prepare for life. Yurii has given up practicing medicine so as not to restrict his freedom to think and write a diary. The Zhivagos settle down to a quiet rustic life. Evgraf drops by suddenly again with offers of help. Yurii still wonders what he is, what he does, and why he is so powerful. All he knows is that he is his half-brother, whom he considers to be his "good genius" and a rescuer. Yurii reveals that he has a heart condition, inherited from his mother. He hears a woman's voice, but it is Lara's, not Tonia's.

Yurii meets Lara again in the public library. They renew their friendship. He begins to visit her at her apartment. The mystery of Strelnikov's identity is finally resolved for Yurii. They talk about him often, concluding that he is not a Communist Party member: He is only trying to exorcise his inability to win Lara's love, so he is taking it out on everybody else. Yurii realizes that his relationship with Lara is unfair to Tonia. He loves Tonia, and he is crushed by a guilty conscience, so he decides to stop seeing Lara. On his return home from the library, he is captured by red partisans, members of the so-called Forest Brotherhood, who require a doctor.

Yurii spends eighteen months in captivity, serving as a doctor but forced also to fire weapons in combat. He shoots mostly at treetops, feeling as though he were shooting at death itself. He tries to escape three times and witnesses many skirmishes between the red and white partisans, as well as examples of untold savagery. On one occasion, he wounds a white partisan boy and nurses him back to health. On another occasion, a distraught red partisan kills his own entire family, fearing what could happen to them if he were killed. The killing of prisoners is common. Yurii meets the son of the Mikulitsyns, a commissar with whom he has violent arguments. Yurii tells him plainly that he does not like the Mikulitsyns and they can all go to the Devil. Yurii finally escapes the Forest Brotherhood and goes to Lara in Yuriatin, instead of going to Tonia in Varikino.

Tonia and the children have returned to Moscow. Waiting for Lara in her apartment, Yurii compares her to Russia as the source of his love for them. He falls ill, and she nurses him back to health. They often talk about Komarovsky and Strelnikov, considering that they have both influenced their lives and made them into Adam and Eve. However, they both express their love for their spouses, Tonia and Pasha. They also blame war for everything. They frequently discuss the revolution, mostly in negative terms. They realize that their time of safety is over and that they cannot escape their destiny.

Yurii suggests that they all go to Moscow, but Lara wants to stay at home until Strelnikov's fate is decided—in case he needs her. A letter arrives from Tonia in Paris telling Yurii that they will never see each other again. Komarovsky appears suddenly. He is now in the new government in the Far East and wants Lara to go there with him because she is in danger. Yurii and Lara return to Varikino instead, with the gift of love for each other. Yurii works on his book of poetry. At night, they hear the wolves howling, coming ever closer. Komarovsky returns, and this time he takes Lara with him because, according to him, Strelnikov has been shot. Yurii agrees that she must go, even though he pines for her terribly. Strelnikov, who has not been shot, appears at Varikino to win Lara back after three years of marriage. After a long talk with Yurii, he shoots himself.

Yurii returns to Moscow in 1922. He marries Marina, the daughter of the porter at Gromeko's home. He soon suffers a heart attack in a streetcar and dies. At the funeral, Lara and Evgraf say their last goodbyes. After leaving the funeral, Lara is arrested on the street and disappears in a concentration camp. Many years later, Yurii's old friends, Dudorov and Gordon, relate that Evgraf raised Lara and Yurii's daughter, Tanya. Dudorov and Gordon enjoy a balmy Moscow evening after the end of the horrible war, hinting at the hopeful future and indestructibility of Russia, as well as of Yurii Zhivago. Yurii's poetry is reprinted in the epilogue of the novel.

"The Story" by Vasa D. Mihailovich

Critical Evaluation:

Doctor Zhivago is the final statement of a writer who lived a full and complex artistic life. Boris Pasternak's father was an accomplished painter, and his mother was a concert pianist. Leo Tolstoy and the composer Aleksandr Scriabin were family friends. Pasternak pursued music in youth but then turned to poetry, a career for which he prepared by studying philosophy at Marburg University. Born of Jewish parents, Pasternak was influenced both by the theology of his ancestors and by Christianity. Though he was relatively free of religious dogma, he was strongly persuaded of the reality of spiritual life, to which, he felt, the artistic impulse was closely related. It is not surprising that *Doctor Zhivago* is a vivid yet complicated and somewhat uneven work.

To observe that *Doctor Zhivago* is a poet's novel is commonplace but nevertheless instructive. Even the work's English translations include remarkably lyric passages that reflect Pasternak's deep love for his native land. The sketches of many people as they live Russian lives early in the twentieth century are especially notable in the first part of the work. Through both parts, there are expressions of opinion, wisely made to come from several of the novel's characters, that reflect the subtle intelligence of the author. The poems of Yurii Zhivago, which conclude the novel, are intended to be an integral part of the whole, exhibiting qualities one might expect of a ranking Russian poet of his century.

On the other hand, there is evidence that *Doctor Zhivago* is the work of a writer who was not thoroughly sure of the novelist's craft. Characters are sometimes drawn with enough care to be memorable only to be more-or-less forgotten. Various incidents in the book are connected to others in ways that are somewhat clumsy. In a writer without Pasternak's ability to make readers suspend disbelief, the coincidences whereby important characters are not only linked but also linked repeatedly and improbably would seem strange. The love story of Zhivago and Lara, surrounded by the circumstances of ordinary life in a more familiar world, would seem too sentimental.

The novel's central concern is the love story of Yurii and Lara. Yurii repeatedly expresses his undying love for Lara even though he is also in love with Tonia. This may seem incongruous, but in a complex character such as Yurii everything is possible. Moreover, he identifies Lara with Russia, thus combining his love for both. At the same time, Yurii is unselfish, as when he allows Lara to go away with Komarovsky, believing that it will be better for her to do so. The story of Yurii and Lara, sentimental though it may be, is one of the greatest love stories in Russian literature.

The novel is also concerned with the nature of life and death, as expressed in Yurii's thoughts on the subject. For him, life is to be lived, not prepared for. Life is continually being reborn even in death, thus making death an integral part of life. In these thoughts and in many other ways, Yurii is connected to Christian idealism. His feelings about life are also related to his thinking about Marxism and revolution in general. As a humanitarian and a believer in constant changes in life, he is at first sympathetic to the revolution, but as it becomes increasingly brutal he turns away from it. His sporadic ambiguity in his stance regarding revolution can be explained on that basis. Thus, life, spirit, and art are the essential elements that Yurii Zhivago struggles to preserve in an epoch with which he feels sympathy but not harmony.

Yurii thinks about literature and the arts in general. Being a poet, he sees life in a poetic way, motivating many of the novel's poetic passages and descriptions. The poems at the end of the novel attest to Yurii's avocation. Living and writing in a restricted society, Pasternak could not avoid referring to the restrictions on artistic freedom. The circumstances surrounding the publication of *Doctor Zhivago*, its critical reception, and the political acrimony that followed have tended to obfuscate thoughtful criticism of the novel, but they cannot be ignored. Pasternak, who had earned a reputation as a poet as early as the 1920's, was not unwilling to serve the revolution if he was allowed intellectual and artistic freedom. These were not allowed, however, and from about 1933 until 1943 he could not publish original poems in the Soviet Union, even though he had not written his novel to make a political statement, nor did he wish to be separated from his people and his homeland.

Ironically, it is the Marxists themselves who have insisted that the artifacts of any human culture include a political dimension. The events of *Doctor Zhivago*, though they might be found politically inconvenient, are the substance of the story. The novel does not reject revolution, political reform, or social justice. It simply records the brutality with which these ideals may be pursued and the difficulty of preserving other ideals—spiritual, personal, or artistic—in a time of violent upheaval. Joseph Stalin's death in 1953 brought about the gradual increase of artistic freedom, as is hinted at the end of the novel.

The most striking of the novel's stylistic devices are its poetic connotations and symbols. The listing of the poems at the end of the novel is one of the few examples of this device in world literature. They do not refer directly to the events in the novel, but the organic connection between the poems and those events can be fathomed. For example, the introductory poem "Hamlet" refers to the irresolute nature of Yurii Zhivago, and "Winter Night" recalls Yurii seeing a candle burning in a window when he was going to a Christmas party, where he saw Lara. There are many instances of biblical and Christian motifs in the poems, such as "Magdalene," a sinful woman, and the concluding poem, "Garden of Gethsemane," which seems to affirm the resurrection, if not of body then of spirit. Other symbols are tied to the novel's events or ideas. The name Zhivago stems from the Russian word *zhit'* ("to live"), underlining Pasternak's idea of Yurii's eternal nature. The name of the town Yuriatin is identified with Yurii. Strelnikov is related to the Russian word *streliat'* ("to shoot") and Komarovsky to *komar* ("mosquito"). The howling of the wolves at Varikino symbolizes the advent of danger. The Rowan Tree is the symbol of life in Russian folklore.

There are also shortcomings. The most glaring is the break between 1912 and 1915. Although *Doctor Zhivago* is not autobiographical and does not require chronology, it describes events affecting the characters, and the three missing years were replete with events important to all of them. Furthermore, some details are too coincidental, such as repeated meetings in different places between Yurii and Lara or Yurii and Strelnikov, sudden visits of Komarovsky and Evgraf, and so forth. It should be pointed out that Pasternak was primarily a poet, not a novelist; moreover, he wanted to make his points by employing such coincidences.

The importance of *Doctor Zhivago* in the history of literature, both Russian and world, can be judged by its artistic value as well as by the circumstances of its publication. It came after a long drought of good literature in Soviet Russia. Pasternak was the first Russian writer after Ivan Bunin to receive the Nobel Prize in the twentieth century. *Doctor Zhivago* also brings to mind the grandeur of Russian literature of the nineteenth century. Social and political issues of the period contained in the novel—potentially a minefield in the artistic sense—elevate the novel from the mediocrity of Socialist Realism prevalent in the Soviet Union by offering a remarkable human story that always attracts readers and remains in their minds.

"Critical Evaluation" by John Higby;
revised by Vasa D. Mihailovich

Further Reading

Erlich, Victor, ed. *Pasternak: A Collection of Critical Essays.* Englewood Cliffs, N.J.: Prentice-Hall, 1978. This collection of essays covers all important facets of Pasternak's work, including short fiction, although the emphasis is on his poetry and *Doctor Zhivago.*

Gifford, Henry. *Boris Pasternak: A Critical Study.* New York: Cambridge University Press, 1977. Follows the stages in Pasternak's life and discusses works written in those stages to establish his achievements as a poet, writer of prose fiction, and translator. Chapters 12 and 13 deal with *Doctor Zhivago.*

Ivinskaya, Olga. *A Captive of Time.* Garden City, N.Y.: Doubleday, 1978. Ivinskaya, Pasternak's love in the last years of his life and the model for the character of Lara in *Doctor Zhivago*, provides a wealth of information about Pasternak and *Doctor Zhivago.*

Mallac, Guy de. *Boris Pasternak: His Life and Art.* Norman: University of Oklahoma Press, 1981. An extensive biography of Pasternak. The second part is devoted to Mallac's interpretation of the most important features of Pasternak's works. *Doctor Zhivago* is discussed in "Toward *Doctor Zhivago*."

Muchnic, Helen. "Boris Pasternak and the Poems of Yurii Zhivago." In *From Gorky to Pasternak.* New York: Random House, 1961. Muchnic discusses the poems appended to the novel as an integral and important part of the novel.

Rowland, Mary F., and Paul Rowland. *Pasternak's "Doctor Zhivago."* Carbondale: Southern Illinois University Press, 1967. This book-length interpretation of *Doctor Zhivago* attempts to clarify allegorical, symbolic, and religious meanings in the novel. Although some interpretations are not proven, most of them are plausible, making for fascinating reading.

Rudova, Larissa. *Understanding Boris Pasternak.* Columbia: University of South Carolina Press, 1997. A general introduction to the full range of Pasternak's works. While the book includes an analysis of *Doctor Zhivago*, Rudova seeks to correct the misconception that this novel was Pasternak's only contribution to world literature.

Sicher, Efraim. "The Father, the Son, and Holy Russia: Boris Pasternak, Hermann Cohen, and the Religion of *Doctor Zhivago.*" In *Jews in Russian Literature After the October Revolution: Writers and Artists Between Hope and Apostasy.* New York: Cambridge University Press, 2006. Describes how Pasternak and other Jews attempted to resolve the conflict between their Judaism and their place in the newly created Soviet Union.

Weir, Justin. *The Author as Hero: Self and Tradition in Bulgakov, Pasternak, and Nabokov.* Evanston, Ill.: Northwestern University Press, 2002. Weir analyzes *Doctor Zhivago*, Mikhail Bulgakov's *Master i Margarita* (1966-1967; censored version; uncensored version, 1973; *The Master and Margarita*, 1967), and Vladimir Nabokov's *Dar* (serial, 1937-1938; book, 1952; *The Gift*, 1963) to describe how character in these three Russian novels is defined as the act of writing itself.

Dodsworth

Author: Sinclair Lewis (1885-1951)
First published: 1929
Type of work: Novel
Type of plot: Social realism
Time of plot: 1920's
Locale: United States and Europe

Principal characters:
SAM DODSWORTH, an American manufacturer
FRAN DODSWORTH, his wife
EMILY, their daughter
BRENT, their son
KURT OBERSDORF, Fran's lover
CLYDE LOCKERT, Fran's admirer
EDITH CORTRIGHT, Sam's friend

The Story:

In 1903, Sam Dodsworth marries Fran Voelker, whom he met at the Canoe Club while he was assistant superintendent at the Zenith Locomotive works. Five years later, Sam became vice president and general manager of production for the Revelation Automobile Company. By 1925, the Dodsworths have two children, Emily, who is about to be married, and Brent, who is studying at Yale. When Sam sells his factory to the Unit Automotive Company, he and Fran decide to go to Europe for a leisurely vacation, a second honeymoon.

The first night out on the S.S. *Ultima*, Sam meets Major Clyde Lockert in the smoking room. Lockert, who says he grows cocoa in British Guiana, quickly becomes friends with Fran and, while Sam looks on like an indulgent parent, squires her about. He continues to see the Dodsworths after they arrive in London. Fran is snobbishly pleased when he takes them to visit his cousins, Lord and Lady Herndon. Between them, Fran and Lockert make Sam feel almost like an outsider. He is a failure at the dinner party the Herndons give, for he is unable to discuss cricket or polo, and he has no opinions about the Russian situation.

One evening, Hurd, manager of the London branch of the Revelation Motor Company, invites Sam to a gathering, along with about thirty representatives of American firms. Sam is surprised to learn that few of them want to go back to the United States except, perhaps, for a visit. They all prefer the leisure and freedom from moral restraint that their adopted land affords. These arguments make Sam see Europe in a different light.

When he returns to the hotel, he finds Fran in tears. Lockert took her out that evening and, on their return, tried to make love to her. Fran, ashamed of the situation and sure that Lockert will laugh at her, asks that they leave for France as soon as possible. They start four days later.

France is a new experience for Sam. When Fran is willing to go sightseeing, he is able to see Paris and observe its people. He is less satisfied when she chooses to be fashionable and take tea at the Crillon with other American tourists. The more he sees of the country, however, the more convinced Sam becomes that he cannot understand the French. In the back of his mind, he is afraid that his inability to accept foreign ways, and Fran's willingness to adopt them, will drive them apart. He feels lonely for his old friend Tubby Pearson, president of the Zenith Bank.

Before long, Fran has many friends among expatriate Americans of the international set. Given her constant visits to dressmakers and a portrait painter, as well as outings with the leisured young men who escort her and her friends, she

and Sam see less and less of each other. When he goes home for his college class reunion that summer, he leaves Fran to take a villa with one of her new friends. He is to join her again in the fall, so that they might go on to the East together.

Back in New York, Sam feels, at first, as if he has become a stranger to the life of noise and hurry he previously took for granted. Nor is he interested in the newest model Revelation that quite competently was developed without his aid. He discovers also that he and his son no longer share common ground. Brent is planning to sell bonds. The newly married Emily, her father observes, is the very capable manager of her own home and needs no assistance. Even Sam's best friend, Tubby Pearson, goes on without him to new poker-playing and golfing companions.

At first, his letters from Fran are lively and happy. Then she quarrels with the friend who shares her villa over one of their escorts, Arnold Israel, a Jew. Sam grows increasingly anxious as he realizes that the man is trailing Fran from one resort to another and that their relationship is becoming increasingly more intimate. He makes sailing reservations and cables his wife to meet him in Paris.

Sam has no difficulty discovering that his wife was unfaithful to him; she admits as much during their stormy reunion in Paris. With the threat that he will divorce her for adultery if she does not agree to drop Israel, he forces her to leave for Spain with him the following day.

The Dodsworths wander across Spain into Italy and, finally, on to Germany and Berlin, and Sam has ample time to observe his wife. Increasingly he notes her self-centeredness, her pretentiousness, but his pity for her restlessness makes him fonder of her. At the home of the Biedners, Fran's cousins in Berlin, the Dodsworths met Kurt Obersdorf, a ruined Austrian nobleman. Kurt takes them to places of interest in Berlin and becomes Fran's dancing companion.

When the news comes that the Dodsworths are grandparents, for Emily now has a boy, they do not sail for home. In fact, they do not tell their friends of the baby's birth because Fran fears that, as a grandmother, she will seem old and faded to them. When Sam goes to Paris to welcome Tubby and his wife, abroad for the first time, Fran remains in Berlin.

Sam and Tubby enjoy themselves in Paris. Then Sam, driven by a longing to see his wife, flies back to Berlin. That night, Fran announces that she and Kurt decided to marry and that she wants a divorce. Sam agrees, on the condition that she wait a month before starting proceedings. Sadly, Dodsworth leaves for Paris and from there goes on to Italy. While he is sitting on the piazza in Venice and reading one of Fran's letters, he sees Edith Cortright, a widow whom the Dodsworths met during their earlier trip to Italy. Edith invites Sam home to tea with her, and on his second visit, he tells her about his separation from Fran.

Sam spends most of the summer with Edith and her Italian friends. He begins to gain a new self-confidence when he finds that he is liked and respected by these new acquaintances, who admire him and are satisfied with him as he is. He grows to love Edith, and they decide to return to America together. Then Sam receives a letter from Fran telling him that she dropped divorce proceedings because Kurt's mother objects to his marriage to a divorced American.

Without saying good-bye to Edith, Sam rejoins Fran, homeward bound. He tries patiently to share her unhappiness and loneliness, but before long, Fran is her old self, implying that Sam is at fault for the failure of their marriage and flirting with a young polo player aboard ship. After breakfast one morning, Sam sends a wireless to Edith, making arrangements to meet her in Venice. When the boat docks in New York, Sam leaves his wife forever. Three days later, he sails again to Italy and to Edith.

Critical Evaluation:

Sinclair Lewis was born into the American middle class, and his novels suggest that he both loved and detested his own kind, a crucial fact in understanding the unevenness of his satirical portraits. The critic Alfred Kazin views Lewis, together with Sherwood Anderson, as new realists—post-World War I reporters freed by the war into a struggle for "freedom of conduct" in middle America. Both writers, liberating forces in American literature of the 1920's, made "transcriptions of average experience," sometimes reproducing it and sometimes parodying it, but always participating in the native culture in the course of revealing its shortcomings. A typical Lewis novel reflects a mixture of scorn and compassion for its characters.

Although Lewis published more than twenty novels, a play, short stories, and sketches between 1914 and his death in 1951, his reputation as an artist eventually came to rest on four novels of the 1920's: *Main Street* (1920), *Babbitt* (1922), *Arrowsmith* (1925), and *Dodsworth* (1929). The protagonists of these works continue to generate interest and empathy because Lewis's feeling for the characters as human beings overrode his abiding skepticism. As a result, these characters are memorable, living individuals whose natures and problems transcend caricature and the topical.

Dodsworth, whose working title was *Exile*, was written in Europe, where Lewis had journeyed in the aftermath of his ruined marriage. While there he found or imagined that he found a culture superior to that of America's half-educated,

anti-intellectual boosters. Lewis's strong if troubled vision of middle America appears to have come from a deep sense of his own inferiority. Although he was the first American to receive the Nobel Prize in Literature, he later remarked that it ruined him; he could not "live up to it." This sense of native inferiority and resulting attempts to ensure self-respect and love are duplicated in Sam Dodsworth's experiences in Europe. Lewis blends autobiography with fiction in a well-controlled third-person narrative technique in *Dodsworth*, focusing primarily on the protagonist and creating a fully realistic account of Sam's travels that simultaneously documents the journeys and reasserts Sam's value as a human being.

Lewis sees Sam idealistically, for the most part, but so skillfully that the romantic and nostalgic are veiled by the realistic surface of events. Sam is the post-Victorian embodiment of American virtue. He is essentially honest, doggedly willing to remain open to new experience, boyish in his sincere if awed appreciation of femininity and womanliness, but reluctant to be henpecked forever. His restrained physical courtship of Edith Cortright entails only kissing her hands. He is reserved, well-mannered, and admirably dignified for an American, even while clutching his Baedeker. By contrast, most other American male characters are presented as inferior if not nefarious. Arnold Israel engages in questionable financial pursuits and is sensual and more European than the Europeans. Tubby Pearson is the perennial adolescent whose idea of humor is to address French waiters as "Goosepeppy" and to ask for fricassée of birds' nests. Brent, the Dodsworths' son, decides to live by selling bonds, hoping to reach the "hundred and fifty thousand a year class."

Most significant in the characterization of Sam, however, is his devotion to a work ethic of substance, which proves to be his salvation. Sam slowly but persistently weighs his values against those of older cultures: England, France, Italy, Spain, and Germany. Europeans know wine, history, women, politics, and are not afraid of things theoretical, even socialism. Therefore, they can just "be," that is, rest in the self-confidence of their familial and cultural heritage. Americans, however, Sam dimly realizes, are born apostles and practitioners of technology. They must "do." Forces beyond their knowledge and control harness their dreams and energies. Their destiny is to build more and better autos, plumbing, and electrical appliances. Sam and Edith decide to return to Zenith to work but not on what Sam calls "kitchy banalities."

Lewis uses architecture as the symbol of Sam's new life and work. In Europe, Sam, becoming absorbed in architecture, observes and sketches bridges, towers, and doorways.

He is impressed by their lines, their strength, their beauty, but he recognizes that they are European. Rather than return to Zenith to build a phony pastiche of villas and chalets in the San Souci development, Sam and Edith talk of building homes for Americans, native to the soil and spirit. Optimistically, Edith cries that the American skyscraper is the only new thing in architecture since the Gothic cathedral. Working together, their future promises to be a sharp contrast to that of the pitiful Fran, to whom all culture was interesting as "social adornment."

Occasionally, Lewis abandons the detached third-person narrative technique to speak directly to the reader, indulge in satirical comments about travelers, and provide a series of descriptions of American tourists complete with names in the comedy of humors tradition. Evident also are some forced metaphors, a few poorly integrated references to "morality hounds" in America or to the absurdities of Prohibition. Nevertheless, Lewis endows the novel with its power basically by making Sam a sympathetic, authentic American whose life matters to him and to the reader.

"Critical Evaluation" by Mary H. Hayden

Further Reading

Bloom, Harold, ed. *Sinclair Lewis*. New York: Chelsea House, 1987. Collection of critical essays on Lewis's work, including an important study of *Dodsworth* by Martin Light, who sees the novel as one of Lewis's strongest achievements and one that resolved the tension in his work between romance and realism. Bloom's introductory essay praises *Dodsworth* as an underrated masterpiece. Includes selected bibliography.

Bucco, Martin, ed. *Critical Essays on Sinclair Lewis*. Boston: G. K. Hall, 1986. Collection of criticism that begins with early reviews and goes on to include later critics. A useful essay by Robert L. Coard analyzes *Dodsworth* as a generic popular novel of the early twentieth century.

Grebstein, Sheldon Norman. *Sinclair Lewis*. New York: Twayne, 1962. Standard introductory study of Lewis, with selected bibliography. Praises *Dodsworth* and *Arrowsmith* as being Lewis's best works for having the best realized and most credible characters.

Hutchisson, James M. *The Rise of Sinclair Lewis, 1920-1930*. University Park: Pennsylvania State University Press, 1996. Focuses on Lewis's career in the 1920's, when he wrote *Dodsworth* and the other novels that earned him the Nobel Prize in Literature. Hutchisson examines the techniques Lewis used to create his novels, focusing on *Dodsworth* in chapter 5.

_____, ed. *Sinclair Lewis: New Essays in Criticism*. Troy, N.Y.: Whitston, 1997. Includes James Williams's essay "Gopher Prairie or Prairie Style? Wright and Wharton Help Dodsworth Find His Way Home," as well as essays on many of Lewis's other novels and an annotated bibliography of Lewis studies from 1977 through 1997.

Lingeman, Richard R. *Sinclair Lewis: Rebel from Main Street*. New York: Random House, 2002. A critical biography that includes analysis of Lewis's novels. Lingeman provides a detailed description of Lewis's unhappy life.

Lundquist, James. *Sinclair Lewis*. New York: Frederick Ungar, 1973. A general study, which places Lewis's novels in their social context and views the writer as someone who contributed to American culture's growing self-awareness. Examines *Dodsworth* as a powerful social document in which Lewis responded to social changes in the United States. Includes selected bibliography.

Schorer, Mark. *Sinclair Lewis: An American Life*. New York: McGraw-Hill, 1961. Thoroughly researched study of Lewis's life and work, an indispensable reference. Explores the autobiographical aspects of *Dodsworth*, which Schorer places in the context of Lewis's role in the transformation of American manners, morals, and intellectual assumptions.

Dog Soldiers

Author: Robert Stone (1937-   )
First published: 1974
Type of work: Novel
Type of plot: Social realism/social criticism
Time of plot: Early 1970's
Locale: Saigon, Vietnam; Southern California; New
     Mexico

Principal characters:
JOHN CONVERSE, a frustrated playwright who goes to
     Vietnam for ideas and ends up smuggling heroin
RAY HICKS, a merchant marine and friend of Converse
     who agrees to transport the heroin to the United States
MARGE, Converse's wife and accomplice
ANTHEIL, a corrupt federal regulatory agent who uses
     Converse to smuggle his heroin
DANSKIN, the most vicious of Antheil's thugs
DIETER BECHSTEIN, Hicks's former *rōshi*, or master of Zen
     Buddhism, and the leader of a failed commune

The Story:

John Converse, once an up-and-coming playwright, has not written a successful play in almost a decade. He begrudgingly works as a sensationalist journalist at his father-in-law's tawdry tabloid, *Nightbeat*. Converse has convinced himself and his employer that an assignment as a foreign correspondent in Vietnam will benefit both the magazine and his own career as a playwright. He has been in Vietnam for eighteen months, working and looking for inspiration to overcome his writer's block. He stays in touch with his wife, Marge, though letters. Marge works at an adult theater and is pronarcotics; the two of them have an open marriage and a young daughter named Janey.

Converse's former lover and present narcotics connection in Saigon is an American named Charmian, a judge's daughter who left Washington after her involvement in a political scandal. After acquiring uncut heroin from Charmian and briefly discussing a plan to smuggle the drug to the United States, Converse joins Jill and Ian Percy for drinks and dinner.

Ian Percy is an Australian agronomist who has been in Vietnam for fifteen years, working for any world organization that would hire him. Converse and Ian enter into an argument about the life and country of Vietnam. Ian takes offense and reacts strongly to Converse's flippant attitude and callous remarks about the war and its victims. Ian maintains that Converse has not been in the country long enough to make jokes about it, and Converse rebuts that his presence at a fragmentation bombing in Cambodia gives him license to say whatever he wants. During dinner, a bomb goes off on the street, shaking the restaurant and sending people outside to survey the damage, count the death toll, and watch the police quickly secure the area with barbed wire.

Converse meets an old acquaintance named Ray Hicks on the American base of My Lat, where they discuss the details of transporting the drugs to the United States. Hicks, a merchant marine on his third tour of duty, is a follower of the philosophies of Friedrich Nietzsche, as well as of Zen Buddhism and the code of the feudal Japanese samurai. A volatile yet highly resourceful man, Hicks delivers the heroin to Converse's house in Berkeley, California, but notices that he is being followed. Soon after he arrives, two men claiming to be special investigators break into the house to seize the drugs.

The men work for Antheil, a corrupt federal agent. Hicks finds out from the men that the heroin deal was arranged by Antheil's connection in Saigon. Following a violent struggle, Hicks contains the men long enough for him, Marge, and Janey to escape. Janey is taken to safety after Hicks explains to Marge that they are in danger and must go into hiding. Hicks drives them deep into the mountains, where he has a vehicle and a hidden arsenal ready. They drive to San Francisco to see Eddie Peace, a sleazy man with many shady connections, who Hicks hopes will be able find a buyer for the heroin.

While Hicks and Marge (who is already a prescription pill addict) are sampling the heroin and waiting to hear from Eddie, Converse arrives home to find his apartment a mess and his wife and daughter gone. Converse is investigating the fate of his family when Danskin and his men abduct him. Attempting to obtain information regarding the whereabouts of their heroin, they drug Converse, beat him, and burn him on a hot stove; they then leave. In the middle of a conversation with the women who temporarily watched after Janey, Converse flashes back to the fragmentation bombing in Cambodia. He recalls an epiphany in which he realized that the physical world is a deathtrap—appropriately so, because human arrogance warrants annihilation.

Hicks and Marge are awakened without warning when Eddie Peace shows up accompanied by a proper-looking young couple named Gerald and Jody. Gerald wants to write a candid and gritty piece on the booming heroin scene, and he feels that he must experience the drug before attempting to write about it. After injecting everyone else with heroin, Hicks purposefully shoots the drug into Gerald's vein, knowing it will cause him to overdose. Too drugged to help her husband, Jody watches the scene with bewilderment. Hicks and Marge speed away, leaving Jody and Eddie to deal with Gerald. Overwhelmed by what has just happened, Marge asks Hicks why he would do something so terrible. Hicks responds that he was an American soldier who watched his fellow patriots die, while Gerald and Jody were simply yuppie "Martians." Hicks thus feels justified in killing Gerald.

Hicks takes Marge into the mountains of New Mexico to the home and former commune of his Buddhist master, or *rōshi*, Dieter. Although Dieter's mountain home is a fortress rigged with lights and speakers to scare off intruders, Dieter maintains that he no longer deals in any type of drug other than psychedelic mushrooms, which he uses for "spiritual" purposes.

Meanwhile, Antheil's men, Danskin and Smitty, have forcefully enlisted Converse to help them reclaim their drugs. Antheil and his men eventually track Hicks, Marge, and the heroin to Dieter's commune, and a face-off on the mountain ensues. Antheil makes Converse tell Marge that they have Janey and will hurt her if she and Hicks do not cooperate. Realizing that Marge is going to relinquish the heroin, Hicks removes it from her bag and replaces it with sand. As Marge makes her way to Converse and Danskin with what she thinks is the heroin, Hicks hides real drugs in a cave. Hicks is shot in the chest, but he reaches Converse and Marge and tells them to take his truck and meet him on the other side of the mountain so he can return and get the heroin. As he makes his way to the appointed meeting place, he begins to philosophize and hallucinate as a result of his blood loss. Converse and Marge find Hicks dead on the tracks and leave both him and the heroin for Antheil to find.

Critical Evaluation:

Written shortly after the end of the Vietnam War, *Dog Soldiers* is Robert Stone's scathing critique of a 1970's counterculture that shifted away from the "peace, love, and happiness" of the 1960's into a degraded generation of heroin addicts. The book's epigraph and title refer to those who suffer under hardship but ultimately possess the will to survive. They are taken from Joseph Conrad's *Heart of Darkness* (1899 serial, 1902 book), a late nineteenth century novel crit-

icizing Belgian imperialism in Africa. Stone lauds both Conrad and Ernest Hemingway as two of his major literary influences, and he references both authors—indirectly through the novel's themes and style and directly within the narrative itself. Winner of the National Book Award in 1975, *Dog Soldiers* retains its position as a highly regarded commentary exposing the Vietnam War's detrimental effects on American idealism.

John Converse goes to Vietnam not for patriotic or idealistic reasons but because he is depressed by his literary failure and disillusioned with life in general. In the eighteen months he is there, he witnesses the death and destruction of war yet deems it a necessary punishment for humanity's hubris. Converse makes the decision to enter the world of drug smuggling partly to impress Charmian and partly to impress himself. He has no agency—no drive to devote his time to positive action—and as a result, the danger involved in drug smuggling appeals to his amoral and fatalistic sensibilities. Converse recruits both his wife and an old merchant marine buddy to aid in his scheme, which quickly falls apart and spirals into an expedition that has dire consequences. The drug hopelessly ensnares Marge, and even Hicks, with his iron will and determined mind, falls prey to the power it represents. Stone's characters are rapidly drawn into the dark subculture of heroin users and suppliers, illustrating the sinister attraction of a substance that was claiming an increasing number of Americans every year.

Both Converse and Hicks are plagued with existential dilemmas throughout the novel. Converse is a selfish, corrupt, and weak man, who is ruled by fear and who is frankly indifferent to the suffering of others. He lacks a moral center and is therefore without compassion. Hicks is Converse's foil: They are equally callous, but Hicks acts out of a strong conviction rather than apathy, so he is the more sympathetic or likeable character. In following Zen Buddhism, Nietzschean philosophy, and the Bushido code of the samurai, Hicks knowingly detaches himself from theistic ideals of crime and punishment. Walking to his death, Hicks philosophizes about nature, power, suffering, and death and comes to believe that he has the ability to absorb his pain and that of others into himself, making him symbolic of Christ. He fights and dies so that Marge and Converse, although not necessarily deserving of his sacrifice, can live.

Stone has stated in an interview that morality is inherent in fiction writing: Every page requires the author to make some kind of decision, and, in making a choice, the author invariably chooses or favors one alternative over another. Within *Dog Soldiers*, those characters that occupy positions of power often abuse that power; this trend represents a comment upon U.S. involvement in the Vietnam War. Moreover, Stone's decision to posit Antheil as Charmian's coconspirator in the drug smuggling ring allows him to illustrate the corruptive power of heroin in the 1970's.

In Stone's portrayal, addictions and monetary prospects infiltrate every aspect of society, as dramatized in the characters of Antheil, the governmental regulatory agent turned drug lord; Gerald, the upper-class writer who feels compelled to explore the underbelly of drug culture; and Marge, who once worked in the Anthropology Department at the University of California but who settles for prescription pills and a job at a porn theater. In the early 1970's, many people viewed the era of war, death, and moral decline surrounding the Vietnam War as apocalyptic. Stone recognized the demoralization of American society that resulted from the occupation of Vietnam and felt it incumbent upon himself to illustrate the steady decline of morality that accompanied the increasing flow of narcotics in the United States.

Lydia E. Ferguson

Further Reading

Elliot, Emory. "History and Will in *Dog Soldiers, Sabbatical*, and *The Color Purple*." *Arizona Quarterly: A Journal of American Literature, Culture, and Theory* 43 (1987): 197-217. Discusses *Dog Soldiers* as a neorealist text in which the characters are devoid of free will as the Vietnam War devastates American idealism.

Giles, James R. "'The Battle of Bob Hope' and 'The Great Elephant Zap': Robert Stone's *Dog Soldiers*." In *The Spaces of Violence*. Tuscaloosa: University of Alabama Press, 2006. An examination of the representation of mental, physical, and social spaces within the novel.

Karagueuzian, Maureen. "Irony in Robert Stone's *Dog Soldiers*." *Critique: Studies in Contemporary Fiction* 24 (1983): 65-73. Engages in a close reading of the irony existent in the names and occupations of the main characters, the narratives of Converse and Hicks, and the overarching story of American culture in relation to the Vietnam War.

Shelton, Frank W. "Robert Stone's *Dog Soldiers*: Vietnam Comes Home to America." *Critique: Studies in Contemporary Fiction* 24 (1983): 74-81. Discusses the novel's Vietnam backdrop as secondary to Stone's portrayal of the war's effect on American society. Argues that themes often associated with war, such as moral conflict and political subterfuge, are beyond the scope of the novel and its critique of Darwinism within a corrupted culture.

Stone, Robert. Interview by Maureen Karagueuzian. *TriQuarterly* 53 (1982): 248-258. Stone discusses literary influences and the themes and ideas present in his work, primarily *Dog Soldiers*. Talks candidly about issues regarding the United States military, existentialism, the religious structure of the world, and the automatic morality that results in fiction writing.

Dog Years

Author: Günter Grass (1927-   )
First published: Hundejahre, 1963 (English translation, 1965)
Type of work: Novel
Type of plot: Social realism
Time of plot: Mid-1920's to mid-1950's
Locale: Free City of Danzig

Principal characters:
EDUARD "EDDI" AMSEL, a scarecrow builder
WALTER MATERN, his "blood" brother and sometime protector
HARRY LIEBENAU, a poet and playwright
URSULA "TULLA" POKRIEFKE, his cruel and promiscuous cousin
JENNY BRUNIES, an orphan who becomes a ballerina
ANTON MATERN, Walter's father
HERR BRAUXEL, a mine owner
SENTA, a black dog
HARRAS, Senta's offspring
PRINZ, Harras's offspring, given to Adolf Hitler

The Story:

Herr Brauxel operates a mine in which no ore is processed, yet Brauxel's employees report for work daily. During morning shifts, Brauxel creates a map of the Vistula, Poland's longest river, which empties into the Baltic Sea in Gdansk. As he shapes the course of the river on his desk out of various objects, Brauxel relates the story of two young friends, Walter Matern and Eduard "Eddi" Amsel, growing up along the Vistula from the mid-1920's to mid-1930's.

Walter is Roman Catholic and the son of a local miller with clairvoyant powers gained from listening to flour mealworms. Eddi is half-Jewish and the son of a prosperous merchant. The boys have exchanged oaths as blood brothers, and Walter, known as the Grinder for his habit of grinding his teeth, acts as protector of pudgy Eddi. The two comrades often play with Walter's black dog, Senta—a German shepherd who is also part wolf—alongside the river where Eddi salvages debris to build lifelike, incredibly effective scarecrows that he rents or sells to local farmers. He invests the money he earns to make even more elaborate and grotesque scarecrows.

Poet-playwright Harry Liebenau, son of a carpenter, writes letters to his cousin Ursula "Tulla" Pokriefke, but he never sends them. Harry's missives relate his memories from the mid-1930's until the end of World War II in 1945. Like the older boys, Harry also has a black dog, Harras, the offspring of Senta.

Harry's letters detail ominous signs of change: Germany has absorbed Danzig, flags with swastikas have blossomed, and Hitler Youth groups are beginning to appear. Harras sires a pup named Prinz, who is presented as a gift to Adolf Hitler. Meanwhile, Walter, after a stint with the communists and a fling as an actor, joins the paramilitary Nazi brown shirts. In disguise, Walter and his comrades attack Eddi, who has been making mechanical figures that mock the Nazis, and knock out all of his teeth.

Eddi, grown wealthy from an inheritance, moves to Berlin under the name Hermann Haseloff and has his teeth replaced with gold dentures (earning him the nickname Goldmouth). As Hermann, he becomes a ballet impresario while coaching his star performer, Jenny Brunies. Walter marches with the German army in the invasion of Poland that begins World War II. He is later wounded, after which he is assigned to an artillery unit in Danzig, where he encounters teenager Harry, an auxiliary.

Harry's cousin Tulla sleeps around, hoping to become pregnant; she eventually does, but has a miscarriage. Jenny's feet are crushed during an Allied air raid, ending her ballet career. Walter deserts to the Allies, while Harry joins the armored infantry and is wounded while participating in many battles. With the war in its final throes, Prinz deserts the doomed Hitler.

Walter is released from a prisoner-of-war camp and wends his way home, intending to settle old scores. A black dog (a disheveled Prinz) follows him, and Walter names him Pluto. Walter, with Pluto, visits former acquaintances, upon whom Walter wreaks revenge. He spreads gonorrhea and fathers a child while sleeping with erstwhile friends' wives and daughters. Meantime, Goldmouth sets up Walter's father, Anton, as a fortune teller. Germany's most important postwar businessmen visit Anton and receive advice that makes them successful. Walter reunites with his father in 1949 and builds an enterprise around the fortune-telling business. In 1953, Anton is kidnapped.

Walter, now unemployed, takes to the road again with Pluto. Not long after Brauxel & Co. introduces miracle glasses that allow youngsters to see adults as they really are, Walter lands a job as an actor on radio. He runs into Harry, who publicly subjects him to a humiliating confession of his sins. Walter deserts Pluto and flees to East Germany by rail. As he travels, he passes scarecrows in Eddi's distinctive style and sees a black dog racing the train.

When Walter arrives in East Berlin, he is met by the dog and a slim chain-smoker called Goldmouth. The two men go barhopping, and Goldmouth eventually reveals himself as Eddi. Walter and Eddi go to Brauxel & Co., where Eddi turns out to be Brauxel as well. The former mine is now a factory where Eddi creates mechanized scarecrows—representing the entire gamut of human emotions—to be released upon the world.

Critical Evaluation:

Dog Years is the third work of the Danzig trilogy, following Günter Grass's first novel, *Die Blechtrommel* (1959; *The Tin Drum*, 1961), and his novella *Katz und Maus* (1961; *Cat and Mouse*, 1963). All three works revolve around the former free state where the author was born and raised, and all deal roughly with the same time period: the years leading up to World War II, the war itself, and the years immediately following the war. A sprawling, dense, difficult work, *Dog Years* is a novel of multiple layers that—prefiguring the theme of the author's later confessional memoir, *Beim Häuten der Zwiebel* (2006; *Peeling the Onion*, 2007)—adds depth, texture, and flavor with each layer penetrated.

At its most basic, *Dog Years* is a rollicking tale of sweeping dimensions in the manner of François Rabelais, Miguel de Cervantes, or Jonathan Swift. By turns deadly serious, playfully philosophical, and mordantly satirical, the novel is first a study of interacting character types. The sensitive artist (Eddi), self-absorbed actor (Walter), naïve poet-playwright (Harry), bubbly ballerina (Jenny), stoic miller (Anton), and the rest are profoundly and individually affected by events over which they have no control. Each is swept up into the prewar fervor of a Teutonic military renaissance under the Nazis, where extraordinary measures become everyday occurrences. Each is churned in the horror of a global conflict that begins triumphantly and ends disastrously for Germany. Survivors are spit into a ruined wasteland and left to fend for themselves. The novel contains passages that have become Grass's trademarks: vivid description and startling brutality.

Grass also uses symbols in the novel. Three primary motifs recur: rivers, scarecrows, and dogs. For Grass, rivers represent ancient constants—indifferent to changing borders—in a fast-moving modern world. Equally important to the plot is the Vistula River, which has a real presence: It delivers the raw materials (dead animals, discarded clothing, broken furniture, and sodden paper that wash up on the dikes) for Eddi's first crude, but strangely effective, scarecrows.

Eddi's scarecrows insightfully capture some brainless aspect of human behavior that is incompatible with nature. Birds instinctively sense the scarecrows' built-in destructive essence and stay away, saving themselves by obviating the need for harsher crop-preserving methods such as nets, guns, or poison. Dogs, particularly the half-wolf line of black German shepherds in the novel, represent a meeting point between humans and nature. Senta, Harras, and Prinz all carry the blood of both wild and domesticated animals and, though usually faithful, can be unpredictable because of this mix.

Dog Years is an especially apt title for the novel, as Grass plays off the words in numerous ways. First, Germany is "going to the dogs" (that is, it is deteriorating, becoming as unruly as a pack of wild animals). Second, at the height of anti-Semitism, those considered inferior were insulted by being compared to dogs, which will eat anything, even their own waste. Third, the war starts in 1939, just after the dog days of summer (a time of stagnation, when animals are most likely to become rabid). Fourth, a person who lives in ease and comfort is said to enjoy a dog's life. Fifth, those persons who survive do so with dogged determination. The term "dog years" reckons seven years of human life as equivalent to one year in a dog's life. In the novel, Grass compares the relative maturity between the two species. As a related point of historical interest, Adolf Hitler did own a German shepherd named Prinz in the early 1920's; Hitler's favorite dog during his years as führer was named Blondi.

The history, governments, politics, and philosophies of Germany and Danzig are woven throughout the novel as well

(Grass supplies several pages of endnotes detailing many of his references). Students of folklore will see a continuous theme of mythology in the novel, especially concerning barbaric pagan Baltic gods—Perkunos, Pilollos, and Potrimpos in particular—reanimated in Eddi's scarecrows. The scarecrows represent the bloodthirsty cult of Nazism. Readers interested in mass psychology will find considerable material of interest, as *Dog Years* is founded on an examination of the German psyche. The novel demonstrates how the national character could permit the possibility of tyrant worship; how it could allow the disenfranchisement, persecution, and elimination of undesirables; how it could encourage the denial of the senses (ignoring railroad cars crammed full of doomed humans, smoke from the fires of crematoriums at concentration camps, and mountains of human bones); and how it could adapt to collective guilt in the wake of the Holocaust.

Grass also employs rich language in *Dog Years*. In telling his many-faceted story, he pays homage to James Joyce's *Ulysses* (1922) by using some of the Irish author's techniques, such as "jamming words together" or mimicking real speech by cutting dialogue midsentence so the reader can mentally fill in missing words. Grass also mixes slang, profanity, distinctly German expressions, puns, and other forms of wordplay. His passages range from choppy and colloquial to eloquent and poetic. His tone alternates from stark realism to surrealism. In style and substance, *Dog Years* offers something for every taste, though the intensity of the flavor will vary according to the discrimination of the individual reader.

Jack Ewing

Further Reading

Mews, Siegfried. *Günter Grass and His Critics: From "The Tin Drum" to "Crabwalk."* New York: Camden House, 2008. A study of the 1999 Nobel laureate's body of work from 1959 to 2005, including *Dog Years*. Criticism of Grass's fiction and politics, particularly in the United States and Germany, has been both vehement and contradictory.

Preece, Julian. *The Life and Work of Günter Grass: Literature, History, Politics.* New York: Palgrave Macmillan, 2004. This biography relates the life of Grass to his fiction, showing how his experiences with the German SS had affected his thought processes first as a writer and later as a social critic and an active political campaigner.

Reddick, John. *The Danzig Trilogy of Günter Grass: A Study of "The Tin Drum," "Cat and Mouse," and "Dog Years."* Geneva, Ill.: Houghton Mifflin Harcourt, 1987. This critical examination of Grass's first three long-fiction works compares central characters, thematic approaches, and symbols and shows how, as a trilogy, the works constitute Grass's unified vision of the causes and effects of the war years and the Holocaust.

Sax, Boria. *Animals in the Third Reich: Pets, Scapegoats, and the Holocaust*. London: Continuum International, 2000. An interesting study that relates directly to *Dog Years*. This book delves into the ways animals have been used in both German myth and Nazi philosophy and practice. Argues that animals helped to shape German culture and politics during the 1930's and 1940's, including the literature of Grass and others.

Taberner, Stuart, ed. *The Cambridge Companion to Günter Grass*. New York: Cambridge University Press, 2009. This overview of Grass and his work was released in the wake of his revelations of his wartime duties with the notorious Waffen SS. Examines both the subsequent critical denunciation of Grass as a hypocrite and his defense by supporters who believe he is a true humanitarian and agitator for human rights.

A Doll's House

Author: Henrik Ibsen (1828-1906)
First produced: Et dukkehjem, 1879; first published, 1879 (English translation, 1880)
Type of work: Drama
Type of plot: Social realism
Time of plot: Nineteenth century
Locale: Norway

Principal characters:
TORVALD HELMER, a bank manager
NORA HELMER, his wife
MRS. LINDE, Nora's old school friend
KROGSTAD, a bank clerk
DR. RANK, a friend of the Helmers

The Story:

On the day before Christmas, Nora Helmer busies herself with last-minute shopping, for this is the first Christmas since her marriage that she does not have to economize. Her husband, Torvald, is made manager of a bank and after the New Year their money troubles are over. She buys a tree and plenty of toys for the children and even indulges herself in some macaroons, her favorite confection, although Torvald does not entirely approve. He loves his wife dearly, but he regards her very much as her own father did, as an amusing doll—a plaything.

It is true that she does behave like a child sometimes in her relations with her husband. She pouts, wheedles, and chatters because Torvald expects these things; he would not love his wife without them. Actually, seven years earlier Nora demonstrated that she had the courage of a mature, loving woman. Just after her first child was born, when Torvald was ill and the doctor said that he would die unless he went abroad immediately, she borrowed the requisite two hundred and fifty pounds from Krogstad, a moneylender. She forged to the note the name of her father, who was dying at the time, and convinced Torvald that the money for his trip came from her father. However, Krogstad was exacting, and since then she devised various ways to meet the regular payments.

When Torvald gives her money for new dresses and such things, she never spends more than half of it, and she finds other ways to earn money. One winter she does copying, which she keeps a secret from Torvald.

Krogstad, who is in the employ of the bank of which Torvald is now manager, is determined to use Torvald to advance his own fortunes. Torvald dislikes Krogstad, however, and is just as determined to be rid of him. The opportunity comes when Christina Linde, Nora's old school friend, applies to Torvald for a position in the bank. Torvald resolves to dismiss Krogstad and hire Mrs. Linde in his place.

When Krogstad discovers that he is to be fired, he calls on Nora and tells her that if he is dismissed he will ruin her and her husband. He reminds her that the note supposedly signed by her father is dated three days after his death. Frightened at the turn matters take, Nora pleads unsuccessfully with Torvald to reinstate Krogstad in the bank. Krogstad, receiving from Torvald an official notice of his dismissal, writes a letter in which he reveals the full details of Nora's forgery. He drops the letter in the mailbox outside the Helmer home.

Torvald is in a holiday mood. The following evening they are to attend a fancy dress ball, and Nora is to go as a Neapolitan fisher girl and dance the tarantella. To divert her husband's attention from the mailbox outside, Nora practices her dance before Torvald and Dr. Rank, an old friend. Nora is desperate, not knowing quite which way to turn. She thinks of Mrs. Linde, with whom Krogstad at one time was in love. Mrs. Linde promises to do what she can to turn Krogstad from his avowed purpose. Nora thinks also of Dr. Rank, but when she begins to confide in him he makes it so obvious that he is in love with her that she cannot tell her secret. However, Torvald promises her not to go near the mailbox until after the ball.

What bothers Nora is not her own fate but Torvald's. She imagines herself already dead, drowned in icy black water, and pictures the grief-stricken Torvald taking upon himself all the blame for what she did and being disgraced for her sake. In fact, Mrs. Linde, by promising to marry Krogstad and look after his children, succeeds in persuading him to withdraw all accusations against the Helmers. She realizes, however, that sooner or later Nora and Torvald will have to come to an understanding.

The crisis comes when Torvald reads Krogstad's letter after their return from the ball. He accuses Nora of being a hypocrite, a liar, and a criminal and of having no religion, morality, or sense of duty. He declares that she is unfit to bring up her children and that she might remain in his household but will no longer be a part of it. When Krogstad's second letter arrives, declaring that he intends to take no action against the Helmers, Torvald's attitude changes, and with a sigh of relief he declares that he is saved.

For the first time, Nora sees her husband for what he is—a selfish, pretentious hypocrite with no regard for her position in the matter. She reminds him that no marriage can be built on inequality and announces her intention of leaving his house forever. Torvald cannot believe his ears and pleads with her to remain, but she declares she is going to try to become a reasonable human being, to understand the world—in short, to become a woman, not a doll to flatter Torvald's selfish vanity. She goes out and, with irrevocable finality, slams the door of her doll house behind her.

Critical Evaluation:

Although Henrik Ibsen was already a respected playwright in Scandinavia before the premiere of *A Doll's House*, it was this work that catapulted him to international fame. The earliest of Ibsen's social-problem plays, this drama must be read in its historical context to understand its impact not only on twentieth century dramaturgy but also on society at large.

Most contemporary theater up to the time, including Ibsen's earlier work, fell into two general categories: the historical romance and the so-called well-made (or "thesis") play. The well-made play was a contrived comedy of manners revolving around an intricate plot and subplots but ultimately suffocated by the trivia of its theme and dialogue as well as by its shallow characterization. There was also the occasional poetic drama—such as Ibsen's *Brand* (1866) and *Peer Gynt* (1867)—but poetic form was often the only distinction between these plays and historical romances, as the content tended to be similar.

Into this dramaturgical milieu, *A Doll's House* injected natural dialogue and situations, abstained from such artificial conventions as the soliloquy or "aside" and observance of the "unities" of time and place, and insisted on the strict logical necessity of the outcome without attempting to wrench events into a happy ending. These theatrical innovations constitute Ibsen's fundamental contribution to the form of realistic drama. This kind of drama emphasizes believability, yet there is no attempt to achieve the comprehensiveness of photographic reality; rather, realism is selective and strives for representative examples in recognizable human experience. Through selectivity, realism implicitly assumes a critical stance. Thus the Helmers' domestic crisis had, and still has, an immediate impact on theater audiences for being potentially true of the audience as well. Drama changed radically after *A Doll's House*, for which reason Ibsen is called the father of modern drama.

Ibsen's influence on twentieth century drama was twofold, for he combined both technique and content in the realism of *A Doll's House*. Specifically, Ibsen elevated playmaking to a level above mere entertainment by validating the respectability of plays about serious social issues. One of the most volatile issues of his day was the position of women, who throughout virtually all of Western society were at that time considered by law and by custom chattel of fathers and husbands. Women were denied participation in public life; their access to education was limited; their social lives were narrowly circumscribed; and they could not legally transact business, own property, or inherit. In the mid-nineteenth century, chafing under such restrictions, some women began to demand autonomy. They pushed for the right to vote and the opportunity for higher education and entry into the professions. By the last two decades of the nineteenth century, this had turned into open defiance, which in turn evoked outrage from many.

Against this turbulent background, Ibsen presented *A Doll's House*. The response was electric. On the strength of the play, suffragists construed Ibsen as a partisan supporter, and their opposition accused the playwright of propagandizing and being an agent provocateur. However, Ibsen was neither a feminist nor a social reformer. Indeed, Ibsen personally deplored the kind of emancipation and self-development that brought women out of the domestic sphere into the larger world; he saw women's proper role exclusively as motherhood. His feminist sympathies were but a facet of his realism. He did no more than try to describe the problems as he saw them; he did not attempt to solve them. Nevertheless, he had a sharp eye and many sharp words for injustice, and it was the injustice of Torvald's demeaning treatment of Nora—a deplorably common occurrence in real life, Ibsen conceded—that provided the impetus for the play.

In the raging debate over the morality of Nora's behavior, however, it is altogether too easy to neglect Torvald's dramatic function in the play. This smug lawyer/bank manager is meant to represent the social structure that decreed an inferior position for women. Torvald is, in effect, a symbol for male-dominated and authoritarian society. Thus he establishes "rules" for Nora—the petty prohibition against macaroons, for one, the requirement that she act like a child and believe in the rightness, empirical as well as ethical, of his view in all matters. (In fact, Ibsen remarks in his "Notes" for the play that men make the laws and judge a woman's conduct from a man's point of view, "as though she were not a woman but a man.") His contemptuous attitude toward Nora's intelligence and sense of responsibility—he calls her his "little lark," his "little squirrel," his "little featherbrain," his "little spendthrift," and so on—actually reflects the prevailing view that many men had of women: that they are owned property, playthings, dolls to be housed in toy mansions and be indulged, but only sparingly.

In this Neanderthal context, it is difficult not to view Torvald as a thoroughgoing villain. Like society, however, Torvald is not completely devoid of redeeming grace, for otherwise Nora would not have married him, or committed forgery at great personal risk and used her utmost ingenuity to protect him from shame. Nora is both sensible and sensitive, despite Torvald's disparaging insinuations, and her awareness of her own worth is gradually awakened as the play unfolds—and with it her sense of individual responsibility. When at last she insists on her right to individual self-development, the spoiled girl-doll becomes a full-fledged woman. She slams the door of the doll house in a gesture symbolic of a biblical putting away of childish things and takes her rightful place in the adult world. Needless to say, that slam shakes the very rafters of the social-domestic establishment, and the reverberations continue in the present. Such a powerful echo makes a powerful drama.

"Critical Evaluation" by Joanne G. Kashdan

Further Reading

Goldman, Michael. *Ibsen: The Dramaturgy of Fear*. New York: Columbia University Press, 1999. Analyzes dialogue, plot, and other elements of Ibsen's plays to demonstrate how he challenges his audience's opinions and expectations. Includes a discussion of *A Doll's House*.

Hornby, Richard. *Patterns in Ibsen's Middle Plays*. Lewisburg, Pa.: Bucknell University Press, 1981. A readable, helpful, and interesting discussion of *A Doll's House* is included in one chapter. Hornby indicates that the play's underlying idea is the "ethical leap" that informs its technical and aesthetic development.

Ledger, Sally. *Henrik Ibsen*. 2d ed. Tavistock, England: Northcote House/British Council, 2008. Includes a close reading of *A Doll's House*, placing the play within its cultural, historical, and intellectual contexts.

Mencken, H. L. Introduction to *Eleven Plays of Henrik Ibsen*. New York: Random House, 1950. Mencken's prose is worth reading for itself and especially so in this case for anyone interested in Ibsen. Mencken lauds *A Doll's House* and declares that it represents the full measure of Ibsen's contribution to the art of drama.

Meyer, Michael. *Ibsen: A Biography*. Garden City, N.Y.: Doubleday, 1971. A well-organized, readable, illustrated source with an annotated index. Includes frequent references to *A Doll's House*, especially in chapter 19. Meyer also discusses the continued focus on Ibsen's view of women's situation in a man's world, on the outcry against *A Doll's House*, and on the monetary return it brought the author.

Moi, Toril. "'First and Foremost a Human Being': Idealism, Theater, and Gender in *A Doll's House*." In *Henrik Ibsen and the Birth of Modernism: Art, Theater, Philosophy*. New York: Oxford University Press, 2006. A reevaluation of Ibsen, in which Moi refutes the traditional definition of Ibsen as a realistic and naturalistic playwright and describes him as an early modernist.

Robinson, Michael, ed. *Turning the Century: Centennial Essays on Ibsen*. Norwich, England: Norvik Press, 2006. Collection of the essays published in the journal *Scandinavica* during the past four decades, including discussions of Ibsen's style, language, and the reception of his plays in England.

Shafer, Yvonne, ed. *Approaches to Teaching Ibsen's "A Doll [sic] House."* New York: Modern Language Association of America, 1985. Useful for both nonspecialists and specialists. Provides a section about the materials available for a study of *A Doll's House* and a section on approaches to teaching it. Provides insight for understanding and interpreting the play.

Templeton, Joan. *Ibsen's Women*. New York: Cambridge University Press, 1997. Templeton examines the women characters in Ibsen's plays and their relationship to the women in the playwright's life and career. Chapter 5, "The Poetry of Feminism," is an analysis of *A Doll's House*.

Unwin, Stephen. *Henrick Ibsen's "A Doll's House": A Study-Guide*. London: Nick Hern, 2007. Focuses on production of the play. Contains a scene-by-scene description of the action and discussion of the play's characters, setting, staging, lighting, costumes, props, and furniture.

Dom Casmurro

Author: Joaquim Maria Machado de Assis (1839-1908)
First published: 1899 (English translation, 1953)
Type of work: Novel
Type of plot: Philosophical realism
Time of plot: Second half of the nineteenth century
Locale: Rio de Janeiro

Principal characters:
BENTO DE ALBUQUERQUE SANTIAGO (DOM CASMURRO), jealous husband
DONA GLÓRIA, mother of Bento
JOSÉ DIAS, member of Dona Glória's household
CAPITU, wife of Bento
EZEQUIEL ESCOBAR, friend of Bento
SANCHA, wife of Escobar
EZEQUIEL, son of Bento and Capitu

The Story:

Now in his fifties, Bento de Albuquerque Santiago is a withdrawn, diffident individual. He has had a successful law career and now lives alone in a comfortable suburb of Rio de Janeiro. Because of his retiring nature, neighbors have given him a nickname of mild mockery: Dom Casmurro, meaning "Lord Solitaire." Bento's father died when Bento was an infant, and the family moved from its plantation to the city. Bento's older brother has also died, and his widowed mother, Dona Glória, is ever attentive to Bento, her only remaining child.

Bento recalls events from his past. As a young boy, he overhears Dona Glória talking to José Dias, a member of her household, who relates that Bento is falling in love with a neighbor girl, Capitu (an abbreviation of Capitolina). Dona Glória, therefore, reconfirms her promise, made after the death of her first son, to send Bento to a seminary. Bento does not want to become a priest, but he enters the seminary. He and Capitu secretly swear they will one day marry.

At the school, Bento makes a new friend, Ezequiel Escobar, whom he admires for his force and masculinity. He confides in Escobar, confessing his passion for Capitu. They elaborate a plan to obtain a papal dispensation from Dona Glória's vow by paying for the education of an orphan. Both boys eventually leave the seminary. Bento becomes a lawyer,

studying in São Paulo. Escobar successfully enters business. Their friendship continues as Bento marries Capitu and Escobar marries Sancha, a friend of Capitu. Eventually, Escobar and Sancha have a daughter, named Capitolina, and Bento and Capitu have a son, whom they name Ezequiel. Dona Glória, who has become fond of Capitu, believes that she has fulfilled her vow, because she did place Bento in the seminary.

In an encounter with Sancha, Bento realizes he has an adulterous attraction to her. Escobar dies suddenly, drowning while swimming. At his funeral, Bento notes the concentrated attention with which Capitu contemplates their dead friend. Bento wonders whether his wife had an affair with Escobar. With the seed of this suspicion planted, as Ezequiel grows, Bento increasingly sees a resemblance between his son and Escobar. He becomes riveted with suspicions of Capitu's infidelity. Attending a production of William Shakespeare's *Othello, the Moor of Venice* (pr. 1604, pb. 1622), Bento does not see the misguided jealousy of the title character. Rather, he becomes more convinced of Capitu's guilt.

As the fury of his jealously mounts, Bento contemplates poisoning himself and then Ezequiel. He tells Ezequiel that the boy is not his legitimate offspring. Following that exchange, he confronts Capitu, making confused accusations against her of infidelity. They agree to a separation. However, to disguise this condition they depart with their son for an excursion in Europe. Capitu and Ezequiel remain in Europe, while Bento returns alone to Rio.

Grown to young manhood, Ezequiel returns to visit his father. He tells him of Capitu's death. Bento's reaction is to continue to note the similarity of Ezequiel to Escobar. The son departs and, on a trip to the Middle East, contracts typhoid and dies. The years pass and other members of Bento's family and entourage die. He is ever more isolated, yet, with the few acquaintances that still know and visit him, he remains fixated on the infidelity of Capitu. It is due to this isolation that his neighbors nickname him Dom Casmurro. Bento resolves to write a narrative of his life, which becomes *Dom Casmurro*.

Critical Evaluation:

Joaquim Maria Machado de Assis, one of Brazil's greatest writers, was born in Rio de Janeiro on June 21, 1839, and raised in straightened circumstances. The biracial Machado de Assis was of small stature and sickly physique. Nonetheless, he was ambitious and persistent, and he possessed an insightful, articulate intelligence and displayed singular qualities of discipline and character. A noted novelist of the time recognized the young Machado de Assis's precocious literary and personal talents and befriended him. Machado de Assis thus entered a literary circle of prominent writers that met at a bookstore, which served also as a publishing house. Employed in government service and rising in the bureaucracy, he married a white Portuguese woman in 1869, the most satisfying relationship of his life. In 1897, he was one of the principal founders of the Brazilian Academy of Letters, elected for life as its first president. Widowed in 1904, he died four years later, on September 29, from complications of chronic intestinal problems.

In numerous genres but especially novels and short stories, Machado de Assis developed an exceptional style and technique that offered precise, penetrating psychological analysis of the ambiguous motives and ironic consequences of human pursuits of love, desire, and material satisfaction. His work may be divided into two phases, an earlier romantic one and a later realist one. His first novel, *Resurreicão* (1872; resurrection) recounts a wealthy young man's love affair, fractured by jealousy, with a beautiful widow. For the rest of the decade, Machado de Assis produced in fiction and for the stage similar works that similarly explored the contradictions and dilemmas of love affairs among bourgeois youth.

After a prolonged illness at the end of the decade, the ro-

mantic writer evolved into a psychological realist. Still writing of romance, he focused on the causes, character, and evolution of an individual's emotions. The first novel in this new vein was *Memórias póstumas de Brás Cubas* (1881; *The Posthumous Memoirs of Brás Cubas*, 1951; better known as *Epitaph of a Small Winner*, 1952), in which a man of little distinction offers a delusional account of the achievements of his life. The work demonstrated Machado de Assis's growing skills in refined character analysis and a narrative dynamic that engaged readers in evaluative involvement. In the 1890's, Machado de Assis published *Quincas Borba* (1891; *Philosopher or Dog?*, 1954; also as *The Heritage of Quincas Borba*, 1954) and *Dom Casmurro*.

Returning to his earlier focus on the theme of jealousy, Machado de Assis analyzes the sentiment in *Dom Casmurro* with singular sophistication and perception. He approaches jealousy in terms of the validity of a character's assessment of circumstances and the trustworthiness of the evidence presented by such a character to readers of his narrative. The novel unfolds from Bento Santiago's perspective, as he recounts the events of his life and marriage. All the information a reader receives comes from the narrator, reflecting his perspective and interests. *Dom Casmurro* represents a culmination of enduring features that Machado de Assis skillfully elaborates and exposes: irony, self-absorption, dissembling, and callousness. The novel repeatedly teaches its readers that self-love and shallow self-absorption defeat needs for intimacy, accomplishment, self-knowledge, and even sanity.

Initially, *Dom Casmurro* seems to be entirely about jealousy, a husband's suspicions about the fidelity of his wife. Ultimately, however, it is about what certainty exists in one person's perception of another, as well as the causes of misunderstanding and its consequences. The involving theme of the work is not just whether Bento can trust Capitu but whether a reader can trust Bento. The novel traces the corrosive consequences of gnawing jealousy by portraying Bento losing love and family as a result of his fear of losing them. The ultimate assertion of the work is that rampant fear of loss causes loss.

The critical acclaim that *Dom Casmurro* has received can be attributed to the extraordinary manner by which Machado de Assis engages a reader as witness and judge of the central character's thoughts and actions.

Machado de Assis makes his readers into active respondents to the narrator, allowing them progressively to grasp the corrosive dilemma in which Bento has isolated himself. Bento's rage against Capitu and his fixation on her supposed infidelity cause his life to end in lonely ruin. He dare not confront the possibility that he wronged her, because it would mean confronting both his own ruin and that of his family. Readers become progressively involved as character witnesses to the self-absorption and weakness that bring about Bento's tortured state. Indeed, the more involved readers become, the more they develop as participants in the work, as evaluators of the narrator's veracity, rationality, and character.

The steadily growing pace of this readerly involvement and evaluation is among the most singular narrative and character features of the novel. Readers actively accompany the denouement of the narrative, becoming increasingly attentive to gestures and diction and alert to perspectives and thematic developments. It is the range and force of Machado de Assis's techniques for engaging readers not only in but also as the dynamics of the unfolding tale that constitute the singular accomplishment of the author's literary craftsmanship.

Machado de Assis has frequently been compared to master writers of his period such as Gustave Flaubert and Henry James. Those writers possessed progressively maturing literary techniques, which dominated their nuanced articulations of psychological insight and narrative complexity. Their need to define the moral axes of their characters motivated the drive to unravel the psychological complexity of individual actions and articulate such insight in subtle, precise prose. However, Machado de Assis leapt almost a century ahead of this time, to the edge of a postmodern dilemma: Where does the judgment of character dissolve into the relativity of any judgment of character? Machado de Assis confronted this dilemma by asserting the fundamental value of connectedness to others, demonstrating that disorientation advances as disconnection deepens. While Machado de Assis's achievement was in literature, his distinction lies in his humanity.

Edward A. Riedinger

Further Reading

Bloom, Harold. "Joaquim Maria Machado de Assis." In *Genius: A Mosaic of One Hundred Exemplary Creative Minds*. New York: Warner Books, 2002. Describes and locates Machado de Assis within a pantheon of major figures in world literature, recognizing how tardy has been recognition of his distinction.

Dixon, Paul B. *Retired Dreams: "Dom Casmurro," Myth, and Modernity*. West Lafayette, Ind.: Purdue University Press, 1989. Examines *Dom Casmurro* in terms of its underlying myths and suggests that the essential tension of the narrative relies on the play between the perspectives of reality and myth.

Fitz, Earl E. *Machado de Assis*. Twayne's World Authors 809. Boston: Twayne, 1989. Offers a concise overview of the life and times of Machado de Assis, summarizing and analyzing his principal works, which include not only novels but also short stories, plays, poetry, and journalism.

Graham, Richard. *Machado de Assis: Reflections on a Brazilian Master Writer*. Austin: University of Texas Press, 1999. Collection of four scholarly articles examining *Dom Casmurro*, Machado de Assis's political writing, and translations into English of his works.

Lisboa, Maria Manuel. *Machado de Assis and Feminism: Re-reading the Heart of the Companion*. Lewiston, N.Y.: Edwin Mellen Press, 1996. Examining nine novels of Machado de Assis, this study initially presents traditional interpretations and assumptions regarding his views on gender interactions, then provides a radical reinterpretation of these relations from a feminist theoretical perspective.

Maia Neto, José Raimundo. *Machado de Assis: The Brazilian Pyrrhonian*. West Lafayette, Ind.: Purdue University Press, 1994. Reviews the two phases (1861-1878 and 1879-1908) of Machado de Assis's fictional production, concentrating on the later phase and especially on the novels *Epitaph of a Small Winner* and *Dom Casmurro*.

Nunes, Maria Luisa. *The Craft of an Absolute Winner: Characterization and Narratology in the Novels of Machado de Assis*. Westport, Conn.: Greenwood Press, 1983. Details the effectiveness of Machado de Assis in creating characters in his novels through development of his narrative techniques and inherited Brazilian cultural traits.

Rabassa, Gregory. "Joaquim Maria Machado de Assis." In *If This Be Treason—Translation and Its Dysfunctions: A Memoir*. New York: New Directions Books, 2005. Noted translator of Spanish and Portuguese relates his experiences in translating numerous authors of modern classics; includes discussion of the subtleties and nuances in Machado de Assis's work.

Schwarz, Roberto. *A Master on the Periphery of Capitalism: Machado de Assis*. Durham, N.C.: Duke University Press, 2001. Analyzes the work of Machado de Assis from a Marxist perspective; scrutinizes *Epitaph of a Small Winner* for its challenges to nineteenth century Brazilian assumptions regarding class, emphasizing the novelist's devastating irony and narrative innovation.

Dombey and Son

Author: Charles Dickens (1812-1870)
First published: 1846-1848
Type of work: Novel
Type of plot: Social realism
Time of plot: Early nineteenth century
Locale: England

Principal characters:
MR. DOMBEY, a wealthy London merchant
PAUL, his son
FLORENCE, his daughter
EDITH GRANGER, his second wife
MR. CARKER, his trusted agent
WALTER GAY, the young man whom Florence loves

The Story:

Mr. Dombey is a stiff, dignified man who rarely shows emotion, but the birth of his infant son, who is named Paul, is cause for rejoicing. Mr. Dombey longed many years for a child who would become the Son of his mercantile firm of Dombey and Son. The fact that Mrs. Dombey dies shortly after the boy's birth does not particularly concern him; his attention centers entirely on the little infant. Mr. Dombey also has a daughter, Florence, but she means nothing to him, for she cannot take a place in the firm.

Little Paul is first given over to a wet nurse, but the woman is considered unreliable and is dismissed. After her dismissal, little Paul is cared for by Mr. Dombey's sister and one of her friends. Despite their vigilant care, however, the boy suffers from poor health. He is listless and never cares to play. At last, Mr. Dombey arranges to have him sent to a home at Brighton, together with his sister, to benefit from the sea air.

Paul loves his sister very much, and they are constant companions, but Paul's love for Florence only makes Mr. Dombey dislike the girl. He resents the fact that she is healthy when his son is not, and he feels that his daughter is coming between him and his son.

One weekend while Mr. Dombey is visiting at Brighton, Walter Gay, a young clerk in his firm, comes to the inn where Mr. Dombey and his children are dining. Some time before, the clerk rescued Florence from an old thief. Now his uncle is about to become a bankrupt, and Walter comes to ask for a loan to save his uncle's shop. Mr. Dombey lets little Paul, then six years old, make the decision. Paul asks Florence what he should do; she tells him to lend the money, and he does.

Shortly afterward, little Paul is placed in a private school at Brighton, where he is to be educated as quickly as possible. The pace of his studies proves too much for him, and before the year is out his health breaks down. Even after his father takes him home to London, he does not seem to grow any better. He dies a few months later, deeply mourned by his father and his sister, although for different reasons.

Mr. Dombey takes his son's death as a personal blow of fate to his plans. His sister and her friend become so concerned about him that they persuade him to take a trip to Leamington with Major Bagstock, a retired officer. While in Leamington, they meet Edith Granger, a young widow whose mother the major knew. Mr. Dombey begins to court Mrs. Granger, seeing in her a beautiful, well-bred young woman who will grace his household and provide him with an heir. Mrs. Granger, coaxed by an aged mother who is concerned for her own and her daughter's welfare, finally accepts Mr. Dombey, although she is not in love with him.

Florence saw young Walter several times since their meeting at Brighton. After her brother's death, she comes to look upon Walter as a substitute brother, despite his lowly station. Their friendship is broken temporarily when Mr. Dombey sends Walter on a mission to the West Indies. Weeks pass, and no word is heard of the ship on which he sailed. Everyone believes that it sank and that Walter drowned.

After Mrs. Granger accepts Mr. Dombey's suit, they begin to make plans for the wedding and for reopening the Dombey house in London. Edith Granger first meets Florence at the house. The two immediately become fast friends, even though Mr. Dombey dislikes his daughter and makes it plain that he does not want his wife to become too fond of the girl.

Mr. Dombey's second marriage is unsuccessful from the start. Edith is too proud to give in to Mr. Dombey's attempts to dictate to her and to his claim upon her as a piece of merchandise, and she resists him in every way. Dombey, who is too dignified to argue with her, begins to send his business manager, Mr. Carker, to tell his wife that he is dissatisfied with her conduct. Carker warns Mrs. Dombey that, unless she obeys Mr. Dombey, Florence will be the one to suffer. Edith thereupon becomes outwardly cool toward her stepdaughter, but she continues to resist her husband. Mr. Carker is dispatched to tell her that Mr. Dombey means to be obeyed in everything.

Edith revolts by ostensibly running off with Mr. Carker, her husband's most trusted employee, who is so far below Mr. Dombey socially that the blow hurts Mr. Dombey even more. When Florence tries to comfort her father, he rebuffs her cruelly, going so far as to strike her. She runs out of the house, knowing she no longer has a home or a father, and finds refuge in the shop owned by Sol Gills, Walter's uncle. Gills disappeared in search of his nephew, and his friend, an old ship's captain, is in charge. Captain Cuttle recognizes Florence and takes her in.

Mr. Dombey learns the whereabouts of his wife and Carker from a young woman whom Mr. Carker seduced and deserted. Mr. Dombey follows the pair to France but fails to locate them. Mr. Carker returns to England after Edith refuses to have anything to do with him. She had her revenge, she says, in ruining him and her husband. Mr. Carker tries to escape into the English countryside, but when he meets Mr. Dombey at a railway station, an accident occurs and Mr. Carker is killed by a train.

Florence continues to stay with Captain Cuttle, hoping that Walter will return, even though everyone gives him up for dead. Her faith is at last rewarded. Walter was picked up by a vessel bound for China. Shortly after his return, he confesses to Florence that he no longer feels toward her like a brother, for she became a woman during his absence. Realizing that she, too, fell in love with him, she accepts his proposal. Walter finds work as a clerk on a ship, and after their marriage, they sail on a ship bound for the East.

The failure of his marriage breaks Mr. Dombey's spirit, and he takes little interest in his firm from that time on. The firm is placed in a difficult position by some of the transactions Mr. Carker handled while he was Dombey's trusted agent. As a result of Mr. Carker's mismanagement and Dombey's lack of interest, the firm goes bankrupt. After the bankruptcy, Mr. Dombey stays alone in his house, sees no one, and gradually drifts into despair.

On the very day that Mr. Dombey decides to commit suicide, Florence returns to London from the East with her one-year-old son, who is named Paul, after his dead uncle. Florence and the baby cheer up Mr. Dombey, and he begins to take a new interest in life. Reconciled to his daughter, he realizes that she always loved him even when he was cruel to her. Walter succeeds in business, and all of them live together happily; his misfortunes make a changed man of Mr. Dombey.

Critical Evaluation:

Dombey and Son, which appeared after *Martin Chuzzlewit* (1843-1844), was Charles Dickens's effort to regain the pop-

ularity he had lost with the publication of his previous novel. *Martin Chuzzlewit*, which had heavily satirized America and Americans, had caused Dickens to lose a great deal of favor, much to Dickens's chagrin, who was by that time in something of a competition for the public's attention with another great Victorian novelist, William Makepeace Thackeray. *Dombey and Son* is unusual in Dickens's work for being set among a higher social level than his previous novels. For the first time, he indicated an interest in and a sympathy for the upper-middle classes and the aristocracy. The story is a very serious one, involving the downfall of a dignified merchant and the painful process by which he learns that love is more powerful than money. As is typical of Dickens, however, there is a large cast of characters providing a rich, sometimes humorous background to the central story.

In *Dombey and Son*, Dickens for the first time attempted to portray the full panorama of English society, from beggar to magnate, from baronet to housemaid. Although less successful than *Bleak House* (1852-1853) in expressing the connections between all levels of society, the novel has a prodigious scope.

The principal theme of the work is the relationship between parents and children, chiefly Mr. Dombey's relationship with Paul and Florence and subordinately those of various parents and their offspring, ranging in social station from Mrs. Skewton and Edith down to Mrs. Brown and her Alice. Each family situation is thrown into relief by contrast with another that is similar in social class yet utterly different in kind. Edith Granger, schooled almost from infancy to be "artful, designing, mercenary, laying snares for men," is shown in contrast with the son of Sir Barnet Skettles, whose parents willingly interrupt his studies at Dr. Blimber's academy in order to enjoy his company during their trip abroad. Mr. Dombey's crude attempt to mold his fragile son to a shape that does his father honor in the world's eyes contrasts with the honest and unpretentious course that Solomon Gills recommends to his nephew Walter: "Be diligent, try to like it, my dear boy, work for a steady independence, and be happy!" The miserable devices of greed that Mrs. Brown urges on her daughter as the only recourse of the poor is proven a lie by the love and warmth shown by Polly Toodle toward her erring son Rob.

The sad ends of Edith, little Paul, and Alice Marwood all result from the corruption of childhood by adult concerns and from the disregard of individuality in children, a view of them as things, counters in a game, or a hedge against destitution or mortality. Mr. Dombey views Paul as a little mirror of his own greatness. He expects his son to reflect himself— that is, to love him as he loves himself. In his stubborn individuality, Paul perceives the merits of Florence and turns to her; Mr. Dombey is amazed and outraged, because he sees Paul as an extension of himself and cannot conceive that the little boy could have a different opinion. In Mr. Dombey's own mind, no blame accrues to himself; he decides that Florence must be the cause of the "distortion" of Paul's feelings. In this way, she falls victim to her father's self-love and becomes the object of his hatred, almost a scapegoat for his repressed feelings of guilt about Paul's death; in his view, she destroyed Paul as a tool capable of advancing his father's self-approbation, the function for which his elaborate education was supposed to have prepared him.

Edith Granger, too, was formed in her youth to fulfill her mother's nasty ambitions. The shining ideal that both Mrs. Skewton and Mr. Dombey urge on their children is a certain standing in the eyes of the world, essentially an adult concern. In contrast, Walter's mentor in his own invincible childishness (he rebukes himself for being "old-fashioned") guides his charge in the path of honesty, which is the natural behavior of childhood. Young Paul is the chief exemplar of this virtue in the novel, and his resistance to corruption is likewise referable to that curious quality of being "old-fashioned." Paul was "born old"; he possesses that wisdom of extreme age that constitutes a return to the innocence of childhood. He is fey and resists classification. His obdurate honesty shows itself in his concern for first principles. When he inquires of his father what money can do and his father proudly replies that money can do anything, little Paul suggests two things it cannot do: bring back his mother or give him health. Then he asks the question again, still more pointedly: "What's money, after all?" as if to direct his father's attention to the extreme paltriness of those things that money can do, to that vain show that nurtures his father's pride. His father takes no notice of it then; it is not for him to learn from a child. Despised, neglected, and thought unfit to prepare for any great purpose, Florence has her brother's memory for a master and educates herself to his truth rather than to her father's ambition.

Dombey and Son is unique among Dickens's novels in its profusion of strongly drawn female characters. Indeed, the author seems intent on ringing the changes on female nature from best to worst. For the most part, these figures though vivid have but one dimension, but two characters evidence a greater depth of understanding than the author had previously achieved in his representation of women. One is the character of Florence, whose states of mind illustrate a classic psychological progression. Rejected by a loved parent, she reasons thus: "I am unloved, therefore unlovable." Her early conviction of unworthiness not only dictates her subse-

quent actions but indeed shapes the main plot of the novel. Florence eventually becomes the figure of ideal womanhood; she even displays talents of a housewife in Solomon Gills's parlor. She is truly good without being saccharine, a major advance in Dickens's treatment of women characters. Miss Tox is even more an unusual creation; Dickens had not previously produced a female character who was at once such an object of satire and so generally sympathetic. She comes in for her share of ridicule for her delusions about Mr. Dombey's intentions and for her genteel pretensions in general, but the author allows her the virtue of her consistency: "poor excommunicated Miss Tox, who, if she were a fawner and a toad-eater, was at least an honest and a constant one. . . ." She is as unlikely a vessel of kindness and simple wisdom as the dandy Toots or the exhausted aristocrat, Cousin Feenix; yet Dickens puts wisdom into their mouths as if to show that although corruption might seem to reign supreme everywhere, truth, though hidden, can flourish and even prevail.

"Critical Evaluation" by Jan Kennedy Foster

Further Reading

Andrews, Malcolm. *Dickens and the Grown-up Child.* Iowa City: University of Iowa Press, 1994. Sees *Dombey and Son* as a reflection of the world through a child's eyes, as well as making "familiar use of the child as an agent of redemption." Describes how Paul Dombey is radically different from earlier male children in Dickens's work.

Armstrong, Frances. *Dickens and the Concept of Home.* Ann Arbor, Mich.: UMI Research Press, 1990. Contains solid information on *Dombey and Son.* Focuses on the creative process of homemaking that increasingly leads Florence outside herself as the novel progresses. Concludes that Florence must make her own home "in the face of mental and physical abuse from the man that should be the center of that home."

Cain, Lynn. *Dickens, Family, Authorship: Psychoanalytic Perspectives on Kinship and Creativity.* Burlington, Vt.: Ashgate, 2008. Focuses on *Dombey and Son* and three other novels that Dickens wrote during the decade beginning in 1843, a period of feverish personal and professional activity. Cain argues that his representation of the family in these novels is a paradigm for his development as an author.

Donovan, Frank. *The Children of Charles Dickens.* London: Leslie Frewin, 1969. Good exploration of the themes of childhood and parenting in *Dombey and Son.* Sees Mr.

Dombey as a classic "rejective parent," whose rejection of Florence is done consciously, whereas his rejection of Paul is unconscious.

Hardy, Barbara. *Dickens and Creativity.* London: Continuum, 2008. Focuses on the workings of Dickens's creativity and imagination, which Hardy argues is at the heart of his self-awareness, subject matter, and narrative. *Dombey and Son* is discussed in chapter 8, "Crises of Imagination in *Oliver Twist, A Christmas Carol, Dombey and Son, Bleak House, Hard Times*, and *The Lazy Tour of Two Idle Apprentices*."

Jordan, John O., ed. *The Cambridge Companion to Charles Dickens.* New York: Cambridge University Press, 2001. Collection of essays with information about Dickens's life and times, analyses of his novels, and discussions of Dickens and language, gender, family, domestic ideology, the form of the novel, illustration, theater, and film.

Paroissien, David, ed. *A Companion to Charles Dickens.* Malden, Mass.: Blackwell, 2008. Collection of essays providing information about Dickens's life and work, including Dickens as a reformer, Christian, and journalist and Dickens and gender, technology, America, and the uses of history. Also includes the essay "*Dombey and Son*" by Brigid Lowe.

Shelston, Alan, ed. *"Dombey and Son" and "Little Dorrit."* Houndsmills, England: Macmillan, 1985. Provides a good introduction to the novel, with information on the origins of *Dombey and Son*, an overview of contemporary critical appraisals, and several important critical studies since 1941.

Dominique

Author: Eugène Fromentin (1820-1876)
First published: 1862 (English translation, 1932)
Type of work: Novel
Type of plot: Psychological
Time of plot: Nineteenth century
Locale: France

Principal characters:
DOMINIQUE DE BRAY, a gentleman
MADELEINE DE NIÈVRES, his beloved
AUGUSTIN, his tutor
OLIVIER D'ORSEL, his friend
JULIE, Madeleine's younger sister, in love with Olivier

The Story:

The narrator of the book first meets Dominique de Bray at Villeneuve. Dominique lives at the large Château des Trembles with his wife and two children. The mayor of the commune, he is shy, unpretentious, and a friend to all in the community. On St. Hubert's Day, Dominique is visited by Olivier d'Orsel, a wealthy, solitary man with captivating manners and a passion for luxury, who retired from social life. A few days after his visit, Olivier tries to commit suicide. This event leads Dominique to tell the narrator about himself.

Orphaned at an early age, Dominique grew up at Villeneuve. In his youth, he became a lover of the outdoors. He was cared for by Madame Ceyssac, his aunt, who provided him with a tutor named Augustin. The two differed greatly in temperament. Dominique was emotional, wild, and loved nature; Augustin was well-read, exact, practical, and apparently oblivious to nature. When he was not tutoring Dominique, he would remain in his room, writing plays and letters. After four years, the time came for Dominique to go away to school. Augustin went to Paris with high hopes of his own success.

Dominique went to live with Madame Ceyssac in her mansion at Ormesson. At school he befriended young Olivier d'Orsel, who also had an estate near Les Trembles. Dominique, who was a good student, helped Olivier with his schoolwork. Too shy to admit it, Dominique fell in love with Madeleine, Olivier's cousin. At night he would spend his time writing poetry. He also kept up a correspondence with Augustin, who warned him against confusing Olivier's love of pleasure with the true goals in life.

Dominique was surprised when Madeleine married Monsieur de Nièvres, a well-established gentleman. After the ceremony Dominique was in despair because he realized that he loved a married woman. After graduation, Dominique and Olivier went to Paris. There they saw Augustin, who grew to like Olivier but had no esteem for him. Olivier, in turn, esteemed Augustin without liking him.

Dominique, trying to forget his love for Madeleine, buried himself in his literary work. He went to libraries and lectures, and he read through the small hours of the night in the belief that the austere routine was good for him. After a few months, however, he burned his writings because he thought them stale and mediocre. Olivier, who saw what Dominique did, told him to find other amusements and affections. Augustin, on the other hand, simply said that he would have to begin again. Augustin, who experienced setbacks of his own, never complained. Having guessed Dominique's love problem, he told him to solve it by plunging into continuous work.

In spite of Augustin's advice and example, Dominique found it impossible to settle to his work. Through Olivier, he met a woman whom he saw steadily for two months. Then he learned that Nièvres and Madeleine were going to Ormesson, and he invited them to Les Trembles for the holidays. Although he never told Madeleine about his love for her, those were happy months for Dominique. That winter Nièvres and Madeleine decided to go to Paris.

Eventually Dominique wanted to make Madeleine admit that they loved each other, but the harder he tried to draw an admission from her the more she pretended to be quite unaware of his intention. One day, when he was determined to tell her of his love, he saw tears in her eyes; he understood then that there was nothing more to be said.

After that day their relationship became relaxed and natural, and Madeleine, wanting to encourage Dominique in his work, began to meet him at the risk of compromising her reputation. After a time, Dominique realized that Madeleine was about to surrender herself to him. He then stopped seeing her, and she became gloomy and irritable. Her reactions made Dominique realize that he deeply troubled her conscience.

Meanwhile, Augustin married. Visiting Augustin in his home, Dominique saw the near-poverty but great happiness in which his former tutor lived. At the same time Olivier, deeply involved with the woman he was seeing, began to hate the world and himself. It became evident that Julie, Madeleine's younger sister, loved Olivier. Olivier, however, claimed that happiness was a myth and refused to think of marrying her; his attitude led to a loss of confidence between Dominique and Olivier.

One night, while Dominique and Madeleine were attending the opera, Dominique caught the glance of his former mistress. Madeleine saw the exchange and later told Dominique that he was torturing her and breaking her heart. That night Dominique, determined to deal honestly with Madeleine, decided to claim her. For the next three weeks, how-ever, she was not at home to him. Frustrated, Dominique moved to new quarters and, as a final effort, tried to escape the life of emotions and concentrate on the logical disciplines of the mind. He read much, saved his money, and published anonymously two volumes of his youthful poetry. He also wrote some political books that were immediately successful. When he evaluated his talents, however, he concluded that he was a distinguished mediocrity.

Several months later, Olivier told Dominique that there was unhappiness at Nièvres, where Madeleine was staying. Julie was ill, and Madeleine herself was not well. Dominique went to Nièvres at once and there found Julie recovering. No longer needed as her sister's nurse, Madeleine, with disregard for propriety, shared three days of supreme happiness with Dominique.

On impulse, after Madeleine led him in a dangerous ride on horseback, Dominique decided to leave as he came, without premeditation or calculation. When he was helping her to fold a large shawl that evening, Madeleine half-fainted into his arms, and they kissed. Dominique felt very sorry for her and let her go. After dinner, Madeleine told him that, although she would always love him, she wanted him to go away, to get married, to take up a new life. That was the last Dominique saw of Madeleine. He returned to Les Trembles and settled down to a quiet country life.

Dominique tells the narrator that the years brought forgiveness and understanding. Augustin, he says, became a respected figure in Paris. Dominique never repented his early retirement; he feels, in fact, that his life is merely beginning.

Critical Evaluation:

Written after Romanticism had flowered and faded in France, *Dominique* is quite similar to the personal memoirs and novels that appeared in early nineteenth century France. François René de Chateaubriand's *René* (1802; English translation, 1813) and Benjamin Constant's *Adolphe* (1816) are examples of novels of this period. Eugène Fromentin's novel is similar to the Abbé Prévost's *Manon Lescaut* (1731) as well, because *Dominique*, like *Manon Lescaut*, has to do with irresistible and destructive passion.

However, *Dominique*'s roots in French literary history go deeper than the Romantic and pre-Romantic eras. In some sense, the novel's hero moves in the tradition of courtly love, worshiping as he does, for at least half the novel, a beautiful woman from afar. Early in his story, Dominique places Madeleine on a pedestal; he admires her, yet he fears approaching her. His status as adoring pseudo-knightly lover is indicated ironically by his name, which derives from the

Latin *dominus*, which suggests that Dominique is a lord of sorts, a man reigning over his own domain. The irony is that Dominique has deep feelings of inferiority and insecurity; he is hardly a lordly or dominating type until he reaches maturity.

The novel opens with a depiction of the mature Dominique, lord of an estate, Les Trembles, married and the father of two children. The novel's first two chapters state the theme of passion versus self-control, and, consequently, service to others. The Dominique whom readers and the first-person narrator of the first two chapters meet is a man of about forty years, known in the environs as a man dedicated to his family and to doing good for others. The lesson he has learned about self-preservation and the importance of dedicating oneself to others is what Dominique talks about in the rest of the novel.

The young Dominique was raised by his aunt in Normandy; he is a young man who loves his native countryside. Without great enthusiasm, he later goes to Paris to pursue his studies and a career as a writer. His friend and counselor in these early years is Augustin, who bears the name of a famous saint and philosopher—which emphasizes his role as the choice of traditional reason, faith, and restraint. Throughout the novel, Augustin serves as Dominique's mentor, offering an example of what one can achieve in life, not through impulse and feeling but by means of discipline. In Dominique's youth, Olivier d'Orsel also opposes Dominque's propensity to self-pity, passivity, passion, and despair. When Dominique, in despair after Madeleine marries the Count of Nièvres, becomes mired in a sense of futility and even destroys his written work, Olivier tries to convince him that love is merely a question of chance—that Madeleine is a unique woman, fated in some way to be the love of his life. Later, however, Olivier is seen to be a less than admirable character, when he spurns the love of Madeleine's sister, Julie. At that point, as Olivier explains to Dominique, he has become very much a selfish, pleasure-seeking man of the world, believing in nothing but his own satisfaction. Much later, ironically, it is Dominique's wife who, believing that doing good and committing oneself to others is one's very reason for living, unknowingly precipitates Olivier's attempted suicide. In contrast, Augustin marries, but with neither the passion Dominique feels for Madeleine, nor the cruel self-interest that motivates Olivier. Dominique despises what he calls the "movement" of life in Paris, the social frenzy that he likens to a whirlpool that threatens those in the Parisian sea with shipwreck. In his frustration with this life and with Madeleine's determination to keep him at an emotional distance, he begins to think of confessing his love

for her. He conceives of an attack, a direct approach to her, thinking in terms of swordplay, a military expedition, a seduction.

Madeleine's vulnerability dissuades Dominique from this brutal attack, although she does, with chagrin, recognize the love Dominique has for her. Oddly enough, Madeleine devotes time and energy to exorcising Dominique's passion for her from his heart—destructive as it is to their well-being. This attempt at a "cure," as Madeleine calls it, fails.

Madeleine's discouragement with Olivier's treatment of Julie and her frustration with her attachment to Dominique comes to a head when Madeleine leads Dominique on a horseback ride through the forest on her estate, excitedly spurs on her mount, and expresses in a brutal fashion the depth and nature of what she feels for Dominique. Her excitement, flushed cheeks, convulsive laughter, and breathless animality when she faces Dominique with her riding crop in her teeth, leads them to a revelation of the dangers unrestrained physical passion holds.

Here is the crisis, and here is where Dominique understands his need for metaphysical and for spiritual rest. At this point in his life and in his relationship with Madeleine, he decides to put his life in order. He decides, first of all, to never see Madeleine again. He then withdraws from the animation of the world, and he returns to his beloved Les Trembles. His marriage ensues.

It is only to be expected that the final image in the novel is that of the sage Augustin, at last a successful public figure and a happy one, who arrives at Les Trembles for a visit.

"Critical Evaluation" by Gordon Walters

Further Reading

Charvet, P. E. "The Romantic Novel." In *The Nineteenth Century, 1789-1870*. Vol. 4 in *A Literary History of France*. New York: Barnes & Noble, 1967. A brief treatment of Fromentin's novel that places it in the context of French Romanticism.

Cruickshank, John. "The Novel of Self-Disclosure." In *The Early Nineteenth Century*. Vol. 4 in *French Literature and Its Background*, edited by John Cruickshank. New York: Barnes & Noble, 1969. Develops the points that the novel is autobiographical and pertinent to Fromentin's stature as a painter. Like other critics, Cruickshank considers the ways in which the novel is both Romantic and post-Romantic.

Howard, Richard. "From Exoticism to Homosexuality." In *A New History of French Literature*, edited by Dennis Hollier et al. Cambridge, Mass.: Harvard University Press,

1994. An interesting placement of *Dominique* in the tradition of exoticism and eroticism in French literature.

Martin, Graham Dunstan. "*Dominique*" and "*Fromentin*." In *The New Oxford Companion to Literature in French*, edited by Peter France. New York: Oxford University Press, 1995. Notes the way in which *Dominique* endorses passion, insofar as the resolution of the conflict between reason and morality is unsatisfactory, and Augustin is a cold figure.

Wright, Barbara. *Eugène Fromentin: A Life in Art and Letters*. New York: Peter Lang, 2000. The first English-language biography relates Fromentin's correspondence to his travel writings, the evolution of his paintings, and the development of his art criticism and fiction.

_____. *Eugène Fromentin: "Dominique."* Glasgow: University of Glasgow, French and German Publications, 2002. A concise, critical overview of the novel by one of Fromentin's biographers.

Don Carlos, Infante of Spain

Author: Friedrich Schiller (1759-1805)
First produced: Don Carlos, Infant von Spanien, 1787; first published, 1787 (English translation, 1798)
Type of work: Drama
Type of plot: Historical
Time of plot: Sixteenth century
Locale: Spain

Principal characters:
DON CARLOS, the heir to the Spanish throne
PHILIP II, the king of Spain and Don Carlos's father
ELIZABETH DE VALOIS, the queen of Spain and Don Carlos's stepmother
MARQUIS DE POSA, Don Carlos's friend
DOMINGO, the king's confessor
DUKE OF ALVA, Philip II's trusted general and minister
PRINCESS DE EBOLI, an attendant to the queen

The Story:

King Philip II of Spain does not wish to trust his son, Don Carlos, with any of the crown's affairs, ostensibly because, even though Don Carlos is twenty-three years old, he is too hot-blooded. Probably the real reason is that Philip, who forced his father, Charles V, from the throne, now fears his own son. The differences and coldness between the king and his son are aggravated by the fact that Philip is married to Elizabeth de Valois, with whom Don Carlos was in love. Indeed, the courtship between the two was sanctioned by France and Spain, until Philip decided to take Elizabeth for himself.

Don Carlos hides his continuing love for Elizabeth, now his stepmother, until his friend, the Marquis de Posa, returns from Flanders, at which time Don Carlos confides in him. The marquis is horrified but swears upon their boyhood friendship to help the prince, if the prince in turn will try to help the people of Flanders escape from the heavy and tyrannic policies forced upon them by Philip through his emissary, the duke of Alva.

Don Carlos goes to his father and pleads that he be made the king's agent in Flanders, declaring that he will act humanely toward the people. Philip refuses to listen and sends

the duke over Don Carlos's protests. He does, however, request that the duke be better disposed toward his son. When the duke goes to speak to the prince, he finds Don Carlos in the queen's antechamber. They have words and fight, until the queen intervenes.

From one of the queen's pages Don Carlos receives a mysterious note and a key to a room in the queen's apartments. Hoping against hope that the queen sent it to him, he goes to the room, an act for which his jealous father would have punished him severely. Instead of the queen, he finds the Princess de Eboli, who sent him the note because she fell in love with him. She asks his help in evading the importunities of the king, who seeks her for his mistress, but Don Carlos repels her advances and thus incurs her anger. When he leaves, he takes with him a letter that the king sent her. Hoping to use the letter as proof that the king is a tyrant and an evil man, he shows it to the Marquis de Posa. The marquis tears up the letter, however, saying that it is too dangerous a weapon and might hurt Don Carlos and the queen more than the king.

In the meantime, the Princess de Eboli, infuriated at Don Carlos's refusal of her love, goes to Domingo, the king's confessor and pander, and tells him of her decision to become Philip's mistress. She also tells about meeting the prince and that he obviously hoped to meet the queen. That information pleases Domingo and the duke of Alva, who want to rid the kingdom of both Don Carlos and the queen.

With the help of the princess, the duke and the confessor lay a trap for Don Carlos and the queen. Becoming suspicious of the conspirators' motives, Philip calls in a man he thinks will be completely honest in solving the problem. Ironically, that man is Don Carlos's friend, the Marquis de Posa. He quickly gains the king's confidence, even though some of his religious ideas are heretical, and he does his best to help Don Carlos. Because the marquis works in secret, Don Carlos considers him disloyal. Other courtiers report to Don Carlos that a file of letters he gave to the marquis were seen in the king's chamber. What Don Carlos hears is true, for the marquis finds it necessary to tell the truth about the letters to clear Don Carlos of the charge of illicit relations with the queen.

Don Carlos, not knowing the truth concerning the marquis's activities, goes to Princess de Eboli to seek her help. The Marquis de Posa, learning of Don Carlos's visit to the princess, enters immediately after the prince. Using the authority given him by the king to arrest Don Carlos, the marquis puts him incommunicado in prison, lest he talk to others who can do him harm. The easiest way to keep Don Carlos safe would be to murder Princess de Eboli, but the marquis does not have the heart to kill her, even when his dagger is at her breast.

Instead of assuming the guilt of murder, the marquis resolves to make himself the victim. The king is convinced that Don Carlos and the queen are involved in a treasonable plot against the crown in Flanders. To clear them, the marquis sends a letter he knows will be put into the king's hands. In it he states that he, the marquis, is the real conspirator. Afterward the marquis has only enough time to go to the prison and reveal his true actions to Don Carlos before a shot is fired through the gratings by an assassin sent by Philip.

Popular wrath and the indignation of the grandees force Philip to release his son, but Don Carlos refuses to leave the prison until his father comes in person to give him back his sword and his freedom. When Philip arrives, in the company of the grandees of the council, Don Carlos confronts him with the marquis's corpse and tells him that he caused the murder of an innocent man. Philip, seeing the truth of the accusation and filled with remorse, becomes ill in the prison and is carried away by the grandees.

A friend reports to Don Carlos that the king and the duke of Alva are enraged by public reaction in favor of the impris-

oned prince. Hoping to lift the yoke of tyranny that his father and the duke of Alva imposed on that country and its people, Don Carlos decides to leave Spain immediately and go to Flanders. Before he leaves, he plans to see the queen once more and tell her of his plans. Donning a mask and the garb of a monk, he goes through a secret passage to the queen's wing of the castle. Once there he walks openly through the corridors to her rooms, able to do so because of a superstition that Charles V, garbed in like manner, haunts the castle. The superstitious soldiers let him pass.

The king, meanwhile, sends for the Cardinal Inquisitor. Asked for his advice, the churchman rebukes Philip for his waywardness in letting the heretic marquis escape proper punishment for so long and then having him killed for political reasons. They discuss also the heresy of the young prince, and Philip resolves to turn his son over to the Inquisition for punishment. Philip leads the cardinal to the queen's apartments, for, having heard reports of the ghost, he guesses who is beneath the disguise. Don Carlos is found with the queen and handed over to the authorities of the Inquisition.

Critical Evaluation:

Friedrich Schiller's dramatic works are often divided into three periods: early, middle, and classical. *Don Carlos*, which took Schiller four years to write and was completed in 1787, is the single play representing the middle period. It is a melodramatic high tragedy written in blank verse, which combines complicated political ideas with a story of doomed love.

In the course of writing *Don Carlos*, Schiller's ideas about the characters changed. Because the first three acts were published in *Die Thalia* between 1785 and 1787 as they were completed, the playwright felt he had to resolve this story line, despite his preference. He would have reworked the play quite differently and created characters more suited to his new ideas had the first acts not already been in the hands of the public. Schiller said of *Don Carlos*, "The parts that first attracted me began to produce this effect in a weaker degree . . . Carlos himself lost my favor, perhaps for no other reason than because I had become his senior, and Posa replaced him. I commenced the fourth and fifth acts with quite an altered heart." The inconsistencies in *Don Carlos* are the result of this change of course. Later in his life, Schiller was extremely critical of *Don Carlos*. In his *Letters upon Don Carlos*, he wrote, "in the first (three) acts I aroused expectations that the last do not fulfill." In the final two acts, Posa does not act in accordance with his earlier course. Initially, he proclaims his loyalty to Carlos; then he seems to ally himself with the king. Probably he could have used that friendship to support his goals of social justice, but when he ruins that possibility the plans for rebellion are destroyed, and all the while Carlos remains in the dark about the greater duties that drive Posa. In the first three acts, Posa is a heroic idealist; in the next acts, he is an unjustified maniac. Even his death, which he feels is purely sacrificial, does not help Carlos, his own greater cause, or anyone else.

Don Carlos was a public success, but critics pointed out some flaws. Schiller's research into the Spanish monarchy of the sixteenth century had shown him several different ways to interpret the same historical moment. He had used Louis-Sébastian Mercier's factual account *Portrait of Phillipe II* (1785), which he translated into German, and for some details he drew on Robert Watson's *History of the Reign of Phillipe II* (1778). Much of the story line for *Don Carlos*, however, comes from César Vichard Saint-Réal's eighty-page *Dom Carlos, Nouvelle Historique* (1672), the least factual of his sources, and as a result Schiller's play may actually contain very little, if any, factual or historical matter.

The most important theme in the play is that of realism versus idealism. Philip represents a harsh and conservative realist who is interested in people only to the extent that they are useful to him; he is not at all interested in improving his subjects' well-being. Posa represents an idealist who strives to improve conditions for all people and to liberate them to a higher plane of existence. One of the most famous lines of this play, in the midst of the most powerful of its compelling scenes, is Posa's statement to the king, "O Give us freedom of thought." In this scene, incidentally, Schiller the philosopher overruns Schiller the poet. In presenting what amounts to a treatise on government, the action and the love story are suspended. The conclusion of the third act reflects the change that Schiller's conception of his characters has undergone, and the attempt in the following acts to justify the importance of his political views as well as to resolve the prince's love for the queen is somewhat disjointed.

The king, a realist, has developed his ideas strictly from experience and observation, as well as from the command of the Church; from these he has determined his rules of judgment and philosophy and mode of action. Posa is attractive to the king because Philip has probably never before met anyone who would not immediately come under his service. Posa claims that his sole motive is to serve others, and this, too, is something the king has not experienced.

Whatever impact Posa might have had on the king is, however, annulled by the entrance of the Grand Inquisitor, who adds another ingredient to the mix of the play when he tells the king that Posa was scheduled to die long ago and the king had in effect taken property away from the Church. The

Grant Inquisitor's presence is amazingly strong. He delineates the proper mentality for a monarch and sets the standard for the realist view that is the king's. The Inquisitor has no tolerance for human beings; he considers people to be a wretched lot of weaklings and fools who should be punished for their inherent flaws by servitude to the Church and the monarchy. The Inquisitor is utterly convinced of his beliefs, and he serves to set the king straight after his interview with Posa that loosens the king's thoughts and lets in a glimmer of light. The Inquisitor serves to nullify that shimmer with his own strong authority, which no one in the play can refute.

"Critical Evaluation" by Beaird Glover

Further Reading

Hammer, Stephanie Barbé. *Schiller's Wound: The Theater of Trauma from Crisis to Commodity*. Detroit, Mich.: Wayne State University Press, 2001. Argues that Schiller was one of the first playwrights to explore the topic of psychological trauma. Analyzes how his plays depict the relationship between pain, spectacle, and money. *Don Carlos* is discussed in chapter 2.

Harrison, R. B. "*Gott ist über mir*: Ruler and Reformer in the Twofold Symmetry of Schiller's *Don Carlos*." *Modern Language Review* 76, no. 3 (July, 1981): 598-611. Discusses structure, symmetry, and characterization in *Don Carlos*. Presents an analysis of Schiller's understanding and use of structure and form.

Kerry, Paul E., ed. *Friedrich Schiller: Playwright, Poet, Philosopher, Historian*. New York: Peter Lang, 2007. Collection of essays that examine Schiller's various vocations, such as a poet, dramatist, historian, prose writer, and philosopher; assesses the status of his work two hundred years after his death.

Martinson, Steven D., ed. *A Companion to the Works of Friedrich Schiller*. Rochester, N.Y.: Camden House, 2005. Collection of essays commemorating the two hundredth anniversary of Schiller's death. Includes discussions of his philosophical aesthetics, lyric poetry, reception in the twentieth century, and relevance to the twenty-first century, as well as analyses of specific works. "Great Emotions, Great Criminals? Schiller's *Don Carlos*" by Rolf-Peter Janz examines this play.

Miller, Ronald Duncan. *Interpreting Schiller: A Study of Four Plays*. Harrogate, England: Duchy Press, 1986. Provides a rigorous criticism and analysis of *Don Carlos*, as well as of *Wilhelm Tell* (1804), *Jungfrau von Orleans* (1801), and *Wallensteins Tod* (1799). Analyzes the plays individually but also compares and contrasts them with one another. Gives some consideration to Schiller's life and times.

Sharpe, Lesley. *A National Repertoire: Schiller, Iffland, and the German Stage.* New York: Peter Lang, 2007. Examines Schiller's influence on the German theater of his time by analyzing his plays' impact on the Mannheim National and Weimar Court theaters, with which he was closely associated. Places his theatrical career in parallel with that of August Wilhelm Iffland, an actor and playwright who eventually produced Schiller's plays at the Berlin National Theatre. Describes the relationship between Schiller and Johann Wolfgang van Goethe as playwrights.

_____. *Schiller and the Historical Character: Presentation and Interpretation in the Historiographical Works and in the Historical Dramas.* New York: Oxford University Press, 1982. Approaches Schiller's works both as histories and as dramas and focuses on defining his historical and philosophical thought. Considers the genre of historical drama and the appropriate approach to analyzing such presentations.

Vazsonyi, Nicholas. "Schiller's *Don Carlos*: Historical Drama or Dramatized History?" *New German Review: A Journal of Germanic Studies* 7 (1991): 26-41. Discusses Don Carlos as both drama and historical drama within the context of Germanic literature.

The Don Flows Home to the Sea

Author: Mikhail Sholokhov (1905-1984)
First published: Tikhii Don, 1928-1940 (partial English translations, 1934 as *And Quiet Flows the Don*; 1940 as *The Don Flows Home to the Sea*; complete English translations, 1942 as *The Silent Don*; 1967 as *And Quiet Flows the Don*)
Type of work: Novel
Type of plot: Historical
Time of plot: 1918-1920
Locale: Russia

Principal characters:
GREGOR MELEKHOV, a soldier
PANTALEIMON PROKOFFIVICH, his father
ILINICHNA, Gregor's mother
PIOTRA, his brother
AKSINIA, his mistress
NATALIA, his wife
KOSHEVOI, a Communist

The Story:

The Germans still carry off flour, butter, and cattle. Every day their trucks roll from the Don through the Ukraine. Various sections of Russia, however, are fighting one another. To the north of the Don Basin, the White Army is driving back the Bolsheviks. Most of the Cossacks are in the White forces, although some are with the Reds.

Gregor and Piotra Melekhov are leaders in the White Army. Piotra, the elder brother, is decidedly anti-Red and wages battle viciously. Gregor is of two minds; perhaps the Reds will bring stable government. Gregor is opposed to pillaging civilians and killing prisoners. As best he can, he keeps his men in hand. When his father and his sister-in-law Daria visit him at the front, he is furious when they take home a wagon load of loot.

In Tatarsk, the Whites are trying to win over the Cossacks to full support of the insurgent cause. In the spring of 1918

there was a great defection of northern Cossacks to the Reds, and the southern Cossacks are only halfhearted in throwing back the Red tide. Koshevoi, a Red sympathizer, is caught when he returns to his home in Tatarsk. His companions are killed, but he is released to join the drovers in the steppes.

Eugene Listnitsky, a rich Cossack from the district, spends a furlough with a brother officer. Eugene is attracted to Olga, the man's wife. After the officer is killed, Listnitsky marries the widow. When he gets home, Aksinia, a woman with a missing arm—and his former mistress—is still there, waiting for him. Eugene wants nothing more to do with her after his marriage. He makes love to her briefly under a currant bush and offers her money to go away. Aksinia is pained but stays. Her husband, Stepan, miraculously alive after years in prison, tries in vain to get her to come home.

Gradually the Cossacks return home; as farmers, they have to till the land. The advancing Red Army passes through the village of Tatarsk. After them comes the political men, and the Red government takes charge. Gregor is glad to be home but has little longing now for Aksinia, who was his mistress before she became Eugene's. After years of fighting Germans and Reds, he is content to be a little reconciled to Natalia, his wife.

Koshevoi is put in charge of the government of Tatarsk, and soon Stockman, a professional Red, comes to help him. In order to consolidate their power, they begin, gradually, seizing a man here and there and spiriting him off to death or imprisonment. They want to arrest Piotra and Gregor. A little afraid to take Piotra, who is friendly with Fomin, a Red commander, they decide to take Gregor. Learning of their intentions in time, Gregor leaves Tatarsk and escapes.

As the political imprisonments and executions increase, the Cossacks revolt. The wrongs they suffered at the hands of the Reds are so great and so many that in a comparatively short time the rebellion is succeeding. Piotra is made a commander immediately. He is a ferocious fighter and ruthless with the Reds. In a skirmish, however, he is captured by the enemy. Koshevoi, now a Communist, steps out from a patrol and kills Piotra without compunction.

After serving under Piotra, Gregor rises to command a division. He is cold with fury toward the Communists and has the reputation of never keeping prisoners alive for long. When the Cossacks begin to imprison Red sympathizers from among civilians, however, he dissents strongly. On one occasion, he even forces open a prison and releases old men and women who are suspected of helping the Reds.

Stockman and the others who were the political rulers of Tatarsk are captured when a Red regiment deserts. Stockman is killed outright, and the others are returned to run a terrible gauntlet at Tatarsk. Daria kills the man she thinks responsible for the death of Piotra, her husband. Koshevoi is not suspected at the time.

Daria recovers from Piotra's death rather speedily and soon is carrying on various affairs. When Gregor comes home on furlough, she even makes tentative love to him. Gregor, however, is tired from fighting and carousing, and he still has bitter memories of Aksinia. Natalia, who heard of Gregor's conduct on his sprees, is cold to him. The day before he is to return to the army, Gregor meets Aksinia at the Don. He thinks of their former love and of her affair with Listnitsky; but the old love is not dead, and he takes Aksinia again.

The Soviet government realizes by May of 1919 that it has a formidable task on its hands and thus increases its forces,

slowly pushing back the insurgent Cossacks. The rebels retreat toward the Don, taking with them crowds of refugees. At last the Cossacks cross the river and hold their positions.

The Reds come through Tatarsk as Natalia is recovering from typhus. Koshevoi is with them; he is indignant that Dunia, Gregor's young sister, is across the Don, for he was long in love with her. Koshevoi's own family is missing, and his father's house was destroyed. He takes pride in setting afire the houses of all the rich landowners in and near Tatarsk.

Gregor, busy as a division commander, takes time to send for Aksinia, and she comes to live near him. Stepan returns, to her embarrassment, and although she does not take him back as her husband, they preserve appearances among the refugee families.

With the arrival of the White Army, the Reds are driven back. Now that the insurgents are incorporated into a regular army, Gregor is demoted to the rank of squadron commander, for he is an uneducated man. The Whites send punitive patrols to punish those who aided the Reds. To the horror of the Melekhovs, all of Koshevoi's relatives are executed. Daria catches syphilis and drowns herself. When Natalia learns of Gregor's return to Aksinia, she refuses to bear him another child. An unskillful abortion is performed, and she bleeds to death.

With increasing Red pressure and desertion from the Cossack ranks, the White Army is going down in defeat. Gregor and Aksinia flee south to try to board a ship. On the way, Aksinia falls ill with typhus and has to be left behind. She later makes her way back to Tatarsk. Gregor cannot leave the country. With nothing better to do, he joins the Reds and fights valiantly against the Poles.

In spite of family protests, Dunia marries Koshevoi, now commissar of the village. When Gregor returns home, Koshevoi at once sets in motion plans to arrest him. Gregor, however, escapes again, joining up with Fomin, a deserter from the Red Army. Fomin tries to rally the Cossacks to revolt against the Communists for levying heavy taxes and collecting grain. The revolt, however, is short-lived. The rebels are killed, and only Gregor goes back to Tatarsk. This time, when Gregor flees, he takes Aksinia with him, but she is killed by a pursuing Red patrol. Gregor throws his weapons into the Don and goes back to his house. Only his son is left to him now, and he will fight no more.

Critical Evaluation:

The Don Flows Home to the Sea is the last half of an immense historical novel, *Tikhii Don*. The novel follows a Don Cossack, Gregor Melekhov, from peacetime czarist Russia through the German-Russian War to the Russian Revolution and the civil war. Although the focal point of the novel is war, the cultural life of Cossack Russia—the roles of men and women in the agrarian family and their love for the land—is equally well portrayed. The length of the work enables a magnificent panorama of history to unfold.

Mikhail Sholokhov intensely loved the Don, the steppe, and the cycles of the seasons, and his poetic language beautifully captures the bond of the Cossacks with their land. Theirs is a peasant's life. They are in tune with the wind, the coming of rain, the swelling and cracking of the frozen Don. Numerous scenes begin with painterly descriptions of landscape, subtle but insistent reminders that it is from the land that life comes. Death, undisguised, is omnipresent. Gory and detailed descriptions of the dying and of the dead are commonplace, but the Don and the steppe survive all tragedies. Sholokhov evokes the sights, sounds, and smells of that earthy existence so vividly that the pain of Cossack uprootedness is totally convincing. Young soldiers who fight valiantly near the Don are ineffectual, lifeless, on foreign soil; refugees wander aimlessly when forced to flee their Don home.

The Melekhov family and the other townspeople of Tatarsk are typical of agrarian society and culture. Roles within family units are assumed unquestioningly, although not always obediently. The head of the Melekhov household, old Pantaleimon Prokoffivich, Gregor's father, is responsible for all who live under his roof: his wife, his sons, their wives and children, and his daughter until she marries. He is the patriarchal authority. Pantaleimon orders the marriage of Gregor and Natalia when he learns of Gregor's affair with Aksinia; Gregor complies. Old Pantaleimon becomes confused about his authority over his sons, however, when their military ranks surpass his.

Pantaleimon expects and demands to be served and respected by women, who are, he assumes, his subordinates. In Cossack society, females are less valued than males and are treated as possessions by husbands. When Stepan Astakhov first learns of the affair between his wife, Aksinia, and Gregor, he returns home to beat, then to stomp on Aksinia as if he were doing a Cossack dance. He is within his rights to thus punish her transgression.

The matriarch of the Melekhov family is Ilinichna, Pantaleimon's wife, who is not only the female head of the household (wife, mother, and grandmother) but also the mother to her sons' wives. The relationship between the mother-in-law and the daughters-in-law is an interesting one. Ilinichna gives orders to Daria, Piotra's wife, and Natalia as a mistress would to servants. The young married women have no rights except as granted by their husbands and mother-in-law.

Children are reared in an extended family, and parental authority is often less than that of the grandparent. The middle generation, sons and daughters-in-law, are treated as overgrown children by the older generation. A major role for the young men is to serve in the military. Service is seen as an honor, a duty that is fulfilled unquestioningly. The process of maturation for young men seems to occur in the military. When Gregor and his friends return home from war, the townspeople comment on how broad-shouldered they have become.

A strain of violence permeates Cossack life. Even during peacetime there is an air of exaggerated rivalry in which anger is expressed overtly. When old Pantaleimon proudly races through the village with his hero son, Gregor, he becomes infuriated with an old woman who scolds him for nearly running over her livestock. His anger could easily lead him to using his whip on her. Wartime violence is seen both on the battlefront and within the civilian population. There is an irony in the reverence a soldier holds for his own mother when he mistreats another's mother; an irony when he who has shared another soldier's wife returns home enraged to find that his wife has been similarly unfaithful.

The length of the novel gives the feeling of the flow of history, not in generalized sweeping trends or wartime strategies, but in a long series of specific circumstances that enables the reader to become involved with numerous major characters and to care about their lives and deaths as much as about the life of the one central figure, Gregor Melekhov. A dead soldier by the side of the road becomes a vital loss, as the reader learns in retrospect from a small diary of the soldier's life and love. The relationship that grows between Podtielkov and Anna Pogodko is another mini-novel that is given life and death within the confines of Sholokhov's world. The deaths that affect Gregor most deeply are those of his and Aksinia's daughter, of Piotra on the battlefield, of Piotra's wife by suicide, of Natalia by an unsuccessful abortion, of Pantaleimon of typhus as a refugee, and, finally, of Aksinia. The reader participates in Gregor's suffering because Sholokhov has fully developed all of these characters.

This long-range focus on history through specific tragedies gives the indelible impression of the war weariness, resignation, and readiness for death that Gregor feels when he finally returns home for the last time. This work and the first part of the narrative, *And Quiet Flows the Don*, have also been published as one book.

"Critical Evaluation" by Mary Peace Finley

Further Reading

Clark, Katerina. "Socialist Realism in Soviet Literature." In *The Routledge Companion to Russian Literature*, edited by Neil Cornwell. New York: Routledge, 2001. Includes discussion of two of Sholokhov's novels, *And Quiet Flows the Don* and *Virgin Soil Upturned*, placing them within the broader context of Soviet social realism.

Ermolaev, Herman. *Mikhail Sholokhov and His Art*. Princeton, N.J.: Princeton University Press, 1982. One of the best studies of Sholokhov and his works by a native scholar trained in the West. *The Quiet Don* is discussed extensively, especially regarding historical sources and Sholokhov's use of them.

Hallett, R. W. "Soviet Criticism of *Tikhiy Don*, 1928-1940." *Slavonic and East European Review* 46, no. 106 (1968): 60-74. A brief but substantive treatment of Sholokhov's difficulties in publishing the novel because the Soviet authorities disliked his objective presentation of the revolution.

Klimenko, Michael. *The World of Young Sholokhov: Vision of Violence*. North Quincy, Mass.: Christopher, 1972. A useful study of Sholokhov's early works, with the emphasis on *The Quiet Don* as the seminal work of the Russian literature about the revolution.

Medvedev, Roy. *Problems in the Literary Biography of Mikhail Sholokhov*. Translated by A. D. P. Briggs. New York: Cambridge University Press, 1977. A former Russian dissident discusses the controversy about the accusations of Sholokhov's plagiarism in writing *And Quiet Flows the Don*.

Mukherjee, G. *Mikhail Sholokhov: A Critical Introduction*. New Delhi: Northern Book Centre, 1992. A bilingual study, in English and Russian. Analyzes Sholokhov's works, considering them within the context of Soviet literature and ideology. Discusses Sholokhov's critical reception.

Murphy, Brian, V. P. Butt, and H. Ermolaev. *Sholokhov's "Tikhii Don": A Commentary*. 2 vols. Birmingham, England: Department of Russian Language and Literature, University of Birmingham, 1997. A detailed discussion of the novel.

Ruhle, Jurgen. "The Epic of the Cossacks." *Literature and Revolution*. Translated and edited by Jean Steinberg. New York: Praeger, 1969. Studies the relationship between literature and revolution, viewing the historical and political background of Sholokhov's *The Don Flows Home to the Sea*.

Simmons, Ernest J. "Sholokhov: Literary Artist and Socialist Realism." In *Introduction to Russian Realism*. Bloomington: Indiana University Press, 1965. Discusses at length the basic dilemma in Sholokhov's creative life—a conflict between art and politics.

Don Juan

Author: Lord Byron (1788-1824)
First published: 1819-1826
Type of work: Poetry
Type of plot: Satire
Time of plot: Late eighteenth century
Locale: Spain, Turkey, Russia, and England

Principal characters:
DON JUAN, a young Spaniard
DONNA INEZ, his mother
DONNA JULIA, his first mistress
HAIDÉE, his second love
THE SULTANA, who covets Juan
CATHERINE, empress of Russia
LADY ADELINE AMUNDEVILLE, Juan's adviser
DUCHESS OF FITZ-FULKE, who pursues Juan
AURORA RABY, pursued by Juan

The Poem:

When Don Juan is a small boy, his father dies, leaving the boy in the care of his mother, Donna Inez. Donna Inez is a righteous woman who made her husband's life miserable. She has her son tutored in the arts of fencing, riding, and shooting, and she attempts to rear him in a moral manner. The young Don Juan reads widely in the sermons and lives of the saints, but he does not seem to absorb from his studies the qualities his mother thinks essential.

At sixteen, he is a handsome lad much admired by his mother's friends. Donna Julia, in particular, often looks pensively at the youth. Donna Julia is just twenty-three and married to a man of fifty. Although she loves her husband, or so she tells herself, she thinks often of young Don Juan. One day, finding herself alone with him, she gives herself to the young man. The young lovers spend long hours together during the summer, and it is not until November that Don Alfonso, her husband, discovers their intrigue. When Don Alfonso finds Don Juan in his wife's bedroom, he tries to throttle him. Don Juan overcomes Don Alfonso and flees, first to his mother's home for clothes and money. Then Donna Inez sends him to Cadiz, there to begin a tour of Europe. The good lady prays that the trip will mend his morals.

Before his ship reaches Leghorn, a storm breaks it apart. Don Juan spends many days in a lifeboat without food or water. At last the boat is washed ashore, and Don Juan falls exhausted on the beach and sleeps. When he awakens, he sees bending over him a beautiful girl, who tells him that she is called Haidée and that she is the daughter of the ruler of the island, one of the Cyclades. Her father, Lambro, is a pirate, dealing in jewels and slaves. She knows her father will sell Don Juan to the first trader who comes by, so Haidée hides Don Juan in a cave and sends her maids to wait on him.

When Lambro leaves on another expedition, Haidée takes Don Juan from the cave and they roam together over the island. Haidée gives jewels, fine foods, and wines to Don Juan, for he is the first man she ever knew except for her father and for her servants. Although Don Juan still tries to think of Donna Julia, he cannot resist Haidée. A child of nature and passion, she gives herself to him with complete freedom. Don Juan and Haidée live an idyllic existence until Haidée's father returns unexpectedly. Don Juan again fights gallantly, but at last he is overcome by the old man's servants and put aboard a slave ship bound for a distant market. He never sees Haidée again, and he never knows that she dies without giving birth to his child.

The slave ship takes Don Juan to a Turkish market, where he and another prisoner are purchased by a black eunuch and taken to the palace of a sultan. There Don Juan is made to dress as a dancing maiden and present himself to the sultana, the fourth and favorite wife of the sultan. She passed by the slave market and saw Don Juan and wants him for a lover. In order to conceal his sex from the sultan, she forces the disguise on Don Juan. Even at the threat of death, however, Don Juan will not become her lover, for he still yearns for Haidée. His constancy might have wavered if the sultana was not an infidel, for she is young and beautiful.

Eventually Don Juan escapes from the palace and joins the army of Catherine of Russia. The Russians are at war with the sultan from whose palace Don Juan fled. Don Juan

is such a valiant soldier that he is sent to St. Petersburg to carry the news of a Russian victory to Empress Catherine. Catherine also casts longing eyes on the handsome stranger, and her approval soon makes Don Juan the toast of her capital. In the midst of his luxury and good fortune, Don Juan grows ill. Hoping that a change of climate will help her favorite, Catherine resolves to send him on a mission to England. When he reaches London he is well received, for he is a polished young man, well versed in fashionable etiquette. His mornings are spent in business, but his afternoons and evenings are devoted to lavish entertainment. He conducts himself with such decorum, however, that he is much sought after by proper young ladies and much advised by older ones. Lady Adeline Amundeville makes him her protégé and advises him freely on affairs of the heart. Another, the duchess of Fitz-Fulke, advises him, too, but her suggestions are of a more personal nature and seem to demand a secluded spot where there is no danger from intruders. As a result of the duchess of Fitz-Fulke's attentions to Don Juan, Lady Adeline begins to talk to him about selecting a bride from the chaste and suitable young ladies attentive to him.

Don Juan thinks of marriage, but his interest is stirred by a girl not on Lady Adeline's list. Aurora Raby is a plain young lady, prim, dull, and seemingly unaware of Don Juan's presence. Her lack of interest serves to spur him on to greater efforts, but a smile is his only reward from the cold maiden.

His attention is diverted from Aurora by the appearance of the ghost of the Black Friar, who once lived in the house of Lady Adeline, where Don Juan is a guest. The ghost is a legendary figure reported to appear before births, deaths, or marriages. To Don Juan, the ghost is an evil omen, and he cannot laugh off the tightness about his heart. Lady Adeline and her husband seem to consider the ghost a great joke. Aurora appears to be a little sympathetic with Don Juan, but the duchess of Fitz-Fulke merely laughs at his discomfiture.

The second time the ghost appears, Don Juan follows it out of the house and into the garden. It seems to float before him, always just out of his reach. Once he thinks he grasped it, but his fingers touch only a cold wall. Then he seizes it firmly and finds that the ghost has a sweet breath and full, red lips. When the monk's cowl falls back, the duchess of Fitz-Fulke is revealed. On the morning after, Don Juan appears at breakfast wan and tired. Whether he overcame more than the ghost, no one will ever know. The duchess, too, comes down, seeming to have the air of one who was rebuked.

Critical Evaluation:

Although Lord Byron said that *Don Juan* was to be an epic, his story does not follow epic tradition. It is a vehicle for digression on any and every subject and person that entered Byron's mind as he wrote. The plot itself is almost a minor part of the poem, for much more interesting are Byron's bitter tirades on England, wealth, power, society, chastity, poets, and diplomats. The poem holds a high place among literary satires, even though it was unfinished at Byron's death.

George Gordon Byron, who became the sixth Lord Byron by inheriting the title from his uncle, William, was born on January 22, 1788. His father, the notorious "Mad Jack" Byron, deserted the family, and young Byron was brought up in his mother's native Scotland, where he was exposed to Presbyterian concepts of predestination, which distorted his religious views throughout his life. In 1801, he entered Harrow, a public school near London; in 1808, he received the master of arts degree from Cambridge; in 1809, he took his seat in the House of Lords. From June, 1809, to July, 1811, Byron traveled in Europe. In 1812, he met Lady Caroline Lamb, who later became his mistress; in 1813, he spent several months with his half-sister, Augusta Leigh, who later bore a daughter who may have been Byron's. Byron married Annabella Milbanke in 1815; she bore him a daughter, Ada, a year later and left him shortly thereafter. In 1816, Byron left England, never to return. That year found him in Switzerland with the Shelleys, where, in 1817, Clare Clairmont bore his illegitimate daughter Allegra. After 1819, Countess Teresa Guicciola, who sacrificed her marriage and social position for Byron, became his lover and comforter. Byron died on April 19, 1824, in Missolonghi, where he had hoped to help Greece gain independence from Turkey. His most famous works are *Childe Harold's Pilgrimage* (1812-1818, 1819), *Manfred* (1817), *Cain: A Mystery* (1821), *The Vision of Judgment* (1822), and *Don Juan*, his masterpiece.

Don Juan, a mock-epic poem written in ottava rima, is permeated with Byronic philosophy. Its episodic plot, narrated in first person by its author, tells the story of young Juan, who, victimized by a narrow-minded and hypocritical mother, an illogical educational system, and his own fallible humanity, loses his innocence and faith and becomes disillusioned. The poem's rambling style allows for Byron's numerous digressions, in which he satirizes many aspects of English life: English government and its officials, religion and its confusions and hypocrisies, society and its foibles, war and its irrationality, woman and her treachery, man and his inhumanity. Even English poets feel the fire of Byron's wrath. Thus Byron has been accused of a completely negative view in *Don Juan*—anti-everything and pro-nothing. The philosophy of *Don Juan* is not wholly pessimistic, however, and its tone is consistently, especially in the digressions, sardonic and tongue-in-cheek. Furthermore, Byron's

flippant refusal to take Juan's story (or life) too seriously and his extensive use of exaggerated rhyme (such as "intellectual" and "hen-peck'd you all") are essentially comic. Thus the zest and the laughter in *Don Juan* belie the statements of despair and lend an affirmation of life despite its ironies; the lapses into lyricism reveal a heart that sings despite the poet's attempts to stifle emotion with sophistication.

In *Don Juan*, Byron's philosophical confusion seems to be caused by his natural affinity for a Platonic, idealistic view, which has been crushed under the weight of a realism he is too honest and too perceptive to ignore. He denies that he discusses metaphysics, but he comments that nothing is stable or permanent; all is mutable and subject to violent destruction. Nevertheless, Byron, in calling the world a "glorious blunder," is not totally blind to its temporary beauties. During the Juan-Haidée romance, the lovers live in an Edenic world of beautiful sunsets and warm, protective caves. Still, Juan's foreboding and Haidée's dream are reminders that nature's dangers always lurk behind its façade of beauty. Even Haidée, "Nature's bride," pursues pleasure and passion only to be reminded that "the wages of sin is death."

Byron's view of the nature of humanity is closely akin to his complex view of natural objects. People have their moments of glory, integrity, and unselfishness. For example, Juan, the novice, does not flee from the horror of battle; he shuns cannibalism even though he is starving; he refuses to be forced to love the sultana; he risks his life to save young Leila. Often Byron emphasizes humanity's freedom of mind and spirit. However, Byron believes that human self-deceit is the chief factor in decadence; false ideas of glory lead to bloodshed. Ironically, Surrow lectures his soldiers on "the noble art of killing"; humanity kills because "it brings self-approbation." In fact, Byron suggests that men are more destructive than nature or God. Still, Byron does not condemn humanity. This is in spite of Byron's opinion that humanity is basically flawed. Lord Henry, the elder sophisticate, is perhaps the best example of the human inability to retain innocence; caught in the trap of his own greed and hypocrisy and of society's political game, Lord Henry finds that he cannot turn back, even though "the fatigue was greater than the profit." Byron also strikes out against political corruption. He had strong hopes for England's budding liberalism: a "king in constitutional procession" had offered great promise in leading the world to political freedom and morality. Byron, however, boldly declares England's failure to fulfill this promise.

Byron does, however, offer positive values in *Don Juan*. He believes that momentary happiness and glory and love are worth living for. Although "A day of gold from out an age of iron/ Is all that life allows the luckiest sinner," it is better than nothing. Humanity must fight, though it knows that it can never redeem the world and that defeat and death are certain. Since hypocrisy is one of the worst sins, people should be sincere. To Byron, the creative act is especially important, for it is humanity's only chance to transcend mortality.

Throughout *Don Juan*, then, one follows humanity through its hapless struggle with life. Born in a fallen state, educated to hypocrisy and impracticality, cast out into a world of false values and boredom, a person follows the downward path to total disillusionment. One learns, however, to protect oneself from pain by insulating oneself with the charred shell of burned-out passion and crushed ideals. Blindly, one stumbles toward that unknown and unknowable end—death. Nevertheless, one goes not humbly but defiantly, not grimly but with gusto.

Therefore, Byron's philosophy, despite its harshness, is one that embraces life, seeking to intensify and electrify each fleeting, irrevocable moment. It is a philosophy of tangibles, though they are inadequate; of action, although it will not cure humanity's ills; of honesty, although it must recognize humanity's fallen state. Although death is inevitable and no afterlife is promised, Byron maintains his comic perspective: "Carpe diem, Juan . . . play out the play."

"Critical Evaluation" by Janet Wester

Further Reading

Bloom, Harold. "Don Juan." In *The Visionary Company: A Reading of English Romantic Poetry*. Rev. ed. Ithaca, N.Y.: Cornell University Press, 1990. Explores how Byron's attempt to straddle the worlds of fallen and reborn humanity places his epic in the same visionary landscape as that of other Romantic poets.

Byron, George Gordon, Lord. *Don Juan*. Edited by T. G. Steffan. New York: Penguin Books, 1986. Excellent edition of Byron's epic, derived from Steffan's four-volume variorum edition. Includes extensive notes, variants, commentary, and bibliography.

Crane, David. *The Kindness of Sisters*. New York: Alfred A. Knopf, 2003. A study of Byron's reputation after death, exploring bitter and conflicting accounts by the wife he divorced and the sister he seduced.

Donelan, Charles. *Romanticism and Male Fantasy in Byron's "Don Juan": A Marketable Vice*. New York: St. Martin's Press, 2000. Views *Don Juan* as a "sensational radical satire," in which Byron exposes the male fantasies behind Romanticism and nineteenth century popular culture. Donelan argues that the poem remains relevant for twenty-first century debates about consumerism, gender, love, power, and liberty.

Franklin, Caroline. *Byron: A Literary Life*. New York: Routledge, 2007. Biography focusing on Byron as a professional writer, recounting the circumstances of how his major poems were produced. Includes numerous references to *Don Juan*, which are listed in the index.

MacCarthy, Fiona. *Byron: Life and Legend*. New York: Farrar, Straus and Giroux, 2002. A biography that reexamines the life of the poet in the light of MacCarthy's assertion that Byron was bisexual, a victim of early abuse by his nurse.

McGann, J. J. *Don Juan in Context*. Chicago: University of Chicago Press, 1976. An analysis of the personal, literary, and historical influences of Byron's epic. Individual chapters discuss the problems of form, development of language, chronology of composition, and the importance of imagination as a creative and analytical faculty.

Ridenour, G. M. *The Style of Don Juan*. New Haven, Conn.: Yale University Press, 1960. Examines the classical theory of styles and its impact on Byron's paradoxical vision and his involvement in the narrative as speaker. Particular attention is paid to the Fall as a metaphor for the creation of art, nature, sexual identity, and a persona.

Stabler, Jane. *Byron, Poetics, and History*. New York: Cambridge University Press, 2002. Stabler maintains that Byron's poetics were a response to contemporary cultural history and to his reception by English readers. She analyzes *Don Juan* and his other works to demonstrate her thesis.

_____, ed. *Palgrave Advances in Byron Studies*. New York: Palgrave Macmillan, 2007. Contains twelve scholarly essays interpreting Byron's work, including discussions of Byron and homosexuality, gender, history, popular culture, war, and psychoanalytic criticism.

Don Juan Tenorio

Author: José Zorrilla y Moral (1817-1893)
First produced: 1844; first published, 1844 (English
    translation, 1944)
Type of work: Drama
Type of plot: Comedy
Time of plot: c. 1545
Locale: Seville, Spain

Principal characters:
DON JUAN TENORIO, a nobleman of Seville
DON DIEGO TENORIO, his father
DON LUIS MEJÍA, an Andalusian gentleman
DON GONZALO DE ULLOA, the comendador of Calatrava
INES DE ULLOA, his daughter
ANA DE PANTOJA, a young woman betrothed to Mejía
MARCOS CIUTTI, Don Juan's servant

The Story:

It is the carnival season in Seville, and the Laurel Tavern is a strange place in which to find gallant young Don Juan Tenorio, when the streets outside are filled with masked merrymakers. He is there with his servant, Marcos Ciutti, to keep a rendezvous with Don Luis Mejía, another gallant, with whom he strikes a wager as to which of them could do the most harm in the next twelve months. That night the bet is to be decided.

Don Gonzalo de Ulloa, the father of the girl whom Don Juan hopes to marry, goes masked to the inn, for he wants to hear with his own ears an account of the wild and villainous deeds attributed to his prospective son-in-law. Don Diego, Juan's father, joins him, masked as well. Several officers, friends of Don Juan and Mejía, are also loitering in the tavern to learn the outcome of the wager, which was discussed in the city for months. Mejía appears promptly, just as the cathedral clock is striking eight.

Good-humoredly, the rivals compare lists of the men they slew in duels and the women they cruelly deceived during the year. Don Juan is easily the victor. Because his roster lacks only two types of women, however, a nun and the bride of a friend, he wagers that he can add both to his list within a week. Fearing that his rival has an eye on Ana de Pantoja, whom he is planning to marry, Mejía sends his servant to call the police. Angered by the evil deeds of which Don Juan boasted, the comendador announces that he will never consent to the young scoundrel's marriage with his daughter Ines. Instead, the girl will be kept safe in a convent. Don Diego disowns his son.

A patrol appears to arrest Don Juan on Mejía's accusations. Other guards summoned by Ciutti take Mejía into custody at the same time.

Through the influence of powerful friends, Mejía is soon freed. He hurries at once to the house of Ana de Pantoja, where he persuades a servant to let him into the house at ten o'clock that night. He intends to keep Don Juan from attempting an entrance. When Ana appears at the balcony, he tells her his plan, and she acquiesces to it.

Don Juan, also released from custody, overhears their conversation, which gives him the idea of impersonating his rival in order to get into Ana's room. Ciutti already bribed Ana's duenna to secure the key to the outer door. To make sure that Mejía is out of the way, Ciutti also hires several men to impersonate the police patrol. These bravos seize Mejía and bind him.

Don Juan next interviews Brigida, the duenna of Ines, and bribes her to deliver a note to the girl in the convent. When the old woman reports that her charge is in love with Don Juan, although she never saw him, the gallant decides that he has time to go to the convent and abduct her before the hour for him to appear at Ana's house.

At the convent, Ines listens abashed as the abbess praises her godliness. Perhaps she was once like that; now she no longer looks forward to taking holy orders. Half-frightened, half-eager, she keeps thinking of Don Juan. The appearance of Brigida with the note upsets her still more, so that when Don Juan appears suddenly at the door of her cell she collapses in a faint. It is easy for him to carry her off in her unconscious state. Don Gonzalo, worried by the young man's boasting and reports of conversations between him and Brigida, arrives at the convent too late to save his daughter. Ines remains unconscious while Don Juan takes her to his house beside the Guadalquiver River. When she comes to, Brigida lies to her, telling her that Don Juan saved her life when the convent caught on fire.

Don Juan returns after he successfully enters Ana's room. Mejía, seeking revenge, comes in pursuit. Don Gonzalo, hoping to rescue his daughter, also appears at the house. Enraged by their insults, Don Juan shoots Don Gonzalo and stabs Mejía. Then he jumps into the river to escape from police who are hammering at his front door. Abandoned by Don Juan, Ines returns to the convent and dies of grief.

Five years later, a sculptor is putting the finishing touches to the Tenorio pantheon. On Don Diego's orders, the family mansion was torn down and the grounds turned into a cemetery for his son's victims. Lifelike statues of the three chief ones—Mejía, Don Gonzalo, and Ines—gleam in the moonlight. Patiently, the sculptor explains his labors to a stranger, who eventually terrifies the craftsman by revealing himself as Don Juan.

Repentant, Don Juan kneels before Ines's monument and begs her to intercede with God for mercy. When he looks up, her statue disappears from its pedestal and Ines herself stands beside him, sent reincarnate from heaven either to bring him back with her to salvation or to be damned with him throughout eternity; he has until dawn to choose their fate. Don Juan, unable to believe that what is happening is real, thinks it a trick of crafty priests.

When two officers who five years before witnessed the outcome of his bet with Mejía come into the graveyard, he laughs at their fear of ghosts; fear has no entry to his heart. After inviting his old acquaintances to have supper with him and hear the story of his adventures, with rash bravado he also extends his invitation to the statue of Don Gonzalo. Only the comendador's presence at the table, Don Juan says, will convince him of a life beyond the grave. The statue keeps its stony silence.

While the trio sit drinking at the table, they hear the sound of knocking, each time nearer, though all the doors are bolted. Then into the room stalks the statue of Don Gonzalo, to tell the skeptic about the life eternal that can be realized through God's mercy. The officers faint, but Don Juan is so courteous a host that before the statue disappears through the wall it invites him to a similar banquet in the cemetery.

Still unconvinced that one moment of repentance can wipe out thirty years of sin, Don Juan refuses to be moved when Ines appears to persuade him to make the right choice. Half believing that the whole affair is a joke concocted by the sleeping officers, he shakes them back to consciousness and accuses them of using him for their sport. They in turn charge him with drugging them. The argument ends in challenges to a duel.

In the half light of early morning, the statues of Ines and Don Gonzalo are still missing from the pantheon of the Tenorio family when Don Juan, melancholy because he killed his old friends in the duel, appears to keep his appointment. His knock at the comendador's tomb transforms it into a banquet table that parodies his own bountiful spread of the night before. Snakes and ashes are the foods, illuminated by the purging fire of God, and ghostly guests crowd around the board. Although Death is on his way, Don Juan still refuses to

repent as Don Gonzalo's statue once more tells him about the redeeming power of heaven.

As Don Juan's funeral procession approaches, Don Gonzalo seizes the sinner's arm and prepares to drag him off to hell. At that moment Don Juan raises his free arm toward heaven. Ines appears and she and Don Juan, both saved, sink together into a bed of flowers scattered by angels. Flames, symbolizing their souls, mount to heaven.

Critical Evaluation:

Don Juan Tenorio, the boastful libertine who defies God in his search for earthly pleasures, is one of Spain's mythical figures. In the legend and in Tirso de Molina's seventeenth century masterpiece *El burlador de Sevilla* (1625?; *The Trickster of Seville*, 1923), time runs out and Don Juan is dragged down into hell. Heaven's justice has been appeased and the fabric of society restored.

In the nineteenth century *Don Juan Tenorio* by José Zorrilla y Moral, on the other hand, Don Juan is given time and is saved, even after death. The difference between the two works lies in the varying perspective of the hero. Although in both works the personality of Don Juan dominates the play, sweeping all other characters aside, Tirso chooses to accentuate in the title the salient trait of his Don Juan's nature, that of gamester, the man who views life as a game and uses people, especially women, as pawns. Tirso's Don Juan is incapable of change or true affection; handsome, magnificently proud, and brave though he may be, he is not complete, not a hero. The Don Juan Tenorio of Zorrilla's play, by contrast, is a hero, the quintessential romantic hero. In one of those rare moments of inspiration, Zorrilla seems to have found the right combination of medieval lore, literary tradition, and the Romantic ideal. *Don Juan Tenorio*, appearing at the very end of the Spanish Romantic movement, resonated with the Spanish people, and every November 1, All Saints Day, the play is still performed throughout the Hispanic world.

Spanish Romantic drama extravagantly rebelled against rigid neoclassicism, and *Don Juan Tenorio*'s only concessions to unity are in the dominance of its protagonist and in its principal theme of salvation through love. It is a long operatic work of seven acts in mixed verse which, although uneven at times, reaches intense melodic heights. The action starts during carnival week in a torch-lit Seville where masked revelers await the participants in a cruel wager, and it ends in a cemetery complete with antithetical vengeful ghosts and cherubs, hellfire and flowers, funeral chants and joyous song. Its acts are titled, each stressing the dominant mood or theme. Act 4, for example, in which Don Juan carries off Ines and has his first chance at redemption, is entitled "The Devil at Heaven's Door," representing the antithesis of the devil and the angel, Don Juan and Ines.

Don Juan, in true Romantic rebel fashion, scoffs at tradition and society's mores until he meets Ines, whom he steals from her convent out of spite. Something in Ines, perhaps her innocence or her obvious adoration of him, mysteriously moves him, or perhaps he sees his only hope of salvation through her. If Don Juan is the archetypal Romantic hero, Ines is the archetypal Romantic heroine. Dreamy, delicate, unaccustomed to the world, shut up in her convent, and almost hypnotized by the force of Don Juan's personality, she forms an ideal image of him that time and death cannot break. She dies from grief after Don Juan's abandonment of her, following her father's death, and then literally sacrifices her own salvation for that of her lover. She may be weak in life, but in death she is forceful enough to make a pact with God.

Theology is not the strong point of *Don Juan Tenorio*. Don Juan is saved after death, even though God generally does not equate a sinner with a saint; an entire life of crime and scandal is rarely blotted away forever by one second of repentance. The moral linchpin of the play, however, is the fact that Don Juan tries to repent; a moment of Gonzalo's scorn and taunting destroys that moment of salvation.

The play, at its most excessive, is melodrama, but it is effective. At times it is as hypnotic as its title character in the kaleidoscopic use of light and sound and changing scenes and in the seductive music of its verse. The extreme contrast between the action, mood, and scene of acts 4 and 5 is a good example of Zorrilla's technique of change and reversal. Act 4 is all passion, light, fire, and motion, but when the reader meets the characters again in act 5, the start of the second half of the play, they have been transformed into lifelike statues in a cemetery dedicated to the victims of Don Juan; their vital force has been converted into frigid marble. The light now is cold; a silver moon shines on a stillness of white and black. There is no movement; even the rhythm of the verse slows down.

The contrasting nature of the scenery and action is the medium for the expression of the work's antithetical themes. All the great dramatic dualities are present—betrayal and faith, damnation and salvation, corruption and innocence, hope and despair, hate and, above all, love. All the excess, all the music, all the disparate images coalesce around this overriding central tenet, that love is dominant, even after death, and can break down even the gates of heaven. This message is certainly one of the principal reasons for the play's continuing popularity.

In contrast to the stern retribution of God's justice in Tirso's *The Trickster of Seville*, here the audience is consoled with the prospect of divine mercy. Another reason for the play's success could be that secretly the audience has always wanted Don Juan to be saved. Even in Tirso's work, in which Don Juan deserves to be punished, it is his fire and passion that are remembered.

"Critical Evaluation" by Charlene E. Suscavage

Further Reading

Arias, Judith. "The Devil at Heaven's Door: Metaphysical Desire in *Don Juan Tenorio*." *Hispanic Review* 61 (Winter, 1993): 15-34. Analyzes the play as a game and deals with the wager underlying the plot. Applies psychological theories of René Girard that show how the character's behavior is an example of mimetic desire, a desire that in Don Juan is "ultimately metaphysical in nature."

Bersett, Jeffrey T. *El Burlado de Sevilla: Nineteenth Century Theatrical Appropriations of "Don Juan Tenorio."* Newark, Del.: Juan de la Cuesta, 2003. Describes the many parodies, imitations, and appropriations of *Don Juan Tenorio* that appeared after the play's debut in 1844.

Feal, Carlos. "Conflicting Names, Conflicting Laws: Zorrilla's *Don Juan Tenorio*." *PMLA* 96 (May, 1981): 375-387. Concludes that the work shows evidence of being an improvisation and enjoys an "exaggerated theatricality" because the figure was "a man in need of an audience." Addresses the myth of Don Juan and compares Zorrilla's and Tirso de Molino's depictions of the legendary character.

Firmat, Gustavo Perez. "Carnival in *Don Juan Tenorio*." *Hispanic Review* 51 (Summer, 1983): 269-281. A structural study that disagrees with Zorrilla's self-criticism of the play. Sees the play's flaws and inconsistencies as "harmonious elements in a coherent, if unusual, design." Concentrates on the letter motif, delivered in a prayer book as a form of masking and unmasking, and the play's reversal of cause-and-effect patterns.

Howe, Elizabeth Teresa. "Hell or Heaven? Providence and Don Juan." *Renascence* 37 (Summer, 1985): 212-219. Describes how Zorrilla's Don Juan expects damnation but gets salvation, the reverse of the situation in Tirso's play. Concludes that Don Juan is the "devil incarnate [and] Satan is a logical extension of the Romantic hero, pursuing self-gratification in defiance of social restraint."

Mandel, Oscar, ed. *The Theatre of Don Juan: A Collection of Plays and Views, 1630-1963.* Lincoln: University of Nebraska Press, 1963. A comprehensive study of the figure of Don Juan, which introduces Zorrilla's version with a thorough overview of his special treatment. Good for understanding the subsequent parodies, burlesques, and other travesties of the play in Spanish-speaking countries. The introductory essay on the legend is particularly insightful.

Schurlknight, Donald E. "Zorrilla and Espronceda: Considerations on Two Stories of Don Juan." In *Spanish Romanticism in Context: Of Subversion, Contradiction, and Politics*. Lanham, Md.: University Press of America, 1998. Compares *Don Juan Tenorio* with Angel de Saavedra Rivas's *Don Alvaro*, placing both plays within the context of nineteenth century Spanish Romanticism. Considers some of the inconsistences and contradictions in *Don Juan Tenorio* and explores the reasons for the play's popularity.

Wright, Sarah. "Repetition Compulsion: Redoing the *Tenorio*." In *Tales of Seduction: The Figure of Don Juan in Spanish Culture*. New York: Tauris Academic Studies, 2007. Traces the appearance of the Don Juan character in Spanish culture and Western theory from its beginnings through the early twenty-first century. Devotes a chapter to *Don Juan Tenorio* and subsequent adaptations of the play.

Don Quixote de la Mancha

Author: Miguel de Cervantes (1547-1616)
First published: El ingenioso hidalgo Don Quixote de la Mancha, part 1, 1605; part 2, 1615 (English translation, 1612-1620)
Type of work: Novel
Type of plot: Mock-heroic
Time of plot: Late sixteenth century
Locale: Spain

Principal characters:
DON QUIXOTE DE LA MANCHA, a knight-errant
SANCHO PANZA, his squire
ALDONZA LORENZO, a farm girl Quixote calls Dulcinea, his "illusionary lady"
PEDRO PEREZ, a village curate
MASTER NICHOLAS, a barber
SAMSON CARRASCO, a young bachelor of arts

The Story:

A retired and impoverished gentleman named Alonzo Quixano lives in the Spanish province of La Mancha. He reads so many romances of chivalry that his mind becomes overwhelmed with fantastic accounts of tournaments, knightly quests, damsels in distress, and strange enchantments, and he decides one day to imitate the heroes of the books he reads and to revive the ancient custom of knight-errantry. Changing his name to Don Quixote de la Mancha, he is dubbed a knight by a publican whose miserable inn he mistakes for a turreted castle.

For armor he dons an old suit of mail that belonged to his great-grandfather. Then, upon a bony old nag he calls Rosinante, he sets out upon his first adventure. Not far from his village he falls into the company of some traveling merchants who think the old man mad and beat him severely when he challenges them to a passage at arms.

Back home recovering from his cuts and bruises, he is closely watched by his good neighbor, Pedro Perez, the village priest, and Master Nicholas, the barber. Hoping to cure him of his fancies, the curate and the barber burn his library of chivalric romances. Don Quixote, however, believes his books were carried off by a wizard. Undaunted by his misfortunes, he determines to set out on the road again with an uncouth rustic named Sancho Panza as his squire. As the mistress to whom he will dedicate his deeds of valor, he chooses a buxom peasant wench famous for her skill in salting pork. He calls her Dulcinea del Toboso.

The knight and his squire sneak out of the village under cover of darkness, but in their own minds they present a brave appearance: the lean old man on his bony horse and his squat, black-browed servant on a small ass, Dapple. The don carries his sword and lance, Sancho Panza a canvas wallet and a leather bottle. Sancho goes with the don because, in his shallow-brained way, he hopes to become governor of an island.

The don's first encounter is with a score of windmills on the plains of Montiel. Mistaking them for monstrous giants, he couches his lance, sets spurs to Rosinante's thin flanks, and charges full tilt against them. One of the whirling vanes lifts him from his saddle and throws him into the air. When Sancho runs to pick him up, Quixote explains that sorcerers changed the giants into windmills.

Shortly afterward he encounters two monks riding in company with a lady in a coach escorted by men on horseback. Quixote imagines that the lady is a captive princess. Haughtily demanding her release, he unhorses one of the friars in an attempted rescue. Sancho is beaten by the lady's lackeys. Quixote betters her Biscayan squire in a sword fight, sparing the man's life on the condition that he go to Toboso and yield himself to the peerless Dulcinea. Sancho, having little taste for violence, wants to get on to his island as quickly as possible.

At an inn, Quixote becomes involved in an assignation between a carrier and a servant girl. He is trounced by the carrier. The don, insulted by the innkeeper's demand for payment, rides away without paying. To his terror, Sancho is tossed in a blanket as payment for his master's debt. The pair come upon dust clouds stirred up by two large flocks of sheep. Quixote, sure that they are two medieval armies closing in combat, intervenes, only to be pummeled with rocks by the indignant shepherds whose sheep he scattered.

At night the don thinks a funeral procession is a parade of monsters. He attacks and routs the mourners and is called Knight of the Sorry Aspect by Sancho. The two come upon a roaring noise in the night. Quixote, believing it to be made by giants, wants to attack immediately, but Sancho judiciously hobbles Rosinante so he cannot move. The next day, they discover that the noise came from the pounding of a mill.

Quixote attacks an itinerant barber and seizes the poor barber's bowl, which he declares to be the famous golden helmet of Mambrino, and his packsaddle, which he believes to be a richly jeweled caparison. Next, the pair come upon a chain gang being taken to the galleys. The don interviews various prisoners and decides to succor the afflicted. He frees them, only to be insulted by their remarks concerning his lady, the fair Dulcinea. Sancho, afraid of what will ensue from their releasing of the galley slaves, leads Quixote into the mountains for safety. There they come upon a hermit, a nobleman, who tells them a long story of unrequited love. Quixote and the hermit fight over the virtues of their respective loves. Deciding to do penance and to fast for the love of Dulcinea, Quixote gives a letter to Sancho to deliver to the maiden. When Sancho returns to the village, Quixote's friends learn from Sancho the old man's whereabouts. They return with Sancho to the mountains, hoping they can trick Quixote into returning with them. The priest devises a scheme whereby a young peasant woman will pose as a princess in

distress. Quixote, all but dead from hunger and exposure, is easily deceived, and the party starts homeward.

They come to the inn where Sancho was tossed in the blanket. The priest explains the don's vagaries to the alarmed innkeeper, who admits that he, too, is addicted to the reading of romances of chivalry. At the inn, Quixote fights in his sleep with ogres and runs his sword through two of the innkeeper's precious wineskins. The itinerant barber stops by and demands the return of his basin and packsaddle. After the party has sport at the expense of the befuddled barber, restitution is made. An officer appears with a warrant for the arrest of the don and Sancho for releasing the galley slaves. The priest explains his friend's mental condition, and the officer departs.

Seeing no other means of getting Quixote quietly home, his friends disguise themselves and place the don in a cage mounted on an oxcart. He is later released under oath not to attempt to escape. A churchman joins the party and seeks to bring Quixote to his senses by logical argument against books of knight-errantry. The don refutes the man with a charming and brilliant argument and goes on to narrate a typical romance of derring-do. Before the group reaches home, they come upon a goatherd who tells them a story and by whom Quixote is beaten through a misunderstanding.

Sometime later the priest and the barber visit the convalescing Quixote to give him news of Spain and of the world. When they tell him there is danger of an attack on Spain by the Turks, the don suggests that the king assemble all of Spain's knights-errant to repulse the enemy. At this time Sancho enters, despite efforts to bar him. He brings word that a book telling of their adventures appeared. The sight of Sancho inspires the don to sally forth again. His excuse is a great tournament to be held at Saragossa. Failing to dissuade Quixote from going forth again, his friends are reassured when a village student promises to waylay the flighty old gentleman.

Quixote's first destination is the home of Dulcinea in nearby El Toboso. While the don waits in a forest, Sancho sees three peasant girls riding out of the village. He rides to his master and tells him that Dulcinea with two handmaidens approaches. Frightened by the don's fantastic speech, the girls flee. Quixote swears that Dulcinea is not enchanted.

Benighted in a forest, the knight and his squire are awakened by the arrival of another knight and squire. The other knight boasts that he defeated in combat all Spanish knights. The don, believing the knight to be mistaken, challenges him. They fight by daylight and, miraculously, Quixote unhorses the Knight of the Wood, who is Samson Carrasco, the village student, in disguise. His squire is an old acquaintance of Sancho. The don declares the resemblances are the work of magicians and continues on his way. Upset by his failure, Carrasco swears vengeance on Quixote.

Sancho fills Quixote's helmet with curds which he procures from shepherds. When the don suddenly claps on his helmet at the approach of another adventure, he thinks his brains are melting. This new adventure takes the form of a wagon bearing two caged lions. Quixote, ever intrepid, commands the keeper to open one cage—he will engage a lion in combat. Unhappily, the keeper obeys. Quixote stands ready, but the lion yawns and refuses to come out.

The don and Sancho join a wedding party and subsequently attend a wedding festival at which the rejected lover tricks the bride into marrying him instead of the rich man she chose. Next, the pair are taken to the Caves of Montesinos, where Quixote is lowered underground. He is brought up an hour later asleep, and, upon awakening, he tells a story of having spent three days in a land of palaces and magic forests where he saw his enchanted Dulcinea.

At an inn, Quixote meets a puppeteer who has a divining ape. By trickery, the puppeteer identifies the don and Sancho with the help of the ape. He presents a melodramatic puppet show which Quixote, carried away by the make-believe story, demolishes with his sword. The don pays for the damage done and strikes out for the nearby River Ebro. He and Sancho take a boat and are carried by the current toward some churning mill wheels, which the don thinks are a beleaguered city awaiting deliverance. They are rescued by millers after the boat is wrecked and the pair are thoroughly soaked.

Later, in a forest, the pair meet a huntress who claims knowledge of the famous knight and his squire. They go with the lady to her castle and are welcomed by a duke and his duchess who read of their previous adventures and who are ready to have great fun at the pair's expense. The hosts arrange an elaborate night ceremony to disenchant Dulcinea, who is represented by a disguised page. To his great discomfort, Sancho is told that he will receive five hundred lashes as his part of the disenchantment. Part of the jest is a ride through space on a magic wooden horse. Blindfolded, the pair mount their steed, and servants blow air in their faces from bellows and thrust torches near their faces.

Sancho departs to govern his isle, a village in the domains of the duke and duchess, while the female part of the household turns to the project of compromising Quixote in his worship of Dulcinea. Sancho governs for a week. He makes good laws and delivers wise judgments, but at the end of a week, he yearns for the freedom of the road. Together he and his master proceed toward Saragossa. Quixote changes their

destination to Barcelona, however, when he hears that a citizen of that city wrote a spurious account of his adventures.

In Barcelona, they marvel at the city, the ships, and the sea. Quixote and Sancho are the guests of Moreno, who take them to inspect the royal galleys. The galley that they visit suddenly puts out to sea in pursuit of pirates, and a fight follows. Sancho is terrified.

There comes to Barcelona a Knight of the White Moon, who challenges Quixote to combat. After the old man is overcome, the strange knight, in reality the student Carrasco, sentences him to return home. Quixote goes back, determined next to follow a pastoral shepherd life. At home, the tired old man quickly declines. Before he dies, he renounces as nonsense all to do with knight-errantry, not realizing that in his high-minded, noble-hearted nature he is a great, chivalrous gentleman.

Critical Evaluation:

It has been said that *Don Quixote de la Mancha* is "the best novel in the world, beyond comparison." This belief was, is, and certainly will be shared by lovers of literary excellence everywhere. Miguel de Cervantes' avowed purpose was to ridicule the books of chivalry that enjoyed popularity even in his day, but he soared beyond this satirical purpose in his wealth of fancy and in his irrepressible high spirits as he pokes fun at social and literary conventions of many kinds. The novel provides a cross-section of Spanish life, thought, and feeling at the end of the chivalric age.

"For my absolute faith in the details of their histories and my knowledge of their deeds and their characters enable me by sound philosophy to deduce their features, their complexions and their statures," says Don Quixote, declaring his expertise in knight-errantry. This declaration affords a key to understanding Cervantes' *Don Quixote de la Mancha*, for it demonstrates both the literal and the symbolic levels of the novel—and the distinction between those levels is crucial to grasping the full import of the story. The literal level is superficial; it is about the misadventures of an eccentric and a fool. The symbolic level, however, probes much deeper; it reveals the significance of these adventures. In fact, the symbolic level deals, as all good literature does, with values. Thus, Quixote's declaration is ironic on the superficial level and, in context, on the level of its true thematic message.

On the literal level, Quixote is eminently qualified by his extensive reading to assert familiarity with the history, the deeds, and the character of virtually every knight whose existence is recorded. Indeed, his penchant for reading books of chivalry is established on the first page of the first chapter of the book. Even his niece and his housekeeper refer frequently to his reading habits. Moreover, the inventory of the don's library, made just before the books are burned, reveals the extent of his collection, and earlier mention of his omnivorous reading leads to the assumption that he has read all of them. Further evidence of Quixote's erudition is his ready knowledge of the rules of knight-errantry and his recalling the legend of Mambrino's helmet in connection with his oath of knighthood. Later, after an encounter with Yanguesan herdsmen, there is evidence, in a very lucid and pragmatic statement for a presumably insane old man, of Quixote's having read Niccolò Machiavelli, followed by the don's citation of the misfortunes that befell his hero, Amadis of Gaul.

Other adventures provide internal evidence of Quixote's knowledge about the history of chivalry. A thrashing by muleteers jogs the don's memory to analogies between his plight and similar outrages visited upon the Marquis of Mantua, Baldwin, Abindarraez, and Don Roderigo de Narvaez. After his lance is broken by a windmill, Quixote remembers the makeshift tree-limb weapon used by Diego Perez de Vargas when the latter's primary weapon was broken in battle. At another time, he explains and defends the code of knight-errantry to fellow travelers, citing Arthurian legend, the ever-present Amadis of Gaul, the stricter-than-monastic rules of knight-errantry, and the noble families of Italy and Spain who contributed to the tradition. In fact, incredible as it may seem, just before the don attacks the herd of sheep, he attributes to each sheep a title and an estate culled from his reservoir of reading—or from his overactive imagination. In addition, to rationalize his own designation as the Knight of the Sorry Aspect, he recalls the sobriquets of other knights-errant. In an attempt to inculcate Sancho Panza with the proper respect for his master, Quixote even relates biographical incidents from the lives of the squires of Amadis of Gaul and Sir Galaor. Significantly, almost craftily, he mentions that Gandalin, Amadis's squire, was also Count of the Firm Isle—a blatant inducement for Sancho to remain in the don's service. Yet, all in all, on the literal level, Quixote's mastery of chivalric lore seems to serve only as a rationalization for his ill luck.

On the symbolic level, more questions are raised than are answered. Quixote claims to have reached a "sound philosophy." Is, however, reliance on reading alone—as he has done—a valid basis for "sound philosophy," or has the don become so absorbed in his books that he is unable to formulate or express the applicability of his reading? Can, for example, literature serve as a basis for understanding reality as Quixote avers? In lieu of a clear-cut answer, Cervantes offers a paradox. Early in the text, Quixote learns from Sancho that the squire has never read any histories because he is illiterate;

but later, trying to divert the don's attention with a story, Sancho, under questioning, admits that although he had not seen the person in question, "the man who told me this story said it was so true and authentic. . . . I could swear on my oath that I had seen it all." The issues of verisimilitude and credibility are not really resolved in this novel. Consequently, these issues generate further questions about distinctions between reality and fantasy. Sancho represents empirical, commonsensical reality; the don stands for whimsy and unfettered imagination. Whose view of the world is more accurate? Cervantes is ambiguous, at best, about the answer. The question endures. Readers are left to ponder this paradox that Emily Dickinson has so succinctly described: "Much madness is divinest sense."

Another issue raised on the symbolic level involves the possible immorality of reading "too many" books. Books, in this sense, are a symbol of education, and this facet of *Don Quixote de la Mancha* may be a veiled protest against censorship in general and the *Index Librorum Prohibitorum* in particular. The literal lesson emphasizes the corruptive power of books (and, therefore, education); however, the symbolic implication—given Cervantes' sympathetic treatment of Quixote—is that books and education are liberating influences on the human psyche. Thus, the symbolic purport of *Don Quixote de la Mancha* may be a parody of the Church's monopoly of literacy in the Middle Ages, with the uninhibited don a foil to the insensitive, book-burning priest.

To be sure, Quixote becomes a tragic figure toward the end of the novel, but not for the failure of his philosophy; rather, it is society's failure to accommodate a deviation from the norm. Herein lies another symbolic level of the novel: society's intolerance of deviance. For Cervantes certainly does not make the don contemptible nor does he treat him with contempt. Such treatment would have been repellent after the tolerance of the first part of the story. Despite the satirical thrust of the novel on the symbolic level, the don himself is a sympathetic character throughout the story. Although he strives to push back time, his efforts are depicted as noble, although futile. The sympathy he evokes is that popular sympathy for the underdog who defies all odds and is broken in the attempt, in contrast to the protagonist who has everything in his favor and succumbs to a surfeit of success.

Cervantes' novel is a complex web of tangled skeins, subject to many more interpretations than those suggested here. Suffice it to say that *Don Quixote de la Mancha* is unequivocally judged the finest Spanish novel ever written and one of the greatest works in world literature.

"Critical Evaluation" by Joanne G. Kashdan

Further Reading

Allen, John J. *Don Quixote, Hero or Fool? A Study in Narrative Technique.* Gainesville: University Press of Florida, 1969. A sound starting place for students of postmodern criticism as it relates to the novel.

Bloom, Harold, ed. *Cervantes's "Don Quixote."* Philadelphia: Chelsea House, 2001. A collection of reprinted essays about the novel that were written by well-known writers and critics, including Thomas Mann, Franz Kakfa, W. H. Auden, Vladimir Nabokov, and Mark van Doren. Includes bibliographical references, an index, and an introduction by Bloom.

Cascardi, Anthony J., ed. *The Cambridge Companion to Cervantes.* New York: Cambridge University Press, 2002. Collection of essays placing Cervantes' life and work within a historical and social context, discussing Cervantes in relation to the Italian Renaissance, and assessing his influence on other writers. Another essay, "*Don Quixote* and the Invention of the Novel" by Anthony J. Cascardi, focuses on the novel.

Close, A. J. *Cervantes and the Comic Mind of His Age.* New York: Oxford University Press, 2000. Analyzes ideas about comedy and comedic writing in the Spanish Golden Age and describes how Cervantes' works reflected these concepts. Includes bibliography and index.

Coover, Robert. "The Last Quixote: Marginal Notes on the Gospel According to Samuel Beckett." In *In Praise of What Persists*, edited by Stephen Berg. New York: Harper & Row, 1983. Coover, a postmodern writer who admires Beckett and *Don Quixote*, connects postmodernism to Cervantes' work.

Entwistle, William J. *Cervantes.* Oxford, England: Clarendon Press, 1969. Essays on Cervantes' life and writing. The essay "The Hero as Pedant" addresses the reception of Cervantes' masterpiece and its rise to the "rank of a work of art." Indexed, with a brief biography and a chronological listing of his works.

Ginés, Montserrat. *The Southern Inheritors of Don Quixote.* Baton Rouge: Louisiana State University Press, 2000. An argument for the presence of Don Quixote, in spirit, in the literature of the American South.

McCrory, Donald P. *No Ordinary Man: The Life and Times of Miguel de Cervantes.* Chester Springs, Pa.: Peter Owen, 2002. A thorough biography based, in part, on original research and unpublished material. McCrory places Cervantes' life within the context of sixteenth and seventeenth century Spanish history. Includes bibliographical references and an index.

Mancing, Howard. *Cervantes' "Don Quixote": A Reference Guide.* Westport, Conn.: Greenwood Press, 2006. An excellent companion for the undergraduate student and for general readers. Individual chapters explore themes, criticism, language and style, publishing history, and other topics. Select bibliographies make this an important resource.

Predmore, Richard L. *The World of Don Quixote.* Cambridge, Mass.: Harvard University Press, 1967. Provides a brief, clear exploration of the complex world of Cervantes' great novel.

Presberg, Charles D. *Adventures in Paradox: "Don Quixote" and the Western Tradition.* University Park: Pennsylvania State University Press, 2001. A study of paradoxes that spans the literary tradition, with a special focus on *Don Quixote.*

Watt, Ian. *Myths of Modern Individualism: Faust, Don Quixote, Don Juan, Robinson Crusoe.* New York: Cambridge University Press, 1996. Watt studies the origins and literary uses of Don Quixote, Don Juan, Faust, and Robinson Crusoe as pervasive myths of the modern individualist world.

Don Segundo Sombra
Shadows on the Pampas

Author: Ricardo Güiraldes (1886-1927)
First published: 1926 (English translation, 1935)
Type of work: Novel
Type of plot: Regional
Time of plot: Late nineteenth century
Locale: Argentina

Principal characters:
DON SEGUNDO SOMBRA, a gaucho
FABIO, a young waif
DON LEANDRO GALVÁN, a rancher
PEDRO BARRALES, a gaucho
PAULA, a pretty young woman and the beloved of Fabio

The Story:

Fabio is a young lad who lives with his two maiden aunts in a small Argentine village. He dislikes his aunts, who feel, in their turn, that he is simply a bother. He is not sure that the two women are truly his relatives, for they pay him little attention as long as he gives them no trouble. Don Fabio Caceres, a rancher, occasionally comes to see the boy and take him into the country for a day, but the man ceases coming when Fabio is about eleven years old.

Fabio grows up to be a mischievous youngster who shows off for the worst element of the town. He knows all the gossip and spends most of his time hanging around the saloons; no one seems to care that he never went to school. The village loafers hint that he is an illegitimate, unwanted child. At best, he seems destined to be a ne'er-do-well who carries a chip on his shoulder in defiance of the rest of the world.

One night, a gaucho rides into the town as Fabio is going home from fishing. The man impresses the boy instantly, and, a little later, Fabio earns the gaucho's interest by warning him of an ambush laid by a knife-wielding bully. The kind words spoken by the gaucho, Don Segundo, go to the boy's heart, and Fabio immediately decides to follow the man when he leaves town. Gathering together his meager possessions, which fortunately include a saddle and two ponies, Fabio goes quietly away without telling anyone where he is going in order to escape his hated aunts. He rides to the ranch belonging to Don Leandro Galván, where he knows Don Segundo is going to spend a few days breaking wild horses.

When he arrives, the boy applies for work and is accepted. By the time Don Segundo is ready to leave the ranch on a cattle drive, Fabio has convinced Don Leandro and Don Segundo that he is a willing worker, and they let Fabio go with the other gauchos on half pay. At the end of the drive, Fabio is doing well in his apprenticeship as a gaucho.

For five years, Fabio continues under the tutelage of Don Segundo. Traveling from ranch to ranch, they work for a number of landowners. From the older man, Fabio learns to care for himself and his horses, to work cattle under various conditions, to live courageously, to get along with all kinds of people, and to have a good time singing songs, dancing, and telling stories. It is more than a way of making a living that the man passes on to the boy; it is an entire culture, a culture as old as the cattle industry and in some respects even older, going back as it does to the culture of Spain.

There are many incidents in their wanderings, including a time when Fabio wins a large amount of money by picking the winning bird in a cockfight when everyone else bets against the bird. That happens in the town of Navarro, a town that remains a lucky place in young Fabio's mind. A long cattle drive to a ranch on the seashore is also an important experience for Fabio. There he finds that he detests the countryside, and he experiences much bad luck; but he falls in love with a young woman there. He picks up quite a respectable string of horses, the tools of the gaucho's trade, and he is very proud of them. In working the cattle at the seashore ranch, however, two of the horses are injured, much to the young gaucho's dismay. One of them is badly gored by a bull, and when Fabio comes across the bull one evening while exploring with another young man, he vows to break its neck. He lassoes the beast and snaps its neck with the shock, but in doing so, he injures himself severely, breaking several bones.

While Fabio remains at the ranch convalescing from his injuries, he falls in love, he thinks, with Paula, a pretty young woman who lives on the place. Unfortunately, she leads him on while she also leads on the rather stupid son of the rancher. The other lad takes advantage of Fabio's crippled arm and attacks him with a knife. Fabio, not wanting to injure the owner's son, to fight over a woman, or to violate the father's hospitality, avoids the other fellow's thrusts until they become deadly. Then with a quick thrust, Fabio slashes the boy's forehead slightly, quickly taking the will to fight out of him. Paula, over whom the fight began, rebukes the crippled Fabio. Disgusted at her and at himself, Fabio, crippled as he is, mounts his horse and rides away to rejoin Don Segundo, who is working at a nearby ranch until Fabio is ready to travel.

Don Segundo and Fabio happen into a small village on a day when people have gathered from miles around to race horses. Fabio bets and loses a hundred pesos, then another hundred, and finally the third and last hundred he possesses. Still not believing that the situation is hopeless, he gambles five of his horses and loses them as well. He comes out of the afternoon's activity a sad young man.

He and Don Segundo are hired to trail a herd of cattle from a ranch near the village to the city to be butchered. It is a long, hard drive, even for experienced gauchos. It is made even more difficult for Fabio by the fact that he has only three horses, for the animals soon become fatigued from the work of carrying him and working the cattle on the road. When the herd stops to rest one afternoon, Fabio decides to see if he can somehow get another horse or two.

While looking about, he finds Pedro Barrales, a gaucho who traveled with him and Don Segundo several times. Pedro Barrales has a letter addressed to Señor Fabio Caceres, which he gives to Fabio. The lad looks blankly at the letter, not believing it is addressed to him, for he thinks he has no surname. Don Segundo opens the letter to find that the maiden aunts are truly Fabio's relatives and that Don Fabio Caceres, who visited him at his aunt's home, is really his father, from whom he inherited a fortune and a large, well-stocked ranch. The news saddens Fabio because he sees that it will take him away from the life he loves. He is angered, too, because he was left so long under the impression that he should be ashamed of his parentage.

Acting upon the good advice of Don Segundo, Fabio returns to his native town, however, and from there to the ranch where he began work under Don Leandro Galván, who now becomes his guardian. When Don Segundo agrees to remain with him for three years on his own ranch, Fabio is willing to settle down. Yet, the three years pass all too swiftly, and at the end of that time, Fabio is exceedingly sad when Don Segundo leaves, answering the gaucho's call to wander.

Critical Evaluation:

The Argentine poet, short-story writer, and novelist Ricardo Güiraldes was born in Buenos Aires in 1886 to a landowning family. He lived his first years in France, returned there often, and died in Paris in 1927. Although he traveled abroad frequently, Güiraldes loved his country, especially the *pampa*, the fertile plains in the province of Buenos Aires, where his family owned a ranch called La Porteña. As a young boy, he spent summers at the ranch among the gauchos, the Argentine cowboys. He learned about gaucho

life and folklore from Don Segundo Ramirez, the man immortalized in *Don Segundo Sombra*, the novel for which Güiraldes received the National Prize for Literature in 1926.

The novel is based on the author's recollections of his early life on the *pampa*. Influenced by works such as Mark Twain's *Adventures of Huckleberry Finn* (1884), the regional and poetic narrative illustrates the experience of growing up in the countryside, having the ideal gaucho as a mentor and role model. *Don Segundo Sombra* symbolizes the *pampa* and its inhabitants and represents the gaucho culture as it once existed, before the invasion of economic and industrial progress in the early twentieth century. Often compared to *El ingenioso hidalgo don Quixote de la Mancha* (1605, 1615; *Don Quixote de la Mancha*, 1612-1620), the novel's gaucho of mythical presence is the last representative of a special kind of life that was disappearing like a shadow but leaving its essence and spirit, becoming more a legend than a way of life.

The coming-of-age story, with the typical structure of a bildungsroman, is told by Fabio through recollections and memories. The twenty-seven chapters may be divided into three parts of nine chapters each. As the reader follows the narrator and protagonist Fabio in his journey toward adulthood, he or she stops with him several times so that he may retrace his steps mentally, in flashbacks. At first, when Fabio is about fourteen years old, one discovers that he considers himself an illegitimate orphan whose unhappy and purposeless life is changed drastically by the arrival of Don Segundo Sombra. Fabio sees his destiny in a nomadic free life, hoping to become a real gaucho. In the second part, Fabio reviews the five years spent learning gaucho skills and overcoming physical and spiritual tests. In the third part, the reader sees him returning to his town of origin, ready to take over his new position as a ranch owner upon the news of his legitimate right to the possessions of his father, who recognizes him as his heir before dying. In the last three chapters, he recalls the departure of Don Segundo, after reviewing his life as a landowner.

The image of Don Segundo is seen through Fabio's eyes. He admires legendary gauchos and transfers his images of them to his mentor, who becomes a hero and father figure for him. Fabio is the protagonist, but Don Segundo is the main character of his recollections. He embodies the virtues of the gaucho Fabio wants to become: laconic, serene, proud, stoic, and respectful of others, prizing freedom above all else. In the journey through the *pampa*, a delinquent, lazy orphan grows up to be an honest, hardworking member of society. His love of unconditional freedom must be given up in order to fulfill his true destiny. At the end of the novel, Fabio learns to accept his fate, having finally found his destiny after traveling physically and mentally in search of his true identity. Don Segundo has taught him to be tough and stoic, fearless and brave, ready to face challenges. With him, Fabio has explored moral and physical attributes that are desirable in a man and has learned the benefits of loyalty, courtesy, understanding, and friendship. Fabio's moments of recollection take place by a stream, a river, and a pond, indicating with the imagery of water the three different stages in the life of Fabio as he moves through this journey of learning. Each kind of water symbolizes life as a current, small at first, gaining strength later, and finally reaching stability as Fabio returns to his origins.

The three moments of recollection—at departure time, during the journey, and at the return—seem to coincide with three figures: Don Segundo, Fabio, and Raucho. Don Segundo represents the past, Fabio the present, and Raucho, Don Leandro Galván's son, the ideal future into which the present is changing. Fabio must learn from the past and accept the future for survival. The novel offers a lesson for the young people of Argentina. Güiraldes uses Don Segundo, the essence and spirit of an authentic Argentina, as a symbol to guide the country into the future. He wants to rescue and keep alive the soul of the nation. Don Segundo becomes the personification of tradition as a guiding light.

The *pampa* provides a stage and a space for Fabio's adventures as a gaucho. The interaction of nature and man provokes emotions that Fabio, the artist as a young man, observes and interprets poetically. The plot is subordinated to the description of nature and rural activities. Lights and colors are captured with impressionistic techniques. The inclusion of songs, traditional stories, proverbs, and colloquial expressions provides realistic authenticity. Even the most realistic scenes, however, are re-created with poetic imagery, characterizing Güiraldes's work as a lyrical novel with striking images.

Don Segundo Sombra, the allegorical farewell to a disappearing national figure and to the literary genre of the gaucho novel, is a classic example of the *novela de la tierra*, or regional novel, also called *criollista*, written in the 1920's in Latin America. The incorporation of the *pampa*, a regional landscape, into fiction expresses the search for authenticity, breaking with traditional models and establishing the foundation of the contemporary Latin American narrative.

"Critical Evaluation"
by Ludmila Kapschutschenko-Schmitt

Further Reading

Alonso, Carlos J. *The Spanish American Regional Novel: Modernity and Autochthony.* New York: Cambridge University Press, 1990. Discusses representative novels, illustrating the search for an indigenous artistic expression. Focuses on the complexity of *Don Segundo Sombra*'s discourse, noting the text's reference to its own process of production.

Bach, Caleb. "Poet of Shadows on the Pampa." *Americas* 54, no. 5 (September-October, 2002): 14. A profile of Güiraldes, providing an overview of his career and literary works and a description of the character of Don Segundo Sombra.

Beardsell, Peter R. "Güiraldes's Role in the Avant-Garde of Buenos Aires." *Hispanic Review* 42, no. 3 (Summer, 1974): 293-309. Explores Güiraldes's participation in the avant-garde movement of the 1920's and shows how this is reflected in his poetry and narrative. Concludes that *Don Segundo Sombra* would not have been possible without the influence of avant-garde literature.

Fitz, Earl E. *Rediscovering the New World.* Iowa City: University of Iowa Press, 1991. Approaches the writings of the Americas as a cohesive literary type. Compares Güiraldes to writers such as Mark Twain and William Faulkner, exploring how their works transcend the local to attain the universal, representing "deep regionalism."

Franco, Jean. *Spanish American Literature Since Independence.* New York: Barnes & Noble, 1973. Compares Fabio's training to a spiritual exercise and emphasizes Don Segundo's spirituality. The regional setting of the novel is seen as conducive to attaining spiritual goals away from the industrialized world.

Güiraldes, Ricardo. *Don Segundo Sombra.* Translated by Patricia Owen Steiner. Pittsburgh, Pa.: University of Pittsburgh Press, 1995. In addition to the text of the novel, this edition contains several critical essays, including discussions of myth and reality in the novel, *Don Segundo Sombra* and the Argentine literary tradition, the gaucho's world, Güiraldes's life and writing, and "*Don Segundo Sombra*: The Life of a Novel."

Vazquez Amaral, José. "Ricardo Güiraldes and the Metaphysical Gaucho: *Don Segundo Sombra.*" In *The Contemporary Latin American Narrative.* New York: Las Americas, 1970. Vazquez discusses Güiraldes's "Argentinity" and the importance of *Don Segundo Sombra* as the summation of the entire literature of the gaucho.

Doña Bárbara

Author: Rómulo Gallegos (1884-1969)
First published: 1929 (English translation, 1931)
Type of work: Novel
Type of plot: Regional
Time of plot: Early twentieth century
Locale: Arauca Valley, Venezuela

Principal characters:
DOÑA BÁRBARA, a beautiful, unscrupulous mestiza
SANTOS LUZARDO, the owner of the Altamira ranch
MARISELA, the illegitimate daughter of Doña Bárbara and Lorenzo Barquero
ANTONIO, a cowboy at the Altamira ranch
THE WIZARD, a rascally henchman of Doña Bárbara
SEÑOR DANGER, an American squatter on the Altamira ranch
DON BALBINO, the treacherous overseer at the Altamira ranch

The Story:

The Altamira ranch is a vast estate in the wildest section of the Arauca River basin of Venezuela, a ranch that was established early in the history of the country's cattle business. Late in the nineteenth century, it was divided into two parts by one of the owners' joint heirs. One part of the ranch kept the old name and went to the male heir of the Luzardo family. The other part went to a daughter who married a Barquero, and it took on the name from the new owner. As the years went by, the two families carried on a feud that killed most of the men on both sides. During the Spanish-American War, the owner of Altamira quarreled with his elder son and killed him; he then starved himself to death. His wife, Doña Luzardo, took her only remaining son to Caracas to rear him in a more civilized atmosphere.

Years go by. Finally the son, Santos Luzardo, decides to sell the ranch, which was allowed to deteriorate under irresponsible overseers. The young man goes into the back country to see the place for himself and to determine what it might be worth. On his arrival, he finds that the neighboring ranch of the Barqueros fell into the hands of Doña Bárbara, a mestiza who was the mistress of the real owner before she ran him off his property. Doña Bárbara is in the process of taking over the Altamira ranch as well, with the help of several henchmen, including Don Balbino, the ranch's overseer. Santos decides to keep the ranch and try to make it prosperous again.

Santos is able to rely on the help of a handful of loyal cowboys who knew him as a child. These include Antonio, a cowboy who was his playmate years before. Santos's first move is to end the feud between himself and the Barqueros. He finds Lorenzo Barquero living in a cabin in a swamp, the only land his mistress did not take from him. After making his peace with Lorenzo and his illegitimate daughter, Marisela, Santos takes them to live at Altamira ranch. Marisela is as beautiful as her mother, Doña Bárbara, and Santos wishes to retrieve her from barbarity.

Most of the cattle was stolen from the Altamira ranch, and only about one hundred head are left. Nevertheless, Antonio sees to it that many hundreds more are allowed to stray into wild country, thus saving them from Doña Bárbara and Señor Danger, an American squatter who is in the process of carving his own ranch out of Altamira land. One of Santos's first acts is to discharge Don Balbino, Altamira's treacherous overseer, who, since he is working for Doña Bárbara and is her lover, thereupon seeks the mestiza's protection.

Santos, who was trained as a lawyer, decides first to try legal means of repossessing the lost parts of his ranch. He goes to the local magistrate and, through his knowledge of the law, forces that official to call in Doña Bárbara and Señor Danger. They are told to permit a roundup of his cattle and to help him, since their herds are intermingled with those from Altamira. They are also told to build fences, since according to the law, they have too few cattle to let them run wild. Doña Bárbara is to help build a boundary fence between her ranch and Altamira. She accepts the decisions with surprisingly good grace. Her henchmen are amazed, for previously she rode roughshod over all opposition. The answer lies in the fact that she is secretly in love with Santos and hopes eventually to inspire his love (and acquire his property) by her beauty.

As the weeks of ranch routine pass, Santos is glad that he brought Marisela to his house, for his efforts to teach her culture keep him from losing touch with civilization. Although his interest in her is only that of a friend and tutor, Marisela falls in love with him.

Along the Arauca River are thousands of herons. When

the birds molt, the people of Altamira go out to collect the valuable plumes; fifty pounds of the feathers are sent to market with two of the cowboys, and Santos intends to use the money from the sale to fence his boundaries. On their way to market, the cowboys are murdered and the feathers stolen. Their loss and the failure of the authorities to track down the culprit cause a great change in Santos. He determines to take the law into his own hands and when necessary to match violence with violence.

His first act is to have three of Doña Bárbara's henchmen captured and sent to prison, for they were long wanted for a number of crimes. A short time later, he receives word from Doña Bárbara, who is torn between her love for him and her wish for power. She tells him that in a certain canyon he will find the thief who took the feathers. Santos goes there in the night and kills the Wizard, Doña Bárbara's most trusted and bloodthirsty henchman.

By this time, Don Balbino, Doña Bárbara's lover, becomes distasteful to her. She has him killed after discovering that it was he who stole the feathers, and, to aid Santos, she throws the blame of the Wizard's murder on Don Balbino. Having recovered the feathers, Doña Bárbara goes to town to sell them for Santos. At the same time, she has documents made out to transfer the disputed lands to their rightful owner. When she returns to her ranch, she finds that her people deserted her; they cannot understand why she turned on her trusted killers. Doña Bárbara rides immediately to Altamira, where she finds Santos talking to Marisela, whose father recently died. Because the girl's love for Santos shows plainly on her face, Doña Bárbara, unseen, draws her revolver to kill her daughter. Her own love for Santos prevents the deed, however, and she rides away without revealing her presence.

Doña Bárbara is not heard from again. The next day, a large envelope is delivered to Santos. In it, he finds a sheaf of documents returning the property she stole from him, and others transferring the Barquero ranch to Doña Bárbara's daughter, Marisela. Shortly afterward, Santos and Marisela marry, and the two ranches that were separated for many years are once again joined under one owner.

Critical Evaluation:

Doña Bárbara is the novel of the *llanos*, the tropical grassland bordering the Orinoco River in the center of Venezuela, a republic almost as large as America's Southwest. The llanos had once supplied the cavalry that filled General Simon Bolívar's revolutionary army's ranks, giving it victory over Spain's Royalist armies during Venezuela's war of independence from Spain. Next to the geography itself, the ranchwoman Doña Bárbara, who symbolizes barbarism, is the most clearly etched character, for she is a wild, dreadful, beautiful half-breed from beyond the remotest tributaries of the Orinoco. Her very name reeks of barbarism. Opposite her is Santos Luzardo, who symbolizes the civilizing energy that is trying to penetrate the llanos's savagery and tame it.

Rómulo Gallegos uses symbols for barbarism, such as the great *tolvaneras*, or whirlwinds, that periodically flay the llanos. There are also rampaging herds of horses and steers; a midnight-black stallion as savage as Satan before Santos tames him; the power of flowing rivers and currents; a fire that scorches the plains and leaves a swath of blackened embers behind; and, evoking the violent spirit of the llanos, the llanero horsemen who threaten to destroy any tendrils of civilization that come within reach. Gallegos describes the area's beauties—the flowers, sunset tints, breezes, white clouds, rains, and pink herons—but ever lurking in the background is the malaria that earlier had nearly depopulated the llanos and had caused the region's inexorable decline.

To some extent, Gallegos uses standard characterizations, but he gives sensitive depictions of the llanero, or cowboy; the boatmen of the Arauca River; the typical military officials and ranch owners; and the itinerant and sometimes rascally Syrian peddlers. Some of Gallegos's sociological types are presented as clearly as if they inhabited an animated museum. Possibly his only near caricature is Señor Danger, a one-dimensional villain intended to represent the Yankee rascal of so many Spanish American novels.

Gallegos develops his plot logically. The book combines interesting subject matter and the author's knowledge of Venezuela to produce a near masterpiece. Gallegos does not exaggerate the human cruelty, his realism is convincing, and there are few distortions. The author did not, however, provide an in-depth study of the range of the llanos's society, and the novel is thus limited at times by an unconscious social prejudice and a certain superficiality. Nevertheless, most of the characters do come alive in the book and are not likely to be forgotten by the reader, for they develop and change subtly but gradually.

The basic themes of *Doña Bárbara* are universal ones. Civilization against barbarism is as dominant a theme here as in Domingo Faustino Sarmiento's *Facundo* (1845), the masterpiece of Argentine literature. Also present are such opposing forces as humans against nature, female against male, cruelty against kindness, justice against oppression, and freedom against bureaucracy.

Doña Bárbara is rich in Venezuelan expressions, idioms, and flavor of speech. Gallegos's style moves effortlessly, without excess words or structural disorganization. *Doña Bárbara*, like other Venezuelan novels, exposes and spotlights national ills. Reform was aided by such writings but was still slow, even after Gallegos himself became president. The author was apparently not strong enough or perhaps lacked enough political acumen to accomplish what was accomplished in the nineteenth century by Argentina's two literary presidents, Bartolome Mitre and Domingo Sarmiento, who were men of action as well as of the pen.

Gallegos's *Doña Bárbara* nevertheless, represents a fine example of that important feature of Venezuelan and Latin American progress—the novel. The broadest and least restricted literary form, mirroring as it does society's ills, the novel is a supple tool in the hands of reformers such as Rómulo Gallegos, who are brave enough to risk political persecution for their writings.

"Critical Evaluation" by William Freitas

Further Reading

Alonso, Carlos J. "'Otra serîa mi historia': Allegorical Exhaustion in *Doña Bárbara*." *Modern Language Notes* 104 (March, 1989): 418-438. Examines symbolic figures and the presence of allegorical constructions in the novel.

Amaral, José Vázquez. "Rómulo Gallegos and the Drama of Civilization on the South American Plains: *Doña Bárbara*." In *The Contemporary Latin American Narrative*. New York: Las Américas, 1970. Discusses the social background of the characters and provides information about the locale and how Gallegos used it to develop his plot.

Brushwood, John S. "The Year of *Doña Bárbara* (1929)." In *The Spanish American Novel: A Twentieth Century Survey*. Austin: University of Texas Press, 1975. Analyzes the novel's characterization and narrative techniques. Situates *Doña Bárbara* in the development of the Spanish American novel.

Englekirk, John E. "*Doña Bárbara*, Legend of the Llano." *Hispania* 31, no. 3 (August, 1948): 259-270. Explains the actual terrain of the novel and compares the real characters with their fictitious counterparts.

Gollnick, Brian. "The Regional Novel and Beyond." In *The Cambridge Companion to the Latin American Novel*, edited by Efraín Kristal. New York: Cambridge University Press, 2005. *Doña Bárbara* is one of the novels discussed in this chapter.

González Echevarría, Roberto. *Myth and Archive: Toward a Theory of Latin American Narrative*. 1990. Reprint. Durham, N.C.: Duke University Press, 1998. Traces the development of Latin American literature and the emergence of the modern novel. Chapter 4 includes numerous references to Gallegos and *Doña Bárbara*.

Henighan, Stephen. "The Reconstruction of Femininity in Gallegos's *Doña Bárbara*." *Latin American Literary Review* 32, no. 64 (July-December, 2004): 29-45. Focuses on gender issues in the novel. Describes how the male protagonist Santos Luzardo, who seeks to bring civilized rationalism to the llanos, is contrasted to the female chieftain Doña Bárbara.

Spell, Jefferson Rea. "Rómulo Gallegos, Interpreter of the Llanos of Venezuela." In *Contemporary Spanish-American Fiction*. New York: Biblo and Tannen, 1968. An excellent starting point for a study of *Doña Bárbara*. Discusses the novel's depiction of the struggle between civilization and barbarism.

Dona Flor and Her Two Husbands

Author: Jorge Amado (1912-2001)
First published: Dona Flor e seus dois maridos, 1966 (English translation, 1969)
Type of work: Novel
Type of plot: Comical realism
Time of plot: Mid-twentieth century
Locale: Salvador, Brazil

Principal characters:
DONA FLOR, a woman who maintains a cooking school from home
VADINHO, her first husband, a vagabond
MIRANDÃO, his scoundrel colleague
DR. TEODORO, Flor's second husband, a pharmacist
DONA ROZALDA, her rancorous mother
DOM CLEMENTE, a parish priest
EDUARDO, her suitor

The Story:

Drunk and in drag, young Waldomiro Guimarães (popularly known as Vadinho) collapses in a public square in Salvador, Brazil, on the Sunday of Carnival. He dies from a life of drinking, gambling, and debauchery. Notified by neighbors, his wife, Florípedes Paiva (Dona Flor), hastens to the scene. Although Vadinho was a conniving scoundrel, during their seven years of marriage, the attractive rake satisfied Flor's needs. His wake is held at home, which serves also as Flor's cooking school, the Academy of Taste and Art, the main source of household income.

Vadinho had frequently absconded with savings from the school's income to finance his nocturnal forays. His companions in chronic carousing now gather at his wake, fondly remembering a carefree vagabond and an easy companion. Only a few members of his family appear, however, and briefly. Later, an elegy circulates in the bars Vadinho had frequented, magnanimously remembering that he was known as Vadinho to "whores" as well as to "friends."

Flor's mother, Dona Rozalda, arrives from her home in the interior of the country. Contriving, manipulative, and acid-tongued, she has been a chronic annoyance for her children. All have tried to escape her, and she now burdens her mourning, youngest daughter. Her dead son-in-law had been her relentless nemesis. One day, while meeting at a local festivity, accompanied by a scoundrel colleague named Mirandão, Vadinho had fooled Rozalda into believing he had prominent social status and ample financial prospects. Rozalda had always connived but failed to achieve social advancement and security through her children.

Vadinho had eyed Rozalda's daughter, Flor, and had tried to seduce the copper-skinned beauty. Finally discovering his pretentions and real intentions, Rozalda then attempted to isolate her daughter from him. The new couple was able to escape, eloping to Salvador, where they were married by a kindly parish priest, Dom Clemente. Infuriated that she has been fooled and abandoned, Rozalda became the embodiment of the vengeful mother-in-law. Vadinhno's defects enraged her, and his successes mocked her.

In the months following Vadinho's death, Flor begins to recover. Her female friends arrange candidates for her remarriage. Among the prospects is Eduardo, who preys on solitary and widowed women, taking advantage of their sentiments and savings. About to victimize Flor, he is exposed by Vadinho's former colleague, Mirandão. Flor retreats from any encounters with men. Increasingly, however, she agonizes from frustrated, unrequited needs.

Flor soon becomes acquainted with the neighborhood pharmacist, Dr. Teodoro, who has impeccable character and integrity. He is unmarried, having for most of his life taken care of his disabled mother, who had recently died. Most of Flor's neighbors encourage the suit. Enamored of Flor, the doctor chastely courts her while duly chaperoned. Charmed by his sobriety and fidelity, she marries him, and they settle in her home, enjoying a contented domesticity. All the neighbors, and Rozalda, approve.

Flor's new husband relieves her personal anxieties and sentimental cravings. However, so methodical is Teodoro that he organizes even their intimate relations, which are scheduled for Wednesdays and Saturdays and, sometimes, for weekend nights and the occasional "double dip" on workday nights. He is an amateur musician, and Flor faithfully accompanies him to the tedious concerts in which he plays. He is displeased that she becomes bored. Friends who gather to commemorate their first anniversary note the devotion and contentment of the couple, Flor's second marriage so strikingly contrasting to the first.

Vadinho appears again in Flor's life in the form of a ghostly recollection that sprawls naked on the conjugal bed. Vadinho seems an occupant of the bed, while her husband is preparing to sleep in it. Tormented by memories of the interludes of passion with Vadinho, she is torn by anxieties of fidelity to her new husband. The worlds of reality and fantasy begin to mingle. On one hand, Flor and her second husband join their resources to buy their rented house in Salvador. On the other hand, the mounting temptations from the memories of her first husband thrust Flor into the world of Afro-Brazilian divination, by which she seeks to charm away temptation. Vadinho seems loosed even in the gambling dens and brothels, making and unmaking fates and fortunes, including those of Mirandão.

Retreating to the interventions of the mythical world, Flor experiences a night of fevered delirium and vivid dreaming, surrendering in frenzied, sensual climax to the passionately remembered Vadinho. In the morning, she awakes to see Teodoro lovingly vigilant over her. She has been satisfied in spirit by her first husband, yet has remained faithful to her second husband who is beside her. She has two husbands: all she wants, and all she needs.

Critical Evaluation:

At the center of Jorge Amado's *Dona Flor Has Two Husbands* are two characters, Flor and the narrator, an omniscient observer. The story is set in Salvador in the Brazilian state of Bahia, but they occupy distinct sectors within the city: a marginal underworld, an urban petty bourgeoisie, and a provincial, small-town interior. Each realm has its own pretensions and survival tactics, and the narrator must be both a knowing intimate and a distanced observer, allowing the characters, with distinctive, though categorized, personalities, to emerge from their respective backgrounds. The narrator's position in turn places the reader in and above the setting as an engaged, sympathetic, yet critical and bemused observer.

Characters such as Dona Flor and Dr. Teodoro form the distinctive environment of Salvador and the novel. They belong to a striving middle class, surviving through discipline, acceptability, and collaboration; suffering intrigues, calamities, and declines; attempting good humor; and bearing the mockery of others. The other population is the underworld, that of Vadinho, Mirandão, and the rakes, scoundrels, gamblers, and prostitutes around them. This is a world of trickery and unctuous flattery, petty gains and dramatic losses, conniving and superstition, fellowship and getting along, and benevolence and knavery.

Among the many ironies suffusing Bahian society and the novel is that of religion. For middle-class Bahia, this religion is Roman Catholicism, organized in parishes and historic churches and supervised by clergy and vigilant sodality ladies. Its adherents pursue fortune and hope, and flee temptation and misfortune by recourse to votive-lit petitions and urgent masses. The underclass resorts to Candomblé, the spiritual synthesis of African gods and myths with Catholicism. Indulgent and easygoing, its followers, nevertheless, must be ever vigilant to trickery and the evil eye. They must themselves take recourse to otherworldly arts, relying on the rituals and incantations of their priests and priestesses.

These two spiritual worlds weave the reality and fantasy that torment, then finally reconcile, Dona Flor in her search for love and marriage. Flor's public and private needs become reconciled in the unique social and spiritual norms of Salvador. In portraying the numerous characters who define this environment, the novel achieves a unique sense of a particular time and place in Brazil, a Latin spirit blended with deep African rhythms. The narrator, joined by the reader, views with irony and some skepticism this landscape and its populace. However, the narrator is filled with the tolerance his compatriots possess, thereby imbuing the reader with his sympathy, even tenderness.

Amado was born on a plantation in Bahia, the historic center of the northeast region and deeply formative of Brazilian society and culture. Bahia's long tradition of slaveholding forged the synthesis of Afro-Brazilian culture, manifest in the religion of Candomblé, the martial art of *capoeira*, and the alluring flavors of Bahian cooking. Although his mother taught him at home to read, Amado's formal educa-

tion began at a Jesuit school in the state capital, where his impressive writing skills were first encouraged.

Amado began his literary career as a high school student, joining the circle of rising young writers in Bahia. He was accepted into law school at the University of Rio de Janeiro at the same time he published his first novel, *O país do carnaval* (1931; "the country of carnival"). Living now in the nation's capital, the young Amado, who survived financially by working as a journalist, became the intimate of a generation of luminaries in modern Brazilian fiction, poetry, and belles lettres, including Vinícius de Moraes, José Américo, Rachel de Queiroz, Gilberto Freyre, Graciliano Ramos, José Lins do Rego, and Rubem Braga.

Amado married in 1934, with the first of his children born the following year. He then published well-received novels, among them *Cacáu* (1933), *Suor* (1934), and *Jubiabá* (1935), which were translated into French and praised by writer Albert Camus. These and other works celebrated the endurance and vitality of the rural, agricultural populace, and lambasted the grinding poverty they endured. Amado joined the Communist Party, following the example of numerous Brazilian intellectuals and cultural figures who opposed the authoritarian rightist regime. Amado was arrested as a political prisoner twice under the regime.

With its overthrow, however, he became a Communist delegate to the assembly that produced the democratic constitution of 1946. In the following decade, however, dismayed by Soviet excesses, he left the party. Beginning in 1958, with the publication of *Gabriela, cravo, e canela* (*Gabriela, Clove and Cinnamon*, 1962), he entered the second phase of his literary career, popularizing worldwide a folk mystique of Bahia and Brazil. *Dona Flor* belongs to this latter phase and is as renowned as *Gabriela, Clove and Cinnamon*. Both novels were made into popular films and television dramas. Amado was elected to the Brazilian Academy of Letters in 1961.

Edward A. Riedinger

Further Reading

Armstrong, Piers. *Third World Literary Fortunes: Brazilian Culture and Its International Reception*. Lewisburg, Pa.: Bucknell University Press, 1999. This rich academic work locates Brazil and Brazilian writers in the realm of Latin American literature, and examines the complicated domestic and international receptions of their works.

Aycock, Wendell, and Michael K. Schoenke. *Film and Literature: A Comparative Approach to Adaptation*. Lubbock: Texas Tech University Press, 1988. Analyzes the comparative context in which *Dona Flor and Her Two Husbands* was made into a film that received international acclaim. Part of a larger study on film adaptations of literary works.

Bognár, Desi K. *Amado: A Personal Account*. Sarasota, Fla.: MNA, 2003. In this short memoir, a Hungarian film historian and critic recounts his experiences with Amado, some of whose novels became successful films.

Brower, Keith H., Earl E. Fitz, and Enrique Martínez-Vidal, eds. *Jorge Amado: New Critical Essays*. New York: Routledge, 2001. A collection of scholarly articles by international specialists on Amado and on Brazilian culture analyzing his life and literary output from various disciplinary perspectives.

Chamberlain, Bobby J. *Jorge Amado*. Boston: Twayne, 1990. A concise, insightful narrative of the life of Amado, with a critique of his collected works and individual novels. Presented by a Brazilian literary specialist working at the peak of the novelist's international acclamation.

Pärssinen, Martti, and Angela Bartens. *For the Sake of the People: Jorge Amado in Memoriam*. Helsinki, Finland: University of Helsinki, 2003. This academic remembrance of Amado by two European scholars of Latin America, testifies to Amado's lasting international acclaim. Examines also his work with popular political and cultural causes.

Wyels, Joyce Gregory. "Boundless Love and Death in Bahia." *Americas* 54, no. 1 (January/February, 2002). A biographical article that discusses Amado's life and death in Bahia, some of his novels, the impact of Salvador, Bahia, on the characters in his fiction, his style of writing, and the plots and themes of his books.

Doña Perfecta

Author: Benito Pérez Galdós (1843-1920)
First published: 1876 (English translation, 1880)
Type of work: Novel
Type of plot: Tragedy
Time of plot: Late nineteenth century
Locale: Orbajosa, Spain

Principal characters:
JOSÉ (PEPE) REY
DOÑA PERFECTA REY, his aunt
ROSARIO, her daughter
DON INOCENCIO, the canon of the cathedral
MARIA REMEDIOS, his sister
JACINTO, María's son

The Story:

The city of Orbajosa, with its 7,324 inhabitants, is proud of its religious atmosphere. It boasts a cathedral and a seminary but possesses nothing else to make it known to the rest of Spain, having no manufacturing. Its only agricultural activity is growing garlic. The leading citizen of Orbajosa is Doña Perfecta Rey, a widow whose wealth is the result of legal victories her brother, an Andalusian lawyer, won over her husband's family. Since her brother has a son, Pepe Rey, and she has a daughter, Rosario, the idea of marriage between the two young people seems a natural arrangement to their elders. It is for this purpose that Pepe is first sent to Orbajosa.

In his busy life as a road construction engineer, Pepe thinks little about matrimony, but he begins to do so after seeing the lovely Rosario. The girl, for her part, is attracted to her cousin, and in the beginning Doña Perfecta, too, is much taken with Pepe.

Doña Perfecta, like the other inhabitants of Orbajosa, is dominated by the Church, and as the town's most exemplary citizen she feels it necessary to be especially devout. Don Inocencio, the canon of the cathedral, has other plans for Rosario. Urged on by his sister, María Remedios, who wants the Rey fortune for her son, Jacinto, Don Inocencio, who is far less innocent than his name implies, begins conniving to end all talk of marriage between the cousins.

Pepe, through his wide travels and training, is unorthodox, though not without regard for religion. Before long, Don Inocencio makes him appear a heretic, and Doña Perfecta, forgetting her indebtedness to his father and ignoring the feelings of her daughter, refuses to let him see Rosario. The girl, made meek by strict education and dominated by her mother, lacks the courage to assert herself in declaring her love for her cousin. Soon everyone in Orbajosa—from the bishop to the working man in the fields—becomes convinced that it is a matter of religious and civic necessity to rid their city of the heretic. The unsuspecting Pepe tries to explain that he has no intention of attacking religion, but his attempts to make his position clear only make matters worse.

Finally, after several stolen interviews with Rosario in the family chapel, Pepe and Rosario decide to run away together. At the very time, however, that the conscience-stricken Rosario is revealing the plan to her mother, María Remedios arrives to warn Doña Perfecta that Pepe is entering the garden. Knowing that Pepe is coming to take Rosario away, Doña Perfecta orders one of her acquaintances to shoot. Pepe falls, mortally wounded. His death drives Rosario insane. Don Inocencio feels himself cut off from the world, and Doña Perfecta dies of cancer. Nobody gains anything, but Orbajosa is convinced it won a victory for the faith.

Critical Evaluation:

Benito Pérez Galdós went to Madrid as a student of law in 1863, but literature and the theater proved more interesting to him than the bar. Early in his literary career, he wrote several novels about politics and social customs. Then, between 1876 and 1878, Pérez Galdós became interested in religion and published three novels dealing with its different aspects: *Doña Perfecta*, the story of a town dominated by the clergy; *Gloria* (1876-1877), a novel about a clash between the Jewish and Christian religions; and *La Familia de Léon Roch* (1878), a story of religious fanaticism that ruined a happy household. All three novels are classified as belonging to the novelist's early period, although they represent a great technical advance over his first attempts.

In *Doña Perfecta*, Pérez Galdós portrays religious intolerance and hypocrisy in a small Andalusian cathedral town removed from the main current of life. The novel graphically presents what Gerald Brennan labeled "the stagnant, stupid, fanatical Spain of the country districts." Pérez Galdós also describes the clash of modern ideas against the walls of bigotry and prejudice. Representative of the new order is the scientifically trained, clear-thinking, outspoken bridge builder Pepe. The old is represented by a wealthy woman so fanatically religious that to save her daughter's immortal soul she would even condone murder.

The shadow of intolerant Doña Perfecta hovers darkly over Orbajosa, just as the cathedral looms over plaza and town. The human beings in the cathedral make it a somber place rather than the mellow, beautiful, hope-inspiring temple of God it could be. Far from attacking religion itself, Pérez Galdós's purpose in writing *Doña Perfecta* is to reform religion. He criticizes Catholicism for its faults but acknowledges that it had once given robust, rural Spain its strength.

Pérez Galdós champions the cause of progress while condemning the abuses of traditionalism, although he is aware that traditionalism could be a life-giving flame.

The novel's characterization is thinner than it is in the author's later works. Father Inocencio clearly symbolizes one of the many types of rural priests of his time, but other characters are not depicted with finesse. Character motivations are also vague at times, and gorgonlike Doña Perfecta herself is one of Pérez Galdós's weaker female characterizations. The characters are not strongly etched because Pérez Galdós viewed them not as individuals but as representatives of their class or profession. Atmosphere and setting are stressed for the same reason. An important element in *Doña Perfecta* is Pepe's hope that human beings can be led upward by education. Pepe Rey thus reflects the views of nineteenth century Spanish intellectual thought that had influenced the author, and as such he is more realistically drawn than many of the other characters in the novel.

Further Reading

Bell, T. E. *Galdós and Darwin*. Rochester, N.Y.: Tamesis, 2006. Traces the influence of Charles Darwin's evolutionary theories and other nineteenth century scientific concepts on Pérez Galdós's literary works.

Cardwell, Richard A. "Galdós' *Doña Perfecta*: Art or Argument?" *Anales Galdosianos* 7 (1972): 29-47. Discusses and questions the idea of the work as a "thesis novel." Focuses on whether Pepe Rey is a liberal martyr to a progressive ideal in a backward rural society.

McGovern, Timothy Michael. *Dickens in Galdós*. New York: Peter Lang, 2000. Compares how Pérez Galdós and Charles Dickens criticize society by creating three types of characters—the religious ascetic, the miser, and the Lazarillo, a type of national savior. Includes bibliography and index.

Scott, Paddy. *Women in the Novels of Benito Pérez Galdós and Ecá de Queiroz*. Lewiston, N.Y.: Edwin Mellen Press, 2008. A feminist analysis of the depiction of women in Pérez Galdós's work, describing how the wives and mothers in his fiction are affected by education, work, religion, and consumerism.

Shoemaker, William H. *The Novelistic Art of Galdós*. 3 vols. Valencia, Spain: Albatros Hispanofila, 1980-1982. Volume 1 offers a broad literary critique of Pérez Galdós's novels in their entirety. Volume 2 discusses each of the novels, providing an overall critique of the specific works, including structure, style, symbolism, and critical consensus.

Varey, J. E. *Doña Perfecta*. London: Grant & Cutler, 1971. A good critical introduction to the novel. Includes a discussion of the novel's situation and characters, as well as its social, moral, and political aspects. One chapter is devoted to the stylistic features of the novel.

Zahareas, Anthony N. "Galdós' *Doña Perfecta*: Fiction, History, and Ideology." *Anales Galdosianos* 11 (1976): 29-58. Focuses on the identification of certain moments in the history of Spain during the nineteenth century that might be related to Pérez Galdós's fictional events. An interesting and enlightening study.

Donald Duk

Author: Frank Chin (1940-)
First published: 1991
Type of work: Novel
Type of plot: Impressionistic realism
Time of plot: 1869 and 1981
Locale: Chinatown, San Francisco; Promontory Point, Utah

Principal characters:
DONALD DUK, a boy about to celebrate his twelfth birthday
KING DUK, his father
DAISY DUK, his mother
VENUS DUK and PENNY DUK, his twin sisters
ARNOLD AZALEA, his friend at school
UNCLE DONALD DUK, Donald's namesake uncle, brother to King Duk
MR. MEANWRIGHT, Donald and Arnold's history teacher
LARRY LOUIE, Donald's tap-dance instructor and self-proclaimed "Chinese Fred Astaire"

The Story:

Donald Duk is approaching his twelfth birthday, as Chinatown in San Francisco prepares for the Chinese New Year. Donald, in turning twelve, will have come full circle by completing his first twelve-year cycle in the Asian lunar zodiac of animal signs. In honor of this event Donald's father, King Duk, a leading Chinatown chef and businessman, has invited Uncle Donald Duk and a Cantonese opera company to visit and perform. Donald daily crosses between American subcultures, from the ethnic enclave of Chinatown to his elite private day school, while imagining himself as a present-day Fred Astaire, tap-dancing through movie scenes.

Donald's family, upholding the Chinese value of hosting guests, friends, and family during the Chinese New Year, invites Donald's Caucasian friend and schoolmate Arnold Azalea to visit. Donald's family, especially his father and uncle, take the opportunity to explain Chinese behavioral patterns and values to Arnold. The boy appreciates these explanations, but Donald himself remains generally bored or embarrassed by his native Chinese culture.

Donald is fascinated with the 108 model airplanes that King Duk is building, emblematic of the 108 outlaw heroes of The Water Margin, a traditional Chinese legend. However,

Donald is aghast when he learns that his father plans not to keep them but to set them afire and launch them from Angel Island in San Francisco Bay at the end of the Chinese New Year's celebration. Past midnight before the dawn of the first day of the New Year, Donald takes one of the smallest model planes, a P26-A Peashooter and goes to the roof of their building in Chinatown, where he meets the bizarre renegade hermit, American Kong. Donald lights the fuse of the plane and watches it flare out.

Donald is seen by the elderly Frog Twins, his neighbors, on the street during his larcenous indulgence of shooting off the plane. They do not seem to inform on him; instead, they buy a kit for him to use to replace the plane. However, his theft is noticed almost immediately by both his father and his uncle, even as his mother purchases a second replacement kit for him to complete. The situation is used by Uncle Donald Duk and by King Duk as a teaching moment for young Donald. They want him to understand family and cultural traditions concerning honesty, honor, and personal courage.

As the days of the New Year continue, King Duk begins to prepare to play the role of Kwan Kung in the opera. He temporarily gives up eating meat, having sexual relations, socializing, talking, and drinking alcohol. He will not even look people in the eye unless he means them harm. The message of his example becomes clear to Donald: Life is serious business, and everyone must take seriously the heroic roles they are expected to play.

Donald begins to have frightening and vivid dreams about Kwan Kung and about various historical events leading up to the Promontory Point, Utah, completion of the transcontinental railroad in 1869. These dreams occur even before Donald and Arnold go to the public library to learn about the Chinese laborers who worked for the Central Pacific railroad and the so-called Big Four businessmen who controlled the California-based central Pacific Railroad: Leland Stanford, Collis Huntington, Mark Hopkins, and Charles Crocker. The role of these Chinese laborers has been undervalued and marginalized by historians, including Mr. Meanwright and Meanwright's professor at Berkeley, whose opinions he repeatedly invokes in his classes. Donald repeatedly dreams himself into the historic event with remarkable accuracy and a clear intent to write a more comprehensive history of the railroad that includes the remarkable and heroic contributions of the Chinese immigrants who built it. He imagines Charles Crocker in a white suit on a white stallion, showing humility as he apologizes to Kwan Kung over workplace issues on the railroad.

During the two weeks of the Chinese New Year celebration, Donald undergoes a rather rapid coming of age, diametrically changing his viewpoint concerning Asian American identity and its context within mainstream American culture. Arnold's parents take a trip to Hawaii, and Arnold becomes a houseguest in the Duk home, allowing cultural features of the New Year celebration to be voiced aloud rather than silently practiced, as Arnold is instructed concerning Cantonese Chinese New Year's traditions. Because it is Donald's totemically important "number-twelve year," Uncle Donald Duk, for example, feels justified in giving away envelopes containing fifty dollars, emphasizing the landmark birthday for Donald as he is on the cusp of manhood.

Early in the morning, Donald sees his father and other restaurant owners shop for fresh fish and vegetables in predawn Chinatown and North Beach. As Donald begins to feel more pride and less embarrassment about his father, his father reciprocates in showing true awe at the dreams with which he believes Donald has been gifted. King Duk is devoted to his Cantonese traditions, but he has never been visited by such dreams as Donald has of the Cantonese Central Pacific Railroad's crews winning the world tracklaying record against the largely Irish Union Pacific crews. The Chinese New Year celebration ends with the family's trip to Angel Island to set off the 108 toy airplanes and the Lantern Festival on the final, fifteenth day of celebration. Donald for the first time takes his place as one of the runners in the dragon.

Critical Evaluation:

Frank Chin has made significant contributions in many genres, including the plays *The Chickencoop Chinaman* (pr. 1972, pb. 1981) and *The Year of the Dragon* (pr. 1974, pb. 1981), the novels *Gunga Din Highway* (1994) and *Donald Duk*, the short-story collection *The Chinaman Pacific and Frisco R.R. Co.* (1988), and the social criticism collection *Bulletproof Buddhists, and Other Essays* (1998). He has also coedited both *Aiiieeeee! An Anthology of Asian-American Writers* (1974) and *The Big Aiiieeeee!* (1991). Despite or possibly because of this "multigenre" success, his novels have perhaps not received the attention that—at least in the case of *Donald Duk*—they eminently deserve. Chin's public and contentious verbal sparring with noted Chinese American novelists Maxine Hong Kingston and Amy Tan has not endeared him or his work to literary critics or college professors, who often—rightfully, most would say—teach Kingston and Tan while perhaps relegating Chin to the role of critic and editor rather than a major voice in the contemporary novel.

In any case, *Donald Duk* works well and can be viewed initially as simply a charming bildungsroman, recounting the coming of age of a precocious, introspective Chinese American young man in San Francisco. However, the text also introduces a palette of Asian American historical events, legacies, and themes, beginning with the nineteenth century exploitation of Chinese laborers, first in the gold fields of California then during the construction of the transcontinental railroad. The distortion of classic Chinese philosophy and literature is eloquently presented in classroom scenes involving Mr. Meanwright, and this dramatization shows clearly the danger of stereotyping and pigeonholing entire cultures through the refractive lens of any single cultural recorder.

Indeed, the statements of Mr. Meanwright provide a barometer for Donald's metamorphosis over the course of the novel. The boy's attitude concerning his personal identity changes during the narrative, as does his relative degree of acceptance of the Cantonese Chinese culture that his father and uncle so faithfully honor. In the opening chapter, for example, Mr. Meanwright simplistically defines the Chinese concept of *tien ming* as passivity; by the end of the text, Donald challenges Mr. Meanwright and redefines his understanding of "the mandate of heaven." As he develops a more complete and comprehensive understanding of *tien ming*, he comes to understand the values and not merely the words and gestures of Cantonese culture.

Although it might initially seem that *Donald Duk* could be viewed as a buddy novel between Donald and his friend Arnold, the latter is no more important than one of Henry James's *ficelles*. That is, he is a character important only in allowing a more important character to incorporate exposition into the novel's dialogue. The focus of the novel is Donald Duk's coming of age as influenced by Uncle Donald Duk and especially by King Duk. King, in his roles both as a respected chef and as a revered actor of Cantonese opera, shows Donald how to be purposeful in life. He teaches the boy how to regard a meal or the acting of a play with the humility, respect, awe, and attention to detail that those activities so richly deserve.

As the fuses of the 108 model airplanes, emblematic of the Thirty-six Stars of Heavenly Spirits and Seventy-two Stars of Earthly Fiends, are lit at Angel Island, each briefly flames out before going dark. They therefore provide a visual image of the central message of the novel, the full understanding of *tien ming*, the mandate of heaven, that "like everything else, it begins and ends with *Kingdoms rise and fall, Nations come and go*, and food." As beautiful and intricate as the toy airplanes are, King Duk constructs them to engage in the purifying act of the New Year: divesting oneself of possessions in a fiery burst. Significantly, once the action is over, King Duk—the great chef, the Cantonese actor, and the doting parent—asks again, "Anybody hungry?" emphasizing as always the importance of food in defining and sustaining human communities, including the customs of hospitality and epicurean expertise.

Richard Sax

Further Reading

Chin, Frank, et al., eds. *Aiiieeeee! An Anthology of Asian-American Writers*. Garden City, N.Y.: Anchor Doubleday, 1975. A landmark anthology that helped to define the flowering of Asian American contemporary writers, though admittedly polemic both in selection of authors and in sociopolitical orientation.

_____. *The Big Aiiieeeee!* New York: Meridian, 1991. An eclectic collection of Asian American writing, headnoted with Chin's own polemic essay, "Come All Ye Asian American Writers of the Real and the Fake."

Goldstein-Shirley, David. "'The Dragon Is a Lantern': Frank Chin's Counter-Hegemonic Donald Duk." *49th Parallel: An Interdisciplinary Journal of North American Studies* 6 (2001). Insightful article that notes the lack of deserved critical acclaim for Chin's first novel and that summarizes most of the principal themes and conflicts of the text.

Goshert, John Charles. *Frank Chin*. Boise, Idaho: Boise State University Western Writers Series, 2003. Brief biography that includes critical evaluations of all of Chin's major works in prose and drama through 2003.

Richardson, Susan B. "The Lessons of *Donald Duk*." *MELUS* 24, no. 4 (Winter, 1999): 57-76. Cultural explication of the significance of the text, noting Chin's deftness in conveying Chinese customs and traditions within a compelling fictional narrative.

Takaki, Ronald. *Strangers from a Different Shore: A History of Asian-Americans*. Rev. ed. Boston: Back Bay Books, 1998. This social history provides a context both for the variety of Asian subcultures in the San Francisco Bay Area and for the significance and impact of the legacy of the Chinese male laborers who in the late 1860's built the Central Pacific portion of the transcontinental railroad.

The Double-Dealer

Author: William Congreve (1670-1729)
First produced: 1693; first published, 1694
Type of work: Drama
Type of plot: Comedy
Time of plot: Seventeenth century
Locale: London

Principal characters:
MELLEFONT, an earnest young man
LORD and LADY TOUCHWOOD, his uncle and aunt
CYNTHIA, his sweetheart
MASKWELL, his false friend

The Story:

Lady Touchwood is infatuated with her husband's nephew, Mellefont, and confesses her ardor to him. Mellefont, who pledged himself to Cynthia, daughter of Sir Paul Plyant, rebukes Lady Touchwood, whereupon she attempts to end her life with his sword. When he prevents her attempt, she vows revenge. Fearing the designs of Lady Touchwood, Mellefont engages his friend Careless to keep Lady Plyant, Cynthia's stepmother, away from Lady Touchwood. Careless reveals his distrust of Maskwell, Mellefont's friend, who is under obligations to Lord Touchwood. Out of sheer spite, Lady Touchwood gives herself to Maskwell. In return, Maskwell promises to help Lady Touchwood by insinuating to Lady Plyant that Mellefont really loves her, not her stepdaughter Cynthia.

Lady Touchwood's plan begins to work. Old Sir Paul Plyant and Lady Plyant express indignation when they are told that Mellefont desires Lady Plyant. Actually, Lady Plyant is flattered and merely pretends anger, but she is nevertheless shocked that Mellefont intends to marry Cynthia for the ultimate purpose of cuckolding Sir Paul. She rebukes him but at the same time tells the puzzled young man not to despair. Maskwell reveals to Mellefont that he is Lady Touchwood's agent in provoking trouble, but he does not reveal his real purpose, which is to create general confusion and to win Cynthia's hand.

Lord Touchwood, refusing to believe that his nephew plays a double game, is scandalized when Lady Touchwood recommends canceling the marriage on the grounds that Mellefont made improper advances to her. Maskwell, instructed by Lady Touchwood, ingratiates himself with Lord Touchwood by saying that he defended Lady Touchwood's honor and prevailed on Mellefont to cease his unwelcome attentions.

Maskwell, to further his plans, tells Mellefont that his reward for assisting in the breakup of Mellefont's marriage to Cynthia is the privilege of bedding with Lady Touchwood. The fake friend pretends that he wishes to be saved from the shame of collecting this reward, and he asks the credulous Mellefont to go to Lady Touchwood's chamber and there surprise him with Lady Touchwood. When Lord Plyant, frustrated by Lady Plyant's vow to remain a virgin, complains to Careless that he does not have an heir, Careless waggishly promises to see what he can do in the matter.

Mellefont, to escape the evil that is brewing, impatiently urges Cynthia to elope with him. Although she refuses, she promises to marry no one but him. When she challenges Mellefont to thwart his aunt and to get her approval of their marriage, he promises to get Lady Touchwood's consent that night.

Lady Plyant, meanwhile, consents to an assignation with Careless. When Lord Plyant appears, Careless gives her, secretly, a note containing directions for their meeting. Lady Plyant, anxious to read Careless's letter, asks her husband for a letter that he received earlier. Pretending to read her husband's letter, she reads the one given her by Careless. By mistake she returns her lover's letter to her husband.

When she discovers her mistake, she reports it in alarm to Careless, but Lord Plyant already read the letter. Lady Plyant insists that it was part of an insidious plot against her reputation, and after accusing her husband of arranging to have it written in order to test her fidelity, she threatens divorce. Careless pretends that he wrote it in Lord Plyant's behalf to test his wife's virtue. Foolish as he is, Lord Plyant is not without suspicion of his wife and Careless.

That night, Mellefont conceals himself in Lady Touchwood's chamber. When she enters, expecting to find Maskwell, Mellefont reveals himself. Lord Touchwood, informed by Maskwell, then appears. When he threatens his nephew, Lady Touchwood pretends that the young man is out of his wits. Not suspecting Maskwell's treachery, Lady Touchwood later tells him of her lucky escape. Maskwell, in a purposeful soliloquy, reveals to Lord Touchwood his love for Cynthia. Duped, the old man names Maskwell his heir and promises to arrange a marriage between Cynthia and the schemer.

Lady Touchwood learns of Maskwell's treachery when

Lord Touchwood tells her that he intends to make Maskwell his heir. Chagrined by her betrayal, Lady Touchwood urges her husband never to consent to Cynthia's marriage with anyone but Mellefont.

Maskwell, still pretending to be Mellefont's friend, makes his final move by plotting with the unwary Mellefont to get Cynthia away from her house. His intention being to marry her himself, he privately tells Cynthia that Mellefont will be waiting for her in the chaplain's chamber. Careless checks Maskwell's carefully laid plans, however, then discloses Maskwell's villainy to the young lovers. Cynthia and Lord Touchwood, in concealment, overhear Lady Touchwood rebuke Maskwell for his betrayal of her, and eventually she tries to stab her lover but is overcome with emotion. Maskwell then reveals the meeting place where Mellefont, in the disguise of a parson, will be waiting for Cynthia. Lady Touchwood, planning to disguise herself as Cynthia, hurries away to meet Mellefont there.

Lord Touchwood, knowing of her plan, puts on a chaplain's habit and confronts his wife when she comes to make overtures to the man she supposes is Mellefont. The whole plot is uncovered and Maskwell, the double-dealer, is unmasked; Mellefont, cleared of all suspicion, takes Cynthia for his own.

Critical Evaluation:

After the great success of his first comedy, *The Old Bachelor* (1693), William Congreve was disappointed at the poor reception of *The Double-Dealer*, which he considered a better play on a more serious theme. Serious it was; like other contemporary comedies, it satirizes the follies and vices of the time, but here the emphasis is on the vices rather than the follies. An unusual combination of Restoration comedy and Jacobean melodrama, the play's action is largely devoted to the intrigues of the villain Maskwell. Audiences were apparently uncomfortable at being forced to take such a long hard look at Machiavellian treachery and romantic knavery at work. As John Dryden pointed out, "The women think he has exposed their bitchery too much and the gentlemen are offended with him, for the discovery of their follies, and the way of their intrigues, under the notion of friendship to their ladies' husbands." Maskwell, in the depth of his resourceful villainy, is reminiscent of William Shakespeare's Iago, and Lady Touchwood compares him to a devil.

Lady Touchwood, of course, is herself a villain, but, as one of the victims of Maskwell's double-dealing, a lesser one. As she reminds Maskwell, her excuse is "fire in my temper, passion in my soul, apt to every provocation, oppressed at once with love, and with despair. But a sedate, a thinking villain, whose black blood runs temperately bad, what excuse can clear?" Unquestionably, the depiction of burning love turning into burning hatred has seldom been as powerful in a work professing to be a comedy as it is in Congreve's play. Lady Touchwood, indeed, has struck some critics as an almost tragic figure. Other indications of the playwright's striving for tragic effect are the unusual number of soliloquies and the play's ending with a piece of moralizing, rather than (as was customary for Restoration comedy) a dance.

Because Congreve's focus of attention is on Maskwell, his hero and heroine are given relatively short shrift. Mellefont and Cynthia are an agreeable pair of lovers, but no more than that. Cynthia is shown to be sensible and sincere, but she has none of the sparkling wit that was to make Congreve's Millamant so admirable. Nor are there any of the almost obligatory battles of wit between hero and heroine. Indeed, Mellefont appears much of the time to be a passive dupe and a fool, so much so that Congreve felt obliged to defend his hero from such charges in the play's dedication.

The plot is original; Congreve was proud that "the mechanical part of [the play] is perfect." Consciously trying to incorporate the three unities into a classical form, he succeeded at least in molding a work that has unity of time (the action is continuous, over a three-hour period) and place (it all takes place in one gallery). As for unity of action, the plot is unusually tight, but there are subplots in the form of the cuckolding of Sir Paul Plyant by Careless and of Lord Froth by Brisk. Indeed, what levity and wit the play has to offer are largely contained in these subplots. The various affectations of the minor characters, the romantic intrigues between the ladies and their gallants, and such brilliantly actable passages as the dialogue between Brisk, Lord Froth, and Careless on whether or not one should laugh at comedies, are ample evidence that Congreve had not forgotten that his prime task as a comic playwright was not to moralize—at least, not overtly—but to entertain.

Further Reading

Birdsall, Virginia Ogden. *Wild Civility: The English Comic Spirit on the Restoration Stage*. Bloomington: Indiana University Press, 1970. Good introduction to *The Double-Dealer* in chapter 7, "Congreve's Apprenticeship." Interprets the play as an exploration of the fate of the gullible in a treacherous world where appearances conceal realities.

Hoffman, Arthur W. *Congreve's Comedies*. Victoria, B.C.: University of Victoria Press, 1993. Stimulating discussion in chapter 2, "The Pessimism of Comedy: *The Double-Dealer*," includes the play's historical background,

John Dryden's protection, and verbal and structural connections with Shakespeare's *Othello, the Moor of Venice* (pr. 1604).

Holland, Norman N. *The First Modern Comedies: The Significance of Etherege, Wycherley, and Congreve*. Cambridge, Mass.: Harvard University Press, 1959. Chapter 13 discusses the combination in *The Double-Dealer* of a serious plot with comic action. Claims that the play is a failure because the hero, the good but naïve Mellefont, is passive while the villain, the worldly wise Maskwell, is an active and successful intriguer.

Owen, Susan J., ed. *A Companion to Restoration Drama*. Malden, Mass.: Blackwell, 2001. Collection of essays discussing the types of Restoration drama, placing these plays within the context of their times, and analyzing works by individual playwrights. There are numerous references to Congreve and his plays, which are listed in the index. His work is also considered in Miriam Handley's essay "William Congreve and Thomas Southerne."

Van Voris, W. H. *The Cultivated Stance: The Designs of Congreve's Plays*. Dublin: Dolmen Press, 1965. Chapter 3 provides a good account of Congreve's imposition of a "mechanically perfect neoclassical order" on the play and a valuable discussion of its characters and political ramifications.

Young, Douglas M. *The Feminist Voices in Restoration Comedy: The Virtuous Women in the Play-Worlds of Etherege, Wycherley, and Congreve*. Lanham, Md.: University Press of America, 1997. Focuses on the female characters in Congreve's plays who demand independence from and equality with men before they commit to courtship or marriage. Devotes a chapter to *The Double-Dealer*.

Dover Beach

Author: Matthew Arnold (1822-1888)
First published: 1867, in *New Poems*
Type of work: Poetry

Matthew Arnold's "Dover Beach" is a poem set near Dover, along the southeast coast of England, where Arnold and his new wife spent their honeymoon in 1851. It is believed that the poet wrote the early draft of "Dover Beach" while here, overlooking the English Channel toward the coast of France, about twenty-six miles away. Arnold and his wife are often considered the models for the speaker and listener in the poem, although any young man and woman could represent the two figures in the tale, caught in a moment of their early lives.

"Dover Beach" is most often classified as a dramatic monologue, a poetic form that Alfred, Lord Tennyson, and especially Robert Browning, found extremely attractive. The monologue, or poem spoken by a single voice, is made dramatic by the presence of a silent audience of one or more listeners, whose responses may be indicated by the speaker, or persona. In this way the poet may be empowered to express views using another person's voice, as William Shakespeare is known for doing.

This strategy may have been particularly attractive to Arnold, for the views of his speaker are diametrically opposed to his own education and upbringing. Matthew was six years old when he was moved into the Rugby School after his clergyman father Thomas Arnold became its headmaster, or principal. As headmaster, Thomas Arnold gained a reputation for educational reform, based on his commitment to the high seriousness of making students aware of the moral as well as the social issues that would make them responsible citizens.

"Dover Beach" has often been read as a kind of seismological record of the shock waves in traditional religion brought about by the New Science in the mid-nineteenth century. The geology of Charles Lyell and others was forcing Europeans and Americans to rethink how life began on the planet. Lyell's discoveries of fossils dating back more than one million years were making it increasingly difficult to accept the traditional notion in the book of Genesis that the world is the work of a creator a mere six or seven thousand years ago. By 1851, when "Dover Beach" was probably written, Charles Darwin, Alfred Russell Wallace, and other scientists had already theorized the essentials of evolution, but it would take Darwin another eight years to publish his findings. Even then, Darwin published *On the Origin of Species by Means of Natural Selection* (1859) only at the urging of his friends, who warned him that others would publish first if he did not set aside his concerns for the devastating moral and spiritual consequences of challenging the traditional story of how life began. It is probably no coincidence that Arnold himself postponed the publication of "Dover Beach" until 1867.

The poem begins with a naturalistic scene, clearly within the Romantic tradition established by William Wordsworth. Like Wordsworth, Arnold understands the elegance and power of simple language: "The sea is calm tonight./ The tide is full, the moon lies fair/ Upon the straits." As often noted, the first stanza contains fourteen lines and the second and third stanzas have six and eight lines, respectively, suggesting the sonnet form, but without its more complicated meter and rhyme systems. From its initial visual images, the first stanza and the subsequent two stanzas move toward the dominance of auditory images. The shift is justified by the obviously limited opportunity to see, even with moonlight, but also by the strong impact of the waves breaking on the beach. By the first stanza's end, the persona, or speaker, has established the poem's central metaphor of the waves' "tremulous cadence slow" to represent an "eternal note of sadness." Additionally, a mere five lines into the poem, the voice has introduced a listener in the scene—telling the reader to "Come to the window"—setting up a tension: Who is the listener? What will be the effect of the melancholy poetic statement on that listener?

This "eternal note" draws the persona further from the directly visualized opening scene with its simple but strong language. The allusion to the ancient Greek tragic dramatist Sophocles offers a context for the speaker's growing "sadness." (Arnold was among one of the last generations for whom a classical education entailed learning ancient Greek and Latin to read the classics in their original languages.) The allusion also draws the poem into the more didactic strategy of a statement—asserting rather than implying meaning—and the deployment of something like allegory—a "Sea of Faith" once at its "flow" but now at its "ebb." This third stanza also reveals evidence of the poet's effort at elevating the language, producing the difficult opening lines in which that sea once "round earth's shore/ Lay like the folds of a bright girdle furled," a choice of words guaranteed to confuse the modern reader. This "girdle" is appropriate to the classical context of Sophocles, but not to the modern world, where it denotes an article of intimate apparel. However, attempts of academics to clarify that meaning have distracted attention from the figurative logic of a sea as a "girdle," or belt, as well as from the unfortunate combination of sounds in "girdle furled." Another issue left unaddressed is the dominance of pessimism in the persona's inability to attend to the logic of this "Sea of Faith": Whatever ebbs will inevitably flow in the future.

The final stanza recalls the earlier reference to the listener—"Ah, love, let us be true/ To one another!"—to focus on the melancholy consequences of the weakening of faith. To the persona, and presumably the poet, the world truly is "a land of dreams," pipe dreams with nothing to believe in, not just God and an afterlife but "joy," "love," and so on. This is Romantic love at its most radical. Without love between a man and a woman, the world is as confusing—and as lethal—as a night battle, fraught with friendly fire. In a sense, Arnold is announcing the big question for the modern world, intent on forcing love to bear the enormous weight of providing human lives with meaning: If love is all humans have, what do they do when they cannot find love, or keep it? It is a question that resonates through the novels, too, of Ernest Hemingway, such as in his *A Farewell to Arms* (1929), or in the contexts of wedding receptions, where some have to suppress the depressing thought, will this be the one of every two marriages that ends in divorce?

"Dover Beach" is the most anthologized text in the English language, and a frequent source of allusions for writers in their own works. One index of the poem's effect on readers of poetry is a poem by American poet laureate Anthony Hecht. In his "Dover Bitch: A Criticism of Life" (1996), Hecht focuses on the silent listener in Arnold's poem, developing her character as a woman who is definitely not the speaker's wife, and identifying the persona in his poem as someone who knew Arnold, the speaker in "Dover Beach." Hecht's poem indicates that the woman responds to Arnold's expression of melancholy, but her first response of sadness is displaced not by erotic desire but by anger at his treating her as "a sort of mournful cosmic last resort." Although Arnold specialists Kenneth and Miriam Allott may attempt to defuse Hecht's parody as "an irreverent *jeu d'esprit*," this is no "witty or humorous trifle." The perceptive Hecht grasps the shabby treatment of the woman by Arnold's speaker, who is using her as a consolation prize for his loss of faith. By implication, Hecht also addresses the sexual mores of Arnold's time, when the young poet could never have lived with his future bride and may well have resorted to Hecht's less respectable female character. Unlike brides in Arnold's day, bridegrooms were not expected to come to the marriage beds as virgins.

Hecht's poem speaks to his confidence in his reader's familiarity with Arnold's poem. That familiarity is evident in the usual catalog of references to "Dover Beach" in popular culture, including in the rock album *Snakes & Arrows* (2007) by Rush, the American film *The Anniversary Party* (2001), Joseph Heller's novel *Catch-22* (1961), Norman Mailer's Vietnam protest book *The Armies of the Night* (1968), and a composition for string quartet and baritone by Samuel Barber. To further demonstrate the poem's continuing influence, reference to "Dover Beach" is included in the climactic scene of Ian McEwan's novel *Saturday* (2005).

Earl G. Ingersoll

Further Reading

Allott, Kenneth, and Miriam Allott. "Arnold the Poet: Narrative and Dramatic Poems." In *Matthew Arnold*, edited by Kenneth Allott. Athens: Ohio University Press, 1976. A useful introduction to Arnold's narrative and dramatic poems by Arnold specialists.

Buckler, William E. *On the Poetry of Matthew Arnold*. New York: New York University Press, 1982. Buckler presents his well-regarded reading of Arnold's poetry.

Caldwell, Lisa. "Truncating Coleridgean Conversation and the Re-Visioning of 'Dover Beach.'" *Victorian Poetry* 45, no. 4 (Winter, 2007): 429-445. Caldwell examines Arnold's "Dover Beach" in the context of Samuel Taylor Coleridge's conversation poems.

Clausson, Nils. "Arnold's Coleridgean Conversation Poem: 'Dover Beach' and 'The Eolian Harp.'" *Papers on Language and Literature* 44, no. 3 (Summer, 2008): 276-304. Clausson discusses Arnold's artistic debt to poet Samuel Taylor Coleridge.

Gollin, Richard M. "'Dover Beach': The Background of Its Imagery." *English Studies* 48 (1968): 493-511. Gollin examines the unity of "Dover Beach," which, he argues, is based in rich imagery.

Roberts, Robin. "Matthew Arnold's 'Dover Beach,' Gender, and Science Fiction." *Extrapolation* 33, no. 3 (Fall, 1992): 245-257. Explores how Arnold's "Dover Beach" has inspired science-fiction writers, arguing, too, that the persona's situation in Arnold's poem is reminiscent of an extraterrestrial world.

Down There

Author: Joris-Karl Huysmans (1848-1907)
First published: *Là-bas*, 1891 (English translation, 1924)
Type of work: Novel
Type of plot: Fantasy
Time of plot: Late nineteenth century
Locale: Paris

Principal characters:
DURTAL, a man of letters
DES HERMIES, a doctor
HYACINTHE CHANTELOUVE, Durtal's mistress
LOUIS CARHAIX, a bellringer
MADAME CARHAIX, his wife
GÉVINGEY, an astrologer

The Story:

Durtal decides to write a biography of Gilles de Rais, the French marshal briefly associated with Joan of Arc, who was the subject of a famous sorcery trial in 1430. His friend des Hermies expresses his delight that Durtal is abandoning the realistic novel, but Durtal wants to apply the methods of modern realism to his task, in spite of the difficulties involved.

Des Hermies takes Durtal to the bell tower of a church and introduces him to the bell ringer Louis Carhaix, who asks to meet him. Carhaix thinks he might be useful to Durtal's research. Durtal describes the early part of Gilles de Rais's life to des Hermies, observing that his excessively luxurious lifestyle alarmed his expectant heirs to petition the king to prevent his selling off parts of the estate. The debts that Gilles de Rais subsequently ran up, Durtal opines, caused him to take an interest in the magical arts, by which means he hoped to

learn the secret of making gold. After his alchemical experiments failed, Durtal claims, Gilles de Rais turned to active Satanism and the mass murder of children.

Having heard Durtal's account, des Hermies raises the subject of modern Satanism and brushes aside Durtal's opinion that there is no such thing, with an assurance that it is rife in contemporary Paris. Durtal thinks that it would help his work enormously to be able to study Satanist rites firsthand. Later, at Carhaix's house, des Hermies offers an account of the uninterrupted descent of a Satanist tradition from the time of Gilles de Rais to modern times. He then begins supplying Durtal with research materials supporting this contention.

Durtal receives an admiring letter from a woman who read his last work of fiction. He replies to it, thus beginning an extensive correspondence that inflames his curiosity considerably. She uses a pseudonym, but he eventually guesses that she might be Hyacinthe Chantelouve, the wife of the historian at whose house he first met des Hermies. This guess is confirmed when she confronts him in Gilles de Rais's castle, where he went to soak up the atmosphere. The two become lovers.

At Carhaix's house des Hermies introduces Durtal to an astrologer named Gévingey, with whom they discuss spiritualism and various other aspects of modern occultism, including the kinds of demon called incubi and succubi. Gévingey names a fallen priest called Canon Docre as an accomplished black magician and suggests that he is an intimate of the Chantelouves. Durtal cannot believe at first that his new mistress is a Satanist, but evidence to that effect begins to accumulate.

After reviewing the record of Gilles de Rais's supposed atrocities, Durtal goes to visit the Chantelouves, where the conversation quickly turns to Satanism and Canon Docre. Durtal's infatuation with Madame Chantelouve is still increasing in intensity, and so is his desire to meet Canon Docre, but he finds some distraction in his continuing discussions with des Hermies and Carhaix on various aspects of magic and demonology, including the exploits of a certain Dr. Johannès, who supposedly freed Gévingey from the evil influence of Docre. He also carries his private account of Gilles de Rais's career forward to the beginning of his trial.

Madame Chantelouve eventually promises to take Durtal to a black mass conducted by Docre. She confesses to being infatuated with the man at one time. While waiting for the appointed time, Durtal completes his account of the trial of Gilles de Rais's, including his lurid confession and extravagant repentance. Madame Chantelouve takes him to the place where the black mass is to be held. He watches with interest but finds the experience rather disappointing; eventually he takes Madame Chantelouve away when she seems to be overcome by the incense that is used. They part on bad terms.

Durtal describes the black mass to des Hermies, Carhaix, and Gévingey, and they discuss its relationship to orthodox religion at some length. Carhaix argues that the prevalence of Satanism is evidence of the decadence and corruption of their society, possibly marking the nearing of its end and the Second Coming of Christ. Durtal agrees that the world is indeed sick and resolves not to have any further contact with Madame Chantelouve—a decision that she eventually accepts in a bitter letter.

Des Hermies tells Durtal more about the virtuous magic of Dr. Johannès and his miraculous cures, but Durtal is as reluctant to credit the power of white magic as he was to credit the power of black. Des Hermies confesses that he remains skeptical, causing Durtal to express a reluctant envy of Carhaix's faith. At Carhaix's house, Durtal adds a brief appendix to his account of Gilles de Rais's career, describing the marshal's execution. The three friends deliver their final verdict on the century that seems to them all to be moving to a sadly ignominious end as "storm-clouds of foul abomination" gather on its horizon. Carhaix alone conserves hope for the future in his vision of a magnificent return of the Holy Spirit.

Critical Evaluation:

Down There is more a debate than a novel. In his most famous work, *À rebours* (1884; *Against the Grain*, 1922), Joris-Karl Huysmans took a flirtatious delight in overturning all conventional evaluations of morality and art in his description of the reclusive Jean Des Esseintes's attempts to live a perfectly decadent life. Durtal is by no means as ambitious a protagonist, and his flirtation with Satanism and Madame Chantelouve is distinctly half-hearted. If Madame Chantelouve is a vampiric succubus—as Durtal briefly suspects—she is not a very effective one.

That is, in the end, the worst charge Durtal brings against Satanism: not that it is evil, but merely that it is inefficient. Its inefficiency is revealed not so much by the fact that Dr. Johannès triumphs over Canon Docre in the war for Gévingey's soul, but by the fact that the visions of grandeur and exoticism that Satanism offers prove in the end to be tawdry. When Durtal finally gets to see the black mass, he finds it sadly lacking in esthetic excitement as well as demoniac power; it is not sufficiently impressive to impose itself upon him, and its failure dispels the illusion that briefly binds him to Madame Chantelouve.

Down There was researched as conscientiously by Huysmans as its imaginary biography of Gilles de Rais was by Durtal, and many commentators have regarded the novel as a *roman à clef*. Paris was full of occultists in Huysmans's time; many of them are cited in the text. Most took their inspiration from the career of Eliphas Lévi (Alphonse Louis Constant), who successfully posed as a practitioner of the occult arts a generation before. The most famous of these would-be magi was Joséphin Péladan, whose Rosicrucian lodge was loudly advertised in his prolific writings. His writings included a long series of novels railing against the decadence of the age and calling for its renewal by a syncretic faith whose architect he desired to be. That Huysmans ever saw an actual black mass is, however, doubtful; Satanism was then, as it is now and always has been, much more a product of lurid fantasies than the active practices of the unholy.

In all probability, the dull truth of the matter is that Gilles de Rais was innocent of all the charges brought against him. Like other victims of famous sorcery trials, he was framed by his enemies, who used the same vicious slanders to discredit and destroy him as the English earlier used to discredit and destroy his companion-in-arms, Joan of Arc. Gilles de Rais's trial was a domestic affair, however, and later generations of the French were content to let his conviction stand so that the Church might use it as a terrible example to those who faltered in the faith. The success of *Down There* as a scary story is an ironic testament to the power of the terrorism of the imagination that killed Gilles de Rais.

It is significant that the flights of fancy on which Durtal and his two friends continually embark are forever being brought down to earth by the kindly attentions of Madame Carhaix, who is always bustling around with supplies of good hot food. She, rather than the devout bell ringer, is the novel's paragon of common sense and virtue. Her unobtrusive presence is testimony to the fact that Huysmans never lost touch with reality while he was in pursuit of his obsession of the moment.

The methodology of Durtal's historical research is explicitly modeled on that of Jules Michelet, a historian who attempted to place himself imaginatively in the shoes of the people of past ages. Michelet wrote a book, *La Sorcière* (1862), about the witch hunts and sorcery trials of the Middle Ages in which he put himself into the shoes of accused witches so as to make them into heroic rebels against the tyranny of an autocratic and misogynist Church. These witches elevated their folk medicine into a kind of Satanism in an expression of ideological resistance. Michelet's book thus became the parent of all the modern scholarly fantasies that insist (falsely) that there was a witch cult, although it was misunderstood and misrepresented by the Church. Durtal's conclusion that Gilles de Rais was eventually driven to madness and remorse by the knowledge that there were no further depths of evil to be plumbed is a fantasy similar to Michelet's, arising from the error of putting a thoroughly modern decadent consciousness into a situation in which it does not belong.

The historical aspects of *Down There* are questionable, but it was not written as history, however, and ought not to be condemned on that account. As a philosophical novel debating the status and worth of religious faith in the decadent Paris of the 1890's, it is fascinating. It explores extremes of hypothetical faith and possible feeling hitherto untreated with such scrupulousness. As a record of Satanism it is completely unreliable, but it remains a remarkably intense examination of the possible utility of Satanism as creed and ritual.

Its conclusion—that Satanism can never be anything but a hollow sham, incapable of delivering any kind of aesthetic or material gratification—is surely secure, no matter how convoluted the argument that led Durtal to its achievement.

Brian Stableford

Further Reading

Baldick, Robert. *The Life of J.-K. Huysmans*. Oxford, England: Clarendon Press, 1955. Rev. ed. Sawtry, England, Dedalus. 2007. A useful biography, which sets *Down There* in the context of Huysmans's own explorations of the occult. In the new edition, Brendan King has extensively revised and updated Baldick's notes to discuss new developments in Huysmansian studies.

Birkett, Jennifer. *The Sins of the Fathers: Decadence in France, 1870-1914*. London: Quartet Books, 1986. A useful study of the Decadent movement. Part 2, chapter 1 discusses Huysmans's work.

Brandreth, Henry R. T. *Huysmans*. London: Bowes & Bowes, 1963. A biographical and critical study. *Down There* is discussed in chapter 4, "The Devil with His Hooked Claw."

Burton, Richard D. E. "Church Prowling: The Back-to-Front Pilgrimage of Joris-Karl Huysmans (1884-1892)." In *Blood in the City: Violence and Revelation in Paris, 1789-1945*. Ithaca, N.Y.: Cornell University Press, 2001. Burton describes how French history from the start of the French Revolution until the end of World War I was filled with outbursts of political violence. He analyzes works by Huysmans and other French authors to show how this violence is reflected in nineteenth century literature.

Hafez-Ergaut, Agnès. *Le Vertige du vide: Huysmans, Céline, Sartre*. Lewiston, N.Y.: Edwin Mellen Press, 2000. A comparison of the work of Huysmans, Louis-Ferdinand Céline, and Jean-Paul Sartre. Hafez-Ergaut maintains that the three French authors are united in their spiritual and philosophical quests and their use of sordid elements to describe the traumatic experiences of modern times.

Lloyd, Christopher. *J.-K. Huysmans and the Fin-de-Siècle Novel*. Edinburgh: Edinburgh University Press, 1990. *Down There* is discussed in terms of its relevance to all four of the book's thematic headings: "Words," "Women," "Monsters," and "Magic."

Schoolfield, George C. *A Baedeker of Decadence: Charting a Literary Fashion, 1884-1927*. New Haven, Conn.: Yale University Press, 2003. Schoolfield analyzes the work of Huysmans and other writers of Decadent fiction. The references to *Down There* are listed in the index.

Dracula

Author: Bram Stoker (1847-1912)
First published: 1897
Type of work: Novel
Type of plot: Horror
Time of plot: Late nineteenth century
Locale: Transylvania and England

Principal characters:
JONATHAN HARKER, an English solicitor
MINA MURRAY, his fiancé
COUNT DRACULA, a mysterious nobleman
DR. JOHN SEWARD, the director of a sanatorium for the
   mentally ill
DR. ABRAHAM VAN HELSING, a Dutch medical specialist
LUCY WESTENRA, Mina's friend
ARTHUR HOLMWOOD, Lucy's fiancé

The Story:

Jonathan Harker, an English solicitor, is apprehensive on his way to Castle Dracula in the province of Transylvania (in what is now Romania). His nervousness grows when he observes the curious, fearful attitude of the peasants and the coachman after they learn of his destination. He is on his way to transact business with Count Dracula, and his mission necessitates remaining at the castle for several days.

Upon his arrival at the castle, Harker finds comfortable accommodations awaiting him. Count Dracula is a charming host, although his peculiarly bloodless physical appearance is somewhat disagreeable to Harker's English eyes. Almost immediately, Harker is impressed with the strange life of the castle. He and the Count discuss their business at night, as the Count is never available during the daytime. Although the food is excellent, Harker never sees a servant about the place. While exploring the castle, he finds that it is situated high at the top of a mountain with no accessible exit other than the main doorway, which is kept locked. He realizes with a shock that he is a prisoner of Count Dracula.

Various harrowing experiences ensue. When Harker secretly explores one of the rooms in the castle, three phantom women materialize and attack him, attempting to bite his throat. Then the Count appears and drives them off, whispering fiercely that Harker belongs to him. Later, Harker thinks he sees a huge bat descending the castle walls, but the creature turns out to be Count Dracula. In the morning, trying frantically to escape, Harker stumbles into an old chapel where a number of coffinlike boxes of earth are stored. He opens one and sees the Count lying there, apparently dead. In the evening, when the Count appears as usual, Harker demands that he be released. The Count obligingly opens the castle door. A pack of wolves surrounds the entrance. The Count laughs maliciously. The next day Harker, weak and sick from a strange wound in his throat, sees a pack cart loaded with the mysterious boxes drive from the castle. Dra-

cula has departed and Harker is alone, a prisoner with no visible means of escape.

Meanwhile, in England, Harker's fiancé, Mina Murray, goes to visit her beautiful and charming friend, Lucy Westenra. Lucy is planning to marry Arthur Holmwood, a young nobleman. One evening, early in Mina's visit, a storm blows up and a strange ship is driven aground. The only living creature aboard is a gray wolflike dog, which escapes into the countryside. Soon afterward, Lucy's happiness begins to fade because of a growing tendency to sleepwalk. One night, Mina follows her friend during one of these spells and discovers Lucy in a churchyard. A tall, thin man bending over Lucy disappears at Mina's approach. Lucy can remember nothing of the experience when she awakens, but her physical condition seems much weakened. Finally, she grows so ill that Mina is forced to call upon Dr. Seward, Lucy's former suitor. Lucy begins to improve under his care, and when Mina receives a report from Budapest that her missing fiancé has been found and needs care, she feels free to end her visit.

When Lucy's condition suddenly grows worse, Dr. Seward asks his old friend Dr. Van Helsing, a specialist from Amsterdam, for his professional opinion. Examining Lucy thoroughly, Van Helsing pauses over two tiny throat wounds that she is unable to explain. Van Helsing is concerned over Lucy's condition, which points to unusual loss of blood without signs of anemia or hemorrhage. She is given blood transfusions at intervals, and someone sits up with her at night. She improves but expresses a fear of going to sleep because her dreams are so horrible.

One morning, Dr. Seward falls asleep outside her door. When he and Van Helsing enter her room, they find Lucy ashen white and weaker than ever. Van Helsing quickly performs another transfusion and she rallies, but not as satisfactorily as before. Van Helsing then secures some garlic flowers and tells Lucy to keep them around her neck at night.

When the two doctors call the next morning, they discover that Lucy's mother removed the flowers because she feared their odor might bother her daughter. Frantically, Van Helsing rushes to Lucy's room and finds her in a coma. Again he administers a transfusion, and again her condition improves. She says that with the garlic flowers close by she is not afraid of nightly flapping noises at her window. Van Helsing sits with her every night until he thinks her well enough to leave. After cautioning her to sleep with the garlic flowers about her neck at all times, he returns to Amsterdam.

Lucy's mother continues to sleep with her daughter. One night, the two ladies are awakened by a huge wolf that crashes through the window. Mrs. Westenra falls dead of a heart attack, and Lucy faints, the wreath of garlic flowers slipping from her neck. Seward and Van Helsing, who has returned to England, discover her half dead in the morning. They know she is dying and call Arthur. As Arthur attempts to kiss her, Lucy's teeth seem about to fasten onto his throat. Van Helsing draws him away. When Lucy dies, Van Helsing puts a tiny gold crucifix over her mouth, but an attendant steals it from her body.

Soon after Lucy's death, several children of the neighborhood are discovered far from their homes, their throats marked by small wounds. Their only explanation is that they followed a pretty lady. When Harker returns to England, Van Helsing goes to see him and Mina. After talking with Harker, Van Helsing reveals to Dr. Seward his belief that Lucy fell victim to a vampire, one of those strange creatures who can live for centuries on the blood of their victims and breed their kind by attacking the innocent and making them vampires in turn. According to Van Helsing, the only way to save Lucy's soul is to drive a stake through the heart of her corpse, cut off her head, and stuff her mouth with garlic flowers. Dr. Seward protests violently. The next midnight Arthur, Dr. Seward, and Helsing visit Lucy's tomb and find it empty, but after Lucy returns the next morning, they do as Van Helsing suggested with Lucy's corpse.

With Mina's help, Seward and Van Helsing thereupon track down Dracula in London, hoping to find him before he victimizes anyone else. They decide their best chance lies in removing the boxes of sterilized earth he brought with him from Transylvania, in which he hides during the daytime. They finally trap Dracula, but he escapes. Before fleeing England, however, Dracula attacks Mina and promises that he will exact his revenge through her. Van Helsing puts Mina into a trance and learns that Dracula is at sea and that it will be necessary to follow him to his castle. Wolves gather about them in that desolate country. Van Helsing draws a circle in the snow with a crucifix, and the travelers rest safely within the magic enclosure. The next morning, they overtake a cart carrying a black box. Van Helsing and the others overcome the drivers of the cart and pry open the lid of Dracula's coffin. As the sun begins to set, they drive a stake through the heart of the corpse. The vampire is no more and Mina is free.

Critical Evaluation:

With his horror novel *Dracula*, Bram Stoker created a work that became something of a symbol for twentieth century society and that, perhaps unlike any other, spawned a range of publications, plays, and motion pictures. The image of the vampire, of course, dates back several thousand years, but Stoker recast the legend in a conventionally Western tradition and provided it with an aura of dark Romanticism reminiscent of John Polidori's *The Vampyre* (1819) and of the voluptuous whisperings of Joseph Sheridan Le Fanu's *Carmilla* (1871). Stoker's novel combined the basic ingredients of the classical horror story with the author's personal experiences and inspiration.

The main character in *Dracula* is based on the historical figure of Vlad Tepes the Impaler, a fifteenth century Walachian prince who ruled Transylvania and Walachia (now Romania) and earned a bloody reputation by spearing domestic criminals and foreign invaders on wooden sticks. He assumed the name Dracula, variously interpreted as "son of the dragon" and "son of the devil," as a further reminder of his powers.

Stoker's book deals with a number of more universal themes as well, including the loneliness of death, the endless allure of erotic love, and an unnerving invocation of insanity. The author, a dreamy visionary with seemingly two sides to his nature, transfers aspects of the hate-love relationship of the vampire state to personal relationships between his characters. That lends a sexually charged underpinning to much of the narrative and creates some of the most gruesome and powerful scenes in the history of the horror novel. Stoker not only employed a series of firsthand accounts (such as diaries, journals, newspaper clippings, and other documents) to tell the story—thus returning to the epistolary technique introduced some years earlier by Wilkie Collins—he also fused several different viewpoints in the narrative. In part because he had little time at his disposal and had to write rapidly, and in part because of the Victorian cultural milieu, he lent a somewhat trite sentimentality to many sections of the book. Fortunately, however, the first few chapters of *Dracula* create a charged atmosphere of suspense that sustains the reader's interest throughout. Stoker also took great care to interlace the narrative elements of the plot; every detail counts and hardly anything is superfluous. Although he relies heavily on direct testimonials, this device also possesses the virtue of imparting an immediate and believable effect. At the time the book was published, reviewers could well still have classified *Dracula* as a traditional gothic horror story because of ingredients such as ships lost at sea, mysterious castles, and vaults resounding with the patter of rats' feet. What is unusual about this novel is the way Stoker treats his themes, the ambiguities in which he cloaks his vampire, and his use of forceful symbolism. *Dracula* has a mysterious and sinister atmosphere heightened by the narrative momentum of the vampire's actions. Stoker offers his readers neither unnameable horror nor the kind of a rationalistic approach that might keep them from succumbing to the supernatural; rather, he concocts a suave combination of the two laced with subtle undertones of cold fear. Nevertheless, he clearly knows how to resort to nightmare horror when the occasion calls for it. Like a true horror writer, he paints with bold and deliberate strokes and as a result creates remarkable and brilliant images. For most of his life, he was deeply involved in theatrical management, and very likely his intimacy with the stage was at least partially responsible for his style. The "big" scenes are elaborate, and there is a dramatic flair to almost every incident. Although Stoker had not originally thought of converting his book into a drama—the only play version given during his lifetime was done for copyright purposes—the blatant melodrama of many of the scenes cries out for stage realization. Most of Dracula's speeches to Harker, for example, are brilliantly dynamic (and have actually been put to good effect by many a filmmaker). Just as effective are the tableaux framed in time, for example the moment when a small band awaits the coming of the Count in Piccadilly or watches Dracula's coffin being driven to his castle. The suspense created by these moments in slow motion is quickly relieved by the almost lightning sequence of events that tends to follow.

Stoker was never taken quite seriously as a novelist, at least not during his lifetime. Perhaps the main accusation against him was that of being a second-rate writer who churned out books and did not seem interested in refining his style. It is nevertheless his achievement that his readers are able to visualize every one of his terrifying details clearly. His blood allegory gathers to itself a host of meanings and a chilling atmosphere in which the most ordinary circumstances begin slipping into the realm of nightmare. It is precisely this ever-mounting anticipation, reeking with primordial awakenings, that creates the special style of *Dracula*. Here the reader is no longer dealing with a receptacle for ingenious devices of terror but with a battleground for searing issues of the body and the soul.

"Critical Evaluation" by Kathryn Dorothy Marocchino

Further Reading

Bloom, Harold, ed. *Bram Stoker's "Dracula."* Philadelphia: Chelsea House, 2003. Collection of critical essays, including discussions of the depiction of gender and sexuality in the novel, *Dracula* and the late Victorian degeneracy crisis, and the novel's rhetoric of reform.

Glendening, John. *The Evolutionary Imagination in Late-Victorian Novels: An Entangled Bank.* Burlington, Vt.: Ashgate, 2007. Examines how Stoker and other late-Victorian novelists dealt with contemporary theories of evolution. The chapter on *Dracula* focuses on evolution and primitivism in the novel.

Hughes, William. *Bram Stoker: Dracula.* New York: Palgrave Macmillan, 2009. Surveys the critical response to the novel from its initial publication to the present day. Focuses on critiques that examine the themes of psychoanalysis and psychobiography; medicine, mind, and body; gender studies; postcolonialism; and Irish studies.

Leatherdale, Clive. *Dracula, the Novel and the Legend: A Study of Bram Stoker's Gothic Masterpiece.* Wellingborough, England: Aquarian Press, 1985. An excellent critical study, which interprets various aspects of *Dracula*, including sexual symbolism, religious themes, occult and literary myth, and political and social allegory.

Murray, Paul. *From the Shadow of "Dracula": A Life of Bram Stoker.* London: Jonathan Cape, 2004. Places *Dracula* within the context of Stoker's life and his entire canon of fiction.

Roth, Phyllis A. *Bram Stoker.* Boston: Twayne, 1982. An introductory overview of Stoker's life and works. Contains an extensive chapter on *Dracula*.

Senf, Carol A., ed. *The Critical Response to Bram Stoker.* Westport, Conn.: Greenwood Press, 1994. An anthology of some of the more interesting critiques of *Dracula* from a scholarly point of view.

Stoker, Bram. *The Essential "Dracula."* Edited by Leonard Woolf and revised in collaboration with Roxana Stuart. Rev. ed. New York: Plume, 1993. Includes the original complete text of *Dracula* with notes, an introductory essay, a selected filmography of major vampire films, commentary by leading horror writers, and new illustrations by Christopher Bing. Features an extensive bibliography.

_____. *The New Annotated Dracula.* Edited by Leslie S. Klinger. New York: W. W. Norton, 2008. Klinger treats *Dracula* as a work of nonfiction, elucidating its plot and historical context and providing numerous annotations. Includes several appendixes, including a Dracula family tree, the novel's film and stage adaptations, and *Dracula*'s reception in academia.

Dragon Seed

Author: Pearl S. Buck (1892-1973)
First published: 1942
Type of work: Novel
Type of plot: Social realism
Time of plot: 1937-1945
Locale: China

Principal characters:
LING TAN, a farmer
LING SAO, his wife
LAO TA, the eldest son
LAO ER, the second son
LAO SAN, the youngest son
PANSIAO, the daughter
ORCHID, Lao Ta's wife
JADE, Lao Er's wife
WU LIEN, the Lings' son-in-law, a city shopkeeper
MAYLI, a repatriated mission teacher

The Story:

Ling Tan and his family all live together on their ancestral farm. In addition to Ling Tan and his wife, Ling Sao, there are three sons and a daughter. Lao Ta, one of the sons, and his wife, Orchid, have two children. Lao Er, another son, and his wife, Jade, are newly married.

While Orchid is the conventional wife and daughter-in-law, Lao Er's wife, Jade, is different. She reveals to her husband that she wants more than what is given and wants to be more than what is expected of a woman. Lao Er is wise enough to realize that his strong-willed, intelligent, thoughtful wife is more blessing than encumbrance and promises that on his next visit to the city he will buy her a book, something no one else in his household ever held.

In the city, Lao Er visits his older sister and her husband Wu Lien. Wu Lien is a shopkeeper, and while Lao Er is visiting, students come to the shop and destroy all the foreign merchandise. They call Wu Lien a traitor. This is one of the earliest indications to the Ling family of the impending Japanese invasion and occupation.

One day Ling Tan is working in his fields when the first Japanese warplanes arrive. They fly over the Lings' village on the way to the city. The Lings are too naïve to know what happened until that night, when Wu Lien brings his entire household with him, seeking refuge. His shop was gutted by a bomb, and much of the city is damaged.

Ling Tan and Lao San go into the city to see the devastation for themselves, and they are caught in an air raid. When Ling Tan gathers his family and asks them what they should do to resist the enemy, Jade and Lao Er announce their wish to flee inland to join the resistance movement. Jade is now carrying their first child. It is decided that while Jade and Lao Er are away the rest of the family will stay and hold on to their land as best as they can.

Streams of refugees pass through the village on their way west, and firsthand accounts of Japanese atrocities prepare Ling Tan and his fellow villagers for what they will have to do when the Japanese come. With the city in ruins and with the last of the Chinese army having fled to the hills, the Japanese march into the area. A marauding group comes to the Lings' village looking for wine and women. Ling Tan sends his family to the fields. Wu Lien's mother, however, is not able to escape in time. She is raped and killed. The house is ransacked.

Ling Tan brings all the women and children in his family to the relative safety of the white missionary woman's compound. He and his sons remain on the farm. The Japanese return and, finding no women in the Ling home, gang-rape the sixteen-year-old Lao San. Filled with hatred, Lao San leaves to join the resistance fighters in the hills.

Meanwhile, Wu Lien does not stay on the farm. He goes back to the city to see what he can salvage of his shop and to see if he can do business with the enemy. Ingratiating himself with the conquerors, Wu Lien is appointed to a post in the new city government. He and his wife and children are then installed in generous quarters provided by the Japanese.

Tired of the monotony in the mission and curious about the new order in the city, Orchid ventures into the city. She is set upon by soldiers, raped, and killed. Ling Sao does not want to stay in the mission any more. Ling Tan comes for her and the two children of Lao Ta and Orchid. Pansiao, however, they leave in the care of the missionary woman, who promises to send her westward to safety and schooling.

The Lings receive news of the birth of Lao Er and Jade's son. Not long after, typhoid hits the village, and Lao Ta's two children are killed. Devastated, Lao Ta goes to the hills, too. Ling Tan and Ling Sao send word to Lao Er and Jade to ask them to return. Ling Tan and Ling Sao start digging a secret cellar. Ling Tan continues to work his land. The Japanese now control the lands and demand most of the harvests. As the Lings' cellar grows, they hide more of their harvests. Digging and expanding the cellar become a daily mission. When Lao Er and Jade and their baby arrive, they can be hidden underground.

With Lao Er and Jade's return, the cellar is large enough for the Ling home to become the village base for the resistance movement. Arms are smuggled in from the hills and stored in the cellar. All three Ling sons are now actively involved in resistance activities. Ling Tan and the other villagers also do their share. They now have the means with which to fight. Whenever they think they can get away with it, they kill the Japanese soldiers who come to the village, carefully hiding the bodies.

With the war, Lao San comes into his own. Previously frail and innocent, he is now a fighter and a ruthless killer. Ling Tan feels that his son needs a wife to tame him. Through Jade, he writes to Pansiao to ask her to find her brother a wife from among the women at the mission. Pansiao sets her sights on the beautiful and spirited MayLi, who returned from abroad and is teaching in her native country. MayLi is intrigued by what Pansiao tells her of Lao San. MayLi leaves the mission and finds her way to the Ling village. She and Lao San are attracted to each other.

After all the devastation through the years, Ling Tan's family is on the rebound. Lao Ta comes home with a new wife. Lao Er and Jade have twin boys. Pansiao, although not at home, is safe and receiving an education. There is hope that Lao San will regain the humanity he lost. He goes inland in pursuit of MayLi.

The occupation continues and the hardships continue for Ling Tan and his family. Steadfastly holding on to his land over the years, Ling Tan also holds on to hope, but he seems to be losing it. Lao Er brings him into the city to listen to the illegal radio broadcast. They hear that China is not alone anymore in fighting the Japanese. They hear that England and the United States are now fighting on their side. Ling Tan weeps for joy.

Critical Evaluation:

Dragon Seed is set in the early years of World War II. More specifically, however, though the Japanese invasion and occupation of China roughly paralleled the war years in Europe and the Pacific, the war specific to China is called the Second Sino-Japanese War. *Dragon Seed* is a chronicle of the war as experienced by the Chinese, in particular the peasants. Their country was conquered and overrun by the Japanese.

Pearl S. Buck, the first American woman to win, in 1938, the Nobel Prize in Literature, is best known for *The Good Earth* (1931). Like *The Good Earth* and many of her other novels, *Dragon Seed* is set in China, where Buck spent much of her early life with her missionary parents. Buck may perhaps be credited with introducing to the American reading public Chinese characters who were more than the figures of ridicule or contempt that had been evident in American fiction. There were a few writers who had written about Chinese or Chinese Americans prior to Buck, but Buck was the first to reach a wide audience.

It is important to note the time in which *Dragon Seed* was published. The United States had recently entered World War II, and on the Pacific front it was, with China, allied against the Japanese. It is debatable whether *Dragon Seed* was intended as propaganda, because Buck had already written extensively about China and the Chinese people. It would seem, however, that in China's war against the Japanese, Buck served to help the Chinese cause. The war novel label that is often attached to *Dragon Seed*, however, must be considered in at least two other contexts. One is the United States' own propaganda war against the Japanese, of which Buck had little choice but to become part. The other is the war against Americans of Chinese ancestry that had lasted sixty years—the Chinese Exclusion Act of 1882, for example, which among other things prohibited the naturalization of Chinese as Americans, was not to be repealed until December, 1943. By default if not by design, the novel is part of these historical contexts.

The novel chronicles one family's struggles against the oppression of a foreign invader. The village and the city in which most of the action takes place are not named; the Ling family can be seen as the symbolic representative of a society built upon the unfailing unity of the family unit. In a time when all the major cities had fallen to the enemy, when the Chinese army was defeated in battle after battle, the rural family, in a country peopled primarily by rural families, seemed to be the last bastion of Chinese resistance.

The main characters are not one-dimensional, but Buck seems so intent on their struggle that the minutest everyday action is always for the cause. The characters do their part in resisting the enemy in whatever way they can, because it is demanded of the times. The "save China" message of the novel is particularly romanticized in the rhapsodic passages about Ling Tan contemplating his land. He and the farmers like him, the people who work the land, seem most deserving of the land. In contrast, the Japanese occupiers are portrayed as having little concept of the land beyond the idea of possession.

In Buck's China, everyone has his or her place. Buck examines the woman's place in the scheme of land, family, and tradition. The novel's women are not all the manipulated creatures they are supposed to be. Ling Sao and Jade are two characters who can be seen as progenitors of the woman warriors to come in later fiction about women of Chinese ancestry. Both are at least the equal of their husbands. Jade and Pansiao are the only two of the Ling family who are literate.

When *Dragon Seed* appeared in 1942, its topicality made it a best seller. Some critics, however, find it simplistic, dated, and romanticized. Reading *Dragon Seed* and trying to gauge its place in literature, it is important to realize that a novel written by an American about China in the context of today's critical assessments is inherently problematic. Does Buck purport to speak for the Chinese better than they can for themselves? Will Chinese be confused with Chinese Americans? When the novel first appeared, there was little differentiation between the two. There was no expression of Chinese American consciousness at a time when American-born Chinese were, by law, not American. *Dragon Seed* is one of the earliest instances of a novel whose characters are Chinese and that was widely read by the American public. As such it is relevant in any study of how American literature portrays characters of Chinese ancestry and how the perception of Americans of Chinese ancestry has evolved.

"Critical Evaluation" by Pat M. Wong

Further Reading

Buck, Pearl S. *My Several Worlds.* New York: John Day, 1954. Buck's autobiography describes vividly her years in China and the impact these experiences had upon her life and work. Discusses her progressive ideas on social issues.

_____. *The Story of "Dragon Seed."* New York: John Day, 1944. This monograph explains how the author came to write the novel. Describes her personal contact with Chinese farming families living near Nanking and her learning of "the horrors of the Japanese invasion."

Conn, Peter. *Pearl S. Buck: A Cultural Biography.* New York: Cambridge University Press, 1996. Attempts to revise the "smug literary consensus" that has relegated Buck to a "footnote" in literary history. Conn does not rehabilitate Buck as a great author but shows how her best work broke new ground in subject matter and is still vital to an understanding of American culture.

Doyle, Paul A. *Pearl S. Buck.* Rev. ed. Boston: Twayne, 1980. Analyzes the plot of *Dragon Seed* to show why the novel is not considered "an artistic success." Compares the work to *The Good Earth.*

Leong, Karen J. *The China Mystique: Pearl S. Buck, Anna May Wong, Mayling Soong, and the Transformation of American Orientalism.* Berkeley: University of California Press, 2005. Leong focuses on three women who were associated with China in the 1930's and 1940's—Buck, actress Anna May Wong, and Mayling Soong, the wife of Chinese leader Chiang Kai-shek—to describe how they altered Americans' perceptions of what it meant to be American, Chinese American, and Chinese.

Liao, Kang. *Pearl S. Buck: A Cultural Bridge Across the Pacific.* Westport, Conn.: Greenwood Press, 1997. Liao analyzes Buck's life, political and social views, and her novels to describe how the author played a key role in improving America's image of China during World War II.

Lipscomb, Elizabeth J., Frances E. Webb, and Peter Conn, eds. *The Several Worlds of Pearl S. Buck: Essays Presented at a Centennial Symposium, Randolph-Macon Woman's College, March 26-28, 1992.* Westport, Conn.: Greenwood Press, 1994. Collection of essays delivered at a conference in which participants sought to reevaluate Buck's work and literary reputation. Several of the essays examine various aspects of *The Good Earth*, while others analyze Buck's portrayal of China and handicapped children and her place in the American literary culture.

Dramatis Personae

Author: Robert Browning (1812-1889)
First published: 1864
Type of work: Poetry

When Robert Browning published *Dramatis Personae*, he was beginning to gain a measure of general esteem in the eyes of the public and of the critics. The year before its publication a three-volume collection of his earlier works had sold moderately well. *Dramatis Personae* added considerably to his popularity, and a second edition was called for before the end of 1864. It is ironic that this volume, the first that can be said to have achieved popular success, contained the first clear signs of the decline of his poetic powers.

It was his first volume of new poems since *Men and Women*, published in 1855. In the interval the pattern of Browning's life had undergone complete transformation. On June 29, 1861, his wife, the poet Elizabeth Barrett Browning, had died. They had made their home in Italy; after her death, Browning returned to England. For years he had been virtually out of touch with the currents of English thought. He plunged into a society that was perplexed by what it had learned and troubled by what it had come to doubt. Browning was soon personally involved in the intellectual and religious controversies of the day.

The changes in his life produced changes in his poetry. His love poems, understandably, became more melancholy. Many of the poems in *Men and Women* have historical settings; all but a few of those in *Dramatis Personae* have contemporary settings. Even when he gives his version of an old tale, as in "Gold Hair," he manages to work in discussion of nineteenth century problems. In general, he was becoming more argumentative, more of a preacher. He still preferred the dramatic mode of utterance but the voice of the poet is often heard behind the dramatic mask.

Two of the important themes in the volume are love and death, frequently juxtaposed. The death of Mrs. Browning may have been an influence on his choice of subjects, but it should not be overestimated; a number of the poems antedate her death. "Prospice," however, written in the fall of 1861, is clearly Browning speaking in his own voice. It is an open affirmation of belief in immortality. When death ends his life, he says, as it has ended hers, "O thou soul of my soul! I shall clasp thee again,/ And with God be the rest!"

In "Too Late" another man grieves over a dead woman, but with a difference. He had never expressed his love for her and now suffers not grief alone but regret at having missed his opportunity. It is a familiar theme in Browning, love unfulfilled through negligence, expressed earlier in "The Statue and the Bust," and, elsewhere in *Dramatis Personae*, in "Youth and Art," and in "Dis Aliter Visum; or Le Byron de Nos Jours." If "Too Late" has an autobiographical element, it is of an inverse order: Browning, unlike the speaker, had not missed his opportunity for love. The speaker of "Too Late" says it would have been better to

> have burst like a thief
> And borne you away to a rock for us two
> In a moment's horror, bright, bloody, and brief,
> Then changed to myself again.

Browning, a sedentary man, had stepped out of character once in his life, when he had spirited a middle-aged poet off to Italy.

Two of the finest poems in *Dramatis Personae*, also love poems, are "Confessions" and "James Lee's Wife" (originally called, misleadingly, "James Lee"). One reason why they are perennially satisfying is that, unlike many poems in the volume, they are free from topical controversy. In "Confessions," one of Browning's shortest dramatic monologues, a dying man recalls, with satisfaction, a love affair of long ago: "How sad and bad and mad it was—/ But then, how it was sweet!" In "James Lee's Wife," the story is that of the death of love. It is a restrained, dignified cry of heartbreak, a skillfully wrought dramatic lyric, the desolate scene and the dying year serving as mute echoes of the speaker's mood.

Of the eighteen poems originally grouped in *Dramatis Personae* (two occasional pieces were later added: "Deaf and Dumb" and "Eurydice to Orpheus"), few are not cluttered with argument. Of these, "James Lee's Wife" and "Confessions" are particularly memorable. "The Worst of It" is mawkish; "May and Death" is pleasant, but slight; "A Face" and "A Likeness" are insignificant. It should not be assumed, however, that the remaining poems, those which serve as vehicles for Browning's beliefs, can all be dismissed as inferior poems.

"Caliban upon Setebos," for example, is not only a statement of Victorian religious belief; it is as well one of Browning's successful poems of the grotesque. The element of controversy is certainly there, as indicated by the subtitle: "Natural Theology in the Island." Browning is satirizing those who, relying too closely on their own resources, posit God in their own image. Caliban is not merely a figure taken from William Shakespeare's *The Tempest* (pr. 1611, pb. 1623); he is also a post-Darwinian figure, a poet's version of the evolutionary missing link. The topical references in the poem do not, however, prevent it from being rated one of Browning's best dramatic monologues.

"A Death in the Desert," another dramatic monologue, is perhaps more seriously marred by its attempts to promote certain religious ideas. Proponents of what was called higher criticism of the Bible—for example, David Friedrich Strauss in *Das Leben Jesu, kritisch bearbeitet* (1835-1836; *The Life of Jesus, Critically Examined*, 1846) and Ernest Renan in *Vie de Jésus* (1863; *The Life of Jesus*, 1864)—had attempted, among other things, to prove that the Gospel of St. John had not been written, as had been assumed, by the beloved disciple. Browning's poem, an imaginative re-creation of John's death, is an argument for the authenticity of the Gospel. It contains a number of Browning's religious positions (for example, a theory about miracles). The fact that it is the dying apostle who gives expression to these ideas is anachronistic: Many of them are clearly indigenous to the middle of the nineteenth century. As a result, the dramatic effect of the poem is appreciably undercut.

The longest poem in *Dramatis Personae*, "Mr. Sludge, 'The Medium,'" is 1,525 lines, or three-eighths of the entire volume. This poem is more successful. It is one of Browning's liveliest character studies, not unworthy of comparison with the great dramatic monologues in *Men and Women*. It, too, is tinged by Browning's growing fondness for argument. Browning satirizes spiritualism, quite a fad in mid-nineteenth century England, by portraying a fraudulent medium whose character is based on an American, Daniel Dunglass Home, whom Browning had met. Moreover, Mr. Sludge, the speaker, gives voice, although inconsistently, to some of Browning's characteristic religious ideas. The propagandizing is done rather subtly, however, and does not strike the reader as being obtrusive.

"Rabbi Ben Ezra" and "Abt Vogler" are similar to "Mr. Sludge" in being good poems as well as statements of opinion with regard to contemporary questions. The first eight sections of "Abt Vogler" are a brilliant tour de force, a lyrical evocation of the exalted spirit of a musician improvising at the keyboard of an organ. The last four sections are not quite so successful, being too flat an exposition of one of Browning's pet theories, the "philosophy of the imperfect":

On the earth the broken arcs; in the heaven,
  a perfect round.
And what is our failure here but a triumph's evidence
For the fullness of the days?

The argumentative element does not predominate; sound and sense are not at odds but in harmony with each other. It was one of Browning's favorites, among his own poems, and it has since been one of the favorites of his readers.

"Rabbi Ben Ezra," another of Browning's most popular poems, is perhaps somewhat less successful than "Abt Vogler." It is unsurpassed, however, as an expression of Browning's own belief in God. The ideas contained in it are typical of Browning. He says, for example: "What I aspired to be,/ And was not, comforts me." The reader is reminded of Andrea del Sarto's dictum in *Men and Women*: "A man's reach should exceed his grasp." Above all, "Rabbi Ben Ezra" is a cogent presentation of Browning's famous and frequently, if too facilely, maligned optimism.

"Gold Hair" is a curious and troubling poem. It relates an old story about the death of a young woman. She had been regarded virtually as a saint; years after her death, however, it is learned that she had been interested in earthly treasure far more than in a heavenly one. Some have objected to the story itself but that, though macabre and a bit cynical, is really unobjectionable. In the last three stanzas Browning simply lectures his readers.

The poet makes no bones about his intention to preach, and the value of his stories begins to decline as they become more and more pointedly the texts for sermons. "Apparent Failure," a lesser poem, finds Browning speaking in his own voice. The story is merely the occasion for moral instruction; it is in Browning's own words, "the sermon's text."

The final poem in *Dramatis Personae*, "Epilogue," gives brief expression to three religious positions current when Browning wrote. The "First Speaker, as David" sums up the High Church, ritualistic position; the "Second Speaker, as Renan" expresses the skepticism of one familiar with higher criticism. The "Third Speaker," Browning himself, answers the first two, calling ceremony unnecessary and belief tenable. Browning's belief, like Alfred, Lord Tennyson's, is sustained by personal feeling rather than by a process of reason. What is really significant about the poem is that it makes no pretense of being dramatic. It sets the pattern for the bulk of his later poems, for Browning's values have changed; controversy now means more to him than writing poems, for poetry has become the vehicle for argument. As a result, the poetry suffers, as some of the poems in this volume and virtually all of the later poems, save "The Ring and the Book," clearly testify.

Further Reading

Browning, Robert. *Robert Browning's Poetry: Authoritative Texts, Criticism*. Selected and edited by James F. Loucks and Andrew M. Stauffer. 2d ed. New York: W. W. Norton, 2007. In addition to a selection of Browning's poetry, this volume contains essays about his work written by nineteenth and twentieth century poets, writers, and critics, including John Ruskin, Gerard Manley Hopkins, Thomas Carlyle, William Morris, and Oscar Wilde.

Crowell, Norton B. *A Reader's Guide to Robert Browning*. Albuquerque: University of New Mexico Press, 1972. Criticisms of "Abt Vogler," "A Death in the Desert," "Caliban," and "Epilogue," with annotated bibliographies following each poem. Includes critical bibliography.

Erickson, Lee. *Robert Browning: His Poetry and His Audiences*. Ithaca, N.Y.: Cornell University Press, 1984. The chapter on *Dramatis Personae* interprets the poet's later work as a departure from the dramatic monologue to works such as "Epilogue to *Dramatis Personae*," in which characters express views on religion. Bibliography includes nineteenth and twentieth century reviews and essays.

Hawlin, Stefan. *The Complete Critical Guide to Robert Browning*. New York: Routledge, 2002. This student sourcebook contains information about Browning's life and times, as well as discussion and criticism of his work. Devotes a chapter to *Dramatis Personae* and *Men and Women*, focusing on the poems about art, religion, and love.

Hudson, Gertrude Reese. *Robert Browning's Literary Life: From First Work to Masterpiece*. Austin, Tex.: Eakin Press, 1992. Two chapters on *Dramatis Personae* describe the circumstances of publication, identify sources of the poems, and ascribe the themes to contemporary religious controversies, especially about higher criticism and spiritualism.

Kennedy, Richard S., and Donald S. Hair. *The Dramatic Imagination of Robert Browning: A Literary Life*. Columbia: University of Missouri Press, 2007. A literary biography, recounting the events of Browning's life, placing it within the context of its times, and offering critical commentary on his poetry. Chapter 28, "The Good of Poetry," provides critical remarks on *Dramatis Personae*.

Tracy, Clarence, ed. *Browning's Mind and Art*. Edinburgh: Oliver & Boyd, 1968. Essays written by well-known Browning critics. The index locates references to some of the poems contained in *Dramatis Personae*.

Ward, Maisie. *Robert Browning and His World: Two Robert Brownings?* 2 vols. New York: Holt, Rinehart and Winston, 1969. The chapter on *Dramatis Personae* discusses Browning's friendship with Benjamin Jowett. Notes religious contrasts in the speakers of the poems.

Woolford, John. *Robert Browning*. Tavistock, England: Northcote House/British Council, 2007. In his time, Browning was called a "grotesque poet." Woolford examines the meaning of this term and how it defines Browning's poetry.

Dream of the Red Chamber

Author: Cao Xueqin (1715?-1763)
First published: Hongloumeng, 1792 (English
   translation, 1958)
Type of work: Novel
Type of plot: Domestic realism
Time of plot: c. 1729-1737
Locale: Peking

Principal characters:
MADAME SHIH, the matriarch of the Chia family
CHIA SHEH, her older son, master of the Yungkuofu, or
   western compound
MADAME HSING, his wife
CHIA LIEN, their son
HSI-FENG "PHOENIX," Chia Lien's wife
YING-CHUN "WELCOME SPRING," Chia Sheh's daughter by
   a concubine
CHIA CHENG, the Matriarch's younger son
MADAME WANG, his wife
CHIA PAO-YU, their son
CARDINAL SPRING, their daughter and an Imperial
   concubine
CHIA HUAN, Chia Cheng's son by his concubine
TAN-CHUN "QUEST SPRING," Chia Cheng's daughter by
   his concubine
TAI-YU "BLACK JADE," the Matriarch's granddaughter and
   an orphan
HSIANG-YUN "RIVER MIST," the Matriarch's
   grandniece
PAO-CHAI "PRECIOUS VIRTUE," Madame Wang's niece
HSUEH PAN, Precious Virtue's brother and a libertine
CHIA GEN, the master of the Ningkuofu, or eastern
   compound
YU-SHIH, his wife
CHIA JUNG, their son
CHIN-SHIH, Chia Jung's wife
HSI-CHUN "COMPASSION SPRING," Chia Gen's sister
HSI-JEN "PERVADING FRAGRANCE,"
CHING-WEN "BRIGHT DESIGN," and
SHEH-YUEH "MUSK MOON," Pao-yu's serving maids

The Story:

Ages ago, in the realm of the Great Void, the Goddess Nugua, whose task it is to repair the Dome of Heaven, rejects a stone that she finds unsuited to her purpose. She touches it, however, so the stone becomes endowed with life. Thereafter it can move as it pleases. In time, it chances on a crimson flower in the region of the Ethereal, where each day it waters the tender blossoms with drops of dew. At last the plant is incarnated as a beautiful young woman. Remembering the stone that showered the frail plant with refreshing dew, she prays that in her human form she might repay it with the gift of her tears. Her prayers are to be granted, for the stone, too, was given life in the Red Dust of earthly existence. At his

birth, the piece of jade is miraculously found in the mouth of Pao-yu, a younger son of the rich and powerful house of Chia, which by imperial favor was raised to princely eminence several generations before.

At the time of Pao-yu's birth, the two branches of the Chia family live in great adjoining compounds of palaces, pavilions, and parks on the outskirts of Peking. The Matriarch, Madame Shih, an old woman of great honor and virtue, rules as the living ancestress over both establishments. Chia Ging, the prince of the Ningkuofu, retired to a Taoist temple some time before, and his son Chia Gen is master in his place. The master of the Yungkuofu is Chia Sheh, the older son of the Matriarch. Chia Cheng, her younger son and Pao-yu's father, also lives with his family and attendants in the Yung-kuofu. A man of upright conduct and strict Confucian morals, he is a contrast to the other members of his family, who grew lax and corrupt through enervating luxury and the abuse of power.

Pao-yu, the possessor of the miraculous jade stone and a boy of great beauty and quick wit, is his grandmother's favorite. Following her example, the other women of the family—his mother, aunts, sisters, cousins, and waiting maids—dote on the boy and pamper him at every opportunity, with the result that he grows up girlish and weak, a lover of feminine society. His traits of effeminacy infuriate and disgust his austere father, who treats the boy with undue severity. As a result, Pao-yu keeps as much as possible to the women's quarters.

His favorite playmates are his two cousins, Black Jade and Precious Virtue. Black Jade, a granddaughter of the Matriarch, came to live in the Yungkuofu after her mother's death. She is a lovely, delicate girl of great poetic sensitivity, and she and Pao-yu are drawn to each other by bonds of sympathy and understanding that seem to stretch back into some unremembered past. Precious Virtue, warmhearted and practical, is the niece of Pao-yu's mother. She is a woman as good as her brother Hsueh Pan is vicious. He is always involving the family in scandal because of his pursuit of maidens and young boys. Pao-yu's favorite waiting maid is Pervading Fragrance. She sleeps in his chamber at night, and it is with her that he follows a dream vision and practices the play of cloud and rain.

When word comes that Black Jade's father is ill and wishes to see her before his death, the Matriarch sends the girl home under the escort of her cousin Chia Lien. During their absence, Chin-shih, the daughter-in-law of Chia Gen, dies after a long illness. By judicious bribery, the dead woman's husband, Chia Jung, is made a chevalier of the Imperial Dragon Guards in order that she might be given a more elaborate funeral. During the period of mourning, Chia Gen asks Phoenix, Chia Lien's wife, to take charge of the Ningkuofu household. This honor gives Phoenix a position of responsibility and power in both palaces. From that time on, although she continues to appear kind and generous, she secretly becomes greedy for money and power. She begins to accept bribes, tamper with the household accounts, and lend money at exorbitant rates of interest.

One day a great honor is conferred on the Chias. Cardinal Spring, Pao-yu's sister and one of the emperor's concubines, advances to the rank of Imperial consort of the second degree. Later, when it is announced that she will pay a visit of

filial respect to her parents, the parks of the two compounds are transformed at great expense into magnificent pleasure grounds, called the Takuanyuan, in honor of the consort's visit. Later, at Cardinal Spring's request, the pavilions in the Takuanyuan are converted into living quarters for the young women of the family. Pao-yu also goes there to live, passing his days in idle occupations and writing verses. His pavilion is close to that of Black Jade, who returns to the Yungkuofu after her father's death.

Pao-yu has a half brother, Chia Huan. His mother, jealous of the true-born son, pays a sorceress to bewitch the boy and Phoenix, whom she also hates. Both are seized with fits of violence and wild delirium. Pao-yu's coffin had already been made when a Buddhist monk and a lame Taoist priest suddenly appear and restore the power of the spirit stone. Pao-yu and Phoenix recover.

A short time later a maid is accused of trying to seduce Pao-yu. After she is dismissed, she drowns herself. About the same time, Chia Cheng is informed that his son turned the love of a young actor away from a powerful patron. Calling his son a degenerate, Chia Cheng almost causes Pao-yu's death by the severity of the beating that the angry father administers.

As Phoenix becomes more shrewish at home, Chia Lien dreams of taking another wife. Having been almost caught in one infidelity, he is compelled to exercise great caution in taking a concubine. Phoenix learns about the secret marriage, however, and by instigating claims advanced by the girl's former suitor she drives the wretched concubine to suicide.

Black Jade, always delicate, becomes more sickly. Sometimes she and Pao-yu quarrel, only to be brought together again by old ties of affection and understanding. The gossip of the servants is that the Matriarch will marry Pao-yu to either Black Jade or Precious Virtue. While possible marriage plans are being discussed, a maid finds in the Takuanyuan a purse embroidered with an indecent picture. This discovery leads to a search of all the pavilions, and it is revealed that one of the maids is involved in a secret love affair. Suspicion also falls on Bright Design, one of Pao-yu's maids, and she is dismissed. Proud and easily hurt, she dies not long afterward. Pao-yu becomes even moodier and more depressed after Bright Design's death. Outraged by the search, Precious Virtue leaves the park and goes to live with her mother.

A begonia tree near Pao-yu's pavilion blooms out of season. This event is interpreted as a bad omen, for Pao-yu loses his spirit stone and sinks into a state of complete lethargy. In an effort to revive his spirits, the Matriarch and his parents decide to marry him at once to Precious Virtue rather than to

Black Jade, who continues to grow frailer each day. Pao-yu is allowed to believe, however, that Black Jade is to be his wife. Black Jade, deeply grieved, dies shortly after the ceremony. Knowing nothing of the deception that was practiced, she felt that she failed Pao-yu and that he was unfaithful to her. The flower, thus, returned to the Great Void.

Suddenly a series of misfortunes overwhelms the Chias as their deeds of graft and corruption come to light. When bailiffs take possession of the two compounds, the usury Phoenix practiced is disclosed. Chia Gen and Chia Sheh are arrested and sentenced to banishment. The Matriarch, who takes upon herself the burden of her family's guilt and surrenders her personal treasures for expenses and fines, becomes ill and dies. During her funeral services, robbers loot the compound and later return to carry off Exquisite Jade, a pious nun. Phoenix also dies, neglected by those she dominated in her days of power. Through the efforts of powerful friends, however, the complete ruin of the family is averted, and Chia Cheng is restored to his official post.

In the end, however, the despised son becomes the true redeemer of his family's honor and fortunes. After a Buddhist monk returns his lost stone, Pao-yu devotes himself earnestly to his studies and passes the Imperial Examinations with such brilliance that he stands in seventh place on the list of successful candidates. The emperor is so impressed that he wishes to have the young scholar serve at court, but Pao-yu is nowhere to be found. The tale is that he became a bodhisattva and disappeared in the company of a Buddhist monk and a Taoist priest.

Critical Evaluation:

Dream of the Red Chamber is a long and extremely complicated domestic chronicle—the novel contains more than four hundred characters—that is at once a lively comedy of manners, a realistic fable of moral seriousness, and a metaphysical allegory. The title is capable of expressing several meanings. For example, it may be translated as "Dreams of Young Maidens," since the younger women of the Chia clan lived in the traditional "red chamber" of a palace compound. The term may also be interpreted as a reference to the metaphor "Red Dust," which in Buddhist usage is a designation for the material world with all of its pleasures, follies, and vices.

On the metaphysical level of the novel, the stone and the flower, originally located in the Ethereal, suffer a fall when they enter earthly reality in the Red Dust. Here the novel may be read as an allegory endorsing a Taoist-Buddhist system of otherworldly values (represented by the mysteriously recurring priest and monk) and rejecting the this-world view of

Confucianism (represented by Chia Cheng). Interestingly, this novel's critique of feudalist and Confucian China won praise from Marxist readers.

The Ethereal stone's fortunes translate into a novel of manners when the stone falls into earthly existence as the protagonist, Chia Pao-yu. In this mode, the novel becomes, through its portrayal of the Chia family, a brilliantly realistic document of upper-class life during the Ching Dynasty. It encompasses financial affairs, sexual aberrations, fraternal jealousies, and tragic suicides. The Chia fortunes reach their apogee when Cardinal Spring becomes the Emperor's concubine. The Takuanyuan Garden, built to honor Cardinal Spring, symbolizes these halcyon days; it becomes the domain of the younger Chia generation led by Pao-yu. In the garden, their way of life is carefree, innocent, almost Edenic, but, just as Pao-yu must grow into adulthood, so evil must invade this Eden. The fall begins when an indecently embroidered purse is found. A general search ensues, scandals surface, a tragic death results. Analogous disasters overtake the family. Their financial dealings incur the Emperor's displeasure; Imperial Guards ransack the Chia compound. Then bandits raid the garden itself. Finally, Pao-yu chooses to deny the folly of this world and to join the Buddhist priest and the Taoist monk, journeying, presumably, to the Ethereal.

The eighteenth century *Hongloumeng*, or *Dream of the Red Chamber*, considered by many scholars as the greatest of Chinese novels, comes closer to Western aesthetics than any Chinese novel written before or after its publication. The book, perhaps first published in 1715, is generally considered to have been written by Cao Xueqin, with the exception of the last forty chapters, which may have been written by Gao E, the editor of the original printed novel. Some critics believe the last forty chapters are less effective rhetorically and were the sole inspiration of Gao E and others; other critics believe that Gao E simply redacted Cao Xueqin's original wording of the last forty chapters. Most scholars agree that, and internal evidence points to, the idea that Cao Xueqin may have drawn upon his own experiences as the son of a once wealthy, powerful family.

Dream of the Red Chamber, with its vast scope and depth, has been called by both Western and Chinese critics a supreme study of psychological realism. The novel is significant for more than its autobiographical elements. The long, complex forward motion of the plot tests ideals in Chinese culture: Confucian teachings, with their tenets about married love, family, overindulgence, sexual obsession, and patriotism; Buddhist and Taoist philosophy, which condemns personal obsessive desire. Although the author's inclusion of diverse Chinese thought may create confusion at times, this does not detract from the story's powerful, rhetorical texture or its readability.

Dream of the Red Chamber uses allegory and symbolism to reflect Cao Xueqin's interest in and study of tradition. Pao-yu, for example, is part of a creation myth. In further allegorical terms, the hero is put into a dream sequence. The author's response to Taoist-Buddhist thought is reflected by the symbolic technique as well as by his response to the Confucian view of the material world.

In addition to the allegory, the author creates settings and actions suggestive of a novel of manners. Thus the highly praised realism of the novel, with its more than four hundred characters, softens the didacticism of allegory, although sometimes it falls into formulaic method. The realism, however, provides a brilliant document of upper-class life during the Ching Dynasty. The fact that the story line does not conclude happily and that Pao-yu, the noble hero, is subject to a series of climactic events toward the end of the book, introduces crucial reflections on compassion and salvation, fulfilling the criteria for serious tragedy. The novel's significant power lies not only in its portrayal of decadent Chinese manners and crushed nobility but also in its incisive treatment of the complexity of human nature.

"Critical Evaluation" by Dorie LaRue

Further Reading

Edwards, Louise P. *Men and Women in Qing China: Gender in the Red Chamber Dream.* Honolulu: University of Hawaii Press, 2001. Uses *Dream of the Red Chamber* as a starting point for analysis of eighteenth century Chinese gender roles, challenging the common assumption that the novel represents some form of early Chinese feminism by examining the text in conjunction with historical data.

Knoerle, Jeanne. *"The Dream of the Red Chamber": A Critical Study.* Foreword by Lui Wu Chi. Bloomington: Indiana University Press, 1972. Evaluates *Dream of the Red Chamber* in aesthetic terms and applies Western literary tenets. Places the novel in perspective within the history of Chinese literature; examines the novel's ethical considerations and its religious and cultural influences. Shows how the tenets of Confucianism, Taoism, and Buddhism are woven together for a unified whole. Knoerle's illumination of the novel's structure and technique is especially helpful.

Wang, Jing. *The Story of Stone: Intertextuality, Ancient Chinese Stone Lore, and the Stone Symbolism in "Dream of the Red Chamber," "Water Margin," and "The Journey to the West."* Durham, N.C.: Duke University Press, 1992. Thorough discussion of the stone symbolism and its relationship to intertextuality, myth, and religion. An excellent section devoted to folk belief systems in the 1600-1899 Qing Dynasty period.

Wu Shih-Ch'ang. *On the Red Chamber Dream.* Oxford, England: Clarendon Press, 1961. Thorough, accessible discussion restricted mainly to textural problems that scholars encountered when they attempted to identify the original, authentic version of the novel. Excellent discussion of the varying and conflicting views concerning authorship.

Xiao, Chi. *The Chinese Garden as Lyric Enclave: A Generic Study of the Story of the Stone.* Ann Arbor: Center for Chinese Studies. University of Michigan, 2001. A history of the garden in Chinese culture and literature, including its symbolism in *Dream of the Red Chamber* and its importance to the Chinese literati during the Qing Dynasty.

Yi, Jeannie Jinsheng. *The "Dream of the Red Chamber": An Allegory of Love.* Paramus, N.J.: Homa & Sekey Books, 2004. Yi analyzes the allegorical and structural role of dreams in the novel, interpreting them as symbols for the impermanent nature of love. She argues that Western literary theory, unless it is seriously modified, is not applicable to Chinese literature.

Yu, Anthony C. *Rereading the Stone: Desire and the Making of Fiction in "Dream of the Red Chamber."* Princeton, N.J.: Princeton University Press, 2001. Yu argues that the novel is a story about fictive representation; through a maze of literary devices, the novel challenges the authority of history and referential biases in reading.

The Dream Songs

Author: John Berryman (1914-1972)
First published: 1969 (complete; originally published
   in *77 Dream Songs*, 1964; and *His Toy, His Dream,
   His Rest*, 1968)
Type of work: Poetry

Begun in 1955, *The Dream Songs* combines two volumes, *77 Dream Songs* (1964) and *His Toy, His Dream, His Rest* (1968). The series of 385 songs is an ongoing, evolving account that mixes historical facts with autobiographical material, current events with philosophy, and archetypal myths with vaudeville humor. John Berryman is often associated with the confessional school of poetry, a style popular in the United States during the 1950's and 1960's and connected with the careers of Berryman's contemporaries Robert Lowell, Randall Jarrell, and Sylvia Plath. The design of *The Dream Songs* (that of a series of lyrics organized around a central motif) has roots in literary tradition, including *Don Juan* (1819-1824, 1826) by the British Romantic writer Lord Byron, and *Cantos* (1930-1970) by the American poet of the twentieth century, Ezra Pound. Berryman cited Walt Whitman, the nineteenth century American poet, as his model, claiming that he designed the poem after Whitman's "Song of Myself" (1855). In 1965, *77 Dream Songs* won a Pulitzer Prize; *His Toy, His Dream, His Rest* won the National Book Award in 1969.

At first glance, the collection seems loose, spontaneous, and improvised, but actually the individual poems are tightly structured, and they adhere technically and thematically to a complex poetic strategy. Each of Berryman's songs consists of 18 lines broken into three stanzas of six lines each. The meter is well regulated, utilizing speech patterns ranging from a parody of beatnik black dialect to baby talk to academic jargon. It takes the attitude of a hip literary insider during the late 1950's and early 1960's. In his 1979 essay "How to Read Berryman's *Dream Songs*," Professor Edward Mendelson points out an even more severe, "arithmetical precision" as a further unifying scheme built around the number seven. He demonstrates "seventy-seven Songs in the first volume . . . 77 x 5 in the completed 385 Songs . . . seven epigraphs; seven Books in all." The songs also suggest a plot, not in a linear episodic sequence of events, but as a quest of the poet's search for himself, seeking a fixed, centered ego.

Books 1 through 3 detail the metaphysical angst of Henry, the main character, recounting events and meditations. Henry is self-obsessed, petty, brilliant, dysfunctional, and damned by his need for meaning, for transcendence. The characters—including friends, enemies and acquaintances—are "zoned!" and "screwed up" or they are intellectual hustlers with their own lives to waste. Mixing slang with formal diction, discordant meter with perfect lyrical rhythms, Berryman combines pedantry with a street-smart style to portray a tragicomical blend of voices, personas, embodied in the polymorphous figure of Henry. In the preface to the one-volume edition of *The Dream Songs* (1969), Berryman writes, "The poem, then, whatever its wide cast of characters, is essentially about an imaginary character (not the poet, not me) named Henry, a white American in his early middle age, sometimes in blackface, who has suffered an irreversible loss and talks about himself sometimes in the first person, sometimes in the third, sometimes even in the second; he has a friend, never named, who addresses him as Mr Bones and variants thereof."

This "irreversible loss" may be traced, despite the disclaimer, to Berryman's own loss of innocence. When Berryman was twelve, his father shot himself to death outside the boy's window. His life after his father's suicide was punctuated by transience and dissolution, although he managed to garner prestigious poetry awards and various teaching positions, notably at Harvard, Princeton, and the University of Minnesota. Married three times, Berryman spent years fighting alcoholism, infidelity, and madness, and finally began to lose faith in his craft as a poet. The incessant strife and psychological turmoil that began so early in his life, and which is so evident in *The Dream Songs*, culminated in his own suicide in 1972.

As the title *The Dream Songs* suggests, the poems are extremely private, subjective, and personal, but as songs they are also by design public, objective, and communal. Many are introspective, confessional, self-incriminating reports from the edge of madness. Others are elegies for Berryman's contemporaries; others read like barstool editorials on political events of the day; still others come off as bitter lectures on the ironies of history. What unites the poems is the strength of the poet's personality. Berryman's genius for detail, his precise phrasing, and his unrelenting insight into the heart of human experience keep *The Dream Songs* from sinking into maudlin self-pity. The work is laced with passionate pessimism, and too often the ironic aside devolves into sour invective; nevertheless, the cynical recitals of spiritual vacuity are tempered by Berryman's stoic resignation, hope bred from despair.

The first song establishes Henry's disillusionment and withdrawal, contrasting his expectations with the reality he finds himself living in. The opening stanza suggests an existential conspiracy, in which "unappeasable Henry" senses that he has been fooled into believing in the possibility of happiness and fulfillment and is suspicious of "a trying to put things over." The second stanza implies that there was a time when Henry had faith in life, when "All the world like a woolen lover/ once did seem on Henry's side." Some event, a "departure," presumably Berryman's father's death, qualifies Henry's sense of a benevolent world ripe with opportunity and promise. He feels exposed, "pried/ open," and in the third stanza seems astounded at the suffering that "the world can bear & be" (playing on the meanings of "bear") amazed that the world can produce and accept his suffering—and "be." Henry is astounded that the world exists at all and that to exist is to suffer. Once in Henry's youth he was "glad/ all at the top, and I sang." He sees life as a constant erosion, in which all endeavors lead to the same conclusion: "empty grows every bed."

The Dream Songs is, at heart, a romantic poem. In the need to discover the root of his failure in an impossible dream of transcendence, Henry becomes a tragic rebel, resenting his freedom as much as he craves it. He is a victim of his own limitations and is haunted by the infinite possibilities of his life. His muse is "Filling her compact & delicious body/ with chicken páprika." After all the strategies and evasions, "life, friends, is boring" and offers as much spiritual nourishment as "a handkerchief sandwich," the only question for Henry is: "Where did it all go wrong?" The punishment of living does not seem to fit the crime of existence. Even though "There sat down, once, a thing on Henry's heart/ so heavy," he is confused by the severity of the penitence he extracts from himself. His crime is against himself, and he complains that he would never "end anyone and hacks her body up/ and hide the pieces, where they may be found."

Book 4, the Op. posth. (opus posthumous section, songs 78-91), describes Henry's symbolic death, as he is "flared out in history." Snuffing out his will, "nourished he less & less/ his subject body." His message from the grave is filled with as much remorse as acrimony. He is both satisfied and bewildered by his condition. In his desire for selflessness, he feels "something bizarre about Henry, slowly sheared off."

As he begins the process of ego extinction, he is left with only "his eyeteeth and one block of memories" which prove "enough for him." After all, he claims, it is "a *nice* pit" and "the knowledge they will take off your hands" keeps him free from the mundane habits—typewriters and deadlines—that infuriate and deaden his life. While he admits that "It would not be easy, accustomed to these things,/ to give up the old world," Henry gives it his best shot. Bound by guilt to experience, he hopes "Henry's brow of stainless steel/ rests free," but unable to absolve himself from the crimes of his conscience, "returning to our life/ adult & difficult," he is "collected and dug up." His return to the world is measured by "accumulated taxes" and wives "glued/ to disencumbered Henry's many ills." Seduced by the opportunity death affords him "to fold/ him over himself quietly," he "muttered for a double rum" and began "with a shovel/ digging like mad, Lazarus with a plan/ to get his own back."

Book 5 continues to catalog his psychic convalescence during a lengthy hospital stay. Caught in a cycle of recovery and relapse, his only recourses are to transform his world or to lose it. Berryman relies on his craft for salvation, in the transforming process of the imagination, rebounding with stoic persistence from one defeat after another. This attempt to impose poetic form on the contingencies of existence culminates for Berryman in book 6, beginning with a sequence of elegies for Berryman's contemporary, American poet Delmore Schwartz, "the new ghost/ haunting Henry most," before continuing through a hodgepodge of meditations, migrations, literary gossip, as "wanderers on coasts lookt for the man/ actual, having encountered all his ghost." The existential travelogue ends in book 7 with the poet in exile— literally—in Ireland, "Leaving behind the country of the dead." In Dublin, surrounded by ghosts, Berryman seems to have discovered a unified voice. The songs become more conversational, less daring. The device of the minstrel from the early songs is abandoned. The delivery becomes almost occasional, resembling letters from the poet to himself. The enervation evident in the later songs of book 7 may, however, be an inevitable result of the theme of the collection. *The Dream Songs* is about the poet's search for the form to contain experience, and therefore to control the world of the self. The shifts in syntax and perspective that mark the early songs are resolved in book 7, and the poet's project—the synthesis of experience and form in the completion of the self—is finished. In fact, the last two songs return to the poet's original source of disillusionment: Berryman as covictim of his father's suicide. The poet makes "this awful pilgrimage" only to "spit upon this dreadful banker's grave/ who shot his heart out." Murderous with grief and anger, he will "ax the casket open ha to see/ just how he's taking it." Berryman's self-destruction, his "final card," may have been merely the poet's last futile attempt to find "a middle ground between things and the soul."

Jeff Johnson

Further Reading

Coleman, Philip, and Philip McGowan, eds. *"After Thirty Falls": New Essays on John Berryman*. Amsterdam: Rodopi, 2007. The contributors to this collection seek to reevaluate and restore interest in Berryman's work. The essays include discussions of Berryman and the twentieth century sonnet and Berryman and Shakespearean autobiography, as well as five essays offering various interpretations of *The Dream Songs*.

Dodson, Samuel Fisher. *Berryman's Henry: Living at the Intersection of Need and Art*. Amsterdam: Rodopi, 2006. Dodson's detailed analysis of *The Dream Works* seeks to provide "the beginning reader and scholar with a map for approaching" the structure and thematic focus of the poem. He includes information about the poem's language, stylistic innovations, epic qualities, and elegiac movement, as well as reproductions of more than thirty draft manuscripts of the work.

Kelly, Richard, and Alan K. Lathrop, eds. *Recovering Berryman: Essays on a Poet*. Ann Arbor: University of Michigan Press, 1993. A broad approach to Berryman's art and life. Includes Lewis Hyde's controversial essay "Alcohol and Poetry: John Berryman and the Booze Talking."

Mariani, Paul. *Dream Song: The Life of John Berryman*. New York: William Morrow, 1990. An exhaustive biography drawing on interviews and anecdotes from Berryman's colleagues and acquaintances. Attempts to connect Berryman's life with his work, stressing autobiographical elements in *The Dream Songs*.

Matterson, Stephen. *Berryman and Lowell: The Art of Losing*. New York: Barnes & Noble, 1987. Explores Berryman's career in the context of his contemporary, Robert Lowell. Discusses the "theme of disintegration" prevalent in Berryman's work.

Mendelson, Edward. "How to Read Berryman's *Dream Songs*." In *American Poetry Since 1960*, edited by Robert B. Shaw. Cheadle Hulme, England: Carcanet Press, 1973. A brief but detailed analysis of *The Dream Songs*, providing an overview of the complete series as well as detailed explications of selected poems; relies less on biographical material than on the more formal poetic structures and strategies.

Thomas, Harry, ed. *Berryman's Understanding: Reflections on the Poetry of John Berryman*. Boston: Northeastern University Press, 1988. Provides a broad cultural context for Berryman's work and a close critical analysis of his poetry.

Drums Along the Mohawk

Author: Walter D. Edmonds (1903-1998)
First published: 1936
Type of work: Novel
Type of plot: Historical
Time of plot: 1775-1783
Locale: Mohawk Valley

Principal characters:
GILBERT MARTIN, a young pioneer
MAGDELANA "LANA" BORST MARTIN, his wife
MARK DEMOOTH, a captain of the militia
JOHN WOLFF, a Tory
BLUE BACK, a friendly Oneida Indian
MRS. MCKLENNAR, Captain Barnabas McKlennar's widow
JOSEPH BRANT, an Indian chief
GENERAL HERKIMER and GENERAL BENEDICT ARNOLD, military leaders against the British
NANCY SCHUYLER, Mrs. Demooth's maid
JURRY MCLONIS, a Tory
HON YOST, Nancy's brother

The Story:

Magdelana Borst, the oldest of five daughters, marries Gilbert Martin and together they start off from her home at Fox's Mill to settle farther west in their home at Deerfield. The time is July, 1776, and the spirit of the revolution reaches into the Mohawk Valley, where settlers who side with the rebels have already formed a company of militia commanded by Mark Demooth. Soon after he comes to his new home, Gil reports for muster day. Some Indians were seen in the vicinity. Also, the militia decides to investigate the home of John Wolff, suspected of being a king's man. Finding evidence that a spy was hidden on the Wolff farm, they arrest Wolff, convict him of aiding the British, and send him to the Newgate Prison at Simsbury Mines.

A few months after their arrival at Deerfield, Gil decides to organize a logrolling to clear his land for farming. The Weavers, the Realls, and Clem Coppernol all come to help with the work. When they are about half finished, Blue Back, a friendly Oneida Indian, comes to warn them that a raiding party of Seneca Indians and whites is in the valley. The settlers immediately scatter for home to collect their few movable belongings, which they might save, and then drive to Fort Schuyler. Lana, who is pregnant, loses her baby as a result of the wild ride to the fort. The enemy destroys the Deerfield settlement. All the houses and fields are burned; Gil's cow is killed; Mrs. Wolff, who refused to take refuge with the people who sent her husband to prison, is reported missing. Gil and Lana rent a one-room cabin in which to live through the winter. With spring coming and needing a job to support himself and Lana, Gil becomes the hired man of Mrs. McKlennar, a widow. The pay is forty-five dollars a year plus the use of a two-room house and their food.

General Herkimer tries to obtain a pledge of neutrality from the Indian chief, Joseph Brant, but is unsuccessful. At the end of the summer, word comes that the combined forces of the British and the Indians, commanded by General St. Leger, are moving down from Canada to attack the valley. The militia is called up, and they set out westward to encounter this army. The attack by the militia, however, is badly timed, and the party is ambushed. Of nearly six hundred and fifty men, only two hundred and fifty survive. The survivors return in scattered groups. Gil receives a bullet wound in the arm. General Herkimer, seriously injured in the leg, dies from his wounds.

After the death of General Herkimer, General Benedict Arnold is sent out to reorganize the army and lead it in another attack—this time against General St. Leger's camp. When Nancy Schuyler, Mrs. Demooth's maid, hears that her brother, Hon Yost, is in the neighborhood with a group of To-

ries, she decides to sneak out to see him. On the way, she meets another Tory, Jurry McLonis, who seduces her. Before she is able to see Hon, the American militia breaks up the band. Hon is arrested but is later released when he agrees to go back to the British camp and spread false reports of American strength. As a result of her meeting with McLonis, Nancy becomes pregnant. About the same time, Wolff escapes from the prison at Simsbury Mines and makes his way to Canada to look for his wife.

The following spring brings with it General Butler's raiding parties, which swoop down to burn and pillage small settlements or farms. Mrs. Demooth torments Nancy constantly because of her condition and one night frightens Nancy so completely that she, in terror, packs a few of her belongings in a shawl and runs away. Her only idea is to try to get to Niagara and find her brother Hon, but she does not get far before labor pains overtake her, and she bears her child beside a stream. An Indian finds her there and takes her with him as his wife. Lana has her child in May. The destruction by the raiding parties continues all through that summer, and the harvest is small. Mrs. McKlennar's stone house is not burned, but there is barely enough food for her household that winter. In the spring, Colonel Van Schaick comes to the settlement with an army, and the militia heads west once again, this time to strike against the Onondaga towns.

Lana has her second child the following August. As a result of the lack of food during the winter, she is still weak from nursing her first boy, Gilly, and after the birth of her second boy, it takes her a long time to recover. The next winter they all have enough to eat, but the cold is severe. During that winter, Mrs. McKlennar ages greatly and keeps mostly to her bed. The raids continue through the next spring and summer. The men never go out to their fields alone; they work in groups with armed guards. One day, after all the men go to the fort, Lana takes the two boys for a walk and then sits down at the edge of a clearing and falls asleep. When she awakens, Gilly is gone. Two Indians are near the house. She puts the baby, Joey, into a hiding place and then searches for Gilly. She finds him at last, and the two of them also crawl into the hiding place. Meanwhile, the two Indians enter the house and set it on fire. Overwhelmed by Mrs. McKlennar's righteous indignation, they carry out her bed for her. They flee when men, seeing the smoke, come hurrying from the fort. Gil and the two scouts, Adam Helmer and Joe Boleo, build a cabin to house them all during the coming winter.

With the spring thaws, a flood inundates the valley. As the waters recede, Marinus Willett comes into the Mohawk Valley with his army, with orders to track down and destroy the British forces under General Butler. Butler's army is already having a difficult time, for British food supplies are running out and wolves kill all stragglers. The militia finally catches up with Butler, harasses his army for several miles, kills Butler, and scatters the routed army in the wilderness. The Mohawk Valley is saved.

Three years later, the war over, Gil and Lana go back to their farm at Deerfield. They now have a baby girl, and Lana and Gil feel content with their hard-won security, their home, their children, and each other.

Critical Evaluation:

During the 1930's, the historical novel became extremely popular. Most of them followed the same pattern: They were long, had many characters, were full of action and realistic detail, and usually ended happily. *Drums Along the Mohawk* has all of these qualities, and it is one of the best of the genre. In 1936, it was on the best-seller list. In his author's note, Walter D. Edmonds defends the genre, noting that the life presented is not a bygone picture, for the parallel is too close to the reader's own. The valley people faced repercussions of poverty and starvation and were plagued by unfulfilled promises and a central government that could not understand local problems. Thus, the valley farmers, in the typically American tradition, learned to fight for themselves and for the land they had worked so hard to wrench from the wilderness.

Contrary to the patriotic myth, the war was not a glorious fight for freedom for all American soldiers. Many fought only because it was necessary to protect their families. They never thought of the American troops in the South and East; that was too remote, while the ever-present threat of immediate disaster was too near. When Captain Demooth says to Gil, "Who gives a damn for the Stamp Tax?" Gil admits that it has not bothered him and asks the key question of most of the farmers: "Why do we have to go and fight the British at all?" The attitude of many of the men conscripted for the militia is "Damn the militia! I need to roof my barn." Yet, as the attacks upon the small settlements begin, they realize that they must band together and fight.

At times, the western settlers wonder which side is the enemy. Denied food, munitions, and the protection of regular troops by the government at Albany, their seed grain commandeered and their fences burned for firewood, the settlers of German Flats become extremely bitter at the indifferent treatment they receive. When the widowed Mrs. Reall, with her many children, tries to collect her husband's back pay, she is denied because he is not marked dead on the paymaster's list. Even though Colonel Bellinger swears that he saw

Reall killed and scalped, the money is withheld. The only alternative she is given is to file a claim before the auditor-general, which must then be passed by an act of Congress. In the meantime, the family must either starve or rely on the charity of others who cannot really afford to help. They find that the Continental currency is practically worthless, but the climax of the colonists' disillusionment with the Congress comes when the residents receive huge tax bills for land that has been abandoned, buildings that have burned, and stock that has been killed. The incredulous settlers realize that the tax list is the one formerly used by the king.

The bestiality of what war does to people dominates the book. As the Indian raids become more ghastly, the Continentals grow more brutal. Scalps are taken by both Indian and white, and the atrocities and mutilations committed by both sides become increasingly barbarous. Yet, in spite of the ever-present atmosphere of horror, fear, and death, Edmonds also presents the forces of life. There is fierce energy in the characters in spite of their hardships. This is seen most clearly in the character of Lana, who, though weakened by starvation, work, and fear, manages to bear and care for her two boys. There is a mystery about her as she nurses and cares for her babies. Although she deeply loves Gil, with the birth of the first child, her role as a mother becomes the most important. Even the rough scout Joe Boleo senses the maternal mystery she exudes. There is also beauty in life itself as seen in the human body and in reproduction. The pregnant Nancy becomes more beautiful as she carries her illegitimate child, and the marriage of young John Weaver to Mary Reall begins another generation when Mary becomes pregnant.

Edmonds's style is free flowing, and he has an excellent ear for natural speech. As omniscient narrator, he goes deeply into the minds of the main characters and captures their reactions to the many events going on about them. All of the main characters have individuality and the gift of life.

The praise that is often given the novel is for the realism that Edmonds achieves by minute detail; however, this is also a weakness. His accounts of the many battles and raids become repetitious, for in the interest of historical truth, he does not want to eliminate anything. Thus, the action becomes blurred because there are so many similar accounts.

Structurally, the book is well handled with the exception of the last chapter, "Lana," which occurs three years after the preceding one. It appears to have been tacked on simply to tie up a few loose ends and to give the story a happy ending. In a book that has proceeded slowly season by season for five years, the three-year interval startles the reader.

The theme of the novel is the strength of those who will

endure anything to achieve the American Dream. Through their own efforts, they hope to earn their land, houses, animals, and the material things necessary to make life easier and more beautiful for themselves and particularly for their children. Lana and Gil begin their marriage with a cow, a few pieces of furniture, and Lana's most valued possession—a peacock feather that, with its mysterious beauty, symbolizes the beauty of the dream. All of this is lost in the war; but in the last chapter, Gil realizes his ambitions. He is farming his own land, he has built a new house, and he owns a yoke of oxen. Lana has her two boys, a baby daughter, security, and even the now battered but still gorgeous peacock feather which the Indian Blue Back returns to her. She is supremely content and secure as she tells herself, "We've got this place. . . . We've got the children. We've got each other. Nobody can take those things away. Not any more."

"Critical Evaluation" by Vina Nickels Oldach

Further Reading

Boxer, Sarah. "W. D. Edmonds Dies at Ninety-four: Author of Historical Novels." *The New York Times*, January 29, 1998. Edmonds's obituary provides information about his life and career.

Edmonds, Walter D. *Tales My Father Never Told*. Syracuse, N.Y.: Syracuse University Press, 1995. Edmonds remi-nisces about his father, who was already an elderly man when his son was born.

Gay, Robert M. "The Historical Novel: Walter D. Edmonds." *The Atlantic Monthly*, May, 1940. Analyzes the structure of the historical novel. Claims Edmonds avoided the common pitfalls of this genre by concentrating on simple characters and powerful narrative, achieving unity and purpose within a complex string of events.

Kohler, Dayton. "Walter D. Edmonds: Regional Historian." *English Journal* 27, no. 1 (January, 1938): 1-11. Comparative analysis of Edmonds's short stories and novels to 1938. Explains the new regionalism movement Edmonds inspired as an exploration of the New York State canal region in colonial times, not as a world separate from the contemporary reader, but as a collection of similar struggles and hopes separated from the present only by time.

Nevins, Allan. "War in the Mohawk Valley." *Saturday Review of Literature* 14, no. 14 (August 1, 1936): 5. Praises the author's ability to represent a realistic view of a region in conflict with Tories and Indians, but laments the novel's absence of any rich characterizations.

Wyld, Lionel D. *Walter D. Edmonds, Storyteller.* Syracuse, N.Y.: Syracuse University Press, 1982. Discusses Edmonds's creation of a new genre, the canal novel, and its impact on subsequent works by others using New York State themes and settings.

Dubliners

Author: James Joyce (1882-1941)
First published: 1914
Type of work: Short fiction

James Joyce, the preeminent experimental modernist, began *Dubliners* with a version of "The Sisters." A first-person narrative, it appeared in a 1904 issue of *Irish Homestead* under the pseudonym Stephen Daedalus. Thus the narrator was part of the story, its now mature protagonist. A character of the same name was already the protagonist of an autobiographical novel-in-progress, *Stephen Hero*, that ultimately became *A Portrait of the Artist as a Young Man* (1914-1915). Stephen Dedalus (why Joyce changed the spelling of the last name is uncertain) would also be a major character in Joyce's masterpiece, *Ulysses* (1922).

Stephen's namesake, Daedalus, the first artist of Greek mythology, is most famous for inventing human flight by combining mundane things—feathers, frames, wax, and knowledge about birds. Like the father of flight, "Stephen Daedalus" uses everyday life in his art, creating soaring insights. Joyce called such insights epiphanies, analogs of the epiphanic belief of New Testament Magi that the manger-housed infant of a Jewish newlywed was their God. Joyce no longer believed in the religious Epiphany but thought art should yield epiphanic insights using mundane facts and events.

Initially, he planned a dozen stories, arranged into four categories. Including a revision of "The Sisters," there would be three stories each, devoted to childhood, adolescence, mature life, and public life. By 1907, he had created a fifth category, married life. Stories on married life were inserted between the stories of adolescence and mature life. "The Sisters," first of the childhood stories, is about a boy's relationship with his teacher, Father Flynn, who just died. The boy's uncle and aunt, who are raising him, and their friend Cotter wonder what happened between the two. The uncle defends Flynn, suggesting that he had a "great wish" for the boy—presumably the priesthood—and the speculation seems to be corroborated by what the boy studied: Latin and priestly duties to the Eucharist and the confessional, in which sinners are absolved in absolute confidentiality. The boy is awed by those duties and, it is suggested, thinks Father Flynn wanted him in the order until he learns through the denials of Flynn's sisters that Flynn spilled sanctified wine, failing in his duty to the Eucharist, and was found paralyzed, helplessly laughing to himself in the confessional. These facts, which Flynn could not share because of a "too scrupulous" duty to the confessional, enable the boy to realize epiphanically that Father Flynn did not intend to awe and to attract but rather to awe and to dissuade him from becoming a priest.

"An Encounter" leads to its protagonist's realization that his attitude toward his fellows has been wanting. Searching for adventure, he and his classmate Mahoney ditch school. The Dillon boys do not join them, and the protagonist takes pleasure in imagining a disciplinarian caning one of them. When a perverse, scholarly old man who disdains common children confesses to the protagonist a delight in administering whippings, the protagonist recognizes a destructive parallel in himself. In "Penitent," he acknowledges the loyal Mahoney as a friend who does not deserve the disdain he felt for him.

"Araby" concludes the childhood group with an epiphanic story about love. The shy protagonist, infatuated with "Mangan's sister," is approached by her one day. She wonders whether he will be going to Araby, a bazaar. She would love to go, she says. When he asks why she cannot, she blames a retreat at her convent. Determined to buy her something, the protagonist goes to the bazaar alone and finds a saleswoman flirting with two men: She claims that she did not say something; they claim that she did. In that context, the love-smitten boy realizes that Mangan's sister had discretely offered to accompany him to the bazaar. Her covert offer would have allowed her to deny doing so if he had teased her about it; too naïve to realize what she was doing, and too shy to say, "Let's go together," he loses the opportunity by assuming she could not go. Crushed, the boy leaves without buying anything.

For the boy, experience yields insight. Protagonists of the remaining narratives, with the possible exception of "The Dead," end benighted. In the subsequent stories of *Dubliners*, epiphanies are reserved for readers.

The adolescents are all failures. Eveline, in the story that bears her name, wants her beau Frank to resemble her dead brother Ernest, who protected her from their violent father. However, doubting Frank's intentions, she fails to determine whether Frank's offer to spirit her to Buenos Aires is earnest or useful. Instead, a frightened animal, she freezes at the boarding ramp of the boat on which Frank leaves.

Jimmy Doyle of "After the Race" thinks he is a companion to the automobile racers he follows. Instead, they bilk the do-nothing butcher's son of his cash. They get him drunk, fleece him at cards, and leave him in a stupor to await "daybreak."

Lenehan and Corley, aging protagonists of "Two Gallants," the final story of adolescence, are even worse off. Lenehan, a leech in a yachting cap, follows in John Corley's wake. Both perpetually need cash, and Corley uses a stratagem to obtain some. While Lenehan eats peas, contemplates marriage to a rich woman, and worries, Corley persuades the homely servant he is servicing to steal from her employer. Thus J. C. (who aspirates the first letter of his name, rendering it Whorely) sells love, and Lenehan is his disciple.

The stories of marriage are no more idyllic. In "The Boarding House," Bob Doran only thinks he sowed wild oats. Meek, he is coerced into marrying Polly Mooney, daughter of "the Madam" who runs the house. Polly, under her mother's eye, allures him, and at the proper moment the Madam demands that Doran save her daughter's honor or face exposure. Fearful, he acquiesces in a marriage that bodes ill from before the start.

Timid Little Chandler of "A Little Cloud" is already married. Father of an infant whom his wife prefers to him, he dreams of becoming a poet. He imagines reviews of his Celtic poems, but no verse issues from him. He would like to emulate his friend Gallaher, who escapes provincial life by becoming a reporter, and when Gallaher visits, Chandler meets him at Corless's, a risqué nightclub that Chandler used to hurry past in trembling excitement. Alas, Gallaher now disdains Ireland. He affects an English accent, dresses like an Englishman, and is touchy about his failure to marry. Chandler sees through Gallaher's bravado briefly but on returning home falls back into blind admiration. His wife upbraids Gallaher for upsetting her "little mannie," and Chandler weeps.

Bulky Farrington of "Counterparts" lashes out instead. A cog in the machine of modern commerce, his physical strength is useless in his job as scrivener. At work, pink, hairless Mr. Alleyne dominates him. Farrington's small wage keeps him subject, and when he wastes the six shillings he gets pawning his watch by standing a round of drinks, an aggravated awareness of his constraints grips him. His attempt to arm-wrestle a circus performer compromises his physical power, and, utterly defeated, he asserts dominance at home by beating his son, blindly striking a blow at himself through his one hope for the future.

The stories of mature life concern people with dismal pasts and no future. Maria of "Clay," a nanny once, reared children who were not hers. A woman who offered motherly attention without the office of mother, she lives now at the Dublin by Lamplight laundry, where women who once sold sex without the office of wife seek shelter. On her way to a visit with her former charge Joe, she is confused by kind words from a tipsy gentleman and disembarks without the plumcake she is bringing. Joe is gracious about it, but his children resent her suggestion that they took the cake. In a game designed to predict the future, they and the girls next door trick Maria into choosing a saucer of clay, suggesting the grave. Joe's wife substitutes a prayer-book, anticipating life in a convent, but the first choice stands. When Maria sings "I Dreamt That I Dwelt," she repeats the nostalgic first verse, leaving out the verse that refers to future love.

James Duffy of "A Painful Case" likewise lacks prospects, but he embraces bleakness. He lives at a distance even from himself, writes about himself in the third person, and, when an opportunity arises to strike up friendships with Mrs. Sinico and her daughter, becomes friendly only with the mother, possibly thinking married women physically unavailable. When she seeks intimate relations, he breaks off the friendship, noting that love between men is impossible because sex must be avoided and friendship with women is impossible because sex cannot be avoided. Disapproving his own impulses, Duffy condemns himself to an isolation that is finalized four years later by Mrs. Sinico's perhaps accidental death.

Not only isolation but absence is the highest presence in "Ivy Day in the Committee Room." At a gathering of political canvassers on the anniversary of Charles Stewart Parnell's death, when all who honor him wear sprigs of ivy, drinking outweighs politics. When Parnell's loyal follower, Joe Hynes, reads his poorly crafted but heartfelt tribute to "Ireland's uncrowned king" (Parnell), the unsympathetic Mr. Croften robs it of value by praising the writing.

Public life, whether artistic, religious, or celebratory, is equally frustrating. Mrs. Kearney of "A Mother" wants to manage her pianist daughter's career but loses sight of her goal. Her dispute with Mr. Holohan over remuneration leads him to deny future employment to the girl.

Father Purdon of "Grace" offers businessmen salvation at a price. Tom Kernan, a drunken salesman, needs to reform, and his friends, led by Mssrs. Power and Cunningham, take him to church, where Purdon's sermon twists the parable of the unjust steward (Luke 16: 8-9) into a "spiritual accountant['s]" call for compromise.

"The Dead," last in the series, combines all categories. Gabriel Conroy, attending a Feast of Epiphany party at the home of his aunts one snowy evening, likes to think of himself as liberated, but he is trapped on many fronts. He imagines that he is genteel, but, when he finds himself alone with Lily, the maid, he is attracted. A college teacher, he married Gretta, a Connacht girl disdained by his now dead mother as "country cute"; he still smarts at the characterization. Imagining himself above politics, he is wounded when his colleague, the political activist Molly Ivors, playfully accuses him of abandoning Ireland. He thinks he disdains his aunts and cousin, but he delivers a speech at the party and carves the goose. He creates a life for Gretta, but she does not play the roles he assigns; when they rent a hotel room her thoughts never approach his erotic imaginings. Gretta is thinking of sickly Michael Furey, who in her teen years exposed himself to the cold for her, worsened, and died. Gabriel, preoccupied with thoughts of being alone with his wife at evening's end, fails to see that for her the evening has been a pining regret over lost youthful love and guilt over Michael's death. Forced to confront his failures, Gabriel, in his own epiphany, sees his living relationship with his wife as less significant than the love of the long-dead Michael, and, in a snowy vision of the living and dead united, resolves to travel westward into Ireland, where he can meet his demise. His understanding, however, is still partial; incomplete recognition can lead to a paralysis as damaging as ignorance.

Joyce was anticipated by the late nineteenth century Russian Anton Chekhov in the writing of apparently plotless stories of everyday life that nevertheless yielded insights into entrapment, frustration, and psychological paralysis. Joyce was first to see such stories as epiphanic and in *Dubliners* produced one of the first collections of stories geographically and thematically linked into a single work of transcendent art.

Albert Wachtel

Further Reading

Bosinelli, Rosa M. Bollettieri, and Harold F. Mosher, Jr., eds. *ReJoycing: New Readings of "Dubliners."* Lexington:

University Press of Kentucky, 1998. The book's fourteen essays provide various interpretations of *Dubliners* as a whole, as well as "The Dead" and "A Little Cloud." Some of the essays examine cliches and repetition, ideology, narrative "cheekiness," and gender issues in the collection.

Brown, Richard, ed. *A Companion to James Joyce*. Malden, Mass.: Blackwell, 2008. Collection of essays, many of which focus on the worldwide influence of Joyce's work, with specific analyses of his impact upon the literature of Ireland, Germany, Japan, India, New Zealand, and France. Vicki Mahaffey examines *Dubliners* in her essay "*Dubliners*: Surprised by Chance."

Bulson, Eric. *The Cambridge Introduction to James Joyce*. New York: Cambridge University Press, 2006. Introductory overview of Joyce's life and work, placing them within the context of Joyce as a modernist, journalist, translator, lecturer, and lover. Chapter 3 analyzes five of Joyce's works, including *Dubliners*, while chapter 4 chronicles his works' critical reception from 1914 through 2005.

Ellmann, Richard. *James Joyce*. Rev. ed. New York: Oxford University Press, 1982. A brilliantly researched biography that traces the stories to their biographical roots.

Kenner, Hugh. *Dublin's Joyce*. Bloomington: Indiana University Press, 1956. Wide-ranging and inventive readings of Joyce's works and sources by an eminent literary critic.

Norris, Margot. *Suspicious Readings of Joyce's "Dubliners."* Philadelphia: University of Pennsylvania Press, 2003. Norris, a noted Joyce scholar, devotes each of the book's fifteen chapters to an analysis of one of the stories in the collection, paying particular attention to their narrative style.

Peake, C. H. *James Joyce: The Citizen and the Artist*. Stanford, Calif.: Stanford University Press, 1977. Comprehensive readings of Joyce as a writer who elucidates his time.

Pierce, David. *Reading Joyce*. New York: Pearson Longman, 2008. Pierce, who has taught and written about Joyce for decades, provides a framework to enable the general reader to understand Joyce's work. He devotes four chapters to explicating some of the stories in *Dubliners*, as well as analyzing the work as a whole.

Thacker, Andrew, ed. *Dubliners: James Joyce*. New York: Palgrave Macmillan, 2006. Some of the book's essays focus on "The Dead," "Araby," "Clay," and "The Sisters," while others analyze *Dubliners* as a whole, including discussions of silences, desire and frustrations, and ideology in the collection.

Wachtel, Albert. *The Cracked Lookingglass: James Joyce and the Nightmare of History*. London: Associated University Presses, 1992. Analyses of the texts as "fictional histories" in which cause and chance prove equally illuminating.

The Duchess of Malfi

Author: John Webster (c. 1577/1580-before 1634)
First produced: 1614; first published, 1623
Type of work: Drama
Type of plot: Tragedy
Time of plot: Sixteenth century
Locale: Amalfi and Milan, Italy

Principal characters:
GIOVANNA, the Duchess of Amalfi
ANTONIO, her second husband
FERDINAND, the duke of Calabria, the duchess's jealous brother
THE CARDINAL, another brother of the duchess
BOSOLA, the brothers' spy and executioner

The Story:

The Duchess of Malfi is a young widow whose two brothers, a cardinal and Ferdinand, the duke of Calabria, are desperately anxious lest she marry again, for they want to inherit her title and her estates. Their spy in her household is Bosola, her master of horse.

The duchess falls in love with her steward, Antonio, and marries him secretly. Later, she secretly bears a son. When the happy father writes out the child's horoscope according to the rules of astrology and then loses the paper, Bosola finds the document and learns about the child. He dispatches a letter immediately to Rome to inform the brothers. The duke swears that only her blood can quench his anger, and he threatens that once he knows the identity of the duchess's lover, he will ruin her completely.

The years pass and the duchess bears Antonio two more children, a second son and a daughter. Antonio tells his friend Delio that he is worried because Duke Ferdinand is too quiet about the matter and because the people of Malfi, not aware of their duchess's marriage, are calling her a common strumpet.

Duke Ferdinand comes to the court to propose Count Malateste as a second husband for the duchess. She refuses. Bosola is not able to discover the father of the duchess's children. Impatient with his informer, the duke decides on a bolder course of action. He determines to gain entrance to the duchess's private chamber and there to wring a confession from her. That night, using a key Bosola gives him, the duke goes to her bedroom. Under his threats, she confesses to her second marriage, but she refuses to reveal Antonio's name. After the duke leaves, she calls Antonio and her loyal servant Cariola to her chamber. They plan Antonio's escape from Malfi before his identity can become known to the duchess's brothers.

The duchess calls Bosola and tells him that Antonio falsified some accounts. As soon as Bosola leaves, she recalls Antonio and tells him of the feigned crime of which she accused him to shield both their honors, and then bids him flee to the town of Ancona, where they will meet later. In the presence of Bosola and the officers of her guard she accuses Antonio of stealing money and banishes him from Malfi. With feigned indignation, Antonio replies that such is the treatment of thankless masters, and he leaves for Ancona. When the duped Bosola upholds Antonio in an argument with the duchess, she feels she can trust him with the secret of her marriage and asks him to take jewels and money to her husband at Ancona. Bosola, in return, advises her to make her own departure from the court more seemly by going to Ancona by way of the shrine of Loretto, so that the flight might look like a religious pilgrimage.

Bosola immediately travels to Rome, where he betrays the plans of Antonio and the duchess to Duke Ferdinand and the cardinal. They thereupon promptly have the lovers banished from Ancona. Bosola meets the duchess and Antonio near Loretto with a letter from Duke Ferdinand that orders Antonio to report to him, since he now knows Antonio to be his sister's husband. Antonio refuses and flees with his older son toward Milan. Bosola takes the duchess back to her palace at Malfi as Duke Ferdinand's prisoner. At Malfi, the duke again visits her in her chamber. He presents her with a dead man's hand, implying that it is from Antonio's corpse. Finally Bosola comes and strangles the duchess. Cariola and the children are also strangled, though not with the quiet dignity with which the duchess accepted her fate. When Bosola asks Duke Ferdinand for his reward, the hypocritical duke laughs and replies that the only reward for such a crime is its pardon.

In Milan, meanwhile, Antonio plans to visit the cardinal's chamber during the night to seek a reconciliation with the duchess's brothers. He intends to approach the cardinal because Duke Ferdinand loses his mind after causing his sister's murder. The cardinal orders Bosola that same evening to seek out Antonio, who is known to be in Milan, and murder him, but Bosola turns on him and accuses him of having plotted the duchess's murder. He demands his reward. When a reward is again refused, Bosola decides to join forces with Antonio to avenge the duchess's death.

That night, all plans miscarry. In the dark, Bosola accidentally murders Antonio, the man he hoped to make an ally in his revenge on Duke Ferdinand and the cardinal. A few minutes later, Bosola stabs the cardinal and is in turn stabbed by the mad Duke Ferdinand, who rushes into the room. Bosola, with his last strength, stabs the duke and they both die. Alarmed, the guards break into the apartments to discover the bodies. Into the welter of blood, a courtier leads the younger son of the Duchess of Malfi and Antonio, whom Antonio took to Milan. He is proclaimed ruler of the lands held by his mother and his uncles.

Critical Evaluation:

Little is known of John Webster's life, although the title page of his pageant, *Monuments of Honour* (1624), calls him a merchant-tailor. In the custom of Jacobean playwrights, he often collaborated, probably with Thomas Dekker, a practice supported by Philip Henslowe, whose *Diary* (1961) gives much information about the theater of the period. Webster's reputation rests almost entirely upon *The White Devil* (c. 1609-1612), and *The Duchess of Malfi*. Both are studies of illicit love, revenge, murder, and intrigues worthy of the Machiavellians that so appealed to Elizabethan and Jacobean audiences.

The Duchess of Malfi is a finer play than *The White Devil*, in part because of the noble character of the duchess herself. Her story has the reputation of being the best poetic tragedy written after William Shakespeare's, and the work reveals Webster's powers to present themes of great moral seriousness in magnificent language while also creating flesh-and-blood characters. Webster and Shakespeare mastered thinking in images so well that the images develop themes and meaning as fully as does the plot.

Some critics have noted that the violence of Webster's revenge-and-blood tragedies may obscure their finer qualities. George Bernard Shaw referred to Webster as "a Tussaud-laureate." Despite the melodramatic or surrealistic qualities of his work, however, few critics underestimate Webster's brilliance as a psychologist. His work shows its descent from Thomas Kyd's *The Spanish Tragedy* (c. 1585-1589), Senecan tragedy, and the medieval morality play, and the dramas reflect a preoccupation with death and the tempestuous history of the Renaissance period. Many of the dramas are set in Italy, the epitome of evil locales to Renaissance English.

The duchess of Malfi was an actual Italian figure, but Webster's immediate source was William Painter's *Palace of Pleasure* (1566), a collection of tediously moral stories, which was in turn based on twenty-five novellas of Matteo Bandello that also provided themes for several plays by Shakespeare and his contemporaries. Painter concentrates on two major sins, or weaknesses: the duchess's sensuality and Antonio's excessive ambition. Bosola is referred to only once in Painter's story. Webster does not alter Painter's version so much as he enlarges it by surrounding the limited world of the lovers with other worlds: the corrupt court of Amalfi and the religious state of Rome. He thereby exposes a universal corruption that expands concentrically beyond the lovers' chambered world. He enlarges and magnifies the role of the villain Bosola and uses him to bind the various worlds together. The resulting revenge tragedy treats the question of personal honor (still tied to feudal values), the political and moral problems of lawlessness, and the supreme question—human vengeance and divine or Providential vengeance.

Webster creates this fallen world through the actions of the duchess, Ferdinand, the cardinal, Antonio, and Bosola, particularizing the questions as to what true love should do in the presence of family pride and social taboos; how an individual can rise in an evil, power-dominated world without undergoing corruption; and, finally, whether people create their own heaven or hell. The topic of free will is both implicit and explicit throughout the play: People are responsible for the choices they make. Webster forces the smaller worlds into collision in the working out of these themes, and tragic destruction ensues. Providence finally asserts its influence through the hope vested in the duchess and Antonio's innocent son.

The duchess of the play is a headstrong but noble woman who says to her executioners: "Pull, and pull strongly, for your able strength/ Must pull down heaven upon me." Nobility notwithstanding, her "passion is out of place," for Antonio is but head steward of her household. In wooing Antonio she denies the chain of being on its social level. Even at the moment when she and Antonio confess their love, they are therefore threatened. In act 1, scene 3 (lines 176-181), she tries to ease his fears:

> ANT.: But for your brothers?
> DUCH.: Do not think of them:
> All discord without this circumference
> Is only to be pitied, not fear'd:
> Yet, should they know it, time will easily
> Scatter the tempest.

Her optimism is that of the pure soul, but she misjudges the power of those outside "this circumference." Her willfulness and passion are lust in the eyes of her brothers, the Church, and society at large. Webster communicates the sweetness of the romance, however, so thoroughly that the lovers are totally sympathetic throughout.

Second to the duchess in importance is Bosola, a symbol of Webster's disgust with an era that admired ambition but provided little opportunity for its honest realization. This melancholy scholar perverts his intelligence to "serve" Ferdinand and the cardinal, representatives of political and ecclesiastical corruption. Bosola's evil actions continue after the duchess's murder so that Webster can complete the theme of corruption. This accounts for the extended action of acts 4 and 5, which some critics have found objectionable. Ultimately, Bosola recognizes his misplaced devotion and his responsibility for the horrors, a recognition too sudden for some readers. Outside Shakespeare's works, however, dramatic characters of the period seldom change gradually, a vestige of the parent morality plays.

Even Ferdinand (who may hide incestuous feelings for his sister) accepts his guilt when he says, "Whether we fall by ambition, blood, or lust,/ Like diamonds, we are cut with our own dust." Ferdinand's marvelous image, which refers to all the characters, is characteristic of the powerful figurative language throughout the play. The image identifies the characters as the most precious of jewels, yet paradoxically made of dust. The place of human beings a little below the angels is secure, Webster declares, only so long as they act in accordance with the moral laws established by Providence. People rise or fall by their own acts. Delio's words that close the play are Webster's imagistic final comment upon the fallen of Amalfi: "These wretched eminent things/ Leave no more fame behind 'em, than should one/ Fall in a frost, and leave his print in snow."

"Critical Evaluation" by Mary H. Hayden

Further Reading

Aughterson, Kate. *Webster: The Tragedies*. New York: Palgrave, 2001. A student guide to Webster's tragedies, analyzing their key moments, scenic and dramatic structures, characters, and imagery. Argues that his plays critique a deceased world of patriarchal and aristocratic politics.

Bloom, Harold, ed. *John Webster's "The Duchess of Malfi."* New York: Chelsea House, 1987. An anthology of eight important articles on the play, including Lisa Jardine's provocative feminist reading. In his introduction, Bloom provides a useful history of the villain-as-protagonist tradition.

Boklund, Gunnar. *"The Duchess of Malfi": Sources, Themes, Characters*. Cambridge, Mass.: Harvard University Press, 1962. A thorough overview of *The Duchess of Malfi*, including a helpful discussion of the narrative sources on which Webster relied. Boklund finds the play unified in its design and provides a highly detailed analysis of the major characters.

Braunmuller, A. R., and Michael Hattaway, eds. *The Cambridge Companion to English Renaissance Drama*. 2d ed. New York: Cambridge University Press, 2003. Although none of the essays in this collection deals specifically with Webster, references to *The Duchess of Malfi* and some of his other plays are listed in the index. These references help place his plays within the broader context of English Renaissance drama.

Jackson, Ken. "'Twin' Shows of Madness: John Webster's Stage Management of Bethlem in *The Duchess of Malfi*." In *Separate Theaters: Bethlem ("Bedlam") Hospital and the Shakespearean Stage*. Newark: University of Delaware Press, 2005. In the Elizabethan era, officials at the Bethlem psychiatric hospital raised funds by charging visitors to view its patients. Webster depicted this visitation practice in *The Duchess of Malfi*, and this chapter discusses that depiction.

Ornstein, Robert. *The Moral Vision of Jacobean Tragedy*. Madison: University of Wisconsin Press, 1960. A substantial chapter on Webster treats the moral vision of *The Duchess of Malfi* and finds spiritual victory, rather than defeat, in the duchess's resolute stand against her brothers.

Peterson, Joyce E. *Curs'd Example: "The Duchess of Malfi" and Commonweal Tragedy*. Columbia: University of Missouri Press, 1978. Argues the controversial thesis that it is the duchess's prideful defiance of order and class that leads to the catastrophe.

Rabkin, Norman, ed. *Twentieth Century Interpretations of "The Duchess of Malfi."* Englewood Cliffs, N.J.: Prentice-Hall, 1968. Presents nine interpretive articles and a number of responding "View Points" on Webster and his play. Rabkin's introductory essay places Webster's work in the context of the decline of tragedy seen in the distinctly unheroic Jacobean society.

Shellist, Elli Abraham. "John Webster." In *A Companion to Renaissance Drama*, edited by Arthur F. Kinney. Malden, Mass.: Blackwell, 2002. In addition to this essay focusing on Webster's plays, this book contains many other essays that describe the Renaissance theater, its actors, and audiences; explain the type of plays presented; and place Renaissance drama in its historical and social context. References to *The Duchess of Malfi* are listed in the index.

Duino Elegies

Author: Rainer Maria Rilke (1875-1926)
First published: Duineser Elegien, 1923 (English translation, 1931)
Type of work: Poetry

For the reader who must rely on a translation of Rainer Maria Rilke's culminating work, the story and the man behind its appearance may overshadow the poem itself. No translation of the elegiac German original can do justice to the philosophy of the man who wrote it or be as deeply affecting as the inspiration that produced the work.

Rilke is often ranked with William Butler Yeats as one of the preeminent poets of the twentieth century. His poetic innovations might, however, be better compared with those of Gerard Manley Hopkins, though in the case of Rilke, experimentation with rhythm and rhyme never took precedence over content. Like Yeats, he often let the content find the form. Of the three, Rilke was the most intuitive, rhapsodic, and mystical, and he was perhaps the most consummate craftsman.

In October, 1911, the poet visited his friend Princess Marie von Thurn und Taxis-Hohenlohe at Duino Castle, near Trieste. He remained at the castle alone throughout the winter until April, and there he composed the first and second elegies and parts of several others. The opening stanza— which begins "Who, if I cried, would hear me among the angelic orders?"—came to him while he was walking in a storm along a cliff two hundred feet above the raging sea, a romantic interlude worthy of an atmospheric passage in a gothic novel. Rilke conceived the plan of all ten elegies as a whole, though ten years elapsed before the poem found its final form.

The first elegy, like the first movement of a musical work, presents the central theme and suggests the variations that follow. From the opening line to the last, Rilke invokes the angels, not those of Christianity but of a special order immersed in time and space, a concept of being of perfect consciousness, of transcendent reality. As a symbol appearing earlier in Rilke's poetry, the angel represents to him the perfection of life in all the forms to which he aspired, as high above humankind as God is above this transcending one. Nearest to this angelic order are the heroes—later he praises Samson—and a woman in love, especially one who dies young, as did Gaspara Stampa (1523-1544), whom Rilke celebrates as a near-perfect example. Like the lover, human beings must realize each moment to the fullest rather than be distracted by things and longings. With this contrast of people and angels, of lovers and heroes, and with the admission of life's transitory nature, the poet suggests the meaning of life and death as well as words can identify such profound things.

If the introduction or invocation is a praise of life, the second elegy is a lament for life's limitations. Mortals must, at best, content themselves with an occasional moment of self-awareness, of a glimpse at eternity. Unlike the Greeks, people in later times have no external symbols for the life within. In love, were humans not finally satiated, they might establish communication with the angels; finally, though, human intuitions vanish, leaving only a fleeting glimpse of reality.

Rilke began the third elegy at Duino and completed it in Paris the following year; during an intervening visit to Spain, he composed parts of the sixth, ninth, and tenth elegies. In the third section, he confronts the physical bases of life, especially love. He suggests that woman is always superior in the love act, man a mere beginner led by blind animal passion, the libido a vicious drive. Sublime love is an end in itself, but

human love is often a means to escape life. Even children have a sort of terror infused into their blood from this heritage of doubt and fear. From this view of mortality, Rilke would lead the child away, as he says in a powerful though enigmatic conclusion:

. . . Oh gently, gently
show him daily a loving, confident task done,—guide him
close to the garden, give him those counter-
balancing nights. . . .
Withhold him.

Perhaps the advent of war made the fourth elegy the most bitter of all, written as it was from Rilke's retreat in Munich in 1915. The theme of distraction, of humankind's preoccupation with fleeting time and time-serving, makes this part a deep lament over the human condition. People are worse than puppets who might be manipulated by those unseen forces, angels. Attempts to force destiny, to toy with fate, cause mortals to break with heaven's firm hold. People must be as little children, delighted within themselves by the world without, and with their attention and energies undivided, alone. Here, they will find the answer to death as the other side of life, a part of life and not the negation or end of it.

The fifth elegy, the last from the standpoint of time, written at the Château de Muzot in 1922, was inspired by Pablo Picasso's famous picture of a group of acrobats. Here again the circumstances of the writing overshadow the real worth of the poem. Picasso's *Les Saltimbanques* was owned by Frau Hertha Koenig, who allowed Rilke the privilege of living in her home in 1915 so that he could be near his favorite painting. Either the poet imperfectly remembered the details of the painting when the poem was finally written or he included the recollections of acrobats who delighted him during his Paris years. Regardless of influences, however, the poem is remarkable in its merging of theme and movement with a painting, emphasizing Rilke's conviction that a poem must celebrate all the senses rather than appeal to eye or ear alone.

The acrobats, symbolizing the human condition, travel about, rootless and transitory, giving pleasure to neither themselves nor the spectators. Reality to the acrobat, as to humankind, is best discovered in the arduousness of the task; routine, though, often makes the task a mockery, especially if death is the end. If death, however, is the other side of life and makes up the whole, then life forces are real and skillfully performed to the inner delight of performers and spectators, living and dead alike.

The hero, Rilke asserts in the sixth elegy, is that fortunate being whose memory, unlike that of long-forgotten lovers, is firmly established by his deeds. Being single-minded and single-hearted, the hero has the same destiny as the early departed, those who die young without losing their view of eternity. The great thing, then, is to live in the flower of life with the calm awareness that the fruit, death, is the unilluminated side of life. For the hero, life is always beginning.

In the seventh elegy, the poet no longer worries about transitory decaying or dying. Now he sings the unpremeditated song of existence:

> Don't think that I'm wooing!
> Angel, even if I were, you'd never come.
> For my call
> is always full of 'Away!' Against such a powerful
> current you cannot advance. Like an outstretched
> arm is my call. And its clutching, upwardly
> open hand is always before you
> as open for warding and warning,
> aloft there, Inapprehensible.

From this viewpoint, Rilke attempts in the eighth elegy, dedicated to his friend Rudolph Kassner, to support his belief in the "nowhere without no," the "open" world, timeless, limitless, inseparable "whole." "We," contrasted to animals, are always looking away rather than toward this openness.

Rilke continues the theme of creative existence in the ninth elegy, possibly begun at Duino but certainly finished at Muzot. He suggests that the life of the tree is superior in felicity to human destiny. People should, perhaps, rejoice in the limiting conditions of mortality by overcoming the negation of the flesh with a reaffirmation of the spirit. Death then holds no fears; it is not opposite to life, not an enemy but a friend. This work possibly represents the author's own recovery from the negating, inhibiting conditions of World War I to a renewed faith in life.

The tenth elegy, the first ten lines of which came to Rilke in that burst of creativity at Duino, contains a satiric portrait of the City of Pain, where man simply excludes suffering, pain, and death from his thoughts; where distractions, especially the pursuit of money, are the principal activities. This semiexistence of the poet contrasts with that in the Land of Pain, Life-Death, where there is continuous progress through insights of a deeper reality to the primal source of joy: "And we, who have always thought/ of happiness climbing,

would feel/ the emotion that almost startles/ when happiness falls." Perhaps Rilke means that by complete submission or attunement to universal forces individuals are suspended or even fall into the "open." This deeply realized philosophy he developed in *Die Sonette an Orpheus* (1923; *Sonnets to Orpheus*, 1936), a work that complements *Duino Elegies*, though it does not surpass it in deep emotional undertones and sheer power of expression.

Taken together, the elegies offer a mural of Rilke's inner landscape. Internalization of travel experiences, the lonely scenery of Duino Castle, the flight of birds, mythological constructs, and other phenomena create a background of timeless "inner space" against which the author projects his coming to grips with the existential polarities of life and death. Progressing from lament to profound affirmation of mortality, the poems glorify the fulfillment of humanity's promise to maintain all things of value through a process of transformation that rescues external nature by placing it in the protected realm of the spirit. The power by which this is accomplished is love. By bringing together earth and space, life and death, all dimensions of reality and of time into a single inward hierarchical unity, Rilke sought to ensure the continuation of humanity's outward existence.

The definitive English translation of the *Duino Elegies* remains the 1939 version produced by J. B. Leishman and the renowned poet Stephen Spender, who established a standard of literary accuracy and fluency that few later translators match. Other useful editions include C. F. MacIntyre's 1961 dual-language version and Elaine Boney's literal 1975 rendering.

Further Reading

Brodsky, Patricia Pollock. *Rainer Maria Rilke*. Boston: Twayne, 1988. A straightforward overview of Rilke's life and works. Chapter 7 explores the *Duino Elegies* and Rilke's other poems of the period. Includes useful primary and secondary bibliographies, notes, and index.

Heller, Erich. "Rilke in Paris." In *The Poet's Self and the Poem: Essays on Goethe, Nietzsche, Rilke, and Thomas Mann*. London: Athlone Press, 1976. The text of a series of lectures originally delivered at the University of London. A brief but perceptive attempt to place Rilke in the context of the major German literary and intellectual figures of his day; pays particular attention to the early elegies.

Komar, Kathleen L. *Transcending Angels: Rainer Maria Rilke's "Duino Elegies."* Lincoln: University of Nebraska Press, 1987. The major English-language study of the *Duino Elegies*. Devotes a chapter to each of the ten elegies and includes a short biographical sketch of Rilke. Includes an excellent bibliography and an index.

Mandel, Siegfried. *Rainer Maria Rilke: The Poetic Instinct.* Carbondale: Southern Illinois University Press, 1965. A landmark study of Rilke's poetic evolution. Of special interest is chapter 1, which provides a fascinating account of the tragedies that shaped the poet's character.

Metzger, Erika A., and Michael M. Metzger, eds. *A Companion to the Works of Rainer Maria Rilke.* Rochester, N.Y.: Camden House, 2001. Collection of essays discussing Rilke's life and analyzing specific works. Kathleen L. Komar, the author of a major study of *Duino Elegies* (above), reexamines the work in her essay "Rethinking Rilke's *Duineser Elegien* at the End of the Millennium."

Nelson, Erika M. *Reading Rilke's Orphic Identity.* New York: Peter Lang, 2005. Analyzes Rilke's poetry within the context of fin-de-siècle literature and as a precursor of modernism and postmodernism. Focuses on his preoccupation with identity and how he reinterpreted the myth of Orpheus in modern psychological and poetic terms.

Paulin, Roger, and Peter Hutchinson, eds. *Rilke's "Duino Elegies": Cambridge Readings.* Riverside, Calif.: Ariadne Press, 1996. Cambridge University faculty members provide ten interpretations of the elegies, analyzing their themes, language, and imagery.

Prater, Donald. *A Ringing Glass: The Life of Rainer Maria Rilke.* New York: Oxford University Press, 1986. A well-documented, scholarly biography derived largely from Rilke's extensive private correspondence. Focuses on the details of the poet's life, with only occasional attention to his work; chapters 4 to 6 cover the period of the *Duino Elegies*' composition. Includes notes, bibliography, and index.

Ryan, Judith. *Rilke, Modernism, and Poetic Tradition.* New York: Cambridge University Press, 1999. Traces Rilke's poetic development from his early aestheticism to his later modernism. Argues that he is not a "solitary genius" but a poet whose work was deeply influenced by the culture of his time.

Dulce et Decorum Est

Author: Wilfred Owen (1893-1918)
First published: 1920, in *Poems by Wilfred Owen*
Type of work: Poetry

Wilfred Owen set his poem "Dulce et Decorum Est" during World War I on the western front in France. His purpose—to protest against the mentality that perpetuates war—is unmistakable, but what sets the work apart from much other antiwar literature is the effectiveness of his tightly controlled depiction of war.

The first fourteen of the poem's twenty-eight lines comprise a sonnet that vividly describes a single terrible moment. The last twelve address the reader directly, explaining the significance or moral of the incident. The speaker is among a company of exhausted men who after a stint at the front are marching unsteadily toward the rear when they are suddenly overtaken by poison gas. After they hastily pull on their gas masks, the speaker sees through the misty lenses that one of them, somehow maskless, is staggering helplessly toward him. He watches the man succumb to the gas, desperately groping the air between them as he drops to the ground, like someone drowning. The third stanza shifts the context to the speaker's dreams. In a single couplet, the speaker declares that in all his dreams he sees that soldier plunging toward him. In the final stanza, he turns to the readers, telling them that if they, too, could have experienced such dreams and watched the soldier dying on the wagon into which the soldiers flung him, they would never repeat to their children "The old Lie: Dulce et decorum est/ Pro patria mori."

Throughout the war, this Latin phrase—a quotation from the Roman poet Horace (*Odes* III. 2.13, 23 and 13 B.C.E.)—was frequently used in inspirational poems and essays. In a letter to his mother, Owen provides the translation, "It is sweet and meet to die for one's country," and he expostulates sarcastically, "*Sweet!* And *decorous!*"

Owen is often judged to be the most remarkable of the group of "war poets" who emerged during World War I. Although "Dulce et Decorum Est" is seldom considered to be technically Owen's finest poem, it is nevertheless among his most famous because it captures so compellingly not only the tribulations of the soldiers who fought in the war but also their belief that the patriotic rhetoric on the home front and the government's refusal to negotiate a peace were more to blame for their suffering than the opposing soldiers. Owen, who was an officer with the Manchester Regiment, planned to publish "Dulce et Decorum Est" in a volume that was to present the truth about the war, which he knew to be utterly at odds with the belligerent cant that appeared daily in newspapers and in magazines in England.

Two drafts of the poem carry the dedication "To Jessie Pope etc" (two other drafts simply say "To a certain Poetess"), suggesting that Owen had originally specifically targeted such individuals as Jessie Pope, whose collection of children's verses, *Simple Rhymes for Stirring Times* (1916), was intended to kindle enthusiasm for the war.

In the end, Owen removed the sarcastic dedication, perhaps to make clear that he wished to address a much broader readership. Most people in England greeted the outbreak of war in August, 1914, with enthusiasm. Wars of recent memory were limited, distant affairs; the people expected adventure and heroism from a contained conflict that would be over by Christmas. Instead, after the second month of the war, when Germany's march on Paris was halted at the Marne, the opposing armies dug themselves into trenches facing each other across a narrow strip known as No Man's Land, a line that stretched across Belgium and France. In part because of the efficiency of machine guns and because tanks were not deployed until near the end of the war, neither side was able to dislodge the other. Millions of men lost their lives in costly and fruitless attempts to break the stalemate; in just one day, July 1, 1916, the great offensive at the River Somme took the lives of sixty thousand men. Rats, lice, and the sight of exposed corpses were inescapable conditions of trench warfare. By the time the war ended, all those who experienced the horrors of trench warfare were forced to abandon their belief in the superiority of European civilization and the idea of European progress.

In the opening lines of "Dulce et Decorum Est," Owen vividly portrays the price of trench warfare, the exhaustion of soldiers who become like old women, "hags," coughing, lame, blind, and deaf. The poet speaks for these individuals who, though they no longer function in tidy military unison, are joined by their shared experience of a nightmare that seems just at the point of being over when the new assault arrives. The deadly gases (at first chlorine, later phosgene and mustard gas) that remain a hallmark of World War I were first used on a large scale on the Western Front. Although soldiers were equipped with respirator masks, more than one million men died from such attacks. The gas, whose effects Owen describes in the second stanza, is the odorless and colorless mustard gas frequently used after July, 1917. Detectable only

by its sting, it gave its victims only seconds to protect themselves and caused severe, often fatal, burns to exposed skin and lungs. Owen also mentions other miseries of the "Great War," such as the unusually heavy rainfalls that turned the fighting zone into a bog in which the men suffered crippling foot ailments and sometimes even drowned.

The poem also expresses "the pity of war," the theme Owen also articulated in the short preface he drafted for the intended collection. English poetry, he explains, is "not yet fit to speak" of heroes, but speaking the truth of war may act as a warning to the next generation. Owen uses the word "pity" in a special sense, one that encompasses a profound fellow feeling for all those who suffer; ultimately, that includes everyone. Hence, his protest against war extends to become a protest against all inhumanity. The ability of Owen's poems to transcend the particular circumstances of their creation was a quality some of his early critics, including the poet Yeats, failed to see. "Dulce et Decorum Est" accomplishes this as effectively as anything Owen wrote, for the focus of its protest is not the pain suffered by a few men but rather the transhistorical "Lie." The horrible death of the gassed soldier exposes the fallacy behind the oft-repeated, high-sounding Latin epigram: The poem's protest is against an abuse of language.

Owen drafted the poem in August, 1917, at the age of twenty-four, while he was convalescing at Craiglockhart War Hospital in Edinburgh. He finished it about one year later, perhaps shortly before his death. The event described in the poem is almost certainly based on actual experience, as Owen reported such "smothering" dreams to his doctor. Recovering from concussion, trench fever, and "shell shock" or "neurasthenia" (terms often used as euphemisms for exhaustion), Owen's stay at Craiglockhart was crucial in his poetic development, in part because he became acquainted with the more experienced soldier-poet Siegfried Sassoon and, even more important, because it gave him a chance to work steadily during a period when his sense of poetic purpose was most urgent.

Owen was deeply concerned about the technical problems involved in the expression of his passionate convictions. Some of his later poems use striking methods such as half rhyme, but in this poem, too, Owen's technical mastery is impressive. The first stanza employs heavy, single-syllable rhymes throughout; to convey exhaustion, Owen breaks up the rhythm, which composes itself in the third line. After several comparatively regular lines, a dramatic shift occurs with the fragmentary syntax of the first lines of the stanza about the gas. The four repeating "um" sounds of those line in the words "fumbling," "clumsy," "someone," "stumbling" produce interior rhymes that create a sudden, panicked sense of double time. After the ellipsis, an eerie, dreamlike calm sets in as the poet coolly, objectively describes the man drowning "as in a green sea." The couplet literally rehearses the moment as do the dreams, and in place of a rhyme it repeats the falling cadence of "drowning" with extraordinary effect, as though poetry itself must stumble and fall at this juncture. The final stanza exploits the steady, relentless rhythm of iambic pentameter for the purpose of "accumulatio," heaping up declarations in couplets that each describe more of what could be seen. "My friend" announces a last turn: a direct accusation against the time-honored, respectable, capitalized "Lie." The extra foot in line 25 shatters the iambic pentameter and produces particularly heavy stresses on the two long syllables of "old Lie," enhancing the resonance of the foreshortened half-line that ends the poem.

In a late revision, Owen substituted lines 23 and 24 ("Obscene as cancer, bitter as the cud/ Of vile, incurable sores on innocent tongues,—") for two lines that introduced a note of eroticism that might have distracted attention from Owen's main purpose ("And think how, once, his head was like a bud,/ Fresh as a country rose, and keen, and young,—") The new lines recall images from Dante's *Inferno* (c. 1320), and their guttural sounds enhance the impression of outrage.

After a year of convalescence, Owen returned to the front in August, 1918. In October, he received the Military Cross, and on November 4, 1918, just one week before the Armistice, he was gunned down on the Sambre Canal. Owen published only five poems during his lifetime, and "Dulce et Decorum Est" was first published posthumously in *Poems by Wilfred Owen* (1920), the eleventh poem in a volume of only twenty-three. His reputation grew rapidly after the publication of Edmund Blunden's 1931 edition of his poems, which included a lengthy memoir. Although the C. Day Lewis edition of Owen's poems is now considered standard, "Dulce et Decorum Est" is often reprinted in versions that differ significantly. In particular, some editors follow Blunden in preferring a manuscript variant of line 8, "Of gas shells dropping softly behind."

Matthew Parfitt

Further Reading

Griffith, George V. "Owen's 'Dulce et Decorum Est.'" *Explicator* 41, no. 3 (1983): 37-39. Provides a detailed reading of the poem, with an emphasis on images of voice. Griffith argues that "Dulce et Decorum Est" is as much a poem about poetry as it is about "the pity of war."

Hibberd, Dominic. *Owen the Poet*. Basingstoke, England: Macmillan, 1986. An illuminating study of Owen's "poethood" based primarily on careful readings of the poems, including "Dulce et Decorum Est."

_____. *Wilfred Owen: A New Biography*. London: Weidenfeld & Nicolson, 2002. Hibberd spent thirty years researching this comprehensive biography, which sheds new light on Owen's family, education, struggles with religion, homosexuality, and experience in World War I. Chronicles his development from a young Romantic poet to the writer who is now considered Britain's national poet of World War I.

Hipp, Daniel W. *The Poetry of Shell Shock: Wartime Trauma and Healing in Wilfred Owen, Ivor Gurney, and Siegfried Sassoon*. Jefferson, N.C.: McFarland, 2005. Describes how the three men used their poetry to recount their experiences in World War I and to recover from the psychological trauma they suffered as a result of that conflict.

Owen, Wilfred. *The Collected Poems of Wilfred Owen*. Edited with an introduction and notes by C. Day Lewis. New York: New Directions, 1964. The definitive edition of Owen's poetry includes juvenilia, notes concerning manuscript variants, and two essential essays by accomplished poets. Also includes a memoir by Edmund Blunden.

Stallworthy, Jon. *Wilfred Owen*. London: Oxford University Press, 1974. This definitive biography sheds valuable light on the context and occasion of "Dulce et Decorum Est."

Welland, Dennis. *Wilfred Owen: A Critical Study*. Rev. ed. London: Chatto and Windus, 1978. In this first and perhaps most influential study of Owen's poetry, Welland argues that "Dulce et Decorum Est," though masterly, is inferior to later, less strident poems, such as "The Sentry."

The Dumb Waiter

Author: Harold Pinter (1930-2008)
First produced: 1959; first published, 1960, in *The Birthday Party*
Type of work: Drama
Type of plot: Absurdist
Time of plot: Mid-twentieth century
Locale: England

Principal characters:
BEN, a hit man
GUS, his fellow hit man

The Story:

Ben and Gus are in a basement room with two beds and a closed serving-hatch between the beds. Ben reads aloud two different stories from the newspaper. Gus complains about the room not having a window, about coming in the dark to a strange place, sleeping all day, doing the job, and going away again in the dark. Ben says that Gus needs hobbies, like his own woodwork. Gus wants Ben to tell him why Ben stopped the car in the middle of the road, when it was still dark, that morning. Ben says that he thought Gus was asleep, that he was not waiting for anything, and that they were too early. When Gus objects that they did as they were told, Ben replies that he, not Gus, took the call. Ben repeats that they were too early but refuses to say more.

Gus wants to know what town they are in (Ben says Birmingham) and, since it is Friday, he wants to go to watch the football team the next day (Ben says there is no time). Gus reminisces about the Birmingham Villa team losing a game in a disputed penalty to the White Shirts. Gus remembers that the other team was from Tottenham, so that the game was in Birmingham. Ben says he was not there, yet he disagrees emphatically about the penalty and denies that the game was in Birmingham. An envelope slides under the door. Gus sees it, unseals it, and finds twelve matches but no writing.

When Ben tells him to "light the kettle," Gus responds that Ben means "light the gas" and "put on the kettle." Ben refuses to back down. When Gus persists, Ben asserts that he is the senior partner and then loses his temper, grabbing Gus by the throat. Gus tries to make tea, but there is a meter on the stove, and neither of them has any money. Gus laments that Wilson did not do well by them, such as leave enough gas available for a cup of tea. He has questions for Wilson but finds Wilson difficult to talk to. Gus wants to know if anyone cleans up after they are gone, and who that would be if so. Another question occurs to him: How many jobs did the two of them do? What if no one ever cleaned up? Ben points out that their employer has departments for everything. The noise of the dumbwaiter descending makes them grab their

revolvers. Gus opens the dumbwaiter and removes a piece of paper that reads "Two braised steak and chips. Two sago puddings. Two teas without sugar."

Ben says the place is probably under new management. Gus wants to know who has it now. A second piece of paper reads "Soup of the day. Liver and onions. Jam tart." Ben looks in the serving hatch but not up it. When Gus puts his finger to his mouth and looks up the hatch, Ben is alarmed. The meager contents of Gus's bag are brought out and put on a plate, but the dumbwaiter has already gone up. Gus questions how a gas stove with three rings can service a busy place? What happens when no one is there? Were those menus coming down and going up for years? The third piece of paper reads "Macaroni Pastitsio. Ormitha Macarounada." Gus puts the plate in the box and calls the contents up the hatch. Ben corrects Gus for shouting.

Gus wants to know if there is another kitchen, other gas stoves. Why, he wonders, did Wilson not get in touch? Does Ben believe that the two of them are unreliable? (Ben says nothing.) The box comes down. The fourth note reads "One Bamboo Shoots, Water Chestnuts, and Chicken. One Char Siu and beansprouts." Their packet of tea is sent back.

A speaking tube is suddenly discovered, and Gus does not understand why he did not see it before. Gus follows Ben's directions—blowing into it, then speaking—but he cannot hear anything. Ben takes the tube and listens and talks into it. The voice on the other end, Ben tells Gus, said everything they sent up was defective. Ben gives Gus his instructions, but he forgets to tell Gus to take out his gun—which Ben never omitted before.

Gus wants to know what they would do if it is a girl—the mess made by the girl on their last job bothered Gus—but Ben replies they will do just the same.

Gus points out that they passed their tests years ago. They took the tests together; they proved themselves. What is he playing these games for? The fifth note reads "Scampi." Gus yells up that they have nothing left. Ben seizes the tube from Gus, hangs it up, goes back to his bed, and picks up the paper. Gus exits left. The whistle on the speaking tube goes off. Ben answers, notes that the usual procedure would be followed, and says they are ready. Ben goes to the left, and the door to the right opens. Ben turns and levels his revolver at the door. Gus stumbles in, stripped of jacket, waistcoat, tie, holster, and revolver. Gus and Ben stare at each other in silence.

Critical Evaluation:

In all likelihood the most original British playwright of the last half of the twentieth century, Harold Pinter wrote not only for the theater but also for radio, television, and film. In his work, Pinter focuses on the individual in relation to others and on the threatening nature of late twentieth century society. In Pinter's world, what one is responsible for is not at all clear. Written at the beginning of Pinter's career, *The Dumb Waiter* presents Ben and Gus, professional hit men, with many hits on their record. It seems, as the play unfolds, that Gus is going to be killed by Ben because Gus asks too many questions. Pinter describes a world in which everything is unreliable, including consciousness, memory, personal relationships, and any kind of social contract. The nature of human beings is at issue in Pinter's plays; he presents them without nostalgia and with no sentimentality.

The extent to which Ben and Gus are responsible for their own lives remains unknown. Is Gus, for instance, acting in good faith to question the life he lives? Or is he acting in good faith when he simply follows orders? What, as a soldier, is he expected to do? Pinter's characters may be simultaneously victors, victimizers, and victims. What is most menacing to the individual occurs by surprise and remains unexplained. However murky the world may appear to the individual and the individual to the world, Pinter's recurrent themes are clear enough: the alienation of the individual from himself or herself, from others, and from the environment; the uncertainty of truth, on any level; the impossibility of interpersonal relationships; the ironies and frequent contradictions of life.

The language of Pinter's plays is often contradictory and uses opposition such as the repeated references to black and white in *The Dumb Waiter*. While Ben reads and rereads the newspaper at any free moment, focusing on what is "down in black and white," Gus, in a stunning non sequitur, finds the black and white crockery thoroughly satisfying. It is the only thing he admires in their present location. Ben accepts what he reads. Gus bets that the newspaper story that Ben reads that says an eight-year-old girl killed a cat is a lie. More likely, the eleven-year-old boy killed the cat and blamed it on

his eight-year-old sister. Ben agrees, but that is the last time he agrees with Gus.

For Pinter, words typically conceal more than they reveal. Silence indicates an inner life, the nature of which may well mystify both the self and others. Ben's silence is opaque, possibly without a self: He reads the newspaper or pursues his hobbies. Since he is not idle, who can criticize him? By carefully describing the outer lives of Ben and Gus, in a seemingly naturalistic manner, Pinter leaves readers and audience members to speculate about the two characters' inner lives.

For Ben, everything is a matter of black and white. The importance to him of the past he shares with Gus remains unknown. Gus continues to be plagued by unanswered questions. These include: Why did Ben stop the car in the middle of the road that morning? Why is an envelope with twelve matches slid under the door when they have no money for the gas meter? Why is there no different method for a hit on a woman? Why does Wilson not treat them better? Why is the suddenly active dumbwaiter making requests of them? Who is upstairs?

The significance of what is not said is as important as what is. What is not said may amount to more emphatic communication than what is stated. Ben, for example, does not like Gus's questions, which is apparent by his silence and by the fact that if he answers, he tends to contradict himself or lose his temper. Pinter's characters are frequently called lower class, and, it is argued, therefore predictably easily frustrated and violent. They defy, in truth, such easy categorization. If Ben is less aware or less intelligent, is that the problem? Is it not rather Ben's lack of courage that threatens Gus, Ben's willingness to victimize anyone and his unwillingness to question, much less to criticize, anyone more powerful? Ben is a "company man" with, it seems, no convictions or restraints to keep him from doing whatever his supervisors want him to do.

With the dumbwaiter becoming active in the middle of the play, Ben accepts as fact—without any questioning—that they must meet the demands that come from above, down in black and white, no matter how unreasonable or increasingly bizarre those demands are. Gus wants to know why. For example, when he and Ben are both in need of their tea, why should they send up their few supplies? Even though Gus sends everything up, he later asks Ben, and then himself, why did they send everything up? Who is upstairs? Why is he playing all these games? Why does not whoever is upstairs understand that they have nothing left? These simple questions, in Pinter's play, become the riddles of existence.

Unlike Gus, Ben does not question. He lives in a black-or-white world in which he seems neither happy nor unhappy but secure. The tube next to the dumbwaiter, through which one alternately listens and talks, does not work for Gus, just as the toilet does not flush for him—until the very end. The tube does work for Ben, who is ready, when his supervisors say so, to do his job. He is even ready to kill his partner when his supervisors instruct him to do so.

Carol Bishop

Further Reading

Baker, William. *Harold Pinter.* London: Continuum, 2008. Brief critical biography examining the themes, patterns, relationships, and ideas that are common to Pinter's life and writings.

Billington, Michael. *Harold Pinter.* London: Faber and Faber, 2007. Critical biography focusing on literary analysis of Pinter's works. Discusses the major plays at length, providing information about their literary and biographical sources.

Burkman, Katherine H. *The Dramatic World of Harold Pinter: Its Basis in Ritual.* Columbus: Ohio State University Press, 1971. A provocative study, with notes, bibliography, and index.

Esslin, Martin. *Pinter: The Playwright.* 6th exp. and rev. ed. London: Methuen, 2000. Comprehensive analytical survey of Pinter's writing career, offering critical commentary on all of his plays.

Hynes, Joseph. "Pinter and Morality." *Virginia Quarterly Review* 68 (Autumn, 1992): 740-752. Examines Pinter's comedy and compares his work to that of Henrik Ibsen and George Bernard Shaw.

Kennedy, Andrew. *Six Dramatists in Search of a Language: Shaw, Eliot, Beckett, Pinter, Osborne, Arden.* New York: Cambridge University Press, 1975. Focuses on Pinter's use of language. Includes bibliography and index.

Raby, Peter, ed. *The Cambridge Companion to Harold Pinter.* New York: Cambridge University Press, 2001. Collection of essays, including discussions of Pinter, politics, and postmodernism; Pinter and the critics; Pinter and the twentieth century theater; and a piece by director Peter Hall about directing Pinter's plays. The numerous references to *The Dumb Waiter* are listed in a separate index of Pinter's works.

Schroll, Herman T. *Harold Pinter: A Study of His Reputation (1958-1969) and a Checklist.* Metuchen, N.J.: Scarecrow Press, 1971. Argues that Pinter's works have lasting significance. Includes bibliography and index.

The Dunciad

Author: Alexander Pope (1688-1744)
First published: 1728-1743
Type of work: Poetry
Type of plot: Mock-heroic
Time of plot: Eighteenth century
Locale: England and the underworld

Principal characters:
DULNESS, a goddess
TIBBALD, hero of the first edition, a Shakespearean scholar
COLLEY CIBBER, hero of the second edition, playwright, producer, and poet laureate

When Alexander Pope set out to criticize the general literary climate of his time and to avenge the slights given his own work by other writers, he took the theme of John Dryden's *Mac Flecknoe* (1682), in which the poetaster Thomas Shadwell is crowned ruler of the Kingdom of Nonsense, and expanded it to make a true mock epic of three books. He added a fourth book when he rewrote the poem in 1742. *The Dunciad* acclaims the goddess Dulness, daughter of Chaos and Night, and her chosen prince. In the first edition the prince of dullness is the scholar Lewis Theobald (Tibbald);

in the second edition he is Colley Cibber, playwright and poet laureate.

This poem lacks the close-knit quality of Pope's other fine mock epic, *The Rape of the Lock* (1712, 1714). *The Dunciad* is longer, and the fact that the hero appears only at intervals explains a certain disunity. Tibbald-Cibber appears at the middle of book 1, is present only as a spectator at the epic games described in book 2, and merely dreams the trip to the underworld, modeled on that of Aeneas in book 4 of Vergil's *Aeneid* (c. 29-19 B.C.E.). The important points in the poem are made in the descriptive passages in these episodes and in conversations that contain criticism of individuals and trends.

Pope relied, for satirical effect, on the classical epic as his model. *The Dunciad*, like *The Rape of the Lock*, begins with a parody of the *Aeneid*:

> The mighty Mother, and her Son, who brings
> The Smithfield Muses to the ear of Kings,
> I sing.

The invocation is appropriately directed not at a muse but at the Patricians, the patrons whose purses inspire dull writing. The dedication to the author's friend Jonathan Swift that follows is an eighteenth century, rather than a classic, convention.

Pope describes in detail the abode of Dulness and the allegorical figures gathered around her throne: Fortitude, Temperance, Prudence, and Poetic Justice, who is weighing truth with gold and "solid pudding against empty praise." The gods are notoriously interested in the affairs of mortals; Dulness looks out upon the ingredients of dull writing and the numerous creators of it. Her eye lights upon the hero, who is raising to her an altar of tremendous tomes of his writing. She anoints him as king of her realm, and the nation croaks Aesop's line, "God save King Log."

In the second book Pope designs appropriate contests for his various groups of enemies. The booksellers race to win a phantom poet. A patron is designated for the poet who tickles best, but he is carried off by an unknown sycophantic secretary. Journalists swim through the muck of the Thames River:

> Who flings most filth, and wide pollutes around
> The stream, be his the Weekly Journals bound;
> A pig of lead to him who drives the best;
> A peck of coals a-piece shall glad the rest.

As a final test the goddess promises her "amplest powers" to anyone who can remain awake as he listens to the verses of "Three College Sophs, and three pert Templars." The book ends with the whole company lying asleep.

Grandiose heroic couplets and numerous parallels with classical visits to the underworld fill the third book. John Taylor, the Water Poet, replaces the ferryman Charon; Elkanah Settle, a Restoration poet, takes Anchises' part in showing the hero the future of Dulness and her offspring. The high point of this book is the crowning of Tibbald-Cibber with a poppy wreath by Bavius, prototype of the worst of poets from ancient times.

The 1742 *Dunciad*, centering on the triumph of Dulness over England, reveals a slightly more mature outlook in the poet than does the earlier version. Tibbald was the object of a vindictive attack, occasioned by his criticism of Pope's edition of William Shakespeare. Cibber is representative of the dull poet; as laureate he was well known for his poor occasional verse. The fourth book is far more concerned with the institutions promoting the rise of dullness than with individuals. The more frequent use of classical names, rather than contemporary ones, indicates the poet's movement toward universality.

The last book is almost an entity in itself. It opens with a new invocation, to Chaos and Night. The pseudo-learned notes, effective satire written by Pope, point out the precedents for a second invocation when an important new matter is introduced. Evil omens presage the coming destruction as Dulness ascends her throne and Cibber reclines in her lap, making his only appearance in this book.

Around the goddess are Science, Wit, Logic, Rhetoric, and other abstractions in chains, reminiscent of several scenes in Edmund Spenser's *The Faerie Queene* (1590, 1596). Various personages appear to tell of Dulness's victory over the many arts and institutions. First to come is a harlot representing the Italian opera; she rejoices in the banishment of Handel to Ireland and the supremacy of chaos in music.

Pope uses an epic simile to describe the nations clustering around the goddess: "orb in orb, congloved are seen/ The buzzing Bees about their dusky Queen." Present are the passive followers of Dulness and those who lead the advance: pompous editors who make mincemeat of good poets with notes and commentary, patrons who set up a bust of a poet after he has died neglected.

A specter, the head of Westminster School, modeled on Milton's Moloch, speaks on the state of education:

> As Fancy opens the quick springs of Sense,
> We ply the Memory, we load the brain,
> Bind rebel Wit, and double chain on chain,
> Confine the thought, to exercise the breath;
> And keep them in the pale of Words till death.

Pope criticizes the hair-splitting grammarians in Aristarchus's boasts that he has turned good verse into prose again. Science is also satirized as the study that loses itself in detail; but Dulness still fears science, for an object of nature is capable of awakening a mind. Religion does not escape; the poet says that it has degenerated into a belief in a mechanistic God, made in humankind's image.

Knowing the state of her kingdom, the goddess celebrates

her mysteries, reflecting Pope's interest in ceremony. As the rites are concluded a state of dullness encompasses the country, schools, government, army. Truth, philosophy, and religion perish as "Universal Darkness buries All."

The Dunciad contains more of the heroic spirit than most other mock epics. Most mock epics are directed toward the amusement of the reader and do not age well past the time in which their jokes are caught without footnotes. *The Dunciad*, however, reveals Pope's passionate conviction that the triumph of dullness was a real danger to art, science, and learning. He chose to deliver his warning to England in a humorous form, but his seriousness about his subject raises the latter part of the fourth book to the level of real heroic poetry.

There are many fine lines of poetry in *The Dunciad*, but it is more diffuse and less brilliant satire than either *Mac Flecknoe* or Pope's own *Epistle to Dr. Arbuthnot* (1735). Missing are the biting, succinct couplets such as Dryden's "The rest to some faint meaning make pretense,/ But Sh—— never deviates into sense" or Pope's lines on Addison, "Damn with faint praise, assent with civil leer,/ And without sneering, teach the rest to sneer."

The greatest deterrent to the modern reader's easy enjoyment of *The Dunciad* is probably the fact that so much of the poet's criticism of contemporary people and issues is almost unintelligible; few names die faster than those of the fifth-rate writers of an era. Nevertheless, the satirical comments on universal conditions remain fresh and pointed. *The Dunciad* is worthy of a high place among mock-heroic poems.

Further Reading

Baines, Paul. *Alexander Pope: A Sourcebook.* New York: Routledge, 2000. Provides biographical information and historical and social context for Pope's life and work. Offers analysis of *The Dunciad* and other works, with suggestions for further reading about each one. Contains critical comment on Pope's poetry, politics, and depiction of gender issues.

Clark, Donald B. *Alexander Pope.* New York: Twayne, 1967. Provides a thorough examination of all of Pope's major works, as well as historical and biographical information.

The bulk of this study comprises interpretations and criticisms of several individual poems.

Goldsmith, Netta Murray. *Alexander Pope: The Evolution of a Poet.* Burlington, Vt.: Ashgate, 2002. Uses modern research on creativity to examine Pope's poetry in relation to his intellectual peers and to explain why he enjoyed spectacular success as a poet in his lifetime.

Ingrassia, Catherine, and Claudia N. Thomas, eds. *More Solid Learning: New Perspectives on Alexander Pope's "Dunciad."* Lewisburg, Pa.: Bucknell University Press, 2000. Collection of critical essays about *The Dunciad*, including discussions of Pope's adaptation of Rabelaisian imagery and satirical purposes in the poem, *The Dunciad* and "mock-apocalypse," and opera, gender, and sexual politics in the work.

Rogers, Pat, ed. *The Cambridge Companion to Alexander Pope.* New York: Cambridge University Press, 2007. Collection of critical essays on various aspects of Pope's life and work, including several pieces about his poetry, as well as discussions of Pope and gender, money, and the book trade. The references to *The Dunciad* are listed in the index.

Rogers, Robert. *The Major Satires of Alexander Pope.* Champaign: University of Illinois Press, 1955. Convincingly argues that each of Pope's satires reflects his own moral concerns about the ethical dilemmas he faced. This comprehensive overview of Pope's satiric poems is essential for any discussion pertaining to the poet's use of irony and wit.

Sitter, John E. *The Poetry of Pope's "Dunciad."* Minneapolis: University of Minnesota Press, 1971. Full-length study concentrates on *The Dunciad*'s imagery, structure, and origins. Use of textual evidence makes the work an excellent starting place for critical analysis.

Williams, Aubrey L. *Pope's "Dunciad": A Study of Its Meaning.* Baton Rouge: Louisiana State University Press, 1955. In order to interpret Pope's meaning and to comment on his imaginative powers, Williams examines the poem from every possible angle. Provides one of the most thorough treatments of *The Dunciad*.

Dune series

Author: Frank Herbert (1920-1986)

First published: 1965-1985; includes *Dune*, 1965; *Dune Messiah*, 1969; *Children of Dune*, 1976; *God Emperor of Dune*, 1981; *Heretics of Dune*, 1984; *Chapterhouse: Dune*, 1985

Type of work: Novels

Type of plot: Science fiction

Time of plot: Eleventh millennium after the founding of the Spacing Guild

Locale: Arrakis, third planet of the star Canopus

Principal characters:

PAUL ATREIDES (MAUD'DIB), the prophet of the Fremen

DUKE LETO ATREIDES, Paul's father

LADY JESSICA, Duke Leto's bound concubine and Paul's mother

ALIA ATREIDES (SAINT ALIA OF THE KNIFE), Paul's sister

GAIUS HELEN MOHAIM, a Bene Gesserit truthsayer

DUNCAN IDAHO, the Atreides' armsmaster

GURNEY HALLECK, the Atreides' retainer

WELLINGTON YUEH, Suk School doctor in the Atreides' service

BARON VLADIMIR HARKONNEN, hereditary enemy of the Atreides

FEYD-RAUTHA HARKONNEN, the baron's nephew and heir

LIET KYNES, Imperial planetologist on Arrakis

CHANI, Kynes' daughter

STILGAR, Fremen leader

EMPEROR SHADDAM IV, ruler of the Imperium

PRINCESS IRULAN, Shaddam's daughter

SCYTALE, a Tlielaxu Face Dancer (shapeshifter)

LETO II, son of Paul and Chani, God Emperor

GHANIMA, daughter of Paul and Chani

MONEO ATREIDES, chamberlain to Leto II

SIONA ATREIDES, daughter of Moneo, who can fade from prescient vision

MILES TEG, commanding general to the Bene Gesserit armies

SHEEANA, girl with the ability to control sandworms

The Story:

In *Dune*, the Atreides household is preparing to relocate from the wet planet Caladan to Arrakis, a desert planet, where Duke Leto is going to take command as the planet's new feudal lord, replacing the Harkonnen household. A mysterious woman arrives to test young Paul, the ducal heir. She is Gaius Helen Mohaim, a member of the Bene Gesserit order, who trained Paul's mother in the order's almost superhuman powers. While Paul proves his ability to surmount agony, the old woman talks to him about philosophy and history.

Paul then meets with Duncan Idaho, Gurney Halleck, and Dr. Wellington Yueh, important members of his father's staff. Hints are planted of the forces that will drive Yueh to betray his employer.

During the actual move, Paul exhibits curiosity about the nature of the Spacing Guild, the guild of navigators who are the only ones capable of overseeing travel between planets. He is firmly warned that he must do nothing to risk the shipping privileges of House Atreides. The Spacing Guild guards its secrets as zealously as any medieval guild, and all other powers in the galaxy are dependent on their navigational skills.

On Arrakis, Paul immediately becomes the subject of awed murmurs on the part of the residents, who have turned to religion for hope during the lengthy reign of the brutal Harkonnens over their world. Their awe is reinforced when Imperial planetologist Liet Kynes takes Paul and Duke Leto into the deep desert to witness spice mining operations, and Paul shows extraordinary perceptivity of the customs and usages of the desert.

Just as the Atreides seem to have settled into their new fief, treachery dispossesses them of it. Dr. Yueh betrays the Atreides, allowing Baron Harkonnen to attack and slaughter the Atreides forces. The baron has taken Dr. Yueh's wife hostage to force his cooperation, but the doctor's real plan is to turn Duke Leto into a suicide assassin, who will be able to kill the baron when he is brought before the gloating victor. Yueh's plan fails, and the baron narrowly escapes.

However, Paul and Jessica are able to escape into the deep desert, where they encounter the Fremen, the fierce people of the sands. Using Bene Gesserit skills, they are able to integrate themselves into the tribe, normally insular and hostile to outsiders. After Paul proves himself in a duel to the death with one of the Fremen tribesmen, he is renamed Maud'Dib after the kangaroo mouse of the desert.

As Paul and Jessica teach the Fremen their Bene Gesserit fighting techniques, the already formidable guerilla fighters become nearly unbeatable and they engage in more open combat against the Harkonnen occupiers. Moreover, Paul and Jessica learn the secrets of Arrakis's most important export commodity, known simply as "spice." A luxury food that has life-extending properties, spice is also necessary to allow the Spacing Guild navigators to predict the future, which is how they are able to navigate ships safely through the myriad dangers of space travel. Without spice, each planet would be isolated and there could be no galactic civilization. Paul and Jessica learn that spice is derived from the excrement of the massive sandworms that inhabit Arrakis—and no other planet, since water is toxic to sandworms.

Paul soon becomes one of their foremost leaders, and in time he is pushed to fight Stilgar for leadership of the tribe. Instead, he refuses and claims his birthright as the Atreides heir and thus the rightful duke of Arrakis. With the desert-hardened, well-trained Fremen under his command, Paul has enough power to rival the emperor himself, whose elite army, known as the Sardaukar, is the basis of his power.

After drinking the Water of Life and gaining his full prophetic powers, Paul forces a final confrontation with both the Harkonnens and the emperor. *Dune* ends on a triumphant note: Paul defeats the killers of his father and takes command of the entire Imperium.

Dune Messiah takes up several years later. The Fremen have engaged in a massive jihad that has ravaged much of the settled galaxy. Paul and his beloved Fremen concubine Chani have no heir, which creates a precarious situation, as various factions jockey for position in the power vacuum created when Paul deposed Emperor Shaddam IV, whose House Corrino had ruled the galaxy for ten millennia. Among these factions are the Bene Gesserit, the Spacing Guild, and the

Tlielaxu, a renegade school for mentats, or human computers. (Computers themselves have been outlawed, so mentats are an important part of galactic society. Paul himself has been trained as a mentat.)

The Tlielaxu are master manipulators of human beings. Their chief representative is Scytale, a shapeshifting "Face Dancer." He brings with him Hayt, who is a ghola, a revenant corpse brought back to life in the mysterious Axolotl Tanks. Specifically, Hayt was once Duncan Idaho, the Atreides swordsmaster who gave his life so that Jessica and Paul could escape.

Hayt is part of an elaborate scheme to entrap Paul and make him dependent upon the Tlielaxu. Through various manipulations in the Imperial Court on Arrakis, involving corrupt courtiers and crippled veterans of the Fremen Jihad, Paul is blinded by a stoneburner, a type of nuclear device. Fremen tradition holds that blinded Fremen must commit suicide by walking alone into the harsh desert. The Tlielaxu had intended to offer Paul metal eyes to restore his sight, thereby gaining control over him. Instead, he turns to his prophetic powers, seeing by prescience as he "remembers" everything that is happening in his present, having foreseen it in the past.

As his son and daughter, Leto and Ghanima, are born at the climax of a pregnancy horribly accelerated, Paul's prescience fails him. Scytale, in another attempt to gain Tlielaxu control of the empire, offers to resurrect Chani as a ghola. Paul refuses. He walks into the desert to die in the manner of the Fremen.

Children of Dune begins a decade later. Young Leto II and his sister Ghanima are growing far beyond their chronological ages as a result of the effects of spice upon their metabolism. They are the objects of superstitious awe and fear among the Fremen, but their positions as the heirs of Emperor Paul make them the targets of the more worldly Great Houses, whose ambitions have not been extinguished by the fury of the Fremen Jihad. In particular, the Princess Wensica, daughter of deposed Emperor Shaddam IV, hopes to place her son Farad'n upon the throne.

To accomplish her goal, Wensica has developed an elaborate scheme to use specially trained Laza tigers to kill the Atreides twins. However, she thinks of them as the children they appear to be, and they use the abilities derived from their ancestral memories to escape. Ghanima is rescued by Stilgar and taken to a Fremen siech stronghold, while Leto flees into the deep desert and begins a journey of discovery that will lead him to the taboo sieches of Jacurutu and Shuloch. He flees the latter with a sabotaged stillsuit, his life's water leaking out into the desert. Out of options, he implements the plan he had seen in many prescient visions and dreaded: He forms a symbiotic relationship with the larval form of the great sandworms of the deep desert.

In this hybrid form, Leto returns to the Imperial Court to confront his aunt Alia, who has become possessed by the ancestral memory of the evil Baron Harkonnen. After defeating her, he begins his reign in his own right. His sister reveals that Leto will eventually "go into the sand." He will survive for millenia.

God Emperor of Dune jumps forward thousands of years, to the end of the reign of Leto II. Over the millenia, he has been able to remake all of galactic society in accordance with his Golden Path, which he believes will enable humanity to survive Kralizek, the Typhoon Struggle that he foresees occurring at the end of time. Central to this plan is his absolute control over the last remaining stores of spice, since the sandworms that generate it have been rendered extinct save for those larval forms encapsulated in his monstrous hybrid form. By doling out or withholding spice according to his pleasure, he is able to reward and punish formerly independent agencies such as the Bene Gesserit, the Spacing Guild, the Tlielaxu biotech masters, and the technologists of Ix.

However tight Leto's control, there is still discontent, and some of it is within his own inner circle. In particular, Siona Atreides, beloved daughter and only child of Leto's chamberlain Moneo, has entangled herself with a group of young rebels who steal a set of journals from Leto's citadel. Leto is aware of her actions, but he believes that he can redirect her energies in accordance to his Golden Path. Thus, instead of having the Fish Speakers, his all-female army and secret police, arrest her, he has her initiated as one of them and assigns an agent personally loyal to him as her companion.

At the same time, Leto is breaking in his latest ghola-clone of Duncan Idaho, one of a long series he has kept as a sort of hobby, a reminder of his youth and his fading humanity. Duncan finds the Fish Speakers disturbing, more so when he is informed he is to be their commander, the sole male among them. As a result, he is quite willing to listen to Siona when she begins calling Leto the Tyrant.

Leto takes Siona on a walk through his tame desert, the Sareer, as his way of sensitizing her to his Golden Path. However, insead of converting her into a loyal follower, as her father Moneo became, the walk serves only to reinforce her determination to see Leto's reign ended and humanity set free to follow its own paths.

After Leto crushes an attempt by the Tlielaxu to assassinate him using Face Dancers, the Ixians take a different approach. They send him a new ambassador, the beautiful Hwi Noiree, who soon beguiles Leto to the point he is besotted.

He announces that he will take her as a bride, and as their wedding procession passes over a bridge, it is ambushed by Siona and Duncan, who topple Leto's royal cart into the river below. Afterward, Siona and Duncan find the dying Leto on the shore, where he tells them that they have served admirably in his plan to return Arrakis to the sandworms, whose larval forms have been freed from his body to burrow into the soil and trap the water, making the planet again inhabitable by the great worms.

Heretics of Dune begins shortly after the framing story for *God Emperor of Dune*. Arrakis has been returned to the desert, and the worms are far more dangerous than they were previously. A young woman named Sheanna has survived the attack of a worm on her family's desert-edge home, and she shows evidence of being able to control the giant worms.

Meanwhile, it appears that Leto's Golden Path was not so perfect as he thought. The Scattered Peoples are coming back, fleeing an enemy so terrible it may yet be able to engulf all of humanity. Among them are the Honored Matres, an offshoot of the Bene Gesserit who use a mode of sexual imprinting to control men. In their desperate fear, the returning refugees begin attacking the very people who are their best hope for succor, lest those peoples refuse to help.

The Bene Gesserit recall from retirement Miles Teg, a legendary commander with Bene Gesserit training. At the same time, they obtain a new ghola-clone of Duncan Idaho from the Tlielaxu, hoping that his wild genes may provide a surprise way of defeating their enemies. Desperate battles wage across the galaxy, and in one of them Arrakis is attacked by massed nuclear weapons, sterilizing it. However, the Bene Gesserit have preserved a number of sandworms and their larval vectors. In *Chapterhouse: Dune* they seek to seed their Chapterhouse world to create a new source for the precious spice. Duncan steals the starship *Ithica* and vanishes into hyperspace, where he sees a mysterious elderly couple, Marty and Daniel, who make a final cryptic comment.

Critical Evaluation:

Dune is noted for being one of the first science-fiction novels to tackle major themes in a literary fashion. While earlier science fiction, such as Isaac Asimov's Foundation trilogy, often handled big themes—such as the engineering of human history—in a diagrammatic way, and through extensive expository prose, Frank Herbert wove his major themes into the fabric of his richly realized world. As a result, *Dune* was an essential turning point in the acceptance of science fiction by at least a portion of the literary establishment.

Members of the establishment began to treat the genre as a worthwhile subject of study.

Ecology is one of the critical themes that Herbert systematically developed, particularly in the first book and to a lesser degree in the second and third books. He did not simply propound the need to understand and care for a world's ecology. He suggested that it might be possible to use one's knowledge of the operation of an ecosystem to actively manage it, even to transform it in ways that would make it more amenable to human life.

The ecological transformation of Arrakis was one of the first examples of terraforming in science fiction, and Herbert's handling of it was even more remarkable. While writers of an earlier generation would have approached it as a technical problem to be solved by square-jawed engineers with massive machines, Herbert made it as much a sociological issue, with an ecologically literate people effecting myriad tiny changes that would ultimately result in major shifts. In its multigenerational scale, the plan becomes the touchstone of hope for an entire culture of oppressed people. Moreover, Herbert significantly complicates matters by specifying that Arrakis became a desert as a result of the introduction of an invasive species, the sandtrout, and that the greening of the desert would have major effects on all of galactic society by disrupting the spice supply.

Culture is another important theme that is developed throughout the *Dune* series. While earlier generations of science-fiction writers generally focused upon individuals and tended to write cookie-cutter societies, Herbert built each of the cultures that appeared in his novels in such a way that readers come away with a greater understanding of the forces that drive an entire society. In particular, the defining beliefs and values that drive people to lose their individuality in a group are given special attention.

Religion had been largely ignored by earlier generations of science-fiction writers, who generally assumed that humanity would outgrow its need for the supernatural and become rationalist, materialist atheists. The only religion in the Foundation trilogy is a sham deliberately promulgated by the First Foundation to better control the technologically regressed populations of several nearby stars, and it is abandoned as soon as technical education resumes on those worlds.

By contrast, Frank Herbert takes seriously the power of religious belief to shape societies and to motivate people to do extraordinary things. The Fremen are nurtured by their religious beliefs amid generations of brutal oppression, and when the tables are turned, they take offense that outsiders do not immediately obey their messiah, Paul. Their offense is so great that it drives them to carry out a terrible jihad that sterilizes worlds and extinguishes civilizations. It is intimated that the Fremen religion was created by the Bene Gesserit as a means of manipulating them, and they accept Paul as their messiah for that reason. However, Paul foreseeing the possibility of the religious jihad, strives desperately to prevent it and is unable to do so, indicating that even fabricated religions may be real social forces beyond the control of any one person or entity.

Herbert drew upon the Muslim religion as inspiration in creating his imagined Fremen religion, the Zensunni. In doing so, he helped bring awareness of Islamic culture and history to many science-fiction readers at the time that Islamic civilization was becoming increasingly important to the United States as a result of American dependency upon Middle Eastern oil.

Dependency on scarce resources and its power over entire civilizations is another major theme in the *Dune* series. Spice, which makes possible travel between the stars and is only found upon Arrakis, can be read as a metaphor for Middle Eastern oil. The brutal scarcity of water on Arrakis is an extreme version of the growing scarcity of freshwater on Earth. Such scarcities become bottlenecks, and those who control them gain great power over their fellow human beings.

Indeed, power is the final major theme of the *Dune* series, especially the ability of power over other human beings to corrupt its weilders. This theme is particularly visible in the second and fourth books, in which the forward-looking heroes of the first and third books have become imprisoned in their own positions of power, making decisions and giving orders that would have been vigorously opposed by their younger selves, because the power they wield has become the center of their lives.

It is the deft handling of these themes in the early *Dune* books that makes those novels outstanding examples not only of science fiction but also of literature in general. The weakness or complete absence of these themes in the fifth and sixth books, by contrast, makes these later works read as if they simply happen to have been set in the *Dune* universe because it was familiar to the author and the fans had demanded further adventures in a much-beloved milleu.

Heretics of Dune and *Chapterhouse: Dune* were to be the first two volumes in a much longer story arc that ended incomplete, much to the frustration of many readers. This nonending was so frustrating that many readers tried to wrest some kind of conclusion out of it, even claiming that Marty and Daniel represented Frank Herbert and his wife releasing the characters into the noosphere. In 1999 Frank Herbert's son Brian, an established author in his own right, announced that he had found some boxes of notes for the seventh *Dune* book. Taking as his collaborator *Star Wars* tie-in novelist Kevin J. Anderson, he produced a two-volume sequel, *Hunters of Dune* and *Sandworms of Dune*. However, many Dune purists do not regard these Dune sequels, nor the two prequel trilogies written by the duo, to be authentic entries in the *Dune* series.

Leigh Husband Kimmel

Further Reading

Clarke, James. *Dune: Frank Herbert.* New York: Spark, 2002. An in-depth analysis of the characters, plot, and themes of the *Dune* books.

Grazier, Kevin R., ed. *The Science of Dune.* Dallas, Tex.: Benbella Books, 2008. A collection of essays on the scientific principles used by Frank Herbert in constructing his imagined world.

Herbert, Brian. *Dreamer of Dune: The Biography of Frank Herbert.* New York: Tor, 2003. Mixes personal reminiscences of Herbert's son with literary criticism.

Herbert, Brian, and Kevin J. Anderson, with Frank Herbert. *The Road to Dune.* New York: Tor, 2005. Includes outtakes from *Dune* and *Dune Messiah*, as well as an earlier working of the ideas of *Dune: Spice Planet.*

Miller, David M. *Frank Herbert.* Mercer Island, Wash.: Starmont House, 1980. A critical study of Frank Herbert's writing, including the *Dune* series.

Dust Tracks on a Road

Author: Zora Neale Hurston (1891-1960)
First published: 1942
Type of work: Autobiography

Principal personages:
ZORA NEALE HURSTON, the narrator
JOHN HURSTON, her father, a carpenter and preacher
LUCY ANN (POTTS) HURSTON, her mother
CHARLOTTE LOUISE MASON (MRS. R. OSGOOD MASON), her patron and benefactor
FRANZ BOAS, a professor of anthropology at Columbia University
FANNIE HURST, a novelist and one of Zora's employers
ETHEL WATERS, a singer and actor

The first eleven chapters of Zora Neale Hurston's *Dust Tracks on a Road* are roughly chronological. Zora is born in Eatonville, Florida, the first all-black town to be incorporated in the United States and where her father serves three terms as mayor. As one of eight children, she grows up in an eight-room house in Eatonville with a five-acre garden and ample opportunities for childhood play. One day in school, when two wealthy white women are visiting, Zora reads flawlessly and is rewarded with boxes of books to read—particularly tales of Greek, Roman, and Norse mythology—thereby advancing her education and stimulating her ability to imagine new worlds.

Zora's mother also encourages her to excel and to maintain a spunky spirit. Accordingly, when Zora's mother dies young, the child suffers grief and remorse, believing that the first phase of her life has ended; she is sent away to school in Jacksonville. When her father quickly remarries—this time to a much younger woman—Zora clashes frequently with her stepmother, whom she regards as an interloper. Eager to live independently, Zora finds employment as a maid, first briefly for a family and then for one year with a singer from Boston who works in a traveling theatrical troupe. These job experiences provide her with greater maturity and self-confidence.

Settling in Baltimore, Zora resumes her education in the high school department of Morgan College, where she excels sufficiently to earn admission to prestigious Howard University in Washington, D.C. Although Zora is unable to keep up with tuition payments after two years, she encounters several influential faculty members who encourage her to publish short stories, which propel her to a scholarship at Barnard College in New York and employment as a secretary to Fannie Hurst. While at Barnard, she becomes a protégé of Franz Boas, who arranges a fellowship that enables Zora to study African American folklore in the South. Her subsequent fieldwork is funded largely by Charlotte Louise Mason, a wealthy white patron with a Park Avenue apartment. This research—in Polk County, Florida; New Orleans; the Bahamas; Mobile, Alabama; British West Indies; Jamaica; Haiti; and elsewhere—results in several successful works, including *Mules and Men* (1935), a pioneering study of African American folklore, and two novels that incorporate these folk traditions, *Jonah's Gourd Vine* (1934) and *Their Eyes Were Watching God* (1937).

The five concluding chapters are thematic essays on various topics: "My People! My People!," which addresses the diversity of African Americans; an appreciation of Fannie Hurst and Ethel Waters as inspirational figures; a meditation on love, including a passionate affair with a man identified only as P.M.P.; her mixed feelings about religion; and a retrospective summation of her life to date.

In 1995, the Library of America published a more complete version of *Dust Tracks on a Road* containing chapters that were rejected by the book's original publisher in 1942. They include a revised version of "My People! My People!" that is harsher in its view of African Americans; "Seeing the World as It Is," which contains critical comments about American democracy and Anglo-Saxons; "The Inside Light—Being a Salute to Friendship," in which Hurston credits the friends in her life while also admitting her personal shortcomings; and "Concert," which describes her role in producing an innovative performance in New York in 1932 of West Indian music and dance.

The factual unreliability of Hurston's autobiography is apparent from the very first page. Although Hurston claims to have been born in Eatonville, Florida, census records attest that she was born some 400 miles away in Notasulga, Alabama. Hurston maintains that her mother married at age fourteen and died when Zora was only nine, but the dates on the family Bible show her mother's age as fourteen when wed and Zora's age as thirteen at the time of her mother's death. Hurston writes that her brothers and sisters were dispersed to other families after the death of their mother and that her father's second marriage collapsed, but census records indicate otherwise. Moreover, many seemingly significant events in Hurston's life—including her continuing closeness to her older brother Bob and his family in Memphis, her work as an editor with the Federal Writers' Project, and even her marriage to Albert Price III—are left out of the autobiography.

Even with its factual errors and omissions, *Dust Tracks on a Road* is a remarkable self-portrait of one of America's best-known black female writers. Without dwelling much on issues of race, Hurston constructs a compelling narrative that (although not literally rags to riches) demonstrates how she is able to overcome poverty, family discord, and personal adversity to become a successful writer, anthropologist, and cultural observer. Presumably written largely for an educated, white audience in the urban north, *Dust Tracks on a Road* presents a vivid and detailed portrait of the black rural south, where Hurston was born and raised and where she conducted most of her fieldwork. In the tradition of the bildungsroman, the book illustrates her maturation from child to adult and the many journeys (both literal and spiritual) along the way.

James I. Deutsch

Further Reading

Boi, Paola. "Zora Neale Hurston's *Autobiographie Fictive*: Dark Tracks on the Canon of a Female Writer." In *The Black Columbiad: Defining Moments in African American Literature and Culture*, edited by Werner Sollors and Maria Diedrich. Cambridge, Mass.: Harvard University Press, 1994. Weighing the book's imaginary elements against its reality, Boi concludes that it is closer to narrative fiction than factual autobiography.

Bordelon, Pam. "New Tracks on *Dust Tracks*: Toward a Reassessment of the Life of Zora Neale Hurston." *African American Review* 31, no. 1 (Spring, 1997): 5-21. Based on archival documents and an interview with one of Hurston's nieces, this carefully researched article provides new biographical information that contradicts some of the alleged facts in *Dust Tracks on a Road*.

Domina, Lynn. "'Protection in My Mouf': Self, Voice, and Community in Zora Neale Hurston's *Dust Tracks on a Road* and *Mules and Men*." *African American Review* 31, no. 2 (Summer, 1997): 197-209. When read together, these two books by Hurston—one classified as autobiography, the other classified as folklore—provide a more complete picture of the author's life.

Hassall, Kathleen. "Text and Personality in Disguise and in the Open: Zora Neale Hurston's *Dust Tracks on a Road*." In *Zora in Florida*, edited by Steven Glassman and Kathryn Lee Seidel. Orlando: University of Central Florida Press, 1991. Argues that Hurston's inventiveness and resourcefulness led her to disguise aspects of her life deliberately in her autobiography.

Robey, Judith. "Generic Strategies in Zora Neale Hurston's *Dust Tracks on a Road*." *Black American Literature Forum 24, no. 4 (Winter, 1990): 667-682. Maintains that Hurston intentionally shifts literary genres—from myth to picaresque to essay—to maintain her independence and authority.

Rodríguez, Barbara. "On the Gatepost: Literal and Metaphorical Journeys in Zora Neale Hurston's *Dust Tracks on a Road*." In *Women, America, and Movement: Narratives of Relocation*, edited by Susan L. Roberson. Columbia: University of Missouri Press, 1998. The structure of Hurston's autobiography reflects her, according to Rodríguez. The first half is primarily metaphorical, using folklore and local legends to suggest Hurston's life story; the second half is more literal, using specific events to document and construct her personal identity.

Snyder, Phillip A. "Zora Neale Hurston's *Dust Tracks*: Autobiography and Artist Novel." In *Critical Essays on Zora Neale Hurston*, edited by Gloria L. Cronin. New York: G. K. Hall, 1998. Because *Dust Tracks on a Road* combines elements of both traditional autobiography and fictional bildungsroman, it allows for multiple interpretations of Hurston's life.

Valkeakari, Tuire. "'Luxuriat[ing] in Milton's Syllables': Writer as Reader in Zora Neale Hurston's *Dust Tracks on a Road*." In *Reading Women: Literary Figures and Cultural Icons from the Victorian Age to the Present*, edited by Janet Badia and Jennifer Phegley. Toronto, Ont.: University of Toronto Press, 2005. Hurston's autobiography reveals much about the books she read and how they affected her career as a scholar and writer.

West, M. Genevieve. *Zora Neale Hurston and American Literary Culture*. Gainesville: University Press of Florida, 2005. Chapter 5 assesses the pressures and factors that led to Hurston's unconventional autobiography and the reviews—both praiseworthy and critical—that appeared at the time.

Dutchman

Author: Amiri Baraka (1934-   )
First produced: 1964; first published, 1964
Type of work: Drama
Type of plot: Political
Time of plot: 1960's
Locale: New York City

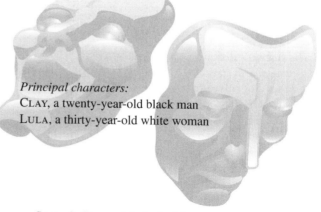

Principal characters:
CLAY, a twenty-year-old black man
LULA, a thirty-year-old white woman

The Story:

Scene 1. Clay and Lula exchange glances as Clay sits inside a subway car pulling into a station and Lula stands outside waiting to board. At first, Clay smiles at Lula "without a trace of self-consciousness," but then he feels a growing sense of embarrassment. The smile that crosses Lula's face is "premeditated." After eating an apple, Lula offers one to Clay. She attempts to engage him in sexual banter, and she ridicules him for adopting the posture and dress of the white middle class, telling him, "You look like death eating a soda cracker." At the same time that Lula makes explicit sexual overtures to Clay, she harasses him about his middle-class identity and his resulting status as a dislocated African American man in America: "Everything you say is wrong. . . . Boy, those narrow-shoulder clothes come from a tradition you ought to feel oppressed by. . . . Your grandfather was a slave, he didn't go to Harvard."

Scene 2. Clay and Lula decide to go to a party together. Lula verbally creates the scenario of a sexual encounter between them. As the conversation continues, Lula becomes more derogatory, her language more racial and aggressive, and she jumps up into a wild dance, shouting slurs at Clay and demanding that he get up to dance and to have sex with her.

Clay tries to calm her down. At first nervously bemused, he becomes more agitated and forceful. When Lula continues to holler epithets and slurs at him, he slaps her hard across the mouth and throws her into a seat. Telling Lula to "shut up and let me talk," Clay then verbally (and figuratively) abuses Lula, stripping her of her delusions of power, insight, and security. He declares that a potentially revolutionary violence underlies African American experience, though it is "for now" present only in the subterranean and indirect modes of jazz and poetry: "If Bessie Smith had killed some white people she wouldn't have needed that music. She could have talked very straight and plain about the world. No metaphors. . . . Just let me bleed you, you loud whore, and one poem vanished."

Lula's response to Clay's furious challenge is cold and detached: "I've heard enough." Clay, too, is suddenly tired, and abruptly he is ready to end the conversation. He turns to leave the subway car, saying, "Looks like we won't be acting out that little pageant you outlined before." As he bends over her to grab his things from the seat, Lula stabs him twice in the chest with a knife. He is dead immediately. Lula turns to the other passengers on the train, both black and white, who sat passively during the entire exchange, and commands them to dump Clay's body from the train and to disembark at the next station. The passengers do as they are told.

Another young African American man boards the subway, carrying his books. "An old Negro conductor," walking through the car, acknowledges the young man with a quick "Hey, brother," then passes Lula "doing sort of a restrained soft shoe." He tips his hat to her and leaves the car. Lula and the young man are left alone.

Critical Evaluation:

Dutchman, an early play by the poet, dramatist, and political writer Amiri Baraka, was written when his name was still LeRoi Jones and at a transitional time for both the playwright and the Black Arts (or Black Aesthetics) movement. *Dutchman* reflects that transition in its aesthetic structure, its political content, and its implied audience.

This transition in African American drama can be characterized as a shift from aesthetics as they were traditionally defined by a primarily white, European-oriented theater community to an explicitly politicized and black nationalist art directed toward and arising from the African American community. Baraka's work throughout the 1960's marks a critical existential shift in stark terms: After winning an Obie Award for *Dutchman* in 1964 (Best Off-Broadway Play), he then in 1968 changed his name to emphasize his African and Kawaida identity and became Imamu Amiri Baraka. At the same time, his shift from artist-activist to black nationalist and Marxist-Leninist socialist critic marked his abandonment of the New York arts scene (including the avant-garde) to focus instead on literary forms deeply tied to African American revolutionary politics. Readers of *Dutchman* who pursue its critical reception will find revealing contrasts in interpretation depending on the political and aesthetic stance of the critic, especially in relation to historical changes and debates within African American liberation politics.

The play itself opens on a subway, "in the flying underbelly of the city," a subterranean metaphor for both the rattling dissonance of American culture and the psychological interior terrain of American racial politics. Baraka sets up the association: "Steaming hot, and summer on top, outside. Underground. The subway heaped in modern myth."

The play consists of two short scenes between the two characters as they ride the subway together. A metaphoric and ironic Eden is suggested when Lula eats an apple and then offers one to Clay. Their first exchange, in which Lula ridicules the image Clay seems to be trying to project, establishes the pivotal issue of power (that is, who controls the conversation) and unveils both Clay's aspirations to the middle class and Lula's moral instability. As the scene proceeds, the tension between them builds. Lula pushes hard, making sexual overtures that are seductive one moment and arrogant and derogatory the next. Clay stays almost entirely reactive to Lula's definition of his identity; he lets her control the conversation while joking to defuse the confrontation, and he refuses to counterattack her verbally. Baraka closes the scene with an explicitly historical and political frame. As Lula declares,

> And we'll pretend the people cannot see you. That is, the citizens. And that you are free of your own history. And I am free of my history. We'll pretend that we are both anonymous beauties smashing through the city's entrails.

The mythic elements of the play deepen in the course of the first scene, even while the dramatic style itself stays naturalistic. Several critics see class and racial struggle as the central themes, with turbulent intensity building in Clay as a symbol of the African American middle class, who must repress black-defined identity in order to assimilate into white-dominated society. In this view, Lula represents the failed moral order of white supremacy, which, although obviously unstable and erratic, remains at least apparently in control. The explicit sexual dynamics and underlying sexual tension represent, in this context, a playing out (and reversal) of racial stereotypes, and Lula's behavior reveals the complex blend of desire and psychosis characteristic of white racism. Other interpretations focus on Clay as representing repressed African American art and artists. Claiming at one point to be "Baudelaire," Clay becomes the Black Aesthetics movement struggling to fit into the constraints of European clothing.

The second scene continues to develop the themes of the first. Clay's revelatory outburst is defined, in the context of a dialogue that was controlled by Lula's fantasies and delusions of power, as a response. Although his self-expression is genuine, deeply realized, and powerful (he speaks both as an artist and as a representative of the African American middle class now alert to its historical dilemma), it leads to his destruction precisely because he chooses to remain in conversation with Lula, whose murderous intolerance of Clay's self-assertion reveals white supremacy in brutal terms. Although Lula is willing to conduct a white liberal charade with Clay, she responds with predictable violence to Clay's potentially revolutionary insight. The second young man and the old conductor present the same dangerous stance toward Lula, who calmly prepares for the next encounter, and as the curtain falls, the audience senses that the cycle is about to begin again. The play's conclusion suggests Baraka's increasingly emphatic call for African Americans to break off conversation both artistically and politically with the failed (and violent) white American culture. In *Dutchman*, Clay's self-defined expression of power and identity leads to his own death. The mythic, symbolic, and historical/political depth in the play makes it clear that Baraka's subterranean travelers are moving beneath, and through, the landscape of American history.

Several issues are important in *Dutchman*. During the 1960's, Baraka increasingly rejected the imperatives of protest literature. Critics pointed to the class politics of the play as indicative of Baraka's emerging socialist critique, and some compared *Dutchman* with the broader sociological analysis of E. Franklin Frazier's *Black Bourgeoisie* (1957). Another key issue concerns the tension in African American cultural politics between claims of racial essentialism (that is, the Black Aesthetics movement as being rooted in racial essence) and pressures toward assimilation into the American middle class. *Dutchman* suggests that the road toward assimilation is the road to individual and collective destruction. A comparative reading of *Dutchman* with other works reveals the complexity and urgency of questions related to African American identity and power. Related to this is the relationship between political ideology and artistic form, the relationship between community identity and the role of drama as political ritual, and the role of art in revolutionary change. The play's title has been called a metaphoric reference to the first slave ships. Baraka's work profoundly engages the implications of history for African American political critique.

Sharon Carson

Further Reading

Anadolu-Okur, Nilgun. *Contemporary African American Theater: Afrocentricity in the Works of Larry Neal, Amiri*

Baraka, and Charles Fuller. New York: Garland, 1997. Describes how the three playwrights created new forms of African American drama. Places their work within the context of the Civil Rights and Black Power movements. Devotes a chapter to analysis of *Dutchman*.

Baraka, Imamu Amiri. *Selected Plays and Prose of Amiri Baraka/LeRoi Jones.* New York: William Morrow, 1979. An important source for reading *Dutchman* in the context of several of Baraka's political essays from the 1960's and 1970's.

Benston, Kimberly W. *Baraka: The Renegade and the Mask.* New Haven, Conn.: Yale University Press, 1976. According to Benston's interpretation, Clay's fate is a tragedy of lost direction and lack of knowledge. In deciding not to kill Lula, he rejects the power and violence that would allow him to dominate the situation; he thus reaffirms his vulnerability and falls victim to Lula's malevolence.

Bigsby, C. W. E. "Black Theater." In *Beyond Broadway.* Vol. 3 in *A Critical Introduction to Twentieth-Century American Drama.* New York: Cambridge University Press, 1985. Bigsby argues that in the context of the early 1960's, the play reflects the self-awareness of a black playwright balancing a successful career as a writer and reflects political necessities that seemed to require actions rather than words.

Brown, Lloyd. *Amiri Baraka.* Boston: Twayne, 1980. Includes a useful chapter on Baraka's drama, with reference to *Dutchman*. Good annotated bibliography.

Effiong, Philip U. *In Search of a Model for African-American Drama: A Study of Selected Plays by Lorraine Hansberry, Amiri Baraka, and Ntozake Shange.* Lanham, Md.: University Press of America, 2000. Effiong describes how the three playwrights devised new forms of drama in order to address the conditions of African Americans, placing their plays within their historical, cultural, and sociopolitical contexts. His discussion includes consideration of Baraka's recurrent use of ritual sacrifices in his plays.

Fabre, Geneviève. "Leroi Jones/Amiri Baraka: An Iconoclastic Theatre." In *Drumbeats, Masks, and Metaphor: Contemporary Afro-American Theatre.* Translated by Melvin Dixon. Cambridge, Mass.: Harvard University Press, 1983. In Fabre's interpretation of *Dutchman*, a paradox of the play is that Lula reveals Clay to himself. His awakening comes too late, because he has already made too many compromises, and too soon, because it is merely individual, rather than communal, and therefore it is ineffectual.

Hudson, Theodore R. *From LeRoi Jones to Amiri Baraka: The Literary Works.* Durham, N.C.: Duke University

Press, 1973. Puts *Dutchman* and other Baraka writings within the framework of his shift from avant-garde literary artist to practicing black cultural nationalist. Provides political and historical context for Baraka's transition; the notes and bibliography point readers to useful articles and interviews from the 1960's and early 1970's.

Lacy, Henry C. *To Raise, Destroy, and Create: The Poetry, Drama, and Fiction of Imamu Amiri Baraka (LeRoi Jones)*. Troy, N.Y.: Whitston, 1981. Includes an excellent and extensive interpretive reading of *Dutchman*. Also provides substantial biographical and political/cultural context, as well as insightful analysis of Baraka's role as inspiration to later African American writers.

Sollors, Werner. *Amiri Baraka/Leroi Jones: The Quest for a "Popular Modernism."* New York: Columbia University Press, 1978. According to Sollors, *Dutchman* combines a realistic look at American society with the absurdist and surrealist traditions of European theater. Lula, although a negative force in the play, expresses many of the playwright's own ideas in his own language.

Watts, Jerry Gafio. *Amiri Baraka: The Politics and Art of a Black Intellectual*. New York: New York University Press, 2001. A critical biography, in which Watts depicts Baraka as a brilliant but derivative writer and an intense but changeable man. Chapter 3, "An Alien Among Outsiders," devotes several pages to *Dutchman*.

The Dynasts
A Drama of the Napoleonic Wars

Author: Thomas Hardy (1840-1928)
First produced: 1914 (abridged version); first published, 1903, 1906, 1908; 1910 (complete)
Type of work: Drama
Type of plot: Historical
Time of plot: 1806-1815
Locale: Europe

Principal characters:
NAPOLEON I
JOSEPHINE, his first wife
MARIE LOUISE, his second wife
KING GEORGE III OF ENGLAND
TSAR ALEXANDER OF RUSSIA
EMPEROR FRANCIS OF AUSTRIA
SIR WILLIAM PITT, prime minister of England
SPIRIT OF YEARS,
SHADE OF EARTH,
SPIRIT OF PITIES,
SPIRIT SINISTER, and
SPIRIT IRONIC, allegorical figures

The Story:

The Spirit of Years, Shade of Earth, Spirit Sinister, Spirit Ironic, Spirit of Pities, and their accompanying choruses forgather somewhere above the earth to watch the larger movements of humans in western Europe in 1805. The design of the Immanent Will manifests itself at the time in Napoleon's preparations for the invasion of England.

In England, Sir William Pitt contends with isolationist members of Parliament to secure proper defense against the invasion, while Napoleon goes to Milan to be crowned king of Italy. The spirits make light of the chicanery and pomp that attends the coronation. The Spirit of Pities descends to earth and disturbs Napoleon by reminding him of his original intention to champion liberty.

At sea, a Pyrrhic victory of the French and Spanish over the English prevents the support required for the planned invasion. On the south coast of England, the Phantoms of Rumor cause great disturbance. A fleet of fishing craft is mistaken for the invasion fleet, and civilians flee from the coastal towns as signal fires flare upon the cliffs and hills.

When Napoleon learns that his admiral, Villeneuve, has returned to Cadiz, he discards his invasion plan and moves eastward against Austria and Russia, countries that Pitt enlisted in the English cause. The Spirit of Years remarks that the ensuing campaign will be a model in tactics for all time. At Ulm, Napoleon defeats the Austrians, who hoped that the English fleet would hold the French forces in northern

France. In London, Pitt, unsuccessful in gaining permission from the king to form a coalition government, visibly declines in health under his terrible burden.

Villeneuve is ordered out of Cadiz. The British under Admiral Horatio Nelson meet the French and Spanish off Trafalgar and defeat them. Nelson is killed in the engagement; Villeneuve subsequently ends his own life in an inn at Rennes. Napoleon defeats the Austrians and Russians at Austerlitz. Then, hearing of the English victory at Trafalgar, he declares his intention to close all continental ports to English ships. He dictates peace terms to Emperor Francis of Austria while attendant Austrian officers stand by in disgust at the sight of a nobody dictating to true royalty. In Paris, the Spirit of Rumor comments on the way Napoleon is uprooting old dynasties and founding new ones.

Pitt being dead and King George III being mentally ill, Charles James Fox negotiates for England with Napoleon for peace, but Napoleon uses the negotiations as a screen for his real plans. He marches on Prussia and defeats the Germans at the Battle of Jena. In Berlin, he decrees that all British ships are barred from continental ports. Napoleon and Tsar Alexander of Russia meet at the River Niemen, where the two draw up a Franco-Russian alliance. During this meeting, Napoleon expresses the desire to cement his various alliances with blood ties. The Spirit of Years remarks ironically that Napoleon is one of the few men who can see the working of the Immanent Will.

Napoleon invades Spain as a friend to help the Spanish gain Portugal. The Spanish Bourbons abdicate and Napoleon's brother, Joseph, is proclaimed king. Bourbon partisans enlist English aid, and an English invasion fleet sails for Portugal.

Back in Paris, Napoleon tells his wife, Josephine, that he wants a divorce. Josephine has given him no children, and he is eager to perpetuate the dynasty he founds. The British invasion of the Iberian Peninsula draws him to Spain to direct the campaign there. Austrian preparations for war induce Napoleon next to invade that country, and he defeats the Austrian forces at Wagram. The British, under the duke of Wellington, hold their own against the French in Spain. At that point, the Spirit Sinister reminds the Spirit Ironic not to sneer for fear Immanent Will will cut short the comedy that is taking place.

A British force is sent to the Scheldt, but the expedition ends disastrously when the army is decimated by miasmal fever. Napoleon, fearful of assassination and still anxious to perpetuate his line, negotiates with the Russians for the hand of a Russian princess and with the Austrians for the hand of Princess Marie Louise. The tsar accepts the offer, but Napo-

leon arranges, through Prince Metternich, a marriage with the Austrian princess, Marie Louise. The marriage is performed with the conspicuous absence of many high clergy; the Russians, feeling insulted, prepare for war. In the meantime, the British in Spain under the duke of Wellington gain a decisive victory at Albuera.

In due time, Marie Louise gives birth to Napoleon's heir. The insane king of England dies after hearing of British successes in Spain. On the continent, war becomes imminent between France and Russia. On the banks of the Niemen, Napoleon receives an evil portent when he is thrown from his horse. The Spirit of Pities foresees misery for the French Grand Army in the Russian campaign. Wellington in Spain defeats the French at Salamanca. Napoleon gains a costly victory over the Russians at Borodino, and the French enter Moscow to find the city deserted and in flames. The French thereupon retreat across snow-covered Russian steppes to Lithuania. Thousands perish from the cold or are killed by harassing Russian cavalry. Napoleon deserts his army and races back to Paris so as to anticipate the news of his failure in Russia. His chief task now is to hold his empire together.

As the British continue their successes in Spain, Austria joins the allies. Napoleon meets defeat at the hands of the Austrians and Prussians at Leipzig. The allies invade France. Napoleon, forced to abdicate, is exiled to Elba, an island in the Mediterranean. Marie Louise and the infant king of Rome go to Austria. The Bourbons reassume the throne of France, and a congress to deliberate on general peace in Europe meets in Vienna.

Napoleon escapes from Elba and returns to Paris at the head of an army he picked up on his way. The allies outlaw Napoleon and prepare to overthrow him again.

A private ball in Brussels is broken up by the news that the French army is nearing the Belgian frontier. Almost overnight, Napoleon organizes and puts into the field a large army, but he fails to separate the British and Prussians in Belgium, and he is brought to utter defeat on the fields south of Waterloo. The Hundred Days ends.

The Spirit of Years points out to the assembled spirits that the human beings below them behave as though they are in a dream, as though they are puppets being drawn by strings manipulated by Immanent Will. The Spirit of Years points to Napoleon in defeat and compares him to a tiny insect on an obscure leaf in the chart of the Ages. When the Spirit of Pities asks for what purpose the events below took place, the Spirit of Irony answers that there is no purpose, for only a dumb thing turns the crank that motivates and directs human behavior.

Critical Evaluation:

In *The Dynasts*, Thomas Hardy realized his lifelong ambition to dramatize the events of the Napoleonic period. He already touched on the subject in his novel *The Trumpet-Major* (1880), and he noted in his journal plans to execute a "Homeric ballad, in which Napoleon is a kind of Achilles." Hardy was an anxious witness to the cultural changes brought about by so-called progress. However, while he regretted such changes as the dissolution of traditions and of folk beliefs, he was at the same time suspicious of conventional religious and social institutions. In *The Dynasts*, he tries, in effect, to "rescue" history by giving comparatively recent human events epic stature.

Much of *The Dynasts* is written in blank verse (unrhymed iambic pentameter), but the work also includes prose passages, lyrics, rhymed couplets, and various other stanza forms. Some critics suggested that Hardy may have chosen verse because a great novel on the subject already existed in Leo Tolstoy's *Voyna i mir* (1865-1869; *War and Peace*, 1886). More probably, Hardy chose an "antique" form to achieve the all-inclusiveness of epic and to claim association with classical epics, such as Homer's *Iliad* (c. 750 B.C.E.; English translation, 1611), which contain all verse forms and represent all levels of human society. Hardy, too, designs his epic to chronicle "the dull peoples and the Dynasts both," seeking to recover the heroic dimension of the human experience.

The greatest obstacle to this goal is what Hardy calls the Immanent Will. In Hardy's cosmology, worldly destiny and ambition are driven by an unconscious, motiveless force rather than by personal initiative or by a watchful, just God. Even the great powers appearing in the drama—Napoleon, Nelson, Wellington—are subject to this force, which works "like a knitter drowsed." Although Hardy denied that it represented a systematic philosophy, *The Dynasts* seems to reinforce the determinism or fatalism prevailing in such earlier novels as *Tess of the D'Urbervilles* (1891). All the characters of the verse drama, whether high-born or humble, are caught in what Hardy calls "satires of circumstance"; whether king, commander, or whore, none seems capable of expressing individual purpose or intention.

To illustrate these satires, Hardy uses a chorus of Spirits or Intelligences. From various perspectives, they comment on the role of the Immanent Will in worldly experience. Themselves subject to the Will, they are free to meddle only superficially in human affairs. They may spread unreliable gossip, as does the Spirit of Rumour, or speak a word or two to an individual in a crisis (for example, to Villeneuve as he considers suicide or to the defeated Napoleon after Waterloo). Only the Spirit of the Pities has any compassion for human misery; the others stand as indifferent, sometimes amused, witnesses to history.

A multitude of human actors crowds the drama. In addition to the key historical figures, Hardy includes many nonspeaking characters whose presence in these events the reader is merely intended to register. (This may be one of the reasons why Hardy stipulated that *The Dynasts* is intended "for mental performance alone.") Some of the more eminent characters serve principally to advance the action. Even Napoleon seems opaque when he makes rhetorical pronouncements; he is most sharply characterized as a victim of the Will: "a solitary figure on a jaded horse." As to the anonymous figures with whom Hardy peoples history, they, too, are caught in the Will's "knitting," as when a group of English deserters cheerfully drink themselves insensible in the ruins of a Spanish farmhouse, waking only when they are overtaken by Napoleon himself.

Hardy's epic vision is panoramic, and his sweeping aerial views of countryside and battlefield are, as the critic John Wain observed, cinematic achievements. Hardy also captures grotesque, anecdotal moments. For example, after Nelson's death at Trafalgar, his body is transported back to England preserved in a keg of rum, which his loyal but thirsty sailors drain before arriving in port. For chronicling such extremes, Hardy develops a curious, even stilted vocabulary that is native neither to poetry nor to prose. At times, he uses the speech of Wessex rustics that is familiar to readers of his novels; panicked at the rumor of Napoleon's approach, English country folk assert that he "lives upon human flesh, and has rashers o' baby every morning for breakfast." The poet invokes a completely different language when his Intelligences speak of the Immanent Will: "These are the Prime Volitions," they explain, "Their sum is like the lobule of a Brain/ Evolving always that it wots not of." In this twentieth century epic, Hardy proves himself to be a virtuoso of metrical form and a keen, if eccentric, observer of historical detail.

"Critical Evaluation" by Sarah A. Boris

Further Reading

Dean, Susan. *Hardy's Poetic Vision in "The Dynasts."* Princeton, N.J.: Princeton University Press, 1977. A thorough and accessible discussion of Hardy's epic vision and of his concept of the Immanent Will.

Kramer, Dale, ed. *The Cambridge Companion to Thomas Hardy.* New York: Cambridge University Press, 1999. An introduction and general overview of all Hardy's work and specific demonstrations of Hardy's ideas and literary skills. Individual essays explore Hardy's biography, aesthetics, and the impact on his work of developments in science, religion, and philosophy in the late nineteenth century. The volume also contains a detailed chronology of Hardy's life and numerous references to *The Dynasts* that are listed in the index.

Maynard, Katherine Kearney. *Thomas Hardy's Tragic Poetry: The Lyrics and "The Dynasts."* Iowa City: University of Iowa Press, 1991. Examines *The Dynasts* in the context of Hardy's shorter poems and helps to define his sense of tragedy in a secular age.

Millgate, Michael. *Thomas Hardy: A Biography Revisited.* New York: Oxford University Press, 2004. This biography enhances and replaces Millgate's 1982 biography, considered to be one of the best and most scholarly Hardy biographies available. Includes bibliography and index.

Page, Norman, ed. *Oxford Reader's Companion to Hardy.* New York: Oxford University Press, 2000. An encyclopedia containing three hundred alphabetically arranged entries examining Hardy's work and discussing his family and friends, important places in his life and work, his influences, critical approaches to his writings, and a history of his works' publication. Also includes a chronology of his life, lists of places and characters in his fiction, a glossary, and a bibliography.

Tomalin, Claire. *Thomas Hardy.* New York: Penguin, 2007. This thorough and finely written biography by a respected Hardy scholar illuminates the writer's efforts to indict the malice, neglect, and ignorance of his fellow human beings. Tomalin also discusses aspects of his life that are apparent in his literary works.

White, R. J. *Thomas Hardy and History.* New York: Barnes & Noble, 1974. An invaluable study of Hardy's treatment of history in *The Dynasts* and elsewhere.

Wickens, G. Glen. *Thomas Hardy, Monism, and the Carnival Tradition: The One and the Many in "The Dynasts."* Toronto, Ont.: University of Toronto Press, 2002. An analysis of the play from the perspective of monism, or the view that reality is one organic whole without any independent parts. Wickens also applies the critical theories of Mikhail Bakhtin to interpret the play.

Wilson, Keith. "*The Dynasts* Adapted: London, Dorset, and Oxford." In *Thomas Hardy on Stage.* New York: St. Martin's Press, 1995. Examines Hardy's involvement with the theater, including the plays he wrote and the works he adapted for the stage.

Wright, Walter F. *The Shaping of "The Dynasts": A Study in Thomas Hardy.* Lincoln: University of Nebraska Press, 1967. Especially useful in assessing Hardy's verse forms as well as his indebtedness to the German philosopher Arthur Schopenhauer.

E

Earth

Author: Émile Zola (1840-1902)
First published: La Terre, 1887 (English translation, 1888)
Type of work: Novel
Type of plot: Naturalism
Time of plot: 1860's
Locale: La Beauce, France

Principal characters:
FOUAN, an old peasant farmer
ROSE, his wife
HYACINTHE, called Jésus-Christ, his older son
FANNY, his daughter
BUTEAU, his younger son
DELHOMME, Fanny's husband
LISE, Fouan's niece and the daughter of Old Mouche
FRANÇOISE, Lise's sister
JEAN MACQUART, a soldier and artisan and later a farm laborer in La Beauce

The Story:

As Jean Macquart finishes sowing each furrow with grain, he pauses and gazes over the wide, rich plain. As far as he can see, farmers are scattering their wheat, anxious to finish sowing before the frosts come. He meets and talks with Françoise about the coming division of old Fouan's property among his sons and son-in-law. In the notary's office, plans for the division are being discussed with anger. Fouan cannot bear to lose the land that took all of his strength to work and that he loved more passionately than his wife. The rent and food he asks in return for his property seem excessive to his children, who, now that the land is within their grasp, intend to keep as much of its yield as possible. Buteau declares that the old man has money saved in bonds. This claim so enrages Fouan that he exhibits some of his old ferocity and authority. Finally, the notary completes the transaction and arranges for the surveyor to divide the land.

Buteau draws the third lot of land. He declares that it is the worst and refuses to take that part of the property. His refusal distresses Lise, Françoise's sister, for Buteau is her lover and she is pregnant. She hoped that when he obtained the land he would marry her.

Old Mouche, the father of Lise and Françoise, has a stroke and dies in his home. As the village women watch by his deathbed, a violent hailstorm lays waste the village crops. The peasants examine the damage by lamplight, their animosities forgotten in their common anguish at this devastation. Lise and Françoise stay in the house after their father's

death. Lise's son is born and still Buteau does not marry her. Jean becomes a constant visitor in the household. Believing that he is attracted by Lise, he proposes to her. Before accepting him, she decides to consult Buteau because of the child. At the autumn haymaking, Jean and Françoise work together. While the girl stands atop the growing rick, Jean forks up bales of hay to her. She is flushed and laughing, and Jean finds himself violently attracted to her. Because he is years older than Françoise, he is greatly upset when he suddenly realizes that it is she who drew him to the house and not Lise.

Jean and the sisters meet Buteau at the market in Cloyes. Because Lise now has property of her own and because he at last accepted his share of land, Buteau decides to marry Lise. Buteau is now delighted by the land, and he plows and sows with vigor and passion, determined never to relinquish one inch of the earth. As the wheat grows, its rolling greenness covers La Beauce like an ocean. Buteau watches the weather as anxiously as a sailor at sea. Although Françoise wishes to have her share of the land decided, Buteau manages to avoid a final settlement.

When Fouan's older son, nicknamed Jésus-Christ, takes to buying brandy with the money that Buteau grudgingly gave his parents as their allowance, Buteau is so infuriated that he strikes his mother to the floor. Rose does not recover, and she dies three days later. That leaves Fouan completely alone. Finally, much against his will, he decides to make his home with Delhomme, his son-in-law.

By harvest time, the green sea of wheat turns to a fiery gold, and the whole village works at the harvest. Meanwhile, Jean is tormented by his desire for Françoise. Finally, exhausted by her struggle to resist his attentions, she yields to him. Buteau, fearing he might lose both the girl and her land, asserts that they can never be married while Françoise is under age.

Fouan is bullied and restricted in Delhomme's home; he has no money for tobacco, and he is allowed little wine. Completely miserable, he goes to live with Buteau and Lise. There he is appalled by Buteau's pursuit of Françoise, whose resistance makes Buteau so angry that even Lise expresses the wish that her sister would surrender in order to have peace once more in the household. Françoise, however, continues proudly to refuse Buteau, and she is gradually transformed into a domestic drudge.

In desperation, Françoise agrees to marry Jean when she is of age. Fouan, drawn into these household quarrels, is no happier than he was with Delhomme. At last, because Buteau and his wife begrudge every mouthful of food that he eats, he accepts Jésus-Christ's offer of a home. Jésus-Christ was the only one of Fouan's children without a passion for land. Although it distresses Fouan to see his hard-won acres go to buy brandy for Jésus-Christ, he enjoys the jokes and the occasional excellent meals cooked in the nearly ruined house by Jésus-Christ's illegitimate daughter.

Before the time of the vintage, Jésus-Christ discovers that his father is spending his bonds on an annuity by which he hopes to acquire some land of his own once more. Amazed, first Fanny and then Buteau try to bribe the old man to return to them. Fouan's relationship with Jésus-Christ is never close again after the discovery.

After a final explosion with Lise, Françoise leaves the house and goes to live with her aunt. It is arranged that she should soon marry Jean and claim her full share of the property. The ill will between the sisters intensifies when the land is divided and Françoise secures the house at auction. Buteau and Lise move to an adjacent house, where Fouan joins them, fearing that Jésus-Christ will steal his bonds.

Jean and Buteau are forced to work side by side in the fields. One day, while Jean is fertilizing the earth, Lise tells Buteau that Fouan suffered a stroke and that she will bring the doctor. To everyone's surprise, the old man recovers. During his illness, however, Lise discovers his bonds. When she refuses to return them, he leaves.

Homeless and desperate, Fouan wanders to Delhomme's farm, where he stays wearily looking into the house. Next, he goes to Jésus-Christ's hovel, but fear and pride again prevent him from entering. That night, during a terrible storm, Fouan,

wretched and exhausted, drags himself around to look once more at the land he owned. Finally his hunger becomes so great that he returns to Buteau, who jeeringly feeds him.

Françoise is pregnant. Enraged by the fear that the property might not revert to him and by the fact that Jean's plow cut into their land, Buteau, aided by Lise, rapes Françoise. With revulsion, the young woman realizes that she always loved him. In her jealousy, Lise knocks Françoise against a scythe in the field, and the blade pierces her abdomen. As she lies dying, Françoise refuses to will her share of the farm to Jean; although he is her husband, she still regards him as an outsider. After her death, Jean is evicted from the land.

Greedy for more money and terrified that the old man will betray the manner of Françoise's death, Lise and Buteau murder Fouan by smothering him with a pillow and then setting fire to his bed. Jean Macquart, having no further ties with La Beauce, decides to become a soldier again. After a final tour of the land, he leaves the region forever. He reasons that if he cannot cultivate the land, he will at least be able to defend the earth of France.

Critical Evaluation:

Émile Zola began as a literary Romantic and an idealist. In his youth, he wrote fairy tales and dreamed of perfect beauty and perfect love. The poverty he experienced early in life, and the general European literary climate, however, brought him to try to picture an imperfect but real "corner of nature."

Earth, the fifteenth volume of the Rougon-Macquarts series, is Zola's horrifying vision of the French peasantry before the Franco-Prussian War. In the relationships between Fouan and his family, Zola consciously adopted the theme of William Shakespeare's *King Lear* (pr. c. 1605-1606, pb. 1608), although the realistic detail with which Fouan is drawn includes none of the nobility of Shakespeare's king. Zola's introduction of Rabelaisian humor in the character Jésus-Christ was an innovation in literary realism. The earth itself dominates the novel, and its beauty and its indifference contrast vividly with the peasants' passionate absorption in possessing the land and with the crimes they commit in order to do so.

A magnificent example of Zola's groping for the authentic details in life, *Earth* can be best understood when placed in the literary context of realism and naturalism. Literary realism developed in the nineteenth century partly as a response to the conditions of modern society. It stressed fidelity to the facts of everyday existence. Scenes, characters, motives, and conflicts were presumably drawn from experiences in life rather than from dreams of other worlds or of the supernatural. Within the realist tradition are distinct and coherent groupings—naturalism is one of them—but it is easier to place a work such as *Earth* in the naturalist tradition than it is to define literary naturalism. In general, however, for the purposes of examining *Earth*, two basic points can be established: Naturalism attempts to portray the actual and significant details of life and especially (though not exclusively) the life of poor and working people, and naturalism most often attempts to uncover those forces in the environment and in the genetic makeup of the individual that determine the course of life.

Earth tries to give an accurate picture of French rural life in the 1860's. This picture is not merely a general account but a brilliantly detailed canvas that conveys the humanity and the density of rural life. The basis of the action of the novel is the division of an old man's land. Much of the novel, therefore, describes the unending, vicious, implacable hatreds and the unyielding tensions that emerge within the farmer's family. Domestic life is described through the conversations, the cooking and cleaning utensils, the jealous glances, and the dirt, cobwebs, and small, damp rooms of the peasant households. The smells of the fields, the manure, the sweat, and the musky odors of water and of age saturate every scene.

The life of the countryside is also explored in relation to the fields, skies, and weather. The division of these fields, the run-down cottages, and the seeding and fertilization of the fields are depicted in meticulous detail. Pages are devoted to storms of various kinds, including a hailstorm, but unlike the Romantics, for whom the excesses of the weather are often merely spectacular, these storms are viewed as destructive and, toward the end of *Earth*, as brutalizing and humbling.

Main events in the harvest are not omitted. Zola sketches a grape harvest, for example, in which the workers pick grapes, stuff themselves, and get sick. In fact, sickness, drunkenness, perversity, and violence are presented as being ever-present in the life of these times. Zola leaves out nothing, including all aspects of the sexual side of life. From the beginning of the novel, where Zola describes a young man and woman working together without embarrassment to help a bull and a cow to mate, the sexual theme is established as a central part of life.

Zola's accumulation of detail from real experience becomes increasingly powerful as the novel advances. These details, linked through action, character, and theme, become the tightly woven, actual fabric of life. Reading *Earth* is, in fact, to be submerged in this life; and this feeling of submersion no doubt accounts for the powerful influence the novel continues to exert. At the same time, Zola's selection of details led to his being accused of presenting only the sordid side of life and of unnecessarily emphasizing the nasty aspects of life. *Earth* was sharply attacked precisely for these reasons when it was first published. Some even thought the novel to be deliberately pornographic. A good argument can be made that these scenes are included not for their shock value but for more serious reasons that are connected to Zola's understanding of science.

The second important feature of literary naturalism—its attempt to portray the underlying forces that shape human destiny—is especially evident in the work of Zola, who understood these forces in a scientific context. The forces were describable, measurable, and inevitable. In his view, in fact, by understanding the genetic and environmental forces working on his characters, and by altering these forces, he could explain his characters scientifically and, at the same time, actually experiment on them and test them in his fiction. Zola did not, however, carry out this experimental procedure vigorously in his novels.

In *Earth*, the forces most evident are those associated with the land. The greed for the land, which is manifest in the character Buteau, overcomes all obstacles. Buteau will have the land or destroy it, himself, and his competitors and family. The power of sex is likewise connected with the earth. The opening scene of the novel deals with the fertilization of the land, and it describes a sexual life "close to the earth." Sexual activity takes place in the fields as well as in the home.

Finally, there is the genetic composition of the characters. Their strengths and weaknesses, determined by the strengths and weaknesses of their ancestors, provide a spectrum of responses to the conditions of rural France. The family thus helps place *Earth* in its proper position in the massive architecture of Zola's Rougon-Macquarts series. Although Zola may have seen his characters as more or less determined by forces outside their control, *Earth* leaves the impression that men and women can, within limits, choose their course in life. It should be said that some other practitioners of naturalist fiction—such as Frank Norris in the United States—took a much more mechanical approach to the so-called scientific forces that shape human life. In Norris's work, the reader is left with the impression that human freedom is simply low farce. In *Earth*, however, Zola does not communicate this sense of a claustrophobic fate. No matter how awful Fouan's end may be, Zola never shifts the responsibility away from Fouan himself. *Earth* certainly demonstrates the limits and the narrowness of the life of the peasant in nineteenth century France, but within those limits, Zola shows that freedom survives and, with freedom, the refreshing possibilities of birth.

"Critical Evaluation" by Howard Lee Hertz

Further Reading

Berg, William J., and Laurey K. Martin. *Émile Zola Revisited*. New York: Twayne, 1992. Focuses on the Rougon-Macquarts series, using textual analysis and Zola's literary-scientific principles to analyze each of the twenty novels.

Brooks, Peter. "Zola's Combustion Chamber." In *Realist Vision*. New Haven, Conn.: Yale University Press, 2005. Zola's novels are among the works of literature and art examined in this study of the realist tradition in France and England during the nineteenth and twentieth centuries.

Brown, Frederick. *Zola: A Life*. New York: Farrar, Straus and Giroux, 1995. A detailed and extensive biography of Zola that discusses his fiction and the intellectual life of France, of which he was an important part. Shows how Zola's naturalism developed out of the intellectual and the political ferment of his time; argues that this naturalism was a highly studied and artificial approach to reality.

Gallois, William. *Zola: The History of Capitalism*. New York: Peter Lang, 2000. Interprets the Rougon-Macquarts novels as a history of capitalism, drawing connections between Zola's novels and the work of economists and sociologists Karl Marx, Max Weber, and Émile Durkheim. Includes bibliography and index.

Grant, Elliott M. *Émile Zola*. New York: Twayne, 1966. Includes an extensive discussion of *Earth* and concludes that the central concept of the novel concerns the cycle of birth, growth, decay, death, and rebirth. Includes poetic descriptions of La Beauce and informative discussions of dramatic action, subthemes, comedy, character, religion, and politics in the novel.

Hemmings, F. W. J. *Émile Zola*. Oxford, England: Clarendon Press, 1966. Intelligent discussion and criticism of Zola's life and works. Sees *Earth* as Zola's novel of nature, with its emphasis on French peasants' passionate and erotic love for the earth. Concludes that the character Buteau is transported to madness by this lust for the soil.

Knapp, Bettina L. *Émile Zola*. New York: Frederick Ungar, 1980. Handbook-style summaries and analysis of the Rougon-Macquarts cycle. Describes the purpose of *Earth* as a realistic depiction of the life of French peasantry: Zola contrasts love of the soil with avarice, possessiveness, immorality, and cruelty. Knapp also discusses the outraged public and critical reaction to the novel.

Nelson, Brian, ed. *The Cambridge Companion to Émile Zola*. New York: Cambridge University Press, 2007. Collection of essays, including discussions of Zola and the nineteenth century; his depiction of society, sex, and gender; and Zola's utopias. Includes a summary of Zola's novels, a family tree of the Rougon-Macquarts, a bibliography, and an index.

Turnell, Martin. *The Art of French Fiction*. New York: New Directions, 1960. Contains a long, informative chapter on Zola. Discusses naturalism and themes of the Rougon-Macquarts cycle. Includes an analysis of *Earth's* fertility imagery.

The Earthly Paradise

Author: William Morris (1834-1896)
First published: 1868-1870
Type of work: Poetry

Of all the poems of William Morris, the most successful, in terms of popularity, is *The Earthly Paradise*, published originally in five thick volumes. Following closely the plan of Geoffrey Chaucer's *The Canterbury Tales* (1387-1400), this composition reveals Morris's attraction to Chaucer's method as well as his sense of beauty. Like Chaucer, Morris found in medieval legends and ancient myths material for his poetic narrative art, and he also found a general plan according to which these unrelated stories could be brought together harmoniously by a technique in which Eastern cultures had long anticipated Chaucer and other Europeans. Unlike Chaucer, whose plan was so large that he could not complete it, Morris, upon an almost equal scale, brought his work to a happy conclusion.

The prologue introduces a company of Norsemen who have fled the pestilence and set sail to seek the fabled Earthly Paradise "across the western sea where none grow old." Not having succeeded in their quest, they have returned "shrivelled, bent, and grey," after lengthy wanderings abroad, to a "nameless city in a distant sea" where the worship of the ancient Greek gods has not died out. In this hospitable city they spend the rest of their lives. Twice each month they participate in a feast at which a tale is told, alternately, by one of the city elders and one of the wanderers. The former tell tales on classical subjects, and the latter draw their tales from Norse and other medieval sources. Thus, of the twenty-four stories, twelve are Greek and classical and twelve are medieval or romantic. Each pair of stories corresponds with one of the twelve months, the first two being told in January, the second two in February, and so on. Thus the long poem is neatly partitioned into twelve books with interpolated prologues and epilogues in the form of lyrics about the progressive changes in nature. *The Earthly Paradise* actually revived in England an enthusiasm for long romances. Despite their high cost, many thousands of Morris's books were sold, and the effect was a favorable one for the new revival of romantic feeling that Morris was fostering in art and decoration as well as in literature. Instead of exhausting Morris, this poetic effort inspired him to embark on other vast projects such as the translation of Homer and Vergil and a modern version of a Scandinavian epic, *Sigurd the Volsung*.

Among the tales told by the wanderers in *The Earthly Paradise*, the most striking is "The Lovers of Gudrun," a version of the Icelandic Laxdaela Saga. It tells of Gudrun, daughter of a great lord in Iceland, who is loved by many men but especially by Kiartan, a youth of manly deeds and kindly disposition. Although Gudrun passionately returns his love, Kiartan, before he will marry her, goes with his bosom friend and cousin Bodli to seek fame in Norway, where he remains some years at the court of Olaf Trygvesson. When Bodli returns alone to Iceland, he yields to his passion for Gudrun and tells her that Kiartan has fallen in love with King Olaf's sister Ingibiarg and will marry her. Convinced of Kiartan's unfaithfulness, Gudrun brokenheartedly marries Bodli. When Kiartan returns to claim his bride, Gudrun curses Bodli, and the desolate Kiartan, half in contempt, spares his life. Despairing and taunted by those about him, Bodli participates in an ambush set up by Kiartan's enemies, treacherously slays his friend, and is in turn killed by Kiartan's brothers. Although Gudrun marries again, what remains indelibly with the reader is Morris's picture of her agonized realization of what, in her faithlessness, she has done:

> She cried, with tremulous voice, and eyes grown wet
> For the last time, what e'er should happen yet,
> With hands stretched out for all that she had lost:
> "I did the worst to him I loved the most."

Morris was a natural creator; that his hand could not outspeed his brain is evidenced by his composing seven hundred lines of poetry in a day. Years after the composition of *The Earthly Paradise* he explained the nonchalant attitude toward the writing of poetry that enabled him to race undaunted through that enormous project: "Waiting for inspiration, rushing things in reliance on inspiration, and all the rest of it, are a lazy man's habits. Get the bones of the work well into your head, and the tools well into your hand, and get on with the job, and the inspiration will come to you."

In spite of its quantity, his poetry has a remarkably high quality. Although somewhat lacking in humor, pathos, and rich humanity, it shows none of the crabbed complaints of many poets. His range of subject matter is as broad as his composition was fluent. The very spacious cycle of stories in *The Earthly Paradise* includes these titles: "The Story of Theseus," "The Son of Croesus," "Cupid and Psyche," "The King's Treasure-House," "Orpheus and Eurydice," "Pygmalion," "Atalanta's Race," "The Doom of King Acrisius," "Rhodope," "The Dolphin and the Lovers," "The Fortunes of Gygis," "Bellerophon," "The Watching of the Falcon," "The Lady of the Land," "The Hill of Venus," "The Seven Sleepers," "The Man Who Never Laughed Again," "The Palace East of the Sun," "The Queen of the North," "The Story of Dorothea," "The Writing on the Image," "The Proud King," "The Ring Given to Venus," and "The Man Born to Be King."

These stories are so arranged that, with the revolving calendar, their temper becomes darker and stronger, developing into a sinister tone at the end. The full effect thus depends upon a continuous and consecutive reading. Conversely, the problem that arises as the reader progresses through this lengthy work is that the embroidery becomes too profuse to be sustained by the fabric. The result is the taint of decoration inherent in the Pre-Raphaelites—too much of beauty, love, languor, everything—so that the reader longs for a little substantial simplicity and cheerfulness. One might, therefore, argue for an occasional and selective reading of the stories, so long as their total scope is kept in mind.

The interludes give readers glimpses into the poet's mind, and these glimpses give evidence that despite his disapproval of introspective poetry, Morris did not always avoid it. While the stories of *The Earthly Paradise* come from all parts of the medieval world, these poems of the months are unequivocally English; they give an admiring description of the land of Morris's birth and life. With variations, they repeat the keynote of the prologue in which he characterizes himself as "the idle singer of an empty day" who has no power to sing of hell or heaven or to make death bearable. By "idle" Morris does not mean "useless" but, rather, one who can, by the scenes he presents, distract from "empty," daily cares. In this manner he acknowledged spiritual emptiness in his time.

Throughout this poetic work there runs a strain of despondency, doubt, and mild skepticism that records the poet's genuine pity for humanity. Although there is in the work an elemental vigor, glorying in youth, power, love, and possessions, these aspects of life are presented primarily through old men's memories. Despite the swift-moving action, the narrative generally seems grandly slow. Neither the tale-tellers nor the actors in the tales are particularly individualized as characters. Finally, readers see a vast, intricate tapestry with its panorama of interwoven figures.

Further Reading

Boos, Florence Saunders. *The Design of William Morris' "The Earthly Paradise."* Lewiston, N.Y.: Edwin Mellen Press, 1990. An analysis of the literary design of *The Earthly Paradise*. Discusses the literary structure of the work, the influences and sources for the poems, and their critical reception.

Calhoun, Blue. *The Pastoral Vision of William Morris: "The Earthly Paradise."* Athens: University of Georgia Press, 1975. Places *The Earthly Paradise* within the genre of the pastoral; this perspective reveals motifs that can be connected to Morris's socialism and artistic endeavors.

Clutton-Brock, Arthur. *William Morris.* New York: Parkstone Press, 2007. Biography chronicling Morris's multifaceted career, including his work as a poet and prose writer.

Helsinger, Elizabeth K. *Poetry and the Pre-Raphaelite Arts: Dante Gabriel Rossetti and William Morris.* New Haven, Conn.: Yale University Press, 2008. Examines the works of the two poet-artists in order to describe the aesthetics of the Pre-Raphaelite movement and its expression in both literature and art. Chapter 8, "Designing *The Earthly Paradise*," focuses on this work.

Hodgson, Amanda. *The Romances of William Morris.* New York: Cambridge University Press, 1987. Examines why Morris used the genre of romance as a vehicle to express his views. A chapter analyzes *The Earthly Paradise* as a romance within the context of Morris's development of this literary form.

Le Bourgeois, John Y. *Art and Forbidden Fruit: Hidden Passion in the Life of William Morris.* Cambridge, England: Lutterworth Press, 2006. An analysis of Morris's life and poetry, describing his attachment to his sister Emma, who was a source of inspiration for his work.

Skoblow, Jeffrey. *Paradise Dislocated: Morris, Politics, Art.* Charlottesville: University Press of Virginia, 1993. Sets *The Earthly Paradise* within the context of modernism and Marxism. Argues that *The Earthly Paradise* expresses a sense of estrangement or dislocation that is a part of modern culture.

Thomas, Jane. "Morris and the Muse: Gender and Aestheticism in William Morris's *Pymgalion and the Image*." In *Writing on the Image: Reading William Morris*, edited by David Latham. Toronto, Ont.: University of Toronto Press, 2007. A close reading of one of the poems in *The Earthly Paradise*.

Tompkins, J. M. S. *William Morris: An Approach to the Poetry.* London: Cecil Woolf, 1988. A complete study of the poetic works, including prose romances, written by Morris. Two chapters are devoted to analysis of *The Earthly Paradise*, examining what the poems reveal about Morris's feelings about society and his life.

Earthsea Trilogy

Author: Ursula K. Le Guin (1929-)
First published: 1968-1972; includes *A Wizard of Earthsea*, 1968; *The Tombs of Atuan*, 1971; *The Farthest Shore*, 1972
Type of work: Novels
Type of plot: Fantasy
Time of plot: Eleventh century after King Morred's coronation
Locale: Earthsea, a realm of islands and ocean

Principal characters:
SPARROWHAWK (true name GED), a wizard and eventually archmage
TENAR, also called Arha, a high priestess
VETCH (true name ESTARRIOL), a village wizard and Ged's friend
OGION THE SILENT, a wizard from Ged's home island, who becomes his mentor
ARREN (true name LEBANNEN), a prince and later King of All the Isles
COB, a sorcerer who delves into the magic of the dead
ORM EMBAR,
KALESSIN, and
YEVAUD, dragons

The Story:

Duny is the last of seven sons of the bronzesmith of the village of Ten Alders, on the island of Gont. His mother dies before he is one year old, and his much older brothers have already left the village. Neglected by his father, Duny runs wild, but his life changes when he hears his aunt use a mysterious word to call a goat off a roof. When Duny uses the word, all the goats in the village follow him and refuse to go away until his aunt gets rid of them. She is the village witch, and she realizes that Duny has an affinity for magic. She explains to him that the mysterious word he used was the true name for goats; everything and everyone in Earthsea has a true, hidden name, and an everyday "use name," and magic is the art of finding and using true names to exert power over things and people.

Duny's aunt teaches him everything that she knows and encourages him to believe that his skills will bring him wealth and power. She does not tell Duny that his skills are far beyond her own. When the island is invaded by Kargish soldiers, Duny uses his power to protect Ten Alders by cloaking it in fog. In doing so, he overstretches himself, falling ill as a result. He is healed by Ogion the Silent, the mage (wizard) of the town of Re Albi, who recognizes Duny's potential and offers to teach him. Later in the year, Ogion gives Duny his true name, Ged (Ged will be known to most people by his adult "use name," Sparrowhawk). Ged returns with Ogion to Re Albi.

Ged is initially disappointed in Ogion's teachings. While his aunt taught him spells and charms and promised him greatness, Ogion performs no unnecessary magic and teaches Ged very little of immediate, obvious value. Instead, the wizard attempts to teach Ged to see the world as a set of interre-

lated parts and to show him that magic has consequences of which every mage must be aware. Names represent power, and spells should not be used lightly. However, Ged is impatient to achieve great things. As a result, he is tempted by the daughter of the lord of Re Albi into finding a spell to summon the spirits of the dead. When Ged secretly consults Ogion's books of spells, he finds the right spell, but even while simply reading it, he seems to have summoned a mysterious black shadow. The shadow is dispelled by Ogion's arrival home, but Ogion realizes that Ged is hungry for overt training in spellcasting and sends him to the School for Wizards on Roke.

At Roke, Ged begins his formal education in the "art magic." Again he learns quickly, his abilities are recognized, and he makes swift progress. He has few friends, however, and his pride makes him quick to see an insult when none is intended. Most of the other students avoid him, but he does not mind. However, what starts as a light-hearted magical duel one night turns to tragedy when Ged believes that he has been mocked by Jasper, another of the students. Ged agrees to summon a dead spirit and uses the spell he first read in Ogion's book. Although he briefly summons the spirit of Elfarran, a beautiful heroine of legend, Ged also releases the black shadow into the world, and it attacks him, severely injuring him physically and mentally. The Archmage Nemmerle repairs the resulting hole in the fabric of the world, but he dies as a result. Ged is ill for many months, and when he recovers sufficiently to resume his studies he has changed greatly, desiring only peace and solitude to study and make amends for his actions.

When Ged finishes his training and becomes a wizard, he is sent to Low Torning, a place under threat from the dragons

of Pendor. He lives peacefully in the village until, while trying to save a dying child, he confronts the shadow once again.
From then on, it haunts his dreams, and he knows that he
must find it. First, he goes to Pendor to remove the threat to
the village in his charge. He is able to negotiate a peace with
Yevaud, the Dragon of Pendor, because he has learned its true
name. Although Yevaud offers to tell him the name of the
shadow, he puts the good of the villagers ahead of his own
and instead makes the dragon promise that it and its offspring
will not bother the people of the Archipelago ever again.

Ged then begins a journey across the Archipelago, trying
to discover the nature of the shadow that haunts him. He is led
to the Court of the Terrenon on Osskil, where he meets
Serret, who is married to the lord of the Terrenon. The
Terrenon is a stone that contains an ancient and evil spirit,
and Ged fears for the woman's safety, until, belatedly, he recognizes her as the daughter of the lord of Re Albi, who plans
to use Ged and the Terrenon for her own ends. Ged escapes,
returns to Ogion at Re Albi, and finally sets out to hunt the
shadow. On the way, he is shipwrecked on an island where an
old man and an old woman abandoned there since childhood
live in extreme poverty,. They help him, and the old woman
gives him part of a ring as a gift. Finally, traveling with his old
friend, Vetch, Ged meets the shadow and subdues it by calling it by his own name, having realized that it is a part of himself and that he needs to embrace it to be healed.

The broken piece of the ring leads Ged to his second adventure in *The Tombs of Atuan*. It is, however, narrated not
from his point of view but from that of Arha, the Eaten One.
Arha is an adolescent girl who is being raised as the priestess
of the Nameless Ones, destined to spend her life at the Place
of the Tombs. She was chosen to be the priestess when very
young, taken from her family, and brought up under the
guardianship of Thar, high priestess of the Twin Ones, and
Kossil, high priestess of the Godking. She is also tended by
Manan, a eunuch. As Arha grows older, she is trained to become the priestess and becomes aware that there are things,
such as the Labyrinth of the tombs, to which she alone has access. However, she is also aware that Kossil wishes to retain
as much power as she can, believing that the Nameless Ones
are no longer active and that only the living Godking now has
any relevance. Arha is desperate to escape because she fears
Kossil (who has already forced Arha to accept the Godking's
prisoners as sacrifices), but she can only find freedom when
she ventures into the parts of the temple where Kossil cannot
go, in particular the Undertomb and the Labyrinth.

One day, Arha finds a young man in the Labyrinth. He is
revealed as Ged, who has come to Atuan to search for the
other part of the ring he had been given. He has discovered

that it is a piece of the lost Ring of Erreth-Akbe. The return to
Havnor of the whole ring will bring about the restoration of
the Lost Rune, signaling the fulfilment of a prophecy and
bringing peace to Earthsea. Ged believes that the lost half lies
in the treasury of the Place of Tombs, but Arha traps him in
the Labyrinth and his powers wane because of the influence
of the Nameless Ones.

Arha decides to help Ged, but she conceals her decision
from Kossil by claiming that the wizard has been sacrificed.
Kossil, however, is suspicious, and Arha is forced to move
Ged deeper into the Labyrinth. Imprisoned in the Treasury,
he locates the missing piece of the ring. Arha returns, knowing that Kossil is aware that Ged has not died and that they
must now leave. Ged unifies the lost ring, and the two of them
escape from the Labyrinth, but the Nameless Ones bring
down the Tombs. Ged has given Arha back her right name,
Tenar. She agrees to travel with him to Havnor to return the
ring, but Ged also agrees that afterward he will take her to
Ogion on Gont, because she wishes to live quietly and atone
for what she sees as her sins.

In the final part of the Earthsea trilogy, *The Farthest
Shore*, Ged has become the archmage at Roke. He receives a
visitor, Arren, Prince of Enlad, who has been sent by his father to report that magic seems to be disappearing from the
world. Sorcerers are losing the ability to cast spells, and people are also forgetting that magic ever existed in the world.
As Arren's father describes it, words seem to have lost their
meaning. The mages on Roke are already aware that this is
happening, but Arren is disappointed that he cannot take an
explanation or solution home to his father. He determines to
stay on Roke and serve the archmage in whatever way possible, but his offer, while not rejected, is not accepted.

The nine masters of Roke and the archmage meet and determine that although the Ring of the Runes of the king has
been returned to Havnor, it is now necessary to find the king
himself to reestablish order in the world. Ged announces that
he will make the journey to discover why magic is vanishing
and that Arren will accompany him. The other mages are reluctant to let him go but finally accept the need. Ged and
Arren begin a journey that takes them through the Archipelago, where they find much evidence of the loss of magic. On
Wathort, they meet with a wizard, Hare, who claims that he
has traded his power for another power, believing that he has
in some way transcended death. With the help of a drug,
hazia, he travels in his own mind to other places. Ged attempts to follow him, but, while in a trance, he is attacked and
robbed, and Arren is kidnapped and sold to slave traders. Ged
finds and releases him, and they continue their journey
through the Archipelago.

Now traveling with a companion, Sopli, they are attacked by islanders on Obehol. Sopli is drowned, Ged is wounded, and the boat, *Lookfar*, drifts out of control. Ged and Arren drift in the boat, dying of thirst, until they are rescued by the Children of the Open Sea, who live on giant rafts in the seas beyond any islands. They nurse Ged back to health, and the two travel with them. Arren is haunted by the fact that he did nothing to help Ged and was afraid of dying, but Ged reassures him. He understands now that magic is vanishing from the world because people are trying to shut out the fear of death, whereas he recognizes that death is a part of life. Someone is teaching them that death can be ignored or overcome. Arren serves as his guide because he is young and afraid of death, whereas Ged himself no longer is.

The dragon, Orm Embar, comes to find Ged, because his people are threatened by a dragonlord. They travel to the island of Selidor, where they confront the mysterious dragonlord, revealed as a man called Cob, whom Ged has met before, when he discovered him using spells to bring back the dead. Cob promises people eternal life but holds power over them, and has styled himself as ruler of the land of the dead. He attacks Ged, but Orm Embar sacrifices his own life for Ged. Ged and Arren follow Cob further into the dead lands, where they discover the hole he has opened between the lands of the dead and the living. Ged uses all of his power to close this hole. Cob, deprived of a way to move between the two lands, joins the ranks of the dead people. Ged and Arren journey back to the land of the living and are rescued there by Kalessin, who takes them back to Roke. Arren is recognized as the new King of All the Isles. Ged, now powerless, retires from the world of "doing," probably to Gont.

Critical Evaluation:

At the heart of the Earthsea Trilogy is a deep concern with the power of words. The magic practiced by the wizards of Earthsea is predicated on knowing and using the correct words and meanings to create effective spells. This reflects Ursula K. Le Guin's wider concerns about the craft of writing and the ways in which language is used. When Ged, in childhood, uses the True Speech to call the goats, he gets into trouble in part because he doesn't understand what he is doing when he says the words, using them indiscriminately. Likewise, when he saves his village through the use of magic, although he is successful it is at great personal cost because he does not fully understand how to use his own power, as he does not yet have all the right words available to him. However, he wins through in part because his motives are pure, in that he seeks to protect his village and his people rather than to gain personal advancement.

This theme points in turn to another significant issue concerning the use of magic. Throughout the trilogy, great emphasis is laid on the fact that "good" magic is not employed for personal gain or self-aggrandizement. While Earthsea's wizards are generally supported by the communities in which they live, the understanding is that the relationship is mutual. The wizard's role is to help the community in whatever ways seem appropriate rather than to accrue personal wealth. Wizards are often paid in kind or else work for nothing. When Ged performs the transformation that releases the black shadow into the world, his act is driven by pride and a desire to prove himself better than others rather than to benefit the world. Ged's subsequent life as a wizard is marked by his need to make redress and destroy the shadow that has come into the world. He has learned compassion, moderation, and humility, key tenets in Taoism, a belief system that Le Guin draws on heavily in constructing her world.

Taoist beliefs are also expressed in the philosophy of balance that shapes Earthsea. The wizard's role is to maintain that balance, and Le Guin continually emphasizes the difference between magic that creates illusion and magic that effects permanent transformation. The consequences of every change that is made as a result of a magical transformation must be considered before the spell is cast. Changes cannot always be undone, and they often bring with them unwanted side effects. While the shadow exists in Earthsea, the world is unbalanced, and it is necessary for Ged to resolve this situation. Ged's quests, first to the Tombs of Atuan to retrieve the piece of the Ring of Erreth-Akbe and later, with Arren, to restore magic to Earthsea, are both driven by the need to keep the world in balance.

Le Guin's own interest in anthropology (her father was the anthropologist Alfred L. Kroeber, best known for his work with Ishi, the "last" Yahi Indian) is demonstrated in the diversity of societies she creates within her work, and in her detailed portrayal of everyday life. One of the most striking aspects of the Earthsea Trilogy is that the majority of the characters are persons of color. Ged is reddish-brown in coloring, and Vetch is black. Only the barbaric peoples of the Kargish islands are white-skinned. Le Guin was one of the first fantasy writers to address issues of ethnicity in this fashion.

Similarly, Le Guin's interests in Taoism and ethnography are expressed in her explorations of different cultures and belief systems: *The Farthest Shore* can, for example, be read as a critique of the effects of Christianity introduced into a world with a very different understanding of the relationship between life and death. Similarly, in *The Tombs of Atuan*, the struggle between Arha and Kossil can be read on a personal level and on a spiritual level, as a polytheistic and a monotheistic religious system vie for a spiritual supremacy that cannot and, indeed, should not be achieved.

Le Guin has been criticized for her portrayal of women in the Earthsea Trilogy. The Wizards' School on Roke is an entirely male preserve, and while women are shown to perform magic, their lack of formal training implies that their magic is of lesser importance, often weaker, and often inimical to maintaining the balance. Women occupy limited roles as homemakers or as duplicitous creatures who seek to undermine men and gain power. Even Arha, as priestess, finds her role circumscribed by a male-dominated religion against which she is seemingly powerless. Le Guin has acknowledged this criticism and has sought to redress the balance in her later novels set in Earthsea, *Tehanu: The Last Book of Earthsea* (1990) and *The Other Wind* (2001), which give more agency to women, in particular, following Tenar in her subsequent life and relationship with Ged. Le Guin's book of short stories set in Earthsea, *Tales from Earthsea* (2001), delves into the history of magic and of Roke, and it explains how women came to be relegated to the place they occupy in Archipelagan society at the time portrayed in the trilogy.

Maureen Kincaid Speller

Further Reading

Bernardo, Susan M., and Graham J. Murphy. *Ursula K. Le Guin: A Critical Companion*. Westport, Conn.: Greenwood Press, 2006. A useful introduction to Le Guin's fantasy and science-fiction writings; includes discussions of individual volumes of the Earthsea Trilogy.

Bloom, Harold, ed. *Ursula K. Le Guin*. New York: Chelsea House, 1986. Contains a wide range of essays on Le Guin's work, including the Earthsea Trilogy.

Cummins, Elizabeth. *Understanding Ursula K. Le Guin*. Columbia: University of South Carolina Press, 1993. Contains a substantial chapter on the Earthsea novels.

Le Guin, Ursula K. *Conversations with Ursula K. Le Guin*. Edited by Carl Freedman. Jackson: University Press of Mississippi, 2008. A compilation of interviews with Le Guin, conducted over a period of twenty-five years, in which the writer discusses many aspects of her writing.

_____. *Dancing at the Edge of the World*. New York: Grove Press, 1989.

_____. *The Language of the Night: Essays on Fantasy and Science Fiction*. London: Women's Press, 1989. Two classic collections of the writer's own essays and articles, which discuss many of the issues raised in her fiction.

East of Eden

Author: John Steinbeck (1902-1968)
First published: 1952
Type of work: Novel
Type of plot: Regional
Time of plot: 1865-1918
Locale: California

Principal characters:
ADAM TRASK, a settler in the Salinas Valley
CATHY AMES, later Adam's wife
CALEB TRASK and ARON TRASK, their twin sons
CHARLES TRASK, Adam's half brother
SAMUEL HAMILTON, a neighbor of the Trasks
LEE, Adam's Chinese servant
ABRA BACON, Aron's fiancé

The Story:

The soil of the Salinas Valley in California is rich, although the surrounding foothills are poor and life shrivels during the long dry spells. The Irish-born Hamiltons, arriving after American settlers displaced the Mexicans, settle on the barren hillside. Sam Hamilton, full of talk, glory, and improvident inventions, and Liza, his dourly religious wife, bring up their nine children there.

In Connecticut, Adam Trask and his half brother Charles grow up in harmony despite the differences in their natures. Adam is gentle and good; Charles is roughly handsome and has a streak of wild violence. After Adam's mother commits suicide, his father marries the docile woman who becomes Charles's mother. Adam loves his stepmother but hates his father, a rigid disciplinarian whose fanatic militarism begins with a fictitious account of his own war career and whose dream is to have a son in the army. He hopes to fulfill his dream through Adam. Charles, whose passionate love for his father goes continually unnoticed, cannot understand this rejection of himself. In despair, he beats Adam almost to death.

Adam serves in the cavalry for five years. Then, although he hates regimentation and violence, he reenlists, for he can neither accept help from his father, who became an important figure in Washington, nor return to the farm Charles now runs alone. Afterward, Adam wanders through the West and the South, serving time for vagrancy, and finally comes home to find that his father has died, making him and Charles rich. In the years that follow, the two brothers live together on the farm. Their bickering and inbred solitude drives Adam to periodic wanderings. Feeling that their life is one of pointless industry, he talks of moving west but he does not do anything about it.

Meanwhile, Cathy Ames is growing up in Massachusetts. She is born unable to comprehend goodness, but she has a sublimely innocent face and a consummate knowledge of how to manipulate and deceive others to serve her own ends. After a thwarted attempt to leave home, she burns down her parents' house, killing them, and leaves evidence to indicate that she was murdered. She becomes the mistress of a man who runs a string of brothels and uses his love for her against him. When he realizes her true nature, he takes her to a deserted spot and beats her savagely. Near death, she crawls to the nearest house—the Trasks'—where Adam and Charles care for her. Adam thinks her innocent and beautiful; Charles, who has an empathetic knowledge of evil, wants her to leave. Cathy, who knows she temporarily needs protection, entices Adam into marrying her. On their wedding night, she gives him a sleeping draught and goes to Charles.

Aware that Charles disapproves of Cathy, Adam decides to carry out his dream of going west. He is so transfigured by his happiness that he ignores Cathy's protests; since she is his ideal of love and purity, he thinks that she cannot disagree with him. Adam buys a ranch in the richest part of the Salinas Valley and works hard to prepare it for his wife and the child she expects. Cathy hates her pregnancy and tries unsuccessfully to abort the child. After giving birth to twin boys, she recuperates for a week; she then shoots Adam, wounding him, and leaves, abandoning her sons.

Changing her name to Kate, Cathy goes to work in a Salinas brothel. Her beauty and seeming goodness endear her to the proprietress, Faye, and Kate gradually assumes control of the establishment. After Faye makes a will leaving Kate her money and property, Kate engineers Faye's death. Making her establishment one that arouses and caters to sadistic tastes, she becomes legendary and rich.

Adam is like a dead man for a year after his wife leaves him, unable to work his land or even to name his sons. Finally, Sam Hamilton awakens him by deliberately angering him. Sam, Adam, and Lee, the Chinese servant and a wise and good man, name the boys Caleb and Aron. The men talk of the story of Cain and Abel, and Lee declares that rejection terrifies a child and leads to guilt and to revenge. Later, after much study, Lee discovers the true meaning of the Hebrew word *timshel* (thou mayest) and understands that the story means in part that man can always choose to conquer evil.

Sam grows old and he knows that he will soon die. Before he leaves his ranch, he tells Adam about Kate and her cruel, destructive business. Adam visits her and suddenly knows her as she really is. Though she taunts him, telling him that Charles is the true father of his sons, and tries to seduce him, he leaves her a free and curiously exultant man. However, he is unable to bring himself to tell his sons that their mother is not dead.

Caleb and Aron grow up very differently. Golden-haired Aron inspires love without trying, but he is single-minded and unyielding; Caleb is dark and clever, a feared and respected leader whom others leave much alone. When Adam moves to town, where the schools are better, Aron falls in love with Abra Bacon, who tells him that his mother is still alive. Aron cannot believe her because to do so will destroy his faith in his father.

About this time, Adam has the idea of shipping lettuce packed in ice to New York. When the venture fails, Aron is ashamed of his father for failing publicly. Caleb vows to return the lost money to his father. As they face the problems of growing into men, Aron becomes smugly religious, which is disturbing to Abra because she feels unable to live up to his idealistic image of her. Caleb alternates between wild impulses and guilt. Learning that Kate is his mother, he begins following her until she, noticing him, invites him to her house. As he talks to her, he knows with relief that he is not like her; she feels his knowledge and hates him. Kate, obsessed by the fear that one of the old girls has discovered Faye's murder, plots ways to destroy this menace. Although Caleb can accept Kate's existence, he knows that Aron cannot. To get the boy away from Salinas, Caleb talks him into finishing high school in three years and beginning college. Adam, knowing nothing of Caleb's true character, is extravagantly proud of Aron.

When World War I breaks out, Caleb goes into the bean business with Will Hamilton and makes a fortune because of food shortages. With growing excitement, he plans an elaborate presentation to his father of the money once lost in the lettuce enterprise. First he tries to persuade Aron, who seems indifferent to his father's love, not to leave college. Caleb presents his money to Adam, only to have it rejected in anger because Adam's idealistic nature cannot accept money made as profit from the war. He wants Caleb's achievements to be like his brother's. In a black mood of revenge, Caleb takes Aron to meet his mother. After her sons' visit, Kate, who is not as disturbed by those she can hurt as she is by someone like Caleb, makes a will leaving everything to Aron. Then, burdened by age, illness, and suspiciousness, she commits suicide.

Aron, unable to face the new knowledge of his parents' past, joins the army and goes to France. Adam does not recover from the shock of his leaving. Abra turns to Caleb, admitting that she loves him rather than Aron, whose romantic stubbornness keeps him from facing reality. When the news of Aron's death arrives, Adam has another stroke. As he lies dying, Caleb, unable to bear his guilt any longer, tells his father of his responsibility for Aron's enlisting and thus his death. Lee begs Adam to forgive his son. Adam weakly raises his hand in benediction and, whispering the Hebrew word *timshel*, dies.

Critical Evaluation:

When John Steinbeck received the Nobel Prize in Literature in 1962, critics considered *The Grapes of Wrath* (1939) his best work, but Steinbeck himself always believed *East of Eden* to be his greatest achievement. The novel disappointed critics upon its first appearance because they were expecting something resembling his previous works. However, in *East of Eden* Steinbeck departed from his usual concise narration to explore complex philosophical and psychological themes about which he had been preparing to write since the late 1930's. As a fictional epic of the area around Salinas, California, where Steinbeck had grown up, the subject is much more personal than that of previous books. In fact, Steinbeck names himself as the grandson of the model for Sam Hamilton. The epic traces the history of two families—one a deteriorating New England family and the other a large family of recent Irish immigrants.

The novel's central theme is the struggle of good against evil, most obviously symbolized by the recurring discussion of the story of Cain and Abel. Steinbeck presents characters in pairs—Adam and Charles, Aron and Caleb, Abra and Cathy—using first initials to identify clearly which characters are inherently good and which must struggle to overcome the seeds of evil within them. Associated with this theme is the Hebrew word *timshel* (thou mayest). In the Old Testament,

God tells Cain that he may overcome evil and gain salvation. *Timshel* does not command that he must overcome evil or guarantee that he will; rather, it provides the opportunity to overcome evil if he chooses to do so. Ironically, it is Lee, the Chinese Presbyterian, who appeals to a group of Confucian scholars to solve the meaning of *timshel*. After learning Hebrew and spending months reading and discussing the Talmud, they give Lee the answer: "Thou mayest." *Timshel* appears again at the end of the novel when Adam, paralyzed by a stroke, whispers the word to Caleb, who has just confessed the evil he has done by taking Aron to meet Kate. The father tells the son, "thou mayest." Hence, the answer to Steinbeck's urgent question—can human beings overcome evil?—is left undetermined.

The philosophical discussion of *timshel* also influences the psychological portions of the novel. Through Steinbeck's explorations of how trying to overcome evil affects the human mind, the reader sees unsettling glimpses of the darkness of the human soul. Customers at Kate's house of prostitution illustrate the varieties of torture and perversion of which the human mind is capable.

"Eden" as symbol for both the biblical garden and the Salinas Valley in Northern California also has ambiguous meaning. Parts of the valley are lush and fertile, but others, like the Hamilton farm, are virtual wastelands—dry and barren. Even the lush Trask ranch is a deceptive ambiguous Eden: Although it is one of the most fertile properties in the county, the fields, orchards, and gardens have been allowed to go wild and the deteriorating old house crumbles to ruins.

In addition to its literary merits, *East of Eden* offers a wealth of social and historical information. In tracing the history of two families, Steinbeck depicts the waves of settlers passing through California, first the Mexicans, then the white Americans, and finally the Irish immigrants. A community cringes at the arrival of its first automobile and gets a lesson on how to crank-start a Ford. New inventions either work (Sam's new windmill) or dreadfully fail (Adam's attempt to exploit icebox railroad freight cars). Through Caleb and Will Hamilton, Steinbeck shows how profitable speculating in food was during wartime, and through Cathy Trask and Kate Ames, he shows a great deal about organized prostitution across the country.

Since the late 1970's, some significant trends developed in the criticism of *East of Eden*. No longer content to say merely that the novel is not like the rest of Steinbeck's work, critics began looking for value in the differences. Whereas earlier novels are more naturalistic, objective, and detached, *East of Eden* is more subjective and personal. Steinbeck remained satisfied with that work's indeterminacy rather than striving to make order where none exists. After a period in which studies focused primarily on the Trask men and Sam Hamilton, criticism turned to some of the peripheral characters, mainly women, and their contribution to the complex fabric of Salinas society. These included perseverant Eliza, Dassie, in whose relaxed dress shop women could laugh and break wind, and Lee, the Trasks' Chinese servant, who is really the voice of wisdom and reason—the mouthpiece for Steinbeck's own views on philosophy and religion. In 1952, readers were not ready for a book like *East of Eden* from an author like John Steinbeck, but the novel seems to age like the fine fermented apple wine in Lee's jug—it gets better with each critical discussion, and its content never diminishes.

East of Eden's psychological explorations of good and evil find predecessors in nineteenth century American novels such as Nathaniel Hawthorne's *The Scarlet Letter* (1850) or Herman Melville's *Moby Dick* (1851). At the same time, in its thorough, almost encyclopedic chronicling of Salinas's places, people, and events, Steinbeck's techniques foreshadow those used by William Kennedy in his Albany novels such as *Ironweed* (1983) and *Quinn's Book* (1988), for example. Steinbeck's comfort with indeterminacy also suggests a connection to other postmodern fiction.

"Critical Evaluation" by Geralyn Strecker

Further Reading

DeMott, Robert J. *Steinbeck's Typewriter: Essays on His Art.* Troy, N.Y.: Whitston, 1997. Three of the essays examine *East of Eden*: "'A Great Black Book': *East of Eden* and *Gunn's New Family Physician*," "'Working at the Impossible': The Presence of *Moby-Dick* in *East of Eden*," and "'This Book to a Man': Charting a Bibliographical Preface to *East of Eden*."

Etheridge, Charles L., Jr. "Changing Attitudes Toward Steinbeck's Naturalism and the Changing Reputation of *East of Eden*: A Survey of Criticism Since 1974." In *The Steinbeck Question: New Essays in Criticism*, edited by Donald R. Noble. Troy, N.Y.: Whitston, 1993. Discusses the novel's disastrous reception in 1952 and its improving critical reputation since.

George, Stephen K., and Barbara A. Heavilin, eds. *John Steinbeck and His Contemporaries.* Lanham, Md.: Scarecrow Press, 2007. A collection of papers from a 2006 conference about Steinbeck and the writers who influenced or informed his work. Some of the essays discuss his European forebears, particularly Henry Fielding and Sir Thomas Malory, and his American forebears, such as Walt Whitman and Sarah Orne Jewett, while other essays compare his work to Ernest Hemingway, William Faulkner, and other twentieth century American writers. Contains two essays on *East of Eden* by Barbara Heavilin, one describing the influence of Fielding on the novel, and the other comparing depictions of good and evil in *East of Eden* and Toni Morrison's *Sula*.

Gladstein, Mimi R. "The Strong Female Principle of Good—or Evil: The Women of *East of Eden*." *Steinbeck Quarterly* 24, nos. 1/2 (Winter/Spring, 1991): 30-40. This significant discussion of women in the novel divides the female characters into the Trask women and the Hamilton women. Calls Abra the principle of good, the second Eve, and the mother of future generations.

Hayashi, Tetsumaro. "The 'Chinese Servant' in *East of Eden*." *San Jose Studies* 18, no. 1 (Winter, 1992): 52-60. On one level, Lee, an ignored, often invisible character, is a stereotypical servant, but he also provides a bridge between the spiritual and material worlds and offers an objective, transcendent view of life. Praises Lee's multifaceted role as servant, manager, surrogate parent, preacher, and scholar.

Meyer, Michael J., ed. *The Betrayal of Brotherhood in the Work of John Steinbeck.* Lewiston, N.Y.: Edwin Mellen Press, 2000. Describes how Steinbeck adapted the biblical story of Cain and Abel in many of his works, most notably in *East of Eden*. Five of the essays examine this novel, including discussions of its depiction of father-son relationships, the significance of Nomos, and the dissolution of the curse of Cain.

Simmonds, Roy S. *A Biographical and Critical Introduction of John Steinbeck.* Lewiston, N.Y.: E. Mellen Press, 2000. Charts Steinbeck's evolution as a writer from 1929 through 1968, discussing the themes of his works and the concepts and philosophies that influenced his depictions of human nature and the psyche. Interweaves details about his writings with accounts of his personal life.

Steinbeck, John. *Journal of a Novel: The "East of Eden" Letters.* New York: Viking, 1969. Steinbeck used this journal, in the form of a letter to his friend and editor Pascal Covici, to work out problems with plot and subject matter. It is an indispensable companion to the novel.

Timmerman, John H. *John Steinbeck's Fiction: The Aesthetics of the Road Taken.* Norman: University of Oklahoma Press, 1986. The chapter on *East of Eden* argues that Cathy is the thematic and structural center of the novel, a Satan figure against whom all others are measured.

Eastward Ho!

Authors: George Chapman (c. 1559-1634), Ben Jonson (1573-1637), and John Marston (1576-1634)
First produced: 1605; first published, 1605
Type of work: Drama
Type of plot: Comedy
Time of plot: c. 1605
Locale: London

Principal characters:
TOUCHSTONE, a goldsmith
MISTRESS TOUCHSTONE, his wife
GERTRUDE, his haughty daughter
MILDRED, his dutiful daughter
FRANCIS QUICKSILVER, his idle and prodigal apprentice
GOLDING, his diligent apprentice
SIR PETRONEL FLASH, a new-made knight
SECURITY, an old usurer
WINIFRED, his young wife
SINDEFY, Quicksilver's mistress

The Story:

Touchstone, a goldsmith, has two daughters, Gertrude, a flutter-brained social climber, and Mildred, a modest, gentle girl. He also has two apprentices, Francis Quicksilver, a fellow as unstable as his name, and Golding, who is steady and conscientious. Caught while trying to slip away from the shop, Quicksilver makes a spirited defense of his way of life, especially of his prodigality among the town gallants. Touchstone answers with a severe moral lecture and points out the exemplary behavior of his fellow apprentice. The lecture is interrupted by a messenger from Sir Petronel Flash, who wishes to make arrangements to marry Gertrude. As soon as Touchstone is out of hearing, Quicksilver abuses the old citizen; Golding defends his master and warns and rebukes Quicksilver.

Mildred, with the help of a tailor and a maid, attires Gertrude elegantly to receive her knight, while Gertrude rattles away, full of herself and contemptuous of her bourgeois family. Touchstone brings in Sir Petronel and concludes the arrangements for the wedding, warning both Gertrude and the knight that they need not expect any gifts beyond the agreed dowry. Gertrude treats him impudently and leaves with the knight, with Mistress Touchstone fluttering in attendance on her soon-to-be-married daughter. After their departure, Touchstone proposes a match between Mildred and Golding.

From the wedding feast Quicksilver returns to the shop drunk, hiccuping and quoting lines from popular plays. Touchstone, losing patience with the fellow, releases him from his indenture and discharges him. After Quicksilver's defiant and staggering exit, Touchstone tells Golding that he, too, will no longer be an apprentice, but a full-fledged member of the guild and his master's son-in-law. At the home of old Security, where Quicksilver and his mistress Sindefy live, the old usurer plots with them to trap Sir Petronel and to

gain possession of Gertrude's property. Quicksilver is to encourage the knight to borrow money for a proposed voyage to Virginia, and both Quicksilver and Sindefy, who is to become Gertrude's maid, are to encourage the bride to put up her land to cover the debt. Before leaving to set his plans in motion, Security delays to bid farewell to his pretty young wife, Winifred.

Sir Petronel confesses to Quicksilver that he has no castle, but that he intends to send his bride on a wild goose chase to an imaginary castle in the country in order to get her out of the way while he carries off old Security's young wife on the Virginia voyage. Security brings in Sindefy and places her with Gertrude as a maid, then takes Sir Petronel to his home for breakfast. Captain Seagull, Scapethrift, and Spendall join Sir Petronel there to make the final plans for the voyage.

As Gertrude prepares for her ride into the country to see her husband's nonexistent castle, Touchstone enters with his other daughter and his new son-in-law, Golding. Gertrude heaps contempt on all three, and Sir Petronel makes disparaging remarks about the groom's lack of nobility. Touchstone distributes a few ironical barbs and leads away the newlyweds. After their departure, Security presents Gertrude with papers, supposedly to cover a loan for new furnishings for the country castle. At Sir Petronel's request she signs the papers without even reading them and sets out in her coach after urging the knight to follow as soon as possible. Sir Petronel and Quicksilver convince Security that the knight is planning to elope with a lawyer's wife; and Security, maliciously delighted at the chance to injure another man, promises to lend them his wife's gown as a disguise. He also feels that lending the gown will be a good way to make certain that his wife does not leave home.

Sir Petronel, the disguised Winifred, Quicksilver, and the

other adventurers ignore storm warnings and set out in their boats for the ship. Security discovers his wife's absence and tries to follow them. Slitgut, a butcher coming to Cuckold's Haven to set up a pair of horns, sees from his elevated vantage point a boat overturned in the waves. A few minutes later old Security crawls ashore, bemoaning the appropriateness of his place of shipwreck. As soon as he creeps away, the butcher sees a woman struggling in the waves and a boy plunging in to save her. The boy rescues a very repentant Winifred, brings her ashore, and offers her shelter and dry clothes. A third victim of the storm is washed ashore at the foot of the gallows—a bad omen, Slitgut thinks. The man is Francis Quicksilver, who passes by cursing his fate. Finally, Sir Petronel and Captain Seagull reach shore and meet Quicksilver. Sir Petronel, losing his money in the water, has no hope of saving his ship, which he expects to be confiscated. Winifred, now dry and freshly dressed, convinces Security that she did not leave home until she began to worry about him. Slitgut makes a few wry remarks about marriage and goes home, unobserved by any of the adventurers.

Touchstone, thoroughly angered by the knight's desertion and by his wife's and daughter's foolishness, turns out Gertrude and Sindefy to shift for themselves, but, bearing his wife as a cross for thirty years, he feels he should continue to do so. Golding, made an alderman's deputy on his first day in the guild, reports that Sir Petronel and Quicksilver are under arrest and the ship is attached. Mistress Touchstone learns her lesson; Gertrude, in spite of her mother's entreaties that she beg forgiveness, treats her father with her customary contempt. Sir Petronel and Quicksilver are brought in by a constable, and Quicksilver is charged with the theft of five hundred pounds, a capital offense. A warrant is also sent out for old Security for his share in the business. Sir Petronel and Quicksilver reach a peak of repentance that makes them the talk of the prison. Golding and the jailer join Mistress Touchstone and her daughters in pleading with Touchstone to show mercy to the offenders; Touchstone is adamant. Finally Golding has himself arrested, sends for Touchstone to come to release him, and arranges for the latter to overhear Quicksilver's ballad of repentance, sung for the edification of other prisoners to the tune of "I Wail in Woe, I Plunge in Pain." Touchstone's heart is moved, and he offers forgiveness to his prodigal son-in-law and prodigal apprentice. Old Security, hearing that a song of repentance works such wonders, rushes up howling a lamentable song in a most lamentable voice; he, too, receives mercy. At Golding's urging, Quicksilver agrees to marry Sindefy. Security returns to Winifred. Even Gertrude forgives her erring husband and asks forgiveness from her father. Thus all differences are reconciled.

Critical Evaluation:

First performed in 1605, *Eastward Ho!* is one of the most remarkably successful collaborative efforts in English literature. The talents of three considerably different playwrights—Ben Jonson, Thomas Marston, and George Chapman—went into its creation. Although Jonson and Marston had cooperated before (as well as having periods of intense, often bitter, competition), *Eastward Ho!* is Chapman's only known collaboration with other dramatists. The almost seamless blend of the three writers' different styles and concerns into a single, coherent play is an outstanding achievement.

The immediate impulse for the collaboration was to compete with the immense popular success of *Westward Ho!* (1604), a comedy of contemporary London life by Thomas Dekker and John Webster that was playing at a rival theater. Several commentators have suggested that a primary reason for the triple collaboration of Chapman, Jonson, and Marston was the need to produce a rival script as quickly as possible. It is likely that the three writers worked on different sections of the drama simultaneously, in order to expedite production.

Although it is impossible to assign definitively acts or scenes to any single one, or even a combination, of the three authors, linguistic and stylistic evidence strongly suggests that Jonson and Marston were largely responsible for the opening and closing sections of the play, where the language is sharper and more satirical, and that Chapman was the author of the middle section, including the major subplot involving Sir Petronel Flash's relationship with Security, the old usurer, and his wife, Winifred. Despite its highly satirical vein, this middle section, critics have noted, has a more genial and accessible humor, characteristic of Chapman's other dramas.

The play as a whole displays a remarkable unity and cohesion that is rarely found in a work by multiple authors. It has been conjectured that much of this unity is the result of an original plan, or outline, and a final revision, probably done either by Jonson himself or with his close supervision. Whatever the case, the play as finally written combines most of the strengths and few of the weaknesses of its three authors.

Eastward Ho! seeks to be a realistic comedy, with characters involved in entertaining but not totally implausible situations. The play's setting was intended to be familiar to its contemporary audience. In a sense, it is a combination of the city comedy play, based on London life, and the comedy of humors, based on individuals who represent types of human personality. In a comedy of humors, the major characters are motivated by their particular ruling passion, or humor (greed, lust, phobias of one kind or another, and so on). The work also has a strong moralistic vein, which was characteristic of the period and which no doubt reflects Marston's and Jonson's satirical viewpoints.

One such expression of views in *Eastward Ho!* was construed as an insult to the Scots in general and by extension to King James I himself, who had recently come to the English throne. The offending passage was the reason for Chapman and Jonson being arrested and imprisoned for a time—although, ironically, it seems likely that Marston was the actual author of the particular lines. He escaped punishment by prompt flight.

A conventional moral framework guides the characters in the play. Touchstone, the London goldsmith, has two apprentices, Quicksilver and Golding. As their names suggest, the two young men have vastly different personalities. Quicksilver is an aimless wastrel who ends the play as a prison inmate. Golding is an ambitious, hardworking lad. Touchstone's two daughters, Gertrude and Mildred, duplicate this pattern: Gertrude, the older, is vain and pretentious and allows herself to be gulled by Sir Petronel Flash. Mildred, engaged to Golding, is chaste and responsible. While some may see Golding and Mildred as too virtuous to be true, and unsympathetic in their relentless goodness and self-conscious morality, they do represent conventional ideas of proper action appropriate to their stations in life, just as Quicksilver and Gertrude are examples from the opposite end of the moral spectrum. By the end of the play, the various characters have received the rewards or punishments due to them and harmony is restored.

The play is also in the tradition of the journey narrative, in which a group of characters come together for a trip and share stories and experiences. In this case, the group is heading east, going down the Thames River for a variety of reasons. For example, Sir Petronel and the two adventurers Scapethrift and Spendall are bound for the new colony of Virginia. Hence the title, *Eastward Ho!*, which parodies the title of the earlier play, whose characters were headed in the opposite direction. Ironically, the trip is even shorter than the one in *Westward Ho!*, in which the travelers are shipwrecked and washed up on the shores of the Thames before they leave London.

Another notable feature about the play is its numerous references and parodies of other theatrical pieces, including a number of William Shakespeare's plays. At one point, the old usurer Security, desperately seeking a way to get down river, cries out, "A boat, a boat, a boat. A full hundred marks for a boat!" In addition to the literary touches, *Eastward Ho!* is remarkable for the number and range of its proverbial allusions, most of them delivered by Touchstone, and many of them heavily moralistic or didactic in tone. The use of these

helps identify Touchstone as an individual character, while the everyday, colloquial flow of the language makes the play more immediate and accessible.

The combination of the two devices of literary allusion and proverbial wisdom draws attention to the play as a self-conscious artifact that is teaching a lesson. In a sense, *Eastward Ho!* comments on its own purpose as a play—to bring the lives of contemporary Londoners to the stage and to draw entertainment and edification from those lives.

"Critical Evaluation" by Michael Witkoski

Further Reading

Braunmuller, A. R., and Michael Hattaway, eds. *The Cambridge Companion to English Renaissance Drama*. New York: Cambridge University Press, 2003. Chapman's plays are discussed in several places in this collection of essays, and these references are listed in the index.

Ingram, Jill Phillips. "Economies of Obligation in *Eastward Ho!*" In *Idioms of Self-Interest: Credit, Identity, and Property in English Renaissance Literature*. New York: Routledge, 2006. Examines the depiction of credit transactions that involve communal trust and a reward for risk-taking in *Eastward Ho!* and other works of English Renaissance literature.

Petter, C. G. Introduction to *Eastward Ho!* London: Ernest Benn, 1973. A brief but highly informative survey of the drama that provides a wealth of information for the serious student and the casual reader. Additional material offers background on contemporary social issues, as well as Jonson and Chapman's imprisonment for their supposed slur on the Scots.

Spivack, Charlotte. *George Chapman*. New York: Twayne, 1967. A general overview of Chapman's life and career, including his role as a collaborator on *Eastward Ho!* Does an excellent job of placing Chapman's dramatic work within the context of his life.

Sullivan, Ceri. "*Eastward Ho!* and Social Catachresis." In *The Rhetoric of Credit: Merchants in Early Modern Writing*. Madison, N.J.: Fairleigh Dickinson University Press, 2002. Focuses on the play's use of language and other devices to depict trade transactions.

Van Fossen, R. W. Introduction to *Eastward Ho!* New York: Manchester University Press, 1979. Examines various elements of the play, including authorship, contents, stage history, staging, and other issues. Includes background material on the plot and a selection of letters by Chapman and Jonson relating to the drama.

Eat a Bowl of Tea

Author: Louis H. Chu (1915-1970)
First published: 1961
Type of work: Novel
Type of plot: Domestic realism
Time of plot: 1941-1949
Locale: Chinatown, New York; Chinatown, San
    Francisco

Principal characters:
WANG BEN LOY, a young Chinese American waiter
WANG WAH GAY, his father
LEE MEI OI, his bride
LEE GONG, her father
AH SONG, her lover

The Story:

Early one morning in New York's Chinatown, two newly-weds awake to the sound of their doorbell. Wang Ben Loy, the young husband, opens their door to find an undesirable figure, a prostitute, from his past. The woman does not believe he is married and only becomes convinced when shown a pair of his wife's underwear on a clothesline. Ben Loy returns to bed with his beautiful wife, Mei Oi, but not to rest. Instead, thoughts of his recent impotence torment him.

Ben Loy is a young, hardworking Chinese American waiter in Stanton, Connecticut. Dominated by a stern Confucian father, Ben Loy finds his only freedom from patriarchal strictures in surreptitiously meeting prostitutes in nearby New York City during his days off work. He and a fellow waiter even expressly rent a hideout in New York, the apartment now tenanted by Ben Loy and his bride.

Ben Loy's father, Wah Gay, had migrated from China several decades before to make his fortune in America, but he eventually ended up running a Chinatown gaming establishment. During his thirty years in America, Wah Gay returned to China once to marry and father a son, returning to New York to work. At age seventeen, Ben Loy joined his father. After Ben Loy reached his twenties and served in the U.S. Army in World War II, his mother wrote his father suggesting that their son marry.

Lee Gong, an old friend and mah-jongg partner of Wah Gay, who led a life similar to Wah Gay's, also wants to marry off his daughter, Mei Oi, who still lives in China. These two elders tacitly arrange a marriage between their children. Ben Loy is then sent to their ancestral village, where he meets Mei Oi; fortunately, the intended couple are attracted to each other. After a happy wedding, followed by a blissful few weeks, the couple leave for Hong Kong, then New York. Much to the newlyweds' dismay, Ben Loy loses his potency once he leaves China. Blaming his previous licentiousness, Ben Loy feels guilty and incompetent; Mei Oi feels undesirable and neglected.

On the couple's arrival in New York, their fathers throw a huge wedding banquet. Many guests hint that the couple is expected to have a child in the next year. Mei Oi becomes depressed and frustrated as time passes and her hopes of conceiving a child dim. It is then that Ah Song, a regular at Wah Gay's establishment, seizes his opportunity. Ah Song is a notorious philanderer who preys on credulous women with tales of exaggerated wealth and protestations of love. He quickly seduces the vulnerable Mei Oi, who soon becomes pregnant. Ben Loy, pleased to save face by his wife's pregnancy, avoids thinking about how their child was conceived.

The secret is exposed, however, when Ah Song is spied leaving Mei Oi's apartment. Gossip spreads rapidly and reaches Lee Gong, who chides his daughter. Then Wang Chuck Ting, the Wang Family Association's president, informs Wah Gay of the situation and advises that the couple move to Stanton to minimize the family scandal. Wah Gay berates Ben Loy, who received intimations of his cuckoldry from the barbershop gossips, and he slaps Mei Oi in anger. Although the couple move to Connecticut, hostile relatives there force them back to New York, where Ah Song and Mei Oi resume their trysts.

On one such rendezvous, the furious Wah Gay ambushes Ah Song and cuts off his left ear. Ah Song presses charges, and Wah Gay hides from the police in an old friend's laundry in New Jersey. Wang Chuck Ting, joined by the Ping On Tong (the association that informally governs Chinatown), then intervenes. With their political clout, this informal judiciary persuades Wah Gay to emerge from hiding and coerces Ah Song to drop charges. Ah Song is then banished for five years. However, the loss of face Lee Gong and Wah Gay suffer because of the scandal forces them to seek anonymity in other states. Ben Loy and Mei Oi also decide to move westward to San Francisco to start a new life. All is forgiven between the couple, and the birth of the baby, whom Ben Loy accepts as his, adds joy to their lives. Free from the oppressive presence of his father, Ben Loy flourishes and seeks remedies for his impotency. He finds a Chinese herbalist who prescribes that he eat a bowl of bitter, medicinal tea regularly. This cure works, Ben Loy regains his virility, and the couple reunites with thoughts of a new baby and renewed life together.

Critical Evaluation:

Eat a Bowl of Tea was neglected for almost two decades until a post-1960's generation of Asian American readers and scholars rediscovered it and acclaimed it the first authentic Chinese American novel. Since then, it has often been reprinted, has been made into a sensitive and entertaining film, and has become an Asian American classic. It is most often praised for its honest realism, classic comic structure, and deeply American themes. Louis H. Chu's novel is the first by a Chinese American insider depicting Chinatown life in a realistic mode. Certainly, more popular works about Chinatown life preceded it, including Lin Yutang's novel *Chinatown Family* (1948) and Chin Yang Lee's *Flower Drum Song* (1957); however, these works depicted Chinatown life in a stereotypical manner. Chu's observation and recording of his Chinatown is, by comparison, more authentic and knowledgeable of life and work in Chinatown.

Unlike Lin and Lee, who neither lived nor worked there, Chinatown is integral to Chu's life and career. Born in Toishan, China, Chu immigrated to America when he was only nine. After graduating from college, he became director of a New York social center, host of the radio program *Chinese Festival*, and executive secretary of Chinatown's Soo Yuen Benevolent Society.

Chu's realism is especially original in his dialogue. Chu renders the language of his Chinatown characters with such a fine ear that one can hear the cadences of Cantonese underlying the broken English and savor the authenticity of the speakers' banter. Early book reviewers who expected Chu's ghetto characters to speak in polite standard English or Hollywood's stereotype of Chinese American speech patterns were bewildered by Chu's raw, unadulterated language.

Chu's novel also faithfully mirrors the "bachelor society" of America's Chinatowns. This society of men without women was created by racist American immigration statutes of the early 1900's forbidding working-class Chinese from bringing wives into the United States, while equally racist miscegenation laws prevented Chinese from marrying Americans and establishing families in America. (Only wealthier Chinese merchants were allowed to bring wives into the

United States.) Thus men such as Wah Gay and Lee Gong left their wives in China while working in America, enjoying a conjugal visit perhaps only once a decade. In the Chinatowns of that period, then, the population was overwhelmingly male, mostly "married bachelors." Hence, a woman like Mei Oi, a war bride of a Chinese American soldier, would be a precious rarity in the Chinatown community.

In addition to its realist qualities, *Eat a Bowl of Tea* is a comic novel of archetypally classic construction. Classic comedy usually depicts a change from one kind of society to another. Initially, the negative characters who obstruct this change control the society; eventually, the incidents of plot that unite the hero and heroine cause a new society to crystallize around the hero. Indeed, the conflict in Chu's novel is one between a society of elders and a society of youth, between the tradition-bound Chinese sojourners (in America to make money) and the new Chinese Americans (in America to stay). Ideologically, the Confucian Chinese ethic of family hierarchy clashes with the American Dream of the individual's right to pursue happiness and identity. Wah Gay and Lee Gong represent the older Confucian sojourner generation, while Ben Loy and Mei Oi represent the younger Chinese American settler generation. Typical of the Confucian father, Wah Gay initially allows Ben Loy no opportunity to develop his individuality, making decisions for Ben Loy's travel, job, and even marriage. Chu shows that this oppressive familial structure breeds hypocrisy. For instance, Wah Gay's playing the role of the moral father is ironic because his means of livelihood, a gambling joint, is more suitable for a gangster than for a model Confucian father. Similarly, Ben Loy keeps up appearances as an obedient, hardworking son, but he secretly resorts to prostitutes as a release.

After Wah Gay's wounding of Ah Song, the Confucian family hierarchy begins to disintegrate as the representatives of the older generation, Lee Gong and Wah Gay, go into exile. The action then focuses on the younger generation, Ben Loy and Mei Oi, as they attempt to rebuild their marriage unencumbered by repressive expectations. The young couple's new sense of family is a loving partnership, not an authoritarian hierarchy. Here, Chu's novel becomes attuned to a profoundly American theme as its young couple moves from the old American East (New York) to the new American West (San Francisco). In so doing, they are following the archetypal journey of the American explorer who voyages westward to seek a second chance at life on new frontiers. Thus, rooting his novel in Chinese America, Chu brings to fruition a work that consorts with themes deep in the American grain: the dream of the individual to pursue happiness and self-actualization, the desire that America be another Eden. *Eat a*

Bowl of Tea is Chu's only published novel, but, with it, he is deservedly designated Chinese America's first novelist, the worthy forerunner of Frank Chin, Maxine Hong Kingston, and Amy Tan.

Jarrell Chua and C. L. Chua

Further Reading

Chan, Jeffrey. Introduction to *Eat a Bowl of Tea*. Seattle: University of Washington Press, 1979. Excellent introduction by a distinguished Chinese American scholar and writer. Praises Chu for his transcription of Cantonese idiom and satirical analysis of Chinatown society. Includes brief biography of Chu.

Eng, David L. "Male Hysteria—Real and Imagined—in *Eat a Bowl of Tea* and *Pangs of Love*." In *Racial Castration: Managing Masculinity in Asian America*. Durham, N.C.: Duke University Press, 2001. Psychoanalytic study of how Asian American masculinity is defined by race and sexuality. Includes a discussion of the representation of masculinity in novels by Chu and David Wong Louie.

Gong, Ted. "Approaching Cultural Change Through Literature." *Amerasia Journal* 7, no. 1 (1980): 73-86. Traces cultural development from Chinese to Chinese American in the work of Monfoon Leong, Louis Chu, and Frank Chin. Examines common themes of the father-son relationship and generational conflict.

Hsiao, Ruth Y. "Facing the Incurable: Patriarchy in *Eat a Bowl of Tea*." In *Reading the Literatures of Asian America*, edited by Shirley Geok-lin Lim and Amy Ling. Philadelphia: Temple University Press, 1992. Places Chu in the tradition of literary debunking of patriarchy. Theorizes that while patriarchy is portrayed as the real villain in the novel, Chu fails to free his own creative imagination from male images of women; patriarchy remains an incurable malady of Chinese society.

Kim, Elaine H. *Asian American Literature: An Introduction to the Writings and Their Social Context*. Philadelphia: Temple University Press, 1982. A groundbreaking book on Asian American literature. Chapter 4, "Portraits of Chinatown," contains an illuminating discussion of the literary and sociological qualities of Chu's novel.

Lee, A. Robert. "*Eat a Bowl of Tea*: Fictions of America's Asia, Fictions of Asia's America." In *Multicultural American Literature: Comparative Black, Native, Latino/a, and Asian American Fictions*. Jackson: University Press of Mississippi, 2003. A study of American ethnic writers, discussing how Chu and other authors address and question the topics of whiteness, autobiography, geography, and prose genres.

Lim, Shirley Geok-lin. "Rescripting Louis Chu's *Eat a Bowl of Tea*: A Chinese American Authentic?" In *Race and the Production of Modern American Nationalism*, edited by Reynolds J. Scott-Childress. New York: Garland, 1999. Examines how race has both helped and hindered the determination of American identity, focusing on several ethnic groups, including Chinese Americans. The essays, including the one on Chu's novel, analyze how race and nationalism are represented in literature and other media.

Shih, David. "*Eat a Bowl of Tea*, by Louis Chu." In *A Resource Guide to Asian American Literature*, edited by Sau-ling Cynthia Wong and Stephen H. Sumida. New York: Modern Language Association of America, 2001. This guide for teachers provides information about fifteen novels, including *Eat a Bowl of Tea*, and six plays written by Asian Americans. The essays discuss publication history, historical context, major themes, and critical issues and offer ideas for teaching each work.

5/3/11